T0189306

Lecture Notes
in Business Information Processing   **402**

More information about this series at http://www.springer.com/series/7911

Marinos Themistocleous ·
Maria Papadaki · Muhammad Mustafa Kamal (Eds.)

Information Systems

17th European, Mediterranean,
and Middle Eastern Conference, EMCIS 2020
Dubai, United Arab Emirates, November 25–26, 2020
Proceedings

 Springer

Editors
Marinos Themistocleous ⓘ
Department of Digital Innovation
School of Business
University of Nicosia
Nicosia, Cyprus

Maria Papadaki
British University in Dubai
Dubai, United Arab Emirates

Muhammad Mustafa Kamal ⓘ
School of Strategy and Leadership
Coventry University
Coventry, UK

ISSN 1865-1348   ISSN 1865-1356 (electronic)
Lecture Notes in Business Information Processing
ISBN 978-3-030-63395-0   ISBN 978-3-030-63396-7 (eBook)
https://doi.org/10.1007/978-3-030-63396-7

This Springer imprint is published by the registered company Springer Nature Switzerland AG
The registered company address is: Gewerbestrasse 11, 6330 Cham, Switzerland

Preface

The European, Mediterranean, and Middle Eastern Conference on Information Systems (EMCIS) is an annual research event addressing the discipline of Information Systems (IS) from a regional as well as a global perspective. EMCIS has successfully helped bring together researchers from around the world in a friendly atmosphere conducive to the free exchange of innovative ideas. EMCIS is one of the premier conferences in Europe and the Middle Eastern region for IS academics and professionals, covering technical, organizational, business, and social issues in the application of information technology. EMCIS is dedicated to the definition and establishment of IS as a discipline of high impact for IS professionals and practitioners. EMCIS focuses on approaches that facilitate the identification of innovative research of significant relevance to the IS discipline, following sound research methodologies that lead to results of measurable impact.

Unlike previous years, the EMCIS 2020 conference was held online due to the developments in the COVID-19 virus which has created a worldwide tragedy. EMCIS 2020's top priority is the health and safety of all participants, considering the expanding spread of COVID-19. The pandemic, the travel bans, movement and gathering restrictions issued by many governments, as well as the restrictions on staff's mobility by many universities and organizations led EMCIS to run the conference online.

This year, we received 161 papers from 37 countries from all continents and 54 of them were accepted with an overall acceptance rate of 34.8%. Portugal leads the table with the most submitted papers followed by Sweden, Greece, France, Poland, Tunisia, Cyprus, and UK. All papers were submitted through the easyacademia.org online review system. Track chairs assigned reviewers and the papers were sent for double-blind review. The papers were reviewed by members of the Conference Committee and/or external reviewers. Track chairs submitted 7 papers and each of these papers were reviewed by a member of the EMCIS Executive Committee and one member of the International Committee. The conference chairs submitted 1 paper in total, which was reviewed by two senior external reviewers each. Overall, 54 papers were accepted for EMCIS 2020 as full papers submitted to the following tracks:

- Big Data and Analytics (6 papers)
- Blockchain Technology and Applications (8 papers)
- Digital Services and Social Media (7 papers)
- Digital Government (4 papers)
- Emerging Computing Technologies and Trends for Business Process Management (2 papers)
- Enterprise Systems (3 papers)
- Information Systems Security and Information Privacy Protection (5 papers)
- Healthcare Information Systems (3 papers)
- Management and Organisational Issues in Information Systems (10 papers)
- IT Governance and alignment (3 papers)
- Innovative Research Projects (3 papers)

The papers were accepted for their theoretical and practical excellence and for the promising results they present. We hope that the readers will find the papers interesting and we are open for a productive discussion that will improve the body of knowledge in the field of IS.

October 2020

Marinos Themistocleous
Maria Papadaki
Muhammad Mustafa Kamal

Organization

Conference Chairs

Maria Papadaki   The British University in Dubai, UAE
Marinos Themistocleous   University of Nicosia, Cyprus

Conference Executive Committee

Muhammad Mustafa Kamal   Coventry University, UK
  (Program Chair)
Vincenzo Morabito   Bocconi University, Italy
  (Publications Chair)
Paulo da Cunha   University of Coimbra, Portugal
  (Publications Chair)
Gianluigi Viscusi (Public   Imperial College Business School, UK
  Relations Chair)

International Committee

Piotr Soja   Cracow University of Economics, Poland
Angelika Kokkinaki   University of Nicosia, Cyprus
Peter Love   Curtin University, Australia
Paulo Melo   University of Coimbra, Portugal
Heinz Roland Weistroffer   Virginia Commonwealth University, USA
Yiannis Charalambidis   University of the Aegean, Greece
Vishanth Weerakkody   University of Bradford, UK
Gail Corbitt   California State University, USA
Miguel Mira da Silva   University of Lisbon, Portugal
Lasse Berntzen   University of South-Eastern Norway, Norway
Marijn Janssen   Delft University of Technology, The Netherlands
Stanisław Wrycza   University of Gdańsk, Poland
Kamel Ghorab   Al Hosn University, UAE
Hemin Jiang   University of Science and Technology of China, China
Luning Liu   Harbin Institute of Technology, China
Slim Kallel   University of Sfax, Tunisia
Walid Gaaloul   Télécom SudParis, France
Mohamed Sellami   Télécom SudParis, France
Celina M. Olszak   University of Economics in Katowice, Poland
Flora Malamateniou   University of Piraeus, Greece
Andriana Prentza   University of Piraeus, Greece
Inas Ezz   Sadat Academy for Management Sciences (SAMS),
      Egypt

Ibrahim Osman	American University of Beirut, Lebanon
Przemysław Lech	University of Gdańsk, Poland
Euripidis N. Loukis	University of the Aegean, Greece
Mariusz Grabowski	Cracow University of Economics, Poland
Małgorzata Pańkowska	University of Economics in Katowice, Poland
António Trigo	Coimbra Business School, Portugal
Catarina Ferreira da Silva	ISCTE – Lisbon University Institute, Portugal
Aggeliki Tsohou	Ionian University, Greece
Paweł Wołoszyn	Cracow University of Economics, Poland
Sofiane Tebboune	Manchester Metropolitan University, UK
Fletcher Glancy	Miami University, USA
Aurelio Ravarini	Università Carlo Cattaneo, Italy
Wafi Al-Karaghouli	Brunel University London, UK
Ricardo Jimenes Peris	Universidad Politécnica de Madrid (UPM), Spain
Federico Pigni	Grenoble Ecole de Management, France
Paulo Henrique de Souza Bermejo	Universidade Federal de Lavras, Brazil
May Seitanidi	University of Kent, UK
Sevgi Özkan	Middle East Technical University, Turkey
Demosthenis Kyriazis	University of Piraeus, Greece
Karim Al-Yafi	Qatar University, Qatar
Manar Abu Talib	Zayed University, UAE
Alan Serrano	Brunel University London, UK
Steve Jones	Conwy County Borough, UK
Tillal Eldabi	Ahlia University, Bahrain
Carsten Brockmann	Capgemini, Germany
Ella Kolkowska	Örebro University, Sweden
Grażyna Paliwoda-Pękosz	Cracow University of Economics, Poland
Heidi Gautschi	IMD Business School, Switzerland
Janusz Stal	Cracow University of Economics, Poland
Koumaditis Konstantinos	Aarhus University, Denmark
Chinello Francesco	Aarhus University, Denmark
Pacchierotti Claudio	University of Rennes, France
Milena Krumova	Technical University of Sofia, Bulgaria
Klitos Christodoulou	University of Nicosia, Cyprus
Elias Iosif	University of Nicosia, Cyprus
Charalampos Alexopoulos	University of the Aegean, Greece
Przemysław Lech	University of Gdańsk, Poland

Contents

Big Data and Analytics

Blockchain Technology and Applications

IT Governance and Alignment

Management and Organisational Issues in Information Systems

Big Data and Analytics

Towards Designing Conceptual Data Models for Big Data Warehouses: The Genomics Case

João Galvão[1]([⊠]) , Ana Leon[2] , Carlos Costa[1] ,
Maribel Yasmina Santos[1] , and Óscar Pastor López[2]

[1] ALGORITMI Research Centre, University of Minho, Guimarães, Portugal
{joao.galvao,carlos.costa,maribel}@dsi.uminho.pt
[2] Research Center on Software Production Methods (PROS), Universitat
Politècnica de València, Valencia, Spain
{aleon,opastor}@pros.upv.es

Abstract. Data Warehousing applied in Big Data contexts has been an emergent topic of research, as traditional Data Warehousing technologies are unable to deal with Big Data characteristics and challenges. The methods used in this field are already well systematized and adopted by practitioners, while research in Big Data Warehousing is only starting to provide some guidance on how to model such complex systems. This work contributes to the process of designing conceptual data models for Big Data Warehouses proposing a method based on rules and design patterns, which aims to gather the information of a certain application domain mapped in a relational conceptual model. A complex domain that can benefit from this work is Genomics, characterized by an increasing heterogeneity, both in terms of content and data structure. Moreover, the challenges for collecting and analyzing genome data under a unified perspective have become a bottleneck for the scientific community, reason why standardized analytical repositories such as a Big Genome Warehouse can be of high value to the community. In the demonstration case presented here, a genomics relational model is merged with the proposed Big Data Warehouse Conceptual Metamodel to obtain the Big Genome Warehouse Conceptual Model, showing that the design rules and patterns can be applied having a relational conceptual model as starting point.

Keywords: Big Data Warehousing · Big data modelling · Conceptual modeling

1 Introduction

Analytical contexts have been highly influenced by Big Data where new challenges arise both in terms of data modeling approaches and technological concerns that must be considered. Traditional Data Warehousing (DWing) systems lost the capacity to handle data with different characteristics, such as high data volumes, produced at high speed and considering different data varieties. To overcome those challenges, as organizations still need structured data repositories supporting decision making tasks, data warehouses are now implemented using Big Data technologies [1, 2].

© Springer Nature Switzerland AG 2020
M. Themistocleous et al. (Eds.): EMCIS 2020, LNBIP 402, pp. 3–19, 2020.
https://doi.org/10.1007/978-3-030-63396-7_1

Due to its novelty, research in Big Data Warehousing (BDWing) has been quite scarce with some works based on unstructured approaches and use case technology-driven solutions [2–5]. The work of [2] overcomes these practices by proposing a structured approach that includes guidelines for the design and implementation of Big Data Warehouses (BDWs). In this paper, the conceptual modeling of BDWs is formalized defining a Big Data Warehouse Conceptual Metamodel (BDW_{CMT}) with the constructs made available in the data modeling approach of [2], and proposes a method that includes patterns and rules to guide practitioners from the BDW_{CMT} to the design of a specific Big Data Warehouse Conceptual Model (BDW_{CM}).

As demonstration case, and due to the complexity of this application domain, the proposed modeling method is applied to Genomics with the aim to implement the Big Genome Warehouse System. This is intended to be implemented using Big Data tools and technologies in the Hadoop Ecosystem, using Hive as the main storage technology, as this is considered the *de facto standard* for DWing in Big Data. This physical implementation in Hive must consider background knowledge inherited from the Big Genome Warehouse Conceptual Model (BGW_{CM}) and from the Human Genome Conceptual Model (HG_{CM}). Both models comply with specific constructs that follow UML Class Diagrams Metamodels, assuming that a system is represented by a model that conforms to a metamodel [6].

The HG_{CM} is the result of a research work on a complex domain where the use of conceptual models has been proved to be a feasible solution for the integration of data coming from heterogeneous and disperse set of genomic sources. One of the most challenging problems in the genomic domain is the identification of DNA variants that could be a potential cause of disease. The huge amounts of available data, characterized by their heterogeneity, either in terms of content and structure, as well as the problems for collecting and analyzing them under a unified perspective has become a bottleneck for the scientific community. In [7], the authors face this problem by presenting a conceptual model that provides the required unified perspective to collect, structure and analyze the key concepts of the domain under a well-grounded ontological basis. Using this background knowledge of the HG_{CM} with the key concepts in this application domain, namely the main identified identities and their relationships, the BGW_{CM} here modeled must conform to the BDW_{CMT}. The aim of this paper is to show how to move from the BDW_{CMT} to the BGW_{CM} using the knowledge explicitly available in the HG_{CM}. A simplification of the HG_{CM} is used in this paper intended to solve a specific task and ease the validation process of this approach. The details about the physical implementation of the BGW_{CM} in Hive is out of the scope of this paper.

The method for data modeling of BDWs proposed in this paper follows an iterative and goal-driven approach that performs a map between the conceptual model of the domain (HG_{CM}) and the BDW_{CMT}. This method considers the main data modeling constructs and proposes the data modeling rules and the data modeling patterns for implementing BDWs. This work is evaluated with the identification of the BGW_{CM}.

This paper is structured as follows. Section 2 presents the related work. Section 3 formalizes the BDW_{CMT}, its main constructs and their characteristics. Section 4 addresses the proposed data modeling rules and patterns, which are instantiated to the Genomics case. Section 5 outlines the presented work and future work.

2 Related Work

Data models are essential in information systems design and development as they ensure that data needs are properly considered [4]. In a traditional organizational environment, relational data models are quite popular and are strictly considering the business requirements. However, in an organizational context making use of Big Data, the ability to process data increases with the use of flexible schemas, and thus the data modeling methods change significantly [8, 9], as the database schemas can change during application runtime according to the analytical needs of the organization [4, 9]. Taking this into consideration, BDWs are significantly different from traditional data warehouses, since schemas must be based on new logical models that allow more flexibility and scalability, hence the emergence of new design and modeling proposals for BDWs [2]. In Big Data, there are multiple challenges when addressing multidimensional data, namely the capability to ensure schema-less or dynamic schema changes, huge number of dimensions and cardinality, recommendations for automatic partitioning and materialization, or real-time processing [3, 10].

The works of [4] and [11] propose an almost automatic design methodology using the key-value model to represent a multidimensional scheme at the logical level, instead of applying the traditional star/snowflakes schemes. Moreover, a multidimensional model is provided by a graph-oriented representation as the basis for the conceptual design of this methodology, aiming at the construction of attribute trees representing facts related to the integrated data source and automatically remodeling these trees based on the restrictions resulting from the requirements analysis phase. Still in the NoSQL realm, the work of [5] proposes three types of translations of a conceptual model to a columnar model, showing the implementation of columnar data warehouses in NoSQL. Additionally, there are works focused on OLAP-oriented technologies for Big Data, being Hive a popular example. The work of [12] proposes a set of rules/guidelines for transforming a traditional dimensional model [13] into a Hive tabular data model for BDWs, adjusting the table's grain to the domain requirements.

A context-independent design and implementation approach for BDWs has been addressed in [2, 14] where several design patterns for modeling performant BDWs were evaluated, targeting advancing decision making with huge amounts of data, collected at high velocity and with different degrees of heterogeneity. In these, a data modeling method is proposed, supporting mixed and complex analytical workloads (e.g., streaming analysis, ad hoc querying, data visualization, data mining).

Research in this area is still relatively ambiguous and yet at an early stage, lacking common approaches [15], reason why this paper proposes a more straightforward rationale for modelling BDWs, supported by the constructs of [2].

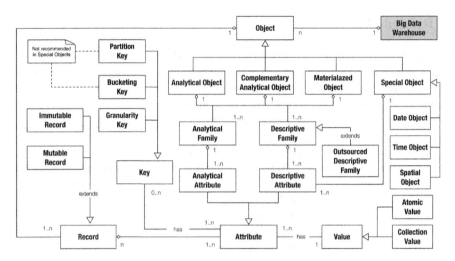

Fig. 1. The BDW's conceptual metamodel

3   The Big Data Warehouse Conceptual Metamodel

In [2], the set of constructs for modelling a BDW were proposed without any formalization in a conceptual metamodel that clearly states how those constructs are organized and how they complement each other in this data system. Extending the work of [2], those constructs are in this paper used to propose the BDW$_{CMT}$, a metamodel that formalizes the elements used to model a BDW (Fig. 1).

Each object in a BDW can be classified as an Analytical Object (AO), a Complementary Analytical Object (CAO), a Materialized Object (MO) or a Special Object (SO). The AOs are subjects of interest in an analytical context, for instance Sales or Products. Usually, objects start as AOs, but as the data modelling approach proceeds, they can turn into CAOs if they are shared by several AOs and if they comply with the characteristics and guidelines presented afterwards in this section. In these cases, the AOs outsource the descriptive families to the CAOs. In a parallelism with Kimball's Dimensional Modeling [13], this type of object is similar to the conformed dimensions of a dimensional data model but capable of combining the concept of aggregated facts for dimensions as well, due to the analytical value of CAOs. The MOs store the results of time-consuming queries aiming to improve the BDW performance by providing pre-aggregated results to the several data consumers, instead of processing heavy aggregations multiple times. Finally, the SOs are of three types: Spatial, Date and Time. They are used to standardize concepts like Date, Time and Space, ensuring that the attributes related to those concepts have the same meaning and format across the BDW. The several objects, excluding the SOs as these are seen as a particular case, include analytical and/or descriptive families, which in their turn include analytical and descriptive attributes, respectively. The attributes include atomic or collection values. The atomic values can be used as (or as part of) the partition, bucketing and/or granularity keys of an object. The records of the objects can be mutable or immutable, allowing or avoiding update operations. These several constructs included in the conceptual metamodel are described in Table 1. Extending the descriptive families, outsourced descriptive families allow relationships between AOs and CAOs. These are useful for having a flexible data modelling approach that enhances the performance of the BDW [14].

Table 1. Description of the BDW's conceptual metamodel constructs

Construct	Class	Description
Object	Represents	Constructs used in the conceptual modeling of a BDW
	Characteristics	Highly performant structures to provide analytical value to decision support scenarios
	Includes	Analytical, complementary analytical, materialized, and special (date, time and spatial) objects
Analytical Object	Represents	Isolated object of a subject of interest for analytical purposes
	Characteristics	Highly denormalized and autonomous structures able to answer queries without the constant need of joins with other data structures
	Examples	Sales, purchases, inventory management, customer complaints, among others
	Includes	Analytical families, descriptive families, records, granularity key, partition key, bucketing (or clustering) key
Analytical Family (including Analytical Attributes)	Represents	A set of attributes with numeric values that can be analyzed using different descriptive attributes (e.g., grouped or filtered by)
	Characteristics	Logical representation of a set of indicators or measures (analytical attributes) relevant for analytical purposes. Can include factual (numeric evidence of something) or predictive (an estimative or a prediction of what could happen) attributes
	Examples	Sold quantity, discount value and sold value
	Includes	Analytical families include analytical attributes
Descriptive Family (including Descriptive Attributes)	Represents	A set of descriptive values that are used to interpret analytical attributes by different perspectives, using aggregation or filtering operations, for example
	Characteristics	A descriptive family is a logical representation of a set of attributes usually used to add meaning to a numeric indicator

(continued)

Table 1. (*continued*)

Construct	Class	Description
	Examples	Customer name, product description and discount type
	Includes	Descriptive families include descriptive attributes
Record	Represents	The set of values for the attributes of an occurrence of an analytical object
	Characteristics	Can be mutable (allow updates) or immutable records (forbid updates)
	Examples	The values that characterize the purchase of a product, by a customer, on a store, with a factual and/or predicted quantity
	Includes	Atomic values (integer, float, double, string, or varchar) or collections (complex structures like arrays, maps, or JSON)
Granularity Key	Represents	The level of detail of records to be stored in an analytical object
	Characteristics	Is defined using one or more descriptive attributes that uniquely identify a record. It may not need to be physically implemented in a data system as a primary key
	Examples	Sales order, product identifier, among others
	Includes	One or more descriptive attributes that uniquely identify a record
Partition Key	Represents	The physical partitioning scheme applied to the data, fragmenting the analytical objects into more manageable parts that can be accessed individually
	Characteristics	Is defined using one or more descriptive attributes (although analytical attributes can also be used) that form the partition key
	Examples	Time and/or geospatial attributes are the most useful ones, as data is typically loaded and filtered in hourly/daily/monthly batches for specific regions or countries
	Includes	One or more descriptive attributes that form the partition key
Bucketing Key	Represents	The physical clustering applied to the data, grouping records of an analytical object
	Characteristics	Is defined using one or more descriptive attributes that form the bucketing key
	Examples	Attributes such as products or customers distributing the data by similar volumes

(*continued*)

Table 1. (*continued*)

Construct	Class	Description
	Includes	One or more descriptive attributes that form the bucketing key
Complementary Analytical Object	Represents	Object that complements other analytical objects, providing an autonomous structure with analytical value that is used to complement the different analytical perspectives provided by the analytical objects
	Characteristics	Object whose granularity key (whole or part of it) is used by other analytical object, meaning that a join between two or more objects is possible
	Examples	Customer account, product, supplier, among others
	Includes	Analytical families, descriptive families, records, granularity key, partition key, bucketing (or clustering) key
Materialized Object	Represents	Object that includes an aggregation of the records of an analytical or complementary analytical object, based on frequent access patterns to the data
	Characteristics	Enhances the performance of frequent queries by performing a pre-aggregation of the data and the pre-computing time-consuming joins between large objects
	Examples	Views on any analytical, complementary analytical and special objects
	Includes	Can be created based on any analytical or complementary analytical objects
Special Object (Time, Date and Spatial Object)	Represents	Objects that include several temporal and/or spatial attributes that complement the analytical objects (or complementary analytical objects)
	Characteristics	Use standard time, date and spatial representations in autonomous objects, avoiding the increase of the size of the analytical or complementary analytical objects
	Examples	Time: hour, minute, second; Date: day, month, year; Spatial: city, country
	Includes	Descriptive families, records, and Granularity keys

Table 2 summarizes a set of guidelines and good practices proposed in [2] for the use of outsourced descriptive families and nested attributes taking into consideration the domain requirements, helping practitioners to identify contexts where the same can be useful.

Table 2. Guidelines for outsourced descriptive families and nested attributes

Construct	Guidelines
Outsourced Descriptive Family	The descriptive family is frequently included in other analytical objects
	The descriptive family has low cardinality, i.e., its distinct records will form a low volume CAO that easily fits into memory, enabling the capability to perform map/broadcast joins in SQL-on-Hadoop engines
	The data ingestion frequency of the resulting CAO is equivalent to the other AOs it is related to
	The CAO resulting from the outsourced descriptive family can provide analytical value by itself
	The records of the CAOs formed by the outsourced descriptive families are recommended to be immutable
Nesting Attributes (in a Collection)	Avoid nested attributes in a collection if there is the need to perform heavy aggregations on that data
	Avoid nested attributes in a collection when using filtering operations based on nested values
	Nested attributes included in a collection are not meant to grow rapidly
	Estimate the collection initial size and its potential growth before adopting nested attributes

4   The Big Genome Warehouse Conceptual Model

The method presented in this paper is based on rules and design patterns that aim to gather the information of a certain application domain mapped in a relational conceptual model, merging it with a BDW_{CMT} in order to obtain a BDW_{CM}. In this work, the method is presented and demonstrated in the Genomics application domain.

4.1   Data Modeling Rules

The data modeling rules are based on a goal-driven approach that identifies the analytical value of the entities present in the conceptual model of the domain and characterizes the data volume and querying frequency of those entities, as this information is later used for applying the data modeling patterns. The three data modeling rules are:

⊙**R1. Entities with High Analytical Value.** Identification of the main entities of the domain, pointing those queried for decision support, providing the main business or analytical indicators. In this process, it is relevant to consider that the approach is goal-driven, so an entity may have a relevant analytical value in a particular domain or business process, being identified as a key entity by this rule, but in other contexts it may only be used for providing contextual information, such as *who* or *what*. In the data modelling perspective, these entities usually receive multiple relationships with the M cardinality (M:1, many-to-one), integrating several concepts of the domain.

⋙**R2. Entities with High Cardinality.** Characterization of entities with high data volume, helping in the process of identifying the entities that are candidates for out-sourced descriptive families, since high cardinality entities are good candidates to denormalization processes, avoiding joins with huge amounts of data. This high cardinality classification of the entities cannot be exclusively based on row counting processes, requiring additional knowledge from the domain. The data engineer with the help of the domain expert should estimate data growing rates based on a deep knowledge of the application domain.

⟳**R3. Entities with Frequent Access Patterns.** Characterization of the entities with frequent access patterns which, combined with R2, point entities that are candidates for MOs, increasing the overall performance of the BDW system.

Taking into consideration the HG$_{CM}$ available at [7] and the constructs and guidelines presented above, the data modeling rules were applied classifying a subset of the entities of this domain attending to R1, R2 and R3 (Fig. 2).

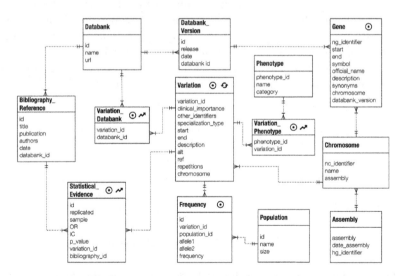

Fig. 2. The human genome conceptual model. Adapted from [7].

4.2 Data Modeling Patterns

The data modeling patterns take into consideration that a BDW is built with the goal of supporting decision-making tasks and that those tasks highly depend on the identified goals or main analytical activities.

This data modeling method has the flexibility that is needed in a Big Data context, allowing the evolution of the models when: i) new business processes/data sources are identified; ii) new data is available for the existing processes/data sources; or iii) new data requirements change the classification of the entities in terms of design rules. As described in Sect. 3, one of the main constructs in the BDW_{CMT} is the concept of AOs. These are highly denormalized and autonomous structures able to answer queries without the constant need of joining different structures. Often based on flat structures, for better performance [14], these completely or mostly flat structures significantly increase the storage size of the BDW, a problem that has even more impact when multiple AOs share the same descriptive families. To face this balance between data volume and processing performance, the proposed data modeling patterns allow for the identification of data models that are: i) highly flexible, as the data engineers have instruments that guide the modeling process, without limiting the human decisions; ii) highly performant, identifying objects that answer the main domain questions considering both data volume and performance concerns; and iii) highly relevant, providing different analytical views on the data under analysis. The design patterns take into consideration the need to identify the different objects in the BDW, their type (AOs, CAOs, MOs or SOs), and the descriptive and analytical families included in those objects.

Considering a traditional relational context in which data is highly normalized and each entity details a specific set of attributes with some level of detail, a BDW uses the same data but denormalizes the data structures as much as possible, without compromising the BDW sustainability in terms of storage space or its usability in terms of performance. In this process, data at different levels of detail can be stored, making available objects that may answer more detailed queries, while others can support aggregated and very performant answers to more general questions (Fig. 3).

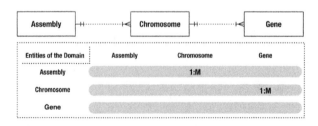

Fig. 3. Levels of detail for the several entities

In Fig. 3, the three entities available in the domain are possible AOs for the BDW and all of them could be included in this data repository using a similar data model (highly normalized). However, the BDW must be aligned with the analytical queries and must consider storage and performance concerns. As an example for a BDW, two possible data models are depicted in Fig. 4.

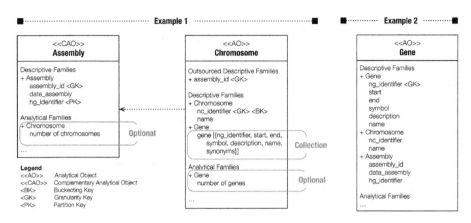

Fig. 4. Examples of possible data models

In Fig. 4, Example 1 includes **Chromosome** as an AO that outsourced a descriptive family, included in a CAO named **Assembly** and nested the descriptive family of **Gene** into a collection, in accordance with the **Chromosome** granularity. Each object has its own granularity and the denormalization must respect that granularity. Example 2 includes a fully denormalized AO called **Gene** with **Chromosome** and **Assembly** as denormalized descriptive families of this object.

Based on the assumption that all the entities present in a data model, such as a relational-based one, are candidate or possible objects in a BDW, the design patterns are:

<<AO>>**P1. Analytical Objects.** Entities classified as of type R1 are identified as possible AOs due to their high analytical value.

<<CAO>>**P2. Complementary Analytical Objects.** Entities can be outsourced to CAOs if they comply with the best practices summarized in Table 2, if they are not classified as of type R2 and if they maintain relationships of cardinality 1:M (one-to-many) with more than one entity of the domain.

<<DF>>**P3. Descriptive Families.** Entities not identified as <<AO>> or <<CAO>> by the design patterns P1, P2 are candidates to be denormalized as descriptive families of AOs or nested to a collection of AOs, in accordance to their granularity. In Fig. 4, Example 1, **Chromosome** includes **Gene** as a collection, as a chromosome includes multiples genes, whereas in Example 2 **Gene** denormalizes **Chromosome** and **Assembly**, as a gene maintains a unitary relationship with a chromosome and an assembly.

<<SO>>**P4. Special Objects.** Entities including temporal and/or spatial attributes point the need for SOs that include the calendar, temporal or spatial descriptive attributes relevant in the application domain.

<<MO>>**P5. Materialized Objects.** Entities of type R3 can be, in addition to the previous patterns, labeled as possible MOs with aggregates usually used in analytical tasks.

Considering the defined patterns and the domain knowledge expressed in the HG$_{CM}$ presented in Fig. 2, which already includes the classification of the entities considering the data modeling rules, it is now possible to integrate the specific characteristics of a BDW with the domain knowledge of the human genome in order to propose the conceptual model of the Big Genome Warehouse (BGW$_{CM}$).

Figure 5 presents a synopsis of the approach that guides practitioners to apply the method and obtain the BGWCM. The entities identified in the domain knowledge are mapped against themselves in a matrix, to identify their common relationships. It also maps the design rules and patterns with the entities of the domain. The application of the data modeling patterns gives a first overview of the main objects of the BDW, which are refined in successive iterations as the data modeling method proceeds.

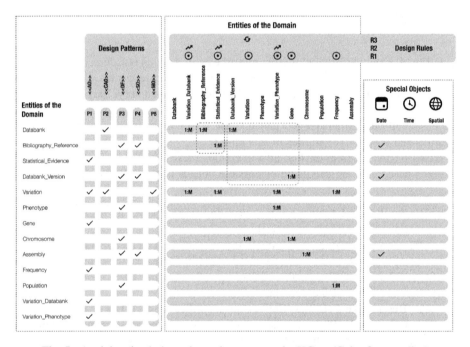

Fig. 5. Applying the design rules and patterns to the HG$_{CM}$ (Color figure online)

In the first step, the application of pattern P1 allows the identification of 6 analytical objects (<<AO>> Variation_Databank, <<AO>> Statistical_Evidence, <<AO>> Variation, <<AO>> Variation_Phenotype, <<AO>> Frequency, <<AO>> Gene). The second step identifies the CAOs, starting by choosing the entities that have more than one 1:M relationships to other entities. In this case, the possible CAOs are Databank, Variation and Chromosome, but only Databank and Variation are classified as CAOs (<<CAO>> Databank, <<CAO>> Variation) since Chromosome alone cannot provide analytical value, complying with the best-practices presented in Table 2. Note that the classification as <<CAO>> can change if the size of the object makes joins inefficient.

Although Databank was not classified by R1, domain experts may show interest in knowing the databanks that are not used in the study of a variation. This is possible with a query that checks records of <<CAO>> Databank not included in <<AO>> Variation_Databank, for instance. In this step, one object previously classified as an AO is now reclassified as a CAO (<<CAO>> Variation) due to its use by other objects.

With the identification of AOs and CAOs, the entities without these classifications are candidates to be denormalized to the AOs or CAOs previously identified (P3), in accordance to their granularity. The fourth step identifies the entities that have relationships with the SOs, namely Date, Time or Spatial. In this, Bibliography_Reference, Assembly and Databank_Version are identified as having relationships with the Date object (P4). In P5, and due to its frequent access pattern, one object is identified as possible candidate to an additional materialized object that answers frequent queries of the application domain, <<MO>> Variation Aggregates.

Following the design patterns, the BGW$_{CM}$ is obtained (Fig. 6). With P1 and P2, 5 AOs and 2 CAOs (<<AO>> Variation_Databank, <<AO>> Statistical_Evidence, <<AO>> Variation_Phenotype, <<AO>> Frequency, <<AO>> Gene, <<CAO>> Databank, <<CAO>> Variation) were identified. Now, the relationships of the entities are analyzed.

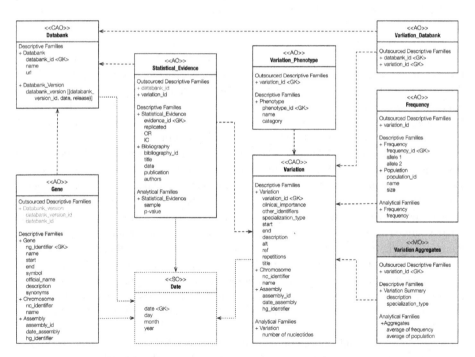

Fig. 6. The big genome warehouse conceptual model (Color figure online)

Starting by Databank, this entity has relationships with Variation_Databank, Bibliography_Reference and Databank_Version, linking <<CAO>> Databank and <<AO>> Variation_Databank. Taking into consideration the domain knowledge, Databank_Version is an entity with a set of properties of Databank which, also, complies with the nested attributes best practices presented in Table 2. For this, Databank_Version is nested and included in the model as a collection of the <<CAO>> Databank. These decisions are left to the data engineer, as the approach is meant to be flexible enough to accommodate the data analysis requirements in the data model that best suits those analytical needs, while complying with the defined data modeling rules and patterns.

Variation_Databank does not have any additional relationship, besides the ones inherited from the application domain, outsourcing the descriptive families of <<CAO> Databank and <<CAO>> Variation. Although this AO only contains outsourced descriptive families without additional descriptive or analytical families, it could be used to perform event tracking analyses, like the variations available in some databanks, or as a coverage table that with <<CAO> Databank allow the identification of databanks that do not include a specific variation (as already pointed). These are usually known as factless fact tables in the Kimball's Dimensional Modeling [13] approach. The same result, with a different approach, can be achieved with a collection of Databank inside <<CAO>> Variation, if the relationship between Variation and Databank is not of high cardinality.

Bibliography_Reference is a candidate to denormalization. As it maintains a relationship with Statistical_Evidence, the information of the entity Bibliography_Reference is denormalized to the <<AO>> Statistical_Evidence as a descriptive family of this object. Additionally: i) as Databank and Bibliography_Reference are related in the application domain, and as Bibliography_Reference is denormalized to the<<AO>> Statistical_Evidence, a relationship between <<AO>> Statistical_Evidence and <<CAO>> Databank is established. This scenario is depicted in red in Fig. 5 and in Fig. 6; ii) as the entity Databank_Version has a relationship with Gene, but it was nested to the <<CAO>> Databank, this object will inherit the relationships of the entity Databank_Version, reason why <<CAO>> Databank is related with <<AO>> Gene, having databank_id and databank_version_id as outsourced descriptive families. This scenario is depicted in blue in Fig. 5 and in Fig. 6; iii) as the entity Variation and all its related entities are already present in the model as objects (independently of their type), there is only the need to establish the relationships between the objects.

Phenotype is denormalized to the <<AO>> Variation_Phenotype, Chromosome is denormalized both to the <<CAO>> Variation and <<AO>> Gene, while Population is denormalized to the <<AO>> Frequency. Lastly, Assembly is denormalized to Chromosome, that was previously included in the objects <<CAO>> Variation and <<AO>> Gene.

Regarding MOs, only Variation is used to propose a MO as an example, <<MO>> Variation Aggregates, which maintains a relationship with <<CAO>> Variation to access details of Variations, in case those are needed.

For the analytical attributes, those can be available in the domain conceptual model or can be created/derived by practitioners in accordance to the queries that need to be answered. Besides the explicit relationships included in the obtained data model

(Fig. 6), those linking AOs, CAOs, MOs and SOs, implicit relationships exist between these objects, allowing join operations between objects that share common attributes. For instance, to know how the variants are distributed in a specific gene, a join can be done between <<AO>> Gene and <<CAO>> Variation, since both share the attributes included in the Chromosome descriptive family.

Following the proposed method, the BGW_{CM} is now identified but not finished. This is seen as a continuous process that refresh the BDW structure as new data requirements or new data sources are available. Based on the method best practices, the data engineer can tune this model based on data access patterns or analytical goals.

Regarding the utility and value of the obtained model, also validating the proposed method, a preliminary analysis about cardiomyopathies was carried out. The data have been extracted and integrated in the Big Genome Warehouse implemented in Hive, using data from different sources and include information about nine well-known related phenotypes which genotypic characteristics are under study. The aim of this study is to identify patterns and similarities among the phenotypes that could help to understand the mechanisms of disease, a task that constitutes a bottleneck in the genomic analysis process. The results of the preliminary analysis, depicted in Fig. 7, show the relationships among the type of variants that occur in the affected chromosomes and the selected phenotypes.

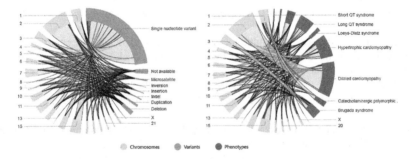

Fig. 7. Variants in the affected chromosomes and phenotypes

Based on these results, it can be concluded that the most interesting genetic components are chromosomes 2, 7 and 15 as these present a huge number of poly-morphisms, mainly associated with Dilated Cardiomyopathy. Following this premise, an extended analysis can be done, focusing on more specific genes and proteins, and helping the experts to extract meaningful insights about these areas of interest.

5   Conclusions

This work extends the knowledge in conceptual modeling applied to Big Data contexts, proposing a conceptual metamodel that formalizes the constructs for designing and implementing BDWs. This paper proposes a method that includes data modelling rules and patterns that guide practitioners from the conceptual metamodel to a specific conceptual model. Due to the challenges of the Genomics domain, the method was demonstrated in this context, being able to provide the Big Genome Warehouse Conceptual Model. As future work, the method must be extended to consider the evolution of the data models when new business processes, data sources or analytical requirements are available. Additionally, best practices must be addressed for the definition of partition or bucketing keys, as these impact the system performance.

Acknowledgements. This work has been supported by FCT – *Fundação para a Ciên-cia e Tecnologia* within the Project Scope: UID/CEC/00319/2019, the Doctoral scholarship PD/BDE/135100/2017 and European Structural and Investment Funds in the FEDER component, through the Operational Competitiveness and Internationalization Programme (COMPETE 2020) [Project nº 039479; Funding Reference: POCI-01-0247-FEDER-039479]. We also thank both the Spanish State Research Agency and the Generalitat Valenciana under the projects DataME TIN2016-80811-P, ACIF/2018/171, and PROMETEO/2018/176. Icons made by Freepik, from www.flaticon.com.

References

1. Krishnan, K.: Data Warehousing in the Age of Big Data. Morgan Kaufmann is an imprint of Elsevier, Amsterdam (2013)
2. Santos, M.Y., Costa, C.: Big Data: Concepts, Warehousing and Analytics. River Publishers, Aalborg (2020)
3. Cuzzocrea, A., Moussa, R.: Multidimensional database modeling: literature survey and research agenda in the big data era. In: 2017 International Symposium on Networks, Computers and Communications (ISNCC), pp. 1–6 (2017)
4. Di Tria, F., Lefons, E., Tangorra, F.: Design process for big data warehouses. In: 2014 International Conference on Data Science and Advanced Analytics (DSAA), pp. 512–518. IEEE (2014)
5. Dehdouh, K., Bentayeb, F., Boussaid, O., Kabachi, N.: Using the column oriented NoSQL model for implementing big data warehouses. In: Proceedings of the International Conference on Parallel and Distributed Processing Techniques and Applications (PDPTA) (2015)
6. Bézivin, J.: On the unification power of models. Softw. Syst. Model. **4**(2), 171–188 (2005). https://doi.org/10.1007/s10270-005-0079-0
7. Reyes Román, J.F., Pastor, Ó., Casamayor, J.C., Valverde, F.: Applying conceptual modeling to better understand the human genome. In: Comyn-Wattiau, I., Tanaka, K., Song, I.-Y., Yamamoto, S., Saeki, M. (eds.) ER 2016. LNCS, vol. 9974, pp. 404–412. Springer, Cham (2016). https://doi.org/10.1007/978-3-319-46397-1_31
8. Embley, D.W., Liddle, S.W.: Big data—conceptual modeling to the rescue. In: Ng, W., Storey, V.C., Trujillo, J.C. (eds.) ER 2013. LNCS, vol. 8217, pp. 1–8. Springer, Heidelberg (2013). https://doi.org/10.1007/978-3-642-41924-9_1
9. Giebler, C., Gröger, C., Hoos, E., Schwarz, H., Mitschang, B.: Modeling data lakes with data vault: practical experiences, assessment, and lessons learned. In: Laender, A.H.F., Pernici, B., Lim, E.-P., de Oliveira, J.P.M. (eds.) ER 2019. LNCS, vol. 11788, pp. 63–77. Springer, Cham (2019). https://doi.org/10.1007/978-3-030-33223-5_7
10. Gil, D., Song, I.-Y.: Modeling and management of big data: challenges and opportunities. Future Gener. Comput. Syst. **63**, 96–99 (2016)

11. Di Tria, F., Lefons, E., Tangorra, F.: GrHyMM: a graph-oriented hybrid multidimensional model. In: De Troyer, O., Bauzer Medeiros, C., Billen, R., Hallot, P., Simitsis, A., Van Mingroot, H. (eds.) ER 2011. LNCS, vol. 6999, pp. 86–97. Springer, Heidelberg (2011). https://doi.org/10.1007/978-3-642-24574-9_12
12. Santos, M.Y., Costa, C.: Data warehousing in big data: from multidimensional to tabular data models. In: Proceedings of the Ninth International C* Conference on Computer Science & Software Engineering, pp. 51–60. ACM, New York (2016)
13. Kimball, R., Ross, M.: The Data Warehouse Toolkit: The Definitive Guide to Dimensional Modeling. Wiley, Hoboken (2013)
14. Costa, C., Santos, M.Y.: Evaluating several design patterns and trends in big data warehousing systems. In: Krogstie, J., Reijers, H.A. (eds.) CAiSE 2018. LNCS, vol. 10816, pp. 459–473. Springer, Cham (2018). https://doi.org/10.1007/978-3-319-91563-0_28
15. Santos, M.Y., Costa, C., Galvão, J., Andrade, C., Pastor, O., Marcén, A.C.: Big data warehousing for efficient, integrated and advanced analytics - visionary paper. In: Cappiello, C., Ruiz, M. (eds.) CAiSE 2019. LNBIP, vol. 350, pp. 215–226. Springer, Cham (2019). https://doi.org/10.1007/978-3-030-21297-1_19

Automating Data Integration in Adaptive and Data-Intensive Information Systems

João Galvão[1]($\boxtimes$) , Ana Leon[2] , Carlos Costa[1] ,
Maribel Yasmina Santos[1] , and Óscar Pastor López[2]

[1] ALGORITMI Research Centre, University of Minho, Guimarães, Portugal
{joao.galvao,carlos.costa,maribel}@dsi.uminho.pt
[2] Research Center on Software Production Methods (PROS), Universitat
Politècnica de València, Valencia, Spain
{aleon,opastor}@pros.upv.es

Abstract. Data acquisition is no longer a problem for organizations, as many efforts have been performed in automating data collection and storage, providing access to a wide amount of heterogeneous data sources that can be used to support the decision-making process. Nevertheless, those efforts were not extended to the context of data integration, as many data transformation and integration tasks such as entity and attribute matching remain highly manual. This is not suitable for complex and dynamic contexts where Information Systems must be adaptative enough to mitigate the difficulties derived from the frequent addition and removal of sources. This work proposes a method for the automatic inference of the appropriate data mapping of heterogeneous sources, supporting the data integration process by providing a semantic overview of the data sources, with quantitative measures of the confidence level. The proposed method includes both technical and domain knowledge and has been evaluated through the implementation of a prototype and its application in a particularly dynamic and complex domain where data integration remains an open problem, i.e., genomics.

Keywords: Big Data · Data integration · Schema matching · Similarity measures

1 Introduction

Data is becoming more and more relevant as decision support in organizations can benefit from retrieving value from the vast amounts of data that are nowadays collected from a wide range of data sources. Many efforts in automating data collection and storage provided the context to have access to a wide range of data sources that can be used to support the decision needs of organizations. Nevertheless, those efforts were not extended to the context of data integration, as many data transformation and integration tasks remain highly manual. This problem is even more critical when we move to a Big Data context in which the volume, variety and velocity of data impose several challenges to this data integration needs.

© Springer Nature Switzerland AG 2020
M. Themistocleous et al. (Eds.): EMCIS 2020, LNBIP 402, pp. 20–34, 2020.
https://doi.org/10.1007/978-3-030-63396-7_2

The problem that motivates this work occurs when new data sources become available and there is the need to integrate this new data into existing data systems. This problem is amplified when those data sources need to be added and removed, in highly dynamical domains due to the variability of the available repositories. In those cases, data engineers need to inspect those data sources to identify the available attributes, their possible values and distribution, assess their quality and then think about their integration in the destination systems. Parts of this work are supported by several tools that can automate data transformation and integration tasks, but data pipelines definition and data modeling (and remodeling) are tasks that are deeply connected to the business knowledge of the data engineer, being often manually performed and highly time consuming.

To overcome these limitations, this work proposes a method for the automatic inference of the appropriate data mapping of new data sources, supporting the data integration process between these data sources and the corresponding destination systems. This method supports data engineers in this process, providing a semantic overview of the data sources, with various quantitative measures of the confidence level of the relationships between the data, taking as input the data sources and the characteristics (e.g., possible values and data distribution) of their several attributes.

This paper is organized as follows. Section 2 presents the related work. Section 3 describes the method for data integration. Section 4 addresses the demonstration case in the genomics field, while Sect. 5 presents the obtained results, and concludes with some proposals of future work.

2   Related Work

In data-intensive systems, general data processing approaches include data extraction, transformation and management with the purpose of making available information to the user [1]. In a Data Warehouse, a data system built to consolidate and make available relevant information for decision support, data from different sources goes through a complex process of data integration that ensures a unified and coherent view of the organizational or application domain data.

Nowadays, with the advent of Big Data, new challenges emerge in Data Warehousing or other data storage systems, as the volume, variety, or velocity of the data require performant solutions able to deal with these data characteristics [2]. In this context, data storage systems need to be seen as flexible, scalable and highly performant systems that use Big Data techniques and technologies to support mixed and complex analytical workloads (e.g., streaming analysis, ad hoc querying, data visualization, data mining, simulations) in several emerging contexts [3]. The data understanding and integration tasks are generally manual-based, supported by tools that give some hints about the available data, but that miss an overall and integrated approach about the data and their characteristics and how a semantic integration of the data sources can be made. Matching entities and attributes of an application domain is usually a human-based time consuming task, which is not suitable for Big Data contexts [4] that must consider highly dynamic environments with data needs that can add or remove data sources in a very dynamic way due to the variability of the available repositories.

The work of [5] highlights a road map for researching in Big Data Management, including data integration and data matching issues. In [6], the authors argue that data matching can be defined as the challenge of proposing a match between elements of two different datasets, with the aim of proposing a unified dataset based on datasets developed and made available in an independent way.

Based in [6, 7], some matching technics are enumerated: (1) Schema matching – based on the comparison between data schemas; (2) Graph matching – based on the comparison of the relations between different elements of the schemas; (3) Usage-based matching – based on the databases' logs that show the users' frequent joins between different datasets; (4) Linguistic matching – based on the name or the description of the elements using similarity on strings; (5) Auxiliary matching – using dictionaries and incompatibility lists; (6) Instance-based matching – using the elements statistics and metadata similarity analysis; and (7) Constraint-based matching – based on data types, values' distributions, foreign keys, unique values, among other constrains.

These different techniques have different degrees of compliance with the data integration tasks, namely in the accuracy and utility of the results. Namely, techniques that address the content of the data tend to have better results, such as the (1) Cosine, (2) Jaccard, (3) Jaro-Winkler, and (4) Levenshtein [8–12] measures.

Due to the characteristics of those measures, mainly analyzing data content in a highly detailed way and comparing all pairs of possible combinations, they may not be the most suited ones for Big Data contexts, if the objective is to compare all pairs of strings and the characters inside them. In some techniques, instead of comparing all sequences of characters, if the comparison is made between strings, the computation of the similarity can be enhanced. This is the case of the Jaccard Index. Based on some of these well-known measures, Zhu et al. [13] present the Set Containment similarity measure, analyzing if a new dataset is contained in an existing one, a measure that is helpful in Big Data contexts. Although the utility of this measure, it cannot be used in an isolated way, as the complexity of the Big Data domain, with a high diversity of new data sources, requires the use of an integrated and automated approach.

In the last years, the scientific community has been addressing the data integration challenge, proposing some works with interesting results. The work of [14] states that the main issues in this area are related with the use of different names and structures for describing the same information. So, the authors propose the use of semantic dictionaries to overcome this problem and verified that, although the obtained time reduction, the dictionary is specific and for a broader use it requires the definition of new ontologies by domain experts. Moreover, a set of data integration frameworks based on ontologies, for unified multidimensional models, are presented in [15, 16].

A semi-automatic approach for Data Warehouses integration with similarity measures applied at a syntactic, semantic and structural level is proposed in [17]. The results of this work show that the proposed similarity methods are not adequate for vast amounts of data, as the ones existing in Big Data contexts.

The KAYAK framework [18] aims to help data scientists in the definition and optimization of the data preparation processes for Data Lakes. This framework uses the available metadata to calculate similarity measures like joinability and affinity. The usage of metadata for the integration of data in Big Data contexts is also explored in [19]. Although their capability to work in Big Data contexts, these works do not address the problem of adapting existing data models and repositories, in a dynamic way, in order to adjust these models and repositories to new data requirements and decision-support needs.

Having addressed the related work and the main limitations of the existing approaches, this paper presents a method for data integration in Big Data contexts that makes use of several similarity measures to identify the inter datasets similarity in an automated way. This method is supported by a prototype that computes the measures and maps the several attributes, in an approach that supports the integration of the several external data sources and in the integration of those data sources with existing data systems.

3 Data Integration in Adaptive and Data-Intensive Information Systems

The method for data integration here proposed assumes that in a Big Data context there is the continuous need for searching new data sources relevant to the organization, application domain or problem at hands. Those data sources are then extracted, analyzed (applying the similarity measures), transformed, validated and loaded to a destination data system that has a unified and coherent view of the data. As the structured practice of this method is here instantiated and evaluated through the implementation of a prototype and its application to a demonstration case, respectively, this section embeds the structured practices proposed for the method in a prototype, presenting its system architecture, with its several components, interfaces and data flows. For the several components, the main technologies used in their implementation are also pointed.

3.1 System Architecture

The Domain Knowledge side, that can be considered an external component of the Data Integration system (Fig. 1), aims to include semantic knowledge in the method using knowledge obtained from a Domain Expert and/or Conceptual Schema. The Conceptual Schema is a domain dependent data model, which may already exist, including the relevant entities of the application domain, their attributes and how the entities are related to each other. It is important to highlight that this conceptual schema provides the context and the ontological background required to perform an accurate validation. In case this schema does not exist, or is not updated, the transformed data can be used to infer such schema or to update it.

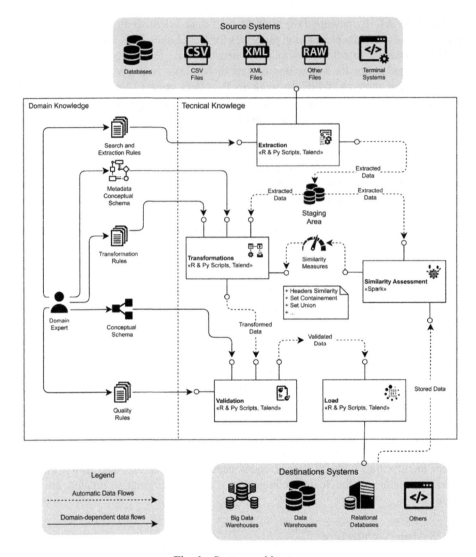

Fig. 1. System architecture

Metadata Conceptual Schemas are general knowledge about how the data should be organized, depending on the Destination System that will store the data. For example, if the data will be stored in a relational database, the Metadata Conceptual Model defines what elements a relational database should have, such as Tables, Attributes, Primary and Foreign Keys, among others. This information is needed to automatically devise the most suited data structure to store the data. In a Big Data context, where file systems, NoSQL, NewSQL, or other data systems can be used, this component ensures that a broad range of destination systems can be used.

For extracting the relevant data, a set of general Search and Extraction Rules needs to be defined by a domain expert, including some guidelines about the relevant data to be found and the extraction rules to be followed, in order to ensure that the data has some value, as the number of potential (existing) data sources is quite high. As an example, and using now the application domain in which the demonstration case will be based, the genomic domain and the supporting information system, the search rules can include guidelines that express the need to find out datasets about the DNA variants associated to the Alzheimer disease. An extraction rule can include constraints such as the format of the information to be retrieved (VCF files, XML, etc.) or the source systems to be considered, ensuring that only data from trusted data sources are used, such as well-known repositories in the genomic domain.

Beside the transformations made to map the attributes, other transformations are usually needed in any data context, in order to clean and to put the data in the appropriate data format. For that, the Transformation Rules includes the set of data-dependent transformation rules needed, such as adding or removing prefixes, normalizing Booleans, among others. Also, dependent on the Domain Knowledge are the Quality Rules, making explicit quality measures that the data must comply in order to be considered in the data integration method. These quality rules can express general data quality measures like handling missing values, noise, outliers, among others.

Looking for relevant data, the proposed method looks for external data sources, collecting data from those systems (Source Systems), using different technological approaches that can include several database drivers, Web Services that can send the output as CSV, XML or other raw format, and Terminal Systems like production machines able to send data in real-time.

Regarding the Technical knowledge, the Extraction component uses the information made available in the Search and Extraction Rules, extracting the identified data into the Staging Area, which in the case of the proposed prototype uses the Hadoop Distributed File System. This Extraction component can be implemented using different scripting languages or specific applications like Talend Open Studio for Big Data, the case in this prototype.

The Metadata Conceptual Schema, the Extracted Data, the Transformation Rules, and the Similarity Measures are inputs of the Transformation component, that will do the transformations needed to map the Extracted Data to the Destination Systems, integrating those external data sources between them and, additionally, with the data already available in the Destination Systems. The Transformation component can be implemented using a scripting language or any available Extraction, Transformation and Loading (ETL) tool, such as Talend.

The Similarity Assessment uses a set of similarity measures to compare two datasets and returns a graph of possible data matches and the corresponding Similarity Measures. As one of the main goals of this work is the use of the similarity measures to automatically identify the data matches, the Similarity Assessment component is further detailed in the next sub-section.

The Validation component uses the Transformed Data, the Quality Rules and the domain Conceptual Schema (when available) to run validation tasks that ensure that the data to be stored in the Destination Systems comply with the domain needs. The Quality Rules can have a lower or higher degree of complexity, requiring different approaches when handling them. In this method, it is proposed that the rules are expressed in a scripting language, in order to be automatically used by the Validation component.

After all the Validation procedures are completed, the Load component is used to send the data to the Destination Systems. This component can be implemented using a scripting language or an ETL tool.

Finally, the Destination Systems component includes the data repositories used as storage components. Several storage technologies can be used, depending on the data characteristics, volume of the data or even organizational technological constraints.

3.2   Similarity Assessment

Given the nature of this work, propose a method for data integration in Big Data contexts, there is the need to identify and implement the similarity measures that allow an automatic data integration process. This component depicted in Fig. 1, central in the proposed method, is now detailed in Fig. 2. The Similarity Assessment component will produce a set of measures that indicate if two attributes are related and, therefore, they can be joined, mapped or merged.

The Similarity Assessment uses new data (Extracted Data) and already existing data (Stored Data), when available in the Destination Systems, comparing the headers (name of the attributes) and the content (different values for those attributes) for the different attributes and computing a set of similarity measures, such as Headers Similarity, Set Containment and Jaccard Index. These are then combined in order to evaluate the similarity of the data sets and how their integration could be achieved. This semantic knowledge is stored in a Similarity Graph. The graph includes edges to express relationships between the attributes and the corresponding computed measures.

In order to support the adequate computation of Headers Similarity, the headers need to be parsed. The rules here applied are defined in the Parsing Rules, and can include tasks such as removing all spaces, removing all special characters, renaming to lowercase, among others. The Headers Similarity computation is done using the Cosine Similarity Measure, which is suitable for contexts where the comparison of a few strings is needed [8].

The analysis of the Content Similarity has two elements that compute three measures. The Set Containment is useful to identify the different data flows that can be followed when looking into the integration of different data sets. For this, the Set Containment measure proposed by Zhu et al. [13] is applied bidirectionally, measuring the set containment from X to Y (Eq. 1) and from Y to X (Eq. 2), as when several external data sources are available, different paths of integration can be followed.

$$SCx(X, Y) = \frac{X \cap Y}{X} \tag{1}$$

$$SCy(X, Y) = \frac{X \cap Y}{Y} \tag{2}$$

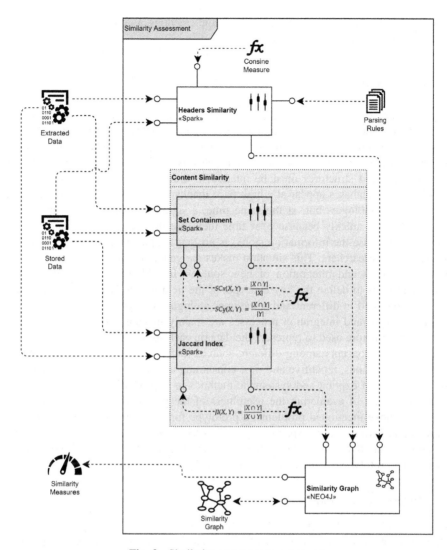

Fig. 2. Similarity assessment component

The use of the Jaccard Index (Eq. 3) is to verify the shared data values between the different attributes of the analyzed data sets.

$$JI(X, Y) = \frac{X \cap Y}{X \cup Y} \tag{3}$$

The implementation of this Similarity Assessment component was done in Spark, using a computational distributed Hadoop platform, and makes available a CSV file with the pairs of all compared attributes and the corresponding computed measures, as well as a Cypher Script that can be used for implementing a graph database with this semantic knowledge in Neo4J.

4 Demonstration

The demonstration case used to validate the Similarity Assessment component is based on the genomic domain, which is characterized by its complexity, what means that the information required to succeed in a complex research is not usually available in only one data source. Frequently, several heterogeneous public databases with different sizes, formats and structures must be queried in order to join all the puzzle pieces together. New databases appear at a high pace thanks to the development of powerful sequencing technologies but, at the same time, a significant number of sources can become obsolete quickly because over time they lose the technological maintenance required or because the information stored is no longer updated affecting its potential usefulness for researchers. This situation makes the genomic domain very dynamic in terms of analysis and integration of new sources. In addition, the lack of a clear ontological basis to define the key concepts of the field means that the same concept can be represented in different and sometimes ambiguous ways.

This analysis and integration processes are mainly manual, which require a deep study of the structure used to represent the data on each source, as well as the mapping of the common concepts among different sources (name, format, etc.). Consequently, the process is tedious, repetitive and time consuming as well as prone to human errors due to the lack of explicit and systematic methods to support it.

With the aim of evaluating the usefulness of the proposed method to help mitigating the above-mentioned problems, a prototype for the Similarity Assessment was developed in Java to run on Apache Spark. This technology was chosen to be capable to deal with data that has Big Data characteristics. The demonstration will be done by running the prototype for the datasets presented in the next subsection.

4.1 Datasets Description

For this work four datasets coming from different sources have been used. The information of each dataset represents DNA variants associated to the risk of suffering Alzheimer's Disease. Each variant is mainly characterized by its structural information (its location in the genome), the change that occurs and the statistical evidence regarding the studies performed over specific populations. Each database provides a different number of attributes that must be integrated in order to provide a global information system that can support the genetic diagnosis of a patient. Next, a brief description of each dataset is provided.

The Ensembl Dataset was extracted from the Ensembl database, developed as a joint project between EMBL-EBI and the Wellcome Trust Sanger Institute. It is composed of 36 attributes that represent data about the location of each variant in the genome, its pathogenicity and statistical information about the different studies found in the literature. Furthermore, the dataset that has called AlzForum has been extracted from the AlzForum database, a repository specialized in the different types of

Alzheimer's Disease and its genetic causes. The dataset includes 14 attributes with data about the location of each variant, its pathogenicity and identifiers to external bibliography resources. This dataset does not include statistical information about the mentioned studies. GWAS dataset was extracted from the GWAS Catalog database, a repository that contains data about different genotype-phenotype association studies. It is composed of 38 attributes focused on the characteristics of each study regarding statistical significance, population and type of study performed. The dataset does not contain information about the pathogenicity of the variants. A least one, the DisGeNet dataset, has been extracted from the DisGeNet database, a repository that contains information about DNA variants associated to different human diseases. It is composed of 16 attributes about the location of the variants in the genome, specific statistics to measure the research interest (relevance) of each variant and identifiers to external bibliography resources.

4.2   Similarity Graph

For the demonstration, four similarity measures were calculated: Header Similarity (HS), Set Containment in both directions (SCx, SCy) and Jaccard Index (JI). The HS measure uses the Cosine Measure comparing the characters inside each header.

The computation of all similarity measures was done for all pairs of attributes between all datasets pairs, resulting in a graph with 1647 relationships between attributes that score at least one measure with a value higher than zero. Due to the complexity of showing the measures in a graph with this amount of relationships, a sample of the Similarity Graph is presented in Fig. 3, including 3 nodes and 3 relationships. The label of each node is the name of the attribute, while the dataset is identified by the pattern of the node's line. The relationships are named as *has_similarity*, meaning that at least one of the similarity measures has a computed value higher than zero, and the measures are represented as a relationship's property.

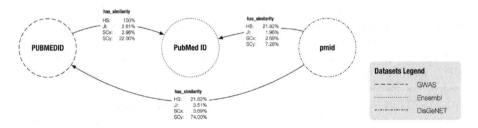

Fig. 3. Sample of the similarity graph

5   Discussion and Conclusions

In order to evaluate the results obtained after the analysis of the four datasets, a comparison between the Similarity Graph and a manual mapping performed by a domain expert was done. With the aim of increasing the legibility when presenting the

results, a filter was applied removing an extensive set of low similarity values: HS >
20 OR (JI > 0 AND SCx > 0 AND SCy > 0).

5.1 Analysis and Discussion of Results

The intersection between the manually mapped graph and the Similarity Graph is
presented in Fig. 4. The result is a set of subgraphs containing 31 nodes and 36
relationships, extending the one presented in Fig. 3, by adding relationships with full
lines that represent the relationships that were manually and automatically detected,
and the dashed lines that represent the relationships that were only manually detected.
Using were identified, even in a complex context were the names of the attributes are
very different. Take, for example, the name of the variant: *Variant name, snpid, SNPS*
and *ID*. By comparing the manually detected relationships (36) with those automatically detected (28), a match rate of 77.7% was achieved, representing a noteworthy
result for a first approach. Other particularly difficult attributes, such as those associated
with the similar and approved using the domain restrictions. This approach, the relevant
entities phenotype, were partially identified. The first analysis of the graph points that
some of the missed relationships could be inferred by transitivity. For example, if
Variant name is similar to *SNPS* and *SNPS* is similar to *ID*, would not be *Variant name*
similar to *ID*? Also, after sharing the results with the domain expert, the pairs (*Reference, Minor allele (ALL)*) and (*Alt, Minor allele (ALL)*) that were not manually
identified, were considered required to do the integration of the different datasets.

To better understand the identified false positives, further analyses were made in
other to identify the False Positive Challenges (FPC). In this context, CM (Content
Measures) stands for all content similarity measures considered in this work (JI, SCx
and SCy). All pairs with HS = 100 and CM = 0 automatically classified were also
manually classified, but there are cases with HS values around 70%–80% that alone
cannot be used to say that two attributes are similar. For example, the pair of attributes
Disease and *diseaseType* with HS = 78% and CM = 0 do not match, as one is the
name of the disease and the other its type (FPC1). Also, comparisons with attributes of
low cardinality tend to increase the number of false positives (FPC2). Higher thresholds
for the metrics reduce the number of the False Positives, but also increase the number
of unmatched pairs (FPC3).

Furthermore, the analysis of results showed the Unmatched Pair Challenges
(UPC) identified in this domain: i) some attributes contain more information than
needed. For instance, the attribute *STRONGEST SNP-RISK ALLELE* has values like
rs144573434-T, including both an alternative allele and a variant identifier. This
situation was noticed by the human domain expert when performing the manual
mapping who identified that the attribute is referring to the allele (UPC1); ii) the range
of values for the attributes are different. For example, the variant identifiers of two
datasets associated to different types of diseases or chromosomes (UPC2); iii) the free
writing of attributes, with values that do not match (UPC3); iv) the lack of patterns or
standards to represent the data that needs prefixes or any other coding (UPC4).

A set of suggestions for future work will be made next in other to overcome the
identified challenges: (FPC1) The addition of a new dimension of analysis for the HS,
like the use of a semantic analysis using word dictionaries, as those could improve the

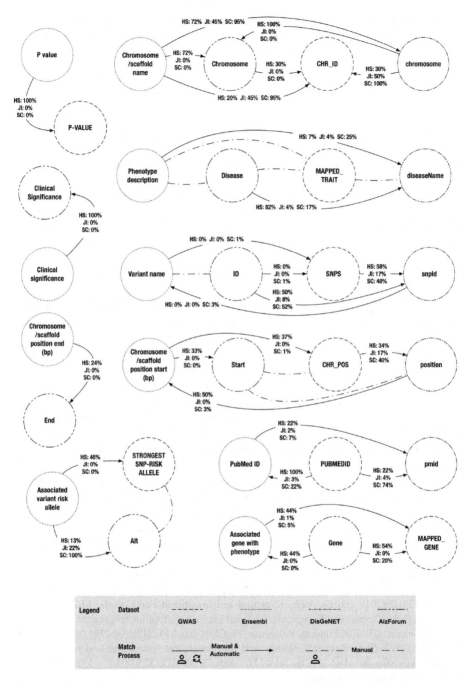

Fig. 4. Graph with manual and automatic mapping relationships

reliability of the HS; (FPC2) Include in the Content Similarity some basic statistics such as the number of district values, frequency distribution, among others; (FPC3) Identify relevant thresholds for filtering the obtained results; (UPC1) Apply rules for data cleaning; (UPC2) Analyze the syntax of the possible values for the attributes with Frequent Pattern Mining techniques (for instance, if two attributes have different values like `rs123456` and `rs654321`, they do not automatically match, but they share the same prefix/syntax, `rs<number>`, meaning that they are likely similar); (UPC3) Identify additional string content measures suitable for Big Data contexts, able to analyze if there is a match between the intersection of the characters of two strings, detecting similarities between two different strings with the same meaning (like `late-onset Alzheimer disease` and `Alzheimer disease`); (UPC4) Identify a set of rules for data cleaning and transformation using frequent pattern detection.

Those suggestions for possible improvements could be applied to the proposed method without the need to adapt it or extend it, just by adding those new metrics or rules.

5.2   Conclusions

This paper highlighted the challenge of the manual effort needed for data integration tasks, namely in highly dynamical domains due to the variability of the available repositories. This work proposes a method capable of automating data integration tasks in adaptive and data-intensive information systems. The instantiation of the proposed method was implemented in Apache Spark to support Big Data contexts.

The evaluation was made by comparing the manual and automatic mapping of the attributes present in four datasets from a particularly complex and dynamic domain: genomics. Besides being satisfactory and showing a high matching rate, the results highlighted some challenges that need to be further addressed, like the occurrence of false positives and the threshold that can be considered to automatically have a certain degree of confidence on the obtained results.

Some improvements were identified for future work, aiming to increase the match rate, highlighting the concept of transitivity that infer the missed relationships, the use of word dictionaries to have a semantic dimension of analysis and the syntax analysis. With these future improvements this method will be applied in other contexts, such as manufacturing, to better understand how the method handles data from other domains.

Acknowledgements. This work has been supported by FCT – *Fundação para a Ciên-cia e Tecnologia* within the Project Scope: UID/CEC/00319/2019, the Doctoral scholarship PD/BDE/135100/2017 and European Structural and Investment Funds in the FEDER compo-nent, through the Operational Competitiveness and Internationalization Programme (COMPETE 2020) [Project nº 039479; Funding Reference: POCI-01-0247-FEDER-039479]. We also thank both the Spanish State Research Agency and the Generalitat Valenciana under the projects DataME TIN2016-80811-P, ACIF/2018/171, and PROMETEO/2018/176. Icons made by Freepik, from www.flaticon.com.

References

1. Krishnan, K.: Data Warehousing in the Age of Big Data. Newnes (2013)
2. Vaisman, A., Zimányi, E.: Data warehouses: next challenges. In: Aufaure, M.-A., Zimányi, E. (eds.) eBISS 2011. LNBIP, vol. 96, pp. 1–26. Springer, Heidelberg (2012). https://doi.org/10.1007/978-3-642-27358-2_1
3. Costa, C., Santos, M.Y.: Evaluating several design patterns and trends in big data warehousing systems. In: Krogstie, J., Reijers, H.A. (eds.) CAiSE 2018. LNCS, vol. 10816, pp. 459–473. Springer, Cham (2018). https://doi.org/10.1007/978-3-319-91563-0_28
4. Bellahsene, Z., Bonifati, A., Duchateau, F., Velegrakis, Y.: On Evaluating Schema Matching and mapping. In: Bellahsene, Z., Bonifati, A., Rahm, E. (eds.) Schema Matching and Mapping, pp. 253–291. Springer, Heidelberg (2011). https://doi.org/10.1007/978-3-642-16518-4_9
5. Santos, M.Y., Costa, C., Galvão, J., Andrade, C., Pastor, O., Marcén, A.C.: Enhancing big data warehousing for efficient, integrated and advanced analytics - visionary paper. In: Cappiello, C., Ruiz, M. (eds.) CAiSE Forum 2019. LNBIP, vol. 350, pp. 215–226. Springer, Heidelberg (2019). https://doi.org/10.1007/978-3-030-21297-1_19
6. Bernstein, P.A., Madhavan, J., Rahm, E.: Generic schema matching. Ten Years Later. PVLDB **4**, 695–701 (2011)
7. Madhavan, J., Bernstein, P.A., Rahm, E.: Generic schema matching with cupid. In: Proceedings of the 27th International Conference on Very Large Data Bases, pp. 49–58. Morgan Kaufmann Publishers Inc., San Francisco (2001)
8. Shirkhorshidi, A.S., Aghabozorgi, S., Wah, T.Y.: A comparison study on similarity and dissimilarity measures in clustering continuous data. PLoS ONE **10**, e0144059 (2015). https://doi.org/10.1371/journal.pone.0144059
9. Xiao, C., Wang, W., Lin, X., Shang, H.: Top-k set similarity joins. In: Proceedings of the 2009 IEEE International Conference on Data Engineering, pp. 916–927. IEEE Computer Society, Washington, DC (2009). https://doi.org/10.1109/ICDE.2009.111
10. Levenshtein, V.I.: Binary codes capable of correcting deletions, insertions and reversals. Soviet Phys. Doklady **10**, 707 (1966)
11. Jaccard, P.: Etude comparative de la distribution florale dans une portion des Alpes et du Jura. Impr. Corbaz, Lausanne (1901)
12. Winkler, W.E.: String Comparator Metrics and Enhanced Decision Rules in the Fellegi-Sunter Model of Record Linkage [microform]/William E. Winkler. Distributed by ERIC Clearinghouse, [Washington, D.C.] (1990)
13. Zhu, E., Nargesian, F., Pu, K.Q., Miller, R.J.: LSH ensemble: internet-scale domain search. Proc. VLDB Endow. **9**, 1185–1196 (2016). https://doi.org/10.14778/2994509.2994534
14. Banek, M., Vrdoljak, B., Tjoa, A.M.: Using ontologies for measuring semantic similarity in data warehouse schema matching process. In: 2007 9th International Conference on Telecommunications, pp. 227–234 (2007). https://doi.org/10.1109/CONTEL.2007.381876
15. Deb Nath, R.P., Hose, K., Pedersen, T.B.: Towards a programmable semantic extract-transform-load framework for semantic data warehouses. In: Proceedings of the ACM Eighteenth International Workshop on Data Warehousing and OLAP, pp. 15–24. ACM, New York (2015). https://doi.org/10.1145/2811222.2811229
16. Abdellaoui, S., Nader, F.: Semantic data warehouse at the heart of competitive intelligence systems: design approach. In: 2015 6th International Conference on Information Systems and Economic Intelligence (SIIE), pp. 141–145 (2015). https://doi.org/10.1109/ISEI.2015.7358736

17. El Hajjamy, O., Alaoui, L., Bahaj, M.: Semantic integration of heterogeneous classical data sources in ontological data warehouse. In: Proceedings of the International Conference on Learning and Optimization Algorithms: Theory and Applications, pp. 36:1–36:8. ACM, New York (2018). https://doi.org/10.1145/3230905.3230929
18. Maccioni, A., Torlone, R.: KAYAK: a framework for just-in-time data preparation in a data lake. In: Krogstie, J., Reijers, H.A. (eds.) CAiSE 2018. LNCS, vol. 10816, pp. 474–489. Springer, Cham (2018). https://doi.org/10.1007/978-3-319-91563-0_29
19. Hai, R., Geisler, S., Quix, C.: Constance: an intelligent data lake system. In: Proceedings of the 2016 International Conference on Management of Data, pp. 2097–2100. ACM, New York (2016). https://doi.org/10.1145/2882903.2899389

Raising the Interoperability of Cultural Datasets: The Romanian Cultural Heritage Case Study

Ilie Cristian Dorobăț[(✉)] and Vlad Posea

"Politehnica" University of Bucharest, Bucharest, Romania
ilie.dorobat@stud.acs.upb.ro, vlad.posea@cs.pub.ro

Abstract. By means of Digital Libraries, entire archives can be made available to users at a click away; but due to the fact that the representation as accurate and as wide as possible of the events in which Cultural Heritage plays an essential role in understanding the past, the metadata aggregators must use data models that satisfy the demands of information. We present the workflow behind the eCHO Framework, a framework which allows users, on the one hand, to sanitize, normalize and interconnect data represented according to LIDO XML Schema, and on the other hand, to take advantage of the representation of metadata through the event-centric approach of Europeana Data Model. Eventually, it is presented the applicability of the use of this framework in the context of identifying the time periods in which took place the most important events in which the Romanian Cultural Heritage have been involved in, statistics that can be extended to the purpose of identifying the lifestyle of the population.

Keywords: Cultural heritage · Digital libraries · Linked data · LIDO · EDM

1 Motivation

Nowadays, when users need more accessible sources of information, digitalization is gaining more and more interest in any domain. Although digital libraries cannot be considered as a substitute for heritage collections, they are an important bridge between cultural heritage institutions and information consumers. The usefulness of digital libraries can be found in the behavior of regular users who needs to be informed about some certain cultural heritage objects (CHOs) that have caught their attention, as well as experts in the field, who need more complex and more accessible information sources.

By identifying the benefits of digitalization of the administrated heritage, cultural institutions have directed their resources towards adopting Linked Data. Unfortunately, for producing Linked Data, the smaller institutions depend on data aggregators such as Europeana [1]. Europeana[1] is the largest digital library in Europe encompassing over 60 million descriptions of CHOs hosted by different European cultural institutions, aggregating metadata acquired from more than 3,000 museums, galleries, libraries and

---

[1] https://www.europeana.eu/portal/en.

© Springer Nature Switzerland AG 2020
M. Themistocleous et al. (Eds.): EMCIS 2020, LNBIP 402, pp. 35–48, 2020.
https://doi.org/10.1007/978-3-030-63396-7_3

archives, hence offering an impressive collection of metadata regarding artworks, artefacts, books, films and music from the National Thesaurus of the European Union member states. For this, it uses an own ontology, the Europeana Data Model (EDM), based on which metadata are represented as a graph, being accessible not only through a user-friendly interface, but also via a programmatic one, by means of a SPARQL endpoint.

For representing metadata, EDM provides two approaches namely: i) *object-centric approach* in which the main focus is on the cultural object itself; ii) *event-centric approach* which allows the emphasize of the relationships between the CHO's described. Sadly, Europeana officially supports only the first approach [2], diminishing the power of digital representation of the CHOs, which, by their specific feature, carry historical connections which might be useful for the understanding of the past.

Due to that a wide part of the European cultural institutions (National Digital Library of Finland[2] [3], Athena Plus[3], German Digital Library[4], Digi Cult[5], etc.) which have digitalized their collection have used the Lightweight Information Describing Objects XML Schema (LIDO) [4], Enhancing the Digital Representation of Cultural Heritage Objects Framework (eCHO)[6] has been developed to facilitate the migration of the smaller institutions to Linked Data, rendering the analysis process more simplistic, focused more on querying the resources than on creating connections.

The current research captures the study done for extending the level of digitalization of cultural institutions which host CHOs, beginning from the presentation of the most relevant projects developed in this direction, followed in Sect. 3 by presenting the research direction. Section 4 is destinated for presenting the used datasets, Sect. 5 is dedicated to the presentation of the workflow behind the eCHO Framework, being followed by a short discussion of how data can be represented through the event-centric approach of EDM. Section 7 describes the most important challenges encountered during the development, followed by presenting of the analysis of the time periods in which the most important events in which Romanian CHOs have been involved, while the final section has been reserved for the presentation of the final remarks and of the direction of further development.

2   Related Work

During CIDOC 2012 Enriching Cultural Heritage conference, Tsalapati et al. presented a scientific study [5] which, on the one hand highlights the premises and stages identified by the authors for facilitating the transition of the datasets structured according to LIDO into Linked Data, and on the other hand exposes the sets of preliminary experiments regarding the interlinking of internal resources with external

---

[2] https://www.digime.fi/en.

[3] http://www.athenaplus.eu.

[4] https://www.deutsche-digitale-bibliothek.de.

[5] http://www.digicult-verbund.de.

[6] https://github.com/iliedorobat/enriching-cultural-heritage-metadata.

data sources like DBpedia or Eurostat. During the study, authors have analyzed the possibility of the direct mapping of the LIDO data structure in properties and classes specific to certain reputable ontologies as CIDOC CRM[7] and EDM.

Thus, starting from the Linked Data principles, in order to translate a dataset represented through a regular data structure, it is mandatory that the defined resources receive a unique identifier which can be extracted from the already existing data, or, when necessary, can be created a new one. The process continues with the identification of the LIDO elements which can be mapped down following the chosen data model, and for those which it is not possible, it has been suggested the defining of new properties and classes specific to the LIDO namespace through the extending of the already existing ones. In addition, for a more detailed representation of the resources, it is also conducted an experiment of mapping these elements in instances of the corresponding resources of the DBpedia knowledge base.

In [1, 4] the authors describe the direction that the Amsterdam Museum adopted towards the implementation of a data model which facilitates the interlinking of hosted collections with other sources of data. Hence, starting from its own digital data management system, the Adlib Museum[8], made the transition towards the EDM. As result, datasets benefited of an improvement regarding the quality of data by the increase of the consistency and interoperability between datasets supplied by different institutions.

Metadata Interoperability system (MINT)[9] provides services for harvesting, mapping and translation of metadata. The aggregation process begins with loading the metadata records in XML or CSV serialization, through one of the HTTP, FTP or OAI-PMH protocol available. After finalizing the loading of datasets, the users will use the visual mapping editor for mapping the records. The visual editor has also a navigation system both in the structure and data of the input scheme, as well as in the target one.

CARARE[10] is an aggregation service developed as an answer to the need of translation of the datasets regarding monuments, buildings, landscape areas and their representations, in a unique format, using as representation method the CARARE Metadata Schema. The system consists in two main components, namely: i) the MINT services used for data mapping and ingestion; ii) the Monument Repository (MORE). The latter is a service destined to store metadata aggregated by providers, facilitating the automatization of the metadata translation in the format used by Europeana for making available for harvesting via an OAI-PHM target [6].

3 Problem Statement

The digitalization of collections is a continuous process which allows cultural institutions migrate physical expositions to the virtual environment. For this, cultural institutions must follow and update datasets to the changes from the standard of the domain.

---

[7] http://www.cidoc-crm.org.

[8] https://www.axiell.com/solutions/product/adlib.

[9] http://mint-projects.image.ntua.gr/museu.

[10] https://pro.carare.eu/doku.php?id=start.

3.1   Research Questions

i. Which is the solution to the complete automatization of the translation process of metadata represented through LIDO into Linked Data?
ii. Which is the solution to the normalization of timestamps?
iii. How can we conserve the events in which cultural goods have been involved in using EDM as reference model?
iv. How can the data represented though LIDO be correlated to the new representation model?

3.2   Paper's Contribution

The present paper aims at offering an overview of the way in which, in the digitalization context, cultural heritage can benefit of the advantages of data migration into Linked Data. Furthermore, the main challenges encountered are analyzed, and in the end, it is presented a practical example of the use of the eCHO Framework for the classification of cultural objects according to different events in which they have been involved and according to the century.

During this process, data are sanitized, normalized, and interconnected; a specific element of this framework being represented by the use of the *event-centric approach* for the representation of the events in which cultural goods have been involved. Thus, unlike the Europeana portal, in which digital representation are targeted towards describing the cultural objects, users will also have the possibility of conserving the events in which a determined cultural object has been involved.

3.3   Research Limitations

An aspect which must be taken into consideration is that the eCHO Framework allows temporarily only the normalization of timestamps expressed in the Romanian language. Therefore, for the normalization of timestamps in other languages, either another model must be added, or this process must be externalized through a service.

Furthermore, the support offered by the framework is only in the direction of translating the records represented through LIDO into Linked Data, using the EDM's *event-centric approach*.

4   Data Source

INP is a Romanian National Public Entity whose objectives, according to the Government Decision no. 593/2011, are to administrate historical monuments to manage their restorative process, to ensure the legislative framework for the protection of historical monuments, as well as to create national databases for archaeological, cultural heritage, intangible cultural heritage and for the associated information resources.

The present research uses the datasets made available by INP on the public Romanian open data portal data.gov.ro[11]. These datasets are represented according to LIDO XML Schema, describing CHOs from a wide range of domains such as Archaeology; Art; Decorative art; Documents; Ethnography; The history of science and technology; History; Metalinguistics; Numismatics; Natural science.

5   Methodology Overview

The present section is reserved to the presentation of the eCHO workflow, followed by the motivation of the implementation of the Linked Data. Figure 1 depicts the process of translation of the metadata from LIDO to Linked Data, beginning with the parsing and storage of the metadata. For this, a standalone component was developed, the LIDO Parser[12], so that this component be used independently not only in this process of translation, but also in any other operations and analysis which users might need.

Once the metadata has been successfully parsed and stored, the process continues with the data curation. In this stage, the calendar dates and the time periods are normalized to a common pattern, the data used for creation of URIs is sanitized, and there are established links between concepts and other vocabularies. Finally, the prepared data is mapped to EDM and users will be able to charge and query the generated set of triplet's *subject-predicate-object* in the semantic data store.

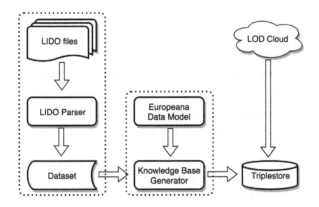

Fig. 1.   The eCHO framework workflow [7].

Even though LIDO is a standard which the online museum objects content creators can use it to represent metadata for describing the museum objects, facilitating the sharing and aggregation of collections and by providing a machine-readable solution for representing museum objects, an ontology offers more advantages in the representation and reuse of data, namely [8, 9]:

---

[11] https://data.gov.ro/dataset?organization=institutul-national-al-patrimoniului.

[12] https://github.com/iliedorobat/LIDO-Parser.

a) the represented knowledge may include semantic structures which detail and define their meaning;
b) the resources may be researched by using a SPARQL endpoint;
c) concepts defined in other ontologies may be reused.

6   Knowledge Base Representation

To represent the knowledge base, EDM makes available two approaches, namely: the object-centric and the event-centric. Like its name, the first approach highlights the description of the CHOs using a series of statements which provide direct links between the described CHO and its characteristics. The latter approach provides a higher level of representation of knowledge by changing the perspective of the description of the CHOs towards the characterization of the various events in which the CHOs have been involved in. Also, EDM allows the coexistence between the two approaches, which determines the increase of the level of detailing.

From a practical point of view, the generation of RDF graphs involve the generation of every RDF graph entity as instances of the classes which EDM uses for representing objects from the real-world. Specifically, for the semantic representation of the real-world objects, EDM considers the differences between the physical object and its digital representations, providing the following three core classes:

a) *edm:ProvidedCHO* for describing the characteristics of the physical objects;
b) *edm:WebResource* for describing the virtual representation of the represented physical object;
c) *ore:Aggregation* for connecting the physical objects to their digital representations.

Likewise, for ensuring a higher degree of detailing, EDM provides the following set of contextual classes as well, through which wider descriptions can be made:

a) *edm:Agent* for describing a private citizen;
b) *foaf:Organization* for describing a legal person (an institution, a governmental or non-governmental organization);
c) *edm:Event* which implements the event-centric approach itself is used for describing an event in which an actor or an object has been involved in;
d) *edm:Place* for describing spatial places;
e) *edm:TimeSpan* for describing time periods and dates;
f) *skos:Concept* for describing various concepts as thesauri, classifications, etc.

7   Data Challenges

Even though LIDO is a very popular standard in the field, which is used for the digital representation of the cultural objects from different domains such as architecture, history, history of technology, etc., the management of the metadata might be cumbersome as an XML schema is nothing else than document syntax constraint specifications and does not provide a method of representation of the connections between the resources. Therefore, the transition from the representation of data in XML format, to the representation based on ontology, is a natural stage for the increase of the degree of data representation.

Nevertheless, as in any other operation of improvement of the process of data representation through their translation using a data structure superior to the one previously used, during the translation process, different situations have been encountered which needed paying high attention to. Amongst the most important such of situations, hereafter called *challenges*, we list: i) timestamp normalization; ii) assigning the URIs for resources; iii) identifying similar resources; iv) handling the cardinality constraints; v) extending the EDM vocabulary.

7.1 Timestamp Normalization

A particular case of URIs definition is encountered in the *lido:displayDate* record type, through which are represented calendar dates and time periods associated to the events in which the CHOs have been involved in. Although, ideally, processing this type of data should not involve significant efforts, in practice, due to the fact the initial data collection was done by human operators without any nomenclator, these data have different shapes. An overview can be found in Table 1, which depicts the five types of time periods identified, starting with values which do not express in any way any type of time period, and continuing with timestamps.

Table 1. Types of time periods and their forms.

Type of time period	Example of time periods*	
unknown	189-45; dinastia xxv; nesemnat; grupa a iv-a; 1(838); 173 [1] etc.	
epoch	pleistocen; epoca de bronz; renaştere etc.	
date[a]	YMD:	1881-08-31; 1857 mai 10 etc.;
	DMY:	09.11.1518; 1 noiembrie 1624 etc.;
	MY:	ianuarie 632 etc.
timespans[b]	centuries:	s:; sec; sec.; secol; secolele; etc.
	millenniums:	mil; mil.; mileniul; mileniului; mileniile
years[c]		

[a]interval, simple date, separated by dash, dot or semicolon.
[b]interval, simple timespan, Arabic numbers, Roman numbers, parts of timespan*: ½; ¼; primul sfert; prima jumatate, etc.
[c]2–4 digits.
*the values are mentioned in the reference language – Romanian language.

As it can be noticed, in the case of calendar dates, these can be found in the format *year-month-day* (YMD), or *day-month-year* (DMY), or *month-year* (MY); all these formats having different forms according to the used separator and to the method the month is expressed. The biggest challenge is represented by the processing of time periods expressed in centuries and millenniums because these forms of representation of time periods are found in various formats. For example, there are cases when for their representation Roman numbers, as well as Arabic numbers are used, or the terms *"century"* and *"millennium"* are not used uniformly, different forms as *"sec"*, *"secol"*, *"secolele"*, etc. being used (all these forms are mentioned in the reference language – Romanian language).

Thus, in order to treat these cases, the use of regular expressions (regexes) has been embraced, through which similar data structures can be identified and regulated so that, the URIs will use only one shape of expressing timespans. Figure 2 depicts an example of regex, namely the regex used to identify chunks which describe periods of time expressed in centuries, using three different colors to highlight each portion of code.

The blue section of code identifies the sequences of characters through which the *"century"* word can be expressed in Romanian (e.g.: *"sec"*, *"secol"*, *"secole"*, *"secolele"*, etc.) and the presence of the prefix *"al"*, which is used in Romanian to express ordinal numbers. The green section depicts the part of the regex that recognizes both the punctuation marks which could be accidentally added by users, and the interval separator *"-"*. The last section identifies the Roman numerals, the suffix *"lea"* used in Romanian to express ordinal numbers and the sequences __AD__ (Anno Domini), respectively __BC__ (Before Christos). The latter is the result of pre-processing of the input using another set of rules which can identify this information.

Thus, we can identify a large series of chunks such as *"sec. iv a hr."*, *"sec. iv p. chr."*, *"sec. iv d chr."*, *"secolul iv"*, *"secolele iv - vii"*, etc. (*"a hr."*, *"p.hr."* and *"d hr."* are the unprocessed values of the sequences __AD__, respectively __BC__). This step of pre-processing is necessary to avoid the use of regexes in the querying data storages for the following considerations: i) the operations which involve regexes are known as being time consuming, especially considering that for the normalization of timestamps a large set of regexes need be applied; ii) users might omit the use of some regexes, which would lead to the alterations of the result.

```
(
    (sec[\w]*)
    ([\., ]+(al[\. ]+){0,1})*
)
[\.,;\?!\- ]*
(
    (
        ?<=
        (^|\A|[\.,;\?!\-(\[= ]+))
        [ivxlcdm]+
        (?=($|\z|[\.,;\?!\-)\] ]+)
    )
    (([- ]*lea){0,1}
    ([\.,;\?!\- ]*(__AD__|__BC__)){0,1}
)
```

Fig. 2. Regex used to identify centuries.

7.2   Assigning the URIs for Resources

Semantic Web, also known as Web of Data, is an improved shape of the Web, where the connections are no longer made between the documents, but directly between the resources. Hence, for the data representation, a standard of semantic knowledge representation, such as RDF, RDFS and OWL, must be used, which, unlike an XML schema, requires the identification of each resource by means of a unique reference. Moreover, since the Web of Data is not only a data storage, but also an environment which may be easily explored by both human operators as well as by machines, the resources identifiers must be URIs, so that the reading of such identifiers may be done easily by both categories of operators. Machines may be programmed to work with URIs, while human operators may identify and distinguish between URIs easier as these are used as names for things [10].

In order to exploit the initial datasets, it has been decided that, in case the LIDO record contains an URI which might describe the record, the former will be considered for use, otherwise, a new URI will be created. For instance, the value of the record *lido: webResourceComplexType* may be used as a candidate URI. As can be seen in Fig. 3, for creating a new URI, the chaining of the defined resource's namespace with the following three elements will be done [7]:

a) the type of defined resource;
b) an optional description, which can be used to delimit two or more elements from the real-world (e.g.: in the case of events, their type may be used);
c) the name of the represented object.

Also, because the name of the resource may contain spaces and special characters, they are replaced with the underscore character ("_"), so that the risk of exposure to security vulnerabilities will be lowered, and humans may easily read these identifiers.

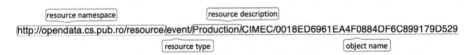

Fig. 3. Example of resource's URI.

7.3   Identifying Similar Resources

An XML schema, being only a set of rules for the constraint of the data representation, does not allow the definition of relations between objects, and in the lack of a unique identifier, the already defined resources cannot be reused. This means that the dataset will be polluted with duplicates of the objects which must be defined again for each record. Fortunately, the translating of LIDO into EDM will solve this problem, but to maintain a high level of data accuracy, it is necessary to identify and reuse the similar resources. By similarity is meant two or more resources which represent the same object from real-world, but which might describe it from different perspective.

For identifying the institutions which host the collection, it has been noted that the unicity is ensured through the value of the record type *lido:legalBodyID*, having the property *lido:type = "CIMEC"*. As far as the dataset's providers are concerned, they have been identified through the record type *lido:legalBodyWeblink*. The weblink can be used in safety for delimitating data providers between them because even if the institutions might have several weblinks, they tend to offer only one, so that there would be avoided confusions regarding the way of accessing the information over the Internet.

In the case of the political entities, these are identified in the LIDO datasets through records of the type *lido:partOfPlace*, having the property *lido:politicalEntity*. If the historical regions and counties are entities whose name is unique in a country, as far as the communes and localities are concerned, these might share the same name if they are part of different counties. Hence, to ensure their differentiation, the name of the county, respectively the name of the county and the name of the commune they are part of has been included in the URIs.

The last type of record which required consolidation operations is represented by the *lido:actorInRole*, which identifies the natural person (*lido:actor* record type) and their role (*lido:roleActor* record type) in the described event. Unfortunately, the only mandatory property is the *lido:actor*, in which, even though the LIDO allows the recording of an unique identifier of the actor through the means of the record type *lido:actorID*, the latter is optional, the only mandatory property being the list of the names an actor might have (*lido:actorNameSet* record type). Therefore, except the name and, eventually of the role, there are no other elements that can be used to disambiguate more actors which share the same name.

7.4   Handling the Cardinality Constraints

Due to the specificities which the EDM has in contrast with LIDO, the translation of the data might have implications for how the described CHOs are represented. A challenge in this respect is to correlate the data on the new representation model, process aiming at the identification of the most appropriate structure of the target data model, which will represent, as accurate as possible, the CHO described through LIDO.

Nevertheless, in some cases, LIDO allows to record an undetermined number of values, but the properties equivalent to EDM restrict the record of only one value per language. For example, in the case of the presenting of an organization, an instance of the class *foaf:Organization* is created, which, according to EDM accepts a single identifier, but, the corresponding LIDO record, *lido:legalBodyID*, allows to register an unlimited number of such identifiers [7]. Hence, to solve this challenge, several options have been identified, namely:

a) the use of the *edm:Agent* class instead of the *foaf:Organization* class;
b) the application of the principle *"first-come, first-served"*;
c) the choice of the most representative identifier.

The generic class *edm:Agent*, which allows to record an unlimited number of identifiers, can be used for the representation of institutions because the *foaf:Organization* is a subclass of the first one. Still, it must be noted that choosing not to use the *foaf:Organization* class will result in losing some specific details. The application of the principle *"first-come, first-served"* is recommended only in case the user has information according to which the identifiers have all the same degree of representativity. A more complex strategy is the choice of the most representative identifier. This assumes that the user analyses the identifiers, and, according to some well-defined rules, establish which identifier is the most representative.

7.5   Extending the EDM Vocabulary

Even though EDM is a data model through which it can be made a representation as clear as possible of the described CHOs characteristics, as well as of the connections between them, in some cases, the vocabulary provided does not cover the current needs of detailing of the presented resources. Yet, one of the most important facilities that this data model offers is the flexibility, that is, the possibility of developing and integrating new features to cover the user's needs.

This flexibility of the data model is provided, on the one hand, by the Europeana staff [4], which can consider the definition of new sets of guidelines or rules applicable to classes and properties already existing, and on the other hand, by its own structure which allows the user to extend the current vocabulary with new specific terms [11, 12]. For the latter approach the following constructs from the RDF Schema will be used: i) *rdfs:subClassOf* to specify the generic class which will be inherited; ii) *rdfs:subPropertyOf* to extend an already existing property. The vocabulary extension mechanism allows applications which use specific metadata to remain interoperable with the generic ones like the Europeana portal [13].

To outline the advantages of extending the vocabulary, Fig. 4 depicts a practical example by which the generic property *dc:description*, is extended to create a more specific property. Thus, through the *openData:displayState* property, users will be able to know exactly what the value *"bună"* (En.: *"good"*) represents, and, at the same time, the metadata integration in the Europeana portal will not suffer.

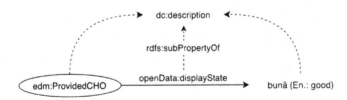

Fig. 4. RDF fragment showing how the application can infer what the CHO's display state is.

8   Experimental Results

As Nicolae Bălcescu, one of the greatest Romanian historians, once said, history represents the cornerstone of a people through which it is mirrored not only the past, but also its present and future [14]. Through the experience of the past, it is easier to a nation to make progress, having a knowledge base of both the perils it has been through, and of the success recorded during its existence.

Nowadays, when technology allows us to implement and use (semi)automatic data analysis tools, inspecting events in which CHOs have been involved becomes a simpler process. Therefore, starting from the datasets made available by INP, using the eCHO Framework, on the one hand, it has been possible to increase the degree of representation of the described elements by interconnecting them using the Semantic Web technologies, and on the other hand, it has been possible to standardize timespans and calendar dates in a unique format which will allow users to easily group events in which CHOs have been involved in.

Having timespans expressed only in centuries, Table 2 presents the top three centuries in which the most events took place; statistics which have been broken down on the three types of events identified in the datasets: i) production for the process of creation; ii) finding for the process of searching; iii) collecting for the process of storing. Thus, it can be noted that the most initiatives of finding valuable CHOs have been carried out in the 20th century, and in a smaller proportion in the successive century. Unfortunately, by themselves these finding events cannot provide information regarding the number of objects identified because the results of the identification may be very different from one event to the other.

As far as the production type events are concerned, the situation is completely different because, by their nature, the production processes involve two factors: the creator and the final product. Hence, by examining the number of production type events, we can remark that, during time, almost half of the CHOs found date during the 18th–20th century, the most significant proportion being assigned to the 19th century. Regarding the rest of 17,155 CHOs found, these have been dated as having different roots, starting from the century 59th B.C. up to the 17th century A.D. Nevertheless, by analyzing not only the result presenting the three types of events, but also the input datasets, it can be determined that there is a discrepancy between the total number of CHOs present in the LIDO datasets (36,132) and the total number of production events identified (34,357).

Table 2. Top three timespans by event type.

Event/Century	21th	20th	19th	18th	Others
Production	–	5,724	8,759	2,719	17,155
Finding	970	6,465	39	–	7
Collecting	14	1,051	13	–	1

Despite the fact that in theory, to each CHO's corresponds a production event, it is possible that in certain cases where to particular CHOs represented through LIDO the record presenting the production event is missing. Therefore, even for most of the events in which CHOs have been involved it has been possible to identify and calculate the century they took place in, there have been cases when determining the century was not possible (3,083 production events and 5 finding events). Among these cases we recall: the lack of the year in the presentation of the calendar date, the presentation of the timespan only as millenniums or as historical periods as Pleistocene, Modern History, etc., situations which have been treated as having undetermined time period.

9 Conclusions and Further Development

The publishing of metadata on Europeana, the largest digital library in Europe, is based on strict rules, using the EDM conceptual model, a model that provides users with both an object-centric approach and a more complex approach, the event-centric approach. Unfortunately, data aggregators are restricted to choosing the first approach because of the lack of the support for representation of the events in which CHOs have been involved, which does only weaken the degree of CHOs representation and the possibility to identity important historical links.

Considering that a wide part of the European cultural institutions which have digitalized their collection have used the LIDO standard, a solution for avoiding the loose of information is the translation of the LIDO datasets to Linked Data using the event-centric approach of the EDM besides the object-centric approach. Therefore, the difference between the eCHO Framework and other mapping frameworks is that eCHO uses for representing the metadata not only the object-centric approach, but also the event-centric. Therefore, eCHO allows users not only the sanitizing, normalizing and interconnecting data but also the preserving the events in which the CHOs have been involved, and, thus, to increase the value of the represented data.

Regarding the direction of further development, the intention is to extend the method of representation of the timespans in order to support the identification not only of the centuries, but also of the years and sequences of centuries and millenniums (the first half, the first quarter, the second one, etc.), to redefine the way of representation of political entities through the interlinking with external sources such as GeoNames and DBpedia, and finally to integrate datasets into the touristic information system Visit Romania Museums [15]. Furthermore, the intention is to extend the analysis done to identify different patterns of lifestyle of the population residing inside the actual boundaries of Romania and not only.

References

1. de Boer, V.: Supporting linked data production for cultural heritage institutes: the Amsterdam museum case study. In: Simperl, E., Cimiano, P., Polleres, A., Corcho, O., Presutti, V. (eds.) ESWC 2012. LNCS, vol. 7295, pp. 733–747. Springer, Heidelberg (2012). https://doi.org/10.1007/978-3-642-30284-8_56
2. Meghini, C., Bartalesi, V., Metilli, D., Benedetti, F.: Introducing narratives in Europeana: a case study. Int. J. Appl. Math. Comput. Sci. **29**(1), 7–16 (2019). https://doi.org/10.2478/amcs-2019-0001
3. Autere, R., Vakkari, M.: Towards cross-organizational interoperability: the LIDO XML schema as a national level integration tool for the national digital library of Finland. In: Gradmann, S., Borri, F., Meghini, C., Schuldt, H. (eds.) TPDL 2011. LNCS, vol. 6966, pp. 62–68. Springer, Heidelberg (2011). https://doi.org/10.1007/978-3-642-24469-8_8
4. de Boer, V., et al.: Amsterdam museum linked open data. Semant. Web **4**(3), 237–243 (2013). https://doi.org/10.3233/SW-2012-0074
5. Tsalapati, E., Simou, N., Drosopoulos, N., Stein, R.: Evolving LIDO based aggregations into linked data. In: The CIDOC Annual Conference, Helsinki (2012)

6. Hansen, H.J., Fernie, K.: CARARE: connecting archaeology and architecture in Europeana. In: Ioannides, M., Fellner, D., Georgopoulos, A., Hadjimitsis, D.G. (eds.) EuroMed 2010. LNCS, vol. 6436, pp. 450–462. Springer, Heidelberg (2010). https://doi.org/10.1007/978-3-642-16873-4_36

7. Dorobăț, I.C., Posea, V.: Enriching the cultural heritage metadata using historical events: a graph-based representation. In: Doucet, A., Isaac, A., Golub, K., Aalberg, T., Jatowt, A. (eds.) TPDL 2019. LNCS, vol. 11799, pp. 344–347. Springer, Cham (2019). https://doi.org/10.1007/978-3-030-30760-8_30

8. Musen, M.A., Schreiber, A.T.: Architectures for intelligent systems based on reusable components. J. Artif. Intell. Med. **7**(3), 189–199 (1995). https://doi.org/10.1016/0933-3657(95)00003-o

9. van Heijst, G., Schreiber, A., Wielinga, B.J.: Using explicit ontologies in KBS development. Int. J. Hum. Comput. Stud. **46**(2–3), 183–292 (1997). https://doi.org/10.1006/ijhc.1996.0090

10. Berners-Lee, T.: Linked Data: Design Issues. https://www.w3.org/DesignIssues/LinkedData.html. Accessed 01 Aug 2020

11. Baker, T., Vandenbussche, P.Y., Vatant, B.: Requirements for vocabulary preservation and governance. Libr. Hi Tech **31**(4), 657–668 (2013). https://doi.org/10.1108/LHT-03-2013-0027

12. Dijkshoorn, C., et al.: The Rijksmuseum collection as linked data. Semant. Web **9**(2), 221–230 (2018). https://doi.org/10.3233/SW-170257

13. Charles, V., Isaac, A. Enhancing the Europeana Data Model (EDM). Technical report, Europeana V3.0 (2015). https://pro.europeana.eu/post/enhancing-the-europeana-data-model-edm. Accessed 01 Aug 2020

14. The Memorial Museum "Nicolae Bălcescu" - quoted from Nicolae Bălcescu. http://memorialulbalcescu.ro/nicolae-balcescu. Accessed 01 Aug 2020

15. Rinciog, O., Dorobăț, I.C., Posea, V. Route suggestion for visiting museums using semantic data. In: Roceanu, I., et al (eds.) eLearning & Software for Education (eLSE 2017), vol. 3, pp. 48–55 (2017). https://doi.org/10.12753/2066-026x-17-180

An Inspection and Logging System for Complex Event Processing in Bosch's Industry 4.0 Movement

Carina Andrade$^{(\boxtimes)}$ ⓘ, Maria Cardoso ⓘ, Carlos Costa ⓘ,
and Maribel Yasmina Santos ⓘ

ALGORITMI Research Centre, University of Minho, Guimarães, Portugal
{carina.andrade,carlos.costa,maribel}@dsi.uminho.pt,
a78439@alunos.uminho.pt

Abstract. Currently, it is possible to have machines producing relevant data to be processed in real-time, facilitating the organizational decision-making. In recent works, we proposed a system that integrates Complex Event Processing (CEP) in the Big Data era, trying to make Industry 4.0 systems more pro-active. Due to its complexity when running in industrial contexts, appropriate monitoring mechanisms need to be ensured to prevent the uncontrolled growth of the system. In this context, this work focuses on proposing a system architecture that will enable an innovative monitoring strategy based on graph analysis, namely the *Intelligent Event Broker* (*IEB*) Mapping and Drill-down System. In this work, it is proposed an inspection and logging strategy for the *IEB that* allows to not only continuously inspect the codebase of the system and fuel an ever-growing Graph Database, but also to strategically store log occurrences to know what is continuously happening. For demonstrating the architecture and design rules, we use a context from Bosch Portugal presenting a flowchart and a graph data model, being the latter a mirror of all the implemented *IEB* components and the relationships between them. This work helps researchers and practitioners in the design and development of CEP systems for Big Data contexts and, especially, the monitoring component of such a complex system.

Keywords: Big data · Complex event processing · Monitoring · Graph database

1 Introduction

Nowadays, several industries are pursuing the adoption of Big Data and Real-time concepts in their enterprises. This need arose, for example, from the current technological evolution that results on a huge amount of data being produced every day by various types of machines inside the shop floor. Once the data is available, the challenge is how to use it to improve the organizations' performance by acting intelligently and without need to wait for human analysis and approvals. The Complex Event Processing (CEP) concept has existed since the 90s, always linked to the need to process various events in a real-time fashion. Nowadays, CEP is being integrated into Big Data contexts due to the need to

© Springer Nature Switzerland AG 2020
M. Themistocleous et al. (Eds.): EMCIS 2020, LNBIP 402, pp. 49–62, 2020.
https://doi.org/10.1007/978-3-030-63396-7_4

process events resulting from real-time data streams that are more frequently available in the organizations.

The *Intelligent Event Broker (IEB)* is proposed in [1] as an innovative system that integrates the CEP and Big Data concepts using a Rules Engine embedded into Spark[1]. The architecture considers the existence of several types of data sources and a component (*Producers*) dedicated to the standardization of the connection to all of them. The events arriving at the system are serialized into classes representing the business entities (*Broker Beans*) that will be subscribed by the *Event Processor* (Spark *Consumers*). This last component can send event data to be aggregated for further Key Performance Indicators (KPIs) calculation in the *Event Aggregator* (supported by Druid[2]). *Consumers* are also directly related to the *Rules Engine* (implemented in Drools[3]) where all the business requirements are defined as strategical, tactical, or operational *Rules*. These three types of *Rules* are translated at runtime by the *Consumers*. The *Triggers* component represents the connection to all the *Destination Systems*, and they will perform certain actions based on the results of the rules verification (e.g., stop a production machine if the last three products registered a failure). The *Predictors and Recommenders* is the component responsible for the application of previously trained Machine Learning models, which are stored in the *Lake of Machine Learning Models*.

Furthermore, it is considered that this kind of system needs closer and rich monitoring capabilities. In this context, a *Mapping and Drill-down System* was previously included in the *IEB* architecture [1], considering a *Graph Database* and a *Web Visualization Platform* to perform the system monitorization. This *Graph Database* will store the data related to the *IEB* codebase that is continuously and automatically inferred, as well as the relationships between them and the logs from the system components that are continuously running. The collected data will be analyzed in a *Web Visualization Platform* already proposed in [2]. Therefore, this work aims to detail this system by proposing an architecture and a set of design rules that will ensure the adequate data collection to feed the *Mapping and Drill-down System*, ensuring the efficient inspection and logging of the *IEB*.

This paper is structured as follows: Sect. 2 presents the related work identified in the literature; Sect. 3 presents the inspection and logging system architecture and a set of design rules; Sect. 4 presents the demonstration case to highlight how the inspection component of the system was implemented, using the Bosch Portugal context; Sect. 5 presents the conclusions and future work.

2 Related Work

Being this a very specific topic inside what is already a very specific research context (i.e., CEP on Big Data contexts), there is a lack of relevant literature and related works. Regarding the existence of systems that integrate the CEP concept in Big Data contexts,

---

[1] https://spark.apache.org/.

[2] https://druid.apache.org/.

[3] https://www.drools.org/.

few works were found in the literature. The work of [3] proposes an architecture (BiDCEP) for a system that integrates the CEP capabilities in the Big Data world. For that, the authors idealized a mixed Big Data Streaming architecture based on the recognized Lambda and Kappa architectures for Big Data. This proposal is summarized as being the extension of these architectures with components that represent the CEP system. The work of [4] presents a prototype named FERARI that aims to process a large number of event streams in a multi-cloud environment. Their proposal is based on four components, each one with distinct goals: a web-based graphical user interface to define CEP concepts; a component to plan the latency and communication between the instances of the inter-cloud; a component responsible for the events processing and a web-based dashboard with reports regarding the processed events. Another architecture to integrate CEP and Big Data using only open source technologies is discussed in [5], using an electronic coupon distribution centre as a demonstration case and giving focus to the technologies selection (uses Apache Kafka as a message broker, HDFS to store the data and a CEP system based on If-Then-Else rules to process the data).

During the analysis of the related work, when looking for the need of systems to monitor a CEP in Big Data contexts, works only revealed the possible use of CEPs to monitor other systems [6, 7]. In this context, proper logging was considered since logs are widely used to indicate the state of the system at runtime, providing the details of the transactions that occur and containing useful information (e.g., name, date, and time of the occurrence [8]), which helps to understand the behaviour of the system. The work of [9] mentions that a log must be recorded in an orderly and controlled manner so that it is human-readable. Nevertheless, its usefulness depends on how the log is applied, proposing much more than debug information and being of considerable value when analyzing the performance of an application [9].

Regarding the monitorization of this kind of systems, this concern was only identified in the FERARI project, with a dashboard component that provides reports about some metadata of the system (e.g., daily events or for the last 4 h) [10], being the focus on the data flows of the system and apparently leaving aside the drill-down into the insights and behaviour from the individual components of the system.

3   The Inspection and Logging System as a *IEB* Mapping and Drill-Down Feeder

Considering the complexity that can arise with the evolution of a system like the *IEB* proposed in [1], especially when running it in industrial contexts, a dedicated system must work in parallel to guarantee the constant and long-term monitoring of the *IEB's* daily operations, ensuring its sustainable and controlled growth.

Taking this into consideration, the **Mapping and Drill-down System** was included in [1] and considers the implementation of two components: i) a **Graph Database** (considered the most adequate database due to the need to deal with the constant evolution of the *IEB* and its potential growth when running with several subjects simultaneously); and, ii) a **Web Visualization Platform** to enable the drill-down over the data, as discussed in [2]. This work is focused on the design of the system that will allow the fueling of the **Graph Database**, to operate as the data source for the **Web**

Visualization Platform, allowing the *IEB* stakeholders and operators to establish relevant relationships and drill-down operations into several occurrences within the system and its components.

3.1   System Architecture

As briefly highlighted in [1], the inspection and logging system architecture present here must ensure the following goals: **G1)** the proper analysis and indexing of the *IEB* codebase; **G2)** appropriate runtime logging mechanisms, to guarantee the storage of all the relevant data about the system components that are constantly working; **G3)** the analysis of the system functionality, recording what happened and when; and, **G4)** the analysis of the system performance (e.g., how many events were produced in ***Producer X***, or consumed by ***Consumer Y***). To ensure that all these defined goals are considered, the system architecture presented in Fig. 1 is divided into two parts:

1. The first part is dedicated to code inspection. For that, the *IEB* codebase (*System Code Repository*) is used as the source for analysis, exploring the folders and files that compose the system and using the ***Code Inspector*** component to collect data to feed the ***Graph Database*** (e.g., collect data to create graph labels, graph nodes, graph nodes' properties and relationships between graph nodes). To collect all the relevant data that will allow the definition of the Graph Data Model (GDM), a set of design rules were defined and are presented in Subsect. 3.2. The implementation of these rules will guarantee the creation of the GDM regardless of how the system is implemented and addressing the previously presented goal **G1)**;

2. The second part is related to logging mechanisms. Here, the *IEB* components already implemented are considered as data sources to provide useful data when they are running. The ***Logger*** component should be embedded in the *IEB* components, logging the time, the events flowing through the system, and the system components execution. The time logs are the key point since time will be a property in the relationships between graph nodes, representing when something happened in the system. Secondary storage is proposed for historical and analytical purposes due to the dimension that the ***Graph Database*** can achieve.

   a. In the ***Historical Storage***, all the raw data history will be available for analytical purposes, when ad hoc queries involving the use of complex interactions and calculations is needed. Here, analytical tools like Hive[4] or Spark can be used to explore the data in the Hadoop Distributed File System (HDFS), and data exploration tools like Zeppelin[5] or Tableau[6] can be used to interact visually with all the raw historical data.

   b. In ***Interactive Storage***, a graph database has the most recent data to drill-down over it and take advantage of the analysis that can be done on graphs. The time frame defined for the data stored in the graph database depends on three factors:

---

[4] https://hive.apache.org/.

[5] https://zeppelin.apache.org/.

[6] https://www.tableau.com/.

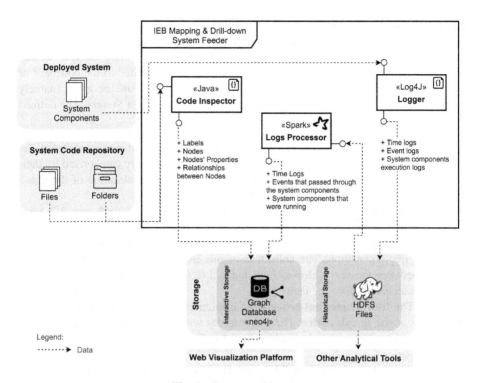

Fig. 1. System architecture

i) the business requirements; ii) the amount of data generated by the system; and, iii) the capacity of the neo4j infrastructure. The **Logs Processor** component will pick up the data from the **Historical Storage** (at predefined periods) to load it into the graph database (**Interactive Storage**). This will guarantee the achievement of the previously presented goals **G2), G3)** and **G4)**.

The architecture presented in Fig. 1 already proposes technologies that can be used for each component (e.g., Spark for the **Logs Processor** component), considering the technological stack already proposed in [1] for the remaining system. Regarding the **Logger** component, Log4j[7] was proposed considering that is an open-source structure, flexible, written in Java and currently commonly used [11]. However, practitioners are free to choose other technologies for their specific implementation of a similar system to monitor their CEP system in Big Data contexts, as the conceptual proposal still holds true.

3.2   Design Rules for the Code Inspector Component

Related to the repository code inspection, several design rules are defined to guarantee that all the relevant *IEB* components are identified and tracked appropriately, as well as

---

[7] http://logging.apache.org/log4j/2.x/.

their relationships. These design rules take into consideration that the result of the code inspection should be a GDM to be implemented in a graph database. Once these design rules are implemented in a piece of software dedicated to inspecting the *IEB*, in any programming language practitioners choose to (ours is in Java due to the codebase of the *IEB*), all the relevant inspection data will be captured to create the graph (namely the inspection part of the graph) for the ***Mapping and Drill-down System***. The defined design rules (DR) are presented as follow:

DR1: The *IEB* components are the 1st level labels. This will guarantee that all the implemented components from the *IEB* (mentioned in Sect. 1) are categorized by their type of component in the architecture, facilitating the future exploration of the graph database (e.g., ***Producers***, ***Rules*** or ***Triggers***).

DR2: The folders' name, where the components were found, are 2nd level labels, if it defines a specific subject for the *IEB*. Considering the variety of subjects that can be implemented in the *IEB*, a clear separation by folders should be made during the implementation. The collection of this information will enable the differentiation between the several topics implemented in the system (e.g., "/producers/alr" or "/consumers/shop-floor-incidents").

DR3: The files' name that reflects the implementation of *IEB* components are the names of the graph nodes. The graph nodes will be the several instantiations of the system components already implemented for the various *IEB* contexts (e.g., ***Producers*** or ***Rules*** for a subject).

DR4: The labels defined in DR1 and DR2 must be associated to the graph nodes identified in DR3. This will guarantee that all the created graph nodes will have at least one label associated, identifying the system component and (in some cases) the subject related to their implementation.

DR5: In the *Broker Beans'* files, their variables and data types are their graph nodes' properties. Considering the importance of this component when representing the data that will flow throughout the system, it is relevant that the ***Broker Beans*** variables and respective data types are collected.

DR6: In the *Broker Beans'* files, if the variable data type is another *Broker Bean*, a relationship between the first identified *Broker Bean* graph node (BB1) and the one identified in the variable data type (BB2) should be created as "BB1 composed_of BB2". Since the ***Broker Beans*** represent the business entities flowing in the system and, in some cases, a business entity can be composed of other business entities, this relationship should be identified.

DR7: In the *IEB* components' files, a relationship between graph nodes should be created when Inheritance or Implementation relationships are identified. For some components (e.g., ***Producers*** or ***Consumers***), the collection of data representing the Inheritance and Implementation between the files that define them is relevant and must be ensured.

DR8: For any system component that instantiates another one, a relationship between the component (Cp1) and the one identified as being instantiated (Cp2) should be created as "Cp1 instantiates Cp2". This step will ensure that all the relationships between the components are stored to generate knowledge about the interaction of the components.

DR9: For the *Consumers*, it should be identified if they verify certain *Rules*, creating a relationship between the *Consumer* (C1) and the Rules Session that is executed (RS1) as "C1 runs RS1" and which *Rule* (Ru1) is verified as "C1 verifies Ru1". With this design rule, it is guaranteed that the *Consumers* running the Rules Session (a set of *Rules* within all the defined *Rules*) and therefore verifying certain *Rules*, are identified, and properly stored in the graph.

DR10: For each *Consumer*, it should be identified if it queries or stores data in the *Event Aggregator* component. A relationship between the *Consumer* (C1) and the used *Event Aggregator* (EA1) should be created as "C1 queries EA1". Moreover, a relationship between the *Consumer* and the *Event Aggregator* where it stores new data (EA2) should be created as "C1 stores_data_in EA2". This design rule identifies an interaction between a *Consumer* and the *Event Aggregator* in both directions: querying and storing data on it.

DR11: For the identified *Triggers*, it should be created a relationship between the *Trigger* (T1) and the *Destination System* (DS1) that will receive the data sent by the *Trigger* as "T1 propagates_data_to DS1". The actions defined in the *Triggers* can send data to different *Destination Systems* identified in the system architecture presented in [1], the reason why each *Trigger* should have a relationship with the graph node that represents the *Destination System* being used in that action.

DR12: Regarding the rules' repository, it should be collected the *Rule*'s name and the *Trigger* fired by the *Rule*, as well as the *Broker Beans* used for the *Rule* verification and to trigger the action. The *Rule*'s names should be saved as graph name nodes and the *Trigger* and *Broker Beans* identified are used for design rules DR13 and DR14. Depending on the Rules Engine being used, different ways for the rules definition can exist (i.e., Drools as a way of defining rules, while other business rules systems may have others). Nevertheless, the *Rules* must be identified and stored in the graph, as well as the *Triggers* and the *Broker Beans* used by them.

DR13: For the *Rules* identified in DR12, it should be created a relationship between the *Rule* graph node (Ru1) and the *Broker Bean* (BB1) used for the *Rule* verification as "Ru1 uses BB1". Moreover, it should be created a relationship between the *Rule* and the graph node that represents the *Trigger* (T1) fired by the *Rule* as "Ru1 fires T1". These relationships will ensure the tracking of which *Broker Beans* are used by the *Rules* verification and which *Triggers* are fired by which *Rule*.

DR14: For the *Triggers* identified in DR12, it should be created a relationship between the *Trigger* graph node (T1) and the *Broker Beans* (BB1) used to take any action as "T1 uses_to_trigger BB1". It is necessary to identify which specific *Broker Beans* are used for the system's actions ensuring the identification of the data that are propagated to the *Destination Systems* (e.g., IoT Gateways or a database to feed Analytical Applications, as identified in [1]).

4 Demonstration Case

In this section, it is presented a demonstration case for the ***Code Inspector*** component of the architecture proposed in Sect. 3. First, it is presented a flowchart that reflects the implementation of the set of design rules defined in Subsect. 3.2, using the *IEB* implementation in the Bosch Portugal ALR[8] data context. Then, for the obtained flowchart, a part of the GDM is demonstrated and explained, resulting from the implementation of the steps in the flowchart. Although the **Logger** and **Logs Processor** components are already being developed, for this paper, this component is defined at the conceptual level, and its demonstration is identified as future work.

4.1   Code Inspector Flowchart

The flowchart (Fig. 2) that represents the implementation of the design rules defined in Subsect. 3.2 is based on the *IEB* system already presented in [1]. To properly interpret this diagram, remember that the *IEB* was implemented using Java and Drools (this last one, as Rules Engine).

In this context, each package represents the implementation of one of the *IEB* components and to save this data, the **Code Inspector** seeks throughout the packages to analyze the implemented code, storing the package name as 1st level label (**DR1**). When inside a package, it searches for *.java* and *.drl* files (Drools files) and for each file, its directory name is saved (if it does not exist yet) as 2nd level label (**DR2**). After that, the file name is saved as the graph node, representing the class that is part of the system implementation (**DR3**). The identified labels are then linked to the created node (**DR4**). All these steps are executed until there are no more packages and no more *.java* or *.drl* files to identify. This will guarantee that the graph nodes and labels needed for the creation of the relationships already exist.

With all the graph nodes already created, the **Code Inspector** starts exploring the files again in the first package. If the selected file is from the **Broker Beans** package, the private variables names and properties are saved as node properties for the graph node previously defined with the same name as the file name being analyzed (**DR5**). If some of the variable's types represent other nodes identified in the **Broker Beans** package, a relationship between the file/graph node being analyzed and the graph node representing the variable type is saved as shown in Fig. 2 (**DR6** - *composed_of* relationship).

For the rest of the *.java* files identified in the packages, if they include a string *"extends"* or *"implements"* followed by another graph name node previously identified, a relationship between the file/graph node being analyzed and the one identified after the mentioned strings are saved as identified in the flowchart (**DR7** - *extends* and *implements* relationships). The string *"new"* followed by another graph name node previously identified will allow the identification of instantiations being carried out by the file under analysis. A relationship is saved as a file/graph node that *instantiates* another graph node (**DR8**). The same happens for the identification of which **Consumers** run the *RulesSession*. In this case, searching for the string *"getStatelessSession"* and saving a relationship as the graph node representing the file being analyzed *runs* the *"ruleSessionName"* (the *getStatelessSession* parameter) identified.

Furthermore, the type of the parameter from the *"executeRules"* method will allow the identification of the **Rules** verified in that session (all the **Rules** waiting for a

---

[8] A system that verifies if a lot can be shipped to the customer.

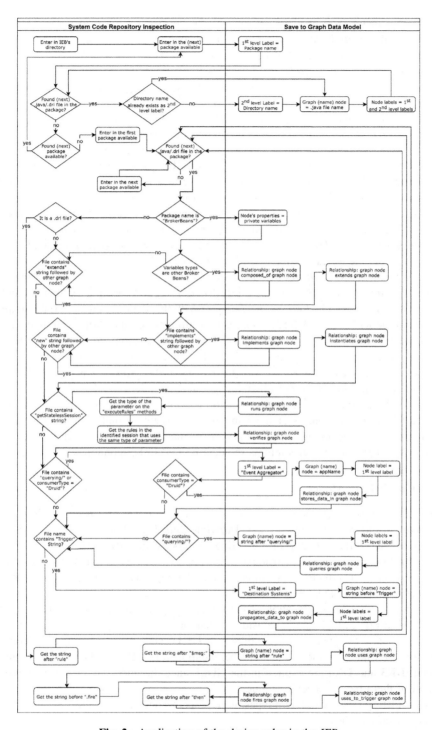

Fig. 2. Application of the design rules in the *IEB*

specific parameter type inside a session will be verified by the **Consumer** - **DR9**). Regarding the **Event Aggregator** component, this one can be queried, and the data can be stored on it. If the file contains the string *"querying/"* or the *"consumerType"* equals *"Druid"*, **Event Aggregator** is saved as 1st level label. For the ones in which the *"consumerType"* equals *"Druid"*: i) the *"appName"* (that represents the **Event Aggregator**) is saved as graph name node; ii) the 1st level label is defined as a label for the created node; and, iii) a relationship is created as the node representing the file being analyzed *stores_data_in* node representing the **Event Aggregator**.

The same happens when the *"querying/"* string is found, being the relationship defined as *queries* instead of *stores_data_in* (**DR10**). On the other hand, if the file name contains the *"Trigger"* string: i) **Destination Systems** is saved as 1st level label; ii) the name before *"Trigger"* is saved as graph name node; iii) the 1st level label is defined for the created node; and, iv) a relationship is created between the node representing the file being analyzed (**Trigger**) and the node created as being the **Destination System** (*"Trigger propagates_data_to Destination System"*) (**DR11**).

Concerning the **Rules** defined in.*drl* files (Drools files), a file exploration process is executed to collect: i) the **Rules** that are in quotes after the *"rule"* string; ii) the **Broker Beans** used for the verification of the rules; iii) the **Trigger** to be fired by the rule; and, iv) the **Broker Bean** to be fired by the **Trigger**. With this data, are created: i) the graph node with the **Rule** name (**DR12**); ii) a relationship between the **Rule** graph node and the **Broker Bean** used for its verification (**DR13**); iii) a relationship between the **Rule** graph node and the **Trigger** that is fired (**DR13**); and, iv) a relationship between the **Trigger** and the **Broker Bean** that was flowing when the **Trigger** was fired (**DR14**).

With the definition of the flowchart, it is possible to understand that the design rules presented in Subsect. 3.2 are easily transformed into small tasks to be coded and applied to the implemented system. Although the system is implemented using Java and Drools, other technologies can be used if the main guidelines are followed, as the application of the design rules returns the data needed to be monitored.

4.2   Graph Data Model

In Fig. 3, it can be seen the representation of the GDM that was obtained from the **Code Inspector** component to support the **Mapping and Drill-down System** (see Subsect. 3.2). Due to the difficulty of presenting here the whole GDM created during this work, this figure only shows an example of the relationships between the possible types of graph nodes. Nevertheless, the whole data model contains sixteen labels, more than fifty nodes and more than sixty relationships.

Before starting the explanation of the nodes (circles) and relationships (edges) of the GDM in Fig. 3, it should be considered that the nodes' backgrounds represent the packages' name (1st level label mentioned in **DR1**), and the lines around the nodes represent the folders' names (2nd level label mentioned in **DR2**) as shown in the figure legend. **DR3** and **DR4** are explicit in the GDM since the nodes are clearly identified and all of them have a specific colour.

Considering this, the different types of graph nodes and relationships between them are described as follow:

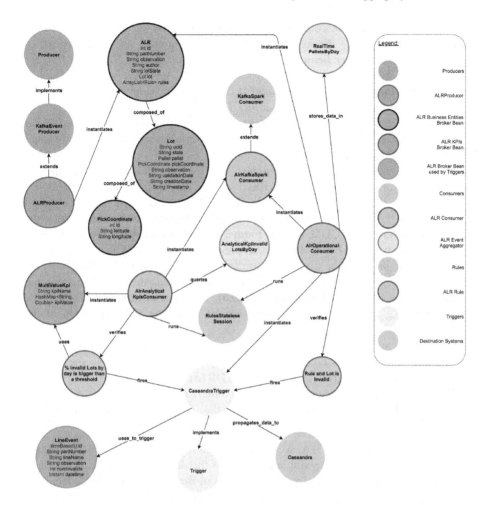

Fig. 3. GDM resulting from the application of the set of proposed design rules (Color figure online)

- The *ALRProducer* extends a generic implementation of a producer developed using Apache Kafka *(KafkaEventProducer)*, which by itself implements the *Producer* interface (**DR7**). This aims to standardize the implementation of the *Producers*, creating a generic class and an interface that reflects the behaviour of every producer in the system.
- Three types of **Broker Beans** can be seen: i) **Broker Beans** representing the business entities that arrive at the system through the events (*ALR*, *Lot* and *PickCoordinate*); ii) **Broker Beans** representing the KPIs calculated by the system (*MultiValueKpi*); and, iii) **Broker Beans** created during the verification of the **Rules** to be later used by the **Triggers** (*LineEvent*). Regarding the **Broker Beans** that represent the business entities, these are instantiated by **Producers** and **Consumers**

(**DR8**). They can also be composed of other **Broker Beans** (an *ALR Broker Bean* is composed of a *Lot Broker Bean* which subsequently is composed of a *PickCoordinate Broker Bean* - **DR6**). The KPIs **Broker Beans** (*MultiValueKpi*) are instantiated by **Consumers** with analytical purposes (*AlrAnalyticalKpisConsumer*) (**DR8**) and they are used by the **Rules** dedicated to the same analytical goals *(% Invalids Lots by day is bigger than a threshold)* (**DR13**). The third type of **Broker Beans** (*LineEvent*) is used by the **Triggers** that propagate them to the **Destination Systems** (**DR14**). For every **Broker Bean**, their variables and data types are identified as node's properties (**DR5**).

- The operational or analytical **Consumers** (*AlrOperationalConsumer* and *AlrAnalyticalKpisConsumer*) instantiate (**DR8**) a specific class (*AlrKafkaSparkConsumer*) that extends the *KafkaSparkConsumer* (**DR7**), being this a specific code design strategy in the *IEB*. Both of them run the *RulesStatelessSession* and verify the defined **Rules** in the GDM (**DR9**). Furthermore, **Consumers** have two types of interactions with the **Event Aggregator** presented in the GDM (e.g., relationship *stores_data_in* between the *AlrOperationalConsumer* and the *RealTimePalletsByDay*, and relationship *queries* between the *AlrAnalyticalKpisConsumer* and the *AnalyticalKpiInvalidLotsByDay* - **DR10**). Finally, **Consumers** instantiate the **Triggers** (e.g., *CassandraTrigger*) that can be fired after the verification of the **Rules** (**DR8**).
- Two **Rules** are defined in the GDM *(% Invalids Lots by day is bigger than a threshold* and *Rule and Lot is Invalid* - **DR12**) with a relationship to the **Trigger** node reflecting that a **Rule** *fires* a **Trigger** (**DR13**).
- Regarding the **Triggers** component, the *CassandraTrigger* implements the *Trigger* interface (**DR7**) and *propagates_data_to* the *Cassandra* **Destination System** (**DR11**).

The detailed GDM (Fig. 3) as well as the design rules identified in the description of the GDM, reflect the successful application of the design rules in the *IEB* system being demonstrated in the Industry 4.0 movement of Bosch Portugal. The codebase of the system was thoroughly analyzed by the authors, comparing it to the generated GDM. With this validation, it was possible to conclude that, as an initial prototype, the data needed to monitor the continuous growth of the system (e.g., new **Producers** or **Consumers**) is adequately identified and captured by the design rules proposed.

Regarding the **Logger** component, the experimental work in progress is currently focused on logging the execution of the *ALRProducer* and the *AlrOperationalConsumer*. The logs are being stored and processed as described in Sect. 3 and the **Web Visualization Platform** [2] is used (with a new design) for the data analysis. In the analysis presented in Fig. 4, it can be seen the *ALRProducer*, the *AlrOperationalConsumer* and the *CassandraTrigger* nodes (green, red and yellow nodes) connected to all the *ALR Broker Beans* nodes (blue). In the future, we will work on extending the GDM presented here with the processed logging information from the *IEB* system.

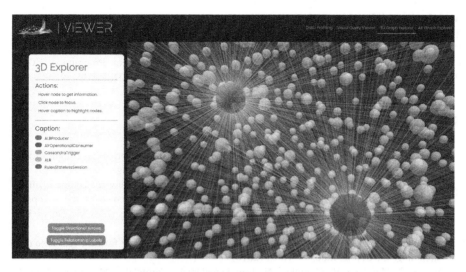

Fig. 4. Data from the *Logger* component presented in the 3D graph explorer of the IEB Web visualization Platform (Color figure online)

5   Conclusions

Given the potential complexity of the *IEB* running in industrial contexts, we consider that adequate monitoring of this system is essential. This monitoring was conceptually considered in the *IEB* system [1] with the proposal of the ***Mapping and Drill-down System*** supported by graph storage and analysis technologies.

In this paper, the architecture for the whole feeding system that will fuel the ***Graph Database*** was presented and discussed considering two main parts: i) the ***Code Inspector***; and, ii) the ***Logger***. This feeding system is responsible for generating the ever-growing graph mentioned above, addressing innovative monitoring capabilities for a CEP in Big Data contexts.

For the ***Code Inspector*** component, the main focus of this work, a set of design rules was defined to ensure that the *IEB* components are continuously and automatically inferred from the codebase, as well the relationships between them. The design rules were applied in a Bosch Portugal demonstration case using the ALR data, showing a flowchart on how to properly inspect the *IEB* codebase, and highlighting the results in a detailed GDM. The design rules were successfully applied to the *IEB* system returning all the useful graph data (labels, nodes, relationships) that is needed to feed the *IEB* ***Mapping and Drill-down System***.

Despite the focus on the *IEB* system being demonstrated in the Bosch Portugal context, we believe that the artefacts and insights provided here, which complement the ones in [1, 2], are conceptually, technically and technologically relevant for several researchers and practitioners in the area. No other system similar to the *IEB* considers the relevance of monitoring using consistent strategies that focus on the evolution and growth of the system when working in production contexts, being this a key point to guarantee the adequate maintenance of the system in many contexts like the industry 4.0 movement.

Acknowledgements. This work has been supported by FCT – Fundação para a Ciência e Tecnologia within the R&D Units Project Scope: UIDB/00319/2020, the Doctoral scholarship PD/BDE/135101/2017 and by European Structural and Investment Funds in the FEDER component, through the Operational Competitiveness and Internationalization Programme (COMPETE 2020) [Project n° 039479; Funding Reference: POCI-01-0247-FEDER-039479].

References

1. Andrade, C., Correia, J., Costa, C., Santos, M.Y.: Intelligent event broker: a complex event processing system in big data contexts. In: AMCIS 2019 Proceedings. Cancun (2019)
2. Rebelo, J., Andrade, C., Costa, C., Santos, M.Y.: An Immersive web visualization platform for a big data context in bosch's industry 4.0 movement. Presented at the european, mediterranean and middle eastern conference on information systems (EMCIS), Dubai, Dec 2019
3. Hadar, E.: BIDCEP: A vision of big data complex event processing for near real time data streaming. In: CAiSE Industry Track (2016)
4. Flouris, I., Manikaki, V., Giatrakos, N., Deligiannakis, A., Garofalakis, M., Mock, M., et al.: FERARI: a prototype for complex event processing over streaming multi-cloud platforms. In: Proceedings of the 2016 International Conference on Management of Data. pp. 2093–2096. ACM, New York (2016)
5. Jha, S., Jha, M., O'Brien, L., Singh, P.K.: Architecture for complex event processing using open source technologies. In: 2016 3rd Asia-Pacific World Congress on Computer Science and Engineering (APWC on CSE), pp. 218–225 (2016)
6. Nguyen, F., Pitner, T.: Information system monitoring and notifications using complex event processing. In: Proceedings of the Fifth Balkan Conference in Informatics. pp. 211–216. Association for Computing Machinery, Novi Sad, Serbia (2012)
7. Jayan, K., Rajan, A.K.: Sys-log classifier for Complex Event Processing system in network security. In: 2014 International Conference on Advances in Computing, Communications and Informatics (ICACCI), pp. 2031–2035 (2014)
8. Nguyen, H.T.C., Lee, S., Kim, J., Ko, J., Comuzzi, M.: Autoencoders for improving quality of process event logs. Expert Syst. Appl. **131**, 132–147 (2019)
9. Gupta, S.: Introduction to Application Logging. In: Gupta, S. (ed.) Logging in Java with the JDK 1.4 Logging API and Apache log4j, pp. 1–9. Apress, Berkeley (2003)
10. Ćurin, T., Bogadi, D., Volarević, M., Štajcer, M., Mihalić, A., Mock, M.: Final Application Scenarios and Description of Test Environment. Hrvatski Telekom (2016)
11. Dickey, D.A., Dorter, B.S., German, J.M., Madore, B.D., Piper, M.W., Zenarosa, G.L.: Evaluating Java PathFinder on Log4J. vol. 15, Carnegie Mellon University (2011)

DECIDE: A New Decisional Big Data Methodology for a Better Data Governance

Mohamed Mehdi Ben Aissa[1(✉)], Lilia Sfaxi[2(✉)],
and Riadh Robbana[2(✉)]

[1] Tunisia Polytechnic School (University of Carthage), Tunis, Tunisia
mehdi_benissa@yahoo.fr
[2] INSAT (University of Carthage), Tunis, Tunisia
lilia.sfaxi@insat.u-carthage.tn,
riadh.robbana@gmail.com

Abstract. Big Data technologies and approaches have an important impact on the organization and governance of the enterprise. With such a high volume of structured & unstructured data, real time and mutualization needs, it is quite complicated to keep a high quality of data by respecting the governance rules and best practices. In addition, new team roles and organization must be applied in order to adapt to the new Big Data decisional constraints. In this direction, we present in this paper an overview of DECIDE, a decisional Big Data Methodology. We focus, particularly, on its team workforce, data quality, storage and governance fundamentals, rules and steps.

Keywords: Big Data Methodology · Analytics · Enterprise systems · Governance · Data quality · Team management · Decision-making

1 Introduction

With the continuous increase of data volume and the need for real time and accurate decision-making, companies rely more and more on Big Data systems and principles to get the best out of their data [1]. These systems are distinguished by the use of federated storage where data from multiple sources are gathered, and where multiple actors are involved in the value creation and consumption. These characteristics, coupled with many shared resources and continuous flows of events and requests, call for a well-defined data governance strategy.

Data Governance is defined as *"a set of policies and procedures adopted in order to manage data in an organization"* [2]. Correct policies are able to protect data from various internal and external risks that can threaten their security and alter their value. At the same time, their application should not be too restrictive that it affects the needed performance and efficiency in value extraction and manipulation [3].

Defining the right data policies in an organization can be of a great impact at the management as well as the technical level. Indeed, an adequate team management policy needs to be defined, to specify the roles and authorizations assigned to each user of the system. The data pipeline needs to be formalized, and storage systems must be consistent and synchronized. All these constraints come with a cost that can be really demotivating for decision makers.

© Springer Nature Switzerland AG 2020
M. Themistocleous et al. (Eds.): EMCIS 2020, LNBIP 402, pp. 63–78, 2020.
https://doi.org/10.1007/978-3-030-63396-7_5

On the other hand, Big Data technologies are evolving, day after day, by offering new features and capacity to deal with the demanding users. However, architects and developers find it increasingly hard to implement adequate solutions for their needs. They try to initiate internal Big Data and decisional projects, which tend to be very complex, with a high level of risk, and the need to involve a big number of actors with various skills. In fact, according to Vidgen et al. [4], the main three management challenges that these companies face in creating value for decision-making are: defining a clear data strategy, finding the right people to conduct a data-driven cultural change, and following information ethics. It is therefore necessary to define the right methodology, that helps organizations address these challenges and determine the desired business and analytics goals [5].

The lack of Big Data decisional methodology with adequate governance rules and fundamentals make it an imperative to define a more comprehensive and adaptable methodology. We refer to this methodology as DECIDE, which stands for **DEC**isional **BI**g **D**ata MEthodology.

2   Literature Review

Several decisional methodologies are defined in the literature [6–8]. These method-ologies are categorized into three types: **requirement-driven** approaches [9–11], that focus on the business users requirements; **data-driven** approaches [12–14], that focus on the underlying data sources to establish the data warehouse design, and **hybrid** approaches [15–19], that combine the advantages of both data- and requirements-driven approaches, by designing the data warehouse according to available data sources, while taking into consideration the requirements of the business users.

The methodologies cited above apply specifically to classical Business Intelligence applications, where data is provisioned from stable and static sources, the data ware-house is centralized and structured, and ETL(Extract-Transform-Load) jobs are com-plex and periodic. But these constraints do not always apply to decisional Big Data projects, where data sources can be unstructured or/and generate data flows with a high velocity. Our approach is more exploratory, where the design of the storage systems and global architecture depend strongly on the data sources that include all sorts of real-time and near-real-time events. This is why we qualify our approach as *Event and Data-driven Approach*, as we are adapting to fast-moving and large-scale data sources.

For decisional projects, some teams, such as in D2D CRC (Data to Decisions Cooperative Research Centers) [20], tend to use Agile principles to organize their work, considering these architectural issues like any other development project.

However, agility is difficult to implement in decisional systems, mainly because of the dimensional modeling's rigidity. In fact, the lack of planning and clear architecture can be a hindrance when designing the system, especially when it comes to defining conformed dimensions. Dimensional modeling requires a global view of the users' needs to define the right model for the data warehouse, and it can be problematic to consider the KPIs (Key Performance Indicators) from a limited set of users. But for Big

Data decisional projects, we are not constrained by a frozen structure of the storage system. Agile methods can be very adequate, as the sources change and evolve constantly, and the user's needs can also vary depending on the type and content of these sources. This is why we opt for *agility* as a basis for our methodology.

On another perspective, Data Mining methods, such as SEMMA, KDD [21] and CRISP-DM [22], can be considered as alternatives for Big Data projects. Contrary to classical BI (Business Intelligence) methodologies, Data Mining methodologies can easily adapt to Big Data projects, thanks to their bottom-up approach helping to apply data discovery to make complex analytics [23]. In fact, their main goal is to understand and discover data, in order to deploy adequate data mining models that will help prediction and decision-making.

Some works [24], tried to adapt these Data Mining methodologies to Big Data constraints. However, these solutions are still very strongly related to the specific case of data mining projects, contrary to our more global solution. On the other hand, pure Data Mining solutions do not take into account all transversal but crucial requirements of Big Data systems, such as DevOps approaches and the choice of the architecture, technologies, tools and roles. In addition, governance is still not the priority of this sort of methodology especially when it comes to data quality, storage design and team workforce considerations.

3   DECIDE and Data Governance Fundamentals

Responsible and effective data management requires attention to three main areas: data governance, which is the overarching framework for maintaining quality; the workforce structure, necessary for operational execution; and the quality elements, metrics and remediation approaches.

Data governance [25] is the pillar of the data management field. It defines a set of rules, processes, roles, policies and standards used to ensure the overall management of the availability, usability, understandability and correctness of the data in the company.

Data governance helps the organization in several aspects [26]: to create a shared understanding of the data, to improve data quality in an efficient and cost effective manner, to represent a clear data mapping in order to locate needed data and have a single version of the truth for business entities, to ensure that the data strategy is compliant with government and corporate regulations, and finally, to continuously improve data management policies by defining proper codes of conduct and best practices.

Figure 1 shows the main activities to encompass in every data governance strategy [26], that we tend to apply at various spots in the overall methodology.

Fig. 1. Data governance activities

4 Overview of DECIDE

The **DEC**isional **BI**g **D**ata MEthodology respects five fundamentals:

- **Agility**: it follows the Agile principles [27].
- **Bottom-up approach**: it is designed independently of specific KPIs.
- **Data and event driven**: it relies on the type and structure of the data sources, and on the various events generated by the environment, to design the data storage.
- **Multi-architectures**: it supports all decisional architectures that respect Big Data constraints.
- **Multi-technologies**: it is designed for any technology or stack.

DECIDE defines four phases: (1) preparation phase, (2) transversal phase, (3) data collection & storage phase, (4) data analysis & presentation phase. Each of these phases is composed of a set of steps, with iterations in the same phase and between phases, showcasing the agility of the methodology. Figure 2 summarizes the main steps and their correlation.

4.1 Preparation Phase

The preparation phase helps to prepare the building blocks of the project. A successful and solid Big Data project should start by defining the initial requirements, considering the target business impact and putting the deployment and automation infrastructure into place.

Initial Requirements Definition. The initial requirements' definition is the result of the first encounters between the development team and the clients. It is done at the

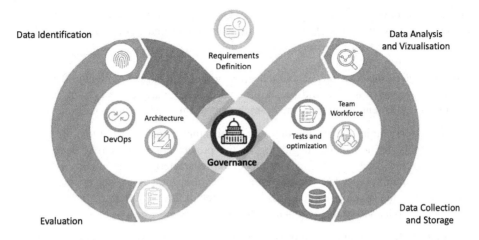

Fig. 2. DECIDE steps

beginning of the project to identify the needs that triggered the implementation of such a system. There are two types of initial requirements:

- **Business requirements**: Where the client states the global needs of the application, and the necessary Business Success Indicators (BSI), to be extracted and represented.
- **Quality requirements**: The definition of the quality requirements justifies many choices, such as the architecture, required tests, or technologies. Several quality attributes can be taken into consideration, such as availability, consistency, security, monitoring, etc.

Agile Approach. Once the requirements and success criteria are defined, the team should produce a first project plan. This first version will be split into different sprints with equal duration, going from one to four weeks. A sprint can include one or many DECIDE steps depending on the context: number of data sources, complexity of the implementation, ecosystem, complexity of the analysis, etc. This part of DECIDE was mainly inspired from the SCRUM methodology [28].

DevOps Approach. Big Data and DevOps are becoming a very close team in big projects. While agility is about adaptation to change and communication, DevOps makes sure that the operations constraints (hardware and deployment environment) are taken into consideration from the beginning at the same level as the functional requirements.

4.2 Transversal Phase

The transversal phase represents recurring actions and operations that occur throughout the execution of the project.

Data Governance. As presented in Fig. 2, Governance is the heartbeat of DECIDE, and not only a step or phase to take into consideration. From an practical point of view, every operation of DECIDE regarding the data life-cycle (extraction, transformation, storage, analysis or linkage) should be recorded and monitored. This enables the construction of the data lineage and the verification of its integrity and confidentiality. A data governance tool should be set up, and used regularly at every step. We recommend implementing an automatic enrichment of this tool during data life-cycle.

Architecture Choice. Choosing the right architecture helps to ensure that the quality requirements defined in the beginning of the project are respected. It depends on several metrics, such as the data and processing characteristics, the quality attributes and the restitution type. The choice of the architecture is not a one-step operation. It is done all over the development phases, as every step of the methodology will contribute in refining your idea of the adequate architecture.

Tests and Optimization. Testing is a critical operation that should occur not only at the end of the project, but also at the end of every step of the methodology. It will determine whether this step needs another iteration, or if we can proceed to the next one. Iterations can be used to optimize code, architectural choices or performance. DECIDE stands out compared to other bottom-up methodologies such as CRISP-DM [22], where the evaluation takes place only at the end of the cycle, instead of at each step, which impacts the agility of the solution and the early detection of faults and design problems.

4.3   Data Collection and Storage Phase

This first phase's purpose is to prepare the environment for the data analysis. This preparation helps mainly in designing the storage system depending on the data to be collected. The design of a system following a bottom-up approach always starts with a data identification step, where various data sources are defined, for immediate use or in anticipation of future needs.

Data Identification. Data can come from many varied physical sources (mainframes, database servers, distributed systems, etc.) that can be of various types (production bases, logs, archived data, etc.). We first need to identify these sources, define their type (streaming, batch or mixed), and reliability. For the latter, a source reliability rating can be used, like for example the *Intelligence source and information reliability rating system* [29], which rates sources from A *"completely reliable"* to E *"unreliable"*. From each identified data source, we list the datasets to be collected by describing their characteristics, such as structuring, type, data sensitivity, frequency and throughput, etc. Cleansing and/or enrichment of datasets improves their quality score and prepares the analytics steps. This is a first data scrubbing phase, done individually for each dataset, and can contain operations like identifying and removing duplicate records. In a Big Data approach, as the cost of storage is very low, it's recommended to keep the different versions of the datasets before and after every data cleansing operation.

Data Storage. During this phase, information about the new datasets are added to the governance tool. All storage layers (data lakes and data stores), and relations between them are defined. Access rules are updated. For example, initial data owners, that had all types of rights over their data, now see these rights reduced to read-only, as only the collection processes can insert or update any existing data. Data owners can also grant read access to other users over their data, to enable value extraction.

Data Collection. In a modern decisional architecture and especially for streaming analytics, fresh data must be collected fast and with a high frequency without impacting the data sources. For each data source and its adequate storage, you have to define the collection processes while taking into consideration the transformation type (pre-load or post-load), the pattern (distributed or centralized) and the execution engine (streaming, batch processes or Change Data Capture paradigm).

4.4   Data Analysis and Presentation Phase

This phase aims to design, implement, test, automate, optimize, present and manage the required analysis. The data collected during the first phase is raw, with a low-density level. This means that it is difficult to exploit it directly or extract information from it natively. In this direction, the next steps allow the end users to explore existing data by building KPIs [30], graphs and dashboards via analytic processes.

Data Analysis. Data users must collect the needs of the end users and decision makers. Each needed analysis is described, along with its attributes, pipeline, the frequency and latency of its operations, its type (OLAP, complex non-linear analysis, machine learning or customized), distribution and scalability, and application pattern (mono- or multi-threading, map-reduce, multi-agent paradigm, etc.). All analytical jobs and flows should be traced in the data governance tool including all the details: input, output, intermediate datasets, workflow and other metadata.

Data Visualization. The aim of data visualization is to restore the results of the processing layer via reports, graphs, dashboards, etc. Data restoration tools and technologies need to use ergonomic and modern features, such as auto-refresh, maps and geo-data, in order to improve as much as possible the user experience. Several choices need to be made, such as the visualization types (reports, graphs, dashboards, etc.), their refresh frequency, whether it is on-demand or pre-built, and other specifications such as their security constraints or multi-tenancy.

Evaluation: Global Optimization and Testing. End-to-end testing and optimization is the step where a complete use case is automatically run on the system, and where KPIs' compliance is evaluated. The key indicators that are considered are: performance, scalability, charge and resilience. This phase will ensure the integration of the different layers, look for the optimization issues and perform the integration, consistency and global performance tests. There is also a possibility to add other data sources and other analysis thanks to the layers' independence. This phase is essential in order to validate the global functional and technical specifications, while taking into consideration other constraints, like: cost, pooling resources, global configuration tuning, etc.

DECIDE is data-centric, and defines the necessary governance activities throughout the entire data life-cycle.

According to Margaret Rouse from TechTarget [31], two of the four pillars of Data Governance are defining the owners and custodians of the data (*Data Team Workforce*), and defining the level of completeness and consistency of the data (*Data Storage* and *Data Quality*). We show hereafter how we apply these concepts in DECIDE.

5 Data Governance Focus in DECIDE

5.1 Storage Design for Better Big Data Governance

Let's imagine new business opportunities that can be implemented via new decisional features, such as customer behavior analytics based on navigation logs and metrics. The problem with classical methodologies is that: (1) unstructured data like logs can't be managed and designed using a multi-dimensional approach, (2) once the data is collected, it is difficult to dynamically add new real time data sources, such as logs in this example, and (3) even if (1) and (2) were possible, the data schema must be modified, and we may have to redesign the warehouse (facts and dimension tables) in order to implement new analytics related to new business needs, which is very costly and can cause a non-negligible down-time of the system.

In addition, the biggest challenge when we have to deal with big data storage remains the governance rules that we have to respect in order to facilitate the usage and accessibility of the different datasets.

Indeed, the storage design must reflect the different storage layers and stores identified and to be implemented for persisting the data, their relationships and the data routing process between them.

In order to overcome these challenges, we propose a storage design to be used in the Data Storage Step (Sect. 4.3). This design aims to keep the archived and time-variant data by keeping a high governance layer. This design is decomposed into four main logical layers or stores [32] (Fig. 3).

- **Integrated raw data lake**: where the data is stored from the sources as it is, conserving their structure, relations and possible redundancies. The main objective of this store is to keep a repository containing all the company's data, without alteration.
- **Integrated refined data lake**: where a denormalized and integrated version of the data is created, after an extraction phase, from the raw data lake.
- **Big Data marts**: which represent a set of dedicated, single subject, schemaon-read, structured and decisional stores. They represent logical views of the data lake, where data having the same function and purpose, and destined to the same users, are consolidated.
- **Serving stores**: which are used to persist the results of the analysis phase. These stores are the only ones made accessible to the decision makers via visualization tools.

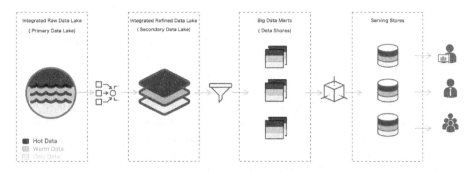

Fig. 3. Big data stores

In this phase, the serving stores can be defined in a preliminary way, using the global information about the types of analysis needed for our requirements. They can later on be changed or refined after the analysis step, in an Agile fashion.

This design aims to keep and trace the different data versions from edge to visualization without any data loss. Data is mutualized, which helps to share the different layers between teams and departments for a better governance.

The architecture of the refined data lake is composed of a set of entities (tables or collections). These entities must be independent and completely noncorrelated, respecting the principles of Big Databases: replication of attributes is thus favored over any dependency relation. The usual normal forms are no longer respected, which makes our refined database *denormalized*. The refined data lake respects these characteristics:

– All the entities should be independent (no physical relationships, no possibility of automatic joins).
– An entity should encapsulate all the dimensions of a specific measure.
– Attributes are never filtered or deleted.
– The new data models are referenced in the data governance tool.

The advantage of this design is that the transformations can be executed via the ELT (*Extract-Load-Transform*) pattern thanks to the Big Data technologies and their high locality level[1] independently of the data sources.

It is important to underline that the raw and refined data lakes are two logical structures of the same global data lake, and should be located in the same physical infrastructure. We notice a physical overhead of non-used or duplicated data between stores during the first implementations. On the other hand, important benefits can be gained from the storage mutualization compared with the data duplication in other approaches. The recommended use of open source Big Data technologies also contributes in costs decrease, thanks to their reduced storage costs and scalability.

---

[1] High locality level: data storage and processing are localized on the same nodes.

5.2   Data Quality

The most important component when it comes to Data Governance is the Data Quality. It is indeed one of the biggest challenges for all companies dealing with a huge amount of data coming from various sources: how to make sure that you are dealing with quality data, while having a data management process that is at the same time *thorough*, *fast* and *cheap*? The thing is, you can't. You can only pick two of these constraints, or try to balance between them all by making compromises. You can choose to let go of some quality metrics in order to save some time and/or money. But to do this, you must, first, define these metrics, and second, prioritize them. In this context, there are no miraculous formulas applicable to all cases when it comes to defining data quality. Each company, depending on their field, size, and available data and technology, has to define the criteria they want to focus on when calculating the data quality score of their data sets. When defining this score, they need to look for the relevant quality metrics they want to focus on. For instance, as defined by the DAMA UK Working Group [33], these metrics can be defined as (but not limited to) *Completeness*, *Uniqueness*, *Timeliness*, *Validity*, *Accuracy* and *Consistency*.

DQS: A New Data Quality Evaluation Metric. We define a formula to compute the data quality of a dataset, called DQS (*Data Quality Score*) [34–36]. We propose the following process:

1. Choose the target quality metrics $M_1, M_2, ..., M_n$
2. For each quality metric M_j:
   a) Associate a weight w_j to the metric, depending on its importance for the company's quality strategy.
   b) For every dimension D_i ($i \in [1..m]$) of the dataset which value is relevant to the chosen metric, define quality rules to be respected in order to conform to the quality metric M_j.
   c) Compute the score of every record regarding the defined rule.
   d) The average of the scores of all records of a dimension D_i is considered to be the score S_i of the dimension.
   e) The quality score S_j of the chosen metric is the average of all the dimension scores of the dataset:

$$S_j = \frac{\sum_{i=1}^{m} S_i}{m} \qquad (1)$$

3. The quality score *DQS* of the data set is the weighted average of all metrics' quality scores:

$$DQS = \frac{\sum_{j=1}^{n} w_j S_j}{\sum_{j=1}^{n} w_j} \qquad (2)$$

This metric can be computed in the Data Identification step (Sect. 4.3).

Applying the DQS to an eCommerce Example. Let's take the example of a simplified e-commerce decisional platform. We want to compute the quality score of a dataset imported from an operational database and composed of three tables, as presented in Fig. 4: *Customer*, *Product* and *Purchase*. We set our target metrics as being the *Freshness* (M_1) and *Completeness* (M_2) of the dataset. We give more importance in our quality strategy to *Completeness* of the information in the dataset rather than to *Freshness* of the purchases, this is why we associate to the metric *Freshness* the weight $w_1 = 1$, while the weight $w_2 = 2$ is associated to *Completeness*.

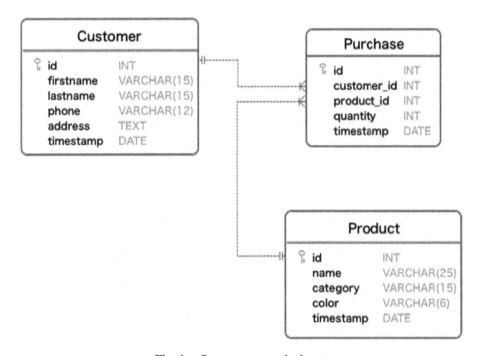

Fig. 4. eCommerce example dataset

For the first metric *Freshness*, we define the following rule: "*a purchase is considered fresh if it was stored less than one year ago*". In this case, the dimension we are concerned with is the *Purchase*, and we focus in particular on its attribute *timestamp*.

We choose to apply a score *1* to any record stored less than a year ago, and *0* otherwise. If we suppose that in our dataset of 50.000 purchases, 10.000 were done the preceding year, then the quality score S_1 for the *Freshness* metric is:

$$S_1 = \frac{10.000}{50.000} = 0,2 \tag{3}$$

As for the metric *completeness*, the quality rule defined in this case is: *"for every table in the dataset, a record is considered complete if all its information are filled"*. As stated in the rule, all the dimensions (*Product, Customer* and *Purchase*) with all their attributes have to be considered. We will apply in this case a score of *1* to every record where all the attributes are defined, *0.5* for records where only one attribute is missing, and *0* if more than one attribute is missing. In this case, let's suppose that among the 50.000 purchases, 20.000 customers and 120 products that we have on our dataset, 34.000 have the score *1*, 30.100 have the score *0.5* and 6.020 have the score *0*. In this case, the quality score S_2 of our dataset for the metric *Completeness* is:

$$S_2 = \frac{34.000 * 1 + 30.100 * 0, 5 + 6.020 * 0}{70.120} = 0,7 \tag{4}$$

Finally, the overall quality score of our dataset is estimated to:

$$DQS = \frac{w_1 * S_1 + w_2 * S_2}{w_1 + w_2} = \frac{1 * 0, 2 + 2 * 0, 7}{3} = 0,33 \tag{5}$$

Quality Improvement Scenarios. In order to improve the quality of this dataset, many cleansing and enrichment processes can be defined. We can for example add, as a metric, the number of clicks on the company's website per product and customer, which will considerably increase the amount of recent data (thus improving the *Freshness* metric), while adding a new attribute that can give more insight about the interest of the customers in the displayed products. A new extraction process must then be defined and the data quality score must be computed again.

As part of the data governance strategy, the computation of the quality score should be done regularly, stored periodically as important metadata, and adequate measures should be taken by the company in order to improve the quality of the internal data. If the considered data sources are external and have a poor-quality score, the data managers should either look for better data sources, or proceed to a cleansing and homogenization phase that can help to improve their quality. A quality score threshold should be defined depending on the needs and expectations of the decision makers.

The cost of this operation can vary depending on the type of dataset and the business context. But, compared to a classical decisional approach, we notice a low additional effort mainly in the first step when the data is identified. This is a part of each data owner's responsibility, who has to keep it updated and to define potential cleansing and enrichment processes in order to improve its data quality score (DQS). Regarding costs and overheads, DECIDE can present a small overhead for the setup and definition of the DQS, but the extraction and needed calculation cost will be the same compared to any other classical approach or methodology. On the other hand, and thanks to this part of DECIDE, the data governance strategy will make it possible to share the data, which will facilitate its usage for more efficient analysis. All team members will have the same data vision and can improve its quality in a collaborative manner. This is very important, especially when we have to deal with external and/or unstructured data sources for better analytics precision. Despite the light overhead of the quality metric's set up, its benefits are clear and will show their results during the DECIDE steps and in the business process.

5.3   Data Team Workforce

Just like any other asset, data needs protection and safeguards, with varying degrees of control and well-defined roles and privileges. It is thus mandatory to define all the actors that are involved in the creation, update, deletion, monitoring, transformation and tractability of the data in its environment: we call it *the data team workforce*.

The team is typically composed of the following actors [37]:

- *Data governance council*: in charge of the strategic view of the data governance plan,
- *Data governance board*: in charge of the tactical view,
- *Data owner(s)*: in charge of defining the requirements and ensuring the data quality and accessibility,
- *Data manager*: usually in the IT department, in charge of implementing the requirements of the data owner and of the management of the infrastructure,
- *Data steward*: in charge of defining the rules and planning the access and delivery of data,
- *Data user*: who has access to the reliable data.

The distribution of the team workforce throughout the different phases and steps of the methodology is represented in Fig. 5. A scaling system from 0 to 10 is defined, representing the implication of every role in each step of the process. 0 means *absent*, while 10 says *essential*.

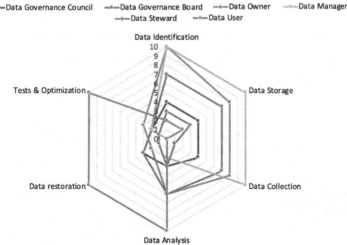

Fig. 5. Team workforce

6 Conclusion

We present in this article DECIDE, a Big Data Decisional Methodology that puts the focus on Data Governance. We recon that DECIDE can be more expensive than classical decisional methodologies when we have to deal with small projects with only one team or less than six members in the same team. However, the medium- and long-term benefits fully cover this overhead thanks to the gain in terms of time to market and refactoring costs in the case of rapidly evolving needs. The governance rules and fundamentals of DECIDE help to keep a solid link between the different teams and their members. In addition, governance shows also its benefits with data mining and exploration use cases, as all lineage and metadata can be accessible for all team members from any place. Indeed, DECIDE enforces a collaborative approach and helps data reuse and analysis.

It is still a real hardship to convince business stakeholders and project managers to apply a big data methodology in their projects, as their main focus is to increase their Return on Investment (RoI). In fact, such methodologies may seem expensive, but their repercussions can be huge in terms of new opportunities, integration of new business needs, taking full advantage of the available data and the team, and reduction of the overall time to market. It is then necessary to find a way to quantify these profits. We intend in a future work to define a method to estimate the overhead and the actual return on investment.

References

1. Koscielniak, H., Puto, A.: Big data in decision making processes of enterprises. Procedia Comput. Sci. **65**, 1052–1058 (2015). International Conference on Communications, management, and Information technology (ICCMIT'2015)
2. Al-Badi, A., Tarhini, A., Khan, A.I.: Exploring big data governance frameworks. Procedia Comput. Sci. **141**, 271–277 (2018). The 9th International Conference on Emerging Ubiquitous Systems and Pervasive Networks (EUSPN-2018)/The 8th International Conference on Current and Future Trends of Information and Communication Technologies in Healthcare (ICTH-2018)/Affiliated Workshops
3. Tallon, P.P.: Corporate governance of big data: Perspectives on value, risk, and cost. Computer **46**(6), 32–38 (2013)
4. Vidgen, R., Shaw, S., Grant, D.B.: Management challenges in creating value from business analytics. Eur. J. Oper. Res. **261**(2), 626–639 (2017)
5. Saltz, J.S.: The need for new processes, methodologies and tools to support big data teams and improve big data project effectiveness. In: Proceedings - 2015 IEEE International Conference on Big Data, IEEE Big Data 2015, pp. 2066–2071 (2015)
6. Abai, N.H.Z., Yahaya, J.H., Deraman, A.: User requirement analysis in data warehouse design: a review. Procedia Technol. **11**(ICEEI), 801–806 (2013)
7. Romero, O., Abello, A.: A survey of multidimensional modeling methodologies. Int. J. Data Warehouse. Min. **5**(2), 1–23 (2009)
8. Selma, K., Ily`es, B., Ladjel, B., Eric, S., Stephane, J., Michael, B.: Ontology-based structured web data warehouses for sustainable interoperability: requirement modeling, design methodology and tool. Comput. Ind. **63**(8), 799–812 (2012)

9. Kimball, R., Reeves, L., Ross, M., Thornthwaite, W.: The Data Warehouse Lifecycle Toolkit: Expert Methods for Designing, Developing, and Deploying Data Warehouses. Wiley, Chichester (1998)
10. Husemann, B., Lechtenborger, J., Vossen, G.: Conceptual data warehouse design. In: 2nd International Workshop on Design and Management of Data Warehouses, Stockholm, Sweden. CEUR-WS.org (2000)
11. Winter, R., Strauch, B.: A method for demand-driven information requirements analysis in data warehousing projects. In: Proceedings of the 36th Annual Hawaii International Conference on System Sciences, 9 pp. IEEE (2003)
12. Moody, D., Kortink, M.: From enterprise models to dimensional models: a methodology for data warehouse and data mart design. In: Proceedings of 2nd International Workshop on Design and Management of Data Warehouses, Stockholm, Sweden. CEUR-WS.org (2000)
13. Jensen, M.R., Holmgren, T., Pedersen, T.B.: Discovering Multidimensional Structure in Relational Data, pp. 138–148. Springer, Berlin (2004)
14. Song, I.Y., Khare, R., Dai, B.: SAMSTAR: a semi-automated lexical method for generating star schemas from an entity-relationship diagram. In: Proceedings of the ACM Tenth International Workshop on Data Warehousing and OLAP, pp. 9–16 (2007)
15. Golfarelli, M., Rizzi, S.: A methodological framework for data warehouse design. In: Proceedings of the 1st ACM International Workshop on Data Warehousing and OLAP - DOLAP '98, pp. 3–9. ACM Press, New York (1998)
16. Boehnlein, M., Ulbrichvom Ende, A.: Deriving initial data warehouse structures from the conceptual data models of the underlying operational information systems. In: Proceedings of the 2nd ACM International Workshop on Data Warehousing and OLAP - DOLAP '99, pp. 15–21 (1999)
17. Bonifati, A., Cattaneo, F., Ceri, S., Fuggetta, A., Paraboschi, S.: Designing data marts for data warehouses. ACM Trans. Softw. Eng. Methodol. 10(4), 452–483 (2001)
18. Cabibbo, L., Torlone, R.: A logical approach to multidimensional databases. In: Schek, H.-J., Alonso, G., Saltor, F., Ramos, I. (eds.) EDBT 1998. LNCS, vol. 1377, pp. 183–197. Springer, Heidelberg (1998). https://doi.org/10.1007/BFb0100985
19. Romero, O., Abello, A.: Multidimensional design by examples. In: 8th International Conference on Data Warehousing and Knowledge Discovery, pp. 85–94 (2006)
20. D2D CRC: Agile Methodologies for Big Data Projects (2018). https://www.d2dcrc.com.au/article-content/agile-methodologies-for-big-data-projects
21. Fayyad, U., Stolorz, P.: Data mining and KDD: promise and challenges. Future Gener. Comput. Syst. 13(2–3), 99–115 (1997)
22. Shearer, C., et al.: The CRISP-DM model: the new blueprint for data mining. J. Data Warehous. 5(4), 13–22 (2000)
23. Provost, F., Fawcett, T.: Data science and its relationship to big data and data driven decision making. Big Data 1(1), 51–59 2013
24. Angée, S., Lozano, S., Montoya-Munera, E., Ospina Arango, J., Tabares, M.: In: 13th International Conference on Towards an Improved ASUM-DM Process Methodology for Cross-Disciplinary Multiorganization Big Data & Analytics Projects, KMO 2018, pp. 613–624, Zilina, Slovakia, 6–10 August 2018, Proceedings (2018)
25. Khatri, V., Brown, C.V.: Designing data governance. Commun. ACM 53(1), 148–152 (2010)
26. Talend Team: What is Data Governance (and Do I Need It)?
27. Beedle, M. et al.: Manifesto for Agile Software Development (2001)
28. Sims, C., Johnson, H.L.: Scrum: A Breathtakingly Brief and Agile Introduction. Dymax, Torrington (2012)
29. United States Army: Human Intelligence Collector Operations. Volume 2–22.3 (2006)

30. TDWI: TDWI BI BENCHMARK REPORT: Organizational and Performance Metrics for Business Intelligence Teams. Technical report (2010)
31. Rouse, M.: Data Governance (DG) (2017)
32. Fowler, M.: Data Lake (2015)
33. Sattler, K.U.: Data Quality Dimensions. Encyclopedia of Database Systems, pp. 1–5 (2016)
34. ShellBlack: Formulas to Create Data Quality Lead Score
35. Evans, P.: Scaling and assessment of data quality. Acta Crystallogr. Sect. D Biol. Crystallogr. **62**(1), 72–82 (2006)
36. White, C.H., Gonzalez, L.R.: The Data Quality Equation—A Pragmatic Approach to Data Integrity (2015)
37. BARC: Data Governance: Definition, Challenges & Best Practices. Technical report, Business Application Research Center (2018)

Towards the Machine Learning Algorithms in Telecommunications Business Environment

Moisés Loma-Osorio de Andrés[1], Aneta Poniszewska-Marańda[2(✉)],
and Luis Alfonso Hernández Gómez[1]

[1] Universidad Politécnica de Madrid, Madrid, Spain
M.loma-osorio@alumnos.upm.es,
luisalfonso.hernandez@upm.es
[2] Institute of Information Technology, Lodz University of Technology,
Lodz, Poland
aneta.poniszewska-maranda@p.lodz.pl

Abstract. We live in times where companies and individuals are dealing with extremely large amounts of data coming from all different kind of sources. This data includes a lot of very valuable information, which, most of the time, cannot be inferred at first sight. Therefore, in today's businesses there is a growing necessity of discovering efficient and useful information out of the data that has been gathered. This is the reason why Machine Learning, a technology that has been developed since mid-20th century, is one of the biggest growing technologies in this last decade, being one of its most popular applications in the field of data. The paper presents an analysis what techniques are available for starting with a Data Science project, how easy they are to implement, and how they can be applied in a real world case. The data that was worked with for this project was gathered from a telecommunications company.

Keywords: Machine learning · Data processing · Machine learning model

1 Introduction

We live in times where companies and individuals are dealing with extremely large amounts of data coming from all different kind of sources. This data includes a lot of very valuable information, which, most of the time, cannot be inferred at first sight. Therefore, in today's businesses there is a growing necessity of discovering efficient and useful information out of the data that has been gathered. This is the reason why Machine Learning (ML) is one of the biggest growing technologies in last decade, being one of its most popular applications in the field of data. Although it can help to interpret the data that has been obtained and getting useful information regarding existing trends, one of the most valuable applications is the ability of predicting future behaviors and trends based on the current ones (predictive model). This way companies not only know how to react to the current situation, but also are able to prepare for any future problems that they might encounter.

In order to get a deep understanding of how these technologies are being used even in traditional companies, we analyzed the data gathered from a company that offers

© Springer Nature Switzerland AG 2020
M. Themistocleous et al. (Eds.): EMCIS 2020, LNBIP 402, pp. 79–96, 2020.
https://doi.org/10.1007/978-3-030-63396-7_6

telecommunication services to their clients, such as phone and internet services, television and movie streaming, and device protection. With this data, different Machine Learning techniques were developed and applied in order to find out if they work properly, to identify which are the main reasons that clients stop hiring the company's services and to predict how likely a new client is to do so, as well as finding out how the company can act in order to stop this from happening.

The main objective of the project is to get a deep understanding of why Machine Learning techniques are being so widely used nowadays in the field of data, why every single company is starting to implement them and what benefits can they obtain from their application, and how a Machine Learning model can be tuned to achieve different results.

The paper presents the study of what techniques are available for starting with a data science project, how easy they are to implement, and how they can be applied in a real world case. The data that was worked with for this project was gathered from a telecommunications company.

The paper is structured as follows. Section 2 presents a short overview of machine learning and data science algorithms. Section 3 describes the model building process with determining the resources and data processing techniques. Section 4 deals with presentation of research methodology and implementation of ML selected methods while Sect. 5 presents the analysis of results of ML methods implementation in the given case.

2 Machine Learning and Data Science Algorithms

Machine learning is an application of artificial intelligence (AI) that provides systems the ability to automatically learn and improve from experience without being explicitly programmed. Machine learning focuses on the development of computer programs that can access data and use it to learn for themselves [1–5].

Machine learning approach involves mostly supervised or semi-supervised techniques. Standard classification methods are applicable, however sequence-based methods that use the whole sentences as sequences of words instead of sets of single words, are more widely used. *Deep learning* is a sub-domain of machine learning that uses neural network architectures, in NER especially valuable are architectures that capture long-term dependencies and operate on data sequences.

Supervised Machine learning techniques are the most common application in Data Science. Starting with a dataset with several entries, we can select a target (output) to make predictions for, based on the rest of the features (inputs). When training the model, the algorithm will stablish relations between the features and the target, and then will use the acquired knowledge to predict new values when faced with new data.

Depending on the type of target that we are trying to predict, it is possible to identify two different categories of algorithms: regression and classification [18]. The main difference between them is the type of target they are trying to predict: regression algorithms are used when the target is a continuous variable, for example, trying to predict the price of a new house; while classification algorithms are used if the target is a discrete value, for example, trying to identify if an incoming email should be classified as spam or not spam. In the problem that is being tackled by this project, the objective is trying to predict if a customer from a company will stop hiring its services or if they will stay, which can be easily identified as a classification problem. In the case of leaving customers in a business environment, this is known as churn prediction. In Machine Learning, classification refers to a predictive modeling problem where a class label is predicted for a given example of input data [2].

In the problem that is being tackled by the project, the objective is trying to predict if a customer from a company will stop hiring its services or if they will stay, which can be easily identified as a classification problem. In the case of leaving customers in a business environment, this is known as churn prediction. Many of machine learning algorithms are used for this kind of problems, such as logistic regression, Naïve Bayes algorithm, k-nearest Neighbors (KNN) algorithm, decision trees. Four of them were implemented for the data gathered from a telecommunications company: random forest [6–8], k-nearest Neighbors [9], extreme gradient boosting [10, 11] and logistic regression [12, 13].

3   Model Building – Resources and Data Processing

Since the nature of the project was data science, there are a few questions needed to answer firstly. First, where do we get the data that will be used in the project? Which programming language should be used to work with it? Which development environment is best suited for this kind of project?

The obvious first step in any data science project is getting the data that will be analyzed and used to train the machine learning model. Though this might seem like a trivial step, sometimes this data is not immediately accessible, depending on its nature. For example, data concerning medical records of patients is usually protected, and this means that it can be a challenge to start a data science project about this topic. Since the objective of this project was to analyze the behavior of clients of a Telecom company, we needed access to personal data from companies, which is rarely shown to the public. Such data was found at Kaggle.com. It contains the following information [14]:

- Customers who left within the last month – column called *Churn*.
- Services that each customer has signed up for – phone, multiple lines, internet, online security, online backup, device protection, tech support, and streaming TV and movies.
- Customer account information – how long they have been a customer, contract, payment method, paperless billing, monthly charges, and total charges.
- Demographic info about customers – gender, age range, and if they have partners and dependents.

The project was developed in *Python* language with the use of *Sckit-learn* library (integrating a wide range of machine learning algorithms for medium-scale supervised and unsupervised problems) and *pandas* library (providing fast, flexible, and expressive data structures designed to make working with "relational" or "labelled" data) [15].

Before starting with the testing of Machine Learning models, it is very important to understand the nature of the data we are working with. A first analysis can reveal some parameters that do not contribute too much to the final result (in this case, whether the customer is going leave the company and hire the services of a different company). Right now, the data is stored in CSV (comma separated values) format, which does not allow for an easy interpretation, so we have to load the data and transform it into an easy to read and manipulate format.

To load the data, we just need to specify the path to the CSV file where it is stored and pass it as an argument to the pandas library method *read_csv*. To check what the data looks like, we can call the DataFrame method *head()*, which returns the first five columns of the DataFrame (Fig. 1). The important thing is to identify which of these columns is the target to predict: in this case, it is the column *Churn*. The fields in this column take only two values: *Yes*, if the customer did not continue hiring the services of the company; or *No*, if they stayed with the company.

```
In [1]: # Load the data as a pandas Data Frame class
        full_data = pd.read_csv('telco-customer-churn.csv')

        # Check the first 5 rows of the data to take a peak at the data
        full_data.head()
```

Out[1]:

	customerID	gender	SeniorCitizen	Partner	Dependents	tenure	PhoneService	MultipleLines	InternetService	OnlineSecurity	...	DeviceProtection	TechSup
0	7590-VHVEG	Female	0	Yes	No	1	No	No phone service	DSL	No	...	No
1	5575-GNVDE	Male	0	No	No	34	Yes	No	DSL	Yes	...	Yes
2	3668-QPYBK	Male	0	No	No	2	Yes	No	DSL	Yes	...	No
3	7795-CFOCW	Male	0	No	No	45	No	No phone service	DSL	Yes	...	Yes
4	9237-HQITU	Female	0	No	No	2	Yes	No	Fiber optic	No	...	No

5 rows × 21 columns

Fig. 1. First five rows of the DataFrame in pandas library

Some of the algorithms used to build the machine learning models in our approach can only predict numerical values, so we need to change the values 'Yes' for '1' and the 'No' values for '0'.

When working with a classification problem, it is important to train the Machine Learning models with data that is balanced, meaning that there needs to be a balance between positive classes (in this case, 1 in the Churn column) and negative classes (0 in the Churn column). In the case of the problem being tackled we had the situation where there is a larger number of non-Churn customers than Churn ones:

- Number of non-Churn customers in the dataset: 5163.
- Number of Churn customers in the dataset: 1869.
- Proportion of Churn vs No Churn: 0.27.

The exact percentage of leaving customers is 27% of the total that is not as extreme as we would like to have, but the performance of the models will still see improvement if we balance this data.

It is important to clarify that data balancing cannot be done to the whole dataset. This is because data has to be divided in training and testing – to train the algorithm and to measure its performance. Both of them are obtained by dividing the original dataset, and balancing the data can only be done to the dataset that will train the model. Otherwise, this would cause a problem known as Data Leakage, since there would be some samples that have been created from already existing data in the testing dataset, which would cause the model to seem much more effective than it really is (fake results). This means that, even though data balancing is being explained before splitting the data, this can only be done afterwards.

Using the SMOTE (Synthetic Minority Oversampling TEchnique) algorithm for balancing the data produced the results presented in Fig. 2.

```
Length of original data is 5625
Length of oversampled data is 8244
Number of no Churn in oversampled data: 4122
Number of Churn: 4122
Proportion of Churn data in oversampled data is 0.5
Proportion of no Churn data in oversampled data is 0.5
```

Fig. 2. Proportion of customers in the training dataset after balancing both classes

4   Research Methodology and Implementation of Selected Methods

After loading, analyzing and preparing the data to work with, it is time to test the selected Machine Learning algorithms indicated in Sect. 2.

The Machine Learning process can be (greatly) simplified in two steps: *training* and *testing* of the model. Since we implement supervised learning algorithms, this means that the training step consists in feeding the model with data where a finite number of feature columns map to a single target column whose values are known in advance.

At this point, we have the modified data split in two different sets: training and validation sets. Both of these are divided in features (X) and target (y – Churn column). The training set is used to fit the different models, which means to stablish relationship between features and target. The validation set is used to evaluate the performance of the model: it uses the validation features set to predict a value for the target set, and then compare these predictions with the real validation targets set, and use different metrics (that was already explained beforehand) of choice to return a performance measure.

This process was done for each of the four models, while changing a few parameters to optimize the results, and then compare the different performance metrics of each models to select the one that gives us the most satisfying results. When trying to improve the performance of each individual model, we performed two main operations: *feature selection*, which consists in finding out which features have lower contribution to the model and getting rid of them to see if it improves its performance; and *hyperparameter tuning*, which means trying several parameter configurations for each algorithm (these parameters are different depending on the way the algorithm works) and find out which combination of parameters works best for each model.

4.1 Random Forest Model

The first model implements Random Forest (RF) classifier algorithm. There are a few parameters that can be set in order to better adapt the model to our data – the considered parameters are: *n_estimators* (number of trees in the forest), *max_depth* (maximum depth of the tree) and *max_features* (number of features to consider when looking for the best split). Firstly, the model with all parameters set at their default values was considered, in order to test if the changes that are made improve on the performance of this basic model. The results are presented in Fig. 3 (top part). The first results with AUC_ROC score equals to 0.7087 are not satisfying. It is because some of the lower ranked features might introduce noise and causing the model to overfit (there are way too many variables to consider).

Therefore, only the first few features were kept to see if the performance of the model improves (Fig. 3, middle part). The recall metric value is now 0.64, an increase of 0.07 point compared to the last case (before deleting some features), which is definitely an improvement. The AUC_ROC value also increases about 0.02 points, once again proving that a large amount of the features were more harmful than helpful to the model.

Finally, some of the parameters were tuned to check to get further improvement. In general, the higher the value of *n_estimators* (number of trees in the ensemble) the more reliable the prediction will be, but the computational cost will also be higher (Fig. 3, bottom part). These results are much more promising than the first ones but Random Forest Algorithm is one of the simpler to implement, so better results with other algorithms are expected.

	precision	recall	f1-score	support
0	0.85	0.85	0.85	1041
1	0.57	0.57	0.57	366
accuracy			0.77	1407
macro avg	0.71	0.71	0.71	1407
weighted avg	0.78	0.77	0.77	1407

AUC_ROC score for this model: 0.7087

	precision	recall	f1-score	support
0	0.87	0.82	0.84	1041
1	0.55	0.64	0.59	366
accuracy			0.77	1407
macro avg	0.71	0.73	0.72	1407
weighted avg	0.78	0.77	0.78	1407

AUC_ROC score for this model: 0.7279

	precision	recall	f1-score	support
0	0.89	0.80	0.84	1041
1	0.55	0.72	0.62	366
accuracy			0.77	1407
macro avg	0.72	0.76	0.73	1407
weighted avg	0.80	0.77	0.78	1407

AUC_ROC score for this model: 0.7556

Fig. 3. Metrics report for Random Forest model and modified Random Forest model with the most important feature

Figure 4. how the ROC curve improved after all the changes we made. The green curve represents the basic model, and the blue one is the model after all the improvements we made to the model and the training data. The red line represents an estimator with 0.5 AUC, which is the score that an estimator that predicted random results (50% of the time class A and 50% class B) would get.

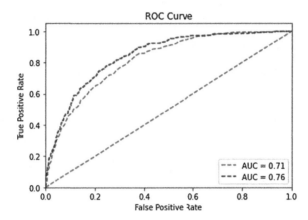

Fig. 4. ROC curves for the basic and improved RF models

4.2   K-Nearest Neighbors Model

K-Nearest Neighbors (KNN) model is the most popular classification algorithm. The same, firstly, default model was tested and then it was improved. By default, the model sets k = 5 (k being number of neighbors). Looking at the values of precision and recall (0.48 and 0.67 respectively) it seems like this model predicts positive classes much more often than it should (less than 50% of predicted positives are actual positives). It finds a fair amount of actual positive classes, but it cannot be considered a good model when looking at these results (Fig. 5, top part).

KNN implements a lazy learning model, which means that it waits for the training data to perform any calculations. This means that removing features from the set can only be done by intuition, so we will use the same ranking as in Random Forest model. Even though it might not be the optimal approach, it is still better than removing features randomly. This time, the best result is achieved when using only the best 8 features (Fig. 5, middle part). Results are improved – recall and AUC_ROC score improve respectively 0.04 and 0.03 points, so even if the deleted features might not have been the optimal ones, the performance of the model is improving rapidly.

So far, all the model tests have been done with a value of k = 5 neighbors which, with such a large training set (around 8000 entries), it is a really low number and can easily lead to wrong predictions. It is necessary to check which K number grants better results for this dataset. In this case, a number between 100 and 120 seems to consistently return the best possible values for both metrics, so when setting the value of K to 117 neighbors, we obtain the results presented in Fig. 5 (bottom part). Setting the number of neighbors to a higher value improves the results of pretty much all the metrics. Focusing on the recall and AUC_ROC, the results have improved greatly, achieving a recall score of 0.81, which is even better than the best score achieved with the Random Forest model. The difference in ROC curves for both KNN models presented in Fig. 6 shows how drastic the improvement actually was.

	precision	recall	f1-score	support
0	0.86	0.75	0.80	1041
1	0.48	0.67	0.56	366
accuracy			0.73	1407
macro avg	0.67	0.71	0.68	1407
weighted avg	0.77	0.73	0.74	1407

AUC_ROC score for this model: 0.7075

	precision	recall	f1-score	support
0	0.88	0.76	0.82	1041
1	0.51	0.71	0.59	366
accuracy			0.75	1407
macro avg	0.69	0.73	0.70	1407
weighted avg	0.78	0.75	0.76	1407

AUC_ROC score for this model: 0.7333

	precision	recall	f1-score	support
0	0.92	0.73	0.81	1041
1	0.51	0.81	0.63	366
accuracy			0.75	1407
macro avg	0.72	0.77	0.72	1407
weighted avg	0.81	0.75	0.77	1407

AUC_ROC score for this model: 0.7721

Fig. 5. Metrics report for K-Nearest neighbors model and modified K-Nearest neighbors model with removed features

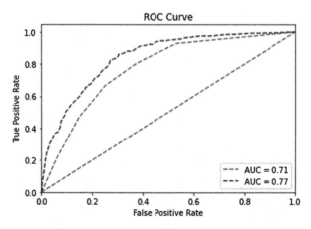

Fig. 6. ROC curves for the basic and improved KNN models

4.3   Extreme Gradient Boosting Model

Extreme gradient boosting (XGB) is a variation of original gradient boosting, one of the more powerful machine learning algorithms developed, and widely used in many data science projects nowadays.

The results obtained for default XGB model are not impressive (Fig. 7, first part). This is because one of the strengths of XGB models are the numerous variables that can be tweaked in order to improve the performance of the algorithm. Some of these parameters include the following [16]: *n_estimators* (number of estimators in the

```
                precision    recall  f1-score   support

            0       0.85      0.86      0.85      1041
            1       0.58      0.55      0.57       366

     accuracy                          0.78      1407
    macro avg       0.71      0.71      0.71      1407
 weighted avg       0.78      0.78      0.78      1407

AUC_ROC score for this model: 0.7058

                precision    recall  f1-score   support

            0       0.92      0.74      0.82      1041
            1       0.52      0.82      0.64       366

     accuracy                          0.76      1407
    macro avg       0.72      0.78      0.73      1407
 weighted avg       0.82      0.76      0.77      1407

AUC_ROC score for this model: 0.7783

                precision    recall  f1-score   support

            0       0.97      0.45      0.61      1041
            1       0.38      0.96      0.54       366

     accuracy                          0.58      1407
    macro avg       0.67      0.70      0.58      1407
 weighted avg       0.81      0.58      0.59      1407

AUC_ROC score for this model: 0.702

                precision    recall  f1-score   support

            0       0.93      0.71      0.81      1041
            1       0.51      0.85      0.64       366

     accuracy                          0.75      1407
    macro avg       0.72      0.78      0.72      1407
 weighted avg       0.82      0.75      0.76      1407

AUC_ROC score for this model: 0.7831
```

Fig. 7. Metrics report for Extreme gradient boosting model and modified Extreme gradient boosting model with deleted features

ensemble), *eta* (weight of each iteration of the loop), *max_depth* (maximum depth of the decision trees), *subsample* (subsample ratio of the training instances).

After a few tests, the following combination of values seems to significantly improve the previous results: n_estimators = 10, eta = 0.1, max_depth = 4, subsample = 0.92. The new obtained results are improved in most metrics, but especially those that we are focusing on. Specifically, recall improved by 0.27 points (which is an extremely high improvement) and AUC_ROC score improved by around 0.07 points (Fig. 7, second part).

Following the tuning of parameters, we will once again try to delete some features in order to see if it can improve the model. Deleting some of the less important columns causes positive effect in the performance of the algorithm. Running the same loop as in previous models returns the value '26' as the number of features to delete in order to maximize the recall value. If we focused only on predicting every single Churn and disregarding every other metric it might be a viable solution, but it is important to find good balance between high recall and rest of the metrics so it seems like deleting features will not help in this instance (Fig. 7, third part).

One alternative option to be considered is setting a value for another parameter: *colsample_bytree*. This works similarly to the subsample feature, but instead of sampling a percentage of the rows in the training data for each iteration of the loop, it does so but for the features (columns). Testing some values, the best results were obtained with a value for this parameter between 0.45 and 0.60. Settling for a value of 0.5 in the end (which at first already seemed like a good choice, since sampling 50% of features each iteration would definitely help in this case, where the training dataset is made of such a large number of features) will grant the following results. Both main metrics have improved after the implementation of this last parameter. So far, this model outperforms the previous one (Fig. 7, fourth part).

Comparing both ROC curve shapes (Fig. 8), it can be appreciated how improved the shape of the final looks compared to the original. This is expected, seeing how XGB is a very popular machine learning algorithm to use in this kind of projects, one of the reasons being the high number of hyperparameters that can be set in order to perfectly fit the data.

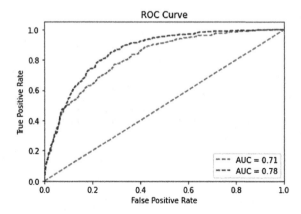

Fig. 8. ROC curves for the basic and improved Extreme Gradient Boosting model

4.4   Logistic Regression

Finally, the Logistic regression (LR) model, commonly used in this type of data science projects, was tested. Firstly, a model with default parameters was trained to get a first grasp of what to expect (Fig. 9, top part). The results are actually pretty decent, even before removing less useful features or tuning some of the hyperparameters. A recall score of 0.81 and an AUC_ROC score of 0.77 are better results than those from previous models even after tuning them.

In this case, the *Recursive Feature Elimination (RFE)* was used to tune the logistic regression model. This was achieved by fitting the algorithm used in the core of the model, ranking features by importance, discarding the least important features, and re-fitting the model. This process is repeated until a specified number of features remains [17]. In order to see which value of features left make for the best improved model, we can run a loop and find the best resulting value for ROC_AUC. In this case, it happens to be nine features out of the 43 original ones.

There is an improvement on the performance, but not as impactful as we could have predicted (since the original result was pretty good to start with). This is as good as it can get, because tuning some of the Logistic Regression hyperparameters does not seem to improve the performance of the model as it did with the rest of the algorithms (Fig. 9, bottom part). The final and original ROC curves are represented in Fig. 10.

	precision	recall	f1-score	support
0	0.92	0.73	0.81	1041
1	0.51	0.81	0.63	366
accuracy			0.75	1407
macro avg	0.72	0.77	0.72	1407
weighted avg	0.81	0.75	0.76	1407

AUC_ROC score for this model: 0.7712

	precision	recall	f1-score	support
0	0.93	0.71	0.81	1041
1	0.51	0.84	0.63	366
accuracy			0.75	1407
macro avg	0.72	0.78	0.72	1407
weighted avg	0.82	0.75	0.76	1407

AUC_ROC score for this model: 0.7754

Fig. 9. Metrics report for Logistic regression model and modified Logistic regression model with deleted feature

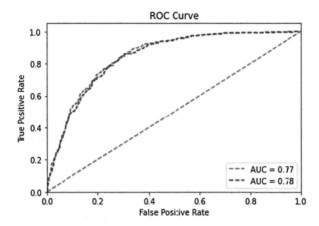

Fig. 10. ROC curves for the basic and improved Logistic regression model

As expected, the performance of the model didn't improve that much even after trying to get the best possible results. This speaks of Logistic Regression as a fairly simple algorithm, that works very well if there is no need to optimize the result for a specific metric.

5 Results and Discussion – Choosing a Machine Learning Model and Its Implementation

After testing four different algorithms and obtaining performance results for all of them, they were compared and one of them was selected to be implemented to tackle the problem of detecting leaving customers in a Telecommunications company environment. While comparing the algorithms, following aspects should be kept in mind:

- There are many metrics used to evaluate the performance of a machine learning model. In our case, the focus was on two metrics: *recall* (to be able to detect as many leaving customers as possible) and *ROC_AUC score* (to get a grasp at how good the model is at distinguishing between positive and negative classes). When testing the different models, we aimed to achieve good balance between these two metrics.
- Only algorithm's metrics performances were taken into account when choosing between models. Other variables, such as overall training and testing speed, do not really matter for this problem, since it does not have real time implications (there is no need for the algorithms to run as fast as possible, sacrificing overall performance).

The results obtained for performances of tested machine learning models are presented in Table 1.

Table 1. Performance metrics results for all tested ML models

	Random forest	KNN	XGBoost	Logistic regression
Recall	0.72	0.81	0.85	0.84
ROC_AUC	0.7556	0.7721	0.7831	0.7754

As expected, Extreme Gradient Boost algorithm performed the best results out of all the tested. The possibility of fine-tuning the hyperparameters to adapt it as well as possible to the data, as well as reinforcing an original weak estimator and transforming it into a strong one are some of the reasons why it is being considered as one of the best performing machine learning algorithms for data science projects. Thus, the chosen final model implements this algorithm, since it is the one which was expected to grant the most reliable results when exposed to new customer's data.

In order to test how this project could be implemented in a real-world case, we created a Python simulation that creates basic synthetic data based on the dataset that has been used to train the model. Originally, the idea behind this project was to use this data as the core dataset for the project, but this idea was quickly discarded, as it is not the best way to evaluate the performance of the different machine learning algorithms. Instead, we used the Kaggle.com dataset to train and test all the models, and then use own program to generate synthetic data bases on this same dataset.

Some considerations were made when developing this program, but in the end this was just a symbolic step in the project, to simulate a real situation where the Machine Learning model is being tested with new data where we don't know yet if the customer will leave or stay. This means that there is no real performance measure to be made with this data, and it is just to recreate a real-world business situation. Still, the objective was to make the synthetic somewhat resembling of the dataset that was used to train the model so that the predictions could be as reliable as they can be. Some of the considerations that were made are the following:

- Gender distribution is 50% between male and female.
- The customer must hire at least one service from the company.
- Probability distribution of the values in different features is similar to the one of the original dataset.
- Monthly charges are calculated based on the number of services the customer has hired.
- Neither monthly nor total charges exceed the minimum or maximum values that were represented in the original data.
- There are some variations added in the calculations of the prices (to add some variance in the dataset).

The Kaggle.com dataset was again used (this time, in its entirety) as training data for the model, while the synthetic data was used as testing set (this time, it is not really labelled as validation data, since it is not used to validate the performance of the model). The steps that are performed to prepare the data are, in order:

- Changing the format of tenure feature values into categorical (from months to range of years, as we already did before) for both training and testing datasets.
- Applying one-hot encoding to both datasets, once again getting rid of the useless features (those that represented no phone service/no internet service).
- Normalizing the numerical columns (once again, monthly and total charges) in both datasets with a MinMax scaler in.
- Applying SMOTE algorithm *only to the training dataset*, in order to balance the data (same number of occurrences for both Churn and no Churn).

Once the data is prepared for the model, next step is defining the latter. As mentioned earlier, the final decision was to create a model that runs an Extreme Gradient Boosting algorithm, with the same parameters that were defined previously when testing the model.

After training the model and computing the predictions, they were added to the synthetic dataset (these steps are represented in Fig. 11) to have the data as organized as possible. The random set of customers and the predicted outcome are presented in Fig. 12.

```
final_model = XGBClassifier(learning_rate=0.1, max_depth=4,
                    subsample=0.92, colsample_bytree=0.33)
xgb_model.fit(final_X_train, final_y_train,
            early_stopping_rounds=10,
            eval_set=[(X_val, y_val)],
            verbose=False)

predictions = xgb_model.predict(final_X_test)

new_data['PredictedChurn'] = predictions
```

Fig. 11. Code cell to obtain the new predictions and joining them with the testing dataset

gender	Male	gender	Female	gender	Male
SeniorCitizen	Yes	SeniorCitizen	No	SeniorCitizen	Yes
Partner	Yes	Partner	Yes	Partner	No
Dependents	No	Dependents	Yes	Dependents	No
tenure	(3, 4)	tenure	(0, 1)	tenure	(1, 2)
PhoneService	Yes	PhoneService	Yes	PhoneService	No
MultipleLines	Yes	MultipleLines	Yes	MultipleLines	No phone service
InternetService	DSL	InternetService	Fiber optic	InternetService	DSL
OnlineSecurity	No	OnlineSecurity	Yes	OnlineSecurity	No
OnlineBackup	No	OnlineBackup	Yes	OnlineBackup	No
DeviceProtection	Yes	DeviceProtection	Yes	DeviceProtection	No
TechSupport	No	TechSupport	No	TechSupport	Yes
StreamingTV	Yes	StreamingTV	Yes	StreamingTV	Yes
StreamingMovies	Yes	StreamingMovies	Yes	StreamingMovies	Yes
Contract	One year	Contract	Month-to-month	Contract	Month-to-month
PaperlessBilling	Yes	PaperlessBilling	Yes	PaperlessBilling	No
PaymentMethod	Credit card (automatic)	PaymentMethod	Electronic check	PaymentMethod	Mailed check
MonthlyCharges	97.82	MonthlyCharges	118.75	MonthlyCharges	65.55
TotalCharges	3691.73	TotalCharges	104.5	TotalCharges	855.43
PredictedChurn	0	PredictedChurn	1	PredictedChurn	1

Fig. 12. Random set of customers and predicted outcome in synthetic dataset

For this first customer, whose features are represented in Fig. 12 the model predicted a value of 0, which means No Churn, or that he will stay with the company. Looking at some of the feature values, we observe he has been in the company for a decent amount of time (between 3 and 4 years), that he has hired DSL over Fiber Optic (which latter correlates to higher churn rates), he has a one year contract (month-to-month usually meant higher churn probability), does not pay by electronic check, and its monthly rates are not in the lower side of the spectrum (which we saw correlated with much higher leaving rates). Thus, the prediction that this customer will stay with the company seems pretty safe.

The second customer (Fig. 12) was predicted to leave by machine learning model. When looking at the data for her, it is no wonder why: tenure value belonging in the first group (which it's indicative of very high churn probability), optic fiber as internet service type, month-to-month contract, electronic check as payment method, low total charges (which were indicative of low tenure and high monthly charges), etc. She ticks almost all the boxes to qualify as a surely leaving customer.

The final customer we are going to look at was also predicted to leave. This time, it is not as obvious as to why, so we have to trust the model on this one. Being a senior citizen and having a monthly contract are some of the most common features in leaving customers, but the rest of parameters should not be too alarming. In this situation, it is important to remember that this model was optimized to maximize its recall value (while still maintaining good overall performance, measured by the AUC_ROC metric), which means that the main objective was to catch as many leaving customers as possible, while probably classifying some customers that had no intention of leaving as Churn.

The model predicted 36% of the customers to be leaving, which is higher than the 27% of confirmed Churn that were present in the original data. This reinforces the notion that the model is over-predicting leaving customers, which is a sacrifice that has to be made in order to catch as many true churn classes.

6   Conclusions

Machine Learning is a technology that is starting to become present in almost every aspect of our lives. While there are uncountable applications of Machine Learning in many different fields, the objective was to explore its applications in the field of data, a field that is also always evolving, and whose applications are extremely important in many aspects of business' life. The goal was to explore how this technology can be used in order to prevent financial losses for a company, which in this case would be losing customers due to several different factors.

While gathering and storing data is a very important step in the data science process, the focus was exclusively on the analysis and obtention of results steps. Testing the performance of different algorithms that are used every day in many data science projects, comparing its results and finding out which one was better suited to tackle this problem was the main focus of the works.

We decided to optimize the model to detect as many leaving customers as possible (while also maintaining a good overall ratio), since this is probably what a company in this situation would want to achieve by using machine learning to analyze its data. We made this assumption based on the thought that, for a company, it is probably much more cost-efficient to propose new offers (such as new physical terminals, new phone or reduction in services' prices) to a larger number of predicted leaving customers, even if some of them had no intention of leaving the company to start with, rather than assuming the loss in revenue if some these clients do end up leaving. This is something that should be discussed with the company, to determine which strategy should be followed to achieve the desired results.

The next works can be cover the implementation of cross-validation technique to improve the performance of the models. This would mean to also implement a pipelines technique to keep the data processing step much cleaner and organized. One possible final step would also be to use multiple machine learning models sequentially with the same data: first optimizing for recall and then for accuracy, in order to further solidify the prediction.

References

1. Alpaydin, E.: Introduction to Machine Learning. 4th edn. MIT Press, Cambridge (2020). ISBN 978-0-262-01243-0
2. Russell, S., Norvig, P.: Artificial Intelligence – A Modern Approach. Pearson, London (2009). ISBN 9789332543515
3. Urbanowicz, R.J., Moore, J.H.: Learning classifier systems: a complete introduction, review, and roadmap. J. Artif. Evol. Appl. **2009**(1), 1–25 (2009). ISSN 1687-6229
4. Zhang, J., Zhan, Z.-H., Lin, Y., Chen, N., Gong, Y.-J., Zhong, J.-H. et al.: Evolutionary computation meets machine learning: a survey. Comput. Intell. Mag. **6**(4), 68–75 (2011)
5. Allahyari, M., Pouriyeh, S., Assefi, M., Safaei, S., Trippe, E., Gutierrez, J.B., et al.: A Brief Survey of Text Mining: Classification, Clustering and Extraction Techniques, University of Georgia, Athens (2017)
6. Rokach, L., Maimon, O.: Data Mining with Decision Trees: Theory and Applications. World Scientific Pub Co Inc., Singapore (2008). ISBN 978-981277171
7. Shalev-Shwartz, S., Ben-David, S.: 18. Decision Trees. Understanding Machine Learning. Cambridge University Press, Cambridge (2014)
8. Rodriguez, J.J., Kuncheva, L.I., Alonso, C.J.: Rotation forest: a new classifier ensemble method. IEEE Trans. Pattern Anal. Mach. Intell. **28**(10), 1619–1630 (2006)
9. Cover, T.M., Hart, P.E.: Nearest neighbor pattern classification. IEEE Trans. Inf. Theory **13**(1), 21–27 (1967)
10. Mason, L., Baxter, J., Bartlett, P.L., Frean, M.: Boosting algorithms as gradient descent. In: Solla, S.A., Leen, T.K., Müller, K. (eds.). Advances in Neural Information Processing Systems, vol. 12, pp. 512–518. MIT Press, Cambridge (1999)
11. Hastie, T., Tibshirani, R., Friedman, J.H.: 10. Boosting and Additive Trees. The Elements of Statistical Learning, 2nd edn., pp. 337–384. Springer, New York (2009). ISBN 978-0-387-84857-0
12. Hosmer, D.: Applied Logistic Regression. Wiley, New Jersey (2013). ISBN 978-0470582473
13. Harrell, F.E.: Regression Modeling Strategies: With Applications to Linear Models, Logistic Regression, and Survival Analysis. Springer, New York (2010). ISBN 978-1-4419-2918-1

14. Telco Customer Churn, Kaggle. https://www.kaggle.com/blastchar/telco-customer-churn/data. Accessed 2020
15. Package Overview, Pandas. https://pandas.pydata.org/docs/\\getting_started/overview.html. Accessed 2020
16. XGBoost Parameters, XGBoost. https://xgboost.readthedocs.io/en/latest/parameter.html. Accessed 2020
17. Brownlee, J.: Recursive Feature Elimination (RFE) for Feature Selection in Python, Machine Learning Mastery. https://machinelearningmastery.com/rfe-feature-selection-in-python/. Accessed 2020
18. Śniegula, A., Poniszewska-Marańda, A., Chomątek, Ł.: Towards the named entity recognition methods in biomedical field. In: Chatzigeorgiou, A., et al. (eds.) SOFSEM 2020. LNCS, vol. 12011, pp. 375–387. Springer, Cham (2020). https://doi.org/10.1007/978-3-030-38919-2_31

Blockchain Technology and Applications

Blockchain Technology for Hospitality Industry

Abhirup Khanna[1(✉)], Anushree Sah[1], Tanupriya Choudhury[1],
and Piyush Maheshwari[2]

[1] University of Petroleum and Energy Studies, Dehradun, India
{akhanna, asah}@ddn.upes.ac.in,
tanupriya1986@gmail.com
[2] The British University in Dubai (BUiD), Dubai, UAE
piyush.maheshwari@buid.ac.ae

Abstract. Blockchain technology and its economic, social, and technological implications, have seen significant upsurge among researchers across the globe. Blockchain has revolutionized the concept of transactions by enhancing their security and efficiency. The blockchain technology is primarily associated with Bitcoin but however, the technology has the potential to go far beyond cryptocurrencies across various verticals. In a recent survey performed by Deloitte, more than 53% of the responds across various industries see blockchain technology as a critical requirement for their respective organizations [4]. The hospitality industry is one such domain where blockchain can prove enormously beneficial. The paper explores major application areas that involve the applicability of blockchain technology in the hospitality industry. The work investigates the implications of blockchain technology in enhancing operational efficiency, increased revenue and improved security and privacy for the hospitality industry. The paper establishes a link between blockchain technology and the hospitality sector and subsequently analyses recent works and case studies. A two-step research study has been introduced to present a systematic review of some of the main contributions in the literature that focuses on the integration of the blockchain technology and hospitality industry. The article adds to an interesting concept of blockchain technology, and its current research trends with respect to the hospitality industry and their various areas of application.

Keywords: Blockchain technology · Travel industry · Hospitality sector · Cryptocurrency · Operations management

1 Introduction

Travel and Tourism industry have a significant role in facilitating economic growth and job creation all across the world. Countries such as Maldives, Seychelles and Bahamas are totally dependent on the tourism sector. According to the World Travel & Tourism Council (WTTC), in 2028, the global travel and tourism sector grew at the rate of 3.9% which being greater than the growth of world GDP for the same year [1]. The resultant of this phenomenal growth contributed $8.8 trillion to the world economy [1]. The tourism industry had undergone drastic transformations since the Internet allowed

© Springer Nature Switzerland AG 2020
M. Themistocleous et al. (Eds.): EMCIS 2020, LNBIP 402, pp. 99–112, 2020.
https://doi.org/10.1007/978-3-030-63396-7_7

customers to search and purchase their respective travel bookings. Companies such as Airbnb, Uber and Oyo are some of the prominent beneficiaries of the advent of internet-based travel bookings. However, the new business model possesses challenges of financial frauds, loss of user data and privacy concerns. For the success of internet-based travel bookings, trust must be the established among all players involved in the travel ecosystem. The advent of Blockchain technology followed by the success of its cryptocurrency Bitcoin has triggered a hype cycle leading to its adoption across various industries. Blockchain aims to address current challenges of tourism industry by ensuring trust, transparency, security and privacy for user transactions. Practitioners from the industry believe that problems such as false reviews, duplicate bookings and data loss can be solved by the integration of Blockchain technology.

Blockchain is a chain of blocks containing immutable data which is managed and governed by multiple nodes in a decentralized manner. Every block in a blockchain is time stamped and connected to one another using cryptographic hash functions. Blockchain technology is generally referred to as distributed ledger technology as it comprises of a distributed ledger which is transparent in nature and requires common consensus among all nodes for updation of data. The three core entities that constitute the blockchain technology are blocks, nodes and miners. Every blockchain comprises of multiple blocks which are used for storing data. Each block has a 256-bit cryptographic hash associated with itself. Miners are entities responsible for creating new blocks in the blockchain. The process of creating blocks in known as mining. The concept of nodes corresponds to the decentralized nature of blockchain. Every node has its own copy of the entire blockchain and adding a new node to the blockchain requires consensus from all nodes making the entire process trusted and verified. According to a survey by Pwc, hospitality industry is among the most promising industries that can benefit from the emergence of blockchain technology [2]. Numerous researchers across the globe are exploring ways and approaches for integration of blockchain and travel sector leading to improved customer experiences. The following are some of the advantages of integrating blockchain technology and hospitability sector.

- *Traveler Identification:* Blockchain aims to revolutionize the way in which customer information is stored and managed. In present times customers are required to show their identification cards at various stages starting from hotel and flight bookings, baggage, immigration clearance and finally hotel check-in. Blockchain provides the user with the ability of paperless identification. It allows user data to be stored on blocks which are secured using cryptographic functions. A new transaction is initiated at every travel stage corresponding to a particular user id. Therefore, creating a hassle-free experience for tourists and moreover helping the local government in knowing the whereabouts of a particular traveler.
- *Prevent Duplicate Bookings:* The implementation of Blockchain, duplicate bookings is a thing of the past. The problem of duplicate booking or overbooking are pertinent during festive and vacation seasons wherein heavy load on centralized payment servers cause multiple bookings by the same user. The problem of centralization may manifest itself in form of multiple bookings of the same entity. One key characteristic of Blockchain is its decentralized nature which prevents any kind of denial of service or single point of failure.

- *Secure & Transparent Transactions:* Blockchain enables financial transactions through the use of cryptocurrencies. The use of cryptocurrency ensures a transaction to be secure and traceable. The risk of transacting fake currency is also mitigated through the use of cryptocurrencies.
- *Authentic & Verified User Ratings:* The best way to gauge the quality of a hospitality service is through its user ratings. But in times of fake reviews, it becomes difficult for users to distinguish a dubious hospitality service provider from the rest [41]. The implementation of Blockchain would ensure authentic and verified user ratings. Blockchain provides the use of a public ledger which is tamper proof and publically available to all users within the chain. Therefore, only genuine reviews from authentic customers are visible to all users.

The rest of the paper is categorized as follows: Sect. 2 elucidates the research methodology. Section 3 presents the detailed literature review of blockchain technology in hospitality industry. Real world case studies discussing implementation of blockchain technology in hospitality industry are discussed in Sect. 4.

2   Methodology

The paper follows a two-step research methodology starting with a broad review of all major contributions in field of blockchain technology. In our primary step, we performed an online search based upon specific keywords like "blockchain", "blockchain technology", "travel industry", "hospitality sector", "blockchain and travel", "blockchain applications in hospitality", etc. We ensured that the keywords were mentioned in a paper's title or abstract. The search led to the identification of 53 research papers. Subsequently, we categorized the papers into three categories "blockchain technology", "blockchain and travel" and "blockchain and hospitality industry". The second step involved filtration of papers based there year of publication. We only selected papers which were published in the past five years i.e. from the year 2015. ScienceDirect [40] and Scopus [36] are the websites used for searching publications. During the entire process we made sure that the papers which we selected were written in English language. Finally, we identified some of the prominent real-world case studies that represent the successful amalgamation of Blockchain technology and the hospitality industry. The figures mentioned in Sect. 5 illustrate publication patterns for the three set of keywords listed. The publication distribution is on the basis of geographical regions and type of publication. Data crunching and subsequent analytics has been performed using tools provided by Scopus [36] (Fig. 1).

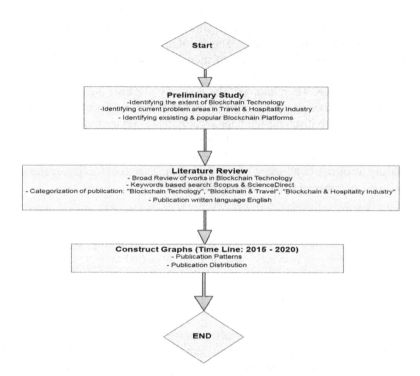

Fig. 1. Research methodology

3 Literature Review: Blockchain Technology and Hospitality Industry

Blockchain technology ensures creation of a democratic system thereby preventing a centralized monopoly of data. Furthermore, it restricts organizations to possess all the world's key information and subsequently preventing them from making new rules and randomly increasing charges of their offered services. The integration of blockchain technology with the travel industry facilitates creation of an immutable and transparent global database comprising of all travel data records. Live access to this database will lead to the conception of an efficient and accurate reservation and payment system devoid of problems of overbooking. Other benefits would involve competitive pricing and real time tracking of supply chain.

The TravelChain [6] project aims to create a modern tourism ecosystem that provides an information base to travelers. The system assists users in finding best deals and ensuring budget trips. The platform enables its users to store their travelling preferences, food choices preferred recreational activities in an encrypted form while remaining anonymous to other users. The integrated pool of data acts as a global decentralized registry allowing service providers to analyze market trends and build on customized solutions that cater to the needs of respective users. TravelChain facilitates its users for sharing their travel experiences in form of reviews on food, accommodation, transportation and entertainment. The entire proposed travel ecosystem runs on Travel Tokens, the means of payment for any financial transaction. Travelers render Travel Tokens in exchange of services being offered. Looking from the business owner's point of view, the platform provides them with an opportunity to attract more customers. Hotel or restaurant owners can assess the requirements of potential customers and subsequently communicate a service option along with requesting for personal information of respective users. Interested users can select their desired services and pay using their e-wallets in form of Travel Tokens.

The authors propose a smart tourism framework named BloHosT (Blockchain Enabled Smart Tourism and Hospitality Management) [7] that allows travelers to interact with various entities in a travel ecosystem. Every tourist can initiate payments through its dedicated wallet identifier which is linked to a cryptocurrency server. A wallet comprises of personal information (user name, photo, previous transaction details) belonging to a tourist. Furthermore, the framework comprises of an immutable ledger that eases the travel experience as it facilitates elimination of the need for carrying any travel documents. The framework allows users to register themselves using a mobile application. Every traveler can have varied cryptocurrency tokens in there wallet along with the ability to exchange them with fellow travelers using the cryptocurrency exchange server. Similar to travelers, business owners and service provides can also register themselves onto the framework. A smart contract layer has been created in order to ensure seamless communication between travelers and service providers. The layer comprises of a series of smart contracts that enable interoperability among tourists and business owners. The framework adopts PoC as a consensus algorithm for validating a user transaction that has been accepted in the Blockchain. In continuation to the smart tourism framework, the authors propose a Deep Learning based framework for providing review ratings for tourist destinations based upon experiences of numerous travelers.

Efficient tracking and monitoring of food items is an integral part of the hospitality industry. Applicability of Blockchain enabled food supply chain management systems could enhance the quality control and ensure food safety for hotels and restaurants. In light of the above proposition, the authors propose a Radio-frequency identification (RFID) and Blockchain enabled agri-food supply chain traceability system [8]. The system categorizes food items into two categories: fruits & vegetables and meat products. The authors make use of RFID technology for implementing data acquisition and circulation along with warehousing activities. Furthermore, Blockchain technology is being implemented for ensuring reliable and authentic data sharing among various supply chain entities. The traceability system is decentralized in nature and ensures increased transparency and real time tracking of food items. The proposed system prevents circulation of fake products by providing a unique id to a food item and encrypting the same.

The authors propose a Blockchain enabled Online Food Ordering System for restaurants and cafeterias [9]. The proposed system aims to simplify online food ordering and helps in reducing long queues and reduction in operational costs. The system enhances operational efficiency and reduces chances of errors as it accepts cryptocurrency tokens as a mode of payment instead of traditional hard cash. The work illustrates the use Ethereum as a platform for creation and management of a private Blockchain. The authors have named their cryptocurrency token as "Foody" which is symbolized by the symbol "F". The platform uses EIP20 as a standard for creating smart contracts. Transger() and totalSupply() are some of the functions that have been incorporated in the smart contract.

The work discusses the use of Blockchain technology for enhancing the operational efficiency of food supply chain [10]. The authors propose a Blockchain model that captures data from various entities in a food supply chain, segregates the same and generates a Food Quality Index (FQI) value for each food item. The FQI value for a particular food item helps in identifying how safe it is for consumption. The proposed model addresses common concerns of adulteration and food wastage. The implementation of Blockchain enhances quality control as each food item is tracked form post-harvest to its distribution across various nodes in the supply chain. A non-permissioned public ledger is used during implementation. Through the proposed model, the authors aim to provide a sustainable Blockchain enabled supply chain that if implemented by restaurant owners can assist them in ensuring quality food items to their respective customers. The implementation advantages of Blockchain include cost effectiveness, standardization and secure information communication. Data such as Producer ID and Date of Production are hashed and subsequently stored in the Blockchain. Each entity in the supply chain upon receiving a product adds its unique id and corresponding date to the Blockchain.

The authors analyze prevalent privacy concerns dealing with online service providers rendering room booking services to tourists and travelers. In order to mitigate such concerns the authors propose a Blockchain enabled privacy preserving model for networked hospitality services [11]. The aim is to ensure privacy preservation for both service providers as well as end users. Threats such as malicious outsider or compromising guest information are successfully dealt with the proposed model. The work utilizes Bitcoin Blockchain as a platform for creating and managing anonymous credentials for any guest accessing the booking website. Using anonymous credentials, both service providers and guests can lease or rent rooms in a secure, anonymous and accountable manner. The credentials are hashed using public key and can be considered

Table 1. Comparative analysis of blockchain publications

Research area	Publication count	Major publications	Research focus	Methodology
Blockchain Technology	26	[14, 16–19, 23]	Applications of Blockchain technology; Advantages & Challenges of Blockchain; Architectures & Frameworks for Blockchain technology	Systematic Review; Qualitative Study; Quantitative Study
Blockchain & Travel	19	[15, 19–21, 24, 25]	Applications of Blockchain technology in: Airline industry; Supply Chain Management; Shared Economy; Currency Exchange	Conceptual Study; Qualitative Study; Quantitative Study
Blockchain & Hospitality Industry	08	[6–11, 26]	Applications of Blockchain technology in: Hotel Room Bookings; Food Supply Chain; Restaurant Payments	Qualitative Study

as Blockchain address. The anonymous credentials help hosts and guest to verify one another without the intervention of a service provider. CoinShuffle [12] is the mixing protocol that is being implemented for anonymous communication between the guest and multiple hosts. Being a peer to peer protocol, CoinShuffle prevents involvement of service provider during any communication between guest and host. A host can verify a genuine guest by examining the Blockchain and vice versa. Proof of work is the consensus algorithm being used for the purpose of validating transactions. Blind signature developed by David Chaum [13] is the cryptographic method (Table 1).

The above table discusses various publications relating to blockchain technology with respect to their research methodology and area of research. The table depicts current extent of research and helps in enhancing the understating of the readers by presenting a comparative analysis of different research themes relating to blockchain technology.

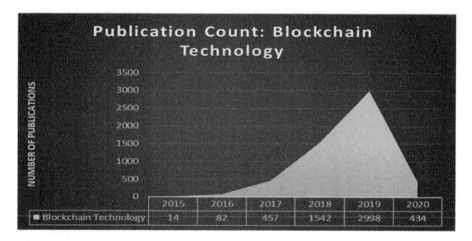

Fig. 2. Year wise Scopus publication count

Figure 2 represents year wise publication count for blockchain technology.

Fig. 3. Publication count comparison

Figure 3 illustrates the comparison between the number of publications relating to "Blockchain and Travel" and "Blockchain and Hospitality Industry". However, it is to be noted, that there wasn't a single publication relating to Blockchain and Hospitality industry for the years 2015, 2016 and 2017 thus reconfirming to the novelty of the respective area.

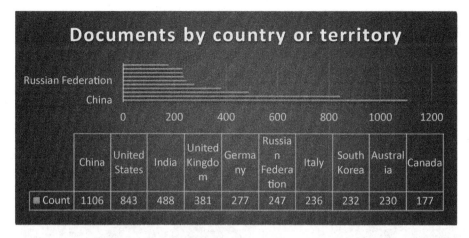

Fig. 4. Publication distribution for "Blockchain Technology"

Figure 4 illustrates the number of publications concerning blockchain technology during the time period of 2015 and 2020. China, United States and India are the top three countries in terms of research for blockchain technology with reference to number of publications.

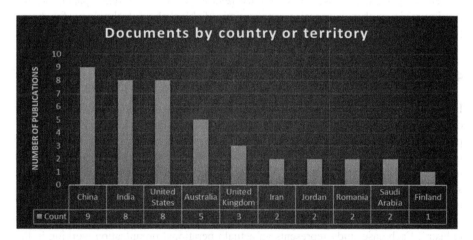

Fig. 5. Publication Distribution for "Blockchain and Travel"

Figure 5 illustrates the number of publications concerning the implementation of blockchain technology in travel industry during the time period of 2015 and 2020. The top three countries continue to be China, Inia and United States but the difference in publication count is drastic when compared with blockchain technology.

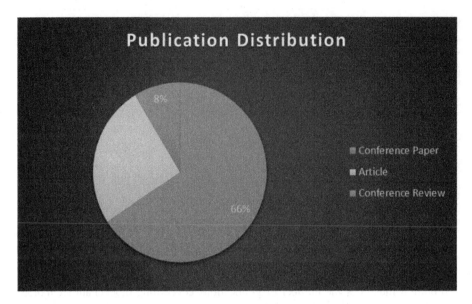

Fig. 6. Publication distribution for publication type "Blockchain and Travel"

Figure 6 describes publication distribution in terms of type publication type such as conference papers, articles and conference review papers. Conference papers are the maximum in umber concerning application of blockchain technology for travel industry.

4   Case Studies

In recent times the travel industry has become a victim of centralized data collector organizations controlling most of the travel data and subsequently generating huge profits. The data can be informed of hotel bookings, flight capacities, supply chain routes, etc. Large collector organizations maintain and distribute such data for manipulating availability of rooms, flights and other travel services. Blockchain offers a solution to this problem by decentralizing the entire travel ecosystem leading to secure user data and increased revenues. The section talks through prominent real-world case studies that discuss the implementation of Blockchain technology in hospitality industry. Each case study represents an actual operational organization working in the domain of travel & tourism industry. The section discusses the procedures and benefits of implementing blockchains.

TUI Group, a German multinational travel agency, is one of the largest travel and tourism companies in the world [31]. In the past few years TUI has lost its market share to some of its contemporaries like Trivago and Booking.com. In an attempt to regain its business, TUI became one of the foremost travel companies to adopt blockchain technology for its booking, reservation and payment systems. The organization decided to implement Ethereum blockchain for access, update and distribution of data relating to hotel capacity thereby removing middlemen companies of the likes of Expedia and Booking.com. Blockchain implementation would help in efficient execution of peak load demands and provide centralized control of bookings. The TUI management expects cost savings after implementation of blockchain technology.

Trippki is a hotel booking platform that uses blockchain technology for managing its customer loyalty reward system [32]. The loyalty service is extremely beneficial as it avoids the role of a third-party organization and provides a direct connection between hotels and customers. Trippki uses the concept of crypto tokens for rewarding its guests once their stay has been completed. Proof of Stay is the consensus algorithm and "TRIP" is the name of the native token used by Trippki. A TRIP is a crypto asset used as a reward point token which can be spent or traded at the owner's discretion. Every guest staying at the hotel or using other hotel services are rendered a TRIP token. The proposed blockchain based reward system is unique in nature as TRIP tokens do not expire and are recorded in the distributed ledger, wherein they can be used for making future bookings, or can be exchanged for cash. In addition to the same, customers are also rewarded for writing reviews. Being a blockchain enabled system fake reviews are eliminated thereby allowing only genuine customers to post reviews. The system enables hotels to identify their shortcomings and be confident about their positive services.

The thought for Beenest was conceived in view of the issues encompassing brought together stages: security, notoriety, and high, certain use fees [33]. Honey bee makes and jam an incentive for has, visitors, judges, and designers inside a decentralized self-ruling association and our decentralized model offers unmistakable points over the dominating, incorporated home sharing model. BeeToken or Beenest is a blockchain home-sharing stage, which associates clients with has and permits clients to organize and pay for remains. Its shared exchanges imply that no commission is charged, while the decentralized idea of the stage gives included security benefits. Beenest means to handle the issues intrinsic in current brought together home-sharing stages. To get this, first investigate what a brought together home sharing stage like Airbnb offers. Beenest essentially charges 0% commissions to hosts and visitors using BEE, on account of savvy contracts mechanizing exchanges that sidestep commission-based stages, money related establishments, and cash categories. As the Bee token is utilized for all exchanges, there are no outside exchange expenses or cash transformation charges, and all investment funds are passed back to the hosts and visitors holding the token. Right now, is characterized as going around utilization charges. Win-win for the clients. To utilize Beenest, clients need to initially join and experience an essential KYC (know your client) procedure to guarantee that clients are genuine and confirmed. Beenest can flawlessly coordinate with outsider authentication stages and connects identities with a weighted value on the Bee notoriety convention.

Winding Tree [34] is a current open source request and response side commercial center for stock following. A few aircraft organizations, including Air New Zealand and Luftansa, have just gone into an association with the stage, with focal points including case of a blockchain booking and stuff an absence of outsider inclusion with booking techniques, and more noteworthy transparent and traceable systems with regards to things following administrations. Winding Tree launched its own coin "Líf" for future money exchanges. The use of a cryptocurrency, in this case, can have some real benefits for international travels involving bookings with different companies operating in various currencies (airline, car rental, insurance, etc.). Such transaction may implicate multiple currency conversions with high fees. A money transfer with Líf will require only one or maximum two that currency exchanges.

5   Conclusion

Blockchain technology is in its early stages when talking about its adoption in the travel industry. Researchers all across the world are working towards creating applications and frameworks involving the applicability of blockchain in the travel and tourism industry. The consequence of the rapid research being conducted in the past few years has led to an increase in acceptance of blockchain thus resulting in new and relevant use cases from within the travel industry. The integration of blockchain ensures enhanced customer data privacy and the facilitation of paperless travel experiences. The paper discusses significant insights to its readers regarding the importance of blockchain technology in the travel and hospitality industry. The aim of the research was to explore blockchain technology from the perspective of the hospitality industry. The research conducted was exploratory in nature and talks through prominent works dealing with the implementation of blockchain in the hospitality industry.

The work identifies the extent of research that has been conducted for the past five years in areas of blockchain technology and its integration with the travel and hospitality industry. The paper presents important case studies from the hospitality industry that help in enhancing the understanding of its readers. Furthermore, it allows all of us to think about further questions to investigate. What are the challenges of the adoption of blockchain technology in the hospitality industry? How integration with blockchain contributes towards revenue generation for the hospitality industry? However, the paper presents itself as an interesting contribution towards existing literature and will assist readers in exploring new avenues and adding advancements to the current scientific research.

References

1. Travel Tourism continues strong growth above global GDP, 25 February 2020 (2020). https://www.wttc.org/about/media-centre/press-releases/press-releases/2019/travel-tourism-continues-strong-growth-above-global-gdp/
2. PricewaterhouseCoopers (n.d.). Blockchain is here. What's your next move? https://www.pwc.com/gx/en/issues/blockchain/blockchain-in-business.html
3. Home (n.d.). https://ethereum.org/
4. Deloitte US: Audit, Consulting, Advisory, and Tax Services. (n.d.). https://www2.deloitte.com/
5. Enterprise blockchain. That actually works (n.d.). https://www.multichain.com/
6. Polukhina, A., Arnaberdiyev, A., Tarasova, A.: Leading technologies in tourism: using blockchain in TravelChain project. In: 3rd International Conference on Social, Economic, and Academic Leadership (ICSEAL 2019). Atlantis Press (2019)

7. Bodkhe, U., Bhattacharya, P., Tanwar, S., Tyagi, S., Kumar, N., Obaidat, M.S.: Blohost: blockchain enabled smart tourism and hospitality management. In: 2019 International Conference on Computer, Information and Telecommunication Systems (CITS), pp. 1–5. IEEE (2019)
8. Tian, F.: An agri-food supply chain traceability system for China based on RFID & blockchain technology. In: 2016 13th International Conference on Service Systems and Service Management (ICSSSM), pp. 1–6. IEEE (2016)
9. Yadav, A., Yadav, D., Gupta, S., Kumar, D., Kumar, P.: Online food court payment system using blockchain technolgy. In: 2018 5th IEEE Uttar Pradesh Section International Conference on Electrical, Electronics and Computer Engineering (UPCON), pp. 1–7. IEEE (2018)
10. George, R.V., Harsh, H.O., Ray, P., Babu, A.K.: Food quality traceability prototype for restaurants using blockchain and food quality data index. J. Clean. Prod. **240**, 118021 (2019)
11. Zhou, H., Niu, Y., Liu, J., Zhang, C., Wei, L., Fang, Y.: A privacy-preserving networked hospitality service with the bitcoin blockchain. In: Chellappan, S., Cheng, W., Li, W. (eds.) WASA 2018. LNCS, vol. 10874, pp. 696–708. Springer, Cham (2018). https://doi.org/10.1007/978-3-319-94268-1_57
12. Privacy for Bitcoin Cash (n.d.). https://cashshuffle.com/
13. Chaum, D.: Blind signature system. In: Chaum, D. (ed.) Advances in Cryptology, p. 153. Springer, Boston (1984). https://doi.org/10.1007/978-1-4684-4730-9_14
14. Crosby, M., Pattanayak, P., Verma, S., Kalyanaraman, V.: Blockchain technology: beyond bitcoin. Appl. Innov. **2**(6–10), 71 (2016)
15. Swati, V., Prasad, A.S.: Application of blockchain technology in travel industry. In: 2018 International Conference on Circuits and Systems in Digital Enterprise Technology (ICCSDET), pp. 1–5. IEEE (2018)
16. Önder, I., Treiblmaier, H.: Blockchain and tourism: three research propositions. Ann. Tour. Res. **72**(C), 180–182 (2018)
17. Zheng, Z., Xie, S., Dai, H., Chen, X., Wang, H.: An overview of blockchain technology: architecture, consensus, and future trends. In: 2017 IEEE International Congress on Big Data (BigData Congress), pp. 557–564. IEEE (2017)
18. Andoni, M., et al.: Blockchain technology in the energy sector: a systematic review of challenges and opportunities. Renew. Sustain. Energy Rev. **100**, 143–174 (2019)
19. Ahram, T., Sargolzaei, A., Sargolzaei, S., Daniels, J., Amaba, B.: Blockchain technology innovations. In: 2017 IEEE Technology & Engineering Management Conference (TEMSCON), pp. 137–141. IEEE (2017)
20. Ozdemir, A.I., Ar, I.M., Erol, I.: Assessment of blockchain applications in travel and tourism industry. Qual. Quant. **54**, 1–15 (2019)
21. Nam, K., Dutt, C.S., Chathoth, P., Khan, M.S.: Blockchain technology for smart city and smart tourism: latest trends and challenges. Asia Pac. J. Tour. Res., 1-15 (2019)
22. Zheng, Z., Xie, S., Dai, H.N., Chen, X., Wang, H.: Blockchain challenges and opportunities: a survey. Int. J. Web Grid Serv. **14**(4), 352–375 (2018)
23. Bai, C.A., Cordeiro, J., Sarkis, J.: Blockchain technology: business, strategy, the environment, and sustainability. Bus. Strategy Environ. **29**(1), 321–322 (2020)
24. Pilkington, M.: Can blockchain technology help promote new tourism destinations? The example of medical tourism in Moldova. The Example of Medical Tourism in Moldova, 11 June 2017 (2017)
25. Vinod, B.: Blockchain in travel. J. Revenue Pricing Manag. **19**(1), 2–6 (2020)

26. Yeh, J.Y., Liao, S.C., Wang, Y.T., Chen, Y.J.: Understanding consumer purchase intention in a blockchain technology for food traceability and transparency context. In: 2019 IEEE Social Implications of Technology (SIT) and Information Management (SITIM), pp. 1–6). IEEE (2019)

27. Morozov, M., Morozova, N.: Innovative staff training strategies for the tourism and hospitality industry. In: 5th International Conference on Economics, Management, Law and Education (EMLE 2019), pp. 393–396. Atlantis Press (2020)

28. Yeasmin, S., Baig, A.: Unblocking the potential of blockchain. In: 2019 International Conference on Electrical and Computing Technologies and Applications (ICECTA), pp. 1–5. IEEE (2019)

29. Zhang, X., Liu, J., Li, Y., Cui, Q., Tao, X., Liu, R.P.: Blockchain based secure package delivery via ridesharing. In: 2019 11th International Conference on Wireless Communications and Signal Processing (WCSP), pp. 1–6. IEEE (2019)

30. Dogru, T., Mody, M., Leonardi, C.: Blockchain Technology & its Implications for the Hospitality Industry. Boston Hospitality Review, Boston University School of Hospitality Administration (2018)

31. Barella, C., Lawrence, G., Baldock, L.: TUI Group – The world's number one tourism business, 27 February 2020. https://www.tuigroup.com/en-en

32. Trippki Home (n.d.). https://trippki.com/

33. Token, T.B.: What is Beenest? How The Bee Token is Revolutionizing The Home Sharing Market, 18 December 2017. https://medium.com/@thebeetoken/what-is-beenest-how-the-bee-token-is-revolutionizing-the-home-sharing-market-8da32d79bbbb

34. Winding Tree - Decentralized Travel Ecosystem (n.d.). https://windingtree.com/

35. Saini, A., Sharma, S., Jain, P., Sharma, V., khandelwal, A.K.: A secure priority vehicle movement based on blockchain technology in connected vehicles. In: Proceedings of the 12th International Conference on Security of Information and Networks, pp. 1–8 (2019)

36. www.scopus.com (n.d.). https://www.scopus.com/

37. Bitcoin futures: an effective tool for hedging cryptocurrencies. Finance Res. Lett. (2019). ISSN 1544-6123. https://doi.org/10.1016/j.frl.2019.07.003

38. Liu, R., Wan, S., Zhang, Z., Zhao, X.: Is the introduction of futures responsible for the crash of Bitcoin?. Finance Res. Lett. (2019). ISSN 1544-6123. https://doi.org/10.1016/j.frl.2019.08.007

39. Open Source Blockchain Technologies (n.d.). https://www.hyperledger.org/

Blockchain in Smart Energy Grids: A Market Analysis

Evgenia Kapassa[1]([envelope]) [iD], Marinos Themistocleous[1] [iD],
Jorge Rueda Quintanilla[2], Marios Touloupos[1] [iD],
and Maria Papadaki[3]

[1] Institute for the Future (IFF), University of Nicosia, Nicosia, Cyprus
{kapassa.e,touloupos.m,themistocleous.m}@unic.ac.cy
[2] Cuerva, Granada, Spain
jruedaq@grupocuerva.com
[3] Faculty of Business and Law, British University of Dubai, Dubai, UAE
maria.papadaki@buid.ac.ae

Abstract. Modern society consumes a huge amount of energy, making the energy industry highly important across the globe. Customers are supplied with the electricity via the energy grid, as part of the utility value chain and pay on per-unit consumed basis. Thus, grid operations and energy prices have little effects on actual energy demand because grid imbalances frequently arise rapidly over very short periods of time, due to imprecise forecasts or unexpected events. Non-predictable renewable energy sources variable generation raises crucial challenges in grid management, making grid defection a rapidly increasing challenge to traditional energy markets. Blockchain technology has been studied to overcome these problems for application in the smart energy grid, and experts agree that it has the potential to change the electricity market. Blockchain and distributed ledger technologies can promote a transparent, secure and decentralized transactions network that will allow new innovative business solutions. Although, the integration of blockchain into the smart energy grid poses some challenges and prohibits the widespread use of blockchain technology in the energy sector. Therefore, in this paper a market analysis was conducted, to investigate the parameters that affect the large-scale adoption of blockchain in smart energy grids. The first part of the paper is setting up the scene, introducing the blockchain and smart grid fundamentals, as well as presenting blockchain's potential impact on different energy use cases. On the second part of the paper the market analysis is presented, providing blockchain technology's market opportunities within the energy grid. The paper ends with a description of threats and market challenges that the technology has to address in order to get through the hype, prove its economic, social and technological potential and eventually be accepted in the mainstream.

Keywords: Blockchain · Distributed ledger technologies · Energy grid · Smart grid · Market analysis

© Springer Nature Switzerland AG 2020
M. Themistocleous et al. (Eds.): EMCIS 2020, LNBIP 402, pp. 113–124, 2020.
https://doi.org/10.1007/978-3-030-63396-7_8

1 Introduction

During the last decade, energy crisis and environmental destruction became two main concerns. Thus, since 2007, the European Union (EU) has committed to reach the 20-20-20 targets. According to the EU [1], greenhouse gas emissions will be decreased by 20% compared to 1990 rates by the end of 2020, 20% of the energy generated will be derived from Renewable Energy Sources (RES), while in total 20% less energy will be used. Additionally, EU expects that greenhouse gas emissions will be reduced by 85–90% by 2050.

As stated in many research studies [2–4], a promising approach for addressing the energy and environmental disruption, is the adoption of smart grid among with the extensive use of RESs. Moving a step forward, over the past few years, blockchain has emerged as a transformative technology in the context of the smart energy grids [5], enabling secure and reliable Peer to Peer (P2P) energy trading between Distributed Energy Resources (DERs) [6–8]. Due to blockchain's nature, a stable, open and decentralized ledger could be established for all data and transactions, related to energy production and consumption. In addition, smart contracts facilitated through blockchain can enable transparent and immutable transactions on the energy grid and promote interconnections between energy producers and energy consumers (i.e. prosumers) in a decentralized and fault-tolerant environment [9, 10]. Thus, a technology such as blockchain, which does not have a centralized trust body, becomes necessary to ensure efficient and reliable energy trading within the smart grid. Nevertheless, the introduction of blockchain into the smart energy grid is also facing some obstacles and prevents the widespread adoption of the technology in the energy sector [11, 12].

Towards this direction, the current work presents a market analysis related to the adoption of blockchain in the area of smart energy grids. Since blockchain in the energy sector is expected to rise in excess of 45% by 2025 [13], the current analysis aims to highlight market opportunities and possible threats that blockchain-enabled energy grids are facing nowadays.

The remaining of the paper is organized as follows. Section 2 presents the blockchain background, while Sect. 3 introduce the incorporation of blockchain in the smart energy grid. In Sect. 4 a market analysis is taking place, considering the opportunities blockchain could provide in the future smart grids, as well as the current threats and challenges the integration of this technology within the grid is facing. Finally, in Sect. 5, we conclude our work.

2 Blockchain Background

Blockchain is one of the most disruptive technology solutions developed in the recent years. In recent years, blockchain has evolved to handle several different types of data. These include information about energy trading, property ownership, national records, outstanding loans, business mergers, shares, stocks and many more [14–17]. Blockchain includes many computers operating together in a decentralized network, leading to a shared infrastructure that consists of distributed computers (i.e. nodes) that are demonstrated in a way that prevents any kind of modification.

Although blockchain performs a wide range of tasks, it is essentially an immutable, decentralized digital ledger. Blockchain holds a permanent record of validated data in a format which is securely encrypted. Each piece of information is encrypted and stored in a data unit called block [18]. Any node with access to this distributed chain of blocks, can "read" it and determine the status of the data that has been shared over the network. For many different blockchain users a node may typically behave as an entry point, but for simplicity purposes we assume that each node represents one user in the network.

The total number of nodes constitutes a P2P network [19]. In order to better understand the P2P transaction process over the blockchain network, it would be helpful to consider as an example the exchange of energy between an energy producer and an energy consumer. The two entities interact via a pair of private-public keys through the blockchain. They use their private keys to approve their energy transactions, and they are recognized via their public key on the network [20]. The transaction is triggered when the producer will request a specific amount of energy to be transacted towards the consumer, identified through its public key. The transaction is then transmitted to all P2P nodes, so that each one can verify it. Once the transaction is verified, a block of data is produced, and attached to previously verified blocks, creating a chain of blocks (i.e. blockchain). Finally, the transaction is completed and confirmed to both the producer and the consumer.

3 Blockchain in the Smart Energy Grid

3.1 Smart Grid

Smart grids are the distribution and transmission systems that use Information Technology (IT), telecommunication and high-level automation resources to significantly increase energy quality and operational efficiency. Due to the high level of aggregate technology, smart grids are able to respond to various demands of modern society, in terms of energy needs and also considering sustainable development [21].

Smart grids represent the revolution in the electric sector and, consequently, the revolution of the world economy. Communication infrastructure eliminates time and reduces distance, connecting people and markets, facilitating new business relationships.

It should be also stated, that the smart grid concept is very so close to the consumers. The innumerable advantages that these intelligent systems can provide for the electrical system, the technological advancement of the equipment and the constant growth of the demand for electric power, drive research on the subject. Smart grid enables real-time metering and bidirectional communication, ensuring the involve of user participation in the power grid. Home appliances (e.g. smart meters, sensors, solar panels, heat pumps etc.) built into smart grids make it possible to determine the power consumption characteristic, allowing the user to control their consumption and reduce their energy tariff costs or adapting their consumptions patterns.

3.2   Blockchain and the Smart Grid

As described in the previous section, smart grids are experiencing a revolutionary shift which is mainly caused by the advent of DERs (e.g. smart meters, sensors etc.). Thus, consideration, discovery and implementation of new paradigms and distributed technologies are becoming necessary. Because of the fundamental design of blockchain, such technology could offer a promising approach for managing decentralized complex energy grids [22–24]. Several technologies and approaches for designing and implementing energy and sustainability platforms have been proposed in the literature, revealing that blockchain technology could act as a game changer in the energy industry [15]. For instance, in study [25], a game-theoretic approach for the demand side management model that incorporates storage components is suggested, and blockchain technology is applied for efficiency and trustworthiness. Additionally, Brooklyn microgrid is one of the first applied systems that facilitate the use of blockchain technology [22]. The whole project is based on P2P energy trading with blockchain, and doesn't need the third party-traditional electricity utility company. Brooklyn microgrid proves blockchain can really be used in practical P2P electricity trading. Moreover, [26] proposed a decentralized on-demand energy supply architecture for miners in the Internet of Things (IoT) network, using microgrids to provide renewable energy for mining in the IoT devices. On the other hand, with the development and popularization of smart city and electric vehicles (EVs), in order to cope with the current situation of the high volume of EV integration, the authors of study [27], with the aim to allow users to actively participate in the energy exchange process, they propose a P2P Electricity Blockchain Trading (P2PEBT) network, based on the existing electric vehicle charging and discharging schemes in the smart grid. An important aspect for both the academia and the industry, is the cyber-physical security of the infrastructure of Battery Energy Storage Systems (BESSs). Towards this direction, the authors in [28], presented a distributed smart-contract based BESS control approach to allow secure operation and stable consensus between the physical and cyber world.

There are several reviews related to blockchain, focusing on various application areas such as finance, IoT, governance, energy and sustainability [29–31]. Along with the previously mentioned applications, the vast growth in energy-related start-ups and research activities (e.g. Flex4Grid, AnyPLACE, BD4OPEM, Energy Shield) indicates that the effect of energy-based blockchain technology can be extended to a number of use cases specific to energy companies' operations and business processes. Some of the main use case implementations and aspects which may be influenced include: a) P2P energy trading [32, 33], Billing services [34], Security and identity management [35, 36], Energy data management [37, 38] and Grid management: [4, 37].

4   Market Analysis

In today's energy ecosystem scientific and technological developments reduce the product and service life-cycles, change business structures and establish new competitors. This growing complexity requires the scope for new business opportunities.

Accordingly, the current section is going to present a market analysis, focusing on market opportunities and current threats and challenges, in order to identify business growth prospects on the market.

4.1   Opportunities

It is obvious by now that blockchain technology has a transformative potential for the energy market. The energy industry take advantage of blockchain in multiple use cases, as it leverages decentralized P2P technology, where both people and energy devices share a common distributed ledger. Thus, blockchain technology is one of the most promising upcoming technological trends in the information technology domain, with a market size valued at USD 1,590.9 million in 2018, and anticipated to grow at a compound annual growth rate (CAGR) of 69.4% from 2019 to 2025, as stated from the relevant report of Grand View Research [22]. Additionally, Gartner stated that by 2025 blockchain technology would generate market value of more than $176 billion, and by 2030 value of $3.1 trillion [23]. Blockchain technology encourages the immutable essence of the operations of the distributed ledger, making energy exchange transactions transparent. Energy-related applications based on blockchain picking up a quick pace, covering many sectors of the industry, and thus creating massive business opportunities. Ms. Litan stated in Gartner that There are many developments in blockchain technology that would change the current paradigm, making Blockchain networks scalable, interoperable and capable of smart contract portability and cross-chain implementations by the end of 2023 [25]. Moreover, very interesting findings were analyzed in a study conducted by Grand View Research, Inc [26]. Below, the most important ones are presented:

- The public segment is forecasted to grow to CAGR of 70% from 2019 to 2025. Such rise can be attributed to the rising willingness of companies or individuals to inculcate open and efficient transactions.
- The Asia Pacific area is expected to witness the fastest growth regional market during the next six years, increasing the adoption of blockchain technology to accelerate global market growth, lower operating costs and optimize business operations.
- Chain Inc., Circle Internet Financial Limited, Digital Asset Holdings, Eric Industries, IBM Corporation, Linux Foundation, Post-Trade Distributed Ledger, R3, Ripple, and Safello are some of the major market players in the blockchain technology.

Many companies (e.g. IBM, Microsoft) have been driving the development of energy-related blockchain applications worldwide over the past few years and it is assumed that others are also working on integrating blockchain solutions, but are still not visible in the energy industry. Moreover, the way blockchain is applied worldwide is influenced by new blockchain projects in various countries and regions. Based on Deloitte's 2019 Global Blockchain Survey, it appears that China, Singapore, Israel and United States are groundbreaking blockchain technology emerging countries, based on their own common objectives and strategies. Figure 1 below, depicts specific blockchain attitudes along many metrics, for the respective countries [27].

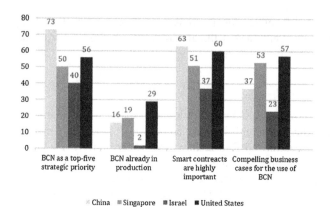

Fig. 1. Blockchain adoption in top emerging countries, Source: [27]

In addition to those major blockchain enablers, Fig. 2 depicts that market participants are migrating towards Blockchain technology. This is justified due to the fact that during 2016 blockchain revenue by area was below $5,000 comparing to $20,000 that it is expected to be until 2025, as described by M. Niranjanamurthy et al. [28].

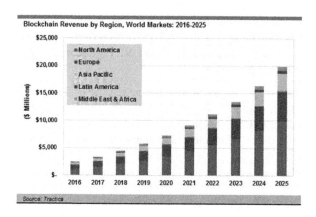

Fig. 2. Blockchain revenue by region (2016–2025), Source: Tractica

4.2 Threats and Challenges

While companies are investigating opportunities to integrate blockchain into their existing business models, or how to adjust current structures and procedures to cooperate with blockchain technology, emerging disrupters have developed their business around blockchain from the beginning. Theoretically, this makes them more flexible and agile than competitors, and less limited by similar challenges that prevent their more advanced competition from embracing them. As the blockchain environment progresses and various use-cases arise, organizations in the energy sectors should face a dynamic and potentially divisive array of problems, as well as new dependencies. The key blockchain market adoption challenges in this area are described below and depicted in Fig. 3.

Fig. 3. Blockchain Market Adoption Challenges

- **Inefficient Technological Design:** While the blockchain technology has several business opportunities, it is still lacking in many technological ways. For instance, some dApps tend to be subjected to miscoding and bugs, leading to limitations and hacking issues within the blockchain network. Additionally, as Deloitte refers in a recent report [39], The problem with many current solutions is that they bypass considerable layers of operation and run services and applications on top of those. Therefore, many different chains are being established by many different organizations, with many different characteristics in a single business market.

- **Scalability:** Scalability is a key barrier when applying blockchain to real business environments. The throughput of a blockchain system is related to the amount of transactions in each block and block time period. The conventional blockchain network, is a "broadcast medium", through which each node relays all transactions. This data transfer mode cannot be extended to accommodate a large number of transactions due to the network bandwidth constraint [40]. The nodes require great processing power and time to calculate the validation algorithms in order to add the block to the blockchain network. According to the study in [41], 30 billion kWh of electricity were expended on handling 30 million transactions, representing about 0.13 per cent of global energy usage. In the energy sector, the amount of transactions per second is very high, especially for large-scale activities, due to thousands of prosumers that are concurrently interested in the energy consumption and production. As a promising solution to this issues, a new blockchain platform called EnergyWeb blockchain, targets the energy market with transaction rates as high as a couple of thousands per second [42].

- **Energy Consumption:** Energy use poses another obstacle for blockchain adoption. The mining process require enormous amount of machine power to solve complex equations, taking more and more energy to conquer that. Miners currently use 0.2%

of total electricity, and if it continues to expand, then miners can take on more power than the planet can produce by 2020. Therefore, it is now becoming one of this network's biggest challenges [43].

- **Cost and Efficiency:** The speed and reliability with which blockchain networks can carry out peer-to-peer transactions comes at a high aggregate cost, higher for certain blockchain forms than others [31]. Moreover, integrating blockchain within the smart grid needs high infrastructural costs in order to re-architect the current grid networks, update smart meters to facilitate transfers by smart contracts, implement blockchain-specific ICT systems and other associated Advanced Metering Interfaces (AMI). For instance, the existing smart grid network, currently uses technology such as telemetry that is much more advanced and much less costly compared to blockchain [44].

- **Privacy and Security:** Security problem and blockchain technology has been discussed intensively. Several professionals and academic experts have argued that blockchain technology is inconsistent with privacy laws like the EU General Data Protection Regulation (GDPR) [32]. Although cryptocurrencies such as Bitcoin provide pseudonymity, other future blockchain implementations allow smart transactions and contracts to be unquestionably connected to established identities, posing serious concerns about privacy and data protection stored and available on the public ledger. Participants who transmit personal data to the blockchain are more likely to be called GDPR *controllers* as they specify the processing information, while blockchain nodes who only collect personal data are more likely to be *processors* as they simply promote the function of the blockchain network. This decision, however, is not easy, because not all blockchain networks function in the same way, and there could be various types of members conducting different activities [33–35].

- **Regulation:** Many organizations are transforming blockchain technology into a transactional tool, without following clear guidelines, resulting to technologies like DLT and blockchain to completely by-pass regulation and tackle inefficiencies in traditional intermediated payment networks entirely. A critical issue for regulators about decentralized structures is who will be kept responsible for violations of law and regulation. This is analogous to the problem of assessing network transparency before blockchain emerges [36]. When it comes to the energy market, the regulatory authorities support the active involvement of users and the emergence of processes for green management practices. However, the existing grid regulatory framework does not accept the exchanging of electricity between prosumers when it comes to massive improvements in the main power grid structure, and does not promote the implementation of the distributed ledger in the process [11].

- **Lack of Adequate Skill Sets:** In addition to the requisite tools and equipment, there is a need for properly qualified personnel to handle the blockchain technologies to be implemented on the energy market. Blockchain technology is relatively recent compared to other technologies and is still developing and few individuals actually have the capacity to support this technology [43].

- **Public Acceptance:** Last but not least, the key challenge associated with blockchain is a lack of technology knowledge, especially in non-banking sectors (e.g. the energy and sustainability sector) and a general lack of understanding of how it functions. The majority of the public is still not aware of the nature of DLTs and its future use. While the technology is making history, attracting more consumers is still not enough.

Distributed ledger technologies and blockchain guarantees trust, immutability/transparency and facilitates disintermediation, as well as providing extra protection for transactions that have been executed. Those are substantial benefits that cannot be overlooked. Although, its cost-of-implementation drawback can be depreciated and minimized in a short period of time, as more expertise is obtained and blockchain becomes a core technology [38].

5   Conclusions

Blockchain technology has attracted significant attention primarily due to the emerging crypto market. Although, the last years researchers are investigating and demonstrating the potential of blockchain in many other sectors, such as finance, IoT, communication technologies and more. Among those, the energy sector is starting a very impressive utilization of blockchain technology, as well. The energy industry, among them, is also making a very remarkable utilization blockchain technology. Blockchain's incorporation into the smart grid requires the society to agree and retain P2P energy transactions within the network. Even if the advantages of blockchain technology within the energy market and specifically the smart energy grids are many, there are still several challenges that need to be passed, in order to fully integrate blockchain technologies within the energy market. Towards this direction, the current paper presents an extensive market analysis, trying to identify possible opportunities and current threats and challenges that need to be addressed. One key point identified through the market analysis is that people are moving towards blockchain technology fast, as in 2016 blockchain revenue by region was below $5,000 and it is predicted to be $20,000 until 2025. On the other hand, though, several challenges were also identified, with the most important ones the regulation and privacy concerns. As clearly identified in the market analysis presented in the current paper, for widespread and large-scale adoption of blockchain in the smart energy grid, industry and the research community will need to work together to tackle the challenges that lie ahead.

Acknowledgements. This work has been partially supported by the PARITY project, funded by the European Commission under Grant Agreement Number 864319 through the Horizon 2020.

References

1. European Commission: 2020 Climate and Energy package (2007) Http://Ec.Europa.Eu/Clima/Policies/Strategies/2020/Index_En.Htm. http://ec.europa.eu/clima/policies/strategies/2020/index_en.htm
2. Aghaei, J., Alizadeh, M.I.: Demand response in smart electricity grids equipped with renewable energy sources: a review. Renew. Sustain. Energy Rev. **18**, 64–72 (2013), Pergamon. https://doi.org/10.1016/j.rser.2012.09.019

3. Poudyal, R., Loskot, P., Nepal, R., Parajuli, R., Khadka, S.K.: Mitigating the current energy crisis in Nepal with renewable energy sources. Renew. Sustain. Energy Rev. **116**, 109388 (2019). https://doi.org/10.1016/j.rser.2019.109388

4. Zhang, M., Eliassen, F., Taherkordi, A., Jacobsen, H.A., Chung, H.M., Zhang, Y.: Energy trading with demand response in a community-based P2P energy market. In: 2019 IEEE International Conference on Communications, Control, and Computing Technologies for Smart Grids, SmartGridComm 2019 (2019). https://doi.org/10.1109/smartgridcomm.2019.8909798

5. Mollah, M.B., et al.: Blockchain for future smart grid: a comprehensive survey. IEEE Internet Things J. 1–1 (2020). https://doi.org/10.1109/jiot.2020.2993601

6. Fotiou, N., Pittaras, I., Siris, V.A., Voulgaris, S., Polyzos, G.C.: Secure IoT Access at Scale Using Blockchains and Smart Contracts. In: 2019 IEEE 20th International Symposium on "A World of Wireless, Mobile and Multimedia Networks" (WoWMoM), pp. 1–6 (2019). https://doi.org/10.1109/wowmom.2019.8793047

7. Asfia, U., Kamuni, V., Sheikh, A., Wagh, S., Patel, D.: Energy trading of electric vehicles using blockchain and smart contracts. In: 2019 18th European Control Conference, ECC 2019, pp. 3958–396 (2019). https://doi.org/10.23919/ECC.2019.8796284

8. Sengupta, J., Ruj, S., Das Bit, S.: A Comprehensive Survey on Attacks, Security Issues and Blockchain Solutions for IoT and IIoT. J. Netw. Comput. Appl. **14**, 102481 (2020).https://doi.org/10.1016/j.jnca.2019.102481

9. Liu, C., Chai, K.K., Zhang, X., Chen, Y.: Peer-to-peer electricity trading system: smart contracts based proof-of-benefit consensus protocol. Wirel. Netw. 1–12 (2019). https://doi.org/10.1007/s11276-019-01949-0

10. Zhang, P., White, J., Schmidt, D.C., Lenz, G., Rosenbloom, S.T.: FHIRChain: applying blockchain to securely and scalably share clinical data. Comput. Struct. Biotechnol. J. **16**, 267–278 (2018). https://doi.org/10.1016/j.csbj.2018.07.004

11. M. Andoni et al.: Blockchain technology in the energy sector: a systematic review of challenges and opportunities. Renew. Sustain. Energy Rev. **100**, 143–174 (2019), Elsevier Ltd. https://doi.org/10.1016/j.rser.2018.10.014

12. L. Herenčić et al.: Overview of the main challenges and threats for implementation of the advanced concept for decentralized trading in microgrids. In: EUROCON 2019 - 18th International Conference on Smart Technologies (2019). https://doi.org/10.1109/eurocon.2019.8861906

13. Nhede, N.: Blockchain in energy market to reach $3 billion by 2025. Smart Energy International (2019). https://www.smart-energy.com/industry-sectors/energy-grid-management/blockchain-in-energy-market-to-reach-3-billion-by-2025/

14. Themistocleous, M., Rupino, P.: Introduction to blockchain and fintech. In: 51st Hawaii International Conference on System Sciences, vol. 9, p. 9981331 (2018). http://hdl.handle.net/10125/50453

15. Themistocleous, M., Stefanou, K., Iosif, E.: Blockchain in solar energy. Cyprus Rev. **30**(2), 203–212 (2018)

16. da Cunha, P.R., Themistocleous, M., Morabito, V.: Introduction to the Minitrack on The Transformational Impact of Blockchain. In: Proceedings of the 52nd Hawaii International Conference on System Sciences (2019). https://doi.org/10.24251/hicss.2019.819

17. Themistocleous, M.: Blockchain technology and land registry. Cyprus Rev. **30**(2), 195–202 (2018)

18. Garfinkel, H., Drane, J.: What is blockchain? (2016). https://blockchainhub.net/blockchain-intro/

19. He, Y., Li, H., Cheng, X., Liu, Y., Yang, C., Sun, L.: A blockchain based truthful incentive mechanism for distributed P2P applications. IEEE Access **6**, 27324–27335 (2018). https://doi.org/10.1109/ACCESS.2018.2821705

20. Massessi, D.: Blockchain Public/Private Key Cryptography in a Nutshell. Medium (2018). https://medium.com/coinmonks/blockchain-public-private-key-cryptography-in-a-nutshell-b7776e475e7c

21. de Oliveira, G.A., Muthemba, L.J., Unsihuay-Vila, C.: State-of-the-art impacts of Smart Grid in the power systems operation and expansion planning. Brazilian Arch. Biol. Technol. **61** (Special issue), 18000400 (2018). https://doi.org/10.1590/1678-4324-smart-2018000400

22. Mengelkamp, E., Gärttner, J., Rock, K., Kessler, S., Orsini, L., Weinhardt, C.: Designing microgrid energy markets: a case study: the brooklyn microgrid. Appl. Energy **210**, 870–880 (2018). https://doi.org/10.1016/j.apenergy.2017.06.054

23. Mylrea, M., Gourisetti, S.N.G.: Blockchain for smart grid resilience: exchanging distributed energy at speed, scale and security. In: Proceedings - 2017 Resilience Week, RWS 2017, pp. 18–23 (2017). https://doi.org/10.1109/rweek.2017.8088642

24. van Leeuwen, G., AlSkaif, T., Gibescu, M., van Sark, W.: An integrated blockchain-based energy management platform with bilateral trading for microgrid communities. Appl. Energy **263**, 114613 (2020). https://doi.org/10.1016/j.apenergy.2020.114613

25. Wang, X., Yang, W., Noor, S., Chen, C., Guo, M., van Dam, K.H.: Blockchain-based smart contract for energy demand management. Energy Procedia **158**, 2719–2724 (2019). https://doi.org/10.1016/j.egypro.2019.02.028

26. Miglani, A., Kumar, N., Chamola, V., Zeadally, S.: Blockchain for internet of energy management: review, solutions, and challenges. Comput. Commun. **151**, 395–418 (2020). https://doi.org/10.1016/j.comcom.2020.01.014

27. Liu, C., Chai, K.K., Zhang, X., Chen, Y., Peer-to-peer electricity trading system: smart contracts based proof-of-benefit consensus protocol. Wirel. Netw. (2019). https://doi.org/10.1007/s11276-019-01949-0

28. Mhaisen, N., Fetais, N., Massoud, A.: Secure smart contract-enabled control of battery energy storage systems against cyber-attacks. Alexandria Eng. J. **58**(4), 1291–1300 (2019). https://doi.org/10.1016/j.aej.2019.11.001

29. Minoli, D., Occhiogrosso, B.: Blockchain mechanisms for IoT security. Internet Things **1–2**, 1–13 (2018). https://doi.org/10.1016/j.iot.2018.05.002

30. Deval, V., Norta, A.: Mobile smart-contract lifecycle governance with incentivized proof-of-stake for oligopoly-formation prevention. In: Proceedings - 19th IEEE/ACM International Symposium on Cluster, Cloud and Grid Computing, CCGrid 2019, pp. 165–168 (2019). https://doi.org/10.1109/ccgrid.2019.00029

31. Li, Y., Yang, W., He, P., Chen, C., Wang, X.: Design and management of a distributed hybrid energy system through smart contract and blockchain. Appl. Energy **248**, 390–405 (2019). https://doi.org/10.1016/j.apenergy.2019.04.132

32. Alam, M.R., St-Hilaire, M., Kunz, T.: Peer-to-peer energy trading among smart homes. Appl. Energy **238**, 1434–1443 (2019). https://doi.org/10.1016/j.apenergy.2019.01.091

33. Long, C., Wu, J., Zhang, C., Thomas, L., Cheng, M., Jenkins, N.: Peer-to-peer energy trading in a community microgrid. In: IEEE Power and Energy Society General Meeting, vol. 2018, pp. 1–5 (2018). https://doi.org/10.1109/pesgm.2017.8274546

34. Alam, M.T., Li, H., Patidar, A.: Bitcoin for smart trading in smart grid. In: IEEE Workshop on Local and Metropolitan Area Networks, vol. 2015 (2015). https://doi.org/10.1109/lanman.2015.7114742

35. Aitzhan, N.Z., Svetinovic, D.: Security and privacy in decentralized energy trading through multi-signatures, blockchain and anonymous messaging streams. IEEE Trans. Dependable Secur. Comput. **15**(5), 840–852 (2018). https://doi.org/10.1109/TDSC.2016.2616861

36. Zyskind, G., Nathan, O., Pentland, A.S.: Decentralizing privacy: using blockchain to protect personal data. In: Proceedings - 2015 IEEE Security and Privacy Workshops, SPW 2015, pp. 180–184 (2015). https://doi.org/10.1109/spw.2015.27

37. Mengelkamp, E., Notheisen, B., Beer, C., Dauer, D., Weinhardt, C.: A blockchain-based smart grid: towards sustainable local energy markets. Comput. Sci. Res. Dev. 33(1–2), 207–214 (2018). https://doi.org/10.1007/s00450-017-0360-9

38. Omar, A.S., Basir, O.: Identity management in IoT networks using blockchain and smart contracts. In: 2018 IEEE International Conference on Internet of Things (iThings) and IEEE Green Computing and Communications (GreenCom) and IEEE Cyber, Physical and Social Computing (CPSCom) and IEEE Smart Data (SmartData), pp. 994–1000 (2018). https://doi.org/10.1109/cybermatics_2018.2018.00187

39. Diloitte: Blockchain Trends for 2020 (2020). https://www2.deloitte.com/content/dam/Deloitte/ie/Documents/Consulting/Blockchain-Trends-2020-report.pdf

40. Xie, J., Yu, F.R., Huang, T., Xie, R., Liu, J., Liu, Y.: A survey on the scalability of blockchain systems. IEEE Netw. 33(5), 166–173 (2019). https://doi.org/10.1109/MNET.001.1800290

41. Digiconomis: Bitcoin Energy Consumption Index. https://digiconomist.net/bitcoin-energy-consumption

42. EnergyWeb: The Energy Web Chain (2019). https://www.energyweb.org/wp-content/uploads/2019/05/EWF-Paper-TheEnergyWebChain-v2-201907-FINAL.pdf

43. Frizzo-Barker, J., Chow-White, P.A., Adams, P.R., Mentanko, J., Ha, D., Green, S.: Blockchain as a disruptive technology for business: a systematic review. Int. J. Inf. Manage. 51, 102029 (2020). https://doi.org/10.1016/j.ijinfomgt.2019.10.014

44. Alladi, T., Chamola, V., Rodrigues, J.J.P.C., Kozlov, S.A.: Blockchain in smart grids: a review on different use cases. Sensors 19(22), 4862 (2019). https://doi.org/10.3390/s19224862

Leadership Uniformity in Raft Consensus Algorithm

Elias Iosif$^{(\boxtimes)}$, Klitos Christodoulou, Marios Touloupou,
and Antonios Inglezakis

Institute For the Future, University of Nicosia, Nicosia, Cyprus
{iosif.e,christodoulou.kl,touloupos.m,inglezakis.a}@unic.ac.cy
https://www.unic.ac.cy/iff/

Abstract. The Raft consensus algorithm constitutes a widely-used algorithm not only in the broader area of distributed systems, ut also in private/permissioned blockchains such as Hyperledger Fabric. A Raft-based distributed system (RDS) strongly relies on leader election, which involves a number of time-related parameters. In the Raft-related literature, the process according to which those parameters are set is an under-researched area. Specifically, the use of the uniform distribution is the dominant approach. Motivated by this realization, in this work, we focus on these time parameters proposing the notion of "leadership uniformity" in combination with a series of performance metrics. Leadership uniformity is based on the desirable characteristic of having equality among the nodes who serve as leaders. The proposed performance metrics are straightforward adaptations of widely-used measurements from broad disciplines such as estimation theory. The experimental results of this work justify the appropriateness of the proposed notion of leadership uniformity. Specifically, the best performance was yielded by the utilization of normal distribution from which the time parameters under investigation were drawn.

Keywords: Consensus algorithms · Blockchain · Raft

1 Introduction

In the field of distributed systems, reliability of services is considered a fundamental challenge, especially in the presence of faulty or Byzantine processes. To achieve reliability of services, consensus algorithms are proposed for enhancing distributed systems with fault tolerance capabilities. A consensus algorithm aims to provide an agreement with regards to the ordering of events, along with presenting to all processes, that participate to the system, a valid common state. Paxos [1] is acknowledged in the literature as the main paradigm of such algorithms. However, the inherent complexity of Paxos has been regarded by many as the main reason for its limited adoption [2]. This complexity has motivated the implementation of a number of variants [3–5]. In this paper we focus

© Springer Nature Switzerland AG 2020
M. Themistocleous et al. (Eds.): EMCIS 2020, LNBIP 402, pp. 125–136, 2020.
https://doi.org/10.1007/978-3-030-63396-7_9

on Raft [6], which was proposed to the literature as an alternative to Paxos [1] cluster of consensus algorithms. In addition to the traditional field of distributed systems, the Raft consensus algorithm is proposed as an alternative to the proof-of-X family of consensus algorithms used in the area of public blockchains [7]. Specifically, the design principles of Raft make it suitable for private or consortium (aka *permissioned*) blockchain systems. For example, the Hyperledger Fabric [8], is considered by many as one of the major proposals for deploying a private/permissioned blockchains fueled by a plug-able consensus algorithm including an implementation of Raft.

A Raft-based distributed system (RDS) strongly relies on the process of leader election. This constitutes a special phase of the overall algorithm and it is controlled by a number of time parameters including the follower timeout. The follower timeout determines the timing of the transition between the default node state (follower) to the state of leader candidate. As such, the follower timeout requires special investigation. Motivated by the significance of the follower timeout, as well as, by the realization that this parameter is under-investigated, in this work we follow an experimental approach, which, to the best of our knowledge, has the following contributions to the Raft-related literature:

1. Proposal of the "leadership uniformity", which is well-aligned with Raft's leadership-centric design and it aims to quantify the equality among nodes that served as leaders.
2. Adaptation of a series of performance measures with respect to leadership uniformity.
3. Experimental investigation of the effect of different probability distributions from which the follower timeout is drawn.

Overall, the main findings from this work aim to further enhance the understanding of Raft's parameter space. Furthermore, the performance metrics discussed in subsequent sections aim to serve as a tool for designers during consensus algorithms development.

The rest of the paper is organized as follows. A brief literature review along with an overview of the Raft algorithm is presented in Sect. 2. The proposed approach is presented in Sect. 3 including a number of performance metrics. The experimental settings and the respective performance scores are reported in Sect. 4 and Sect. 5, respectively. Section 6 concludes this work.

2   Literature Review and Background

This section is organized into two parts. Firstly, we briefly discuss the consensus algorithms landscape through a literature review. Lastly, we present the internal mechanics of Raft.

Specifically, Sect. 2.1 explores the Raft-related literature in an attempt to highlight the motivation behind Raft, and further relate it with the area of blockchain technologies. In the broader area of distributed systems (including blockchains) the agreement on data/information shared between nodes is known as "consensus". Nodes need to collaborate with each other in order to make decisions on the basis of shared data/information. For the specific case of applications based on shared ledgers (including blockchains), this agreement takes the form of globally recognized ledger of transactions that are validated and, thus, trusted (e.g., see [9–11]). The set (cluster) of nodes should function as a coherent whole being able to survive (i.e., preserve a proper operational mode including the integrity of shared data/information) even in the presence of individual failures (i.e., when a number[1] of nodes crashed).

Following from the above, Sect. 2.2 details the Raft-specific background information that relates to the present work. Raft [12] was proposed as an easy to built, easy to understand fault-tolerant consensus algorithm[2]. A fundamental design characteristic of Raft, is the leader-centric design where the consensus relies heavily on a leader election process which carries the responsibility of reaching agreements. The leadership lasts for a (short) period of time which is parameterizable. In a nutshell, all client requests arriving in the network, are handled by the current leader. A client can be regarded as any machine being connected to the network which, however, is not eligible for serving as a leader (i.e., it consumes information without having the opportunity to play a role in the consensus that guarantees the integrity of the information). The above topics are further elaborated below.

2.1   Literature Review

Paxos is a fundamental paradigm of a consensus algorithm in the area of fault-tolerant distributed system [1]. The problem that Paxos successfully solved is summarized as follows: let a set of processes that propose values; the consensus algorithm should choose and verify only one value among the proposed ones. However, Paxos is considered by several researchers complex to understand and, therefore, hard to implement. Indicative descriptions of those difficulties are presented in [13–15].

After Paxos, several related research studies have been performed such as the work demonstrated in [16]. The authors have presented a series of design decisions for the creation of a fault-tolerant database using the Paxos algorithm. Furthermore, Paxos is considered by many as the "father" of the Raft consensus algorithm [6]. The complexity of the Paxos algorithm is used to serve educational purposes on state machine replication. The need for having an easy–to–understand consensus algorithm, which can be used not only for systems development but also for education purposes, created the conditions for the proposal of Raft.

Recent technological advancements with the introduction of blockchain technologies (including consensus algorithms) pose a series of educational challenges in training courses, especially in mixed student groups (e.g., student from engineering and business backgrounds). These challenges are detailed in [17] along

---

[1] In many cases, this number should be less than the 50% of total number of nodes.
[2] Raft can only tolerate crash failures and not malicious nodes.

with a series of recommendations. Specifically, Raft's authors introduced new techniques compared to Paxos, including feature decomposition and state space reduction. Numerous investigations have been conducted, analysing the performance of Raft, e.g., [18]. Other research attempts have demonstrated Raft variants such as the realization of a dynamic Raft cluster [19], introducing the dynamic utilization of resources and the concept of disqualified nodes. Furthermore, Raft has been tested in several use cases such as in distributed Software Defined Networks (SDNs) [20]. In [20], a thorough overview of Raft is provided along with a discussion regarding the implementation of SDN controller platforms in OpenDaylight [21] and ONOS [22].

Since Raft was introduced for the development of distributed fault-tolerant systems, with the rise of the blockchain and Distributed Ledger Technologies (DLTs), researchers have also introduced Raft in different blockchain systems such as Quorum [23] and Hyperledger Fabric [8]. Among the numerous approaches that appear in the literature, the work presented in [18] highlights consensus as a challenging problem in blockchain systems. This work is concerned with a study on the efficiency of Raft in non-negligible packet-loss rate networks. The authors proposed a detailed computational model that is used to evaluate the possibility of crashing the distributed network. Moreover, the work reported in [24], demonstrates a non Byzantine fault–tolerant algorithm called KRaft. KRaft is similar to Raft retaining most of its structure and it can be used in private blockchain systems. KRaft utilizes the K-Bucket node relationships in the Kademlia protocol [25].

In [26], the performance of the Quorum blockchain was evaluated followed by an investigation regarding the support of different consensus algorithms. The main findings propose that in a permissioned setting, where participants are known, it is unnecessary to use a consensus algorithm such as Proof–Of–Work (PoW); which is used in public blockchains like Bitcoin [9]. It seems that algorithms similar to Raft are better suited in private settings. However, this goes against the open-participation, and decentralized philosophy adopted by public blockchains. A recent study presented in [27] suggests the investigation of the interplay between the decentralization degree, that characterize a blockchain system, and the underlying consensus algorithm. For the case of non-public permissioned blockchains [27] constitutes one of the first experimental approaches towards this direction. Specifically, it is reported that the decentralization degree of the Ripple protocol can be determined as a function of the adversarial attacks or network faults. Under certain conditions the centralization degree of private/permissioned networks can be relaxed.

2.2   Raft: Background

As stated above, the nodes in a distributed system need to agree on the shared data/information. Enabling consensus in a fault-tolerant environment is also essential for the development of decentralized applications (abbreviated as dApps) that are deployed over a blockchain [28]. Being inline with this spirit, the main characteristic of the Raft algorithm is the provision of consensus in fault-tolerant distributed systems and dApps [12]. The notion of fault, refers to the case of node crashes excluding any Byzantine faults. In addition, Raft was proposed as a clearer alternative to Paxos, as well as, to provide a deeper understanding on how consensus can be accomplished in distributed systems. This was motivated by the widely-accepted view according to which its predecessor, Paxos [29], was considered difficult to understand and adopt (mainly due to the respective design complexity).Raft was intended to be more understandable by separating the logic of Paxos in a more comprehensible way. Furthermore, Raft was formally proven to be safe while offering some additional features.I n particular, Raft provides an inclusive way for handling a state machine in a set of nodes. Thus, the agreement on the same series of state transitions is achieved. The background information regarding Raft is presented in subsequent sections focusing on: (i) the election of leaders; (ii) the replication of the (shared) log; and (iii) a series of safety features. For completeness we note that this work relies on [6,30] where the algorithm is explained in detail.

Leader Election. According to [31], in non-faulty conditions, a node in a cluster can remain in one of the following states {follower, candidate, leader} during a certain time unit. The default state is "follower". Any node can become leader through the transition by the "candidate" state. The leader node transmits messages (also referred to as heartbeats or pulses) to other nodes declaring its leadership. That is, it lets the rest nodes know that an active leadership exists. When a follower signals a time-out while waiting for a pulse from the leader, a leader election phase may take place. Specifically, the timed-out node switches to the "candidate" state, votes for itself, and issues a number of Remote Procedure Calls (RPC). The aforementioned RPC calls are labeled as "RequestVotes", meaning that votes from the rest nodes are needed in order the candidate to become the leader. This phase can result into one of the following three outcomes:

1. By gaining the majority of votes, the candidate becomes the leader.
2. If vote majority is not reached, the phase may end without assigning leadership and the candidate returns to the state of "follower".
3. In case of multiple candidates, the leader is determined by the respective term number which is an index denoting whether the node is updated with respect to the shared data (also referred to as the replicated log).

Log Replication. Raft breaks down the "consensus problem" by introducing the leader election as a separate process in combination with the log replication and safety. The replicated log cannot be manipulated while it supports append–only entry storage. The log exists in every node enabling tolerance to faults, as well as, high availability.

The leader is responsible for having replicas of the logs on all nodes. Requests can be sent to the leader by the clients, which can be regarded as read/write commands to be executed with effect on the shared log. After a successful write operation, a new entry is appended to the leader's log, and this change is forwarded to the followers via an "AppendEntries" RPC message. If a follower (or more) is unavailable, the leader will retry sending the "AppendEntries" RPC until the change is adopted by all followers. A log entry typically contains three fields as follows:

1. **Command**: Denotes the command requested by the client.
2. **Index**: Specifies the position of the entry in the log.
3. **Term number**: Encodes the relative[3] time.

As stated in [12], the logs can become unreliable in the event of leader crash. In this case, the latest version of the (available) log is identified and taken into account.

Safety. The following safety features are supported by Raft:

1. **Election safety:** Only one leader can exist in the context of a term.
2. **Leader append-only:** The leader can perform only append operations in the log (i.e., no substitutions and/or deletions).
3. **Log matching:** Two logs are considered to be identical up to an index, if they have an entry that corresponds to the same index and term.
4. **Leader completeness:** The leaders' logs contain the log entries that were committed in previous terms.
5. **State machine safety:** When a node attaches a log entry to its state machine, then other nodes can not apply any changes to it.

In the sections that follow, we focus on *timeouts* that play a key role in leader election (briefly described in Sect. 2.2). Firstly, we introduce a series of definitions followed by the description of the experimental setup and the respective performance results. These results are reported for various performance metrics and different timeout configurations.

3   Model

In this section, we provide a series of definitions regarding the characterization of an RDS (see Sect. 3.1). Those definitions are used for introducing a series of performance metrics in order to quantify the leadership uniformity of the respective RDS (see Sect. 3.2).

3.1   Definitions

At each any point in time, an RDS can be characterized by the following model:

$$RDS = (N, \ D_f, \ D_c, \ g(t_f, t_c)), \tag{1}$$

---

[3] In a message–passing distributed system a global clock does not apply [32], so, the timings are encoded as (numerical) indices.

where, N is the number of nodes in RDS, D_f is the distribution used for setting the follower timeout t_f, and D_c is the distribution from which the candidate timeout t_c is drawn. In addition, $g(t_f, t_c)$ denotes a function reflecting the relation between t_f and t_c. Note that the model defined by (1) is focused on the critical timeouts that determine the election phase of the Raft algorithm. That is, this model is not meant to encode an exhaustive description of all Raft's parameters (i.e., parameters that apply in addition to the election phase).

For a cluster of N nodes, the following sequence is defined

$$(n_{1,L}, n_{2,L}, ..., n_{i,L}, ..., n_{N,L}) \quad \text{for} \quad i = 1, ..., N, \tag{2}$$

where, $n_{i,L}$ denotes the absolute frequency (i.e., number of times) with which the i-th node, n_i, was elected as leader ($n_{i,L} \in \mathbb{Z}_0^+$). The sequence of frequencies can be treated as a set of unordered values as, by design, the ordering of nodes does not play any role in the election phase.. This "bag-of-leadership-frequencies" can be directly used for computing basic yet informative measurements as explained next.

3.2 Performance Metrics

Here, four metrics are defined meant to quantify the leadership uniformity and used as performance metrics. Those metrics can be organized in two categories: (i) variation of leadership frequencies, and (ii) divergence from ideal leadership.

Variation of Leadership Frequencies. Two intuitive measurements of the variation of the leadership frequencies in (2) are the standard deviation (denoted as *Std*) and variance (denoted as *Var*). Semantically, a desirable leadership uniformity implies low variation of leadership frequencies. In an ideal scenario, all participating nodes should be characterized by equal $n_{i,L}$ values. As the RDS under investigation approaches the ideal leadership uniformity, the respective *Std* and *Var* of (2) tend to zero.

Distance from Ideal Leadership. The second category of performance metrics relies on the idea of measuring the (average) distance from the ideal leadership uniformity. The latter is denoted by $\bar{n}_L$ and is defined as:

$$\bar{n}_L = \frac{T}{N}, \tag{3}$$

where, T stands for the number of successful election trials (rounds), i.e., trials in context of which exactly one leader has been elected. Based on this definition, we can adopt the notion of mean absolute error (a widely-used measurement applied in various disciplines such as estimation theory [33]) as follows:

$$MAE = \frac{1}{N} \sum_{i=1}^{N} |n_{i,L} - \bar{n}_L|. \tag{4}$$

The meaning of "error" is equivalent to the meaning of the distance of $n_{i,L}$ from the ideal value $\bar{n}_L$. A variation of (4) can be defined as follows:

$$MSE = \frac{1}{N} \sum_{i=1}^{N} (n_{i,L} - \bar{n}_L)^2. \tag{5}$$

Similarly to the case of *MAE*, *MSE* is motivated by the commonly used measurement of mean squared error. In general, *MSE* is a fundamental criterion that is widely-used in the broad context of optimal estimators [33]. As the RDS under investigation tends to the ideal leadership uniformity, the respective *MAE* and *MSE* scores tend to zero.

The quadratic operations used in *Var* and *MSE*, are meant to "amplify" the respective differences in an attempt to facilitate the comparison of the considered distributions from which the timeouts are drawn.

4   Experiments

The experimental setup used throughout the experiments reported by this work is described as follows.

1. Number of nodes (N): In total, five nodes were utilized which constitutes a typical cluster size according to the Raft reference paper [6]. For the sake of clarity, we note that the $N = 5$ configuration deals with the number of nodes that can be deemed as candidate leaders (and therefore being responsible for system's consensus) and it does not limit the number of nodes that can participate in the overall network as clients. For example, we may have five nodes deemed as candidate leaders along with thousands (or more) of other nodes acting as clients. The latter type of nodes are not eligible for leadership and they can only exchange information with the leader.
2. Distributions from which the timeouts are drawn (D_f, D_c): The uniform distribution is widely used in numerous Raft-related works, while it seems that other distributions are less-researched. Motivated by this gap, the focus of this work is the investigation of the role of two additional distributions, namely, *normal* and *lognormal*, for the case of follower timeout. The normal distribution was chosen due its vast applicability for modeling various phenomena. The employment of the lognormal distribution was motivated by the observation that the latency of nodes in distributed systems can be modeled by distributions that belong to the lognornal family. For example, an indicative early study can be found in [34], while a more recent lognormal-based modeling is presented in [35].

For the case of candidate timeout, t_c, a uniform distribution was used taking values in the [0,500] ms interval. Regarding the follower timeout, t_f, and the normal/lognormal distributions, the following three cases were investigated: (i) $\bar{t}_f = 50$ ms, (ii) $\bar{t}_f = 500$ ms, and (iii) $\bar{t}_f = 5000$ ms, where $\bar{t}_f$ stands for the mean value of the respective distribution. These timeout values imply a linear relationship (as a possible form of $g(t_f, t_c)$) between follower and candidate timeouts. The standard deviation, σ, of those distributions was set to $\frac{1}{4}\bar{t}_f$. For the case of t_f's uniform distribution, the following range was used $[\bar{t}_f - 2\sigma, \bar{t}_f + 2\sigma]$. In order to compare the performance yielded for the aforementioned experimental settings, the metrics defined in Sect. 3.2 were used for 100 successful election trials. All experiments reported were performed by extending *pyraft*, a Python-based implementation of Raft[4].

5   Analysis of Performance

In this section, the performance of the Raft consensus algorithm is presented with respect to *leadership uniformity* using four evaluation measurements, namely, *Std*, *Var*, *MAE*, and *MSE*. Regarding the normal and lognormal distributions, the respective scores are reported for the following cases (also referred to as $\bar{t}_f$ scenarios): (i) $\bar{t}_f = 50$ ms, (ii) $\bar{t}_f = 500$ ms, and (iii) $\bar{t}_f = 5000$ ms. Also, the performance yielded by the uniform distribution is also presented.

Table 1. Follower timeout: leadership uniformity ($\bar{t}_f = 50$ ms).

Distribution	Std	Var	MAE	MSE
Uniform	8.53	72.80	11.20	172.80
Normal	**6.90**	**47.60**	**10.80**	**147.60**
Lognormal	10.00	100.00	12.40	200.00

Table 1 demonstrates the performance scores for the case of $\bar{t}_f = 50$ ms. The best performance is achieved by the normal distribution, while the utilization of the lognormal distribution exhibits the lowest scores. As expected –and by definition– all four metrics are correlated. However, *Var* and *MSE* are characterized by larger ranges compared to *Std* and *MAE* amplifying the performance differences among the distributions under comparison. Regarding $\bar{t}_f = 500$ ms, the performance analysis is presented in Table 2. Similarly to the previous case, the best results are yielded by the normal distribution. Slightly different observations hold when increasing the follower timeout. These are presented for the

Table 2. Follower timeout: leadership uniformity ($\bar{t}_f = 500$ ms).

Distribution	Std	Var	MAE	MSE
Uniform	8.72	76.00	12.00	176.00
Normal	**6.07**	**36.80**	**10.40**	**136.80**
Lognormal	6.08	37.00	12.00	209.60

---

[4] https://pypi.org/project/pyraft/.

Table 3. Follower timeout: leadership uniformity ($\bar{t}_f = 5000\,\text{ms}$).

Distribution	Std	Var	MAE	MSE
Uniform	**8.07**	**65.20**	**11.60**	**165.20**
Normal	8.94	80.00	12.80	180.00
Lognormal	11.15	124.40	13.60	224.40

$\bar{t}_f = 5000\,\text{ms}$ case as shown in Table 3. In this case, the uniform distribution constitutes the top performing distribution followed by the uniform and lognormal distribution.

Overall, the top performance was achieved for the middle $\bar{t}_f$ scenario (i.e., $\bar{t}_f = 500\,\text{ms}$) that achieved $MSE = 136.80$. An example where the effectiveness of MSE is clearly shown, is the comparison between the normal and lognormal distribution, as shown in Table 2. According to Std and Var, the two distributions exhibit slight differences (e.g., 6.07 vs. 6.08 for Std). However, this difference is emphasized when using MSE, i.e., 136.80 vs. 209.60.

6   Conclusions

In this work, we explored an under-investigated aspect of the Raft algorithm. This aspect deals with the setting of follower timeout that constitutes a critical parameter for the leader election phase. In addition, the notion of leadership uniformity was proposed based on the idea that all nodes should be granted equal leadership roles. This is well-aligned with the core spirit of Raft according to which the consensus is managed by the (current) leader. With regards to leadership uniformity we have shown the straightforward adaptation of a number of intuitive performance metrics. Those metrics provided a comprehensive quantification of performance with respect to leadership uniformity. The experimental results suggest that the MSE performance metric is more descriptive compared to MAE and Std. The variance of leadership frequencies, Var, exhibits similar behavior with MSE. A key finding of the present work is the observation that the normal distribution yields the best performance when the average follower timeout, $\bar{t}_f$, is kept less than 1s. This was verified for $\bar{t}_f = 50\,\text{ms}$ and $\bar{t}_f = 500\,\text{ms}$. For those timeouts, the superiority of the normal distribution over the uniform distribution can be attributed to the fact that all timeouts according to the latter distribution are equiprobable. This finding contributes to the Raft-related literature where the utilization of uniform distribution seems to be the usual (i.e., default) choice.

Future work deals with the automatic estimation of the distribution parameters. In this context, we also aim to investigate the dynamic selection of the optimal timeout. This will require the employment of a machine learning based component which should be trained on the network characteristics (e.g., based on the relative differences of nodes' timeouts). Last but not least, we aim to explore the effect of other distributions exhibiting asymmetric characteristics (skewness).

Acknowledgement. This research was funded by the Ripple's Impact Fund, an advised fund of Silicon Valley Community Foundation (Grant id: 2018-188546).

References

1. Lamport, L.: The part-time parliament. In: Concurrency: The Works of Leslie Lamport, pp. 277–317 (2019)
2. Howard, H., Schwarzkopf, M., Madhavapeddy, A., Crowcroft, J.: Raft refloated: do we have consensus? ACM SIGOPS Oper. Syst. Rev. **49**(1), 12–21 (2015)
3. Lamport, L., Massa, M.: Cheap Paxos. In: International Conference on Dependable Systems and Networks, 2004, pp. 307–314. IEEE (2004)
4. Lamport, L.: Fast paxos. Distrib. Comput. **19**(2), 79–103 (2006)
5. Mazieres, D.: Paxos made practical (2007)
6. Ongaro, D., Ousterhout, J.: In search of an understandable consensus algorithm. In: 2014 USENIX Annual Technical Conference, pp. 305–319 (2014)
7. Bano, S., et al.: SoK: consensus in the age of blockchains. In: Proceedings of the 1st ACM Conference on Advances in Financial Technologies, pp. 183–198 (2019)
8. IBM: Build and run a smart contract on a Hyperledger Fabric network with the Raft ordering service (2020)
9. Nakamoto, S., Bitcoin, A.: A Peer-to-peer Electronic Cash System. Bitcoin (2008). https://bitcoin.org/bitcoin.pdf
10. Wood, G., et al.: Ethereum: a secure decentralised generalised transaction ledger. Ethereum Proj. Yellow Pap. **151**(2014), 1–32 (2014)
11. Schwartz, D., Youngs, N., Britto, A., et al.: The Ripple protocol consensus algorithm. Ripple Labs Inc. White Pap. **5**(8) (2014)
12. Howard, H.: ARC: analysis of raft consensus. Technical report UCAM-CL-TR-857, University of Cambridge, Computer Laboratory (2014)
13. Meling, H., Jehl, L.: Tutorial summary: Paxos explained from scratch. In: Baldoni, R., Nisse, N., van Steen, M. (eds.) Principles of Distributed Systems. OPODIS 2013. Lecture Notes in Computer Science, vol. 8304, pp. 1–10. Springer, Cham (2013). https://doi.org/10.1007/978-3-319-03850-6_1
14. Chand, S., Liu, Y.A.: What's live? understanding distributed consensus. arXiv preprint arXiv:2001.04787 (2020)
15. Liu, Y.A., Chand, S., Stoller, S.D.: Moderately complex Paxos made simple: high-level specification of distributed algorithm. Computing Research Repository (2017)
16. Chandra, T.D., Griesemer, R., Redstone, J.: Paxos made live: an engineering perspective. In: Proceedings of the twenty-sixth annual ACM symposium on Principles of distributed computing, pp. 398–407 (2007)
17. Themistocleous, M., Christodoulou, K., Iosif, E., Louca, S., Tseas, D.: Blockchain in academia: where do we stand and where do we go? In: Proceedings of the 53rd Hawaii International Conference on System Sciences (2020)

18. Huang, D., Ma, X., Zhang, S.: Performance analysis of the raft consensus algorithm for private blockchains. IEEE Trans. Syst. Man Cybern. Syst. **50**(1), 172–181 (2020)
19. Nakagawa, T., Hayashibara, N.: Resource management for raft consensus protocol. Int. J. Space-Based Situated Comput. **8**(2), 80–87 (2018)
20. Sakic, E., Kellerer, W.: Response time and availability study of RAFT consensus in distributed SDN control plane. IEEE Trans. Netw. Serv. Manage. **15**(1), 304–318 (2017)
21. : The Linux Foundations Projects. OpenDaylight (2019)
22. Open Networking Foundation (2019)
23. Quorum: Home. Quorum (2020)
24. Wang, R., Zhang, L., Xu, Q., Zhou, H.: K-Bucket based Raft-like consensus algorithm for permissioned blockchain. In: 2019 IEEE 25th International Conference on Parallel and Distributed Systems (ICPADS), pp. 996–999 (2019)
25. Kademlia: a design specification. XLattice (2019)
26. Baliga, A., Subhod, I., Kamat, P., Chatterjee, S.: Performance evaluation of the Quorum blockchain platform. arXiv preprint arXiv:1809.03421 (2018)
27. Christodoulou, K., Iosif, E., Inglezakis, A., Themistocleous, M.: Consensus crash testing: exploring Ripple's decentralization degree in adversarial environments. Future Internet **12**(3), 53 (2020)
28. Ren, L., Ward, P.A.S.: Distributed consensus and fault tolerance mechanisms. In: Li, K.-Ch., Bertino, E., Chen, X., Jiang, H. (eds.) Essentials of Blockchain Technology. 1st edn. (2019)
29. Lamport, L., et al.: Paxos made simple. ACM Sigact News **32**(4), 18–25 (2001)
30. Ongaro, D.: Consensus: bridging theory and practice. Ph.D. thesis, Stanford University (2014)
31. Arora, V., Mittal, T., Agrawal, D., El Abbadi, A., Xue, X., et al.: Leader or majority: why have one when you can have both? improving read scalability in Raft-like consensus protocols. In: 9th {USENIX} Workshop on Hot Topics in Cloud Computing (HotCloud 17) (2017)
32. Coulouris, G.F., Dollimore, J., Kindberg, T.: Distributed Systems: Concepts and Design. Pearson Education (2005)
33. Kay, S.M.: Fundamentals of Statistical Signal Processing. Prentice Hall PTR (1993)
34. Almeida, V., Bestavros, A., Crovella, M., De Oliveira, A.: Characterizing reference locality in the www. In: Fourth International Conference on Parallel and Distributed Information Systems, pp. 92–103. IEEE (1996)
35. Underwood, R., Anderson, J., Apon, A.: Measuring network latency variation impacts to high performance computing application performance. In: Proceedings of the 2018 ACM/SPEC International Conference on Performance Engineering, pp. 68–79 (2018)

Positive and Negative Searches Related to the Bitcoin Ecosystem: Relationship with Bitcoin Price

Ifigenia Georgiou[1(✉)], Athanasia Georgiadi[2], and Svetlana Sapuric[1]

[1] School of Business, University of Nicosia, Nicosia, Cyprus
{georgiou.i,sapuric.s}@unic.ac.cy
[2] School of Business, University of Nicosia,
Cyprus and Hellenic Open University, Patras, Greece
nasiageor@yahoo.gr

Abstract. In this study, we investigate whether public awareness of positive or negative possible incidents pertaining to the bitcoin ecosystem are related to bitcoin price and we model bitcoin price volatility taking into consideration public awareness. We take a middle-of-the-road approach, by using a simpler – and thus less data demanding - proxy for public awareness compared to studies that have used complex models that include many parameters to capture the relationships and factors in the ecosystem, but at the same time, a richer approach compared to approaches that simply use the volume of searches for "bitcoin" and its "price" as a proxy in their models. Specifically, we use six different Google Trends queries as proxies in our models: three searches for positive incidents, and three for negative ones. We employ a dataset with monthly price data that covers the time period from September 1st 2011 to December 31st 2019 and we use GARCH and EGARCH models to test whether public awareness of positive or negative possible incidents pertaining to the bitcoin ecosystem is related to bitcoin price and to model price volatility. Results show that majority of our proxies of public awareness are significantly related to price. Moreover, our EGARCH model has detected an asymmetry pertaining to the price volatility's reaction to price news, specifically an "anti-leverage effect", that is, the price volatility is more sensitive to good financial news rather to bad news. In addition, we detected a significant effect of both old and novel news.

Keywords: Bitcoin · Bitcoin ecosystem · Cryptocurrency · Bitcoin price · Bitcoin volatility · Asymmetry · Media · Public awareness · Google trends

1 Introduction

Not long after bitcoin started trading, its value drivers, and what is behind its price fluctuations got into the spotlight. In a déjà vu way, just like it happened back in the dot.com glory days, both scholars and investors started looking for the drivers of bitcoin prices; they searched not only among economic measures but in non-financial metrics as well. Bitcoin's price behaviour could perhaps not be explained by formal economic theory as bitcoin is a digital currency not affected by macroeconomic variables in the

© Springer Nature Switzerland AG 2020
M. Themistocleous et al. (Eds.): EMCIS 2020, LNBIP 402, pp. 137–150, 2020.
https://doi.org/10.1007/978-3-030-63396-7_10

way conventional currencies are, as [29] argued. Bitcoin value drivers have been sought in several places: from technical factors such as its hash rate as a proxy for the technical difficulty for mining bitcoins [6, 21, 22, 30], to its alleged status as a "safe haven" – a suggestion that has been examined with conflicting results (see [7, 9, 30]), to its utility as a portfolio diversification tool [10]. Consequently, [15] found that bitcoin price was largely driven by supply and demand and argued that standard financial exchange models may partly explain changes in the price of bitcoin. Bitcoin's supply is determined by its algorithm and its demand is driven by the investors' expected profit from buying and selling bitcoins; there is no interest rate or other pecuniary benefits. These features make bitcoin a speculative asset that attracts speculative investors governed by short-termism [28]. Moreover, a lot of scholars have studied bitcoin's apparently high price volatility [2, 3, 13, 41]. This volatility came to enhance bitcoins' reputation as a speculative investment [45].

As it appears the bitcoin ecosystem is a technical, social, and economic phenomenon, is highly complex and includes a number of entities and relationships that interact to eventually affect its price. The mapping of this ecosystem is still a work in progress; a relatively small number of studies have recently focused on capturing the Bitcoin ecosystem, its players and their roles, the entities and relationships and how they are affected and interact (see for example [18, 34, 43], and that due to the dynamic nature of bitcoin and the rapid fluctuations in its prices, it would make sense that the factors that affect its price change over time [30]. A few studies attempted to link the price of bitcoin to incidents related to its ecosystem. A stream of studies focused on the role of media, conventional or social, in the determination of bitcoin's price and volatility [8, 33, 35, 38]. [29] argues that the frequency of online searches for bitcoin is a good substitute for measuring interest and popularity, an idea that had previously been applied to the stock market [39]. Indeed, a strong positive relationship existed between the price of bitcoin and the search frequency for bitcoin on Google and Wikipedia [29, 30]. Other studies have demonstrated a relationship between bitcoin price and Google searches, Twitter or other media (see [15, 20, 21, 25, 26]). Some studies looked into specific types of news, such as political news [28], and news on cyberattacks relating to bitcoin [5, 15]. Perhaps the reason that publicity is important is because this is what affects the market's confidence in this new concept which in turn affects the price, thus poor publicity can potentially lead to sudden price declines and potential collapse [24]. However, [40] has demonstrated empirically that public confidence in the system is growing strong despite adverse incidents. [12] on the other hand, suggest that specific news categories such as news about the bitcoin ecosystem such as mining and bans can affect cryptocurrency prices significantly.

In this study, we take a middle-of-the-road approach, by using a simpler – and thus less data intensive - proxy for public attention compared to studies that have used complex models that include many parameters to capture the relationships and factors in the ecosystem that can capture the attention of the market (see for example [12] or [21])[1], but a richer approach than for instance [29] that simply uses the search for the

---

[1] Indicatively, [12] examined 1054 news sources, created 22 categories and used cluster analysis to reduce them to six; [21] employ eleven variables in their elaborate sentiment analysis methodology.

term "bitcoin" and its "price" as a proxy in their models. Specifically, we use six different Google Trends queries as proxies in our models. For balance, we use three search queries for "positive" and three for "negative". The search queries for positive incidents, are "bitcoin + legal", "bitcoin + security" and "bitcoin + profit" and the search queries for negative incidents, are "bitcoin + illegal", "bitcoin + fraud", "bitcoin + loss". We use an EGARCH model to see whether public awareness of positive or negative possible incidents related to the bitcoin ecosystem are related to bitcoin price and to model price volatility. Results showed that most of our proxies are statistically significant and moreover, the EGARCH model has detected an asymmetry - specifically an "anti-leverage effect". In addition, a significant effect of both old and novel news was detected.

This introduction is followed by a description of the background that leads to the development of our hypotheses in Sect. 2. Further, the methodology in presented in Sect. 3, and the empirical results are presented in Sect. 4. Finally, Sect. 5 concludes.

2 Background and Motivation of Hypotheses

[8] suggest that the erratic movements of bitcoin price are caused by the attention of the media to this new phenomenon and by market speculation. Indeed, the price and volume of bitcoin transactions seemed to be guided by the people's beliefs about it and its popularity [33, 35, 38]). [29] argues that the frequency of online searches for bitcoin is a good substitute for measuring interest and popularity. In a similar way that [39] found that the volume of Google search queries about terms related to the financial market was reflected in the current state of the stock market, and that search volume could predict future market trends, [29] found a strong positive relationship between the price of bitcoin and the search frequency for bitcoin on Google and Wikipedia; the growing interest in bitcoin seems to lead to increased demand, which leads to bitcoin price increase. In addition, the study finds that the relationship is reciprocal and bi-directional, which means that price also affects public interest [29]. The strong relationship between public interest and bitcoin price is further confirmed by [30]. [20] examined the relationship between Google Trends, Twitter and the price of bitcoin and discerned a "social circle" at work: when the price rose, the search volume increased, leading to a higher number of tweets, which in turn further pushed the price upwards. Moreover, a negative relationship between Google search and the price of bitcoin was also observed, indicating that a large increase in searches could lead to a decrease in prices the next day [20]. [25] found a moderate relationship between "emotional signal" posts on Twitter and the price of bitcoin. The findings were more pronounced for negative emotions and signs of uncertainty, which led bitcoin to price decreases. [21] showed that the Twitter sentiment ratio is positively correlated with bitcoin prices and that the number of Wikipedia search queries and the hash rate have a positive effect on the price of bitcoin. [15] found a positive relationship between Wikipedia searches and price when bitcoin was a relatively new phenomenon, but in recent years Wikipedia searches have had no effect on the price of bitcoin. [26] also found that an interaction between the sentiment of the media and the price of bitcoin exists, and that there is a tendency for investors to overreact to the news in a short period of time.

Some studies have looked at specific news and incidents and their relationship with bitcoin price. For example, news about political incidents and statements have been found to affect bitcoin price [28]. News regarding security breaches and cyberattacks were also considered: [15] argue that bitcoin is more vulnerable than traditional currencies and that cyber-attack news could reduce bitcoin's attractiveness to investors. [5] investigated the crash of the large bitcoin trading platform Mt. Gox, which collapsed after a major security breach in 2014. Finally, several authors have argued that the price of bitcoin is related to the public confidence in this new concept. As a result, poor publicity around it can lead to sudden price declines and potential collapse [24]. However, [40] has demonstrated empirically that adverse incidents in the bitcoin ecosystem have little or no effect on bitcoin price volatility, suggesting that public confidence in the system is growing despite its shortcomings. [12] examining six different news category groups and how they affected prices in four cryptocurrencies, suggest that there are news categories that affect their prices and in particular news about the bitcoin ecosystem such as mining and bans that affect its price significantly.

Several studies have attempted to map the complexity of the bitcoin ecosystem, as a technical, social and economic phenomenon, articulating the interactions among a vast number of entities and relationships that can eventually affect its price. [34] have presented a causal loop diagram of the bitcoin ecosystem, which captures entities, relationships, and variables, demonstrating its complexity. The basic categorization of the factors adopted by [34] is summarised into the following four categories: (a) Factors affecting the quantity of bitcoin, (b) technical factors pertaining to the protocol, (c) factors unrelated to the protocol, and (d) factors affecting bitcoin's social contract. The numerous entities, regardless of the category they fall into, interact, form relationships and influence each other. In addition, an incident related to one of the entities can positively affect some factors and negatively affect others. Moreover, the timing of the incidents, the intensity and the duration can significantly alter the effect. It should also be noted that the incidents do not affect all users in the same way. Furthermore, the power of users to influence the price of bitcoin is not uniform among users. Traditional, online, and social media reproduce news that promote market awareness. The system is so complex that it is particularly difficult to pinpoint and isolate specific incidents that affect most of those stakeholders who, based on their roles in the ecosystem, can either directly or indirectly significantly affect the price of bitcoin. To capture this complexity, it is important to use a proxy that captures the awareness of the public about a possible incident. Focusing on the announcement or publication of a relevant piece of news will not do. The point in time when the incident is perceived and the reaction time cannot be automatically deduced from the time and date of announcement or publication of the news. To cause an action – let alone a price response – a piece of news should reach the public and make it aware enough of its possible consequences. This is expressed at the time of the search. For this reason, we use the Google searches as a proxy for public awareness. [39] that studied the relationship between Google searches and the course of the stock market, demonstrated that there are Google search patterns that can be interpreted as "early warning signs" for stock market trends.

Indeed, the present study focuses primarily on a widely used medium, i.e. Google, and specifically, Google Trends that captures the stage during which the user decides to be informed and seek information about a possible incident in the bitcoin ecosystem, and into two main categories of incidents for the bitcoin, positive and negative. More specifically we focus on the following possible incidents to proxy public awareness: (1) legalization –using the keyword "legal", (2) security, and (3) profit as positive incidents, and as negative ones we use (4) illegal, (5) fraud, and (6) loss- damage using the keyword "loss". Specifically, our first hypothesis is:

H1: Public awareness regarding negative (positive) incidents pertaining to the bitcoin ecosystem as these can be proxied by Google searches can be negatively (positively) related to bitcoin price.

Further, following previous studies (see [32, 41, 44]) who study the returns of Bitcoin, we hypothesize that there is an "anti-leverage" effect, i.e. the effect that unexpected increases in price have on bitcoin price volatility is higher than the effect decreases in price have.

H2: Bitcoin price volatility increases more when there are unexpected increases in price rather than decreases.

Furthermore, because in markets where there is no reliable fundamental methodology to measure intrinsic value such as the Bitcoin market, participants rely on technical analysis [2], we hypothesize that both old and fresh financial news are related to volatility.

H3: Both old and novel news about changes in price are related to bitcoin price volatility.

3 Data and Methodology

3.1 Data

We use monthly bitcoin prices for the time period from September 1st, 2011 (from when data is available) to December 31st, 2019 drawn from the online source investing.com. We use data on the monthly volume of searches for the key concepts/keywords under investigation that were performed on Google - the largest global search engine – as given by Google Trends[2]. We chose not to use the Wikipedia search platform because as demonstrated by [15], despite the positive relationship between Wikipedia searches and the price of bitcoin during the period when it was a relatively new phenomenon, from 2014 onwards Wikipedia searches had no effect on the price of bitcoin. These findings agree with [30]. Keywords have been chosen to represent categories of incidents that are considered to be of particular importance to the bitcoin ecosystem. An effort was taken to

---

[2] Google, according to Nielsen, collects more than 60% of online queries, which makes it the leader in search engines. People feel quite comfortable with Google, so they express themselves without hesitation, even for taboo ideas. The Google Trends tool can provide data related to Google search queries and in this way, intrinsic or specific people's interests can be easily retrieved compared to other research methods where researchers may not have such capabilities to achieve similar or same results. Therefore, Google Trends can serve as a research tool due to the reliability and leadership of Google in this field. Google Trends was introduced in 2006 by Google. However, it does contain data from 2004 onwards. It is open access and free to all people [31].

balance the negative with the positive incidents with respect to weight, thus words of similar weight and range were chosen. For example, the word "Loss" widely covers the concept of loss and may have been used for loss-damage from bitcoin but also for loss of wallets or even data or transactions. Respectively, the word "Security" can cover many areas of security, from the anonymity of users, transactions, network, etc. In this way it was sought to cover wider and more balanced advantages and disadvantages as well as related risks such as security issues, fraud, legality. In the search queries we used the "+" to combine keywords in order to ensure that searches contain both keywords. Specifically, we collect the monthly data pertaining to the following searches: queries representing positive incidents, i.e. "bitcoin + legal", "bitcoin + security" and "bitcoin + profit", as well as for negative incidents i.e. "bitcoin + illegal", "bitcoin + fraud", "bitcoin + loss" are drawn from the Google Trends website. These data do not represent absolute search volume numbers because they are normalized and presented on a scale from 0 to 100.

Monthly data are used, with the assumption that public awareness regarding a possible incident (positive or negative) is not immediately reflected in the price of an asset. While [8] argue that changes in bitcoin prices are caused by media attention, [40] who studied negative incidents related to the bitcoin ecosystem, finds that these have little or no effect on price changes. On the other hand, [26] found that a relationship between the sentiment in the media and the price of bitcoin exists, and that there is a tendency for investors to overreact to the news within a short period of time. Studies that have tried to interpret changes in bitcoin prices by linking them to posts and/or social media posts have yielded conflicting results [8, 26, 28, 40].

3.2   Models

We use GARCH and EGARCH models to test whether public awareness of positive or negative psible incidents pertaining to the bitcoin ecosystem are related to bitcoin price and to model price volatility. The ARCH – GARCH family of models are considered a standard in the finance literature for modelling currency and cryptocurrency volatility (see for example [1, 14, 16, 17, 19, 23, 27, 41]). In this paper we include variables representing negative and positive searches as a proxy of public awareness in the mean equation and we model the variability of the price using the GARCH (1.1) and EGARCH (1.1) models. The specific models were selected using the ARCH-LM that detected conditional heteroscedasticity on the first-time lag.

The mean equation in both the GARCH (1.1) and the EGARCH (1.1) model has price as the dependent variable and the volume of the different Google searches as independent variables. We run separate models for negative and positive Google searches to avoid multicollinearity issues. The mean equation is used to test H1.

The GARCH (1.1) modelling of volatility is expressed as follows:

$$h_t = \gamma_0 + \gamma_1 * u_{t-1}^2 + \delta_1 * h_{t-1}. \tag{1}$$

The EGARCH (1.1) modelling of volatility is expressed as follows:

$$logh_t = a_o + \delta 1 * \frac{|u_{t-1}|}{\sqrt{h_{t-1}}} + \gamma_1 * \frac{u_{t-1}}{\sqrt{h_{t-1}}} + \alpha_1 logh_{t-1}. \tag{2}$$

Where the coefficient γ_1. in the equation measures the asymmetry or leverage effect, and the $\delta 1$ coefficient captures the effect of current and lagged price information. While the GARCH (1.1) model is used as a reference, the EGARCH (1.1) is used to test H2 (γ_1 coefficient) and H3 ($\delta 1$ and $\alpha 1$ coefficients).

4 Empirical Results

4.1 Trend Analysis and Descriptive Statistics

The graphs *in* Fig. 1, show the evolution of bitcoin prices for the time period 1/9/2001–31/12/2019 in parallel with the evolution of the "negative" (Fig. 1) and "positive" (Fig. 2) searches. Notably, the "negative" (Fig. 1) searches follow the price pattern quite closely, at least until the peak of bitcoin price towards the end of 2017, with searches for "bitcoin + loss" dominating the other two searches "bitcoin + illegal" and "bitcoin + fraud" which almost coincide. In December 2017, when the price of bitcoin peaks, the search for the negative possible incidents under study also peaks. However,

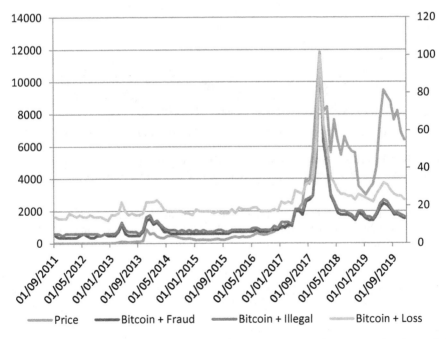

Fig. 1. Bitcoin Price – Fraud – Illegal -Loss: Evolution of bitcoin prices for the period 1/9/2001–31/12/2019 in parallel with the evolution of the "negative" searches

after the peak comes a gradual decline in the price of bitcoin followed by small price fluctuations and a parallel decrease in the interest in negative incident searches by investors. Interestingly, when bitcoin price rises again in July 2019 the searches do not follow in the same magnitude. The search "bitcoin + loss" is again above the two others. The evolution of the "positive" searches (Fig. 2) follow almost the same path. The searches for "bitcoin + Security" dominate the other two searches "bitcoin + legal" and "bitcoin + profit". The searches "bitcoin + legal" are the second most popular after the searches for "bitcoin + security". In a similar way with the negative incident keywords, at the time of the bitcoin price peak in December 2017, the searches using the positive keywords also peak. What follows next is also similar to the case of negative incident keyword search in Fig. 1.

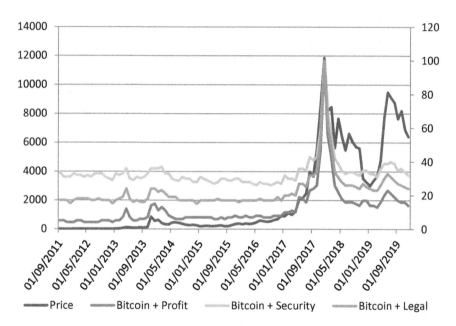

Fig. 2. Bitcoin Price – Profit – Security – Legal: Evolution of bitcoin prices for the period 1/9/2001–31/12/2019 in parallel with the evolution of the "positive" searches

Table 1 summarizes the descriptive statistics of the bitcoin price and the Google searches. Notably, the most searches are for "bitcoin + security" and least are for "bitcoin + fraud".

Table 1. Descriptive Statistics on bitcoin price and positive and negative searches

	Bitcoin Price (€)	Negatives			Positives		
		Bitcoin + Loss	Bitcoin + Fraud	Bitcoin + Illegal	Bitcoin + Profit	Bitcoin + Security	Bitcoin + Legal
Mean	2,124.15	21.75	10.95	12.27	12.26	33.68	22.49
Median	426.60	18.00	6.00	7.00	7.50	32.00	18.00
Mode	3.80	17.00	5.00	7.00	7.00	33.00	17.00
Standard deviation	3,007.78	11.40	12.48	12.42	12.46	9.26	10.97
Minimum	2.20	12.00	3.00	4.00	4.00	26.00	15.00
Maximum	11,850.30	100.00	100.00	100.00	100.00	100.00	100.00

4.2 Garch and Egarch Results

The results shown in Table 2 pertaining to the mean equation of the GARCH (1.1) model with the negative incidents show that the coefficients of the variables representing the search "bitcoin + loss" and the variable representing "bitcoin + fraud" are statistically significant at the 0.01 and 0.10 levels respectively. The latter is consistent with our first hypothesis, that public awareness regarding negative (positive) incidents pertaining to the bitcoin ecosystem can be negatively (positively) related to bitcoin price. Contrary to our first hypothesis, "bitcoin + loss" is positively related to price. These results are consistent with the results of the asymmetric GARCH model, EGARCH, (Table 3) for the negative incidents. The "bitcoin + illegal" is not statistically significant.

For the positive incidents, in the mean equation the coefficients of the variable "bitcoin + profit" is statistically significant at the 0.01 level in both the GARCH (1.1) (Table 2) and the EGARCH (1.1) (Table 3) model. In the EGARCH (1.1) model (Table 3) the terms "bitcoin + security" and "bitcoin + legal" are also statistically significant at the 0.01 level; the former negatively – which is inconsistent with our hypothesis, while the latter positively, which is consistent with our hypothesis. These terms are not statistically significant in the GARCH (1.1) model (Table 2).

Although these results do not outright confirm our first hypothesis with respect to the public awareness regarding negative (positive) incidents being negatively (positively) related to bitcoin price, they do demonstrate a strong relationship between public awareness as this is expressed by the Google searches and bitcoin price, a result that confirms prior studies that used different metrics for public awareness (see for example [15, 21, 26, 29, 30, 39]).

In the variance equation of the GARCH (1.1) model, both the coefficients ARCH and GARCH, are statistically significant at the 0.01 level for both the positive and the negatives searches (Table 2). This indicates the existence of a time-varying conditional variance for bitcoin prices. The sum of the ARCH and GARCH coefficients is greater than one in the negatives model and close to one for the positives model, which indicates that there are very significant variance shocks in both cases.

Table 2. GARCH (1.1) Analysis Results

	GARCH negatives			GARCH positives		
	Coefficients	z	Prob.	Coefficients	z	Prob.
Mean equation						
Constant	−3701.593	−6.106***	0.000	289.277	0.105	0.917
BITCOIN FRAUD	−158.748	−1.850*	0.064			
BITCOIN ILLEGAL	17.901	0.200	0.842			
BITCOIN LOSS	281.267	5.232***	0.000			
BITCOIN SECURITY				−57.045	−0.281	0.779
BITCOIN LEGAL				50.998	0.262	0.793
BITCOIN PROFIT				133.770	13.472***	0.000
Variance equation						
Constant	199232.700	3.260***	0.001	1632044.000	3.391***	0.001
ARCH	1.451	4.248***	0.000	1.104	1.979**	0.048
GARCH	−0.172	−2.795***	0.005	−0.235	−2.553**	0.011
Adjusted - R - squared	0.284			0.444		

***, **, *: Statistically significant at the 0.01, 0.05, and 0.1 level of significance.

Notably, in the variance equation of the EGARCH (1.1) (Table 3) the coefficient γ is positive and equal to 0.976 and 0.585 for the negative and the positive incidence models respectively, and statistically significant at the 0.01 level in both cases. This means that volatility increases more when there are unexpected increases in price than it does when there are decreases in price. This is the so-called "anti-leverage effect", which is also noted by [10, 41]. This is consistent with our second hypothesis.

In the EGARCH (1.1) model with the positive incidences (Table 3), the coefficient $\delta 1$ is not statistically significant, but the coefficient $\alpha 1$ is statistically significant at the 0.01 level. This shows the effect of old news on bitcoin prices. For the positive incidents EGARCH (1.1) model $\delta 1$ is statistically significant at the 0.05 while the coefficient $\alpha 1$ is statistically significant at the 0.01 level. This denotes the effect of both the old and novel news on bitcoin price. This is consistent with our third hypothesis, and with the assertion of [2] that point out that in markets where there is no reliable fundamental methodology to measure intrinsic value such as the Bitcoin market, participants rely on technical analysis.

Notably, the adjusted R^2 for the positive incidents GARCH (1.1) model (Table 2) is 44.4%, while for the model for the negative incidents is 28.4% which shows that the model with the positive incidents can explain more of the variability in prices. Similarly, The R^2 adjusted of the positives model is 53.4% which is higher from the corresponding 19.2% of the model with the negative incidents for the EGARCH (1.1) model (Table 3).

Table 3. EGARCH (1.1) Analysis Results

	EGARCH negatives			EGARCH positives		
	Coefficients	z	Prob.	Coefficients	z	Prob.
Mean equation						
C	−5374.153	−9.701***	0.000	40.678	0.523	0.601
BITCOIN FRAUD	−418.099	−4.561***	0.000			
BITCOIN ILLEGAL	97.881	0.925	0.355			
BITCOIN LOSS	441.057	8.962***	0.000			
BITCOIN SECURITY				−141.768	−50.966***	0.000
BITCOIN LEGAL				249.304	18698.330***	0.000
BITCOIN PROFIT				36.197	10.176***	0.000
Variance equation						
$\alpha 0$	5.816	5.444***	0.000	1.396	2469.073***	0.000
$\delta 1$	0.549	1.380	0.168	0.415	2.260**	0.024
$\gamma 1$	0.976	3.585	0.000	0.585	4.599***	0.000
$\alpha 1$	0.528	6.682***	0.000	0.865	96.315***	0.000
Adjusted - R - squared	0.192			0.534		

***, **, *: Statistically significant at the 0.01, 0.05, and 0.1 level of significance.

5   Conclusions and Discussion

5.1   Conclusions

In this study we investigate how the bitcoin price is related to the awareness of the public of possible positive and negative incidents of the bitcoin ecosystem. To do this, we study the relationship of negative and positive Google searches pertaining to bitcoin with the bitcoin price and the volatility of bitcoin price using GARCH (1,1) and EGARCH (1,1) models for the time period from September 1st, 2001 to December 31st, 2019. We find that during the period of our study, there is a statistically significant relationship between the bitcoin price and the search criteria we investigated (both for the negative and positive search proxies). This further adds to the literature that public perception of the whole bitcoin ecosystem is related with the bitcoin price (see for example [15, 21, 26, 29, 30, 39]). Moreover, our EGARCH model has detected an asymmetry pertaining to the price volatility's reaction to price news, specifically the price volatility is more sensitive to good financial news rather to bad news. This so-called an "anti-leverage effect", has been discussed by [36]. It has also been observed in a number of empirical studies (see for example [32, 44]). [44] give a speculative markets explanation to this phenomenon, while [10, 41] who study this for bitcoin in particular a "bitcoin as a safe haven" explanation, and an ideological explanation respectively. In addition, our results revealed the effect of both old and novel news on bitcoin prices, a phenomenon that highlights [2] assertion that in lack of a reliable fundamental methodology to measure intrinsic value in a market, participants rely on technical analysis.

5.2 Limitations

While Google holds the lion's market share in most of the world [42] things are different in at least two particular countries, China and Russia. Google and China have a long history of censorship; the search engine Baidu holds the largest market share in China. In Russia, Yandex remains the dominant search engine for the country and many of its neighbours [37]. As a result, for a large part of the population, which is also a significant percentage of active users and miners of bitcoin - China dominates bitcoin mining, with 65% of bitcoin hash power residing within the country [4] - search data has not been included.

In addition, due to the anonymity of bitcoin users and the high degree of concentration [11], it is difficult to pinpoint the small number of users who own the largest percentage of bitcoin and can therefore take decisions that can impact its price significantly. It could be possible that incidents of the ecosystem that can be relevant to the wider market have little or no effect on the decisions of these influential bitcoin mega-users.

5.3 Future Research

Using raw data instead of the normalized scale data of the Google trends tool could perhaps increase the accuracy of the awareness proxy. In addition, an event analysis with daily data could provide further insights.

Further, it would be interesting to explore the correlation of multiple events happening simultaneously over certain periods and the contribution of their impact. Finally, using search data that provides information about the geographic area the searches come from, combined with the ability to identify wallet and public domain addresses to generate information on which areas of the world are more sensitive to which incidents in the bitcoin ecosystem and their market reaction.

References

1. Auer, R., Claessens, S.: Regulating cryptocurrencies: assessing market reactions. BIS Quart. Rev. 51–65 (2018)
2. Balcilar, M., Bouri, E., Gupta, R., Roubaud, D.: Can volume predict Bitcoin returns and volatility? A quantiles-based approach. Econ. Model. **64**, 74–81 (2017)
3. Baur, D.G., Dimpfl, T.: Excess volatility as an impediment for a digital currency (2018). SSRN 2949754

4. Bitcoin Mining Network, The Report. https://coinshares.com/research/bitcoin-mining-network-june-2019
5. Bolici, F., Rosa, S.D.: Mt.Gox is dead, long live bitcoin! In: Torre, T., Braccini, A.M., Spinelli, R. (eds.) Empowering Organizations. LNISO, vol. 11, pp. 285–296. Springer, Cham (2016). https://doi.org/10.1007/978-3-319-23784-8_22
6. Bouoiyour, J., Selmi, R.: What does bitcoin look like? Ann. Econ. Financ. **16**(2), 449–492 (2014)
7. Bouoiyour, J., Selmi, R.: The price of political uncertainty: evidence from the 2016 U.S. Presidential Election and the U.S. Stock Markets. arXiv:1612.06200v2 (2017)
8. Bouoiyour, J., Selmi, R., Tiwari, A., Olayeni, O.: What drives bitcoin price? Econ. Bull. **36** (2), 843–850 (2016)
9. Bouri, E., Molnár, P., Azzi, G., Roubaud, D., Hagfors, L.: On the hedge and safe haven properties of bitcoin: Is it really more than a diversifier? Financ. Res. Lett. **20**, 192–198 (2017)
10. Bouri, E., Molnár, P., Jalkh, N., Roubaud. D.: Bitcoin for energy commodities before and after December 2013 crash: diversifier, hedge or safe haven? Appl. Econ. **49**(50), 5063–5073 (2017b)
11. Brar, H.K.: Bitcoin's 99 Problems = No Future? Medium (2018). https://medium.com/@orbify.io/bitcoins-99-problems-6c44a360c1d0
12. Cankaya, S., Alp, E., Findikci, M.: News sentiment and cryptocurrency volatility. In: Hacioglu, U. (ed.) Blockchain Economics and Financial Market Innovation: Financial Innovations in the Digital Age. Springer, Cham (2019)
13. Cermak, V.: Can bitcoin become a viable alternative to fiat currencies? An empirical analysis of bitcoin's volatility based on a GARCH model (2017)
14. Chu, J., Chan, S., Nadarajah, S., Osterrieder, J.: GARCH modelling of cryptocurrencies. J. Risk Financ. Manage. **10**(17), 1–15 (2017)
15. Ciaian, P., Rajcaniova, M., Kancs, D.: The economics of bitcoin price formation. Appl. Econ. **48**(19), 1799–1815 (2016)
16. Corbet, S., Katsiampa, P.: Asymmetric mean reversion of bitcoin price returns. Int. Rev. Financ. Anal. (2018, in Press)
17. Corbet, S., Larkin, C.J., Lucey, B.M., Meegan, A., Yarovaya, L.: The volatility generating effects of macroeconomic news on cryptocurrency returns. SSRN (2018)
18. Cusumano, M.A.: The bitcoin ecosystem. Commun. ACM **57**(10), 22–24 (2014)
19. Dyhrberg, A.H.: Bitcoin, gold and the dollar–A GARCH volatility analysis. Financ. Res. Lett. **16**, 85–92 (2016)
20. Garcia, D., Tessone, C., Mavrodiev, P., Perony, N.: The digital traces of bubbles: feedback cycles between socio-economics signals in the bitcoin economy. J. Roy. Soc. Interface **11** (99), 1–28 (2014)
21. Georgoula, I., Pournarakis, D., Bilanakos, C., Sotiropoulos, D., Giaglis, G.: Using time-series and sentiment analysis to detect the determinants of bitcoin prices. In: MCIS 2015 Proceedings, p. 20 (2015)
22. Hayes, A.: Cryptocurrency value formation: an empirical analysis leading to a cost of production model for valuing bitcoin. In: MCIS 2015 Proceedings, p. 4 (2015)
23. Hayes, A.: Cryptocurrency value formation: an empirical study leading to a cost of production model for valuing bitcoin. Telematics Inf. **34**(7), 1308–1321 (2017)
24. Johansson, S., Malin, N.T.: The price volatility of bitcoin. a search for the drivers affecting the price volatility of this digital currency. Master thesis. Umeå: Umeå School of Business and Economics (2014)
25. Kaminski, J., Gloor, P.A.: Nowcasting the bitcoin market with Twitter signals. ArXiv, abs/1406.7577 (2014)

26. Karalevicius, V., Degrande, N., De Weerdt, J.: Using sentiment analysis to predict interday bitcoin price movements. J. Risk Financ. **19**(1), 56–75 (2018)
27. Katsiampa, P.: Volatility estimation for bitcoin: a comparison of GARCH models. Econ. Lett. **158**, 3–6 (2017)
28. Kjærland, F., Meland, M., Oust, A., Øyen, V.: How can bitcoin price fluctuations be explained? Int. J. Econ. Financ. Issues **8**(3), 323–332 (2018)
29. Kristoufek, L.: Bitcoin meets Google trends and Wikipedia: quantifying the relationship between phenomena of the Internet era. Sci. Rep. **3**(3415), 1–7 (2013)
30. Kristoufek, L.: What are the main drivers of the bitcoin price? Evidence from wavelet coherence analysis. PLoS ONE **10**(4), e0123923 (2015)
31. Liolios, E.: Google Trends as a predictive tool for the sales of the Apple. Master thesis. International Hellenic University (2015)
32. Ludvigson, S.C., Ng, S.: The empirical risk–return relation: a factor analysis approach. J. Financ. Econ. **83**(1), 171–222 (2007)
33. Mai, F., Bai, Q., Shan, Z., Wang, X., Chiang, R.: From bitcoin to Big Coin: the impact of social media on bitcoin performance. In: 36th International Conference on Information Systems, 13–16 December, Fort Worth (2015)
34. Majakivi, A.: Modeling the bitcoin ecosystem. Master of Science in Technology thesis. Aalto University, Espoo Finland (2019)
35. Matta, M., Lunesu, I., Marchesi, M.: The predictor impact of Web search media on bitcoin trading volumes. In: 7th International Joint Conference on Knowledge Discovery, Knowledge Engineering and Knowledge Management (IC3K), vol. 01, pp. 620–626 (2015)
36. Nelson, D.: Conditional heteroskedasticity in asset returns: a new approach. Econometrica **59**(2), 347–370 (1991)
37. Newton, E.: International search engines you should know and optimizing for them, brightedge.com (2020)
38. Polasik, M., Piotrowska, A., Wisniewski, T., Kotkowski, R., Lightfoot, G.: Price fluctuations and the use of bitcoin: an empirical inquiry. Int. J. Electron. Commer. **20**(1), 9–49 (2015)
39. Preis, T., Moat, H.S., Stanley, H.: Quantifying trading behavior in financial markets using Google trends. Sci. Rep. **3**, 1684 (2013)
40. Pryzmont, P.: An empirical study of how bitcoin related incidents impact its price volatility. Thesis in Master of Business Administration. Dublin: National College of Ireland (2016)
41. Sapuric, S., Kokkinaki, A., Georgiou, I.: The relationship between bitcoin returns, volatility and volume: asymmetric GARCH modeling. J. Enterprise Inf. Manage. (2020)
42. Statista. https://www.statista.com/statistics/220534/googles-share-of-search-market-in-selected-countries/
43. Wörner, D., Von Bomhard, T., Schreier, Y.P., Bilgeri, D.: The bitcoin ecosystem: disruption beyond financial services? (2016)
44. Wu, L.: Reverse return-volatility asymmetry, and short sale constraints: evidence from the Chinese markets. Presented at the EFMA Annual Meeting (2017)
45. Yermack, D.: Is Bitcoin a real currency? An economic appraisal. In: Handbook of Digital Currency, pp. 31–43. Academic Press (2015)

LOKI Vote: A Blockchain-Based Coercion Resistant E-Voting Protocol

Marwa Chaieb[1(✉)] and Souheib Yousfi[2]

[1] Faculty of Sciences of Tunis, Tunis, Tunisia
chaiebmarwa.insat@gmail.com
[2] National Institute of Applied Science and Technology, Tunis, Tunisia
souheib.youssfi@gmail.com

Abstract. Creating an online electronic voting system that ensures coercion-resistance and end-to-end verifiability at the same time, has constituted a real challenge for a long period of time. The notion of coercion-resistance was first introduced by Juels, Catalano, and Jakobsson (JCJ) in 2005. Since that time, several research papers have appeared to address the main issue of JCJ scheme (the quadratic complexity of verifying credentials). The majority of these systems have been based on the availability of a secure web bulletin board. Despite this widespread requirement, the notion of an append-only web bulletin board remains vague, and no method of constructing such a bulletin board has been proposed in those papers. Our paper fills the gap and proposes an end-to-end verifiable e-voting protocol based on Blockchain technology. In this research work, we propose a Blockchain-based online electronic voting protocol that ensures all the security requirements expected from secure and democratic elections. Our proposal is inspired from the scheme proposed by Araùjo and Traoré in 2013, which is based on the work of JCJ and has a linear complexity. Called *LOKI Vote*, our scheme is practical for large scale elections and ensures a strong privacy for voters by using a variety of cryptographic primitives. Additionally, our protocol enhance the complexity of the old coercion resistant systems by using a new mix network, called Low Latency Anonymous Routing Protocol, which is characterized by a lower complexity and a higher level of security. Finally, we formally prove the security of LOKI Vote using the automated verification tool, ProVerif, and the Applied Pi-Calculus modeling language.

Keywords: Online electronic voting · Coercion-resistance · Blockchain · LOKI · Anonymous credential · Low Latency Anonymous Routing Protocol · Formal security proofs

1 Introduction

Voting is the backbone of every democratic society. Traditional voting systems suffer from several issues mainly the high cost in both money and time and

© Springer Nature Switzerland AG 2020
M. Themistocleous et al. (Eds.): EMCIS 2020, LNBIP 402, pp. 151–168, 2020.
https://doi.org/10.1007/978-3-030-63396-7_11

the lack of transparency and verifiability throughout the voting process. Taking advantages from the proliferation of internet, several online electronic voting protocols have appeared to overcome the limitations of traditional voting systems. Such a system has to ensure an exhausted list of security requirements. This list includes: *Eligibility:* Only eligible and registered voters can participate to the election; *Completeness:* All valid votes are counted correctly; *Soundness:* Invalid votes should be easy to detect and discard; *Robustness:* The protocol can tolerate a certain number of misbehaving voters; *Fairness:* No early results that could influence other voters decisions are made available; *Integrity:* Ballots are not altered or deleted during any step of the election; *Vote-and-go:* A voter does not need to wait for the end of the voting phase or trigger the tallying phase; *Privacy:* It should be impossible to link a vote to a voter without his/her help; *Universal verifiability:* Any interested party should be able to verify the correct computation of the final tally from submitted ballots; *Receipt-freeness:* A voter cannot construct a receipt allowing him/her to prove to a third party that he voted in a particular way. This would also prevent vote selling; *Coercion-resistance:* Even when a voter interacts with a coercer, the coercer can not be sure of whether the voter obeyed his demand or not.

Designing an online e-voting system that guaranties all the above requirements remains difficult. Indeed, there is always a compromise between end-to-end verifiability and privacy. Coercion-resistance is a strong notion of privacy that has been defined for the first time by Juels, Catalano, and Jakobsson (JCJ) in 2005 [1]. Their proposed system is based on fake and valid anonymous credentials and has a quadratic complexity when tallying votes. Based on this work, several proposals have been appeared to surmount this inherent complexity. These voting systems rely on a public bulletin board (PBB), where they post votes and other public parameters, without however specifying how this can be implemented. They make the assumption that this public bulletin board ensures the end-to-end verifiability, fairness, and correctness of the election process. Thus, public bulletin boards must have the following properties: (1) *Distributed architecture* to withstand Distributed Denial Of Service (DDOS) attacks, (2) *Time stamped* to reference data by their dates of publication, (3) *Immutable* to ensure resistance against adding, removing or altering posted data and finally (4) *Universally verifiable* to ensure a high level of transparency. These are exactly the main characteristics of Blockchain technology. Blockchain is a distributed ledger that operates without the need to a trusted party. It can be seen as a digital, decentralized, public and large register where all exchanges made between its users are recorded in a public and secure way. In this paper, we propose a coercion resistant Blockchain-based online electronic voting protocol, called *LOKI Vote*.

Contributions: Our contributions can be summarized as follow:

- Based on the work of Araùjo and Traoré [2], we design an online electronic voting protocol that satisfies the above security requirements and has a linear complexity when tallying votes,

- Called *LOKI Vote*, our proposed system is based on Blockchain technology to ensure end-to-end verifiability and integrity of the election process,
- *LOKI Vote* is designed to be implemented over Loki[1] platform. This Blockchain-based platform comes with a novel mix network, called Low Latency Anonymous Routing Protocol (LLARP), that has a lower complexity than some existing mix networks and fix their vulnerabilities,
- Finally, we formally evaluate the security of the protocol, using ProVerif and Applied Pi-Calculus.

Paper Organization: Our paper is organized as follow: in the next section, we review some of the existing coercion resistant schemes. Section 3 presents the cryptographic primitives and technologies used in our protocol. Section 4 is a detailed description of *LOKI Vote* and its different stakeholders and phases. We discuss the security of our proposed scheme in Sect. 5 and finally Sect. 6 is dedicated to the conclusion and a set of perspectives.

2   Related Work

In this section, we give an overview of some e-voting schemes that are, or claimed to be, coercion resistant. We start by describing three protocols from the literature that are interesting for our work and did not use Blockchain technology (1, 2 and 3). Then, we present two online e-voting systems based on Blockchain technology and claimed to be coercion resistant (4 and 5). We evaluate the security of these systems in Table 2.

1. **Coercion Resistant Electronic Elections (CREE)** [1]: In their paper, Juels, Catalano, and Jakobsson (JCJ) give the first formal definition for coercion-resistance and propose the first coercion resistant e-voting system. Their scheme relies on a secret random string "σ" that serves as an anonymous credential for eligible voters. Each eligible voter gets a valid anonymous credential during the registration phase, after verifying his/her eligibility by an authority called Registrar (R). To vote, each voter encrypts his/her anonymous credential, using a modified version of El-Gamal cryptosystem, and sends it with his/her ballot to a public bulletin board (PBB). Authors make the assumption that the PBB is universally accessible, to which every party can write and read data but no one can alter or delete information from it. After the end of the voting phase, an authority called Talliers (T) perform a blind comparison (using Plaintext Equivalence Test PET [3,4]) between hidden credentials and a list L of encrypted credentials published by R alongside the plaintext names of registered voters. The list of hidden credentials and L are passed through a re-encryption mix network [5,6] before being compared to each other. T retain only votes that their corresponding credentials match an element of L, according to PET. Finally, T decrypt all eligible valid votes and tallies the final result.

---

[1] https://loki.network/wp-content/uploads/2018/10/LokiWhitepaperV3_1.pdf.

The JCJ scheme ensures coercion-resistance thanks to the use of anonymous credentials σ. Indeed, when a voter V_i is under coercion, he/she can simply select and reveal a random group element σ_i', claiming that this is the credential σ_i. As the coercer is unable to distinguish between a valid credential and a fake one, he can not be sure if the coerced voter obeyed to his demand or not.

The main drawback of JCJ's scheme is its quadratic complexity in the number of voters during the tallying phase (when verifying the validity of credentials). This issue makes the scheme unrealistic since it can not be employed in a real-world context. Even so, the protocol is widely discussed and taken as a starting point for further improvements [2,7–11].

2. **Towards Practical and Secure Coercion Resistant Electronic Elections (TPSCREE)** [9]: To overcome the drawbacks of JCJ scheme, authors propose a new coercion resistant election approach with linear complexity. This solution relies on the BBS group signature scheme [12]. In their paper, authors first describe an attack on Schweisgut scheme [13] (which is also based on the work of JCJ) and prove that it is not coercion resistant as claimed since a coercer can verify later if the coerced voter obeyed to his demand and gave him a valid credential or not. Then, they propose their voting scheme and prove, formally, that is coercion resistant and suitable for large scale elections. The proposed protocol is based on the same cryptographic primitives as JCJ proposal, namely: a public bulletin board [14], the modified El-Gamal cryptosystem proposed by JCJ [1], a universally verifiable mixnet [6,15], a set of zero knowledge proofs [16,17] and PET [3]. It unfolds in the following stages: *Registration Phase:* the registrars verify the eligibility of every voter and provides him/her by a credential that has the following form (A, r, x) where $A = (g_1 g_3^x)^{1/(y+r)}$, g_1 and g_3 are public parameters, x is a secret value, y is the private key of R and r is a random value; *Voting Phase:* each voter encrypts his/her vote and credential and casts them via a PBB, including with them a set of proofs to justify the validity of the voting tuple; *Tallying Phase:* the talliers record voting tuples from the PBB, verify the validity of each one, eliminate duplicates and tuples with invalid credentials, then decrypt the remaining votes and count the election final result. When under coercion, a voter gives a fake credential to the coercer. A fake credential has the following form (A, r, x') where $x \neq x'$.

This protocol presents two main issues. (1) A set of malicious registrars have the possibility to provide ineligible voters by valid credentials. Thus, the final tally may include valid but illegitimate votes. (2) It is impossible to run another election, that has a different list of eligible voters from the first one, without performing the registration phase another time because authorities do not have the possibility to revoke credentials that are no more eligible.

3. **A Practical Coercion Resistant Voting Scheme Revisited (PCRVSR)** [2]: In 2013, R. Araùjo and J.Traoré pointed out the drawbacks of the previous scheme [9] and propose a revisited version to overcome these issues. They add some modifications in the election process to make the verification of votes eligibility and credential revocation possible. To resolve

the first issue, the registrars construct and publish a list L_2, during the registration phase, that contains $< E_T[A], ID_{voter} >$ for each registered voter, where T is the public key of the talliers. During the tallying phase, talliers compare valid credentials in the voting tuples with the list L_2 and count only votes that their credentials match an element from L_2. To resolve the second one, the registrars generate for each new election new key pair and use it to generate new credentials. They calculate the new credentials from the new private key and a list L_1 that retains the couple $< E_R[g_1 g_3^x], ID_{voter} >$ for each voter. The list L_1 is published on the PBB during the first election. The new credentials have the following form $(A' = (g_1 g_3^x)^{1/(y'+r')}, r', x)$, where r' is a random number, y' is the new secret key of the Registrars and x is the same secret value given to the voter during the first time registration.

4. **Platform-Independent Secure Blockchain-based Voting System (PISBVS)** [18]: It is an independent e-voting system implemented on a Byzantine Fault Tolerance consensus [19] based Blockchain. Authors claim that their solution does not rely on a centralized trusted party to compute and publish the election final result, but they still need to trust an administrator to decrypt the sum of votes and upload the result to the Blockchain. They use Paillier cryptosystem to encrypt votes before publishing them on the election Blockchain. It recalls proof of knowledge to ensure correctness and consistence of votes, and Short Linkable Ring Signature (SLRS) to guarantee voters privacy. However, this protocol does not ensure voters eligibility since a voter can register him/herself by simply providing his/her e-mail address, ID number or an invitation URL with a password and these mechanisms are not sufficient to verify the eligibility of a voter. In addition, authors claim to ensure coercion-resistance under the following assumption "*it is assumed that no one stand behind a voter or uses digital devices to record the voting process. We do not take the physical voting environment security into our consideration*". Thus, referring to the definition of coercion-resistance given by JCJ [1], this protocol is not coercion resistant. A coercer can vote in the place of a voter if he knows the voter's secret key. The coerced voter cannot provide a fake secret key to the coercer because a vote with a fake secret key is rejected by the voting smart contract.

5. **Efficient, Coercion-Free and Universally Verifiable Blockchain-based Voting (ECFUVBV)** [20]: It is a Blockchain-based e-voting protocol, claimed to be secure and coercion-resistance without the need to use valid and fake credentials. It uses a randomizer token, a tamper resistant device that can be instantiated with smart cards or Trusted Platform Module (TPM) [21] enabled devices. Authors use Bitcoin to ensure verifiability. Its tallying phase has a linear complexity. It unfolds in the following phases: *Setup:* the election authority generates its public and private keys along with other system parameters; *Register:* a voter V_i interacts with the registrar R to get a pair of public/private keys along with a signed commitment C_i on values s_i, r_i generated by V_i's token randomizer. The voter's credential is the signed version of the commitment using the voter's private key; *Vote:* each voter encrypts its choice v using a one-time key K_i. Then, he/she computes a proof

π_i to prove knowledge of r_i using zero-knowledge Succinct Non-interactive ARguments of Knowledge (zk-SNARKs) [22]. He/She casts a tuple that has the following form $< \pi_i, s_i, E_{K_i}(v) >$ via the election Blockchain; *Tally:* the election authority checks the validity of each ballot posted on the blockchain using π_i and eliminates ballots with invalid proofs. It also eliminates duplicates using the element s_i. Then, it decrypts votes using K_i, which are published by voters alongside with the value s_i to facilitate matching the key to her previously transmitted encrypted vote, and computes the final result. In this paper, authors suppose that the coercer and the voter are not side-by-side. All that the attacker can do is to issue instructions and ask for proof of compliance. Accordingly to the definition of coercion-resistance of JCJ [1], plus the fact that the voter can vote only once, this scheme is not coercion resistant.

3   Basic Notions

In this section, we give an overview of the main cryptographic primitives and technologies used in our protocol.

3.1   El-Gamal Cryptosystem

The proposed protocol uses a threshold version of El-Gamal cryptosystem proposed by JCJ in [1]. In this scheme, the key pair is constructed by cooperation between n authorities. It requires t out of n authorities to decrypt a ciphertext. As proved in [1], this modified version of El-Gamal is semantically secure under the Decision Diffie Hellman (DDH) assumption [23]. This variant can be described by the following steps:

- **Key Generation:** Let $\mathbb{G}$ be a cyclic group of order a prime number q, in which the DDH assumption holds. We denote the public key by y and it is represented by the following tuple: $y = (g_1, g_2, h)$; where $h = g_1^{x_1} g_2^{x_2}$. Its corresponding private key is the couple (x_1, x_2); where $x_1, x_2 \in \mathbb{Z}_q$.
- **Encryption:** The ciphertext of a message $m \in \mathbb{G}$ is represented by the following tuple: $E_y[m] = (\alpha, \beta, \gamma) = (m \cdot h^r, g_1^r, g_2^r)$; Where r is a random number from $\mathbb{Z}_q$.
- **Decryption:** m is obtained from (α, β, γ) using the following formula: $m = \alpha/(\beta^{x_1}\gamma^{x_2})$

3.2   Proof of Knowledge

Our protocol recalls the Non-Interactive Zero Knowledge Proof (NI-ZKP) [24] during the voting phase to prove the validity of the tuple formed by the voter.

Zero Knowledge Proofs (ZKP) [25] are cryptographic primitives that allow one party, called "prover", to prove to another party, called "verifier", that he knows a secret without revealing the secret itself or any additional secrets. NI-ZKP [26,27] is a variant of ZKP in which no bidirectional interaction between the prover and the verifier is needed .

3.3 Group Signature Scheme of Boneh, Boyen and Shacham

In their paper [12], Boneh, Boyen and Shacham presented a short group signature scheme. Its security relies on the Strong Diffie-Hellman (SDH) [28] and Decision Linear (DL) [12] assumptions.

Our proposed e-voting protocol uses the BBS group signature scheme, presented in Sect. 8 of the paper [12], as anonymous credentials for eligible voters. This scheme can be described as follow: Let $\mathbb{G}$ be a cyclic group of order a prime number q, in which the DDH assumption holds, $g_1, g_2 \in \mathbb{G}$ are two random generators, y is a secret key, and $r, x \in \mathbb{Z}_q$ are two random numbers. The signature is represented by the tuple (A, r, x) where $A = (g_1 g_2^x)^{1/(y+r)}$.

3.4 Loki

Loki[2] is a platform based on Monero[3] Blockchain. It proposes significant modifications on Monero source code to ensure a high degree of privacy and provide a model for anonymous transactions and decentralized communication. The main drawbacks of Monero Blockchain are the significant bandwidth and disk space that its node operators require plus the fact that they are not rewarded for their work. To fix this problem, Loki comes with a novel node reward scheme that provides economic incentives for node operators, called *Service Nodes*. These service nodes ensure the privacy and the security of the network. This technology has been proposed to provide internet neutrality, digital anonymity and censorship-resistant suite of tools allowing people to communicate in a private and secure way. This is why Loki can be used in various areas especially when we need to ensure a high level of privacy and anonymity, such as in e-voting systems.

Loki recalls several cryptographic primitives namely *Ring Signature* [29] to obfuscate the true history of transaction outputs, *Stealth Address* [30] to ensure the unlinkability between the receiver true public key and his transactions and *Ring Confidential Transactions* [31] to obfuscate transaction amounts. This Blockchain-based platform also uses the proof of work consensus algorithm to validate transactions and construct blocks. It opts for a different way of block reward distribution: 45% of the block reward are reserved for miner, 50% for service node and 5% for governance operations. The main role of service nodes is to operate the Low Latency Anonymous Routing Protocol[4], which is an anonymous mixnet, and form the Lokinet, which is a fully decentralized network that does not rely on any trusted authority. The Low Latency Anonymous Routing Protocol (LLARP) is a private routing layer created by Loki. It is an hybrid between The Onion Routing (TOR)[5] and Invisible Internet Protocol (I2P)[6]. It fixes vulnerabilities of TOR and I2P protocols and provides a higher level of

---

[2] https://loki.network/wp-content/uploads/2018/10/LokiWhitepaperV3_1.pdf.

[3] https://www.allcryptowhitepapers.com/wp-content/uploads/2018/05/monero-whitepaper.pdf.

[4] https://github.com/loki-project/loki-network.

[5] https://www.torproject.org/.

[6] https://geti2p.net/en/.

security and distribution than any existing routing protocol. To better understand how LLARP works, we recall TOR and I2P protocols. The advantages and disadvantages of each protocol are summarized in Table 1.

Table 1. Advantages and disadvantages of TOR and I2P

	The Onion Routing (TOR)	Invisible Internet Protocol (I2P)
Advantages	+ Provides an anonymous network,	+ Provides an anonymous network,
	+ Preserves internet privacy,	+ Uses a Distributed Hashing Table (DHT) instead of directory authorities,
	+ Performs better at evading state level firewalls,	+ Allows both TCP and UDP traffics
	+ Ensures a high level of censorship Resistance	
Disadvantages	- It is an hierarchical network,	- Problems of performance and lack of Bandwidth,
	- Relies on a group of directory Authorities (centralized servers),	- Tunnels are short lived,
	- Trusting claimed capacity,	
	- Allows only TCP traffic,	- Irresistant to Sybil attacks
	- Irresistant to Sybil attacks	

TOR and I2P are operated by volunteers, which can cause problems of security, reliability and performance. In fact, a network constructed from financial incentives can achieve a greater resilience against attacks, while providing a more reliable service. This is what proposes LLARP by using a Distributed Hashing Table (DHT) based on Blockchain technology. This Blockchain-based DHT allows service nodes to act as routers in the network and they are rewarded for their work. LLARP also opts for packet switched based routing instead of tunnel based-routing to allow better load balancing and redundancy in the network. To avoid Sybil attacks, LLARP allows only service nodes to route packets, and they are rewarded for their honesty.

4   Protocol Description

We propose a coercion resistant online e-voting system that uses Blockchain technology and designed to be implemented over Loki. Called *LOKI Vote*, our protocol provides an end-to-end verifiability by using a Blockchain-based public bulletin board to display all public values and offer a persistent view to all voters. In this section, we present the different entities involved in *LOKI Vote* as well as its different phases.

4.1   Entities

Our protocol involves three main entities:

- *Registration authorities (RAs)*: They cooperate and generate a new key pair (R, R') for each new election, generate and publish the election parameters on the Blockchain during the setup phase, verify the eligibility of every person wishing to register to the election, during the registration phase, and provide only eligible voters by anonymous credentials which are constructed by cooperation between all RAs. In addition, they cooperate to construct and publish two lists L_1 and L_2 which serve later, respectively, for credential revocation and verification of votes eligibility. Finally, they help the tallying authorities to verify the validity of credentials during the tallying phase.
- *Tallying authorities (TAs)*: They cooperate and generate a key pair $(\mathscr{T}, \mathscr{T}')$ during the setup phase, read voting tuples from the election Blockchain, verify, decrypt and compute eligible and valid votes during the tallying phase. Finally, they publish the final tally on the Blockchain.
- *Eligible voters (V)*: Every eligible voter (V_i) has a unique valid credential per election to vote with, and can generate an unlimited number of fake credentials to use them when he/she is under coercion. He/she has the right to vote more than once before the end of the voting phase and only his/her last and valid vote is counted.

Every entity in our protocol has a read and write access to our election Blockchain, which is considered as a public bulletin board and ballot box. Also, observers and election organizers have the right to access the Blockchain and supervise the election to ensure the correctness of the election process.

4.2   Phases

Our protocol unfolds in four phases: setup, registration, vote and tally. There are two ways to perform the setup and the registration phases, depending on whether it is the first time the protocol is runned (the first election) or more.

Setup Phase

Setup for the first election: This phase is described by Fig. 1.

1. RAs start by generating the following election parameters and publish them on the election Blockchain: $\mathbb{G}$ a cyclic group of order a prime number q, in which the Decision Diffie Hellman problem holds; g_1, g_2, g_3 and $o \in \mathbb{G}$ four random generators. They also cooperate and generate their key pair (R, R'), where $R = g_3^y$ is the public key and $R' = y$ is the private one. A Modified El-Gamal threshold [1] key pair $(\mathscr{R}, \mathscr{R}')$ is also generated by cooperation between all RAs. Finally, they publish the public parts on the election Blockchain.
2. TAs cooperate and generate a key pair of Modified El-Gamal threshold $(\mathscr{T}, \mathscr{T}')$, where $\mathscr{T} = (g_1, g_2, h = g_1^{x_1} g_2^{x_2})$ is the public part and $\mathscr{T}' = (x_1, x_2)$ is the secret one. They publish their public key on our Blockchain.

Fig. 1. Setup Phase, First Election

Setup for the Second (or more) Election: For each new election, RAs create a new random generator $o' \in \mathbb{G}$. If we have no need to revoke the old credentials, RAs publish the same election parameters as the first ones, with replacing o by o' (Fig. 2).

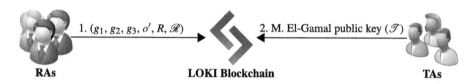

Fig. 2. Setup Phase, Second or more Election, Without Revocation

Otherwise, they generate a new key pair (R_1, R_1'), where $R_1 = g_3^{y_1}$ and $R_1' = y_1$ and publish all public parameters on the election Blockchain (Fig. 3). The new key pair is used for credential revocation.

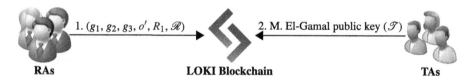

Fig. 3. Setup Phase, Second or more Election, With Revocation

Registration Phase

Registration for the First Election: Every person who has the right to vote and wishes to do so, physically moves to the nearest polling station and provides his/her identity card to the registration authorities (RAs). These authorities verify his/her eligibility and provides him/her by a valid and anonymous credential if he/she is eligible to participate to the election. Otherwise, the registration phase fails. Figure 4 illustrates a successful registration phase. The credential is calculated by cooperation between the registration authorities and is used by the voter to cast a vote during the voting phase. To calculate the credential, RAs generate two random numbers $r, x \in \mathbb{Z}_q$, use their shared private key y and calculate $A = (g_1 g_3^x)^{1/(y+r)}$. The credential is formed by the tuple (A, r, x) where x is the secret part of the credential. After registering all eligible voters, RAs cooperate and generate two lists:

- $L_1 = < E_{\mathscr{R}}[g_1 g_3^x], ID_{voter} >$ contains, for each voter, the ciphertext of $(g_1 g_3^x)$ using their public key $\mathscr{R}$ with the corresponding unique voter identifier ID_{voter}. This list will serve later for credential revocation.
- $L2 = < E_{\mathscr{T}}[A], ID_{voter} >$ contains, for each voter, the ciphertext of A using TAs public key $\mathscr{T}$ with the corresponding unique voter identifier ID_{voter}. This list serves for verification of credentials eligibility.

Finally, RAs publish L_1 and L_2 on the election Blockchain.

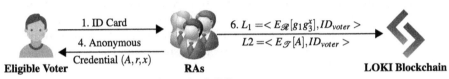

1. ID Card
4. Anonymous Credential (A, r, x)
6. $L_1 = < E_{\mathscr{R}}[g_1 g_3^x], ID_{voter} >$
$L2 = < E_{\mathscr{T}}[A], ID_{voter} >$

Eligible Voter   **RAs**   **LOKI Blockchain**

2. Check voter's eligibility
3. Cooperate and generate a credential
5. Cooperate and generate L_1 and L_2

Fig. 4. Registration phase, first election.

Registration for the Second (or More) Election: For each new election, and if there is one or more credentials to revoke, RAs need to update credentials for voters who still have the right to vote. From the list L_1 and their new shared private key y_1, they calculate the new valid anonymous credentials. By inspecting the values ID_{voter}, the RAs identify voters that can vote in the new election. For each of these voters, RAs choose randomly $r_1 \in \mathbb{Z}_q$ and calculate his/her new valid credential $\sigma_1 = (A_1, r_1, x)$, where $A_1 = (g_1 g_3^x)^{1/(y_1+r_1)}$ and x is the same secret value given to the voter during his/her first time registration. At the end of this phase, RAs publish on the election Blockchain the lists $L_3 = < (A_1, r_1), ID_{voter} >$ and $L_4 = < E_{\mathscr{T}}[A_1], ID_{voter} >$. This phase is illustrated by Fig. 5.

1. $L_1 = < E_{\mathscr{R}}[g_1 g_3^x], ID_{voter} >$
3. $L_3 = < (A_1, r_1), ID_{voter} >$
$L_4 = < E_{\mathscr{T}}[A_1], ID_{voter} >$

RAs   **LOKI Blockchain**

2. Cooperate and generate L_3 and L_4.

Fig. 5. Registration Phase, Second or more Election

Voting Phase. To cast a vote, each eligible voter constructs a voting tuple that contains his/her encrypted vote, his/her encrypted credential and a set of Non-Interactive Zero Knowledge Proofs that prove the correctness of the tuple. It has the following form: $< E_{\mathscr{T}}[V], E_{\mathscr{T}}[A], E_{\mathscr{T}}[A^r], E_{\mathscr{T}}[g_3^x], o^x, \mathscr{P} >$ Where $\mathscr{T}$ is the public key of TAs, V is the choice of the voter, A, r, and x constitute the voter's credential and $\mathscr{P}$ is composed of a set of NI-ZKP. These proofs are constructed by using standard techniques such as [16] and contain: P_1: Proof of validity of the encrypted vote V; P_2: Proof of knowledge of the plain-text related to $E_{\mathscr{T}}[A]$; P_3: Proof of knowledge of the plain-text related to $E_{\mathscr{T}}[A^r]$; P_4: Proof of knowledge of the plain-text related to $E_{\mathscr{T}}[g_3^x]$; P_5: Proof related to the value of A to ensure that is different from 1; P_6: Proof of knowledge of the discrete logarithm of o^x in the basis o and its equality to the discrete logarithm of the plain-text related to $E_{\mathscr{T}}[g_3^x]$ in the basis g_3. This phase is illustrated by Fig. 6. The voter has the right to cast more than one tuple before the end of the voting phase and only his/her last valid vote is counted. When he/she is under coercion, the voter generates $x' \neq x$ and constructs a tuple using the value of x' instead of x. If it is not the first election, the voter uses o' instead of o and his/her new valid credentials σ_1 that he/she received from the RAs during the registration phase.

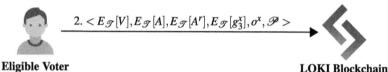

Eligible Voter

1. Generates and constructs the voting tuple.

$2. < E_{\mathscr{T}}[V], E_{\mathscr{T}}[A], E_{\mathscr{T}}[A^r], E_{\mathscr{T}}[g_3^x], o^x, \mathscr{P} >$

LOKI Blockchain

Fig. 6. Voting phase

Tallying Phase. After the end of the voting phase, the tallying authorities read all voting tuples from our election Blockchain and proceed to the tallying process. They start by checking the validity of every tuple proofs and discard the ones with invalid proofs. Then, they eliminate duplicates using the attribute o^x (or o'^x if it is not the first election) included in each tuple, using a hash table. As all voting tuples were sent through LOKI network, they have been passed through the LLARP mix network (see section 3.4 for more details). At this step, each voting tuple has the following form: $< E'_{\mathscr{T}}[V], E'_{\mathscr{T}}[A], E'_{\mathscr{T}}[A^r], E'_{\mathscr{T}}[g_3^x] >$. Using the three last elements of each tuple, TAs cooperate with RAs and check the validity of the anonymous credentials. They proceed as follow:

- Using their shared secret key y, RAs cooperate and calculate $E'_{\mathscr{G}}[A]^y$ which is equal to $E'_{\mathscr{G}}[A^y]$ thanks to El-Gamal homomorphic property. Then, they perform the following multiplication: $E'_{\mathscr{G}}[A^y] \cdot E'_{\mathscr{G}}[A^r] = E'_{\mathscr{G}}[A^y \cdot A^r] = E'_{\mathscr{G}}[A^{y+r}]$. The first equality is obtained by using the homomorphic property of El-Gamal cryptosystem.

- TAs cooperate and perform the following multiplication, in which they also use the homomorphic property of El-Gamal: $E'_{\mathscr{G}}[A^{y+r}] \cdot E'_{\mathscr{G}}[g_1]^{-1} \cdot E'_{\mathscr{G}}[g_3^x]^{-1} = E'_{\mathscr{G}}[A^{y+r} \cdot g_1^{-1} \cdot g_3^{-x}]$. The result $E'_{\mathscr{G}}[A^{y+r} \cdot g_1^{-1} \cdot g_3^{-x}]$ is denoted C. Then, TAs execute the PET to determine whether C is an encryption of 1 or not. If it is the case, the credential is judged valid and the corresponding tuple passes to the next step. Indeed, a valid credential has the following form $\sigma = (A, r, x)$ where $A = (g_1 \cdot g_3^x)^{1/(y+r)}$ so we have $A^{y+r} = g_1 \cdot g_3^x$ thus $A^{y+r} \cdot g_1^{-1} \cdot g_3^{-x} = 1$. Otherwise, the credential is judged invalid and the voting tuple is discarded.

The next step consists on verifying the eligibility of votes by using the element $E'_{\mathscr{G}}[A]$ included on each voting tuple and the list L_2. We recall that $L_2 = <E_{\mathscr{G}}[A], ID_{voter} >$ was published on the election Blockchain by RAs during the registration phase. At this step, and after being passed through the LLARP mix network, we obtain $L'_2 = < E'_{\mathscr{G}}[A], ID'_{voter} >$. By using a hash table, TAs compare $E'_{\mathscr{G}}[A]$ coming on each voting tuple to each $E'_{\mathscr{G}}[A]$ included on the list L'_2 and maintain only tuples that match an element from L'_2. Finally, TAs cooperate and decrypt all votes of the retained list, using their shared secret key $\mathscr{G}'$, and compute the election final result.

We mention that if it is not the first election, y is replaced by y_1, A and r are replaced, respectively, by A_1 and r_1 and L_2 by L_4.

5   Security Evaluation

In this section, we discuss, formally and informally, the security of our proposed scheme.

5.1   Informal Security Evaluation

We start by evaluating our protocol against the list of security requirements presented in the Introduction section. We resume this evaluation in Table 2.

- Eligibility: *LOKI Vote* includes a face to face registration phase, in which the RAs verify the eligibility of every voter and provides only eligible ones by valid credentials. At the end of this phase, RAs publish the list L_2 of all registered voters. Thus, everyone can verify the validity of this list. In addition, during the tallying phase, TAs count only votes that match an element from L_2.

- Completeness: TAs ensure that all valid votes are counted correctly and give proofs for the correctness of their work.
- Soundness: This property is ensured by using the set of proofs included in each voting tuple. Indeed, TAs discard all tuple with invalid proofs from the final tally.
- Robustness: Our proposed protocol is resistant to the misbehavior of malicious voters.
- Fairness: All votes are encrypted, using the TAs public key $\mathscr{T}$, before being cast. Thus, no one, except TAs, has the possibility to decrypt votes and get partial results before the official tally. We mention here that the decryption private key is constructed by cooperation between all TAs. So, we need to trust only one TA to ensure fairness.
- Integrity: The fact of casting and storing votes and the other voting data in the Blockchain safeguard them from being altered or deleted thanks to the immutability property of Blockchain technology.
- Vote-and-go: *LOKI Vote* does not need the voter neither to wait for the end of the voting phase nor to trigger the tallying one. He can simply cast a vote and quiet the voting system.
- Privacy: This property is ensured by using the Loki platform, which is built on the top of Monero Blockchain. Monero is characterized by the anonymity of its transactions since it uses ring signature and ring confidential transactions primitives. Thus, we can not link a transaction to its sender. Consequently, we can not link a voter to his/her vote.
- Universal verifiability: This property in ensured by using Blockchain technology as a public bulletin board. Except the registration phase, all our protocol phases are on chain. Thus, voters, election organizers, observers and any interested party have the possibility to watch the voting process and verify the correctness of each step as well as the final tally.
- Receipt-freeness: From all public data, which are written on the election Blockchain, the voter can not construct a receipt that reflects his/her vote.
- Coercion-resistance: *LOKI Vote* is inspired from the scheme [2], which is formally proved coercion resistant. This property is ensured by using the BBS signature scheme $\sigma = (A, r, x)$ as anonymous credentials for eligible voters. When they are under coercion, voters disclose a random value x' instead of x and pretend that $\sigma' = (A, r, x')$ is the valid credential. Since the voter has the right to vote more than once, he/she has the possibility to cast another vote when he/she is lonely and uses his/her valid credential. The coercer has no possible way to verify if the voter obeyed to his instructions or not.

Table 2. Security Evaluation of CREE, TPSCREE, PCRVSR, PISBVS, ECFUVBV and *LOKI Vote*

	CREE	TPSCREE	PCRVSR	PISBVS	ECFUVBV	LOKI vote
Eligibility	✗	✗	✓	✗	✓	✓
Completeness	✓	✓	✓	✓	✓	✓
Soundness	✓	✓	✓	✓	✓	✓
Robustness	✗	✗	✗	✓	✓	✓
Fairness	✓	✓	✓	✓	✓	✓
Integrity	✗	✗	✗	✓	✓	✓
Vote-and-go	✓	✓	✓	✓	✓	✓
Privacy	✓	✓	✓	✓	✓	✓
Universal verifiability	✓	✓	✓	✓	✓	✓
Receipt-freeness	✓	✓	✓	✓	✓	✓
Coercion-resistance	✓	✓	✓	✗	✗	✓

5.2 Formal Security Evaluation

In this part, we perform an automated security analysis using the verification tool ProVerif [32]. It is an automatic symbolic protocol verifier, capable of proving *reachability properties*, *correspondence assertions*, and *observational equivalence* [33] of a given protocol described in Applied Pi-Calculus [34]. This modeling language is a variant of the Pi-Calculus extended with equational theory over terms and functions and provides an intuitive syntax for studying concurrency and process interaction. The Applied Pi-Calculus allows us to describe several security goals and to determine whether the protocol meets these goals or not. We use the classical intruder model and the standard modeling of the security properties proposed by Dreier et al. [35] in our ProVerif code.

Because of the limitation on the number of pages, we put all ProVerif codes online[7]. We define the following queries to prove votes secrecy, voters' authentication and votes privacy and give the results of executing the codes, and the time it takes ProVerif to prove the properties in Table 3.

- **Verification of votes secrecy:** To capture the value of a given vote, an attacker has to intercept the values of the parameter *Vote*. Thus we use the following query:

```
query attacker(Vote)
```

- **Verification of voters authentication:** Authentication is captured using correspondence assertions. The protocol is intended to ensure that the TAs verify the eligibility of all voters by verifying the validity of their credentials. Therefore, we define the following events and query:

---

[7] https://drive.google.com/drive/folders/1rJRUAuOdnRHLo40umY6Lq9CRrYwZBLw3?usp=sharing.

```
event  ValidCred.
event  CredentialVerification.
query  event(ValidCred)==>event(CredentialVerification).
```

- **Verification of votes privacy:** To express votes privacy we prove the observational equivalence property between two instances of our process that differ only in the choice of votes. To do that, we use `choice[V1,V2]` to represent the terms that differ between the two instances. Likewise, we use the keyword `sync` to express synchronization which help proving equivalences with choice since they allow swapping data between processes at the synchronization points.

Table 3. ProVerif results and execution times.

Properties	Result	Time
Vote secrecy	Proved	0.007 s
Voter authentication	Proved	0.009 s
Vote privacy	Proved	0.089 s

6   Conclusion

We have proposed an end-to-end verifiable, coercion resistant and secure Blockchain-based online e-voting protocol. LOKI Vote is based on the work of Araùjo and Traoré [2] and uses Loki platform. It recalls several cryptographic primitives namely NI-ZKP, Modified El-Gamal, BBS signature and LLARP mix network. It has a linear complexity which makes it practical for large scale elections. We have also proved, formally by using ProVerif, the security of our protocol. Future work will be devoted to implement and evaluate the performance and scalability of the proposed protocol.

References

1. Juels, A., Catalano, D., Jakobsson, M.: Coercion-resistant electronic elections. In: Atluri, V., di Vimercati, S.D.C., Dingledine, R., (eds.) Proceedings of the 2005 ACM Workshop on Privacy in the Electronic Society, WPES 2005, Alexandria, VA, USA, 7 November 2005, pp. 61–70. ACM (2005)
2. Araújo, R., Traoré, J.: A practical coercion resistant voting scheme revisited. In: Heather, J., Schneider, S., Teague, V. (eds.) Vote-ID 2013. LNCS, vol. 7985, pp. 193–209. Springer, Heidelberg (2013). https://doi.org/10.1007/978-3-642-39185-9_12
3. Jakobsson, M., Juels, A.: Mix and match: secure function evaluation via Ciphertexts. In: Okamoto, T. (ed.) ASIACRYPT 2000. LNCS, vol. 1976, pp. 162–177. Springer, Heidelberg (2000). https://doi.org/10.1007/3-540-44448-3_13

4. MacKenzie, P., Shrimpton, T., Jakobsson, M.: Threshold password-authenticated key exchange. In: Yung, M. (ed.) CRYPTO 2002. LNCS, vol. 2442, pp. 385–400. Springer, Heidelberg (2002). https://doi.org/10.1007/3-540-45708-9_25
5. Furukawa, J., Sako, K.: An efficient scheme for proving a shuffle. In: Kilian, J. (ed.) CRYPTO 2001. LNCS, vol. 2139, pp. 368–387. Springer, Heidelberg (2001). https://doi.org/10.1007/3-540-44647-8_22
6. Neff, C.A.: A verifiable secret shuffle and its application to e-voting. In: Reiter, M.K., Samarati, P. (eds.) CCS 2001, Proceedings of the 8th ACM Conference on Computer and Communications Security, Philadelphia, Pennsylvania, USA, 6–8 November 2001, pp. 116–125. ACM (2001)
7. Weber, S.G., Araújo, R., Buchmann, J.A.: On coercion-resistant electronic elections with linear work. In: Proceedings of the The Second International Conference on Availability, Reliability and Security, ARES 2007, The International Dependability Conference - Bridging Theory and Practice, 10–13 April 2007, Vienna, Austria, pp. 908–916. IEEE Computer Society (2007)
8. Clarkson, M.R., Chong, S., Myers, A.C.: Civitas: toward a secure voting system. In: IEEE Symposium on Security and Privacy (S&P 2008), 18–21 May 2008, Oakland, California, USA, pp. 354–368. IEEE Computer Society (2008)
9. Araújo, R., Ben Rajeb, N., Robbana, R., Traoré, J., Youssfi, S.: Towards practical and secure coercion-resistant electronic elections. In: Heng, S.-H., Wright, R.N., Goi, B.-M. (eds.) CANS 2010. LNCS, vol. 6467, pp. 278–297. Springer, Heidelberg (2010). https://doi.org/10.1007/978-3-642-17619-7_20
10. Spycher, O., Koenig, R., Haenni, R., Schläpfer, M.: A new approach towards coercion-resistant remote e-voting in linear time. In: Danezis, G. (ed.) FC 2011. LNCS, vol. 7035, pp. 182–189. Springer, Heidelberg (2012). https://doi.org/10.1007/978-3-642-27576-0_15
11. Rønne, P.B., Atashpendar, A., Gjøsteen, K., Ryan, P.Y.A.: Coercion-resistant voting in linear time via fully homomorphic encryption: towards a quantum-safe scheme. CoRR abs/1901.02560 (2019)
12. Boneh, D., Boyen, X., Shacham, H.: Short group signatures. In: Franklin, M. (ed.) CRYPTO 2004. LNCS, vol. 3152, pp. 41–55. Springer, Heidelberg (2004). https://doi.org/10.1007/978-3-540-28628-8_3
13. Schweisgut, J.: Coercion-resistant electronic elections with observer. In: Krimmer, R. (ed.) Electronic Voting 2006: 2nd International Workshop, Co-organized by Council of Europe, ESF TED, IFIP WG 8.6 and E-Voting.CC, 2nd–4th August 2006. Castle Hofen, Bregenz, Austria, vol. P-86, pp. 171–177. LNI, G I (2006)
14. Cachin, C., Kursawe, K., Shoup, V.: Random oracles in constantinople: practical asynchronous byzantine agreement using cryptography. J. Cryptol. 18(3), 219–246 (2005)
15. Furukawa, J., Sako, K.: An efficient publicly verifiable mix-net for long inputs. IEICE Trans. 90-A(1), 113–127 (2007)
16. Okamoto, T.: Provably secure and practical identification schemes and corresponding signature schemes. In: [36], pp. 31–53
17. Chaum, D., Pedersen, T.P.: Wallet databases with observers. In: [36], pp. 89–105
18. Yu, B., et al.: Platform-independent secure blockchain-based voting system. In: Chen, L., Manulis, M., Schneider, S. (eds.) ISC 2018. LNCS, vol. 11060, pp. 369–386. Springer, Cham (2018). https://doi.org/10.1007/978-3-319-99136-8_20
19. Androulaki, E., et al.: Hyperledger fabric: a distributed operating system for permissioned blockchains. In: Oliveira, R., Felber, P., Hu, Y.C., (eds.) Proceedings of the Thirteenth EuroSys Conference, EuroSys 2018, Porto, Portugal, 23–26 April 2018, pp. 30:1–30:15. ACM (2018)

20. Dimtiriou, T.: Efficient, coercion-free and universally verifiable blockchain-based voting. IACR Cryptology ePrint Archive **2019**, 1406 (2019)
21. Brickell, E.F., Camenisch, J., Chen, L.: Direct anonymous attestation. In: Atluri, V., Pfitzmann, B., McDaniel, P.D. (eds.) Proceedings of the 11th ACM Conference on Computer and Communications Security, CCS 2004, Washington, DC, USA, 25–29 October 2004, pp. 132–145. ACM (2004)
22. Gennaro, R., Gentry, C., Parno, B., Raykova, M.: Quadratic span programs and succinct NIZKs without PCPs. In: Johansson, T., Nguyen, P.Q. (eds.) EURO-CRYPT 2013. LNCS, vol. 7881, pp. 626–645. Springer, Heidelberg (2013). https://doi.org/10.1007/978-3-642-38348-9_37
23. Boneh, D.: The decision Diffie-Hellman problem. In: Buhler, J.P. (ed.) ANTS 1998. LNCS, vol. 1423, pp. 48–63. Springer, Heidelberg (1998). https://doi.org/10.1007/BFb0054851
24. Desmedt, Y.G. (ed.): CRYPTO 1994. LNCS, vol. 839. Springer, Heidelberg (1994). https://doi.org/10.1007/3-540-48658-5
25. Goldwasser, S., Micali, S., Rackoff, C.: The knowledge complexity of interactive proof systems. SIAM J. Comput. **18**(1), 186–208 (1989)
26. Blum, M., Feldman, P., Micali, S.: Non-interactive zero-knowledge and its applications (extended abstract). In: Simon, J., (ed.) Proceedings of the 20th Annual ACM Symposium on Theory of Computing, 2–4 May 1988, Chicago, Illinois, USA, pp. 103–112. ACM (1988)
27. Blum, M., Santis, A.D., Micali, S., Persiano, G.: Noninteractive zero-knowledge. SIAM J. Comput. **20**(6), 1084–1118 (1991)
28. Boneh, D., Boyen, X.: Short signatures without random Oracles. In: Cachin, C., Camenisch, J.L. (eds.) EUROCRYPT 2004. LNCS, vol. 3027, pp. 56–73. Springer, Heidelberg (2004). https://doi.org/10.1007/978-3-540-24676-3_4
29. Rivest, R.L., Shamir, A., Tauman, Y.: How to leak a secret: theory and applications of ring signatures. In: Goldreich, O., Rosenberg, A.L., Selman, A.L. (eds.) Theoretical Computer Science. LNCS, vol. 3895, pp. 164–186. Springer, Heidelberg (2006). https://doi.org/10.1007/11685654_7
30. Diffie, W., Hellman, M.E.: New directions in cryptography. IEEE Trans. Inf. Theor. **22**(6), 644–654 (1976)
31. Noether, S., Mackenzie, A.: Ring confidential transactions. Ledger **1**, 1–18 (2016)
32. Blanchet, B.: Automatic verification of security protocols in the symbolic model: the verifier ProVerif. In: Aldini, A., Lopez, J., Martinelli, F. (eds.) FOSAD 2012-2013. LNCS, vol. 8604, pp. 54–87. Springer, Cham (2014). https://doi.org/10.1007/978-3-319-10082-1_3
33. Delaune, S., Kremer, S., Ryan, M.: Verifying privacy-type properties of electronic voting protocols. J. Comput. Secur. **17**(4), 435–487 (2009)
34. Abadi, M., Blanchet, B., Fournet, C.: The applied pi calculus: mobile values, new names, and secure communication. J. ACM **65**(1), 1:1–1:41 (2018)
35. Dreier, J., Lafourcade, P., Lakhnech, Y.: A formal taxonomy of privacy in voting protocols. In: Proceedings of IEEE International Conference on Communications, ICC 2012, Ottawa, ON, Canada, 10–15 June 2012, pp. 6710–6715. IEEE (2012)
36. Brickell, E.F. (ed.): CRYPTO 1992. LNCS, vol. 740. Springer, Heidelberg (1993). https://doi.org/10.1007/3-540-48071-4

Blockchain for Smart Cities: A Systematic Literature Review

Ifigenia Georgiou$^{(\boxtimes)}$, Juan Geoffrey Nell, and Angelika I. Kokkinaki

School of Business, University of Nicosia, Nicosia, Cyprus
{georgiou.i,nell.j,kokkinaki.a}@unic.ac.cy

Abstract. We use a systematic literature review methodology to answer the following questions pertaining to smart cities and blockchain: (i) Why was blockchain chosen as the solution? (ii) What blockchains are being considered for use in smart cities and why? and (iii) What blockchain based applications are being researched for smart cities? Our results - based on 45 peer-reviewed academic studies all published in journals that met pre-defined search criteria - show that increased security, privacy, and trust are the reasons most cited in the literature for the use of blockchain for smart cities. Consortium, Hybrid, Private, and Public blockchains are discussed with respect to their suitability for smart cities applications, and finally, we discuss smart cities blockchain applications from the literature using a taxonomy based on the framework defined by Silva et al. [40]. In conclusion, this study highlights the current blockchain challenges and future research opportunities, including the need to change the current mindset of centralized control and trusted third parties to a more participative engagement model across smart cities.

Keywords: Smart cities, blockchain · Blockchain · Distributed ledger technology (DLT) · Internet of Things (IoT) · Sharing economy · Decentralization · Smart contracts · Systematic literature review

1 Introduction

Rapid urbanization and ICT developments have been applied and lead to the origin of the concept of smart city [10]. [14] theorized that a smart city is "when investments in human and social capital and traditional transport and modern ICT communication infrastructure fuel sustainable economic growth and a high quality of life, with wise management of natural resources, through participatory governance". [6] and [16] included areas such as smart governance, smart mobility, smart living, smart use and management of natural resources, smart citizenship and smart economy; these elements are even further expanded upon by [45], who proposed the elements of smart citizenship, smart healthcare, smart grid, smart transportation, supply chain management, smart business, smart home, smart government and smart education.

According to [4] massive efforts are still needed to enable services to connect to one another and to gain real value through such connectivity. [40] expand on the challenges and include integration and interoperability of systems in the application layer, infrastructure and information security concerns, privacy and confidentiality, cyber-

© Springer Nature Switzerland AG 2020
M. Themistocleous et al. (Eds.): EMCIS 2020, LNBIP 402, pp. 169–187, 2020.
https://doi.org/10.1007/978-3-030-63396-7_12

attacks and the exponential growth of data. [4] confirm that new forms of database design will be required that can be distributed at a city-wide scale and that data collection will rely on crowdsourcing to elicit the preferences of citizens and enable the city to engage in social experimentation around what we know and how we address key urban problems. And this is where blockchain becomes relevant. The United Nations, in their 2018 Revision explicitly point out – in "Goal 11" that "blockchain provides an opportunity to collaborate in a transparent secure way across the many components of smart cities, ensuring sustainability and accountability" [43]. Sustainability improvement is one of the goals of smart cities.

[45] point out that although smart cities and blockchain have been studied extensively in previous works, these two important areas have traditionally been thus far researched separately, and they provide a survey of the state-of-the-art blockchain technology that can be applied in smart cities. To the best of our knowledge, [45] that focused on providing a taxonomy of blockchain-based solutions in smart cities is the first and only attempt to look into the field of blockchain applications to smart cities. We extend this work into two important ways: first, we focus on specific additional questions such as why blockchain was used as the solution, and what blockchains have been considered; secondly, our study differs in scope as we employ a systematic literature review methodology that derives data from journals that meet pre-defined search criteria.

Specifically, the aim of this study is to provide a systematic review of the literature on blockchain application for smart cities to answer the following research questions (i) Why was blockchain chosen as the solution? (ii) What blockchains are being considered for use in smart cities and why? and (iii) What blockchain based applications are being researched for smart cities? The results of our study are potentially useful to researchers in the fields of blockchain and smart cities, but also to practitioners such as urban planners and governments.

The remaining of this paper is structured as follows: Sect. 2 outlines the methodology followed for the systematic literature review. Section 3 presents the findings from the three research questions. Section 4 concludes.

2 Methodology

A systematic literature review methodology is used, which is a process for searching existing literature, evaluating and analysing the literature to report on findings and evidence to allow conclusions to be reached about what is known and not known in the area being researched [11]. The systematic literature review follows pre-defined steps. The first step is to formulate the research questions. We have already presented the questions in the Introduction. The second step is to identify appropriate keywords and formulate the search strings. The main keywords used were "blockchain" and "smart city", representing the main topics in our research. To ensure that all relevant academic articles were included, it was decided to include variations of the two terms, that is, "distributed ledger" or "DLT" for "blockchain", and "smart district", "digital city", and "smart towns" for "smart city". Step 3 involved identifying the data sources and setting inclusion and exclusion criteria for the search. The following electronic database sources were searched based on their wide acceptance and respectability among the academic community: (a) Scopus, (b) Science direct, and (c) IEEE Explore digital library. The inclusion criteria used are: (a) papers written in the English language, and (b) the search terms had to be present in the title or keywords or abstract to ensure that the results were narrowly focused on the topic. The search was conducted across all years. The exclusion criteria specified that only papers published in peer-reviewed academic journals are to be included in the systematic literature review; therefore, all other publications are to be excluded. Step 4 involved entering the search strings in the chosen databases and apply the inclusion and exclusion criteria defined in the previous step. This process provided 641 results. In Step 5 these 641 papers were then further evaluated and screened. Papers that were duplicated or where the full text was not available or papers that focused on solely on improving the blockchain or Bitcoin technology were then removed. The above process resulted in a list of 60 unique, relevant papers, selected based on a review of the title, keywords, abstract and document type where available. The last screening required reading the full paper to ensure that the paper did provide insight on the research questions. Research papers were explicitly excluded when the focus was on improving the blockchain technology itself, literature reviews, or when the paper did not focus on any particular use case. This left us with 42 studies. Next, the references of these papers were checked to ensure that any relevant articles that satisfy our criteria were not missed. Three papers were introduced based on this cross-referencing process. Data from the resulted 45 papers were populated into a data collection table to facilitate a content analysis focusing on answering the research questions. Figure 1 provides a visual representation of the steps 1–5 described above.

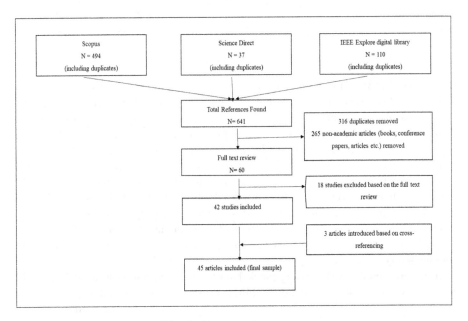

Fig. 1. Data mapping process

3   Results

The final step of the systematic review process is the descriptive review of the literature, followed by the thematic analysis. As the concept of smart cities is new, few papers were published prior to 2018. Through these years, there is gradual evolvement of the focus of research from smart contracts towards a more thorough examination of blockchain applications relevant in use cases of smart cities. Geographically - based on the first author's location - most studies originate from Asia; specifically, most papers originate from China, followed by South Korea and then India. The remaining of this section focuses on the main research questions and the relevant findings based on the systematic literature review.

3.1   Why was Blockchain Chosen as the Solution?

Table 1 highlights the key reasons that blockchain was proposed as a potential solution including increased security, the decentralized nature of the blockchain, and its trustworthiness due to immutability. Privacy was also cited, despite transparency of transactions.

Table 1. Reasons for implementing blockchain applications

Reason for blockchain	No. of papers	Citation
Increased security	32	[1–3, 7, 9, 11–13, 15, 17–20, 22, 25–27, 29, 31–34, 36, 37, 39, 41, 42, 44, 46, 48, 50]
Privacy	16	[9, 11–13, 19, 23, 25, 26, 28, 29, 32, 39, 41, 49–51]
Trust	14	[5, 8, 12, 17, 19, 23, 24, 27, 28, 31, 35, 42, 47, 51]

Blockchain for Increased Security. Security was the top reason cited for the use of blockchain. Due to the massive volume of data, the stakeholders involved and necessary controls, smart cities require high levels of security. Blockchain would improve security across Internet of Things (IoT) in a smart city and sharing economy. This view was reinforced by [2, 3, 11, 13, 19, 22, 29, 32, 34, 39, 41]; and [27].

[33] provide a framework to be used across the IoT ecosystem to detect potential attacks by monitoring and analyzing all the traffic data based on blockchain, while [28] argues that using blockchain to secure IoT is not a suitable solution due to the significant computer power and cost that this entails. [18] propose a 'bubble of trust' where secure virtual zones are created to enable communication of IoT devices. [15] focused on secure IoT device management to ensure integrity, data availability and confidentiality.

In the transport industry, using blockchain to enable secure sharing of Internet of Vehicles (IoV) data was researched by [46] and [8]. [48] focus on solving the security issues of vehicular ad hoc networks (VANETs) through the Block-SDV project, whereas [37] point out that blockchain can be used to build a secure, autonomous transport system for autonomous vehicles. [44] discuss the use of blockchain to implement secure energy delivery services for electric vehicles and energy nodes involving both the transport and energy industry.

In the energy industry, [1] and [31] discuss a secure blockchain-based electrical energy trading system. [7] and [50] discuss secure energy trading for electric vehicles.

In the medical industry, [9] research using blockchain to enable secure sharing of patient medical records with patients, providers, and third parties, whereas [20] focused on securing patient and provider identities.

[25] also suggest that blockchain can provide improved security for user identities. Other studies focus on blockchain for securing information in the casino and entertainment industry [26], blockchain for smart campus cybersecurity [13], and manufacturing supply chain security [36].

Blockchain for Improved Privacy. Identity and access management could be controlled through blockchain [23]. [25] presented a privacy preservation technique to protect user identity, while [13] focused on the social contract enforcement of identity privacy. [51] presented "Reportcoin" blockchain-based incentive anonymous reporting system to combat privacy issues in reporting law violations. [9] define a privacy-preserving framework for access control and interoperability. [11] propose a privacy-preserving blockchain for the analysis of big data in healthcare. Scalability problems and data leakage was a concern in [13].

[28] discusses the "questionable" privacy formats used by central authorities, while [39] in a more technical paper explores the Privacy-Preserving Support Vector Machine training over blockchain-based encrypted IoT data in smart cities. Machine learning based privacy-preserving fair data trading was explored by [49].

The use of blockchain to tackle IoT-related privacy issues is proposed by [19, 29, 32, 38, 41] proposed using a Proof-of-Work scheme to ensure privacy in IoT. [50] discussed the privacy challenges Internet of Vehicles (IoV).

Increased Trust. User trust in the entire system is critical [5]. Trust can be seen from two different perspectives: One perspective is as a result of the inherent blockchain attributes of transparency, immutability and auditability which ensure data integrity [8, 23, 27, 31, 51]. The other perspective emerges from the need to obtain network consensus before a transaction can be committed and the decentralised nature of blockchain technology which results in removing the need to trust centralized third parties [12, 17, 19, 23, 24, 28, 35, 42, 47]. As explained by [51] "blockchain converts trust in people or institutions into trust in the system".

Other Reasons. The concept of blockchain applications for Loyalty and Reward programmes was covered by eight papers. [5] created UniMeCoin for incentive mechanism services. [30] proposed loyalty programmes for local and international travel, and [8] introduced blockchain as a traceable and irreversible mechanism for incentives. Loyalty programmes also received some attention in relation to motivating citizens to participate in the collection and sharing of data [8]; [46], the reporting of issues [51], and validation of data [20].

Six studies cited Peer to Peer (P2P) as a reason for selecting a blockchain solution. Disintermediation [30], better interaction with customers [30] and Decentralized Apps (DApps) based on Peer-to-Peer (P2P) transactions [12] were amongst the more generic applications of blockchain for P2P. Furthermore, [42] presented an approach where no one can unilaterally take actions on behalf of the community. [20] researched the use of blockchain for distributed P2P ASP for IoT, and [31] presented a P2P prosumer-chain energy exchange methodology.

Another important reason cited for using blockchain as a solution was efficiency (see [20, 23, 36]).

The remaining studies focus on currency/token management (see [13, 26, 30, 44, 46] and [27] focus on incentives. Provenance was conceptually discussed by [26]. Lastly, [30] focus on records and rights management; [20] on clinical research and data monetisation, while with [26] look at Notarisation.

3.2   What Blockchains are Being Considered for Use in Smart Cities?

Of the 45 papers analysed, only 16 mentioned a particular type of blockchain, four referred to a public blockchain, seven referred to a private blockchain, one referred to a hybrid and four to a consortium. A summary is shown in Table 2.

Ethereum is the predominant platform, proposed by 12 of the 17 papers that referenced a particular blockchain as a solution, this is possibly due to most of the papers incorporating smart contracts, 31 of 45 papers, as an integral component of the blockchain for smart cities. There were three Non-specified Consortium papers, and one Consortium solution using BigChainDB; One Non-Specified Hybrid solution, one custom public/private blockchain, and one non-specified Ethereum solution. The public blockchains were split amongst Ethereum (two, one Tangle, and one unspecified). Ethereum had seven papers with Private blockchain as the solution.

Table 2. Blockchain types used in Research

Type of blockchain	Blockchain referenced	% of total	Citation
Consortium	Not specified	16%	[7, 8, 50]
Consortium	BigChainDB	5%	[24]
Hybrid	Not specified	5%	[23]
Private	Ethereum	37%	[5, 9, 15, 29, 33, 36, 38]
Private	Ethereum and hyperledger blockchain	5%	[32]
Public	Ethereum	11%	[18, 25]
Public	Tangle (DAG)	5%	[13]
Public	Not specified	5%	[51]
Private and public	Custom based on ethereum	5%	[26]
Not specified	Ethereum	5%	[28]

Public Blockchain. Ethereum Public Blockchain was selected by two studies. [25] attempted to solve the issue of public blockchains being computationally expensive, demanding high bandwidth and extra computational power, and not generally considered completely suitable for most resource constrained IoT devices meant for smart cities. They propose a framework of modified blockchain models allowing for additional privacy and security properties making IoT application data and transactions more secure and anonymous over a blockchain-based network. [18] looked at creating a decentralised blockchain-based authentication system for IoT – both human to device, and device to device. This approach relies on the security advantages provided by blockchain, and will alleviate malicious users, and bring about the following blockchain advantages: decentralised, robust against falsification and alteration, autonomous, smart contracts, scalable. Private blockchain was considered, but disregarded due to the limitations it presented to the above advantages. Ethereum was selected as it has the second greatest ledger in the world, secure, uses smart contracts, accommodates the creation of decentralized applications, (dApps), and it is followed by a big community [18].

[13] suggest Tangle that takes into account constant delays and a random selection algorithm to enforce social contracts and to implement control systems focusing on dynamic deposit pricing; the desired level of compliance is enforced by a pricing signal following a predetermined set of rules.

[51] combine smart contracts with zero knowledge proof to propose a novel Blockchain-based incentive mechanism in ReportCoin, a novel efficient and practical blockchain-based incentive anonymous reporting system that guarantees user identity privacy and reporting message reliability. A public blockchain was suggested because of the openness and transparency, tamper-resistance and decentralization.

Custom Blockchain (Private/Public). [26] specifically focused on how blockchain technology can be applied to logistics management in integrated casinos and entertainment (ICE). "TransICE", an open, automated, and transparent platform, consisting of two parts, the Shipment Pricing and Scheduling process, and the Pickup, Shipping and Delivery process. They have selected a hybrid model to keep financial transactions are stored on the public blockchain.

Non-specified Ethereum. [28] developed a universal blockchain framework for urban governance that can be used globally and that is Ethereum-based. Off-blockchain preparatory process will be app-based and will inform the on-blockchain smart contract. This on-and-off-blockchain combination is called Group2Group (G2G) system of peers and alleviates pressure on the public blockchain.

Private Ethereum. Ethereum Private Blockchain was selected by eight authors. [29] wanted to leverage off the advantages of confidentiality, integrity, authentication, authorization, trust, verification, information storage, and management, availability challenges need to be addressed. They used Ethereum virtual machine to implement the blockchain distributed network and healthcare insurance claims is taken as an example to test the proposed solution, and the results indicated trust management and security and privacy challenges were addressed [29]. The [29] framework is based on the principle that all the participants are connected in a distributed way to pre-registered entities.

[5] propose a fully centralized version of the blockchain implementing the proof of authority consensus mechanism, creating public auditability through UniMeCoin,

where one single miner is involved in the blockchain under the control of the University of Messina. After the pilot, the decision was taken to migrate to a consortium-chain network in which more partners are involved in the management of UniMeCoin by hosting additional miners [5].

[9] designed Ancile, a permission-based framework that utilises smart contracts access control and obfuscation of data, to be implemented over existing systems; it utilises specific Ethereum tools to create a system that is both cost and storage effective, in an attempt to prevent data breaches of the private information of patients.

[32] present a blockchain and IoT-based Cognitive Edge Framework to support security-and privacy-oriented smart contract services for the sustainable IoT-enabled sharing economy in mega smart cities. The framework offers a sustainable incentive mechanism for a Multi-access edge computing (MEC)-based sharing economy system, which leverages the blockchain and off-chain framework to store immutable ledgers [32].

[33] looked at the security architecture based on the Mininet emulator for an IoT network to prevent cyber-attacks by implementing a decentralized security architecture based on Software Defined Networking (SDN) coupled with a blockchain technology for IoT network in the smart city that relies on the three core technologies of SDN, blockchain, and Fog and mobile edge computing in order to detect attacks in the IoT network more effectively.

[38] proposes a novel hybrid network architecture for the smart city simulated on top of a private Ethereum blockchain network, by leveraging Software Defined Networking and blockchain technologies through a two-part architecture: core network and edge network.

[36] investigated a private Ethereum blockchain-based distributed framework for Automotive Industry in a smart city, and propose a blockchain-based distributed framework, which includes a novel miner node selection algorithm for the blockchain-based distributed network architecture. Simulations using real time data of mined blocks from litecoinpool.org, to test feasibility demonstrated that the proof-of-concept model can be used for wide range of future smart applications [36].

[15] propose a private blockchain-based device management framework that consistently inspects the integrity of the device timely, providing secure and guaranteed device updates and storing the results to keep improper management and updating to cause losses to a smart city.

Consortium/Hybrid. [7] propose a blockchain-based secure energy trading scheme for electric vehicles (EVs), where a blockchain is used to validate EVs' requests. The miner nodes in the blockchain consortium validate the requests on the basis of energy requirements, time of stay, dynamic pricing, and connectivity record, providing transaction security and privacy protection without relying on a trusted third-party to carry out verification.

[50] propose a consortium blockchain-enabled secure energy trading framework for EVs to develop a distributed, privacy-preserved, and incentive-compatible demand response mechanism for IoEV. Challenges, such as a lack of and incentive mechanism, privacy leakage, and security threats are addressed.

[23] introduce a novel scalable architecture that is based on a distributed hybrid ledger model allowing for refined and secure management of data generated and

processed in different geographical and administrative units of a city. A proof of concept mechanism is used, which highlights the need to keep and process citizen data at the local level. The proposed architecture provides secure and privacy protected environment for citizen participatory applications.

[24] conducted an experiment named#SmartME on BigchainDB and designed and implemented a trust-less smart city data acquisition, storage and visualization system layer on top of the #SmartME stack, which was tested in a real-world smart city scenario, by running it on the #SmartME deployment available in the city of Messina.

[8] introduce a trustless, privacy preserving consortium blockchain that includes a smart contract for automatic data sharing and computing cost. Simulations show that the proposed algorithm is scalable, truthful, individually rational, and can maximize the social welfare with low social cost and low computational complexity.

3.3 What Blockchain Based Applications are Being Researched for Smart Cities?

Every eligible paper was reviewed so as to be categorized based on the high-level components defined by the research of [40] (Fig. 2). The classification into components was based on best fit and the stated use case(s). Sometimes they would fall in more than one category; for example, [26] discuss applications for integrated resorts which may be considered as a small city that includes healthcare, transport, logistics, supply chains, hospitality etc.

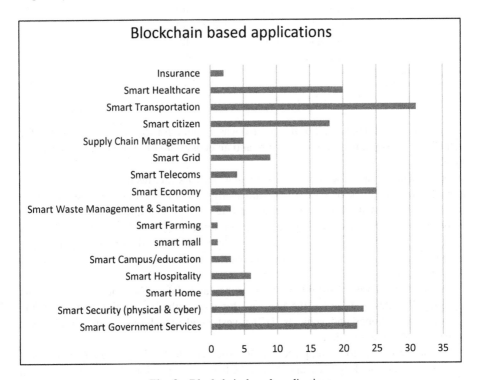

Fig. 2. Blockchain based applications

Below is a detailed breakdown of the top six major themes, comprising 80% of the use cases identified in the research.

Smart Transportation/Mobility. Smart Transportation/Mobility has the highest amount of use cases researched for smart cities, Table 3 lists the use cases and the papers referring to them.

Table 3. Transportation/mobility applications

Application	Citation
Smart transportation/mobility	[17, 24, 26, 32, 36–38, 12]
Electric vehicles	[7, 44]
Automotive loyalty/incentives programs	[36, 44, 8]
Parking	[5, 38]
Car pooling	[5]
Logistics	[21, 26]
Ride sharing/bike sharing	[35, 37]
Data sharing	[41]
Drones	[20]
Environment data using taxi infrastructure	[5]
Traffic data	[5]
Automotive automated payments	[36]
Mobile crowdsensing	[46]
Vehicle registration and maintenance services	[36]
Vehicle and smart phone communications	[48]
Vehicular network	[37]
Smart roads	[18]

The concept of Traffic and traffic control was a theme for [5], which covered "traffic lights" and "car-pooling", "Infrastructure and an ecosystem of potholes" was discussed by [5]

In a research paper focusing on a vehicular network architecture in smart city [38] looked into vehicle resource discovery and sharing, intelligent transport systems which communicate with the home, and incorporating ride sharing and scheduling into the home and vehicular network, as part of a smart home. [44] also looked into integrating electric vehicles into smart homes. [44] also focused on the data management application of the vehicular energy network (VEN), and renewable energy (RE) transportation.

[5] researched the possibilities of environmental data collection using taxi data (speed, GPS, etc). [48] noted the use case for data gathering on the communication between smartphones and vehicles. [17] investigated data forensics in IoT and [18] focus on IoT authentication.

"Smart transportation", supported by logistics and technology is another potential use case under the Logistics and Supply Chain classification. Both [26] and [46] investigated mobile crowdsensing recognising that incentives will be implemented to encourage the automotive crowdsensing. [21] and [26] researched mobility logistics in the pharmaceutical and gaming industries respectively.

Smart Economy. Applications for the smart economy was the second most researched topic, with 25 use cases by different authors. Those are shown in Table 4.

Table 4. Smart economy applications

Application	Citation
Virtual currencies	[5, 26, 30, 50, 51]
Payments	[5, 30, 36, 37]
Loyalty and rewards	[21, 44, 8]
Marketplace	[7, 35, 49]
Investing	[25, 28]
Financial transactions and trades	[17]
Sharing economy	[42]
Econometric Models	[28]
Clinical research and data monetisation	[20]
Smart economy	[12]

Many papers were on the introduction of new virtual currencies as a trading token [50], incentives and rewards token [5, 30, 51] or as e-money across an entire ecosystem [26].

[36] researched the automated payment process in the automotive industry in a smart city and as part of their research into an IoT service ecosystem for smart cities, [5] looked at payments (parking, university services, voting). In the casinos and entertainment industry, their entire research on using blockchain as a platform for the integrated casino and entertainment industry which can be seen as a mini smart city, and also explored financial transactions as a generic concept.

Investing use cases focused to real estate investing [25] and smart malls [38]. Loyalty and rewards incentives is a critical element of influencing participation and engagement with stakeholders in a smart economy and was discussed by [21]. A financial framework for energy delivery for vehicular networks was discussed by [44]. [8] looked into a quality-driven auction based incentive mechanism.

Finance was one of the topics tackled by [17] whilst looking into blockchain technology and its integration with IoT. [49] explored data trading in the big data market, with a specific focus on machine learning and preserving financial privacy. Where [1] researched a smart energy grid based on blockchain technology, whereby energy providers and private citizens can freely exchange energy both as consumers and prosumers.

Smart Security (Physical and Cyber). Smart security is a critical element of a smart city - the entire premise of a smart city is that it is enabled by technology and technology is at high risk of cyber-attacks (Table 5). The most prominent use cases for smart security is around securing information and data. Eight papers focused on secured information management and exchange with [37] describing a model allowing vehicles within a network of vehicles to discover and share their resources and data securely.

[44] examine secure energy delivery services for electric vehicles and energy nodes. [34, 39, 46, 49], and [27] all focused on securing IoT data, whereas [22] were interested in ensuring the security of the collection and trading of data on the network. [28] explored blockchain as the next enabling network, illustrating how blockchain technology can used to connect data processing technologies securely for IoT.

Identity management was the second highest subtopic in security with 5 papers exploring the topic in more detail. In the research into a decentralized blockchain-based authentication system for IoT, [18] noted a use case for Identity and Access Management related to the IoT. Authentication of the integration between a decentralized identity management and distributed credential storage was researched by [17] and by [30] in their smart tourism research where they explicitly noted an integrated identity management network. Tornado was identified as a potential enabler and integrator for blockchain in IoT.

Another sub-topic within secure identity management is the sharing economy. [32] present a blockchain and IoT-based cognitive edge framework for sharing economy services in a smart city. [3] with a focus on healthcare, looked at the data management of firmware detection and self-healing though IoT. This has a huge impact on the Identity management aspect of smart security.

Identity management is also highlighted as a potential use case within logistics and supply chain management by [17], where they looked at blockchain technology and its integration with IoT and found that decentralized identity management, as well as distributed credential storage created good use cases.

Table 5. Smart security (physical and cyber) applications

Application	Citation
Secured information/data management and exchange	[22, 27, 34, 37, 39, 44, 46, 49]
Identity management	[15, 18, 30, 32, 41, 20]
Detect and mitigate security attacks in IoT	[24, 33, 29]
Firmware detection, updates and self-healing IoT	[3, 15]
Data forensics	[17]
Big data auditing	[47]
Secure communication in a distributed environment	[19]
Anonymous reporting	[51]

The remaining use cases included research into a blockchain-based secure device management framework for an IoT network in a smart city, focusing on device management and firmware updates [15]. This research aligned to the paper by [24] around the design of a trustless smart city system where they looked at the acquisition, storage and consumption of sensor data. Additionally [19] researched emerging technologies for sustainable smart city network security, looking at secure communication in a distributed environment, whereas [44] researched a blockchain-based secure incentive scheme for energy delivery in a vehicular energy network, to be integrated into the IoT through the management of devices at home, vehicle, and city.

Smart Government. Governmental services and administration can be trusted, secured, be more transparent and encouraging citizen participation on a blockchain (see Table 6). [21] examines loyalty and rewards platforms, birth and death registries, court case files, property registration, local business registration and voting platforms. [5] also included voting platforms among other applications.

Both [5, 28] made cases for the need of policies, rules, laws, regulations and standards to govern smart cities, and the availability of these on the blockchain. Citizen engagement and participation within smart cites and government was the main point of [28] that discussed use cases for citizens to submit their urban needs onto the blockchain encouraging involvement in policy decisions. [28] also focused on geographical information systems, econometric models, mayors' dashboards and statistical projections. Finally, [22], who discussed an immutable log of events and management of access control to government data.

Table 6. Smart government applications

Application	Citation
Administration including court case files and building information	[21, 28]
Policies, rules, laws, regulations, standards	[28, 5]
Crowdsensing and crowdsourcing	[20, 5]
Voting platforms	[21, 5]
Infrastructure and an ecosystem of services	[5]
Incentive mechanisms	[5]
Registrations (Birth and death, property, local business)	[21]
Citizen data (sharing)	[23]
District area monitoring and safety	[24]
Urban budgeting	[24]
Social compliance	[13]
Log of events and management	[22]
Geographic information system	[28]
Mayors dashboards	[28]
Statistical projections	[28]
Crisis mapping and recovery	[20]

Smart Healthcare. Smart healthcare has also garnered a lot of interest (Table 7). [2] and [9] refer to opportunities in healthcare at a high level. [17] delves deeper into the topic in combination with IoT and describes financial, transactional and trade within intelligent healthcare networks. [18] researches the concept of secure virtual zones (bubbles) where things can identify and trust each other. This creates opportunities for hospitals, healthcare and medical use cases.

[32] are more focused on a sharing economy including smart health services and [26] include smart health in their study of use cases for integrated casino and entertainment. [20] researched various applications in healthcare including medical fraud detection, mechanisms for validating, crediting and rewarding crowdsourced geotagged data, public health surveillance and wearables.

Table 7. Smart healthcare applications

Application	Citation
Smart healthcare	[2, 9, 17], [26, 32, 18]
Collection, processing and storage of healthcare data	[20]
Transparent pharmaceutical and medical device supply chains	[21, 20]
Secure sharing of data	[41, 20]
Remote patient monitoring	[11]
Single electronic health record for the citizens	[21]
Smart hospital	[38]
Clinical research and data monetization, medical fraud detection, public health surveillance, wearables	[20]
Healthcare insurance claims	[29]

Smart Citizenship. This pertains to the social element of smart cities where citizen participation and engagement play a major role (Table 8). [35] focusing on this social element to smart cities, explored citizen co-creation, both at the neighbourhood-scale, as well as bi-directional, and city-wide. [35] also brought in the social aspects of using a smart city platform for societal value exchange and co-creation, named WeValue. [28] additionally targeted the "people's layer" for urban technologies, and Geographical Information Systems.

[5] and [23], specifically looked at "citizen participation" in terms of listing issues, sharing data, and participation in governmental decision-making. Only one paper focused on education falling into the "smart people" subcategory [13].

Table 8. Smart citizenship applications

Application	Citation
Citizen participation and engagement	[23, 24, 28, 35]
Energy trading & marketplace	[1, 2, 7, 50]
Crowdsensing (problem reporting)	[5, 51]
Incentives and rewards	[5, 21]
Sharing economy	[35, 42]
Remote patient monitoring	[11]
Smart living	[17]
Smart people (education)	[12]

Other Classifications. Energy grid applications for "energy exchange" is a popular use case for blockchains. [1] and [31] explore citizens as prosumers, trading energy between providers, prosumers and consumers of smart homes. [35] noted that a smart city platform for societal value exchange may be utilised for energy-savings. [12] researched smart governance, smart living and smart economy of energy management and [1] looked at the data associated with energy trading and a sustainable electrical energy transaction ecosystem between prosumers and consumers of smart homes. [44] proposed a blockchain-based incentive scheme for energy delivery in vehicular energy network creates a case for integrated wireless power transfer technology into the smart home and building in incentive schemes through intelligent reporting. Both [21] and [5] found notable use cases for the use of blockchain in "Renewable energy" within their research.

Another topic of interest was waste management. [18] as well as [24] focused on waste management and sanitation, whilst [5] explored blockchain as an option for payments for waste management in smart cities. [24] focused on the mobility of waste management services.

Smart homes was another interesting topic investigated. [17] in their study on the authentication of blockchain technology and its integration with IoT, explore IoT for smart lives and smart homes. [36] had an architectural approach to smart homes within the smart city.

Supply chain management is mentioned in association with applications of blockchain technology to logistics management in integrated casinos and entertainment [26] automotive industry in a smart city [36], and with the applications of blockchain technology in smart city development in [21] where they looked specifically at pharmaceutical supply chains.

4 Discussion and Conclusions

The intersection of blockchain and Smart Cities has the potential of creating sustainable smart cities aligned to the United Nations sustainable cities and communities' goal. This is also a worth exploring complex topic which spans across multiple disciplines. In this study we employ the methodology of systematic literature review to analyse 45 academic papers published in 33 different journals mostly within the Computer Science field, to answer three research questions.

The first question is why blockchain was chosen as the solution. The main reasons cited were security, privacy, and trust. Security was the top reason cited for the use of blockchain. Due to the vast volume of data, the stakeholders involved, and the necessary controls, smart cities require a very high level of security. Privacy issues involve identity privacy, healthcare privacy, privacy when reporting crimes, privacy issues in Internet of Vehicles. Trust, another reason cited, is enhanced by transparency, immutability and auditability, and the ability to have trustless systems.

The second question concerned the type of blockchain suggested. The most popular type was private blockchain. Public blockchains have been also suggested, as well as Non-specified Ethereum, Private Ethereum, and Consortium/Hybrid.

The third question focuses on the blockchain applications that are being researched for smart cities and to answer that the [40] framework for the thematic taxonomy of applications is applied. Our findings show that smart cities blockchain applications focus on smart transportation, smart economy, smart security, smart government, smart healthcare and smart citizenship applications, creating important links between the social, economic and industry elements of smart cities. Moreover, in reviewing the literature, it became clear that often studies tended to focus on smaller subsets of a smart city; so, a "Smart City" is a conglomeration word for "Smart Places". These include smart campuses, smart suburbs, smart hospitals, integrated casinos, smart malls, etc. but the concept can also expand to include a whole country. The 'place' becomes the centrepiece of the model, and there are six smart themes, facilitated through different blockchains (Fig. 3). The six themes of this taxonomy each have applications associated to it. The breakdown of each as follows: Economy, which has the applications Sharing, Investing and Market-place associated; Environment, associated with Mobility, Energy, and Telecoms; Governance, with its associated Laws & Regulations, and Record Keeping; Services, associated with Education, Healthcare, Insurance, and Waste Management; Security, and its associated Identity Management, and Data Security; and, Citizen, associated with Rewards and Incentives, Participation & Engagement, and Reporting.

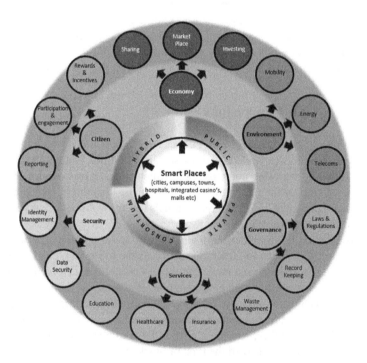

Fig. 3. Graphical view of blockchain based applications

Some of the challenges that emerged are that blockchain solutions need to be carefully thought through and implemented as the very attributes that make blockchain desirable for smart cities could also create challenges that need to be overcome, including the need for notaries, quality data input, regulatory privacy and the ability to be forgotten, additionally future research is needed around blockchain scalability, standards and interoperability across multiple blockchains to enable a holistic ecosystem that brings together all the elements of a smart city.

Enabling the smart citizen as a contributor, prosumer and decision maker within smart cities is particularly inspiring and encouraging. Blockchain based applications within the smart city context are steadily gaining more momentum; however, it has to be noted that they are still in an evolution state. Significant developments and change management will be required to position blockchain based applications for smart cities as an opportunity for transparency, trust and participative citizenry.

In conclusion, opportunities that blockchain based applications can bring to smart cities are discussed, across all sectors and industries. Current blockchain challenges and future research opportunities have been highlighted, including the need to change the current mindset of centralized control and trusted third parties to a more participative engagement model across smart cities.

The smart city is a relatively new concept, and certainly an evolving one and there is a high likelihood that many research papers have been omitted due to researchers classifying their research using alternative terms and not the terms specifically targeted with this study. The selected keywords and databases used for the research may have resulted in missing relevant literature, however the results covered a broad range of use cases and the references of the selected papers were also checked to minimize the inadvertent omission of any papers.

References

1. Alessandra, P., et al.: Smarter city: smart energy grid based on blockchain technology. Int. J. Adv. Sci. Eng. Inf. Technol. **8**(1), 298–306 (2018)
2. Altulyan, M., Yao, L., Kanhere, S.S., Wang, X., Huang, C.: A unified framework for data integrity protection in people-centric smart cities. Multimedia Tools Appl. **79**, 4989–5002 (2019). https://doi.org/10.1007/s11042-019-7182-7
3. Banerjee, M., Lee, J., Choo, K.-K.R.: A blockchain future for internet of things security: a position paper. Digit. Commun. Netw. **4**(3), 149–160 (2018)
4. Batty, M., et al.: Smart cities of the future. Eur. Phys. J. Spec. Top. **214**, 481–518 (2012)
5. Bruneo, D., et al.: An IoT service ecosystem for smart cities: the #SmartME project. Internet Things **5**, 12–33 (2019)
6. Caragliu, A., Del Bo, C., Nijkamp, P.: Smart cities in Europe. J. Urban Technol. **18**, 65–82 (2011)
7. Chaudhary, R., et al.: Best: blockchain-based secure energy trading in SDN-enabled intelligent transportation system. Comput. Secur. **85**, 288–299 (2019)
8. Chen, W., Chen, Y., Chen, X., Zheng, Z.: Toward secure data sharing for the IoV: a quality-driven incentive mechanism with on-chain and off-chain guarantees. IEEE Internet Things J. 1 (2019)

9. Dagher, G.G., Mohler, J., Milojkovic, M., Marella, P.B.: Ancile: privacy-preserving framework for access control and interoperability of electronic health records using blockchain technology. Sustain. Cities Soc. **39**, 283–297 (2018)
10. Denyer, D., Tranfield, D.: Producing a systematic review (2009)
11. Dwivedi, A.D., Gautam, S., Dhar, S., Singh, R.: A decentralized privacy-preserving healthcare blockchain for IoT. Sensors **19**(2), 326 (2019)
12. Fernandez-Carames, T.M., Fraga-Lamas, P.: Towards next generation teaching, learning, and context-aware applications for higher education: a review on blockchain, IoT, Fog and edge computing enabled smart campuses and universities. Appl. Sci. **9**(21), 4479 (2019)
13. Ferraro, P., King, C., Shorten, R.: Distributed ledger technology for smart cities, the sharing economy, and social compliance. IEEE Access **6**, 62728–62746 (2018)
14. Giffinger, R., et al.: Smart Cities: Ranking of European Medium-Sized Cities. Vienna University of Technology, Vienna (2007)
15. Gong, S., et al.: Blockchain-based secure device management framework for an internet of things network in a smart city. Sustainability **11**(14), 3889 (2019)
16. Gori, P., Parcu, P.L., Stasi, M.: Smart Cities and Sharing Economy (2015)
17. Hadi, F.A., et al.: A vision of blockchain technology and its integration with IOT: applications, challenges, and opportunities; from the authentication perspective. J. Theor. Appl. Inf. Technol. **97**(15), 4048 (2019)
18. Hammi, M.T., Hammi, B., Bellot, P., Serhrouchni, A.: Bubbles of trust: a decentralized blockchain-based authentication system for IoT. Comput. Secur. **78**, 126–142 (2018)
19. Jo, J.H., Sharma, P.K., Sicato, J.C.S., Park, J.H.: Emerging technologies for sustainable smart city network security: issues, challenges, and counter measures. J. Inf. Process. Syst. **15**(4), 765–784 (2019)
20. Kamel Boulos, M.N., Wilson, J.T., Clauson, K.A.: Geospatial blockchain: promises, challenges, and scenarios in health and healthcare. Int. J. Health Geogr. **17**(25) (2018)
21. Karale, S., Ranaware, V.: Applications of blockchain technology in smart city development: a research. Int. J. Innov. Technol. Explor. Eng. **8**(11S) (2019)
22. Khan, M.A., Salah, K.: IoT security: review, blockchain solutions, and open challenges. Future Gener. Comput. Syst. **82**, 395–411 (2018)
23. Khan, Z., Abbasi, A.G., Pervez, Z.: Blockchain and edge computing-based architecture for participatory smart city applications. Concurr. Comput. Pract. Exp. (2019)
24. Khare, A., et al.: Design of a trustless smart city system: the #SmartME experiment. Internet Things (2019)
25. Kumar, S.E., Talasila, V., Pasumarthy, R.: A novel architecture to identify locations for real estate investment. Int. J. Inf. Manag. (2019)
26. Liao, D.-Y., Wang, X.: Applications of blockchain technology to logistics management in integrated casinos and entertainment. Informatics **5**(4), 44 (2018)
27. Liu, Y., et al.: Tornado: enabling blockchain in heterogeneous internet of things through a space-structured approach. IEEE Internet Things J. **7**(2), 1278–1286 (2020)
28. Marsal-Llacuna, M.-L.: Future living framework: is blockchain the next enabling network? Technol. Forecast. Soc. Chang. **128**, 226–234 (2018)
29. Mohanta, B.K., Jena, D., Satapathy, U.: Trust management in IOT enable healthcare system using ethereum based smart contract. Int. J. Sci. Technol. Res. **8**(9) (2019)
30. Nam, K., Dutt, C. S., Chathoth, P., Sajid Khan, M.: Blockchain technology for smart city and smart tourism: latest trends and challenges. Asia Pac. J. Tour. Res. (2019)
31. Park, L.W., Lee, S., Chang, H.: A sustainable home energy prosumer-chain methodolgoy with energy tags over the blockchain. Sustainability (2018)
32. Rahman, A., et al.: Blockchain and IoT-based cognitive edge framework for sharing economy services in a smart city. IEEE Access **7**, 18611–18621 (2019)

33. Rathore, S., Kwon, B.W., Park, J.H.: BlockSecIoTNet: blockchain-based decentralized security architecture for IoT network. J. Netw. Comput. Appl. **143**, 167–177 (2019)
34. Sa, B., Umamakeswari, A.: Role of blockchain in the internet-of-things (IoT). Int. J. Eng. Technol. **7**(2.24), 109–112 (2018)
35. Scekic, O., Nastic, S., Dustdar, S.: Blockchain-supported smart city platform for social value co-creation and exchange. IEEE Internet Comput. **23**(1), 19–28 (2018)
36. Sharma, P.K., Kumar, N., Park, J.H.: Blockchain-based distributed framework for automotive industry in a smart city. IEEE Trans. Industr. Inf. **15**(7), 4197–4205 (2019)
37. Sharma, P.K., Moon, S.Y., Park, J.H.: Block-VN: a distributed blockchain based vehicular network architecture in smart city. J. Inf. Process. Syst. **13**(1), 184–195 (2017)
38. Sharma, P.K., Park, J.H.: Blockchain based hybrid network architecture for the smart city. Future Gener. Comput. Syst. **86**, 650–655 (2018)
39. Shen, M., et al.: Privacy-preserving support vector machine training over blockchain-based encrypted IoT data in smart cities. IEEE Internet Things J. **6**(5), 7702–7712 (2019)
40. Silva, B.N., Khan, M., Han, K.: Towards sustainable smart cities: a review of trends, architectures, components, and open challenges in smart cities. Sustain. Cities Soc. **38**, 697–713 (2018)
41. Singh, S.K., Rathore, S., Park, J.H.: BlockIoTIntelligence: a blockchain-enabled intelligent IoT architecture with artificial intelligence. Future Gener. Comput. Syst. (2019)
42. Sun, J., Zhang, K.: Blockchain-based sharing services: what blockchain technology can contribute to smart cities. Financ. Innov. **2**(26), 1–9 (2016)
43. United Nations, Department of Economic and Social Affairs, Population Division:. World Urbanisation Prospects: The 2018 Revision (ST/ESA/SER.A/420). United Nations, New York (2019)
44. Wang, Y., Su, Z., Zhang, N.: BSIS: blockchain-based secure incentive scheme for energy delivery in vehicular energy network. IEEE Trans. Industr. Inf. **15**(6), 3620–3631 (2019)
45. Xie, J., et al.: A survey of blockchain techology applied to smart cities: research issues and challenges. IEEE Commun. Surv. Tutor. **21**(3), 2794–2830 (2019)
46. Yin, B., et al.: An efficient collaboration and incentive mechanism for internet of vehicles (IoV) with secured information exchange based on blockchains. IEEE Internet Things J. **7**(3), 1582–1593 (2020)
47. Yu, H., Yang, Z., Sinnott, R.O.: Decentralized big data auditing for smart city environments leveraging blockchain technology. IEEE Access **7**, 6288–6296 (2018)
48. Zhang, D., Yu, F.R., Yang, R.: Blockchain-based distributed software-defined vehicular networks: a dueling deep Q-learning approach. IEEE Trans. Cogn. Commun. Netw. **5**(4), 1086–1100 (2019)
49. Zhao, Y., et al.: Machine learning based privacy-preserving fair data trading in big data market. Inf. Sci. **478**, 449–460 (2019)
50. Zhou, Z., Wang, B., Guo, Y., Zhang, Y.: Blockchain and computational intelligence inspired incentive-compatible demand response in internet of electric vehicles. IEEE Trans. Emerg. Top. Comput. Intell. **3**(3) (2019)
51. Zou, S., et al.: Reportcoin: a novel blockchain-based incentive anonymous reporting system. IEEE Access **7**, 65544–65559 (2019)

Blockchain in Digital Government: Research Needs Identification

Demetrios Sarantis[1]([✉]), Charalampos Alexopoulos[2],
Yannis Charalabidis[2], Zoi Lachana[2], and Michalis Loutsaris[2]

[1] Operating Unit on Policy-Driven Electronic Governance, United Nations University, Guimarães, Portugal
sarantis@unu.edu
[2] Department of Information and Communication Systems Engineering, University of the Aegean, Samos, Greece
{alexop,yannisx,zoi,mloutsaris}@aegean.gr

Abstract. The so-called disruptive technologies play an important role in shaping the next generation of digital government: Government 3.0. This new stage places the focus on the data-driven and evidence-based decision and policy making. The prerequisite in achieving this stage is the seamless access to government data. The use of blockchain supports the interoperability-by-default concept in the creation of public services. At the same time blockchain is addressing another important problem governments facing across all over the world, namely, low level of citizens' trust. In this paper, the authors review literature and projects on blockchain as a tool for improving interoperability and trust in Government 3.0 and they outline the issues for further research in the area, taking into consideration the knowledge collected in existing projects and the opinions of experts in the domain. The research needs are synthesized a) by analysing recent EU-funded projects involving blockchain and b) by drawing a future scenario, which is evaluated by experts to formulate further research needs. Finally, fifteen research needs are identified for blockchain in digital government.

Keywords: Blockchain · Digital government · Distributed ledger technologies · Research needs

1 Introduction

Blockchain (BC) is "a distributed ledger that maintains a continually growing list of publicly accessible records, cryptographically secured from tampering and revision" [1]. BC technology can be used to improve the quality of government services [1] by ensuring greater transparency and accessibility of government information [2], by increasing interoperability through information-sharing across different organizations and assistance in building an individual credit system [3]. BC-based platforms can be used to give citizens or even businesses [4] access to reliable government information, which can in turn strengthen the government's credibility. Moreover, within the BC system, every transaction is recorded, which makes it easy to trace the parties

M. Themistocleous et al. (Eds.): EMCIS 2020, LNBIP 402, pp. 188–204, 2020.
https://doi.org/10.1007/978-3-030-63396-7_13

authorizing transactions and understand the scope of the transaction. It also means that data can be more easily and safely transferred between different organizations and promoting the integration of information amongst different organizations. Ølnes [5] reveals that storing certificates on the blockchain is a cost-effective way of storing and securing vital information. Thus, social benefits such as a more collaborative society could be a result of BC technology (BCT) usage in government [6].

Different scholars provide literature reviews of the use of BCT in government. Ølnes [5] shows that the majority of articles dealing with BCT focus primarily on the technology behind bitcoin and until 2015 there are few publications relative to BCT in government in the literature databases (including bitcoin, crypto currency technology, eGovernment, electronic government, e-Government etc.). The author suggests that in order to be a potential valuable technology for use in public sector, BCT needs to be more than a payment solution.

Generally, as OPSI [7] mentioned BCT has three goals to be achieved. These goals are: (a) Reduce or eliminate the need of a central authority, (b) Eliminate central points of failure and (c) Enable trust among people who don't know each other to directly conduct transactions.

As it was noted BCT is often used as a solution for the improvement of public services. Recent case studies include BCT for digital payments [8], providing academic certificates stored on the BCT at the University of Nicosia [9], a sovereign government–backed identity credential as a pilot (e-ID card) in Dutch [10] and healthcare, pensions, government performance, food safety and government divisions, all of which have close relationships with individuals' livelihood in China [11]. Furthermore, Dubai wants all government documentation to be transacted digitally by using blockchain. According to the Dubai blockchain strategy, government believes that adopting blockchain technology will save 5.5 billion dirham [12]. Also, NCSL [13] estimates that 10 percent of global GDP will be stored on BCT by 2027.

It is evident that blockchain is gaining momentum since the scientific community deals with the issue from different perspectives. It is also a relatively new topic in the digital government domain, and it lacks systematic review on the research directions towards the realisation of its true benefits. This paper tries to fulfil this gap identifying research needs and building a scenario around vehicles' life cycle management unveiling the true potential of the technology under study.

The remainder of this paper goes as follows: Sect. 2 presents the research method underlying our research; Sect. 3 illustrates the results of the analysis of the existing implementation of BTC, and the scenario analysis; Sect. 4 presents the identified research needs; finally, Sect. 5 concludes the paper.

2   Research Method

In the context of the research, a "research need" is a gap identified by relevant stakeholders as important and, if addressed, it will help to resolve a specific real-world problem [14]. A "specific real-world problem" in this paper refers to challenges of using blockchain elements in digital public service provisioning, where citizens should be engaged. The identification of research needs is done by employing two research methods: project analysis and scenario analysis.

Project analysis involved the study and synthesis of active and completed European Union (co-)funded projects applying blockchain technology in the public services. A total of sixteen projects were identified based on keyword search ('blockchain*') in the European Union's CORDIS database. The projects were analysed to identify research needs using the gap analysis method [15]. The addressed needs included topics that were researched in the project, while the identified research needs spotted gaps that were not necessarily researched or in any way addressed by the project. Such needs may relate to the 'future directions' mentioned in final reports or other deliverables of the projects.

The Scenario Technique is a common method to explore possible future developments in various fields of industry, commerce, and government [16, 17]. It was used in a number of digital government-related research projects as a tool for roadmapping and prognosis [18–21]. Scenarios are narrative texts (often accompanied by diagrams) describing the future state or situation in a specific domain [22]. They can provide different perspectives and viewpoints on the problem, which allows better understanding of potential future developments [23]. As such, scenarios are particularly useful for complex problems involving multiple stakeholders and dealing with a high degree of uncertainty as they allow considering multiple possible directions of the domain's evolution [19, 24]. Scenarios are generated by experts and/or through interactive workshops with relevant stakeholders. Then, each scenario is subsequently analysed to identify relevant topics or facets of research, again using a schema for the systematic analysis [25]. The next section summarises the main findings from the project and scenario analysis.

3 Analysis of Research Method

3.1 Project Analysis

A total of 16 blockchain-related projects (active and completed European Union (co-) funded projects) have been identified (presented in ANNEX I).

The current state of research around blockchain considers the following main topics:

- The creation of decentralized and distributed solutions and ecosystems, in favour of democratic engagement, transparency, citizen empowerment, security, data protection, and privacy.
- Concerns around the efficiency of the public services, the awareness about blockchain and its usefulness for societal problems.
- Implications, benefits, challenges and risks in the use of blockchain solutions for the creation of a digital society, for smart cities, cyber-physical systems, and infrastructure, including digital rights, risks propensity, use of appropriate governance models, consensus mechanisms and applications design.
- The challenges around legal aspects, ethics, and regulation of cryptocurrencies, financial services, and blockchain solutions.

- Benefits, challenges, and risks in the use of the technology for land registry, circular economy, collaborative economy, waste management, and e-voting.

3.2 Scenario Analysis

The following scenario has been generated by experts through interactive workshops with relevant stakeholders during the implementation of research project entitled 'Scientific foundations training and entrepreneurship activities in the domain of ICT - enabled Governance' (GOV3.0). This scenario is subsequently analysed to identify relevant topics or facets of blockchain research, using a schema for the systematic analysis.

A vehicle's life includes a variety of possible actions such as service, rent, accident involvement and resale. Apart from vehicle owner, several other stakeholders (e.g. companies, public sector organisations etc.) get involved during those actions. During vehicle's resale, for example, the parties involved in the agreement should follow a specific process, fill specific documents and satisfy some obligations (e.g. tax payment). In this transaction there is always a risk of intentional or unintentional information provision from one of the stakeholders. The buyer should ensure that the seller provides the correct certificate in order to avoid possible trouble with law (e.g. stolen car). On the other hand, the seller should ensure that the buyer undertakes the future obligations of the vehicle by registering it on the proper public organization [26] (Fig. 1).

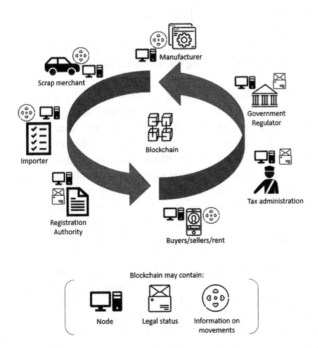

Fig. 1. Scenario "blockchain for vehicle lifecycle management"

Blockchain technology can be applied to implement a solution that can reliably assure the integrity of the transaction [26]. Transaction's data is stored in a blockchain and creates one shared record of the vehicle history. In this way data consistency, integrity and completeness are assured and possible issues likes fraud, mistakes and operational costs are minimized. Responsible public authority is the only stakeholder that controls and can update the registration information in the blockchain. Responsible public authority initiates the blockchain process by assigning vehicle ownership to the manufacturer. The manufacturer adds the model, chassis number and relevant information of the vehicle. Vehicle's resale is securely completed when seller initiates it, by using the chassis number of the vehicle, the byer's ID and the terms of the resale such as price, place and date of the transaction. The byer is instantly notified and can accept or reject the deal. When the byer fulfils all transaction's terms, the seller of the vehicle can complete the deal and transfer the ownership to the buyer. The advantages of this solution are achieved due to cryptography, consensus mechanisms, real time transactions and full transparency of vehicle's data [26].

4   Synthesis of Research Needs

Research, in the area of blockchain, needs to consider different aspects, such as scalability, security, data privacy, governance models, and legal issues, like the following:

- Identify the main challenges and needs to enable governments to create a scalable distributed network with blockchain technology.
- Identify how regulation should address the benefits of blockchain for society and how to reduce the risks for citizens.
- Characterization of a successful digital society from the perspective of the universal declaration of human rights and digital rights and evaluation of the contribution of blockchain.
- Potential use of blockchain for managing online identity and personal data in a citizen-friendly and privacy-aware way, considering data protection by design and privacy by default, giving citizens the control of their data and the possibility to authorization and disallowance of access to data in different situations.
- The role of the stakeholders in the ethics and governance model of blockchain solutions and its involvement in smart contracts and solution design process.
- Identification of success factors and main challenges in the use of blockchain for the circular economy, waste management, critical energy infrastructure protection, and security, electronic voting, biometric, and health data.
- Influence of blockchain for security issues in the context of smart cities projects.
- Advancements in the legal aspects regarding cryptocurrencies.
- The influence of big tech companies in the financial system of the future, possible scenarios, and how to deal with them. Regulation aspects for big tech companies dealing with cryptocurrencies globally.
- Implications and challenges of computational law
- Information asymmetry around big tech companies, collective risks for society, and the contribution of distributed and decentralized systems using blockchain.

- Compliance of blockchain technology with General Data Protection Regulation and how to deal with the right to be forgotten.
- Regulation of facial recognition and surveillance technology.
- Benefits, challenges, and capabilities development in public and private partnership of blockchain projects.
- Leapfrog in the use of blockchain by the government in developing countries.

The primary training needs are not only relative to blockchain technology, but they should also be linked to the new opportunities, challenges, and problems addressed by the technology, like the following:

- Definition of main concepts: blockchain technologies, smart contracts, governance models, consensus mechanisms, privacy by design solutions.
- Applications of BC in different areas: smart cities, cyber-physical systems and infrastructure, education, financial services, land registry, and e-voting, presenting the potential, risks, and challenges.
- Opportunities addressed by BC: citizen empowerment, appropriate governance models, ecosystem management, data protection, and privacy literacy, transparency in blockchain solutions, characterization of citizen digital rights and digital society, legal frameworks, involvement of stakeholders in governance models and smart contract design, public and private partnerships and the development of competencies.
- Challenges and problems addressed by BC: the centralization of the internet, scalability of blockchain solutions, information asymmetry in the context of big tech companies, regulations, compliance with general data protection regulation, myths, and realities around cryptocurrencies, how to deal with smart contracts and computational law.

5   Conclusions and Limitations

This study has conducted an analysis landscaping of BCT use in the public sector. Our findings indicate that BCT is starting to be considered as an enabling technology that can contribute to the openness and transparency of services in the public sector for many different services. Newest application scenarios could allow even waste management and fake news detection, as well as immigrants' identities provision and health records' management that could never been falsified. At the level of public administrations, record keeping constitutes the most widely used application area of BCT due to a series of advantageous technical properties related to the creation/verification of records, namely, speed, security, and transparency. Furthermore, this study concludes on the following results: (a) there is no standard way of implementing BCT in the public sector; (b) the preferable BCT type is the private one, since it offers better control and avoids scalability issues, (c) most of the current cases of BCT in the public domain have been applied to services, improving transactional and registry functionality, while in all cases (based on blockchain's capabilities) interoperability can be enhanced.

The identified research needs indicate directions for future research in the domain of digital governance. When explored, they will allow citizen engagement promotion and effective, efficient and attractive Government 3.0 services implementation. While some of the identified research directions (e.g. how regulation should address the benefits of blockchain for society) have been studied extensively, in some other domains (e.g., the role of the stakeholders in the ethics and governance model of blockchain solutions), more systematic focus on the digital government is needed to address the particular challenges.

Finally, some limitations of the current research need to be spotted. The project analysis was limited to the EU-funded projects, so projects from outside Europe and those funded by other organisations or private businesses were excluded. The use of scenario analysis mitigated this limitation to some extent by collecting further research needs not covered in the projects. Still, it should be acknowledged that in the paper, we do not aim at providing a comprehensive list of the research gaps in the domain. The identified fifteen research needs can serve as a suggestion for researchers aiming to advance blockchain in digital governance, underlining the areas where our understanding is still lacking

Acknowledgments. This paper is a result of the project "SmartEGOV: Harnessing EGOV for Smart Governance (Foundations, methods, Tools)/NORTE-01-0145-FEDER-000037", supported by Norte Portugal Regional Operational Programme (NORTE 2020), under the PORTUGAL 2020 Partnership Agreement, through the European Regional Development Fund (ERDF).

A Appendix

Acronym, Call, URL	Project description	Identified research needs	Identified training needs
ANITA (H2020), HTTP://WWW. ANITA-PROJECT. EU/	ANITA aims at improving investigation capabilities of LEAs by delivering a set of tools and techniques to efficiently address online illegal trafficking of counterfeit/falsified medicines, NPS, drugs, and weapons	- Systematic literature review about initiatives to deal with the use of cryptocurrencies for illegal activities - Advancements in the mitigation of the use of cryptocurrencies for online illegal trafficking	- Advancements in the mitigation of the use of cryptocurrencies for online illegal trafficking

(continued)

(continued)

Acronym, Call, URL	Project description	Identified research needs	Identified training needs
ARTICONF (H2020), HTTP://ARTICONF. EU/	ARTICONF addresses issues of trust, time-criticality and democratisation for a new generation of federated infrastructure, to fulfil the privacy, robustness, and autonomy related promises that proprietary social media platforms have failed to deliver so far	- Identification of the main problems with centralized social media, including issues related to privacy, predictability of behaviour, information asymmetry and the lack of transparency of business model - Opportunities and barriers for the use of blockchain for decentralized social media services	- Presentation of the main problems with centralized social media, including issues related to privacy, predictability of behaviour, information asymmetry and the lack of transparency of business model - Presentation of the benefits of decentralized social media and how blockchain can support it
CO3 (H2020), HTTP:// WWW. PROJECTCO3.EU/	CO3, Digital Disruptive Technologies to Co-create, Co-produce and Co-manage Open Public Services along with Citizens, aims at assessing the benefits and risks of disruptive technologies, namely: blockchain, augmented reality, geolocated social network, liquid democracy tools and gamification, in the co-creation, co-production and co-management of public services with citizens as PAs partners	- Identification of success factors and benefits for citizens in the use of blockchain technology for co-creation, co-production and co-management of public services. Suggestion to use multiple case studies research	- The benefits, risks and challenges in the use of blockchain for the co-creation, co-production and co-management of public services

(continued)

(continued)

Acronym, Call, URL	Project description	Identified research needs	Identified training needs
COHUBICOL(ERC), HTTP://WWW.COHUBICOL.COM/	COHUBICOL (Counting as a Human Being in the Era of Computational Law) will investigate how the prominence of counting and computation transforms many of the assumptions, operations and outcomes of the law	- Implications and challenges of computational law - History and advancements of computational law - Assumptions in the relation of smart contracts and computational law	- Computational law: history, advancements, challenges, risks and benefits - Smart contracts and computational law
D-CENT (FP7), HTTP://WWW.DCENTPROJECT.EU/	D-CENT (Decentralised Citizens ENgagement Technologies) was a Europe-wide project bringing together citizen-led organisations that have transformed democracy in the past years, and helping them in developing the next generation of open source, distributed, and privacy-aware tools for direct democracy and economic empowerment	- Analyse the impact of the centralization of the Internet in democracy and society - Identify the influence of decentralized and distributed platforms and free and open source solutions in democratic engagement - Verify how blockchain technology can be used as a distributed platform to citizen empowerment and transparency - Identify the privacy requirements to give citizens the control of their data in blockchain projects	- The journey of the centralization of the internet and its effects for society and democracy - Present the initiatives and trends related to the decentralization of platforms - The role, benefits and risks of blockchain in the context of distributed systems used by citizens - Requirements and pitfalls of data privacy in governmental blockchain solutions

(continued)

(*continued*)

Acronym, Call, URL	Project description	Identified research needs	Identified training needs
DECENTER (H2020), HTTP://WWW. DECENTER-PROJECT.EU/	DECENTER is a research and innovation project aiming to deliver a robust Fog Computing Platform, covering the whole Cloud-to-Things continuum, that will provide application-aware orchestration and provisioning of resources, driven by methods of Artificial Intelligence. The underlying infrastructure will span across borders into a federation, and will utilize blockchain and Smart Contracts to reach secure processing, automated operation and timely delivery of responses	- The use of smart contracts to customized service level agreements, its potential, challenges and risks	- Smart contracts, definitions, potential and barriers to its use
DECODE (H2020), HTTP:// DECODEPROJECT. EU/	DECODE will explore how to build a data-centric digital economy where data that is generated and gathered by citizens, the Internet of Things (IoT), and sensor networks is available for broader communal use, with	- Systematic literature review about the effect of the centralization of the Internet and big tech companies in innovation - The potential use of blockchain for managing online identity and personal data in a citizen-friendly and privacy-aware way	- Citizen digital rights - Open source and free software: differences, history, principles, computer user freedom, community and standards - Digital democracy - The effect of the centralization of the

(*continued*)

(*continued*)

Acronym, Call, URL	Project description	Identified research needs	Identified training needs
	appropriate privacy protections	- The potential of blockchain for decentralised ecosystems, sustainable and commons-based economy - The collective benefits of data protection and the collective risks of the lack of data protection - Information asymmetry around big tech companies and collective risks for society - Compliance of blockchain technology with General data protection regulation - Data protection by design and by default: Suggestion of multiple case study research	Internet in innovation - Information asymmetry around big tech companies and collective risks for society - The potential use of blockchain for managing online identity and personal data in a citizen-friendly and privacy-aware - General data protection regulation and blockchain: compliance and assumptions - Data protection by design and by default
DEFENDER (H2020), HTTP://DEFENDER-PROJECT.EU/	DEFENDER will adapt, integrate, upscale, deploy and validate a number of different technologies and operational blueprints with a view to develop a new approach to safeguard existing and future European CEI operation over cyber-physical-	- Contributions of blockchain for critical energy infrastructure protection and security	- Benefits of blockchain for critical energy infrastructure protection and security

(*continued*)

(continued)

Acronym, Call, URL	Project description	Identified research needs	Identified training needs
	social threats, based on a) novel protective concepts for lifecycle assessment, resilience and self-healing offering "security by design" and b) advanced intruder inspection and incident mitigation systems		
MARKET4.0 (H2020), HTTP://MARKET40. EU/	MARKET4.0 provides a peer-to-peer marketplace for 'plug & produce', a reference implementation and domain-specific implementation for three key equipment manufacturing markets. It improve the sales power of production equipment SMEs by allowing them to "plug" into the marketplace and "produce" solutions for their customers	- Systematic literature review about the security issues of cryptocurrencies	- Definition of cryptocurrencies, its developments, problems and potential - Myths and reality around cryptocurrencies - Regulation of cryptocurrencies
M-SEC (H2020), HTTP://WWW. MSECPROJECT.EU/	The M-Sec smart city platforms will be distributed and robust, and based on IoT, cloud, Big Data and blockchain technologies. Through this trusted infrastructure, IoT	- Systematic literature review about the influence of blockchain for security in the context of smart cities projects	- Definition, challenges and risks of smart cities - The use of blockchain for smart cities

(continued)

(*continued*)

Acronym, Call, URL	Project description	Identified research needs	Identified training needs
	stakeholders will be empowered to develop and operate new IoT applications for smart cities on top of smart objects		
P2PMODELS (ERC), HTTP://P2PMODELS. EU/	P2P Models is a large research project focused on building a new type of Collaborative Economy organizations, which are decentralized, democratic and economically sustainable harnessing the potentials of the blockchain	- Identification of self-enforcing rules for automatic governance and economic rewarding, in the use of blockchain for collaborative economy - Identification of factors influencing users empowerment in blockchain applications for collaborative economy	- Definition of agent-mediated organizations for collaborative communities - Opportunities, challenges and risks with the use of blockchain for collaborative economy
POSEID-ON (H2020), HTTP://WWW. POSEIDONPROJECT. EU/	The aim of the POSEIDON Project system is to eliminate legionella infection risks in every kind of water distribution and HVAC (heating, ventilation and air conditioning) systems	- Benefits of blockchain to end users for enabling data protection by design and by default	- Data protection by design and by default: history, technical and governance requirements, advancements
PTWIST (H2020), HTTP://WWW. PTWIST.EU/	PTwist aims to design, deploy, and validate an open platform which will twist plastic reuse practices, by boosting citizens awareness, circular economy practices, and sustainable	- Identification of success factors and main challenges in the use of blockchain for circular economy and/or waste management. Suggestion to do a	- Presentation of cases of open source and blockchain solutions for circular economy and/or waste management. Presentation of the main benefits and

(*continued*)

(*continued*)

Acronym, Call, URL	Project description	Identified research needs	Identified training needs
	innovation inline with the new plastics economy vision	multiple case studies research - Identify the factors influencing the implementation of open source solutions using blockchain for circular economy and/or waste management	challenges with the use of the technology for this purpose
QUALICHAIN (H2020), HTTP:// QUALICHAIN-PROJECT.EU/	QualiChain targets the creation, piloting and evaluation of a decentralised platform for storing, sharing and verifying education and employment qualifications and focuses on the assessment of the potential of blockchain technology, algorithmic techniques and computational intelligence for disrupting the domain of public education, as well as its interfaces with private education, the labour market, public sector administrative procedures and the wider socio-economic developments	- Potential use of blockchain for education and employment qualifications management - Identification of needs and requirements from the different stakeholders for the governance model and for the design of the solution	- Potential use of blockchain for the creation of ecosystems, with different stakeholders and requirements - Process for the involvement and requirements gathering from the stakeholders in the definition of a governance model for a blockchain solution

(*continued*)

(continued)

Acronym, Call, URL	Project description	Identified research needs	Identified training needs
SONNETS (H2020), HTTP://WWW. SONNETS-PROJECT. EU/	SONNETS' aims at renovating the way the public sector operates by suggesting a concrete set of actions that will place the public sector in the front line of tackling societal challenges, armoured with the right ammunition and with the right people that could take over the necessary tasks and activities	- How to increase the efficiency of public services in the identification, monitoring and early detection of societal needs - Propose a methodology to support the timely awareness of emerging technologies and their usefulness for societal problems	- Lessons learnt from developed countries with the use of blockchain for public services that can be useful for the leapfrog of developing countries
TITANIUM (H2020), HTTP://WWW. TITANIUM-PROJECT.EU/	TITANIUM has researched, developed, and validated novel data-driven techniques and solutions designed to support Law Enforcement Agencies (LEAs) charged with investigating criminal or terrorist activities involving virtual currencies and/or underground markets in the darknet	- Advancements in the legal aspects regarding cryptocurrencies - The influence of big tech companies in the financial system of the future, possible scenarios and how to deal with them - Regulation aspects for big tech companies dealing with cryptocurrencies globally - Legal and ethical framework for investigations of crime and terrorism on the internet: controversies and concerns	- The challenge to deal with the use of cryptocurrencies for money laundering and other illegal activities - Legal frameworks and compliance of cryptocurrencies

References

1. Hou, H.: The application of blockchain technology in e-government in China. In: 2017 26th International Conference on Computer Communications and Networks, ICCCN 2017 (2017). https://doi.org/10.1109/ICCCN.2017.8038519
2. Atzori, M.: Blockchain technology and decentralized governance: ithe state still necessary? (2015)
3. Alexopoulos, C., Charalabidis, Y., Androutsopoulou, A.: Benefits and obstacles of blockchain applications in e-government. In: Proceedings of the 52nd Hawaii International Conference on System Sciences, pp. 3377–3386 (2019)
4. Engelenburg, S.V., Janssen, M., Klievink, B.: Design of a software architecture supporting business-to-government information sharing to improve public safety and security: combining business rules, events and blockchain technology. J. Intell. Inf. Syst. (2017). (forthcoming)
5. Ølnes, S.: Beyond bitcoin enabling smart government using blockchain technology. In: Scholl, H.J., et al. (eds.) EGOVIS 2016. LNCS, vol. 9820, pp. 253–264. Springer, Cham (2016). https://doi.org/10.1007/978-3-319-44421-5_20
6. Swan, M.: Blockchain: Blueprint for a New Economy. O'Reilly Media, Inc., Newton (2015)
7. OPSI: Blockchain and its Use in the Public Sector (2018). https://oecd-opsi.org/wp-content/uploads/2018/06/Blockchains-Unchained-Slides.pdf
8. Kastelein, R.: EU Parliament Approves Blockchain and Cryptocurrency Task Force, 30 May 2016. http://www.the-blockchain.com/2016/05/30/eu-parliamentapproves-blockchain-and-cryptocurrency-task-force/
9. Narayanan, A., Bonneau, J., Felten, E., Miller, A., Goldfeder, S.: Bitcoin and Cryptocurrency Technologies: A Comprehensive Introduction. Princeton University Press, Princeton (2016)
10. Alexandre, A.: R3 Partners With Dutch Tech Company to Pilot Blockchain-Based Digital IDs (2018). https://cointelegraph.com/news/r3-partners-with-dutch-tech-company-to-pilot-blockchain-based-digital-ids
11. Gervais, A., Karame, G.O., Wüst, K., Glykantzis, V., Ritzdorf, H., Capkun, S.: On the security and performance of proof of work blockchains. In: Proceedings of the 2016 ACM SIGSAC Conference on Computer and Communications Security, pp. 3–16. ACM (2016)
12. Dubai Blockchain Strategy (2018). https://smartdubai.ae/en/Initiatives/Pages/DubaiBlockchainStrategy.aspx
13. NCSL: Blockchain Technology: An Emerging Public Policy Issue. LegisBrief, vol. 25, no. 44 (2017). http://www.ncsl.org/documents/legisbriefs/2017/lb_2544.pdf
14. Chang, S.M., Carey, T.S., Kato, E.U., Guise, J.M., Sanders, G.D.: Identifying research needs for improving health care. Ann. Intern. Med. 157, 439–445 (2012)
15. Pucihar, A., Bogataj, K., Wimmer, M.A.: ICT related eGovernment research: a methodology to analyse gaps and identify future research topics. In: Pinterič, U., Svete, U. (eds.) E-governance and e-business at the service of customer, pp. 229–241. FDV, Ljubljana (2007)
16. Ratcliffe, J.: Scenario building: a suitable method for strategic property planning? Prop. Manag. 18(2), 127–144 (2000)
17. Peterson, G.D., Cumming, G.S., Carpenter, S.R.: Scenario planning: a tool for conservation in an uncertain world. Conserv. Biol. 17(2), 358–366 (2003)
18. Xiaofeng, M., Wimmer, M.A.: eGovRTD2020 operational roadmapping methodology. In: Codagnone, M.A., Wimmer, C. (ed.s) Roadmapping eGovernment Research: Visions and Measures Towards Innovative Governments in 2020, pp. 31–34. MY Print snc di Guerinoni Marco & C., Clusone (2007)

19. Janssen, M., et al.: Scenario building for e-government in 2020: consolidating the results from regional workshops. In: Proceedings of Annual Hawaii International Conference System Sciences, pp. 296–297 (2007)
20. Majstorovic, D., Wimmer, M.A.: Future scenarios of ICT solutions for governance and policy modelling. In: ACM International Conference Proceeding Series (2014)
21. Ronzhyn, A., Spitzer, V., Wimmer, M.A.: Scenario technique to elicit research and training needs in digital government employing disruptive technologies. In: Proceedings of dg.o 2019: 20th Annual International Conference on Digital Government Research (dg.o 2019), 18 June 2019, Dubai, United Arab Emirates (2019)
22. Johnson, K.A., et al.: Using participatory scenarios to stimulate social learning for collaborative sustainable development. Ecol. Soc. **17**(2) (2012)
23. Carroll, J.M.: Five reasons for scenario-based design. In: Proceedings of the 32nd Hawaii International Conference on System Sciences, pp. 1–11 (1999)
24. Berkhout, F., Hertin, J., Jordan, A.: Socio-economic futures in climate change impact assessment: using scenarios as 'learning machines'. Glob. Environ. Change (2002)
25. Janssen, M., Van Der Duin, P., Wimmer, M.A.: Methodology for scenario building. In: Codagnone, C., Wimmer, M.A. (eds.) Roadmapping eGovernment Research: Visions and Measures towards Innovative Governments in 2020, pp. 21–27. MY Pring snc di Guerinoni Marco & C, Clusone (2007)
26. Berryhill, J., Bourgery, T., Hanson, A.: Blockchains unchained (2018)

An Exploratory Study of the Adoption of Blockchain Technology Among Australian Organizations: A Theoretical Model

Saleem Malik[1(✉)], Mehmood Chadhar[1], Madhu Chetty[1],
and Savanid Vatanasakdakul[2]

[1] School of Engineering, IT, and Physical Science, Federation University,
Ballarat, Australia
{smalik, m.chadhar, madhu.chetty}@federation.edu.au
[2] Information Systems, Carnegie Mellon University, Doha, Qatar
savanid@cmu.edu

Abstract. Scholarly and commercial literature indicates several applications of Blockchain Technology (BCT) in different industries e.g. health, finance, supply chain, government, and energy. Despite abundant benefits reported and growing prominence, BCT has been facing various challenges across the globe, including low adoption by organizations. There is a dearth of studies that examined the organizational adoption of blockchain technology, particularly in Australia. This lack of uptake provides the rationale to initiate this research to identify the factors influencing the Australian organizations to adopt BCT. To achieve this, we conducted a qualitative study based on the Technology, Organization, Environment (TOE) framework. The study proposes a theoretical model grounded on the findings of semi-structured interviews of blockchain experts in Australia. The proposed model shows that the organizational adoption of blockchain is influenced by perceived benefits, compatibility, and complexity, organization innovativeness, organizational learning capability, competitive intensity, government support, trading partner readiness, and standards uncertainty.

Keywords: Blockchain · Theoretical · Adoption · TOE · Australia

1 Introduction

Blockchain (BCT), widely known for Bitcoin and other cryptocurrencies, is a technology that works as a platform for decentralized transactions and data management. Transaction systems such as those found in banks are centralized, while the BCT is a decentralized system that provides secure, immutable, and timestamped data transmission over a peer to peer network without the involvement of any controlling intermediary [1]. BCT provides solutions to overcome many issues in today's digital business world, for example, lack of trusted partnership, security breaches, cyber-crimes, and frauds, which are the main hurdles in flourishing the digital industries. BCT paves the path for a paradigm shift from central control to distributed and decentralized authority by decomposing the governance structure and thus enables better decision

© Springer Nature Switzerland AG 2020
M. Themistocleous et al. (Eds.): EMCIS 2020, LNBIP 402, pp. 205–220, 2020.
https://doi.org/10.1007/978-3-030-63396-7_14

making [2]. There are several benefits of BCT reported for different industries such as finance, healthcare, supply chains, government, and energy [3, 4]. The BCT has also been contributing to the global trade volume [5, 6] and has the potential to revolutionize the world [7]. Google reported BCT among its top trends [8]. The Gartner, Forbes, Economist, and Fortune have also included BCT in its megatrends. Various global leading organizations, for example, IBM, Walmart, Microsoft have been finding ways to utilize BCT to enhance their business process and value [6, 9]. Despite all this, the review of scholarly and commercial literature reveals that blockchain is not adopted heavily by organizations all over the globe, and there exists a research gap to find the rationale for its low adoption [10–14]. This gap motivated us to investigate the factors that influence the adoption of BCT, particularly in Australia.

1.1 Why Did We Choose Australia?

Australia has been working with BCT for a long time and has highly invested to find ways to utilize BCT to offer e-services. One of its research agencies, CSIRO's Data61, has been developing national blockchain through which the Australian government has plans to integrate its different departments to coordinate and share their data. [15, 16]. The Australian government has recently started a BCT pilot project for trading water rights [17]. Recently it has developed a roadmap for BCT adoption. According to this roadmap, "the Australian government has provided support and funding for the government, private sector, and researchers, to foster innovation and collaboration around blockchain, through programs such as Austrade business missions to international markets; the Entrepreneur's Programme; Australian Research Council Grants; and Business Research and Innovation Initiative pilots" [18].

There is great support for BCT at the private level. Blockchain Australia, formerly known as the Australian Digital Commerce Association (ADCA), has actively been promoting the adoption of BCT among Australian organizations [19].

The Economist Intelligence Unit (EIU), a world reliable body, ranked Australia first in its technology readiness index [20], indicating that it has all the required infrastructure to embrace new technology like BCT. However, having all this support from the government and private sector, the Australian organizations have not adopted BCT heavily [21–23]. In other words, there is a definite need to address the key research question:

"What are the factors that influence the adoption of BCT among Australian organizations?"

The rest of the paper is as follows. Section 2 reports the literature review. Section 3 explains the theoretical foundations. Section 4 demonstrates the research methodology of this paper. Divided further into three subsections, the Sect. 5 elaborates the proposed research model and the impact of factors related to technological, organizational, and environmental contexts of the TOE framework. Section 6 concludes the paper, reports theoretical and practical contributions, and mentions the limitations of the research.

2   Literature Review

Most of the studies that explored BCT adoption are either conceptual or address the issue from an individual perspective and lack empirical evidence. For example, Streng [24], Duy, Hien [25], Parino, Beiró [26], and Batubara, Ubacht [27] proposed BCT use cases for organizations and governments. Kokina, Mancha [28] presented an overview of the BCT practices adopted by different accounting firms. A similar study was conducted by Taufiq, Hidayanto [29]. Wang, Chen [30] proposed a maturity model. However, their model is not derived from empirical evidence. Kamble, Gunasekaran [31] investigated factors influencing individuals to BCT adoption in the supply chain industry. Supranee and Rotchanakitumnuai [32] conducted a similar study in the Thai automotive industry. Another conceptual study in the supply chain was conducted by Kshetri and Loukoianova [33]. Few studies that investigated BCT adoption from an organizational perspective include: Holotiuk and Moormann [34] investigated the factors influencing organizational adoption of BCT in the finance industry of Germany. However, they did not include BCT-specific aspects and developed a general framework, based on the existing knowledge of adoption. Wong, Leong [10] conducted a similar study for the adoption of BCT among Malaysian SMEs in the supply chain business. Clohessy and Acton [35] explored the impact of top management support, organization size, and organizational readiness on the adoption of BCT in Ireland. Their study is limited to three selective factors only. Albrecht, Reichert [36] investigated the implementation of BCT in the energy sector. However, they do not provide any information about how the factors mentioned in their study influence the organizations to adopt BCT.

From the above literature review, it has become apparent that there exists no study that explores the factors influencing BCT adoption among Australian organizations.

3   Theoretical Foundations

The present study uses a theoretical lens approach suggested by Creswell and Creswell [37] and Strauss and Corbin [38]. They recommend the use of this approach when the phenomenon under investigation is unknown and unarticulated, and literature is scarce on the topic. This is very relevant to the adoption of BCT in Australia. The theoretical lens approach requires using a well-established theory as a starting point for further investigation of the phenomenon, but the researchers are encouraged to go beyond and do not confined with the starting theory only. They should be open to accepting any of the new findings coming out of the whole inquiry process. This approach, also known as theory elaboration [39], helps researchers to extract new insights that further extend the theory. This approach helps to shape the type of questions being asked, provides directions on how to collect and analyze the data, and gives information about the issues. Many of the past studies have utilized this approach to investigate the adoption of different technologies e.g. e-commerce [40], ICT [41], and business analytics [42].

To find an appropriate theory for exploring BCT adoption, we conducted an extensive literature review and observe that the adoption of technology occurs either at the individual level or at the organizational level. For the individual level adoption, researchers use various theories and models including the Theory of Reasoned Action (TRA), the Theory of Planned Behaviour (TBA), the Technology Acceptance Model (TAM), and Unified Theory of Acceptance and Use of Technology (UTAUT) enlisted in [43, 44]. The organizational level theories include the Technology-Organizational-Environment (TOE) framework [45], Diffusion of Innovation (DoI) [46], and the Institutional Theory [47].

The institutional theory emphasizes the role of the inter-organizational relationship in the organizational decision to adopt new technology; the DoI theory demonstrates that technology adoption is a linear process and the organizational decision to adopt new technology is influenced by the technological and organizational characteristics; the TOE framework states that the organizational decision to adopt new technology is influenced by the three contextual factors, namely, technology, organization, and environment. Compared to the other organizational theories, the TOE framework provides a better foundation to explain the organizational adoption of new technology because it overcomes or supplements the shortcomings of those theories [48]. Most of the organizational theories are considered as a variant of the TOE framework that further divide or extend dimensions of the TOE framework [49]. For example, the TOE framework comprises the technological and organizational contexts, which are part of the DoI theory. In addition, it contains the inter-organizational aspect of the Institutional Theory into its "Environment Context". Due to the robustness and comprehensiveness, many researchers used the TOE framework to explore the adoption of different technologies such as ERP [50], IoT [51], e-business [52]. Oliveira and Martins [48] and Baker [53] provided a review of the studies that utilized the TOE framework to examine the adoption technologies e.g. EDI, Open Systems, and RFID, etc. These empirical pieces of evidence provided us the rationale to select the TOE framework as a starting point to explore the factors influencing the adoption of BCT among Australian organizations.

4 Research Methodology

The study uses a qualitative research approach by conducted the semi-structured interviews of BCT experts and decision-makers working with different organizations in Australia. Considering the novelty of BCT and scarcity of literature on the organizational adoption of BCT among Australian organizations, we find qualitative research very appropriate to find the answer of the research question, as advised by Yin [54]. Soja, Themistocleous [55] suggests to carry out this kind of research by conducting the interviews of 'experts' in the subjects. We employed semi-structured interviews because of they provide flexibility and power to extract rich insights, identifying, and understanding viewpoints, making clarifications, and collecting supplementary information [54]. The interviewees for this study were selected very carefully based on the following predefined qualifying criteria: (1) they should be expert of BCT and have a minimum of three-five years of knowledge/experience, and (2) they should be working as decision-making position such as CEO, CTO etc. with organizations, which had adopted BCT or in the process of BCT adoption. We reached the potential participants through using multiple online platforms such as LinkedIn, Google, BCT related groups on Facebook, and snowball sampling methods. We also used our professional network. Although, the interviews were the main source of the primary data collection, however, the findings of this study were strengthened with the secondary data that were either provided by the participants or were collected through different online sources including websites of participants' organizations, government reports, white papers, literature. This triangulation of data enhances the reliability and validity of the findings [54]. We kept continuing to conduct interviews until the data saturation arrived i.e. new insight stopped coming out from the interviews. We conducted 23 online interviews. Every interview: lasted 30–60 min; recorded with the consent of the interviewees; conducted by a team of two persons, authors of this research who having extensive BCT knowledge, to remove intrinsic biases; transcribed and analyzed after its completion. After every interview, the participants were requested to confirm the major findings of the interview. later, they were provided a transcribed copy of the interview. An interview guide was prepared to ask specific questions. The guide comprised the interview questions that were mainly derived from the TOE framework. However, the participants were encouraged to report any of the factors pertinent to the organizational adoption of BCT in Australia. Organization-specific questions were also included in the interview guide. Table 1 shows the details of the participants and their organizations.

Table 1. Summary of the participants and organizations

Organizations	Participants	Interviews
IT	CEOs, Founders, Software Engineer, System Analyst, CTO, Project Manager	8
Finance	CEO, Founder, CTO	3
Travel	CEO, Technical Analyst	2
Education	Director	1
Government	Senior Computer Forensics Officer	1
Consulting	CEOs, Project Manager, Solution Architect	4
Legal	CEOs, Director	4
Total		23

We followed the guidelines of Strauss and Corbin [38] for the analysis of interview data using QSR NVivo tool. We performed multiple iterations of data analysis to extract relevant and valid findings. The underlying concepts were drawn by examining the transcribed interviews line-by-line. The identified concepts were grouped into different categories based on their similarity and differences. Finally, the categories were mapped with the TOE framework.

5 Proposed Theoretical Model

Based on the findings derived from the interview data, the study proposes a theoretical model (Fig. 1) that describes the factors affecting the organizational adoption of BCT in Australia. The model shows that the organizational adoption of BCT is influenced by the technological context, organizational contexts, and the environmental context. The technology context includes perceived benefits, perceived compatibility, and perceived complexity; organizational context consists of organization innovativeness, organizational learning capability, and top management support; environmental context contains competition intensity, government support, trading partner readiness, and standards uncertainty.

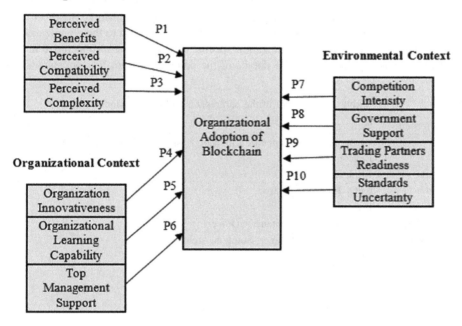

Fig. 1. Proposed theoretical model for the organizational adoption of BCT

The following sub-sections further explain the relationship of the TOE factors with the organizational adoption of BCT.

5.1 Technology Context

Perceived Benefits. Perceived benefits refer to the degree to which an organization perceives benefits from the use of technology. Many of the past studies consistently reported the positive influence of perceived benefits of different new technologies on their adoption among organizations. For example, Chwelos, Benbasat [56] and [57–59] studied the impact of perceived benefits on EDI, SCM, and B2B-commerce. AlBar and Hoque [60] reported a positive role of ERP advantages on its adoption. Barnes III and Xiao [61] say that an organization adopts BCT when it perceives that BCT will bring improvements to its business. Wong, Leong [10] says that organizations adopt BCT when they expect increased transparency and security in their business. Many benefits of using BCT are reported in the recent IS literature, for instance, transparency among transactions, improved accountability, fraud reduction, security, auditability, and traceability [62]. Therefore, we propose that:

P1. The more benefits of BCT are perceived, the more likely an organization will adopt BCT.

Perceived Compatibility. Perceived compatibility of technology refers to the perception of an organization towards its suitability with its values and technological infrastructure. It is considered an important factor for the adoption of new technology. If technology is more compatible with the existing needs of an organization, it has more likelihood of being adopted [63]. Kühn, Jacob [64] state that if BCT is not compatible with the organization's IT infrastructure, there are fewer chances of its adoption. Sadhya and Sadhya [65] state that the adoption of BCT requires organizations to procure or develop BCT related solutions that interoperate with their present legacy systems or transform their existing systems to be BCT compatible. They further mentioned that the use of BCT requires the consumption of extra energy, extra storage capacity, and skilled professional. Therefore, an organization, willing to adopt BCT, should make its existing infrastructure compatible with the aforementioned requirements of BCT. If BCT is not fit with the existing business processes, organizations will be unwilling to adopt [66]. We put forward the following proposition:

P2. The more compatibility of BCT with the existing system is perceived, the more likely an organization will adopt BCT.

Perceived Complexity. Perceived complexity refers to the degree to which organizations perceive technology is difficult in using and understanding. The adoption of technology is affected by the extent of simplicity or difficulty of using a particular technology [67]. If more complex a technology appears, organizations are unlikely to adopt it. For instance, Huang, Janz [57] found that the complexity of EDI negatively influenced organizations' intention to adopt I-EDI technology. The perceived complexity of technology makes organizations anxious about whether their employees would be able to understand and use a particular technology. Since the BCT appears analogous to inter-organizational systems like EDI, the past studies report the similar impact of perceived complexity on BCT adoption among organizations. Wong, Leong [10] found that the technical complexity of BCT was a challenge to Malaysian organizations to understand that adversely affected their decision to the adoption of BCT. The use of BCT requires public and private keys, hashing of blocks, and obscure addresses etc., which are considered complex processes by organizations [65]. Clohessy and Acton [35] reported the perceived complexity of BCT a barrier that negatively affects the organizational adoption of BCT. This leads to proposing the following:

P3. The more complex BCT is perceived, the less likely an organization will adopt BCT.

5.2 Organizational Context

Organizational Innovativeness. Innovativeness refers to the willingness and ability of an organization to adopt new technology for continuous improvement in its services [68]. Thong and Yap [69] relate organizational innovativeness to the management's acceptance of new ideas and technology. Newby, Nguyen [70] state that the innovativeness of an organization plays a significant role in its decision to adopt an innovation. In the case of BCT, we noted the organization that adopted it has a culture of openness to new ideas as stated by Venkatesh and Bala [71]. They further indicate that if there is a culture of innovativeness, an organization is more likely to adopt the inter-organizational system. Since BCT is an inter-organizational system, hence, we can hypothesize that:

P4. The more *innovative an organization is, the more likely it will adopt BCT.*

Organizational Learning Capability. Organizational Learning Capability (OLC) refers to an organization's ability to acquire new knowledge from its internal and external environment, and then store, disseminate, and implement that knowledge into its business decisions [72]. Organizational learning and information technology supplement each other [73]. Woiceshyn [74] states that the adoption of new technology depends on the capability of an organization to learn. Organizational learning provides an environment wherein organizations create new ideas, new knowledge is shared and applied that consequently leads to the adoption of an innovation [75] and Berta, Teare [76]. Takian, Sheikh [77] and [78] report the enabling role of organizational learning in the adoption of HER and ERP systems. Svetlik, Stavrou-Costea [79] demonstrates that OLC comes through the experimentation, risk-taking that is closely related to BCT. Kulkarni and Patil [80] state that the learning culture of an organization significantly influences the adoption of BCT. Therefore, we propose that:

P5. The more capable an organization to learn, the more likely it will adopt BCT.

Top Management Support. Top management is considered essential to the adoption of new technology. Haneem, Kama [81] show an influential role in the adoption of Master Data Management System adoption among Malaysian organizations. Koster and Borgman [82] indicate how management support positively influences the adoption of BCT in the Netherland. Similar results of the leadership support in organizational adoption of big data, ERP systems were found by [83, 84]. Hughes, Park [85] report that if the management is not supportive, BCT adoption within an organization is not possible. This is further supported by Houston, Acton [86] and Clohessy, Acton [87] regarding BCT adoption in Ireland. One of our interviewees reported, *"our organization adopted BCT because our management was very supportive and actively involved BCT related activities"*. Based on this piece of evidence, we propose that:

P6. *The more support top management provides, the more likely an organization will adopt BCT.*

5.3   Environment Context

Competition Intensity. Competition intensity (also called competitive or external pressure) refers to the degree that an organization feels pressure from its competitors in the market [88]. It forces organizations to adopt new technology quickly to perform their business better and gain a competitive advantage over their competitors. Sun, Cegielski [89] showed a significant role of competitive pressure in the organizational adoption of big data technologies. Zhu, Kraemer [90] mentions that technologies like BCT that provide information transparency and operational efficiency help organizations to maintain a competitive edge. Therefore, organizations tend to adopt those technologies. Competition intensity has long been recognized in the past studies on the adoption of inter-organizational systems like BCT, e-business, and EDI as an important driver [91, 92]. Wong, Leong [10] showed that competitive pressure played an important role in the adoption of BCT among Malaysian organizations. Barnes III and Xiao [61] postulated that when a business invests in BCT, competitors might follow suit and adopt BCT to maintain their competitive position. Kulkarni and Patil [80] reported competition intensity as a strong positive factor in the adoption of BCT among Indian organizations. Therefore, it is reasonable to propose:

P7. *The greater the intensity of competition, the more likely an organization will adopt BCT.*

Government Support. Government support is considered a major driving force in the organizational adoption of new technology [93]. Governments develop policies, regulations, and set up facilities that encourage organizations to adopt new technology. Lack of government regulations about new technology like BCT impedes organizations to adopt it [94]. Mills and Newbold [95] showed the positive influence of government support in the adoption of HER technology. Chong, Man [96] and Ilin, Ivetić [97] reported that the organizational adoption of big data technologies and ERP systems is not possible without the support of the government. Government positive and legitimate environment for new technology persuade organizations to its adoption. Koster and Borgman [82] state that government support speeds up the adoption of BCT among organizations. Some other studies [10, 80] have also reported government support a significant indicator for the successful adoption of BCT. This leads to propose:

P8. *The more support government provides, the more likely an organization will adopt BCT.*

Trading Partner Readiness. BCT, similar to any inter-organizational system like EDI requires strong collaboration and interaction among the trading partners [98]. The value of such inter-organizational systems is achieved at its fullest when all the trading partners have adopted it [91]. An organization alone can not decide the adoption of an inter-organizational system until its trading partners are financially and technologically ready for it [91]. Chang and Chen [99] states that the actions of an organization to adopt an inter-organizational system are dependent on the actions of its trading partners. Many studies have reported that trading partners play an important role in the adoption of inter-organizational systems, for instance, EDI, SCM, and e-commerce [100–102]. Since every organization has a different level of its financial resources and IT skills, therefore, when an organization is motivated to adopt an inter-organizational system can not adopt it due to the un-readiness of its trading partners [56]. Zhu, Kraemer [103] reports that a lack of trading partner readiness significantly inhabits organizations to adopt an inter-organizational system. Kühn, Jacob [64] state that an organization adopts BCT when its trading partners are ready to share their data over the BCT network. Hence, considering the positive impact of trading partner readiness on the organizational adoption of inter-organizational systems like BCT, we propose that:

P9. The more technically and financially trading partners are ready, the more likely an organization will adopt BCT.

Standards Uncertainty. Standards uncertainty has a substantial impact on the adoption of new technology like BCT because organizations feel reluctant to adopt a technology for which there exist no established standards in the market [71]. Organizations feel confident to adopt new technology when standards related to that technology become de-facto standards in the market [104]. To be compliant with the standards specification, organizations require substantial changes in their business processes. Standards uncertainty obstruct organizations to accurately predict whether the standards associated with new technology would become stable overtime or not. Venkatesh and Bala [71] state that the technologies that are still evolving significantly like BCT and their use vary from industry to industry; it is hard to estimate the certainty pertinent to their relevant standards. Consequently, it creates fear, among organizations, of losing investments due to adopting an uncertain technology. In the case of BCT, there are no clear standards regarding data privacy, funds transfer, smart contracts that impede organizations to its adoptions. Kühn, Jacob [64] found that standards uncertainty prohibit organizations to adopt BCT. This is further supported by Clohessy and Acton [35]. Sadhya and Sadhya [65] reports standards uncertainty a barrier inhibiting large-scale adoption of BCT. They further state that industry standards increase network effects that ultimately result in speedy adoption of BCT among organizations. These perspectives lead to the following proposition:

P10. The more uncertainty of BCT standards, the less likely an organization will adopt BCT.

6 Discussion and Conclusion

The study explores the factors affecting the adoption of BCT among Australian organizations and proposes a theoretical model. To achieve this, we employ a qualitative approach by using the theoretical lens of the TOE framework and conduct interviews of BCT experts and the decision-makers working with the organizations that had adopted BCT or in the process of adopting BCT. The proposed model conceptualizes and articulates all the relevant factors, which influence the adoption of BCT by organizations in Australia. The model shows that the adoption of BCT is influenced by the technological context (perceived benefits, compatibility, and complexity), organizational context (organization innovativeness, organizational learning capability, top management support), and environmental context (competition intensity, government support, trading partners readiness, and standards uncertainty) of an organization. The model validates the findings of the past studies, reports some new insights, and contributes to the existing body of knowledge both theoretically and practically.

From the theoretical perspective, the study extends the TOE framework by adding the BCT-related variables into its three main contexts from an Australian perspective. The theory-driven and data grounded model reported in this study describes the factors; most of them, for example, organization innovativeness, organization learning capability, trading partner readiness, and standards uncertainty, which were not reported in the prior studies of BCT adoption. Most of the past research on IT adoption used the TOE framework quantitatively; this study validates the TOE framework qualitatively. From the practical perspective, the model would help not only the Australian government and the organizations to address issues pertinent to the adoption of BCT in Australia. It would also provide guidelines to the multinational organizations, willing to expand their BCT products and services in Australia, to understand the adoption of BCT in Australia. The model would also provide valuable insights to the organizations when they decide to supplement their existing technologies with the BCT. The marketing and consulting firms could use the proposed model to understand the factors, which are important to reaching their audiences more efficiently. Although the research model is developed for identifying the factors in BCT adoption by the organizations in Australia, the model can be applied in BCT adoption in other countries having similar characteristics to Australia like New Zealand.

Despite the above-mentioned theoretical and practical contributions, the study has some limitations that create opportunities for future research. First, the proposed model is derived from the interviews of a small number of experts. Second, the study focuses on the Australian perspective only. In the future, a quantitative study will be conducted with a larger sample size to validate the proposed model and increase its external validity.

References

1. Nakamoto, S.: Bitcoin: a peer-to-peer electronic cash system (2008)
2. Aste, T., Tasca, P., Di Matteo, T.: Blockchain technologies: the foreseeable impact on society and industry. Computer **50**(9), 18–28 (2017)
3. Friedlmaier, M., Tumasjan, A., Welpe, I.M.: Disrupting industries with blockchain: the industry, venture capital funding, and regional distribution of blockchain ventures. In: Venture Capital Funding, and Regional Distribution of Blockchain Ventures, 22 September 2017. Proceedings of the 51st Annual Hawaii International Conference on System Sciences (HICSS) (2018)

4. Makridakis, S., Christodoulou, K.: Blockchain: current challenges and future prospects/applications. Future Internet **11**(12), 258 (2019)

5. Forum, W.E.: Trade Tech – A New Age for Trade and Supply Chain Finance, pp. 1–16 (2018)

6. Research, W.G.: Blockchain Market Shares, Market Strategies, and Market Forecasts, 2018 to 2024 (2018)

7. Ganne, E.: Can blockchain revolutionize international trade?. World Trade Organization (2018)

8. Google: Global news trends (2017). https://trends.google.com/trends/yis/2017/GLOBAL/. Accessed 01 Nov 2018

9. Council, B.: Top 10 companies that already adopted blockchain (2018). https://www.blockchain-council.org/blockchain/top-10-companies-that-have-already-adopted-block chain/. Accessed 20 Jan 2019

10. Wong, L.-W., et al.: Time to seize the digital evolution: adoption of blockchain in operations and supply chain management among Malaysian SMEs. Int. J. Inf. Manag. 101997 (2019)

11. Deloitte: Deloitte's 2018 global blockchain survey (2018)

12. PWC: PwC's Global Blockchain Survey 2018 (2018)

13. Woodside, J.M., Augustine Jr., F.K., Giberson, W.: Blockchain technology adoption status and strategies. J. Int. Technol. Inf. Manag. **26**(2), 65–93 (2017)

14. CA: The Future of Blockchain (2017)

15. DFAT: Advancing Australia's blockchain industry (2018)

16. Austrade: Australian Blockchain Mission to Consensus 2018, A.T.a.I. Commission, Editor (2018)

17. CRCNA: Australian government in Water Ledger blockchain for trading water rights (2020). https://crcna.com.au/research/projects/improving-water-markets-and-trading-through-new-digital-technologies. Accessed 2020

18. DISER: The National Blockchain Roadmap. pp. 1–52 (2020)

19. Australia, B.: Promoting blockchain innovation in Australia (2020). https://blockchainaustralia.org/. Accessed 2020

20. Unit, E.I.: Preparing for disruption Technological Readiness Ranking, pp. 1–21 (2018)

21. ACS: Blockchain 2030, A Look at the Future of Blockchain in Australia. Australian Computing Society (2019)

22. Ward, O., Rochemont, S.: Understanding Central Bank Digital Currencies (CBDC). Institute and Faculty of Actuaries (IFoA) (2019)

23. Australia: Opportunities and implications of blockchain in Australia (2016)

24. Streng, M.: Blockchain–the case for market adoption of the distributed ledger. In: Linnhoff-Popien, C., Schneider, R., Zaddach, M. (eds.) Digital Marketplaces Unleashedpp, pp. 65–70. Springer, Heidelberg (2018). https://doi.org/10.1007/978-3-662-49275-8_9

25. Duy, P.T., et al.: A survey on opportunities and challenges of blockchain technology adoption for revolutionary innovation. In: Proceedings of the Ninth International Symposium on Information and Communication Technology (2018)

26. Parino, F., Beiró, M.G., Gauvin, L.: Analysis of the bitcoin blockchain: socio-economic factors behind the adoption. EPJ Data Sci. **7**(1), 38 (2018)

27. Batubara, F.R., Ubacht, J., Janssen, M.: Challenges of blockchain technology adoption for e-government: a systematic literature review. In: Proceedings of the 19th Annual International Conference on Digital Government Research: Governance in the Data Age. ACM (2018)

28. Kokina, J., Mancha, R., Pachamanova, D.: Blockchain: emergent industry adoption and implications for accounting. J. Emerg. Technol. Acc. **14**(2), 91–100 (2017)

29. Taufiq, R., Hidayanto, A.N., Prabowo, H.: The affecting factors of blockchain technology adoption of payments systems in Indonesia banking industry. In: 2018 International Conference on Information Management and Technology (ICIMTech). IEEE (2018)
30. Wang, H., Chen, K., Xu, D.: A maturity model for blockchain adoption. Financ. Innov. **2** (1), 12 (2016)
31. Kamble, S., Gunasekaran, A., Arha, H.: Understanding the blockchain technology adoption in supply chains-Indian context. Int. J. Product. Res. 1–25 (2018)
32. Supranee, S., Rotchanakitumnuai, S.: The acceptance of the application of blockchain technology in the supply chain process of the Thai automotive industry. ICEB (2017)
33. Kshetri, N., Loukoianova, E.: Blockchain adoption in supply chain networks in Asia. IT Prof. **21**(1), 11–15 (2019)
34. Holotiuk, F., Moormann, J.: Organizational adoption of digital innovation: the case of blockchain technology (2018)
35. Clohessy, T., Acton, T.: Investigating the influence of organizational factors on blockchain adoption. Indus. Manag. Data Syst. (2019)
36. Albrecht, S., et al.: Dynamics of blockchain implementation - a case study from the energy sector. In: Proceedings of the 51st Hawaii International Conference on System Sciences (2018)
37. Creswell, J.W., Creswell, J.D.: Research Design: Qualitative, Quantitative, and Mixed Methods Approaches. Sage Publications, Upper Saddle River (2017)
38. Strauss, A., Corbin, J.: Basics of Qualitative Research. Sage Publications, Upper Saddle River (1990)
39. Fisher, G., Aguinis, H.: Using theory elaboration to make theoretical advancements. Org. Res. Methods **20**(3), 438–464 (2017)
40. Dwivedi, Y.K., Papazafeiropoulo, A., Scupola, A.: SMEs' e-commerce adoption: perspectives from Denmark and Australia. J. Enterp. Inf. Manag. (2009)
41. Leung, D., et al.: Applying the technology-organization-environment framework to explore ICT initial and continued adoption: an exploratory study of an independent hotel in Hong Kong. Tour. Recreat. Res. **40**(3), 391–406 (2015)
42. Ramanathan, R., et al.: Adoption of business analytics and impact on performance: a qualitative study in retail. Prod. Plan. Control **28**(11–12), 985–998 (2017)
43. Lai, P.: The literature review of technology adoption models and theories for the novelty technology. JISTEM-J. Inf. Syst. Technol. Manag. **14**(1), 21–38 (2017)
44. Taherdoost, H.: A review of technology acceptance and adoption models and theories. Procedia Manuf. **22**, 960–967 (2018)
45. Tornatsky, L., Fleischer, M.: The Process of Technology Innovation. Lexington Books, Lexington (1990)
46. Rogers, E.M.: Diffusion of Innovations. Simon and Schuster, New York (2003)
47. DiMaggio, P.J., Powell, W.W.: The iron cage revisited: institutional isomorphism and collective rationality in organizational fields. Am. Soc. Rev. 147–160 (1983)
48. Oliveira, T., Martins, M.F.: Literature review of information technology adoption models at firm level. Electron. J. Inf. Syst. Eval. **14**(1), 110 (2011)
49. Verma, S., Bhattacharyya, S.S.: Perceived strategic value-based adoption of big data analytics in emerging economy. J. Enterp. Inf. Manag. (2017)
50. Pan, M.-J., Jang, W.-Y.: Determinants of the adoption of enterprise resource planning within the technology-organization-environment framework: Taiwan's communications industry. J. Comput. Inf. Syst. **48**(3), 94–102 (2008)
51. Schmitt, G., et al.: Smart contracts and internet of things: a qualitative content analysis using the technology-organization-environment framework to identify key-determinants. Procedia Comput. Sci. **160**, 189–196 (2019)

52. Yeh, C.-H., Lee, G.-G., Pai, J.-C.: Using a technology-organization-environment framework to investigate the factors influencing e-business information technology capabilities. Inf. Dev. **31**(5), 435–450 (2015)
53. Baker, J.: The technology–organization–environment framework. In: Dwivedi, Y., Wade, M., Schneberger, S. (eds.) Information Systems Theory, vol. 28, pp. 231–245. Springer, New York (2012). https://doi.org/10.1007/978-1-4419-6108-2_12
54. Yin, R.K.: Case Study Research and Applications: Design and Methods. Sage Publications, Upper Saddle River (2017)
55. Soja, P., et al.: Determinants of enterprise system adoption across the system lifecycle: exploring the role of economic development. Inf. Syst. Manag. **32**(4), 341–363 (2015)
56. Chwelos, P., Benbasat, I., Dexter, A.S.: Empirical test of an EDI adoption model. Inf. Syst. Res. **12**(3), 304–321 (2001)
57. Huang, Z., Janz, B.D., Frolick, M.N.: A comprehensive examination of internet-EDI adoption. Inf. Syst. Manag. **25**(3), 273–286 (2008)
58. Kuan, K.K., Chau, P.Y.: A perception-based model for EDI adoption in small businesses using a technology–organization–environment framework. Inf. Manag. **38**(8), 507–521 (2001)
59. Saunders, C.S., Clark, S.: EDI adoption and implementation: a focus on interorganizational linkages. Inf. Resour. Manag. J. (IRMJ) **5**(1), 9–20 (1992)
60. AlBar, A.M., Hoque, M.R.: Factors affecting cloud ERP adoption in Saudi Arabia: an empirical study. Inf. Dev. 0266666917735677 (2017)
61. Barnes III, B.W., Xiao, B.: Organizational adoption of blockchain technology: an ecosystem perspective. Technology **12**, 15 (2019)
62. Grover, P., et al.: Perceived usefulness, ease of use and user acceptance of blockchain technology for digital transactions–insights from user-generated content on Twitter. Enterp. Inf. Syst. **13**(6), 771–800 (2019)
63. Alshamaileh, Y., et al.: Understanding the determinants of enterprise resource planning adoption in Jordan. In: 2017 8th International Conference on Information Technology (ICIT). IEEE (2017)
64. Kühn, O., Jacob, A., Schüller, M.: Blockchain adoption at German logistics service providers. In: Artificial Intelligence and Digital Transformation in Supply Chain Management: Innovative Approaches for Supply Chains. Proceedings of the Hamburg International Conference of Logistics (HICL), vol. 27. epubli GmbH, Berlin (2019)
65. Sadhya, V., Sadhya, H.: Barriers to adoption of blockchain technology (2018)
66. Kalaitzi, D., Jesus, V., Campelos, I.: Determinants of blockchain adoption and perceived benefits in food supply chains (2019)
67. Awa, H.O., Uko, J.P., Ukoha, O.: An empirical study of some critical adoption factors of ERP software. Int. J. Hum.-Comput. Interact. **33**(8), 609–622 (2017)
68. Tajeddini, K., Trueman, M., Larsen, G.: Examining the effect of market orientation on innovativeness. J. Mark. Manag. **22**(5–6), 529–551 (2006)
69. Thong, J.Y., Yap, C.-S.: CEO characteristics, organizational characteristics and information technology adoption in small businesses. Omega **23**(4), 429–442 (1995)
70. Newby, M., Nguyen, T.H., Waring, T.S.: Understanding customer relationship management technology adoption in small and medium-sized enterprises. J. Enterp. Inf. Manag. (2014)
71. Venkatesh, V., Bala, H.: Adoption and impacts of interorganizational business process standards: role of partnering synergy. Inf. Syst. Res. **23**(4), 1131–1157 (2012)
72. Jerez-Gómez, P., Céspedes-Lorente, J., Valle-Cabrera, R.: Organizational learning and compensation strategies: evidence from the Spanish chemical industry. Glob. Bus. Org. Excell. **26**(3), 51–72 (2007)

73. Malik, S., Chetty, M., Chadhar, M.: AIS Electronic Library (AISeL)
74. Woiceshyn, J.: Technology adoption: organizational learning in oil firms Jaana Woiceshyn. Org. Stud. **21**(6), 1095–1118 (2000)
75. Hua, Y., Chan, I.: Development of a conceptual model for organizational learning culture and innovation diffusion in construction. In: Proceedings of the 29th Annual ARCOM Conference. The Association of Researchers in Construction Management (ARCOM) (2013). The Proceedings' website is located at http://www.arcom.ac.uk/-docs/proceedings/
76. Berta, W., et al.: The contingencies of organizational learning in long-term care: factors that affect innovation adoption. Health Care Manag. Rev. **30**(4), 282–292 (2005)
77. Takian, A., Sheikh, A., Barber, N.: Organizational learning in the implementation and adoption of national electronic health records: case studies of two hospitals participating in the National Programme for Information Technology in England. Health Inform. J. **20**(3), 199–212 (2014)
78. Chadhar, M., Daneshgar, F.: Organizational learning and ERP post-implementation phase: a situated learning perspective. J. Inf. Technol. Theory Appl. (JITTA) **19**(2), 7 (2018)
79. Svetlik, I., et al.: Measuring organisational learning capability among the workforce. Int. J. Manpower (2007)
80. Kulkarni, M., Patil, K.: Block chain technology adoption for banking services-model based on technology-organization-environment theory (2020). SSRN 3563101
81. Haneem, F., et al.: Determinants of master data management adoption by local government organizations: an empirical study. Int. J. Inf. Manag. **45**, 25–43 (2019)
82. Koster, F., Borgman, H.: New kid on the block! Understanding blockchain adoption in the public sector. In: Proceedings of the 53rd Hawaii International Conference on System Sciences (2020)
83. Catherine, C., Abdurachman, E.: ERP system adoption analysis using TOE framework in Permata Hijau Group (PHG) Medan. Int. J. Enterp. Inf. Syst. (IJEIS) **14**(3), 91–105 (2018)
84. Angwar, H.: Understanding the determinants of big data adoption in India: an analysis of the manufacturing and services sectors. Inf. Resour. Manag. J. (IRMJ) **31**(4), 1–22 (2018)
85. Hughes, A., et al.: Beyond bitcoin: what blockchain and distributed ledger technologies mean for firms. Bus. Horiz. (2019)
86. Houston, M., et al.: Organisational factors that influence the blockchain adoption in Ireland: a study by JE Cairnes School of Business & Economics in association with the Blockchain Association of Ireland (2018)
87. Clohessy, T., Acton, T., Rogers, N.: Blockchain adoption: technological, organisational and environmental considerations. In: Treiblmaier, H., Beck, R. (eds.) Business Transformation Through Blockchain, pp. 47–76. Springer, Cham (2019). https://doi.org/10.1007/978-3-319-98911-2_2
88. Zhu, K., Kraemer, K.L., Dedrick, J.: Information technology payoff in e-business environments: an international perspective on value creation of e-business in the financial services industry. J. Manag. Inf. Syst. **21**(1), 17–54 (2004)
89. Sun, S., et al.: Understanding the factors affecting the organizational adoption of big data. J. Comput. Inf. Syst. **58**(3), 193–203 (2018)
90. Zhu, K., Kraemer, K.L., Xu, S.: The process of innovation assimilation by firms in different countries: a technology diffusion perspective on e-business. Manag. Sci. **52**(10), 1557–1576 (2006)
91. Iacovou, C.L., Benbasat, I., Dexter, A.S.: Electronic data interchange and small organizations: adoption and impact of technology. MIS Q. 465–485 (1995)
92. Zhu, K., Kraemer, K.L.: Post-adoption variations in usage and value of e-business by organizations: cross-country evidence from the retail industry. Inf. Syst. Res. **16**(1), 61–84 (2005)

93. Tan, M., Teo, T.S.: Factors influencing the adoption of internet banking. J. Assoc. Inf. Syst. **1**(1), 5 (2000)
94. Zamani, E.D., Giaglis, G.M.: With a little help from the miners: distributed ledger technology and market disintermediation. Ind. Manag. Data Syst. **118**(3), 637–652 (2018)
95. Mills, M., Newbold, S.K.: Creating a governmental policy framework for adoption of an electronic health record. Stud. Health Technol. Inform. **146**, 678–682 (2009)
96. Chong, W., Man, K., Rho, S.: Big data technology adoption in Chinese small and medium-sized enterprises. In: Proceedings of the International MultiConference of Engineers and Computer Scientists (2015)
97. Ilin, V., Ivetić, J., Simić, D.: Understanding the determinants of e-business adoption in ERP-enabled firms and non-ERP-enabled firms: a case study of the Western Balkan Peninsula. Technol. Forecast. Soc. Chang. **125**, 206–223 (2017)
98. Werner, F., et al.: Blockchain adoption from an interorganizational systems perspective–a mixed-methods approach. Inf. Syst. Manag. 1–16 (2020)
99. Chang, H.-L., Chen, S.-H.: Assessing the readiness of internet-based IOS and evaluating its impact on adoption. In: Proceedings of the 38th Annual Hawaii International Conference on System Sciences. IEEE (2005)
100. Yee-Loong Chong, A., et al.: Influence of interorganizational relationships on SMEs'e-business adoption. Internet Res. **19**(3), 313–331 (2009)
101. Shang, R.-A., Chen, C.C., Liu, Y.-C.: Internet EDI adoption factors: power, trust and vision. In: Proceedings of the 7th International Conference on Electronic Commerce. ACM (2005)
102. Chong, A.Y.-L., et al.: Do interorganisational relationships and knowledge-management practices enhance collaborative commerce adoption? Int. J. Prod. Res. **51**(7), 2006–2018 (2013)
103. Zhu, K., Kraemer, K., Xu, S.: Electronic business adoption by European firms: a cross-country assessment of the facilitators and inhibitors. Eur. J. Inf. Syst. **12**(4), 251–268 (2003)
104. David, P.A., Greenstein, S.: The economics of compatibility standards: an introduction to recent research. Econ. Innov. New Technol. **1**(1–2), 3–41 (1990)

Digital Government

Analyzing a Frugal Digital Transformation of a Widely Used Simple Public Service in Greece

Sophia Loukadounou[✉], Vasiliki Koutsona, and Euripidis Loukis

Department of Information and Communication Systems Engineering,
University of the Aegean, Samos, Greece
{icsdm618009,icsdm618008,eloukis}@aegean.gr

Abstract. The digital transformation of public services has been traditionally one of the main targets of digital government research and practice; however, it has focused mainly on the digital transformation of complex public services, based on the development of highly sophisticated and costly information systems (IS) for this purpose. Nevertheless, considerable public value can be generated through the digital transformation of widely used simpler public services as well, as it can result in huge savings of both public servants' and citizens' time, as well as improvements in the quality of these services. Furthermore, due to the financial resource constraints that governments of most countries face, it is important that this is implemented at a low cost, adopting a 'frugal innovation' approach. In this direction this paper: a) describes the 'frugal' low-cost digital transformation of a widely used simple public service in Greece, the 'certification of authenticity of signature', which is applied in two special forms, the 'formal declaration' and the 'authorization'; b) evaluates these novel e-services, based on an extension of 'Diffusion of Innovation' theory with an additional trust-related dimension, using both qualitative and quantitative techniques, and finally drawing interesting conclusions of wider interest and applicability.

Keywords: Digital transformation · Digital innovation · Frugal innovation · Digital public services · Diffusion of innovation · Greek Government

1 Introduction

Though innovation had been initially associated with resource-rich private firms of developed countries, subsequently there has been much interest among both researchers and practitioners in the development of lower cost innovation by private firms in the resource constrained contexts of developing countries, and later developed ones as well, and this gave rise to the development of 'frugal innovation' [1–7]; it is defined as 'a resource scarce solution (i.e., product, service, process, or business model) that is designed and implemented despite financial, technological, material or other resource constraints, whereby the final outcome is significantly cheaper than competitive offerings (if available) and is good enough to meet the basic needs of customers' [3]. Information systems (IS) can be important drivers or enablers of frugal innovation,

© Springer Nature Switzerland AG 2020
M. Themistocleous et al. (Eds.): EMCIS 2020, LNBIP 402, pp. 223–237, 2020.
https://doi.org/10.1007/978-3-030-63396-7_15

especially low-cost ones [5–7]. Considerable research has been conducted in this area of frugal innovation, motivated by the resource scarcity in the developing countries (in which live a large share of world's population), and also in some of the developed ones as well (especially in times of economic crises that repeatedly occur in market-based economies); this research investigates the inputs (resources), the success factors, the impediments and also the outputs (resulting low-cost products and services) of frugal innovation. A comprehensive review of this research on frugal innovation is provided in [2]. However, the research that has been conducted in this area concerns only frugal innovation in the private sector, while frugal innovation in the public sector has not been researched, despite the pressure that government agencies of most countries face to offer 'more with less': to provide more services, through traditional and digital channels, and also digitally transform the existing services, with continuously decreasing budgets [8, 9].

The digital transformation of public services has been traditionally one of the main targets of digital government research and practice [10]; however, it has focused so far mainly on the digital transformation of complex public services, such as taxation and social insurance - welfare ones (for instance see the main e-government services defined by the eGovernment Benchmark Reports of the European Commission, such as the most recent one [11]), based on the development of highly sophisticated information systems (IS), which are costly, take time and necessitate lengthy and complex procurement procedures. Nevertheless, considerable public value can be generated through the digital transformation of simpler public services as well, which are widely used by citizens, as it can result on one hand in huge savings of both public servants' and citizens' time, and on the other hand in significant improvements in the quality of the services offered to the citizens' and the jobs of the public servants (improving their work composition by eliminating mundane routine tasks). Furthermore, due to the financial resource constrains that governments of most countries face, as mentioned above, it is important that this digital transformation is implemented at a low cost, adopting a 'frugal innovation' approach.

In this direction this paper makes two contributions:

a) It describes the 'frugal' low-cost digital transformation of a widely used simple public service in Greece, the 'certification of authenticity of signature', which is applied in two special forms, the 'formal declaration' and the 'authorization'; it is based on a simple and low cost IS, which exploits existing authentication services of the well-established and highly mature taxation and banking information infrastructures of Greece.

b) It evaluates these novel e-services, based on an extension of the 'Diffusion of Innovation' theory with an additional trust-related dimension, using both qualitative and quantitative techniques, and finally drawing interesting conclusions concerning the frugal development of digital government and digital transformation of public services in national contexts of lower economic and technological development.

In the following Sect. 2 the background of this study is outlined, while in Sect. 3 the digital transformation of the abovementioned simple public service is presented.

The methodology of the evaluation of the new e-services is described in Sect. 4, followed by the results in Sect. 5, and the conclusions in the final Sect. 6.

2   Background

2.1   Public Sector Innovation

Although historically private sector firms have been more active with respect to innovation in their products, services and processes, the increasing problems and needs of modern societies as well as the emerging digital technologies are drivers of substantial innovation in the public sector organizations as well [12–18]. According to Windrum [12] the most usual types of innovation in the public sector concern the services they offer to society: 'service innovation' is defined as the introduction of a new service product or an improvement in the quality of an existing one, while 'service delivery innovation' is defined as the use of new or altered ways of delivering services to citizens, or otherwise interacting with them (including the use of digital channels for this purpose). Another important type of innovation in the public sector they define is the 'administrative and organizational innovation', which changes the organizational structures and routines by which front office staff produce services and/or back office staff support front office services. In the same study [12] have been defined three more types of innovation that are specific to the public sector: 'conceptual innovation', defined as the development of new world views that challenge assumptions that underpin existing service products, processes and organizational forms; 'policy innovations', which concern changes in the shared understanding of a social problem or need, the policy instruments and the roles of the policy actors; and 'systemic innovation' that involves new or improved ways of interacting with other organizations and knowledge bases. Chen et al. [13] developed a typology of innovations in public sector organizations, based on two dimensions: the 'innovation focus' (which can be strategy, capacity and operations) and the 'innovation locus' (which can be internal and external); so this typology includes six types of public sector innovations concerning mission, management, services (internal innovations), as well as policy, partner and mechanisms/platforms for citizen collaboration (external). Hartley et al. [17] propose and analyze three strategies for public sector innovation: a New Public Management oriented one, which emphasizes market competition; a neo-Weberian state oriented one, which emphasizes organizational entrepreneurship; and a collaborative governance oriented one, which emphasizes multi-actor engagement across organizations in the private, public, and non-profit sectors.

The digital technologies can be important drivers or enablers of incremental or even radical innovations in government agencies, concerning their processes, tasks, internal as well as external communication, services, or even business models, and also their relationships with citizens and other government agencies, which can lead to their 'digital transformation' [8, 9]. However, extensive research is required concerning the exploitation of this transformative potential of digital technologies in the public sector, and the realization of all these aspects of its digital transformation, in a context of financial resources scarcity, adopting as much as possible cost-efficient 'frugal innovation' approaches. Our study contributes in this direction.

2.2 Diffusion of Innovation

Furthermore, extensive research has been conducted for identifying factors that affect positively or negatively the diffusion of innovations, which has developed several diffusion models, with the most established and widely used of them being the 'Diffusion of Innovation' (DOI) theory of Rogers [19]; according to it the main characteristics of an innovation that affect its diffusion are:

- relative advantage (the degree to which an innovation is perceived as better than the idea it supersedes);
- compatibility (the degree to which an innovation is perceived as being consistent with the existing values, past experiences, and needs of potential adopters);
- complexity (the degree to which an innovation is perceived as difficult to understand and use);
- trialability (the degree to which an innovation may be experimented with on a limited basis);
- observability (the degree to which the results of an innovation are visible to others).

Furthermore, previous research has revealed that the adoption of both commercial e-services (such as e-commerce and e-banking ones) and non-commercial e-services (including public sector e-government ones) is influenced significantly by the degree of trust of the potential user to the technology and the provider of the e-service [11, 20–24]. In particular, this research concludes that the technology-mediated nature of the provision of e-services, and the lack of face-to-face interaction between the service consumer and the service provider (and especially of visual and physical clues) generate risk perceptions and uncertainties to the former; these can affect negatively the adoption of e-services, if they are not counter-balanced by consumer trust, meant as consumer's confidence in the ability, integrity and honesty of the provider, as well as the reliable operation of the whole technological and operational infrastructure. Citizens' trust is particularly important for the adoption of e-government services; a comprehensive review of relevant literature is provided by [24]. For all the above reasons our theoretical foundation for the evaluation of the new e-service is an extension of the DOI with the trust dimension.

3 Digital Transformation of a Simple Service

In this section is described the digital transformation of a simple (from a citizen/user perspective, based on the number and the complexity of the steps to be performed) and widely used public service: the 'certification of authenticity of signature', which is applied in two special forms: the 'formal declaration' and the 'authorization'. It is estimated that about thirty million performances of it were performed manually each year[1]. Initially is described its traditional paper-based form (in 3.1), and then its digital transformation (i.e. the new corresponding e-services) (in 3.2).

---

[1] According to "Certificate of Authentication: estimation of annual transactions and cost in Greece", submitted by Koutsona V. & Loukadounou S. in partial fulfillment of the requirements for master's degree in eGov, http://www.dgrc.gr/material_el/studies_el/gnisio-ypografis-metrisi-ke-ypologismos-synolikou-etisiou-kostous-gia-ti-chora/, 2020 .

3.1   Certification of Authenticity of Signature: Paper-Based Form

The 'certification of authenticity of a signature' is a public service provided in Greece, which is applied for the confirmation of the identity of the citizen signing a document, in order to certify the authenticity of the signature (i.e. that the stated signatory and holder of the document's statements is authentic, true and genuine, and not a different person from the stated one) [25]. In the paper-based form of this service the citizen visited a Citizens' Service Centre (CSC) branch or a Police Station, presented his/her identity card and signed on the document before a designated employee. The employee then made an annotation in the document with the details of the deed that was conducted by stamping the document. This process could be applied in any type of document, with no restrictions, and the content of it was not examined by the employee. The document's scope, therefore, was private. The activity diagram of the conventional paper-based service is shown in Fig. 1.

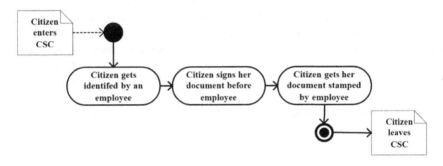

Fig. 1. Activity diagram of the conventional paper-based services

The certificate of authenticity of signature was applied in two special forms widely used: the 'formal declaration' and the 'authorization'. The 'formal declaration' was a legal document that was addressed to the public administration or an individual in order to provide information about the citizen for a legal requirement when no other evidence was available about it (e.g. having fulfilled an obligation). In such a document, the citizen declared under the law that they were personally accountable for their allegations and that they are susceptible to the legal penal sanctions if the allegations are false. The text of the document had no restrictions on its form and language in which it was drafted. The signatory is initially identified by a designated employee, and then the signature's authentication was applied/stamped on the document, which rendered it a formal legal document, with no time limit set for its usage. The formal declaration has been widely used in Greece due to the limited interoperability among the IS of different government agencies, which does not allow one government agency to access data stored in the IS of another one.

The 'authorization' was a written statement with which a person declared that they wish to be represented by someone else (for a specific activity concerning the public or private sector), and it was widely used in the public as well as the private sector. The personal details of the authorized person were indicated, as well as the description of the work they would perform for the grantor. The document could be used only once, and it expired with the fulfilment of the deed for which it had been authorized. It did not require a special form. Revoking it involved a relevant statement to the authorized person. The authentication of the signature was applied to the authorization document, after the identification of it by a designated employee, making the document a formal legal document; however, there were cases for which the representation required the power of attorney from a notary public.

3.2   The New e-Services

In order to use the new formal declaration and authorization e-services is initially required access to gov.gr via an internet-connected device. Both e-services include a web form with a set of steps that guide the users through each process. Following authentication, the users fill in their personal details, the declaration or authorization text and the name of the receiver. Upon submitting the form, an electronic document is created, with the above provided details embedded. A hash code and a QR code for the document are created as well. Both codes are used as a means of document validity verification: the hash code is suitable for verifying the electronic file, while the QR code is appropriate for its printed version. The electronic document can then be either

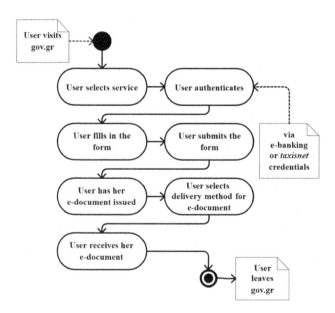

Fig. 2. Activity diagram of the new e-services

delivered as a URL via email and SMS to the users or saved locally. Also, the authorization issuance service provides revoking functionality. The activity diagram of the formal declaration and authorization e-services is shown in Fig. 2.

These declarations and authorizations are stored in a public sector server of the GRNET and can be verified by the receivers. In particular, the validity of a formal declaration or an authorization can be verified by the receiver, regardless of its form (which can be electronic or printed). For electronic documents, one could provide their hash code in a special form in gov.gr. For their printed version, one could scan their QR code via smartphone. The portal provided functionality for QR code scanning as well. Should the verification be successful, the receiver could access the online version of the document.

Only authenticated users can use these digital public services. In Greece there are limited public/private key authentication infrastructures, as well as limited use of digital certificates/signatures. For these reasons the implementation of user authentication for these e-services drew on the most mature nationwide authentication ICT infrastructures: the taxation (Ministry of Economy) and banking ones. In fact, two-factor authentication is applied within two discrete steps. Initially the users, if they are using these e-services for the first time, log in using their e-banking credentials to the banking ICT infrastructure. Their personal details as well as their mobile phone number are retrieved from it and recorded in gov.gr, since banks' data are regarded as highly accurate and reliable. This provides the user with the future options to log in using either their e-banking or their government taxation e-services (taxisnet) credentials. The second authentication step involves the users receiving a code number on their mobile phones (accessed from their e-banking accounts), which has to be submitted back in gov.gr. The whole process provides a highly reliable way of users' authentication, which did not require any complex and costly developments, but uses the most mature existing nationwide ICT infrastructures for authentication: the banking and taxation ones.

These e-services were internally developed in the public sector, by 'GRNET S.A.', a governmental company that provides various public bodies with network, cloud computing and ICT infrastructure services, by its existing internal personnel, leveraging their knowledge and expertise (concerning both technology and public sector processes and specificities), without employing any external human resources. Also, these e-services are hosted in the cloud infrastructures of the GRNET. This enabled on one hand the rapid development of these e-services, avoiding the lengthy and complex public procurement procedures defined by relevant legislation (usually resulting in high 'transaction costs'), and on the other hand the high-quality and low-cost operation and maintenance of these services in a central government cloud ICT infrastructure. For the above reasons the development and operation cost of the above e-services was quite low, so they can be definitely characterised as 'frugal innovations'.

4   Evaluation Methodology

The e-services described in the previous sections were evaluated using a combination of qualitative and quantitative techniques. Initially one of the researchers, who was an active employee in a CSC branch during the time of the study, conducted qualitative discussions with 22 citizens, who preferred accessing the services via the conventional physical channel rather than the digital one. The purpose of those discussions was to gain a better understanding of possible underlying barriers that prevented those citizens from using the new e-services.

Then a survey was conducted, using a questionnaire, based on an extension of the DOI with an additional trust-related dimension (see Sect. 2.2). It consists of three sections. In the first section the initial question asked the participants whether they had used at least one of the e-services (question A1), followed by a question concerning the frequency of making formal declarations or authorizations through the traditional physical channel (i.e. by visiting a CSC branch) before the new e-services were made available (question A2).

In the second section ten evaluation questions (all to be answered in a Likert scale 1–5) were included. Respondents that would not answer positively in the first question, could not have access to the evaluation section. Initially there were two questions for measuring the general satisfaction of the respondent with the e-services (question B1), as well as his/her intention to use them in the future (question B3). Also, there were seven questions designed carefully for assessing to what extent the respondent believes that these e-services have the first three characteristics defined by the DOI (relative advantage – question B2, complexity – questions B4, B8, B9, compatibility – questions B5, B6, B7), as they obviously have the other two (trialability and observability). Then followed a question (B10) concerning the level of trust the respondents felt towards the public sector, in terms of acknowledging the novel outcome of the e-services as valid (i.e. accepting the formal declaration/authorization issued electronically as valid). In the third section seven demographic-related questions were included, and also a question asking the respondent to write comments/remarks about these e-services in free text (question C8).

The above survey questionnaire was developed as an online Google Form. It was launched on the 14th of June 2020 and lasted for a week. The questionnaire link was distributed via social media and emails. 1274 responses were submitted, with 493 of them reporting that they had used both the manually and the digitally delivered services, so they were allowed to answer the evaluation questions of Sect. 2; so our analysis focused on these responses, while the remaining 781 ones were excluded as non-relevant. Detailed demographics of the above 493 respondents can be found in Tables 1 and 2. We can see in Table 1 that among our citizens' sample there was an almost equal representation of the genders, with most of them having higher education,

Table 1. Demographics of the sample

Age	18–30	31–55				>55	
	8.9%	68.2%				22.9%	
Gender	Male	Female				Other	
	51.0%	48.5%				0.5%	
Educational background	Primary	Second.	Vocat.		Higher	5	
	0.0%	6.3%	8.9%		81.1%	3.7%	
Occupation	1	2	3	4	5	6	7	8
	3.0%	10.5%	26.2%	36.7%	13.2%	4.9%	3.3%	2.2%

Table 2. Physical channel usage frequency

Question	1	2	3	4
How often did you visit a CSC branch to issue formal declarations/authorizations before the e-services were made available?	75.5%	21.3%	1.8%	1.4%

and belonging to the 31–55 years age group. In Table 2 we can see that most of them were rarely visiting a CSC branch to issue formal declarations or authorizations, before the e-services were made available.

5   Results

The initial qualitative part of our study based on discussions with 22 citizens, which revealed some interesting barriers to the use of these e-services. The most extensively mentioned barriers were poor awareness of the e-services' existence as well as lack of digital skills. A group of citizens raised a concern regarding the use of their internet banking credentials for authenticating in these digital public services, as they believed that revealing their internet banking credentials might pose risks of their misuse by government (e.g. for taxation or other purposes); this reveals an important mistrust in the government concerning the way of use of this banking-related data provided by the citizens, which affects negatively the attitude of citizens towards the use of these e-services. Moreover, another group of them preferred accessing the conventional services, because the text-to-be-declared by them was in such a special form (e.g. tables, images) that could not be accepted as an input to these e-services. This reveals that these e-services can meet the basic relevant needs of citizens, but cannot meet some more complex ones that may appear.

The survey results are shown in Table 3. We can see that 87.2% of respondents were either satisfied or very satisfied with the e-services, and 92.7% of them would continue using them in the future. Therefore, overall satisfaction and intention to use the e-services in the future were particularly high. Furthermore, 93.3% of the participants perceived these e-services as better or much better than the conventional paper-based ones provided through physical channels. So, the relative advantage of this innovation seems to be perceived as exceptionally high. Also, 84.8% of the participants

Table 3. Evaluation survey results

Question	1	2	3	4	5
Overall satisfaction					
How satisfied are you with the online service for issuing a formal declaration/authorization?	0.2%	1.8%	10.8%	41.0%	46.2%
Intention in future use					
Would you prefer to issue exclusively online a formal declaration/authorization via gov.gr in the future?	0.6%	1.6%	5.1%	21.5%	71.2%
Relative advantage					
Compared to the conventional way, how is the online service for issuing a formal declaration/authorization?	0.0%	1.2%	5.5%	31.6%	61.7%
Complexity					
How easy is the online service process for issuing a formal declaration/authorization?	0.4%	1.8%	13.0%	42.0%	42.8%
How satisfied are you with the means available to complete the text of a formal declaration/authorization in gov.gr?	0.2%	3.9%	17.2%	51.7%	27.0%
How satisfied are you with the means available for delivering the issued formal declaration/authorization to you? (sending by email, sending by SMS, save on the PC)	0.6%	0.8%	6.5%	45.2%	46.9%
Compatibility					
How compatible is this online service with the way you make transactions with the public sector?	7.7%	29.6%	14.2%	35.5%	13.0%
How compatible is this online service with the way you make transactions with the private sector?	2.0%	13.0%	22.9%	44.2%	17.9%
How satisfied are you with using taxisnet and internet banking credentials to authenticate yourself in the service?	2.8%	8.1%	9.9%	43.1%	36.1%
Trust					
How confident do you feel that the public body - receiver will accept the formal declaration/authorization issued electronically as valid?	1.8%	13.2%	14.8%	44.8%	25.4%

assessed the e-services as easy or very easy to use. In fact, 78.7% of the users were satisfied or very satisfied with the available text input features and 92.1% were satisfied or very satisfied with the available delivery ways of the electronic documents. Therefore, on the continuum of complexity - simplicity the innovation was perceived as highly simple and easy.

Regarding the compatibility of these e-services with past experiences concerning transactions within the public sector, 48.5% of the participants perceived using the specific e-services as either familiar or very familiar to them, but a considerable percentage of 37.3% of them perceived it as either unfamiliar or very unfamiliar. Regarding past experiences with transactions with the private sector 62.1% of the participants perceived using the specific e-services as either familiar or very familiar, while 15% perceived it as either unfamiliar or very unfamiliar to them. Therefore, these new e-services are to some extent compatible with the ways respondents transact with the private sector. Furthermore, they find the authentication procedure compliant with the ones they use for the taxation system taxisnet and the internet banking, since 79.2% of the respondents were at least satisfied with the use of taxisnet and internet banking credentials for authentication in these e-services.

Finally, with respect to trust, 25.4% of the respondents were completely certain and 44.8% of them were rather certain that the issued electronic documents would be acknowledged as valid by the public body – receiver; 14.8% were feeling neither certain nor uncertain whether the electronic documents were accepted, while 13.2% were rather uncertain and 1.8% were completely uncertain. Therefore 70.2% of the respondents perceive high or very high level of 'technical/operational' trust in these e-services, believing that they will finally work smoothly, and the recipients-receivers of these electronically issued formal declaration/authorizations (mainly rather conservative government agencies) will accept them as valid. However, a substantial number of respondents did not completely trust that the public sector would be flexible enough to welcome the novel outcome of these e-services, even though it was legally valid.

In the free text comments/remarks respondents point out some interesting aspects of these e-services:

– they are less time consuming and more convenient than the use of the conventional ones, since no commute and no waiting time were required, while the digital channel was accessible 24/7 from anywhere with an Internet connection available;
– they are more inclusive, in terms of reduced mobility affected groups, such as older people or people with certain disabilities;
– Greek nationals living abroad can benefit from them;
– however, people with no digital skills are excluded from their use, contributing to an increase of 'digital divide';

– though any identification document can be used as a means of identification of the citizens who accessed the services via the physical channel, this does not hold for the digital channel; it requires having internet banking credentials in one of the four Greek systemic banks, which constitutes a limitation, given the low level of internet banking use in Greece.

6 Conclusions

In the previous sections has been described and evaluated the low-cost 'frugal' digital transformation of a widely used simple public service, the 'certification of authenticity of signature', which is applied in two special forms: the 'formal declaration' and the 'authorization'. It has been based on the 'internal' development (by a public sector organization, the GRNET) of a simple and low cost IS, which exploits existing well established and mature taxation and banking ICT infrastructures (widely used and highly trusted by citizens) for users' authentication, addressing in this 'smart' way the limited adoption of digital certificates/signatures in Greece. Furthermore, these e-services are hosted in the central government cloud ICT infrastructure of the same organization, which results in high-quality and low-cost operation and maintenance of them. A first evaluation of these e-services has found that they possess to a good extent the necessary characteristics for wide diffusion according to the DOI:relative advantage, low complexity and compatibility. Also, it revealed a high level of 'technical/operational' trust in these new e-services, but also lower level of trust concerning the use by the government of the banking-related data provided by the users (perceiving risks of possible misuse of them for other purposes). Furthermore, it identified some weaknesses of these e-services with respect to the capabilities they provide for meeting some more sophisticated needs of the users beyond the basic ones (e.g. formal declarations and authorizations involving special forms of content, such as tables, images, etc.; and also risks of increasing 'digital divide').

Our study has significant implications for research and practice in the areas of 'frugal' digital innovation in the public sector, and especially 'frugal digital transformation' of government services and agencies, especially concerning simple but widely used public services. It reveals that the importance of trust for the adoption of such innovations, indicating that the widely used classical DOI theory [19] sometimes has to be extended with trust-related dimensions, and this is quite useful for future relevant research. Furthermore, our study creates some new practically useful knowledge in the above two areas, filling existing gaps, and revealing a generally applicable model by government agencies for low-cost 'frugal' digital innovation and transformations in the public sector: it leverages to the highest possible extent existing public and private sector mature ICT infrastructures, as well as 'internal' public sector knowledge and expertise, human resources and assets (such as equipment and systems, as well as data and digital registries concerning citizens, firms, cars, etc.). This model can be quite useful for designing and implementing similar public sector innovation and transformations in the future, in conditions of scarcity of government financial resources both in developing and developed countries, by exploiting the extensive functionalities and data of large and mature government IS.

Appendix – Survey Questionnaire

A. Formal Declaration / Authorization				
A1	Have you made a formal declaration or authorization via gov.gr			
	1. No		2. Yes		
A2	How often did you make formal declarations or authorizations by visiting a Citizens Service Centre branch before the new online services were made available?			
	1. Rarely	2. 1 - 5 times a month	3. 6 - 10 times a month	4. More than 10 times a month
B. Evaluation of the Online Services				
B1	How satisfied are you with the online service for issuing a formal declaration / authorization?			
	1. Very dissatisfied	2. Rather dissatisfied	3. Neutral	4. Rather satisfied	5. Very satisfied
B2	Compared to the conventional way, how is the online service for issuing a formal declaration / authorization?			
	1. Much worse	2. Rather worse	3. Similar	3. Rather better	4. Much better
B3	Would you prefer to issue exclusively online a formal declaration / authorization via gov.gr in the future?			
	1. Definitely no	2. Probably not	3. Maybe	4. Probably yes	5. Definitely yes
B4	How easy is the online service process for issuing a formal declaration / authorization?			
	1. Very difficult	2. Rather difficult	3. Moderate	4. Rather easy	5. Very easy
B5	How compatible is this online service with the way you make transactions with the public sector?			
	1. Quite incompatible	2. Rather incompatible	3. Neutral	4. Rather compatible	5. Quite compatible
B6	How compatible is this online service with the way you make transactions with the private sector?			
	1. Quite incompatible	2. Rather incompatible	3. Neutral	4. Rather compatible	5. Quite compatible
B7	How satisfied are you with using taxisnet and web banking codes to authenticate yourself in the service?			
	1. Very dissatisfied	2. Rather dissatisfied	3. Neutral	4. Rather satisfied	5. Very satisfied
B8	How satisfied are you with the means available to complete the text of the formal declaration/authorization on gov.gr? (free text, forms)			
	1. Very dissatisfied	2. Rather dissatisfied	3. Neutral	4. Rather satisfied	5. Very satisfied
B9	How satisfied are you with the means available of handling the formal declaration /authorization on gov.gr? (sending by email, sending by SMS, save on the PC)			
	1. Very dissatisfied	2. Rather dissatisfied	3. Neutral	4. Rather satisfied	5. Very satisfied
B10	How confident do you feel that the recipient-receiver will accept the formal declaration/authorization issued electronically as valid?			
	1. Uncertain	2. Rather uncertain	3. Neutral	4. Rather certain	5. Certain
C. Other Information				
C1	How often do you shop online?			
	1. Never	2. Rarely	3. Occasionally	4. Often	5. Very often
C2	How often do you use e-banking?			
	1. Never	2. Rarely	3. Occasionally	4. Often	5. Very often
C3	How often do you use online transactions with the public sector?			
	1. Never	2. Rarely	3. Occasionally	4. Often	5. Very often
C4	Age			
	1. 18-30	2. 31-55		3. >55	
C5	Gender			
	1. Male	2. Female		3. Other	
C6	Educational background			
	1. Primary education	2. Secondary education	3. Vocational education	4. Higher education	Other
C7	Occupation			
	1. Unemployed	2. Student	3. Private sector employee	4. Public servant	5.Freelancer	6. Business owner	7. Retired	8. Other
C8	Comments			
	Optionally fill in any comments you want to make about your answers or anything related to the digital services of the formal declaration and authorization			

References

1. Weyrauch, T., Herstatt, C.: What is frugal innovation? Three defining criteria. J. Frugal Innov. **2**(1), 1–17 (2016). https://doi.org/10.1186/s40669-016-0005-y
2. Hossain, M.: Frugal innovation: a review and research agenda. J. Clean. Prod. **182**, 926–936 (2018)
3. Hossain, M., Simula, H., Halme, M.: Can frugal go global? Diffusion patterns of frugal innovations. Technol. Soc. **46**, 132–139 (2016)
4. Agarwal, N., Grottke, M., Mishra, S., Brem, A.: A systematic literature review of constraint-based innovations: state of the art and future perspectives. IEEE Trans. Eng. Manag. **64**(1), 3–15 (2017)
5. Ahuja, S., Chan, Y.: Beyond traditional IT-enabled innovation: exploring frugal IT capabilities. In: Twentieth Americas Conference on Information Systems (AMCIS), Savannah (2014)
6. Ahuja, S., Chan, Y.: The enabling role of IT in frugal innovation. In: Thirty Fifth International Conference on Information Systems, Auckland (2014)
7. Tan, F., Ky, D., Barney, T.: Toward a process theory of IT-enabled frugal innovation: the role of organizational bricolage in Koufu Singapore. In: Pacific Conference on Information Systems, Taiwan (2016)
8. Pedersen, K.: E-government transformations: challenges and strategies. Transform. Gov. People Process Policy **12**(1), 84–109 (2018)
9. Mergel, I., Edelmann, N., Haug, N.: Defining digital transformation: results from expert interviews. Gov. Inf. Q. **36**(4), 1–16 (2019)
10. Alruwaie, M., El-Haddadeh, R., Weerakkody, V.: Citizens' continuous use of eGovernment services: the role of self-efficacy, outcome expectations and satisfaction. Gov. Inf. Q. **37**(3), 1–11 (2020)
11. European Commission: eGovernment Benchmark 2019 - Empowering Europeans Through Trusted Digital Public Services. Publications Office of the European Union, Luxemburg (2019)
12. Windrum, P.: Innovation and entrepreneurship in public services. In: Innovation Public Sector Services: Entrepreneurship, Creativity and Management, pp. 3–20. Edward Elgar, Cheltenham UK (2008)
13. Chen, J., Walker, R., Sawhney, M.: Public service innovation: a typology. Publ. Manag. Rev. (2019)
14. Torugsa, N., Arundel, A.: Complexity of innovation in the public sector: a workgroup-level analysis of related factors and outcomes. Publ. Manag. Rev. **18**, 392–416 (2016)
15. Walker, R.M.: Innovation type and diffusion: an empirical analysis of local government. Publ. Adm. **84**, 311–355 (2006)
16. Moore, M., Hartley, J.: Innovations in governance. Publ. Manag. Rev. **10**, 3–20 (2008)
17. Hartley, J., Sørensen, E., Torfing, J.: Collaborative innovation: a viable alternative to market competition and organizational entrepreneurship. Publ. Adm. Rev. **73**, 821–830 (2013)
18. Torfing, J., Ansell, C.: Strengthening political leadership and policy innovation through the expansion of collaborative forms of governance. Publ. Manag. Rev. **19**, 37–54 (2017)
19. Rogers, E.: Diffusion of Innovations, 5th edn. The Free Press, New York (2003)
20. Hsu, M.H., Chuang, L.W., Hsu, C.S.: Understanding online shopping intention: the roles of four types of trust and their antecedents. Internet Res. **24**(3), 332–352 (2014)
21. Mpinganjira, M.: Use of e-government services: the role of trust. Int. J. Emerg. Mark. **10**(4), 622–633 (2015)

22. Fakhoury, R., Aubert, B.: Citizenship, trust, and behavioural intentions to use public e-services: the case of Lebanon. Int. J. Inf. Manag. **35**(3), 346–351 (2015)
23. Mou, J., Shin, D.H., Cohen, J.F.: Trust and risk in consumer acceptance of e-services. Electron. Commer. Res. **17**, 255–288 (2017)
24. Alzahrani, L., Al-Karaghouli, W., Vishanth Weerakkody, V.: Analysing the critical factors influencing trust in e-government adoption from citizens' perspective: a systematic review and a conceptual framework. Int. Bus. Rev. **26**(1), 164–175 (2017)
25. Administrative procedure code 45B/1999, Greek Republic (1999)

Why are Rankings of 'Smart Cities' Lacking? An Analysis of Two Decades of e-Government Benchmarking

Mariusz Luterek[(✉)]

Department of Journalism, Information and Book Studies, University of Warsaw,
Warsaw, Poland
m.luterek@uw.edu.pl

Abstract. This paper aims to discuss current approaches to smart city rankings following the main thesis that two decades of e-government benchmarking should be used as a source of inspiration on how to evaluate smart government. We use critical analysis of selected smart-city and two major e-government rankings for this purpose. As our findings show, smart city rankings are lacking for several reasons: there is no consensus on what a smart city is, there are no defined development stages, smart city rankings tend to use quantity indicators or concentrate on the supply-side, and they often suffer from dimension or company biases and often lack methodological transparency.

Keywords: e-Government · Digital government · e-Government ranking · Benchmarking

1 Introduction

The general understanding of e-government is that it "employs technology, particularly the Internet, to enhance the access to and delivery of government information and services to citizens, businesses, government employees, and other agencies" [1]. However, the number of associated concepts has grown significantly through the years (e.g.: e-inclusion [2], e-participation [3], ubiquitous service delivery [4], open government [5], transparency [6], Big Data [7]). Consequently, although e-government is being globally benchmarked for two decades now, it still faces challenges, partly due to changing technological and political environments forcing continuous development. Researchers disagree on what indicators describe the phenomenon the best and what methodology should be used (quantitative vs. qualitative) [8]. However, the consensus is that those rankings should include data referring to both supply and demand-side [9], with the addition of usability benchmarks defined through content analysis [10], as a way to evaluate user-centered approach [11].

A smart city is understood here as intelligent solutions that allow modern cities to enhance the quality of the services provided to citizens in the urban environment [12]. Similarly to e-government, it is a complexed concept, continuously challenged by the rise of new ideas (e.g., ubiquitous city [13], resilient city [14], sustainable city [15]). It is not surprising, as the smart government is sometimes seen as the next level of e-

© Springer Nature Switzerland AG 2020
M. Themistocleous et al. (Eds.): EMCIS 2020, LNBIP 402, pp. 238–255, 2020.
https://doi.org/10.1007/978-3-030-63396-7_16

government development [16], and extension of the traditional four stages e-gov model, including catalog, transaction, vertical integration, and horizontal integration [17]. In this approach Big Data and data analytics (data-driven government), combined with super-applications, can lead to the emergence of a more proactive decision-making government – which is a form of smart government and provides services under the idea of Government as a Platform [18]. The main difference is that e-government refers mostly to the provision of information and services at a larger scale and is anchored at the national level (especially in the technological and legal contexts) [19], while the smart city concept refers to urban environments.

With over two decades of e-government rankings, the research community has produced a lot of output [20] on how to measure and what to measure [21], and what is the purpose of the measurement [22]. However, it still has not reached a consensus on the topic. There is a visible diversity, but also incoherence of benchmarks, which are being sometimes accused of being disconnected from traditional "analog" context [23], providing limited informational value [24], focusing on the provision-side [25], lacking in capturing the essence of quality of services provision [26, 27] as well as user's attitudes [28], and not providing data on how the government is changing through the usage of ICT [19]. Successful implementation of e-government is, for some, related to the existence of proper strategies and development plans, thus underlying another set of contextual political indices [29], and to others it is related solely to the level of investment in ICT infrastructure [30]. Additionally, a gradually changing technological environment calls for constant adjustment of related indices [31, 32], especially in the case of developing countries where the affordability of technology becomes an important factor [33]. That's why there is a lot of scientific discussion on bench-marking's statistical aspects [8, 23], but it also makes the general approach to how to measure digital government even more important – defining the stages of e-gov development we want to use in benchmarking models [34].

Smart city benchmarking leads to a new set challenges, as it covers a much broader spectrum of problems related to data acquisition and analysis, opening doors to dis-cussing its influence on a selected dimension (e.g., city's health system [35] or sus-tainability [36]), given institution [37] or cities from a specific country [38, 39]. In 2016 [40] identified 26 smart city benchmarking tools, and the number is growing.

The relation between e-government and smart government benchmarking is not often discussed, although it does not go unnoticed, especially in the context of local administration [41]. Furthermore, local e-government services tend to be included in smart city benchmarking indicators.

This paper aims to discuss current approaches to smart city rankings following the main thesis that two decades of e-government benchmarking should be used as a source of inspiration on how to evaluate smart government. For this purpose, we use critical analysis of selected smart-city and e-government rankings to foster discussion on how to assess smart phenomena.

The remainder of this paper is organized as follows. First, we discuss the methodological approach and limitations; then, we describe selected smart city rank-ings, followed by a deeper analysis of e-government rankings. Finally, we identify areas in which smart city rankings are lacking.

2 Justification and Methodological Approach

This paper is the result of the work done as a part of a larger research project on "Smart City Research and Library and Information Science", and as a result, our analysis is conducted from the library and information science point of view. Our underlying hypothesis is that citizen re-orientation gives more space for public libraries and information specialists to participate actively in "smart" initiatives.

We have found that existing smart city rankings are lacking, and using them as a source for objectively identified research sample is very problematic, thus the need to discuss the subject.

Our thesis is that two decades of e-government benchmarking should be used as a source of inspiration on how to evaluate smart cities. For this purpose, we use the critical analysis of selected smart-city and e-government rankings.

Identification of existing smart cities rankings was done by the usage of the phrase "smart city ranking" in the Google search engine, which led not only to finding rankings with "smart city" phrase in their titles, but also those which were referred to as a "smart city ranking" by media, city officials and fellow researchers. The following criteria were used in the final selection of the rankings for further analysis. Each ranking had to 1) include indicators referring to each smart city dimension defined by [12], thus excluding one-dimensional rankings, 2) have at least one ranking published, 3) include a methodological statement, and 4) have a global reach. The sample discussed below includes Top 50 Smart City Governments [42], Global Cities Index [43], IMD Smart City Index [44], Sustainable Cities Index [46], Smart Cities Index [47], and IESE Cities in Motion Index [48]. The analysis included the following criteria: 1) the number of indices used, 2) scope of indices used, 3) type of indices used, 4) entity responsible for the ranking's creation, and 5) clarity of the methodological statement.

e-Government rankings were purposely selected. Both EU's [52] and UN's [80] surveys fulfill the following criteria: 1) long history, with multiple rankings published, 2) presence of clear and detailed methodological statements, 3) recognition by the scientific community (which was verified by searches in both Scopus and Web of Science databases). The analysis included five main aspects: 1) the number of indices used, 2) scope of indices used, 3) type of indices used, 4) types of objects selected for evaluation, and 5) changes introduced to the methods used over time and the reasoning for them.

Finally, e-government rankings are used as a reference point for smart city rankings for two main reasons. Firstly, those concepts overlap, with the provision of e-government services, access to public information, and open government incorporated into the smart city concept. Secondly, the e-government phenomenon, just like the smart cities concept many years later, started as heavily IT-oriented and became over time more citizen-centered. This change brought many challenges for e-government rankings, as technology indicators are based on much more easily collectible data. Lessons learned from how e-government rankings handled human-centricity could be used to improve smart city rankings.

3   Smart City Rankings

The first attempt to rank cities on their "smartness" in 2007 was limited geographically and referred only to medium-size cities, with the assumption that they differ from other urban environments [12]. Characteristics defined then, namely: smart economy, smart people, smart governance, smart mobility, smart environment, and smart living, are still being used as the reference point for researchers and policy-makers. What makes a city smart, according to global rankings?

Top 50 Smart City Governments [42], published by Eden Strategy Institute and ONG&ONG, is a unique approach to ranking smart cities. It underlines the way city officials are implementing smart solutions in their municipalities. For that purpose, authors identify three smart city dimensions: scope (from the concepts based on a few landmark projects to those based on hundreds of small projects), scale (referring to the size of the project, defined geographically or population-wise), and integration (whether an integrated or decentralized approach is used). Cities are ranked based on ten factors: vision, leadership, budget, financial incentives, support programs, talent-readiness, people centricity, innovation ecosystems, smart policies, and track record. Unfortunately, there is no detailed information on the ranking process, what indicators are used, and how the authors actually understand those factors. For example, the very vague explanations provided, e.g., in the case of people centricity- "a sincere, people-first design of the future city" - only create more questions – in this case, how to quantify sincerity? A similar flaw was identified in the case of the Global Cities Index [43], which is published together with Global Cities Outlook ranking (with Index referring to current performance and Outlook describing future potential). It is based on five dimensions: 1) business activity (30%), 2) human capital (30%), 3) information exchange (15%), 4) cultural experience (15%) and 5) political engagement (10%), using 27 metrics in total, to rank 25 cities out of 130 analyzed. Authors, however, do not provide a detailed list of indicators used for this purpose. Instead, they use generic labels: for example, 'human capital' stands for 'education levels'. Finally, there is the IMD Smart City Index, prepared by the IMD World Competitiveness Center in cooperation with the Singapore University of Technology and Design, and it is the newest addition to the growing number of attempts to quantify this phenomenon. As the authors claim, its uniqueness comes from a holistic approach that allows the capture of the perceptions of those who live and work in the smart cities, understood as "an urban setting that applies technology to enhance the benefits and diminish the short-comings of urbanization" [44]. It is based on 120 surveys conducted on randomly chosen citizens in each of 102 cities included in the ranking [45]. However, the methodological note does not explain: 1) how (or why) those cities were selected for the survey, 2) how the random selection of respondents was managed, 3) what are the characteristics of respondents in each city. Furthermore, the questionnaire itself is not provided, and the small number of respondents from each city limits the possibility of drawing scientifically justified conclusions on this basis.

The Sustainable Cities Index [46], published by the global design and consultancy firm Arcadis, ranks 100 cities in three main categories: people (13 indicators), planet (11 indicators), and profit (7 indicators) and is constructed by a three-stage averaging process. Some of them are complex indicators; for example, "transport infrastructure" from the profit category includes: congestion (primary source of data - TomTom Traffic Index), rail infrastructure (World Metro Database, Metrobits.org), airport satisfaction (World Airport Awards), transport economic opportunity (financial statements of transport providers) and transport public finances, with a combined weight of 15%. Surprisingly, there is no specific explanation of how those sub-indicators influence final scoring. In general, it is a very well documented methodology, based on data from reputable sources and rationale for each indicator used. Simultaneously, the sub-indicators used in Sustainable Cities Index (also called Citizen-Centric Cities) make it a very human-centric ranking, making it people-dimension biased.

Smart Cities Index by Easy Park Group [47] analyzes 500 cities with medium to high recognition in the United Nations Human Development Index, using 24 factors to list 100 top cities. The final score is based on 5 dimensions: 1) transport and mobility (22.5%), 2) sustainability (12.5%), 3) governance (15%), 4) innovation economy (5%), 5) digitisation (17.5%), 6) living standard (10%), 7) cybersecurity (7.5%), and 8) expert perception (10%). Each indicator comes with a clear label and data source statement. Detailed analysis of indicators used proves that the Smart Cities Index is very technology-oriented. Furthermore, assigning the highest weight to transport and mobility dimension is unfounded and could only be explained by company bias, as Easy Park Group is a company selling solutions for parking.

IESE Cities in Motion Index [48], prepared by the IESE Business School, University of Navarra, covers 174 cities from 80 countries. It uses the total of 106 indicators, grouped in nine dimensions: 1) economy (e.g., number of calendar days needed so a business can operate legally, hourly wage in the city, Uber presence), 2) human capital (e.g., international movement of higher-level students, expenditure on leisure and recreation per capita), 3) social cohesion (e.g., number of public and private hospitals and health centers, suicide rate), 4) environment (e.g., total renewable water sources, percentage of the rise in temperature in the city during the summer forecast for 2100 if pollution caused by carbon emissions continues to increase), 5) governance (e.g., number of research and technology centers, e-Government Development Index), 6) urban planning (e.g., number of bike-rental or bike-sharing points, number of people per household). 7) international outreach (e.g., number of McDonald's chain restaurants, number of hotels per capita), 8) technology (e.g., number of LinkedIn users, broadband subscriptions per 100 inhabitants) and 9) mobility and transportation (e.g., estimation of traffic inefficiencies such as long journey times, length of the metro system). Each indicator is provided with a detailed description, including information on the unit of measurement and the source of the data used. As a result, the conceptual framework of the ranking is broad and - at the same time - very well defined and properly-documented. It doesn't seem to favor any dimension, highlights every aspect of the city's life. However, its over-complexity makes it hard to understand why one city scores higher than another.

4   e-Government Rankings

e-Government rankings vary in scope, and similarly to smart city rankings, can favor one aspect over others. For example, the Global e-Government Survey analyses municipal websites' content in selected cities [49], while both SIBIS and eUSER concentrated on the usage and e-inclusion [25]. In some cases, although e-government evaluation is done in a broader context, it is not supported by a deepen explanation of the methodology [50]. This paper will focus on two e-government rankings, one global, prepared by the United Nations, and one with more limited geographical coverage, prepared for the European Commission.

4.1   European Union's Ranking

The first report published in October 2001 [51] and the sixteenth published in 2019 [52] European Union's measurement of e-government development is the longest systematic approach to benchmarking digital government. It started as a measurement exercise for the 15 member states of the EU, Iceland, Norway, and Switzerland, with additional countries added in the following years to accommodate the Union's enlargements from 2004, 2007, and 2013. Such time span also led to many method-ological adjustments, reflecting a technological change in the e-gov provision and political goals set up at the EU's level in consecutive strategies. Consequently, it is possible to identify three main stages of this benchmarking process, with the most significant change introduced in the third stage.

Stage one includes reports published between October 2001 and June 2006, pre-senting a benchmark study of 20 most common public services, 12 provided for citizens (income taxes, job search, social security benefits, personal documents, car registration, application for building permission, declaration to the police, public libraries, birth and marriage certificates, enrollment in higher education, announcement of moving and health-related service), and 8 for businesses (social contribution for employees, corporate tax, VAT, registration of a new company, submission of data to the statistical office, customs declaration, environment-related permits, and public procurement). Services were scored based on their on-line development level: 1) information (no on-line interaction possible), 2) one-way interaction (downloadable forms), 3) two-way interaction (submittable forms), and 4) transaction (full electronic case handling). An additional binary indicator was also introduced, ranking services as level 0 (levels 1–3) and 1 (full electronic case handling). Apart from separate rankings for each of the 20 public services, those reports presented aggregated results for each country, as well as for both end-user groups (citizens and businesses) [53].

Benchmarking e-government in the European Union during stage one was heavily relying on the data on the digitalization of public services. Consequently, it provided information on the availability of public services – so supply-side, and not their actual usage – demand-side [9], as laid down by the eEurope Strategy [54]. Furthermore, as defined here, the availability is strictly IT-related and describes the level of the development of the proper infrastructure at the central level, which does tell nothing about its actual availability at the municipal level. In other words, although a country can score 4 for the service, it cannot be provided in most of its territory. In fact, for local administrations to be able to be efficient in the e-government world, those systems need to be functional, easy to implement and cheap to maintain, capable of interconnecting with existing back-office systems (so come with a proper level of interoperability), and citizen and employee-friendly [55]. Additionally, the benchmarking framework used here refers neither to the quality of the service delivery (and user's experience) nor its impact on the government's day-to-day operation [56]. It is surprising, as many studies prove a low correlation between overall government efficiency and e-government [57]. The supply-driven approach to benchmarking digital government led to even more critique, as it was understood that it would not result in the widely expected outcomes, and more user-oriented action plans are needed [25]. As a result, the new i2010 strategy took a different turn [58] and, consequently, the report from 2006, in the section "The Future of eGovernment Measurement" announced the change of the benchmarking approach, with special attention paid to comparison between supply and use of on-line public services [53].

The benchmarking model used in stage two (September 2007 - December 2010) is built upon the model used in previous years with an addition of new level five of on-line development of public services: 5) personalization (pro-active, automated). It refers to the extent to which the on-line provision of some of the 20 previously defined services (in case of several services, it is impossible to reach level 5) is based on a new model of front and back-offices integration, the re-use of available data and pro-active service delivery (e.g., pre-filling data in the application forms) [59].

Additionally, a completely new indicator – user-centricity - was introduced to complement the two existing sophistication and full-online availability indices. The assumption was that it would provide more user-related information on transactional services. However, supply-driven data were used to benchmark the demand-side of e-government provision. It included four sub-indicators: 1) Legally Binding eID (is there a legally binding eID system in place), 2) Number of data fields (how many mandatory and not pre-filled data fields must be completed by the user?), 3) Multi-channel access (is there a least one other channel used for the service delivery?) and 4) Compliance with accessibility standards (is there any accessibility statement or logo referring to international guidelines?) [59], all of which describe how the service was designed and not how it is used. The definition of sub-indicator 4) makes it even more questionable, as it associates a statement or a logo with actual compliance with accessibility standards. In fact, it only proves knowledge of service providers on the existence of those standards, and not their effective implementation.

The evolution of the measurement method in the following years led to addressing some of those concerns. For example, Since 2009, special focus was put on e-procurement service [60], analyzed in-depth in the dedicated report from 2008, and identified as a high impact area of e-government [61]. In 2010 the 20 services metrics were applied at NUTS levels for the first time, providing more reliable data on eGovernment performance across regional and local administrations [62].

The user-centricity indicator was replaced with *user experience* indicator in 2009, consisting of five sub-indicators: 1) Accessibility (this time determined by automated web-crawler analysis limited to national portals) 2) Usability (multi-channel provision, progress tracking, help functionality, privacy protection), 3) User Satisfaction Monitoring (limited to feedback intake and reporting on it), 4) One-stop-shop approach (availability of 20 basic services on the principal portal), 5) User-focused portal design (use of target groups, thematic or life-events based organization of information) [60]. In the report from 2010, the indicator was reshaped again and redesigned to include the following criteria: 1) Transparency of service delivery (tracking service provision, indication of time duration for service completion, etc.), 2) Multichannel service provision, 3) Privacy Protection, 4) Ease of use (existence of supporting mechanisms, like FAQ; possibility to add additional documents to the form), 5) User satisfaction monitoring (presence of appropriate monitoring mechanisms) [62].

Table 1. Composition of the user-centricity indicator.

2007 [59]	2009 [60]	2010 [62]
1. Legally Binding eID 2. Number of data fields 3. Multi-channel access 4. Compliance with accessibility standards	1. Accessibility 2. Usability 3. User satisfaction monitoring 4. One-stop-shop approach 5. User-focused portal design	1. Transparency of service delivery 2. Multi-channel access 3. Privacy protection 4. Ease of use 5. User satisfaction monitoring

The most problematic aspect of this indicator – its supply-side context – remained unaddressed. Ease of use is verified by the provision of FAQs, and user satisfaction is limited to providing feedback mechanisms, with no information if this feedback is even used to improve e-government services.

Stage three of EU's benchmarking of e-government includes reports published between 2012 and 2019, shifting attention towards selected life events and baskets of services related to them with bi-annual coverage – the approach first tested in the previous report [62]. Life events offer a new approach to benchmarking, as they allow collection and analysis of more complex, cross-cutting data sets, involving multiple channels and service owners. The trinity of services analyzed in 2012 included: starting and early trading of a business, losing and finding a job, and studying. The assessment of life events is done by mystery shoppers, who go through the experience of the given life event [63].

Demand-side was included through data collected from a representative sample of respondents (survey of 27 questions in five subject areas: user profile, usage of e-government, user satisfaction, perceived benefits and barriers in using digital government), and supply-side through assessment of five key technology enablers (electronic identification, e-documents, base registries, security, and single sign-on) [64]. It is an excellent example of how to benchmark well-developed systems, where digital services are already available on-line, and the main problem is the effectiveness of their provision. However, at this stage, European reports are often described as *pilot studies*, and their methodology and scope change several times - for example, in 2011, benchmark pilot on open government and transparency, which was a global hot topic in digital government back then, was published [65] and influenced how this aspect is measured in the following years.

Top-level benchmarks used in this stage are e-government maturity (per life event and top-level benchmark), cross-border mobility (are public services available on-line for foreign EU citizens?), effective government (does government succeed in satisfying on-line users, achieve re-use and fulfill expectations?), transparent government (are public organizations transparent, how do they manage personal data?), key enablers (are key IT enables integrated into live event service models?) and user-centric government (on-line availability and usability of services) [64]. While in 2012, some of those top-benchmarks were described by sets of sub-indicators with no actual top-benchmark (e.g., transparent government included only three separate numbers for service delivery, public organizations, and personal data), in 2014, that was only the case of "effective government" top benchmark [63]. Starting from 2017, the mobility benchmark is replaced by two separate indicators to describe cross-border availability of services for businesses and citizens [66].

Table 2. Top-level benchmarks used in country sheets

	2012 [64]	2014 [63]	2015 [67]	2016 [68]	2017 [66]	2018 [69]	2019 [52]
Maturity	X						
Mobility	X	X	X	X	B/C	B/C	B/C
Effectiveness	X	X					
Transparency	X	X	X	X	X	X	X
User centricity	X	X	X	X	X	X	X
Key enablers	X	X	X	X	X	X	X

The basked of life events benchmarked till 2019 included: 1) business start-up and early trading operations (covering 33 services needed in this business event, from registering a company to hiring employees), 2) family life (services for the typical young family, from marriage to renovating a house), 3) losing and finding a job (unemployed applications for additional benefits and allowances, job search – a total of 22 services), 4) studying (14 services, from higher education enrolment to portability of grants), 5) regular business operations (11 services, from human resources to refund of VAT), 6) moving (from deregistering to registering new permanent address and move notifications to public offices and utilities), 7) owning and driving a car (12 services – from buying and selling a vehicle to getting a driver's license) and 8) starting a small claim procedure [52].

4.2   UN e-Government Survey

The main goal of the Survey, which has 11 editions published between 2001 and 2020, is to provide data on how digital government can support implementing Sustainable

Development Goals, currently within the 2030 Agenda, which makes the reasoning behind this benchmarking similar to the one conducted for European Union – supporting policymaking and implementation. The analysis of the reports also proves a switch of approach from technology to human orientation. At first, e-government was understood as utilizing the internet and the world-wide-web for delivering government information and services to citizens [70], seen as a historic opportunity, especially for developing countries [71], thus limiting it to the use of all ICTs by the government to provide information and services to citizens [72]. Starting from 2005, reports underline the advantages of digitalization: efficient government management of information; better service delivery; and empowerment of the people through access to information and participation in public policy decision-making [73] or improving transparency and accountability in government functions and allowing for cost savings in government administration [74]. In other words, e-government is being deployed not only to provide citizen services but also to increase public sector efficiency and enhance its capacity [75].

Another significant shift comes with the 2012 report, as it goes beyond service delivery towards a framework for smart, inclusive, and sustainable growth for future generations [76]. In the following years, the focus goes to the use and application of ICTs in public administration to streamline and integrate workflows and processes, effective management of data and information, and expanding communication channels for engagement and empowerment of people [77], thus improving the relationship between citizens and government and making public services delivery more effective, accessible and responsive to people's needs [78]. Finally, benchmarking focuses on deploying e-government to build resilient societies and sets out the necessary preconditions [79].

UN's benchmarking model is based on the assessment of the e-government performance of member states relative to one another, with each report dedicated to special issues – from e-inclusion [73] to sustainability [78]. For this purpose, it uses the E-Government Development Index (EGDI), based on three groups of indicators: 1) telecommunication infrastructure (based on data obtained from the International Telecommunications Union), 2) use of ICTs (with data provided by the UNESCO), and 3) on-line services and content (data collected by the group of researchers in a survey under the supervision of the UNDESA), which define general methodological framework used throughout the years [79]. Unlike the EU's ranking, the UN's goes through evolutionary and not revolutionary changes, which are reflected by adjustments in the form of using different sub-indicators and/or assigning them new weights, and not by introducing a completely new idea for the benchmarking. It can be misleading while comparing results between the years, as a reader has to be aware of those little methodological changes, but at the same time makes it much easier to understand the general philosophy behind the research.

On-Line Services and Content. The first report, based on the analysis of over 1900 national government websites, grouped countries into five categories, which are similar to stages of e-government development used in early EU's reports: 1) emerging (few independent sites with limited, basic, static information), 2) enhanced (sites are regularly updated), 3) interactive (downloadable forms), 4) transactional (websites accept payment) and 5) seamless (total integration of services) [70]. In the following years, each stage had higher requirements, reflecting the general development of the internet and related technologies. In 2003 "seamless" was replaced with "networked presence" [71] and "connected" in 2008 [74], both of which better describe this category. In 2010 the model was simplified and reduced to four stages by removing the "interactive" category [75]. The role of those pre-defined stages has decreased consistently since then - the 2014 report just mentions them [77], and they are entirely omitted from 2016 [78].

Telecommunication Infrastructure included several indicators describing penetration of selected ICTs: personal computers, internet hosts, telephone lines, mobile phones, and televisions (with the context of web TV) and one user indicator – a percentage of the population using the internet [70]. The first change in this indicator comes in 2003, with "internet hosts" being replaced with "internet users" [71], then in 2008, televisions and on-line population were dropped and fix broadband was introduced [74], personal computers were replaced in 2012 with fixed broadband facilities [76] for one year, and with wireless broadband from 2014 [77], and telephone lines were finally dropped in 2020 [80].

Human Capital was based on two pre-existing sub-indices: Human Development Index (describes the state of the society in the context of education, economy, and healthcare) and Information Access Index (utilizes data collected by Freedomhouse International and Transparency International), as well as one urbanization sub-index (urban as a percentage of the total population) [70]. It was completely redone in the 2003 report and based solely on adult literacy rate and education gross enrolment ratio [71] and expanded in 2014 by the addition of another two sub-indicators: expected years of schooling and mean years of schooling [77].

5   Why Are 'Smart City' Rankings Lacking?

UN's and EU's e-Government rankings share many similarities, highlighting the main disadvantages of smart city rankings. Both come with strong and transparent methodological background, use existing data as well as purposely collected data, have clear, measurable goals which were at first tied to development stages of e-government services, and now describe a specific *experience* that users have while interacting with digital government. They also ignited the research community to discuss the problem of the e-government measurement and improved over time on the basis of that discussion. Why are smart city rankings lacking in comparison?

There is No Consensus on What a Smart City Actually is. It is a concept discussed for over twenty years [81], yet it remains fuzzy [82], with a plethora of definitions to choose from [83], which makes defining a conceptual framework for the measurement much more challenging. There is no clear goal for evaluation with no clear understanding of what this phenomenon is and what it means to be smart. Some of those smart city rankings discussed above don't even use the word "smart" in their title, referring to, e.g., sustainability instead.

Lack of Clear Development Stages. Both e-government rankings are based on specific development stages, which are set in technological and political contexts. While one-way interaction and two-way interaction in the provision of public services are easily definable and measurable, in the case of smart government, the emphasis is on the dimensions [12], models [84], paths [81], or vaguely identifiable generations [85], and not development stages. Additionally, the EU's ranking is tied to strategic goals presented in consecutive strategies for developing information society, and UN's is connected to Sustainable Development Goals, which define benchmarks to measure.

Quantity over Quality. Smart city rankings are using mostly simple indicators based on pre-existing data. For example, "cost of a monthly transport ticket" [47] provides no information on the quality of public transportation, and "number of facilities" does not describe the quality of services provided by those facilities. It is even not clear how to interpret the change of such indicators over time – is a decrease or increase of 'number of facilities' the desired change? The main advantage of those indices is that they are based on pre-existing, easily acquirable data.

Supply-Side Orientation. It is a natural consequence of the problem stated above. Pre-existing data come from statistical offices, local public institutions, or bodies collecting them for their own purposes, not with the smart city concept in mind. It is also true for UN's ranking in the case of telecommunication infrastructure and human capital sub-indicators. Still, even here, one-third of the final score comes from data collected by the dedicated group of researchers "instructed and trained to assume the mindset of an average citizen user in assessing sites. Thus, responses were generally based on whether the relevant features could be found and accessed easily, not whether they, in fact, exist but are hidden somewhere in the site(s)" [80]. With the same concept implemented in the EU's ranking, it is safe to assume it is the best option for measuring the experience of living in a smart city and including user-side in the benchmarking framework.

Lack of Methodological Transparency. It is probably the most unexpected outcome of our analysis, as several smart city rankings provide an only general statement on their methodological framework. Furthermore, those that explain what indices they use and the reasoning behind it often use many composite indicators, prepared by other bodies. For example, [48] uses the Health index, Gini index, or Global Peace Index, among others, which forces the reader to search for their detailed methodological background in other sources. Furthermore, while analyzing changes over time in the ranking, the user has to be aware of possible methodological adjustments introduced by, e.g., Walk Free Foundation in their Global Slavery Index.

Dimension Bias. One of the approaches we could take with such a complex object of the measurement as the "smart city" is its simplification by favoring one of the smart city dimensions identified in 2007 [12]. It is the case of [46] and its environmental bias, or [44] and its bias towards people dimension - putting a "smart city" staple on the ranking doesn't make it a smart city ranking.

Company Bias. Finally, it is also important to consider who is responsible for the creation or funding of a given ranking. With the most prominent IT companies like

IBM or Ericsson being very active in the field of smart cities, the reasoning behind the chosen methodological framework may be biased. [47] could be identified as 'dimension bias,' as it favors transport, but the fact that it is prepared by EasyPark Group, a company offering technological solutions for parking, sheds a different light on the reasoning behind such orientation.

6 Conclusions

Technological determinism, which is the leading paradigm in problem-solving in everything information related since WWII, is proven to be lacking. The main advantage of ICT orientation of e-government and smart city benchmarking is the availability of comparable data and ease of analysis. In contrast, proper inclusion of social context (ease of usage, satisfaction, etc.) requires respondents' involvement and refers more to the quality of services provided.

With over twenty years of experience, e-government rankings have found their way to achieve – still challenged – a balance between the supply-side and demand-side by introducing a methodological framework allowing to measure the quality of *experience* while being in contact with the public sector. Unfortunately, smart city rankings are yet to find their way to that level of maturity. They tend to rely on pre-existing data and measure the quantity and are not fully transparent when explaining the methodology behind their benchmarks.

From the researcher's point of view, smart city rankings present limited value as a source of representative samples for research in this domain. The question is if, without political context, which heavily influences both the UN's and EU's rankings, it is possible to create a strong, objective, and widely accepted smart-city benchmarking methodology.

References

1. Jaeger, P.T.: The endless wire: E-government as global phenomenon. Gov. Inf. Q. **20**(4), 323–331 (2003)
2. Echeverria, J., Unceta, A.: Citizenship and participation in the European Electronic space. Arbor-Ciencia Pensam. Y Cult. **188**(756), 725–732 (2012)
3. Panopoulou, E., Tambouris, E., Zotou, M., Tarabanis, K.: Evaluating eParticipation sophistication of regional authorities websites: the case of Greece and Spain. In: Electronic Participation: Proceedings of the 1st IFIP WG 8.5 International Conference, ePart 2009, vol. 5694. Linz, Austria, pp. 67–77, 07 December 2009
4. Bwalya, K.J., Mutula, S.M.: E-government: Implementation, Adoption and Synthesis in Developing Countries. Degruyter, Boston
5. Bremer, E.S.: Incorporation by reference in an open-government age. Harv. J. Law Publ. Policy **36**(1), 131–210 (2013)
6. Lemieux, V.L., Trapnell, S.E., Worker, J., Excell, C.: Transparency and open government: reporting on the disclosure of information. In: 5th Conference on E-Democracy Open Government (CeDEM 2015), vol. 7, no. 2, pp. 75–93, June 2015

7. Ho, A., Bender, K., Steenson, J., Roche, E.: Big data and local performance management: the experience of Kansas City, Missouri. In: Chen, Y.-C., Ahn, M.J. (eds.) Routledge Handbook on Information Technology in Government, pp. 95–107. Routledge, New York (2017)

8. Whitmore, A.: A statistical analysis of the construction of the United Nations e-Government development index. Gov. Inf. Q. 29(1), 68–75 (2012)

9. Waksberg-Guerrini, A., Aibar, E.: Towards a network government? A Critical Analysis of current assessment methods for e-government. In: Wimmer, M.A., Scholl, J., Grönlund, Å. (eds.) EGOV 2007. LNCS, vol. 4656, pp. 330–341. Springer, Heidelberg (2007). https://doi.org/10.1007/978-3-540-74444-3_28

10. Baker, D.L.: Advancing e-government performance in the United States through enhanced usability benchmarks. Gov. Inf. Q. 26(1), 82–88 (2009)

11. Bertot, J.C., Jaeger, P.T.: User-centered e-government: challenges and benefits for government Web sites. Gov. Inf. Q. 23(2), 163–168 (2006)

12. Giffinger, R., Fertner, C., Kramar, H., Kalasek, R., Pichler-Milanović, N., Meijers, E.: Smart cities: ranking of European medium-sized cities, Vienna (2007)

13. Lee, J., Lee, H.: Developing and validating a citizen-centric typology for smart city services. Gov. Inf. Q. 31(S1), S93–S105 (2014)

14. Papa, R., Galderisi, A., Vigo Majello, M.C., Saretta, E.: Smart and resilient cities a systemic approach for developing cross-sectoral strategies in the face of climate change. Tema-J. L. Use Mobil. Environ. 8(1), 19–49 (2015)

15. Vázquez, D.G., Gil, M.T.N.: Sustainability in smart cities: the case of Vitoria-Gasteiz (Spain) – a commitment to a new urban paradigm. In: Carvalho, L.C. (ed.) Handbook of Research on Entrepreneurial Development and Innovation Within Smart Cities, pp. 248–268. Information Science Reference, Hershey (2017)

16. Bernardino, S., Santos, J.F.: Building smarter cities through social entrepreneurship. In: Carvalho, L.C. (ed.) Handbook of Research on Entrepreneurial Development and Innovation Within Smart Cities, pp. 327–362. Information Science Reference, Hershey (2017)

17. Andersen, K.V., Henriksen, H.Z.: E-government maturity models: extension of the Layne and Lee model. Gov. Inf. Q. 23(2), 236–248 (2006)

18. Lemke, F., Taveter, K., Erlenheim, R., Pappel, I., Draheim, D., Janssen, M.: Stage models for moving from e-government to smart government. In: Chugunov, A., Khodachek, I., Misnikov, Y., Trutnev, D. (eds.) EGOSE 2019. CCIS, vol. 1135, pp. 152–164. Springer, Cham (2020). https://doi.org/10.1007/978-3-030-39296-3_12

19. Schellong, A.R.M.: Benchmarking EU e-government at the crossroads: a framework for e-government benchmark design and improvement. Transform. Gov. People, Process Policy 4(4), 365–385 (2010)

20. Jovanovska, M.B.: Demarcation of the field of e-government assessment. Transylvanian Rev. Adm. Sci. (48), 19–36 (2016)

21. Young-Jin, S., Seang-tae, K.: e-Government concepts, measures, and best practices. In: Al-Hakim, L. (ed.) Global e-Government: Theory, Applications and Benchmarking, pp. 340–369. Idea Group Inc., Hershey (2007)

22. Skargren, F.: What is the point of benchmarking e-government? An integrative and critical literature review on the phenomenon of benchmarking e-government. Inf. Polity 25, 67–89 (2020)

23. Janowski, T., Durkiewicz, J.: Towards synthetic and balanced digital government benchmarking. In: HICCS (2020). http://hdl.handle.net/10125/64000. Accessed 30 June 2020

24. Potnis, D.D., Pardo, T.A.: Mapping the evolution of e-Readiness assessments. Transform. Gov. People, Process Policy 5(4), 345–363 (2011)

25. Kunstelj, M., Jukić, T., Vintar, M.: Analysing the demand side of e-government: what can we learn from Slovenian users? In: Wimmer, M.A., Scholl, J., Grönlund, Å. (eds.) EGOV 2007. LNCS, vol. 4656, pp. 305–317. Springer, Heidelberg (2007). https://doi.org/10.1007/978-3-540-74444-3_26

26. Magoutas, B., Halaris, C., Mentzas, G.: An ontology for the multi-perspective evaluation of quality in e-government services. In: Wimmer, M.A., Scholl, J., Grönlund, Å. (eds.) EGOV 2007. LNCS, vol. 4656, pp. 318–329. Springer, Heidelberg (2007). https://doi.org/10.1007/978-3-540-74444-3_27

27. Jansen, A., Ølnes, S.: Benchmarking eGovernment quality: whose quality are we measuring? In: Electronic Government and Electronic Participation: Joint Proceedings of Ongoing Research and Projects of IFIP WG 8.5 EGOV and ePart 2013, vol. 221. Koblenz, Germany, pp. 43–53 (2013)

28. Siskos, E., Malafekas, M., Askounis, D., Psarras, J.: e-Government benchmarking in European Union: a multicriteria extreme ranking approach. In: Collaborative, Trusted and Privacy-Aware e/m-Services. 12th IFIP WG 6.11 Conference on e-Business, e-Services, and e-Society, pp. 338–348 (2013)

29. Gonçalo P.D.: Policy matters? An analysis of outliers in the UN e-Government index. In: ECDG 2019 19th European Conference on Digital Government, pp. 10–18 (2019)

30. Das, A., Singh, H., Joseph, D.: A longitudinal study of e-government maturity. In: 15th Pacific Asia Conference on Information Systems (PACIS 2011), pp. 1–12 (2011)

31. Máchová, R., Lněnička, M.: Reframing e-government development indices with respect to new trends in ICT. Rev. Econ. Perspect. **15**(4), 383–411 (2015)

32. Wahid, J.A., Shi, L., Saleem, K.: Incorporation of social media indicator in e-government index. In: 5th International Conference on Communication and Information Processing, pp. 201–209 (2019)

33. Tassabehji, R., Hackney, R., Maruyama, T.: Evaluating digital public services: a contingency value approach within three exemplar developing countries. Inf. Technol. People **32**(4), 1021–1043 (2019)

34. Janssen, M., van Veenstra, A.F.: Stages of growth in e-government: an architectural approach. Electron. J. e-Gov. **3**(4), 193–200 (2005)

35. Boulos, M.N.K., Tsouros, A.D., Holopainen, A.: 'Social, innovative and smart cities are happy and resilient': insights from the WHO EURO 2014 International Healthy Cities Conference. Int. J. Health Geogr. **14** (2015)

36. Marsal-Llacuna, M.-L.: City indicators on social sustainability as standardization technologies for smarter (citizen-centered) governance of cities. Soc. Indic. Res. **128**(3), 1193–1216 (2015)

37. Maheshwari, D., Janssen, M.: Reconceptualizing measuring, benchmarking for improving interoperability in smart ecosystems: the effect of ubiquitous data and crowdsourcing. Gov. Inf. Q. **31**(S1), S84–S92 (2014)

38. Jurevičienė, D., Biekšaitė, A.: Valuation of Lithuanian cities's smartness. Econ. Cult. **17**(1), 104–115 (2020)

39. Noori, N., De Jong, M., Hoppe, T.: Towards an integrated framework to measure smart city readiness: the case of Iranian cities. Smart Cities **3**, 676–703 (2020)

40. Anthopoulos, L., Janssen, M., Weerakkody, V.: A Unified Smart City Model (USCM) for smart city conceptualization and benchmarking. Int. J. Electron. Gov. Res. **12**(2), 77–93 (2016)

41. Batlle-Montserrat, J., Blat, J., Abadal, E.: Local e-government benchlearning: impact analysis and applicability to smart cities benchmarking. Inf. Polity **21**(1), 43–59 (2016)

42. Top 50 Smart City Governments. Eden Strategy Institute, ONG&ONG Pte Ltd. (2018). https://static1.squarespace.com/static/5b3c517fec4eb767a04e73ff/t/5b513c57aa4a99f62d168e60/1532050650562/Eden-OXD_Top+50+Smart+City+Governments.pdf. Accessed 05 May 2019
43. Hales, M., Pena, A.M., Peterson, E., Dessibourg-Freer, N.: A question of talent: how human capital will determine the next global leaders. 2019 Global Cities Report. ATKearney (2019)
44. Bris, A., Chee, C.H., Lanvin, B.: Sart city index (2019). https://www.imd.org/globalassets/wcc/docs/smart_city/smart_city_index_digital.pdf. Accessed 12 Dec 2019
45. Bris, A., Chee, C.H., Lanvin, B.: Smart city index methodology (2019). https://www.imd.org/globalassets/wcc/docs/smart_city/smart_city_index_methodology_and_groups.pdf. Accessed 12 Dec 2019
46. Batten, J.: Citizen centric cities. the sustainable cities index 2018. Arcadis (2018). https://www.arcadis.com/media/1/D/5/%7B1D5AE7E2-A348-4B6E-B1D7-6D94FA7D7567%7DSustainable_Cities_Index_2018_Arcadis.pdf. Accessed 20 Jun 2019
47. Smart Cities Index 2019. EasyPark Group (2019). https://www.easyparkgroup.com/smart-cities-index/. Accessed 05 May 2019
48. Berrone, P., Ricart, J.E.: IESE cities in motion index (2019). https://media.iese.edu/research/pdfs/ST-0509-E.pdf. Accessed 07 Dec 2019
49. Holzer, M., Manoharan, A.P., Melitski, J., Moon, M.J.: Global E-Government Survey (2018-19). National Center for Public Performance, Boston (2020)
50. Obi, T., Iwasaki, N.: A Decade of World e-Government Rankings. IOS Press BV, Amsterdam (2015)
51. Wauters, P., Kerschot, H.: Web-based survey on electronic public services: results of the second measurement: April 2002. Summary report. Cap Gemini Ernst & Young (2002). https://administracionelectronica.gob.es/pae_Home/pae_OBSAE/Posicionamiento-Internacional/Comision_Europea_OBSAE/benchmark-egovernment.html. Accessed 15 Jun 2020
52. van der Linden, N., eGovernment benchmark 2019: empowering europeans through trusted digital public services. Background report. Capgemini, IDC, Sogeti, and Politecnico di Milano (2019). https://administracionelectronica.gob.es/pae_Home/pae_OBSAE/Posicionamiento-Internacional/Comision_Europea_OBSAE/benchmark-egovernment.html. Accessed 15 June 2020
53. Wauters, P., Colclough, G.: On-line availability of public services: how is Europe progressing? Web based survey on electronic public services. In: Report of the 6th Measurement. Capgemini (2006). https://administracionelectronica.gob.es/pae_Home/pae_OBSAE/Posicionamiento-Internacional/Comision_Europea_OBSAE/benchmark-egovernment.html. Accessed 15 June 2020
54. eEurope - an information society for all. European Commission, COM(1999) 687 final (1999). https://eur-lex.europa.eu/legal-content/EN/TXT/HTML/?uri=URISERV:l24221&from=EN. Accessed 15 June 2020
55. Koussouris, S., Charalabidis, Y., Gionis, G., Tsitsanis, T., Psarras, J.: Building a local administration services portal for citizens and businesses: service composition, architecture and back-office interoperability issues. In: Wimmer, M.A., Scholl, J., Grönlund, Å. (eds.) EGOV 2007. LNCS, vol. 4656, pp. 80–91. Springer, Heidelberg (2007). https://doi.org/10.1007/978-3-540-74444-3_8
56. Wauters, P.: Benchmarking e-government policy within the e-Europe programme. Aslib Proc. **58**(5), 389–403 (2006)
57. Bavec, C., Vintar, M.: What matters in the development of the e-government in the EU? In: Wimmer, M.A., Scholl, J., Grönlund, Å. (eds.) EGOV 2007. LNCS, vol. 4656, pp. 424–435. Springer, Heidelberg (2007). https://doi.org/10.1007/978-3-540-74444-3_36

58. i2010 – A European Information Society for growth and employment. European Commission, COM(2005) 229 final (2005). https://eur-lex.europa.eu/legal-content/EN/TXT/PDF/?uri=CELEX:52005DC0229&from=EN. Accessed 15 June 2020
59. Wauters, P., Nijskens, M., Tiebout, J.: The user challenge benchmarking the supply of online public services 7th measurement. Capgemini (2007). https://administracionelectronica.gob.es/pae_Home/pae_OBSAE/Posicionamiento-Internacional/Comision_Europea_OBSAE/benchmark-egovernment.html. Accessed 15 June 2020
60. Colclough, G., Tinholt, D.: Smarter, faster, better egovernment. 8th benchmark measurement. CAPGEMINI, RAND EUROPE, IDC, SOGETI AND DTI (2009). https://administracionelectronica.gob.es/pae_Home/pae_OBSAE/Posicionamiento-Internacional/Comision_Europea_OBSAE/benchmark-egovernment.html. Accessed 15 June 2020
61. Codagnone, C.: Benchmarking on-line public services. To develop and improve the eGovernment indicators, second year contract: final report. RSO SPA, IDC Italy (2008). https://administracionelectronica.gob.es/pae_Home/pae_OBSAE/Posicionamiento-Interna cional/Comision_Europea_OBSAE/benchmark-egovernment.html. Accessed 15 June 2020
62. Colclough, G., Tinholt, D., Lörincz, B.: Digitizing public services in Europe: putting ambition into action. 9th benchmark measurement. Capgemini, IDC, Rand Europe, Sogeti and DTi (2010). https://administracionelectronica.gob.es/pae_Home/pae_OBSAE/Posicionamiento-Internacional/Comision_Europea_OBSAE/benchmark-egovernment.html. Accessed 15 June 2020
63. Tinholt, D., van der Linden, N.: Delivering the European advantage? 'How European governments can and should benefit from innovative public services'. Final Background Report. Capgemini, IDC, Sogeti, IS-practice (2014). https://administracionelectronica.gob.es/pae_Home/pae_OBSAE/Posicionamiento-Internacional/Comision_Europea_OBSAE/benchmark-egovernment.html. Accessed 15 June 2020
64. Tinholt, D., van der Linden, N.: Public services online 'digital by default or by detour?' Assessing user centric eGovernment performance in Europe – eGovernment benchmark 2012. Final insight report. Capgemini, IDC, Sogeti (2012). https://administracionelectronica.gob.es/pae_Home/pae_OBSAE/Posicionamiento-Internacional/Comision_Europea_OBSAE/benchmark-egovernment.html. Accessed 15 June 2020
65. Tinholt, D., Lörincz, B.: 2011 eGovernment benchmark pilot on open government and transparency measuring the potential of eGovernment to foster open government and transparency in Europe. Capgemini, IDC, Rand Europe, Sogeti and DTi (2011). https://administracionelectronica.gob.es/pae_Home/pae_OBSAE/Posicionamiento-Internacional/Comision_Europea_OBSAE/benchmark-egovernment.html. Accessed 15 June 2020
66. van der Linden, N., Tinholt, D.: eGovernment benchmark 2017. Taking stock of user-centric design and delivery of digital public services in Europe. Capgemini, IDC, Sogeti, and Politecnico di Milano (2017). https://administracionelectronica.gob.es/pae_Home/pae_OBSAE/Posicionamiento-Internacional/Comision_Europea_OBSAE/benchmark-egovernment.html. Accessed 15 June 2020
67. Tinholt, D., van der Linden, N.: Future-proofing eGovernment for a digital single market. Final insight report. Capgemini, IDC, Sogeti, and Politecnico di Milano (2015). https://administracionelectronica.gob.es/pae_Home/pae_OBSAE/Posicionamiento-Internacional/Comision_Europea_OBSAE/benchmark-egovernment.html. Accessed 15 June 2020
68. Tinholt, D., van der Linden, N.: eGovernment benchmark 2016. A turning point for eGovernment development in Europe? Capgemini, IDC, Sogeti, and Politecnico di Milano (2016). https://administracionelectronica.gob.es/pae_Home/pae_OBSAE/Posicionamiento-Internacional/Comision_Europea_OBSAE/benchmark-egovernment.html. Accessed 15 June 2020

69. van der Linden, N., Tinholt, D.: eGovernment benchmark 2018: securing eGovernment for all. Capgemini, IDC, Sogeti, and Politecnico di Milano (2018). https://administracionelectronica. gob.es/pae_Home/pae_OBSAE/Posicionamiento-Internacional/Comision_Europea_ OBSAE/benchmark-egovernment.html. Accessed 15 June 2020

70. Ronaghan, S.A.: Benchmarking e-Government: a global perspective. United Nations, Division for Public Economics and Public Administration (2002). https://publicadministration.un.org/ en/research/un-e-government-surveys. Accessed 30 June 2020

71. Bertucci, G., Hafeez, S.: UN global e-Government survey 2003. United Nations, Department of Economic and Social Affairs (2003). https://publicadministration.un.org/en/research/un-e-government-surveys. Accessed 30 June 2020

72. Bertucci, G., Hafeez, S.: UN global e-Government readiness report 2004. United Nations, Department of Economic and Social Affairs (2004). https://publicadministration.un.org/en/ research/un-e-government-surveys. Accessed 30 June 2020

73. Bertucci, G., Hafeez, S.: UN global e-Government readiness report 2005. United Nations, Department of Economic and Social Affairs (2005). https://publicadministration.un.org/en/ research/un-e-government-surveys. Accessed 30 June 2020

74. Bertucci, G.: United Nations e-Government Survey 2008. United Nations, New York (2008)

75. Qian, H.: United Nations e-Government Survey 2010. United Nations, New York (2010)

76. Qian, H., Kauzya, J.-M., Aquaro, V.: United Nations e-Government Survey 2012. United Nations, New York (2012)

77. Qian, H., Aquaro, V.: United Nations e-Government Survey 2014. United Nations, New York (2014)

78. Zhu, J., Barthélemy, M.: United Nations e-Government Survey 2016. United Nations, New York (2016)

79. Aquaro, V., Barthélemy, M., Schweinfest, S.: United Nations e-Government Survey 2018. United Nations, New York (2018)

80. Aquaro, V.: e-Government Survey 2020 Digital Government in the Decade of Action for Sustainable Development. Department of Economic and Social Affairs, United Nations, New York (2020)

81. Mora, L., Angelidou, M., Reid, A.: The current status of smart city research: exposing the division. In: Komninos, N., Kakderi, C. (eds.) Smart Cities in the Post-Algorithmic Era, pp. 17–35. Edward Elgar Pub. (2019)

82. Barth, J., et al.: Informational urbanism. a conceptual framework of smart cities. In: Proceedings of the 50th Hawaii International Conference on System Science (HICSS-50), Waikoloa Village, Hawaii, USA, pp. 2814–2823 (2017)

83. Albino, V., Dangelico, R.M., Berardi, U.: Smart cities: definitions, dimensions, performance, and initiatives. J. Urban Technol. 22(1), 3–21 (2015)

84. Anthopoulos, L.G.: The rise of the smart city. In: Anthopoulos, L.G. (ed.) Understanding Smart Cities: A Tool for Smart Government or an Industrial Trick?, pp. 5–45. Springer, Cham (2017). https://doi.org/10.1007/978-3-319-57015-0_2

85. Cohen, B.: The 3 generations of smart cities. Fast Company (2015). https://www. fastcompany.com/3047795/the-3-generations-of-smart-cities. Accessed 30 June 2020

Citizens' Perceptions of Mobile Tax Filing Services

Tinyiko Hlomela and Tendani Mawela$^{(\boxtimes)}$ (iD)

University of Pretoria, Hatfield, South Africa
tghlomela44@gmail.com, tendani.mawela@up.ac.za

Abstract. This study aimed to identify the user acceptance determinants of a revenue services agency mobile filing application. The study used the UTAUT model which was adapted by introducing privacy and trust factors to understand taxpayers' perceptions towards the mobile filing application. Data was collected through a survey conducted with taxpayers. The results of the study provide empirical evidence on m-Government and in particular the adoption of mobile filing of tax returns. The results highlight that prior experience with using electronic filing systems has a direct effect on the intention of taxpayers to accept and use the revenue services' mobile filing application to submit their tax returns. These effects are moderated by certain facilitating conditions, effort expectancy and social influence from important stakeholders in a citizen's context. The study puts forward recommendations towards enhancing the uptake and impact of mobile government services.

Keywords: e-Government · m-Government · e-Filing · UTAUT · m-Filing

1 Introduction

Information and Communication Technologies (ICT's) have altered the manner in which government's communicate and offer services to their citizens. The ongoing growth in mobile technology, particularly the high penetration of mobile phones that have internet access and smart phones provide governments with a channel to enhance electronic government (e-Government) and deliver government services to citizens effectively [1]. This introduction of mobile technology has brought about the development of mobile government (m-Government) services. M-Government is the use of wireless mobile devices to exchange information and services by public administration with business, citizens and other government institutions [2].

This study sought to understand the perspectives of citizens on m-Government solutions through a case study based in the Republic of South Africa (RSA). The RSA government has acknowledged the core benefits associated with e-Government [3]. The literature indicates that e-government initiatives are often plagued by low adoption by civilians [4]. With the extensive usage of mobile phones in developing countries such as RSA and the upward internet penetration, the prospect to grow e-Government services and reach through the use of mobile technology is significant [5]. This study explores m-Government services acceptance and use with a particular focus on mobile tax filing (m-filing) services. The main research question is:

© Springer Nature Switzerland AG 2020
M. Themistocleous et al. (Eds.): EMCIS 2020, LNBIP 402, pp. 256–269, 2020.
https://doi.org/10.1007/978-3-030-63396-7_17

Which factors influence tax payers' acceptance and use of the SARS m-filing application?

2 Literature Review

2.1 Mobile Government Drivers and Benefits

With the increasing popularity of mobile communication devices, m-government services have become essential for improving citizen to government communication [1]. The drivers and enablers of m-government include the global proliferation of mobile phones and internet access, availability of affordable smart phones, and also the notion that mobile phones are easy to use [6]. It is argued that mobile technology infrastructure is easier to setup compared to wired technology infrastructure. Additionally, mobile technology capabilities have advanced over the years offering various features and functionality [7].

Public service delivery by governments has been transformed by the emergence of m-Government [8, 9]. M-Government is an extension of e-Government, it is the delivery of information and services to citizens and organisations through the use of mobile devices [10]. The paper by [11] highlights that governments in developing countries are investing in providing more access to information and services for businesses, citizens, and civil servants through wireless technology. Mobile technology infrastructure and services may help provide a solution to the absence of wired ICT infrastructure in developing countries [12]. M-Government is proving to be a viable option for providing citizens and businesses with further access to e-Government [1].

According to [13], m-Government applications can provide individual personalised services to citizens. Mobile government supports timeous information delivery and offers several advantages to citizens such as: convenience; always on; they may access it from anywhere coupled with time and cost-savings [14–17].

2.2 Mobile Government Challenges

Several challenges are noted in the efforts by government institutions to provide m-Government including: different mobile phones complexity challenges, lack of secure networks to guarantee secure services, complying with privacy and legal issues and selecting the applicable and appropriate services to be provided on mobile platforms [8, 11]. Also [18] highlight barriers such as high access costs including data and recharge rates, technology accessibility and a lack of standards to implement m-Government initiatives.

According to [18] the successful implementation of m-Government also requires: a national government strategy supported by leadership, investment in physical wireless infrastructure, human capacity development and skills. Additionally m-Government faces challenges of being vulnerable to attacks due to the mobility of the devices. Also limitations such as the capacity of mobile devices, limitations on screen size, user interface and content have been highlighted [19].

2.3   Mobile Government Case Study Overview

RSA has made a commitment to the use of ICT's towards the goals of socioeconomic progress and service delivery. The government has put forward various plans and expansive budgets for the delivery of e-Government programs across national, provincial and local government sectors. RSA is faced with challenges when it comes to effective and sufficient delivery of services to their citizens [12]. M-government services may provide a solution to the access limitation and challenges in RSA's e-Government deployment [12].

A significant e-Government project for RSA is the South African Revenue Services (SARS) agency e-filing system [20, 48]. The primary aim of the e-filing system is to enable taxpayers and tax advisors to electronically submit their tax returns and payments. The traditional approach of submitting tax returns is still available to taxpayers e.g. visiting a SARS office. However, e-filing was aimed at improving the service through providing a quicker and more efficient service [20]. The e-filing service enables individual taxpayers, tax consultants and various organizations to sign up for e-filing and conclude transactions with SARS electronically [21, 48]. The e-filing system has resulted in improved turnaround times for the processing of tax returns. In 2018 the majority of payments to SARS were made through the e-filing payments channel accounting for 76.1% of the value of all taxpayer payments for the financial year 2017–2018 [21].

Mobile phone penetration in RSA is amongst the highest within developing countries [22]. Accordingly [18] argue that m-Government may be considered a complementary part of improving information and service delivery to citizens. According to [23] the delivery and service quality of e-Government may be improved by using m-Government. SARS has subsequently implemented a mobile filing (m-filing) application. Evidence of research on m-Government and m-filing of tax returns in developing countries is limited. There is scant research regarding the acceptance and use of m-filing services in the literature. This study aimed to identify the user acceptance determinants of the SARS m-filing application.

3   Theoretical Foundation of the Study

We leaned on the UTAUT framework to support the study's objectives. It is highlighted by [24] that UTAUT suggests that effort expectancy, performance expectancy and social influence predict behavioural intention towards Information Technology acceptance and use. The UTAUT model further suggests that behavioural intention and facilitating conditions predicts usage behaviour in the acceptance and use of information technology [25] and the model has been used to evaluate various IT applications [26].

We appended to the UTAUT model by including privacy and trust of government as factors to explore the determinants of SARS m-filing application acceptance and use by South African taxpayers. It is argued that building user trust may help the process of mobile services acceptance and usage. This is achieved by ensuring privacy on user data such as personal information. Ensuring protection of user personal information will bolster trust levels. Similar to the studies by [29] and [30] we incorporated privacy and trust as a moderator to understand m-government acceptance and use.

Additionally, the alterations we made to the UTAUT model are as follows; in this study behavioural intention is used for showing the actual outcome on usage of m-filing system. Also [27] and [28] based their research models on UTAUT, and they excluded gender, and age moderators from their models due to the unbalanced distribution, these moderating effects were also excluded in this study for the same reason. Our proposed model that is primarily based on [31] is seen in Fig. 1.

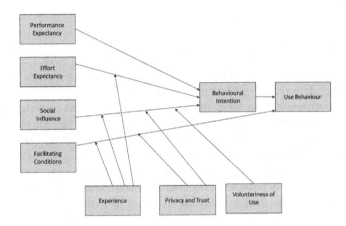

Fig. 1. Research model based on UTAUT

4 Research Methods

The research study adopted a positivist philosophical paradigm. The research approach was exploratory and quantitative. A cross sectional survey questionnaire was used to collect data. It comprised of 38 questions with a 5-point Likert scale that were informed by extant literature and based on the UTAUT which supported construct validity. Ten hypotheses aligned to the UTAUT [31–34] were proposed and evaluated as outlined in Sect. 5.3. Judgement sampling was adopted and involves actively identifying the most relevant sample to answer the research questions, who in this context were citizens that are taxpayers. It is reported that RSA has a narrow tax base and in 2019 approximately 5% of citizens paid 97% of all income tax [47]. This study aimed to target registered tax payers specifically. Similar to [35] this study also used snowball sampling to obtain the applicable respondents. The selected taxpayers resided in Gauteng Province the economic hub of the country and referred the questionnaire to other taxpayers after completing the questionnaire. The questionnaire was self-administered by respondents electronically.

The reliability of the research instrument was tested using the Cronbach's alpha. The overall alpha coefficient for all the items is 0.87 suggesting that the items have relatively high internal consistency. The results of the quantitative data were analysed using structural equation modelling (SEM) and Regression Analysis techniques [36,

37]. The Spearman rank-order correlation was used to measure the relationship between the independent and dependent variables. A total number of 150 questionnaires were initiated online of which a valid completion rate of 67% was achieved, providing a total of 88 valid completed questionnaires to be analysed for the exploratory study.

5   Research Results

5.1   Descriptive Statistics

Performance Expectancy
It was found that 8 out of 10 (84.2%) of respondents felt that SARS m-filing application will be more efficient than the existing paper-based approaches to tax filing. Very few either disagreed (6.6%) or were uncertain (9.2%). 90.8% felt that SARS m-filing application would help them file taxes in less time, with very few who were neutral (7.9%) or disagreed (1.3%). This majority (90.8%) also had the perception that SARS m-filing application would streamline the process of filing taxes. 64% also believed that SARS m-filing application system can opt for a taxation calculation approach that offers them the highest tax refund and monetary gains, with 19.7% who were uncertain about this issue and less than 20% who disagreed. Generally, the vast majority of respondents (96%) indicated that they feel that using SARS m-filing application will be helpful to them, compared to very few (3.9%) who were negative about this.

Social Influence
Social Influence is the extent to which persons see that significant persons believe they should make use of the system. The section seeks to address whether Social Influence will have a positive effect on the intention to use SARS m-filing application to file tax returns by the taxpayers. The vast majority - 96.1% of respondents did not think that SARS m-filing application conflicts in anyway with their former method of filing taxes. Very few either were uncertain (4%) - a negligible proportion and no one indicated that they disagreed. Eight out of ten (81.6%) felt that their colleagues and friends appear to be happy with some of the advantages of using the SARS m-filing application. 17.1% were neutral and negligible proportions of the respondents were in disagreement (1.3%). Just over 82.9% of respondents indicated that they had experienced that more of their colleagues and friends are using the m-filing application to submit their taxes. One in ten was neutral (10.5%) while very few (6.6%) indicated they never noticed this aspect.

Also, eight out of ten (82.9%) felt that their friends and colleagues are happy with the benefits of using the SARS m-filing application. One in ten (13%) were uncertain about this while very few indicated they were not satisfied with this aspect. Eight to nine out of ten respondents (86.8%) seemed to trust the experience of their family, friends and colleagues with using the SARS m-filing application. 11.8% were uncertain on this issue while almost no one disagreed. Also, three quarters of the respondents (75%) think that the media have offered good reviews about the SARS m-filing application, a quarter were uncertain about this aspect. Nine out of ten respondents (92%) believed that progressive and efficient solutions provided by public administrators could convince them to accept and use the SARS m-filing application. They thought that specialists in associated fields were confident about m-filing and thought highly of the SARS m-filing application (88%). Research participants thought that people in their personal networks believe that adopting m-filing was advantageous (86.8%). Respondents also indicated that they used m-filing because it was promoted as more efficient in comparison to paper-based tax filing (80.3%), a fifth were uncertain on this.

Privacy and Trust

Privacy and Trust has been proven to moderate the relationship between Social Influence and the dependent construct behavioural intention. This section seeks to address whether the positive effect of Social Influence on the intention to use SARS m-filing application to file tax returns is moderated by privacy and trust. Almost nine out of ten (88.2%) indicated that they felt assured and comfortable that SARS has implemented the appropriate safety procedures and protocols to safeguard personal information, with very few who were either uncertain (9.2%) or disagreed (2.6%). Slightly above half (55%) of the respondents did not trust the m-filing system with any of their personal and financial information, compared to a third (32.9%) who indicated they did trust the m-filing system with information. 11% respondents were uncertain whether they trusted the m-filing system with any of their personal and financial information or not. The vast majority (93.4%) of respondents trusted the m-filing system while very few were uncertain (2.6%) or disagreed (4%). Furthermore, between eight and nine out of ten (86.9%) indicated that they trusted the m-filing system with their personal information. A few were either uncertain (9.2%) or were in disagreement (4%).

Voluntariness of Use

Voluntariness of use is the degree to which an individual recognises that he or she can decide to use or not to use IT. The section seeks to address whether the positive effect of Social Influence on the intention to use SARS m-filing application to file tax returns is moderated by Voluntariness of use. Almost nine out of ten (88.2%) could quite easily access and trial the SARS m-filing application prior to making a choice on whether to accept and use the application, very few respondents (12%) were not in agreement with this aspect. Nine out of ten (93.4%) of respondents felt that they have adequate opportunities to acquire knowledge about the m-filing application prior to making a decision to accept and use it. Very few did not agree to this (7%). This majority (86.8%) also believed that they could frequently trial the m-filing application prior to accepting and using it, one in ten (10.5%) was undecided.

Effort Expectancy

Effort expectancy is the extent to which the system is easy to use for individuals. We sought to understand whether Effort Expectancy will have a positive effect on the intention to use SARS m-filing application. The vast majority of respondents (92.1%) felt that the SARS m-filing application is simple to use, with very negligible proportion who did not feel so. Respondents believed that they could seamlessly submit their taxes with the SARS m-filing application. They also felt it was straightforward and easy to learn how to use SARS m-filing application, no respondent disagreed.

Experience

Experience is defined as the past use of IT systems. This section seeks to address whether the positive effect of Facilitating Conditions (FC) on the Use Behaviour of SARS m-filing application to file tax returns is moderated by experience, such that the effect is stronger for taxpayers who have more experience in using IT. The vast majority of respondents (93.4%) believe they are able to use the SARS m-filing application completely. They felt that if they were so inclined, they are fully able to use the SARS m-filing application (92.1%). A similar proportion (92.1%) felt that even if they do not obtain direct instructions, they were capable of using the SARS m-filing application. Due to this, they seem to feel comfortable using the m-filing system on their own.

Behavioural Intention

Behavioural Intention consists of Performance Expectancy, Social Influence and Effort Expectancy. The majority of respondents were in agreement with all the aspects in this dimension. Over 90% believed that the SARS m-filing application is worth using (96.1%) that if they were so inclined, they would be fully capable of operating the SARS m-filing application (92.1%). They felt that even if they do not obtain direct instructions, they were capable of using the SARS m-filing application (92.1%). Almost everybody in the sample felt they were comfortable in using the m-filing system on their own (97.4%).

Facilitating Conditions

Facilitating Conditions is the extent to which a person believes the use of the system is supported by an organisation. This section seeks to address whether Facilitating Conditions (FC) will have a positive effect on Use Behaviour of SARS m-filing application to file tax returns by the taxpayers. The majority of respondents (96.1%) felt that the tools and resources required to use m-filing were readily available. However, half of them (52%) would like to use m-filing but don't have access to the relevant tools and resources. They indicated that looking ahead, they will continue to use or consider using the SARS m-filing application (97.4%). The results show that nine out of ten (90%) have internet access at home to connect to m-filing. They would use their phone to access m-filing (89.5%).

5.2   Hypothesis Testing

We examined the relationship between the factors that influence citizens to use the m-filing solution through paired t-tests for paired observations. This was done through ten hypothesis tests. We tested the null hypothesis against the hypothesis that there is no relationship that exists between Behavioral Intention (BI) and its explanatory factors, experience (Exp.), privacy & trust (PT) and voluntariness of use (VU) as moderators. In the upcoming section we share and discuss the results.

5.3   Discussion of the Findings

Research Hypothesis Results

H1: Performance Expectancy (PE) will have a positive effect on the intention to use SARS m-filing application to file tax returns by the taxpayers. We found that there is a direct positive relationship between PE and BI, suggesting that Performance Expectancy could have as much as 4 times potential/likelihood to positively affect BI. In performance expectancy, the majority (90.8%) had the perception that m-filing would streamline the process of submitting their taxes. Fewer, (64%) believed that SARS m-filing application is able to choose the taxation calculation approach that yields the highest monetary gain for them. Descriptive results indicate that Behavioural Intention sub scale had the highest mean score, indicating strongest agreement in its factors. In this scale, the majority of respondents (96%) indicate that they feel that using the SARS m-filing application will be helpful to them. Almost everybody in the sample felt they were comfortable in using the m-filing system on their own (97.4%). Six out of ten (64%) also believed that SARS m-filing application can apply the taxation calculation approach that yields the highest monetary gain for them. These findings show that taxpayers with high performance expectancy are more likely to be interested in the acceptance and use of m-Government services, particularly m-filing in the context of this study. These results are consistent with other studies [31, 38–40]. The findings therefore support the proposed hypothesis, that performance expectancy is an influential factor on the use and acceptance of the SARS m-filing application.

H2: Effort Expectancy (EE) will have a positive effect on the intention to use SARS m-filing application for filing tax returns by the taxpayers. The results indicate a direct positive relationship between Effort Expectancy (EE) and Behavioral Intention (BI), suggesting that EE could have as much as 2 times potential/likelihood to positively affect BI - acceptance and use of the SARS m-filing application. Descriptive statistics indicate that effort expectancy (EE) had strongest agreement. Respondents felt that the SARS m-filing application is easy to understand and operate, with very negligible proportion who did not feel so. The finding is similar to other studies [31]. As a result of this finding, it is expected that taxpayers who are technically skilled are most likely to use the SARS m-filing application, and therefore most likely to adopt m-filing services.

H3: Social Influence (SI) will have a positive effect on the intention to use SARS m-filing application to file tax returns by the taxpayers. There is a direct positive relationship between Behavioral Intention (BI) and Social Influence (SI), suggesting that SI could have as much as 4 times potential to positively affect BI. These results are consistent with extant literature [41]. With regards to SI-the vast majority -nine out of ten (96.1%) respondents did not think that m-filing conflicts with their previous ways of submitting their taxes. They think that the media has offered good reviews regarding the SARS m-filing application, a quarter were uncertain about this aspect.

H4: Facilitating Conditions (FC) will have a positive effect on the intention to use SARS m-filing application to file tax returns by the taxpayers. The results found that there is a direct positive relationship between Behavioral Intention (BI) and Facilitating Condition (FC), suggesting that FC could have up to 6 times potential to positively affect Behavioral Intention. These results are consistent with literature such as: [42] and [43], that facilitating conditions have a significant impact on predicting behavioural intention. In Facilitating Conditions, respondents generally agreed with the factors within the sub scales. It was seen that the majority of respondents (96.1%) felt that the tools and resources required to use m-filing were readily available. However, half of them (52%) would like to use m-filing but don't have access to the necessary tools and resources.

The following hypotheses were proposed based on the moderating effects of privacy and trust:

H5: The positive effect of Social Influence (SI) on the intention to use SARS m-filing application to file tax returns is moderated by Privacy and Trust (PT), such that the effect is stronger for tax payers who trust the infrastructure and the government entity managing the infrastructure. Contrary to this, the results suggest that that there is no relationship between and SI and PT as a moderator. These results are consistent with prior research [44]. On privacy and trust, the majority (93.4%) of respondents trusted the m-filing application but were afraid of hackers and other internet threats. Slightly above half (55%) of the respondents did not trust the m-filing application with any of their personal and financial information.

H6: The positive effect of Facilitating Conditions (FC) on use behaviour of SARS m-filing application to file tax returns is moderated by privacy and trust, such that the effect is stronger for tax payers who trust the infrastructure and the government entity managing the infrastructure. Contrary to this hypothesis, the results suggest that that there is no relationship between and FC and PT as a moderator. This is inconsistent with other studies which found that the trust of the people in m-Government agencies will significantly influence their intention to use their e-services.

H7: The positive effect of Social Influence (SI) on the intention to use SARS m-filing application to file tax returns is moderated by voluntariness of use, such that the more voluntary the behaviour, the more one's attitude toward intention to use and usage. Opposite to this, the results suggest that that there is no relationship between and SI and VU as a moderator. However, the most important factor in VU was that nine out of ten (93.4%) of respondents felt that they have adequate opportunities to gain knowledge about the m-filing application prior to making a decision about accepting and using it.

H8: The positive effect of Facilitating Conditions (FC) on the use behaviour of SARS m-filing application to file tax returns is moderated by experience, such that the effect is stronger for tax payers who have more experience in using IT. The results suggest that that there is some relationship between experience and FC as a moderator. The implication of these results is that through factors of experience, FC could have up to 4 times as much indirect positive effect on the intention to use SARS m-filing application to file tax returns. Descriptive results indicate that the most important factor in experience was that respondents are able to utilize the SARS m-filing application fully. The finding is consistent with other studies [39, 40, 45].

H9: The positive effect of Effort Expectancy (EE) on the intention to use SARS m-filing application to file tax returns is moderated by experience, such that the effect is stronger for tax payers who have more experience in using IT. The results suggest that that in this study there was no evidence of a relationship between experience and EE and as a moderator. These findings are inconsistent with the findings of [46] who found that effort expectancy's effect on behavioural intention changed depending on experience.

H10: The positive effect of Social Influence (SI) on the intention to use SARS m-filing application to file tax returns is moderated by experience, such that the effect is stronger for tax payers who have more experience in using IT. The results suggest that that there is some relationship between experience and Social Influence as a moderator. The implication of these results is that through factors of experience, SI could have up to 3 times as much indirect positive effect on intention to use SARS m-filing application to file tax returns.

Correlation and Regression Analysis

Correlation results were of moderate magnitude and indicate moderate associations and not relationships between factors of Behavioural Intention. Notably, Privacy and Trust (PT) (rs = 0.398; $p < 0.05$) and voluntariness of use (VU) (rs = 0.308; $p < 0.05$) have moderate positive associations with BI –acceptance and use of SARS m-filing application. These results imply that an increase in the three moderator factors, experience, privacy & trust and voluntariness of use are likely to result in a unit increase in the acceptance and use rate (BI) of the m-filing solution, with a modest magnitude of effect. It is only Experience (Exp) which has a strong positive association with BI (rs = 0.526; $p < 0.05$).

To test for possible causal relationships, we now discuss the results from a regression analysis. First, we focus on the factors on the intention of taxpayers to use SARS m-filing application to submit their tax returns, with Privacy and Trust as a moderator. The results indicate that there is a positive causal relationship between Facilitating Conditions (FC) (b = 0.25; $p < 0.05$), Effort Expectancy (EE) (0.29; $p < 0.05$), and Social Influence (SI) (b = 0.38; $p < 0.05$). A unit increase in Facilitating Condition, Effort Expectancy and Social Influence is likely to lead into an increase in Privacy and Trust (PT), Social Influence having the strongest effect (38%), followed by Effort Expectancy (29%) and lastly FC (25%). Performance expectancy seems not to have any effect on Privacy and Trust. The implication of these results is that the three exogenous factors here have a direct effect on Privacy and Trust, implying they are likely to have an indirect effect on Behavioural Intention.

Next, we also looked at the factors on the intention of taxpayers to use SARS m-filing application to submit their tax returns, with Voluntariness of Use as a moderator. The results indicate that there is a positive causal relationship between Effort Expectancy (b = 0.27; $p < 0.05$) and SI (b = 0.34; $p < 0.05$). A unit increase in Effort Expectancy, Social Influence is likely to lead into an increase in Voluntariness of Use, with Social Influence having the strongest effect (34%), followed by Effort Expectancy (27%). Performance expectancy and Facilitating Conditions seem not to have any effect on Voluntariness of Use at 5% significant level. The implication of these results is that the two exogenous factors here have a direct effect on Voluntariness of Use, implying they are likely to have an indirect effect on Behavioural Intention.

Additionally, factors on the intention of taxpayers to use SARS m-filing application to submit their tax returns, with Experience as a moderator were considered. The results indicate that there is a strong positive causal relationship between Effort Expectancy (b = 0.41; p < 0.05). A unit increase in Effort Expectancy is likely to lead into an increase in experience, the strongest effect so far (41%). Although Performance Expectancy is not significant, it provides an insight that it is the only factor that had negative tendency on another (experience). The implication of these results is that Effort Expectancy has a direct strong effect on experience, implying it is likely to have an indirect effect on Behavioural Intention.

6   Conclusion, Recommendations and Future Research

6.1   Concluding Remarks

This study investigated the factors that influence the intention to accept and use the SARS m-filing system by taxpayers and was on a model informed by UTAUT. The results shows that privacy and trust as well as voluntariness of use seem not to have any effects on Behavioural Intention-the beta coefficient are very negligible and the p-values are far greater than the conventional levels. The findings showed that only one factor (experience) had statistically significant results, with as much as 45% positive effect on Behavioural Intention. In addition, Facilitating Conditions could have up to 6 times likelihood to positively affect Behavioural Intention. A unit increase in Facilitating Conditions, Effort Expectancy and Social Influence is likely to lead into an increase in Privacy & Trust, Social Influence having the strongest effect (38%), followed by Effort Expectancy (29%) and lastly Facilitating Conditions (25%). A unit increase in Effort Expectancy, Social Influence is likely to lead into an increase in Voluntariness Use, with Social Influence having the strongest effect (34%), followed by Effort Expectancy (27%). Lastly, a unit increase in Effort Expectancy is likely to lead into an increase in experience, the strongest effect so far (41%). Also, contrary to the objectives, privacy and trust and voluntariness of use seem not to have any effects on Behavioural Intention - the beta coefficient are very negligible and the p-values are far greater than the conventional levels.

Based on the results, it is suggested that government entities should ensure future m-government systems are designed with ease of use as a priority. It is recommended that authorities should also look at educating the citizens on how to use the m-government applications and offer opportunities to trial the systems. Additionally there should be a focus on strengthening their technological and application support by providing support personnel and resources such as online tutorials and subject matter experts. The findings of the study may assist government agencies such as SARS to enhance the acceptance and usage of their mobile government systems. This study contributed to the literature on the technology acceptance in a developing country context. It highlighted the utility of the UTAUT in research investigating factors that influence m-government acceptance. The model used for this study, was a modified version of the UTAUT model and thus contributes to existing literature on technology acceptance.

6.2   Limitations and Future Research

This study excluded the gender and age moderators, future research may include them and additional variables as they can provide further understanding of mobile filing acceptance. The exploratory study was conducted within the Gauteng province. A larger sample across all RSA provinces is recommend for future studies. Additionally a comparative study across various developing countries and regions may yield interesting lessons. We also recommend qualitative approaches including focus groups with citizens to further understand their perceptions on m-government.

References

1. Dwivedi, Y.K., Sahu, G.P., Rana, N.P., Baabdullah, A.M.: Citizens' awareness, acceptance and use of mobile government services in india: an exploratory research. In: Proceedings of the 11th International Conference on Theory and Practice of Electronic Governance, pp. 236–239 (2018)
2. Ishmatova, D., Obi, T.: M-government services: user needs and value. I-WAYS-J. E-Gov. Policy Regul. **32**(1), 39–46 (2009)
3. Mpinganjira, M.: E-government project failure in Africa: lessons for reducing risk. Afr. J. Bus. Manag. **7**(32), 3196–3201 (2013)
4. Munyoka, W.: Exploring the factors influencing e-Government use: empirical evidence from Zimbabwe. Electron. J. Inf. Syst. Eval. **22**(2) (2019)
5. Wentzel, J.P., Diatha, K.S., Yadavalli, V.S.S.: An application of the extended technology acceptance model in understanding technology-enabled financial service adoption in South Africa. Dev. Southern Afr. **30**(4–5), 659–673 (2013)
6. Dixit, A.: Governance institutions and economic activity. Am. Econ. Rev. **99**(1), 5–24 (2009)
7. Germanakos, P., Samaras, G., Mourlas, C., Christodoulou, E.: Innovative personalization issues for providing user-centric mGovernment services. In: Proceedings of the Second European Conference on Mobile Government (Euro mGov 2006), Brighton, August 2006, pp. 30–31 (2006)
8. Amailef, K., Lu, J.: m-Government: a framework of mobile-based emergency response systems. In: 2008 3rd International Conference on Intelligent System and Knowledge Engineering, November 2008, vol. 1, pp. 1398–1403. IEEE (2008)
9. Rana, N., Janssen, M., Sahu, G.P., Baabdullah, A., Dwivedi, Y.: Citizens' perception about m-government services: results from an exploratory survey. In: Proceedings of the 52nd Hawaii International Conference on System Sciences, January 2019, pp. 3356–3365 (2019)
10. Lee, S.M., Tan, X., Trimi, S.: M-government, from rhetoric to reality: learning from leading countries. Electron. Gov. Int. J. **3**(2), 113–126 (2006)
11. Mengistu, D., Zo, H., Rho, J.J.: M-government: opportunities and challenges to deliver mobile government services in developing countries. In: 2009 Fourth International Conference on Computer Sciences and Convergence Information Technology, November 2009, pp. 1445–1450. IEEE (2009)
12. Nkosi, M., Mekuria, F.: Mobile government for improved public service provision in South Africa. In: 2010 IST-Africa, May 2010, pp. 1–8. IEEE (2010)
13. Snellen, I., Thaens, M.: From e-government to m-government: towards a new paradigm in public administration. Administrative innovation, international context and growth. Formez, Gianni Research, pp. 1–33 (2008)

14. Singh, A.K., Sahu, R.: Integrating Internet, telephones, and call centers for delivering better quality e-governance to all citizens. Gov. Inf. Q. **25**(3), 477–490 (2008)
15. Sheng, H., Trimi, S.: M-government: technologies, applications and challenges. Electron. Gov. **5**(1), 1 (2008)
16. Babullah, A., Dwivedi, Y.K., Williams, M.D.: Saudi citizens' perceptions on mobile government (mGov) adoption factors. In: UKAIS, April 2015, p. 8 (2015)
17. Ntaliani, M., Costopoulou, C., Karetsos, S.: Mobile government: a challenge for agriculture. Gov. Inf. Q. **25**(4), 699–716 (2008)
18. Maumbe, B.M., Owei, V., Alexander, H.: Questioning the pace and pathway of e-government development in Africa: a case study of South Africa's Cape Gateway project. Gov. Inf. Q. **25**(4), 757–777 (2008)
19. Isagah, T., Wimmer, M.A.: Mobile government applications: challenges and needs for a comprehensive design approach. In: Proceedings of the 10th International Conference on Theory and Practice of Electronic Governance, March 2017, pp. 423–432 (2017)
20. Van Rooyen, E., Van Jaarsveld, L.C.: A South African developmental perspective on e-government. J. Publ. Adm. **38**(3), 236–252 (2003)
21. South African Revenue Services (SARS): Tax Statistics for 2018 (2018). https://www.sars.gov.za/AllDocs/Documents/Tax%20Stats/Tax%20Stats%202018/Tax%20Statistics%202018.pdf
22. Reinecke, R., Coulson, D., Thinyane, H.: E-democracy through mobile monitoring: participatory journalism. Rhodes Journal. Rev. **2012**(32), 50 (2012)
23. Bailey, A., Minto-Coy, I., Thakur, D.: IT governance in e-government implementations in the Caribbean: key characteristics and mechanisms. In: Rusu, L., Viscusi, G. (eds.) Information Technology Governance in Public Organizations, pp. 201–227. Springer, Cham. (2017)
24. Taiwo, A.A., Downe, A.G.: The theory of user acceptance and use of technology (UTAUT): a meta-analytic review of empirical findings. J. Theor. Appl. Inf. Technol. **49**(1) (2013)
25. Alam, M.Z., Hu, W., Barua, Z.: Using the UTAUT model to determine factors affecting acceptance and use of mobile health (mHealth) services in Bangladesh. J. Stud. Soc. Sci. **17**(2) (2018)
26. Al-Shafi, S., Weerakkody, V., Janssen, M.: Investigating the adoption of eGovernment services in Qatar using the UTAUT model. In: AMCIS 2009 Proceedings, p. 260 (2009)
27. Van Schaik, P.: Unified theory of acceptance and use for web sites used by students in higher education. J. Educ. Comput. Res. **40**(2), 229–257 (2009)
28. Tan, P.J.B.: Applying the UTAUT to understand factors affecting the use of English e-learning websites in Taiwan. Sage Open **3**(4), 1–12 (2013)
29. Hung, S.Y., Chang, C.M., Yu, T.J.: Determinants of user acceptance of the e-Government services: the case of online tax filing and payment system. Gov. Inf. Q. **23**(1), 97–122 (2006)
30. Min, Q., Ji, S., Qu, G.: Mobile commerce user acceptance study in China: a revised UTAUT model. Tsinghua Sci. Technol. **13**(3), 257–264 (2008)
31. Venkatesh, V., Morris, M.G., Davis, G.B., Davis, F.D.: User acceptance of information technology: toward a unified view. MIS Q. 425–478 (2003)
32. Brown, S.A., Dennis, A.R., Venkatesh, V.: Predicting collaboration technology use: integrating technology adoption and collaboration research. J. Manag. Inf. Syst. **27**(2), 9–54 (2010)
33. Liu, L., Nath, H.K.: Information and communications technology and trade in emerging market economies. Emerg. Mark. Finance Trade **49**(6), 67–87 (2013)
34. Khechine, H., Lakhal, S., Pascot, D., Bytha, A.: UTAUT model for blended learning: the role of gender and age in the intention to use webinars. Interdisc. J. e-Learn. Learn. Objects **10**(1), 33–52 (2014)

35. Alfalah, A., Choudrie, J., Spencer, N.: Older adults adoption, use and diffusion of e-government services in Saudi Arabia, Hail City: a quantitative study. In: Proceedings of the 50th Hawaii International Conference on System Sciences, pp. 2953–2962 (2017)
36. Grace, J.B.: Structural equation modeling for observational studies. J. Wildl. Manag. **72**(1), 14–22 (2008)
37. Cheng, E.W.: SEM being more effective than multiple regression in parsimonious model testing for management development research. J. Manag. Dev. **20**(7), 650–667 (2001)
38. Venkatesh, V., Bala, H.: Technology acceptance model 3 and a research agenda on interventions. Decis. Sci. **39**(2), 273–315 (2008)
39. Davis, F.D.: Perceived usefulness, perceived ease of use, and user acceptance of information technology. MIS Q. 319–340 (1989)
40. Venkatesh, V., Davis, F.D.: A theoretical extension of the technology acceptance model: four longitudinal field studies. Manag. Sci. **46**(2), 186–204 (2000)
41. Bertot, J.C., Jaeger, P.T., Grimes, J.M.: Using ICTs to create a culture of transparency: e-government and social media as openness and anti-corruption tools for societies. Gov. Inf. Q. **27**(3), 264–271 (2010)
42. Gillwald, A., Moyo, M., Christoph Stork, D.: Understanding what is happening in ICT in South Africa: a supply- and demand-side analysis of the ICT sector (2012). https://media.africaportal.org/documents/Policy_Paper_7_-_Understanding_what_is_happening_in_ICT_in_South_Africa.pdf
43. Alshehri, M., Drew, S., AlGhamdi, R.: Analysis of citizen's acceptance for e-government services: applying the UTAUT model. In: IADIS International Conferences Theory and Practice in Modern Computing and Internet Applications and Research (2013)
44. Horst, M., Kuttschreuter, M., Gutteling, J.M.: Perceived usefulness, personal experiences, risk perception and trust as determinants of adoption of e-government services in The Netherlands. Comput. Hum. Behav. **23**(4), 1838–1852 (2007)
45. Thong, J.Y.: An integrated model of information systems adoption in small businesses. J. Manag. Inf. Syst. **15**(4), 187–214 (1999)
46. Venkatesh, V., Zhang, X.: Unified theory of acceptance and use of technology: US vs. China. J. Glob. Inf. Technol. Manag. **13**(1), 5–27 (2010)
47. Kruger, A.: SA's problem of a narrow tax base and high taxes, Moneyweb. https://www.moneyweb.co.za/news/south-africa/sas-problem-of-a-narrow-tax-base-and-high-taxes/
48. Jankeeparsad, R.W., Jankeeparsad, T.R., Nienaber, G.: Acceptance of the electronic method of filing tax returns by South African tax payers: an exploratory study. J. Econ. Financ. Sci. **9**(1), 120–136 (2016)

Knowledge Graphs for Public Service Description: The Case of *Getting a Passport* in Greece

Promikyridis Rafail and Tambouris Efthimios[(✉)]

Department of Applied Informatics,
University of Macedonia, Thessaloniki, Greece
{mis18002, tambouris}@uom.edu.gr

Abstract. An important part of electronic Government is the provision of high quality Public Services (PS) to citizens. Towards this goal, the European Commission has proposed the Core Public Service Vocabulary (CPSV), as a PS data model to be used across the public sector. CPSV is adequate for use in the case of simple PS however its effectiveness is questionable in the case of complex PS. A complex PS is one having many (often complicated) rules interrelating its concepts, e.g. dictating citizens have to submit different documents to invoke a PS based on their profiles and circumstances. The aim of this paper is to investigate the use of Knowledge Graphs (KG) for providing personalized information on PS modeled using CPSV. For this purpose, we develop and evaluate a KG for PS "*Get a passport*" in Greece as a proof-of-concept to study mapping of CPSV to KG. For simplicity, we limit our scope to developing a KG that can provide the input documents and the relevant cost required for obtaining a passport by citizens based on their profile and circumstances. Free software GRAKN.AI was employed for the development of the KG.

Keywords: E-government · Knowledge graph · Public service provision · CPSV · Get a password · Grakn

1 Introduction

During the past 20 years, electronic Government (eGov) has become a political priority worldwide [1–3]. To a large extent, eGov refers to the provision of better Public Services (PS). Increased PS quality is related to personalised, citizen-oriented services.

PS provision is based on an underlying *PS model*, i.e. a data model proposed for describing and/or developing PS. A PS model includes concepts such as title, description, cost, legal framework, required documents (input), output etc. Adopting a universal, standard PS model could accelerate eGov systems development thus saving billions of Euros [4] and resolve eGov interoperability obstacles, which cost 68 billion Euros per year to the EU economy [5]. Recently, EC and EU member states introduced Core Public Service Vocabulary (CPSV) as a proposed standard PS model to be used across the EU. CPSV has high potential to resolve significant interoperability problems however its use is limited. Recent research revealed that although CPSV is useful for simple PS it is not equally useful to accommodate complex PS [4, 6]. A *complex PS* is

© Springer Nature Switzerland AG 2020
M. Themistocleous et al. (Eds.): EMCIS 2020, LNBIP 402, pp. 270–286, 2020.
https://doi.org/10.1007/978-3-030-63396-7_18

one having many (often complicated) rules interrelating its concepts, e.g. dictating citizens have to submit different documents or suffer different costs to invoke a PS, based on their profile or other legal conditions.

PS provision can be divided into two phases: the informative phase where citizens (or businesses) seek information about PS (e.g. documents to be submitted, cost etc.) and the performative phase where they actually invoke the PS and obtain its result [7]. In this paper we concentrate on the PS informative phase.

Information about PS is often provided by public authorities in their websites or using PS catalogues. This approach however faces significant challenges, as these websites do not provide personalised information particularly regarding complex PS.

Recently, knowledge graphs (KG) have started to attract attention due to their interesting characteristics [8]. KG can help citizens, employees and public servants make better decisions by identifying knowledge faster and easier [9]. KG inherently support rules thus seem a potentially interesting technology for providing personalized information on complex PS. This however has not been yet exploited particularly for PS based on CPSV.

The aim of this paper is to investigate the use of KG for providing personalized information on PS modeled using CPSV. More specifically, we develop and evaluate a KG for PS *Get a passport* in Greece as a proof-of-concept to study mapping of CPSV to KG. For simplicity, we limit our scope to developing a KG that can provide the input documents and the relevant cost required for obtaining a passport by citizens based on their profile and circumstances. For this reason, our study does not include all CPSV concepts e.g. Output, Public Organization etc. For KG development the free software GRAKN.AI was employed.

The rest of this paper is structured as follows. Section 2 outlines background work related to methods for providing personalized PS information, CPSV, Knowledge Graphs and Grakn. Section 3 presents the methodology. Section 4 illustrates the development of a KG for "Getting a passport" in Greece. Finally, conclusions are drawn in Sect. 5.

2 Background Work

2.1 Methods for Providing PS Information About Public Services

Information about PS is often provided in websites or PS catalogues. An example is www.passport.gov.gr providing information about getting a Greek passport. National one-stop government portals also contain PS information including PS descriptions. Dialogue-based systems have been also investigated by researchers (e.g. [10]) and operationally used by the public sector, e.g. benefits.gov in the USA. Interactive Voice Response (IVR) systems and chatbots [11] have also been employed by public authorities for the same purpose [12].

2.2   Core Public Service Vocabulary

In 2013, the European Commission (EC) in the framework of ISA and ISA^2 programs, proposed the Core Public Service Vocabulary (CPSV) [13] as a modular, extensible, context, syntax and technology-neutral PS data model. Based on CPSV, an Application Profile (CPSV-AP) [14] was developed in 2014 that exploits Linked Open Data (LOD) as an underpinning technology. An Application Profile is a specification that reuses terms from other standards, adding more specificity by identifying mandatory, recommended and optional elements, as well as by defining controlled vocabularies to be employed. The main objective of CPSV-AP is the description of public services and life or business events for the Points of Single Contact which each Member State had to implement in the context of the EU Services Directive (2006/123/EC).

Figure 1 illustrates an extract of CPSV-AP. This diagram contains only those classes with particular interest for our study, namely *Public Service* that represent the PS itself, *Evidence* that represents the needed input documents for invoking the PS, *Cost* that represents the PS cost, and *Rule* that represents a document that sets out the specific rules, guidelines or procedures that the PS follows (it is noted that CPSV-AP does not envisage instances of the Rule class as machine-readable business rules).

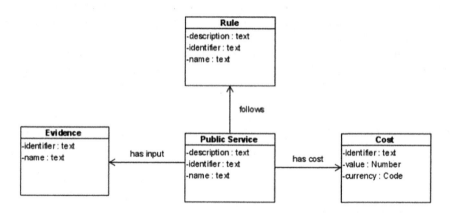

Fig. 1. Extract of CPSV-AP ver. 2.2.1 (adapted from [13])

CPSV has been used in a number of EU members states [15–19]. For example, Belgium has used CPSV-AP to centralize different regional sources into one user-centric portal. Estonia has extended and used CPSV-AP to address local needs. Finland, Ireland, Italy, Portugal, Spain, Netherlands and Slovakia have also used CPSV-AP to create a national data model. Finally, in Greece, the Region of Epirus has used CPSV-AP to model their public services [6].

2.3   Knowledge Graphs

The term *Knowledge Graph* is increasingly used after it was introduced by Google in 2012. Since then, a number of researchers have attempted to formally define it.

According to [20] *"Knowledge graphs are large networks of entities, their semantic types, properties, and relationships between entities."* In other words, a KG represents knowledge using a graph structure. The main elements of a KG are four. *Entities* are the nodes of the graph. *Attributes* are the properties of the entities, i.e. a piece of information that characterizes entities. *Relations* connect two or more entities and are represented as arcs in the graph. The last and most important concept of a KG are rules. The use of rules largely determines the behavior of a graph. *Rules* enable the discovery and derivation of new knowledge that would otherwise be difficult to detect. In order to define a KG, its entities, attributes, relations and rules have to be defined.

In Fig. 2a simple KG is presented as an example. *Public Service, Public Organization* and *Country* are entities; *identifier* and *name* are attributes; *is located at* and *has competent authority* are relations of the KG. A simple rule of the KG suggests that if a PS has a Public Organization (PO) as competent authority and this PO is located at a specific country, then the PS itself is located at the same country too.

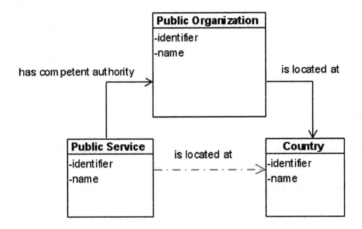

Fig. 2. Knowledge graph example

KG has been used in the public sector in various occasions. For example, Zaragoza city council, since 2003 has been developing its own KG [21] to improve its public service system. KG can also support decision making and sustainability of public finances [22]. In Korea to secure government transparency a KG has been created using open government data [23]. KG have been also employed to address challenges related to overload that can occur from massive government open data [24]. KG have been also used as tools to analyse and supervise government spending [25].

2.4   GRAKN.AI

GRAKN.AI is a free-to-use software application for developing KG [26]. It contains two major parts, Grakn and Graql. *Grakn* is a database in the form of a KG used to model complex datasets [27]. *Grakn schema* is an important part of a Grakn KG that describes the nature of data that are stored in the database as well as how these are structured [26]. It also provides a high level data structure that offers high integrity and data consistency, thus enabling responses to complex queries. After its creation, a KG schema needs to be populated with data in order to become functional (queryable) and produce results (answers to the queries). *Graql* is the language used by the user to interact with the knowledge graph using queries. Using this language, it is possible to obtain and process the stored knowledge from Grakn. More specifically, queries can be formulated that correspond to some action, such as inserting or deleting entities and relationships, calculating useful information about the graph, statistics etc.

Grakn is mainly operated through the computer console. Once the Grakn installation file has been downloaded and unzipped, the Grakn's server [26] can be started from the console. As long as the server runs, KG can be created and edited in one or more workplaces (keyspaces). There are two options to create a KG. The first is to define every entity, attribute, relation and rule through the console. The second is to create a file with all concepts of the schema and upload it also via console. The same two options also apply to populate the KG schema with data. Querying of the KG can be done through the console. Grakn also offers the Grakn Workbase [26]. This software application is an interface that offers visual display of a KG, creation and editing of a KG as well as querying of a KG. Concluding, once the Grakn's server has been up and running we can connect from any computer with Grakn and Grakn Workbase by using the appropriate host and port numbers.

3 Methodology

The methodology is based on design science research method and includes the following steps.

Step 1. Analyze the "Get a Passport" Service. In this step, information about PS *"Get a Passport"* is gathered and studied. All information is obtained from passport.gov, which is the official website providing information about getting a passport in Greece. This information provides a solid understanding of the PS that is essential for the next steps. For simplicity, we concentrate on input documents and relevant costs based on citizens profile and circumstances.

Step 2. Construct KG Schema. Based on CPSV model constructed in the previous step, we develop a KG schema for *"Get a Passport"*. This includes the construction of rules, which is the most challenging activity in the process.

Step 3. Implement KG in Grakn. In this step, the KG is implemented in Grakn.ai. The language used to create the KG and relevant queries is Graql.

Step 4. Populate KG with Data. In this step, we populate the KG schema with actual data for the PS, i.e. on citizen's profile, input documents, and costs.

Step 5. Construct Usage Scenarios. In this step, we construct three usage scenarios to demonstrate the practical use of the constructed KG.

Step 6. Evaluate KG. In this step, the KG is used and evaluated. The evaluation is performed by undergraduate and postgraduate students using a variation of the Technology Acceptance Model (TAM) that was developed for that purpose.

4 A Knowledge Graph for "Get a Passport"

4.1 Analysis of "Get a Passport" Based on CPSV-AP Model

The following information is obtained for the PS.

Public Service: The PS under investigation is *"Get a passport"* in Greece.

Evidence: There are 16 different input documents needed for executing this PS. The exact input documents needed depend on the profile and circumstances of the citizen. Some input documents are identification card, birth or marital status certificate, photographs adhering to specific technical requirements etc.

Cost: The cost can be 84.40 Euros, 73.60 Euros, 68.80 Euros, 63.40 Euros or 58 Euros. The cost depends on the passport duration and whether the citizen applies for a new passport or to renew an existing passport.

Rules: Here, we include all other information that is important to determine which are the needed Evidences and Costs depending on the citizen's circumstances.

Firstly, there are four main categories based on the citizen's need to obtain a passport, namely:

- Issuance of a new passport
- Passport renewal
- Replacement of a valid passport
- Issuance of a new passport due to theft or loss

The age of the citizen is also an important consideration. The input documents differ for various ages and relevant age categories. The relevant categories are:

- Adults
- Minors
- Minors under 12
- Minors from 12 to 14
- Minors under 14
- Minors over 14

Moreover, there are additional categories to which a citizen may belong, as follows:

- Permanent resident of another country (besides Greece)
- Completed military obligations (for males only)
- Conviction by court order
- Temporary ban on leaving the country
- Unfulfilled technical requirements of the photo (due to health condition)

Clearly, most of these cases can be combined e.g. Passport renewal for an adult with permanent resident of another country and uncompleted military obligations.

4.2   Construct KG Schema

The starting point to construct the KG schema is the extract of the CPSV model presented in Fig. 1. Thus, the first draft of the KG schema includes three entities (Public Service, Evidence and Cost), their attributes and their relations. The next and most important activity is the creation of rules. The analysis of the previous step revealed a number of rules that link citizen's profile and circumstances with relevant evidences and cost. We use the entity Rule to accommodate this information.

During the construction of rules, the need to introduce additional concepts emerged. Specifically, a need to also store information on the profile and circumstances of the citizen who is interested to get a passport was identified. To accommodate this need we included a new Entity in out KG schema, called *Citizen*. The creation of attributes for the entity Citizen was also a necessity for the creation of the KG schema. Citizens must include attributes to inform on the categories they belong. Therefore, we decided to introduce all relevant information as attributes of the citizen. The attributes of the entity Citizen are shown in Table 1 (Appendix A). It should be noted that other designs are also possible. However, the proposed one is deemed as appropriate as our main objective was to produce a working KG schema and not necessarily an optimal one.

Furthermore, the entity Evidence in the KG schema had to be slightly different from the one in CPSV-AP. More specifically, in the KG schema we defined the attribute *name* as the unique identifier and not the attribute *identifier*. The reason is that we wanted more than one input documents to have the same identifier. These identifiers depend on the category to which the citizen belongs. For example, input documents required in all cases have identifier equal to "1"; input documents required only for citizens over 12 years of age have identifier equal to "1t"; input documents required only for citizens who want to issue a passport for first time have identifier equal to "1a"; input documents required only for citizens who want to renew their passport have identifier equal to "3", etc. In addition, some new relations were also introduced. These relations can be found at Table 2 (Appendix A). Concluding, the rules that we defined in the schema of the "*Get a passport*" KG are presented at Table 3 (Appendix A). The final KG schema constructed is shown in Fig. 3. In all figures from Grakn Workbase the background color changed from black to white both for better illustration as well as to preserve ink in the case of printing this paper.

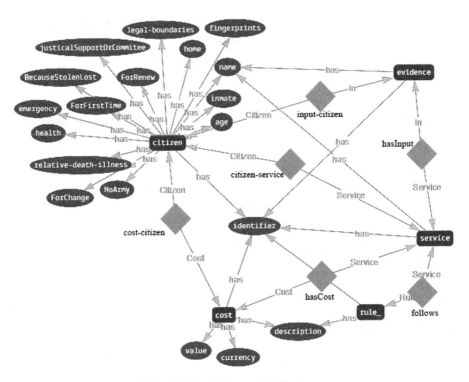

Fig. 3. "Get A Passport" KG schema

4.3   Implement KG in Grakn

In this section the implementation of the KG is presented. The schema of the KG was already conceptually created, so we could start by implementing either the entities or the attributes. Using the results of our analysis in terms of Entities, Attributes and Relationships, we first create attributes (name and type).

The following code example (in Graql) demonstrate how attribute *identifier* is defined.

```
define identifier sub attribute,
      datatype string;
```

Afterwards, we create the entities and assign the created attributes on them. The following code example (in Graql) demonstrates how entity *Cost* is defined.

```
define cost sub entity,
      plays Cost,
      key identifier,
        has value,
        has currency,
      has description;
```

Next, we implement relationships. The following code example (in Graql) demonstrates how relation *hasCost* is defined.

```
define hasCost sub relation,
      relates Service,
        relates Cost;
```

The following code example (in Graql) demonstrates how a rule (namely *auto-relation*) is defined.

```
define auto-relation sub rule,
        when {
        $h1 isa citizen;
        $ser isa service;
        }, then {
(Citizen: $h1, Service: $ser) isa citizen-service;
        };
```

4.4   Populate KG with Data

To import the data to the KG's schema we use the query language Graql. The following three code examples demonstrate how data are inserted in the KG.

Example 1 shows the code for Evidence ID card.

```
insert $in2 isa evidence, has identifier "1t", has name
  "Two-sided photocopy of police identifier card on the
                same page";
```

Example 2 shows the code for Evidence photographs.

```
insert $in3 isa evidence, has identifier "1", has name "A
    recent (last month) 4x6cm color photo of specific
technical specifications, printed on analog photo paper,
  without the use of inkjet or laser technology.";
```

Example 2 shows the code for Cost 84.40 Euros.

```
insert $cost5Y isa cost, has identifier "5Y", has
        currency "Euro", has value 84.40;
```

4.5   KG Usage Scenarios

In this section, three usage scenarios are presented to illustrate the use of the developed KG. In the first scenario, we assume an adult citizen who wishes to obtain a new passport due to theft of the previous passport. This citizen does not belong to any special category, so the only information that is entered is age and name (a nickname that the citizen chooses for interacting with the system).

To import this citizen's data in the KG, we use the following code:

```
$citizen1 isa citizen, has identifier "1", has name
"Rafail", has age 26, has BecauseStolenLost "yes";
```

Then, with the following query the KG will automatically obtain the necessary documents the citizen must provide to invoke the PS as well as the relevant cost:

```
match $x isa input-citizen; $y isa cost-citizen; get;
```

The result shown by the graph is depicted in Fig. 4.

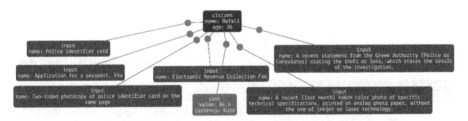

Fig. 4. Matched inputs and cost for Scenario 1

In the second scenario, we assume a minor citizen with permanent residence abroad who wishes to obtain a new passport for the first time.

To import this citizen's data in the KG, we use the following code:

```
$citizen6 isa citizen, has identifier "6", has name
"Susan", has age 10, has ForFirstTime "yes", has home
"NoGR";
```

After running the same query as in the first scenario, the system returns the answer presented in Fig. 5.

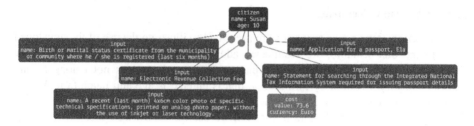

Fig. 5. Matched inputs and cost for Scenario 2

In the third scenario, the citizen is an adult who wants to renew his passport, he has permanent resident abroad and has not fulfilled his military obligations.

To import this citizen's data in the KG, we use the following code:

```
$citizen5 isa citizen, has identifier "5", has name
"Paul", has age 33, has ForRenew "yes", has home "NoGR",
has NoArmy "yes";
```

Running the same query as in the other scenarios, the system returns the answer shown in Fig. 6.

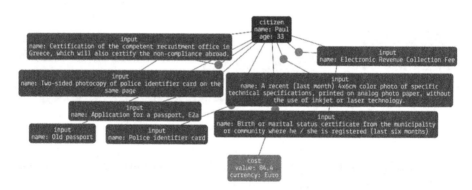

Fig. 6. Matched inputs and cost for Scenario 3

4.6   Evaluation of the KG

For the evaluation, a twenty question Technology Acceptance Model (TAM) [28] based questionnaire was used. These questions are intended to evaluate (a) Perceived ease of use and (b) Perceived usefulness. According to TAM, (a) Perceived ease of use is defined as *"the degree to which an individual believes the using a particular system would be free from physical and mental effort"* and (b) Perceived usefulness is defined as *"the degree to which an individual believes that using a particular system would enhance his or her job performance"* [29]. For this purpose, ten questions evaluate

(a) and ten evaluate (b). Furthermore, the answers were a seven-point scale from strong disagreement to strong agreement and the questionnaire was implemented using Google forms.

Twenty one both undergraduate and postgraduate students participated in the evaluation. Initially, information about KG in general and the three usage scenarios shown in the previous section were presented to students. Based on that, the students were asked to evaluate the KG completing the TAM-based questionnaire.

The tenth question of the questionnaire is related to the perceived ease of use, specifically it states "*Overall, I consider that the use of KG seems easy.*" Three students strongly agree, two disagree and the rest are in the neutral zone. Also, twelve students believe that the interaction with KG requires small spiritual effort, eleven students believe that finding information for PS is easy with KG, six students believe that the process of learning to use KG is easy.

The twentieth question of the questionnaire is related to the perceived usefulness, specifically it states "*Overall, it seems useful to use KG to obtain information about Public Services*". Sixteen students agree with this.

In conclusion, the answers of this questionnaire were overall encouraging. The participants found KG a useful and easy to use tool for obtaining information about Public Services. The participating students also consider dealing with KG requires small spiritual effort.

5 Conclusions and Future Work

The aim of this paper was to investigate the use of Knowledge Graphs (KG) for providing personalized information on PS modeled using CPSV. For this purpose, a KG for part of PS "*Get a passport*" is presented based on CPSV. The analysis results suggest that KG can offer significant benefits for providing personalized information of complex PS. This is mainly due to KG's ability to model rules enabling them to accommodate complex PS. However, there are still significant challenges to overcome before KG can be used in an operational environment. For example, the whole process of KG development is still complicated and thus cumbersome for public servants. In addition, easy-to-use ICT tools are still missing for public servants to create KG at a large scale.

We should further note that although the study produced promising results, it nevertheless has a number of limitations. First, for simplicity we restricted our work to a small number of classes from CPSV model. Thus, the whole CPSV model should be used for creating the KG. Also, we analyzed only one PS, thus additional PS should be studied. In addition, our development experience and knowledge was gained from using GRAKN.AI thus additional platforms should be investigated. Furthermore, the evaluation of our KG was done by a small number of students so we cannot conclude on how useful and important KG are perceived by citizens in general.

Future work includes working further with KG to overcome this study's limitations. In addition, we are working towards the development of a chatbot which would greatly simplify data entry into the KG thus making it more user-friendly. Additional work includes enhancing CPSV model to incorporate machine-readable rules. By inferring rules, logic could be applied to the data, thus giving access to new knowledge that is not obvious.

Appendix

See Appendix Table 1, 2, and 3

Table 1. Attributes of citizen entity

Attributes	Definition/description
identifier	Represents a unique identifier for every citizen that uses the Public Service
name	The name of the citizen
age	Represents the age of the citizen
home	Represents the permanent residence of the citizen. If it's in Greece or not and it can take "GR or NoGr" as values
health	Represents the health situation of the citizen. Specifically, it refers to the condition of his face and if his photograph follows the technical standards
relative_death_illness	Declares if the citizen applied for a passport, because of death or illness of a close relative
inmate	Represents if a citizen is an inmate or not
fingerprints	Declares if it's possible or not, taking fingerprints of the specific citizen
legal_boundaries	Declares if the citizen has legal issues that do not allow him to leave the borders of the country
ForFirstTime	Declares if the citizen applies for a passport for the first time
ForChange	Declares if the citizen applies for a new passport because of inappropriateness of his old one
ForRenew	Declares if the citizen applies for a renewal of his passport
BecauseStolenLost	Declares if the citizen applies for a new passport because his old one is lost or stolen
emergency	Declares if the citizen applies for a passport because he is critically ill or he is critically injured or he lost a close relative, from death or disappearance or his property is destroyed due to a physical disaster
justicalSupportOrCommitee	Declares if the citizen applies for a passport because he is a person in a committee or judicial assistance
NoArmy	Declares if the citizen has fulfilled military obligations

Table 2. New relations of the model

Relations	Definition/description
input-citizen	Links an input with a citizen
citizen-service	Links a citizen with the Public Service
cost-citizen	Links a cost with a citizen

Table 3. Rules of the KG "Get a Passport"

Rule	Definition/description
emergency-passport	Determines if the situation is an emergency and the passport has to be produced within a working day
auto-relation	Creates an automatic link between a citizen and the Public Service as soon as the citizen is in need of the specific Public Service
citizen-input1	Determines if a citizen should be connected with inputs with identifier "1"
citizen-input11	Determines if a citizen should be connected with inputs with identifier "1t"
citizen-input-First-Time	Determines the connection between a citizen and inputs with identifier "1a". In case a citizen wants to apply for a new passport for the first time
citizen-input-Renew	Determines the connection between a citizen and inputs with identifier "2a". In case a citizen wants to renew his old passport
citizen-input-Renew1	Determines the connection between a citizen and inputs with identifier "3". In case a citizen wants to renew his old passport
citizen-input-Change	Determines the connection between a citizen and inputs with identifier "3a". In case a citizen wants to replace his old passport
citizen-input-Change2	Determines the connection between a citizen and inputs with identifier "3". In case a citizen wants to replace his old passport
citizen-input-Lost-Stolen	Determines the connection between a citizen and inputs with identifier "4a". In case the citizen wants to apply for a new passport because his old passport is lost or stolen
citizen-input-Lost-Stolen1	Determines the connection between a citizen and inputs with identifier "9". In case a citizen wants to apply for a new passport because his old passport is lost or stolen
citizen-input-NoGR	Determines the connection between a citizen and inputs with identifier "2". In case the citizen has a permanent residence outside Greece
citizen-input-army	Determines the connection between a citizen and inputs with identifier "7". In case the citizen is an adult, has permanent residence outside Greece and has fulfilled military obligations
citizen-input-eyes	Determines the connection between a citizen and inputs with identifier "6". In case the citizen has a health situation and the technical standards of the photo are not fulfilled

(*continued*)

Table 3. (*continued*)

Rule	Definition/description
citizen-input12	Determines the connection between a citizen and inputs with identifier "10". In case the citizen's age is "<= 12"
citizen-input-supCom	Determines the connection between a citizen and inputs with identifier "4". In case the citizen is a person in a committee or judicial assistance
citizen-input-legal	Determines the connection between a citizen and inputs with identifier "5". In case the citizen can't leave from the country due to legal issues
cost3m	Determines the connection between a citizen and a cost with identifier "3 M". In case the citizen is an inmate and the produced passport has three months duration
cost5y	Determines the connection between a citizen and a cost with identifier "5Y". In case the citizen has age ">14" and the produced passport has five years duration
cost3y	Determines the connection between a citizen and a cost with identifier "3Y". In case the citizen has age "<=14" and the produced passport has three years duration
cost8m	Determines the connection between a citizen and a cost with identifier "8 M". In case it's impossible to take fingerprints and the produced passport has eight months duration
costChange	Determines the connection between a citizen and a cost with identifier "change". In case the citizen wants to replace his old passport
cost13m	Determines the connection between a citizen and a cost with identifier "13 M". In case the citizen can't leave from the country due to legal issues, he is critically ill or he is critically injured or he lost a close relative, from death or disappearance or his property is destroyed and the produced passport has thirteen months duration
passOut	Determines the connection between a Public Service and an output when the Public Service is already connected with a cost. The identifier of the cost has to be the same with the identifier of the output

References

1. European Commission: eEurope - An information society for all (1999). http://eur-lex.europa.eu/legal-content/EN/TXT/HTML/?uri=LEGISSUM:l24221&from=EN. Accessed 15 May 2020
2. European Commission: Europe 2020: A strategy for smart, sustainable and inclusive growth (2010). http://eur-lex.europa.eu/LexUriServ/LexUriServ.do?uri=COM:2010:2020:FIN:EN:PDF. Accessed 15 May 2020
3. USA Government: American Recovery and Reinvestment Act (2009). http://www.gpo.gov/fdsys/pkg/BILLS-111hr1enr/pdf/BILLS-111hr1enr.pdf. Accessed 15 May 2020
4. Gerontas, A., Peristeras, V., Tambouris, E., Kaliva, E., Magnisalis, I., Tarabanis, K.: Public service models: a systematic literature review and synthesis. IEEE Trans. Emerg. Top. Comput. (2019). https://doi.org/10.1109/tetc.2019.2939485

5. Madrid, L.: The Economic Impact of Interoperability - Connected Government. Microsoft (2012)
6. Gerontas, A., Tambouris, E., Tarabanis, K.: On using the core public sector vocabulary (CPSV) to publish a "citizen's guide" as linked data. In: 19th Annual International Conference on Digital Government Research: Governance in the Data Age. ACM International Conference Proceeding Series (2018)
7. Peristeras, V.: The Governance Enterprise Architecture-GEA-for Reengineering Public Administration. Ph.D. Thesis, University of Macedonia, Greece (2006)
8. Augello, A., Pilato, G., Vassallo, G., Gaglio, S.: A semantic layer on semi-structured data sources for intuitive chatbots. In: Proceeding of the Second International Workshop on Intelligent Interfaces For Human-Computer Interaction (IIHCI), pp. 760–765 (2009)
9. Pan, J.Z., Vetere, G., Gomez-Perez, J.M., Wu, H. (eds.): Exploiting Linked Data and Knowledge Graphs in Large Organisations, p. 281. Springer, Heidelberg (2017). https://doi.org/10.1007/978-3-319-45654-6
10. Tambouris, E., Tarabanis, K.: A dialogue-based, life-event oriented, active portal for online one-stop government: the OneStopGov platform. In: The Proceedings of the 9th Annual International Digital Government Research Conference (dg.o), pp. 405–406. ACM Press (2008)
11. Petriv, Y., Erlenheim, R., Tsap, V., Pappel, I., Draheim, D.: Designing effective chatbot solutions for the public sector: a case study from Ukraine. In: Chugunov, A., Khodachek, I., Misnikov, Y., Trutnev, D. (eds.) EGOSE 2019. CCIS, vol. 1135, pp. 320–335. Springer, Cham (2020). https://doi.org/10.1007/978-3-030-39296-3_24
12. European Commission: Architecture for public service chatbots. ISA Programme, PwC EU Services (2019). https://joinup.ec.europa.eu/sites/default/files/news/2019-09/ISA2_Architecture%20for%20public%20service%20chatbots.pdf. Accessed 16 July 2020
13. European Commission: Core Public Service Vocabulary specification, ISA Programme (2013). https://joinup.ec.europa.eu/sites/default/files/distribution/2013-06/Core%20Public%20Service%20Vocabulary%20specification%20v1.01.pdf. Accessed 16 July 2020
14. PwC Services: Definition and development of a data model for description of the services related to key business events CPSV-AP (2014). https://joinup.ec.europa.eu/solution/core-public-service-vocabulary-application-profile/distribution/cpsv-ap-specification-v100-docx. Accessed 16 July 2020
15. European Commission - DG DIGIT - ISA Programme, About Core Public Service Vocabulary Application Profile. https://joinup.ec.europa.eu/solution/core-public-service-vocabulary-application-profile/about. Accessed 26 Sep 2020
16. Peristeras, V., Gerontas, A., Stamlakou, A.: Report of methodology and guidance for modelling and publishing administrative processes Administrative Reform Technical Assistance in Greece (2019)
17. Renda, A., Simonelli, F., Iacob, N., Campmas, A.: Evaluation Study supporting the interim evaluation of the programme on interoperability solutions for European public administrations, businesses and citizens (ISA²) (2019). https://www.ceps.eu/wp-content/uploads/2019/06/NO0119341ENN.en_.pdf. Accessed 26 Sep 2020
18. PwC EU Services: Open data and e-government good practices for fostering environmental information sharing and dissemination (2019). https://www.unece.org/fileadmin/DAM/env/pp/a_to_i/Joint_UNECE-EEA_workshop/Draft_OD_EGOV_GP_.pdf. Accessed 26 Sep 2020
19. PwC EU Services: APIs for CPSV-AP based Catalogue of Services (2019). https://joinup.ec.europa.eu/sites/default/files/news/2019-09/ISA2_APIs%20for%20CPSV-AP%20based%20Catalogue%20of%20Services_0.pdf. Accessed 26 Sep 2020

20. Kroetsch, M., Weikum, G.: Journal of Web Semantics: Special Issue on Knowledge Graphs (2016). https://www.websemanticsjournal.org/search?q=+Special+Issue+on+Knowledge+Graphs

21. Espinoza-Arias, P., Fernández-Ruiz, M.J., Morlán-Plo, V., Notivol-Bezares, R., Corcho, O.: The Zaragoza's knowledge graph: Open data to harness the city knowledge. Information (Switzerland) 11(3), 129 (2020). https://doi.org/10.3390/info11030129

22. Cifuentes-Silva, F., Fernández-Álvarez, D., Labra-Gayo, J.E.: National budget as linked open data: new tools for supporting the sustainability of public finances. Sustainability (Switzerland) 12(11), 4551 (2020). https://doi.org/10.3390/su12114551

23. Kim, H.: Interlinking open government data in Korea using administrative district knowledge graph. J. Inf. Sci. Theor. Pract. 6(1), 18–30 (2018). https://doi.org/10.1633/JISTaP.2018.6.1.2

24. Wang, P., Li, Z., Li, Z., Fang, X.: A government policy analysis platform based on knowledge graph. Paper presented at the 2019 2nd International Conference on Artificial Intelligence and Big Data, ICAIBD 2019, pp. 208–214 (2019). https://doi.org/10.1109/icaibd.2019.8836979. www.scopus.com

25. Simperl, E., et al.: Towards a knowledge graph based platform for public procurement. In: Garoufallou, E., Sartori, F., Siatri, R., Zervas, M. (eds.) MTSR 2018. CCIS, vol. 846, pp. 317–323. Springer, Cham (2019). https://doi.org/10.1007/978-3-030-14401-2_29

26. Grakn Labs Ltd.: GRAKN.AI. https://grakn.ai. Accessed 15 May 2020

27. Stichbury, J.: Get Started with GRAKN.AI (2017). https://blog.grakn.ai/get-started-with-grakn-ai-72bb210f915c. Accessed 15 May 2020

28. Lee, Y., Kozar, K., Larsen, K.: The technology acceptance model: past, present, and future. Commun. Assoc. Inf. Syst. 12 (2003). https://doi.org/10.17705/1CAIS.01250. Accessed 16 July 2020

29. Davis, F.: User acceptance of information technology: system characteristics, user perceptions and behavioural impacts. Int. J. Man Mach. Stud. 38, 475–487 (1993)

Digital Services and Social Media

e-Commerce Websites and the Phenomenon of Dropshipping: Evaluation Criteria and Model

Jacek Winiarski[1] and Bartosz Marcinkowski[2(✉)]

[1] Division of Electronic Economy, University of Gdansk, Sopot, Poland
jacek.winiarski@ug.edu.pl
[2] Department of Business Informatics, University of Gdansk, Sopot, Poland
bartosz.marcinkowski@ug.edu.pl

Abstract. In the contemporary highly competitive digital commerce market, it is easy to miss new online ventures being launched and those that go away. The success of such a venture is highly dependent on the quality of an e-commerce platform. Even more so in the case of dropshipping-based business models, where similarly-profiled businesses are intensively working on acquiring customers to sell goods delivered by the same distributors. Many criteria, frameworks, and models for assessing e-commerce platforms were developed to date, yet applying those directly to dropshipping ventures leave some important areas unexplored. The study scrutinizes the factors that make an e-commerce platform stand out to effectively attract customers in a highly competitive market. Design Science Research approach was used to deliver a dropshipping-oriented evaluation model extension. Business cases for new criteria and proposals for e-commerce platform features designed to address inefficiencies in IT solutions currently operating in the market were provided.

Keywords: e-Commerce · Dropshipping · Website evaluation · Evaluation criteria · Design Science Research

1 Introduction

Dropshipping might be considered a business model for e-commerce logistics in which the company that hosts an e-commerce platform has the sole task of acquiring customers, effectively acting as a middleman [L] is in fact [1]. Their orders are passed along to distributors (e.g. wholesalers or manufacturers) who are tasked with handling all the activities related to delivering the ordered product to a given customer. It is the difference between the wholesale and retail price that is the source of profit for the dropshipping service provider. The relative ease of launching and operating an e-commerce venture in line with the principles of dropshipping constitutes its great advantage. Therefore, such a business model proves to be quite popular in contemporary global markets – market size for dropshipping was reported at over USD 100 billion in 2018, with a Compound Annual Growth Rate predicted at 28.8% by 2025 [GVR] is in fact [2]. The dropshipping service provider does not require its own warehouses [R] is in fact [3] and is not forced to tie up the capital with the goods

M. Themistocleous et al. (Eds.): EMCIS 2020, LNBIP 402, pp. 289–300, 2020.
https://doi.org/10.1007/978-3-030-63396-7_19

offered via its e-commerce platform. Finally, the assortment that did not find its buyer does not constitute a direct burden on the seller.

The mechanics behind dropshipping-oriented platforms are relatively straightforward from a purely IT perspective. It is required to build and launch a scalable online platform that shall advertise products delivered by one or more suppliers and handle business processes related to ordering. The database of such a platform is required to be subjected to frequent synchronization with the databases of cooperating wholesalers in order to monitor stock levels, update prices, and introduce new product offerings. There are IT vendors on the market who offer Application Programming Interfaces (API) to databases recording products offered by many wholesalers. In such a situation, the primary challenge for an e-commerce business that takes advantage of the dropshipping business model is to offer its customers a platform that streamlines the purchase of a basket of goods and makes it significantly more attractive compared to other ventures that supply goods from the same business partners.

The primary motivation for us was to investigate the dimensions of competitiveness for online stores that sell goods in line with the principles of dropshipping. The goal of the research is to scrutinize the factors that make an e-commerce platform stand out to effectively attract customers in a highly competitive market. To achieve that, it was essential to identify the individual features of a dropshipping-based distribution and translate them into the specific functionality of the software that supports this type of distribution. After the introduction, the literature review is performed. Subsequently, research questions are developed, and the research approach is presented. The findings of the study are introduced and discussed next, followed by conclusions.

2 Literature Review

There is little doubt that website evaluation is a multi-criterion undertaking. One might argue that the most natural criterium for assessing e-commerce platforms relates to Graphical User Interface (GUI) properties – such as functionality, usability, or user-friendliness. In this regard, Yates explores the needs of website users with disabilities, concluding that while there is an obvious rationale behind developing accessible and usable online platforms, the costs behind successfully delivering such platforms made this aspect highly undervalued when the study was conducted [4]. Upon completing three-stage studies of selected websites that included automated accessibility evaluation, expert-led manual heuristic evaluation, and blind user tests, Goncalves et al. came up with a list of recommendations aimed at enhancing accessibility and usability of e-commerce platforms [5]. Diaz et al. discard several usability metrics and propose 39 individual usability metrics grouped into 10 usability aspects, provide quantitative measures, and validate them through interviews with usability experts [6]. Whereas they did not explore a practical application of the proposed method, it might potentially be adapted to assessing dropshipping platforms should the authors increase the portfolio of metrics considering the specific properties of dropshipping websites. On the other hand, Zafiropoulos and Vrana propose a website evaluation framework intended solely for assessing websites that provide hotel services [7]. Their approach uses the Hierarchical Cluster Analysis (HCA). The method establishes 65 evaluation components grouped under the specificity of hotel services. The proposed solution is an example of a strictly profiled framework.

Nevertheless, most models, frameworks, and evaluation scales go beyond the assessment of the aforementioned features. Technical criteria emerge as one of the leading priorities – in particular those that enable evaluating such aspects as lag-free website loading and operation [8–11] as well as security and privacy-related criteria [8, 10–13]. It is in fact the E-S-QUAL scale for assessing the quality of electronic services [8] that emerged as one of the most widely acknowledged models, which enable identifying strengths and weaknesses of given websites and uncovering room for improvement. It covers all previously discussed criteria with a four-dimensional, 22-item scale and comes with a complementary E-RecS-QUAL set of criteria. The latter is designed to address features that only need to be used when digital sale processes were not completed seamlessly, and inquiries, issues, complaints, or compensations need to be handled. Al-Khalifa proposed a solution called the Mobile University Evaluation Framework (MUEF) taking into account the requirements of W3C Mobile Web Best Practices [9]. The author selected the websites of two universities to validate the proposed method. The websites were rated by two experts who addressed individual criteria using the Likert scale. Chua and Goh performed a study aimed at assessing the quality of world libraries' web portals [10]. They used selected elements of established solutions – such as WebQual and E-SERVQUAL. The assessment method covered three categories: System Quality, Information Quality, and Service Quality. Variables for each of these categories were provided, including Usability, Responsiveness, Ease of Access, and Privacy for evaluating the System Quality. The proposed method was validated via a survey by three experts. A framework for measuring the acceptance of websites profiled for the tourism industry (websites for purchasing the services of low-cost airlines in particular) was delivered by Khalifah et al. [11]. The generic E-QUAL method was expanded to include protection and privacy. Abidi et al. dealt with the problems of applying Web Services Composition Engineering (WSCE) and Web Services Composition (WSC) to the framework called PASCO [12]. Personalization and security issues were the most important dimensions examined. The correctness of the PASCO proposal was verified during the examination of websites of selected banks. Finally, Qi et al. submitted a proposal to evaluate websites across three areas: Website Usefulness, Website Service Quality, and Website Physical Accessibility [13]. The validation of the proposed model was not addressed in the article and no in-depth characteristics of the measures were proposed.

It is marketing that is another essential aspect of assessing e-commerce portals – all the more important in the context of dropshipping. Thus, Sulova proposed a system of indicators for assessing online store websites [14]. The indicators have been grouped into the following sets: visitability of a website, specific e-commerce indicators, functionality of a website, e-commerce platform in terms of a marketing tool. A method for calculating a qualitative metric was proposed that utilizes such variables as no. of visits, no. of unique visitors, returns, time on site, bounce rate, top-exit pages, pages viewed/visitors, top-visited pages, traffic source, an top visitors/country. The proposed method, despite a robust set of indicators, does not cover dropshipping-specific features and constitutes a viable candidate for presenting an extension in that regard.

It should be noted that while some of the proposals are conceptual in nature (e.g. [6, 13]), many schemes are supported by an extensive mathematical apparatus – just to mention [15–17]. Chiu et al. proposed a new hybrid Multiple Attribute Decision Making (MADM) model based on a number of previous solutions [15]. The contribution identified the lack of customer satisfaction with service in the online store as a research gap. The next element of MADM was to formulate a recommendation to modify the website under review to introduce changes that would lead to the required level of acceptability. Yi et al. noted that in assessing customer satisfaction regarding the use of websites, criteria (vectors) such as time and space are not taken into account [16]. High-order subspace analysis based on non-negative Tucker decomposition is performed to enable customer satisfaction evaluation. The proposed model is used to assess several of the most popular Chinese websites by three experts. Kang et al. proposed a framework that represents multiple criteria decision-making methods [17]. They integrate a fuzzy hierarchical TOPSIS method and E-S-QUAL scale for evaluating business-to-customer e-commerce websites. The proposed assessment method features seven stages. The study was concluded with sensitivity analysis and validation of results.

Last but not least, attempts to evaluate web portals in the context of dropshipping emerge. Singh et al. highlight the most important stages of establishing dropshipping activities on the Internet [18]. The authors discuss the importance of (1) proper e-commerce platform operation; (2) correctly configured CSV files; and (3) well-deployed MySQL solutions. They analyze the IT-related implications associated with the Minimum Advertising Price (MAP), i.e. the amount the supplier is not willing to go below. The solutions proposed in the article might be considered guidelines for entrepreneurs who deploy IT services for an online store that operates in line with the principles of dropshipping. Vellve and Burgos dive into the specifics of online dropshipping services in Spain [19]. They reveal that this type of activity is associated with a high level of the so-called annual cart abandonment rates above (63%, measured on an annual basis) as well as high returns (6%) on invoiced goods. The authors of the article propose several solutions that are designed to minimize these two phenomena from an IT point of view.

3   Research Questions Development

The literature review revealed that the scientific community came up with a number of criteria, frameworks, and models for assessing e-commerce platforms. The aforementioned models substantially differ in their abstraction level and focus – from very generic models that cannot be directly implemented in business practice, to heavily profiled ones that lean towards a specific perspective, e.g. the challenge of website performance. That being said, diving into the evaluation criteria for e-commerce platforms and confronting them with the daily practice of businesses operating in line with dropshipping principles led to the conclusion that related research shows a clear trend towards traditional e-commerce solutions. Therefore, the criteria naturally neglect the features that are distinctive for the dropshipping phenomenon. Whereas a number of universal criteria – which constitute the core of many analyzed models – are undoubtedly useful for evaluating e-commerce platforms taking into account this phenomenon, the multi-faceted look at e-commerce solutions from the perspective of many actors reveals some deficiencies in existing frameworks. Thus, in our humble opinion, we are dealing with a dropshipping-related research gap.

To fill this research gap, the following research questions were posed:

RQ1:   What is the difference in the mechanics of goods distribution between traditional e-commerce ventures and those that operate in line with the principles of dropshipping?

RQ2:   What additional functionalities and/or features should the software for dropshipping online stores be equipped with compared to IT solutions that support the traditional e-commerce business models?

4   Research Approach

In our study, the literature review accomplished constituted a basis for conducting a series of five semi-structured in-depth interviews with dropshipping practitioners who run their businesses in Poland, EU. The feedback, in turn, fueled the Design Science Research (DSR) approach. Given that both dropshipping – and e-commerce in general – are dynamic phenomena, expert knowledge enabled us to capture the most up-to-date knowledge. The review itself addressed both mainstream models for e-commerce evaluation as well as the phenomenon of dropshipping itself. The Google Scholar service was selected owing to its particularly wide indexing range. The following search strings were used to narrow down the contents of Google Scholar library: (1) website evaluation framework; (2) evaluation e-commerce; (3) evaluation web service economics; and (4) dropshipping.

The DSR method enables contributing to both practice and theory in the course of solving a vast portfolio of practical challenges [20]. It shares core characteristics with Action Research, emphasizing coming up with implementable solutions [21] – yet no joint intervention with the staff of the business engaged in the research is called for. Peffers et al. argue that the design-centric approach may be considered a distinctive feature of Information Systems research among other business academe and brings a set of widely accepted features to the table [22]:

- delivering an artifact that captures domain-specific knowledge with a degree of generalization;
- incorporating a specifically-defined or loosely-defined process for motivating and determining a problem, designing a solution, and evaluating it;
- focus on conceptualizing based on a review of domain-related knowledge created so far rather than ad-hoc solving instantiated problems.

As established by Thakurta et al. in course of charting the DSR discourse through a comprehensive literature review that covered as many as 293 cases, (1) the artifact palette proves to be very broad and includes such types of artifacts as methods (42.7%), models (22.2%), systems (13.7%), constructs (6.8%), frameworks (6.1%) or architectures

(2.0%), whereas (2) 27.6% of artifacts might be classified as fully ready for use after their implementation and validation [23]. Thus, our research falls within mainstream DSR research. To increase the robustness of our study, we took advantage of several guidelines by Hevner et al.: we set up a problem space for the design process, designed a purposeful artifact that delivers a streamlined solution and yields utility to a specific problem domain, we ensured its internal consistency and formalized it, initiated the evaluation process, and finally reported the outcomes of DSR to all potential parties involved [24].

5   Findings

The research conducted resulted in filling some of the gaps that remain upon applying widely acknowledged website evaluation criteria to a dropshipping setting. As a result, an artifact – i.e. the dropshipping-oriented E-S-QUAL/E-RecS-QUAL model extension – was built. Confronting the experiences of the practitioners with the proposals submitted, among others, in [6, 14, 19] allowed for streamlining the list of potential dropshipping-centric criteria.

In order not to unduly complicate the description of the overall model, we put focus on stating business cases for each extending evaluation criteria proposal and related e-commerce platform features while keeping the nature of generic variables and dimensions intact. The artifact takes advantage of the *Core* service quality scale and the *Recovery* service quality scale (Fig. 1) originally proposed by Parasuraman et al. [8]. Within the former, the generic criteria that comprise the *Fulfillment* dimension were supplemented with a couple of dropshipping-oriented criteria, i.e. *Suggesting product replacements to streamline delivery costs* as well as *Delivery time- and location-driven shipping*. As the software behind traditional e-commerce ventures and those that operate in line with the principles of dropshipping differ in a number of ways, the inclusion of a brand-new dimension (*Market Recognition*) proved justified. This extending core dimension features a few specific criteria: (1) *product price juxtaposition mechanics that hints a new competitive price proposal automatically*; (2) *management of multi-instance advertising campaigns*; and finally (3) *wizard for creating customized product descriptions*.

5.1   Suggesting Product Replacements to Streamline Delivery Costs

When purchasing more than one product, the platform should automatically propose potential substitutes for selected goods that are not available from a specific distributor in order to reduce the total logistics costs and produce a more attractive package in terms of total price (customer-oriented functionality).

Business Case. The vast majority of e-commerce websites operating on the principles of dropshipping sell goods offered by various wholesalers and/or manufacturers. The functionality discussed refers to a situation when a customer puts more than one product in a basket, and the assortment to be delivered comes from suppliers located in different geographical locations. In such a situation, it is necessary to process the order by sending more than one shipment to the customer or sending the ordered goods to a single location – and repackaging those before finally forwarding the goods to the final recipient. Both of these scenarios address the issue of buying goods from more than one supplier, yet result in increased delivery costs.

e-Commerce Platform Features Required. It is recommended that the software that enables a dropshipping e-commerce venture suggested substitutes offered by a single supplier upon a customer selects goods from different suppliers. It is desirable that the substitutes were in a similar price range (or cheaper) and had main features consistent with the original product. Putting such practice into operation would result in decreasing the total amount of the transaction borne by the customer by the cost of at least a single redundant shipment.

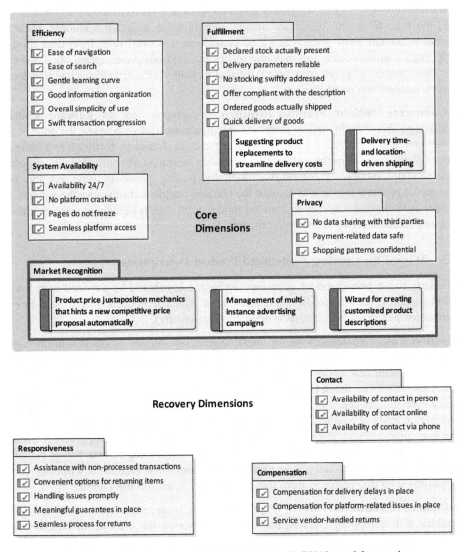

Fig. 1. Dropshipping-oriented E-S-QUAL/E-RecS-QUAL model extension

5.2   Product Price Juxtaposition Mechanics that Hints a New Competitive Price Proposal Automatically

The pricing of goods offered via the platform ought to be automatically confronted with identical products marketed by other online stores. The software is to automatically suggest a competitive price for each of the products sold (administrator-oriented functionality).

Business Case. In practice, many e-commerce stores operating in line with the principles of dropshipping sell goods provided by the same wholesalers or manufacturers. IT services vendors provide APIs that enable access to data from many distributors in an integrated form. A natural consequence of this state of affairs is that target pricing for retail customers across different dropshipping businesses might be alike or even uniform. This occurs quite frequently given the current level of technological maturity and the need to devote significant manual workflows to maintain a rational pricing model – but flat retail prices cannot be considered a general rule. Individual dropshipping e-commerce ventures may have different wholesale prices agreed upon due to the sheer volume of goods from given distributors sold via their platforms and translate this advantage into retail pricing.

e-Commerce Platform Features Required. We propose that the software behind operating a dropshipping online store was able to automatically juxtapose the price of a given item that is planned for sale (as well as the ones already in distribution) with the prices of the same item throughout the competing ventures. This functionality should automatically propose a competitive price for putting goods for sale via the e-commerce platform taking into account the planned margin and supervise the valuation model used. Should a deviation from the model occur due to significant price changes at competitors, alerting should be accounted for.

5.3   Wizard for Creating Customized Product Descriptions

Similarly to the pricing model, dropshipping businesses should be provided with low-effort support in creating/modifying tailored descriptions of products offered via their e-commerce platforms (administrator-oriented functionality).

Business Case. Wholesalers and/or manufacturers who supply products sold through dropshipping online stores supplement their offerings with databases, from which the store's software can automatically download product information. Through such an interface, extensive datasets are exchanged – just to mention product descriptions, accompanying images, specifications, keywords, and customer reviews. Lack of customization leads to a situation in which numerous dropshipping sites offer the sale of the same products with identical photographs and comments – what negatively impacts the credibility and recognition of the venture. Even considering the mechanics behind Internet search engines only, it is vital for a business that product descriptions and keywords used differentiated from those commonly found on the Internet.

e-Commerce Platform Features Required. It is recommended that the software that enables a dropshipping e-commerce venture supported the creation of customized descriptions of products sold with intensive use of keyword-based phrase generators and description style/layout wizards. This functionality should enable creating one's own descriptions and automatically compare them with the descriptions of the same products offered by other online stores.

5.4   Delivery Time- and Location-Driven Shipping

To make the platform functionality more inclusive for business customers robust and cover specialized goods, enabling placing multi-scale purchase orders for various customer-side locations with fixed dates of delivery might be considered (customer-oriented functionality).

Business Case. According to the domain-related literature, the dropshipping e-commerce logistics business model is predisposed to handle the sale of specialized goods – including perishable ones (such as flowers or food) and those that require dedicated storage conditions. In the process of distributing these kinds of products, a dropshipping e-commerce venture bears neither the cost of acquiring specialized storage spaces nor the risk of losses related to the unsold lot that needed to be recycled. Specialized goods sale might also imply a setting in which the buyer requires delivery of the purchased assortment under one order to different destinations with different delivery times (this applies to e.g. groceries ordered centrally by chains of retail stores). Purchase that falls into this category is usually planned by a recipient well in advance and sometimes features a set of related deliveries. In such a case, traditional, siloed e-commerce solutions and a multitude of shipping methods at one's disposal lead to the practical impossibility of ensuring any kind of delivery synchronization.

e-Commerce Platform Features Required. The software for operating a dropshipping store is to enable the customer to purchase numerous products as a single order or a meta-order, where the composition of items is inherited per facility with an option of adjusting the quantity and pick-up location. For individual (sub-) orders it should be possible to indicate different dates of their actual delivery.

5.5   Management of Multi-instance Advertising Campaigns

Global dropshipping businesses face the need to simultaneously manage multiple advertising campaigns carried out in different online locations (administrator-oriented functionality).

Business Case. As stated before, many dropshipping stores offer the same products at similar prices. One of the ways to increase sales through a given e-commerce platform is a properly prepared and executed advertising campaign that will encourage customers to carry out the purchase transaction through a specific online store. In practice, dropshipping sellers place numerous ads addressing the same product on the Internet, yet lack the technological maturity to monitor and adjust them properly.

e-Commerce Platform Features Required. Dropshipping IT solutions should be able to automate the process of advertising campaign preparation, placing ads in preferred Internet-based channels, and tracking their impact. The management of advertising campaigns should make it possible to assess the effectiveness of each of the advertisements launched in order to, inter alia, discontinue those that do not generate the revenues required.

6   Conclusions

Electronic commerce is an economic phenomenon accompanied by continuous growth – in 2019 alone, in the USA its volume increased by 14.9% and is reported to grow even more in 2020 [25]. Dropshipping is currently one of the most intensively developed forms of sales via the Internet. That being said, the owners of dropshipping businesses encounter some barriers specific to this form of trade. To gain a competitive advantage, they expect as much support from IT tools at their disposal as possible.

The paper contributes to digital commerce theory by re-assessing a series of website evaluation criteria that date as far back as the E-SERVQUAL method and its further iterations in light of the dropshipping phenomenon – just to mention E-S-QUAL and E-RecS-QUAL scales. It was revealed that whereas the latter scale was found adequate to evaluate e-commerce solution features aimed at handling alternative scenarios of digital sale processes as well as some supporting business processes in the dropshipping context, the core dimensions necessitated additional criteria. Both business cases for new criteria that address leading divergences between e-commerce business models in place (RQ1) and draft system requirements related to e-commerce platform features designed to address inefficiencies in IT solutions currently operating in the market constitute implications for practice as well. Five additional criteria were included, three of which establish a new dimension – Market Recognition. Thus, we addressed RQ2 by recommending a set of dropshipping-specific features that future iterations of the software behind such a business model might be equipped with.

Like virtually any research, this study has a few limitations. First of all, while the design process of the artifact closely followed the guidelines [24], no prototype of the e-commerce solution profiled for dropshipping was built at this stage of research, and the validation of the artifact is pending. A wide audience's feedback ought to be collected to assess the usefulness of individual components proposed in this work at a multi-national scale. Secondly, as long as the study explored and developed the functionality directly related to interfacing an e-commerce platform with numerous IT solutions of suppliers that are covered by the dropshipping business model, the issues of interface reliability, data cleansing, and retransmission upon failure were not discussed.

The next step will be further research on identifying IT-related options for addressing the difficulties encountered in conducting dropshipping activities. Subsequently, the method proposed in this paper is to be developed, enabling the assessment of e-commerce tools available on the market in terms of their suitability in dropshipping. The proposed model will be evaluated by specialists and then applied in practice. The ultimate goal of the solution sought is to increase the number of customers using dropshipping services.

References

1. Zając, D.: Dropshipping as logistics business model of e-commerce. Logistyka **4**, 5069–5074 (2014)
2. Varma, R.: Dropshipping Market Size, Share & Trends Analysis Report by Product (Toys, Hobby & DIY, Furniture & Appliances, Food & Personal Care, Electronics & Media, Fashion), by Region, and Segment Forecasts, 2019–2025. Market research report, Grand View Research (2019)
3. Reszka, L.: Multicriteria optimisation methods in logistics on the example of warehouse location. J. Posit. Manage. **9**(3), 3–16 (2018)
4. Yates, R.: Web site accessibility and usability: towards more functional sites for all. Campus Wide Inf. Syst. **22**(4), 180–188 (2005)
5. Goncalves, R., Rocha, T., Martins, J., Branco, F., Au-Yong-Oliveira, M.: Evaluation of e-commerce websites accessibility and usability: an e-commerce platform analysis with the inclusion of blind users. Univ. Access Inf. Soc. **17**(3), 567–583 (2017)
6. Diaz, E., Flores, S., Paz, F.: Proposal of usability metrics to evaluate e-commerce websites. In: Marcus, A., Wang, W. (eds.) HCII 2019. LNCS, vol. 11586, pp. 85–95. Springer, Cham (2019). https://doi.org/10.1007/978-3-030-23535-2_6
7. Zafiropoulos, C., Vrana, V.: A framework for the evaluation of hotel websites: the case of Greece. Inf. Technol. Tourism **8**(3), 239–254 (2006)
8. Parasuraman, A., Zeithaml, V.A., Malhotra, A.: ES-QUAL: a multiple-item scale for assessing electronic service quality. J. Serv. Res. **7**(3), 213–233 (2005)
9. Al-Khalifa, H.S.: A framework for evaluating university mobile websites. Online Inf. Rev. **38**(2), 166–185 (2014)
10. Chua, A.Y.K., Goh, D.H.: A study of web 2.0 applications in library websites. Libr. Inf. Sci. Res. **32**(3), 203–211 (2010)
11. Khalifah, Z., Wong, C.B., Hashim, N.H.: A review of website quality framework for low cost carrier. Am. J. Econ. **3**(5C), 143–149 (2013)
12. Abidi, A., Fakhri, M., Essafi, M., Ghazela, H.B.: A comprehensive framework for evaluating web services composition methods. Int. J. Web Inf. Syst. **15**(3), 324–345 (2019)
13. Qi, S., Ip, C., Leung, R., Law, R.: A new framework on website evaluation. In: Proceedings of the 2010 International Conference on E-Business and E-Government, pp. 78–81. IEEE Computer Society, Washington (2010)
14. Sulova, S.: A system for e-commerce website evaluation. In: Proceedings of the 19th International Multidisciplinary Scientific GeoConference SGEM 2019, pp. 25–32. SGEM World Science, Sofia (2019)
15. Chiu, W.Y., Tzeng, G.H., Li, H.L.: A new hybrid MCDM model combining DANP with VIKOR to improve e-store business. Knowl. Based Syst. **37**, 48–61 (2013)
16. Yi, W., Dong, P., Wang, J.: Customer satisfaction evaluation model of e-commerce website based on tensor analysis. In: Proceedings of the 8th International Conference on E-Business, Management and Economics ICEME 2017, pp. 6–10. ACM, New York (2017)
17. Kang, D., Jang, W., Park, Y.: Evaluation of e-commerce websites using fuzzy hierarchical TOPSIS based on E-S-QUAL. Appl. Softw. Comput. **42**, 53–65 (2016)
18. Singh, G., Kaur, H., Singh, A.: Dropshipping in e-commerce: a perspective. In: Proceedings of the 9th International Conference on E-Business, Management and Economics ICEME 2018, pp. 7–14. IEDRC, Hong Kong (2018)
19. Vellve, F.J.S., Burgos, S.L.M.: Dropshipping in e-commerce: the Spanish case. Esic Mark. Econ. Bus. J. **49**(2), 285–310 (2018)

20. Stal, J., Paliwoda-Pekosz, G.: Fostering development of soft skills in ICT curricula: a case of a transition economy. Inf. Technol. Develop. **25**(2), 250–274 (2019)
21. Marcinkowski, B., Gawin, B.: A study on the adaptive approach to technology-driven enhancement of multi-scenario business processes. Inf. Technol. People **32**(1), 118–146 (2019)
22. Peffers, K., Tuunanen, T., Niehaves, B.: Design science research genres: introduction to the special issue on exemplars and criteria for applicable design science research. Eur. J. Inf. Syst. **27**(2), 129–139 (2018)
23. Thakurta, R., Müller, B., Ahlemann, F., Hoffmann, D.: The state of design – a comprehensive literature review to chart the design science research discourse. In: Proceedings of the 50th Hawaii International Conference on System Sciences, pp. 4685–4694. AIS. Atlanta (2017)
24. Hevner, A.R., March, S.T., Park, J., Ram, S.: Design science in information systems research. MIS Q. **28**(1), 75–105 (2004)
25. Lipsman, A., Liu, C.: US Ecommerce 2020 – Coronavirus Boosts Ecommerce Forecast and Will Accelerate Channel-Shift. Market research report, eMarketer (2020)

E-Learning Improves Accounting Education: Case of the Higher Education Sector of Bahrain

Abdalmuttaleb M. A. Musleh Al-Sartawi[(✉)] [iD]

Ahlia University, Manama, Bahrain
amasartawi@hotmail.com

Abstract. The aim of current research is to investigate the impact of e-learning on the performance of accounting students at universities in the Kingdom of Bahrain. A questionnaire was distributed to accounting employees and students. The results indicated that e-learning enhancing students' performance and their employability skills. This study recommends that the higher education institutions of the Kingdom of Bahrain expand the e-learning context and connect learners with accounting professions.

Keywords: E-learning · Education · Accounting education · Skills · Bahrain

1 Introduction

The accounting profession changed many times among the years because of the changes in the global markets and the way of running businesses that need specific skills in the accountant to deal with the new era requirements like artifactual intelligence, cybersecurity, knowledge-based economy, and the digital economy [3, 4]. Accountants became responsible for maintaining the intellectual capital and to disclose about in different ways, which request them to be more aware of the technology as it is one of the important pillars of the intellectual capital [5, 6]. Accordingly, the employability skills of the accounting graduates have changed to provide the market with will-prepared and more professionals accountants to deal with the technology. As a result, many schools around the world effectively depending on online accounting education [18] Online education provides learners flexible time management, cost effective traveling, and a balance between their personal and professional life [2, 19] But the question is how we can measure online course learning effectiveness. Such a scholarly inquiry remains under scant investigation. In recent years, accounting firms are more willing to hire accounting graduates with some online accounting coursework [16]. With the marketability of accounting degrees and the growing demands, more accounting courses are offered online. One of three main issues related to online accounting education is how to assess the learning quality and outcome of the online education experience in an accounting course [11]. [15] compares the learning effectiveness of online accounting education with traditional in-class teaching; and revealed that the traditional classroom environments generate more favorable learning effectiveness with more advanced outcome for higher level of accounting courses than in the

© Springer Nature Switzerland AG 2020
M. Themistocleous et al. (Eds.): EMCIS 2020, LNBIP 402, pp. 301–315, 2020.
https://doi.org/10.1007/978-3-030-63396-7_20

online teaching-learning delivery mode. The delivery method, whether online or traditional, is not so important in the introductory accounting courses [15]. Accounting education is globally the biggest fields, and in the Kingdom of Bahrain. Many students enroll in accounting major in the higher education sector for various reasons; hence the aim of this study to identify if e-learning positively or negatively affects the accounting education at the higher education level within the Kingdom of Bahrain. Also, it would be prosperous to inquire on the e-learning methods applied in the higher education accounting majors.

This paper is arranged as the follows. Section 2 is about published literature review. Section 3 discusses the methods that were employed for data collection. Section 4 discusses the results, and finally, Sect. 5 provides the conclusion and recommendation.

2 Literature Review

The term blended learning is used in academic teaching and business. According to [10] it is difficult to conclusively determine if blended learning is a unique learning environment or only a combination of traditional classroom teaching and online classes. [11] find the definition of blended learning in the literature on the subject to be somewhat controversial. However, this does not prevent blended learning from gaining popularity both in the world of academia and professional business training. The term appeared for the first time on March 5, 1999, when a company in Atlanta advertised courses in the press and referred to them as blended learning courses [13]. The blended learning approach assumes the use of new teaching techniques which utilize the internet technology while maintaining the traditional approach, which is a direct (face to face) contact between students and the teacher. [22] define blended learning as a coherent combination of e-learning and traditional teaching in order to achieve the intended educational aims. According to [12] blended learning refers to a combination of classes conducted in the traditional way with on-line classes. The American Society for Training and Development recognized blended learning as one of the ten most important trends in the broadly understood business knowledge transfer. In the academic world, the blended learning approach is more and more often discussed during a variety of conferences and in scientific journals [21]. Many universities point out the numerous advantages of teaching with the use of this method. Blended learning can be considered a leading trend in university education whose potential has not been fully exploited yet. According to the forecasts of The Journal of Asynchronous Learning Networks, in the nearest future, 80–90% of all ongoing courses will be organized as a combination of traditional and e-learning classes.

This paper is focused on accounting courses which are perceived as difficult academic subjects demanding systematic work. Assuming that, in the nearest future, graduates of blended learning accounting courses will be recruited by many corporations as accounting staff, a profile or at least several desirable qualities of an "accounting" graduate can be denoted such as conscientiousness, independence and creativity. Moreover, a graduate will be required to continue education and self-education in order to maintain competence at a sufficiently high-level Teaching solely in a traditional way and teaching solely online are two completely opposite teaching methods. Each of them has some advantages and disadvantages. Blended learning, which is a mixture of the two, combines most advantages of traditional teaching and distant learning and few drawbacks. Therefore, it seems to be the optimum form of instruction suited to universities. An additional advantage of this approach is the ability to personalize the teaching process so that it would meet the needs of different audiences with varied preparation for subjects. It remains questionable what percentage of e-learning classes is necessary for a course to be considered blended learning. According to the Sloan Consortium, it is 30–79% of the teaching hours [17, 23].

Comparative studies are a popular approach to investigating the problem of teaching with the use of blended learning. Classes carried out entirely in the traditional manner are treated as a reference point and are then compared with the distant learning classes. The latter can be conducted entirely via the internet (online learning) or partially so (blended learning). [15] conducted a study concerning the level of effectiveness of the accounting course and students' satisfaction with it among MBA students. The scholars classified students into two groups. The first one comprised student participating in the classes conducted in the traditional form. The second group of students attended a blended- learning course where the extent of traditional classes was limited. Both forms of teaching were appreciated by the students who pointed out their advantages and disadvantages. Blended learning approach was very positively assessed by the students. Most of them expressed their willingness to participate in other courses conducted with the use of this method. However, the students found instructions given during traditional classes easier to follow. Blended learning classes allowed the students to gain an appreciation of the concepts in the field. They also noted that their analytical skills had significantly improved.

In another study, [15] examined students' opinions on the teaching of accounting. The students were asked to evaluate the differences between traditional classes and those which applied blended learning. According to the research results, blended learning should be regarded as an attractive combination of the traditional and on-line teaching methods. Blended learning reduces some of the disadvantages of the classes conducted solely on-line. The students positively assessed the teamwork and the fact that teachers could answer their questions more promptly. It seems, however, that the blended approach does not offer instant communication and steady interaction between teachers and students. According to the students, it is also important to split classes into the traditional and e-learning ones in appropriate proportions [13].

[1] divided students of accounting into two groups: one group participated in traditional classes and the other in a blended learning course. The average grades of the students taking part in the blended learning course proved to be significantly higher. According to the author, it was since they took responsibility for their own learning to a larger extent. This form of teaching made students more active. They asked questions more often, although this was not mandatory. They were also observed to get more involved in the teaching process and to take greater responsibility for the learning results. The study does not consider variables such as students' intelligence or other factors like gender, etc. The blended learning approach was not only more flexible in terms of the time and space, but it also created a habit of ongoing self-learning process which is useful for the entire working life period of an individual. [17] analyzed blended learning and distance learning as two methods of teaching considering the

students' retention rate1, satisfaction and their achievements. Blended learning proved to be much more efficient in terms of student retention, while students' achievements were generally similar in both forms of teaching. The level of satisfaction was relatively high for blended learning and distance learning: most students were satisfied with the way the courses were conducted.

[19] carried out a study among financial accounting students. They proposed to employ a new, dual approach to the delivery of course material to assess students' satisfaction with distance learning and their perception of its effectiveness. Students were able to shift between traditional, live lectures and live lectures viewed over the Internet. The results showed that the students reported a relatively lower level of satisfaction with the distance-learning component, as well as diminished effectiveness in mastering the distance-learning course material.

The mainstream of empirical research concerning blended learning focuses on the costs and benefits of this form of teaching. The benefits include: flexible time of learning, better teaching results, more intensive interaction between the students and the teacher, greater students' involvement, positive impact on the university's reputation due to the enhancement of the educational offer and reduction of the education costs (classrooms costs, faculty and students' time and travel costs). It is not without significance that this form of teaching also provides a new, more active, educational "experience", as compared to the traditional teaching and allows the acquisition of knowledge in a new information environment which offers many different forms of activity.

According to [18] the application of e-learning tools forces students to become self-reliant in the search for information, selection of important information, its processing, and eventually its critical evaluation and formulation of their own opinions. [22] indicate the following as representing added value of e-learning classes: higher level of cooperation between students in solving the group assignments, as well as participating in discussion forums, which increases the sense of social involvement and raises the level of satisfaction with the course attendance. Stronger social ties between members of the group are created during this type of classes. They are often long-lasting and continue outside the classroom [2]. The above-mentioned benefits for students on an emotional level and stronger social ties result in a smaller number of drop-out students [14], which also means financial benefits for the university. [21] distinguishes three main benefits resulting from the use of blended learning approach: greater teaching efficiency, improved accessibility and convenience of studying for students and reduction of costs for universities.

[17] draw attention to several potential benefits of the use of blended learning in the teaching of accounting: the reduction of working time for lecturers at university, more efficient use of working time for students. An increased range of courses conducted with the use of e-learning is an important argument for students while choosing the academic program and making decisions about studying in a university. [20] carried out a study concerning the teaching process with the use of blended learning at the University of Granada. The research was conducted among 1,400 students. The results confirmed the contention that blended learning contributed to the reduction in dropout rates and improved the final examination results. The students' perception of blended learning is associated with their final grades depending on the blended learning

activities, the age, previous experience and the frequency of class attendance. [1] states that combining traditional classes and classes conducted with the use of e-learning is a desired teaching method. A study carried out at the Yildiz Technical University in Istanbul confirmed that this form of teaching is of great interest. It increases students' motivation and their responsibility for the learning process. However, according to students' opinions, the way in which teaching materials are distributed and some methods of conducting classes need improvement. An appropriate proportion of traditional and e-classes also seemed to be important. Students indicated the 50%–50% approach as a good solution.

In 2008 and 2009, the University of Winchester successfully introduced many courses using blended learning techniques in financial management and accounting [9]. The university also conducted research on the perception of this type of classes by the students. The students' attitude toward this teaching approach was positive, which is in line with the results of other studies. An increase in the involvement of students in the educational process was observed. Resources and institutional practices were the essential factors of success in this process at university level. The results of empirical studies indicate that the initial negative evaluation of distance learning, compared to traditional methods has disappeared over the last years [15]. Positive changes in the e-learning accounting courses over the years were confirmed by the study conducted by [16]. They referred to the design of the course, its content or interactivity.

[9, 10] made a review of empirical studies which proved that courses using the blended learning approach were not worse at achieving teaching aims than the traditional ones. Currently, blended learning can be evaluated as a more efficient method, provided that students are responsible for managing their time, they are able to deal with the technical problems which can occur during e-classes, teachers have experience and devote sufficient time to the development of e-courses and contact with students, the university strives to support the educational process with advice on e-courses methodological content and infrastructure. The university's organizational culture, openness to change and willingness to help faculty and students are important in order to achieve success in blended learning. A survey is another research approach in studies concerning e-learning as an educational tool. Surveys make it possible to measure the quality of the educational process and its benefits and drawbacks according to the students' opinions. The results of a series of surveys [2, 14, 15] carried out in different environments suggest that students still prefer direct contact with the teacher, the commands delivered in the classroom is answered in more explicit terms, and students can ask questions directly, rather than via email or discussion forums. These are arguments against the form of teaching that consists only of e-classes, which seems a worse solution than blended learning. However, it should be noted that the above-mentioned studies were conducted 6–8 years ago and reluctance to use Web tools seems to have considerably decreased since then.

Current research conducted by [20] among 120 students of economics indicate that, at present, students do not have problems with the application of the internet technologies and are willing to participate in courses which use the blended learning approach. Some of the most popular tools used during blended learning classes included videos, PowerPoint presentations, texting, email, discussion forums and online activities. Research on determining the opinions of students in terms of quality and overall satisfaction with the e-classes was conducted by [12]. The research was carried out among a group of 48 students of medicine with the use of a questionnaire and interviews. The analysis of empirical data showed that students who appreciate learning together (in a group) are generally more satisfied with the e-learning than other students. The level of students' satisfaction was also affected by the structure of the course, the emotional support they got from the teacher and the implemented communication tools. The perception and evaluation of blended learning courses by students is heavily associated with the effects of education. [2] conducted extensive surveys among 577 students in a large academic center. The final assessment of the course was assumed as a dependent variable while independent variables included the level of satisfaction with the course, the facilities offered by the course and the level of engagement and the evaluation of the results by the students. Research results indicate that all the above independent variables are positively correlated with students' assessment and the level of satisfaction is the most important. Survey results also indicate that students less familiar with computer techniques also receive worse grades upon the completion of the course.

The blended learning approach is not free from drawbacks. Even though the idea of blended learning has been known for a long time, still many organizations continue to have a problem with its effective implementation. There is an objective need for training people who are using the platforms which enable the use of distance learning techniques [18]. Issues related to the choice of technology and software should be treated with utmost importance in the decision-making process while creating an e-learning platform. The choice of the platform itself may be crucial in terms of the effectiveness of online education. [20, 25] believe that the methods of conducting academic classes in the form of e-learning are developing very dynamically. However, they are often used for the sake of technology itself rather than for teaching purposes. For e-learning courses to be successful, many requirements must be met. An important one is the appropriate experience of the teacher. It is essential to coordinate the need for incurring expenditure on information technology. [1] stress the significance of modern technology in an effective online learning process and the availability of tools such as video conferences. Immediate response within the framework of the educational process is important but it can also be automatic without teacher participation.

[9, 10, 23] believe that modern teaching techniques such as blended learning is very important thru virtually shared knowledge between students and instructors [15]. They are still being developed conceptually, methodologically and analytically. However, their practical implementation is not uniform for many subjects and academic disciplines. Difficulties can also arise when deciding on the proportion of traditional and e-classes. The decision should be made considering students' expectations and the requirements they must fulfill [14].

Bahrain as one of the middle eastern countries is focusing in developing the online education which can be clearly traced through the expanded size of capital invested in the knowledge-based economy and by developing the corporate governance system [7, 8, 24] in order to achieve the vision of 2030 which needs graduates who are technically skilled, self-oriented and willing to serve the community which can be achieved through the independent online learning and education.

3   Research Methodology

The research design is the procedures that the researcher follows in order to get answers to the questions of the research in order to fulfil the objectives assigned to the research on what is the relationship between the banks' credit ratings and its profitability in the Kingdom of Bahrain. Research design is the logical and systematic planning and directing of the research. The research uses the statistical nature. The primary data has been collected through a questionnaire that is specially designed to meet the objectives of this research study. On the other hand, the secondary data were taken from different journals, articles, textbooks, and websites. Together, the primary and secondary data will be used and analyzed to reach the conclusions of the research study. This research study has been done using the statistical nature method where it describes the impact of e-learning on accounting education at universities in the Kingdom of Bahrain. The data was collected through questionnaire that is designed to meet the objectives of the research study and the analysis has been done using Microsoft Excel. The convenience sampling method has been chosen by the researchers to reach the conclusions of the research study in hand where the units were chosen according to the researchers' convenient The researchers have followed the convenience sampling technique for the survey to reach a conclusion for the research study. The table presents the sample of the analysis techniques used in this research (Table 1).

Table 1. Sample techniques analysis

Technique used	Simple average method
Charts	Pie charts
Sample size	One hundred
Data collection method	Questionnaire
Mode of collection	Direct, telephone, e-mails

This research did not consider all the variables into consideration in the research model. For this reason, the limitation of the research is that the results generated from this research is generalized and that the opinions from the questionnaire may not be reflecting the true pinions of the sample population as they might not be expressing their actual opinions. The current research is focused on the relationship between two variables: e-learning (independent variable) and accounting based education (dependent variable). Thus, the research hypothesis will be: (1) Null Hypothesis (H0): E-learning has an impact on accounting education in the Kingdom of Bahrain, and (2) Alternative Hypothesis (H1): E-learning does not have an impact on accounting education in the Kingdom of Bahrain.

4   Data Analysis and Findings

This section presents the complete analysis of the data that was statistically collected. The researchers used descriptive statistical analysis in order to interpret and analyses the data collected to be able to reach clear conclusions and results. The researchers, in this chapter, will employ descriptive data analysis to identify what each item or statement corresponds to and to know what the responses to these items imply and how they lead to the research findings. This chapter also includes the questionnaire item analysis. The researcher focused on the analysis of the demographics of the sample population in the first part of the questionnaire. This part included analysis of the gender, age, education, and work experience of the individuals within the sample size. One hundred and five questionnaires were distributed by the researchers to individuals within the sample population while only one hundred were returned which provides a response rate of 95% (Table 2).

Table 2. Statistics of the gender variable

Gender	Number	Frequency
Male	60	60%
Female	40	40%
Total	100	100%

The sample that the questionnaire was distributed to consisted of 60% males and 40% females as it can be seen from the above chart (Table 3).

Table 3. Statistics of the age variable

Age	Number	Frequency
Below 30 years	30	30%
From 30 to 40	20	20%
From 40 to 50	40	40%
More than 50	10	10%
Total	100	100%

When analyzing the age variable of the sample population, 30% of the population were below thirty years old, 20% of ages between 30 and 40 years old, 40% of the sample population were of ages between 40 and 50 years old, and 10% of the population were above fifty years (Table 4).

Table 4. Statistics of the education variable

Education	Number	Frequency
Bachelors	40	40%
Masters	20	20%
PhD	10	10%
Other	30	30%
Total	100	100%

The education level of the sample population indicated that 40% of the sample hold a bachelor's degree, 20% are holding a master's degree, 10% are holding a PhD, and the remaining 30% of the sample population hold other professional certificates such as ACCA, CPA, and CMA (Table 5).

Table 5. Statistics of the work experience of the sample

Experience	Number	Frequency
Below 7 years	30	30%
From 7 to 12 years	30	30%
From 12 to 20 years	20	20%
More than 20 years	20	20%
Total	100	100%

The sample population included 30% of employees who have less than seven years of experience, another 30% who have working experience between 7 to 12 years, another 20% have working experience between 12 to 20 years, and another 20% who have more than twenty years of working experience. The researchers conduct the analysis of the parts of the questionnaire that has been distributed and included ten items divided into two sections. In this section, the researchers exploit the descriptive statistical analysis to show the percentages of responses of each item after it has been analyzed (Table 6).

Table 6. Statistics of availability of accounting e-learning materials

Availability of accounting e-learning materials	Number	Frequency
Strongly agree	40	40%
Agree	30	30%
Neutral	10	10%
Disagree	10	10%
Strongly disagree	10	10%
Total	100	100%

When the sample population were asked whether their universities had e-learning materials for the accounting major, 40% strongly agreed, 30% agreed to this research statement, and 10% of the sample population were neutral about the statement. However, 10% disagreed that their university had available e-learning materials for the major of accounting at their universities.

Table 7 Statistics of Updating Accounting E-learning Content.

Table 7. Statistics of updating accounting e-learning content

Updating accounting e-learning content	Number	Frequency
Strongly agree	30	30%
Agree	50	50%
Neutral	10	10%
Disagree	10	10%
Strongly disagree	0	0%
Total	100	100%

The above table shows 30% of the sample population stated that the accounting e-learning contents were updated by faculty members on regular basis. Another 50% of the population agrees to this statement. 10% of the population were indifferent about this regard and 10% disagree that the faculty members update the contents of accounting e-learning on regular basis (Table 8).

Table 8. Statistics of Accounting e-learning training and awareness

Accounting e-learning training and awareness	Number	Frequency
Strongly agree	40	40%
Agree	30	30%
Neutral	20	20%
Disagree	10	10%
Strongly disagree	0	0%
Total	100	100%

40% of the sample population strongly agree that training and awareness about the accounting e-learning at the university has been provided to the students, another 30% agrees to this statement. 20% of the sample population had no opinion about this statement, and 10% of the sample population disagrees about this research statement (Table 9).

Table 9. Statistics of understanding how to utilize accounting e-learning content

Understanding how to utilize accounting e-learning content	Number	Frequency
Strongly agree	30	30%
Agree	30	30%
Neutral	20	20%
Disagree	10	10%
Strongly disagree	10	10%
Total	100	100%

The sample population has agreed to the statement that faculty members and students understand how to utilize the accounting e-learning material available at the university where the agreement rate is 60% distributed as 30% strongly agreeing and 30% agreeing. 20% of the sample population had no opinion about this statement while 20% disagreed with regards to this research statement (Table 10).

Table 10. Statistics of importance of accounting e-learning

Importance of accounting e-learning	Number	Frequency
Strongly agree	40	40%
Agree	20	20%
Neutral	20	20%
Disagree	10	10%
Strongly disagree	10	10%
Total	100	100%

40% of the sample population strongly agree that accounting e-learning is important, another 20% of the sample population agree about this statement. Another 20% of the population are neutral about this statement. However, 10% disagree about the indicated research statement and 10% strongly disagree with it (Table 11).

Table 11. Statistics of easiness of using accounting e-learning contents

Easiness of using accounting e-learning contents	Number	Frequency
Strongly agree	30	30%
Agree	40	40%
Neutral	10	10%
Disagree	10	10%
Strongly disagree	10	10%
Total	100	100%

When the sample population were asked whether it is easy to use the accounting e-learning materials available at their universities, 40% strongly agreed regarding this indication, 30% agreed to this research statement, and 10% of the sample population were neutral. However, 20% disagreed about this research statement (Table 12).

Table 12. Accounting e-learning and students understanding

Accounting e-learning and students understanding	Number	Frequency
Strongly agree	30	30%
Agree	50	50%
Neutral	10	10%
Disagree	10	10%
Strongly disagree	0	0%
Total	100	100%

The above table shows 30% of the sample population indicated that accounting e-learning material and content help accounting students to understand the topics they are studying in an effective manner. Another 50% of the population agrees that it helps students in understanding their studies more effectively. 10% of the population had a neutral opinion about this research statement while 10% disagreed about it (Table 13).

Table 13. Statistics of importance of e-learning for accounting study process

Importance of e-learning for accounting students studying process	Number	Frequency
Strongly agree	40	40%
Agree	40	40%
Neutral	10	10%
Disagree	10	10%
Strongly disagree	0	0%
Total	100	100%

40% of the sample population strongly agrees that e-learning is an important and essential part in the accounting students' course of studies, another 40% agrees to this research statement. 20% of the sample population had no opinion about this statement, and 20% of the sample population disagrees about this research statement (Table 14).

Table 14. Statistics of accounting e-learning and students performance

Accounting e-learning and students performance	Number	Frequency
Strongly agree	40	40%
Agree	30	30%
Neutral	20	20%
Disagree	10	10%
Strongly disagree	0	0%
Total	100	100%

40% of the sample population has strongly agreed on the statement that students perform better because accounting e-learning materials are available to them during their studies, another 30% agreed to this research statement. However, 20% of the sample population were indifferent about this statement and the remaining 10% disagreed about the given research statement (Table 15).

Table 15. Statistics of accounting e-learning and students' GPA

Accounting e-learning and students' GPA	Number	Frequency
Strongly agree	30	30%
Agree	40	40%
Neutral	20	20%
Disagree	10	10%
Strongly disagree	0	0%
Total	100	100%

70% of the sample population agrees that accounting e-learning availability help in improving the GPA of accounting students distributed between 30% who strongly agree and 40% who agree. 20% of the sample population were neutral about this research statement and 10% disagreed to this statement of the research. From this data analysis, it was revealed that e-learning and students' performance are closely related. It has also been found that e-learning is positively related with the performance of students at universities in the Kingdom of Bahrain. This has been concluded because there is a high acceptance range of accounting e-learning and the performance of accounting students. As a result, the null hypothesis will be accepted which indicates that e-learning has a positive impact on accounting students' performance at universities in the Kingdom of Bahrain.

5 Conclusions and Recommendations

The research study was conducted to identify the impact that e-learning has on the performance of accounting students at universities in the Kingdom of Bahrain. The study showed that there is a strong relationship between e-learning and accounting students' performance. It has also been found that e-learning has a positive impact on accounting students' performance in Kingdom of Bahrain where they seem to have more effective understanding of the topics they study. The research study also found that faculty members and students find that e-learning is important part of the accounting studies. Moreover, the research study identified that universities provide awareness and training to their students about the accounting e-learning material and content and how to use them and that faculty members update the content of e-learning on regular basis. As a result, all of the above has given the indication that accounting e-learning actually helps in improving the performance of accounting students at universities in the Kingdom of Bahrain which gave the conclusion that accounting e-learning is very important to universities in the Kingdom of Bahrain and that it is highly related and correlated positively with the students' performance and their GPA. The following are recommendations that are determined after the results of this research study: (1 universities in the Kingdom of Bahrain should continue to stress on the importance of accounting e-learning contents to the improvement of the performance and GPA of students who study accounting, (2) universities should give more training about e-learning after the students commence their accounting studies in the university, and (3) it is important to update the content of accounting e-learning in order to cope with the changes and trends in accounting.

References

1. Abraham, A.: Student-centred teaching of accounting to engineering students: comparing blended learning and traditional approaches. Faculty Commerce-Papers, Univ. Wollongong **435**, 1–11 (2007)
2. Akkoyunlu, B., Soylu, M.Y.: A study of student's perceptions in a blended learning environment based on different learning styles. Educ. Technol. Soc. **11**(1), 183–193 (2008)
3. Al-Sartawi, A.: Information technology governance and cybersecurity at the board level. Int. J. Crit. Infrastruct. **16**(2), 150–161 (2020)
4. Al-Sartawi, A.: Ownership structure and intellectual capital: evidence from the GCC countries. Int. J. Learn. Intellect. Capital **15**(3), 277–291 (2018)
5. Al-Sartawi, A.: Corporate governance and intellectual capital: evidence from Gulf Cooperation Council countries. Acad. Acc. Financ. Stud. J. **22**(1), 1–12 (2018)
6. Al-Sartawi, A.: Social Media disclosure of intellectual capital and firm value. Int. J. Learn. Intellect. Capital (2020). Accepted article
7. Al-Sartawi, A.: Does it pay to be socially responsible? Empirical evidence from the GCC countries. Int. J. Law Manag. **62**(5), 381–394 (2020)
8. Al-Sartawi, A., Sanad, Z.: Institutional ownership and corporate governance: evidence from Bahrain. Afro-Asian J. Finance Acc. **9**(1), 101–115 (2019)
9. Arbaugh, J.B., Desai, A., Rau, B., Sridhar, B.S.: A review of research on online and blended learning in the management disciplines: 1994–2009. Org. Manag. J. **7**(1), 39–55 (2010)

10. Arbaugh, J.B., Godfrey, M.R., Johnson, M., Pollack, B.L., Niendorf, B., Wresch, W.: Research in online and blended learning in the business disciplines: key findings and possible future directions. Internet High. Educ. **12**(2), 71–87 (2009)

11. Bliuc, A.M., Goodyear, P., Ellis, R.A.: Research focus and methodological choices in studies into students' experiences of blended learning in higher education. Internet High. Educ. **10**(4), 231–244 (2007)

12. Bonk, C.J., Graham, C.R. (eds.): Handbook of Blended Learning: Global Perspectives, Local Designs. Pfeiffer Publishing, San Francisco (2012)

13. Catalano, H.: The opportunity of blended-learning training programs in adult education - ascertaining study. Procedia – Soc. Behav. Sci. **142**, 762–768 (2014)

14. Chandra, V., Fisher, D.L.: Students' perception of a blended web-based learning environment. Learn. Environ. Res. **12**, 31–44 (2009)

15. Chen, C.C., Jones, K.T.: Blended learning vs. traditional classroom settings: assessing effectiveness and student perceptions in an MBA accounting course. J. Educ. Online **4**(1), 1–15 (2007)

16. Concannon, F., Flynn, A., Campbell, M.: What campus-based students think about the quality and benefits of e-learning. Br. J. Educ. Technol. **36**(3), 501–512 (2005)

17. Cottrell, D.M., Robison, R.A.: Case 4: blended learning in an accounting course. Q. Rev. Distance Educ. **4**(3), 261–269 (2003)

18. Dziuban, C., Moskal, P., Hartman, J.: "Higher education, blended learning, and the generations: knowledge is power: no more. Elements of quality online education: engaging communities. Sloan Center for Online Education, Needham (2005)

19. Emelo, R.: The new way to blend learning. Train. J. **11**, 23–26 (2014)

20. Flynn, A., Concannon, F., NíBheacháin, C.: Undergraduate students' perceptions of technology-supported learning: the case of an accounting class. Int. J. E-Learn. **14**(4), 427–444 (2005)

21. Graham, C.R., Allen, S., Ure, D.: Benefits and challenges of blended learning environments. In: Encyclopedia of Information Science and Technology, pp. 253–259. IGI Global, Hershey (2005)

22. Guzer, B., Caner, H.: The past, present and future of blended learning: an in depth analysis of literature. Procedia – Soc. Behav. Sci. **114**, 4596–4603 (2014)

23. Reyad, S., Al-Sartawi, A., Badawi, S., Hamdan, A.: Do entrepreneurial skills affect entrepreneurship attitudes in accounting education? High. Educ. Skills Work-Based Learn. **9**(4), 739–757 (2019)

24. Sanad, Z., Al-Sartawi, A.: Investigating the relationship between corporate governance and internet financial reporting (IFR): evidence from Bahrain Bourse. Jordan J. Bus. Adm. **12**(1), 239–269 (2016)

25. Themistocleous, M., Christodoulou, K., Iosif, E., Louca, S., Tseas, D.: Blockchain in Academia: where do we stand and where do we go? In: Proceedings of the Fifty-third Annual Hawaii International Conference on System Sciences, (HICSS 53), 7–10 January 2020, Maui, Hawaii, USA. IEEE Computer Society, Los Alamitos (2020)

Influence of Website Design on E-Trust and Positive Word of Mouth Intentions in E-Commerce Fashion Websites

Pedro Manuel do Espírito Santo[1] and António Trigo[2,3(✉)]

[1] Polytechnic Institute of Coimbra, ESTGOH, Rua General Santos Costa,
3400-124 Oliveira do Hospital, Portugal
pedro.santo@estgoh.ipc.pt
[2] Polytechnic Institute of Coimbra, ISCAC, Quinta Agrícola, Bencanta,
3040-316 Coimbra, Portugal
antonio.trigo@gmail.com
[3] Centro ALGORITMI, University of Minho, 4804-533 Guimarães, Portugal

Abstract. The online sales channels of fashion stores, like the physical stores, aim to capture and retain customers. In the case of online sales channels, such as e-commerce fashion websites, success depends on the confidence that customers have in their use and reputation, which can be assessed through customers' intentions to convey positive opinions about the website. Studies in the literature state that the design of the website, both in terms of its visual aspect and usability, contributes to increasing the confidence and positive word of mouth (WOM) intentions defined as information and/or rumour sharing between individuals of customers. This study seeks to validate this hypothesis regarding fashion e-commerce websites. To this end, a survey-type study was conducted involving 220 customers of e-commerce fashion websites. The results of the study support the hypothesis that website design contributes to generating trust in it, and consequently positive WOM intentions.

Keywords: Online shopping · E-commerce fashion websites · Website design · E-trust · Positive WOM intentions

1 Introduction

The fashion industry is one of the main engines of the world economy, moving about 1.3 trillion dollars annually and employing about 300 million people worldwide [1]. Data compiled by The Fashion and Apparel Industry Report reveal that global e-commerce fashion revenues are expected to increase from \$481.2 billion in 2018 to \$712.9 billion in 2022 [2].

Top retailers, like Mango, Zara, H&M, and Privalia, have their online stores and are also creating mobile applications for making online purchases (around 20% of the online purchases reported in these retailers is made via mobile phone) [3]. It is not only the big brands that bet on online, but this is also a preferred channel for smaller players that can reach a wider audience, for example, the case of Spanish fashion luxury market

© Springer Nature Switzerland AG 2020
M. Themistocleous et al. (Eds.): EMCIS 2020, LNBIP 402, pp. 316–330, 2020.
https://doi.org/10.1007/978-3-030-63396-7_21

companies that have internationalized by creating a website or by building up their e-commerce operations [4].

In short, the online bet is now transversal to all companies in the fashion industry, either through individual efforts or through online sales aggregation platforms such as Farfetch or Zalando. As an example of the commitment to online one of the largest European fashion companies, Zalando, from 2015 to 2017, increased the number of employees associated with the digital infrastructure from 800 to 1700, representing 1 in 7 employees of its workforce [5].

Recently, the issue of social distance imposed by COVID-19 has triggered the use of online channels, in activities where it was not usual to use them, such as the purchase of food or medical consultations [6, 7]. Concerning the fashion industry, although the major brands had already made the transition online, they experienced with COVID, on the one hand, the abrupt drop in sales in physical stores such as those existing in shopping centres (United States had a drop of 52% year-over-year [8]), and, on the other hand, the surge in online sales (e.g. Nike increased 30% of its sales through digital channels), although not offsetting the decline in-store sales [9].

Online sales are therefore increasingly assuming a leading role for companies in the fashion sector, and great care must be taken in developing these platforms, both online and mobile. This concern translates into issues, such as the visual appearance of the website, the usability of the website, and how the information about the product is made available [10–12].

Given this effort in the development of e-commerce fashion websites, which are visually appealing, both at the level of the website and at the level of the product presentation and functional, it becomes imperative to study whether or not these factors impact the trust of customers in the website (e-trust) and positive word of mouth (WOM).

The rest of the paper is structured as follows. First, we present a literature review and a research model, and after we present the methodology and results. At the end of the paper, we discuss the results and show the conclusions.

2 Literature Review and Research Model

In e-business, websites are the main point of contact with the customer, and an e-business cannot be successful without this channel for launching products, making sales, launching advertising campaigns and connecting to customers, being for many retailers the main centre of their digital marketing strategy [13].

Given the importance of this channel for customer relations, those responsible for the development of this channel in companies should pay close attention to the characteristics this channel and should have in order to influence the initial purchase decision and repurchasing intention, customer satisfaction, and consequently, the customer's loyalty and positive WOM intentions [4, 14–16].

2.1   Product Information

Information provided by e-commerce websites about products helps customers on purchasing decisions [17]. Product information should be detailed and may include features such as name, price, size, materials, photographs, videos, user opinions, among others, in order to allow the customer to assess the quality and usefulness of the product and, consequently, assist in making a purchasing decision. In-depth and comprehensive information allows the customer to predict the quality and usefulness of a product [18].

According to Mir-Bernal et al. [4] the most important criterion for brand awareness is the product information that ecommerce websites make available online, highlighting this study the need for care in the visual aspect of the product, recommending, for example, the inclusion of at least two photographs of the product and a zoom photograph on the product, something that happens in e-commerce sites like Springfield or Farfetch.

The presentation of complete information both at the product information level and at the product presentation level is therefore very important. More and better information available on the websites leads to customers being able to interact with the product and the more they interact, the more likely they are to express positive opinions about it [19].

2.2   Website Aesthetics

The visual aspect of a website encompasses all aspects associated with the website's overall graphical look, which include among others, colour schemes, fonts used, contrast, and/or photo quality. The visual aspect of a website, as mentioned in the introduction, is the key element to get the customer's attention in the first moment, so it has deserved a lot of attention, both from the professionals who develop the websites/interfaces, having in recent years appeared a new professional area called User eXperience (UX) design, consider has one of the most crucial factors for e-commerce [20], as well as in the area of behaviour and social sciences to better understand, which elements hold the customer's attention and make him/her stay in that website and not leave [21, 22].

Recent studies have also shown that the visual appearance of the website increases customers' satisfaction and trust, two key factors that foster customers' loyalty and positive WOM intentions [12, 23, 24].

2.3   Website Usability

The usability of websites in the context of this work focuses on the concept proposed by Flavián et al. [11], which refers to the ease of navigating or making transactions (purchases) on the website perceived by the customer. Usability is frequently associated with ease of use, a critical factor for the development of e-commerce and for achieving customer satisfaction [25].

Usability is also related to the UX design concept mentioned above, but in the present context, it is separated from the visual appearance of the website mentioned above, that is, while the usability focuses on the functions and the way they are provided to the customer the appearance of the website focuses on the beauty and visual appeal and the website. Similar to the website visual appeal, the usability of a website is fundamental to its success by affecting the decisions and purchases of customers [11] and contributing to their retention [14].

If we take into account that in e-commerce websites there is no physical contact of the buyer with the seller and product, i.e. everything is done without anyone's help, website functionalities as product catalogue, search engine, price comparisons, shopping carts, etc., become fundamental in the success of user interaction with the website and purchase intention [15, 21].

2.4   E-trust

The Internet has allowed the physical business to be online [26]. In this type of commerce, it is not possible to try the products or observe them directly. In this context, relationships are built through trust in brand and trust in website (e-trust). E-trust can be defined as a qualified reliance on the information that customers get from the website so that they feel confident in doing business online [27].

E-commerce can increase the value of a business in many ways, but there are still some obstacles to overcome [28], notably the ones associated with uncertainties and risks. Trust mitigates the uncertainties and risks associated [29] with e-commerce and both academics and professionals recognize the relevance of e-trust and its influence on consumer decision making [30]. E-trust is one of the relevant determinants for websites to be truly successful.

Ou and Sia [31] consider that trust is associated with something positive and good such as belief, benevolence, and empathy between the parties. In the online environment, trust has multiple dimensions such as trust in the seller, trust in the Internet as a distribution channel and trust in the online regulatory environment [26].

Trust is described as the psychological state of mind [32] and is defined as the willingness of one party to be vulnerable to the actions of another party based on the expectation that the other party will carry out an important action, regardless of the ability to control that action. In online commerce, e-trust refers to the degree to which customers believe that a website, through the technology and quality of its services, will facilitate the transaction process [33].

In this context, the brand and website can reduce uncertainty and consequently increase online trust [34]. The work of Urban et al. [35] states that e-trust is generated when the design is pleasing and the information translates safety into the business that customers want to do.

The websites are presented as the communication channel between customers and online stores where their aesthetic and usability characteristics take on a leading role [28]. In this sense, trust appears in scientific studies as a mediator between the characteristics of online stores and consumer behaviour [29].

Customers' assessment of whether the characteristics of a website that meets their needs reflect an overall perception of excellence of the website [28]. Thus, if customers believe that using a website provides them with utility in comparison to others, the website can be perceived as reliable for the customer [29]. In addition, the balance between the features of websites, their visual appeal and aesthetics demonstrate the capacity and professionalism of the online store, which increases e-trust [29]. In this sense, our study will propose the following research hypotheses:

- H1: Website design has a positive effect on e-trust
- H1a: Product information has a positive effect on e-trust
- H1b: Website aesthetics has a positive effect on e-trust
- H1c: Website usability has a positive effect on e-trust

2.5   Word of Mouth

The word of mouth (WOM) is a source of information that influences consumers' purchasing decisions [36]. This influence is due to the exchange of information between people who trust each other.

Existing literature on WOM indicates that when brand information is accurate and correct it is easier for the customer to understand and interpret this information, increasing the intention of positive WOM by customers [37]. Thus, the characteristics of websites play a central role in WOM intention, where not only the website's usability is of vital importance, but also the website's aesthetics [32]. In this sense, we present the following research hypotheses:

- H2: Website design has a positive effect on WOM
- H2a: Product information has a positive effect on WOM
- H2b: Website aesthetics has a positive effect on WOM
- H2c: Website usability has a positive effect on WOM

Trust is a significant antecedent of a member's desire to exchange information online [36]. Lien and Cao [38] found that trust in online messages (e-trust) positively influences customers' intention to write or share positive WOM intentions. In this sense, we intend to test the following research hypothesis:

- H3: E-trust has a positive effect on WOM.

2.6   Research Model

The proposed model has five constructs and seven hypotheses, which have been generated from the relations of these five constructs (see Fig. 1).

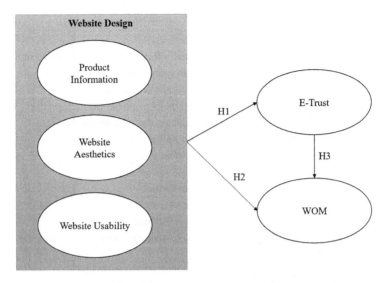

Fig. 1. Research model and hypothesis

3   Method

To validate the proposed model, a survey was conducted among customers of online fashion stores (e-commerce websites).

3.1   Measures

The data were collected through a self-administered survey. The survey had two phases: the first one asks participants to think about a fashion brand that has an online store; the second one has the constructs' items who were adapted to the context from previous studies. To measure the constructs' items, we used Pham and Ahammad [17] and Cebi [39] items for website design (PRI – Product information, AES – Website aesthetics, and USA – Website usability). E-Trust (ETR) was measured through items used by Cyr [40] and Escobar-Rodríguez and Bonsón-Fernández [3]. The scale adopted for Word of Mouth (WOM) were adapted from Brown [24] (Table 1). All the items used in this study were measured using a 5-point Likert scales, ranging from strongly disagree (1) to strongly agree (5).

Table 1. Survey instrument

Construct	Measuring variables
PRI	PRI1 – This website presents updated information on products and trends
	PRI2 – This website has good quality photos of the products
	PRI3 – This website can clearly show the colours of the product
	PRI4 – This website shows all the colours available for each product
	PRI5 – This website shows all available sizes of each product
	PRI6 – This website clearly informs product prices
AES	AES1 – This website design is attractive to me
	AES2 – I like the colour scheme of this website
	AES3 – This website has a nice font theme
USA	USA1 – This website is easy to use
	USA2 – I can easily find products on this website
	USA3 – I can easily remember how to find each page when I visit the website next time
ETR	ETR1 – I trust the information presented on this website
	ETR2 – I trust the transaction process on this website
	ETR3 – I can trust this website
WOM	WOM1 – I say positive things about this website to other people
	WOM2 – I recommend this website to anyone who seeks my advice
	WOM3 – I encourage friends and relatives to do more shopping at this website

3.2   Sample

The sample has 220 valid questionnaires. On Table 2 we show that 65.0% are female and most of the observations (N = 200; 90,91%) originate from individuals below 40 years old. Many of them (N = 166; 74,45%) have higher qualifications (Table 2).

Table 2. Demographic profiles (N = 220)

Variables	Category	N	%
Gender	Male	77	35.00%
	Female	143	65.00%
Age	≤ 20	20	9.09%
	20–29	135	61.36%
	30–39	45	20.45%
	40–49	15	6.82%
	≥ 50	5	2.27%
Education	Primary school studies	1	0.45%
	Secondary school studies	53	24.09%
	High school	166	75.45%

The top 5 e-commerce fashion websites identified by the study participants were: Zara (18%); Berska (9%); Fashionnova (6%); Nike (5%) and Mango (4%).

4 Results

We choose Partial Least Squares – Structural Equation Modelling (PLS-SEM) because it enables the researchers to assess causal relationships among items and causal relationships of latent constructs. The PLS-SEM is appropriate for exploratory research and does not require normality of data [41]. PLS-SEM is executed in two steps: first, analysis to reliability and validity (measurement model) and secondly analysis to relations between constructs. The PLS-Algorithm was executed on SMART PLS v3.2.8 soft-ware [42].

4.1 Reliability and Validity

A preliminary data analysis was conducted to validate VIF – Variance Inflactor Factor, which is below the threshold and therefore there is no multicollinearity (VIF < 5) and to validate the Skewness (Sk) and Kurtosis (Ku), which reveal that the items do not diverge from normality (Sk < 3; Ku < 7) [41].

Construct Validity and Reliability
To achieve construct validity and reliability standardized item loadings (λ) were analysed for all reflexive constructs above the minimum threshold value of 0.7 (see Table 3) [43], which were acceptable for further analysis.

Table 3. Items, Descriptive Statistics, and coefficient loadings (N = 220)

Construct	Measuring variables	Mean	Std dev	λ	t-values
PRI	PRI1	4.085	0.681	0.787	19.039
	PRI2	4.121	0.689	0.806	22.274
	PRI3	3.987	0.755	0.822	25.274
	PRI4	3.955	0.819	0.738	16.340
	PRI5	4.063	0.767	0.787	19.214
	PRI6	4.099	0.727	0.782	14.705
AES	AES1	3.942	0.697	0.872	39.465
	AES2	3.852	0.709	0.853	27.124
	AES3	4.009	0.584	0.829	24.679
USA	USA1	3.870	0.719	0.866	43.244
	USA2	3.834	0.766	0.837	21.118
	USA3	3.821	0.795	0.798	23.126
ETR	ETR1	3.860	0.682	0.920	61.495
	ETR2	3.861	0.730	0.930	52.892
	ETR3	3.897	0.698	0.911	34.781
WOM	WOM1	3.950	0.692	0.897	49.847
	WOM2	3.523	0.933	0.858	37.055
	WOM3	3.825	0.752	0.892	44.431

λ – standardized values

Table 4 shows that Average Variance extracted (AVE) (ranging from 0.620 to 0.847) and composite reliability (CR) (ranging from 0.873 to 0.943) are above the threshold values (AVE > 0.5; CR > 0.7). These values showed convergent validity for all constructs.

Table 4. Reliability and convergent validity

	Cronbach α	ρA	CR	AVE
PRI	0.877	0.880	0.907	0.620
AES	0.810	0.811	0.888	0.725
USA	0.782	0.789	0.873	0.696
ETR	0.910	0.914	0.943	0.847
WOM	0.859	0.871	0.914	0.779

AVE = Average Variance extracted; CR = Composite Reliability;

Discriminant Validity

Discriminant validity has been confirmed in three steps. First, through the Fornell and Larcker criteria [44] it was verified that the correlations between latent constructions are below than values of the square root diagonals of the AVE (Table 5). In the second step, the discriminant validity was analysed through the cross-loadings criterion. Table 6 shows a comparison of the column loadings. Each indicator exhibits that indicator's loadings on its construct is higher in all cases compared to all its cross-loadings with other constructs. Finally, in the third step, the discriminant validity was examined through the Heterotrait-Monotrait (HTMT) ratio of correlations and, as can be seen in Table 7 the HTMT values are below 0.90 [45]. Therefore, discriminant has been established between variables.

Table 5. Discriminant validity: Fornell and Larcker criterion [44]

	PRI	AES	USA	ETR	WOM
PRI	0.787				
AES	0.655	0.851			
USA	0.589	0.653	0.834		
ETR	0.621	0.679	0.521	0.920	
WOM	0.447	0.624	0.589	0.635	0.883

Table 6. Cross-loadings

	PRI	AES	USA	ETR	WOM
PRI1	**0.787**	0.436	0.511	0.429	0.334
PRI2	**0.806**	0.567	0.455	0.502	0.340
PRI3	**0.822**	0.528	0.456	0.541	0.343
PRI4	**0.738**	0.437	0.387	0.457	0.297
PRI5	**0.787**	0.607	0.484	0.462	0.426
PRI6	**0.782**	0.503	0.487	0.532	0.365
AES1	0.511	**0.872**	0.569	0.551	0.567
AES2	0.479	**0.853**	0.491	0.560	0.496
AES3	0.674	**0.829**	0.602	0.621	0.527
USA1	0.507	0.597	**0.866**	0.439	0.575
USA2	0.479	0.520	**0.837**	0.400	0.434
USA3	0.486	0.511	**0.798**	0.463	0.453
ETR1	0.592	0.687	0.520	**0.920**	0.551
ETR2	0.550	0.600	0.471	**0.930**	0.615
ETR3	0.571	0.582	0.443	**0.911**	0.591
WOM1	0.493	0.627	0.580	0.642	**0.897**
WOM2	0.317	0.491	0.476	0.491	**0.858**
WOM3	0.354	0.519	0.494	0.532	**0.892**

Table 7. Discriminant validity HTMT ratio

	PRI	AES	USA	ETR	WOM
PRI					
AES	0.769				
USA	0.710	0.815			
ETR	0.691	0.787	0.614		
WOM	0.504	0.739	0.707	0.712	

4.2 Hypothesis Testing

The hypotheses are tested through the PLS-SEM with bootstrapping resample (5000 subsamples). Table 8 shows that 5 hypotheses are supported and 2 are not supported.

Table 8. Structural theory results

		β	t values	p-values	95% confidence interval	Hypothesis
H1a	PRI → ETR	0.295	4.531	0.000	[0.168…0.426]	Supported
H1b	AES → ETR	0.450	6.383	0.000	[0.309…0.586]	Supported
H1c	USA → ETR	0.052	0.734	0.463	[−0.091…0.183]	Not supported
H2a	PRI → WOM	−0.141	1.883	0.060	[-0.286…0.013]	Not supported
H2b	AES → WOM	0.249	2.958	0.003	[0.078…0.408]	Supported
H2c	USA → WOM	0.303	4.538	0.000	[0.179…0.445]	Supported
H3	ETR → WOM	0.397	4.207	0.000	[0.209…0.583]	Supported

5 Discussion

In the context of online commerce, our study aimed to test the effects of website design on e-trust and the WOM.

The hypothesis test aimed, to verify the influence of the website's design on e-trust (H1), to verify the influence of the website's design on positive WOM intentions (H2), and to verify the influence of e-trust on positive WOM intentions (H3).

On e-commerce websites, clear and accurate product information helps customers reduce uncertainty [35]. The results of this study confirm that product information influences e-trust ($\beta_{PRI \rightarrow ETR} = 0.295$; t = 4.531; p < 0.01). The H1a hypothesis is supported by our study.

Our study found the aesthetics of the website, has positive effects on e-trust ($\beta_{AES \rightarrow ETR} = 0.450$; t = 6.383; p < 0.01), which supports the H1b hypothesis. These results are framed by the work of Kim and Peterson [29], which suggests visual appeal and aesthetics as synonymous of online stores' competence. These authors state that attractive online stores with high visual appeal contribute to online confidence. Chou et al. [12] also suggested that e-trust leading to WOM can be affected by website design. In another study in which 571 online responses were analysed, Cyr 2013 [40] demonstrated that an effectively designed website in terms of its visual elements may attract online users, leading to an increase in customer trust in an online vendor.

Our study found no significant relationship between usability and e-trust. The H1c hypothesis was not supported by our study ($\beta_{USA \rightarrow ETR} = 0.052$; t = 0.734; p > 0.05). If on the one hand usability is understood as a predictor of trust in websites, through the ease of use and easy of navigation on websites, we understand that, because our sample has 75% of customers with higher education qualifications, they consider usability to be something that already exists. The more educated individuals have greater Internet and e-commerce related skills. Thus, e-commerce fashion websites have high usability perceived by customer, which leads them to consider usability as a given fact. Thus, e-commerce fashion websites do not vary much in terms of usability perceived by customer which leads us to accept the result of not corroborating the H1c hypothesis.

The information on products presented on the website, when accurate, contributes to the WOM intention of customer [37] however, our study found no evidence to conclude in the same direction ($\beta_{PRI \rightarrow WOM} = 0.141$; t = 1.883; p > 0.05), therefore, not validating the H2a hypothesis. The fact that our study finds no evidence for this relationship may be because the product information presented on websites is shared when customer trust this information [33] and, this may be the justification for the direct effects of product information on the WOM. Product information could promote WOM if trust takes a mediating role for customer [29].

The results obtained in our study support the H2b hypothesis ($\beta_{AES \rightarrow WOM} = 0.249$; t = 2.958; p < 0.01), which is in line with other studies in literature such as the study by Almeshal and Alhidari [32], in which the authors state that the aesthetics of the website influences WOM by customer.

Usability affects the behaviors and attitudes towards a website, referring Almeshal and Alhidari [32] that the website usability positively affects the WOM. Our study supports this statement, since H2c hypothesis is supported ($\beta_{USA \rightarrow WOM} = 0.303$; $t = 4.538$; $p < 0.01$).

The exchange of information is based on the costumer's trust in the information sharing partners [38]. Our study obtained evidence to support the H3 hypothesis ($\beta_{ETR \rightarrow WOM} = 0.397$; $t = 4.207$; $p < 0.01$) concluding that WOM is influenced by e-trust.

6 Conclusion

The model used to confirm the importance of the e-commerce fashion websites' characteristics in costumer behaviour, namely in terms of e-trust and positive WOM intentions, obtained values of R^2 above 0.2 [43] ($R^2_{ETR} = 0.508$; $R^2_{WOM} = 0.515$), an acceptable value, confirming other studies in the literature [3, 21, 40].

This work demonstrates that the characteristics of websites influence confidence in e-commerce stores as shown by the literature [29]. This influence is due to the information presented about the products, but also to the aesthetics and usability of the website. Another conclusion of our study is evidenced in the relationship between the characteristics of the website and positive WOM intentions as shown by other studies [32]. It was concluded that the characteristics of websites in the fashion sector influence the positive WOM by their customer and that this positive WOM depends on the confidence that each costumer has in the online store.

WOM is recognized as a relevant variable for online stores to influence more customers [36, 37]. Therefore, this research presents itself as relevant to business practice, since our study emphasizes that online fashion stores should give importance to the design of the e-commerce website, specifically regarding the aesthetics and usability of the website. Furthermore, the appealing presentation of products and information presented about them produce significant effects on customer' positive WOM intentions. Therefore, e-commerce fashion online stores must focus their efforts on improving their website features.

Although the study found valid results, these were subject to some limitations. Among the limitations found, it was identified that the sample consisting of young individuals with high school education may have limited the results. More educated individuals have greater skills related to the Internet and e-commerce, which leads them not to perceive usability as an obstacle to using e-commerce fashion websites, adapting easily to them for shopping. Therefore, it is proposed to carry out studies with different samples in online commerce in the field of fashion or to seek studies in other sectors using e-commerce. In these studies, new variables can also be included, such as the satisfaction variable with the online shop.

References

1. Gazzola, P., Pavione, E., Pezzetti, R., Grechi, D.: Trends in the fashion industry. The perception of sustainability and circular economy: a gender/generation quantitative approach. Sustainability **12**, 2809 (2020). https://doi.org/10.3390/su12072809

2. Shopify: Fashion Industry Report (2019)
3. Escobar-Rodríguez, T., Bonsón-Fernández, R.: Analysing online purchase intention in Spain: fashion e-commerce. IseB **15**(3), 599–622 (2016). https://doi.org/10.1007/s10257-016-0319-6
4. Mir-Bernal, P., Guercini, S., Sádaba, T.: The role of e-commerce in the internationalization of Spanish luxury fashion multi-brand retailers. J. Glob. Fashion Mark. **9**, 59–72 (2018). https://doi.org/10.1080/20932685.2017.1399080
5. Cadieux, S., Heyn, M.: The journey to an agile organization at Zalando. McKinsey Co. 1–12 (2018)
6. Hobbs, J.E.: Food supply chains during the COVID-19 pandemic. Can. J. Agric. Econ. (2020). https://doi.org/10.1111/cjag.12237
7. Yan, A., Zou, Y., Mirchandani, D.A.: How hospitals in mainland China responded to the outbreak of COVID-19 using information technology–enabled services: an analysis of hospital news webpages. J. Am. Med. Inform. Assoc. (2020). https://doi.org/10.1093/jamia/ocaa064
8. Shelley, E.K.: Apparel and accessories suffer a catastrophic 52% sales decline in March. In: Forbes (2020). https://www.forbes.com/sites/shelleykohan/2020/04/16/apparel-and-accessories-suffer-a-catastrophic-52-percent-decline-in-march-sales/#2120ed8c1b5b. Accessed 16 July 2020
9. Gerstell, E., Marchessou, S., Schmidt, J., Spagnuolo, E.: How COVID-19 is changing the world of beauty (2020)
10. Park, E.J., Kim, E.Y., Funches, V.M., Foxx, W.: Apparel product attributes, web browsing, and e-impulse buying on shopping websites. J. Bus. Res. **65**, 1583–1589 (2012). https://doi.org/10.1016/j.jbusres.2011.02.043
11. Flavián, C., Guinalíu, M., Gurrea, R.: The role played by perceived usability, satisfaction and consumer trust on website loyalty. Inf. Manag. **43**, 1–14 (2006). https://doi.org/10.1016/j.im.2005.01.002
12. Chou, S., Chen, C.-W., Lin, J.-Y.: Female online shoppers. Internet Res. **25**, 542–561 (2015). https://doi.org/10.1108/IntR-01-2014-0006
13. Harris, C.: The Fundamentals of Digital Fashion Marketing. Bloomsbury Publishing, London (2017)
14. Pee, L.G., Jiang, J., Klein, G.: Signaling effect of website usability on repurchase intention. Int. J. Inf. Manag. **39**, 228–241 (2018). https://doi.org/10.1016/j.ijinfomgt.2017.12.010
15. Chen, Y.-H., Hsu, I.-C., Lin, C.-C.: Website attributes that increase consumer purchase intention: a conjoint analysis. J. Bus. Res. **63**, 1007–1014 (2010). https://doi.org/10.1016/j.jbusres.2009.01.023
16. Loureiro, S.M.C., Cavallero, L., Miranda, F.J.: Fashion brands on retail websites: customer performance expectancy and e-word-of-mouth. J. Retail. Consum. Serv. **41**, 131–141 (2018). https://doi.org/10.1016/j.jretconser.2017.12.005
17. Pham, T.S.H., Ahammad, M.F.: Antecedents and consequences of online customer satisfaction: a holistic process perspective. Technol. Forecast. Soc. Chang. **124**, 332–342 (2017). https://doi.org/10.1016/j.techfore.2017.04.003
18. Wolfinbarger, M., Gilly, M.C.: eTailQ: dimensionalizing, measuring and predicting etail quality. J. Retail. **79**, 183–198 (2003). https://doi.org/10.1016/S0022-4359(03)00034-4
19. Chung, K., Shin, J.: The antecedents and consequents of relationship quality in internet shopping. Asia Pac. J. Mark. Logist. **22**, 473–491 (2010). https://doi.org/10.1108/13555851011090510
20. Bonastre L., Granollers T.: A set of heuristics for user experience evaluation in E-commerce websites. In: ACHI 2014 - 7th International Conference on Advances in Computer-Human Interaction, pp. 27–34 (2014)

21. Ganguly, B., Dash, S.B., Cyr, D., Head, M.: The effects of website design on purchase intention in online shopping: the mediating role of trust and the moderating role of culture. Int. J. Electron. Bus. **8**, 302 (2010). https://doi.org/10.1504/IJEB.2010.035289
22. Shaouf, A., Lü, K., Li, X.: The effect of web advertising visual design on online purchase intention: an examination across gender. Comput. Hum. Behav. **60**, 622–634 (2016). https://doi.org/10.1016/j.chb.2016.02.090
23. Verkijika, S.F., De Wet, L.: Understanding word-of-mouth (WOM) intentions of mobile app users: the role of simplicity and emotions during the first interaction. Telemat Informatics **41**, 218–228 (2019). https://doi.org/10.1016/j.tele.2019.05.003
24. Brown, T.J.: Spreading the word: investigating antecedents of consumers' positive word-of-mouth intentions and behaviors in a retailing context. J. Acad. Mark. Sci. **33**, 123–138 (2005). https://doi.org/10.1177/0092070304268417
25. Tandon, U., Kiran, R., Sah, A.: Analyzing customer satisfaction: users perspective towards online shopping. Nankai Bus. Rev. Int. **8**, 266–288 (2017). https://doi.org/10.1108/NBRI-04-2016-0012
26. Lee, S., Jeon, S., Kim, D.: The impact of tour quality and tourist satisfaction on tourist loyalty: the case of Chinese tourists in Korea. Tour. Manag. **32**, 1115–1124 (2011). https://doi.org/10.1016/j.tourman.2010.09.016
27. Thakur, R., Summey, J.H.: e-Trust: empirical insights into influential antecedents. Mark. Manag. J. **17**, 67–80 (2007)
28. Agag, G.M., El-Masry, A.A.: Why do consumers trust online travel websites? Drivers and outcomes of consumer trust toward online travel websites. J. Travel Res. **56**, 347–369 (2017). https://doi.org/10.1177/0047287516643185
29. Kim, Y., Peterson, R.A.: A meta-analysis of online trust relationships in e-commerce. J. Interact. Mark. **38**, 44–54 (2017). https://doi.org/10.1016/j.intmar.2017.01.001
30. Prasad, S., Gupta, I.C., Totala, N.K.: Social media usage, electronic word of mouth and purchase-decision involvement. Asia-Pac. J. Bus. Adm. **9**, 134–145 (2017). https://doi.org/10.1108/APJBA-06-2016-0063
31. Ou, C.X., Sia, C.L.: Consumer trust and distrust: an issue of website design. Int. J. Hum. Comput. Stud. **68**, 913–934 (2010). https://doi.org/10.1016/j.ijhcs.2010.08.003
32. Almeshal, S.A., Alhidari, A.M.: Consumers' value perception and value construction: the case of bottled water in the Middle East. J. Food Prod. Mark. **24**, 982–998 (2018). https://doi.org/10.1080/10454446.2018.1458676
33. Banerjee, S., Bhattacharyya, S., Bose, I.: Whose online reviews to trust? Understanding reviewer trustworthiness and its impact on business. Decis. Support Syst. **96**, 17–26 (2017). https://doi.org/10.1016/j.dss.2017.01.006
34. Park, J., Gunn, F., Han, S.-L.: Multidimensional trust building in e-retailing: cross-cultural differences in trust formation and implications for perceived risk. J. Retail. Consum. Serv. **19**, 304–312 (2012). https://doi.org/10.1016/j.jretconser.2012.03.003
35. Urban, G.L., Amyx, C., Lorenzon, A.: Online trust: state of the art, new frontiers, and research potential. J. Interact. Mark. **23**, 179–190 (2009). https://doi.org/10.1016/j.intmar.2009.03.001
36. Wang, T., Yeh, R.K.-J., Chen, C., Tsydypov, Z.: What drives electronic word-of-mouth on social networking sites? Perspectives of social capital and self-determination. Telemat. Inform. **33**, 1034–1047 (2016). https://doi.org/10.1016/j.tele.2016.03.005
37. Sijoria, C., Mukherjee, S., Datta, B.: Impact of the antecedents of eWOM on CBBE. Mark. Intell. Plan. **36**, 528–542 (2018). https://doi.org/10.1108/MIP-10-2017-0221
38. Lien, C.H., Cao, Y.: Examining WeChat users' motivations, trust, attitudes, and positive word-of-mouth: evidence from China. Comput. Hum. Behav. **41**, 104–111 (2014). https://doi.org/10.1016/j.chb.2014.08.013

39. Cebi, S.: Determining importance degrees of website design parameters based on interactions and types of websites. Decis. Support Syst. **54**, 1030–1043 (2013). https://doi.org/10.1016/j.dss.2012.10.036

40. Cyr, D.: Website design, trust and culture: an eight country investigation. Electron. Commer. Res. Appl. **12**, 373–385 (2013). https://doi.org/10.1016/j.elerap.2013.03.007

41. Hair, J., Black, W., Babin, B., Anderson, R.: Multivariate Data Analysis: Global Edition, 8th edn. Annabel Ainscow, New York (2018)

42. Ringle, C.M., Wende, S., Becker, J.M.: SmartPLS 3. SmartPLS, Bönningstedt (2015)

43. Chin, W.W.: The partial least squares approach to structural equation modeling. Mod. Methods Bus. Res. **295**, 295–336 (1998)

44. Fornell, C., Larcker, D.F.: Evaluating structural equation models with unobservable variables and measurement error. J. Mark. Res. **18**, 39 (1981). https://doi.org/10.2307/3151312

45. Henseler, J., Ringle, C.M., Sarstedt, M.: A new criterion for assessing discriminant validity in variance-based structural equation modeling. J. Acad. Mark. Sci. **43**(1), 115–135 (2014). https://doi.org/10.1007/s11747-014-0403-8

When Persuasive Technology Gets Dark?

Tobias Nyström[1]($\boxtimes$) and Agnis Stibe[2,3]

[1] Uppsala University, Uppsala, Sweden
tobias.nystrom@im.uu.se
[2] Métis Lab, EM Normandie Business School, Paris, France
[3] INTERACT Research Unit, University of Oulu, Oulu, Finland

Abstract. Influencing systems and persuasive technology (PT) should give their users a positive experience. While that sounds attractive and many rush implementing novel ideas things such as gamification, a serious professional and scientifically rich discussion is needed to portray a holistic picture on technology influence. Relatively little research has been aimed at exploring the negative aspects, outcomes, and side effects of PT. Therefore this research aims at addressing this gap by reviewing the existing knowledge on dark patterns, demonstrating how intended Pt designs can be critically examined, introducing the Visibility-Darkness matrix to categorize and locate dark patterns, and proposing a Framework for Evaluating the Darkness of Persuasive Technology (FEDPT). The framework is instrumental for designers and developers of influential technology, as it clarifies an area where their products and services can have a negative impact on well-being, in other words, can become harmful to the users.

Keywords: Dark patterns · Design · Evaluation · Framework · Negative · Persuasive technology · Visibility-Darkness matrix

1 Introduction

Like most technological advancements, an introduction and use of persuasive technology (PT) can have both beneficial and harmful effects on the users. Game experience has recently gained rapid popularity as an enabler of persuasion, as it drives the engagement by using game elements. Oftentimes, game experience is the catalyst for increasing the efficiency of the designed and intended persuasion. However, when it comes to real-life implementations, all technologies can potentially be used for good or bad. Moreover, the study of unintended negative consequences of behavioral interventions is growing and becoming an important research area [16,17,38,48].

In persuasion and computer game research, the harmful effects on people are often labeled as "the dark side" [4,12,23,28,31], and the issues of ethics are rarely explored [30]. Therefore, it is important to thoroughly study both direct and indirect effects of PT in the context of darkness.

© Springer Nature Switzerland AG 2020
M. Themistocleous et al. (Eds.): EMCIS 2020, LNBIP 402, pp. 331–345, 2020.
https://doi.org/10.1007/978-3-030-63396-7_22

Previous research on negative user effects and human behavior (e.g. the dark side and persuasive backfiring) calls for further exploration [4,48]. This research aims at advancing this essential but relatively uncharted area of PT. Thus, the research question for this work is: *When and how can PT get dark?* To address this question, the Visibility-Darkness matrix is proposed and used to identify PT that can be classified as manipulative or designed with bad intentions.

The paper is structured in six sections. The background in Sect. 2 presents the concept of PT, its negative sides, and dark patterns. In Sect. 3 an outline of search results is being mapped into the Visibility-Darkness matrix. A validation of the framework by using use case is shown in Sect. 4 followed by a discussion in Sect. 5. Finally in Sect. 6 conclusions and future research paths are given.

2   Background

2.1   Persuasive Technology

The design and use of PT for transforming human behavior can be done in various forms, for example, to help smoking cessation, exercising frequently, driving less and biking more [26]. Fogg defined persuasion in the context of persuasive computers as "an attempt to shape, reinforce, or change behaviors, feelings, or thoughts about an issue, object, or action" [18]. Later in the context of using computers as persuasive technologies (captology) Fogg [19] define persuasion "as an attempt to change attitudes or behaviors or both (without using coercion or deception)", the intended change and planned persuasive effects are central in captology. As coercion is an antonym of persuasion, any technology using force should be labeled as coercive technology. Adding deception to the definition as does not make the PT unproblematic, as ethical issues often emerge in the design phase [40]. Important to note is that both coercion and deception can be a subjective experience for an individual. One popular example of a PT is the use of gamification to change behavior (e.g. persuade towards sustainability see [39]). Commonly gamification is defined as the use of game elements in a non-game context [13] or as a process of providing affordances for gameful experiences which support the customers' overall value creation [27]. Gamification is usually rich with applying points, badges, leaderboards and often includes progress bars, quests, avatars, and performance graphs.

2.2   Possible Pitfalls When Designing Persuasive Technology

A literature search using Scopus and Web of Science (2018-10-05) with the keywords ("persuasive technolog*" OR "persuasive system*") AND (dark* OR backfir* OR negative OR ethics OR manipulation OR exploitation) was conducted. It was done to identify prior findings about negative outcomes (and synonyms like backfire, backfiring, darkness, dark side, ethics, exploitation, and manipulation) of persuasive technolog(y/ies)/system(s). Scopus returned 90 papers and Web of Science returned 45 papers and the total number of unique papers was 98. The key inclusion criteria was defined as: peer-reviewed research that address negative effect(s) of PT on individual users. In the first round after reading the abstracts, 32 papers were chosen as candidates, thus further read in detail. In the second round, the whole paper was read and 18 papers fulfilled the key inclusion criteria, so had relevance for this research, see Table 1.

Table 1. Papers exploring pitfalls of persuasive technology

Id	Theme	Id	Theme
[5]	Awareness of unintended outcomes	[6]	Privacy and designer responsibility
[22]	Responsiblity and ethical consideration	[24][25]	Morally acceptable
[29]	Ethical consideration of adaptable PT	[30]	Ethical framework gamification
[35]	Applicability of discourse ethics on PT	[36]	Applying discourse ethics on PT
[42]	Awareness - lack of understanding and commitment	[43]	Ethical acceptability of PT
[45]	PT design concerns privacy, autonomy, and coercion	[47]	Design guidelines by using discourse ethics
[48]	Awareness and a taxonomy for PT	[49]	Investigate the moral acceptability of machine persuasion
[53]	Autonomy and volunteerism to PT	[55]	Autonomy and volunteerism to PT
[56]	Critical design questions to assess value, action, and goal		

By reading the papers a few themes where discovered. A number of papers [5,6,22,30,45,55] discuss the ethics and responsibility of PT from different viewpoints. Unintended outcomes of PT are discussed e.g. compusuasion is Atkinson's [5] term for unintended behavior change. Fogg's [19] focus on the intended outcome of PT and omission of unintended outcome of PT is problematic since the latter could have a large impact. According to Atkinson [5], the designer of PT should take responsibility for unintended, unforeseen, and unpredicted outcome, although they could not categorically be seen as belonging to persuasion.

Berdichevsky and Neuenschwander [6] explore the ethics of PT by suggesting a systematic approach and develop a framework for evaluating the ethics of the interaction of persuader, PT and the persuaded. They also display a flowchart that shows how ethical responsibility is connected to predictable/unpredictable intent and intended/unintended outcomes. As a summary, their work outlines ten principles for ethical design of PT. Gram-Hansen [22] also explores ethics of

PT, especially the impact of ubiquitous technology, as it probably is the most efficient way to change user's behavior. The problem with ubiquitous technology is that it could change human behavior without proper disclosure. This calls for an ethical consideration during the whole design process and evaluation of both the original intention and the practical application. Kim and Werbach [30] identified several ethical issues that needs to be addressed. The issues are framed into four categories: exploitation, manipulation, harms, and (detrimental to) character. These four issues could be the base to formulate a framework for evaluation. Reitberg et al. [45] looked at PT design concerns related to ethics. The TV Companion application (aimed to persuade users towards healthy TV consumption) is critically evaluated. When designing PT, three design areas should be considered "autonomy and free choice", "coercion versus reflection", and "surveillance and privacy". Verbeek [55] researched the perils of ambient intelligence and PT. Technology is not only a neutral enabler of behaviors, but it also shapes how people act and experience reality. Thus, PT requires reconsidering the concept of human freedom and our understanding of both moral and casual responsibility. The author elaborates on the responsibility of both the user and the designer.

Another area of concerns is about what in PT is morally and ethically acceptable [24,25,29,43,49]. Guerini et al. [24] have researched the moral implications and actions of autonomous artificial agents, e.g., adaptive PT. The authors emphasize that flexibility is important for PT through adapting a persuasive strategy to fit the situation and the character of the persuaded. Ham and Spahn [25] looked at the physiological effects and moral acceptability of persuasive robots. An important issue to consider is alternative persuasive strategies and what means to reach the aim. The importance to identify persuasive principles and attention to ethical consideration is emphasized. Page and Kray [43] used focus groups to understand relevant ethical aspects of PT in the context of healthy living. The result showed three factors that people value when determining the ethical acceptability of PT, namely the commissioner, the recipient, and the means of delivery. Text messages were seen as more acceptable and electrical shock or bank account restrictions most unethical. Interesting to notice is that electric shock could sometimes be justified. Stock et al. [49] researched adaptive PT to gain better understanding of the moral acceptability of the communicative action conducted by PT to reach its goal of persuading. One interesting finding is that people do not seem to evaluate the moral acceptability of machine persuasion differently compared to human persuasion, despite the fact that a priori most answered that machine persuasion could not be morally accepted. The persuasive system should be flexible with persuasion strategies and adaptive to the persuaded. Kaptein and Eckles [29] showed concerns regarding adaptive persuasive systems, as they rarely disclose the system's ability to adapt to individual differences and that a system trained in one context could be used in other unexpected ways. The systems could create persuasion profiling of an individual, and this may become ethically challenging, as the personal data could be distributed and shared between systems without any consent from the user.

Privacy of PT is also something that needs attention [6,35]. Leth et al. [35] showed valid ethical concerns that PT could contribute to the surveillance of individuals. The authors discuss how Berdichevsky and Neuenschwander's framework and Fogg's stakeholder analysis could be used as a help to ethical problems, because many systems could be used for surveillance, depending on the context, and for some this possibility might be quite tempting. The persuasive system should not violate individual privacy.

Researchers [45,53] are also interested in the volunteerism of PT. Timmer et al. [53] wrote about an important ethical issues for PT, e.g., persuasive systems that are used at work could, depending on context and viewpoint, be seen as mandatory. Thus, the system use would not be perceived as voluntary, and group pressure at work could influence users. Ethically responsive PT should preserve the autonomy of an individual, and this is something the designer of PT must consider.

Another theme that concerns the design of PT, is about guidelines and evaluation [6,36,45,47,56]. Spahn [47] and Linder [36] both apply discourse ethics to PT as a way to understand the ethics of this technology. Spahn derives various criteria from discourse ethics for usage and design of PT, so these criteria could be used as a guideline. Linder elaborates on the assessment of PT, as it is a medium for the designer, the engineer, or authority to change the user's behavior towards planned goals. The principals of discourse ethics could be a way to reflect PT, but Linder also demonstrates the limitation of discourse ethics. Yetim [56] use value-based practical reasoning and argumentation schemes as a foundation to build a framework for practical discourse. The questions are remapped into practical-, ethical-, and moral discourse and could be used when designing, evaluating, and critically assesses the goals, values, and actions of a persuasive system. Stibe and Cugelman [48] have demonstrated how PT could backfire and calls for a discussion concerning negative outcomes of PT. To aid this discussion, they have developed the "Intention-Outcome" and risk managing "Likelihood-Severity" matrices, as well as a taxonomy for categorizing persuasive backfire. de Oliveira and Carrascal [42] proposed new approaches when designing PT to highlight necessary ethical concerns and to wake the awareness of both designers and users of PT. They explored three approaches: an enforced prevention (e.g. guidelines provided by government or organizations), an encouraged prevention (e.g. voluntary certification), and a remediation-based approach (e.g. tools for users to reveal, identify, and remove or mitigate the bias of PT).

2.3   Dark Patterns and Computer Game

Design pattern as a concept was introduced by Christopher Alexander as a solution that is proven and reusable for an architectural design problem [2]. Design patterns have, for example, been used in interaction design [10], software engineering [21], and game design [8], as a reusable solution for problems in a specific context. A pattern solution often captures more solutions in preference of one exact solution. Dark patterns were introduced by Harry Brignull when he cataloged (on darkpatterns.org) different types of interfaces that trick users into doing things that are not in their best interest [11].

Hence, a dark pattern design could be defined as: *the craft of purposefully designing patterns that damage the well-being of the users.*

Related to that, Zagal et al. did research on dark game design patterns, which can be seen as unethical and questionable [58]. Linehan et al. developed dark design patterns for anti-health games [37]. The negative experiences for players are likely to happen without their consent and against their best interest. Dark patterns are design strategies that are used to benefit developers more than the target audience, e.g., using unethical applications, such as coercion, deception, and fraud. Any design pattern becomes dark at the moment when it intentionally unbalances the well-being gains towards the creator of Pt and away from its users.

3   Visibility-Darkness Matrix

To explore the dark side of behavioral designs, Stibe and Cugelman [48] have introduced the Intention-Outcome matrix that has four quadrants. Target behavior is the primary intended positive behavioral outcome being designed for. Surprise behavior is a positive behavioral outcome that was not intended, however is a complementary benefit of the behavioral design that contributes to the well-being of users. Backfiring includes several negative outcomes, like a side effects, when the target behavior is achieved, but the design also triggers unintended negative outcomes.

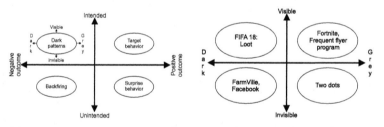

(a) The Intention-Outcome matrix (extended from [48]).

(b)   Visibility-Darkness   matrix with examples.

Fig. 1. Matrices of darkness

As an extension of the Intention-Outcome matrix (Fig. 1a), we propose to uncover the deeper dimensions for classifying dark patterns, which is the fourth quadrant (upper left) of the Intention-Outcome matrix. Dark patterns often are made invisible to the users of influencing systems. For example, websites can hide their true intentions of why they collect user information. Sometimes, partial information is made available in small print way down the structure of a website. Such approach makes dark patters to be less visible to the users. In a few occasions, some of the information describing a dark pattern is made quite visible to the users, however many of them tend to be careless while rushing through their chosen PT, so they pay little to none attention. Dark patters also can be of various intensity, meaning they can have different sizes of impact on users and their desired outcomes while interacting with PT. Some of the dark patterns may leave a very small footprint on user experience, while others can seriously challenge personal well-being of individual users. There are persuasive designs that tend to increase addiction, for example, which is a very dark pattern as such. Other interaction design patterns may not be that dark, for example, only collecting user information and then emailing updates to subscribers without their proper consent. That still is a dark pattern in the shade of grey, but not pitch-dark.

Thus, we propose subdividing the dark patterns quadrant into a matrix that contrasts the visibility of dark patterns (visible to invisible) with the shade of darkness (grey to dark). Based on that, we introduce the Visibility-Darkness matrix Fig. 1b. Further, we provide and discuss examples as illustrations for the four quadrants of the Visibility-Darkness matrix.

Visible-Grey Quadrant: Here we have PT designed to be beneficial for the users, but an outcome may not be as good as it is presented for the individuals. In other words, the potential benefits are clearly emphasized, while all potentially inconvenient extras are given as undebatable. Thus, everything looks like to be visible, however there seems to be an unfair divide of gains between the designer and the users. For example, different bonus systems, such as frequent flyer miles and alike. Users may often get manipulated into buying more products or service than necessary. Traditional bonus systems usually rely on badges and leaderboards, i.e. different levels that give benefits and increase status (upgrades, lounges). Participants at times need to spend a certain amount of money to keep their current level. Also, the previously earned bonus points may have an expire date that would clearly encourage users to buy, rent, or fly extra to keep the points Fortnite is a free-to-play video game by Epic Games that became a viral phenomenon in year 2018. The in-game store offers outfit customization, dance moves, etc. to make the game more fun to play. Fortnite's in-game currency is V-bucks (1000 V-buck cost US$9.99). V-bucks can also be earned through completing game missions. The customization does not bring any competitive advantage against other players. The game developers are regularly introducing new game enhancements, persuading people to continue playing. Many players are young and feel persuaded to buy the same things as their friends, therefore the total amount of money spent on the game after a while can become high. Although, the game brings enjoyment to players, the outcome may not be always that beneficial for them. For example, a sort of game addiction may emerge, as well as a form of coercion for parents to buy V-bucks.

Invisible-Grey Quadrant: Here we have PT designed with features that may not be clearly seen or properly understood by the users. At the same time, such implementations by definition are also aimed at bringing more benefits to the designers versus the users. In other words, not only the gains are skewed towards the designers, but they also try hiding their intentions under the surface of misleading user interaction. An example here is a mobile game called Two Dots that is developed by PlayDots and available on Google Play and App Store. The game is quite minimalistic in design. When a user loses a game, pressing a green button usually means to continue. However, once all the available lives are lost, the user is seeing a familiar green box, but now it means to pay US$ 0.99 to continue [54]. This could be classified as a learned conditioned stimulus, when users press the green button by a reflex to continue the game despite a small "x" is available for canceling that action.

Invisible-Dark Quadrant: Here we have PT designed with an intention that is not clearly visible, as well as the potential damage to the users may be quite large. This quadrant is actually the place, where the darkest patterns can hide. Because they can be very dark and well camouflaged at the same time. By definition, here the designers would be abusing the weaknesses of human nature. Zynga is a game company that produced Facebook games like FarmVille, allowing players to use microtransactions for buying in-game benefits. These kind of Facebook games has been criticized for being designed for revenue and multiply users in every possible way [20]. Ian Bogost created a game "Cow Clicker" that mimics the social games on Facebook in a satiric way. He criticizes the compulsive and time destroying elements of such games [9].

Facebook uses confidential algorithms for persuading users to read and interact with their news feed on the platform [14]. The algorithm that recommends news could act in Facebook's best interest and not the user's well-being. Bessi et al. [7] found that Facebook users typically engage with information that confirms with their thinking. That could increase the chance of addiction to the social media site. This gives rise for a new relationship between machines and humans transforming the prioritization of news and their interpretation [14].

Visible-Dark Quadrant: Here we have PT designed with an intention that can look dubious to the users. Electronic Arts is the maker of FIFA 18 a football game, where players can buy "Loot packs" to increase their chance to beat opponents. The loot pack's content is randomized, many game players say they need to buy loot packs to stay competitive. They claim that the game design is "pay-to-win" and unfair. Some people are also suffering from game addiction similar to gambling, by spending much money on loot packs. Ther is an ongoing debate in Sweden about the ethics and the mechanics of the game, as it is almost coercive to buy the loot packs [51,52]. FIFA 18 is not unique, there are other games where loots are used: Valve's "Counter-Strike: Global Offensive (CS GO)", and Blizzard's "Overwatch". CS Go have Lootmarket.com where players can buy items from loots.

Popularity have gained free games and apps with inbuilt "motivation" to pay for premium content later. A Swedish newspaper reported that children were able (without security codes) to buy in-game items for US$ 5550 during one month by playing The Smurfs' village [1]. There are numerous free games that allow players to buy in-games item to boost performance. If friends are buy boosts, social dynamics can motivate others to buy boosts. An example of such a game is Candy Crush Saga, with items to unlock next level, or to boost gameplay. After losing lives, instead of waiting a certain time to get a new life the player can pay to continue playing. The game players may have invested a lot of time in the game and hence have inner incentives and motivation to pay the fee to continue. Some game levels are extremely difficult, so the game could be designed with an intention that the players have to buy in-game items in order to enjoy the game and keep up with other players.

Evaluation of the Darkness of PT. Fogg [19] recommended 7 steps that designers can use to evaluate the ethical nature of PT by its outcome, methods, and intentions. Berdichevsky and Neuenschwander [6] developed a framework to evaluate the ethics of PT. It's focus is on interaction between persuader, PT, and persuaded person. Because the persuader designs and creates PT, which can be seen as a technical mediation, see Latour [32], that uses persuasive methods on the persuaded person, resulting in an outcome (both predictable and unpredictable). Thus, we adapted this framework for evaluation of the PT darkness (see Fig. 2).

The designer of PT creates an experience with a set goal. PT uses different game mechanics depending on the context, e.g., resources, feasibility and time frame, etc. The well-being is the outcome of PT that constitute a benchmark for the evaluation using the Visibility-Darkness matrix. It is important to not regard technology as a neutral instrument, because, in a social context, it is value-laden [50], and aims at transforming user's behavior.

Fig. 2. Framework for evaluating the darkness of persuasive technology (FEDPT).

Below the FEDPT is used to elaborate on the previous given examples for the Visibility-Darkness matrix:

Visible-Grey - Well-Being: The users think something is beneficial for them, however may end up with something that is not in their best interest. PT may have clear visible rules, but a holistic result and the well-being impact for the user is difficult to foreseen completely. The users may think they have chosen the best option but most benefits might go to the PT owner.

Invisible-Grey - Well-Being: In this case, the PT design is aimed at getting users hooked and react to stimulus in a certain way, without providing all relevant information appropriate. Later, this is used in making people follow a learnt behavior, which may not bring any well-being to the user. The PT designer has implemented options and the user can try complaining, but might not do so if the micro-transaction has a low perceived value. The PT designer takes a calculated risk on users willingness to recover their loss.

Invisible-Dark - Well-Being: The user may not really understand possible outcomes or purpose of PT, as it seems to be a repetitive and never-ending game. The user could get hooked by friends into using social games with no real challenge (just wait and click), and then waste time and perhaps money by purchasing all in-game items. With an aim of increasing interaction and revenue, hidden algorithms can persuade and change the way users interact on a social network site. The algorithm could transform how the users are interpreting news. A PT designer may optimize their news and increase their impact, the logic is hidden from the users so they are left to the grace of PT designers.

Visible-Dark - Well-Being: Although, the user can see and understand the purpose of PT, they still can be easily hooked and get addicted. After a conscious reflection that actually may feel as a manipulation into "wasting" more time and money. This should be especially well controlled and monitored for PT aimed at children, where the designers should have an even larger responsibility, therefore necessary to aim for the highest degree of trustworthiness.

4 Use Case

The FEDPT is validated thru use case methodology. Use case is a method that gives a foundation for higher-level verification. The interaction sequences between users of a system and the system related to a specific goal is represented through the use cases. One research article that reflects similar system design is selected for the validation as a use case can show possible system activities in the interaction between a system and users.

The persuasive system design (PSD) model have four persuasive system principles: primary task support, dialogue system support, perceived credibility, and social support [41]. Case studies should focus on contemporary issues in real life and be grounded on the managerial or organizational level [57]. Using a use case conforms to the purpose of using case studies in qualitative research where it has been argued that case studies could be used to test theory within the positivist paradigm [15,33,34] and to synthesize insight from previous research what Seddon and Scheepers calls theory building [46]. Support carrying out of the user's primary task principles includes reduction, tunneling, personalization, tailoring, self-monitoring, simulation, and rehearsal. System principles to support implementing computer-human dialogue includes liking, praise, rewards, reminders, suggestion, similarity, and social role. System principles that gives system credibility consists of credibility, trustworthiness, surface, real-world feel, expertise, authority, third-party endorsements, and verifiability. And finally, the system principles belonging in the social support category are social comparison, social facilitation, normative influence, competition, social learning, cooperation, and recognition. The use-case diagram of FEDPT mapped with PSD is shown in Fig. 3. PSD is crucial and chosen for the use case since it could be considered fundamental in designing and evaluating persuasive systems and PT. The PSD in the context of FEDPT gives a clearer awareness for the designer of the goal of wellness and the possible dangers of dark and unintended outcomes. The actor in the use case aims towards well-being goals for the persuasive system.

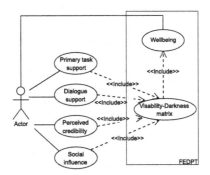

Fig. 3. Use case of PSD with FEDPT.

5 Discussion

When taking a closer look into the dark side of PT, many patterns become recognizable, as they make people addicted to what they use or game experiences they have. Although, the creators of such PT would argue that their designs are intended to keep users engaged, in many cases it goes beyond what might be perceived as positive contributions to well-being. There must be a clearer way for everyone to see and recognize how their PT engagements interplay with their own well-being. One could suggest John Rawl's "veil of ignorance" [44], hence the designers should not design PT that they would not use themselves. That is similar to Berdichevsky and Neuenschwander's "the golden rule of persuasion", the designer should not create PT that persuade to something they themselves would not like to be persuaded to do. Ultimately, such requirements and vision shall be a prerequisite for the PT scholars and professionals, so incorporated as an essential part of their design and development processes. Research has shown how UX design practitioners are tempted by the dark (pattern) side to implement dubious design [23].

More than ever before, it now becomes very important to engage PT designers to create a common understanding of how the essentials of their work are influencing and determining the lives of millions. The scientific work that we have outlined in this paper contributes to sharper understanding of how the design and strategical choices of the PT experience can potentially appear to be harmful for the well-being of users. The FEDPT, including the Visibility-Darkness matrix, shall now be very instrumental for many PT scholars and practitioners to assess their designs and evaluate possible negative effects on the users and the overall user experience. Although, it could be argued that a sinister designer of dark PT could use the FEDPT to enhance the darkness, the FEDPT reveal and makes the dark patterns a shared knowledge. All the stakeholders of PT, i.e. scholars, users, designers, professionals, etc. can now use FEDPT to evaluate PT and perhaps also certify the persuasive user experiences as not having a negative impact on well-being.

Particular care should be taken when designing PT for children. There should be requirements of extra safety mechanism for in-game purchases (something that Alha et al. [3] noticed for free-to-play games). The focus on extrinsic rewards should be kept at a minimum, as such rewards are often useless in the real life, regardless of their ability to boost self-confidence or perceived status. Also devices get increasingly connected, the Internet of things (IoT), thus the designers should be careful when designing PT that takes advantage of these new capabilities such as continuously collecting data in a secure manner and respecting the right to privacy. PT such as gamification is popular so companies unfortunately started implementing it without properly understanding the essence of game mechanics, flow, immersion, and story. That often can result in PT that does not go in line with the intended positive goal or result in negative outcomes.

6   Conclusions and Future Research

A proper and meaningful discussion around and research on the negative consequences of PT and behavioral change designs has now become inevitable, when thinking and caring about our collective future well-being. Many scholars and practitioners have already raised related concerns over the last years. More importantly, such debate must be an integral part of all efforts aimed at designing technology for influencing human behavior. Scholars are now encouraged to co-create new scientific knowledge by using, applying, and extending the proposed FEDPT framework and the Visibility-Darkness matrix. Practitioners are urged to include this work into their daily processes for designing PT and delivering products and experiences. Particularly, we invite interested researchers and practitioners of PT to join our work by providing additional examples of dark patterns. There is a need to continue exploring and monitor emerging forms of dark PT, so to advance the knowledge and refining the proposed framework. For example, we need a clearer discussion on ways for differentiating examples of visible versus invisible and grey versus dark patterns. Having such fundamental work progressing, we shall be able to create a taxonomy of dark patterns, including sharper guidelines for classifying designs that produce negative outcomes.

References

1. Aftonbladet: Barnens ipad spel kostade 50 000 kr (2011). www.aftonbladet.se/nyheter/article12846738.ab. Accessed 7 Feb 2018
2. Alexander, C.: A Pattern Language: Towns, Buildings, Construction. Oxford University Press, Oxford (1977)
3. Alha, K., Koskinen, E., Paavilainen, J., Hamari, J., Kinnunen, J.: Free-to-play games: professionals' perspectives. In: Proceedings of Nordic Digra 2014 (2014)

4. Andrade, F.R.H., Mizoguchi, R., Isotani, S.: The bright and dark sides of gamification. In: Micarelli, A., Stamper, J., Panourgia, K. (eds.) ITS 2016. LNCS, vol. 9684, pp. 176–186. Springer, Cham (2016). https://doi.org/10.1007/978-3-319-39583-8_17
5. Atkinson, B.M.C.: Captology: a critical review. In: IJsselsteijn, W.A., de Kort, Y.A.W., Midden, C., Eggen, B., van den Hoven, E. (eds.) PERSUASIVE 2006. LNCS, vol. 3962, pp. 171–182. Springer, Heidelberg (2006). https://doi.org/10.1007/11755494_25
6. Berdichevsky, D., Neuenschwander, E.: Toward an ethics of persuasive technology. Commun. ACM **42**(5), 51–58 (1999)
7. Bessi, A., et al.: Users polarization on Facebook and Youtube. PloS One **11**(8), e0159641 (2016)
8. Björk, S., Holopainen, J.: Patterns in Game Design. Charles River Media Inc., Rockland (2004)
9. Bogost, I.: Blog: Cow clicker - the making of obsession (2018). bogost.com/blog/cowclicker1/. Accessed 10 Feb 2018
10. Borchers, J.O.: A pattern approach to interaction design. AI Soc. **15**(4), 359–376 (2001)
11. Brignull, H.: Darkpatterns.org (2018). darkpatterns.org. Accessed 9 Apr 2018
12. Callan, R.C., Bauer, K.N., Landers, R.N.: How to avoid the dark side of gamification: ten business scenarios and their unintended consequences. In: Reiners, T., Wood, L.C. (eds.) Gamification in Education and Business, pp. 553–568. Springer, Cham (2015). https://doi.org/10.1007/978-3-319-10208-5_28
13. Deterding, S., Dixon, D., Khaled, R., Nacke, L.: From game design elements to gamefulness: Defining "gamification". In: MindTrek 2011, pp. 9–15. ACM, New York (2011)
14. DeVito, M.A.: From editors to algorithms. Digit. J. **5**(6), 753–773 (2017)
15. Eisenhardt, K.M.: Building theories from case study research. Acad. Manage. Rev. **14**(4), 532–550 (1989)
16. Etkin, J.: The hidden cost of personal quantification. J. Cons. Res. **42**(6), 967–984 (2016)
17. Fishbach, A., Choi, J.: When thinking about goals undermines goal pursuit. Organ. Behav. Hum. Decis. Process. **118**(2), 99–107 (2012)
18. Fogg, B.: Persuasive computers: perspectives and research directions. In: CHI 1998, pp. 225–232. ACM Press/Addison-Wesley Publishing Co., New York (1998)
19. Fogg, B.: Persuasive Technology: Using Computers to Change what We Think and Do. Morgan Kaufmann, Burlington (2003)
20. Gamasutra: Zynga: the future, or just a bit of it? (2010). www.gamasutra.com/blogs/DavidHayward/20100315/4670/Zynga_The_Future_Or_Just_A_Bit_Of_It.php. Accessed 12 Feb 2018
21. Gamma, E., Helm, R., Johnson, R., Vlissides, J.: Design Patterns: Elements of Reusable Object-Oriented Software. Addison-Wesley, Boston (1995)
22. Gram-Hansen, S.B.: Persuasive everyware-possibilities and limitations. In: 14th World Multi-Conference on Systemics, Cybernetics and Informatics: WMSCI 2010, pp. 254–260. International Institute of Informatics and Systemics (2010)
23. Gray, C.M., Kou, Y., Battles, B., Hoggatt, J., Toombs, A.L.: The dark (patterns) side of UX design. In: CHI 2018, pp. 534:1–534:14. ACM, New York (2018)
24. Guerini, M., Pianesi, F., Stock, O.: Is it morally acceptable for a system to lie to persuade me? In: Artificial Intelligence and Ethics: Papers from the 2015 AAAI Workshop, vol. WS-15-02, pp. 53–60 (2015)

25. Ham, J., Spahn, A.: Shall i show you some other shirts too? The psychology and ethics of persuasive robots. In: Trappl, R. (ed.) A Construction Manual for Robots' Ethical Systems. CT, pp. 63–81. Springer, Cham (2015). https://doi.org/10.1007/978-3-319-21548-8_4

26. Hamari, J., Koivisto, J., Pakkanen, T.: Do persuasive technologies persuade? - A review of empirical studies. In: Spagnolli, A., Chittaro, L., Gamberini, L. (eds.) PERSUASIVE 2014. LNCS, vol. 8462, pp. 118–136. Springer, Cham (2014). https://doi.org/10.1007/978-3-319-07127-5_11

27. Huotari, K., Hamari, J.: Defining gamification: a service marketing perspective. In: MindTrek 2012, pp. 17–22. ACM, New York (2012)

28. Hyrynsalmi, S., Smed, J., Kimppa, K.K.: The dark side of gamification: how we should stop worrying and study also the negative impacts of bringing game design elements to everywhere. In: Proceedings of the 1st International GamiFIN Conference, pp. 96–104. CEUR Workshop Proceedings (2017)

29. Kaptein, M., Eckles, D.: Selecting effective means to any end: futures and ethics of persuasion profiling. In: Ploug, T., Hasle, P., Oinas-Kukkonen, H. (eds.) PERSUASIVE 2010. LNCS, vol. 6137, pp. 82–93. Springer, Heidelberg (2010). https://doi.org/10.1007/978-3-642-13226-1_10

30. Kim, T.W., Werbach, K.: More than just a game: ethical issues in gamification. Ethics Inf. Technol. 18(2), 157–173 (2016)

31. Kuonanoja, L., Oinas-Kukkonen, H.: Recognizing and mitigating the negative effects of information technology use: a systematic review of persuasive characteristics in information systems. In: Müller, S.D., Nielsen, J.A. (eds.) SCIS 2018. LNBIP, vol. 326, pp. 14–25. Springer, Cham (2018). https://doi.org/10.1007/978-3-319-96367-9_2

32. Latour, B.: On technical mediation. Common knowl. 3(2), 29–64 (1994)

33. Lee, A.S.: A scientific methodology for MIS case studies. MIS Quart. 13, 33–50 (1989)

34. Lee, A.S., Baskerville, R.L.: Generalizing generalizability in information systems research. Inf. Syst. Res. 14(3), 221–243 (2003)

35. Leth Jespersen, J., Albrechtslund, A., Øhrstrøm, P., Hasle, P., Albretsen, J.: Surveillance, persuasion, and panopticon. In: de Kort, Y., IJsselsteijn, W., Midden, C., Eggen, B., Fogg, B.J. (eds.) PERSUASIVE 2007. LNCS, vol. 4744, pp. 109–120. Springer, Heidelberg (2007). https://doi.org/10.1007/978-3-540-77006-0_15

36. Linder, C.: Are persuasive technologies really able to communicate?: some remarks to the application of discourse ethics. Int. J. Technoethics (IJT) 5(1), 44–58 (2014)

37. Linehan, C., Harrer, S., Kirman, B., Lawson, S., Carter, M.: Games against health: a player-centered design philosophy. In: CHI EA 2015, pp. 589–600. ACM, New York (2015)

38. Lupton, D.: Self-tracking modes: reflexive self-monitoring and data practices. In: Imminent Citizenships: Personhood and Identity Politics in the Informatic Age - Workshop. SSRN (2014)

39. Nyström, T.: Gamification of persuasive systems for sustainability. In: 2017 Sustainable Internet and ICT for Sustainability (SustainIT). IEEE (2017)

40. Oinas-Kukkonen, H.: A foundation for the study of behavior change support systems. Pers. Ubiquit. Comput. 17(6), 1223–1235 (2013)

41. Oinas-Kukkonen, H., Harjumaa, M.: Persuasive systems design: key issues, process model, and system features. Commun. Assoc. Inf. Syst. 24, 28 (2009)

42. de Oliveira, R., Carrascal, J.P.: Towards effective ethical behavior design. In: CHI EA 2014, pp. 2149–2154. ACM, New York (2014)

43. Page, R.E., Kray, C.: Ethics and persuasive technology: an exploratory study in the context of healthy living. In: Proceedings of the First International Workshop on Nudge & Influence Through Mobile Devices, vol. 690, pp. 19–22. CEUR-WS (2010)

44. Rawls, J.: A Theory of Justice. Revised edn. Harvard University Press, Cambridge (1999)

45. Reitberger, W., Güldenpfennig, F., Fitzpatrick, G.: Persuasive technology considered harmful? An exploration of design concerns through the TV companion. In: Bang, M., Ragnemalm, E.L. (eds.) PERSUASIVE 2012. LNCS, vol. 7284, pp. 239–250. Springer, Heidelberg (2012). https://doi.org/10.1007/978-3-642-31037-9_21

46. Seddon, P.B., Scheepers, R.: Generalization in is research: a critique of the conflicting positions of Lee & Baskerville and Tsang & Williams. J. Inf. Technol. **30**(1), 30–43 (2015)

47. Spahn, A.: And lead us (not) into persuasion...? persuasive technology and the ethics of communication. Sci. Eng. Ethics **18**(4), 633–650 (2012)

48. Stibe, A., Cugelman, B.: Persuasive backfiring: when behavior change interventions trigger unintended negative outcomes. In: Meschtscherjakov, A., De Ruyter, B., Fuchsberger, V., Murer, M., Tscheligi, M. (eds.) PERSUASIVE 2016. LNCS, vol. 9638, pp. 65–77. Springer, Cham (2016). https://doi.org/10.1007/978-3-319-31510-2_6

49. Stock, O., Guerini, M., Pianesi, F.: Ethical dilemmas for adaptive persuasion systems. In: AAAI 2016, pp. 4157–5161. AAAI Press (2016)

50. Sundström, P.: Interpreting the notion that technology is value-neutral. Med. Health Care Philos. **1**(1), 41–45 (1998)

51. Sveriges Radio: SR 3 - radio news: Fifa 18 loot packs part 1 (2018). sverigesradio.se/sida/avsnitt/1031434. Accessed 8 Feb 2020

52. Sveriges Radio: SR 3 - radio news: Fifa 18 loot packs part 2 (2018). sverigesradio.se/sida/avsnitt/1034069. Accessed 8 Feb 2020

53. Timmer, J., Kool, L., van Est, R.: Ethical challenges in emerging applications of persuasive technology. In: MacTavish, T., Basapur, S. (eds.) PERSUASIVE 2015. LNCS, vol. 9072, pp. 196–201. Springer, Cham (2015). https://doi.org/10.1007/978-3-319-20306-5_18

54. User testing blog: dark patterns: the sinister side of UX (2015). https://www.usertesting.com/blog/dark-patterns-the-sinister-side-of-ux/. Accessed 10 Apr 2020

55. Verbeek, P.P.: Ambient intelligence and persuasive technology: the blurring boundaries between human and technology. NanoEthics **3**(3), 231 (2009)

56. Yetim, F.: A set of critical heuristics for value sensitive designers and users of persuasive systems. In: ECIS 2011 (2011)

57. Yin, R.K.: Case Study Research: Design and Methods, Sixth edn. Sage publications, Oaks (2017)

58. Zagal, J.P., Björk, S., Lewis, C.: Dark patterns in the design of games. In: Proceedings of the Conference on Foundations of Digital Games 2013 (2013)

Influential Nodes Prediction Based on the Structural and Semantic Aspects of Social Media

Nesrine Hafiene[1,2]([✉]), Wafa Karoui[1,3], and Lotfi Ben Romdhane[1,2]

[1] Université de Sousse, Laboratoire MARS—Modeling of Automated Reasoning Systems, LR17ES05, ISITCom, 4011 Sousse, Tunisia
hafiene.nesrine@gmail.com, karoui.wafa@gmail.com,
lotfi.ben.romdhane@gmail.com
[2] Université de Sousse, ISITCom, 4011 Sousse, Tunisia
[3] Université de Tunis El Manar, Institut Supérieur d'Informatique,
2080 Ariana, Tunisia

Abstract. A key problem in social media is the identification of influential nodes and the analysis of how these nodes are reflected in the graph structure evolution. Influence prediction is an important issue in social networks. Most of the existing methods aim to predict interactions between individuals for static networks, ignoring the dynamic feature of social networks. In order to solve this problem, we propose a new approach to detect influential nodes taking into consideration the structural and semantic evolution of social networks. First, we find the influential nodes within a period of time by using an incremental algorithm. Then, by exploring the structural and semantic aspects of social networks, we predict the future influential nodes.

Keywords: Dynamic social networks · Influence prediction · Social network analysis

1 Introduction

Since the recent emergence of social media such as Facebook and Twitter in the past few years, more and more people pay attention to social networks. A social network is a social structure composed of a set of social actors where nodes represent individuals or even other entities embedded in a social context and where edges reflect the interaction, cooperation or influence between entities.

People's relationships are continuously evolving, new edges and vertices are added over time to the graph and old ones can be removed. Social networks are highly dynamic. As a key issue of social networks, prediction has attracted more and more attention, as prediction of links is important for mining and analyzing social network evolution.

One of the interesting issues addressed in social network analysis, allowing the understanding of the evolution of social networks, concerns the problem of

© Springer Nature Switzerland AG 2020
M. Themistocleous et al. (Eds.): EMCIS 2020, LNBIP 402, pp. 346–359, 2020.
https://doi.org/10.1007/978-3-030-63396-7_23

prediction. It consists of predicting future associations between a pair of nodes knowing that there is no link between them in the current state of the graph.

Social networks are not static but are dynamically changing at an exponential rate with regular changes (*e.g.* nodes and edges additions/deletions). Similar to the regular network structure changes, node attributes often change automatically, the modification of online user posts is a classic example. With both topology and attribute changes, we refer to such networks as dynamic social networks. The aim of our work is to quantify the influence of individuals within a period of time by using a new approach and to find influential individuals in a such manner that we can predict the influence of each user with a high precision. The contributions of this paper are:

1. To propose an incremental algorithm to detect influential nodes taking into consideration the structural evolution of social networks,
2. To present a new influential nodes prediction method for dynamic networks based on the egocentric networks detected in the first contribution and the semantic similarity of the nodes extracted from those networks.

The rest of this paper is organized as follows. In Sect. 2, we discuss the related work. Our proposed method is given in Sect. 3. Experimental results are presented in Sect. 4. Finally, we conclude our work and present some future work in Sect. 5.

2   Related Work

This section discusses the review of different researches done on the prediction problem in the literature. In this paper, we have classified the problem of prediction into two approaches namely: Link prediction and User influence prediction like described in Fig. 1. We have classified the existing approaches based on the different measures used in the prediction problem (see Table 1).

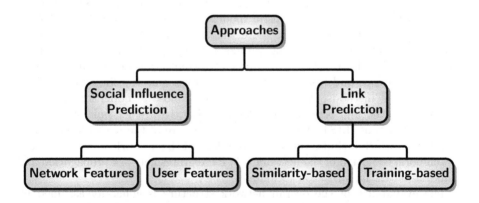

Fig. 1. Approaches of prediction problem

2.1 Link Prediction Approaches

The link prediction problem has several applications [2], such as link analysis, bioinformatics, information retrieval, tracking temporal topics [17] or the identification of influential nodes [7]. In particular, predicting future links is useful for understanding the network evolution. The evaluation measures used in the field of link prediction are embraced from other fields of research, i.e. classification, retrieval information [16].

The estimation of future connections is useful for the understanding of the evolution of the network and communication. In social media networks, for example, promising links that do not yet exist will facilitate user engagement and interaction, which also affects the structure of the network. In addition, the network structure influences the interaction or the spread of information. For example, future friendships could be predicted when analyzing social networks or predicting future co-authors in a collaborative network. Existing link prediction approaches can be divided into similarity based and learning-based approaches. Similarity based approaches consist of measuring the similarities between a pair of nodes through various similarity metrics, and using the similarity scoring as a classification to predict the relation between two nodes in the future.

In [3], the authors show that the analysis of user-to-user evaluations can be considerably reinforced by taking into account the similarity of user characteristics such as the degree to which their contributions to the site involved similar content, or involve interactions with a common set of other users. Learning-based methods have difficulties in selecting features and unbalancing performance groups, and are affected by computational costs and capacity constraints, so it is not ideal for large and dynamic networks. In order to predict the relation, the authors [15] evaluated six different social attributes in the context of face-to-face communication networks. Language and country are the two attributes that play an important role in communication prediction. They have observe that people prefer to contact those people who are similar in language and region.

Some traditional machine learning models including classifiers (Markov chains, SVM, etc.) and probabilistic models (Markov Random Fields, Bayes model, etc.) can thus be used to solve this problem. Li et *et al.* suggested a graph-based learning model using profile features (i.e. book title, education, age, introduction, keywords, etc.) to predict a connection in the bipartite network between user and item [10]. In order to overcome the limitations of the Learning-based methods, Aggarwal *et al.* [20] propose a model for predicting links with spatial and temporal precision (LIST), to predict links in series of networks over time. LIST characterizes the structure of the network as a function of time, which includes the spatial topology of the network at each time and the temporal evolution of the network. LIST integrates network propagation and temporal matrix factorization techniques.

The availability of the overall network structure is generally assumed by existing link prediction algorithms. However, this assumption is unfeasible since real-world networks are always large-scale and measured in terabytes or even petabytes. This fact makes them difficult to store and recall before link prediction takes place.

2.2 Social Influence Prediction Approaches

Due to the massive data and the public availability of the popular social media system, researchers recently became interested in studying the influence of users on social networks. The study of the issue has a reasonable meaning in our real life. It helps marketing strategies to target the most influential people to maximize the selling process.

Social influence is everywhere, not only in our real life, but also on social media. The term social influence usually refers to the phenomenon according to which one person's emotions, opinions, or behaviours are affected by others.

All the existing mesaures allow users to be ranked at a certain instant or period of time from existing data. Over time, these rankings can change considerably, leaving a trail of historical data that can be used to make social influence predictions. To predict influential users, we can extract information from metrics such as the ones given in Table 1. Some studies have estimated user influence from the network structure perspective to measure social networking potentials of social media users. As shown in [12], people tend to create new relationships with people that are closer to them on a social graph.

Users, in online social networks, not only make new friends but also seek and share information. Users tend to create relationships with people that are similar to them along certain profile attributes, such as gender, education and religion. When a user shares a message, his/her contacts can be influenced to re-post that information. A new idea to quantify user influence is introduced in [21]. The user's influence is described as the potential of his actions that motivates others to republish or respond to his messages. This description calculates influence by taking into account both the quantity of posted messages and their popularity. In [1], the authors suggest a novel user similarity for the evaluation of social networks regarding to network structure and profile attributes. The authors implement two distinct similarity metrics, namely network and profile similarity, and demonstrate how these two measures can be combined to find user similarity.

Qiu *et al.* [14] developed an end-to-end framework named DeepInf, motivated by the recent success of deep neuron networks in a wide variety of computing applications. DeepInf uses the local network of a user to learn its latent social representation as an input into a graph neural network. To integrate both network structure and user features into a neural network, the authors design strategies. Given the active action of the near neighbors of a user and their local structural details, the objective of the authors is to predict the user's action status.

2.3 Preliminaries and Problem Statement

The prediction is an important problem in social networks. Many of the existing approaches attempt to predict interactions between individual in static networks,

Table 1. Classification of measures used in the prediction problem

Apps		Techniques	Characteristics	Refs
Link Prediction	Similarity-based	Common Neighbors (CN)	It is simple and intuitive. It is necessary to use common neighbors to predict links.	[3, 15]
		Jaccard Coefficient (JC)	Intersection against union. Normalizes the similarity of common neighbors in comparison to total neighbors.	
		Adamic Adar (AA)	Give high weight to common neighbors having few neighbors.	
		Preferential Attachement (PA)	It prefers high-degree nodes to be linked. Not sufficient for finding connections between nodes of lower degrees.	
		Resource Allocation (RA)	New nodes are likely to be connected to higher-degree nodes. In dense areas, it provides bad results.	
	Training-based	Support Vector Machines (SVM)	A set of supervised learning strategies for the identification of classification, regression, and outliers.	[10, 20]
		Markov chains	A statistical model that can be used in predictive analytics and is highly based on the principle of probability.	
		Logistic Regression (LR)	It is used based on one or more predictor variables to predict the class (or category) of individuals	
Social Influence	User features	Profiles attributes	Locate a user's private information through analyzing network connections and social networks groups.	[5, 19]
		Social actions	Use the actions of historical users (comments, retweets, etc.) as training data in various methods and use the learned model to predict future user actions.	
	Network features	Coreness centrality	The average length of the shortest distance in the graph between the node and all other nodes.	[8, 9]
		Katz centrality	The total number of nodes that can be linked via a path is calculated.	
		Clustering coefficient	It calculates how well a node's neighbors are connected.	
		Eigenvector centrality	It assigns relative scores based on high scores to all nodes in the network.	
		PageRank centrality	In online information retrieval, the PageRank approach is generalized	

ignoring the dynamic structure of social networks. In this paper, we propose a prediction method that explores the dynamic topology of social networks.

Given a set of influential nodes identified in our first phase, our aim is to predict the collection of influential nodes that can be generated in the future. In the first phase of our proposed approach, we study the evolution of the network between t1 and t2. In the second phase, we look to predict with precision taking into consideration the structural evolution of the graph the influential nodes that will be modified during the interval time t1 (or t2) at a given future time t. Our aim is to predict the presence of an influential node in the new set of nodes at the time $t + 1$, taking into account the node's features. We denote the dynamic social network as a sequence of networks at different timestamps: $DSN = \{G^1, G^2, ..., G^t\}$, where: G^t represents the snapshot of network at time t, and $G^t = (V^t, E^t)$, whith V^t denoting the set of nodes in G^t and E^t denoting the set of edges in G^t. We will assign a set of interests for each user that will describe it. Such interests are described as an attributes vector $X_i = \{x_{i1}, ..., x_{ij}\}$, where X_{ij} is the value taken by the attribute j of the vertex v_i. In this work, we adopt the following definitions:

Definition 1. *Influential Nodes (Inf^t). It represents the set of influential nodes detected from G^t after a succession of updates. Therefore $Inf^t = \{S_1^t, S_2^t, ..., S_{k^t}^t\}$, where: k^t represents the number of influential nodes in G^t and S_i^t represents the ith nodes in G^t.*

Definition 2. *Subgraph ($SubG^t$). It represents the set of subgraphs in the time interval ΔG^{t+1} from t to $t + 1$. These subgraphs are composed by nodes and edges added/removed over a well determined time interval.*

Definition 3. *Influential egocentric network $G' = (V', E')$. It represents the influential area as an aggregation of egocentric networks detected from DSN based on Inf^t. The egocentric network contains an "ego" which consists of the influential nodes and nodes influenced by the ego which are called "alters".*

3   Semantic and Structural Influential Nodes Prediction

The proposed approach looks to detect the most influential nodes in dynamic social networks. It is interested in the structural and semantic aspects of the network. For this reason, the main idea is to propose a two-phase approach. Indeed, the first phase of our approach explains the structural evolution of the network, the second phase focuses on the semantic aspect by presenting the proposed prediction model.

3.1   Phase 1

In the first phase, by applying metrics, we begin to identify the influential nodes detected in the original graph. During the second step, we attempt to detect the change in the structure of the network since the network is dynamic then the edges and nodes change.

It's very expensive to measure influential nodes from scratch after each update, which inspires us to develop a structural approach to updating influential nodes in dynamic social networks. The main objective of this phase is to identify the different subgraphs detected between two different timestamps. Based on the relation between the subgraph observed in time t and the previously observed influential nodes, we propose three types of changed elements.

To start, the proposed approach detects the influential nodes in the original graph. In the first step, we propose to use SND algorithm [6]. On the one side, it exploits the relationships between the network's nodes and, on the other side, the attributes characterizing them. In the second step, we seek to detect the change in the structure of the network. As the network is dynamic, the edges and nodes evolve over time. Thus the already identified influential nodes in the original graph will change over time. In the third step, we present our updating strategies for the subgraphs that have been observed between two consecutive timestamps.

In this step, we propose to divide the social network observed in time t into a collection of egocentric networks G' that are connected together to better classify the changed areas. Every egocentric network contains a node of "ego" (influential node) and nodes affected by (and between) this ego, called "alters" (see Fig. 2). We can observe the influential region by using the egocentric network. We define the following three strategies to update the influential node based on the observed subgraphs.

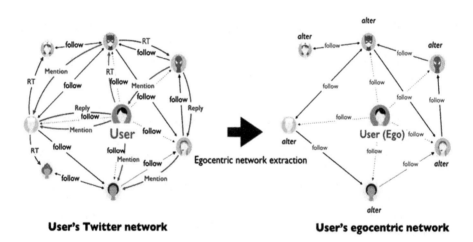

User's Twitter network   **User's egocentric network**

Fig. 2. Example of an egocentric network

1. **Strategy to update the completly separate type**
   In this type all $SubG^i$ added nodes are new ones. We just consider the new $v \in Inf^{t+1}$ added node if they change the marginal gain of any node that is not in G'.

2. **Strategy to update the Completely reliant type**
   In this type, edges added between nodes are considered. Second, we use ego-centric networks to identify the influential nodes. Then, to classify the influential nodes affected by this update, we caculate the closeness centrality [13] between added edges and ego nodes. Finally, we change the influence degree of the ego node. Equation 1 is used to calculate the influence degree of a node where V_u is the set of nodes influenced by u in G^t and N^t is the set of nodes in G^t.

$$\sigma(u) = \frac{V_u}{N^t} \tag{1}$$

3. **Strategy to Update the Mixed type**
   In this type, we consider adding/removing new and old nodes. Thus, we need to measure the average relation strenght of nodes in $N(v)$ (respectively $N'(v)$) with each node in G (respectively G'), where $N(v)$ denotes the neighbors of v and $N'(v)$ is the set of neighbors of v in G'. The value of $sim^t(v, u)$ represents the Jaccard's coefficient used to calculate the semantic similarity between two nodes v and u. If the division of $S_v^{G'}$ (see Eq. 2) by $S_v^{G'}$ (see Eq. 3) exceeds 1, then we added v to G' and we change the influence degree of the ego node.

$$S_v^{G'} = \sum \left(\frac{\sum_{u \in N'(v)} sim^t(v, u)}{|N'(v)|} \right) \tag{2}$$

$$S_v^{G} = \sum \left(\frac{\sum_{u \in N(v)} sim^t(v, u)}{|N(v)|} \right) \tag{3}$$

3.2   Phase 2

In this phase, our aim is to collect the required data that our learning model can be trained. In the first phase and based on the observed subgraphs between two timestamps, we tried to update the influential nodes. The proposed prediction model is described in Fig. 3. The formation of new influential nodes is predicted from the topology of a social network obtained from the evolutions of the network during the test period. In the data acquisition process, an egocentric network (output of our first contribution) is generated based on the observed influential nodes. From this input graph, information relating to the influential nodes found in the egocentric network is extracted. Our proposed approach is summarized as follows: First, we apply SND algorithm to identify the influential nodes in the original network. Second, we adopt our proposed strategies to update the influential nodes based on the structure evolution of the social network between two consecutive timestamps. Then, we propose a model for the prediction of the future influential nodes via exploring the semantic aspect of social networks Fig. 3.

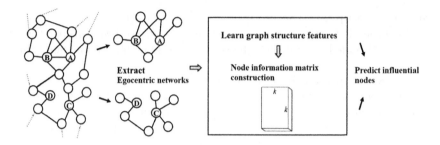

Fig. 3. The influence prediction model

After updating the graph, we identify the influential node A as shown in Fig. 4. We extract respectively the two observed egocentric networks of A ego-centric network 1 and egocentric network 2. We suppose that A is an influential node. We have 2 influential area of A. The node A has 10 friends observed in two areas (Black nodes). We suppose that we have two strangers nodes u and v. Our objective is to predict, based on the semantic similarity between the influential nodes A and the two strangers' ones, which is the favourable node that can be added to the influential area of A. To do that, we need to calculate the semantic similarity between the influential node A and the two stranger nodes u and v. We have associated the link between two nodes of the egocentric network with the weight which is defined by the semantic similarity of their information given in the following equation:

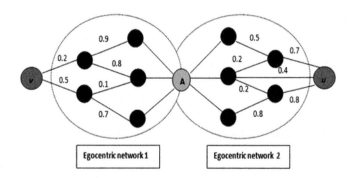

Fig. 4. Illustratif example of the semantic aspect

$$sim^t(x, y) = \frac{|n_x \cap n_y|}{|n_x \cup n_y|} \qquad (4)$$

Semantic similarity compares the center of interests stored in the attributes vector associated with two social network users, to determine how much they are similar. The easiest way is to compute the semantic similarity of all the paths between an ego node I and a stranger node x (see Eq. 5).

$$NS(I,x) = \frac{Log(\sum_{Paths \in E'_{(I,x)}} sim(I,x))}{Log(2.\sum_{Paths \in E'_{(I)}} sim(I))} \qquad (5)$$

Stranger u has 3 common friends with user A and the egocentric network contains 9 edges, stranger v also has 3 common friends with A and 6 edges within the egocentric network. The network similarity between A and u is then NS(A, v) = Log(3.9)/Log(2 * 9.1) = 0.46, while NS(A, u) = Log(5.1)/Log(2 * 9.1) = 0.65. Our metric favors u as it is connected to a stronger influential area around A than v.

4   Experiments

We test the effectiveness and efficiency of the proposed approach on real dynamic networks where each node has been associated with a set of centers of interest. Experiments were conducted to provide a comparison between the proposed structural and semantic approach and those discussed in the literature.

4.1   Datasets

We evaluated the proposed approach on three real-world networking datasets. We assume that the evolution of each network is an evolving network with two timestamps. Table 2 gives information about these networks.

Table 2. Datasets

Name	Nodes	Edges	Corresponding site
Facebook	4039	88234	https://snap.stanford.edu/
Email	10,029	139,264	http://konect.uni-koblenz.de/
NetHEPT	15,200	31,400	https://arxiv.org/

4.2   Algorithms and Parameters

Algorithms. We compared our algorithm with two algorithms called UBI [4] and Local D&U [18] to improve dynamic influence of social networks. UBI's main aim is to classify the important nodes based on those previously identified, rather than locate them from an empty set. Local D&U's main objective is to classify influential nodes in dynamic networks by exploiting a local detection and updating strategy. In this paper we used Local D&U's first step to calculate the fraction of the activated nodes. Since, it provides nodes with larger degree centrality having a higher influence on their neighbours, then those nodes can be considered as seed nodes [11]. The selected seed nodes can be used to spread the influence based on the relationship strength between nodes because if the neighbours of a node v strongly follow the node then v can be considered as an influential node.

Parameter Settings. For UBI, we vary the maximal number of seed nodes k from 40 to 100 respectively in each timestamp by 20. In our experiments, the marginal gain of a node is selected empirically by a threshold θ which vary from 0.1 to 1 by 0.1. A larger value of θ leads to a significant change on the influence of the k selected seed nodes. Thus, the marginal gain of a node v depends on the influence of seed nodes over those nodes that v influences.

4.3 Results

Dynamic networks are generated between two timestamps based on each original network and the changed elements. A dynamic network can be generated between 40 and 100 timestamps and updated using the updating strategy and the prediction model.

Evolution of the Influence Degree. We can observe from Tables 3, 4 and 5 that our approach achieves better values of influence degree than those of both UBI and Local D&U algorithms.

We may observe that the values of influence degree obtained with our approach and with Local D&U have shown some variation compared to UBI. The value of the influence degree obtained with algorithm and that of the Local D&U algorithm are close. Local D&U algorithm takes into account the evolution of

<table>
<tr><td colspan="4" align="center">**Table 3.** Email</td></tr>
<tr><td>Time</td><td>UBI</td><td>Local D&U</td><td>Our approach</td></tr>
<tr><td>40</td><td>0,016</td><td>0,11</td><td>**0,12**</td></tr>
<tr><td>60</td><td>0,035</td><td>0,1</td><td>**0,11**</td></tr>
<tr><td>80</td><td>0,032</td><td>0,109</td><td>**0,112**</td></tr>
<tr><td>100</td><td>0,065</td><td>0,111</td><td>**0,12**</td></tr>
</table>

<table>
<tr><td colspan="4" align="center">**Table 4.** Facebook</td></tr>
<tr><td>Time</td><td>UBI</td><td>Local D&U</td><td>Our approach</td></tr>
<tr><td>40</td><td>0,02</td><td>0,08</td><td>**0,08**</td></tr>
<tr><td>60</td><td>0,032</td><td>0,085</td><td>**0,089**</td></tr>
<tr><td>80</td><td>0,044</td><td>0,089</td><td>**0,1**</td></tr>
<tr><td>100</td><td>0,065</td><td>0,09</td><td>**0,1**</td></tr>
</table>

Table 5. NetHEPT

Time	UBI	Local D&U	Our approach
40	0,055	0,059	**0,06**
60	0,088	0,054	**0,08**
80	0,1	0,058	**0,12**
100	0,112	0,058	**0,13**

nodes and edges in each time interval to change the degree of influence of the important nodes. Our algorithm should have a greater degree of control. Thus, the first phase of our proposed approach allows us to cover a large number of influential nodes in any type of network. UBI aims to follow dynamically a set of influential nodes in such a way that the degree of influence is maximized at any time. Therefore, where the current snapshot differs considerably from the previous one, the UBI algorithm reaches a low influence degree.

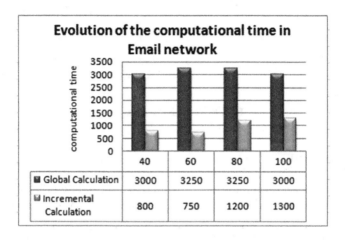

Fig. 5. Email network

Evolution of the Computational Time. From Fig. 5, we can note that in the incremental calculation process, the computational time of our proposed approach is more stable that results when using the global calculation version of our approach. This can be explained by the smallness number of changed elements between two consecutive timestamps. In this experiment, we compare our approach based on the two calculation process: the global and incremental versions of our proposed approach.

In the global calculation version, we calculate the influence degreee of important nodes globally (in all the network) based on our approach. In the incremental calculation version of our approach, we only need to update the influence degree of the modified elements. From Fig. 6, we can observe that, while using our proposed approach in the incremental version, the computational time varies overall timestamps while using the global calculation version is almost constant. This is due to the considerable variation in the nodes degrees in NetHEPT network. There are multiple nodes of various degrees which are added and/or removed at each timestamp. Thus, the calculation varies with each timestamp. Therefore, in the case of small and large social networks, our proposed solution based on incremental calculation version produces good results.

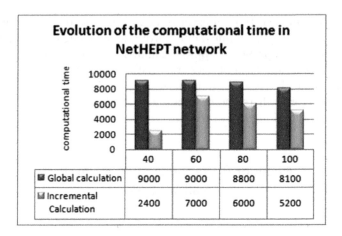

Figure content (table within figure):

	40	60	80	100
Global calculation	9000	9000	8800	8100
Incremental Calculation	2400	7000	6000	5200

Fig. 6. NetHEPT network

5   Conclusion

In this paper, a structural and semantic approach to update influential nodes in dynamic social networks is proposed. The main idea is to propose a two-phase approach. Indeed, the first phase of our approach explains the structural evolution of the network, and the second phase focuses on the semantic aspect by presenting the proposed prediction model. Thus, the proposed approach presented in this paper is efficient and effective. Its efficiency is proved with experiments based on the influence degree and computational time on three real dynamic social networks. In future work, we would like to explore the machine learing models to study the dynamic evolution of both the network structure and the user's features. It is also important to analyze the optimal duration of the training period in dynamic social networks.

References

1. Akcora, C.G., Carminati, B., Ferrari, E.: User similarities on social networks. Soc. Netw. Anal. Min. **3**(3), 475–495 (2013)
2. Al Hasan, M., Zaki, M.J.: A survey of link prediction in social networks. In: Aggarwal, C. (ed.) Social Network Data Analytics, pp. 243–275. Springer, Boston, MA (2011). https://doi.org/10.1007/978-1-4419-8462-3_9
3. Anderson, A., Huttenlocher, D., Kleinberg, J., Leskovec, J.: Effects of user similarity in social media. In: Proceedings of the Fifth ACM International Conference on Web Search and Data Mining, pp. 703–712 (2012)
4. Chen, X., Song, G., He, X., Xie, K.: On influential nodes tracking in dynamic social networks. In: Proceedings of the 2015 SIAM International Conference on Data Mining, pp. 613–621 (2015)
5. Ding, Z., Jia, Y., Zhou, B., Han, Y., He, L., Zhang, J.: Measuring the spreadability of users in microblogs. J. Zhejiang Univ. Sci. C **14**(9), 701–710 (2013)

6. Hafiene, N., Karoui, W.: A new structural and semantic approach for identifying influential nodes in social networks. In: International Conference on Computer Systems and Applications (AICCSA), pp. 1338–1345. IEEE (2017)

7. Hafiene, N., Karoui, W., Ben Romdhane, L.: Influential nodes detection in dynamic social networks: a survey. Expert Syst. Appl. **159**, 113642 (2020)

8. Hajian, B., White, T.: Modelling influence in a social network: metrics and evaluation. In: 2011 IEEE Third International Conference on Privacy, Security, Risk and Trust and 2011 IEEE Third International Conference on Social Computing, pp. 497–500. IEEE (2011)

9. Jin, X., Wang, Y.: Research on social network structure and public opinions dissemination of micro-blog based on complex network analysis. J. Netw. **8**(7), 1543 (2013)

10. Li, X., Chen, H.: Recommendation as link prediction in bipartite graphs: a graph kernel-based machine learning approach. Decis. Support Syst. **54**(2), 880–890 (2013)

11. Lü, L., Zhou, T., Zhang, Q.-M., Stanley, H.E.: The H-index of a network node and its relation to degree and coreness. Nat. Commun. **7**(1), 1–7 (2016)

12. McPherson, M., Smith-Lovin, L., Cook, J.M.: Birds of a feather: homophily in social networks. Ann. Rev. Sociol. **27**(1), 415–444 (2001)

13. Morone, F., Makse, H.A.: Influence maximization in complex networks through optimal percolation. Nature **524**(7563), 65 (2015)

14. Qiu, J., Tang, J., Ma, H., Dong, Y., Wang, K., Tang, J.: DeepInf: social influence prediction with deep learning. In: Proceedings of the 24th ACM SIGKDD International Conference on Knowledge Discovery & Data Mining, pp. 2110–2119 (2018)

15. Samad, A., Islam, M.A., Iqbal, M.A., Aleem, M., Arshed, J.U.: Evaluation of features for social contact prediction. In: 2017 13th International Conference on Emerging Technologies (ICET), pp. 1–6. IEEE (2017)

16. Samad, A., Qadir, M., Nawaz, I., Islam, M.A., Aleem, M.: A comprehensive survey of link prediction techniques for social network. EAI Endorsed Trans. Indust. Netw. Intell. Syst. **7**(23), e3 (2020)

17. Sendi, M., Omri, M.N., Abed, M.: Discovery and tracking of temporal topics of interest based on belief-function and aging theories. J. Ambient Intell. Hum. Comput. **10**(9), 3409–3425 (2019)

18. Wang, S., Cuomo, S., Mei, G., Cheng, W., Nengxiong, X.: Efficient method for identifying influential vertices in dynamic networks using the strategy of local detection and updating. Future Gener. Comput. Syst. **91**, 10–24 (2019)

19. Xiao, F., Noro, T., Tokuda, T.: Finding news-topic oriented influential twitter users based on topic related hashtag community detection. J. Web Eng. **13**(5&6), 405–429 (2014)

20. Yu, W., Cheng, W., Aggarwal, C.C., Chen, H., Wang, W.: Link prediction with spatial and temporal consistency in dynamic networks. In: IJCAI, pp. 3343–3349 (2017)

21. Zhou, J., Wu, G., Tu, M., Wang, B., Zhang, Y., Yan, Y.: Predicting user influence under the environment of big data. In: 2017 IEEE 2nd International Conference on Cloud Computing and Big Data Analysis (ICCCBDA), pp. 133–138. IEEE (2017)

Determinants of the Intention to Use Online P2P Platforms from the Seller's Perspective

Nuno Fortes[✉], Adriana Pires, and Pedro Manuel do Espírito Santo

Polytechnic Institute of Coimbra, ESTGOH, Oliveira do Hospital,
Rua General Santos, 3400-124 Costa, Portugal
{nuno.fortes,adriana.pires,pedro.santo}@estgoh.ipc.pt

Abstract. The exponential growth of online peer-to-peer (P2P) platforms paved the way for large-scale commerce between individuals. This work aims to evaluate the determinants of the intention to use these platforms by the sellers for the transaction of products and services, contributing to fill a gap in the literature. The results confirmed all the hypotheses of the research model, allowing us to conclude that the intention to use is strongly explained by performance expectation, habit, trust, and innovativeness. From the study it is possible to draw relevant implications for the academic world, as well as for the management of P2P platforms.

Keywords: P2P platforms · Intention to use · Performance expectation · Habit · Trust · Innovativeness · Seller

1 Introduction

The explosion of the Internet and subsequent applications has permanently changed the form of traditional commerce [1]. Companies took advantage of their know-how to serve their customers even better, capitalize on the advantages brought by their online presence, expand their focus market and modernize their way of selling. The Internet has changed the way business has been done, with shorter sales cycles, reduced costs, and improved service quality [2].

With regard to private consumers, the Internet provided not only the advantage of purchasing products or services at more affordable prices, but also the possibility to carry out commercial transactions themselves, thus creating peer-to-peer (P2P) businesses, also known as consumer-to-consumer (C2C) businesses. The emergence of these platforms paved the way for large-scale trade between individuals [3].

On these platforms, where users can take on both the role of consumer and supplier [4], there is an exact match between what the consumer wants to buy and what the seller has to offer. Correspondence must be carried out at the right time, as long as the need for both exists, and at a reasonable price, depending on the type of good or service in question [5]. It is also possible for the consumer to assume a central role in the business, announcing the product or service he wishes to acquire, bearing the burden of selling under the responsibility of the seller. Hawlitschek et al. refer that these platforms establish the match between supply and demand, facilitate research, communication, initiation of transactions and even payment [3].

M. Themistocleous et al. (Eds.): EMCIS 2020, LNBIP 402, pp. 360–369, 2020.
https://doi.org/10.1007/978-3-030-63396-7_24

Although there is an exponential growth in the appearance of P2P platforms, there is a limited amount of research on behavioural, strategic and technical issues that explain the success, failure and impact that these services will have on existing industries and on the economy in general [6–8]. In order to fill this gap, the present work has the main objective of identifying the factors that influence the intention to use P2P online platforms for the sale of products and services.

This work is divided into 4 fundamental parts. The first concerns the theoretical framework of the research problem, which will culminate in the presentation of the research model. Then, the methodology that guided the empirical study will be presented. In the following chapter, the results obtained will be described. Finally, the results will be discussed and the conclusions drawn.

2 Theoretical Framework

2.1 P2P Platforms

Electronic commerce has seen a major transformation in the last decade, with a clear predominance of B2B businesses, as opposed to B2C businesses, which had proliferated until then [7]. Information technology has enabled the appearance of P2P activities to obtain, give and share goods, access and services [6] that have become an attractive and profitable option for families and individuals [4].

With the emergence of digital intermediaries, communities and social ties are no longer restricted to the offline world, and from the moment it became a habit to shop, conduct bank transactions and date via Internet platforms, the risk of sharing products and providing services has become more reduced [9].

It is still not clear enough what factors are driving and which are preventing participation in P2P platforms [7]. Habibi et al. indicate the main motivation for cost reduction [10] and Hawlitschek et al. add to this motivation the idea that these platforms are a more social, variable, sustainable, convenient, anti-capitalist and cheaper alternative than traditional markets [7].

2.2 Formulation of Hypotheses

Since P2P platforms fit into e-commerce, the determinants of the intention to use these platforms do not differ much from e-commerce in general [11].

Within the scope of the Unified Theory of Acceptance and Use of Technology (UTAUT) and UTAUT 2, performance expectation is defined as the degree to which an individual believes that the use of technology will help him to improve his performance, assuming himself as one of the main determinants of the intention to use technology [12, 13]. Liu and Yang concluded about the importance of performance expectation in the sharing economy, especially on P2P platforms, and identified that it has a positive impact on the intention to use it [14].

Thus, we can affirm that an individual who intends to obtain benefits in the use of this type of platforms to transact their products or services, will certainly develop a strong motivation to use them as an alternative of others that will provide them with lower returns. Thus, we deduce the following hypothesis:

H1: Performance expectation has a positive influence on the intention to use P2P platforms.

Within the scope of UTAUT 2, Venkatesh et al. defined habit as the degree of automation with which an individual tends to use a technology as a consequence of learning, having concluded that it is a significant determinant of the intention to use that technology [13]. Regarding the use of P2P platforms, Hawlitschek et al. referred that previous experience and familiarity are commonly seen as catalysts for their use in the future [15]. Thus, it is expected that an individual who accumulates experience in the use of P2P platforms develops automatisms that results in a significant desire to use them again in the future. Thus, we propose the following hypothesis:

H2: Habit has a positive influence on the intention to use P2P platforms.

The online selling process is especially loaded with uncertainty, as products cannot be touched or inspected and non-contextual tips, such as tone of voice, expressions or body language, which can be used to judge the seller's honesty, are also absent [16]. Therefore, trust assumes a central role in businesses developed in an online environment. Pavlou defined trust as the belief that the other party will behave in a socially correct manner and, in doing so, will fulfil its role, without taking advantage of vulnerability [17]. In his study, Pavlou concluded that trust is the most influential factor in the intention to make a transaction [17].

In the context of P2P platforms, trust is the basis of the relationship between the consumer-seller and the consumer-buyer, having even been dubbed by some authors as the currency of these platforms [14]. Hawlitschek et al. referred that, in transactions developed between consumers, P2P platforms assume a role of mediator, being able to print more or less trust in the transaction [14]. These authors also concluded that trust in platforms is higher in consumer-sellers than in consumer-buyers. On the other hand, Görög assumed that feedback and reputation systems can increase trust among participants and be the key to the success of these platforms [18].

Just as trust in sellers is a crucial factor and a prerequisite for buyers to use P2P platforms [15], trust in buyers is also expected to be a determining factor in the intention to use P2P platforms by vendors. As such, we formulate the following hypothesis:

H3: Trust has a positive influence on the intention to use P2P platforms.

Rogers defined innovativeness as the degree to which an individual adopts an innovation earlier than others [19]. In turn, Goldsmith and Hofacker conceptualized innovativeness as a person's predisposition to try a new product or service [20].

Several studies have shown a positive correlation between innovativeness and the frequency of online shopping [21–24]. The study by Blake et al. goes further by concluding that innovativeness is a predictive factor of the quantity and diversity of online purchases [21]. More recent works have shown the positive influence of innovativeness in the intention to adopt remote mobile payments [25], in the intention to use P2P payment systems [26] and in the intention to purchase online [27]. Thus, given that P2P platforms can be considered as an innovation compared to traditional e-commerce websites, it is expected that individuals with a higher degree of innovativeness will have a greater motivation to use these platforms. Thus, we proceed with the following hypothesis:

H4: Innovativeness has a positive influence on the intention to use P2P platforms.

2.3   Research Model

The proposed research model, consisting of 5 constructs and the 4 hypotheses formulated above, is represented in Fig. 1.

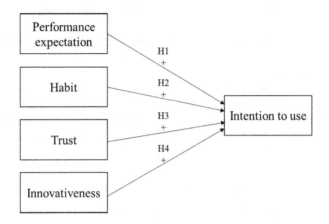

Fig. 1. Research model.

3   Methodology

The methodology used in this work is of a quantitative nature, because we seek to test hypotheses which are grounded on cause and effect relationships between variables.

The study population was made up of Portuguese Internet users, who made sales in the last year through online P2P platforms.

For reasons of cost savings and quick data collection, the sample was non-random, of convenience, having been constituted through a snowball approach on social networks. The sample collected was composed of 100 individuals, who were mostly male (55%), had between 30 and 49 years old (68%) and completed higher education (60%).

Data collection was performed using an online questionnaire, which was composed of previously validated scales for the 5 constructs included in the research model. Performance expectation (PE) and habit (HAB) were measured using the scales proposed by Venkatesh et al. [13]. In turn, trust (TR) was measured using the Leonard scale [28], while innovativeness (INNOV) was measured using the Goldsmith and Hofacker scale [20]. Finally, purchase intention (INT) was measured using the scale proposed by Hamari et al. [6].

All scales consisted of 3 items and were measured using 7-point Likert scales (from 1 – strongly disagree to 7 – strongly agree).

Prior to the launch of the questionnaire, a pre-test was carried out, in order to assess the clarity and sequencing of the questions, as well as the functioning of the online data collection platform. As a result of the pre-test, slight changes were made to the formulation of some questions.

4   Results

The statistical treatment of the data was carried out using partial least squares structural equation modelling (PLS-SEM) with the SmartPLS 3.0 software. The use of this methodology is justified because it is highly efficient in the estimation of parameters, even in small samples, and does virtually no assumption about the distribution of data [29]. The statistical significance of the model parameters was obtained through bootstrapping with 5000 iterations [30].

Initially, the reliability, convergent validity and discriminant validity of the measurement model were evaluated. Table 1 shows the loadings of the measurement indicators and the respective p-values, as well as the cross loadings. All loadings are above the minimum value of 0.7 [31] and statistically significant at the 0.1% level, which shows its reliability.

Table 1. Loadings and cross loadings.

Items	Loadings	p-values	Cross loadings				
			PE	HAB	TR	INNOV	INT
PE1	0,955	<0,001		0,708	0,694	0,467	0,813
PE2	0,959	<0,001		0,727	0,668	0,439	0,791
PE3	0,976	<0,001		0,749	0,689	0,463	0,817
HAB1	0,951	<0,001	0,705		0,628	0,654	0,747
HAB2	0,959	<0,001	0,715		0,647	0,538	0,736
HAB3	0,962	<0,001	0,748		0,661	0,594	0,790
TR1	0,972	<0,001	0,676	0,658		0,563	0,720
TR2	0,970	<0,001	0,663	0,618		0,586	0,744
TR3	0,970	<0,001	0,727	0,687		0,623	0,785
INNOV1	0,942	<0,001	0,444	0,570	0,589		0,625
INNOV2	0,951	<0,001	0,461	0,639	0,573		0,640
INNOV3	0,907	<0,001	0,420	0,532	0,544		0,648
INT1	0,900	<0,001	0,823	0,677	0,705	0,547	
INT2	0,955	<0,001	0,756	0,732	0,739	0,689	
INT3	0,935	<0,001	0,761	0,801	0,715	0,671	

Table 2 shows the average variance extracted (AVE), the composite reliability (CR) and the correlations of each latent variable. CR values are much higher than the minimum recommended value of 0.6 [31], varying between 0.951 and 0.980, which allows us to conclude that all constructs have adequate reliability. On the other hand,

AVEs vary between 0.866 and 0.943, clearly above the minimum threshold point of 0.5 [31, 32], which attests to their convergent validity. Finally, according to the Fornell-Larcker criterion, the discriminant validity of each construct is confirmed, since the square root of the AVE is greater than the absolute value of the correlations with the other constructs [33]. The use of the HTMT criterion, also confirms the discriminant validity, since the HTMT values are less than 0.9 [34]. In addition, according to Table 1, cross-loadings are less than the loadings in each item, which reinforces the discriminant validity [31].

Table 2. AVE, CR and correlations between constructs.

| | AVE | CR | Correlations (HTMT) | | | | |
			PE	HAB	TR	INNOV	INT
PE	0,928	0,975	0,963				
HAB	0,916	0,970	0,756	0,957			
			(0,789)				
TR	0,943	0,980	0,710	0,675	0,971		
			(0,734)	(0,700)			
INNOV	0,871	0,953	0,474	0,622	0,609	0,933	
			(0,502)	(0,662)	(0,642)		
INT	0,866	0,951	0,838	0,792	0,773	0,684	0,930
			(0,890)	(0,843)	(0,817)	(0,739)	

Note: the diagonal contains the square root of the stroke; the correlations between the constructs are shown outside the diagonal; HTMT values are shown in parentheses.

Figure 2 shows the structural model, whose evaluation was made using the sign, magnitude and statistical significance of the of the structural relations parameters, as well as by the explained variance (R^2) of the endogenous latent variable [31]. All relations have parameters with a sign compatible (positive) with that predicted in the research model and are statistically significant at the 0.1% level. The performance expectation has the strongest effect on the intention to use ($\beta = 0.473$; $p < 0.001$), followed by innovativeness ($\beta = 0.254$; $p < 0.001$).

In this way, the results allow the confirmation of the 4 hypotheses proposed in the research model. Analyzing the explained variance of the endogenous latent variable, it appears that the intention of use is explained in 83.2% by performance expectation, habit, trust, and innovativeness, a value that can be considered quite high.

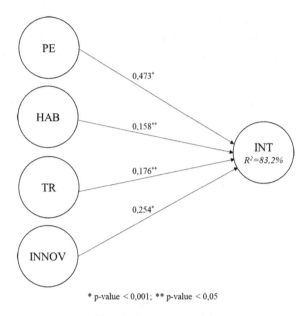

* p-value < 0,001; ** p-value < 0,05

Fig. 2. Structural model.

5   Discussion of Results and Conclusions

5.1   Discussion of Results

This study aimed to understand the causes that determine the intention to use online P2P platforms by sellers.

To answer to this objective, we proposed a research model composed of 4 hypotheses. The empirical validation of the model was carried out through a quantitative study, which surveyed a sample of 100 individuals, through an online questionnaire. The results obtained confirmed all the hypotheses proposed.

Hypothesis 1 established that the performance expectation had a positive influence on the sellers' intention to use P2P online platforms. The results obtained confirmed this hypothesis, in addition to revealing that the performance expectation is the determinant that has the strongest effect on the intention to use. Thus, the conclusions of the studies by Venkatesh et al. [12], Venkatesh et al. [13] and Liu and Yang [14] are reinforced, concluding that individuals who have higher expectations in terms of improving their performance in selling products or services through online P2P platforms are those who are more likely to come to use these platforms.

In hypothesis 2, the positive influence of habit on the intention to use P2P online platforms was evaluated. The results obtained in the empirical study corroborated this hypothesis, meeting the conclusions of the works by Venkatesh et al. [13] and Hawlitschek et al. [15]. As such, we can affirm that the greater the degree of automation with which the individual tends to use a P2P platform to sell products or services as a result of learning, the greater the motivation to come to use it.

Hypothesis 3 proposed that trust had a positive influence on the intention to use P2P online platforms. The results confirmed this hypothesis, corroborating the conclusions of the works by Pavlou [17] and Hawlitschek et al. [7]. In this way, we can assure you that sellers' trust in buyers is a fundamental ingredient in the intention of doing business online, especially on P2P platforms.

The latter hypothesis proposed that innovativeness had a positive influence on the intention to use P2P online platforms. The results obtained corroborate this hypothesis, meeting the conclusions of the works by Blake et al. [21], Citrin et al. [22], Goldsmith [23, 24], Slade et al. [25], Lara-Rubio et al. [26] and Hebbar et al. [27]. As such, we can conclude that individuals who are more likely to try new products or services are those who are more likely to become sellers on P2P online platforms.

5.2 Study Contributions

From a theoretical point of view, this work presents the contribution of proposing and empirically fully validating a research model that identifies the determinants of the intention to use P2P online platforms by the Portuguese sellers, helping to fill the lack of studies in this area [6–8]. It is also noteworthy the high explanatory capacity of the model, which explains more than 80% the variance in the intention to use.

In practical terms, this study indicates that the strategy of P2P online platform operators must be based on (1) improving their performance, (2) developing an environment favourable to the consolidation of trust between sellers and buyers and (3) innovating. The fact that the performance expectation is the most relevant factor in the intention to use indicates that P2P platforms should invest in the development of features that allow sellers to achieve maximum performance when selling their products and services.

On the other hand, the valuation of the trust factor points to the need for P2P platforms to invest in measures that mitigate risk, such as certification by third parties, the provision of feedback forums or the provision of insurance associated with transactions. The focus on platform innovation should be an aspect to take into account, as we know that the individuals with the greatest propensity for innovation are most likely to use these platforms. We believe that platforms that provide high performance, have an environment of trust and implement a strategy of continuous improvement, with permanent innovation, will have a greater probability of success and will develop stronger user routines in their users.

5.3 Limitations and Suggestions for Future Research

The limitations of this study are mainly due to the size and type of sample collected. The sample is small in size and has a non-probabilistic nature, which does not allow generalizing the results of the study. In future investigations, it would be important for the empirical study to allow the collection of a larger sample with sociodemographic characteristics that would provide a more reliable representation of the study population.

Future studies could apply this model in specific P2P platforms and in different categories of products or services, in order to understand if the model is robust in different contexts.

In order to deepen the motivations for the intention of using P2P platforms to sell products or services, a qualitative study would be advisable, through in-depth individual interviews or focus groups.

References

1. Chen, D.N., Jeng, B., Lee, W.P., Chuang, C.-H.: An agent-based model for consumer-to-business electronic commerce. Expert Syst. Appl. **34**(1), 469–481 (2008)
2. Geraldo, G.C., Mainardes, E.W.: Estudo sobre os fatores que afetam a intenção de compras online. REGE - Revista de Gestão **24**(2), 181–194 (2017)
3. Hawlitschek, F., Notheisen, B., Teubner, T.: The limits of trust-free systems: a literature review on blockchain technology and trust in the sharing economy. Electron. Commer. Res. Appl. **29**, 50–63 (2018)
4. Apte, U.M., Davis, M.M.: Sharing economy services: business model generation. Calif. Manag. Rev. **61**(2), 104–131 (2019)
5. Dervojeda, K., et al.: The Sharing Economy: Accessibility Based Business Models for Peer-to-Peer Markets. European Commission, Directorate-General for Enterprise and Industry, Brussels (2013)
6. Hamari, J., Sjöklint, M., Ukkonen, A.: The sharing economy: why people participate in collaborative consumption. J. Assoc. Inform. Sci. Technol. **67**(9), 2047–2059 (2016)
7. Hawlitschek, F., Teubner, T., Weinhardt, C.: Trust in the sharing economy. Swiss J. Bus. Res. Pratice **70**(1), 26–44 (2016)
8. Mitchell, A., Strader, T.J.: Introduction to the special issue on "sharing economy and on-demand service business models". IseB **16**(2), 243–245 (2018). https://doi.org/10.1007/s10257-018-0373-3
9. Bucher, E., Fieseler, C., Lutz, C.: What's mine is yours (for a nominal fee) – exploring the spectrum of utilitarian to altruistic motives for Internet-mediated sharing. Comput. Hum. Behav. **62**, 316–326 (2016)
10. Habibi, M.R., Davidson, A., Laroche, M.: What managers should know about the sharing economy. Bus. Horiz. **60**(1), 113–121 (2017)
11. Chang, W.L., Wang, J.Y.: Mine is yours? using sentiment analysis to explore the degree of risk in the sharing economy. Electron. Commer. Res. Appl. **28**, 141–158 (2018)
12. Venkatesh, V., Morris, M.G., Davis, G.B., Davis, F.D.: User acceptance of information technology: toward a unified view. MIS Q. **27**(3), 425–478 (2003)
13. Venkatesh, V., Thong, J.Y., Xu, X.: Consumer acceptance and use of information technology: extending the unified theory of acceptance and use of technology. MIS Q. **36**(1), 157–178 (2012)
14. Liu, Y., Yang, Y.: Empirical examination of users' adoption of the sharing economy in china using an expanded technology acceptance model. Sustainability (2071–1050), **10**(4), 1–17 (2018)
15. Hawlitschek, F., Teubner, T., Gimpel, H.: Consumer motives for peer-to-peer sharing. J. Clean. Prod. **204**, 144–157 (2018)
16. Yoon, H.S., Occeña, L.G.: Influencing factors of trust in consumer-to-consumer electronic commerce with gender and age. Int. J. Inf. Manage. **35**(3), 352–363 (2015)

17. Pavlou, P.A.: Consumer acceptance of electronic commerce: Integrating trust and risk with the technology acceptance model. Int. J. Electron. Commer. **7**(3), 101–134 (2003)
18. Görög, G.: The definitions of sharing economy: a systematic literature review. Management (18544223), **13**(2), 175–189 (2018)
19. Rogers, E.M.: Diffusion of Innovations, 4th edn. Free Press, New York (1995)
20. Goldsmith, R.E., Hofacker, C.F.: Measuring consumer innovativeness. J. Acad. Mark. Sci. **19**(3), 209–221 (1991)
21. Blake, B.F., Neuendorf, K.A., Valdiserri, C.M.: Innovativeness and variety of Internet shopping. Internet Res. **13**(3), 156–169 (2003)
22. Citrin, A., Sprott, D., Silverman, S., Stem, D.E.: Adoption of Internet shopping: the role of consumer innovativeness. Ind. Manag. Data Syst. **100**(7), 294–300 (2000)
23. Goldsmith, R.E.: How innovativeness differentiates online buyers. Q. J. Electron. Commer. **1** (4), 323–333 (2000)
24. Goldsmith, R.E.: Using the domain specific innovativeness scale to identify innovative Internet consumers. Internet Res. **11**(2), 149–158 (2001)
25. Slade, E.L., Dwivedi, Y.K., Piercy, N.C., Williams, M.D.: Modeling consumers' adoption intentions of remote mobile payments in the United Kingdom: extending UTAUT with innovativeness, risk, and trust. Psychol. Mark. **32**(8), 860–873 (2015)
26. Lara-Rubio, J., Villarejo-Ramos, A.F., Liébana-Cabanillas, F.: Explanatory and predictive model of the adoption of P2P payment systems. Behav. Informa. Technol. 1–14 (2020). https://doi.org/10.1080/0144929X.2019.1706637
27. Hebbar, S., Kamath, G.B., Mathew, A.O., Kamath, V.: Attitude towards online shopping and its influence on purchase intentions: an urban Indian perspective. Int. J. Bus. Innov. Res. **22** (3), 326–341 (2020)
28. Leonard, L.N.: Attitude influencers in C2C e-commerce: buying and selling. J. Comput. Inform. Syst. **52**(3), 11–17 (2012)
29. Hair Jr., J.F., Sarstedt, M., Hopkins, L., Kuppelwieser, G.V.: Partial least squares structural equation modeling (PLS-SEM): an emerging tool in business research. Eur. Bus. Rev. **26**(2), 106–121 (2014)
30. Hair, J.F., Ringle, C.M., Sarstedt, M.: PLS-SEM: indeed a silver bullet. J. Mark. Theory Pract. **19**(2), 139–151 (2011)
31. Götz, O., Liehr-Gobbers, K., Krafft, M.: Evaluation of structural equation models using the partial least squares (PLS) approach, Chapter 29. In: Vinzi, V.E., Chin, W., Henseler, J., Wang, H. (eds.) Handbook of Partial Least Squares: Concepts, Methods and Applications. Springer, Berlin (2010)
32. Hair, J., Black, W., Babin, B., Anderson, R.: Multivariate Data Analysis: A Global Perspective. Pearson, Upper Saddle River (2016)
33. Fornell, C., Larcker, D.F.: Evaluating structural equation models with unobservable variables and measurement error. J. Mark. Res. **18**(1), 39–50 (1981)
34. Henseler, J., Ringle, C.M., Sarstedt, M.: A new criterion for assessing discriminant validity in variance-based structural equation modeling. J. Acad. Mark. Sci. **43**(1), 115–135 (2015)

Social Media Impact on Academic Performance: Lessons Learned from Cameroon

Josue Kuika Watat[1]([⊠]) [iD], Gideon Mekonnen Jonathan[2] [iD],
Frank Wilson Ntsafack Dongmo[3],
and Nour El Houda Zine El Abidine[4]

[1] AMBERO Consulting GmbH, 61476 Kronberg Im Taunus, Germany
josuewatat@gmail.com
[2] Stockholm University, Stockholm, Sweden
gideon@dsv.su.se
[3] Ministry of Secondary Education, Yaounde, Cameroon
ntsafackf@yahoo.fr
[4] Institut Superieur de Gestion de Tunis, Tunis, Tunisia
noorzinelabidine@gmail.com

Abstract. The continuously improving Internet penetration in the continent, coupled with the increasing number of smartphone users in Africa has been considered as the reasons for the adoption of social media among students and other adolescents. Even though this development has been recognizing in the literature, only a few studies have investigated the acceptance, use, and retention of social media for academic purposes. However, findings of prior studies suggest that the use of social media has an influence on academic performance. To address the lack of knowledge on the adoption of social media among students, this study aims to explore the factors that are related to students' acceptance and use of social media. We attempt to extend the Technology Acceptance Model by integrating relational engagement, Perceived Satisfaction, as well as the Perspective of the Use of Social Media in Education. The proposed theoretical model was evaluated using quantitative data collected from 460 students in Cameroon. We applied PLS-SEM technique to test the hypotheses and the theoretical model. Implications of the findings, as well as future research directions, are presented.

Keywords: Social media · Academic performance · TAM · Relational commitment · Africa

1 Introduction

In recent years, the use of social media among university students in sub-Saharan Africa has grown rapidly, thanks to the continuing Internet penetration and access to smartphones. It has been noted that the use of social media plays a role in strengthening the social and academic bonds that may exist between stakeholders at the university. This, in turn, is beneficial for building an essential educational eco-system. Previous

© Springer Nature Switzerland AG 2020
M. Themistocleous et al. (Eds.): EMCIS 2020, LNBIP 402, pp. 370–379, 2020.
https://doi.org/10.1007/978-3-030-63396-7_25

studies, for instance [1–4], have widely explored the use of social media and how it affects the academic performance of University students from diverse backgrounds. Although social media plays an important communication lever for students which fosters an effective sharing of educational content between users, its influence on academic performance has so far remained an under-exploited area of research. For example, a study conducted by Lau [5] in 2017 reports that social media has been the cause of several academic failures. Thus, it is of paramount importance to investigate how social media is accepted and used by students. To address the gap in the literature, this study aims to explore the factors that are related to students' acceptance and use of social media. To start with, we develop a research model based on the extant literature on social media and education to meet the research objectives.

This paper is structured as follows. In the next section, we develop our theoretical model and formulate the hypotheses based on the existing literature. The following section presents the research methodology—data collection and analysis methods, as well as the procedures, followed to evaluate the proposed research model and test the hypotheses. The subsequent section presents the results of the study. Finally, the conclusion briefly summarises the findings of the study and presents limitations as well as opportunities for future research.

2   Theoretical Background

The theoretical representation proposed in this research (Fig. 1) is an extension of the Technology Acceptance Model (TAM) with Perceived Satisfaction, Perspective of Social Media in Education, and Relational Commitment. The TAM model was proposed by [6, 7] to measure the potential for adoption and use of technology by individuals, and to identify the necessary reforms that need to be carried out for wider acceptance by users. The authors state that *"the goal of TAM is to provide an explanation of the determinants of computer acceptance that in general is capable of explaining user behaviour across a broad range of end-user computing technologies and user populations, while at the same time being both parsimonious and the theoretically justified"* [7].

The TAM has been widely used in emerging literature related to social media and education. For example, [8] made use of TAM by branching out subjective norms to explore the use of social media by 145 business students at an elite management school in Mumbai, India. Besides, researchers investigated the perception of teachers in initial training to use social media in the performance of their duties given the important place occupied by technology within the education sector. Akman and Turhan [9] also investigated the perception of 142 students on the adoption of Web 2.0 technologies for social learning. In a context strongly influenced by political, religious and economic trends, [10] extended TAM to assess the level of acceptance of social media for e-learning among Lybian academic institutions. Also, [11] extended the TAM model by incorporating engagement and collaborative learning as a construct to measure the inclusion of social media in the collaborative learning system and engagement of different stakeholders in universities in Malaysia.

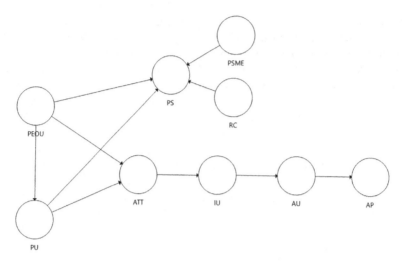

Fig. 1. Research model

Drawing from the foundations of the emerging literature on social media and education, we propose the following hypotheses in the context of social media and academic performance in university systems that find it difficult to adopt technology truly:

H_1: Perceived Ease of Use has a significant positive effect on Perceived Usefulness.
H_2: Perceived Ease of Use has a significant positive effect on Attitude.
H_3: Perceived Ease of Use has a significant positive effect on Perceived Satisfaction.
H_4: Perceived Usefulness has a significant positive effect on Attitude.
H_5: Perceived Usefulness has a significant positive effect on Perceived Satisfaction.

Besides, we emphasize that the perspective of social media in education plays a key role in the acceptance, use and effects of social media in education. Moreover, several studies have shown to what extent the perspective of social media in education plays an important role in the emerging literature on information systems [12].

Kanthawongs et al. [12] discover that Relational Commitment is a big part of user satisfaction with Facebook acceptance in education. Thus, we make use of previous research and suggest that in the context of economies in search of emergence, marked by a low acceptance and use of technologies, Relational Commitment remains a key factor in the process of acceptance, use. and satisfaction. In this context, therefore, we suggest the following hypotheses:

H_6: Perspectives of Social Media in Education has a significant positive effect on Perceived Satisfaction.
H_7: Relational Commitment has a significant positive effect on Perceived Satisfaction.
H_8: Attitude has a significant positive effect on Intention to Use.
H_9: Intention to Use has a significant positive effect on Actual System Use.
H_{10}: Actual System Use has a significant positive effect on Academic Performance.

3   Methodology

The study uses a survey questionnaire which was performed on Google form. The questionnaire's link was distributed through several social media students' groups. Data was collected from 460 (46.74% males and 53.26% females) students from public and private higher institutions in Cameroon. The items of each construct of the research model were adapted from prior studies of the extant literature about the subject. A total of 33 items were used to measure the nine variables of the structural research model. Besides the demographic profile, all the items were measured using a 7-point Likert Scale ranging from 1 to 7. SmartPLS, version 3.2.6 was used for data analysis. It is a PLS-SEM tool, to evaluate structural equations modelling (SEM) which helps researchers to assess the adequacy of the theoretical model and verify hypotheses.

Table 1. Demographic characteristics of respondents

Profile	Description	Frequency	%
Gender	Male	215	46.74
	Female	245	53.26
Age	15–17	4	0.88
	18–25	333	72.39
	26–35	116	25.21
	36–45	7	1.52
	46–60	0	0
Degree	Undergraduate	195	42.39
	Postgraduate	250	54.34
	PhD	15	3.26
Type of higher institutions	Public	211	45.87
	Private	249	54.13
Experience in use of social media	Between 1–3	38	8.26
	Between 4–6	138	30
	Between 7–9	144	31.3
	Between 9–10	57	12.40
	More than 10	83	18.04
Most frequently use social media	WhatsApp	237	51.52
	Facebook	42	9.13
	Twitter	112	24.35
	Instagram	12	2.61
	Wikipedia	16	3.48
	YouTube	28	6.09
	Pinterest	3	0.65
	Snapchat	5	1.07
	LinkedIn	5	1.07

Following the demographic statistics (Table 1), a total of 460 students completed the survey questionnaire. All fields of the survey were mandatory to avoid missing data. Of the 460 respondents, 215 were men (46.74%). It is an average distribution. As for age, the majority of respondents 97.60%, are between 18 and 35 years old while 72.39% is situated between 18 and 25. The participants' average age was between 18 and 25, which corresponds to individual's inclination to use information technologies services such as social media intensively.

4   Results

Table 2 presents our constructs along with measurement items and corresponding values for loadings, composite reliability as well as average variance extracted (AVE). We can observe that the values of Composite Reliability are above 0.7, and the figures for AVE are above 0.5. Regarding the items, we can notice that the only loading below the value of 0.7 is the item PSME. However, this is not likely to compromise the validity of the construct. Apart from this single case, all the items used in our study have a value of higher than 0.7. Thus, the thresholds specified in the literature are respected for the values mentioned above [13, 14]. Therefore, we can include all constructs in the proposed research model.

Table 2. Outer loadings, composite reliability (CR) and average variance extracted (AVE) values of the constructs.

Constructs	Items	Loadings	CR	AVE
Academic Performance (AP)	AP1	0.897	0.932	0.774
	AP2	0.915		
	AP3	0.820		
	AP4	0.885		
Attitude (ATT)	ATT1	0.852	0.869	0.691
	ATT2	0.901		
	ATT3	0.732		
Intention to Use (IU)	IU1	0.881	0.912	0.775
	IU2	0.889		
	IU3	0.870		
Perceived Ease of Use (PEOU)	PEOU1	0.891	0.927	0.810
	PEOU2	0.908		
	PEOU3	0.900		
Perceived Satisfaction (PS)	PS1	0.884	0.897	0.685
	PS2	0.797		
	PS3	0.846		
	PS4	0.779		

(continued)

Table 2. (*continued*)

Constructs	Items	Loadings	CR	AVE
Perspectives of Social Media in Education (PSME)	PSME1	0.782	0.834	0.560
	PSME2	0.742		
	PSME3	0.603		
	PSME4	0.846		
Perceived Usefulness (PU)	PU1	0.843	0.917	0.689
	PU2	0.834		
	PU3	0.820		
	PU4	0.812		
	PU5	0.842		
Relational Commitment (RC)	RC1	0.791	0.925	0.713
	RC2	0.864		
	RC3	0.859		
	RC4	0.853		
	RC5	0.852		
Actual System Use (AU)	AU1	0.863	0.877	0.781
	AU2	0.904		

In Table 3, the values associated with Composite Reliability go up to 0.932, which exceeds the threshold of 0.7 [14]. For Cronbach's alpha values, the associated values go up to 0.903, thus exceeding the threshold of 0.7 [14]. These values show a strong internal coherence as well as the reliability of the constructs which form our research model. For AVEs, Table 3 shows values up to 0.810, which is above the acceptable threshold of 0.5 [14]. Concerning the values obtained, we can affirm that the convergent validity of our model is confirmed.

Table 3. Construct reliability and validity

	Cronbach's alpha	rho_A	CR	AVE
AP	0.903	0.920	0.932	0.774
ATT	0.780	0.839	0.869	0.691
AU	0.721	0.735	0.877	0.781
IU	0.855	0.855	0.912	0.775
PEOU	0.883	0.884	0.927	0.810
PS	0.846	0.853	0.897	0.685
PSME	0.735	0.774	0.834	0.560
PU	0.887	0.887	0.917	0.689
RC	0.900	0.906	0.925	0.713

Table 4. Discriminant Validity

	AP	ATT	AU	IU	PEOU	PS	PSME	PU	RC
AP	**0.880**								
ATT	0.619	**0.831**							
AU	0.685	0.589	**0.883**						
IU	0.667	0.799	0.654	**0.880**					
PEOU	0.673	0.463	0.552	0.525	**0.900**				
PS	0.699	0.688	0.594	0.659	0.567	**0.828**			
PSME	0.586	0.625	0.470	0.564	0.487	0.759	**0.749**		
PU	0.762	0.689	0.633	0.727	0.697	0.674	0.586	**0.830**	
RC	0.378	0.363	0.330	0.321	0.318	0.396	0.366	0.350	**0.844**

As shown in Table 4 the discriminant validity of our research model is supported. It is measured by making a comparison between the data in the correlation matrix and the square root of the AVEs in the diagonals. This involves checking whether each value of the square root of the AVEs is greater than the intercorrelation with the values of the other constructs. [15–17].

Table 5. Structural model testing hypothesis using bootstrapping

	Original sample (O)	Sample mean (M)	Standard deviation (STDEV)	T statistics ($|O/STDEV|$)	P values
H1: PEOU => PU	0.697	0.696	0.041	17.216	0.000****
H2: PEOU => ATT	−0.034	−0.035	0.074	0.457	0.648
H3: PEOU => PS	0.096	0.101	0.062	1.545	0.123
H4: PU => ATT	0.712	0.712	0.058	12.200	0.000****
H5: PU => PS	0.273	0.264	0.067	4.088	0.000****
H6: PSME => PS	0.524	0.527	0.045	11.647	0.000****
H7: RC => PS	0.078	0.083	0.048	1.630	0.104
H8: ATT => IU	0.799	0.801	0.025	31.834	0.000****
H9: IU => AU	0.654	0.656	0.041	16.156	0.000****
H10: AU => AP	0.685	0.686	0.034	19.974	0.000****

****$P < 0.001$

In Table 5, we can observe that the p-values of all of the hypotheses of our study. Thus, these findings support hypotheses H_1, H_4, H_5, H_6, H_8, H_9 and H_{10} while hypotheses H_2, H_3 and H_7 are not supported (Table 6).

Table 6. Hypotheses testing results

Hypothesis	Test results
H_1: Perceived Ease of Use has a significant positive effect on Perceived Usefulness.	Supported
H_2: Perceived Ease of Use has a significant positive effect on Attitude.	Not supported
H_3: Perceived Ease of Use has a significant positive effect on Perceived Satisfaction.	Not supported
H_4: Perceived Usefulness has a significant positive effect on Attitude.	Supported
H_5: Perceived Usefulness has a significant positive effect on Perceived Satisfaction.	Supported
H_6: Perspectives of Social Media in Education has a significant positive effect on Perceived Satisfaction.	Supported
H_7: Relational Commitment has a significant positive effect on Perceived Satisfaction.	Not supported
H_8: Attitude has a significant positive effect on Intention to Use.	Supported
H_9: Intention to Use has a significant positive effect on Actual System Use.	Supported
H_{10}: Actual System Use has a significant positive effect on Academic Performance.	Supported

The present study provides support for the Technology Acceptance model in the context of the use and impact of social media on academic performance. The results show that Perceived Ease of Use positively influences Perceived Usefulness. Besides, perceived usefulness positively influences attitude and perceived satisfaction which is in line with [12, 18]. However, our study did not confirm a positive effect of perceived ease of use on attitude and perceived satisfaction, and in the other hand, of relational commitment on perceived satisfaction.

5 Conclusions, Limitations and Future Research Directions

The objective of this research was to propose an extension of the TAM model by incorporating Perceived Satisfaction, the Perspective of the Use of Social Media in Education, Relational Engagement, as well as academic performance. The aim was to explore the acceptance of social media in an educational context where technology has not yet reached its cruising speed. The data were collected from students in Cameroon and analysed through the software SmartPLS Version 2.8 to assess the research hypotheses of the proposed theoretical representation. The findings show strong support for the Technology Acceptance Model when it comes to using social media in universities and thus assessing the consequences on Academic Performance. The study also found a strong correlation between Relational Commitment and Perceived Satisfaction when using social media.

However, this study bears some limitations. The first one is the absence of a qualitative approach in this study to explain the findings. A mixed-method approach with both qualitative and quantitative methods could have provided more detailed information for a better understanding of the influence of social media on academic performance in higher education in African countries. The second limitation relates to the geographical restriction of the study area to only Cameroon. Broadening the study to other African countries, and specifically, sub-Saharan ones such as francophone (Ivory Coast, Senegal, Chad etc.) and anglophone (Nigeria, Ghana, Kenya etc.) could have improved our findings to make a better generalisation. This is a setback to be considered in future research attempts. Lastly, future works should take in to account additional adoption constructs, especially big five personality traits such as Openness, Neuroticism, Extraversion. These traits are fundamental to understand users' psychological status since the use of ICT remains new in several sectors of life in sub-Saharan Africa. Besides, future studies might include access to the internet, network infrastructure, and connection costs might to the list of variables that could explain the adoption of social media among students in the region.

References

1. Al-Rahmi, W.M., Yahaya, N., Alamri, M.M., Alyoussef, I.Y., Al-Rahmi, A.M., Kamin, Y. B.: Integrating innovation diffusion theory with technology acceptance model: supporting students' attitude towards using a massive open online courses (MOOCS) systems. Interact. Learn. Environ. 1–13 (2019). https://doi.org/10.1080/10494820.2019.1629599
2. Cha, K., Kwon, S.: Understanding the adoption of e-learning in south Korea: using the extended technology acceptance model approach. KEDI J. Educ. Policy 15(2) (2018)
3. Tarhini, A., Hone, K., Liu, X.: Measuring the moderating effect of gender and age on e-learning acceptance in England: aa structural equation modeling approach for an extended technology acceptance model. J. Educ. Comput. Res. 51(2), 163–184 (2014)
4. Yeou, M.: An investigation of students' acceptance of Moodle in a blended learning setting using technology acceptance model. J. Educ. Technol. Syst. 44(3), 300–318 (2016)
5. Lau, W.W.: Effects of social media usage and social media multitasking on the academic performance of university students. Comput. Hum. Behav. 68, 286–291 (2017)
6. Davis, F.D.: Perceived usefulness, perceived ease of use, and user acceptance of information technology. MIS Q. 13, 319–340 (1989)
7. Davis, F.D., Bagozzi, R.P., Warshaw, P.R.: User acceptance of computer technology: a comparison of two theoretical models. Manage. Sci. 35(8), 982–1003 (1989)
8. Dhume, S.M., Pattanshetti, M.Y., Kamble, S.S., Prasad, T.: Adoption of social media by business education students: application of technology acceptance model (tam). In: 2012 IEEE International Conference on Technology Enhanced Education (ICTEE). pp. 1–10. IEEE (2012)
9. Akman, I., Turhan, C.: User acceptance of social learning systems in higher education: an application of the extended technology acceptance model. Innov. Educ. Teach. Int. 54(3), 229–237 (2017)
10. Elkaseh, A.M., Wong, K.W., Fung, C.C.: Perceived ease of use and perceived usefulness of social media for e-learning in Libyan higher education: a structural equation modeling analysis. Int. J. Inform. Educ. Technol. 6(3), 192 (2016)
11. Al-Rahmi, W.M., Othman, M.S., Yusuf, L.M.: Social media for collaborative learning and engagement: adoption framework in higher education institutions in Malaysia. Mediterr. J. Soc. Sci. 6(3 S1), 246 (2015)

12. Kanthawongs, P., Kanthawongs, P., Chitcharoen, C.: Factors affecting perceived satisfaction with facebook in education. International Association for Development of the Information Society. pp. 188–194 (2016)
13. Sun, H., Zhang, P.: An exploration of affect factors and their role in user technology acceptance: mediation and causality. J. Am. Soc. Inform. Sci. Technol. **59**(8), 1252–1263 (2008)
14. Hair, J.F., Sarstedt, M., Ringle, C.M., Mena, J.A.: An assessment of the use of partial least squares structural equation modeling in marketing research. J. Acad. Mark. Sci. **40**(3), 414–433 (2012)
15. Chin, W.W., et al.: The partial least squares approach to structural equation modeling. Mod. Methods Bus. Res. **295**(2), 295–336 (1998)
16. Chin, W.: How to write up and report pls analyses. In: Handbook of Partial Least Squares: Concepts, Methods and Application. Esposito Vinzi, V pp. 645–689 (2010)
17. Fornell, C., Larcker, D.F.: Structural equation models with unobservable variables and measurement error: Algebra and statistics. J. Mark. Res. (JMR) **18**(3) (1981)
18. Ibili, E., Resnyansky, D., Billinghurst, M.: Applying the technology acceptance model to understand Maths teachers' perceptions towards an augmented reality tutoring system. Educ. Inform. Technol. **24**(5), 2653–2675 (2019)

Emerging Computing Technologies and Trends for Business Process Management

Towards Applying Deep Learning to the Internet of Things: A Model and a Framework

Samaa Elnagar$^{(\boxtimes)}$ and Kweku-Muata Osei-Bryson

Information Systems, Virginia Commonwealth University, Richmond, USA
{elnagarsa,kmosei}@vcu.com

Abstract. Deep Learning (DL) modeling has been a recent topic of interest. With the accelerating need to embed Deep Learning Networks (DLNs) to the Internet of Things (IoT) applications, many DL optimization techniques were developed to enable applying DL to IoTs. However, despite the plethora of DL optimization techniques, there is always a trade-off between accuracy, latency, and cost. Moreover, there are no specific criteria for selecting the best optimization model for a specific scenario. Therefore, this research aims at providing a DL optimization model that eases the selection and re-using DLNs on IoTs. In addition, the research presents an initial design for a DL optimization model management framework. This framework would help organizations choose the optimal DL optimization model that maximizes performance without sacrificing quality. The research would add to the IS design science knowledge as well as the industry by providing insights to many IT managers to apply DLNs to IoTs such as machines and robots.

Keywords: Deep Learning · Internet of Things · Deep learning optimization · Edge Computing · DL tunneling

1 Introduction

With the emergence of Artificial Intelligence (AI) especially Deep Learning (*DL*) methods, there has been much focus on giving IoT devices the knowledge and the inference capabilities of humans. Internet of Things (*IoTs*) could be in the form of *End* and *Edge* devices. a Deep Learning Networks (*DLNs*) could be applied to various *IoTs* such as robotics, self-driving vehicles, augmented reality, and digital assistance [1].

On the one hand, *DL* models are known for their computational cost and complexity, so they are mostly run on servers on the cloud [2]. On the other hand, *end devices (e.g.* smart sensors*)* and *edge devices* (e.g. routers) are often battery powered, have limited memory, processing and energy resources to store and process data. Applying *DL* models to *IoT* is challenging, in a manner that is similar to attempting to fit a giant elephant in a tight limited tunnel. DLNs have to be optimized and compressed to fit to IoTs limited computational sources. In addition, the optimization of the IoTs themselves is also necessary in terms of memory and hardware optimization [3].

© Springer Nature Switzerland AG 2020
M. Themistocleous et al. (Eds.): EMCIS 2020, LNBIP 402, pp. 383–398, 2020.
https://doi.org/10.1007/978-3-030-63396-7_26

*IoT*s provide businesses with the leverage of allowing data generated from customers to be included in their decision-making processes [4] that led to the development of the *Edge Computing* paradigm [5]. The development of optimization algorithms for *DLN*s could empower *IoT* with many cognitive abilities [6]. However, there is a lack of guidance on how to choose the appropriate *DLN* and optimization model to be applied according to different settings. Therefore, the main focus of this research is the development of a model for optimizing *DL* to be applied on *End* and *Edge* devices? Our two major objectives are:

1. To build an *DL* optimization model that provides an end-to-end modeling for applying *DLN* to IoTs according to specific contextual settings.
2. To provide the foundational bricks for building a Deep Learning Optimization Model Management Framework (DLOM)^2 that maximizes value gained from applying the presented model.

The research adds to IS body of knowledge by creating an optimization model that connects two emergent yet important paradigms: *DL* and *IoT*. In addition, the paper sheds light on the issues related with optimizing *DL* models for *IoT*. The target audience for this research are IT practitioners who are eager to apply the *DL* to edge and end devices, but they are concerned about how to choose the convenient models to be applied to their environments.

Why Is There A Need for DL Modeling for IoT? *DL* modeling is fueled by the increasing need to embed *DL* to *IoT* (end and edge devices) and the complexity of transferring *DL* to such limited capacity devices [7]. In addition, changing a DL model (its network structure and hyper-parameters) to fit a customized environment is an exhaustive empirical inquiry [8].

Applications of *DLN*s to *IoT* are endless. For example a small robot that applies object recognition could double the production rates and reduce human errors significantly [9]. In order to embed *DLN*s to *IoT*s (edge and end devices), optimizing *DLN*s is necessary. *DLN*s optimization targets not only reducing DL model size, but also optimizing the memory and computational requirements of *IoT*s to accelerate the inference on these limited devices.

2 Background and Review of Previous Related Research

2.1 Overview on Edge Computing and Internet of Things (IoT)

According to O'Connor [10], the *IoT* refers to "computing devices often with sensor capability to collect, share, and transfer data using the Internet" (p. 80). *IoT*s have many strategic benefits such as increasing automation and error rates, enhancing trust in asset management and providing greater predictability in risk-based decision-making [11]. The success of the *IoT*s and the huge amount of data generated from these devices created the need for *Edge computing* [5] in which data processing are performed near network edge, rather than centralized computing on the cloud. *Edge Computing (EC)* was developed to solve latency, network decency, costs, security, and privacy [12].

2.2   Overview on Deep Learning Model Management Systems (DL-MMS)

Research on model management in the area of edge computing and *IoT* are relatively few. A Model Management System (*MMS*) supports the creation, compilation, reuse, evolution, and execution of mappings between schemas represented in a wide range of meta-models [13]. The most challenging research question in developing *MMS* is how to support mappings between many popular metamodels.

Gupta [14] developed iFogSim to model *IoT* and Fog environments to measure the impact of resource management techniques in terms of latency, network congestion, energy consumption, and cost. However, the iFogSim didn't address the modeling of *DLNs* nor IoT as hardware. The research only focused on resource management policies in terms of network, RAM consumption, and execution time.

Ko et al. [15] presented a modeling framework for *Edge Computing (EC)* that provides useful guidelines, provisioning and planning. Unfortunately, the research focused on networking topologies only. There have been some recent attempts to address *DL* model management in both academia and industry, such as ModelHub, ModelDB, MLflow [8]. Unfortunately, most of these approaches either require a considerable amount of customization or they are limited to a specific commercial platform. In addition, none of them are targeting *IoT* devices.

ModelDB [16] is one of the early systems that aimed at addressing *DL* model management issues, and it comes very close to our solution in its functionality. However, ModelDB is tailored for specific machine learning models, and provides limited support for *DLNs*. ModelHub [8] is a high-profile deep learning management system that proposes a domain specific language to allow easy exploration of models, a model versioning system, and a deep-learning-specific storage system. It also provides a cloud-based repository. Schelter et al. [17] provided an automated tool to extract the model's metadata with an interactive visualization to query and compare experiments.

2.3   Gap in Literature

The findings of literature could be summarized in two directions: modeling for *EC* as a networking paradigm which moves computation near end devices; and modeling of the deep learning models to be applied to devices with high computational resources. However, none of the modeling techniques aggregated *DL* optimization for *IoT*. *DL* optimization modeling is more complicated than general *DL* modeling, where choosing the network best hyper parameter is just one sub problem in the *DL* optimization schema. Therefore, the proposed model management system is the first to provide modeling for *DL* optimization for *IoT*.

2.4   Objectives for DL Optimization

In this section, we are pointing out the pillars for *DL* Optimization which are *Privacy and Security, Compression, Quantization, and Hardware Optimization*

Privacy and Security: There is always a tradeoff between privacy, computational complexity and response delay as shown in Fig. 1. On the server side, shielded execution or assigning a secure enclave for custom models to be trained on the cloud server [18]. On the edge side, CryptoNets [19] and fog-based nodes are used to encrypt data.

Compression: compression aims to reduce the massive size of *DL* networks. One of the popular compression methods is the *Pruning* technique that eliminates the connections between neurons to directly reduce the feature map width and shrink the network size. However, removing neurons might be dramatically challenging because it will change the input of the following layer [20]. *Tensor Decomposition (TD)* is also used to further reduce the network weight especially for convolutional kernels which can be viewed as a 4D tensors. *TD* is derived by the intuition that there is a significant amount of redundancy in the 4D tensor [21].

Fine-tuning is another method used to train custom models with a generative objective, followed by an additional training stage with a discriminative objective. The underlying assumption is that a reasonably good result on the large training data set already puts the network near a local optimum in the parameter space so that even a small amount of new data is able to quickly lead to an optimum [22]. *Knowledge Distillation (KD)* [23] is another compression technique that involves training a quantized neural network (student model) with the help of a full-precision pre-trained network (teacher model). The compressed student model can take the benefit of transferring knowledge from the teacher model.

Quantization: Quantization aims at compacting the number of bits required to store the *DLN* weights usually from 64 bit to 8 bits [24]. Quantization of the *DLN* without training is a fast process but the accuracy of the resultant network is particularly low compared to quantized networks after training [25]. However, it remains an open problem as to what is the best level of quantization that won't hurt accuracy for a given network [26].

Hardware Optimization: Since *IoT*s are resource limited, hardware specs of *IoT* must be chosen carefully. The adoption of Field Programmable Gate Arrays (FPGA) offers 2-bit ternary and 1-bit binary *DLN*s which resulted in as high as 90% by pruning because FPGAs designed for extreme customizability [3].

Google's Tensor processing Unit *(TPU)* is powering a wide range of Google real time services. *TPU* often delivers 15x to 30x faster inference than CPU or GPU, and even more per watt power at a comparable cost level. Its outstanding inference performance originates from major design optimizations: Int8 quantization, *DNN*-inference-specific CISC instruction set, massively parallel matrix processor, and minimal deterministic design [27].

2.5   Knowledge Management Challenges for DL Optimization

The knowledge acquired by *DL* is in the form of tacit knowledge that cannot be converted to a mathematical formula or a logical model to be applied to other different problems. Let's at first summarize what are the major objectives for optimizing *DL* models as mentioned in the overview discussed earlier. We can conclude that there are six main objectives. Three are to be maximized which are *performance, reliability and security*. Another three are to be minimized which are *cost, latency, and complexity* as shown in Fig. 1. Unfortunately, there is no single solution that could overcome all these challenges. A solution might have a positive effect on one objective but negative effect on others as shown in Table 1. For example: pruning as an optimization technique enhances performance but increases latency. So, there is always a tradeoff between different objectives (e.g. tradeoff between performance and cost).

To elaborate the optimization methodologies and related issues, we divided the methodologies on the cloud side or the server side and the client side or the *IoT* side as shown in Fig. 2. The green shapes are the optimization methodologies and the red circles are the issues related to these methodologies. So, in case of no optimization method is used, bottlenecks, latency and performance degradation will occur [28]. When fine tuning is applied, a *discriminative objective* function should be applied, otherwise we will have training imbalance [29]. Compression techniques are trying to decrease the *DLN* size by shrinking weights, connection and layers. However, removing too much of the network could affect the *DLN* throughput and response time. Shielding for the company *DLN*s on cloud servers provides security but also increases performance overhead.

On the client side, optimizing the IoT device could be achieved by choosing a powerful processor, decent memory, and fast communication channels. However, without correct optimization on the cloud side, there are potential memory allocation problems, inference latency which decrease throughput and traffic overhead [30].

Table 1. Effects of optimization methods on different DL optimization objectives.

Optimization method	Performance	Latency reduction	Cost reduction	Complexity reduction	Reliability	Privacy
Pruning	+	−	+	+	+	0
Knowledge distillation	−	−	+	+	+	0
Quantization	−	+	+	+	−	0
Fog computing	+	−	−	−	+	+
Shielded execution	+	−	−	−	+	+
Tensor decomposition	−	+	+	+	−	0
Hardware optimization	+	+	−	−	+	0

(+) means to increase; (−) means to decrease; (0) means has no effect.

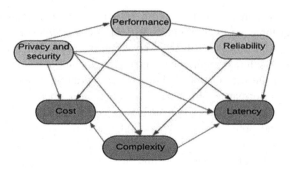

Fig. 1. DL optimization objectives.

3 Research Methodology

We are following a design science methodology called *complexity control* perspective for the design of the *DL* optimization Model [31]. This perspective is built upon the uncertainty of understanding the sociotechnical nature of complex systems. Therefore, we consider the proposed design as an initial iteration in a series of upcoming design iterations where the design is subject to change in each iteration. Based on the *complexity control* perspective, kernel theories are used to just predict how a particular design artifact will perform in the application environment. The supporting theoretical perspective for building the artifact should focus on the *information exchange* [32] and effective modeling.

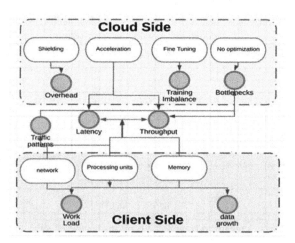

Fig. 2. Issues with each optimization methodology. (Color figure online)

To establish the rigor of the research, we built the DL optimization modeling schemas based on the established model of DM^3 ontology [13]. In addition, the developed schema not only contains the technical methodologies used in the optimization process, but also encompass quality metrics to evaluate different models [33]. The summary of the research activities of this research based on [34] design guidelines is summarized in Table 2:

Table 2. DSR guidelines-based activities of this research

DSR Guideline	Activity of this research project
Design as an artefact	Development of a DL optimization modeling schema for modeling DLNs application to IoT
Design evaluation	in this stage of the research program, the artefacts will be evaluated using illustrative example
Research rigor	Building the artefact based on established theories and utilization of established modeling techniques such as DM^3 [13]
Design as a search process	Research on DL, IoT, MMS, EC and other relevant literature in order to identify appropriate techniques & other results that could be used to inform the design of the procedure

4   Proposed Solution

4.1   The DL Optimization Model Schema

The *DL* optimization modeling lifecycle exposes several knowledge management challenges such as: a) managing many different models and their settings, b) large storage footprints of learned parameters, c) comparing models, d) selecting the best optimization techniques both in server and cloud side, and e) sharing models with others. Therefore, the first essential step is building a unified schema that structures the optimization process and eases the management processes. Abstracting the main classes of the *DL* optimization schema, it will be divided into modeling the *DLN* itself, modeling optimization techniques, and modeling end and edge device hardware as shown in Fig. 3. The proposed schema consists of six classes as shown in Table 3. However, the developed modeling schema is subject to change through the design iterations according to the *complexity control* perspective discussed earlier.

The first class of the *DL* optimization modeling schema is the *Model Class* that encompasses information about the previous models (meta-data) such as the date the model was built, the purpose (business focus), and the total cost. The *Model Class* is to ease the compare and contrast of different models and retrieval of models based on business focus and planned cost. The most important attribute in the *Model Class* is *Rating*. The *Rating* attribute is provided by the users who rate the model based on six objectives of *performance, reliability, security, cost, latency, and complexity*. All objectives have a fixed measure scale from 1 to 5 where 1 is the worst and 5 is the best. The first three objectives (i.e. *performance, reliability,* and *security*) are forward scaled, while the other three (i.e. *cost, latency, and complexity*) are reverse scaled. The rating attribute will help new users prioritize their preferences and it will ease the selection of the appropriate model.

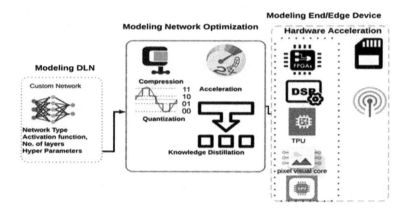

Fig. 3. DL optimization model components.

The *Cloud Configuration Class* encompasses the settings for the main *DLNs* on the cloud such as security protocols and cost plan. This class is important as running models on the cloud is costly and prone to security threats. The *End devices Specifications Class* provides information on the *IoT* technical specifications. The *Main DLN Class* aims at modeling the DLN specifications on the cloud which includes the network name, no. of layers, weights, hyper parameters, activation, and loss functions. For example: *DLN* is ResNet-50, activation is SoftMax, input and output layer size are 300.

The *Optimization Class* records the optimization techniques used such as the Tensor Decomposition and Quantization. The *Optimization Class*, the *Cloud Configuration Class and Main DLN Class* target the IT specialists to gain information about the technical requirements needed to implement DL optimization models. The *DL* Optimization model schema could be visualized as an ontology or a knowledge graph as in Fig. 4.

4.2 Performance Measures Class

The *Performance* class might be the most important class in the *DL* optimization model schema that nominates different models over others. The performance class is built upon the previous performance criteria discussed in the literature:

- The root-mean-square error (RMSE), mean absolute relative difference (MARD), and Mean Average Precision (mAP) that serve as the primary indicators to evaluate DLN accuracy [1].
- The vital performance goal of *DL* modeling for *IoT* is to decrease inference latency. Automated services relying on inference are required to respond in near real time. For example: self-driving cars require less than 200 ms inference time [27]. Latency is divided into two metrics: inference time and system response time.

- Throughput: measures the completed work amount against the time consumed. It also used to measure the performance of a processor, memory or network interaction [18].
- Energy watts to be measured in Watts, memory is measured in MB.
- Stability [35] (variance in accuracy for the same target). Stability could be measured by calculating the variance in the average accuracy measured every day for a certain period.

Table 3. Basic classes of the DL optimization model schema

Performance class	End devices specs. class	Main DLN class	Optimization class	Cloud conf. class	Model class
System latency	Name	Name	Quantization	Host address	Year created
Inference latency	CPU, GPU	Training dataset	KD	Response time	Rating
Accuracy	Memory	Hyper parameters	TD	Shielded execution	Application area
Stability (variance in accuracy for the same target)	Camera	Activation/loss functions	Pruning	Security protocols	Total cost
Average power consumption	DL mobile framework	No of layers	Fine-tuning	Cost plan	Purpose
Throughput	Price	No. of input/outputs	Algorithms	Backup-address	No. IoT devices

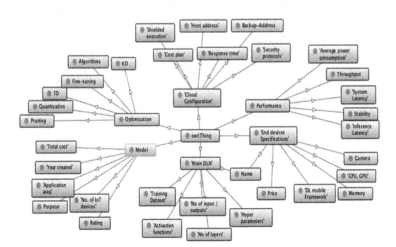

Fig. 4. The ontological representation DL optimization model schema

5   The DL for IoT Model Management Framework (DLOM^2)

Since *DL* optimization for *IoT* is still an emerging field, our model management framework might be one of the earliest attempts to address *DL* optimization for *IoT*. The model management system is not just a knowledge base for *DL* models, but also a prediction platform. Due to the limited knowledge about how to mix and match different optimization techniques to maximize *DL* modeling objectives, existing amalgamation of optimized *DL* techniques represents a rich knowledge repository that can be used to analyze, explore and create new models.

This knowledge repository keeps the optimized *DL* models saved according to the *DL* optimization schema presented earlier. The knowledge repository will ease querying of models based on different criteria using SPARQL. The architecture of DLOM^2 consists of four main components: *Cloud-based Repository, Graphical User Interface (GUI), Decision support system (DSS)*, and *a DL Modeling Network* as shown in Fig. 5.

5.1   Graphical User Interface (*GUI*)

The *GUI* is responsible for providing an interactive user interface to help them select the best *DL* model. The *GUI* is responsible for taking modeling requests and displaying results to the user. In the modeling request, several criteria will be chosen to select the best optimization *DL* model. The modeling request is sent to the *DSS* to select the best model. The *GUI* is also responsible for displaying suggested *DL* models along with explanation for the suggestion made.

5.2   Cloud Repository

The cloud repository is responsible for storing different *DL* optimization models based on the *DL* optimization schema provided earlier. However, it might be very complicated with all the information in a single repository. For example: it is not wise to store *DL* hyper parameters (technical, hard to read knowledge) along with performance metrics (human friendly knowledge). Therefore, there are four different repositories where each repository is responsible for storing certain classes to ease *management, maintenance and replication*. The four repositories are the DLN parameters repository, the client-side configurations repository, the server-side configurations repository, and the model and performance repository.

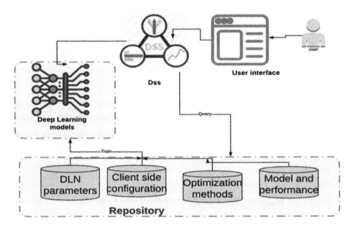

Fig. 5. The DLOM^2 architecture.

5.3 The DL Modeling Network

Since there are no predefined criteria to design the best optimization *DL* models, an *unsupervised DL* approach is needed to explore the patterns of the development of different *DLN* optimization models. Training a *DL* model will help to understand how *DLN* optimization models could be created. So, a *DL* network is trained with different optimization models previously stored in the repository. The optimization models are saved in the repository according to the schema introduced in the previous section. An example of how the *End devices Specs* class will look like according to the schema:

<End_devices_Specs >< Name > Raspberry   pi   3 </Name >< price > 70 </ price >< DLFramework > MobileNet V3 </DLFramework >< Memory > 8 GB </ Memory >< Camera > 16 MP </Camera > <CPU ></CPU ></End_devices_ Specs>

This model will be the training input for the DL modeling network. The *DLN* should be able analyze what are the combinations of optimization techniques that could maximize a certain criterion. The *DLN* should also infer the connection between the optimization techniques used in previous models to create new models that could even achieve better performance than existing models. However, it needs a huge number of successful optimization models to train such *DL* network.

DSS: The *DSS* simply retrieves existing models based on criteria submitted by the users. If more than one model retrieved. Then, the DSS let the users elucidate their preferences to further filter the retrieved models. Finally, the user decides whether to adopt one of the filtered models or to ask the DL network to predict a new model that would fit in the user requirement. The workflow of the DSS is shown in Fig. 6.

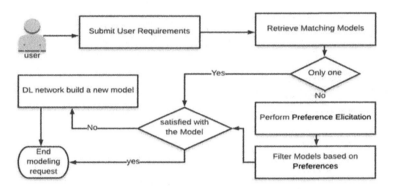

Fig. 6. The workflow of the DSS processes.

As shown in the figure, the selection criteria would have some mandatory requirement that would be the decision objectives. At first, relevant models are selected from the repository by querying the model that matches the user criteria. Next, the user should perform *Preference Elicitation* [36] to prioritize the desired set of objectives by giving weights to each objective in correspondence to other objectives as follows:

Decision Criteria: Let Prf_j, Rel_j, Sec_j, Cst_j, Lat_j, *and* Cmp_j be the values of the *performance, reliability, security, cost, latency, and complexity* respectively objectives for model $j \in J$, where the set J includes all of the models in the repository. Let w_{Prf}, w_{Rel}, w_{Sec}, w_{Cst}, w_{Lat}, w_{Cmp} be the weights for the *performance, reliability, security, cost, latency, and complexity* respectively objectives. The overall score for model j would be calculated as in Eq. 1:

$$Ovrl_j = w_{Prf} * Prf_j + w_{Rel} * Rel_j + w_{Sec} * Sec_j + w_{Cst} * Cst_j + w_{Lat} * Lat_j + w_{Cmp} * Cmp_j \tag{1}$$

The models could be ranked based on $Ovrl_j$, $j \in J$. In case that using queries didn't retrieve a model that matches the selection criteria, the DSS could send the selection criteria to the DLN modeling to create an optimization model that match the selection criteria. The DSS accordingly will select this new model as the optimum model. Then, the DSS will save a copy of the new model configurations in the repository.

6   Illustrative Example

In this section, we are going to explain how the framework works and what are expected inputs and outputs. A medical company ABC used the DLOM^2. The modeling request process goes through six steps where each step represents a class in the optimization model schema presented in Table 3. At step 1, the company determines the nature of the project and related attributes as in Figs. 7a. The company selected that the model cost should not exceed \$14 k for 10 end devices. The company has no certain specifications provided for IoT.

Then, at step 2, the company selects the attributes of the *Main DLN* as shown in Fig. 7b. Repeatedly, the user goes through the six classes of the *DL* modeling schema where each class represents a GUI interface. In the following steps, the user is asked if there are any preferences in specifying cloud server, end device specifications, and minimum accepted performance. Based on the requirements submitted by user, the framework builds a SPARQL query that encompasses all the requirements and turn them to query parameters to search for the matching models from the repository as shown in query 1, where "*apparea*" is the business focus and "*cost*" is the representing the budget.

Query 1:SELECT * WHERE { ?apparea a type: apparea; ?cost a type: cost FILTER (?no > = ?Nodevice)

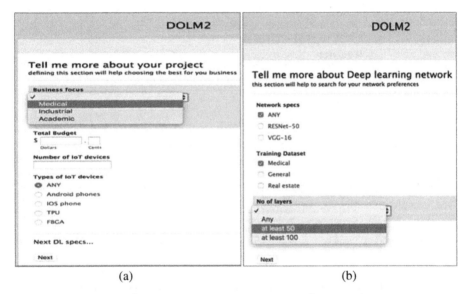

(a)   (b)

Fig. 7. (a) DOLM² modeling request step 1 (b) DOLM² modeling request step 2

The query retrieved three models that match the requirements submitted by the user. So, further refinement for results should be performed. In the next step, *Preference Elicitation* is performed to identify the user top priorities. For each Objective, a pairwise comparison operation is performed to determine the weights of each of the six objectives w_{Prf}, w_{Rel}, w_{Sec}, w_{Cst}, w_{Lat}, w_{Cmp}.

Each pairwise comparison has four possible weights of *Equal Importance, Weak Importance, Stronger Importance, Absolute importance* as shown in Fig. 8a. For example: performance has a preference over the cost and complexity, while latency has a weaker importance than security and cost. Substituting the values of the six rating dimensions Prf_j, Rel_j, Sec_j, Cst_j, Lat_j, and Cmp_j respectively to Eq. 1 using the weights submitted by the user.

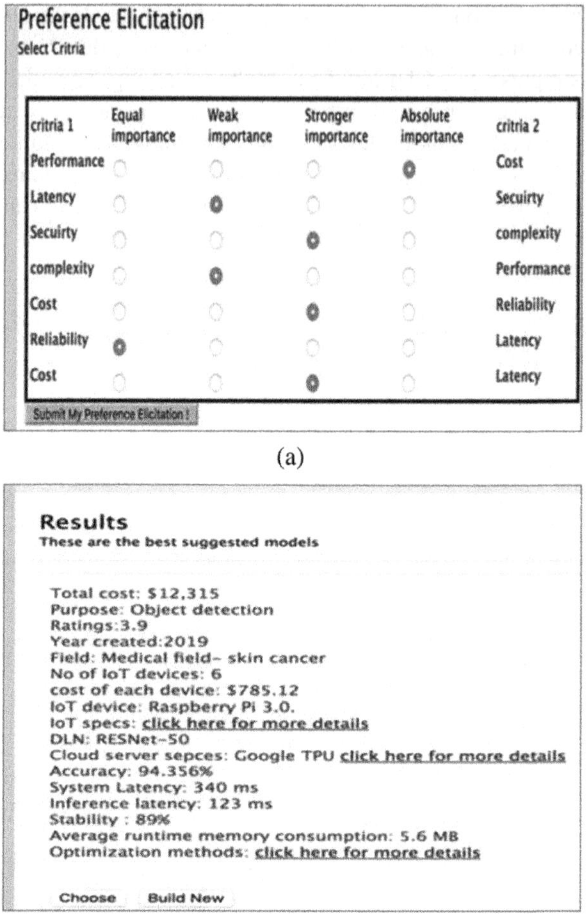

Preference Elicitation

Select Critria

critria 1	Equal importance	Weak importance	Stronger importance	Absolute importance	critria 2
Performance	○	○	○	◉	Cost
Latency	○	◉	○	○	Secuirty
Secuirty	○	○	◉	○	complexity
complexity	○	◉	○	○	Performance
Cost	○	○	◉	○	Reliability
Reliability	◉	○	○	○	Latency
Cost	○	○	◉	○	Latency

Submit My Preference Elicitation !

(a)

Results

These are the best suggested models

Total cost: $12,315
Purpose: Object detection
Ratings:3.9
Year created:2019
Field: Medical field– skin cancer
No of IoT devices: 6
cost of each device: $785.12
IoT device: Raspberry Pi 3.0.
IoT specs: click here for more details
DLN: RESNet–50
Cloud server sepces: Google TPU click here for more details
Accuracy: 94.356%
System Latency: 340 ms
Inference latency: 123 ms
Stability : 89%
Average runtime memory consumption: 5.6 MB
Optimization methods: click here for more details

Choose   Build New

(b)

Fig. 8. (a) Preference elicitation step. (b) Selected model results

Next, the DSS select the model with the highest $Ovrl_j$ as in Fig. 8b. However, the framework let the user decide whether to adopt the suggested model or to use the *DLN* to suggest a new model. If the user selected to build a new one, the requirements submitted by the user are sent to the *DL Modeling Network* to build a new model.

7   Discussion and Conclusion

Despite the complexity of *DL* models, it is no longer unreasonable to find an *IoT* device that can perform *DL* tasks. Thanks to *DL* and *IoT* optimization techniques which compress and accelerate *DL* models to fit into the tight computational tunnel of *IoTs* as end and edge devices. However, there are a myriad of optimization techniques but there is no certain criteria that selects the best optimization techniques to be applied to an

IoT. In addition, there are no certain optimization approach that could achieve all possible optimization objectives. This paper has two objectives. The first is to develop a DL for IoT optimization schema that joins the required optimization methods to ease model creation, selection, reuse and sharing. In addition, the paper put the abstract constituents to a *DL* optimization model management framework that could help the selection and creation of new *DL* optimization models according to user goals.

Thus, instead of using the mix and match methodologies to select the best optimization methods, the framework selects or creates new models based on the modeling history stored in the framework repository. However, there is some limitations in the paper, the first is that the proposed framework is considered an initial abstract design iteration and it needs further work to be completed. Future work is to follow an action research approach and ground theorizing to complete developing the framework. In other words, the design of the framework should be revisited to reflect the theoretical, strategic and business objectives to adopt *DLN*s for *IoT*s. Then, the instantiation and evaluation of the framework should reflect the best theoretical ground of the design.

References

1. Li, K., et al.: Convolutional recurrent neural networks for glucose prediction. IEEE J. Biomed. Health Inform. **24**, 603–613 (2019)
2. Wu, J., et al.: PocketFlow: An Automated Framework for Compressing and Accelerating Deep Neural Networks (2018)
3. Synced. Deep Learning in Real Time – Inference Acceleration and Continuous Training (2017)
4. Boos, D., et al.: Controllable accountabilities: the internet of things and its challenges for organisations. Behav. Inform. Technol. **32**(5), 449–467 (2013)
5. Elnagar, S., Thomas, M.: Federated Deep Learning: A Conceptual Model and Applied Framework for Industry 4.0 in Americas Conference on Information Systems 2020. AIS (2020)
6. Shi, W., et al.: Edge computing: vision and challenges. IEEE Internet Things J. **3**(5), 637–646 (2016)
7. Gharibi, G., et al.: Automated management of deep learning experiments. In: Proceedings of the 3rd International Workshop on Data Management for End-to-End Machine Learning. ACM (2019)
8. Miao, H., et al.: Towards unified data and lifecycle management for deep learning. In: 2017 IEEE 33rd International Conference on Data Engineering (ICDE). IEEE (2017)
9. Lyu, L., et al.: Fog-embedded deep learning for the internet of things. IEEE Trans. Ind. Inform. PP(99), 1–1 (2019)
10. O'Connor, Y., et al.: Privacy by design: informed consent and internet of things for smart health. Procedia Comput. Sci. **113**, 653–658 (2017)
11. Lunardi, W.T., Decision support IoT framework: device discovery and stream analytics (2016)
12. Li, H., Ota, K., Dong, M.: Learning IoT in edge: deep learning for the Internet of Things with edge computing. IEEE Netw. **32**(1), 96–101 (2018)
13. Li, Y., Thomas, M.A., Osei-Bryson, K.-M.: Ontology-based data mining model management for self-service knowledge discovery. Inform. Syst. Front. **19**(4), 925–943 (2017)

14. Gupta, H., et al.: iFogSim: a toolkit for modeling and simulation of resource management techniques in the Internet of Things, Edge and Fog computing environments. Softw.: Pract. Exp. **47**(9), 1275–1296 (2017)

15. Ko, S.-W., Han, K., Huang, K.: Wireless networks for mobile edge computing: spatial modeling and latency analysis. IEEE Trans. Wireless Commun. **17**(8), 5225–5240 (2018)

16. Vartak, M., et al.: Model DB: a system for machine learning model management. In: Proceedings of the Workshop on Human-In-the-Loop Data Analytics. ACM (2016)

17. Schelter, S., et al.: Automatically tracking metadata and provenance of machine learning experiments. In: Machine Learning Systems workshop at NIPS (2017)

18. Kunkel, R., et al.: TensorSCONE: a secure TensorFlow framework using Intel SGX. arXiv: 1902.04413 (2019)

19. Gilad-Bachrach, R., et al.: Cryptonets: Applying neural networks to encrypted data with high throughput and accuracy. In: International Conference on Machine Learning (2016)

20. Hanson, S.J. Pratt, L.Y.: Comparing biases for minimal network construction with back-propagation. In: Advances in neural information processing systems (1989)

21. Yang, Z., et al.: Deep fried convnets. In: Proceedings of the IEEE International Conference on Computer Vision (2015)

22. Alsing, O.: Mobile Object Detection using TensorFlow Lite and Transfer Learning (2018)

23. Hinton, G., Vinyals, O., Dean, J.: Distilling the knowledge in a neural network. arXiv:1503. 02531 (2015)

24. Han, S., Mao, H., Dally, W.J.: Deep compression: Compressing deep neural networks with pruning, trained quantization and huffman coding. arXiv:1510.00149 (2015)

25. Goncharenko, A., et al.: Fast adjustable threshold for uniform neural network quantization. arXiv:1812.07872 (2018)

26. Jacob, B., et al.: Quantization and training of neural networks for efficient integer-arithmetic-only inference. In: Proceedings of the IEEE Conference on Computer Vision and Pattern Recognition (2018).

27. Zhang, X., Wang, Y., Shi, W.: pcamp: Performance comparison of machine learning packages on the edges. in {USENIX} Workshop on Hot Topics in Edge Computing (HotEdge 18) (2018)

28. Niu, W., et al.: 26 ms Inference Time for ResNet-50: Towards Real-Time Execution of all DNNs on Smartphone. arXiv:1905.00571 (2019)

29. Bhunia, A.K., et al.: Query-based Logo Segmentation. arXiv:1811.01395 (2018)

30. Frajberg, D., et al. Accelerating Deep Learning inference on mobile systems. In: International Conference on AI and Mobile Services. Springer (2019)

31. Gregor, S., Hevner, A.R.: Positioning and presenting design science research for maximum impact. MIS Q. **37**, 337–355 (2013)

32. Chang, S.-K.: Information exchange theory and man-machine interaction. In: 1982 21st IEEE Conference on Decision and Control. IEEE (1982)

33. Elnagar, S., Yoon, V., Thomas, M.: An automatic ontology generation framework with an organizational perspective. In: Proceedings of the 53rd Hawaii International Conference on System Sciences (2020)

34. Hevner, A., et al.: Design science research in information systems. MIS Q. **28**(1), 75–105 (2004)

35. Minitab: What is measurement stability (2018) https://support.minitab.com/en-us/minitab/ 18/help-and-how-to/quality-and-process-improvement/measurement-system-analysis/ supporting-topics/other-gage-studies-and-measures/what-is-measurement-stability/

36. Chen, L., Pu, P.: Survey of preference elicitation methods (2004)

HapiFabric: A Teleconsultation Framework Based on Hyperledger Fabric

Hossain Kordestani[1,2(✉)] ⓘ, Kamel Barkaoui[2] ⓘ, and Wagdy Zahran[1]

[1] Department of Research and Innovation, Maidis SAS, Chatou, France
{hossain.kordestani,wagdy.zahran}@maidis.fr
[2] Centre d'études et de recherche en informatique et communications,
Conservatoire National des Arts et Métiers, Paris, France
kamel.barkaoui@lecnam.net
http://www.maidis.fr
https://cedric.cnam.fr

Abstract. Due to longevity, the world population is getting older; this leads to an enormous number of patients with chronic diseases. Their vulnerability in facing viral and bacterial diseases, in particular in the case of the outbreak of the coronavirus, promotes teleconsultation since the latter reduces their physical interactions and consequently, their chance of contamination. Teleconsultation is considered more economical, comfortable, and practical compared to face-to-face consultations. Due to the criticality of the data and process in teleconsultation, there are numerous concerns, in particular in terms of reliability and security. Moreover, similar to all financial systems; the transparency concerns are also prominent in teleconsultation. To this end, we propose HapiFabric, a teleconsultation framework based on Hyperledger Fabric. Our proposed framework exploits this blockchain technology to improve security, reliability, and transparency of teleconsultation workflows. Without losing generality, we prioritize the elderly and patients with chronic diseases in HapiFabric becasue of their vulnerability. Our innovative teleconsultation workflows cooperate with a telemonitoring service to provide comprehensive medical care at the patients' homes. We exploited Hapicare, an existing healthcare monitoring system with self-adaptive coaching using probabilistic reasoning, as one of the main participants of HapiFabric which provides telemonitoring services. Moreover, HapiFabric has other participants, namely patients, doctors, insurance, and auditors. We have opted for off-chain data storage of medical data using the InterPlanetary File System (IPFS). We evaluate the HapiFabric framework using two scenarios.

Keywords: Teleconsultation · Blockchain · Medical workflow · BPMN · Hyperledger Fabric · IPFS

This work was supported by the French National Research and Technology Agency (ANRT)[CIFRE Reference number 2018/0284].

M. Themistocleous et al. (Eds.): EMCIS 2020, LNBIP 402, pp. 399–414, 2020.
https://doi.org/10.1007/978-3-030-63396-7_27

1 Introduction

The emergence of technology has important impacts on several application domains, including ambient assisted living [13,15,18], rehabilitation [14], and healthcare [10,11,16,17]. In the healthcare domain, the necessity of a teleconsultation system is inevitable, especially with the outbreak of coronavirus (SARS-CoV-2) in 2020. As the governments implement lockdowns to stop the contamination cycles of this lethal virus, access to medical care become more difficult. The need is more critical for the elderly and people with chronic diseases prone to deaths because of coronaviruses [23]; they are also in need of regular visits to their doctors. In normal days, there is 0.6 consultation per year for each aged person [27]. However, the need for consultation arises during a health crisis. On the other hand, access to clinicians is not evenly distributed; people living in suburbs and small towns might require long trips to visit their doctors, which puts them at higher risk of contamination. Therefore, teleconsultation have recently achieved a huge amount of attention to deal with these challenges.

Besides the health benefits of teleconsultations during viral outbreaks, remote treatments tend to be economically and environmentally better solutions as they remove the need to travel for medical treatments.

Moreover, patients favor teleconsultation, given the aforementioned benefits and more comforts. A six-month pilot run of teleconsultation services[22] supports this claim, as it received full satisfaction from the patients. In this pilot run, more than one-third of patients opted for teleconsultation, who had averagely saved 66 min of travel in avoiding 49 km to the doctors' office. In [22], as well as the direct costs of a face-to-face consultation, the indirect ones are also discussed, particularly the costs related to the travel and absence from work of the accompanying persons. Although the teleconsultation system discussed in the aforementioned study focuses on specialist radiotherapy services, seemingly the results can be generalized for different types of teleconsultations. For example, TELEDIABE [5] is dedicated to patients who have diabetes; yet received similar positive feedbacks from its users. For each teleconsultation using TELEDIABE, the patients averagely saved 115 min and 80 euros.

Although teleconsultation has undeniable benefits over face-to-face consultations, there are various concerns that slow the deployment of such systems. These concerns can be generally categorized into two classes: (1) the security of medical information and (2) the financial aspects of such systems. One of the most tangible examples of the former class of concerns is the confidentiality of the data in transit required for teleconsultation; e.g., medical files, prescription, and video calls. Because of the criticality of medical information, they are used to be stored in an isolated network; however, for a teleconsultation, this practice is no longer applicable, which raises this concern of confidentiality. The latter class of concerns roughly exists in most online financial systems; however, teleconsultation is arguably more complicated. In common online systems only consists of providers and consumers; contrarily, in the teleconsultation, insurance acts as a third actor. Various approaches have been studied to address the aforementioned concerns; one of the recent technologies that can be applied for handling these concerns is blockchain technology. The latter is a chain of data blocks to form a decentralized data structure; the blocks in the blockchain are linked together using cryptographic algorithms. Blockchain is intrinsically considered secure, reliable, consistent, and transparent [9]. Hence, it is a perfect fit for the infrastructure of teleconsultation services.

To the best of our knowledge, only a few studies had used blockchain technology for teleconsultation; the closest existing approach is DermoNet [12], which is telemedicine specific for dermatology. However, given the importance of security of medical data, many studies have been carried out to secure Electrical Health Records (EHRs) [24,25,28]. In [25], encrypting the records over the network while preserving a balance between the patients' privacy and data confidentiality. Similarly, FHIRChain is proposed in [28] which integrates blockchain technology in HL7-FHIR. The latter stands for Health Level 7-Fast Healthcare Interoperability Resources, is a standard for exchanging EHRs created by HL7 [8]. FHIRChain has improved HL7-FHIR in terms of modularity, integrity, access control, and trust; these improvements are because of intrinsic features of blockchain. Another approach of using blockchain is proposed in [24], which applies blockchain technology for aggreation of EHRs coming from different sources and implementing a content-based access control for patients. The benefits of these approaches in securing EHRs are indisputable; in particular they can be used even for telemedicine as well as other medical services. However, they fail to get the most of blockchain technology; in particular the transparency and modularity of medical workflow which are vital for addressing the concerns on financial aspects as well as the security concerns of teleconsultations. In DermoNet [12], blockchain technology is applied to avail the management of patients' data as well as vast access to specialists to the patients. Although DermoNet is a promising tool for its purpose, i.e., telemedicine for dermatology, it lacks the requirements for integrating with other health services, such as monitoring.

In this paper, we propose *HapiFabric*, a teleconsultation framework based on Hyperledger Fabric[1]; this framework couples with our previous work *Hapicare* [11] to provide holistic medical care for patients, in particular, the elderlies and the patients with chronic diseases. Hapicare is a healthcare monitoring system with self-adaptive coaching using probabilistic reasoning. Since the elderly and patients with chronic diseases were the target population of Hapicare, and they are vulnerable in face-to-face medical visits, we continue to prioritize them in HapiFabric. The proposed framework can be also useful for the general use and the benefits of the general public. Hapicare provides medical telemonitoring services for the patients when they are at their homes; in the case of a need for the intervention of a doctor, HapiFabric provides the infrastructure of a teleconsultation. Moreover, if doctors decide that their patients require continuous monitoring during a teleconsultation on HapiFabric, they can prescribe Hapicare. Hence, HapiFabric is coupled with Hapicare by design. Consequently, Hapicare is an additional actor in the HapiFabric framework for data collection required remote examination. HapiFabric and Hapicare are complementary to each other

---

[1] https://www.hyperledger.org/use/fabric.

and coupled together to improve the health of patients at their homes; Fig. 1 illustrates the interactions between these two frameworks.

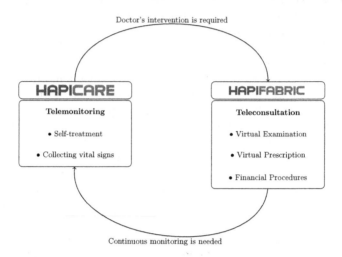

Fig. 1. The interaction between Hapicare and HapiFabric

The main contributions of *HapiFabric* are as follows:

- A framework for teleconsultation with modularity, security, reliability, and transparency using blockchain technology
- Use of Hyperledger Fabric as a private blockchain
- An innovative teleconsultation coupled with telemonitoring: in HapiFabric, we introduce teleconsultation services to add doctors' supervision to complete the telemonitoring in Hapicare.

The remainder of this paper is structured as follows: in Sect. 2, the principles of the blockchain are described. The details of the HapiFabric framework, is explained in Sect. 3. Two scenarios are provided and discussed in Sect. 4 to evaluate the HapiFabric framework. Lastly, conclusion and future works are presented in Sect. 5.

2   From BitCoin to Hyperledger Fabric

Blockchain belongs to Decentralized Ledger Technology (DLT) [20], which is a consensus of replication, share, and synchronization of data. The distribution can be completely decentralized without central data storage. Fundamentally, blockchain is a data structure formed by linked lists of blocks, chains of blocks. Each block stores a replication of data, as they all are distributed and shared across a peer-to-peer network. The connection between the blocks is via hash values and digital signature, which are one-way cryptographic functions; hence,

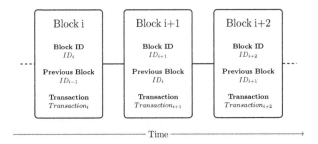

Fig. 2. A schema of blockchain network

modification of a block is only possible if all the blocks after that are modified [21]. Figure 2 depicts a schema of blockchain, in which the ID_i is a cryptographic signature based on the contents of ith block; i.e., any change in the contents of this block would invalidate that signature. The most popular application of blockchain is a peer-to-peer anonymous cash system, named BitCoin [19].

Although blockchain was around for some years, with BitCoin's success, the background technology has also gained more attention; in other words, researchers try to apply blockchain in various domains. However, in BitCoin, the transactions are simple cryptocurrency transfer. To use blockchain for more complex transactions in other domains, structured scripting for application development in blockchain is needed, which promotes the second generation of blockchain. In which, *Smart contracts* have been introduced to enable using blockchain for workflows. Smart contracts can be defined as a program in which its execution is triggered once a transaction occurs. This feature is useful for enforcing required actions upon different transactions, e.g., enforcing tax-payment upon the purchase of a product or service. Ethereum [6] is second-generation blockchain platform; which features smart contracts. In Ethereum, a modified version of the blockchain is used, i.e., it consists of state machines. Each transaction causes a change in the state. In other words, the next state depends on the data of the current state and the current transaction. For instance, in a finance system, the states are balance sheets of members of that system, and transactions are any activities that affect the states of the system. E.g., "Alice has 2 euros, and Bob has 5 euros" is a state, while "Bob transfers 1 euro to Alice" is a transaction which will change the state to the new state of "Alice has 3 euros, and Bob has 4 euros." In Ethereum, each script's execution would cost a fee depending on the complexity of the script referred to *gas*. Although Ethereum improves the blockchain platform to use more complex transactions, however, in Ethereum, similar to blockchain, all the nodes have a copy of the entire states; they are designed to be public; although they can be set up in a private network, any members of that network have access to node contents. They provide anonymity and transparency to the fullest, but the tradeoff is privacy and scalability; which makes them unsuitable for the application that a controlled transparency is required. Although this limitation can be mitigated

Table 1. A simplified overview of comparison between Hyperledger Fabric versus Ethereum [26]

Criterion	Ethereum	Hyperledger fabric
Type of membership	Permissionless and Permissioned	Only Permissioned
User Identifications	Decentralized Anonymous Users	Centralized, the nodes are known
Sybil attack protection	Using huge power required for computing proof-of-work	Using identity management
Latency	Poor-up to 1 h	Depends of implementation-matter of milliseconds
Throughput	15 transactions per second	More than 10,000 with the existing implementations
Temporary forks	Possible (might lead to double-spending attacks)	Not pssible
Consensus finality	No	Yes
Consensus Protocol	Proof-of-Work [6]	Practical Byzantine Fault Tolerance [26]
Smart Contract Language	Solidity [6]	Go and Java [26]
Scalability [7]	Less scalable	More scalable

with the installation of Ethereum in a private manner; it rests another limitation in its throughput, as it is limited to only 7 to 15 transactions per second [2]. To this end, another approach is private blockchain networks, commonly known as permissioned blockchain. The latter features protocols for authentication, authorization, and permission of actions. They often have central identity management and hence are not ideal for a very large number of nodes. However, their throughput can be more than 10,000 transactions per second [26], which is incomparable with the throughput of BitCoin and Ethereum. *Hyperledger Fabric* is an implementation of permissioned blockchain for running smart contracts, using familiar technologies [3]. For instance, the smart contracts in Hyperledger Fabric are called *Chaincode*, and they can be written in Go[2] or Java languages[3]. Hyperledger Fabric is built on a modular architecture and allows scalable consensus mechanism which enhance the global scalibilty of the application use case. Table 1 presents an overview of differences between the Ethereum and Hyperledger Fabric. In which, *Sybil attack* is an attack wherein the attacker creates

---

[2] https://golang.org/.
[3] https://www.java.com/.

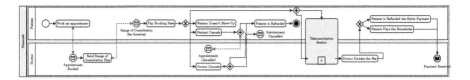

Fig. 3. The simplified process model of a financial aspects of a teleconsultation session

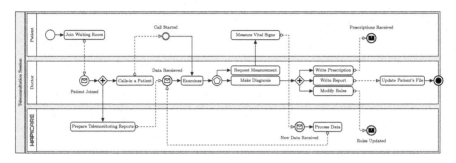

Fig. 4. The simplified process model of a teleconsultation session

numerous fake identities to affect the system. Moreover, *consensus finality* is the affirmation that blocks in the blockchain are final and will not be revoked.

The Hyperledge Fabric is a permissioned network, the nodes are all identified and can have three roles, namely *Clients*, *Peers*, and *Ordering Service Nodes*, defined as follows [3]:

- *Clients* submit the proposal of transactions.
- *Peers* execute the proposals of transactions, and validate them. Peers keep blockchain ledgers. The latter contains the immutable records of transactions. Only a subset of peers, namely the endorsing peers (also known as endorsers) can execute the proposals. The committing peers (also known as committers) validate the transactions.
- *Ordering Service Nodes* (also known as orderers) collects the transactions that are approved by endorser and distribute them between the committers.

3   HapiFabric

Given the aforementioned challenges in the workflow, namely the security and modularity concerns, and the properties of Hyperledger Fabric, we introduce HapiFabric, a teleconsultation framework coupled with telemonitoring exploiting Hyperledger Fabric. We have opted for this blockchain technology. It provides more flexibility and throughput, which are vital for our application.

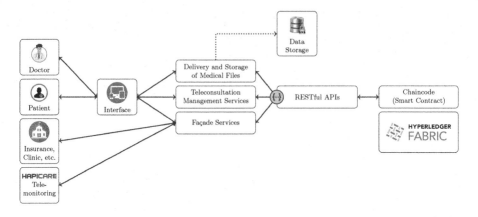

Fig. 5. Architecture of HapiFabric Framework

3.1 Architecture

The general architecture of HapiFabric is depicted in Fig. 5. The chaincodes are the core of blockchain applications built on Hyperledger Fabric; we use the Representational state transfer (REST) interface for accessing these codes. There are generally three types of REST application programming interfaces (APIs): (1) APIs used for the management of medical files; e.g., delivery and storing of them; (2) APIs used for teleconsultation management; e.g., appointment management, scheduling, document sharing, and video conferencing; and (3) Façade APIs used for organizational access; e.g., telemonitoring and insurance. Doctors and patients can use the APIs through the web interface.

3.2 Participants and Assets

A typical teleconsultation service consists of a doctor who gives out the consultation and a patient who receives that. Mapping a typical teleconsultation into Business Process Model and Notation (BPMN) consists of two actors, and the shared resources can be agendas, waiting room, video call channel, prescription, and report. In HapiFabric, as we couple teleconsultation with telemonitoring, we have an additional actor, which brings additional shared resources.

The main members of the BPMN of HapiFabric, commonly known as participants, are listed as follows:

- *Doctors* provide teleconsultation. Doctors hold the video conference sessions, author prescriptions reports, and compose medical rules.
- *Patients* use HapiFabric to receive teleconsultation.
- *Hapicare* [11] provides telemonitoring services to the patients. This participant consumes collected data from the patient and the medical rules from the doctor and provides analyzed data to the doctor and some coaching to the patient.

- *Insurance companies* interact with doctors for reimbursements. This member share financial assets with doctors and patients.
- *Auditors* examine the transactions, e.g., fiscal auditors.
- *Clinics* act as the intermediate between doctors and patients.

The main resources used in the BPMN of HapiFabric, usually known as assets, are the followings:

- *Agenda* is the group of assets related to doctors' available time-slots and the booked ones by the patients.
- *Video channel* is used as a medium of teleconsultation. This asset is shared between the doctor and the patient of a teleconsultation session.
- *Virtual waiting room* is a place resembling doctors' waiting room; that holds the patients who are online and waiting to be called in.
- *Prescription* is one of the primary outcomes of teleconsultation sessions. This asset could contain some drug names, their dosages, and their use guidelines. Presciptions could also include some additional diagnostic steps, such as blood exams.
- *Payment* is the group of assets related to the financial transaction, including payment card details, prepayment amounts, and fees.
- *EHRs* are the medical files of patients, which include all the visit reports.
- *Monitoring reports* are the products of *Hapicare* telemonitoring services. This asset contains vital signs, symptoms, and other information about the patients during their stays at home.
- *Monitoring rules* are based on the expert knowledge used in *Hapicare*. The rules are used to analyze captured data and provide suitable coaching based on the medical conditions.

3.3 Teleconsultation Workflow

Teleconsultation is defined as medical consultation services provided at distance. Multiple workflows form a teleconsultation service. The followings are the main workflows in teleconsultation:

1. Agenda management: The doctor provides a list of his/her available times, and the patient selects and books one of them.
2. Virtual examination and prescription: The doctor asks the patient for symptoms and exam results for his/her diagnosis and consequently providing a prescription.
3. Finance management: The doctor bills the patient based on the type of consultation, based on the insurance plan of the patient, the sum will be paid to the doctor via the patient and the insurance company.
4. Income share: The amount might be received by a clinic, which would share the amount with the doctor and the infrastructure provider.

An overview of third workflow is shown in Fig. 3; in which the second workflow is depicted as a box. Before the teleconsultation session starts, a few prerequisite steps happen: a doctor previously has provided some time-slot for the times at which he/she is available for teleconsultation sessions; then a patient upon his/her will or based on the suggestion of Hapicare books one of them. It is common in medical consultation that the exact fee is not decided until the end of the session, as different types of consultations cost differently. At the time of booking the appointment, the patient would select a reason for consultation; on that basis, a range of consultation fees are provided. One of the doctors' concerns is false bookings; i.e., since the procedure of booking is very simple, malicious users book the time-slots of a doctor without the intention of using them; it blocks real patients from accessing the doctors. To this end, one common practice is prior payment; since the exact consultation fee is not decided in the booking time, the patient would pay a defined fee enough to discourage false booking. Either party can cancel the appointment, resulting in the refunding the prepayment. Upon concluding the teleconsultation session, the doctor decided a consultation fee; if this fee is lower than the prepayment, the extra amount is returned to the patient; otherwise, the patient pays the difference. Once the doctor has received the payment, it will be stored in his/her logbook for future reference for insurance reimbursements and fiscal aspects.

The core of teleconsultation is the *virtual examination and prescription* workflow; the simplified process model of this core workflow is shown in Fig. 4. The core workflow, depicted as a box in Fig. 3 and detailed in 4, starts on the time of appointment. The patient logs-in the system to join the virtual waiting room. Similar to physical consultation, a waiting room is vital to provide flexibility for doctors to spend enough time with each patient. Upon joining each patient, the doctor is notified, and the waiting room is updated. The doctor (or his/her secretary) can always check who is in the waiting room, consultation reasons and scheduled appointments, and how long patients are online in the waiting room. This information allows the doctor to manage better his/her time to visit all the patients in a timely manner.

Moreover, Hapicare starts preparing all the data about the patient who has joined the waiting room. Once the doctor selects a patient to start the video call, this data is transferred to the doctor to help him to have holistic information about the patient. The doctor examines the Hapicare file and asks some questions; he/she might ask for additional measurements. The patient can provide them using his/her connected sensors. After measuring the vital signs, Hapicare will collect the information and transfer them to the doctor. Once the doctor has enough information about the patient to make a diagnosis; he/she would typically write a prescription for the patient; the prescription might include additional diagnosis steps, such as blood exams or referral letters for a specialist. The doctor would also write some reports in the medical file of the patient. If necessary, he/she might also update some of the telemonitoring rules in Hapicare, based on his/her diagnosis; with the conclusion of the teleconsultation session, the rest general workflow (see Fig. 3) continues with *the doctor deciding a consultation fee*.

The workflow is dynamic and might differ based on the needs. For example, a doctor can impose some regulations to charge last-minute cancellations. Moreover, given the pace of advancement in technology and consequently, the change of procedures, it is inevitable to have changes in the workflows of teleconsultation. For example, in the near future, with the necessary infrastructure, the prescription might be sent directly to an online pharmacy. The patient receives his medications at his home. The dynamicity of teleconsultation workflows calls for an adaptable system to consider such charastric.

On the other hand, there are various security concerns to be considered regarding teleconsultation. The most critical concern is the confidentiality of data; because the teleconsultation inevitably involves some confidential information, such as medical files of patients. Other security concerns include the availability of teleconsultation services, the integrity of prescription and reports, the integrity of payment logbook, and transparency of prescription history. To this end, we use blockchain technology to address the challenges mentioned above in teleconsultation. Given the comparison discussed in Table 1, Hyperledger Fabric better suits the requirements of teleconsultation, as it provides access control and a higher level of performance.

3.4 Storage

In HapiFabric, there are two groups of data; the transactional data, which are arguably equivalent to logs in traditional systems, and the functional data which include medical files, profiles, appointment data. The blockchain data structure is optimized for the validation of transactions; it is not best suited for storing a large amount of data [1]. Hence, we opted for off-chain data storage for the functional data. IPFS [4] stands for InterPlanetary File System, a decentralized file system that allows access, storage, and security of files on a distributed network. Given its characteristics, IPFS is a common practice for off-chain data storage. Hence, in HapiFabric, we use IPFS for storing the functional data; and use chaincodes for the access control.

3.5 Chaincode

Chaincodes are the core of the HapiFabric; we use Go for developing the chaincodes. The main chaincodes related to the functionalities of HapiFabric are as follows:

- *Agenda Management* are the transactions related to doctors' availability and their booking by the patients. Both parties can update the appointment assets and submit them to the system.
- *Payment Management* is a group of transactions that are related to payments. That includes the prepayment by the patient, the decision of fee by the doctor, and paying the outstanding amount by the patient. Hence, both parties can write in this transaction to submit to the system.

– *Treatment* is the transaction that includes the treatment plan of the doctor; in other words, it is a combination of Hapicare rules, prescriptions, and consultation reports. Doctors write this transaction.
– *Telemonitoring* is the transaction that records the reports of patients during their stay at home. Hapicare writes this transaction.

Blockchains, including Hyperledger Fabric, operate on the principle of assets, participants, and transactions. Hence, upon creating, updating, or deleting any of the assets, participants, and transactions, Hyperledger Fabric records this event and appends it to the immutable logbook on the distributed ledger. The trails provide transparent details of operations in the network, which are useful for the auditors.

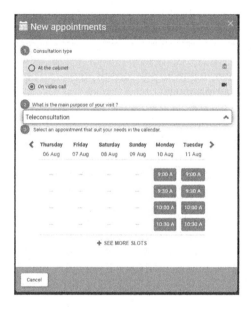

Fig. 6. Patient's view of the appointment selection

4   Use Case

HapiFabric is in the continuation of Hapicare; they are complementary to each other (see Fig. 1). The proposed framework is evaluated using two different scenarios. The screenshots of the

4.1   Scenario - 1

In this scenario, we follow the use-case discussed in [11]. The doctor and the patient use Hapicare as a telemonitoring system and HapiFabric as a teleconsultation system. Jack is a patient of Dr. Smith; he had been diagnosed with diabetes about two years ago. Recently, Dr. Smith has prescribed him to switch to insulin. Hapicare monitors Jack's vital signs and symptoms to make sure his blood sugar stays normal. Hapicare records multiple hyperglycemia; it then suggests Jack to take an appointment using HapiFabric based on the analysis of the measurements. Dr. Smith has provided time-slots for teleconsultation, and Jack selects one of them for booking (see Fig. 6). Dr. Smith requests a prepayment of 5 euros to discourage false bookings. Once Jack selects a time-slot and pays the prepayment amount, the appointment transaction and payment transactions are executed and committed in Hyperledger Fabric.

Fig. 7. Doctor's view of the virtual waiting room

At the time of appointment, Jack joins the waiting room; Dr. Smith will get notified of his presence, and he can call him in (see Fig. 7). Dr. Smith accesses the *telemonitoring* transactions that include the reports of Jack's frequent hyperglycemia. Moreover, he also accesses the *treatment* transactions to know his course of treatment. Dr. Smith concludes to prescribe Jack for an additional dosage of insulin. He also writes an additional rule for Hapicare to monitor him more closely for the coming days for symptoms of hypoglycemia. This new prescription and the new medical rule, are written into the treatment transactions and committed in Hyperledger Fabric. Dr. Smith decides the fee of consultation is 25 euros by writing into the payment transactions. Jack would pay the difference in the HapiFabric web interface.

4.2 Scenario - 2

Jill, 62 years old, had a mild heart attack recently. Her doctor, Dr. Brown, has recently been diagnosed with COVID-19. However, Dr. Brown's condition is not severe, but he opted for teleconsultation to avoid the risks of contamination. Dr. Brown asks Jill to take an appointment on HapiFabric to follow-up her treatment. During the teleconsultation, Dr. Brown understands that Jill's children have stopped visiting her because of the lockdown related to COVID-19; there is no person to take care of Jill's health situations. Hence, Dr. Brown prescribes Jill to use Hapicare to monitor her conditions continuously. In this case, Jill's treatment transaction has been updated and submitted to the Hyperledger Fabric. The appointment and financial processes are similar to the previous scenario.

4.3 Discussion

In the given scenarios, the cooperation between the two telemedicine solutions, namely HapiFabric and Hapicare [11], is shown. In the first one, Hapicare would redirect the patient to HapiFabric when a doctor's intervention was required; and in the second scenario, the doctor has prescribed Hapicare to monitor the patient at home using HapiFabric.

HapiFabric has two sources of added values: (1) telemedicine services and (2) Hyperledger Fabric. The scenarios show how telemedicine helps patients without any replacement at their maximum comfort. In particular, teleconsultation saves both parties' time and money, as they avoid the trips to the clinic or doctors' office. Another bold benefit of teleconsultation is during health crisis and viral outbreaks, as it promotes a healthier solution for medical consultation.

Hyperledger Fabric has easily configurable access control, which promotes the confidentiality and privacy of the medical data. The trails are tamper-proof; hence auditors can quickly look up the logbooks to see for the events in Hapi-Fabric. Moreover, Hyperledger Fabric enables modularity; hence the dynamic changes in HapiFabric are straight-forward. Because of the architecture of Hyperledger Fabric which splits the execution of chaincodes (smart contracts), Hapi-Fabric can also perform well in scale.

5   Conclusion

The population is growing old across the globe; almost all of the elderly suffer from chronic diseases. Managing them is necessary and costly; hence, it is vital to use technology to deal with this challenge. The outbreak of the coronavirus in 2020 has pointed the importance of remote medical care. Although telemonitoring is vital for managing patients at their homes, yet in many cases, it is not sufficient. In other words, telemonitoring brings e-nurses to the patients' homes; but sometimes it is important to bring doctors, too. Teleconsultation can be considered as an efficient approach for this matter. It has multiple advantages over traditional face-to-face consultations; including removing the time and costs of travel to the doctors' office and removing the physical contact, which increases the chance of contamination. In this paper we have proposed Hapi-Fabric, a framework for a teleconsultation service coupled with telemonitoring service. HapiFabric is a BPM implementation of teleconsultation service over Hyperledger Fabric technology. The latter is a permissioned blockchain technology that provides access control in addition to transparency, and security to our framework. In this paper, we have discussed two scenarios to show how HapiFabric and Hapicare can cooperate, and how HapiFabric exploits blockchain technology to deliver teleconsultation service. In terms of research perspectives to this study, an interesting topic is to formally model the HapiFabric workflows and verify their strength against various attacks. Another interesting research direction to explore is to deploy HapiFabric for use in the real world to receive feedback from doctors and patients.

References

1. A Blockchain Platform for the Enterprise - hyperledger-fabricdocs master documentation. https://hyperledger-fabric.readthedocs.io/en/release-2.0/index.html
2. Sharding-FAQs. https://eth.wiki/sharding/Sharding-FAQs, library Catalog: eth.wiki
3. Androulaki, E., et al.: Hyperledger fabric: a distributed operating system for permissioned blockchains. In: Proceedings of the Thirteenth EuroSys Conference, pp. 1–15, April 2018. https://doi.org/10.1145/3190508.3190538. http://arxiv.org/abs/1801.10228
4. Benet, J.: IPFS - Content Addressed, Versioned, P2P File System, p. 11
5. Bertuzzi, F., et al.: Teleconsultation in type 1 diabetes mellitus (TELEDIABE). Acta Diabetologica **55**(2), 185–192 (2018). https://doi.org/10.1007/s00592-017-1084-9
6. Buterin, V.: Ethereum white paper: a next-generation smart contract and decentralized application platform (2014). https://github.com/ethereum/wiki/wiki/White-Paper
7. Dinh, T.T.A., Wang, J., Chen, G., Liu, R., Ooi, B.C., Tan, K.L.: BLOCKBENCH: a framework for analyzing private blockchains, March 2017. arXiv:1703.04057
8. HL7: summary - FHIR v4.0.1. http://hl7.org/fhir/summary.html
9. Iansiti, M., Lakhani, K.R.: The truth about blockchain, p. 11
10. Kordestani, H., Barkaoui, K., Zahran, W.: HapiChain: a blockchain-based framework for patient-centric telemedicine. In: Proceedings of 8th IEEE International Conference on Serious Games and Applications for Health (SeGAH), August 2020
11. Kordestani, H., et al.: Hapicare: a healthcare monitoring system with self-adaptive coaching using probabilistic reasoning. In: 2019 IEEE/ACS 16th International Conference on Computer Systems and Applications (AICCSA), pp. 1–8. IEEE. Abu Dhabi, United Arab Emirates, November 2019. https://doi.org/10.1109/AICCSA47632.2019.9035291. https://ieeexplore.ieee.org/document/9035291/
12. Mannaro, K., Baralla, G., Pinna, A., Ibba, S.: A blockchain approach applied to a teledermatology platform in the sardinian region (Italy). Information **9**(2), 44 (2018). https://doi.org/10.3390/info9020044. http://www.mdpi.com/2078-2489/9/2/44
13. Mojarad, R., Attal, F., Chibani, A., Amirat, Y.: Automatic classification error detection and correction for robust human activity recognition. IEEE Robot. Autom. Lett. **5**(2), 2208–2215 (2020). https://doi.org/10.1109/LRA.2020.2970667
14. Mojarad, R., Attal, F., Chibani, A., Amirat, Y.: Context-aware adaptive recommendation system for personal well-being services. In: Proceedings of 32nd International Conference on Tools with Artificial Intelligence (ICTAI), November 2020
15. Mojarad, R., Attal, F., Chibani, A., Amirat, Y.: A context-aware hybrid framework for human behavior analysis. In: Proceedings of 32nd International Conference on Tools with Artificial Intelligence (ICTAI), November 2020
16. Mojarad, R., Attal, F., Chibani, A., Amirat, Y.: A context-based approach to detect abnormal human behaviors in ambient intelligent systems. In: Proceedings of the European Conference on Machine Learning and Principles and Practice of Knowledge Discovery in Databases (ECML-PKDD), September 2020
17. Mojarad, R., Attal, F., Chibani, A., Amirat, Y.: A hybrid context-aware framework to detect abnormal human daily living behavior. In: Proceedings of IEEE World Congress on Computational Intelligence (WCCI), July 2020

18. Mojarad, R., Attal, F., Chibani, A., Fiorini, S.R., Amirat, Y.: Hybrid approach for human activity recognition by ubiquitous robots. In: IEEE/RSJ International Conference on Intelligent Robots and Systems (IROS), pp. 5660–5665, October 2018. https://doi.org/10.1109/IROS.2018.8594173. ISSN: 2153-0866
19. Nakamoto, S.: Bitcoin: a peer-to-peer electronic cash system, p. 9 (2008)
20. Natarajan, H., Krause, S., Gradstein, H.: Distributed Ledger Technology and Blockchain. World Bank (2017). https://doi.org/10.1596/29053. https://elibrary. worldbank.org/doi/abs/10.1596/29053._eprint: https://elibrary.worldbank.org/ doi/pdf/10.1596/29053
21. Nofer, M., Gomber, P., Hinz, O., Schiereck, D.: Blockchain. Bus. Inf. Syst. Eng. 59(3), 183–187 (2017). https://doi.org/10.1007/s12599-017-0467-3
22. O'Cathail, M., Aznar-Garcia, L., Bentley, R., Patel, P., Christian, J.: Teleconsulta-tions bringing specialist radiotherapy services to patients. Radiother. Oncol. 133, S894 (2019). https://doi.org/10.1016/S0167-8140(19)32081-X
23. Paget, J., et al.: Global mortality associated with seasonal influenza epidemics: new burden estimates and predictors from the GLaMOR Project. J. Global Health 9(2), 020421 (2019). https://doi.org/10.7189/jogh.09.020421. http://jogh. org/documents/issue201902/jogh-09-020421.pdf
24. Pukas, A., Smal, V., Zabchuk, V.: Software based on blockchain technology for consolidation the medical data about the patients examination, p. 5 (2018)
25. Vora, J., et al.: BHEEM: a blockchain-based framework for securing electronic health records. In: 2018 IEEE Globecom Workshops (GC Wkshps), pp. 1–6. IEEE, Abu Dhabi, United Arab Emirates, December 2018. https://doi.org/10. 1109/GLOCOMW.2018.8644088. https://ieeexplore.ieee.org/document/8644088/
26. Vukolić, M.: Hyperledger fabric: towards scalable blockchain for business, p. 18 (2015)
27. Wang, Y., Hunt, K., Nazareth, I., Freemantle, N., Petersen, I.: Do men consult less than women? An analysis of routinely collected UK general practice data. BMJ Open 3(8), e003320 (2013). https://doi.org/10.1136/bmjopen-2013-003320. http://bmjopen.bmj.com/lookup/doi/10.1136/bmjopen-2013-003320
28. Zhang, P., White, J., Schmidt, D.C., Lenz, G., Rosenbloom, S.T.: FHIRChain: applying blockchain to securely and scalably share clinical data. Comput. Struct. Biotechnol. J. 16, 267–278 (2018). https://doi.org/10.1016/j.csbj.2018.07.004. https://linkinghub.elsevier.com/retrieve/pii/S2001037018300370

Enterprise Systems

Evaluating the Utility of Human-Machine User Interfaces Using Balanced Score Cards

Saulo Silva and Orlando Belo[(⊠)]

ALGORITMI R&D Centre, Department of Informatics, School of Engineering,
University of Minho, Braga, Portugal
saulo.silva@ifg.edu.br, obelo@di.uminho.pt

Abstract. Evaluating the utility of Human-Machine Systems' User Interfaces is not trivial. Several evaluation methods can be used to investigate if the behaviour of the user interface complies with best practices of Human-Machine Interface Design. Even when is possible to agree on which methods to use to conduct the evaluation, defining the utility requires evaluating the interface under analysis toward the company's goals, or mission. This paper investigates how the utility, perceived by end users of interfaces, can be captured by a research instrument, as well as be represented by a structured approach based on Usability evaluation and Balanced Score Cards methodology. This is an alternative demarche for accessing the Usability of a Software System, and the main goal is helping designers and administrators to maintain and improve their systems.

Keywords: Usability · Balanced scorecards · Interactive systems · User interfaces

1 Introduction

Today, universities' libraries provide websites for consulting information, which can be referred to as User Interface [1] of a Human-Machine System, i.e., a computer system that supports interaction between humans and computers. When websites are designed according to the best practices in the engineering of Human-Machine Systems, they can be valuable tools for its users, fulfilling their needs and expectations, assisting them in accomplishing their tasks with the system. Consequently, providing a well designed website is of major importance for Companies and Universities, which seek supporting their strategic goals. Different aspects can be considered for determining if a website is well designed, such as reliability and security, for instance [2]. However, when evaluating from the user point of view, usability is an important aspect to consider [3, 4], especially when the web usability evaluation methods and techniques are grouped among those requiring end user participation. Therefore, this work focus on evaluating a library website according to usability aspects, with end user involvement, which are often university staff, such as professors, researchers and students. According to [3], end users of library websites have high expectations on respect to its performance when they are carrying particular tasks, with especial attention to how easy is to use it, how efficient is the outcome, and finally how satisfied they are. Even when a website is

© Springer Nature Switzerland AG 2020
M. Themistocleous et al. (Eds.): EMCIS 2020, LNBIP 402, pp. 417–432, 2020.
https://doi.org/10.1007/978-3-030-63396-7_28

evaluated against the constructs mentioned hitherto, a company/university designer might find it challenging measuring the level of utility of the resource. That is, to provide quantified evidence that the usability evaluation constructs (e.g., usefulness, satisfaction, effectiveness, or efficiency) are perceived toward the company's goals, or mission.

In this paper we propose the use of *Balanced Score Cards* (BSC), to monitor and follow the utility of the systems whose user interface needs being constantly evaluated and improved (e.g., library websites). The Balanced Scorecards method is a multidimensional approach that takes advantage of the multiplicity of information resources existing today, to provide an expanded view of company's values and align them with their internal processes. Consequently the contribution of this paper is to provide a structured approach to assess the perceived utility of a user interface. In order to achieve that we addressed the following research question: what is the level of perceived utility of the library website by end users, according to usability assessment?

To help answering the research question, the perceived usability of a library website is investigated with the assistance of a research instrument based on three underlying concepts, namely Effectiveness, Efficiency and Learnability as well as Balanced Scorecards. The rest of this paper is organised as follows: Sect. 2 addresses the underlying theory that supports Usability Testing and Balanced Scorecards, Sect. 3 presents the design of the research as well as information about research goals, Sect. 4 presents information about the Evaluation the Usability of a User Interface with BSC, Sect. 5 presents the findings, and considerations about the limitations of the research, and, finally, Sect. 6, presents conclusions and future work.

2   Related Work

Usability is accounted as one of the several assessment tools available the Software Engineering tool's belt for evaluating User Interfaces of computer systems, *Human-Machine Interaction* (HMI) community continuously contribute for the activity in the research field, e.g., coining different yet complementary definitions for the term. For Nielsen Usability is a quality attribute, measuring user interfaces easiness level [5]. This is supported by [6], whose work reveals positive correlation between Usability and Quality. Standards and regulations might provide their own definitions, e.g., ISO 9241-11 considers tree constructs when evaluating a specified product's context of use, namely Effectiveness, Efficiency and Satisfaction [7]. Still in the context of ISO 9241-11, Effectiveness refers to the completeness at which users achieve specified goals; Efficiency refers to the resources used in completing a task; and Satisfaction reveals positive attitudes toward using the system. When considering the model for the framework used as research instrument, we noticed that the literature provides evidence of strong positive correlation between Satisfaction with Effectiveness and Efficiency [8]. Due to these findings, the construct of Satisfaction was excluded from the framework used as research instrument. Instead of Satisfaction, the construct of Learnability is selected as part of the research instrument. This construct is based on Software Engineering aspects, such as the usability model proposed by Nielsen in the early 1990 [9], referring to as the capability of systems being easy to use by casual users [10], or ISO/IEC 9126 [11], referring to as the capability of software products to make possible that users learn how to use it. Learnability is identified in several studies as fundamental characteristic for Usability [10, 12–14].

Web usability evaluations are generally performed with and without end user participation. After the process is performed, and the system design is consequently improved, a company/university might find difficult to measure the level of utility of the resource. That is, to provide quantified (cardinal) evidence that the usability evaluation constructs (e.g., Usefulness, Satisfaction, Effectiveness, or Efficiency) are perceived toward the company's goals, or mission. The construct of Utility might have a continuum of possible conceptualisations, as observed by [15], often tied to subjective preference for particulars. Therefore, is necessary to establish a common ground, such as the definition of utility provided by Jacob Nielsen [9], which suits computer software design applied to web design. In his definition, utility means the match between task requirements and product functionality, or the ability of the system to help the user carry out a set of tasks [16]. The presentation of Utility information can make use performance indicators. Due to the increasingly business competitiveness, the evaluation of performance in business environments, which is a topic of research that has been received great attention over the years, has lead to the adoption of *Management Information Systems* (MIS). While MIS provide important resources for decision-making, control, analysis and visualisation of information regarding the company and its processes, they also creates new management challenges, namely the ability to understand the new decision models and their methods [17]. The use of indicators of performance in MIS supports manager's decision-making processes. Indicators have the potential to cooperate with the company's view alignment and processes organisation around their goals.

Some researchers have concerns about the impact of such indicators in the management of companies, claiming that traditionally they are built on the top of financial information, and therefore, provide few hints about other processes [17]. Others consider the importance of using non-financial indicators (e.g., customer relationships, organisational culture) when evaluating the business performance [18]. Apart from that discussion, managers still have difficulties on the necessary methodology to deal with such kind of indicators and advance for the need of solutions that might correlate complex issues such as flexibility, accuracy or speed, in simple but meaningful number. Kaplan and Norton have investigated how to improve the concept of control system with information beyond the traditional financial dimension [17]. As result, in the early 90s they developed the BSC framework. They were interested in indicators that summarized information such as i) financial and non-financial, ii) internal and external, iii) business performance and iv) current results and future of the company, which could link the company's goals with well-defined strategy, one that can help employees to achieve the goals through concrete actions. BSC can be considered a structured approach to evaluate the performance and enforce the company's vision and mission, by agreeing in perspectives and measures that are monitored individually. The following processes are implemented to obtain information using BSC (Fig. 1):

- Process to convert the vision: it allows for the management team to obtain a consensus in terms of the company's vision and strategy.

- Process of communicating and bonding: it allows for the management team to communicate the company's vision and strategy in order that they bond it to the personal and individual objectives.
- Process of business planning: it allows the companies to plan about their plan of action and resources.
- Process of strategic learning: it allows the companies to perform strategic learning.

The company's strategies are converted into BSC components, such as strategic objectives, indicators, goals and action programs, which are the depth of the analysis, usually represented in four perspectives. Each perspective of analysis should provide indicators, which are measured according to a measurement scale defined according to the process.

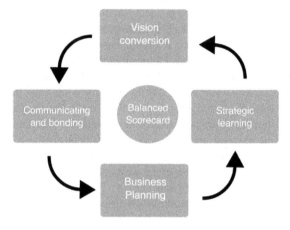

Fig. 1. Processes in BSC [17].

According to [17], BSC (usually) supports four perspectives, namely Resources, Community, Internal Processes and Personal. Figure 2 illustrates how the perspectives correspond to the strategic view.

BSC constitutes into a multidimensional approach, one that assist companies in adopting a wider spectrum of analysis of their internal processes, providing an expanded view of its values, aligned with such processes. Evidence of the benefits for using BSC in the field of software engineering is provided by [18], who evaluated the utility of a Data Warehousing System.

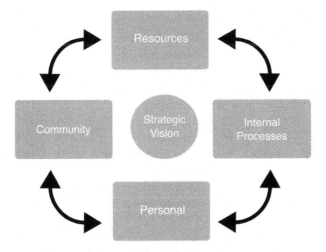

Fig. 2. Template dimensions in BSC framework [17].

3 The Evaluation Approach

A. *Research Goals and Object of Research*

The present research investigates the perceived utility of a library website through the Usability constructs of Effectiveness and Efficiency, according to ISO 9241-11 [7], as well as through the construct of Learnability, based on the Usability Model proposed by Nielsen [10]. The object of research in question, i.e., the library website, is a service that makes possible for end users to conduct bibliographic research in different databases, such as the university's thesis and dissertations, as well as in other databases available for the academic community. The library website is mainly targeted for students, researchers and university staff. The participants that we have addressed in this research are part of two groups, namely students and researchers (Table 1).

Table 1. Characteristics of the respondents.

Characteristic	Category	Freq.	%
Gender	Female	7	20%
	Male	28	80%
	Prefer not declare	–	–
Age	18–24	30	86%
	25–30	2	6%
	31–40	2	6%
	41–50	–	–
	51–60	1	3%

(*continued*)

Table 1. (*continued*)

Characteristic	Category	Freq.	%
Status	Graduation/master student	33	94%
	PhD student	2	6%
	Professor/researcher	–	–
Level of computer skill	Intermediate level	5	14%
	Advanced level	19	54%
	Expert level	11	31%
Use frequency	Daily or almost daily	35	100%
-	Once or twice a week	–	–
	Once or twice a month	–	–
	Once or twice a year	–	–

We decided to design our research instrument in the form of a survey, which is used to collect necessary data to analyse. The survey uses closed questions to collect the information, as opposed to open-ended questions, which the responder is free to provide his/hers own answers to the questions. In this case, we rely on the Likert scale to transform order points into a linear scale [19] to address two groups of information:

1) Demographic information, also referred to as filter questions, enabling to explore the characteristics of the different study groups;
2) Research questions information, also referred to as usability evaluation instrument, directly related with the usability evaluation model in the context of academic libraries, proposed by [12].

Usually the scale rating ranges from 5, 7 and 9 points. We decided to design our instrument using the 7 points scale, as we can see in Table 2. The research survey is designed to collect information in a monthly basis periodicity. The measurement framework is presented in Table 3.

Table 2. Likert Scale defined for the research instrument [19].

(1) I strongly disagree	(2) Disagree	(3) Slightly disagree	(4) I do not agree or disagree	(5) Slightly agree	(6) I agree	(7) I totally agree
(Do not answer at all to the required)	(Serves with failed the minimum required)	(Meets partially below the expectations)	(Neither agree or disagree)	(Meets partially above the expectations)	(Meets completely the expectations)	(Above the expectations)

B. *Interface Evaluation Process*

The web software *BSC Designer* is used for implementing the BSC. It allows the implementation of strategic maps, strategic objectives, indicators, data entrance and normalisation of data. The data visualisation is possible by the means of several graphical representation elements, such as dashboards, graphics (e.g., pie, bar, etc.). The data for analysis is collected using the instrument research previously identified.

The word 'usability' refers to methods for improving ease-of-use during the design process. It is based on human psychology and user research and in general refers to the quality of the interaction between the user (human operator) and the system being operated, where a set of factors such as time taken to perform tasks, errors made during the interaction, among others, might be considered [20]. The causal framework usability (depicted in Fig. 3) proposed by [21] intends to highlight the multiplicity of usability constituents, or guidelines and standards for web design [22]. As the usability of a system has the potential to impact how the user accomplishes his/her tasks with the system, it is relevant to use all methods and tools to understand its underlining complexity and subsequently improve the interactive system's user interfaces.

Table 3. Measurement framework

Category	Attributes	Method	Metric (%)	Measurement scale	Value
Characteristics of the respondents	Gender	Research survey	Gender	F/M/ND	1 (Female), 2(Male), 3 (Prefer not declare)
Characteristics of the respondents	Age	Research survey	Age category	5-point	1 (18–24), 2 (25–30), 3(31–40), 4(41–50), 5 (51–60)
Characteristics of the respondents	User status	Research survey	Status	3-point	1 (Graduation/Master Student), 2 (PhD Student), 3 (Professor/Researcher)
Characteristics of the respondents	User level of computer skill	Research survey	Level of computer skill	3-point	1 (Intermediate level), 2 (Advanced level), 3 (Expert level)
Characteristics of the respondents	Frequency of computer's use	Research survey	Frequency of computer's use	4-point	1 (Daily or Almost Daily) 2 (Once or Twice a Week) 3 (Once or Twice a Month) 4 (Once or Twice a Year)
Effectiveness	Six questions related to the construct	Research survey	Level of general effectiveness	7 point	1 (I strongly disagree), 7 (I totally agree)
Efficiency	Six questions related to the construct	Research survey	Level of general efficiency	7 point	1 (I strongly disagree), 7 (I totally agree)
Learnability	Six questions related to the construct	Research survey	Level of general learnability	7 point	1 (I strongly disagree), 7 (I totally agree)

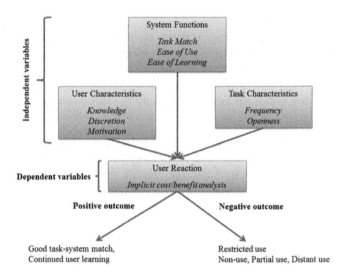

Fig. 3. Usability causal framework by [21].

The literature reported several methods [23] to verify the perceived usability level of a system, namely the questionnaire for User Interface Satisfaction (QUIS) [24], the computer System Usability Questionnaire (CSUQ) [25], the system Usability Scale (SUS) [26], Words, adapted from Microsoft's Product Reaction Cards [27], Website usability evaluation questionnaire [28], or the Usability Evaluation Model in the context of academic libraries [12]. To support the research variables from the perspectives for the BSC, we chose using the Usability Evaluation Model and associated evaluation survey tool proposed by [12], tailored to academic libraries websites.

4 Using Balanced Scorecards

As BSC presents a multidimensional approach that helps the practitioner to consider a wide variety of aspects in the evaluation of the company's mission, we consider it for supporting the evaluation of the utility of User Interfaces of interactive systems, which has the potential to improve the level of task accomplishment from the user with the referred system. Figure 4 depicts the strategic map defined for the BSC, which identifies the relationships between the perspectives and the strategic objectives.

The initial design approach for the BSC perspectives is based on four perspectives, namely *Financial, Client, Internal Processes* and *Learning and Growth*. However, Kaplan and Norton suggest that those perspectives should be used as a template, not as a strait jacket. In this sense, this work defines three perspectives that we believe are sufficient to translate our mission, namely the perspectives of Community, Internal Processes, and Learning and Growth (Fig. 4) (Table 4).

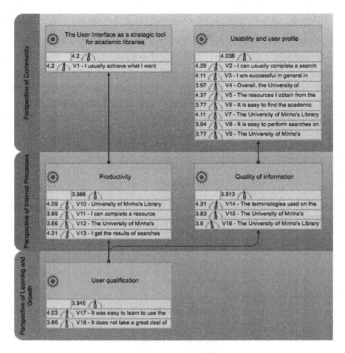

Fig. 4. The BSC strategic map with indicators defined for this project. Adapted from BSC designer.

In the perspective of Community, two strategic objectives are defined, along with their indicators and objectives, in order to attest the level of coupling between system and modelled processes, as well as to verify the user's difficulties of utilisation, respectively. In the perspective of Internal Processes, two strategic objectives are defined, along with their indicators and objectives, for verifying the level of user's productivity, as well as to verify the user's perception of system information. The perspective of Learning and Growth has one strategic objective defined, along with its indicators and objective, having the goal to check user's qualification level.

Table 4. Description of the Perspectives and strategic objectives.

Strategic objectives	Indicators	Objectives
Perspective of community		
The user interface as a strategic tool for academic libraries	Decision-making process	Increase the importance of the User Interface for the Universities
Usability and user profile	Task completeness	Decrease the difficulties of utilisation
	Information findability	
	Overall usefulness	
	Usefulness of resources	
	Easiness of resources	
	General usability	
	Easiness of task	
	Understandability of menus	
Perspective of internal processes		
Productivity	Coverability of topics	Increase level of user's productivity
	Quickness of task completion	
	Design satisfaction	
	Quickness of results presentation	
Quality of information	Understandability of terminologies	Decrease time of user recovering from errors
	Availability of help functions	
	Information organisation	
Perspective of learning and growth		
User qualification.	Learnability level	Increase user qualification
	Training level for initial use of system	

5 Result Analysis

The overall given value for the variables are composed by the pair [order point/representation in the linear scale], in which the order point is obtained by verifying the *mode* value of each research topic, and the representation in the linear scale can be obtained by consulting Table 2. In the first strategic objective of the "Perspective of Community", we verify the user perception about the User Interface as a strategic tool for academic libraries. The value measured for the variable V1 is presented in the Table 5. This intends to measure the user perception about task achievement using the user interface in question. Nielsen highlights that the ability of user's completing tasks are a relevant indicator of success rates. In this sense, the result indicates that users *"Neither agreeing or disagreeing"* on the UI supporting their decision-making processes (Support for decision-making process indicator).

Table 5. Topics of the strategic objective "The User Interface as a strategic tool for academic libraries".

Variables	Topics	Overall average	Overall average for strategic objective
V1	I usually achieve what I want using the University of Minho's Library web site	4,0	4,0

The "Usability and user profile" strategic objective presents an enlarged number of topics, aiming to verify the user's perception of usability aspects. The values measured for the variables V2 to V9 are presented in the Table 6. Those variables measure how the system's usability meets their expectations. Users reported *"Neither agreeing or disagreeing"* on the variables V5 and V4, which investigates the perception of usefulness of the website (Overall usefulness and Usefulness of resources indicators). The literature frequently correlates lack of usefulness with low user adoption. About a general level of facility for finding resources, users reported *"Neither agreeing or disagreeing"* on variables V3 and V8 (Information findability and Easiness of task indicators) and *"Meets partially above the expectations"* on variable V6 (Easiness of resources indicator). This is one of the most relevant measurements in usability, and is frequently correlated with quality design of products. In general, users *"Neither agree or disagree"* on the General usability indicator (V7). On V9, users report *"Neither agreeing or disagreeing"* in the facility to understand the website menus (Understandability of menus indicator). Menu Design is a relevant topic, which presents guidelines for good design for helping users to find content and features. Along with accuracy, completeness helps to evaluate how effective the user goals can be achieved. In variable V2, users reported *"Neither agreeing or disagreeing"* on the Task completeness indicator, about success on completing a search task using the investigated website.

Table 7 present the topics of the "Productivity" strategic objective. Variables V11 and V13 are concerned with aspects about the speed of achieving a certain goal, which is frequently correlated with efficiency in the literature. Users accounted *"Neither agreeing or disagreeing"* for Quickness of task completion indicator and *"Meets partially above the expectations"* for Quickness of results presentation indicator.

Table 6. Topics of the strategic objective "Usability and user profile".

Variables	Topics	Overall average	Overall average for strategic objective
V2	I can usually complete a search task using the University of Minho's Library web site	4,0	4,0
V3	I am successful in general in finding academic resource(s) using the University of Minho's Library web site	4,0	
V4	Overall, the University of Minho's Library web site is useful in helping me find information	4,0	
V5	The resources I obtain from the University of Minho's Library web site are usually useful	4,0	
V6	It is easy to find the academic resources that I want on the University of Minho's Library web site	5,0	
V7	The University of Minho's Library web site is easy to use in general	4,0	
V8	It is easy to perform searches on the University of Minho's Library web site	4,0	
V9	The University of Minho's Library web site offers easy-to-understand menus	4,0	

Variable V12 investigates the design of the website in question, and is indeed a difficult topic for the casual, non-designer user, to evaluate. Respondents reported *"Neither agreeing or disagreeing"* on the Design satisfaction indicator. Coverage of topics is a relevant topic for any university's library, since its main mission is to deliver a wider range of information for its selected and highly exigent public. In the variable V10, users reported *"Neither agreeing or disagreeing"* that the website covered sufficient topics based on their exploration (Coverability of topics indicator).

In Table 8 we can see the information related to the "Quality of Information" strategic objective. As part of a good user experience with any user interface, documentation resources such as user Manuals, Reference Sheets, and Help Functions directly in the User Interface might be provided for users, containing appropriate terminologies for the website's audience. Variables V14 to V16 investigates the user perception about the terminologies used in the website and available help functions. Respondents declared *"Neither agreeing or disagreeing"* on indicators 'Understandability of terminologies', 'Availability of help functions' and 'Information organisation'.

Table 7. Topics of the strategic objective "Productivity".

Variables	Topics	Overall average	Overall average for strategic objective
V10	University of Minho's Library web site usually covers sufficient topics that I try to explore	4,0	4,0
V11	I can complete a resource finding task quickly using the University of Minho's Library web site	4,0	
V12	The University of Minho's Library web site is well designed to find what I want	4,0	
V13	I get the results of searches quickly when using the University of Minho's Library web site	5,0	

Next, in Table 9, we present the topics of "User qualification" strategic objective. Variables V17 and V18 investigates user perception about the level of facility to learn and become proficient with the universities' website. This is a relevant aspect of usability. Products (e.g., websites) that are easy to learn are frequently considered easy to use. Users reported "*Neither agreeing or disagreeing*" on both website being easy to learn (Learnability level indicator) and demanding few effort to become proficient (Training level for initial use of system indicator), respectively.

Table 8. Topics of the strategic objective "Quality of information".

Variables	Topics	Overall average	Overall average for strategic objective
V14	The terminologies used on the University of Minho's Library web site are easily understandable	4,0	4,0
V15	The University of Minho's Library web site has appropriate help functions	4,0	
V16	The University of Minho's Library web site provides well-organized help information for new users	4,0	

BSC methodology enables frequent data input for each variable measurement, which makes possible continuously monitoring the selected topics. For the evaluated period, users report "*Neither agreeing or disagreeing*" on the perceived utility of the website, according to the presented model, which allows the achievement of the main goals of this paper.

Table 9. Topics of the strategic objective "User qualification".

Variables	Topics	Overall average	Overall average for strategic objective
V17	It was easy to learn to use the University of Minho's Library web site	4,0	4,0
V18	It does not take a great deal of effort for new users to become proficient with the University of Minho's Library web site	4,0	

Although this research is applied for a number of academic members, we understand that involving more categories other than students and researchers among the universe of respondents (e.g., university staff, library and department employees, etc.) would have the potential to increase not only the size of the sample but also to increase the spectre of opinions. Collecting information from enlarged representative group would have the potential to increase the feedback regarding the usability aspects that were considered, and even consider different aspects that need to be investigated. The same could apply to extend the participation for members of different courses at the university.

6   Conclusions and Future Work

With the increasingly number of users, companies that relies their processes in websites need accurate, reliable and quick feedback about their working. This paper investigated how the perceived utility of those websites can be captured by a research instrument, as well as be represented by a structured methodology, intending to help system designers and administrators to maintain and improve their systems. We achieved the proposed goals of this paper, by providing evidence that the level of utility of a website perceived by users can be verified in terms of Effectiveness, Efficiency and Learnability. We also provided evidence that the BSC methodology is able to provide quantified (cardinal) evidence about the utility of the website in question, captured by the research instrument.

Future improvements in this research include using an automated instrument of analysis, in a way that the results can be updated automatically within a shorter period of time, as well as increase the universe of responders. As selecting the best indicators from the Engineering of User Interfaces is also hard work, future improvements in the research model with more relevant investigation keys might support the investigation of other relevant questions. Another possibility would be to investigate another type of user interface, such as in critical systems. The usability investigation of the University of Minho Library website was responded by a public composed by 94% of graduation/master students, which declared daily or almost daily computer's use frequency, 54% of them claiming to possess advanced level of computer knowledge (Informatics/Computer Science field). Small recommendations can be made to reinforce the items variables V12 and V16 (Design satisfaction and Information organisation indicators). In general they account for providing well-organized help information for new users and for the web site being well designed to find the information users are seeking.

Acknowledgement. This work was supported by Conselho Nacional de Pesquisa (CNPq), COMPETE: POCI-01-0145-FEDER-007043, and by FCT – Fundação para a Ciência e Tecnologia within the R&D Units Project Scope: UIDB/00319/2020. We also thank Instituto Federal de Educação, Ciência e Tecnologia de Goiás (IFG).

References

1. Benyon, D.: Designing interactive systems: a comprehensive guide to HCI, UX and interaction design (2014)
2. Fernandez, A., Insfran, E., Abrahão, S.: Usability evaluation methods for the web: a systematic mapping study. Inf. Softw. Technol. **53**(8), 789–817 (2011)
3. Okhovati, M., Karami, F., Khajouei, R.: Exploring the usability of the central library websites of medical sciences universities. J. Librarianship Inform. Sci. **49**(3), 246–255 (2017)
4. Djamasbi, S., Siegel, M., Tullis, T.: Generation Y, web design, and eye tracking. Int. J. Hum Comput Stud. **68**(5), 307–323 (2010)
5. Kous, K., Pušnik, M., Heričko, M., Polančičm G.: Usability evaluation of a library website with different end user groups. J. Librarianship Inform. Sci. 0961000618773133 (2018)
6. Bevan, N.: Usability is quality of use. Adv. Hum. Factors Ergon. **20**(2003) 349–349 (1995)
7. ISO/IEC (International Organization for Standardization): Standard 9241: Ergonomic Requirements for Office Work with Visual Display Terminals (VDT)s, Part 11. Guidance on Usability (1998). https://www.iso.org/obp/ui/#iso:std:iso:9241:-11:ed-1:v1:en. Accessed 20 Jan 2019
8. Joo, S.: How are usability elements-efficiency, effectiveness, and satisfaction-correlated with each other in the context of digital libraries? Proc. Am. Soc. Inform. Sci. Technol. **47**(1), 1–2 (2010)
9. Nielsen, J.: Usability 101: Introduction to Usability (2003)
10. Nielsen, J.: Usability inspection methods. In: Conference Companion on Human Factors in Computing Systems, pp. 413–414. ACM (1994)
11. ISO/IEC (International Organization for Standardization): Standard 9126: Software Engineering Product Quality, parts 1, 2 and 3 (2001)
12. Joo, S., Lin, S., Lu, K.: A usability evaluation model for academic library websites: efficiency, effectiveness and learnability. J. Libr. Inform. Stud. **9**(2), 11–26 (2011)
13. Brinck, T., Gergle, D., Wood, S.D.: Usability for the Web: Designing Web Sites that Work. Elsevier, San Diego (2001)
14. Guenther, K.: Assessing Web Site Usability (2003)
15. Simons, T.: Speech patterns and the concept of utility in cognitive maps: the case of integrative bargaining. Acad. Manag. J. **36**(1), 139–156 (1993)
16. Keinonen, T.: Designers, Users and Justice. Bloomsbury Publishing, London (2017)
17. Kaplan, R.S., Norton, D.P.: The Balanced Scorecard: Translating Strategy into Action. Harvard Business Press, Boston (1996)
18. Martins, I., Belo, O.: A balanced scorecard approach for evaluating the utility of a data warehousing system. In: European, Mediterranean, and Middle Eastern Conference on Information Systems, pp. 633–645. Springer, Cham (2017)

19. Babbie, E.: The Basics of Social Research. Wadsworth, New York (1999)
20. Issa, T., Isaias, P.: Sustainable Design. Springer, London (2015)
21. Eason, K.D.: Towards the experimental study of usability. Behav. Inform. Technol. 3(2), 133–143 (1984)
22. Bevan, N.: Guidelines and standards for web usability. In: Proceedings of HCI International, vol. 2005, Lawrence Erlbaum (2005)
23. Root, R.W., Draper, S.: Questionnaires as a software evaluation tool. In: Proceedings of the SIGCHI conference on Human Factors in Computing Systems, pp. 83–87. ACM (1983)
24. Chin, J.P., Diehl, V.A., Norman, K.L.: Development of an instrument measuring user satisfaction of the human-computer interface. In: Proceedings of the SIGCHI Conference on Human Factors in Computing Systems, pp. 213–218. ACM (1988)
25. Lewis, J.R.: IBM computer usability satisfaction questionnaires: psychometric evaluation and instructions for use. Int. J. Hum.-Comput. Inter. 7(1), 57–78 (1995)
26. Brooke, J.: SUS: a "quick and dirty" usability scale.In: Jordan, P.W., Thomas, B., Weerdmeester, B.A., McClelland, A.L. (eds.) Usability Evaluation in Industry. Taylor and Francis, London (1996)
27. Benedek, J., Miner, T.: Measuring desirability: new methods for evaluating desirability in a usability lab setting. Proc. Usability Prof. Assoc. 2003(8–12), 57 (2002)
28. Tullis, T.S., Stetson, J.N.: A comparison of questionnaires for assessing website usability. In: Usability Professional Association Conference, vol. 1 (2004)

Enterprise Systems, ICT Capabilities and Business Analytics Adoption – An Empirical Investigation

Niki Kyriakou[✉], Euripidis Loukis[✉],
and Michail Marios Chatzianastasiadis[✉]

Department of Information and Communication Systems Engineering, University
of the Aegean, Samos, Greece
{nkyr, eloukis, mchatz}@aegean.gr

Abstract. Business Analytics (BA) has attracted great interest among firms of most sectors worldwide, as it enables a more advanced and valuable exploitation of firms' data assets, beyond operations, for the supporting of decision-making. However, though numerous firms take some first steps in this area, most of them make limited use of BA in some of their activities, and cannot advance to a more extensive adoption of BA throughout their activities, so they do not exploit the full potential of it. For this reason, some first research has been conducted on BA adoption and factors affecting it, however more research is required on this topic. Our study makes a contribution to this research stream, by investigating empirically the effect of the extent of enterprise systems (such as ERP, CRM and SCM ones) adoption, as well as the degree of development of firm's ICT capabilities, distinguishing between technological and management ones, on the extent of BA adoption. It has been based on the Technology, Organization and Environment (TOE) framework. We have used data collected from 363 Greek firms from both manufacturing and services sectors through a questionnaire, from which ordinal regression models are estimated. It has been concluded that both the adoption of enterprise systems, as well as the development of firm's ICT capabilities, and especially the ICT management capabilities, affect positively the extent of BA adoption.

Keywords: Business analytics · ICT adoption · Enterprise systems · ICT capabilities

1 Introduction

Firms, all over the world, are called upon to cope with a highly complex, globally competitive and dynamic business environment, and in order to address the multiple challenges it poses they are increasingly adopting and using various digital technologies to increase their efficiency and effectiveness (Aydiner et al. 2019). Among these technologies are definitely the enterprise systems (ES), defined as large and complex software packages that provide comprehensive support and integration of various business functions (Rainer et al. 2016; Laudon and Laudon 2019; Roztocki et al. 2020); the most important kinds of ES are the Enterprise Resource Planning (ERP), the

© Springer Nature Switzerland AG 2020
M. Themistocleous et al. (Eds.): EMCIS 2020, LNBIP 402, pp. 433–448, 2020.
https://doi.org/10.1007/978-3-030-63396-7_29

Customer Relationship Management (CRM) and the Supply Chain Management (SCM) ones. These ES systems aim mainly to support firms' daily operations, however they offer only some limited decision support capabilities. This gave rise to the development of a 'second generation' of business information systems, oriented mainly towards decision support, which aim to support and enhance firms' decision making, through various kinds of sophisticated analysis of operational data, referred to as 'Business Analytics' (BA) systems. BA can be defined as "techniques, technologies, systems, practices, methodologies, and applications that analyze critical business data to help an enterprise better understand its business and market and make timely business decisions" (Nam et al. 2019).

BA has attracted great interest among firms of most sectors, as it enables a more advanced and valuable exploitation of firms' data assets, beyond operations, for the support of decision-making, by providing a better description and understanding of firm's previous activities and operations (descriptive analytics), as well as predictions of future evolutions and behaviors (predictive analytics), and also recommendations for future actions (usually recommending optimal selections among existing alternatives) (prescriptive analytics) (Aydiner et al. 2019). However, though numerous firms take some first steps in this area, most of them cannot progress further, so they make limited use of BA in some of their activities, but cannot advance to a more extensive adoption of BA throughout their activities, and therefore do not exploit the full potential of it (Ransbotham et al. 2016; Nam et al. 2019). For this reason, some first research has been conducted on BA adoption and factors affecting it, which investigates the effects of some firm's internal and external factors on BA adoption (a review of it is provided in Sect. 2). However, much more research is required in order to obtain a better understanding of the drivers and the barriers to the adoption of BA by firms (Nam et al. 2019), by investigating the effects of a wider range of firm's internal and external factors on BA adoption.

Our study makes a contribution in this direction, by investigating empirically the effects of two technological factors that have not been examined before on the extent of BA adoption by firms:

- the extent of enterprise systems (such as ERP, CRM and SCM ones) adoption,
- and also the degree of development of firm's ICT capabilities (Ravichandran and Lertwongsatien 2005; Gu and Jung 2013; Garrison et al. 2015), distinguishing between technological and management ones.

It has been based on the well-established and widely used Technology, Organization and Environment (TOE) framework of technological innovation adoption (Tornatzky and Fleischer 1990; Baker 2011). We use data collected from 363 Greek firms from both manufacturing and services sectors through a questionnaire, from which ordinal regression models are estimated. These models have as dependent variable the extent of BA adoption, and as independent variables: the extent of enterprise systems adoption (technological factor), the degree of development of firm's ICT capabilities (technological and management ones); and also firm's general and ICT-related human capital, innovativeness, size and sector (organizational factors), and finally the price and non-price competition (environmental factors).

This paper consists of five sections. The following Sect. 2 reviews previous relevant literature, and then Sect. 3 formulates the research hypotheses. In Sect. 4 our method and data are described, and then in Sect. 4 our results are presented and discussed. The final Sect. 5 summarizes conclusions and proposes future research directions.

2   Literature Review

For the reasons mentioned in the Introduction some first research has been conducted concerning the factors that affect the adoption of BA. Most of these studies have been based on the Technology, Organization and Environment (TOE) framework, and investigate the effects of some firms' technological, organizational and environmental characteristics on the adoption of BA by them.

Malladi (2013) estimates a model of factors affecting the extent of organizational adoption of Business Intelligence and Analytics (BIA) technologies, concluding that perceived benefits from these technologies, technology sophistication in terms of data infrastructure, sectoral knowledge intensity and size affect positively the extent of BIA adoption, while the lack of relevant industry standards hinders its adoption. A similar study is presented by Malladi and Krishnan (2013), concluding that high level of data infrastructure sophistication has a positive impact on the use of BIA systems, while data management challenges as well as challenges concerning data integration and attraction/management of talented human resources prevent their use; also large organizations are more inclined to use BIA. With respect to the external environment, competitive intensity impacts positively the extent of BIA adoption, but environmental dynamism has no effect on it.

Boonsiritomachai et al. (2016) found that factors affecting the level of BI adoption by SMEs include the Relative Advantage it provides, its perceived complexity, the availability of organizational resources, the innovativeness of the owners and managers, as well as the competitive pressure, and vendor selection; on the contrary, it was found that the compatibility of BI with firm's needs and culture, the absorptive capacity of the firm and the ICT knowledge of the owners and managers do not affect the level of BI adoption. Puklavec et al. (2017) also focus on SMEs, and consider the adoption of BI systems as a process consisting of three stages, evaluation, adoption and use, investigating the factors affecting each of them. They find the perceived cost effectiveness of BI has a negative impact in the BIS adoption and use stage; also, if BI is part of ERP systems this has a positive impact in all three stages of BI adoption. At the organizational level, it follows that management support has a significant positive impact in the BI evaluation and use stages, and rational decision-making culture has a significant and negative impact only for the evaluation stage. Moreover, the existence of a project champion has a positive effect in all three stages of BI adoption. High-Quality Organizational Data is another positively important factor for the use stage, while organizational readiness has a positive impact in the evaluation and adoption stages. Finally, it is worth noting that the external support has been found to be not important.

Recently Nam et al. (2019) investigate factors affecting BA initiation, adoption and assimilation stages. They found that firm's data infrastructure affects all these stages, while data quality management affect the adoption and assimilation stages. The existence of management-related obstacles (concerning big changes and extensive training required, as well as difficulties in integrating BA into firm's processes and decision-making) prevent adoption and assimilation, while the organizational centralization of BA exploitation has negative impact in the assimilation stage. Finally, the competitive pressure faced by the firm affects positively the BA initiation stage, but none of the other stages, while government support affects none of these stages.

Summarizing, some studies have been conducted concerning the factors that affect BA adoption, which investigate the effects of some internal and external factors; however, further research is required in order to obtain a better understanding of BA adoption, its drivers as well as barriers, investigating of wider range of internal factors (firm's characteristics) and also external factors (characteristics of firm's external environment) on the extent of BA adoption. Our study makes a contribution in this direction, by investigating two widely debated in IS research factors, ES adoption and ICT capabilities, with respect to their impact on BA adoption.

3 Research Hypotheses

Our study, as mentioned in the Introduction, has as theoretical foundation the TOE framework: we have developed research hypotheses about the effects of one technological factor (extent of ES adoption), five organizational factors (ICT capabilities, general human capital, ICT-related human capital, innovativeness and size), and two environmental factors (price and non-price competition), on the extent of BA adoption.

3.1 Technological Factors

As mentioned in the Introduction, firms are increasingly adopting various kinds of ES (Rainer et al. 2016; Laudon and Laudon 2019; Roztocki et al. 2020), such as ERP, CRM and SCM systems, which support their main activities and functions, and enable collecting extensive data about them. These data constitute the main 'raw material' for applying the techniques of BA (such as reporting, dashboards, data-warehousing, prediction models, etc.), which aim to convert these data into meaningful information that can be useful for decision making. In particular, the development and use of the above main kinds of ES by firms involves the collection of a large volume of data derived from all the in-house and inter-company functions they automate, coordinate and manage. In particular, ERP systems, which support all operations and business interfaces, are a source of data concerning sales, supplies, production, financial management, human resources management, etc. CRM systems offer more specialized data about existing and potential customers' needs and preferences, as they provide support capabilities for pre-sale, post-sale, and customer service operations in general. SCM systems allow the collection of a large volume of specialized external data about the firm's supply chain activities, concerning not only relevant internal activities, but also suppliers', affiliates' and customers' ones. Therefore, we expect that larger extent of ES adoption will result in availability of higher volumes of data concerning firm's activities and functions, and therefore in more capabilities and opportunities for making highly beneficial use of BA techniques across more firm's activities and functions, which will lead to larger extent of BA adoption. So, our first research hypothesis is:

Hypothesis 1: *The extent of enterprise systems (ES) adoption has a positive effect on the extent of BA adoption.*

3.2 Organizational Factors

IS research has revealed that for the efficient and effective adoption of digital technologies by firms and the generation of business value from them quite important is the development of ICT-related capabilities (Ravichandran and Lertwongsatien 2005; Gu and Jung 2013; Garrison et al. 2015); the relevant literature distinguishes two kinds of such capabilities: technological ones, concerning mainly the development, modification and integration of applications, and managerial ones, concerning strategic planning of the use of these technologies closely associated with firm's overall strategic planning, co-operation between firm's ICT units and personnel with the business ones, as well as co-operation with firm's ICT vendors. With respect to ICT technological capabilities, the adoption of BA often requires combining/integrating data from several different applications, and also developing new decision-support applications using these data, or modifying existing applications in order to exploit these data for providing new decision support functionalities. The development or customization of BA solutions is a unique case for every firm, or even for every different need of the same firm, that requires special treatment, which might make it quite expensive and difficult, if the firm relies exclusively on outsourcing; so if the firm has relevant internal capabilities, this can lead to better and less costly BA solutions. Therefore, we expect that higher degree of such ICT technological capabilities will reduce the cost of BA development, and at the same time improve its quality, so will finally increase the extent of BA adoption. Thus, our second research hypothesis is:

Hypothesis 2: *The degree of development of firm's ICT-related technological capabilities has a positive effect on the extent of BA adoption.*

Furthermore, highly important is the identification of opportunities for highly beneficial BA use that addresses the particular problems, challenges and needs of each specific firm (which might be quite different from the ones of other firms); this necessitates close cooperation between on one hand firm's ICT units and personnel (who have knowledge about the existing BA technologies, systems and practices and on the other hand the business ones (who have knowledge about firm's activities, functions, as well as their problems, challenges and needs, and will finally use BA). The existence of good internal relations between the staff of firm's ICT and the staff of its business units that use ICT for supporting their tasks creates a high level of mutual understanding, trust, interdependence and finally co-operation. This can be the best source of ideas for identifying valuable, rare and difficult to imitate by other firms combinations of data from different sources, as well as decision-support functionalities based on them (e.g. highly valuable reports, dashboards, key performance indicators, predictions, optimizations, etc.); furthermore, this is going also to be very important for the implementation of the above ideas, and the production of highly beneficial BA solutions that meet business users' needs, and are user friendly. Also, this might necessitate highly sophisticated exploitation of existing ICT infrastructure, and especially applications, and use of advanced features of them that had never been used before. Developing a good and deep relationship with ICT suppliers of hardware, software and networks, characterized by extensive exchange of information and knowledge, mutual understanding, trust and a positive attitude, will enable us to acquire from them the required knowledge about the above advanced features, resulting finally in higher levels of efficiency with respect to BA systems development.

Furthermore, IS research has extensively emphasized the importance and impact of adopting a strategic approach to ICT and connecting it with overall strategy, and revealed the high usefulness of ICT strategic planning and alignment between the ICT unit of the firm and its business units (Chan and Reich 2007; Leidner et al. 2011; Wu et al. 2015). So, if a firm has a good ICT strategic planning and alignment capability it can identify valuable strategic opportunities for BA use, which can support or even enhance its strategy, and provide strong support from higher hierarchical levels of the firm for their implementation, leading finally to larger extent of BA adoption. Summarizing, we can expect that higher degree of these ICT management capabilities will enable the identification of more valuable opportunities of BA use, as well as their efficient and effective implementation, so it will finally increase the extent of BA adoption. Thus, our third research hypothesis is:

Hypothesis 3: *The degree of development of firm's ICT-related management capabilities has a positive effect on the extent of BA adoption.*

Furthermore, in order to formulate a more complete BA adoption model, we have developed some more research hypotheses, concerning the effects on BA adoption of some factors that have been found in previous innovation research to affect positively the adoption of technological innovation: human capital (distinguishing between general and ICT-related human capital), innovativeness, size and competition (distinguishing between price and non-price competition).

The relationship between human capital and innovation has been traditionally investigated and discussed extensively in many previous studies (Aghion and Howitt 1998; Barro 1999; Arvanitis et al. 2013). Business human resources are the driving force of all kinds of innovation, as it is a key factor for acquiring business skills to identify new needs and requirements as well as external knowledge absorption skills, which enables firms to create new knowledge and apply it for making valuable innovations (Vandenbussche et al. 2006; Vinding 2006; Lopez-Garcia and Montero 2012). Thus, taking into account the requirements of BA technologies for business personnel who have: i) a good knowledge and understanding firm's activities and processes, as well as their problems, challenges and needs, ii) ability to 'associate' them with the results and outputs that the existing BA techniques can provide, and therefore identify opportunities, and identify opportunities of using these techniques for addressing the above problems, challenges and needs, iii) and high level of abilities to use BA results for making decisions, we can expect that higher levels of 'general' human capital (e.g. higher share of employees having higher education) will result in larger extent of BA use. Thus, our fourth research hypothesis is:

Hypothesis 4: *Firm's human capital has a positive effect on the extent of BA adoption.*

The complexity of processes of modern firms requires ICT personnel to have advanced ICT skills, as well as business understanding of firm's activities and processes, in order to make innovative use of ICT in the different business areas of the firm (Arvanitis et al. 2013). The advantage provided by competent ICT personnel is therefore vital for the effective adoption of new innovative ICT, so they constitute firm's ICT-related human capital critical for technological innovations. With respect to BA firm's ICT personnel is highly important for monitoring evolutions in BA technologies, identifying the ones that might be useful for the firm, disseminating them to business personnel, and collaborating with them in order to identify valuable BA use opportunities, as well as for implementing them efficiently and effectively. However, ICT personnel have multiple duties related to the operation, management and support of the users of existing applications and systems, the development of new ones, and the management of several ICT projects in progress, usually in collaboration with external partners and consultants (Shih et al. 2011). Therefore, it is necessary to have a sufficient number of ICT personnel, so that these the above necessary and urgent ICT tasks can be completed, and at the same time there is some time left for creative thinking concerning the introduction of new innovative technologies, including BA. Innovation research has traditionally emphasized the importance of 'slack resources' for innovation (Nohria and Gulati 1996). So, our fifth research hypothesis is:

Hypothesis 5: *Firm's ICT-related human capital has a positive effect on the extent of BA adoption.*

The innovativeness of top management and their support has been identified as an important factor for the adoption of many technological innovations (e.g. see Low and Chen (2011) for cloud computing adoption), including BA (Boonsiritomachai et al. 2016; Puklavec et al. 2017). In this study we investigate the wider concept of innovativeness at the level of the whole firm, manifested through the frequent introduction of new products and services. If a firm is innovative it has a culture of and familiarity with searching for, learning and experimenting with new ideas and technologies, managing their inherent problems and risks, and finding solutions for overcoming them; furthermore, their personnel exhibits low level of 'resistance to change'. We expect that these will facilitate and assist the adoption of BA as well, so our sixth research hypothesis is:

Hypothesis 6: *Firm's innovativeness has a positive effect on the extent of BA adoption.*

The size of organizations has been systematically associated positively with business innovation, with larger organizations appearing to be more innovative than smaller ones, as they have more financial and human resources for this (Malladi and Krishnan 2013; Rogers 2003; Mytinge 1968; Mahler and Rogers 1999). Previous studies traditionally show that the level of complexity that firms have to cope with in order to achieve their smooth and efficient operation is proportional to their size; however, proportional to their size are also their organizational resources, and especially their economic resources, that can be made available for the introduction of innovative technological infrastructures (Geroski 2000; Rogers 2003). Large firms, due to economies of scale are able to adopt technologies with the lowest increase of costs per unit compared to small and medium-sized firms. Also, due to the great complexity large-scale firms face at all levels of their operations, they are necessarily turning to integrating innovations to cope with these challenges, and BA can be quite useful for this. Furthermore, large firms have more extensive and complex activities and processes, and also larger volumes of data, so they have stronger motivation to use the latter for gaining a better insight into the former, which can be useful for improving and optimizing them. Furthermore, previous studies have found that the degree of availability of organizational resources, and relevant organizational readiness, has a positive impact on the adoption of BA technologies (Puklavec et al. 2017; Boonsiritomachai et al. 2016). Hence, the firm's size is expected to have a positive effect on the extent of adoption of BA, so our next research hypothesis is:

Hypothesis 7: *Firm's size has a positive effect on the extent of BA adoption.*

3.3   Environmental Factors

Previous innovation research has traditionally dealt with the impact of competition on firms' innovation activities, concluding that intense competition between firms leads to an increase in the adoption of innovations (e.g. Mansfield 1968; Mansfield et al. 1977; Arvanitis et al. 2013). In this study we distinguish between two dimensions of competition. The first one relates to the competition that the firms face with respect to the prices of products and services (price competition), while the second one relates to all other axes of competition, beyond price, such the quality of products and services, the ability to customize them to special needs of customers, the introduction of new products and services, the provision of support services, etc. (non-price competition). Competition intensity has been found in previous studies to promote BA adoption (Malladi and Krishnan 2013; Boonsiritomachai et al. 2016, Nam et al. 2019). Higher competition, both price and non-price one, put pressure on firms to increase their efficiency, as well as to improve the quality of their products and services, and meet to the highest possible extent the needs of their customers; these increase firms' propensity to exploit better their data assets, through advanced processing of them using BA techniques, for the above purposes. Thus, our final research hypotheses are:

Hypothesis 8: *The intensity of price competition has a positive effect on the extent of BA adoption.*

Hypothesis 9: *The intensity of non-price competition has a positive effect on the extent of BA adoption.*

Our research model is shown in Fig. 1.

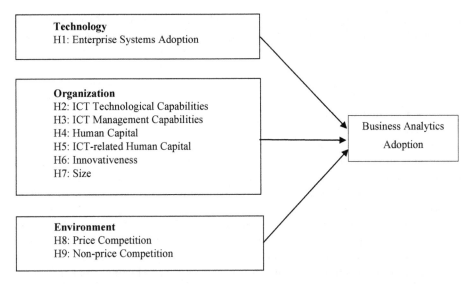

Fig. 1. Research model

4   Data and Method

This study was based on data collected from 363 Greek firms, through a survey, conducted in cooperation with ETH Zurich and ICAP SA, a leading Greek business information and consulting firm, titled "Innovation - Use of Information Technology and Cloud - Effects of the Economic Crisis on Greek Enterprises". We received from ICAP SA a random sample of Greek firms of all sizes from the most advanced sectors of the Greek economy (food and beverages, footwear, papermaking, ICT production, electronics, shipbuilding and repairs, construction, tourism, telecommunications and hospital services). The research team developed the questionnaire and sent it via e-mail to the CEOs of these firms, asking them to return it completed via the electronic form, fax or email within one month. From the respondent firms 52.9% are small businesses (1–49 employees), 36% are medium-sized ones (with 50–249 employees) and the remaining 11.2% are large enterprises (with more by 250 employees).

In order to test the research hypotheses formulated in the previous section we used data concerning a subset of the questions of the above questionnaire, which are shown in the Appendix.

Our dependent variable is the extent of BA adoption (BA_AD), which is measured in a 5-points Lickert scale (where 5 = to a very large extent, 4 = to a large extent, 3 = to a moderate extent, 2 = to a small extent, 1 = not at all).

Our technological independent variable is the extent of ES adoption (ES_AD), which is calculated as the average of three variables assessing the extent of adoption of an ERP, a CRM and a SCM system respectively (measured in the same 5-points Likert scale). The degree of development of firm's ICT technological capabilities (ICT_TC) is calculated as the average of three variables assessing the degree of having capability for: a) rapid internal implementation (by the ICT staff of the firm) of various changes in the application software of its IS in order to meet new requirements; b) rapid internal development (by the ICT staff of the firm) of new software applications in order to meet new requirements; c) rapid internal implementation (by the ICT staff of the firm) of various interconnections/integrations of existing applications, so that there is interoperability of them (= one application can use data and functionality of other applications). All these variables are measured in a 5-points Lickert scale (where 5 = to a very high degree, 4 = to a high degree, 3 = to a moderate degree, 2 = to a low degree, 1 = not at all). The degree of development of firm's ICT management capabilities (ICT_MC) is calculated as the average of three variables assessing the degree of having capability for: i) good cooperation, mutual understanding and trust between the ICT staff of the firm and the staff of the other business units that use ICT; ii) good cooperation, trust and exchange of information with the ICT suppliers (of hardware/software/networks), as well as support from them for solving all relevant problems; iii) ICT strategies and plans which are connected with the overall strategies and plans of the firm (ICT business alignment).

The general human capital has been measured through the share of firm's personnel who are graduates of higher education (HC), while the ICT-related human capital has been measured by the number of firm's ICT personnel divided by total number of firm's personnel (ICT_HC). Firm's innovativeness has been measured through the extent of firm's strategy including the introduction of new products and services with significant innovations (INNOV), measured in the same 5-points Likert scale used for measuring the dependent variable BA_AD. The size of the firm is quantified through a dummy variable based on firm's number of employees in full-time equivalents, taking value 1 for small-sized firms with less than 50 employees, 2 for medium-sized firms with 50 to 249 employees and 3 for large-sized firms with 250 or more employees (D_SZ). Also, we used another sector dummy variable (D_SECT), taking value 0 for service sectors firms and 1 for manufacturing or construction sectors firms.

Finally, the two environmental independent variables, intensity of price and non-price competition, were measured both in 5-points Likert scales (where 5 = very strong, 4 = strong, 3 = moderate, 2 weak, 1 = very weak) (P_COMP and NP_COMP).

Based on the above data we estimated ordinal regression models having the following specification:

$$BA\_AD = b_0 + b_1 * ES\_AD + b_2 * ICT\_C + b_3 * HC + b_4 * ICT\_HC + b_5 * INNOV + b_6 * COMP + b_7 * D\_SZ + b_8 * D\_SECT + e$$

Since there was high level of correlation between the two competition independent variables P_COMP and NP_COMP it was not possible to include both of them in one regression model as independent variables, as this would lead to multi-collinearity problems (unreliable estimations of their corresponding bi coefficients) (Greene 2018), so we estimated one model with the former, and another model with the latter as independent variable. The same happens with the two ICT capabilities' independent variables ICT_TC and ICT_MC, so we estimated one model with the former, and another model with the latter as independent variable, and also an additional one with their average ICT_C as an overall measure of firm's ICT capabilities. So, we estimated $2 \times 3 = 6$ ordinal regression models in total.

5   Results - Discussion

The estimated ordinal regression models are shown in Table 1. The statistically significant bi at the 1%, 5% and 10% levels are denoted with asterisks (***, ** and * respectively).

Table 1. Results from the regression models.

Variable	Model 1	Model 2	Model 3	Model 4	Model 5	Model 6
ES_Adoption	1,287***	1,284***	1,239***	1,242***	1,248***	1,248***
	(,120)	(,120)	(,122)	(,122)	(,121)	(,121)
Size	,582***	,552***	,503***	,481***	,512***	,488***
	(,173)	(,172)	(,177)	(,176)	(,177)	(,176)
Sector	−,318	−,311	−,299	−,287	−,312	−,301
	(,223)	(,224)	(,224)	(,225)	(,224)	(,224)
Human Capital	,440	,357	,297	,222	,373	,291
	(,406)	(,406)	(,411)	(,412)	(,408)	(,408)
ICT Human Capital	−,212	−,227	−,205	−,200	−,308	-,309
	(,491)	(,492)	(,480)	(,481)	(,489)	(,491)
ICT Capabilities					,349***	,346***
					(,124)	(,124)
ICT Technological Capabilities	,197**	,208**				
	(,100)	(,100)				
ICT Management Capabilities			,383***	,361***		
			(,125)	(,124)		
Innovativeness	,150	,261	,204	,321	,168	,285
	(,280)	(,281)	(,281)	(,281)	(,280)	(,281)
Price Competition	,212*		,239*		,220*	
	(,104)		(,104)		(,104)	
Non-Price Competition		−,106		−,093		−,099
		(,096)		(,097)		(,096)

We can see that the extent of ES adoption has a statistically significant positive effect on the extent of BA adoption, so research hypothesis 1 is supported. This indicates that the adoption of ES, such as ERP, CRM and SCM ones, generates large amounts of data concerning various different firm's activities and processes, which are of comprehensive, integrated and of high quality, so the basis and 'raw material' for building high value BA applications that summarize these data and extract useful knowledge from them, providing substantial support for making better and more evidence-based decisions. Comparing the correlations of the extent of BA adoption with the extent of adoption of ERP, CRM and SCM reveals that the CRM one has the highest value, followed by the SCM one, and finally the CRM one. Therefore, the extensive data about our interactions with existing as well as potential customers, and their needs and preferences, generated by CRM systems are strong drivers for the development of BA applications that extract from them valuable knowledge (having the form of advanced reports, dashboards, customer clusters and segments, relevant predictions, etc.) concerning our markets, which can be very useful for increasing our sales. Also, the extensive data concerning our supply chain activities generated by SCM systems are strong divers for the development of BA applications enabling the identification of inefficiencies in these activities, which can be very useful for reducing our operating costs.

Also, we can see that the degree of development of ICT technological capabilities, ICT management capabilities, and also overall ICT capabilities, have a statistically significant positive effects on the extent of BA adoption, so research hypotheses 2 and 3 are supported. By comparing the corresponding bi, and also the correlations with the dependent variable, it can be concluded that the positive effect of firm's ICT management capabilities on the extent of BA adoption is higher than the one of ICT technological capabilities. This indicates that firms having good capabilities in managing ICT usage, initially by carefully planning their exploitation, by developing ICT strategic plans, which support and enhance firm's overall strategic plans (ICT strategic alignment) (Chan and Reich 2007; Leidner et al. 2011; Wu et al. 2015), and then by establishing an effective co-operation of the ICT unit with the business units (who use ICT for their work) as well as with ICT vendors, will be better positioned for identifying highly valuable opportunities of BA use and then implementing the corresponding BA applications. They will be able to identify strategic BA applications, and also to exploit and combine both the business-related knowledge of their business units and personnel, with the BA-related knowledge of their ICT units and personnel, in order to identify a variety of valuable opportunities of BA use for supporting and improving decision-making in a multitude of firm's activities and processes. Also, they will be able to acquire knowledge from their ICT vendors for exploiting efficiently and effectively their existing ICT infrastructure (e.g. existing hardware, software, data, networks, etc.) in order to build to realize these opportunities and build the corresponding BA applications at a low cost and with good quality. These are going to lead to a more extensive development and use of BA within the firm. Furthermore, firms having good ICT technological capabilities, concerning applications development, modification and integration/interconnection, will be able to integrate existing data and applications, which is of critical importance for the development of highly valuable BA applications, which combine data from different activities and functional areas, and provide holistic pictures, quite useful for evidence-based decision-making.

On the contrary, from Table 1 we can see both the general and the ICT-related human capital variables do not have statistically significant effects on the extent of BA adoption, so research hypotheses 4 and 5 are not supported. This is not in agreement with previous research finding that human capital, both generic and ICT-related, affect positively innovation (see research hypotheses 4 and 5 in Sect. 3); it possibly reflects lack of awareness and knowledge about BA of the highly educated personnel, as well as the ICT personnel, of the Greek firms, and also lack of direction and motivation of them by higher management towards BA exploitation. Similarly, firm's general innovativeness does not have statistically significant effect on the extent of BA adoption, so research hypothesis 6 is not supported. This probably indicates that the adoption of BA required quite different skills, attitudes and mentalities from the ones required from the 'classical' products and services innovation activity of firms (e.g. the change of decision-making style from mainly intuitive towards a more evidence-based one). The size has a statistically significant effect on the extent of BA adoption, so research hypothesis 7 is supported; this in agreement with our expectations and the findings of relevant innovation literature (see arguments for research hypothesis 7 in Sect. 3).

Finally, we can see that the intensity of price competition has a statistically significant positive effects on the extent of BA adoption, while the intensity of non-price competition does not have a statistically significant effect; so, research hypothesis 8 is supported, but research hypothesis 9 is not supported. This probably indicates that Greek firms perceive BA mainly as a means of identifying inefficiencies and reducing their operating costs, and much less as a means of improving the quality of their products and services, and customer service. This is in agreement to some extent with previous studies on the factors affecting BA adoption finding that competition intensity is a driver of BA adoption (Malladi and Krishnan 2013; Boonsiritomachai et al. 2016; Nam et al. 2019).

6 Conclusions

In the previous sections has been presented a study that contributes to the research on the factors that affect the extent of BA adoption, by investigating the effects of two factors that had not been examined before: the extent of ES adoption, and the degree of development of firm's ICT capabilities, distinguishing between technological and management ones. For this purpose, we have specified a BA adoption model, based on the TOE framework, which includes as independent variables the above two factors, and also (for the completeness of our model) some additional factors that have been found in previous innovation research to affect positively the adoption of technological innovation: human capital (distinguishing between general and ICT-related human capital), innovativeness, size and competition (distinguishing between price and non-price competition).

We have found that both the extent of ES adoption, and the degree of development of firm's ICT capabilities (and especially the ICT management ones) have a positive impact on BA adoption. Furthermore, we have found that the intensity of price competition, as well as size, impact positively the extent of BA adoption. On the contrary, firm's human capital, both the generic and the ICT-related ones, general innovativeness, and non-price competition, do not have any effect on the extent of BA adoption of the Greek firms.

Future research should look into the effects on more variables – firm's characteristics concerning the three dimensions of the TOE framework (technological, organizational and environmental). As far as the technological dimension is concerned, various other new digital technologies or other technologies (e.g. production ones) need to be studied. Regarding the organizational dimension, it is necessary to examine the relationship between the adoption and use of BA technologies with decision-making styles of the firm, the characteristics of its processes (e.g. their complexity), its structures (e.g. the degree of centralization of decision-making), its strategic choices and business plans. With regard to the environmental dimension, it is necessary to examine the effects on BA adoption of other characteristics of firm's external environment, such as its dynamism, complexity, etc. These should be examined in different kinds of national contexts, characterized by different levels of economic and technological development, as well as culture.

Appendix

Variable	Question
BI_BA adoption	To what extent are Business Analytics systems used in your firm? (= software that supports advanced forms of processing business data, which lead to the creation of useful reports, as well as various types of models, aiming at the support of decision-making)
ERP adoption	To what extent are Enterprise Resource Planning (ERP) systems, used in your firm?
CRM adoption	To what extent are Customer Relationship Management (CRM) systems used in your firm?
SCM adoption	To what extent are Supply Chain Management (SCM) systems used in your firm? (=software that supports the electronic exchange of information with customers, suppliers and business partners, such as inventory levels, orders, production, shipments, invoices, etc.)
Size	Number of firm employees
General Human Capital	Percentage of the personnel of your firm who are Graduates of Higher Education
ICT Personnel	Number of qualified ICT specialists of your firm
ICT Technological Capabilities	To what degree does your firm have: a) Capability of rapid internal implementation (by the ICT staff of your firm) of various changes in the application software of your information systems in order to meet new requirements; b) Capability of rapid internal development (by the ICT staff of your firm) of new software applications in order to meet new requirements; c) Capability of rapid internal implementation (by the ICT staff of your firm) of various interconnections/integrations of existing applications, so that there is interoperability of them (=one application can use data and functionality of other applications)
ICT Management Capabilities	To what degree does your firm have: a) Good cooperation, mutual understanding and trust between the ICT staff of your firm and the staff of the other business units that use ICT, b) Good cooperation, trust and exchange of information with your ICT suppliers (of hardware/software/networks), as well as support from them for solving all relevant problems; c) ICT strategies and plans which are connected with the overall strategies and plans of the firm (ICT business alignment)

(continued)

(continued)

Variable	Question
Innovativeness	To what extent does your business strategy include introduction of new products/services with significant innovations
Price Competition	How intensive is the competition you face from other firms with respect to price (price competition)
Non-Price Competition	How intensive is the competition you face from other firms with respect to other competition dimensions beyond price, such as quality of products/services, adaptation to specific customer needs (customization), introduction of new products/services, provision of support services, etc. (non-price competition)

References

Aghion, P., Howitt, P.: Endogenous Growth Theory. MIT Press, Cambridge (1998)

Arvanitis, S., Loukis, E., Diamantopoulou, V.: Are ICT, Workplace Organization, and Human Capital Relevant for Innovation? A Comparative Swiss/Greek Study (2013)

Aydiner, A.A., Tatoglu, E., Bayraktar, E., Zaim, S., Delene, D.: Business analytics and firm performance: the mediating role of business process performance. J. Bus. Res. **96**, 228–237 (2019)

Baker, J.: The technology-organization-environment framework. In: Dwivedi, Y., Wade, M., Schneberger, S. (eds.) Information Systems Theory: Explaining and Predicting Our Digital Society, pp. 231–246. Springer, New York (2011). https://doi.org/10.1007/978-1-4419-6108-2_12

Barro, R.J.: Human capital and growth in cross-country regressions. Swedish Econ. Policy Rev. **6**(2), 237–277 (1999)

Boonsiritomachai, W., McGrath, G.M., Burgess, S.: Exploring business intelligence and its depth of maturity in Thai SMEs (2016)

Chan, Y.E., Reich, B.H.: IT alignment: what have we learned? J. Inf. Technol. **22**, 297–315 (2007)

Garrison, G., Wakefield, R.L., Kim, S.: The effects of IT capabilities and delivery model on cloud computing success and firm performance for cloud supported processes and operations. Int. J. Inf. Manage. **35**(4), 377–393 (2015)

Geroski, P.: Models of technology diffusion. Res. Policy **29**, 603–625 (2000)

Greene, W.: Econometric analysis -, 8th edn. Pearson, USA (2018)

Gu, J.W., Jung, H.W.: The effects of IS resources, capabilities, and qualities on organizational performance: an integrated approach. Inf. Manag. **50**(2–3), 87–97 (2013)

Laudon, K.C., Laudon, J.P.: Management Information Systems: Managing the Digital Firm, 16th edn. Pearson Education Limited, New York (2019)

Leidner, D., Lo, J., Preston, D.: An empirical investigation of the relationship of IS strategy with firm performance. J. Strat. Inf. Syst. **20**(4), 419–437 (2011)

Lopez-Garcia, P., Montero, J.M.: Spillovers and absorptive capacity in the decision to innovate of spanish firms: the role of human capital. Econ. Innov. New Technol. **21**(7), 589–612 (2012)

Low, C., Chen, Y.: Understanding the determinants of cloud computing adoption. Ind. Manag. Data Syst. **111**(7), 1006–1023 (2011)

Mahler, A., Rogers, E.M.: The diffusion of interactive communication innovations and the critical mass: the adoption of telecommunications services by German Banks. Telecommun. Policy **23**, 719–740 (1999)

Malladi, S.: Adoption of business intelligence & analytics in organizations – an empirical study of antecedents. In: Proceedings of the Nineteenth Americas Conference on Information Systems, Chicago, Illinois, 15–17 August (2013)

Malladi, S., Krishnan, M.S.: Determinants of usage variations of business intelligence & analytics in organizations – an empirical analysis. In: Proceedings of the Thirty Fourth International Conference on Information Systems, Milan, Italy, 15–18 December (2013)

Mansfield, E.: Industrial Research and Technological Innovation. Norton, New York (1968)

Mansfield, E., Rapoport, J., Romeo, A., Villani, E., Wagner, S., Husic, F.: The Production and Application of New Industrial Technology. Norton, New York (1977)

Nam, D., Lee, J., Lee, H.: Business analytics adoption process: an innovation diffusion perspective. Int. J. Inf. Manage. **49**, 411–423 (2019)

Nohria, N., Gulati, R.: Is slack good or bad for innovation. Acad. Manag. J. **39**(5), 1245–1264 (1996)

Puklavec, B., Oliveira, T., Popovic, A.: Understanding the determinants of business intelligence system adoption stages: an empirical study of SMEs (2017)

Rainer, R.K., Prince, B., Watson, H.J.: Management Information Systems, 4th edn. Wiley, New York (2016)

Ransbotham, S., Kiron, D., Prentice, P.K.: Beyond the hype: the hard work, behind analytics success. MIT Sloan Manag. Rev. **57**(3), 3–16 (2016)

Ravichandran, T., Lertwongsatien, C.: Effect of information system resources and capabilities on firm performance: a resource-based perspective. J. Manag. Inf. Syst. **21**(4), 237–276 (2005)

Rogers, E.M.: Diffusion of Innovations. Free Press, New York (2003)

Roztocki, N., Soja, P., Weistroffer, H.R.: Enterprise systems in transition economies: research landscape and framework for socioeconomic development. Inf. Technol. Dev. **26**(1), 1–37 (2020)

Shih, S., Jiang, J., Klein, G., Wang, E.: Learning demand and job autonomy of IT personnel: impact on turnover intention. Comput. Hum. Behav. **27**(27), 2301–2307 (2011)

Tornatzky, L.G., Fleischer, M.: The processes of technological innovation. Lexington Books, Lexington (1990)

Vandenbussche, J., Aghion, P., Meghir, C.: Growth, distance to frontier and composition of human capital. J. Econ. Growth **11**(2), 97–127 (2006)

Vinding, A.L.: Absorptive capacity and innovative performance: a human capital approach. Econ. Innov. New Technol. **15**(4–5), 507–517 (2006)

Wu, S.P., Straub, D.W., Liang, T.P.: How information technology governance mechanisms and strategic alignment influence organizational performance: insights from a matched survey of business and IT managers. MIS Q. **39**(2), 497–518 (2015)

Evaluation of Cloud Business Intelligence Prior to Adoption: The Voice of Small Business Enterprises in a South African Township

Moses Moyo[✉] and Marianne Loock

University of South Africa, Pretoria, South Africa
mosesm50@gmail.com, loockm@unisa.ac.za

Abstract. The purpose of this qualitative study was to provide an insight into how small business enterprises from a South African township evaluated cloud business intelligence solutions and the challenges faced. The study found that despite limited knowledge in security evaluation and lack of easy-to-use techniques for small business enterprise, decision makers conducted basic and unsystematic evaluation of cloud business intelligence prior to adoption. Unsystematic security evaluation was mainly on data security, access control functionalities such as authentication, cloud service providers' security, trust and reliability and financial risks. The study concluded that an easy-to-use security evaluation framework for cloud business intelligence solution tailored for small business enterprises was a necessity to overcome challenges among enterprises in South African townships in order to enhance good security practices when adopting cloud services.

Keywords: Security evaluation · Data security · Cloud business intelligence · Small business enterprises

1 Introduction

The acceptance and use of cloud business intelligence solutions (CBIs) are not yet consolidated in South Africa, therefore, it is relevant to question their adoption by small business enterprises (SBEs). CBIs can be used as some decision support systems to strategically increase business viability by reducing operational disruptions and competition among (SBEs) [1, 2]. However, several security challenges deprive SBEs of the benefits these technologies, particularly in townships where there is scarce information technology (IT) specialists [3]. With the growing awareness and acceptance of cloud services among South African SBEs, the need for security evaluation becomes a vital process to undertake when adopting CBI [4]. Without conducting security evaluation, there is a possibility that SBEs can adopt and use CBIs without evaluating security risks, a practice that may expose the enterprise information system to cyber security threats and risks. Apparently, the problem is that, many CBIs are still novel to SBEs who have limited knowledge of inherent security vulnerabilities, threats and risks that need to be assessed [5]. This is worsened when CBIs depend on cloud computing technologies that are prone to several security threats and breaches which compromise

© Springer Nature Switzerland AG 2020
M. Themistocleous et al. (Eds.): EMCIS 2020, LNBIP 402, pp. 449–460, 2020.
https://doi.org/10.1007/978-3-030-63396-7_30

information systems and potentially jeopardise enterprise operations, viability and competitiveness [6]. With several South African SBEs adopting and using cloud services, data breaches also increase exponential resulting in the loss of millions of Rands in revenue annually [7, 8]. A report by [9] shows that, close to 60% of the cyber-attacks in South Africa target SBEs. These reports underscore that SBEs migrating data to the cloud cannot be spared of data breaches and therefore, the need for these enterprise to be cautious when adopting CBIs.

The problem is that whenever SBEs in townships decide to adopt and use any new technologies the owners and managers of these enterprises, who are not security specialists, assume responsibilities in security evaluation. Consequently, basic knowledge in security evaluation among decision makers becomes a crucial requirement for selecting appropriate and secure CBIs. Currently, there is scarce information about how SBEs select the CBIs they use to support business activities.

The purpose of this study is to contribute to existing knowledge on the security evaluation of CBIs among disadvantaged SBEs in South African townships by critically examining the practices of these enterprises when adopting cloud services. This qualitative study was designed to answer the following research questions:

a. *What security evaluation techniques do SBEs use when selecting cloud business intelligence prior to adoption?*
b. *What challenges do SBEs face in implementing the evaluation techniques?*
c. *What do SBEs consider to be important aspects in security evaluation of CBIs?*

The structure of the article is as follows: Sect. 2: Review of related works; Sect. 3: Research design and methods, Sect. 4: Analysis of results and interpretations; Sect. 5: Discussions of findings and Sect. 6: Conclusions and limitations.

2 Review of Related Works

CBI combines a cloud computing platform and BI technology in a user-friendly, flexible and cost-effective manner to support fast decision making in an enterprise [10]. SBEs in South African townships with weak financial resources and limited IT knowledge to acquire and implement traditional business intelligence (BI) can benefit from CBIs. Dashboards and reports present results in formats that are easy to interpret and facilitate actionable decision-making without involving expensive data analytics experts [11]. However, security vulnerabilities, threats and risks in the cloud environments pose as main challenges [3, 6]. Cloud computing security should be the core reason to inspire SBEs to adopt the use of cloud services [6, 11]. Ideally, CBIs should be more secure than on-premise information systems because CSPs are supposed to be specialised in providing security in the cloud [12]. Conversely, literature by [13] and [14] shows that security in cloud environments is difficult to attain due to vulnerabilities in the technologies used and increasing cyber threats. With SBEs gradually realising the importance of CBIs as decision support systems, adopting these technologies without proper security evaluation defeats the intended purposes.

Adopting CBIs and migrating data to the cloud is a big decision that requires SBEs to evaluate a range of security aspects and other functionalities that are crucial to the enterprise operations [1]. Security evaluation entails analysis of a solution to determine its degree of compliance with a stated security model, security standard, or specification [15]. Similarly, [16] posits that security evaluation plays an important role in identifying existing threats and potential vulnerabilities of the system so as to avoid them in future systems. SBEs need to perform security evaluation in order to verify that security measures and functionalities are in place accurately and effectively comply with the individual user's security requirements. Furthermore, CBIs security evaluation can be used to verify CSPs security trust, assurance and reliability in service provision [10]. Presently, there is very thin literature on security evaluation of cloud services by SBEs particularly in South Africa. This study is vital in providing knowledge and insights on personal experiences of SBEs decision making on CBIs evaluation prior to adoption. Findings from the empirical study will narrow the knowledge gap of security evaluation by SBEs in township that public and academic researcher could have been taking for granted.

3   Research Design and Data Collection Method

This study utilised a qualitative design for the researcher to interact with participants in their natural settings where they were free to express their experiences about the phenomenon being studied [17], security evaluation in CBIs. A purposive sample of five decision makers from SBEs already using ITs to support business operations was used. Participants with experience in IT systems and basic knowledge in cloud services were regarded as rich source of information relevant to CBIs being investigated [18]. The use of a purposive sample was supported by [19] who argues that it was effective in attaining data saturation with a few participants. The inclusion criteria were based on the knowledge of CBIs and the intention to adopt by SBEs already using IT systems to support business operations.

Face-to-face semi-structured interviews were done to collect data from the selected participants. The use of semi-structured interview guide provided the researcher with an opportunity to understand the security evaluation from the point of view of decision makers. The interview sessions lasted an average of 30 min.

3.1   Ethical Issues

An ethical clearance was obtained from the relevant institution before data collection. Prior to the interview, each participant signed the consent form which stipulated ethical issues such as privacy of identity, anonymity and confidentiality of participants, protection of participants and other researchers from harm, voluntary participation and withdrawal and avoiding the use of deception. Participants were identified as P1, P2, P3, P4 and P4.

3.2 Trustworthiness

In ensuring trustworthiness and credibility, we followed recommendations by [20] of asking interviewees to confirm at the end of the interview and data transcriptions that they agreed with the transcripts.

4 Analysis and Interpretation of Results

Qualitative data analysis was conducted using Atlas ti 8 following thematic analysis method [21]. Themes and sub-themes important to this article were those that related to the evaluation of CBIs and the challenges that decision makers faced.

4.1 Evaluation Strategies Used by Decision Makers in Selecting Cloud Business Intelligence Solutions

The attestations highlight how decision makers assessed CBIs to be adopted. The evaluation strategies used included active assessment of security features in CBIs, asking for information from friends and CSPs, searching for information about CBIs from internet and using trial versions.

Assessing Data Security in Cloud Business Intelligence Solutions. Although participants were non-IT specialists, the need to assess data security in CBIs was regarded as very important to decision makers:

> 'I do my own evaluation bit by bit, comparing different solutions looking for possible security weaknesses in the interface, data conversions, data retrieval', [P1].
> 'I use trial or free versions to check if security features work and also to find out if the system support data migration easily. I do not want to struggle when moving data to the cloud', [P3].
> 'I check how secure the systems is in terms of interface used, particularly what takes place during logging-in and logging-out. Ideally, I would want to check how many users can access my account if I leave the app without logging out', [P5].

The extracts show that security evaluation centres on vital information about data security in the application. It is also clear that decision makers make effort to check applications for security weaknesses. These findings show that decision makers evaluating data security in CBIs was a key strategy which should be done to protect business assets.

Using Information About Cloud Service Providers to Assess Security, Trust and Reliability in Service Provision. CSPs play a crucial role in providing CBIs as service hence the need to evaluate CBIs by examining the history of security, trust and reliability of the providers. The extracts confirm this:

> 'I make background checks of a providers to see how reliable they are in providing the services and how they performed in terms of security. I also use discussion forums to check what is being said about the app I am interested in', [P2].
> 'I look for formation on previous data breaches which occurred with provider...how they were dealt with.... I request information from providers on how safety of data storages', [P4].

Consulting colleagues to get information and advice on new IT solutions and what to do was another strategy suggested by partipcants:

'I prefer to consult my colleagues whenever there is new technology I want to use then I decide from what they say...I compare what my colleagues tell me with what I find from the internet concerning the new technologies. I visit web sites of service providers to familiarise myself with their product', [P5].

The four attestations show a growing need for decision makers to be initiative in the evaluation of IT solutions to support their decision making process for the adoption. Easy access to information about CBIs and CSPs can make it feasible for decision makers to find and learn much about the solutions they intend to adopt.

Using Checklists to Evaluate Cloud Business Intelligence Solutions. The use of checklists in the evaluation of CBIs prior to adoption was raised by two participants only. This shows that decision makers were not aware of existing tools that could be used to guide them when evaluating CBIs:

'I use checklists from the Web to assess how secure the app is and how to use it. Checklist guides me on those vital aspects of the cloud I should evaluate. At least I get an idea of what should be done although some of the guidelines are too difficult to follow', [P3].

'There are many checklists one can use to evaluate cloud services, the problem is that they are specific to certain product and not others. All the same they are important as a starting point. It is different from adopting a solution without assessing it', [P5].

The use of checklists by some of the decision makers in evaluating CBIs highlighted the importance of having an easy-to-use evaluation tool for non-IT end users. This would encourage them to try things out on their own or with minimum assistance from specialists.

Inspecting Physical Security of Data Centres Participants indicated that decision makers preferred to ascertain how secure the physical infrastructure was against various natural disasters, burglary and unauthorised access.

'I am not confident with cloud technologies; I cannot take any chance without assessing physical security of the place where the data will be stored. It is my desire to check whether the service provider has the capabilities of protecting the computers where data will be kept', [P1].

The situation becomes difficult when it comes to physical security in the cloud as it is difficult to access the place where data is stored and check how secure it. All now depends on how trustworthy the provider is. I would like to visit the site where data is stored so that I see how secure it is and who access the data [P2].

Assessing of physical security of data centres was viewed as an important aspect of security evaluations in CBIs which decision makers could conduct to ascertain the security of their data.

4.2 Description of Challenges Faced in the Evaluation of Cloud Business Intelligence

Although decision makers were forthcoming which strategies in evaluating CBIs, challenges faced were counterproductive to their efforts. Three main challenges were identified from the interviews with participant as presented.

Limited Knowledge on How to Evaluate Security in Cloud Business Intelligence Solutions. Excerpts from participants show that limited knowledge in assessing CBIs by decision makers was a major challenge that stifled their effort to recommend the adoption of cloud services. The two excerpts below support this finding;

Without the know-how of cloud technologies, it's difficult to tell which cloud business intelligence is safe to adopt. I have little technical knowledge about security and how to evaluate IT solutions. Something may appear appealing but hiding threats, [P2].

Lack of evaluative skills of emerging information technologies is detrimental to the enterprise as we continue to rely on old methods of data management. In my opinion, being able to use an app is much easier than evaluating it. With people like me, if the app is working everything is fine, [P4].

This finding shows that decision makers value knowledge and skills for evaluating IT solutions for business use, but they acknowledge having limited knowledge to accurately assess CBI security measures as setback. Without basic knowledge in security evaluation of CBIs, decision makers would not be able to select the appropriate application.

Inadequate Knowledge of Existing Tools Used in the Evaluation of the Cloud Business Intelligence Solutions by Decision Makers. Extracts from participants 3 and 5 reveal that decision makers faced challenges related ignorance of tools suitable for use in evaluating CBIs.

I am not sure if we have simple techniques to guide small business in selecting cloud services. I think small businesses are treated like large businesses in IT solutions. It is difficult for use to assess cloud business intelligence advanced techniques and tools for big companies, [P3].

It is difficult for us small businesses to select cloud services because we cannot systematically evaluate them properly due to lack of tools for that purpose. .... everyone thinks we should follow the big businesses even if there are very clear differences in our needs, [P5].

From these attestations, participants were aware of differences between SBEs and large business needs and that the existing evaluation tools are designed for latter. The assertions confirm that SBEs expect to have evaluation tools tailored for these enterprises.

Difficult in Getting Relevant Information from the Cloud Service Providers About the Cloud Business Intelligence Solutions. Although participants alleged that they used information from various sources to evaluate CBIs, finding such information from CSPs and vendors was difficult. Some of the information was misrepresenting the solutions and outdated. The extracts illustrate the claims:

It is difficult to find the right information about cloud apps from the Web because providers do not cooperate. Some attract customers with fancy marketing language but offering service with deplorable results, [P1].

I realised that some of the sites offering business intelligence are never updated for a long time. I doubt if they still offer the solutions. ... I avoid such providers, ... the trend is noticeable in many situations where the offers are exaggerated making it difficult to tell the appropriateness of the services from the little information available, [P2].

The finding shows the importance of historical and current information about CBIs and CSP in the evaluation process. However, the inability of CSPs to provide such information makes it difficult for decision makers to evaluate CBIs on their own. Information from outdated web sites and challenges in accessing current information deterred decision makers from conducting proper evaluation of CBIs.

4.3 Important Aspects Considered When Evaluating Cloud Business Intelligence Solutions

Participants suggested four aspects that should be considered when decision makers decided to evaluate CBIs.

Examining the Level of Knowledge and Skill Needed to Operate or Use the Application. The level of knowledge and skills needed to use CBIs was an important area to evaluate so that decision makers avoid making mistakes that lead to breach security procedures in the applications.

> *It is important to check how easy it is to use or learn to use the apps before I make costly mistakes. I would avoid any apps difficult to use or subscribe. I do not want to spend much time learning to use new apps...I do not want to make mistakes that corrupt information..., [P2].*
> *I want to maintain my business in good working condition...so any solution I want to use should be perfect and should not provide glitches, the time I take to learn the solution is important.... it tells me how difficult it is. ...skills needed to use the application without making blunders is important to consider in this case, [P4].*

These two utterances illustrate that decision makers regarded knowledge about how CBIs worked crucial in the evaluation process. The amount of effort needed to use or learn how to use the solution was very important in the evaluation process.

Data Security, Portability and Application Interoperability in the Clouds. Some participants expressed that decision makers should prioritise data security, portability and application interoperability when evaluating CBIs.

> *I look at how sensitive the data is and decide which one to put on the cloud... I make sure that it is safe to use and that my information and data will be protected especially when it is on the Web where the chances of information being corrupted or stolen is always high, [P2].*
> *The first thing I may consider is checking whether data can be uploaded to the cloud storage without being converted to another format and ... the new system can open the data files without corrupting it.... data remains unchanged during migration for future use, [P4].*

These assertions show that data security and portability should be major considerations when migrating sensitive data to the cloud. There was need to consider how data integrity was maintained during migration to the cloud.

Security Functionalities and Compliance of Cloud Business Intelligence Solutions. Some excerpts conveyed the notion that decision makers should expected certain security functionalities to be available in CBIs and should consider checking their deployment and effectiveness prior to adoption.

> *I will be interested in features used to protect data during migration and while being stored in the cloud, [P3].*
> *I will consider the functionality in the app, how they are deployed and used by end users. ...I expect cloud service providers to comply with security regulations but some can flout these regulations as they wish, [P4].*

This finding confirms that decision makers should be concerned with key security features, functionalities and how secure they were. Decision makers were also supposed to consider providers compliant to security standards.

Financial Risks Associated with the Cloud Business Intelligence Solution. Financial benefits than risks arising from security data breaches and system unavailability were very important considerations recommended in the evaluation process. The extracts illustrate the need for such considerations:

> It is wise to look at financial benefits of the app to the enterprises first and then look at the pitfalls. At times, one can be blinded by many benefits and overlooks risks which surface when using the application, [P1].
> I will consider financial risks of using cloud business intelligence...if I am to subscribe to a service provider, I want assurance that service disruptions will not prejudiced the enterprise in any way, [P4].

Financial risks that arise from additional subscription fees imposed on the enterprise on supposedly free app were important considerations.

> I am sceptical of financial risks incurred from supposedly free product that demands payment when in use or one is locked out. ...evaluation should check for such payments to avoid disruptions, [P5].

Decision makers were supposed to take into account financial risks due to losing control of sensitive data to CSPs and litigations.

> Storing data in the cloud is giving up control to providers who can do whatever they want with it. ... financial loses arise if the provider's employees access and leak sensitive data to the public. Paying for legal costs is one thing we cannot afford, [P3].

The findings show a multiple of aspects that led to potential financial risks should be considered during the evaluation process of CBIs. Possible unethical practice by some service providers and their employees were financial risks with negatively impact profits that SBEs would avert. Ligations arising from leakages of sensitive enterprise by CSPs and their employees compelled SBE to consider assurance from the CSP on the security financial responsibilities.

5 Discussion of Findings

In this section, discussions of findings are made for each research question.

5.1 What Security Evaluation Techniques Did SBEs Use When Selecting Cloud Business Intelligence Prior to Adoption?

The findings show that decision makers conducted unsystematic security evaluation in cloud services as a managerial obligation to safeguard enterprise information assets. The key strategies involved assessing access control, authentication and security functionalities using interfaces of CBIs, as recommended by [5]. Similarly, [2] suggest that SBE should use of trial versions to verify the claims made by CSPs in providing secure applications. Decision makers used CSPs' history information in providing security, trust and honouring contracts in the evaluation process. This finding was consistent with existing literature by [22] who emphasise the importance of getting reports about security posture of CSPs. Decision makers consulted friends and at times IT specialist for advice on the security of CBIs they were interested in before adoption. Consultation during the evaluation of new technologies is a good practice within social network of business persons and makes it easy for decision makers to have up-to-date information [23]. However, information shared in networks by friends may not flow to others out of the network thereby delaying the evaluation process. Another danger is circulating inaccurate information among SBEs facing similar problems and the may not be applicable to needs of other enterprises. The use of checklists in security evaluation is a standard practice [24], increasingly used for self-sustenance among SBEs. These findings show basic unsystematic security evaluating of CBIs prior to adoption by SBEs was a good initiative is security good practice.

5.2 What Challenges Did SBEs Face in Implementing the Evaluation Techniques?

Decision makers face three major challenges in security evaluation of CBIs namely: 1) limited knowledge to systematically evaluate CBI; 2) lack of knowledge about appropriate tools for evaluating CBIs for SBEs; and 3) difficulties in getting relevant information from the CSPs about the CBIs. These findings showed that decision makers appreciated the importance of basic knowledge in security evaluation for them to be actively involved in the selection of CBI solutions. According to [2] posit that knowledge about security evaluation of IT solutions is crucial in assisting users in selecting appropriate solutions for their enterprises. Existing evaluation tools were difficult for decision makers to use as they required technical knowledge in security evaluation. SBEs require CBIs which are easy-to-use without requiring much training [5]. A difficult-to-use CBI was construed as a security challenge which led users to make mistakes that result to security breaches. Decision makers found it difficult to get current information about CBIs from CSPs who did not respond to enquiries, or provided outdated information on their web sites. Previous studies in IT solution evaluations emphasise on the importance of accurate information needed when evaluating new technologies [23]. Without correct up-to-date information about CBIs, it was difficult for decision makers to proceed with evaluations.

5.3 What Did SBEs Consider to Be Important Aspects in Security Evaluation of CBIs?

Several considerations were recommended for successful CBIs evaluating by SBEs. Decision makers were aware that the cloud was prevalent of data security breaches and therefore prioritised evaluation of CBIs vulnerabilities and threats that would affect data portability and application interoperability. A study by [23] encourages potential cloud service users to evaluate data security, portability and application interoperability to avoid frustrations of data and vendor lock-in. CSPs fail to provide tools, techniques and standard data formats, services or interfaces for clients to manage data and service portability due differences in technologies used [10]. This consideration was important for decision makers to make beforehand, to ensure data integrity and availability.

Operational security functionalities, features and ratings of CBIs can be used in the evaluation process. These aspects intended to show decision makers how secure the CBIs behaved when in use [3]. Poor-quality CBIs can be very costly and difficult to rectify once the contract is operational. Consequently, decision makers needed to evaluate this aspect prior to the adoption of CBIs. This shows the extent to which decision makers mistrusted CSPs in providing quality and secure CBIs.

The evaluation of cloud deployment model particularly public clouds was another important consideration that should be made. CSPs provide different public clouds that pose data and application portability challenges that SMEs might find it difficult to resolve by themselves [25]. CSP security, trust and reliability were considered important for evaluation because these were part of contractual obligations. One of the major expectations of enterprises from CSPs is the trust in keeping data safe and providing services as stipulated in the contracts [1]. Decision makers could assess reliability by checking the performance of a CSP against the service level agreement over a duration of a year using information from publications or requested by clients [26]. Adopting CBIs from untrusted and unreliable CSPs can lead to financial loss which SBEs seek to avoid.

Financial risks were found to be important aspect that should be evaluated. Different CSPs use their own pricing models which the SBEs should check to avoid running into unnecessary costly financial risks that may lead to unforeseen financial risks [27]. This would assist decision makers to select reliable CSPs with competitive pricing schemes. The level of knowledge and skills needed to operate or use the applications was also considered important when evaluating CBIs because it ultimately affected data security when the user accidentally used the application wrongly. This finding is supported by [4] who posit that an easy to learn and use application tends to lead to fewer security breaches by users compared to a difficult one.

6   Conclusions and Limitations

The study concluded that: 1) the security evaluation strategies used by SBEs were unsystematic and were characterised by the use of unorthodox means; 2) decision makers faced challenges of limited knowledge in security evaluation, lacked knowledge of tools for evaluating CBIs; inability to get correct and up-to-date information from the CSPs needed for CBIs evaluation; and 3) decision makers considered data security, portability and interoperability in the clouds; operational and security functionalities and ratings of CBIs; environment where CBIs were used, financial benefits and risks of the CBIs and CSP trust and reliability as the most important areas to evaluate. The study also concluded that security evaluation of CBIs by SBEs was very important and the enterprises required assistance to overcome challenges in evaluation tools and increase in basic security knowledge need to conduct basic evaluations.

Limitations of the study were that of the sample used was too small to generalise to a large population of other townships in South Africa. Based on the findings of this study, a security evaluation framework for CBIs tailored for SBEs was needed to improve good practice among these enterprises. The findings of this study have implications on the future design and developing security evaluation tools appropriate for use by SBEs intending to adopt different cloud applications. The study recommended similar study with a bigger sample from SBEs across south Africa in order to formulate a security evaluation framework suitable for these enterprises.

References

1. Wise, L.: Evaluating business intelligence in the cloud (2016). http://www.cio.com/article/3041639/business-intelligence/evaluating-business-intelligence-in-the-cloud.html
2. Herwig, V., Friess, K.: Integrating business intelligence services in the cloud: a conceptual model. In: Khosrow-pour, M.H. (ed.) Business Intelligence: Concepts, Methodologies, Tools and Applications, pp. 572–584. IGC Global (2016)
3. Llave, M.R.: Business intelligence and analytics in small and medium-sized enterprises: a systematic literature review. Int. J. Bus. Intell. Res. **10**(1), 19–41 (2019)
4. Moyo, M., Loock, M.: Small and medium-sized enterprises' understanding of security evaluation of cloud-based business intelligence systems and its challenges. In: Venter, H., Loock, M., Coetzee, M., Eloff, M., Eloff, J. (eds.) ISSA 2018. CCIS, vol. 973, pp. 133–148. Springer, Cham (2019). https://doi.org/10.1007/978-3-030-11407-7_10
5. Indriasari, E., Prabowo, H., Meyliana, K., Hidayanto, A.N.: Key benefits of cloud business intelligence: a systematic literature review. Int. J. Mech. Eng. Technol. **9**(13), 819–831 (2018)
6. Patil, S.S., Chavan, R.: Cloud business intelligence: an empirical study. Stud. Indian Place Names UGC Care J. **27**, 747–754 (2020)
7. Niekerk, B.V.: An analysis of cyber-incidents in South Africa. African J. Inf. Commun. **20** (2017), 113–132 (2017)
8. IBM Security, Cost of a Data Breach Report 2020 (2020). https://www.ibm.com/security/digital-assets/cost-data-breach-report/
9. TechCentral, South Africa's vulnerability to cyberattacks (2019). https://techcentral.co.za/south-africas-vulnerability-to-cyberattacks/90051/
10. Cloud Security Alliance, Cloud Computing Top Threats in 2016 (2016). http://oemhub.bitdefender.com/top-threats-to-securing-the-cloud
11. Elmalah, K., Nasr, M.: Cloud business intelligence. Int. J. Adv. Netw. Appl. **10**(6), 4120–4124 (2019)
12. Alia, M., Khana, S., Vasilakos, A.: Security in cloud computing: Opportunities and challenges. Inf. Sci. (NY) **2015**(305), 357–384 (2015)
13. Khan, N., Al-Yasiri, A.: Framework for cloud computing adoption: a roadmap for SMEs to cloud migration. Int. J. Cloud Comput. Serv. Archit. **5**(56), 258–269 (2015)
14. Dresner, H.: Cloud Computing and Business Intelligence Market Study Licensed to Domo (2017). https://www.domo.com/blog/wp-content/uploads/2018/04/2018-Wisdom-of-Crowds-Cloud-Computing-BI-Market-Study-Licensed-to-Do.pdf
15. Encyclopedia.com, Security Evaluation (2020). https://www.encyclopedia.com/computing/dictionaries-thesauruses-pictures-and-press-releases/security-evaluation
16. Heyszl, J., Schütte, J.: Security Evaluation (2018). https://www.aisec.fraunhofer.de/en/fields-of-expertise/security-evaluation.html
17. Bradshaw, C., Atkinson, S., Doody, O.: Employing a qualitative description approach in health care. Res. Glob. Qual. Nurs. Res. **4**(1–8) (2017)

18. Vasileiou, K., Barnett, J., Thorpe, S., Young, T.: Characterising and justifying sample size sufficiency in interview-based studies: systematic analysis of qualitative health research over a 15-year period. BMC Med. Res. Methodol. **18**(148), 125–136 (2018)
19. Kaushik, V., Walsh, C.A.: Pragmatism as a research paradigm and its implications for Social Work research. Soc. Sci. **8**(9) (2019)
20. Polit, D., Beck, T.: Nursing research, generating and assessing evidence for nursing practice, 10th edn. Lippincott Williams and Wilkins, Philadelphia (2017)
21. Clarke, V., Braun, V.: Teaching thematic analysis: overcoming challenges and developing strategies for effective learning. Psychology **26**(2), 120–123 (2013)
22. Majhi, S.K., Dhal, S.K.: A study on security vulnerability on cloud platforms. Phys. Procedia **78**(2016), 55–60 (2016)
23. Salim, S., Sedera, D., Sawang, S., Alarifi, A., Atapattu, M.: Moving from evaluation to trial: how do SMEs start adopting Cloud ERP? Australas. J. Inf. Syst. **2015**(19), S219–S254 (2015)
24. Agostino, A., Soilen, S.K., Gerritsen, B.: Cloud solution in business intelligence for SMEs – vendor and customer perspectives. J. Intell. Stud. Bus. **3**(2013), 5–28 (2013)
25. Bach, M.P., Celjo, A., Zoroja, J.: Technology acceptance model for business intelligence systems: preliminary research. Procedia Comput. Sci. **100**(2016), 995–1001 (2016)
26. Cloud Industry Forum: 8 criteria to ensure you select the right cloud service provider (2019). https://www.cloudindustryforum.org/content/8-criteria-ensure-you-select-right-cloud-service-provider
27. Chaudhari, N., Al-Yasiri, A.: A cloud security approach for data at rest. Int. J. Cloud Comput. Serv. Archit. **5**(1), 11–16 (2015)

Healthcare Information Systems

Hospital Information Systems: Measuring End-User Satisfaction

Fotis Kitsios[1], Maria Kamariotou[1(✉)], Vicky Manthou[1], and Afroditi Batsara[2]

[1] Department of Applied Informatics, University of Macedonia, Thessaloniki, Greece
`kitsios@uom.gr`, {`mkamariotou,manthou`}`@uom.edu.gr`
[2] 424 Military Hospital, Thessaloniki, Greece
`abatsara@yahoo.gr`

Abstract. As problems with health workers' acceptance and satisfaction are now regarded among the most significant barriers to the diffusion of IS within health settings, the purpose of this paper is to examine which factors affect the level of satisfaction of medical and nursing staff with the use of information systems in the 424 Military Hospital in Northern Greece and especially the impact of gender and age on users' satisfaction. A total of 257 questionnaires were collected from 3 clinics. Results show that the participants in the survey are satisfied with the usefulness of the Information System as well as the ease of use of the Information System to a large extent. However, the respondents expressed little satisfaction with the provision of the necessary instructions for the execution of the work, but a better level of satisfaction with the ability of the technical support staff to provide quality services.

Keywords: Hospital information systems · User satisfaction · Nursing · Acceptance · Health

1 Introduction

Nowadays, the health sector experiences different challenges and fundamental changes. Demands are placed on nursing institutions around the world to reconsider their core functions and find new ways to reorganize their business to offer efficient and effective services, reduce their operating costs and become more competitive while providing more and high-quality patient care services [38].

The modern challenges faced by nursing homes are numerous, which include the problem of managing the huge volume of health information produced and circulated and the need to find new methods - techniques to reorganize and improve their business activities. They also have the problem of reducing excessive costs in order to manage their finance rationally and also the problem of providing better quality and personalized health services that are based on evident practice [13, 31, 37].

The use of traditional information systems in sharing the sheer volume and variety of health information has caused problems in providing patient care. The progressive development of informatics has made the managers of hospitals recognize information

© Springer Nature Switzerland AG 2020
M. Themistocleous et al. (Eds.): EMCIS 2020, LNBIP 402, pp. 463–479, 2020.
https://doi.org/10.1007/978-3-030-63396-7_31

technology as a powerful tool that can enhance their productivity. Many hospitals around the world are in the process of applying electronic health information to support patient care [1].

In addition, the information society has changed the doctor-patient model from the medical-central era to the patient-central one, through e-health. E-health does not only provide patients with high-quality health services but also helps to streamline the resources of health systems [13]. Health information systems are those that allow the collection, storage, management, analysis and exchange of information and data of patients in the context of clinical practice [20].

Nursing staff is important when it comes to using health information systems because they are the key providers of patient care, which includes carrying out medical evaluation, diagnosis and intervention. Nurses need to quickly process information about different patients and interpret them directly to design quality care. Therefore, it is imperative to design information systems that can aid the nurses in their duties for better coordination of patient care activities [1].

The two most important areas reported by nursing staff in the use of information systems are the development of real-time feedback systems for nurses and the impact of the information system on nursing care and patients' outcomes [9]. Several studies have shown that in most cases the internal environment of hospitals is the main factor that negatively affects the effort of nursing institutions to introduce new information systems that can be used to modernize their business processes. This could be as a result of most health professionals not having (e.g. doctors, nurses, executives, IT staff, etc.) the basic knowledge or skills of IT, their inability to understand the basic capabilities and limitations of technology, and their inability to understand how these new systems are harmonized in the hospital's work environment [34].

Users' satisfaction of any Hospital Information System development and implementation project is an important research topic which can be explained by the response of healthcare professionals to the use of Information Systems in healthcare. Current research [32, 33] concluded that more satisfied users are have been associated with deeper levels of engagement with a system's functionality, which is significant to achieving higher-order benefits from Information Systems implementations. In healthcare, nurses and medical staff comprise the largest group of workers. Therefore, it is important to interact frequently with Hospital Information Systems in order to handle the appropriate information [2, 10, 14, 39]. Unfortunately, health workers have numerous concerns about IS usage and its implications for their work. Problems with health workers' acceptance and satisfaction are now regarded among the most significant barriers to the diffusion of IS within health settings [10].

Thus, the purpose of this paper is to examine which factors affect the level of satisfaction of medical and nursing staff with the use of information systems in the 424 Military Hospital in Northern Greece and especially the impact of gender and age on users' satisfaction. A total of 257 questionnaires were collected from 3 clinics at the 424 Military Hospital in Northern Greece.

The layout of this paper is as follows sections: The next section, after a brief introduction to this area, is the theoretical background in respect of the satisfaction in healthcare systems. Section 3 explains the methodology, while Sect. 4 shows survey findings. Finally, conclusions are presented in Sect. 5 and the paper ends.

2 Theoretical Background

An information system is designed not only to support the access and collaboration of health professionals with a variety of patients' information but also to promote the quality of health care through coordinated information exchange. Today, the main goal of any health information system is to manage information from all activities related to health care, including planning, monitoring, coordination and decision making. Information systems are mainly used in hospitals to make patients' files readily available, to aid easy access to patient care information, to reduce the time spent waiting for diagnostic information, such as laboratory results, and to improve certification procedures and test results [21, 22, 36]. They are very necessary to meet the growing demands of health care and related diagnostic, therapeutic and administrative burdens, to support better patient care planning and to make better clinical or administrative decisions. Real-time access, exchange and retrieval of clinical data from the information system have helped to improve clinical documentation, reduce the overlap of care services and support decision-making on patient care [1].

Since the advent of information systems development, many health department managers and healthcare designers have tried to identify factors that affect the quality of patient care. Many believe that the quality of health care is enhanced through the information collected and managed through information systems. The quality of information and information systems are linked to effective, timely and appropriate care services provide, low health risks, effective normalization of clinical and administrative tasks, such as communication with patients, their families and other professionals, monitoring of patients by health professionals, and achieving the objectives of community health planning and health management [1, 30].

The value of the information comes from the changes it makes in making decisions, so the quality of information is defined as the data that are suitable for the use of respective users. Healthcare environments are increasingly dependent on information; the volume of data collected, stored and used has increased significantly, as well as health care workers' dependence on computers. Health care information and related data have been growing rapidly over the past decade. Today's health information has become more functional and complex than previous information. However, larger and more complex data are not necessarily better data. The most important issue in this area is the use of high-quality information to improve patient care. Thus, health information can be more effective when the data are of high quality [1, 7, 28].

A good health information system collects data from all relevant partners to ensure that information users have access to reliable, valid, useful, understandable and comparable data. Therefore, an information system is not only considered good due to its ability to provide accessible, reliable and valid information but also due to its ability to present information in a useful and understandable way [6, 26]. In many cases, the data quality problem is not addressed immediately. Unless the burdens and incentives around data collection are addressed, data quality will remain poor, and also concentrating on a data warehouse will not improve the quality of data. Technology can help improve data quality, but data quality is not primarily a technological problem. Investing in advanced electronic storage is of limited value if poor data quality is largely a function of the weight of existing data collection processes and the lack of incentives for accurate reporting. Research by [16] found that nursing staff in Iranian hospitals are moderately satisfied with the quality provided by the information system. At the same time, it was found that the quality of user interfaces also led to moderate satisfaction of the nursing staff. Therefore, the ease in using an information system and the way the system interacts with the users are determinants of users' satisfaction, i.e. nursing staff.

[24] in a survey, found that perceived ease of use determined the satisfaction of nurses with the use of an information system. It was found that the factors that significantly affect the satisfaction of the nurses included perceived usefulness in aligning the quality of the system, perceived usefulness in aligning the quality of information, perceived ease of use in aligning the quality of the system and perceived ease of use in aligning the quality of information. However, the perceived usefulness in aligning the quality of services did not have a significant effect on the satisfaction of the nurses [8, 11].

[1] in their research, show that an important determinant of nurses' satisfaction with an information system is their views about the use of such a system in patient care, based on the evaluation of both information and system quality. So far, the most important issue for the successful implementation of an information system is the acceptance and use of technology by end-users. The research findings suggest that nurses have widely accepted the use of an information system as a necessary element of their daily practice in providing patient care. The results of this study suggest that the first condition for quality patient care is accurate and accessible information. In hospitals, the information system provides an electronic health record that becomes a repository of data and information collected about patient care. This often forces nurses to have the ability to use information systems to document their activities and to recognize these systems as powerful tools for obtaining more complete and accurate information for better patient care. The results of the study showed that the quality of information regarding accuracy and completeness is an important predictor of the use of information in the process of patient care. Therefore, the quality of information should be a priority of organizational control in terms of improving patients' performance and patient care. Certain system features, such as timeliness and reliability, are associated with the use of a system in providing good patient care. Access to real-time access, exchange and retrieval of clinical data reduce the overlap of care services and improve the quality of patient care, especially through the longer time they leave nurses for care-related work rather than bureaucratic procedures [3, 17].

In the research of [4, 16] the results show that the coexistence of the perception of nurses about the performance of information systems and their technological ability to succeed in nursing care has a positive impact on nurses' satisfaction with the use of information systems. As a result, the satisfaction of nurses will increase with the improvement of nursing care performance. The performance of nursing care in measuring organizational benefits has two-component structures: the quality of clinical care and patient safety. The performance of nursing care refers to the assessment of nurses' belief that the use of an information system affects the quality of clinical care and patient safety. The quality of clinical care refers to the evaluation of nurses in providing high-quality care in terms of accurate prediction of patients' outcomes, and objective assessments of patient care quality. Patient safety refers to the evaluation of nursing care that does not adversely affect the health of patients, which is assessed as a whole by the outcomes of patients [27].

It should be noted that the demographic characteristics of health professionals are an important determinant of their satisfaction with the use of an information system. For example, research by [19] found that age and years of experience had a significant effect on the acceptance of an information system. In the study younger and less experienced people had lower levels of satisfaction, as they believed that the system was too slow, not user-friendly or difficult to use, provided inadequate, inaccurate and sometimes uninformed information, increased the time patients spent in the hospital and did not improve the quality of patient care, and that the educational materials did not help.

Similarly, [18] reported that young nursing staff with few years of experience was less satisfied with an information system. In contrast, [5] found in his research that the determinants of satisfaction with an information system were the study staff's ability to use computers and their level of education, not their gender and age.

3 Methodology

To assess the satisfaction of medical and nursing staff with the use of information systems, a questionnaire was drafted. A total of 257 questionnaires were collected from medical staff working at 3 clinics (Clinics of the Pathology Department, Surgery Clinics and Special Closed Departments) at the 424 Military Hospital in Northern Greece. The instrument used 5-point Likert-scales to operationalize the following constructs: perceived ease of use, perceived usefulness, user experience, system quality, service quality and satisfaction. The perceived ease of use construct measured the extent to which user easily uses the functions of the system, and the extent to which user easily learns and with clear operation description. Another indicator is the perceived usefulness construct which measures how useful the hospital information system is considered to be by the users. The user experience construct measures the users' experience of computers use, and how this can have an influence on their intention of reusing it in the future. Characteristics such as information system efficiency, response time, speed of providing services and system security and effectiveness are measured as well. Service quality is evaluated by the users' perspective on handling information and managing capability of hospital information systems problems. The items were derived from [2, 8, 10, 12, 23]. Much of the bias in the standard deviation is in fact removed by the use of the degrees of freedom. Analysis of the data was carried out using Mann-Whitney and Kruskal-Wallis tests.

4 Results and Discussion

A correlation analysis is performed to determine whether the views of the study participants about information systems are influenced either by their demographic profile or by their computer skills. The effect of gender on the respondents' views about information systems was initially tested using the Mann-Whitney test. Then, the Kruskal-Wallis test was used to examine the effect of age on the respondents' views about information systems. Tables 1 and 2 present the results of the analysis.

Table 1. Correlation between gender and satisfaction.

	Gender	N	MeanRank	p-value
The Information System allows you to quickly get the information you need	Male	95	134.78	0.271
	Female	161	124.80	
	Total	256		
The Information System improves the efficiency and effectiveness of your work	Male	95	127.09	0.743
	Female	162	130.12	
	Total	257		
Overall, how satisfied are you with the usefulness of the Information System	Male	95	126.54	0.734
	Female	161	129.66	
	Total	256		
Learning to use the Information System is easy	Male	95	139.83	0.036
	Female	161	121.81	
	Total	256		
Skills required for the use of the Information System	Male	95	146.04	0.002
	Female	161	118.15	
	Total	256		
Overall, how satisfied are you with the ease of use of the Information System	Male	95	135.77	0.193
	Female	161	124.21	
	Total	256		
The Information System is reliable	Male	95	120.16	0.142
	Female	161	133.42	
	Total	256		
Someone can trust the Information System	Male	95	133.51	0.369
	Female	161	125.54	
	Total	256		
The Information System contains Information Technology which helps in data sharing	Male	95	126.35	0.708
	Female	161	129.77	
	Total	256		
Overall, how satisfied are you with the level of confidentiality of the Information System	Male	95	132.42	0.485
	Female	161	126.19	
	Total	256		
Overall, how satisfied are you with the performance of the Information System	Male	95	132.65	0.466
	Female	161	126.05	
	Total	256		
You have direct access to the Information System	Male	95	137.96	0.123
	Female	162	123.74	
	Total	257		

(*continued*)

Table 1. (*continued*)

	Gender	N	MeanRank	p-value
The Information System includes the necessary transactions which can be completed online	Male	95	138.11	0.119
	Female	162	123.66	
	Total	257		
The Information System is properly organized	Male	95	131.38	0.675
	Female	162	127.60	
	Total	257		
Overall, how satisfied are you with providing the necessary instructions to perform your tasks	Male	95	126.75	0.826
	Female	160	128.74	
	Total	255		
You find all the information you need	Male	95	132.78	0.452
	Female	161	125.97	
	Total	256		
You have access to the information you need	Male	95	138.23	0.112
	Female	162	123.59	
	Total	257		
The information is constantly updated	Male	95	137.06	0.143
	Female	162	124.27	
	Total	257		
The information including in the Information System is presented clearly	Male	95	133.59	0.418
	Female	162	126.31	
	Total	257		
The Information System provides high quality information	Male	95	128.81	0.973
	Female	162	129.11	
	Total	257		
The information provided by the Information System is understandable and easy to read	Male	95	142.09	0.019
	Female	162	121.32	
	Total	257		
Overall, how satisfied are you with the quality of the information provided	Male	95	129.64	0.840
	Female	161	127.83	
	Total	256		
The technical support staff is always kind with the users	Male	95	131.97	0.537
	Female	161	126.45	
	Total	256		
The technical support staff understands users' needs	Male	95	132.72	0.445
	Female	161	126.01	
	Total	256		
Overall, how satisfied are you with the quality of service provided by the technical support staff	Male	94	129.40	0.801
	Female	161	127.18	
	Total	255		
Only users who should have access to the Information System have access to it	Male	95	136.54	0.169
	Female	161	123.76	
	Total	256		
Access to the Information System is limited	Male	95	146.21	0.002
	Female	161	118.05	
	Total	256		

(*continued*)

Table 1. (*continued*)

	Gender	N	MeanRank	p-value
The Information System is protected from unauthorized access	Male	95	144.15	0.006
	Female	161	119.27	
	Total	256		
Overall, how satisfied are you with the level of security of the Information System	Male	95	145.36	0.002
	Female	160	117.69	
	Total	255		
Overall, how satisfied are you with the technological capabilities required for the Information System	Male	94	139.48	0.031
	Female	160	120.46	
	Total	254		
The Information System is effectively aligned with the needs of nurses, doctors and management	Male	95	132.40	0.552
	Female	162	127.01	
	Total	257		
The Information System is efficiently aligned with the needs of nurses, doctors and management	Male	95	137.31	0.144
	Female	162	124.13	
	Total	257		
Overall, how satisfied are you with the Information System	Male	95	133.40	0.439
	Female	162	126.42	
	Total	257		
Using the Information System, you can offer treatment and medicines to patients at the right time	Male	95	141.17	0.038
	Female	162	121.86	
	Total	257		
Using the Information System, you can offer accurate and competent care services to patients	Male	95	133.93	0.397
	Female	162	126.11	
	Total	257		
Using the Information System, you can offer with respect hospital services	Male	95	135.46	0.228
	Female	161	124.39	
	Total	256		
Using the Information System, you can help relieve patients	Male	95	124.42	0.531
	Female	160	130.13	
	Total	255		
You can achieve accurate patient identification	Male	95	131.66	0.650
	Female	162	127.44	
	Total	257		
Using the Information System, you can accurately identify and respond to changes in the condition of patients	Male	95	137.57	0.143
	Female	162	123.97	
	Total	257		
Overall, how satisfied are you with the performance of the nursing care you provide through the use of the Information System	Male	95	134.78	0.271
	Female	161	124.80	
	Total	256		

Table 2. Correlation between age and satisfaction.

	Age	N	MeanRank	p-value
The Information System allows you to quickly get the information you need	21–30	68	134.57	0.643
	31–40	115	122.60	
	41–50	71	130.94	
	>=51	1	93.00	
	Total	255		
The Information System improves the efficiency and effectiveness of your work	21–30	68	136.07	0.153
	31–40	116	119.03	
	41–50	71	135.39	
	>=51	1	223.00	
	Total	256		
Overall, how satisfied are you with the usefulness of the Information System	21–30	68	127.46	0.007
	31–40	115	115.07	
	41–50	71	147.85	
	>=51	1	242.00	
	Total	255		
Learning to use the Information System is easy	21–30	68	144.85	0.023
	31–40	115	122.73	
	41–50	71	118.80	
	>=51	1	242.50	
	Total	255		
Skills required for the use of the Information System	21–30	68	157.99	0.000
	31–40	115	119.75	
	41–50	71	111.00	
	>=51	1	245.00	
	Total	255		
Overall, how satisfied are you with the ease of use of the Information System	21–30	68	140.90	0.078
	31–40	115	124.76	
	41–50	71	119.23	
	>=51	1	245.50	
	Total	255		
The Information System is reliable	21–30	68	118.12	0.250
	31–40	115	125.82	
	41–50	71	141.21	
	>=51	1	113.00	
	Total	255		
Someone can trust the Information System	21–30	68	135.32	0.365
	31–40	115	121.38	
	41–50	71	130.65	
	>=51	1	203.00	
	Total	255		
The Information System contains Information Technology which helps in data sharing	21–30	68	138.78	0.332
	31–40	115	124.83	
	41–50	71	123.97	
	>=51	1	46.00	
	Total	255		

(*continued*)

Table 2. (*continued*)

	Age	N	MeanRank	p-value
Overall, how satisfied are you with the level of confidentiality of the Information System	21–30	68	146.36	0.033
	31–40	115	125.21	
	41–50	71	116.14	
	>=51	1	42.00	
	Total	255		
Overall, how satisfied are you with the performance of the Information System	21–30	68	145.59	0.030
	31–40	115	117.29	
	41–50	71	129.84	
	>=51	1	33.50	
	Total	255		
You have direct access to the Information System	21–30	68	140.15	0.186
	31–40	116	121.62	
	41–50	71	129.95	
	>=51	1	31.50	
	Total	256		
The Information System includes the necessary transactions which can be completed online	21–30	68	132.23	0.132
	31–40	116	120.60	
	41–50	71	139.38	
	>=51	1	19.00	
	Total	256		
The Information System is properly organized	21–30	68	132.10	0.136
	31–40	116	121.54	
	41–50	71	138.07	
	>=51	1	11.50	
	Total	256		
Overall, how satisfied are you with providing the necessary instructions to perform your tasks	21–30	67	138.19	0.186
	31–40	116	123.59	
	41–50	70	125.41	
	>=51	1	11.00	
	Total	254		
You find all the information you need	21–30	68	130.13	0.306
	31–40	115	122.13	
	41–50	71	136.71	
	>=51	1	39.00	
	Total	255		
You have access to the information you need	21–30	68	140.01	0.059
	31–40	116	118.56	
	41–50	71	135.37	
	>=51	1	11.50	
	Total	256		
The information is constantly updated	21–30	68	139.12	0.110
	31–40	116	121.69	
	41–50	71	131.11	
	>=51	1	11.50	
	Total	256		

(*continued*)

Table 2. (*continued*)

	Age	N	MeanRank	p-value
The information including in the Information System is presented clearly	21–30	68	146.46	0.007
	31–40	116	115.58	
	41–50	71	134.09	
	>=51	1	9.00	
	Total	256		
The Information System provides high quality information	21–30	68	140.33	0.014
	31–40	116	114.94	
	41–50	71	140.63	
	>=51	1	35.00	
	Total	256		
The information provided by the Information System is understandable and easy to read	21–30	68	151.13	0.011
	31–40	116	124.03	
	41–50	71	114.56	
	>=51	1	98.50	
	Total	256		
Overall, how satisfied are you with the quality of the information provided	21–30	67	146.49	0.022
	31–40	116	118.87	
	41–50	71	127.13	
	>=51	1	10.50	
	Total	255		
The technical support staff is always kind with the users	21–30	68	134.06	0.726
	31–40	115	126.58	
	41–50	71	123.83	
	>=51	1	175.50	
	Total	255		
The technical support staff understands users' needs	21–30	68	127.03	0.135
	31–40	115	137.53	
	41–50	71	113.94	
	>=51	1	96.50	
	Total	255		
Overall, how satisfied are you with the quality of service provided by the technical support staff	21–30	68	134.61	0.343
	31–40	114	119.80	
	41–50	71	132.22	
	>=51	1	186.50	
	Total	254		
Only users who should have access to the Information System have access to it	21–30	68	151.01	0.003
	31–40	115	114.20	
	41–50	71	129.91	
	>=51	1	15.50	
	Total	255		
Access to the Information System is limited	21–30	68	139.15	0.169
	31–40	115	122.37	
	41–50	71	124.85	
	>=51	1	241.50	
	Total	255		

(*continued*)

Table 2. (*continued*)

	Age	N	MeanRank	p-value
The Information System is protected from unauthorized access	21–30	68	143.71	0.007
	31–40	115	112.25	
	41–50	71	137.25	
	>=51	1	214.00	
	Total	255		
Overall, how satisfied are you with the level of security of the Information System	21–30	68	136.72	0.100
	31–40	114	116.75	
	41–50	71	134.72	
	>=51	1	213.50	
	Total	254		
Overall, how satisfied are you with the technological capabilities required for the Information System	21–30	67	130.90	0.747
	31–40	114	121.81	
	41–50	71	131.57	
	>=51	1	133.00	
	Total	253		
The Information System effectively is aligned with the needs of nurses, doctors and management	21–30	68	127.42	0.339
	31–40	116	132.91	
	41–50	71	123.92	
	>=51	1	16.50	
	Total	256		
The Information System is efficiently aligned with the needs of nurses, doctors and management	21–30	68	130.22	0.326
	31–40	116	131.86	
	41–50	71	122.97	
	>=51	1	14.50	
	Total	256		
Overall, how satisfied are you with the Information System	21–30	68	127.50	0.348
	31–40	116	132.29	
	41–50	71	124.88	
	>=51	1	13.50	
	Total	256		
Using the Information System, you can offer treatment and medicines to patients at the right time	21–30	68	148.73	0.031
	31–40	116	122.34	
	41–50	71	120.51	
	>=51	1	34.50	
	Total	256		
Using the Information System, you can offer security in the use of medicines	21–30	68	127.73	0.094
	31–40	116	120.58	
	41–50	71	143.51	
	>=51	1	34.00	
	Total	256		
Using the Information System, you can offer accurate and competent care services to patients	21–30	68	122.67	0,225
	31–40	116	125.35	
	41–50	71	140.52	
	>=51	1	36.50	
	Total	256		

(*continued*)

Table 2. (*continued*)

	Age	N	MeanRank	p-value
Using the Information System, you can offer with respect hospital services	21–30	68	141.58	0.130
	31–40	115	120.59	
	41–50	71	128.36	
	>=51	1	31.50	
	Total	255		
Using the Information System, you can help relieve patients	21–30	68	121.25	0.357
	31–40	114	126.24	
	41–50	71	136.70	
	>=51	1	43.50	
	Total	254		
You can achieve accurate patient identification	21–30	68	131.38	0.333
	31–40	116	123.55	
	41–50	71	135.30	
	>=51	1	24.50	
	Total	256		
Using the Information System, you can accurately identify and respond to changes in the condition of patients	21–30	68	136.24	0.404
	31–40	116	125.60	
	41–50	71	127.22	
	>=51	1	29.50	
	Total	256		
Overall, how satisfied are you with the performance of the nursing care you provide through the use of the Information System	21–30	68	134.57	0.643
	31–40	115	122.60	
	41–50	71	130.94	
	>=51	1	93.00	
	Total	255		

The results of the analysis show that the participants in the research are satisfied with the usefulness of the Information System, and also with the ease of use of the Information System. Ease of use and utility of an information system has been found by other surveys [15, 18, 24, 25, 29, 35] as important determinants of user satisfaction.

However, the respondents expressed little satisfaction with the provision of the necessary instructions for the execution of their work, but are fully satisfied with the training given to health workers by the technical support staff to provide quality services. The provision of quality services by health workers based on the training they receive is an important determining factor of the satisfaction of users of health information systems as well as health professionals [10].

Also, a small degree of satisfaction was expressed with the quality of information provided, the degree of security of the Information System and the technological capabilities of the Information System. However, a significant number of studies [1, 10] have demonstrated the importance of the quality of the information provided by an information system, in terms of validity, reliability, security and timely information, which are presented and easy to manage. Data protection is also an important part of an information system.

In addition to the above, a small degree of satisfaction was found with the nursing care provided through the use of the Information System. However, the quality of an information system is linked to the support of effective, timely and appropriate care services [1]. Some studies [1, 4, 9, 25] has also focused on reconciling the performance of information systems and their technological capabilities in terms of nursing outcomes.

The lowest level of satisfaction was found in the case of the nursing care provided through the use of the information system and the training given to health staff by technical support staff to provide quality services. These results mean, first and foremost, that health professionals need to understand the importance and benefits of using an information system, that there should be programs to help them develop the skills to use this system, and that they should improve the information system, especially in terms of the quality of the information provided by the system.

Another finding of this study is that gender, age, years of experience, position, and computer skills affect the level of satisfaction of the respondents with the information system. These findings are consistent with the findings of [18, 19], which revealed that age and years of service are determinants of the satisfaction of health professionals with the use of an information system. Also, Bahnassy's (2015) research [5] revealed that the ability and availability of computer and computer skills, in general, affect users' level of satisfaction with information systems. However, the findings of this study are in contrast with the results of Bahnassy's (2015) study [5], which showed that gender and age are factors that affect the level of health professionals' satisfaction with the use of an information system.

5 Conclusion

Thus, the purpose of this paper was to examine which factors affect the level of satisfaction of medical and nursing staff with the use of information systems in the 424 Military Hospital in Northern Greece and especially the impact of gender and age on users' satisfaction.

This paper provides important implications for theory and practice. The contribution of this paper is that it helps healthcare professionals to understand the significant dimensions of satisfaction in order to improve the quality of Hospital Information Systems. The health worker's perception of the service and system quality plays significant role in achieving healthcare professionals' satisfaction and the causal relationship between the service quality and satisfaction has been an important topic of discussion. Accordingly the satisfaction resulting from the whole process of using Hospital Information Systems can be considered as overall satisfaction. This overall satisfaction combines various components of system quality such as technical, functional, infrastructural, interpersonal and environmental. Thus, training of health workers is needed to enhance positive attitudes about Hospital Information Systems and take advantage of these systems. Once critical variables were identified, teaching strategies could be designed for specific nursing populations to achieve maximum outcomes.

Finally, by extending these results with an importance-performance analysis, future researchers can also examine which specific system attributes should be in highest priorities, which attributes must be maintained, and which are of lower priority. This could be investigated because different outcomes are probably associated with different system attributes.

References

1. Abdul Rahman, A., Takhti, H.K., Abedini, S., Abedini, S.: Impact of hospital information systems on patient care: Nurses' perceptions. Canadian J. Nurs. Inform. (CJNI) **6**, 1–9 (2012)
2. Aggelidis, V.P., Chatzoglou, P.D.: Hospital information systems: measuring end user computing satisfaction (EUCS). J. Biomed. Inform. **45**, 566–579 (2012)
3. Atinga, R.A., Abekah-Nkrumah, G., Domfeh, K.A.: Managing healthcare quality in Ghana: a necessity of patient satisfaction. Int. J. Health Care Qual. Assur. **24**, 548–563 (2011)
4. Ayatollahi, H., Langarizadeh, M., Chenani, H.: Confirmation of expectations and satisfaction with hospital information systems: a nursing perspective. Healthcare Inform. Res. **22**, 326–332 (2016)
5. Bahnassy, A.A.: Nurses' satisfaction with the use of health information system (HIS) in A Saudi Tertiary Care Medical Center. Int. J. Adv. Res. Comput. Sci. Softw. Eng. **5**, 56–61 (2015)
6. Borkan, J., Eaton, C.B., Novillo-Ortiz, D., Rivero Corte, P., Jadad, A.R.: Renewing primary care: lessons learned from the Spanish health care system. Health Aff. **29**, 1432–1441 (2010)
7. Caiata-Zufferey, M., Abraham, A., Sommerhalder, K., Schulz, P.J.: Online health information seeking in the context of the medical consultation in Switzerland. Qual. Health Res. **20**, 1050–1061 (2010)
8. Chang, M.Y., Pang, C., Tarn, J.M., Liu, T.S., Yen, D.C.: Exploring user acceptance of an e-hospital service: an empirical study in Taiwan. Comput. Stand. Interf. **38**, 35–43 (2015)
9. Cipriano, P.F., Hamer, S.: Enabling the ordinary: more time to care. Nurs. Technol. Inf. Syst. **8**, 2–4 (2014)
10. Cohen, J.F., Coleman, E., Kangethe, M.J.: An importance-performance analysis of hospital information system attributes: a nurses' perspective. Int. J. Med. Inform. **86**, 82–90 (2016)
11. Drosos, D., Tsotsolas, N., Zagga, A., Chalikias, M.S., Skordoulis, M.: MUlticriteria satisfaction analysis application in the health care sector. In: 7th International Conference on Information and Communication Technologies in Agriculture, Food and Environment (HAICTA), pp. 737–754, Kavala, Greece (2015)
12. Handan, Ç.A.M.: The role of information technology in patient satisfaction. Turkish Econ. Rev. **3**, 91–102 (2016)
13. Handayani, P.W., Hidayanto, A.N., Pinem, A.A., Sandhyaduhita, P.I., Budi, I.: Hospital information system user acceptance factors: user group perspectives. Inform. Health Soc. Care **43**, 84–107 (2018)
14. Jandavath, R.K.N., Byram, A.: Healthcare service quality effect on patient satisfaction and behavioural intentions in corporate hospitals in India. Int. J. Pharm. Healthcare Mark. **10**, 48–74 (2016)
15. Kaba, B.: Validating measurements of perceived ease comprehension and ease of navigation of an online learning technology: improving web based learning tool adoption and use. Int. Trans. J. Eng. Manag. Appl. Sci. Technol. **2**, 287–301 (2011)

16. Kahouei, M., et al.: Nurses' perceptions of usefulness of nursing information system: a module of electronic medical record for patient care in two university hospitals of Iran. Mater Sociomed. **26**, 30–34 (2014)

17. Kamra, V., Singh, H., De Kumar, K.: Factors affecting patient satisfaction: An exploratory study for quality management in the health-care sector. Total Qual. Manag. Bus. Excell. **27**, 1013–1027 (2016)

18. Khajouei, R., Abbasi, R.: Evaluating Nurses' satisfaction with two nursing information systems. CIN: Comput. Inform. Nurs. **35**, 307–314 (2017)

19. Khalifa, M.: Evaluating nurses acceptance of hospital information systems: a case study of a tertiary care hospital. Stud. Health Technol. Inform. **225**, 78–82 (2016)

20. Kitsios, F., Kamariotou, M., Manthou, V.: Hospital information systems planning: strategic IT alignment in healthcare. In: Sakas, D.P., Nasiopoulos, D.K. (eds.) Strategic Innovative Marketing, Springer Proceedings in Business and Economics, pp. 203–209. Springer, Cham (2019). https://doi.org/10.1007/978-3-030-16099-9_25

21. Kitsios, F., Stefanakakis, S., Kamariotou, M., Dermentzoglou, L.: E-service evaluation: user satisfaction measurement and implications in health sector. Comput. Stand. Interf. J. **63**, 16–26 (2019)

22. Kitsios, F., Papadopoulos, T., Angelopoulos, S.: A roadmap to the introduction of pervasive Information Systems in healthcare. Int. J. Adv. Pervasive Ubiquitous Comput. **2**, 21–32 (2010)

23. Lee, T.T., Lee, T.Y., Lin, K.C., Chang, P.C.: Factors affecting the use of nursing information systems in Taiwan. J. Adv. Nurs. **50**, 170–178 (2005)

24. Lin, H.C.: Nurses' satisfaction with using nursing information systems from technology acceptance model and information systems success model perspectives: a reductionist approach. CIN: Comput. Inform. Nurs. **35**, 91–99 (2017)

25. Lin, H.C., Chiou, J.Y., Chen, C.C., Yang, C.W.: Understanding the impact of nurses' perception and technological capability on nurses' satisfaction with nursing information system usage: a holistic perspective of alignment. Comput. Hum. Behav. **57**, 143–152 (2016)

26. Liu, C.F., Tsai, Y.C., Jang, F.L.: Patients' acceptance towards a web-based personal health record system: an empirical study in Taiwan. Int. J. Environ. Res. Public Health **10**, 5191–5208 (2013)

27. Manolitzas, P., Grigoroudis, E., Matsatsinis, N.F.: Using multicriteria decision analysis to evaluate patient satisfaction in a hospital emergency department. J. Heath Manag. **16**, 245–258 (2014)

28. Naidu, A.: Factors affecting patient satisfaction and healthcare quality. Int. J. Health Care Qual. Assur. **22**, 366–381 (2009)

29. Ohk, K., Park, S.B., Hong, J.W.: The influence of perceived usefulness, perceived ease of use, interactivity, and ease of navigation on satisfaction in mobile application. Adv. Sci. Technol. Lett. **84**, 88–92 (2015)

30. Oroviogoicoechea, C., Watson, R., Beortegui, E., Remirez, S.: Nurses' perception of the use of computerised information systems in practice: questionnaire development. J. Clin. Nurs. **19**, 240–248 (2010)

31. Owusu Kwateng, K., Appiah, C., Atiemo, K.A.O.: Adoption of health information systems: health professionals perspective. Int. J. Healthcare Manage (2019, in press)

32. Sebetci, Ö.: Enhancing end-user satisfaction through technology compatibility: an assessment on health information system. Health Policy Technol. **7**, 265–274 (2018)

33. Shabbir, A., Malik, S.A., Janjua, S.Y.: Equating the expected and perceived service quality. Int. J. Qual. Reliab. Manag. **34**, 1295–1317 (2017)

34. Shabbir, A., Malik, S.A.: Measuring patients' healthcare service quality perceptions, satisfaction, and loyalty in public and private sector hospitals in Pakistan. Int. J. Qual. Reliab. Manag. **33**, 538–557 (2016)

35. Shen, C.C., Chiou, J.S.: The impact of perceived ease of use on Internet service adoption: the moderating effects of temporal distance and perceived risk. Comput. Hum. Behav. **26**, 42–50 (2010)

36. Sindakis, S., Kitsios, F.: Entrepreneurial dynamics and patient involvement in service innovation: developing a model to promote growth and sustainability in mental health care. J. Knowl. Econ. **7**(2), 545–564 (2014). https://doi.org/10.1007/s13132-014-0228-1

37. Vest, J.R., Jung, H.Y., Wiley Jr., K., Kooreman, H., Pettit, L., Unruh, M.A.: Adoption of health information technology among US nursing facilities. J. Am. Med. Dir. Assoc. **20**, 995–1000 (2019)

38. Wright, A., et al.: Problem list completeness in electronic health records: a multi-site study and assessment of success factors. Int. J. Med. Inform. **84**, 784–790 (2015)

39. Zarei, E., Daneshkohan, A., Pouragha, B., Marzban, S., Arab, M.: An Empirical study of the Impact of Service Quality on patient Satisfaction in private Hospitals Iran. Global J. Health Sci. **7**, 1–9 (2015)

Performance Evaluation of ANOVA and RFE Algorithms for Classifying Microarray Dataset Using SVM

Sulaiman Olaniyi Abdulsalam[1], Abubakar Adamu Mohammed[1],
Jumoke Falilat Ajao[1], Ronke S. Babatunde[1],
Roseline Oluwaseun Ogundokun[2], Chiebuka T. Nnodim[2],
and Micheal Olaolu Arowolo[1(✉)]

[1] Kwara State University, Malete, Nigeria
[2] Landmark University, Omu-Aran, Nigeria
arowolo.olaolu@lmu.edu.ng

Abstract. A significant application of microarray gene expression data is the classification and prediction of biological models. An essential component of data analysis is dimension reduction. This study presents a comparison study on a reduced data using Analysis of Variance (ANOVA) and Recursive Feature Elimination (RFE) feature selection dimension reduction techniques, and evaluates the relative performance evaluation of classification procedures of Support Vector Machine (SVM) classification technique. In this study, an accuracy and computational performance metrics of the processes were carried out on a microarray colon cancer dataset for classification, SVM-RFE achieved 93% compared to ANOVA with 87% accuracy in the classification output result.

Keywords: SVM-RFE · ANOVA · Microarray · SVM · Cancer

1 Introduction

In biological learning, Next-generation sequencing (NGS) has been expansively utilized. General NGS information is the Ribonucleic Acid sequencing (RNA-seq); it is utilized to test the anomalies of mRNA expression in ailments. In difference with microarray advancements, microarray talks about significant data that presents explicit inventiveness of narrative protein isoforms with various compound scopes of uncovered qualities.

Microarray has become an expansively utilized genome-wide expression profile for figuring substance cells, because of their capacity of determining potential heterogeneities in cell populaces [1]. Since the advancement of RNA tasks as a notable intermediary among genome and proteome, finding and estimating gene expression have been the unmistakable conduct in biological science [2]. There is no foremost prospective or good channel for the assorted variety of claims and analysis state in which microarray can be utilized. Researches and adoption of systematic methodologies on living being and their objectives have advanced [3].

M. Themistocleous et al. (Eds.): EMCIS 2020, LNBIP 402, pp. 480–492, 2020.
https://doi.org/10.1007/978-3-030-63396-7_32

A flourishing microarray study must have a major prerequisite of creating information with the possibilities of responding to biological inquiries of concern. This is practiced by characterizing an investigational aim, series intensity and replicating reasonable biological plans under examination and by advancement of sequencing research, ensuring that information achievement does not end up being tainted with redundant views. One critical part of the microarray information is the expulsion of the scourge of high-dimension, for example, noises, commotions, repetition, redundancy, immaterial as well as irrelevant data, among others [4]. Because of high-measurement of biological information challenges, dimension reduction techniques are vital. Microarray information has turned out to be a potential high-throughput procedure to simultaneously profile transcriptomes of substantial information [5]. Microarray has key advantages, for example, the capacity to spot narrative transcripts, precision, and dynamic range [6]. Thousands of quality genes are simultaneously communicated and expressed in microarray, expression levels of genes are usually difficult, finding an effective low-dimensional representation of microarray information is important. A few dimension reduction methods utilized for gene expression data analysis and information investigation to expel noises related to explicit information exist [7]. Although many dimensionality reduction methods have been proposed and developed in this field, yet this study proposes efficient feature selection methods, by ranking the feature genes and selecting key to tackle principal drawbacks of high dimensional data. Overcoming this limitation, this study introduces an efficient implementation of SVM classification combined with the selected informative genes. This study proposes a simple method for preprocessing datasets, for informative dispersal of samples with a more credible classification result.

This study proposes a computational dimensionality reduction technique using ANOVA and RFE, to deal with the issue of curse of high dimensionality in gene expression space and analyzes SVM kernel classification methods. This study exhibits the robustness of this technique regarding to noises and sampling on RNA-Seq Anopheles Gambiae dataset.

2   Materials and Methods

2.1   Dataset Used for Analysis

Colon cancer dataset was used for this experiment, it contains an expression of 2000 genes with highest minimal intensity across 62 tissues, derived from 40 tumor and 22 normal colon tissue samples. The gene expression was analyzed with an Affymetrix oligonucleotide array complementary to more than 6,500 human genes. The gene intensity has been derived from about 20 feature pairs that correspond to the gene on the DNA microarray chip by using a filtering process. Details for data collection methods and procedures are described [8], and the data set is available from the website http://microarray.princeton.edu/oncology/.

MATLAB (Matrix Laboratory) is utilized to perform the experiment, due to its ease and beneficial programming environment for engineers, architects, scientists, researchers, among others. MATLAB is a multi-worldview numerical processing environment and exclusive programming language created by MathWorks. It permits framework controls, plotting of functions and information, execution of algorithms, production of User Interfaces, and interfacing with projects written in different languages, such as; C, C++, C#, Java, Fortran and Python [9]. The principle point of this study is the prediction of the RNA-Seq technology utilizing the MATLAB tool by utilizing the colon database. Table-1 demonstrates a concise description of the dataset.

2.2   Experimental Methodology

This study summarizes the proposed framework in Fig. 1 below. The fundamental idea is to predict machine learning task on high dimensional microarray data, for cells and genes into lower dimensional dataset. The plan is adjusted to fetch out important data in a given dataset by utilizing ANOVA and RFE feature selection methods and evaluate the performance of colon cancer microarray dataset on SVM classification algorithm.

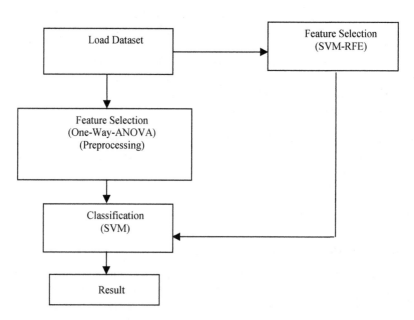

Fig. 1. Proposed framework.

Microarray data is the next generation sequencing technology to think about in transcriptome. It is utilized as an option to microarrays for gene expression analysis, without the need to earlier realize the RNA/DNA succession. RNA-seq offers progressively precise information and applications including identification of gene fusion, variations, alternative joining, post-transcriptional changes as well as analysis of small

RNAs, such as; tRNA or miRNA profiles [10–12]. A total image of the RNA/DNA substance can be gotten from low quantity biological samples. A few expository advances are basic for an effective portrayal and evaluation of the transcriptome. Bioinformatics tools are proposed for quality control, information handling, annotation, quantification and representation for translation and biological science investigation for understanding gene information.

2.3   Analysis of Variance (ANOVA)

ANOVA algorithm simplifies the value of intensity as a sum of components. ANOVA algorithm helps in normalization and gene-specific model. The normalization eliminates properties due to total differences in intensity among diverse arrays. ANOVA normalization is trivial and basically deducts the mean of the log-transformed intensity from each array and refer to the distorted and normalized intensity values as Y [13]. ANOVA test is used to compare the 'multiple means' values of the dataset, and visualize whether there exists any significant difference between mean values of multiple groups (classes). The statistic for ANOVA is called the F-statistic, which can be calculated using following steps [14, 35, 36]:

$$F-score = BMS/WMS \tag{1}$$

The input to the algorithm is a matrix of the form N × M, where N is the total number of feature sets and M is the number of samples in the dataset.

2.4   Recursive Feature Elimination (RFE)

Guyon introduce RFE [15], RFE makes feature selection by iteratively training a set of data with the current set of features and eliminating the least significant feature indicated. In the linear case, the separating hyperplane (decision function)is $D(\vec{x}) = (\vec{w} \cdot \vec{x}) + b$. The feature with the smallest weight w^2 contributes the least to the resulting hyperplane and can be discarded. Due to the heavy computational cost of RFE, several variants have been introduced to speed up the algorithm. Instead of removing only one least important feature at every iteration, removing a big chunk of features in each iteration will speed up the process. The goal is to remove more features during each iteration, but not to eliminate the important features. [16].

2.5   Classification

A few classification algorithms exist, for example, Logistic Regression, SVM, K-Nearest Neighbor, among others [17]. After reducing the dimensional complexity of data, the subsequent stage is the classification procedure. Classification is the fundamental goal; the analyzed data is classified. Two SVM kernels techniques were utilized: Polynomial Kernel and Gaussian Kernel. The results of the algorithms are analyzed and compared based on computational time, training time and performance metrics such as accuracy.

2.6   Support Vector Machine (SVM)

SVM is a learning machine algorithm presented by Vapnik in 1992 [18]. The algorithm works with the point of finding the best hyperplane that isolates between classes in the input space. SVM is a linear classifier; it is created to work with nonlinear problems by joining the kernel ideas in high-dimensional workspaces. In non-linear issues, SVM utilizes a kernel in training the data with the goal of spreading the dimension widely. When the dimensions are tweaked, SVM will look for the optimal hyperplane that can separate a class from different classes [19] (Chang, and Lin 2011). As indicated by the adoption of Aydadenta and Adiwijaya (2018) [18], the procedure to locate the best hyperplane utilizing SVM is as follows:

i. Let

$$y_i \in \{y_1, y_2, \ldots, y_n\}, where \ y_i \ is \ the \ p - attributes \ and \ target \ class \ z_i \in \{+1, -1\}$$

ii. Assuming the classes +1 and −1 can be separated completely by hyperplane, as defined in Eq. 2 below

$$v \cdot y + c = 0 \tag{2}$$

From Eq. (2), Eqs. (3) and (4) are gotten:

$$v \cdot y + c \geq +1, for \ class + 1 \tag{3}$$

$$v \cdot b + c \leq -1, for \ class - 1 \tag{4}$$

Where, y is the input data, v is the ordinary plane and c is the positive relative to the center field coordinates.

SVM intends to discover hyperplanes that maximizes margins between two classes. Expanding margins is a quadratic programming issue that is solved by finding the minimal point. The advantage of SVM is its capacity to manage wide assortment of classification problems in high dimensional data [20].

Compared to other classification methods, SVM is outstanding, with its exceptional classification adequacy [21]. SVM is grouped into linear and non-linear separable. SVM's has kernel functions that change data into a higher dimensional space to make it conceivable to perform seperations. Kernel functions are a class of algorithms for pattern analysis or recognition. Training vectors xi is mapped into higher dimensional space by the capacity Φ. SVM finds a linear seperating hyperplane with the maximal in this higher dimension space. $C > 0$ is the penalty parameter of the error term.

There are several SVM kernels that exist such as; the polynomial kernel, Radial basis function (RBF), linear kernel, Sigmoid, Gaussian kernel, String Kernels, among others. The decision of a Kernel relies upon the current issue at hand, since it relies upon what models are to be analyzed, a couple of kernel functions have been found to function admirably in for a wide assortment of applications [22]. The prescribed kernel function for this study is the SVM-Polynomial Kernel and Gaussian Kernel.

SVM-Gaussian Kernel

Gaussian kernel [23] compare to a general smoothness supposition in all k-th order subordinates. Kernels coordinating a certain prior recurrence substance of the data can be developed to reflect earlier issues in learning. Each input vector $\underline{x}$ is mapped to an interminable dimensional vector including all degree polynomial extensions of $x's$ components. For instance, a polynomial kernel model features conjunction up to the order of the polynomial. Radial basis functions permit circles in contrast with the linear kernel, which permits just selecting lines (or hyperplanes).

$$K(y_a, y_j) = (\gamma y_a^S y_b + q)^e, \gamma > 0 \tag{5}$$

For instance, polynomial kernel is the least complex kernel function. It is given by the inner product *(a, b)* in addition to a discretionary constant K.

$$K(y_a, y_b) = y_a^S y_b \tag{6}$$

In SVM kernel functions, γ, a, and b are kernel parameters, RBF is the fundamental kernel function due to the nonlinearly maps tests in higher dimensional space unlike the linear kernel, it has less hyper parameters than the polynomial portion.

$$K(y_a, y_b) = \exp(-\gamma ||y_a, y_b||^2), \gamma \rangle 0 \tag{7}$$

3 Related Works

Dimensionality reduction approaches have established important consideration recently, with evolving new algorithms and variant combinations. SVM has engrossed researchers' interests due to its viable performance in classification and intrinsic capability.

A dimensionality reduction model was proposed [4] for zero inflated single cell gene expression analysis, they built a dimensionality reduced technique, zero inflated factor analysis (ZIFA), which expressly models the dropout attributes, and demonstrate that it improves modelling precision on biological and simulated datasets. They modified the PPCA and FA framework to represent dropout and deliver a safe technique for the dimensionality reduction of single-cell gene expression data that gives robustness against such vulnerabilities.

Without dropouts, the method is basically equal to PPCA or FA. Hence, users could utilize ZIFA as an immediate substitute with the advantage that it will consequently represent dropouts while remedial endeavors might be required with standard PCA. There procedure varies from methodologies, for example, the numerous variations of strong PCA, which mean to show corrupted perceptions. ZIFA regards dropouts as genuine perceptions, not exceptions, whose event properties have been described utilizing an observationally educated factual model.

A novel hybrid dimension reduction method was proposed [24], for small high dimensional gene expression datasets with information intricacy principle for cancer classification. Their study addressed the restrictions inside the setting of Probabilistic PCA (PPCA) by presenting and building up new and novel methodology utilizing most extreme entropy covariance matrix and its hybridized smoothed covariance estimators. To diminish the dimensionality of the data and pick the quantity of probabilistic PCs (PPCs) to be held, they further presented and created observed Akaike's information criterion (AIC), consistent Akaike's information criterion (CAIC), and the information theoretic measure of complexity (ICOMP) rule of Bozdogan. Six openly accessible undersized benchmark informational collections were breaking down to demonstrate the utility, adaptability, and flexibility of their methodology with hybridized smoothed covariance matrix estimators, which does not decline to play out the PPCA to diminish the measurement and to do regulated characterization of malignancy bunches in high measurements. Their proposed technique can be utilized to take care of new issues and difficulties present in the investigation of NGS information in bioinformatics and other biomedical applications.

A feature selection for cancer classification for disease utilizing microarray data expression was proposed [25]. This paper used information on microarray gene expression level to decide marker genes that are pertinent to a sort of malignancy. They researched a separation-based element choice strategy for two-gather grouping issue. So as to choose marker genes, the Bhattacharyya separation is actualized to quantify the uniqueness in gene expression levels. They used SVM for classification with utilization of the selected marker genes. The execution of marker gene selection and classification are represented in both recreation studies and two genuine information analyses by proposing a new gene selection method for classification based on SVMs. In the proposed method, they firstly ranked every gene according to the importance of their Bhattacharyya distances between the two indicated classes. The optimal gene subset is chosen to accomplish the least misclassification rate in the developed SVMs following a forward selection algorithm. 10-fold cross-validation is connected to locate the optimal parameters for SVM with the final optimal gene subset. Subsequently, the classification model is trained and built. The classification model is evaluated by its prediction performance for testing set. The execution of the proposed B/SVM technique with that of SVM-RFE and SWKC/SVM gives normal misclassification rate (1.1%) and high normal recovery rate (95.7%).

An Alzheimer's infection determination by utilizing dimensionality reduction was proposed [26], based on KNN classification algorithm for analyzing and classifying the Alzheimer malady and mild cognitive mutilation are available in the datasets. Their study gave more precision rate, accuracy rate and sensitivity rate to give a better output. This paper proposed a narrative dimensionality reduction based KNN classification Algorithm dissected the Alzheimer's illness present in the datasets. With the algorithm, the dataset was separated into 3 classes; first class having the Alzheimer's disease (AD), second class was having the normal outcome, third class having the mild cognitive impairment. The information's were taken from the researcher's data dictionary - Uniform Data Set (RDD-UDS).

The relative investigations between the current PNN classification procedures with the proposed KNN classification demonstrated that high measure of normal accuracy, sensitivity, specificity precision, recall, jaccard and dice coefficients furthermore diminish the information dimensionality and computational multifaceted nature. Their future work, stated that the feature extraction and classification algorithm will improve the classification performance.

PCA and Factor Analysis for dimensionality reduction of bio-informatics data was proposed [27], they utilized the dimensionality reduction model of bioinformatics information. These systems were applied on Leukemia dataset and the number of attributes was decreased. An investigation was exhibited on reducing the number of attributes using PCA and Factor Analysis. Leukemia data was used for the analyses. PCA was carried out on the dataset and 9 components were chosen out of the 500 components. The Factor Analysis was used to extract the critical features.

A simulation study for the RNA-Seq data classification was proposed [28], they contrasted a few classifiers including PLDA renovation, NBLDA, single SVM, bagging SVM, CART, and random forest (RF). They analyzed the impact of a few parameters, for example, over-dispersion, sample size, number of genes and classes, differential expression rate, and the transform technique on model performances. A broad modeled study was conducted and the outcomes were contrasted using the consequences of two miRNA and two mRNA exploratory datasets. The outcomes uncovered that expanding the sample size, differential expression rate and transformation method on model presentation. RNA-Seq data classification requires cautious consideration when taking care of data over-scattering. They ended up that count-based classifier, the power changed PLDA and as classifiers, vst or rlog changed RF and SVM classifiers might be a decent decision for classification.

A neural network algorithm to reduce the dimensions of single cell RNA-Seq data was proposed [9], containing a few new computational complexities. These incorporate inquiries concerning the best strategies for clustering scRNA-Seq data, how to recognize unique cells, and deciding the state or capacity of explicit cells dependent on their expression profile. To address these issues, they created and tested a technique based on neural network (NN) for the analysis and recovery of single cell RNA-Seq data. They showed different NN structures, some of which fuse prior biological learning, and utilized these to acquire a reduced dimension representation of the single cell expression data. They demonstrate that the NN technique enhances earlier strategies in the capacity to accurately group cells in analyses not utilized in the training and the capacity to effectively derive cell type or state by questioning a database of a huge number of single cell profiles. Such database queries (which can be performed utilizing a web server) will empower researchers to better characterize cells while investigating heterogeneous scRNASeq tests.

A review of recent ongoing advancements in PCA as a strategy for diminishing the dimensionality of RNA-Seq datasets was proposed [29], for expanding interpretability and yet limiting data misfortune by making new uncorrelated factors that progressively maximize variance. This study presented the essential thoughts of PCA, talking about what it can, can't do and after that depict a few variations of PCA and their application.

4   Results

The colon cancer dataset extracted were classified, the classification results obtained show the features capability for classifying the colon's status. The average classification accuracy, which is using features with ANOVA and RFE are recorded in tabular form below. The proposed methodology was applied to the publicly available colon cancer database, the classification algorithm applies SVM kernel by utilizing MATLAB tools to implement the model.

Using ANOVA as a dimensionality reduction method, 416 features where fetched from the 2001 attributes of colon cancer dataset obtained from Alon, 2001 [8]. Using ANOVA, the output of the analysis is a statistically significant difference between group means. The significance value is 0.05 which is the mean length of time to complete the spreadsheet problem between the different courses taken.

ANOVA is appropriate when the model holds, have a single "treatment" with, say, k levels. "Treatment" may be interpreted in the loosest possible sense as any categorical explanatory variable. There is a population of interest for which there is a true quantitative outcome for each of the k levels of treatment. The selected features a processed for classification.

A supervised SVM kernel classifier methods, is among the most well-established and popular machine learning approaches in bioinformatics and genomics, 10-folds cross validation was used to evaluate the execution of the performance of the classification models, using 0.05 parameter holdout of data for training and 5% for testing to check the accuracy of the classifiers.

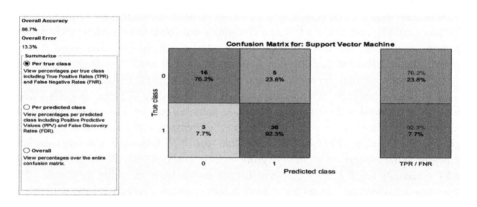

Fig. 2. Confusion matrix and performance metrics for SVM-ANOVA

To each of the classifiers, a basic supervised learning assessment protocol is carried out. In particular, the training and testing stages are assessed as a 10-fold cross validation to eliminate the sampling bias. This protocol is implemented using MATLAB. The reported result of assessment is based on the computational time and performance metrics (Accuracy, Sensitivity, Specificity, F-score, Precision and Recall) [30–34].

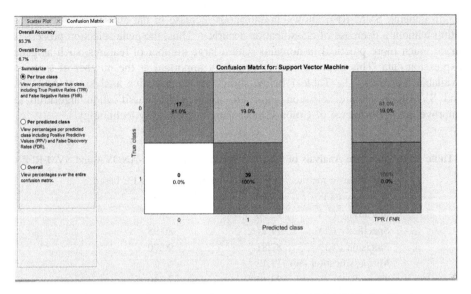

Fig. 3. Confusion matrix and performance metrics for SVM-RFE classification

Figure 2 and Fig. 3 shows the confusion matrix table comprising of the TP, TN, FP and FN which are used extensively for the evaluation of the performance metrics.

RFE-SVM algorithm was used to fetch out relevant data in the colon cancer dataset, 868 features were selected. SVM-RFE improve the computational performance of recursive feature elimination by eliminating chunks of features at a time with as little effect on the quality of the reduced feature set as possible. The RFE algorithm is implemented using an SVM to assist in identifying the least useful gene(s) to eliminate. Using SVM-RFE, the selected data was classified and accomplish 93.3% Accuracy.

In this study, data analysis of a well-known dataset colon cancer dataset by Alon [8], consisting of expression levels of 2000 genes describing 62 samples (40 tumor and 22 normal colon tissues, was analyzed using MATLAB tool. The dataset was used to compare the performance of the One-Way-ANOVA and SVM-RFE. The dataset was trained and tested. A different number of genes were selected by each of the algorithms, 416 and 868 respectively. The SVM was trained on the training data that was trimmed to the selected genes from each algorithm respectively. The SVM model produced was evaluated by its performance to predict the class labels (since cross validation results on the training data tend to be optimistic). Comparisons of the two algorithms in terms of prediction rate and time required are made. A comparison between ANOVA and SVM-RFE is also performed. The performance of ANOVA was comparable to the SVM-RFE algorithms in terms of prediction accuracy rate (each achieving around 87% and 93% accuracy on the test data). Experiment on the Alon colon cancer data sets also show that ANOVA has similar performance when compared with SVM-RFE with respect to accuracy, when comparing computational time, ANOVA is much faster than the SVM-RFE.

In general, SVM-RFE allows an enormous increase in the efficiency of the algorithm without a decrease of classification accuracy. Thus, the gene selection process is made much more practical in domains with a large number of features, such as gene expression data. This improvement is especially important as the number of samples available increases. The Table 1 below shows the comparative analysis of ANOVA and SVM-RFE feature selection algorithm using SVM classification algorithm to improve the performance of Colon Cancer data in microarray technology.

Table 1. Comparative Analysis of the Classification of One-Way-ANOVA and SVM-RFE

Performance metrics	ANOVA-SVM based	SVM-RFE based
Accuracy (%)	86.70	93.33
Sensitivity (%)	92.30	100
Specificity (%)	77.27	80.95
Precision (%)	87.81	90.70
Misclassification (%)	13.12	6.67
Time (Sec)	23.1409	7.340

The performance analysis of classification using Support Vector Machine on colon cancer dataset shows that, SVM-RFE feature selection technique method achieves necessary higher value in the datasets on performance parameters such as the accuracy, timing, sensitivity, specificity, and prediction when compared to the ANOVA feature selection method. When the dataset is of high dimensional, by application of dimensionality reduction, some valuable data are considered and the accuracy of an algorithm increases by removing unnecessary data. The feature selection algorithm using ANOVA for high dimensional datasets plays an important role, it improves the performance of feature extraction methods, and SVM-RFE also enhances the classification algorithm "SVM" performance, in terms of accuracy, sensitivity, specificity and precision.

5 Conclusion

In the past few years, remarkable works have been done on the innovation of microarray, improvement as far as the execution measurements and productivity that are extraordinarily influenced by exploratory plan, activity and the data analysis forms are in trends to enhance the performance. cancer is a deadly insect comprising of various kinds. Small sample sizes of high dimensionality are main characteristics of microarray data and they are challenging data analysis criterion. The significance of classification of colon cancer into gatherings has prompted numerous researches. By examination, this study classifies a colon cancer data by using SVM on reduced dimensional data that employs RFE and ANOVA algorithms. The experiment accomplished a comparable result that shows that SVM-RFE outperforms ANOVA-SVM with 93%. Further studies should be conducted to improve performance of Machine Learning based methods by using more data and hybridized models.

References

1. Aaron, T.L., Davis, J.M, John, C.M.: A step-by-step workflow for low-level analysis of single-cell RNA-seq data. Research **1**(5), 1–62. https://doi.org/10.12688/f1000research.9501.2

2. Ana, C., et al.: A survey of best practices for RNA-seq data analysis. Genome Biol. **17**(13), 1–19 (2016). https://doi.org/10.1186/s13059-016-0881-8

3. Levin, J.Z., et al.: Comprehensive comparative analysis of strand-specific RNA sequencing methods. Nat. Methods **7**, 709–715 (2010)

4. Pierson, E., Yau, C.: ZIFA: dimensionality reduction for zero-inflated single-cell gene expression analysis. Genome Biol. **16**, 241–257 (2015)

5. Dongfang, W., Jin, G.: VASC: dimension reduction and visualization of single-cell RNA-seq data by deep variation autoencoder. Genom. Proteom. Bioinform. (2018). https://doi.org/10.1016/j.gpb.2018.08.03

6. Junhyong, K.: Computational Analysis of RNA-Seq Data: From Quantification to High-Dimensional Analysis. University of Pennsylvania, pp. 35–43 (2012)

7. Bacher, R., and Kendziorski, C.: Design and computational analysis of single-cell RNA-seq experiments. Genome Biol. **17**(63) (2016)

8. Alon, U., et al.: Broad patterns of gene expression revealed by clustering analysis of tumor and normal colon tissues probed by oligonucleotide arrays. Proc. Natl. myAcad. Sci. USA 8; **96**(12), 6745–6750 (1999)

9. Chieh, L., Siddhartha, J., Hannah, K., Ziv, B.: Using neural networks for reducing the dimensions of single-cell RNA-Seq data. Nucleic Acids Res. **45**(17), 1–11 (2017). https://doi.org/10.1093/nar/gkx681

10. Mariangela, B., et al.: RNA-seq analyses of changes in the Anopheles gambiae transcriptome associated with resistance to pyrethroids in Kenya: identification of candidate-resistance genes and candidate-resistance SNPs. Paras. Vector **8**(474), 1–13 (2015). https://doi.org/10.1186/s13071-015-1083-z

11. https://figshare.com/articles/Additional_file_4_of_RNA-seq_analyses_of_changes_in_the_Anopheles_gambiae_transcriptome_associated_with_resistance_to_pyrethroids_in_Kenya_identification_of_candidate-resistance_genes_and_candidate-resistance_SNPs/4346279/1

12. Bezanson, J., Karpinski, S., Shah, V., Edelman, A.: Julia: a fast-dynamic language for technical computing (2012). arXiv:1209.5145

13. Gary, A.C.: Using ANOVA to analyze microarray data. Biotechn. Future Sci. **37**(2), 1–5 (2018)

14. Mukesh, K., Nitish, K.R., Amitav, S., Santanu, K.R.: Feature selection and classification of microarray data using MapReduce Based ANOVA and KNN. Procedia Comput. Sci. **54**, 301–310 (2015)

15. Ding, Y., Dawn, W.: Improving the performance of SVM-RFE to select genes in microarray data. BMC Bioinform. **2**(12), 1–11 (2015)

16. Shruti, M., Mishra, D.: SVM-BT-RFE: An improved gene selection framework using Bayesian T-test embedded in support vector machine (recursive feature elimination) algorithm. Karbala Int. J. Modern Sci. **1**(2), 86–96 (2015)

17. Rimah, A., Dorra, B.A., Noureddine, E.: An empirical comparison of SVM and some supervised learning algorithms for vowel recognition. Int. J. Intell. Inf. Process. (IJIIP) **3**(1), 1–5 (2012)

18. Aydadenta, H., Adiwijaya: On the classification techniques in data mining for microarray data classification. In: International Conference on Data and Information Science, Journal of Physics: Conf. Series vol. 971. pp. 1–10 (2018). https://doi.org/10.1088/1742-6596/971/1/012004

19. Chang, C., Lin, C.: LIBSVM: a library for support vector machines. ACM TIST. **2**(3), 27

20. Soofi, A.A., Awan, A.: Classification techniques in. machine learning: applications and issues. J. Basic Appl. Sci. **13**, 459–465 (2017)

21. Khan, A., Baharudin, B., Lee, L.H., Khan, K.: A review of machine learning algorithms for text-documents classification. J. Adv. Inf. Technol. **1**(1), 1–17 (2010)

22. Bhavsar, H., Panchal, M.H.: A review on support vector machine for data classification. Int. J. Adv. Res. Comput. Eng. Technol. (IJARCET) **1**(2), 185–189 (2012)

23. Devi, A.V., Devaraj, D.V.: Gene expression data classification using support vector machine and mutual information-based gene selection. Procedia Comput. Sci. **47**, 13–21 (2015)

24. Esra, P., Hamparsum, B., Sinan, Ç.: A novel hybrid dimension reduction technique for undersized high dimensional gene expression data sets using information complexity criterion for cancer classification. Comput. Math. Methods Med. **1**, 1–14 (2015). https://doi.org/10.1155/2015/370640

25. Wenyan, Z., Xuewen, L., Jingjing, W.: Feature selection for cancer classification using microarray gene expression data. Biostat. Biometr. J. **1**(2), 1–7 (2017)

26. Balamurugan, M., Nancy, A., Vijaykumar, S.: Alzheimer's disease diagnosis by using dimensionality reduction based on KNN classifier. Biomed. Pharmacol. J. **10**(4), 1823–1830 (2017)

27. Usman, A., Shazad, A., Javed, F.: Using PCA and factor analysis for dimensionality reduction of bio-informatics data. (IJACSA) Int. J. Adv. Comput. Sci. Appl. **8**(5), 515–426 (2017)

28. Gökmen, Z., et al.: A comprehensive simulation study on classification of RNASeq data. PLoS ONE J. **12**(8), 1–24 (2017)

29. Ian, T.J., Jorge, C.: Principal component analysis: a review and recent developments. Philosoph. Trans. Math. Phys. Eng. Sci. **374**, 1–21 (2017)

30. Nathan, T.J., Andi, D., Katelyn, J.H., Dmitry, K.: Biological classification with RNA-Seq data: Can alternative splicing enhance machine learning classifier? bioRxiv. doi:http://dx.doi.org/10.1101/146340 (2017)

31. Keerthi, K.V., Surendiran, B.: Dimensionality reduction using Principal Component Analysis for network intrusion detection. Perspect. Sci. **8**, 510–512 (2016)

32. Sofie, V.: A comparative review of dimensionality reduction methods for high-throughput single-cell transcriptomics. Master's dissertation submitted to Ghent University to obtain the degree of Master of Science in Biochemistry and Biotechnology. Major Bioinformatics and Systems Biology, pp. 1–88 (2017)

33. Elavarasan, Mani, K.: A survey on feature extraction techniques. Int. J. Innov. Res. Comput. Commun. Eng. **3**(1), 1–4 (2015)

34. Divya, J., Vijendra, S.: Feature selection and classification systems for chronic disease prediction: a review. Egyptian Inform. J. (2018). https://doi.org/10.1016/j.eij.2018.03.002

35. Awotunde, J.B., Ogundokun, R.O., Ayo, Femi E., Ajamu, Gbemisola J., Adeniyi, E.A., Ogundokun, E.O.: Social media acceptance and use among university students for learning purpose using UTAUT model. In: Borzemski, L., Świątek, J., Wilimowska, Z. (eds.) ISAT 2019. AISC, vol. 1050, pp. 91–102. Springer, Cham (2020). https://doi.org/10.1007/978-3-030-30440-9_10

36. Ogundokun, R.O.: Evaluation of the scholastic performance of students in 12 programs from a private university in the south-west geopolitical zone in Nigeria. Research **8** (2019)

Telemedicine in Shipping Made Easy - Shipping eHealth Solutions

Eleni-Emmanouela Koumantaki[1], Ioannis Filippopoulos[2,3],
Angelika Kokkinaki[3], Chrysoula Liakou[4], and Yiannis Kiouvrekis[1,3(✉)] (iD)

[1] University of Thessaly, Volos, Greece
yiannis.kiouvrekis@gmail.com, kiouvrekis.y@uth.gr
[2] Hellenic American University, Athens, USA
[3] University of Nicosia, Nicosia, Cyprus
[4] Fleet Medical Advisor Angelicoussis Group, Athens, Greece

Abstract. This research study aims to highlight the main weak and strong points of existing telemedicine technologies as well as to propose the creation of a new, innovative and financially efficient system of telemedicine which can be used in the maritime industry. In addition to main applications and details of the new system, the article describes and expounds on necessary equipment as well as personnel training.

Keywords: Telemedicine · Navy · Naval · Naval medicine

1 Introduction

Telemedicine allows for the administration of remote medical care; it is defined as the administration of medical care over great distance through the application of medical expertise in combination with communication and IT technology. This field involves clinical medicine, i.e. diagnosis, treatment and evidence based medicine as well as its academic applications, which involve research, training and experimentation [12].

Electronic medicine and m-health, which involve medical care administered over mobile phone, is increasingly applied in the administration of medical care both in the public and the private sector [9]; however, when it comes to telemedicine's use in the maritime industry, its application and development is still rather limited.

1.1 Telemedicine – Definition, Applications and Operations

Telemedicine involves the general application of communication and IT technologies in administering clinical medical care over distance [12]. Thanks to internet and satellite-based communications, it is feasible nowadays for smaller clinics to send electrocardiograms, x-rays and other images to urban hospitals for the purposes of consultation. Over time, it became possible to record direct connections

© Springer Nature Switzerland AG 2020
M. Themistocleous et al. (Eds.): EMCIS 2020, LNBIP 402, pp. 493–505, 2020.
https://doi.org/10.1007/978-3-030-63396-7_33

of patients to practitioners, even though at a high cost per use, given the high prices of video conferencing equipment [5].

In certain instances, consultation over a smartphone can serve as a substitute for in-person consultation with a medical practitioner. The application of telemedicine in healthcare is not confined exclusively in the administration of medical care.

1.2 Telemedicine and the Maritime Industry

Telemedical practice can take on many different forms depending on available technology or the application used for transmission and the time required to send and receive said transmissions [9].

In its most basic form, images and data are transmitted with a certain degree of delay, as the user needs to take a picture by means of a conventional or digital camera, save it as an image file and then send it. Remote interactive communication constitutes the next stage in telemedical practice. This stage involves audio-visual consultation with the help of HD screens, digital cameras and digital stethoscopes.

In order for a telemedicine system to be complete and efficient, it is necessary to integrate all pieces of technology required for clinical examination, remote training and exchange of information, both between private citizens and between private citizens and government agencies [14]. A system of this type can be described as follows (Fig. 1):

Fig. 1. Optimization of telemedicine infrastructure and interface

1.3 Issues Arising from Storing and Transferring of Data

Sensitive data protection is a topical issue which is frequently brought up in the related discourse concerning general healthcare issues. Healthcare institutions have been required to digitize all their files in order to allow for direct information exchange and taking prompt action in cases of emergency.

The EU has already taken measures in order to limit risks involving the lack of regulation and protection of personal data. These issues have been largely addressed through the application of the General Data Protection Regulation (GDPR) 2016/679, which lays down clear rules for personal data protection while upholding EU core freedoms – the freedom of movement of people, goods, capital and services over borders.

The GDPR sections relevant to this study include (EU 2016):

- Section 36 of the introduction, dealing with the protection of personal data pertaining to current, past or future health status of the data subject as well as data derived from testing, treatment, etc.
- Section 45 of the introduction, which sets a derogation in case of potential hazzards posed to public health, e.g. if there are fears of a contagious disease spreading (a parameter also referred to in section 52).
- Section 53, which refers specifically to authorizing experts or health authorities with access to data of natural persons, if a risk to those persons' health has been established.
- Section 63, which gives the right to natural persons to demand access to their health data, including history, examination results, etc.
- Section 91, which authorizes healthcare professionals and lawyers with access to such data, as long as a) it is deemed necessary and b) data processing does not occur on a large scale.
- Article 4, section 15, wherein data concerning health is defined as "personal data related to the physical or mental health of a natural person, including the provision of health care services, which reveal information about his or her health status".
- Article 9, which prohibits processing of data which could reveal information concerning the health of a natural person while taking into consideration the aforementioned derogations.

1.4   Limitations and Weaknesses of Existing Systems

The application recommended has been designed to be useable both by professionals and by non-experts, such as ship passengers. It is intended to be easy to download and run on smartphones or tablets by providing identification and accurate information on the ship. However, it appears that there are several ethical and practical issues concerning data transfer and the use of digital files (examination results, x-ray images, etc.) in particular [6, 7].

This raises the question whether the quality benefits of telemedicine in the maritime industry are financially efficient. As is usually emphasized, a high degree of accuracy and efficiency is important. The sender must exchange data with the receiver and specialized agencies must be notified. This ensures that the appropriate health care is provided. Quantity benefits are also substantial, as costs of docking and moving patients are lowered, benefiting both governments and businesses [10].

1.5   Medical Data Encryption

According to existing legislation and in accordance with GDPR provisions, medical data exchanged must be encrypted in all instances. Data encryption is a requirement for safeguarding citizens' private and professional lives, since their social status, career, etc. could otherwise be placed in jeopardy. Patients suffering from serious, non-contagious diseases, HIV-seropositive individuals, etc. are at particular risk of facing social stigma and discrimination [4].

Proposed solutions include data standardization, classification and safe encoding of information, standardization of the data transfer process as well as the utilization of an internal system which would involve encoding the data pertaining to the subject and the digital file and standardizing the communication procedure. This would both lower risks and increase benefits [15].

1.6   Presentation of the New e-Health and m-Health System Designed for Use on Marine Vessels

The system will utilize e-mobile services for a) locating the marine vessel, b) locating the healthcare facility nearest to it and c) simplifying the process of data transfer and exchange by means of a digital database. The application will be effective both in the case of ships with specialized equipment and that of smaller ships utilizing only a basic satellite system. The application's basic functions are designed in a way that renders interception of data impossible. In accordance with GDPR 2016/679, medical data can be accessed by (EU 2016):

– The authorities (hence coast guard officers) and the ship's captain, in case of an emergency or an incident which could pose a public health hazzard, namely an outbreak of an infectious or contagious disease on a ship located far away from a medical center or station.
– A healthcare professional, e.g. the ship physician.
– The patients themselves, in the event of extraordinary circumstances, namely if a crew member or the ship physician is unavailable due to an accident, e.g. an explosion, becoming trapped, etc.

The application must uphold the current European Regulation on personal data and in no way contravene any European legislation or member-state legislation to the jurisdiction of which the ship is subject (EU 2016). In accordance with existing international law, it is vital to hold appropriate authorization. Therefore, it is crucial for the application to utilize the appropriate systems of encoding concerning [15]:

– Data reading,
– Information exchange,
– Communication,
– Data storage.

The general idea is that the program will allow users to identify as one of the following:

1. Medical professional (physician/surgeon).
2. Nursing staff or healthcare professional in general (paramedical staff).
3. General staff.
4. Passenger.

In case the application is utilized by an unauthorized crew member, it must be ensured that the subject's data will not be accessible, i.e. that access is denied and a specialized signal is subsequently sent to the nearest medical center, where a member of the medical staff or a government employee will be taking charge of remote support [11].

A key point is that the application will be making use of a multilingual software which will provide basic terminology. The subject must be in a position as to describe their condition, while the software will provide the ability to search for the nearest physicians able to deal with the case according to the key-words provided [2].

If results do not match or if the user is unable to accurately specify their condition, in order to prevent further risks and complications, it is necessary to facilitate direct connection to medical centers providing general practitioner services. This will render the application easy to use even for non-experts.

2 Description

Initially, the application must enable the user to "input" information, namely to manually type a description of their condition. If the application is sufficiently advanced, filled in information can take the form of a text message, e.g.: "Trouble breathing and intense throat pain". Otherwise, the user will have to navigate through a fixed list of incident types, e.g. "Emergencies-Breathing problems-Trouble breathing + Pain-Throat-Intense".

Subsequently, the application must specify the incident, whether it has been input following the previous or the latter method. The incident will be specified through a coded sequence, which can be subsequently sent out.

In addition to other functions, the application must contain a list of instructions to be given in the event of an emergency. These instructions can involve anything, ranging from Allergic Shock to CPR. Instructions will ideally be given through voice guidance and figures, so as to enable the user to promptly comprehend how to administer first aid.

The application should also cross-examine input data with the subject's history; this cross-examination could be performed through accessing the subject's Individual Electronic Health File.

Following cross-examination, the application will encode the incident in a format suitable for sending out to the nearest Healthcare Center.

There should be more than one method of transmitting an incident report; therefore, the encoding format should be simple, so that it can be transmitted even by Morse code. The application should ideally be able to transmit an incident report in any of the following ways:

- Satellite Communication
- Digital Signal
- Analog Signal
- Low frequency (Morse).

After receiving the signal, the Healthcare Center will be able to respond using the same application. In practice, this means that the method of response input, encoding and transmission out should be the same.

The application will subsequently decode the response and will either give instructions following a fixed list or will relate the physicians' instructions verbatim. A provision should be made in the event of delay in transmitting or receiving the signal, so that the application automatically sends a notification to the respective Coast Guard in order for the patient to be transferred without delay to a medical facility. The aforementioned proposed features are in compliance with ISO 27001 "Information Security Management in Shipping", also the procedure proposed is based on general telemedicine principles. First, the user will be able to select among specific categories and enter the data, which will be assessed by the application itself. Following this, the nearest center will be located and a signal will be sent to it along with the encrypted data.

Menu selection will include entries of the following:

A) sex, age and medical history.
B) incident category.
C) body part where the patient feels pain, discomfort or irritation (e.g. shoulder, wrist, foot, chest, etc.).
D) symptom selection.

After submitting any relevant data to the application, a card will return listing location, health professional, staff member or passenger ID, topic, a summary of the incident, justification and a reference code, which will refer to a preliminary diagnosis. The following is an example of a complete entry card (Fig. 2):

Incidence no i.e. 31	Local coordinates (i.e. 51° 28' 38" N)¹
	Ship: i.e. Bella 2
	ID: Ship doctor: Dr. A. Moussadi i.e. X9838922, Konstantina Bellianidi
	Topic: Ophthalmological condition
	Summary: optic nerve disorder
	Justification: swollen eye, allergic reaction
	Code: H47.C03

Fig. 2. A basic presentation of the application

3   e-Health and m-Health: Practical Applications

3.1   Kit Presentation

Before a ship can be cleared for departure, it is necessary for it to be stocked with essential medical supplies and equipment to facilitate administration of telemedicine and general medical services. The needs in provisions and equipment depend on the number of passengers. Every ship physician as well as the ship's captain are supplied with a Kit containing the basic tools needed to determine a prompt diagnosis and notifiy the nearest medical center [4].

A provisional version of that Kit will include the following equipment (their function will be elaborated on later) (Fig. 3):

Fig. 3. Basic Kit

This basic Kit should include [1]:

1. A mobile touch screen computer with the capacity to run the software used. Given the modern technology used, the computer should meet the following specifications:
   - Windows 10 or MAC or Linux Operating System.
   - Word processing software compatible with the aforementioned Operating Systems, such as Microsoft Office^{TM} or Open Office©.
   - Wifi adapter and Bluetooth connectivity.
   - USB 2.0 and USB 3.0 ports.
   - A minimum requirement of an i3 processor at 2.0 GHz.
   - Graphics card and sound card.
2. A digital stethoscope compatible with the Kit's mobile computer.
3. A pulse oximeter.
4. A digital oscilloscope.
5. An ultrasound machine.

6. A multipurpose dermatoscope.
7. A microphone and speaker.
8. An HD camera.

As previously mentioned, this application should be easy for everyone to use, whether it is the ship physician, a crew member and/or a passenger. In addition, the application should be useable in all fields of medicine, e.g. a) telecardiology, b) teleophthalmology, c) teledermatology, d) teleradiology, e) telepsychiatry, as well as in incidents that should be addressed by a gynecologist, pediatrician or a general practitioner.

In the interests of a more accurate diagnosis, live video (audio-visual) communication is established between the ship and the land service center. Concerning the x-rays, it should be noted here that all information is transferred via the Internet – a feature supported by the application. The satellite connection technology, which will be utilized, is the Mobile Satellite Communication (MOST), which will allow for two-way communication between sender and receiver through the SatCOM series. The main advantage here is that communication can be achieved by using a mobile phone through both Ku and Ka frequency bands. This method enables the terminal station to transfer information to mobile terminals. Furthermore, transmission, reception as well as polarization is made possible through the use of stabilization systems and miniature antennas.

3.2   Drivers and Encryption Process Presentation

In the interests of patient data protection and non disclosure of the ship's location, telemedicine allows for total encryption. This is deemed necessary to fully protect the ship owning company's interests as well as passenger data. Therefore, it is essential for the application to employ an encryption system which both the ship physician and the captain can comprehend [3].

Related materials will include a specialized application form or a declaration of honor by virtue of which a passenger or a crew member will consent to allow access to their personal digital data or to any database which would contain their personal data. The international encoding system ICD 10, as utilized in the SNOMED approach, will be employed to encrypt the data [15].

This system will form the basis to set a commonly accepted framework in order to classify medical conditions and to establish a common "vocabulary" which is in use in medical science. This achieves a twofold benefit: a) on the one hand, data is classified in such a manner as to ensure that a non-expert will not gain direct access to a patient's personal information and, b) on the other hand, the program which will serve as the basis for the application will be capable of "reading" a code and thus retrieve any relevant information [13].

Information can also be transmitted through Morse signals following communication with a physician. In this instance, the physician will contact the staff of the nearest center and, in case the connection was lost or interrupted, a distress signal "describing" the incident will be sent out to the authorities [13] (Fig. 4).

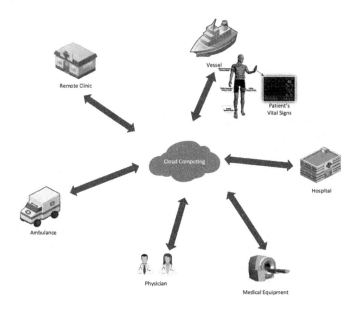

Fig. 4. Presentation of the system employed by the application. Source: Liu 2013

The following is the usual classification method based on ICD standards employed in SNOMED, which provides common encoding guidelines for several types of incidents [15]:

It becomes evident that this type of encoding requires additional materials explaining the method of encoding to those unfamiliar with it. The system described above will be adapted to the new application. The first part of the code remains unchanged and, therefore, Latin numerals will be used to provisionally specify a condition or a probable category of conditions. To this end, the symbols I–XX (1–20) will be used [15]:

A number between 0–99 is entered to specify the information input. The numbers indicate different conditions relating to the first category [13]. Furthermore, a separate serial number will be used to indicate the gravity of the condition, ranging from 00 (indicating a non-serious condition) to 99 (indicating an extremely serious condition) [8].

Based on this input, the program will subsequently combine this information into a common program which we have named "Careta-Careta" for the sake of our example. In simple script, the program will encrypt data as follows:

Code:

```
    clc
disp 'welcome to careta-careta'
disp 'please calm down and tell me what happened'

No=input('please input incident number');
ID=input('doctors id');
```

```
disp 'insert local coordinates'
lat=input ('latitude');
lon=input ('longitude');
Coor=[lat;lon];

prompt = 'Insert Patient Name';
Name = input(prompt,'s');
if strcmp(inp,'CBA')
    fprintf('answer is 1');
elseif strcmp(inp,'BAC')
    fprintf('answer is 0');
end
disp 'Describe the incident'
prompt = 'Please input roman letter code, from the list
 provided in the instructions:';
inp = input(prompt,'s');
if strcmp(inp,'CBA')
    fprintf('answer is 1');
elseif strcmp(inp,'BAC')
    fprintf('answer is 0');
end
S=input ('please input symptoms combination (00-99)');
disp 'Select the causality factor'
disp 'Select a letter from the list'
disp 'T-topography, M-Morphology, L-living organism, C-chemical
 agent, F-function, O-occupation'
disp 'D-diagnosis, P-procedure, G-general, A-physical agents'
prompt= ('Please input one of the above letters:');
F = input(prompt,'s');
if strcmp(inp,'CBA')
    fprintf('answer is 1');
elseif strcmp(inp,'BAC')
    fprintf('answer is 0');
end

L=input('Where did the incident occur?');
Lo=input('Please be more specific');
E=input ('Do i need to know anything else?');
X=cell(1,6);
C{1,1}=inp;
C{1,2}=S;
C{1,3}=F;
C{1,4}=L;
C{1,5}=Lo;
```

```
C{1,6}=E;
disp 'encryption is complete'
disp 'please wait'

disp 'coordinates are:'

disp (Coor)
disp 'incident no:', No
disp 'Doctor id:', ID
disp 'Patient Name:', Name
disp 'incident code is:'
disp (C)
```

In the case of the example presented in previous subsection

```
Incidence no
i.e. 31
Local coordinates
Ship: i.e. Bella 2
ID: Ship doctor: Dr. A. Moussadi
i.e. X9838922,
Konstantina Bellianidi Topic: Ophthalmological condition Summary:
 optic nerve disorder Justification: swollen eye, allergic reaction
```

Thus, the program will give the following:

```
    welcome to careta-careta
please calm down and tell me what happened
please input incident number 31
doctors id X9838922
ID=input('doctors id');
doctors id 9838922
insert local coordinates
latitude 51.2838
longitude 34
Insert Patient Name Konstantina Bellianidi
Describe the incident
Please input roman letter code, from the list provided
 in the instructions: IV
please input symptoms combination (00-99) 32
Select the causality factor
Select a letter from the list
T-topography, M-Morphology, L-living organism, C-chemical agent,
 F-function, O-occupation
D-diagnosis, P-procedure, G-general, A-physical agents
Please input one of the above letters: A
Where did the incident occur? 4
```

```
Please be more specific 3
Do i need to know anything else? 0
encryption is complete
please wait
coordinates are:
   51.2838
   34.0000

incident no:

No =

     31

Doctor id:

ID =

     9838922

Patient Name:

Name =

   ' Konstantina Bellianidi'

incident code is:
   ' IV'    [32]    ' A'    [4]    [3]    [0]
```

Communication is encrypted using the respective codes. The Kit will also include: - Lists of basic terms. - The classification list. - An application manual.

4   Conclusions

The aim of this paper is to propose a new application which can be used to administer remote medical assistance to crew members or passengers on marine vessels. This application intends initially to meet the needs of patients on freight ships and subsequently to find use in the greater context of naval medicine. A great number of factors were taken into consideration in the stage of its planning and application, including legislation, existing technology, standard practices as well as potential circumstances which could have an effect on the nature of the maritime industry in the future.

References

1. Anliker, U., et al.: AMON: a wearable multiparameter medical monitoring and alert system. IEEE Trans. Inf. Technol. Biomed. **8**(4), 415–427 (2004). https://doi.org/10.1109/TITB.2004.837888
2. Apostolakis, I., Valsamos, P., Varlamis, I.: Decentralization of the Greek national telemedicine system. In: Healthcare Information Systems and Informatics: Research and Practices, pp. 278–296. IGI Global (2008)
3. Doarn, C.R., et al.: Evolution of telemedicine in Russia: the influence of the space program on modern telemedicine programs. Telemed. J. e-Health **9**(1), 103–109 (2003)
4. European Society of Radiology (ESR): The new EU general data protection regulation: what the radiologist should know. Insights Imaging **8**(3), 295–299 (2017)
5. Flodgren, G., Rachas, A., Farmer, A.J., Inzitari, M., Shepperd, S.: Interactive telemedicine: effects on professional practice and health care outcomes. Cochrane Database Syst. Rev. (9) (2015). https://doi.org/10.1002/14651858.CD002098.pub2. Art. No.: CD002098
6. Graschew, G., Roelofs, T.A., Rakowsky, S., Schlag, P.M.: Design of satellite-based networks for u-health-GALENOS, DELTASS, MEDASHIP, EMISPHER. In: 2007 9th International Conference on e-Health Networking, Application and Services (June 2007)
7. Graschew, G., et al.: Globalization of healthcare by virtualization of hospitals. Berlin: Second UN International UN Spider Workshop: "Disaster Management and Space Technology" - Bridging the Gap (2000). https://www.slideshare.net/ISCRAM/globalisation-of-healthcare-by-virtualisation-of-hospitals-presentation
8. World Health Organization: How to use the ICF: a practical manual for using the international classification of functioning, disability and health (ICF). Exposure draft for comment. WHO, Geneva (October 2013)
9. Latifi, R.: Telemedicine for Trauma, Emergencies, and Disaster Management. Artech House, Norwood (2011)
10. Mermelstein, H., Guzman, E., Rabinowitz, T., et al.: The application of technology to health: the evolution of telephone to telemedicine and telepsychiatry: a historical review and look at human factors. J. Technol. Behav. Sci. **2**, 5–20 (2017)
11. M-healthintelligence: How to design and develop a mobile health application. https://mhealthintelligence.com/features/how-to-design-and-develop-a-mobile-health-application. Accessed 29 Sep 2020
12. Sood, S., et al.: What is telemedicine? A collection of 104 peer-reviewed perspectives and theoretical underpinnings. Telemed. e-Health **13**(5), 573–590 (2007)
13. Spackman, K., Campbell, K., Côté, R.: SNOMED RT: a reference terminology for health care. In: Proceedings of the AMIA Annual Fall Symposium. American Medical Informatics Association (1997)
14. Subba Rao, S.: Integrated health care and telemedicine. Work Study **50**(6), 222–229 (2001)
15. Tsipouras, M., Giannakeas, N., Karvounis, E., Tzallas, A.: Medical Informatics. Hellenic Academic Libraries Link, Athens (2015). http://hdl.handle.net/11419/2975

Information Systems Security and Information Privacy Protection

Game-Based Information Security/Privacy Education and Awareness: Theory and Practice

Stylianos Karagiannis[1,2(✉)] ⓘ, Thanos Papaioannou[1,3] ⓘ,
Emmanouil Magkos[1] ⓘ, and Aggeliki Tsohou[1] ⓘ

[1] Department of Informatics, Ionian University, Plateia Tsirigoti 7,
49100 Corfu, Greece
{skaragiannis, thanospapa, emagos, atsohou}@ionio.gr
[2] Beyond Vision, 3830-352 Ílhavo, Portugal
[3] PDMFC, 1300-609 Lisboa, Portugal

Abstract. This paper reviews and assesses classical and novel methods and tools towards engaging students and workforce in the concepts of information security and privacy. We investigate the theoretical basis for deploying a game-based approach for security/privacy learning and awareness, and assess state-of-the-art tools and methods that could be used as part of a challenge-based or game-based framework for learning, including serious games, CTF platforms, escape rooms, puzzle/interactive books and Alternate Reality Games (ARGs), while also identifying key-elements and important aspects that should be taken into consideration when designing a security and privacy learning/awareness program. For each of the above approaches and tools' categories, we highlight their potential for using them for education and awareness of information security and privacy.

Keywords: Game-based learning · Gamification · Information security · Privacy awareness · Education

1 Introduction

Nowadays, public and private sector maintain high interest in information security and privacy awareness training programs, usually struggling as well to recruit enough workforce specialized in cybersecurity [1, 2] to support such efforts. In the industry and the literature there is a significant tendency for using entertaining approaches such as Gamification, Games for Learning (G4L) and Game-Based Learning (GBL) for achieving high information retention rates for the trainees [3]. Organizations usually cannot afford large-scale programs to enhance information security and privacy awareness of their employees [4] and create appropriate related exercises. The topics are usually focused exclusively on advanced concepts and, in the end, the programs fail to meet the specific learning goals regarding beginners or non-IT professionals and therefore not all existing relevant programs on the market provide the appropriate deployment flexibility. As a result, modern educational tools must be extended, to be adaptive and meet personal needs [5–7]. Even though recent research has started to

© Springer Nature Switzerland AG 2020
M. Themistocleous et al. (Eds.): EMCIS 2020, LNBIP 402, pp. 509–525, 2020.
https://doi.org/10.1007/978-3-030-63396-7_34

focus on gamification-based approaches for security and privacy education [8–11], much work still needs to be done in this area.

This paper reviews and investigates methods and tools to engage students and workforce in concepts of information security and privacy, facilitating knowledge acquirement in the area, while enhancing security and privacy awareness. It also provides new insights regarding gamification and game-based learning activities offered for security and privacy awareness. To this end, we conduct a literature review with a focus on serious and tabletop games, escape rooms, puzzles/interactive books and Alternate Reality Games (ARGs), and identify key-elements and important aspects that must be taken into consideration when designing gamified or game-based learning/awareness experiences in the areas of information security and privacy. We provide a taxonomy for classifying the most popular tools and approaches while also investigating the theoretical basis for deploying a game-based approach for learning. For each of the above approaches and tools' categories, even for those that do not directly address the security and privacy topics, we highlight their potential for using them for awareness and training purposes, along with key-factors that are important when designing and developing such approaches. The corresponding playful approaches that exist in the field of security and privacy learning are limited in number but also in a variety of implementations. To concretize their categorization, to expand their systematic use and to promote the development of new implementation ideas, we present a classification of those that already exist and are used.

The research paper is organized as follows: In Sect. 2 the main learning theories and pedagogic approaches for motivated learning are presented based in novel approaches of using gamification and game-based learning emphasizing in computer security and privacy. In Sect. 3 we provide a taxonomy and analysis of the existing gamification and game-based learning approaches extending to computer security education and awareness. Finally, Sect. 4 concludes the paper and discusses future work.

2   Theories and Approaches for Motivated Learning

Modern learning approaches and researchers tend to agree that teaching environments that meet the needs of the learning theory of constructivism are more effective [12]. Constructivism asserts that learning is an idiosyncratic activity for the learner [13]. This theory is found in psychology and explains how individuals construct knowledge and learn from their experiences [14]. Constructivists consider the individual as an active procreator in the learning process [15–18]. This view contradicts other learning theories, in which learning is simply the transfer of knowledge from one person to another [13]. If the phenomenon of learning is sought to be explained through constructivism, then learning environments should be created in which the learner is exposed to the cognitive material to be studied [19]. Other scientists have argued that the focus should be also on the social and cultural context in which the individual is growing up. Vygotsky's argument that social interaction generates cognitive development is clearly evident in the definition of the zone of proximal development as *"the distance between the actual developmental level as determined by independent problem-solving and the level of potential development as determined through problem-solving under adult guidance or in collaboration with more capable peers*" [20, 21]. This was considered as a modern direction called social constructivism, according to which personal thinking is formulated on social interaction. According to social constructivism any successful learning can take place only if individuals are motivated internally and are involved in the construction of knowledge.

2.1 Framework for Gamification and Game-Based Learning

According to McGonigal (2011), people in modern times express a prolonged discontent with everything that happens in real life, while enjoying satisfaction and positive emotions in a playful environment [9, 22]. There are two key terms for the use of games, and especially of computer games, for educational purposes: Gamification and Game-Based Learning. The term "gamification" was introduced by Pelling (2003), even though the word has only been widely used in the last decade [23]. A commonly adopted definition is "The process of game-thinking and game mechanics to engage users and solve problems" from Zichermann and Cummingham [24]. Deterding et al. (2011) argued that gamification is *"the use of game design elements in non-game contexts"*, implying that gamification is more related to the game elements of an activity rather than playfulness [25]. Yang summarizes the above arguments in order to separate the meaning of the two terms in the following definition: *"Gamification relates to gaming techniques while game-based learning carries the learning through the form of games"* [3]. Finally, the properties for the effectiveness and quality of using games for cognitive learning processes are mentioned in various frameworks [26–29]. Important aspects that are included on such approaches are presented in Table 1. Considering the theoretical framework for learning, we argue that the aspects could include more features and enhance more the learning impact. Therefore, we came to the compilation/extension of the framework resulting in the following table that presents an extended research vision in this field.

Table 1. Existing selected aspects from frameworks, gamification and game-based approaches

	Aspects	Description
Design features	Realism	Real-world scenarios must be reproduced providing hands-on labs
	Role orientation and adaptability	Adapt the training to the role of each trainee according to personal skills
	Zone of proximal development	Balance between the effort and what participants could accomplish. Reflect to the participants' skills, knowledge and experience. Present relevant topics creating sub-tasks
	Workforce diversity	Difference in terms of culture, knowledge, skills and experience. Personalized scenarios enhance the teamwork
	Learning goals	Mapping to official curriculum knowledge topics and addressed skills. Matching to learning taxonomies (e.g. NICE)

(continued)

Table 1. (*continued*)

	Aspects	Description
	Extent on other IT topics	Not only cybersecurity skills must be present, but the participants must be able to understand other technical topics as well
	Adversary emulation	Deployment of malicious, attack and defense roles, during the training
Required experience	Workforce diversity	Difference in terms of culture, knowledge, skills and experience. Personalized scenarios enhance the teamwork
	Flow of use	The rate and complexity that the information is presented in connection to the experience of the participants
	Zone of proximal development	The zone of knowledge proof is important to consider the personal characteristics of the participants
Subjective factors	Usability	Ease of access and high usability rates
	Fun	Storytelling elements, intrinsic and extrinsic rewards along with other gamification elements will enhance this aspect
	Information retention	Maintain the knowledge and skills for a long time. Conduct assessments and competitions
Game mechanics	Supervision	Monitor and assess the progress of each trainee
	Growth	Steady growth of new exercises related to new cyberthreats and technology evolution
	Collaborative learning	The teams will be responsible for maintaining the best approaches. Each member has a specific role
	Self-directed learning	Maintain basic technical skills following the guidelines and learning paths. Collaborative learning will enhance this process
	Single and multiplayer	Opportunity for the participants to join or create a team. Self-directed and self-development must be also present
	Scoreboard	Scoreboard is important to include details about the teams and individual scoreboard for each participant and to connect with official scoreboards providing evidence of the participation.
	Leaderboard	Leaderboards are important to include Most Valuable Player (MVP) and to promote the best players for each of the different individual topics
	Progress bar	Progress bars for each security/privacy scenario is important for enhancing the situational awareness of the participants and to help in terms of supervision
	Supervision	Includes features that are related to supervision such as the scoreboard from the managers perspective, logfiles, announcement capabilities and support tickets, among others
	Teamworking and competitiveness	Scoring and reward system focused on self-improvement and encouraging team working

(*continued*)

Table 1. (*continued*)

	Aspects	Description
Expected outcomes	Active participation	Team discussions, short-written exercises, debates and learning by teaching actions. Being critical, negotiable, and reflective
	Engagement	High levels of engagement are expected when the scenarios are realistic, the environment responsive as well as the assignments are put in efficient way
	Habituation	Information retention is easier to achieve from repetitive tasks, however, the participants must be exposed to unspecified and unpredictable cases and challenges to assess their responses in real-time situations
	Increase privacy awareness	Self-assessment methods must be designed and deployed to increase privacy awareness using specific scenarios
	Increase security awareness	Demonstrate acquired skills and knowledge. Relate to experiences and personalized scenarios including targeted and understandable context
	Information retention	Maintain the knowledge and skills for a long time. Conduct assessments and competitions

2.2 Novel Theories (Game-Based) for Information Security/Privacy Learning

Most novel approaches related to information security/privacy education tend to be based on the learning theory of constructivism and Vygotsky's Zone of Proximal Development, where the lecturer's role is to guide and facilitate the total process and help students to achieve their goals [30–32]. More specifically, there is an increasing demand for enhancing the learning process with high levels of interactivity, important for improving the learning experience [33]. Research carried out in the early years of internet expansion has shown that traditional learning theories, like behaviorism and cognitivism, are popular to support learning with technology [34]. However, these approaches focus on the transfer of knowledge, and on the value of text and dialogue between learners and tutors. The use of virtual worlds, combined with text, voice, vision and a sense of physical presence, enhances interactivity and therefore promotes learning experience through social interaction, stronger engagement and motivation, and enhances the development of meta-level thinking skills [35].

For enhancing security and privacy awareness, context is usually delivered using methods including, but not limited to, classroom-style training, posters and presenting content through websites and newsletters. Khan et al. 2011, regarding the effectiveness of the different security awareness methods, highlighted that group discussions and educational presentations are the most effective [36, 37]. To this extent, computer games also have been used in security training as they motivate and draw attention from the users allowing them to participate and acquire knowledge within a given scenario [38]. More specifically the researchers mention the positive outcomes of computer games regarding the change of attitude however they fail similarly on finding details related to change of the behavior.

Nowadays, most learning methods focus on delivering content theoretically. In contrary, experiential workshops could be deployed identifying specific attack vectors while observing the behavior of the trainees. Therefore, measuring the risk, defining the exposures and extracting data related to the level of awareness that required from the trainees, will eventually lead to a successful and useful awareness programs. Privacy awareness requirements could be different for the data subject, processor or controller. For example, the multidimensional model of Information Privacy Awareness (IPA) [39] is a directive approach that considers different aspects of enhancing and measuring privacy awareness. According to this approach privacy awareness could be described in three different types such as knowledge/literacy, understanding and projection.

Proposed Future Avenues for Research and Practice. Integrating gamification and story-telling elements into the learning process seems challenging. Learning goals should be directly related to the official curriculum and practices. Therefore, the challenges could integrate linear and non-linear scenarios for fulfilling specific learning goals, considering the audiences attributes such as background knowledge and according to their social and working environment. Furthermore, storytelling elements could be integrated choosing various themes which will apply to the audience accordingly. Novel methods could be applied to replace instructive learning processes and to present the main learning context as well to include a variety of options for enhancing security and privacy awareness. For example, tabletops are appropriate for initializing group discussions or approaches such as escape rooms which engage participants in team-based activities. Group discussions and educational context can be delivered by various novel approaches such as interactive and puzzle books providing self-directed learning and self-assessment methods. Including literacy metrics is important for acquiring sufficient knowledge and demonstrating the acquired knowledge and skills along with the possible behavior change. Privacy literacy assessment considers the following dimensions [38]:

a. Practices of Organizations, Institutions, and Online Service Providers
b. Technical Aspects about Online Privacy and Data Protection
c. Laws and Legal Aspects of Online Data Protection in Germany
d. Directives on Privacy and Data Protection
e. User Strategies for Individual Online Privacy Control
f. Ways to deal with privacy threats.

Some case examples for stimulating the learning outcomes towards security and privacy awareness include the following topics: password management, email handling and viruses, phishing attacks, web browsing behavior, updates and awareness, Security Protocols Compliance, operating systems and security, physical security (e.g. exposed peripherals), smartphone security (third-parties, privilege and access management, disclosures), geolocation data (location awareness), risks regarding published media (photos, text, sound), data handling (distinction between personal and sensitive data).

For addressing the above, we first investigated and analyzed the existing learning theories of behaviorism, cognitivism and constructivism, as well as pedagogies that focus on Gamification and Game-Based learning. Subsequently, the primary researcher tested and reviewed existing Gamification and Game-Based tools and approaches and for each approach we created a classification explaining the specifics of each approach and their specific attributes. In the next sections, we extracted the key-benefits and drawbacks of each approach and we present challenges and future work gaps taking into consideration the discussed learning theories.

3 Challenge-Based and Gamification-Based Tools for Computer Security Education and Awareness

Creating learning experiences which appeal to personalized characteristics, specific skillset and background knowledge is expected to improve the motivation rates of the learning programs and enhance learning outcomes [5]. Maintaining high motivation levels in the topics of information security is difficult, due to issues deriving from the absence of participants' skills and technical experience, while such educational programs require large effort from smaller organizations [4]. Our purpose is to investigate and extract the key-elements of the existing approaches.

3.1 Capture the Flag (CTF) Platforms and Cyber Ranges

Capture the Flag (CtF) competitions have a similar logic to the traditional CtF outdoor games, with the difference being that the game takes place in the digital world; instead of fields, each team has to protect and attack vulnerable systems and the flags are alphanumeric strings. Well known approaches for enhancing the learning process also include the use of vulnerable virtual systems [40, 41]. Such approaches are also used in CtFs; however, the challenges can be also deployed individually with the option to be an important tool for creating self-directed learning experiences. For extending such approaches, cyber ranges have been lately developed and are used together with CtF challenges for creating exercises related to information security [1, 41–44]. Examples include approaches that are published in Vulnhub[1] including popular exercises such as Metasploitable[2] from Rapid7. The benefits from using virtualization techniques include the ability to create realistic security scenarios, customization capabilities and the ability to create challenges that relate to the learning goals.

We tested some of the existing CTF approaches that include hands-on labs and provide security challenges and we classified them depending if they a platform, challenges and they are offered as commercial products. The results of our analysis are provided in Table 2. Some of them include management tools as others include ready-to-deploy challenges or embed the challenges inside the developed platform.

---

[1] vulnhub.com/.

[2] rapid7.com/.

Proposed Future Avenues for Research and Practice. Although CtF platforms are easy to deploy, it is typically hard to match them with existing learning topics and therefore more research is required to provide methods that reduce such efforts. Most CtF challenges are focused on bug hunting, skills' testing while few are focused on the learning perspectives. Therefore, it is usually hard for beginners or non-IT employees to follow such practices as the unguided progress suits mostly to advanced learners, since a lot of technical concepts are usually included on the CtF challenges. Finally, we propose to include basic guidance and introduction to fundamental concepts, for better meeting the learning goals and for novice participants to engage more to the learning process.

3.2   Serious Games and Computer Games Integrating Educative Context

A few commercial computer games are thematically based on cybersecurity topics, naming Hacknet[3], Uplink[4] and NITE Team4[5] among others. More specifically, NITE Team4 is mostly related to the approach of Game for Learning (G4L) since the learning goals are not clearly stated. For instance, in CyberCIEGE[6] which is a serious game, the learning goals are clear and relate to network security and security awareness [36]. There are two distinct categories of serious games; computer games integrating information from cybersecurity topics and serious games as described below:

1. **Computer games integrating cybersecurity context.** Hacknet is a simulation hacking computer game using a Linux bash shell and featuring real-world networks and real-like system infrastructure. Not only the Linux commands are similar, but a set of toolkits for penetration testing and ethical hacking like the real ones are presented [10]. Another example is the pc game Uplink, where the learning outcomes include the introduction to network commands and including realistic commands deriving from UNIX along with other basic terminology used in cybersecurity. The main difference between Hacknet and NITE Team4, is that methods presented in the game are more realistic. Furthermore, the in-game context is embedded with extra educational material regarding real-world information such as real ethical hacking tools, penetration testing methods and educational information regarding various cybersecurity concepts and terminology.
2. **Serious Games.** Examples include CyberCIEGE, Cyphinx[7] and Cyberprotect[8] which are focused on cyber defense [8, 10, 36, 45–48]. The main goal of such approaches is to prepare workforce including system engineers, software developers, system designers and network administrators and increase their security awareness.

---

[3] hacknet-os.com/.

[4] introversion.co.uk/.

[5] niteteam4.com/.

[6] nps.edu/web/c3o/cyberciege/.

[7] cybersecuritychallenge.org.uk/.

[8] sgschallenge.com/cyber-protect/.

Table 2. Existing CtF approaches

CtF approaches	Platform	Challenges	Commercial
FBCTF; CTFd; Mellivora; OpenCtF; Nightshade; RootTheBox	✓	–	✗
Hacker101	✓	✓	✓
VulnHub; OverTheWire; Metasploitable	✗	✓	✗
CTF 365	✓ Paid version	✓	✗ Free trial
HacktheBox	✓ Paid version	✓	✗ Missing features
TryHackMe	✓	✓	✓

Proposed Future Avenues for Research and Practice. Approaches like serious games and computer games, focused on computer security/privacy learning, could be extended and include high immersion rates by providing the appropriate context, themes and storytelling elements. In addition, novel gaming mechanics could be integrated specifying learning goals and outcomes. Extra tools could be developed for providing extra customization, scenario generation and integration with real-world challenges in connection with official curriculums (e.g. academic environment). The context and learning environment can be easily customized to provide the important stimuli that matches to the participants, achieving active learning through exploration and enhancing the social interaction and collaboration which are the basic tenets of constructivism.

3.3   Tabletop Games

Most table-top games focus on acquiring familiarity related to terminology used in information security. Not only card games could be developed but a large variety of posters and other media for meeting the learning requirements accordingly. Examples include the following:

1. **Control-Alt-Hack:** Control-Alt-Hack is a card game for increasing security awareness. The game mechanics and designed content is engaging, encouraging interest in computer security. Research findings have been positive in terms of increasing security awareness and privacy awareness [49, 50].
2. **[d0x3d!]:** [d0x3d!] is an open source card game designed for informal computer security education [10, 51]. The game is cooperative, and players assume the role of white-hat hackers, with the main task of retrieving digital assets from an adversarial network. The card game is released in three different forms [47, 52] and the main benefit is the possibility for creating realistic network and system topologies.
3. **Elevation of Privilege:** An easy and entertaining way from Microsoft for getting started in threat modelling using frameworks such as STRIDE and DREAD [53, 54].

4. **OWASP Cornucopia:** Cornucopia introduces threat-modelling ideas into development teams focused on web application weaknesses with the suits being based on the structure of OWASP Security Coding Practices (SCP) [46, 48, 51].
5. **Escape Rooms in a Box:** Some of the examples include The Werewolf Experiment[9], EXIT[10], and iDventure[11] Unfinished case of Holmes, among others. Such approaches do not include direct educative context but usually cultivate problem-solving skills and sharp the mind.

Advantages that tabletops include are the rich social elements they provide, as well as their appropriateness for team-based learning, encouraging debates and criticism [50, 55]. Therefore, with tabletops it seems easier to provide educative context related to threat modeling, as well as for increasing security and privacy awareness.

Proposed Future Avenues for Research and Practice. For tabletops and more specifically card games to become useful as educational tools, specific design principles must be taken into consideration. For example, the learning goals should be specified, and approaches must focus on collaborative learning and team discussions. Therefore, the tenets of constructivist pedagogy match to this approach promoting communication, collaboration and with the game-based learning design attributes. Finally, extra tools could be developed for enabling customization capabilities in the design phase of a game as a construction framework to be easier to create new cases and provide appropriate walkthroughs.

3.4   Alternate Reality Games (ARG)

ARGs combine real-world artifacts with puzzles and clues that are hidden on websites or on physical form combining themes that derive from movies or books.

Such approaches usually include strong storytelling elements and hidden messages increasing the total engagement capabilities using digital or physical media such as mobile applications or books. Positive outcomes include the enhancement of critical thinking and increasement of problem solving with puzzles, riddles and quizzes. The context of ARGs might include concepts from simple puzzles or advanced concepts that require knowledge topics extended but not limited on cryptanalysis and code exploitation. ARGs are a combination of a simulated environment and real-world context and it is possible to be designed for formal learning purposes [56–58]. We identified and reviewed existing ARG approaches, which we classify into four categories depending on their purpose and who provides them (e.g., workforce, marketing campaigns) and the results of this classification are provided in Table 3.

---

[9] escaperoominabox.com.

[10] kosmosgames.co.uk.

[11] idventure.de.

Table 3. Existing ARG approaches and developed examples

ARG approach	Description	Examples
Mysterious and anonymous; activism	Participants are invited to test their problem-solving skills for them to communicate with the organizers of a mystery group that created the challenges	Cicada 3301; Tengri 137
Official workforce recruitment	Official organizations created also similar challenges featuring ARG elements	Can You Crack It[a] (GHCQ); The Codebreaker Challenge (NSA); Project Architeuthis (U.S. Navy).
Gaming industry; prices and rewards; marketing	Marketing and promotional purposes; engagement	Order of 10 (Nvidia), Sombra ARG (Blizzard)
ARGs and computer games	Gaming industry including ARG elements	The black watchmen[b]

[a]canyoucrackit.co.uk/.
[b]blackwatchmen.com/.

Proposed Future Avenues for Research and Practice. ARGs and Cyber Ranges could be combined and create an engaging learning environment, focusing on team-working and triggering discussions that could eventually build strong interrelationships between the participants. Potential pedagogic benefits include the student autonomy, peer learning and scenarios that embed problem-solving and personal discovery having the benefit to extend from the virtual world to the real world. Possible positive outcomes include for the participants to think out of the box and to cultivate the ability to combine problem-solving skills that extend from IT to other topics as well.

3.5   Puzzle/Interactive Books

Interactive or puzzle books could include dynamic context, quizzes, puzzles, riddles and other various challenges in order to test the skills of the reader. More specifically, puzzles could engage the readers and embed appropriate educational context or used for assessing the skills of the readers. We identified four types of interactive/puzzle books, which are presented in Table 4.

Proposed Future Avenues for Research and Practice. Various educational kits feature learning goals focusing on self-directed learning using puzzles and quizzes. Such approaches could be aligned on skills development and knowledge acquirement in various topics from cybersecurity to other IT topics. The pedagogic benefit includes the possibility to use of books in its traditional form, jointly with the enrichment provided by other embedded physical or digital material.

Table 4. Different approaches of interactive books

Approach	Description	Examples
Quizzes	Quiz books focused on specific skills and problem-solving capabilities	GCHQ Puzzle Book; Bletchley Park Brainteasers
Interactive books	Integration of smartphone applications, puzzles along with challenges with topics of cryptography and steganography	Journal 29; Trip 1907; Codex Enigmatum; Miracle 47; Initiation
Escape rooms in a book	Escape rooms could be converted also into books	The Great Sherlock Holmes; The Escape Book
Journals that spark extreme creativity	Includes books that are missing specific information and it is up to the reader to fill it with personal information, comments, or conclusions. Self-discovery and self-improvement,	Put Your Worries Here: A Creative Journal for Teens with Anxiety; Wreck This Journal Everywhere

3.6 Escape Rooms

A promising type of game that has emerged in recent years is the escape room, where a small group tries to "escape" a predetermined time facing a variety of puzzles and challenges. A main reason for the game's popularity is its cooperative nature and its challenges, giving the chance to the players to communicate directly with each other in the real world. The room's theme creates a unique atmosphere that, combined with the time that counts, the kind of challenges, the decoration, and even the background music, emotionally engages the player and arouses his curiosity and excitement. [56]. Escape rooms are intended to support teambuilding, improve critical thinking and test problem solving skills for groups of all kinds, simulating real environments and could be either virtual (computer games, smartphone applications) or physical. Other approaches extend to puzzle and interactive books or integrating VR elements. We identified three materializations of escape rooms that differ significantly from one another, and they include physical, virtual or focused learning techniques (Table 5). The above approaches could also be combined to create a more engagement environment, providing rich media elements and interactivity. Some of the approaches are focused on learning and training such as CGI CyberCon[12] Escape Room.

Admittedly, there are not many examples of similar games or activities that involve so many human skills [59, 60]. Regarding the use of escape rooms in the field of information security, in the Autonomous University of Barcelona [61], activities based on a real-life escape room were designed to motivate students and improve their knowledge acquisition in the courses of computer networks and information security. It

---

[12] https://www.cgi.fi/fi/cybercon.

Table 5. Deployment approaches for escape rooms

Approach	Description	Examples
Physical	Maintain physical media, include riddles puzzles and combining technological elements to present the appropriate context	Spy Catcher; World of Escapes
Virtual	Virtual and digital media or online platforms that relate to hacking and cyberthreats	Livingsecurity Cyber Escape Room; Insecure Security Awareness; Thales Cyber Escape Room
Focused on learning and training	Totally focused in succeeding and define the learning outcomes	Escape Room; CGI CyberCon Escape Room; Cyber Escape Room

is claimed that results were *extremely positive* as students had increased motivation and willingness to learn [61].

Proposed Future Avenues for Research and Practice. Escape rooms could simulate a Cyber Range to enhance security and privacy awareness. The approach would be either virtual or physical. Furthermore, escape rooms could be considered as the infrastructure for deploying all the above approaches and challenges. Finally, tools for enabling extra customization capabilities could be embedded ensuring the integration with CtF challenges and for integrating the aforementioned approaches. Escape rooms are based in shared environments that set the bases for active learning and social constructivism, providing the learning context bypassing any complex technical terms to reach ordinary people and public interest.

4   Conclusions

In this paper we reviewed and investigated novel methods and tools to engage students, employees and trainees in security/privacy programs for education and awareness. After including a brief presentation of traditional and modern learning theories which can be used for creating educational games, we developed a classification of the most popular implementations of gamification and game-based learning tools and approaches that relate to information security and privacy. Some of these tools do not directly address the security and privacy topics; however, we highlight their potential for using them for such purpose. For each tool/approach, we present potential proposed future avenues for research and practice extracting important aspects to consider when designing a learning/awareness program. This results in a baseline framework for creating customized games, featuring pre-generated scenarios and to include realistic security scenarios.

We are aware that changing the subjects' actual behavior after the proposed challenges is difficult. Especially in the topics of privacy and considerable the increase of privacy awareness, security and privacy literacy could change the subjects' attitude, but this does not mean that their behavior will eventually change [62, 63]. For acquiring such outcomes real-time assessments are important to include in the participants' daily work and to monitor their daily operation periodically. Using the ZKP the gamification elements that are presented in this paper, we can design and implement such cases and expand beyond the existing gamified or game-based learning approaches. Future work includes the creation and mapping of case-based scenarios that relate to information security and privacy learning and awareness, as part of a framework that will combine the best elements of the state-of-the-art challenge-based and gamification-based approaches.

References

1. Beuran, R., Chinen, K., Tan, Y., Shinoda, Y.: Towards effective cybersecurity education and training. Research report (School of Information Science, Graduate School of Advanced Science and Technology, Japan Advanced Institute of Science and Technology). IS-RR-2016, pp. 1–16 (2016)
2. Caballero, A.: Security Education, Training, and Awareness. Elsevier, Amsterdam (2017)
3. Becker, K.: Choosing and Using Digital Games in the Classroom – A Practical Guide. Springer, Heidelberg (2016). https://doi.org/10.1007/978-3-319-12223-6
4. Berger, H., Jones, A.: Cyber security & ethical hacking for SMEs. In: ACM International Conference Proceeding Series. Part F1305 (2016)
5. Schiaffino, S., Amandi, A.: Intelligent user profiling. In: Bramer, M. (ed.) Artificial Intelligence An International Perspective. LNCS (LNAI), vol. 5640, pp. 193–216. Springer, Heidelberg (2009). https://doi.org/10.1007/978-3-642-03226-4_11
6. Liegle, J.O., Woo, H.-G.: Developing adaptive intelligent tutoring systems: a general framework and its implementations. In: Proceedings of 2001 Informing Science Conference, pp. 392–397 (2001)
7. Sottilare, R.A., Brawner, K.W., Sinatra, A.M., Johnston, J.H.: An updated concept for a generalized intelligent framework for tutoring (GIFT). GIFTtutoring.org. pp. 1–19 (2017)
8. Hendrix, M., Al-Sherbaz, A., Bloom, V.: Game based cyber security training: are serious games suitable for cyber security training? Int. J. Serious Games. 3, 53–61 (2016)
9. Mora, A., Riera, D., Gonzalez, C., Arnedo-Moreno, J.: A literature review of gamification design frameworks. In: VS-Games 2015 - 7th International Conference on Games and Virtual Worlds for Serious Applications (2015)
10. Gonzalez, H., Llamas, R., Ordaz, F.: Cybersecurity teaching through gamification: aligning training resources to our syllabus. Res. Comput. Sci. 146, 35–43 (2017)
11. Beltran, M., Calvo, M., Gonzalez, S.: Experiences using capture the flag competitions to introduce gamification in undergraduate computer security labs. In: Proceedings - 2018 International Conference on Computational Science and Computational Intelligence, CSCI 2018, pp. 574–579 (2018)
12. Bada, M., Creese, S., Goldsmith, M., Mitchell, C., Phillips, E.: Improving the effectiveness of CSIRTs, vol. 42 (2014)
13. Olusegun, S.: Constructivism learning theory: a paradigm for teaching and learning. IOSR J. Res. Method Educ. 5, 2320–7388 (2015). Ver. I
14. Bereiter, C.: Constructivism, socioculturalism, and Popper's world 3. Educ. Res. 23, 21–23 (2015)
15. von Glasersfeld, E.: Cognition, construction of knowledge, and teaching. Synthese 80, 121–140 (1989)

16. von Glasersfeld, E.: A Constructivist Approach to Teaching. In: Steffe, L.P., Gale, J. (eds.) Constructivism in Education, pp. 3–15. Lawrence Erlbaum Associates Publishers, NJ (1995). ISBN-13 978-0805810950
17. Chen, C.: A constructivist approach to teaching: implications in teaching computer networking. Inf. Technol. Learn. Perform. J. **21**, 17–27 (2003)
18. Steffe, L.P., Thompson, P.W.: Steffe, L.P., Thompson, P.W.: Teaching experiment methodology: underlying principles and essential elements. In: Lesh, R., Kelly, A.E. (eds.) Research Design in Mathematics and Science Education, pp. 267–307. Erlbaum, Hillsdale (2000)
19. Tam, M.: Constructivism, instructional design, and technology: implications for transforming distance learning. J. Educ. Technol. Soc. **3**(2), 50–60 (2000)
20. Vygotsky, L.S.: Interaction between learning and development. Read. Dev. Child. **23**, 34–41 (1978)
21. Crawford, K.: Vygotskian approaches to human development in the information era. Educ. Stud. Math. **31**, 43–62 (1978)
22. Leaning, M.: A study of the use of games and gamification to enhance student engagement, experience and achievement on a theory-based course of an undergraduate media degree. J. Media Pract. **16**, 155–170 (2015)
23. Zichermann, G., Cunningham, C.: Gamification by Design: Implementing Game Mechanics in Web and Mobile Apps. O'Reilly Media Inc., Newton (2011)
24. Deterding, S., O'Hara, K., Sicart, M., Dixon, D., Nacke, L.: Gamification: using game design elements in non-gaming contexts. In: Conference on Human Factors in Computing Systems – Proceedings, pp. 2425–2428 (2011)
25. Yang, Y.: Three questions to ask before you embark on gamification. eLearn **2014**, 4 (2014)
26. Laamarti, F., Eid, M., El Saddik, A.: An overview of serious games. Int. J. Comput. Games Technol. **2014**, 15 (2014). https://doi.org/10.1155/2014/358152. Article ID 358152
27. Chou, Y.: Actionable Gamification: Beyond Points, Badges, and Leaderboards. Packt Publishing Ltd., Birmingham (2015)
28. de Freitas, S., Oliver, M.: How can exploratory learning with games and simulations within the curriculum be most effectively evaluated? Comput. Educ. **46**, 249–264 (2006)
29. Dondi, C., Moretti, M.: Quality in eLearning and quality of learning games. In: Digital Game Based Learning: Proceedings of the 4th International Symposium for Information Design, June 2 2005. Stuttgart Media University (2006)
30. Kim, B., By, V., Jackson, R., Karp, J., Patrick, E., Thrower, A.: Social constructivism social constructivism emphasizes the importance of culture and context in understanding what occurs in. Emerging Perspectives on Learning, Teaching and Technology (2006)
31. Kalina, C., Powell, K.C.: Cognitive and social constructivism: developing tools for an effective classroom. Education **130**(2), 241–250 (2009)
32. Chaiklin, S.: The zone of proximal development in Vygotsky's analysis of learning and instruction. Vygotsky's Educ. Theory Cult. Context **1**(2), 39–64 (2003)
33. Chan, S.C.H., Wan, J.C.L., Ko, S.: Interactivity, active collaborative learning, and learning performance: the moderating role of perceived fun by using personal response systems. Int. J. Manag. Educ. **17**, 94–102 (2019)
34. de Freitas, S., Rebolledo-Mendez, G., Liarokapis, F., Magoulas, G., Poulovassilis, A.: Learning as immersive experiences: using the four-dimensional framework for designing and evaluating immersive learning experiences in a virtual world. Br. J. Educ. Technol. **41**, 69–85 (2010)
35. Facer, K., Joiner, R., Stanton, D., Reid, J., Hull, R., Kirk, D.: Savannah: mobile gaming and learning? J. Comput. Assist. Learn. **20**, 399–409 (2004)

36. Cone, B.D., Irvine, C.E., Thompson, M.F., Nguyen, T.D.: A video game for cyber security training and awareness. Comput. Secur. **26**, 63–72 (2007)
37. Zeissig, E.M., Lidynia, C., Vervier, L., Gadeib, A., Ziefle, M.: Online privacy perceptions of older adults. In: International Conference on Human Aspects of IT for the Aged Population (2017)
38. Trepte, S., et al.: Reforming european data protection law (2015)
39. Correia, J., Compeau, D.: Information privacy awareness (IPA): a review of the use, definition and measurement of IPA. In: Proceedings of the 50th Hawaii International Conference on System Sciences, pp. 4021–4030 (2017)
40. Schreuders, Z.C., Shaw, T., Shan-A-Khuda, M., Ravichandran, G., Keigh-ley, J., Ordean, M.: Security scenario generator (SecGen): a framework for generating randomly vulnerable rich-scenario VMs for learning computer security and hosting CTF events. In: ASE 2017 (2017)
41. Noor Azam, M.H., Beuran, R.B.: Usability evaluation of open source and online capture the flag platforms. Informe de investigación (Escuela de Ciencias de la Información, Escuela Superior de Ciencia y Tecnología, Instituto Avanzado de Ciencia y Tecnología de Japón). IS-RR-2018 (2018)
42. Ford, V., Siraj, A., Haynes, A., Brown, E.: Capture the flag unplugged: an offline cyber competition. In: Proceedings of the Conference on Integrating Technology into Computer Science Education, ITiCSE, pp. 225–230 (2017)
43. Pham, C., Tang, D., Chinen, K., Beuran, R.: CyRIS: a cyber range instantiation system for facilitating security training, pp. 251–258 (2016)
44. Beuran, R., Pham, C., Tang, D., Chinen, K.I, Tan, Y., Shinoda, Y.: Cytrone: an integrated cybersecurity training framework. In: ICISSP 2017 - Proceedings of the 3rd International Conference on Information Systems Security and Privacy, January 2017, pp. 157–166 (2017)
45. Thomps, M., Irvine, C.: Active learning with the CyberCIEGE video game. In: 4th Workshop on Cyber Security Experimentation and Test, CSET 2011, pp. 1–8 (2011)
46. Denning, T., Lerner, A., Shostack, A., Kohno, T.: Control-Alt-Hack: the design and evaluation of a card game for computer security awareness and education. In: Proceedings of the ACM Conference on Computer and Communications Security, pp. 915–928 (2013)
47. Denning, T., Shostack, A., Kohno, T.: Practical lessons from creating the Control-Alt-Hack Card game and research challenges for games in education and research. In: Usenix (2014)
48. Mirkovic, J., Dark, M., Du, W., Vigna, G., Denning, T.: Evaluating cybersecurity education interventions: three case studies. IEEE Secur. Priv. **13**, 63–69 (2015)
49. Gondree, M., Peterson, Z.N.J.: Valuing security by getting [d0x3d!] experiences with a network security board game. In: 6th Workshop on Cyber Security Experimentation and Test, CSET 2013 (2013)
50. Flushman, T.R., Gondree, M., Peterson, Z.N.J.: This is not a game: early observations on using alternate reality games for teaching security concepts to first-year undergraduates. In: 8th Workshop on Cyber Security Experimentation and Test, CSET 2015 (2015)
51. Gondree, M., Peterson, Z.N.J., Denning, T.: Security through play. IEEE Secur. Priv. **11**, 64–67 (2013)
52. Shostack, A.: Elevation of privilege: drawing developers into threat modeling. In: USENIX Summit on Gaming, Games, and Gamification in Security Education, pp. 1–15 (2014)
53. Thompson, M., Takabi, H.: Effectiveness of using card games to teach threat modeling for secure web application developments. Issues Inf. Syst. **17**, 244–253 (2016)
54. Hart, S., Margheri, A., Paci, F., Sassone, V.: Riskio: a serious game for cyber security awareness and education. Comput. Secur. **95**, 101827 (2020)

55. Mcdonald, J., et al.: Designing authentic cybersecurity learning experiences: lessons from the cybermatics playable case study. In: Proceedings of the 52nd Hawaii International Conference on System Sciences, vol. 6, pp. 2507–2516 (2019)
56. Wiemker, M., Elumir, E., Clare, A.: Escape room games: can you transform an unpleasant situation into a pleasant one? Game Learn. **55**, 55–68 (2015)
57. Clarke, S.J., Peel, D.J., Arnab, S., Morini, L., Keegan, H., Wood, O.: EscapED: a framework for creating educational escape rooms and interactive games to for higher/further education. Int. J. Serious Games **4**, 73–86 (2017)
58. Nicholson, S.: Creating engaging escape rooms for the classroom. Child. Educ. **94**, 44–49 (2018)
59. Mcgonigal, J.: Reality is broken: why games make us better and how they can change the world. Penguin **10**, 51–73 (2011)
60. Blohm, I., Leimeister, J.M.: Gamification: design of IT-based enhancing services for motivational support and behavioral change. Bus. Inf. Syst. Eng. **5**, 275–278 (2013)
61. Borrego, C., Fernández, C., Blanes, I., Robles, S.: Room escape at class: escape games activities to facilitate the motivation and learning in computer science. J. Technol. Sci. Educ. **7**, 162–171 (2017)
62. Kokolakis, S.: Privacy attitudes and privacy behaviour: a review of current research on the privacy paradox phenomenon. Comput. Secur. **64**, 122–134 (2017)
63. Pötzsch, S.: Privacy awareness: a means to solve the privacy paradox? In: Matyáš, V., Fischer-Hübner, S., Cvrček, D., Švenda, P. (eds.) Privacy and Identity 2008. IAICT, vol. 298, pp. 226–236. Springer, Heidelberg (2009). https://doi.org/10.1007/978-3-642-03315-5_17

Big Data Analytics in Healthcare Applications: Privacy Implications for Individuals and Groups and Mitigation Strategies

Paola Mavriki[✉] and Maria Karyda[✉]

Department of Information and Communication Systems Engineering, University of the Aegean, 83200 Karlovassi, Samos, Greece
{pmavriki,mka}@aegean.gr

Abstract. Big data analytics in healthcare present a potentially powerful means for addressing public health emergencies such as the COVID-19 pandemic. A challenging issue for health data to be used, however, is the protection of privacy. Research on big data privacy, especially in relation to healthcare, is still at an early stage and there is a lack of guidelines or best practice strategies for big data privacy protection. Moreover, while academic discourse focuses on individual privacy, research evidence shows that there are cases such as mass surveillance through sensing and other IoT technologies where the privacy of groups needs also to be considered. This paper explores these challenges, focusing on health data analytics; we identify and analyse privacy threats and implications for individuals and groups and we evaluate recent privacy preserving techniques for contact tracing.

Keywords: Big health data analytics · Privacy · Group privacy

1 Introduction

The widespread availability of Internet access, the explosive growth in mobile devices, sensor networks, healthcare applications, social media networks etc. constantly generate vast amounts of structured, unstructured and semistructured data [1]. Big data related to public health include biological, geospatial, electronic health records, personal monitoring, effluent data, social media posts, blogs in health subjects, etc. [2, 3].

Analytics refers to techniques used to analyse and acquire intelligence from big data, the process of researching massive amounts of complex data in order to reveal hidden patterns or identify secret correlations [4, 5].

The use of big data in healthcare appears attractive [6] as big data is unlocking novel opportunities to understand public health [2]. Big data analytics may be used for a wide range of purposes (e.g. clinical decision support, health insurance, disease surveillance, population health management etc.) [7]. For example, contact tracing is an established part of the response to any contagious disease outbreak [8]. According to Nanni et al. [9], personal big data able to describe the movement of people in great

© Springer Nature Switzerland AG 2020
M. Themistocleous et al. (Eds.): EMCIS 2020, LNBIP 402, pp. 526–540, 2020.
https://doi.org/10.1007/978-3-030-63396-7_35

detail, could provide a potentially powerful means for addressing public health emergencies such as the COVID-19 pandemic. However, one of the most challenging issue related to big health data is privacy [5, 7, 10].

Health information is considered as one of the types of personal information the public consider most sensitive [11]. Furthermore, the biomedical applications of big data, are considered as particularly ethically challenging due to the sensitivity of health data and fiduciary nature of healthcare [12]. Even more, it seems that privacy concerns potentially may be a significant impediment in using big health data for the benefit of the public health. For instance, in the case of the COVID-19 pandemic, one of the most ambitious uses of massive-scale citizen data ever attempted [13] health research combined with various tracing measures potentially may result in saving many lives. Research evidence indicates that big data analytics may be used with success for limiting the risk of spreading the new Corona virus [14]. But a recent survey [8] shows that privacy concerns are limiting the efficacy of the various tracing measures taken by governments. People hesitate to participate in these procedures expressing the need to be assured that their personal information is protected. As Nanni et al. [9] state, 'give more data, awareness and control to individual citizens, and they will help COVID-19 containment'. Particularly in the case of public health emergencies, there is a need for enhancing privacy of individuals and groups while reassuring them that their data is protected when used for big data analytics.

The study on big data privacy is still at a very early stage and at the moment there is not a clear view of the best strategies to protect privacy in big data [15, 16]. Furthermore, while, academic and public discourse on privacy focuses on the individual level, several authors [17–19] argue that, since most people are not targeted by profiling as individuals, but as members of specific groups, the privacy of these groups needs also to be further examined. According to Taylor et al., [19] genetic profiling, policy intervention for behavior change or security or mass surveillance through sensing technologies are only some example where it is clear that individual privacy is not enough. Also, as mentioned in [20], to ensure the right to privacy and of informational self-determination as democratic values, we need new legal and data management frameworks that empower users beyond their individual agency, taking into account the evidence of collective aspect of privacy.

Exploring these issues, we conducted an extensive literature review related to applications of big data analytics in healthcare and associated privacy issues. We examined several relevant big data techniques (e.g. mobile tracking technologies for monitoring, predictive algorithms, automated profiling, aggregation techniques) analysing simultaneously the involved privacy issues for individuals and groups. Furthermore, for a deeper understanding of the impact of tracking technologies on privacy, we investigated recent research related to the use of big data analytics for limiting the spread of the new virus Corona. We identified and analysed several privacy threats and implications for individuals and groups. Moreover, we examined and evaluated several related privacy-preserving methods proposed in the literature.

The remaining paper is structured as follows: the next Section investigates the background in regard to applications of big data in healthcare and related privacy issues while Sect. 3 examines privacy challenges in the healthcare context and explores the case of combating COVID-19 with big data analytics. Section 4 identifies and examines privacy threats for individuals and groups while Sect. 5 evaluates privacy preserving techniques for contact tracing. We conclude in Sect. 6 with a discussion and conclusions.

2 Background: Applications of Big Data in Healthcare and Privacy Issues

Several studies are focusing on privacy and security issues related to electronic health records (EHR). In [21] the authors consider that the protection of patients' privacy can be achieved with anonymisation and encryption while with regard to the key security goals, access control policy, user access management and monitoring can significantly help to ensure the confidentiality and integrity of personal health information. Similarly in regard to EHR systems, in [22] the authors point on ensuring privacy and security through enhancing administrative control and monitor physical and system access. Furthermore, Malay [23] expresses concerns with regard to surveillance and EHRs. The author mentions that although the Health Insurance Portability and Accountability Act (HIPPA) affords notable protections for most private information, accidental breaches of patient privacy have occurred while he believes that improved security measures, won't stop the dissemination of misinformation that stems from overdiagnosis, miscoding, and surveillance bias.

One of the most comprehensive studies in regard to privacy issues related to medical data analytics is by Price and Cohen [24]. The authors examine among others the role of the patient in the data collection and access and the extent of an individual's data which should be available for use in predictive analytics without her consent. They also illustrate possible uses of big data which raise ethical and legal questions; and argue that 'the ethical analysis will depend heavily on the type of data, including its identifiability; who will be accessing it; and for what purpose'.

Related to ethics and practices of consent and privacy for clinical genomics and personalised medicine in [25], the authors consider that the risks of re-identification, informational harms, and data security vulnerabilities are issues that need to be better addressed in the clinical setting to reconcile the unpredictable pathway of research and practice in the networked information society. Privacy issues related to genomic information are also discussed in [24]. The authors express concerns in regard to discrimination based on health data while they consider that the laws (e.g. GINA, ADA PPACA) have important limits. They conclude that 'striking the right balance—protecting privacy so that patients are comfortable providing their data, but not allowing privacy to drive secrecy that reduces validation and trust in the potential benefits arising from those data—will be a tricky challenge for proponents of big data, machine learning, and learning health systems'.

Another stream of research focuses on healthcare sensor data generated through quantified self-tracking devices, biosensors, wireless Internet-of-things devices. In [26] the authors claim that is important that the privacy concerns regarding wearable technologies relate to both the users of those technologies and others in surrounding environments.

Medical IoT devices produce an increasingly large volume of increasingly diverse real-time data, which is highly sensitive with severe consequences in the case of privacy violations. According to Sun et al. [27], security and privacy of data collected from medical IoT devices, either during their transmission to a cloud or while stored in a cloud, are major unsolved yet concerns. The authors also investigate existing solutions to security and privacy issues and argue that research related to the effective protection of data security and privacy at all stages of data flow is needed. Furthermore [28] examines telemonitoring which is an emerging area with growing interest to collect sensitive personal and private data. In the authors' opinion, since the data involved in the telemonitoring setting are sensitive from a privacy point of view, privacy preserving technologies are needed in order to protect patients' privacy and increase compliance and adoption.

Furthermore, over the past two decades, there is a massive growth in online social support group/community for people facing health concerns, activity [29] and a stream of research is related to information disclosure in online health communities. The health online communities are also rich sources of qualitative data for health researchers raising several ethical questions, especially pertaining to privacy and informed consent [30–33].

Concluding, most of the research in privacy from the health community focuses on medical data publishing and is, therefore, database-centric [28] while studies focusing on big data applications in the health area and associated privacy issues are still scarce. In addition, related to privacy protection, the vast majority of the authors' arguments are based on the informational self-determination principle. However, as specified by [34], these principles have proved less useful with the rise of data analytics and machine learning. There are privacy harms for which individual control offers no protection such as in the case of decision-making based on group classifications, or in the case of new and unexpected inferred insights from data that individuals have intentionally disclosed, or when an individual's sensitive personal information is derived through analysing data revealed by others in their social network etc.

3 Privacy Challenges in the Healthcare Context

Privacy is a complex issue, difficult to define and restrict within limits due to multiple interests at stake and many actors involved [18, 35, 36].

Several authors argue that privacy has to be conceptualized according to context and environment. In Nissenbaum's opinion [37], physicians, patients, tests and treatment, symptoms, insurance forms, illnesses, diagnoses, and medications are some of the constitutive elements of the healthcare context which have a particular structural arrangement including also roles or capacities in which people act.

Medical privacy refers to having personal information about one's health status unaccessed and having one's personal sensorial space (autotopos) unaccessed in the context of medical settings [38, 39]. As Phillips et al. [38] specify 'medical context is an important home for privacy' as people typically do not like anyone knowing about their disease, particularly when it comes to certain disease that carry more stigma with them. Medical relationships are of particular concern due to the patient being in a vulnerable (and trusting) state [12]. Policymakers, patients, and physicians seem to accept the principle of health privacy exceptionalism according to which health information deserves a higher level of privacy protection than most other types of data.

Analysing data for decision-making or for discovering trends in various areas is not new. The scale of data in combination with advanced analytics technologies however, brings privacy risks into a whole new level. The privacy challenges become more complex 'growing together with the technological capabilities of the analytics' and letting behind the data protection principles which remain the same [40]. Through quantification the vast and amount of any kind of data (numbers, texts, pictures etc.) uploaded by every user in any area is transformed in elements that can be analysed [41] blurring the boundaries between private and public.

In addition, privacy scholars are beginning to recognize that privacy problems raised by group level inferences produced from algorithmic aggregation of individuals are different from those related to individuals identifying [19, 42, 43]. In previous work [44, 45] in a different context, we also elaborate on the importance and the role of group privacy. The members of a social group have the same social identity. They identify themselves in the same way and have the same definition of who they are, what attributes they have, and how they relate to and differ from specific outgroups [46]. Salience is typically defined as a combination of the readiness to adopt an identity and the relevance of an identity to a given situation [47]. Grouping algorithms "are designing" automatically group identities according the goals and the contexts of processing personal or open data. Thus, the salient characteristics which create the group in this case is not a result of social processes but an automatic procedure. Extending Floridi's interpretation of information privacy [12], in the big era data, in some cases, there is no difference between a group's information sphere and the group's identity. Thus, group privacy violations may be described as a form of aggression toward the group's identity.

3.1   Case Study: Fighting Against COVID-19 Pandemic with Big Data

The COVID-19 pandemic broke out in December 2019 Wuhan, and rapidly has spread across the rest of the world posing unprecedented challenges for every country's healthcare system [48, 49]. COVID-19 has already caused at the time of writing this paper many times more cases than the previous coronavirus-induced public health emergencies of international concern, the 2002–2003 severe acute respiratory syndrome (SARS) outbreak, and the COVID-19 numbers are expected to grow.

In addition to medical measures, non-pharmaceutical measures have proven to be critical for delaying and containing the spread of the virus [50]. Contact tracing is a well-established part of the response to any contagious disease outbreak. In the traditional way it requires a large number of public health fieldworkers to contact family, friends, coworkers and other contacts of infected individuals, to interview them to find out about their potential contacts in turn. Therefore, the attention and resources have been focused on finding ways to automate parts of this process by taking advantage of the fact that a majority of citizens carry smartphones, IoT devices, and wearable technology which integrate GPS chips capable of precise location tracking and Bluetooth radios which can sense the proximity between devices, [8, 13].

Countries have been using various ways to enable contact tracing. In Israel, legislation was passed to allow the government to track the mobile-phone data of people with suspected infection. South Korea's Centers for Disease Control and Prevention deployed the contact tracing system, known as the COVID-19 Smart Management System, that uses data from security camera footage, credit card records, even GPS data from cars and cellphones to trace the movement of individuals with COVID-19 [48]. In Taiwan, within a 72-h period was built a system whereby a mobile health declaration pass was then sent via SMS to phones using a local telecom operator, which allowed for faster immigration clearance for those with minimal risk. Also, on February 18, the government announced that all hospitals, clinics, and pharmacies in Taiwan would have access to patients' travel histories [14].

Researchers and governments have started to collaborate with mobile network operators, to estimate and visualize the effectiveness of control measures. The Yuhang District in Hangzhou City first developed and launched a smartphone mini-program, known as "Health Barcode", to replace traditional, paper-based access permits; the program was implemented within two weeks of the nation-wide lockdown, on 7 February 2020. Health Barcode enables a dynamic epidemic risk management of the new Corona disease using individual self-report health status and travel history in combination with big data from aviation, railway and ground transportation systems, social media, COVID-19 database, and mobile GPS and payment records to retrace individuals' movement. Complex and sophisticated artificial intelligence (AI) and machine learning algorithms are then employed to retrace the movement of the infected person and all persons in close contact, feeding into individual risk assessment of three levels - low, medium, and high [49, 51]. Singapore, was one of the first countries to be affected by the new Coronavirus, and for a while was the country with the highest COVID-19 numbers outside of China from 5 February 2020 to 18 February 2020. Early detection of cases through surveillance and aggressive contact tracing around known cases has helped to contain spread of the outbreak in Singapore. Together with other measures, they allow the COVID-19 outbreak to be managed without major disruption to daily living [52, 53].

Also, many EU countries are currently working on applications aimed at facilitating the fight against the COVID-19 crisis. Some of them are based on geolocation, such as Coronamadrid and StopCovid19 in Spain, whereas others are based on the Bluetooth technology known as a "digital handshake", such as Stopp-CoronaApp in Austria, StopCovid in France, ProteGo in Poland or an app being developed by the NHS in the United Kingdom [54].

Undoubtedly tracking and controlling the spread of the new Coronavirus may save many lives. However, to achieve this with the help of advanced technologies, a centralized (health) authority needs detailed information from both healthy individuals and diagnosed patients. Consequently, these approaches result in privacy concerns [55]. Concluding, research shows that sensitive big health data is increasingly used and processed through tracking, monitoring, surveillance, personalisation technologies for new knowledge generation, profiling and predictions raising new privacy concerns. On one hand, these processes undoubtedly bring crucial benefits to the public health [56] but on the other hand, they may lead to new complex privacy problems with significant consequences which we investigate next.

4 Privacy Threats for Individuals and Groups

Privacy Threats Associated to Surveillance
One of the most debated category of privacy threats stemming from big data analysis is related to surveillance. Privacy harm can also occur in the absence of a human agent. For example, in the case of monitoring with mobile tracking techniques which governments deploy for combating epidemics, the perception of observation that people experience is permanent while people need solitude, among others, for their mental health. This category of harms relates to the consequences of the loss of control over personal information and it also conveys anxiety, embarrassment, fear, etc. [57, 58].

In the case of the current at the time of writing COVID-19 emergency, all limitation strategies require analysis of diagnosed carriers of the virus location trails in order to identify other individuals at risk for infection [55, 59]. When tracking through mobile technologies are combined with facial recognition technology and big data, sophisticated artificial intelligence can theoretically pinpoint anyone, anytime, anywhere, and what they have done [60]. When identified, diagnosed individuals often face harsh social stigma and persecution [59], often considered worse than the disease. Privacy threats can stem from hackers or governments violating individual privacy for unrightful use, criminal activities, or political surveillance [60].

Privacy Threats Associated to Predictions
Another category of privacy threats stems from the use of big data to make predictions. For example, mobile apps providers collect personal data in order to provide users with information about their fitness or health status (e.g. heart condition, dietary habits, etc.) that help to identify or predict health attributes. These data can be valuable to insurance companies and/or other providers (e.g. sports centers, dietary consultants, etc.) who may target specific users [40]. Also, tendencies to depression can be inferred through Facebook and Twitter usage, moreover, Google has attempted to predict flu outbreaks as well as other diseases and their outcomes while Microsoft can likewise predict Parkinson's disease and Alzheimer's disease from search engine interactions. Furthermore, Amazon's Alexa might be able to infer health status based on speech patterns [61]. When these data sets are cross-referenced with traditional health information, as big data is designed to do, it is possible to generate a detailed picture about a person's health, including information the person may never have disclosed to a healthcare provider.

Moreover, the nature of big data's dynamic analytical tools is such that the privacy problems of predictive algorithms are often themselves unpredictable, and their effects may not even be fully understood by their programmers [6]. In addition privacy violations related to wireless body sensors may cause the humiliation and the embarrassment of the patient if a miscommunication occurs [60].

Privacy Threats Associated to Automated Profiling
Profiling with big data analytics may raise problems that are different from the problems that may be raised by forms of statistical profiling. The relations found using data mining are not necessarily causal or they may be causal without being understood. In this way, the scope of profiles that are discovered may be much broader (only a small

minority of all statistical relations is directly causal) with unexpected profiles in unexpected areas [62].

Identifying individuals is not necessary for group profiling to occur and peoples' privacy may be violated without their identity being disclosed. Groups might be targeted in epidemiological searches [63]. In [43] there are examples of specific group inference technologies that may threat individual and group privacy such as the case of Strava fitness application and the case of 'Community - Aware Trending Topics Analysis'.

Moreover, in the case of COVID-19 identities of local businesses such as cafes, shops etc. may be divulged when a virus carrier's location trail is released in public. Public association with the path of a diagnosed carrier, as examples from China and South Korea show, damages local businesses. At a time of heightened vulnerability due to the economic stress which often coincides with an epidemic, these businesses may suffer significant financial hardship and possibly collapse [59]. In this case the whole group of people with roles in the business experience (among others) the same kind of harm (financial) which stems from disclosing the identity of a collective entity: the business. In addition, one of the major developments in technology from 1990 to 2002 which framed the privacy debates was the Human Genome Project's unlocking of the genetic code, with enormous promise for use in developing new pharmaceutical medications, family planning, and health care [11]. Beside the fact that a genome sequence may lead to revealing the identity of a person, one individual's genome can reveal information about other individuals. When multiple individuals share aspects of genetic architecture, they form a 'genetic group' [19, 64].

Group specificity distinguishes group members from other random members, implying the existing of a special group and the common privacy. Even if the individual is protected, message from group members still carries the group specificity. 'Once the mass fragments are excavated and pieced together as integrated information, the group privacy will be exposed in the end'. Consequently, protecting the individual privacy of group is far from enough [19, 65].

Privacy Threats Associated to Aggregation
The last category of threats examined here is related to the aggregation of data. Medical data is coming from traditional sources but also from smartphone applications, data brokers, social networks, Internet searches, environmental data, ambient sensors, wearables, consequently health data reaches beyond the doctor's office and the hospital into everyday life. Big data analytics is able to correlate relationships between health and buying habits, movement tracking, sleeping habits, social relations, and more. People's medical data may be sold to third parties, for targeted marketing, for personalised pricing or for developing artificial intelligence tools that can be applied in unknown ways in the future [39]. In addition, privacy standards for electronic health records apply to entities of health plans, healthcare clearinghouses, and health care providers; in contrast, it is unclear whether these regulations will apply to organizations that are not so characterized, but who still receive personal health information from individuals or by generating it through big data [6].

In addition, individuals freely disclose medical and other sensitive information about themselves in published memoirs, in social media postings, and in forums devoted to illnesses, medical procedures, prescription medications, and alternative medicine. [66]. Researchers have found that people with stigmatized health problems are drawn to online support groups/communities because these groups and communities help them to manage stigma [29]. However, privacy concerns can hamper user participation and knowledge/information sharing [30]. These concerns are justified by the introduction of sophisticated prediction algorithms that not only analyse individual behaviours but make inferences about consumers' intimate psychological traits and states [67]. For example, Facebook was recently criticized for analysing teenagers' emotional or mental state using their Facebook profiles. While Facebook said it does not currently use such inferences for targeting, even the collection of such data raised consumers' ethical concerns [68].

Concluding, research evidence suggests that health information which is one of the most highly protected types of personal information will be increasingly vulnerable in the context of big data and predictive analytics [69]. The violation of health privacy may have severe implications as there are related to the life itself. New technologies such as personalisation, tracking, monitoring, surveillance technologies for new knowledge generation, profiling, predictions etc. magnify the consequences of known privacy threats while their pose new problems rising legal and ethical concerns as well. Finally, research evidence indicates that in some cases (such as genomics, monitoring through mobile tracking technologies, profiling etc.) protecting individual privacy is not enough hence there is a need to consider the privacy protection on group level as well. In the next Section we evaluate privacy-preserving methods for contact tracing.

5   Privacy-Preserving Techniques

Information privacy challenges may have a technical nature and also depend on political and judicial decisions [70]. In addition, the gathering of medical data raise ethical privacy questions [24] which are not discussed here due space limitation.

As specified in [48], in the case of a health emergency such as the COVID-19 crisis, the goal is to reduce the information which may be inferred by each of the above parties while still achieving the public health goal of informing people of potential exposures to help slow the spread of the disease. The authors examine the Singaporean app Trace-Together and found that it works well in the case of snoopers in public places and the users' privacy from each other but it does not in the case of the authorities. In the absence of a fully decentralised peer-to-peer system, any information sharing among phones with the app installed will have to be mediated by some coordinating servers. Without any protective measures (e.g. based on cryptography), the coordinating servers are given an inordinate amount of knowledge hence with the use of cryptography protocols app-based contact tracing can be accomplished without completely sacrificing privacy. The authors also show that with just minor modifications to the Singaporean app, a polling-based direct contact tracing solution allows for some anonymity from authorities.

The privacy-preserving technique proposed in [55] to control the spread of a virus in a population is based on private set of intersection between physical contact histories of individuals (that are recorded using smart phones) and a centralized database (run by a health authority) that keeps the identities of the positive diagnosed patients for the disease. The individuals may receive warning messages indicating their previous contacts with a positive diagnosed patient while neither of the parties that involve in the protocol obtain any sensitive information about each other. Furthermore, in [71] the authors present a modular approach with several alternatives and trade-offs to achieve contact tracing in a privacy preserving manner. They also indicate that the leakage of private information thought previously as inevitable is purposeless because the identities used for warning at-risk users from the information that is broadcast locally and can be observed by other users are dissociated. The authors also show some additional protective measures which may be implemented by using existing techniques.

Also, Yasaka et al. [72] propose a peer-to-peer smartphone app for contact tracing that does not use personal data, such as location. Their also developed a prototype of this app, which is open source and publicly available as well as a computer simulation model that demonstrates the potential of the app to impact the course of a pandemic. In the authors' opinion this app could potentially be applied to the COVID-19 pandemic as well as others in the future to achieve a middle ground between drastic isolation measures and unmitigated disease spread.

Furthermore, the frameworks developed by Google and Apple, which used the idea conceived by the Decentralized Privacy-Preserving Proximity Tracing (DP-3 T) protocol and are being implemented in countries including Germany, Italy, Japan and many U.S. states, meanwhile, create no accessible archive of contact or location data and also hide completely the users' identities [13]. Bradford et al. [54] examined the compatibility of the proposed Apple/Google Bluetooth Exposure Notification System and associated applications with Western privacy and data protection principles, including the EU General Data Protection Regulation (GDPR). In their opinion the Apple/Google ENS will fall within the governance system of the GDPR and can be operated in a way that is compatible with the GDPR rules.

Moreover, related to group privacy, in [43], the authors indicate that the means to protect privacy are so focused on personal privacy that they ignore or even may unintentionally reveal group privacy. K-anonymity, for example almost by design, reveals group characteristics, and thus may compromise group privacy. Yang et al. [65] propose a method of 'anti-data mining on group privacy information'. Transforming the clustering process by adding and swapping, the group specificity is altered and the data mining becomes ineffective.

In generally, technological mechanisms to protect privacy are focused on individual level. Traditional approaches are based on the idea of hiding the individual in the crowd an aggregating data to protect information about an individual [43].

Finally, anonymisation is frequently seen as the minimum requirement necessary to protect data subjects' privacy in aggregating data [12], but one of the increased privacy risks introduced by big data is that it can be used to re-identify apparently de-identified data [63].

6 Discussions and Conclusions

When it comes to health privacy, the literature reveals two main categories of contradictory opinions. On one hand, health privacy is seen in literature as a special type of privacy which deserves a special attention and a higher level of protection than other types of data [39] while on the other hand, authors [73] consider that restrictive policies on data are in some cases barriers for innovative and valid epidemiological research.

Yet, there is a third category of opinions which "stays in the middle" of the two "extremes" and accept that privacy cases are resolved by balancing the private interest (e.g. personal autonomy) and the common interest (e.g. public health) related to a particular privacy violation. However, confirming Sloot's [74] opinion, we suggest that this kind of rationale is not applicable in the age of big data, as in many cases massive amounts of personal data are gathered without a pre-established goal. Furthermore, it is often unclear how certain data gathering and processing initiatives improve societal interest.

We identify in this work several privacy threats stemming from the use of advanced technologies for surveillance, new knowledge generation, profiling and predictions in the health area. Moreover, we show in this paper a new aspect of privacy on a collective level which according to several authors [18, 19, 43] it justifies at least ethical considerations. We examine group privacy underlining the importance of the identity of the groups and we indicate that even if the individual privacy of a group member is preserved, he/she may experience harms stemming from privacy violations related to the group he/she belongs to. We suggest that there are privacy violations which involve in the same way all the members of the group with the same kind of harms for all the members of the group. For example, the disclosure of the identity of a business that is related to a positive case of Corona disease provokes among others financial loss for everyone involved. Further research related to group privacy may follow a "back forth" approach through examining first in detail the implications of a privacy violation related to more than one individual. If the consequences are the same kind for all the members of the group while their personal privacy is protected, it may be assumed that is probably a case of group privacy violation. Furthermore, as Taylor [75] claims these problems underline the need for a new ethical approach to research with regard to group-level information. Demographic-level research is fundamentally changing and evolving to offer ever more possibilities for categorisation, by a wider group of potential analysts.

Summarising, research evidence indicates that in the case of big data analytics in health context, in particular in the case of health emergencies such as the COVID - 19 crisis, there is a need among others to find solutions to protect privacy while using big data analytics for combating the disease which is also an urgent necessity. We indicate in this paper several relevant privacy preserving methods proposed in literature. Also, as specified in [76], large-scale collection of data could help curb the COVID-19 pandemic, but it should not neglect privacy and public trust. Best practices should be identified to maintain responsible data-collection and data-processing standards at a global scale.

References

1. Russom, P.: Big data analytics. TDWI best practices report, fourth quarter. vol. 19, p. 40 (2011)
2. Mooney, S.J., Pejaver, V.: Big data in public health: terminology, machine learning, and privacy. Annu. Rev. Publ. Health **39**, 95–112 (2018)
3. Raghupathi, W., Raghupathi, V.: An overview of health analytics. J. Health Med. Informat. **4**, 2 (2013)
4. Gandomi, A., Haider, M.: Beyond the hype: Big data concepts, methods, and analytics. Int. J. Inf. Manag. **35**, 137–144 (2015). https://doi.org/10.1016/j.ijinfomgt.2014.10.007
5. Jain, P., Gyanchandani, M., Khare, N.: Big data privacy: a technological perspective and review. J. Big Data **3**(1), 1–25 (2016). https://doi.org/10.1186/s40537-016-0059-y
6. Crawford, K., Schultz, J.: Big data and due process: toward a framework to redress predictive privacy harms. BCL Rev. **55**, 93 (2014)
7. Abouelmehdi, K., Beni-Hssane, A., Khaloufi, H., Saadi, M.: Big data security and privacy in healthcare: a Review. Procedia Comput. Sci. **113**, 73–80 (2017). https://doi.org/10.1016/j.procs.2017.08.292
8. Simko, L., Calo, R., Roesner, F., Kohno, T.: COVID-19 contact tracing and privacy: studying opinion and preferences. arXiv:2005.06056 [cs] (2020)
9. Nanni, M., et al.: Give more data, awareness and control to individual citizens, and they will help COVID-19 containment. arXiv preprint arXiv:2004.05222 (2020)
10. Chirita, A.D.: The Rise of Big Data and the Loss of Privacy. Social Science Research Network, Rochester (2016)
11. Westin, A.F.: Social and political dimensions of privacy. J. Soc. Issues **59**, 431–453 (2003). https://doi.org/10.1111/1540-4560.00072
12. Mittelstadt, B.D., Floridi, L.: The ethics of big data: current and foreseeable issues in biomedical contexts. Sci. Eng. Ethics **22**(2), 303–341 (2015). https://doi.org/10.1007/s11948-015-9652-2
13. Fahey, R.A., Hino, A.: COVID-19, digital privacy, and the social limits on data-focused public health responses. Int. J. Inf. Manag. 102181 (2020)
14. Wang, C.J., Ng, C.Y., Brook, R.H.: response to covid-19 in taiwan: big data analytics, new technology, and proactive testing. JAMA **323**, 1341–1342 (2020). https://doi.org/10.1001/jama.2020.3151
15. Soria-Comas, J., Domingo-Ferrer, J.: Big data privacy: challenges to privacy principles and models. Data Sci. Eng. **1**(1), 21–28 (2015). https://doi.org/10.1007/s41019-015-0001-x
16. Yu, S.: Big privacy: challenges and opportunities of privacy study in the age of big data. IEEE Access **4**, 2751–2763 (2016). https://doi.org/10.1109/ACCESS.2016.2577036
17. Floridi, L.: Group privacy: a defence and an interpretation. In: Taylor, L., Floridi, L., van der Sloot, B. (eds.) Group Privacy. PSS, vol. 126, pp. 83–100. Springer, Cham (2017). https://doi.org/10.1007/978-3-319-46608-8_5
18. Mittelstadt, B.: From individual to group privacy in big data analytics. Philos. Technol. **30**, 1–20 (2017). https://doi.org/10.1007/s13347-017-0253-7
19. Taylor, L., Floridi, L., van der Sloot, B.: Group Privacy: New Challenges of Data Technologies. Springer, Cham (2016). https://doi.org/10.1007/978-3-319-46608-8
20. Garcia, D., Goel, M., Agrawal, A.K., Kumaraguru, P.: Collective aspects of privacy in the Twitter social network. EPJ Data Sci. **7**(1), 1–13 (2018). https://doi.org/10.1140/epjds/s13688-018-0130-3

21. Fernández-Alemán, J.L., Señor, I.C., Lozoya, P.Á.O., Toval, A.: Security and privacy in electronic health records: a systematic literature review. J. Biomed. Inform. **46**, 541–562 (2013)

22. Sahney, R., Sharma, M.: Electronic health records: a general overview. Curr. Med. Res. Pract. **8**, 67–70 (2018)

23. Malay, D.S.: Electronic health records, privacy, and surveillance. J. Foot Ankle Surg. **52**, 561–562 (2013)

24. Price, W.N., Cohen, I.G.: Privacy in the age of medical big data. Nat. Med. **25**, 37–43 (2019)

25. Chow-White, P.A., MacAulay, M., Charters, A., Chow, P.: From the bench to the bedside in the big data age: ethics and practices of consent and privacy for clinical genomics and personalized medicine. Ethics Inf. Technol. **17**(3), 189–200 (2015). https://doi.org/10.1007/s10676-015-9373-x

26. Thierer, A.D.: The internet of things and wearable technology: addressing privacy and security concerns without derailing innovation. Adam Thierer, The Internet of Things and Wearable Technology: Addressing Privacy and Security Concerns without Derailing Innovation. 21 (2015)

27. Sun, W., Cai, Z., Li, Y., Liu, F., Fang, S., Wang, G.: Security and privacy in the medical internet of things: a review. Secur. Commun. Netw. **2018** (2018)

28. Abbas, A., Khan, S.U., Zomaya, A.Y.: Introduction to large-scale distributed computing in smart healthcare. In: Khan, S.U., Zomaya, A.Y., Abbas, A. (eds.) Handbook of Large-Scale Distributed Computing in Smart Healthcare. SCC, pp. 1–7. Springer, Cham (2017). https://doi.org/10.1007/978-3-319-58280-1_1

29. Wright, K.B.: Communication in health-related online social support groups/communities: a review of research on predictors of participation, applications of social support theory, and health outcomes. Rev. Commun. Res. **4**, 65–87 (2016). https://doi.org/10.12840/issn.2255-4165.2016.04.01.010

30. Kordzadeh, N., Warren, J.: Communicating personal health information in virtual health communities: an integration of privacy calculus model and affective commitment. J. Assoc. Inf. Syst. **18** (2017). https://doi.org/10.17705/1jais.00446

31. Oh, S.: The characteristics and motivations of health answerers for sharing information, knowledge, and experiences in online environments. J. Am. Soc. Inform. Sci. Technol. **63**, 543–557 (2012). https://doi.org/10.1002/asi.21676

32. Petersen, C., Lehmann, C.U.: Social media in health care: time for transparent privacy policies and consent for data use and disclosure. Appl. Clin. Inform. **9**, 856–859 (2018). https://doi.org/10.1055/s-0038-1676332

33. Zhang, X., Liu, S., Chen, X., Wang, L., Gao, B., Zhu, Q.: Health information privacy concerns, antecedents, and information disclosure intention in online health communities. Inf. Manag. **55**, 482–493 (2018). https://doi.org/10.1016/j.im.2017.11.003

34. Mulligan, D.K., Koopman, C., Doty, N.: Privacy is an essentially contested concept: a multi-dimensional analytic for mapping privacy. Philos. Trans. Roy. Soc. A: Math. Phys. Eng. Sci. **374**, 20160118 (2016)

35. Margulis, S.T.: Three theories of privacy: an overview. In: Trepte, S., Reinecke, L. (eds.) Privacy Online, pp. 9–17. Springer, Heidelberg (2011). https://doi.org/10.1007/978-3-642-21521-6_2

36. Petronio, S.: Boundaries of Privacy: Dialectics of Disclosure. SUNY Press, Albany (2012)

37. Nissenbaum, H.: Contextual integrity up and down the data food chain. Theor. Inquiries Law **20**, 221–256 (2019)

38. Phillips, A.M., de Campos, T.C., Herring, J.: Philosophical Foundations of Medical Law. Oxford University Press, Oxford (2019)

39. Véliz, C.: Medical privacy and big data: a further reason in favour of public universal healthcare coverage (2019)
40. D'Acquisto, G., Domingo-Ferrer, J., Kikiras, P., Torra, V., de Montjoye, Y.-A., Bourka, A.: Privacy by design in big data: an overview of privacy enhancing technologies in the era of big data analytics. arXiv preprint arXiv:1512.06000 (2015)
41. Mai, J.-E.: Big data privacy: the datafication of personal information. Inf. Soc. **32**, 192–199 (2016). https://doi.org/10.1080/01972243.2016.1153010
42. Floridi, L.: The ontological interpretation of informational privacy. Ethics Inf. Technol. **7**, 185–200 (2005). https://doi.org/10.1007/s10676-006-0001-7
43. Suh, J.J., Metzger, M.J., Reid, S.A., El Abbadi, A.: Distinguishing group privacy from personal privacy: the effect of group inference technologies on privacy perceptions and behaviors (2018). https://doi.org/10.1145/3274437
44. Mavriki, P., Karyda, M.: Big data in political communication: implications for group privacy. Int. J. Electron. Gov. **11**, 289–309 (2019)
45. Mavriki, P., Karyda, M.: Automated data-driven profiling: threats for group privacy. Inf. Comput. Secur. (2019)
46. Hogg, M.A., Sherman, D.K., Dierselhuis, J., Maitner, A.T., Moffitt, G.: Uncertainty, entitativity, and group identification. J. Exp. Soc. Psychol. **43**, 135–142 (2007). https://doi.org/10.1016/j.jesp.2005.12.008
47. Huddy, L.: From group identity to political cohesion and commitment. In: Oxford Handbook of Political Psychology, pp. 737–773 (2013)
48. Cho, H., Ippolito, D., Yu, Y.W.: Contact tracing mobile apps for COVID-19: privacy considerations and related trade-offs. arXiv:2003.11511 [cs] (2020)
49. Lin, L., Hou, Z.: Combat COVID-19 with artificial intelligence and big data. J. Travel Med. (2020)
50. Oliver, N., et al.: Mobile phone data and COVID-19: missing an opportunity? arXiv preprint arXiv:2003.12347 (2020)
51. Mozur, P., Zhong, R., Krolik, A.: In coronavirus fight, china gives citizens a color code, with red flags (2020). https://www.nytimes.com/2020/03/01/business/china-coronavirus-surveillance.html
52. Guy, J.: Singapore rolls out coronavirus contact-tracing device for people without smartphones – CNN. https://edition.cnn.com/2020/06/29/asia/tracetogether-tokens-singapore-scli-intl/index.html. Accessed 26 July 2020
53. Lee, V.J., Chiew, C.J., Khong, W.X.: Interrupting transmission of COVID-19: lessons from containment efforts in Singapore. J. Travel Med. **27** (2020). https://doi.org/10.1093/jtm/taaa039
54. Bradford, L.R., Aboy, M., Liddell, K.: COVID-19 Contact Tracing Apps: A Stress Test for Privacy, the GDPR and Data Protection Regimes. Social Science Research Network, Rochester (2020)
55. Demirag, D., Ayday, E.: Tracking and controlling the spread of a virus in a privacy-preserving way. arXiv:2003.13073 [cs] (2020)
56. Bates, M.: Tracking disease: digital epidemiology offers new promise in predicting outbreaks. IEEE Pulse **8**, 18–22 (2017)
57. Calo, R.: The boundaries of privacy harm. Ind. LJ. **86**, 1131 (2011)
58. Solove, D.J.: A Taxonomy of Privacy. Social Science Research Network, Rochester (2005)
59. Raskar, R., et al.: Apps gone rogue: maintaining personal privacy in an epidemic. arXiv preprint arXiv:2003.08567 (2020)
60. Lenert, L., McSwain, B.Y.: Balancing health privacy, health information exchange, and research in the context of the COVID-19 pandemic. J. Am. Med. Inform. Assoc. **27**, 963–966 (2020)

61. Wachter, S.: Normative challenges of identification in the internet of things: privacy, profiling, discrimination, and the GDPR. Comput. Law Secur. Rev. **34**, 436–449 (2018). https://doi.org/10.1016/j.clsr.2018.02.002

62. Custers, B.: Data dilemmas in the information society: introduction and overview. In: Custers, B., Calders, T., Schermer, B., Zarsky, T. (eds.) Discrimination and Privacy in the Information Society, pp. 3–26. Springer, Heidelberg (2013). https://doi.org/10.1007/978-3-642-30487-3_1

63. Terry, N.P.: Protecting patient privacy in the age of big data. UMKC L. Rev. **81**, 385 (2012)

64. Cowie, M.R., et al.: Electronic health records to facilitate clinical research. Clin. Res. Cardiol. **106**(1), 1–9 (2016). https://doi.org/10.1007/s00392-016-1025-6

65. Yang, F., Tian, T., Yao, H., Zhao, X., Zheng, T., Ning, M.: Anti-data mining on group privacy information. In: Zu, Q., Hu, B. (eds.) HCC 2017. LNCS, vol. 10745, pp. 481–491. Springer, Cham (2018). https://doi.org/10.1007/978-3-319-74521-3_51

66. Allen, A.: Privacy and Medicine (2009)

67. Matz, S.C., Netzer, O.: Using big data as a window into consumers' psychology. Curr. Opin. Behav. Sci. **18**, 7–12 (2017)

68. Matz, S.C., Appel, R.E., Kosinski, M.: Privacy in the age of psychological targeting. Curr. Opin. Psychol. **31**, 116–121 (2020)

69. Boyd, D., Crawford, K.: Critical questions for big data. Inf. Commun. Soc. **15**, 662–679 (2012). https://doi.org/10.1080/1369118X.2012.678878

70. Karyda, M., Gritzalis, S., Hyuk Park, J., Kokolakis, S.: Privacy and fair information practices in ubiquitous environments: research challenges and future directions. Internet Res. **19**, 194–208 (2009). https://doi.org/10.1108/10662240910952346

71. Bagdasaryan, E., et al.: Ancile: enhancing privacy for ubiquitous computing with use-based privacy. In: Proceedings of the 18th ACM Workshop on Privacy in the Electronic Society, pp. 111–124. Association for Computing Machinery, London (2019). https://doi.org/10.1145/3338498.3358642

72. Yasaka, T.M., Lehrich, B.M., Sahyouni, R.: Peer-to-peer contact tracing: development of a privacy-preserving smartphone app. JMIR mHealth uHealth **8**, e18936 (2020)

73. Wartenberg, D., Thompson, W.D.: Privacy versus public health: the impact of current confidentiality rules. Am. J. Publ. Health **100**, 407–412 (2010). https://doi.org/10.2105/AJPH.2009.166249

74. van der Sloot, B.: How to assess privacy violations in the age of Big Data? Analysing the three different tests developed by the ECtHR and adding for a fourth one. Inf. Commun. Technol. Law **24**, 74–103 (2015). https://doi.org/10.1080/13600834.2015.1009714

75. Taylor, L.: Safety in numbers? Group privacy and big data analytics in the developing world. In: Taylor, L., Floridi, L., van der Sloot, B. (eds.) Group privacy, pp. 13–36. Springer, Cham (2017). https://doi.org/10.1007/978-3-319-46608-8_2

76. Ienca, M., Vayena, E.: On the responsible use of digital data to tackle the COVID-19 pandemic. Nat. Med. **26**, 463–464 (2020). https://doi.org/10.1038/s41591-020-0832-5

A Multiple Algorithm Approach to Textural Features Extraction in Offline Signature Recognition

Jide Kehinde Adeniyi[1(⊠)], Tinuke Omolewa Oladele[2],
Noah Oluwatobi Akande[1], Roseline Oluwaseun Ogundokun[1],
and Tunde Taiwo Adeniyi[3]

[1] Department of Computer Science, Landmark University,
Omu-Aran, Kwara State, Nigeria
{adeniyi.jide,akande.noah,
ogundokun.roseline}@lmu.edu.ng
[2] Department of Computer Science, University of Ilorin,
Ilorin, Kwara State, Nigeria
oladele.to@unilorin.edu.ng
[3] National Assembly, Abuja, Nigeria
Adekitos2@gmail.com

Abstract. Signature is a biometric trait that has piqued the interest of researchers. This is due to its high rate of acceptability. Offline signature in particular, has been around for a while and hence its suitability as a biometric trait. This paper proposes an offline signature recognition system using a multiple algorithm approach. The system accepts handwritten signature, filters the signature and crops the signature region. The Local Binary Pattern (LBP) of the signature image is then obtained. After this, Grey Level Co-occurrence Matrix (GLCM) is applied. Statistical features are then extracted. The difference in the stored features and the extracted features was obtained. The output is compared with a threshold for discrimination. This research aims at improving the performance of offline signature recognition using its textural features. The designed system gave an FRR and FAR of 8.6%, 4.6% respectively for MYCT signature database and 8.8%, 5.2% for GPDS signature database.

Keywords: Offline signature · Local binary patter · Grey level co-occurrence matrix · False acceptance ratio · False rejectance ratio

1 Introduction

Individual identification in the past used to be performed with the aid of password, PIN (Personal Identification Number) and so on) [13]. However, issues arising from forgetfulness, theft amongst others has led to the need for a better way of identification [9, 13]. Biometrics emerged to alleviate some of the challenges of the traditional identification methods. Biometrics is the use of an individual's characteristics (Physical or behavioural) for identification. There are several biometric traits, however, they are generally grouped into three (3) categories [5]. These categories are Physiological,

© Springer Nature Switzerland AG 2020
M. Themistocleous et al. (Eds.): EMCIS 2020, LNBIP 402, pp. 541–552, 2020.
https://doi.org/10.1007/978-3-030-63396-7_36

behavioural and Chemical [5, 8]. A Physical biometric trait uses a physical characteristic of an individual for recognition, some examples include iris, palmprint, hand geometry, and so on. Chemical biometrics uses a chemical characteristic for identification, and an example is body odour. Behavioural characteristics uses an individual's behavioural characteristics for identification [17]. Amongst the behavioural biometrics is the Signature. [6] defines signature as the legal mark of an individual. While signature's biometric performance is low compared to some of its peers, its acceptance is high [7, 8]. Its uses ranges from bank transactions to document validation [9]. Signature can be replicated falsely by others and this is termed signature forgery. Signature forgery can either be random (without prior knowledge of the signature), unskilled (with less practice of the forged signature) and skilled (with proper practice of the signature being forged). Random signature forgery is the easiest to identify while skilled forgery is the most difficult to identify [18].

Signature recognition can either be online or offline. Online signature are individual signatures obtained on digital tablets. Data are obtained as the user writes on the tablet. Offline signatures are obtained from hardcopy scanned (or snapped) into the computer [20, 22]. Online signature performs better than offline signatures because of the various features extracted during the signing process (such as co-ordinates, pressure, pen angle and others) [5, 20]. However, Offline signature is still more widely used than Online signature [22]. Hence the need to improve this biometric method. Several approaches have been proposed for offline signature; however, most approaches have been limited to the co-ordinates, edges and curvature of the signature [5, 8, 9]. Recent trends in offline signature is examining the use of textural features for signature recognition. Hence, this paper presents a texture-based offline signature recognition system.

2   Related Work

Offline Signature recognition has been an area of interest for a while with researchers exploring this biometric method so as to increase its accuracy. Researchers have focused on the binarization of offline signatures so as to extract features from this biometric. This section examines some of the approaches to signature recognition. [13] examined both Offline and Online signature recognition respectively. For the Offline signature, filtering was performed to reduce noise in the signature image. Binarization and thinning were both done to make the signature image compact. For the Online signature, preprocessing was not necessary as data were obtained as the user writes on the digital tablet. The stroke co-ordinates were used as features for the Offline signature while the co-ordinates, pressure of pen and time to complete signature were used as features for Online signatures. The PCA was used to extract relevant features from the feature set and Manhattan Distance (MD) was used for matching.

A classification method to detect forged signatures from the authentic signature was presented [10]. In this approach, binarization was the first step performed. Smoothing is performed to remove unconnected pixels from the signature image. To avoid variation in image thickness, thinning was performed. The last step in the preprocessing stage crops out the actual signature area. Global features, slant features and textural features were collected from the binary image. Fine random forest model was used for classification.

An approach consisting of four major steps was proposed by [18]. These steps are: preprocessing, features extraction, features selection and feature verification. Median filter was used for noise removal. Otsu method and morphological operations were used to segment the signature image. Global features (width, height and area of signature) and Local features (slope, signature centroid, angle and distance) were extracted. Genetic algorithm was used for the feature selection, and the support vector machine performs the verification.

[9] used Local Binary Pattern (LBP) and Binary Statistical Image Features (BSIF) for Offline features extraction. Kernel Neural Network was used classification. In their Offline signature verification system, the signature image is converted to its binary representation before the LBP and BSIF is applied.

[6] examined Online signature verification using Dynamic Time Warping for features extraction. Smoothing, rotation and normalization were performed as preprocessing steps. Coordinate, pressure, altitude and azimuth were extracted during the signature capture.

From the reviewed literature, LBP has been credited with its ability to extract image features even under varying pixel intensities. Combining this trait with a statistical function that has the ability to produce a global representation of the features extracted would certainly improve the recognition rate of this biometric trait.

3 Proposed Method

The proposed method is examined in this section. The proposed method is made up of the following steps: Acquisition, Preprocessing, Features extraction, Matching. The system can undergo two stages and they are the Enrolment stage and Recognition stage. The features extracted from an individual's signature is saved as a template in the enrolment stage while the recognition stage states whether a signature is genuine or not. Figure 1 depicts the block diagram of the system.

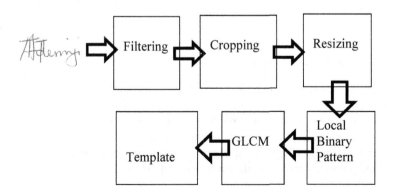

Fig. 1. Block diagram of the system

The first step is the acquisition of signature image after which is preprocessing. Preprocessing is the second step in this system and it is primarily aimed at preparing the signature image for features extraction. The steps involved in preprocessing the signature image in this system are filtering, cropping and resizing.

3.1 Signature Image Filtering

Gaussian Filter was applied to remove noise from the signature images. The blurred image is obtained from the original image using the Eq. 1 [13]:

$$G(a, b; \sigma) = \frac{1}{2\pi\sigma^2} e^{-\left(\frac{a^2 + b2}{2\sigma^2}\right)} \tag{1}$$

with a as the distance horizontally, b being the distance vertically and σ is the standard deviation (σ^2 the variance).

3.2 Signature Image Cropping

After the noise in the image is removed, cropping is performed so as to rid the image of unwanted pixels (background) surrounding the signature. The algorithm used to crop out the signature area is as follows:

Input: An array of the grey value of an image.

a. Start
b. Locate the coordinate of the first non-white pixel (x, y), moving from left to right, beginning at the top.
c. Locate the coordinate of the first non-white pixel (x, y), moving from left to right, beginning at the bottom.
d. Locate the coordinate of the first non-white pixel (x, y), moving from top to bottom, beginning from the left.
e. Locate the coordinate of the first non-white pixel (x, y), moving from top to bottom, beginning from the right.
f. Copy pixels within the boundary specified by the pixels obtained from step b, c, d and e above.
g. end

3.3 Signature Image Resizing

The images are resized to 100 by 80. There are several methods for resizing. However, bicubic interpolation was used in this system because it examines 16 data points in the neighbourhood of the interpolation region. This improves its result because more pixels are examined compared to cubic interpolation [13].

Bicubic interpolation uses an up-sampling distance Z to estimate pixels not known for the interpolation process as shown in Fig. 2 [13].

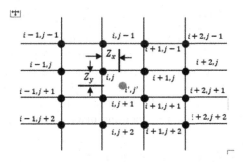

Fig. 2. Sample pixels of an image

At (i',j') in Fig. 2, the interpolated pixel is obtained with Eq. 2 below.

$$
f_{i'j'} = \begin{bmatrix} f_{i-1,j-1} & f_{i,j-1} & f_{i+1,j-1} & f_{i+2,j-1} \\ f_{i-1,j} & f_{i,j} & f_{i+1,j} & f_{i+2,j} \\ f_{i-1,j+1} & f_{i,j+1} & f_{i+1,j+1} & f_{i+2,j+1} \\ f_{i-1,j+2} & f_{i,j+2} & f_{i+1,j+2} & f_{i+2,j+2} \end{bmatrix} \begin{bmatrix} W_{-1}Z_x \\ W_0Z_x \\ W_1Z_x \\ W_2Z_x \end{bmatrix} [W_{-1}Z_y \quad W_0Z_y \quad W_1Z_y \quad W_2Z_y] \quad (2)
$$

where $Z_y = j' - j, Z_x = i' - i$ and $f_{i,j}$ means the pixel at (i,j). For weights $W_{-1}(Z), W_0(Z), W_1(Z), W_2(Z)$, they are given as

$$
W_{-1}(Z) = \frac{-Z^3 + 2Z^2 - Z}{2} \quad (3)
$$

$$
W_0(Z) = \frac{3Z^3 + 5Z^2 - 2}{2} \quad (4)
$$

$$
W_1(Z) = \frac{-3Z^3 + 4Z^2 + Z}{2} \quad (5)
$$

$$
W_2(Z) = \frac{Z^3 - Z^2}{2} \quad (6)
$$

4   Features Extraction

For features extraction, the local binary pattern and grey level co-occurrence matrix is proposed. The local binary pattern is a grey image features extraction method that is resistance to changes in intensity. This is proposed so as reduce the effect of the colour of the pen used.

4.1   Local Binary Pattern

Local binary pattern (LBP) is a textural feature extraction method that uses the grey version of an image. It examines a pixel, uses it as threshold for categorizing its neighbours as 1 or 0 and computes the decimal value of the binary representation of the neighbouring pixels in a clockwise manner [11, 15]. This is shown in Fig. 3. If the centre pixel is greater than any neighbouring pixel, the pixel is set to 0. If the center pixel is less than or equal to the neighbouring pixel is set to 1.

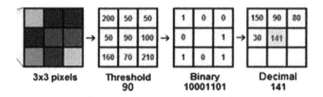

Fig. 3. Figure showing the operation of LBP

Hence, the LBP of a given pixel is denoted as [16, 19]:

$$LBP_A(i,j) = \sum_{h=0}^{A-1} s(g_h - g_c)2^h \qquad (7)$$

$$s(k) = \begin{cases} 1, k \geq 0 \\ 0, k < 0 \end{cases} \qquad (8)$$

Where i,j is the location of the pixel at the centre, A are the 8 neighbouring pixels, g_c is the grey value of the center pixel, g_h is the grey value of the neighbouring pixel, $s(k)$ is a sign function of a sequence k defined in Eq. (8). The feature vector LBP_A is a histogram of 2^A Local Binary Pattern of image pixels.

4.2   Grey Level Co-occurrence Matrix

Grey Level Co-occurrence Matrix (GLCM) is used for analyzing textural information of an image [1]. It is a statistical technique that give detailed descriptions about spatial relationship of pixels [1, 2]. It examines the relationship between two pixels at a time, and is sometimes termed the reference and neighbour pixel. The separation is made by the second order statistics [3, 4, 21]. Second order means they consider the relationship between groups of two pixels in the original image. First order texture measures are statistics calculated from the original source (image), like variance, and do not consider relationship between pixels. It is computed using the displacement and orientation between surrounding pixels [12, 17].

Let P be a normalized symmetric GLCM. Let μ_x, μ_y, σ_x and σ_y be the means and standard deviations of P_x and P_y respectively, of the partial probability density functions. Let $P_{x+y}(i)$ be the probability of co-occurrence matrix coordinates summing to $x+y$. The features used in this research include [4, 17]:

Contrast: This is also known as "sum of square variance" or "inertia". It is obtained using equation [1, 3]:

$$Contrast = \sum_{i,j=0}^{N-1} P_{i,j}(i-j)^2 \tag{9}$$

Dissimilarity: Unlike contrast, dissimilarity weight increases linearly [1]

$$Dissimilarity = \sum_{i,j=0}^{N-1} P_{i,j}(i-j) \tag{10}$$

Homogeneity:

$$Homogeneity = \sum_{i,j=0}^{N-1} P_{i,j}(i-j) \tag{11}$$

Angular Second Moment:

$$ASM = \sum_{i,j=0}^{N-1} P_{i,j}^2 \tag{12}$$

Energy: This is the square root of the Angular Second Moment (ASM)

$$Energy = \sqrt{\sum_{i,j=0}^{N-1} P_{i,j}^2} \tag{13}$$

Entropy:

$$Entropy = \sum_{i,j=0}^{N-1} P_{i,j}(-\log P_{i,j}) \tag{14}$$

Correlation Texture Measure: This computes the linear dependency of a grey level with those of its neighbors.

$$Entropy = \sum_{i,j=0}^{N-1} P_{i,j} \left[\frac{(i-\mu_i)(j-\mu_j)}{\sqrt{(\sigma_i^2)(\sigma_j^2)}} \right] \tag{15}$$

Where variance (μ) and standard deviation σ is $\mu_i = \sum_{i,j=0}^{N-1} i(P_{i,j})$,

$$\mu_j = \sum_{i,j=0}^{N-1} j\left(P_{i,j}\right),$$

$$\sigma_i^2 = \sum_{i,j=0}^{N-1} P_{i,j}\left(i - \mu_i\right)^2,$$

$$\sigma_j^2 = \sum_{i,j=0}^{N-1} P_{i,j}\left(i - \mu_j\right)^2,$$

$$\sigma_i = \sqrt{\sigma_j^2},$$

$$\sigma_j = \sqrt{\sigma_j^2}$$

5 Matching

The system made use of Euclidean distance for matching. The Euclidean distance of the GLCM features extracted from the enrolled signature image and the features extracted for the verification process is used for matching. The obtained value is compared with the stated threshold for verification. The Euclidean distance is expressed in Eq. 16 [23, 24]:

$$d_{ij} = \sqrt{\sum_{k=1}^{n} \left(x_{ik} - x_{jk}\right)^2} \tag{16}$$

For two samples $X_i = \left(X_{i1}, X_{i2}, \ldots, X_{in}\right)^T$ and $X_i = \left(X_{j1}, X_{j2}, \ldots, X_{jn}\right)^T$.

6 Experimental Result

For evaluating the performance of the method suggested above, online database of signatures and manually collected signatures were used. Repetitive collection was used for the enrollment process. Repetitive collection here entails extracting the GLCM features multiple times (5 times in this system) and averaging the results of each GLCM feature. MYCT and GPDS offline signature database were used. For the evaluation of the performance of the system, the False Acceptance Ration (FAR), False Rejectance Ratio (FRR) and the Accuracy of the system were used. FAR is the ratio of falsely accepted signature and the total false signature submitted. FRR is the ratio of genuine signature rejected and the total genuine signature submitted. Both FAR and FRR are usually represented in percentage. Accuracy is also used in some researches because it is obtained from both the FAR and the FRR and it is given in Eq. 17 [13].

Figure 4 shows the Equal Error Rate (EER) of the system. It is a graph of the thresholds against their FAR and FRR. It usually denotes the optimal threshold for which both the FAR and the FRR are fairly represented. It is used in obtaining the threshold for the system. The threshold at which the FAR and FRR crosses each other is the threshold at which both are low (without one being extremely high and the other very low).

Fig. 4. Handwritten signature samples

$$Accuracy = 100 - \frac{(FAR + FRR)}{2} \tag{17}$$

The prototype of the system was developed using Matblab R2015a on an intel core i7 laptop with a processor of 2.20 GHz and a RAM of 4 GB.

6.1 MYCT Dataset

MYCT is a publicly available database of biometric images, that is widely used for biometric system testing. Ministerio de Ciencia y Tecnologı́a, Spanish Ministry of Science and Technology was partially responsible for funding the biometric image collection from four academic institutions [14]. After testing this system, a FAR of 4.6% and an FRR of 8.6% was obtained.

6.2 GPDS Dataset

GPDS (Digital Signal Processing Group) is group at the University of las Palmas de Gran Canaria that specializes in research related to biometrics, one- and two-dimensional pattern recognition and behaviour characterization through audio and video. They have available signature database for signature biometric system testing. It consists of 4000 sets of signature images, each with 30 forged and 24 genuine. After testing the system with randomly selected forged images and genuine images, a FAR of 5.8% and an FRR of 8.8%. Some Handwritten signature samples used are shown Fig. 4:

Table 1 summarizes the FAR, FRR and accuracy of the system and Fig. 5 shows the Equal Error Rate graph of the system.

A comparison of the obtained result with other relevant papers is shown in Table 2.

Table 1. Result obtained from testing the system.

Database	FAR (%)	FRR (%)	Accuracy
MYCT	4.6	8.6	93.3
GPDS	5.2	8.8	92.7

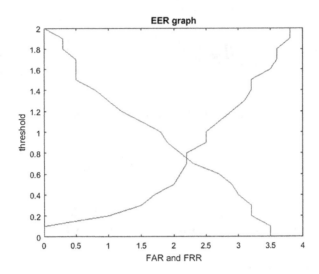

Fig. 5. The Equal Error Rate (EER) graph of the system

Table 2. Comparison of result with existing results in the literature.

Paper		FAR (%)	FRR (%)	Acc. (%)
Chandra and Maheshkar [25]	**MYCT**	8.76	9.83	93.84
	GPDS	7.36	8.84	90.56
Jadhav [27]	**GPDS**	1.92	13.79	85.66
Pushpalatha et al. [26]	**GPDS**	9.34	4.9	88.34
Proposed	**MYCT**	**4.6**	**8.2**	**93.3**
	GPDS	**5.2**	**8.8**	**92.7**

7 Conclusion

This work presented the design of a textural features extraction method for signature recognition using a multi-algorithmic approach. The signature used for testing were obtained from MYCT handwritten signature databased and GPDS handwritten signature database. The obtained images were preprocessed by removing noises from them, cropping out the actual signature area and resizing the signature image. Gaussian filter was used for noise removal and resizing was performed using bicubic interpolation. The Local Binary Pattern of the image was generated and the Grey Level Co-occurrence Matrix was computed. A number of statistical properties of the Grey Level Co-occurrence Matrix were computed. The Manhattan distance was applied to the difference obtained from the test signature and the store template. The obtained result is then compared with the system threshold so as to verify whether the signature is genuine or not. The results obtained after testing the system showed that the textural feature extracted from signature images using the fusion LBP and the GLCM is better than those obtained from using only LBP or GLCM. Hence, the use of a statistical method for feature selection (GLCM) after applying LBP for features extraction gives a better feature set than when LBP is used alone. For future research, a look at the fusion of textural features, curvature features and stroke co-ordinates-based features to improve the performance of this biometric trait is a viable direction.

References

1. Aferi, F.D., Purboyo, T.W., Saputra, R.E.: Cotton texture segmentation based on image texture analysis using gray level co-occurrence matrix (GLCM) and Euclidean distance. Int. J. Appl. Eng. Res. **13**(1), 449–455 (2018)
2. Gade, A.A., Vyavahare, A.J.: Feature extraction using GLCM for dietary assessment application. Int. J. Multimedia Image Process. (IJMIP) **8**, 2 (2018)
3. Hall-Beyer, M.: GLCM Texture: A Tutorial v. 3.0, March 2017. University of Calgari (2017). https://doi.org/10.11575/prism/33280
4. Josuttes, A., Zhang, T., Vail, S., Pozniak, C.: Parkin, I.: Classification of crop lodging with gray level co-occurrence matrix. In: IEEE Winter Conference on Applications of Computer Vision (2018). https://doi.org/10.1109/WACV.2018.00034
5. Masoudnia, S., Mersa, O., Araabi, B.N., Vahabie, A., Sadeghi, M.A., Ahmada-badi, M.N.: Multi-representational learning for offline signature verification using multi-loss snapshot ensemble of CNNs. Expert Syst. Appl. (2019). https://doi.org/10.1016/j.eswa.2019.03.040
6. Patil, B.V., Patil, P.: An efficient DTW algorithm for online signature verification. In: International Conference on Advances in Communication and Computing Technology (ICACCT) (2018)
7. Rateria A., Agarwal S.: Offline signature verification through machine learning. In: UPCON 2018 5th IEEE Uttar Pradesh Section International Conference on Electrical, Computer and Electronics (2018)
8. Diaz, M., Ferrer, M.A., Impedovo, D., Malik, M.I., Pirlo, G., Plamondon, R.: A perspective analysis of handwritten signature technology. ACM Comput. Surv. **51**(6) (2019)
9. Hezil, H., Djemili, R., Bourouba, H.: Signature recognition using binary features and KNN. Int. J. Biometrics **10**(1) (2018)
10. Jayaraman, M., Gadwala, S.B.: Writer-independent offline signature verification system. In: Balas, V.E., Sharma, N., Chakrabarti, A. (eds.) Data Management, Analytics and Innovation. AISC, vol. 839, pp. 213–223. Springer, Singapore (2019). https://doi.org/10.1007/978-981-13-1274-8_17
11. Kumra, S., Rao, T.: A novel design for a palm prints enabled bio-metric system. IOSR J. Comput. Eng. (IOSRJCE) **7**(3), 1–8 (2012)
12. Mohebian, R., Riahi, M.A., Yousefi, O.: Detection of channel by seismic texture analysis using grey level cooccurrence matrix based attributes. J. Geophys. Eng. **15**(5), 1953–1962 (2018). https://doi.org/10.1088/1742-2140/aac099
13. Olabode O., Adeniyi J.K., Akinyede, R.O., Oluwadare S.A.: A signature identification system with principal component analysis and Stentiford thinning algorithms. Int. J. Comput. Technol. **14**(9) (2015)
14. Ortega-Garcia J., et al.: Biometrics on the internet MCYT baseline corpus: a bimodal biometric database. IEE Proc.-Vis. Image Sig. Process. **150**(6) (2003). https://doi.org/10.1049/ip-vis:20031078

15. Priya, T.V., Sanchez, G.V., Raajan, N.R.: Facial recognition system using local binary pattern (LBP). Int. J. Pure Appl. Math. **119**(15), 1895–1899 (2018)
16. Rachapalli, D.R., Kalluri, H.K.: Texture driven hierarchical fusion for multi-biometric system. Int. J. Eng. Technol. **7**(4), 33–37 (2018)
17. Rajapaksa S., et al.: Modified texture features from histogram and gray level co-occurence matrix of facial data for ethnicity detection. In: IEEE 2018 5th International Multi-Topic ICT Conference (IMTIC) (2018). https://doi.org/10.1109/IMTIC.2018.8467231
18. Sharif, M., Khan, M.A., Faisal, M., Yasmin, M., Fernandes, S.L.: A framework for offline signature verification system: best features selection approach. Pattern Recogn. Lett. (2018). https://doi.org/10.1016/j.patrec.2018.01.021
19. Singh, S., Kaur, A.: Off-line signature verification using sub uniform local binary patterns and support vector machine. In: International Conference on Chemical Engineering and Advanced Computational Technologies (ICCEACT 2014) (2014). https://doi.org/10.15242/iie.e1114033
20. Sthapak, S., Khopade, M., Kashid, C.: Artificial neural network based signature recognition & verification. Int. J. Emerg. Technol. Adv. Eng. **3**(8) (2013)
21. Valentin, P., Kounalakis, T., Nalpantidis, L.: Weld classification using gray level co-occurrence matrix and local binary patterns. In: IEEE International Conference on Imaging Systems and Techniques (IST) (2018). https://doi.org/10.1109/IST.2018.8577092
22. Yadav, D., Saxena, C.: Offline signature recognition and verification using PCA and neural network approach. Int. J. Sci. Res. Dev. **3**(9) (2015)
23. Pandit, S., Gupta, S.: A comparative study on distance measuring approaches for clustering. Int. J. Res. Comput. Sci. **2**(1) (2011)
24. Zhang, Y., Xu, Y., Bao, H.: Offline handwritten signature recognition method based on multifeatures. J. Converg. Inf. Tech. (JCIT) **8**(5) (2013)
25. Chandra, S., Maheshkar, S.: Static signature verification based on texture analysis using support vector machine. Int. J. Multimedia Data Eng. Manag. **8**(2) (2017). https://doi.org/10.4018/ijmdem.2017040103
26. Pushpalatha, K.N., Gautam, A.K., Raviteja, K.V., Shruthi, P., Srikrishna, A.R., Yuvaraj, P.: Signature verification using directional and textural features. In: IEEE 2013 International Conference on Circuits, Controls and Communications (CCUBE) (2013). https://doi.org/10.1109/ccube.2013.6718560
27. Jadhav, T.: Handwritten signature verification using local binary pattern features and KNN. Int. Res. J. Eng. Technol. (IRJET) **6**(4) (2019)

Modified Least Significant Bit Technique for Securing Medical Images

Roseline Oluwaseun Ogundokun[1]([⊠]) [iD],
Oluwakemi Christiana Abikoye[2] [iD], Sanjay Misra[3],
and Joseph Bamidele Awotunde[2] [iD]

[1] Department of Computer Science, Landmark University,
Omu Aran, Kwara State, Nigeria
ogundokun.roseline@lmu.edu.ng
[2] Department of Computer Science, University of Ilorin, Ilorin,
Kwara State, Nigeria
[3] Department of Electrical and Information Engineering, Covenant University,
Ota, Ogun State, Nigeria

Abstract. The confidentiality and safety of patient records is a significant concern for medical professionals. So protections must be placed to guarantee that illegal individuals do not have access to medical images (Patient's description). Hence, the objective of this study is to secure digital medical images being transmitted over the internet from being accessed by an intruder. The study, therefore, proposed a modified Least Significant Bit (LSB) algorithm implemented on a MATLAB 2018a programming environment, and the proposed system was compared with the existing system using three performance metrics which are PSNR. MSE and SSIM. The result showed that the proposed approach outperformed the current standard methods by producing a more robust, high capacity, and highly imperceptible stego image. The comparative analysis conducted also showed that the PSNR valve is higher, and MSE value is lower when compared with existing systems. It was concluded that the projected technique accomplishes excellently in making the medical image transmitted to be more secured, robust, and invisible, thereby making the communication to be unnoticeable by an intruder or attacker.

Keywords: Steganography · Medical image · Least significant bit · PSNR · MSE · SSIM

1 Introduction

These days, the growing of information technology, particularly systems such as mobile communication, the computer network, and digital interactive program applications, has unlocked innovative possibilities for steganography and concealing procedures for information [1]. Data security has been a critical topic in recent years as a product of the massive developments in information technologies as well as the tremendous rise in computer networks used by data transmission and receiving [2, 28]. Researchers then concentrated on developing data security systems, and experiments

© Springer Nature Switzerland AG 2020
M. Themistocleous et al. (Eds.): EMCIS 2020, LNBIP 402, pp. 553–565, 2020.
https://doi.org/10.1007/978-3-030-63396-7_37

were carried out to refine existing strategies and introduce new ones to secure data from hackers [3]. Cryptography is a tool used to confirm the details of a message by scrambling the message in such a way that nobody can decode apart from the individual who has the undisclosed password. It also a means of ensuring that messages were not altered throughout the communication cycle. Many methods for encoding and decoding messages to secure them have been developed, nevertheless with the emergence of the internet, these methods became inefficient [3]. New techniques were, therefore, necessary to resolve this problem, and this led to the advent of the principle of steganography [4–6].

Steganography refers to know-how and the ability to hide messages or any communication between the source and the destination of the undisclosed message via an electronic channel transferring the message [7–10]. The term (steganography) arising out of (steganos) denoting (concealed) and (graph) denoting (script) denotes (hidden writing) [11, 12]. Steganography is a way of covering coded communications in a plain concealment medium such as stegograms so that the presence of the hidden messages would not be revealed to an accidental observer [13–17, 49, 50]. Using steganographic strategies, material that is perceptually and statistically undetectable can be contained inside images, audio, video documents, or text. The electronic object is the utmost well-known concealment medium because of its extreme level of verbosity [18, 19]. The equivalent technique could be utilized in video steganography to entrench a communication into all the video edges [20, 21]. Audio steganography integrates the message as noise in a concealment acoustic medium at a rate of recurrence that is below the normal listening range [22]. It's discovered that steganography disguises the presence of hidden communication, equating steganography with cryptography [23], while cryptography masks the meaning of the hidden communication [1].

Therefore, the objective of this study is to secure digital medical images being transmitted over the internet or an electronic medium from being accessed by an intruder. The study, therefore, proposed a modified Least Significant Bit algorithm implemented on a MATLAB 2018a programming environment and submitted to conduct a comparative analysis of the developed system with the existing system using three performance metrics which are PSNR. MSE and SSIM.

The remaining part of the paper are prearranged as follows: Sect. 2 discussed the related research works, Sect. 3 described the proposed method for this study, the datasets used for the implementation of the system and the stages with the algorithms utilized for performance, Sect. 4 discussed the results obtained from the implementation of the system, and this also showed the interfaces of the performance. The qualitative evaluation metrics used for the developed system analysis and the comparative analysis of the developed system with previous researches were discussed in Sect. 5. This investigation was concluded in Sect. 6.

2   Related Works

Several studies have investigated the various Steganography image approaches utilized to conceal messages in concealment objects [24–27]. The critical problem of communication concealing methods is to embed the most significant volume of communication in the cover object while maintaining consistency, including the reliability and power of the system in challenging hackers with electronic attacks. Several techniques and methods have been proposed to mask image data due to the immense number of visual imageries on the internet and as well as the straightforwardness of managing imageries in a concealment procedure [29–31].

To this end, scholars have tried to use new methods to deal with the accelerated evolution of concealing strategies to obtain specific outcomes. Researchers recently concentrated on enhancing the hiding mechanism in images by utilizing diverse approaches, for instance, LSB.

The LSB structure is prevalent plus is the utilization of Images to conceal data. This approaches the concealment medium specifically by modifying the least essential bit size to insert the details about the undisclosed communication and make it very difficult to identify the evolving mechanism in the medium from the people's eyes. Hence, it a robust technique to add hidden knowledge by effecting imperceptible changes in the cover object [32, 33].

[34] proposed the Manipulating Alteration Path approach where the image was divided into multiple clusters comprising n pixels to inject the undisclosed file into (2n + 1)-ary encryption. The amount of a particular pixel within a category was raised or decreased by one during the insertion phase. Their method's drawback is the reduced concealment object features because the group size had two pixels.

[35] proposed a structure to develop the so-called EMD process (IEMD). Compared to the standard EMD approach, this system collected a significant volume of data without compromising the concealment object features. This process transformed the undisclosed communication into an undisclosed digit in an 8-ary encrypting structure and inserted all secret communication into a collection of two pixels.

[36] proposed a system for improving the conventional EMD approach by embedding secret messages in all pixels using every pixel in the image. The entrenched material in the picture was duplicated when contrasted with the traditional method in the process. Utilizing the approach overpowered the detrimental features of the EMD system plus integrated the best volume of facts as long as maintaining the image characteristics.

[37] proposed an Opt EMD structure to what end the association amid the number of pixels (n) in the whole cluster with the number of payloads contained in the image was used to minimize the image distortion. This scheme achieved high efficiency, but the volume of the payload was affected.

[38] introduced a scheme using the methods of encoding Huffman, affine cypher, and Knight Tour. The undisclosed communication was scrambled and compacted in the procedure utilizing affine encryption and Huffman encoding, after that the new message was entrenched into a concealment object using LSB and Knight's tour approaches.

The item was translated into the colour space of YCbCr, and the undisclosed communication was inserted in the Cb part.

[39] brought forward a system utilizing better techniques for coding EMD and Huffman. This approach compacts the mystery message using Huffman coding; after that, the mystery cypher was encoded in an image utilizing the EMD approach, whereas the collection of pixels used for entrenching was divided into two subcategories of 2 and 3 pixels successively to maximize the payload beyond effecting the concealment object characteristics.

[40] implemented a data hiding structure that would calculate the sum of the I structure contained in the image utilizing the EMD process. The undisclosed message in this scheme was represented using (cn-ary). Then, utilizing C of diverse approaches to change its rate after that the set of (n) pixels was used to enclose the undisclosed communication in it.

[41] recommended a structure utilizing the LZW technique to minimize the magnitude of undisclosed details and raise the payload then use the Knight tour system as well as EMD structure to incorporate new knowledge into the concealment picture.

[42] set out a framework for developing the EMD process. The picture was separated into n pixels in the scheme and was utilized to implant 2kn-ary figures in the core section. The technique of Image Steganography was proposed by combining the methods of cryptography and steganography in this investigation. First, Vigenere cypher and Huffman encrypting were used to scramble and compact undisclosed communication. This means preserving the details and raising the size of the unknown communication for integration into the concealment picture utilizing the EMD procedure. Using the Knight tour scheme and arbitrary function, it was then enhanced to improve robustness and reliability by selecting the wedges and clusters used to enclose the secret communication into a particular pixel. This as well helps to maintain the stego-picture consistency and brought it nearer to the camera cover.

To ensure internet stability, [43] established a new LSB replacement scheme using stego-key guidance. The system's payload and imperceptibility were models as a search issue for optimization. Finally, using a messy map, the critical information was arbitrarily inserted into the cover image. The recovery of classified information requires all procedures being reversed. The technique got 44.09db and 0.97 respectively as PSNR and SSIM.

[48] recommended image steganography established on integrated files plus inverted bit LSB replacement. The research intended to deliver three layers of security moderately than entrenching the file's bit straight forward into the concealment object. The pixels were engendered arbitrarily via a pseudo-random number generator after the undisclosed communication is concealed inside the concealment object utilizing an inverted LSB approach.

The findings from the review show that the standard LSB steganography has mostly been used for hiding information, and it has shown that it had some limitation of perceptibility, distortion, the cover image is not robust.

3   Material and Method

3.1   Proposed Method

The need to develop reliable mechanisms for transmitting and receiving information through a contact channel is a significant issue. An innovative method is anticipated to cover the medical image by changing the LSB steganography approach to mask a considerable volume of records and given the accuracy of stego-images succeeding incorporating the medical image into the file. This provides an extreme degree of confidentiality in concealing the details inside the cover picture and through the method's intensity in the digital occurrence situation. Such elements are confrontations facing the technique of hiding messages in photographs.

The stages of the projected method comprise

Embedding Procedure: The medical image is entrenched within the concealment object by utilizing a modified LSB procedure called Circular Shift LSB and gives an output called stego image which is an image hiding the medical image in it.

Extraction Process: The stego image is detached out of the stego image using the modified LSB procedure called the Circular Shift algorithm.

3.2   Materials

Data Availability.
The medical images which are mammogram images exploit in this investigation are openly obtainable at mini-MIAS: http://peipa.essex.ac.uk/pix/mias/.

Sample Medical Images.
Figure 1 displays the sample medical images, which are a mammogram used for the testing of the developed system.

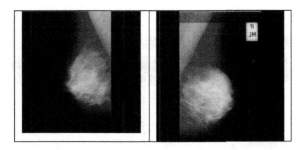

Fig. 1. Sample medical image

3.3   Proposed Method Algorithms

Embedding Algorithm

Input: Medical image, Cover object, Stego key
Output: Stego image
Phase 1: Enter the medical image and the stego key
Phase 2: Read the given message of the medical image
Step 3: Change the pictures to ASCII arrangement
Phase 4: Embed the ASCII format into the cover image using the modified LSB algorithm called Circular Shift Method
Phase 5: Produce a stego image

Extracting Algorithm

Input: Stego image, Stego key
Output: Medical image, Cover image
Phase 1: Enter the stego image and the stego key
Phase 2: Read given stego image
Phase 3: Change the picture to ASCII arrangement
Phase 4: Extract the ASCII format from the stego image utilizing the projected system algorithm called Circular Shift Method
Phase 5: Produce the medical image and the initial cover image

4   Results and Discussion

The study exploits the use of MATLAB for the implementation of the proposed technique, the system also employed medical images for the testing of the system. The following interfaces display the results from the performance of the developed system.

4.1   Embedding Phase of the System

Figure 2 shows the proposed system interface for the secured medical information system.

Fig. 2. The interface of the system

Figure 3 displays the interface showing the procedure of the embedding technique.

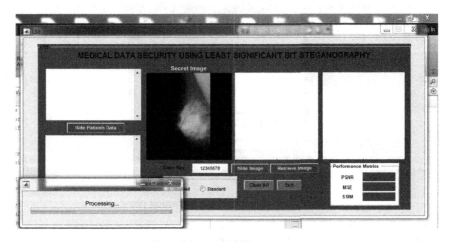

Fig. 3. Embedding process in progress

Figure 4 shows the interface displaying the result of the embedding stage of the system. This demonstrates the initial concealment object and the steganographic image (that is object hiding the patient's information).

Fig. 4. The interface of embedding result

4.2 Extracting Phase of the System

Figure 5 displays the extraction phase for the scheme, and here the stego key for access to the secured patient information is entered.

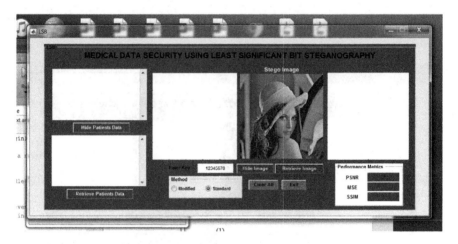

Fig. 5. The interface of the extraction phase

Figure 6 shows the folder from where the saved stego image is being stored and picked for extraction.

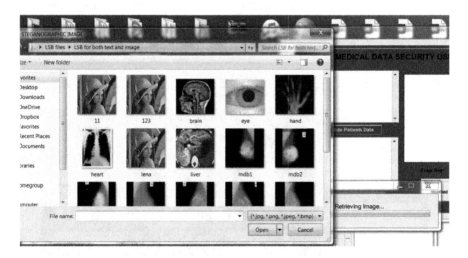

Fig. 6. The interface of folder having the message sent

Figure 7 displays the extraction phase of the projected scheme, and the confidential information is shown on the retrieve message and also the initial cover message.

Fig. 7. The interface of the extraction phase

5 Qualitative Evaluation Metric

Mean square error (MSE), peak signal-to-noise ratio (PSNR), normalization of cross-correlation (NCC), structural similarity index (SSIM), plus histogram are generally utilized to assess the characteristics of stego-images virtually [44]. In this investigation, the authors used three out of the metrics; for instance, the MSE, PSNR, and SSIM.

Mean Square Error (MSE).
This tests the quality of a stego image by determining the variation amid the concealment object and the stego image [45].

$$MSE = \frac{1}{mn} \sum\nolimits_{0}^{m-1} \sum\nolimits_{0}^{n-1} c - s^2 \tag{1}$$

m and n are the entered images number of rows and columns correspondingly, C is the cover-object while S is the stego-image.

Peak Signal to Noise Ratio (PSNR).
The PSNR calculates the rate at which the encoded information in the decibel (dB) variable distorts a stego-image as a result. A more excellent PSNR value represents the advanced stego-image efficiency and is measured as [46].

$$PSNR = 10 log\left(\frac{255^2}{MSE}\right) \tag{2}$$

Where 255 is the utmost pixel value in both stego-image plus concealment object.

Structural Similarity Index (SSIM).
SSIM contrasts two equivalent pictures using their configurations to values ranging from -1 to 1. The closest the SSIM is to 1 the. The resemblance between the two images given and is determined [47].

5.1   Comparative Evaluation

Three qualitative evaluation metrics were used for the comparative analysis with previous researches, and these were used in comparing with two earlier pieces of research which are Younus & Hussain, 2019, and Bhardwaj & Sharma, 2016.

Table 1. Comparative analysis of the developed system with previous works

Methods	Payload	PSNR value	MSE value	SSIM value
Younus & Hussain [2]	32.768 bytes	58.12	——	——
Bhardwaj & Sharma [48]	24.964 bytes	51.98	0.2499	——
Proposed System	32.768 bytes	82.35	0.0744	0.99

Table 1 illustrates the values of PSNR, MSE, and SSIM for Younus & Hussain, (2019), Bhardwaj & Sharma, (2016), and the proposed system. It displays the value of payload, PNSR value, MSE value, and SSIM. Consequently, it was deduced that the PSNR value is higher than 30 which is 82.35 and the MSE value is increased with 0.0744, which signifies that the suggested approach is ideal at entrenching the medical image inside the concealment object by implanting a considerable quantity of medical images within it and maintaining the concealment object quality. The SSIM value is similar to 1, which means that the stego image is the same as the initial concealment image of good quality.

6   Conclusion

The critical aim of steganography techniques is to hide a vast volume of details within an image without compromising the appearance of the picture. The robustness and reliability of these systems also offer protection against cyber threats. For this study, an innovative technique was recommended, which is the circular shift (Modified LSB) steganography technique to mask the medical image within cover images. The proposed scheme was tested utilizing PSNR, MSE, and SSIM to determine the consistency and utilizing the embedding degree to exam the payload. The analytical findings indicate that the suggested scheme's efficiency and payload are higher than conventional approaches. Furthermore, the protection and robustness of the presented process were considered to be satisfactory in the face of electronic attacks. The system can be checked in future works by producing other electronic threats, and other techniques can be used for random selection as well.

References

1. Attaby, A.A., Ahmed, M.F.M.M., Alsammak, A.K.: Data hiding inside JPEG images with high resistance to steganalysis using a novel technique: DCT-M3. Ain Shams Eng. J. **9**, 1965–1974 (2018). https://doi.org/10.1016/j.asej.2017.02.003

2. Younus Z.S., Hussain, M.K.: Image steganography using exploiting modification direction for compressed, encrypted data. Journal of King Saud University–Computer and Information Sciences, an article in press (2019). https://doi.org/10.1016/j.jksuci.2019.04.008

3. Morkel, T., Eloff, J., Olivier, M.: An overview of image steganography. In: Proceedings of the Fifth Annual Information Security South Africa Conference (ISSA2005), Sandston, South Africa (2005)

4. Rehman, A., Alqahtani, S., Altameem, A., Saba, T.: Virtual machine security challenges: case studies. Int. J. Mach. Learn. Cybern. **5**(5), 729–742 (2013). https://doi.org/10.1007/s13042-013-0166-4

5. Kumar, V., Kumar, D.: Performance evaluation of modified colour image steganography using discrete wavelet transform. J. Intell. Syst. (2017). https://doi.org/10.1515/jisys-2017-0134

6. Younus, Z.S., Younus, G.T.: Video steganography using knight tour algorithm and LSB method for encrypted data. J. Intell. Syst. (2019) https://doi.org/10.1515/jisys-2018-0225

7. Habibi, M., Karimi, R., Nosrati, M.: Using SFLA and LSB for text message steganography in 24-bit RGB colour images. Int. J. Eng. **2**(3), 68–75 (2013)

8. Tejeshwar, G.: Colour image steganography using LZW compression and fisher-yates shuffle algorithm. Int. J. Innovative Res. Dev. **3**(6), 54–61 (2014)

9. Ranjani, J.J.: Data hiding using pseudo magic squares for embedding high payload in digital images. Multimedia Tools Appl. **76**(3), 3715–3729 (2016). https://doi.org/10.1007/s11042-016-3974-1

10. Taha, A., Hammad, A., Selim, M.: A high capacity algorithm for information hiding in Arabic text. Journal of King Saud University, pp. 1–8 (2018) https://doi.org/10.1016/j.jksuci.2018.07.007

11. Kalra, M., Singh, P.: EMD techniques of image steganography a comparative study. Int. J. Technol. Explor. Learn. **3**(2), 385–390 (2014)

12. Hashim, M., Rahim, M.: Image steganography based on odd/even pixels distribution scheme and two parameters random function. J. Theor. Appl. Inf. Technol. **95**(22), 5977–5986 (2017)

13. Christiana, A.O., Oluwatobi, A.N., Victory, G.A., Oluwaseun, O.R.: A secured one time password authentication technique using (3, 3) visual cryptography scheme. J. Phys. Conf. Ser. **1299**(1), 012059 (2019)

14. Marvel, Jr, Boncelet, C., Retter, C.: Spread spectrum image steganography. IEEE Trans. Image Process. **8**, 1075–83 (1999)

15. Akande, N.O., Abikoye, C.O., Adebiyi, M.O., Kayode, A.A., Adegun, A.A., Ogundokun, R. O.: Electronic medical information encryption using modified blowfish algorithm. In: Misra, S. (ed.) ICCSA 2019. LNCS, vol. 11623, pp. 166–179. Springer, Cham (2019). https://doi.org/10.1007/978-3-030-24308-1_14

16. Memon N, Chandramouli R. Analysis of LSB based image steganography techniques. In: Proceedings of IEEE ICIP (2001)

17. Abikoye, O.C., Ojo, U.A., Awotunde, J.B., Ogundokun, R.O.: A safe and secured iris template using steganography and cryptography. Multimedia Tools and Appl. **79**(31), 23483–23506 (2020). https://doi.org/10.1007/s11042-020-08971-x

18. Marvel, Jr, Boncelet, C., Retter, C.: Spread spectrum image steganography. IEEE Trans. Image Process. **8** 1075–83 (1999)
19. Memon N, Chandramouli R.: Analysis of LSB based image steganography techniques. In: Proceedings of IEEE ICIP (2001)
20. Morimoto, N., Bender, W., Gruhl, D., Lu, A.: Techniques for data hiding. IBM Syst. J. **35**, 313–316 (1996)
21. Doerr, G., Dugelay, J.L.: Security pitfalls of frame-by-frame approaches to video watermarking. IEEE Trans. Signal Process. Suppl. Secure. Media **52**, 2955–2964 (2004)
22. Gopalan K.: Audio steganography using bit modification. In: Proceedings of the IEEE International Conference on Acoustics, Speech, and Signal Processing (ICASSP '03), vol. 2 (6), pp. 421–24 (2003)
23. Anderson, R., Petitcolas, F.: On the limits of steganography. IEEE J. Select Areas Commun. (J-SAC) **16**, 474–481 (1998)
24. Kutade, P., Bhalotra, P.: A survey on various approaches of image steganography. Int. J. Comput. Appl. **109**(3), 1–5 (2015)
25. Prajapati, H., Chitaliya, N.: Secure and robust dual image steganography: a survey. Int. J. Innovative Res. Comput. Commun. Eng. **3**(1), 534–542 (2015)
26. Kalaivanan, S., Ananth, V., Manikandan, T.: A survey on digital image steganography. Int. J. Emerg. Trends Technol. Comput. Sci. **4**(1), 30–33 (2015)
27. Hussain, M., Hussain, M.: A survey of image steganography techniques. Int. J. Adv. Sci. Technol **54**, 113–124 (2013)
28. Idakwo, M.A., Muazu, M.B., Adedokun, E.A., Sadiq, B.O.: An extensive survey of digital image steganography: state of the art. J. Sci. Technol. Edu. **8**(2), 40–54 (2020)
29. Chang, C., Tai, W., Chen, K.: Improvements in EMD embedding for large payloads. In: Third International Conference on International Information Hiding and Multimedia Signal Processing (IIH-MSP 2007), pp. 473–476. ACM (2007)
30. Cheddad, A., Condell, J., Curran, K., McKevitt, P.: Digital image steganography: survey and analysis of current methods. Signal Process. **90**, 727–752 (2010). https://doi.org/10.1016/j.sigpro.2009.08.010
31. Maniriho, P., Ahmad, T.: Information hiding scheme for digital images using difference expansion and modulus function. J. King Saud Univ.-Comput. Inf. Sci. 1–13 (2018). https://doi.org/10.1016/j.jksuci.2018.01.011
32. Chan, C., Cheng, L.: Hiding data in images by simple LSB substitution. Pattern Recogn. **37**, 469–474 (2004). https://doi.org/10.1016/j.patcog.2003.08.007
33. Shjul, A., Kulkarni, U.: A secure skin tone based steganography using wavelet transform. Int. J. Comput. Theory Eng. **3**(1), 16–22 (2011)
34. Zhang, X., Wang, S.: Efficient stenographic embedding by exploiting modification direction. IEEE Commun. Lett. **10**(11), 781–783 (2006). https://doi.org/10.1109/LCOMM.2006.060863
35. Lee, C., Wang, Y., Chang, C.: A steganography method with high capacity by improving exploiting modification direction. In: IEEE Third International Conference on Intelligent Information Hiding and Multimedia Signal Processing (IIHMSP), pp. 497–500. (2007) https://doi.org/10.1109/IIH-MSP.2007.62
36. Jung, K., Yoo, K.: Improved exploiting modification direction method by modulus operation. Int. J. Signal Process. Image Process. Pattern. **2**(1), 79–87 (2009)
37. Lin, K., Hong, W., Chen, J., Chen, T., Chiang, W., n et al. Data hiding by exploiting the modification direction technique using optimal pixel grouping. In: IEEE 2010 2nd international Conference on Education Technology and Computer (ICETC) (2010). https://doi.org/10.1109/ICETC.2010.5529581

38. Mohsin, A.T.: A New Steganography Technique Using Knight's Tour Algorithm, Affine Cipher, And Huffman Coding (Master Thesis). Faculty of Computer Science and Information Systems, Universiti Teknologi Malaysia (2013)
39. Ahmad, A., Sulong, G., Rehman, A., Alkawaz, M., Saba, T.: Data hiding based on improved exploiting modification direction method and huffman coding. J. Intell. Syst. **23**(4), 451–459 (2014). https://doi.org/10.1515/jisys-2014-0007
40. Lee, C., Chang, C., Pai, P., Liu, C.: Adjustment hiding method based on exploiting modification direction. Int. J. Netw. Secur. **17**(5), 607–618 (2015)
41. Alsaffawi, Z.S.Y.: Image steganography by using exploiting modification direction and knight tour algorithm. J. Al-Qadissiya Comput. Sci. Math. **8**(1), 1–11 (2016)
42. Saha, S., Ghosal, S., Chakraborty, A., Dhargupta, S., Sarkar, R., Mandal, J.: Improved exploiting modification direction-based steganography using dynamic weightage array. Electron. Lett. **54**(8), 498–500 (2018). https://doi.org/10.1049/el.2017.3336
43. Walia, G.S., Makhija, S., Singh, K., Sharma, K.: Robust stego-key directed LSB substitution scheme based upon the cuckoo search and chaotic map. Optik **170**, 106–124 (2018)
44. Preishuber, M., Hütter, T., Katzenbeisser, S., Uhl, A.: Depreciating motivation and empirical security analysis of chaos-based image and video encryption. IEEE Trans. Inf. Forensics Secur. **13**(9), 2137–2150 (2018)
45. Atawneh, S., Almomani, A., Al Bazar, H., Sumari, P., Gupta, B.: Secure and imperceptible digital image steganographic algorithm based on diamond encoding in the DWT domain. Multimedia Tools Appl. **76**(18), 18451–18472 (2017). https://doi.org/10.1007/s11042-016-3930-0
46. Wang, Z., Zhang, X., Yin, Z.: Joint cover-selection and payload allocation by steganographic distortion optimization. IEEE Signal Process. Lett. **25**(10), 1530–1534 (2018)
47. Kumar, V., Kumar, D.: A modified DWT-based image steganography technique. Multimedia Tools Appl. **77**(11), 13279–13308 (2017). https://doi.org/10.1007/s11042-017-4947-8
48. Bhardwaj, R., Sharma, V.: Image steganography based on complemented message and inverted bit LSB substitution. Procedia Comput. Sci. **93**, 832–838 (2016). https://doi.org/10.1016/j.procs.2016.07.245
49. Christiana, A.O., Oluwatobi, A.N., Victory, G.A., Oluwaseun, O.R.: A secured one time password authentication technique using (3, 3) visual cryptography scheme. In: Journal of Physics: Conference Series, vol. 1299, no. 1, p. 012059, IOP Publishing (2019)
50. Abikoye, O.C., Akande, N.O., Garuba, A.V., Ogundokun, R.O.: A secured one time password authentication technique using (3, 3) visual cryptography scheme (2019)

A New Text Independent Speaker Recognition System with Short Utterances Using SVM

Rania Chakroun[1,3(✉)] and Mondher Frikha[1,2]

[1] Advanced Technologies for Image and Signal Processing (ATISP) Research Unit, Sfax, Tunisia
chakrounrania@yahoo.fr
[2] National School of Electronics and Telecommunications of Sfax, Sakiet Ezzit, Tunisia
[3] National School of Engineering of Sfax, Sfax, Tunisia

Abstract. Recent advances in the field of speaker recognition have proved to highly outperform algorithms. However this performance degrades when limited data are presented. This paper presents examples on how Support Vector Machines (SVM) can improve speaker recognition for short utterance data duration. The main contribution in this approach is the use of new vectors when training and testing data are limited. We show how different kernels function of SVM can be used to validate the new approach with different speakers from different databases.

Keywords: Speaker recognition · Speaker verification · Speaker identification · SVM

1 Introduction

Biometric systems are essentially pattern recognition systems which operate by acquiring biometric data from an individual. Instead of the use of passwords and PIN codes which can be forgotten or stolen or using signatures which can be easily forged, body characteristics such as voice, face, fingerprints and gait have been considered as discriminative features which cannot be easily stolen or forged [1]. Human relationships are essentially based on communication between individuals. The speech in both its written and spoken form supports all aspects of human interactions. In fact, individuals can communicate with one another employing only the human vocal apparatus. Hence, the acoustic signal of human speech carries not only what is being said but also embodies individual characteristics of the speaker such as speaking styles, the speaker specific characteristics and emotions, the speaker accent, the state of health of the speaker, transmission channel properties,…etc. Every person possesses a unique voice and even when the same person says the same words, the resulting sounds can't be identical. Among the important directions in speech analysis research we find the field

---

R. Chakroun—No academic titles or descriptions of academic positions should be included in the addresses. The affiliations should consist of the author's institution, town, and country.

© Springer Nature Switzerland AG 2020
M. Themistocleous et al. (Eds.): EMCIS 2020, LNBIP 402, pp. 566–574, 2020.
https://doi.org/10.1007/978-3-030-63396-7_38

of speaker recognition. This domain has received much attention from the scientific community since many years up to the present day. Indeed, the most used in society and least importunate biometric measure is that of human speech.

In this article, we refer to speaker recognition systems which utilize human speech to recognize an individual [2]. In the past decade, numerous speaker recognition algorithms have been developed in literature [3]. However, the performances of these speaker recognition systems have usually been drastically degraded when limited data are presented.

To decrease the problem of speaker recognition based on short utterances, this article introduces a new robust speaker recognition system, which is based on new cepstral features combining between the well known state of the art Mel Frequency Cepstral Coefficients (MFCC) [3, 22] together with new robust features called Power Normalized Cepstral coefficients (PNCC) that proves to be lately efficient and successful for speech and speaker recognition applications [31–34]. We evaluate the effectiveness of these combined features on speakers taken from TIMIT [16] and VoxCeleb2 [15] databases.

The rest of this paper is organized as follows. In Sect. 2, Support Vector Machines technique is explained, Sect. 3 describe related works in speaker recognition field and explain the utility of the proposed approach, experimental protocol is presented in Sect. 4, Experimental results are demonstrated in Sect. 5 and conclusions are drawn in Sect. 6.

2   Support Vector Machines

2.1   Linear Support Vector Machines

An SVM is a classifier based on hyperplane separators. Considering the problem of separating a set of m training vectors $S = \{\{(x_i, y_i)\}$, where $x_i \in R^n$ is a vector of features, $y_i \in \{1, -1\}$ is a class label and i = $\{1,...,m\}$, into two different classes, with a separating hyperplane having the following equation:

$$wx + b = 0 \tag{1}$$

This hyperplane must maximize the margin, that's why it should satisfy the following conditions:

$$y_i(\omega.x_i) + b \geq +1 \forall i \in \{1,...,m\} \tag{2}$$

The best separating hyperplane must maximize the margin M given by the equation:

$$M = \frac{2}{\|\omega\|} \tag{3}$$

In fact, the optimal hyperplane is the one that minimizes:

$$\phi(\omega) = \frac{1}{2}\omega.\omega \tag{4}$$

2.2 Non-linear Support Vector Machines

When the set of training vectors of two classes are non-linearly separable, Cortes and Vapnik [8] use new variables ξ_i to measure the miss-classification errors, with $\xi_i >= 0$.

For the solution of the optimisation problem, a minimization of the classification error is needed [9]. The optimal hyperplane must satisfy the following inequalities:

$$(\omega.x_i) + b \geq +1 - \xi_i, \text{ si } y_i = +1 \tag{5}$$

$$(\omega.x_i) + b \leq -1 + \xi_i, \text{ si } y_i = -1 \tag{6}$$

In this case, the optimal hyperplane is determined by the vector ω which tries to minimize the following function:

$$\phi(\omega, \xi) = \frac{1}{2}\omega.\omega + C\sum_{i=1}^{m} \xi_i \tag{7}$$

Where $\xi = (\xi_i, \ldots, \xi_m)$ and C are constants.

2.3 Kernel Support Vector Machines

When a linear boundary is inappropriate, the principle of the SVM consists in throwing the learning vectors in a high dimensional space to be able to find an optimal hyperplan.

SVM replaces the input data (x_i, x_j) with a kernel function $K(x_i, x_j)$ to constructs an optimal hyperplane in the new space. The kernel function maps the input data via an associated function Φ into a high dimensional feature space in which the mapped data can be separated linearly.

Although the existence of different kernel functions, the following functions are the most known:

- Linear: $K(x_i, x_j) = x_i^T x_j$
- Polynomial: $K(x_i, x_j) = (\gamma x_i^T x_j + r)^d, \gamma > 0$.
- Radial Basis Function (RBF): $K(x_i, x_j) = \exp(-\gamma \|x_i - x_j\|^2), \gamma > 0$.

Where γ, r and d are kernel parameters.

3 Related Works

For classification problems, we find that most paradigms referred to one of two families: generative models such as Gaussian Mixture Models (GMM) or discriminative classifiers like SVM. The generative models need only to train data samples from the class or target speaker and make a statistical model which describes the target speaker distribution. However, discriminative classifiers require training data for both the target and imposter speakers and generating an optimal separation between the different speakers.

Most of state-of-the-art speaker recognition systems depend on the generative training of GMM. In fact, the problem has traditionally been interpreted by directly modelling the spectral content of the speech with GMM [10]. However, the generative training of the Gaussian mixture models doesn't directly optimize the classification performance. That's why it was interesting to develop alternative discriminative approaches which address directly the classification problem [11, 12]. Some other latest works recur to the use of the neural networks technique [4]. In fact, deep neural networks (DNN) have been used for speaker verification systems [4–7].

Popular in the recent advances in speaker recognition field, the increasing adoption of SVMs, which have demonstrated to be a novel effective method for speaker recognition applications [13], [26–30]. In fact, owing to the kernel which represent the main design component in an SVM, this classifier is able to find an appropriate metric in the SVM feature space relevant to the classification problem [14]. Generally, these systems conduct to comparable or superior performances than generative methods with much less training data.

Even so, most techniques have been applied to related problems such as speaker verification, and there is a lack of effective recognition method for the short utterance text independent speaker identification task.

For speaker recognition applications, the process of feature extraction presents another fundamental phase for speaker recognitions. Indeed, this step is essential to capture the speaker specific characteristics [23]. State of the art applications use appropriate features where the most successful are the Linear Prediction Coefficients (LPCs) [17], Perceptual Linear Prediction (PLP) coefficients [20], and the latest successful and well known are spectral features which have become popular are the MFCCs Coefficients. They allow obtaining high level of performance due to the use of perceptually based Mel spaced filter bank processing of the Fourier Transform and the particular robustness to the environment and flexibility that can be achieved using cepstral analysis [3, 22].

Recently the use of the PNCC coefficients proves a great efficiency in the domain of speech recognition and also for speaker recognition applications [31–34].

In this work, we try to enhance the performance of the proposed system by using both combined MFCC and PNCC features. Thus, we profit from the robustness of both features for the task of speaker recognition. The resultant combined feature vectors are evaluated for a speaker identification system when only short utterances are available and the proposed system performance is compared against results obtained with baseline systems.

4 Experiments

4.1 Test Database

We performed our experiments using the TIMIT Dataset. The TIMIT corpus is comprised of recordings of 630 speakers (438 male, 192 female [16]) using eight major dialects of American English. Table 1 illustrates the different dialect region of TIMIT database and their respective code. For each speaker, there are ten different utterances over a clean channel. The dataset contains about 5.25 h of audio file in wav format. The sampling frequency of the utterances is 16 kHz with 16-bit resolution. The recordings are single-channel, and the mean duration of each utterance is 3.28 s.

Table 1. The different dialect regions of TIMIT database.

Dialect region	Code
New England	DR1
Northern	DR2
North Midland	DR3
South Midland	DR4
Southern	DR5
New York City	DR6
Western	DR7
Army Brat	DR8

The second set of experiments is performed using speakers from the VoxCeleb2 database [15]. This corpus contains over a million utterances from a large pool of speakers. TIMIT corpus contains clearly read speech, while VoxCeleb2 has more background noise and overlapping speech.

4.2 Acoustic Features

In our experiments, we used cepstral features extracted from the speech signal using a 25 ms Hamming window with an overlap of 10 ms. 12 MFCC Coefficients together with log energy are calculated every 10 ms. Delta and double delta coefficients were then calculated to obtain a 39-dimensional final vector. This feature vector is the most efficient in the literature [3]. We use also 39-dimensional PNCC feature vectors.

4.3 SVM Systems

The classification is realized with SVM which proved their efficiencies with regard to the other systems of classification in our domain [3, 18].

We used two SVM kernel functions in our experiments. The first one is the linear kernel. The second system uses the radial basis function kernel.

To compare our results with other approaches, we have performed two different kernel systems with low-dimensional vectors and limited training data. In fact, unlike Dehak [19] who used NIST SRE 2006 corpus where the train and test utterances contain 2.5 min of speech on average, we used utterances with a mean duration of about 3 s from TIMIT and VoxCeleb2 databases. Besides, we used MFCC features which prove their efficiency in speaker recognition [3] instead of Linear Frequency Cepstral Coefficients (LFCC) which are widely criticized because of the not linear character of the speech [21]. Moreover, as in [3], we use 39 MFCC features extracted from the speech signal instead of 60-dimensional feature vectors which are almost used in [24, 25].

Referring to the protocol suggested in [3], we use 64 speakers. For TIMIT database, we divide the utterance spoken by each speaker into 8 utterances per speaker for training and 2 utterances for testing. After that we further reduced the training duration and we use only 3 utterances per speaker for training and 2 utterances for testing. For VoxCeleb2 database, the first set of experiments is dealt with about 24 s for training and 6 s for testing. The second set of experiments is dealt with about 10 s for training and 6 s for testing.

5 Results and Discussion

We examine the performance of speaker recognition systems described previously by carrying out experimental evaluations as follows. We use two baseline systems, the first one is based on the use of MFCC features, the second baseline system is based on the use of PNCC features, and the proposed system is based on both combined MFCC and PNCC features.

The different systems for speaker recognition were implemented and evaluated with a series of experiences. For each kind of kernel, we varied its various parameters to find the values which give the optimal learning. After achieving the phase of learning, we make a set of experiences in the phase of test.

We start by presenting the first set of experiments in Table 2. For TIMIT database, we give the speaker identification rates (IR) found with linear and RBF kernels with 8 utterances per speaker for training and 2 utterances for testing. For VoxCeleb2 database, we give the results obtained with 24 s for training and 6 s for testing

From the experimental results, we notice that the use of the SVM systems with RBF kernel achieves the best identification rates.

If we compare our results to the results obtained with the baseline systems, we can remark that the proposed system outperforms the results obtained with standard MFCC coefficients and PNCC features. In fact the use of combined features allow to obtain 100% of correct identification rates against only 97.66% and 99.22% respectively with PNCC and MFCC features with TIMIT database. The results are also ameliorated for VoxCeleb2 database which attain 93.75% of correct identification rates against only 88.28% and 89.06% respectively with MFCC and PNCC features.

For further comparison, a second set of experiments was developed with shorter training duration. In fact, we use only 3 utterances for training and 2 utterances for

Table 2. Speaker identification rates with SVM-based systems using RBF and linear kernels.

Systems	TIMIT		VoxCeleb2	
	Linear kernel	RBF kernel	Linear kernel	RBF kernel
SVM baseline system with MFCC	92.18	99.22	71.88	88.28
SVM baseline system with PNCC	96.88	97.66	77.34	89.06
SVM proposed system with MFCC-PNCC	98.96	100	82.81	93.75

testing For TIMIT database and about 10 s for training and 6 s for testing with VoxCeleb2 database. The results are illustrated in Table 3.

Table 3. Speaker identification rates with SVM-based systems using RBF and Linear kernels with reduced training duration.

Systems	TIMIT		VoxCeleb2	
	Linear kernel	RBF kernel	Linear kernel	RBF kernel
SVM-baseline system with MFCC	81.25	96.09	70.31	73.44
SVM baseline system with PNCC	86.72	96.88	71.88	78.13
SVM proposed system with MFCC-PNCC	94.53	98.43	79.69	90.63

The results obtained highlight the influence of the use of short utterances in our system with limited data in the training phase. Compared to the results obtained with baseline approaches, it is clear to remark that the proposed features outperform the standard ones and allow obtaining 98.43% of correct identification rates with the RBF kernel against only 96.88% and 96.09% respectively with PNCC and MFCC coefficients. The same remark is also validated with VoxCeleb2 database which attain 90.63% of correct identification rates against only 73.44% and 78.13% respectively with MFCC and PNCC coefficients.

6 Conclusions and Perspectives

In this paper, we present a new enhanced system based on the SVM approach for speaker recognition task. This system has focused on the formulation of new features looking for recognizing speakers with much reduced information. In fact we don't need to use additional training dataset as in traditional algorithms. Besides, we don't require incorporating further complex algorithms. We plan the proposed features with other approaches under different conditions.

References

1. Jain, A., Ross, A., Prabhakar, S.: An introduction to biometric recognition. IEEE Trans. Circ. Syst. Video Technol. **14**(1), 4–20 (2004)
2. Reynolds, D.: An overview of automatic speaker recognition technology. In: Proceedings of IEEE International Conference Acoustics Speech Signal Processing (ICASSP), vol. 4, pp. 4072–4075 (2002)
3. Togneri, R., Pullella, D.: An overview of speaker identification: accuracy and robustness issues. In: IEEE Circuits And Systems Magazine, vol. 11, no. 2, pp. 23–61 (2011) ISSN: 1531-636X
4. Snyder, D., Ghahremani, P., Povey, D., Garcia-Romero, D., Carmiel, Y., Khudanpur, S.: Deep neural network-based speaker embeddings for end-to-end speaker verification. In: 2016 IEEE Spoken Language Technology Workshop (SLT), pp. 165–170. IEEE (December 2016)
5. Zhang, S.X, Chen, Z., Zhao, Y., Li, J., Gong, Y.: End-to-end attention based text-dependent speaker verification. arXiv preprint arXiv:1701.00562 (2017)
6. Variani, E., Lei, X., McDermott, E., Moreno, I.L., Gonzalez-Dominguez, J.: Deep neural networks for small footprint textdependent speaker verification. In: 2014 IEEE international conference on acoustics, speech and signal processing (ICASSP), pp. 4052–4056. IEEE (2014)
7. Heigold, G., Moreno, I., Bengio, S., Shazeer, N.: End-to-endtext-dependent speaker verification. In: 2016 IEEE international conference on Acoustics, speech and signal processing (ICASSP), pp 5115–5119. IEEE (2016)
8. Cortes, C., Vapnick, V.: Support vector networks. Mach. Learn. **20**, 1–25 (1995)
9. Kamppari, S.O., Hazen, T. J.: Word and phone level acoustic confidence scoring. In: Proceedings of IEEE International Conference on Acoustics, Speech, and Signal Processing (2000)
10. Reynolds, D.A., Quatieri, T.F., Dunn, R.: Speaker verification using adapted gaussian mixture models. Digital Signal Process. **10**(1–3), 19–41 (2000)
11. Keshet, J., Bengio, S.: Automatic Speech and Speaker Recognition: Large Margin and Kernel Methods. Wiley, Hoboken (2009)
12. Louradour, J., Daoudi, K., Bach, F.: Feature space mahalanobis sequence kernels: application to svm speaker verification. IEEE Trans. Audio Speech Lang. Process. **15**(8), 2465–2475 (2007)
13. Campbell, W.M.: Generalized linear discriminant sequence kernels for speaker recognition. In: Proceedings of the International Conference on Acoustics Speech and Signal Processing. pp. 161–164 (2002)
14. Campbell, W.M., Sturim, D.E., Reynolds, D.A.: Support vector machine using GMM supervectors for speaker verification. IEEE Signal Process. Lett. **13**(5), 308–311 (2006)
15. Chung, J.S., Nagrani, A., Zisserman, A.: Voxceleb2: deepspeaker recognition. In: Proceedings of Interspeech 2018, pp. 1086–1090 (2018)
16. Reynolds, D.A.: Automatic speaker recognition using gaussian mixture speaker models. Lincoln Lab. J. **8**(2), 173–192 (1995)
17. Atal, B.: Effectiveness of linear prediction characteristics of the speech wave for automatic speaker identification and verification. J. Acoust. Soc. Am. **55**, 1304 (1974)
18. Jourani, R. Reconnaissance automatique du locuteur par des GMM à grande marge", UT3 Paul Sabatier (2012)

19. Dehak, R., Dehak, N., Kenny, P., Dumouchel, P.: Linear and non linear kernel GMM supervector machines for speaker verification. In: Proceedings of Interspeech, Antwerp, Belgium, pp. 302–305 (2007)
20. Mammone, R., Zhang, X., Ramachandran, R.: Robust speaker recognition: a feature-based approach. IEEE Signal Process. Mag. 13(5), 58–71 (1996)
21. Pitsikalis, V., Maragos, P.: Some advances on speech analysis using generalized dimensions. In: ISCA Tutorial and Research Workshop on Non-Linear Speech Processing (NOLISP) (2003)
22. Poddar, A., Sahidullah, M., Saha, G.: Speaker verification with short utterances: a review of challenges, trends and opportunities. IET Biometrics 7(2), 91–101 (2017)
23. Chakroun, R., Frikha, M.: Robust features for text-independent speaker recognition with short utterances. Neural Comput. Appl. 32(17), 13863–13883 (2020). https://doi.org/10. 1007/s00521-020-04793-y
24. Dehak, N., Karam, Z., Reynolds, D., Dehak, R., Campbell, W., Glass, J.: A channel-blind system for speaker verification. In: Proceedings of ICASSP, pp. 4536–4539, Prague, Czech Republic, May 2011
25. Dehak, N., Kenny, P., Dehak, R., Dumouchel, P., Ouellet, P.: Front-end factor analysis for speaker verification. IEEE Trans. Audio Speech Lang. Process. 19(4), 788–798 (2011)
26. Zhang, W.Q., Zhao, J., Zhang, W.L., et al.: Multi-scale kernels for short utterance speaker recognition. In: Proceedings of ISCSLP 2014, pp. 414–417
27. McLaren, M., Matrouf, D., Vogt, R., Bonastre, J.-F.: Applying svms and weight-based factor analysis to unsupervised adaptation for speaker verification. Comput. Speech Lang. 25(2), 327–340 (2011)
28. Rao, W., Mak, M.W.: Construction of discriminative kernels from known and unknown non-targets for PLDA-SVM scoring. In: 2014 IEEE international conference on acoustics, speech and signal processing (ICASSP), pp. 4012–4016. IEEE (2014 May)
29. Chakroun, R., Frikha, M.: New approach for short utterance speaker identification. IET Signal Process. 12(7), 873–880 (2018)
30. Chakroun, R., Frikha, M.: Efficient text-independent speaker recognition with short utterances in both clean and uncontrolled environments. Multimedia Tools Appl. 79, 21279–21298 (2020). https://doi.org/10.1007/s11042-020-08824-7
31. Kim, C., Stern, R.M.: Power-normalized cepstral coefficients (PNCC) for robust speech recognition. IEEE/ACM Trans. Audio Speech Lang. Process. 24(7), 1315–1329 (2016)
32. Nayana, P. K., Mathew, D., Thomas, A.: Performance comparison of speaker recognition systems using GMM and i-vector methods with PNCC and RASTA PLP features. In: 2017 International Conference on Intelligent Computing, Instrumentation and Control Technologies (ICICICT), pp. 438–443. IEEE (2017 July)
33. Al-Kaltakchi, M.T., Woo, W.L., Dlay, S.S., Chambers, J.A.: Study of fusion strategies and exploiting the combination of MFCC and PNCC features for robust biometric speaker identification. In: 2016 4th International Conference on Biometrics and Forensics (IWBF), pp. 1–6. IEEE (March 2016)
34. Shi, X.Y., Jing, X.X., Zeng, M., Yang, H.Y.: Robust speaker recognition based on improved PNCC and i-vector. Comput. Eng. Des. 4, 42 (2017)

Innovative Research Projects

Artificial Intelligence for Air Safety

Rajesh Gandadharan Pillai$^{(\boxtimes)}$, Poonam Devrakhyani, Sathvik Shetty,
and Deepak Munji

Toulouse Business School, Place Alphonse Jourdian, Cedex 7,
CS 66810 Toulouse, France
{r.gangadharan.pillai, p.devrakhyani,
s.shetty, d.munji}@tbs-education.org

Abstract. Safety is a vital aspect of aviation industry, and emphasis has been made by all stakeholders in the industry to ensure aviation safety. Strict safety and regulatory procedures are adapted during all phases of aviation including design and development, manufacturing, operations, maintenance and ground services. Still, accidents and incidents persist in aviation, resulting in loss of human life and huge losses to airlines and aircraft OEMs. Artificial intelligence is an evolving domain, which has gained lot of importance during the last decade, predominantly due the capacity of AI systems to handle and process huge amount of data and implement complex algorithms. This paper is indented to improve the aviation safety with the prudent use of artificial intelligence. The paper focuses on how the effects of the factors like pilot fatigue, adverse weather and false warnings, which affect aviation safety, can be mitigated with the use of artificial intelligence.

Keywords: Artificial intelligence · Machine learning · Smart cockpit assistant · Aviation safety

1 Introduction and Applications of AI in Aviation

Artificial intelligence is a topic, gaining popularity across industries and has a lot of applications in the aviation domain. The concept of AI has originated in 1950s, but the influence of AI has increased recently due to its improved capabilities.

With technologies like Micro Electro Mechanical Systems (MEMS) in sensors and Very Large-Scale Integration (VLSI) in the semiconductors, terabytes of data can be collected and easily stored. Powerful data processing algorithms have evolved for digital signals, image & speech processing that can efficiently process complex data. The advanced control systems are capable of executing complex nonlinear controls at near to real time conditions. The data communication techniques have advanced and now terabytes of data can be shared securely between stakeholders. With all these evolutions & capabilities, AI can influence the aviation industry in an emphatic way. Artificial intelligence has a lot of applications in the aviation industry and can be used in design & development, production, operations, maintenance and customer support [1].

In design, the future of aviation will be unmanned vehicles powered by AI techniques like machine learning and deep learning. The use of AI has already started in

M. Themistocleous et al. (Eds.): EMCIS 2020, LNBIP 402, pp. 577–594, 2020.
https://doi.org/10.1007/978-3-030-63396-7_39

military aviation and unmanned aerial vehicles are performing tasks that are dull, dirty and dangerous with less human involvement. The stringent regulatory requirements of civil aviation have not allowed artificial intelligence into flying activities yet.AI has huge potential in air traffic management, and can reduce the workload of pilots and air traffic controllers [2]. AI algorithms can be used to predict flight delays, trajectory prediction [3] and improving wake separation during landing and enhanced airspace management [4]. AI can be very useful in Customer Relationship Management, where a customer receives better service with AI tools [5]. Airports can use intelligent techniques like face recognition for passenger check-in. With AI, the maintenance concept of aircraft can change from time-based maintenance, where the aircraft goes for maintenance at scheduled intervals, to condition based maintenance, where the aircraft goes for maintenance when a failure is predicted. This paradigm shift, powered by AI tools can improve the availability of aircraft for flying and reduce the downtime.

Application of AI for aviation safety is a very less investigated topic, but with its immense capabilities, AI can definitely improve aviation safety. This paper provides the insights towards the improvement of air safety with the prudent use of artificial intelligence.

2   Research Methodology

Air, safety, which affects all stakeholders in aviation despite advancements in technologies, is a significant concern in aviation. The authentic air accident and incident data, required for the research was collected from sources like National Transportation Safety Board (NTSB). Qualitative studies were carried out to find the practical problems affecting aviation safety, with interviews with pilots and maintenance technicians. Interviews were conducted with test pilots, who fly the experimental prototypes to understand how efficiently they handle an emergency situation compared to commercial pilots. The pilot workload was accessed with the help of standard operating procedures from aircraft manuals and correlated with the flying experience of one of the authors. Scope of artificial intelligence in the problem was worked out by brainstorming and literature surveys. A potential solution for the factors that affect safety was conceptualized be the professional experience of the researchers and concepts of artificial intelligence. The onboard system architecture were conceptualized & validated by professional experience of the authors in design and development of aircraft systems. The research methodology adapted is described in Fig. 1. The core idea of the research was to provide a concept based on Artificial Intelligence that can be further developed by extensive research and retrofitted on the aircrafts to enhance air safety in a cost effective way.

3   Air Safety

Safety is generally considered as a technical parameter, but in reality, is it is a factor affecting every stakeholder of the industry. The International Civil Aviation Organization, (ICAO) the apex body of international air transport, states "one of the key

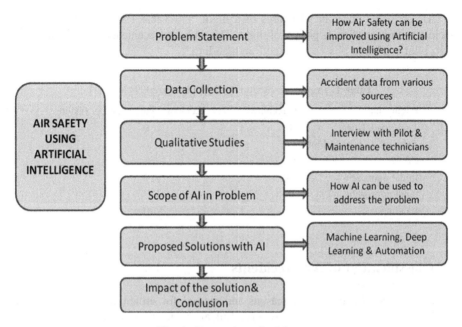

Fig. 1. Research methodology

elements to maintaining the vitality of civil aviation is to ensure safe, secure, efficient and environmentally sustainable operations at the global, regional and national levels." An accident can affect designers, aircraft & equipment manufacturers, regulatory authorities, airlines and ultimately, the passengers. Figure 2 shows the accidents, fatal accidents & fatalities in civil aviation from 2014 to 2018.

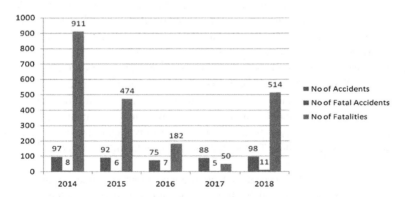

Fig. 2. Number of air accidents, fatal accidents and fatalities

Despite the advances in technology and use of modern aircrafts, 98 accidents occurred in scheduled commercial air transport operations in year 2018. Out of these 11 of the accidents were fatal and has resulted in 514 fatalities in the year 2018 [6].

Air accidents occur in all phases of a flight, and Table 1 shows summary of air accidents during different phases of flight. This indicates accidents occur more during high pilot workload phases of takeoff and landing.

Table 1. Air accidents during flight phases, 2009–2018 [7]

Flight phase	Percentage of fatal accidents	Percentage of fatalities
Taxi/Load/Tow	10	0
Take off & Initial climb	12	6
Cruise	14	31
Initial approach	4	12
Final approach	25	27
Landing	24	10

4 Classification of Air Accidents

Accidents happen due to many reasons and reasons for some crashes like Malaysian Airlines MH 370 still remains mystery. But air accidents have evolved over time. During the initial phases of aviation, the aircrafts consisted of more of mechanical systems with linkages and parts which were prone to failure and less electronics. So, the accidents in the early stages of aviation were mostly machine faults. With the advances in electronics, the aviation has changed drastically and with technologies like fly by wire, there are hardly any mechanical linkages in the aircraft. The modern era aircraft is a complex machine with sensors, microprocessors and data communication systems. The level of sophistication in the aircraft has made the machine safer and reliable, but still the accidents continue. In many cases, the complexity of the machine is more than what an average human brain can adapt and has resulted in accidents. As per analysis carried by Boeing, machine faults resulted in 80% of accidents during the beginning of the century, but with evolution of technology, human errors cause 80% of the accidents [8].

In addition to human faults and machine faults, weather plays an important role in air accidents. The weather at 40,000 feet altitudes is unpredictable with endless air movements. Tornados, ice, thunderstorms, lightning, hail, clear air turbulence, volcanic ashes are a few of the weather hazards that have caused losses in aviation. Aviators still consider weather as a major threat to aviation safety, apart from the human and machine faults. Some of these factors are mitigated with the use of advanced weather radars (Fig. 3).

Figure 4 shows the major weather factors contributing to incidents during different flight phases. Visibility (caused by fog, heavy rain or snowfall) is the most critical factor for accidents during the takeoff, climb and landing phases, where the terrain is much closer to the aircraft. Rain is the second major factor in the take-off, approach and landing phases. Clear Air Turbulence has effect during the cruise phase only.

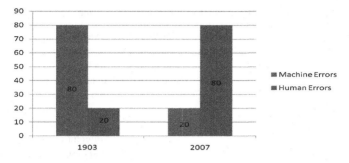

Fig. 3. Evolution of aircraft accidents

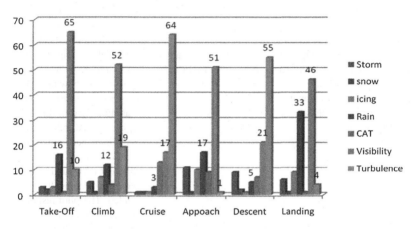

Fig. 4. Contribution of weather factors (in percentage) to air accidents for various flight phases 1967–2010 [9]

5 Analysis of Air Accidents

A detailed analysis of few accidents was carried out using the data from National Transportation Safety Board, and other reports published by accident investigation agencies. A brief of the accidents analyzed is provided in Table 2.

The factors contributing to air accidents can be broadly classified into human causes, machine faults and bad weather.

Human Errors

Human errors leading to accidents can be pilot error or the errors made by the maintenance crew. In many instances, like AirAsia 8501 accident, a wrong maintenance action followed by incorrect pilot responses have lead to accidents. To correlate with the accidents occurring at different phases of flight, the pilot workload in the different phases of flight was analyzed. It can be broadly divided into on ground activities, takeoff activities, in flight activities, landing procedures and ground activities after landing. The maximum workload occurs during the takeoff and landing phases and distraction or emergencies during these phases become critical and lead to accidents.

Table 2. Brief of air accidents analyzed

Accident/Incident	Date	Airline	Reason
Ethiopian Airlines flight, Boeing 737 MAX 8, crashed near Ejere, Ethiopia, shortly after takeoff from Addis Ababa Bole International Airport, Ethiopia killing 157 people	March 10, 2019	Ethiopian airlines flight 302	Accident investigation is still under progress. Preliminary data shows an angle of attack sensor error and incorrect pilot response to it. The left and right airspeed readings were showing different readings. The pilot response to the warnings differed from the assumptions of pilot responses made by Boeing during the functional hazard analysis carried out during the design phase
Lion Air flight 610, Boeing 737 MAX 8, crashed in the Java sea shortly after takeoff from Soekarno- Hatta International Airport, Jakarta, Indonesia killing 189 people	Oct 29, 2018	Lion air flight 610	Accident investigation is still under progress. Angle of attack sensor was showing error between the sensors and there was difference in the left and right airspeed indicators. The same issue had happened during the previous flight with a different crew, and pilots flew the aircraft manually and landed. The pilot response to the sensor warning was different in each case [10]
Air Canada flight 759 (Airbus A 320–211) was cleared to land on runway 28R at San Francisco Airport. Instead, it descended to 100 feet on taxiway C and flew over four airplanes were waiting to take off	July 7, 2017	Air Canada flight 759	Flight crew misidentified taxiway C as the intended landing runway. This was result of the crewmembers' lack of awareness and fatigue. The captain and the first officer were fatigued during the flight, being awake for hours and circadian disruption. The first officer, focused on cockpit tasks, couldn't effectively monitor the approach and recognize that the airplane was not aligned with the intended landing runway [11]
Indonesia AirAsia Flight 8501 (Airbus A 320) operated by AirAsia C, a subsidiary of AirAsia was operating from	28 Dec 2014	Air Asia Flight 8501	A soldered electrical connection in the plane's Rudder Travel Limiter Unit was cracked, likely for a year, resulting in

(*continued*)

Table 2. (*continued*)

Accident/Incident	Date	Airline	Reason
Surabaya, Indonesia, to Singapore. During the flight, the aircraft crashed into the Java Sea, killing all 162 people on board			intermittent cockpit warnings. The data indicated this event happened 23 times during a year. But it was solved by resetting the system, rather than identifying the root cause, the solder crack. On the accident day, the warning appeared four times during flight. First three times it was cleared as per procedures. When the warning appeared for the fourth time, captain was frustrated & decided to reset to the Flight Augmentation Computer circuit breakers. He had seen a ground engineer doing this &believed this could be done in flight also, without knowing its repercussion in-flight. The aircraft stalled, lost control and crashed [12]
An airbus A 330–200, flying from Rio de Janeiro to Paris crashed in Atlantic ocean	1 June 2009	Air France AF 447	Pitot probes were blocked by ice in cruise. The crew become progressively de-structured, by warnings likely never understood that it was faced with a "simple" loss of three sources of airspeed information [13]

Even though only 20% of a flight is spent in landing or take-off phase, most fatal accidents happen in these phases. Summary of analysis of pilot errors that have resulted in accidents are summarized in the Table 3.

The findings from the analysis of the accidents are provided below:

- Multiple alerts and indications in the cockpit increase the pilot's workload and make it difficult to identify the high priority procedure. At times, assistance should be provided to pilots to decide on the highest priority action. This is extremely critical during the critical flight phases of takeoff and landing.
- Many warnings that appear in the cockpit are false alarms and it's only the experience and skill of the pilot in analyzing the situation correctly avoids an accident. This is lacked by many new pilots.

Table 3. Crew factors in air accidents [14]

Si no	Factor	Effect
1	Loss of situational awareness	Situational awareness is ability of humans to combine data into meaningful information (perception), understand the meaning of the information (comprehension) and use it to plan the activity (projection). The loss of situational awareness leads to incorrect response to a situation and lead to accidents
2	Spatial disorientation	Spatial disorientation is the inability of the pilot to maintain awareness of his & aircraft's orientation, position and trajectory relative to the earth. Many accidents were results of spatial disorientation
3	Crew fatigue	The crew fatigue can be result of insufficient rest or the end phase of the flight is affected circadian body clock. This prevents the pilot from taking the correct decisions and slower neuro motor response
4	Crew workload	Full attention of the crew is required during takeoff and landing phases. Diversion of attention due to additional work like an emergency increases the pilot workload
5	Incorrect responses	There are cases where crew does not adhere to emergency procedures as suggested by the flight manual and has taken incorrect actions leading to accidents

- Manufacturers assume that pilots respond in the same way to emergency conditions as accessed by the functional hazard analysis carried out during the design, but the combined effect of alerts and indications are sometimes not evaluated. The combined effects might impact pilots' recognition and lead to accidents as seen in many accidents analyzed.
- The circadian body clock does not adapt fully to altered schedules such as night work and the landing phase of a flight may be during the circadian body low, where the ability of the crew to act promptly becomes compromised.

Maintenance Errors

Errors made by the maintenance crew have also resulted in many accidents. The main points evolved from interview of maintenance crew are:

- It is extremely difficult to identify airframe damages that accumulate over a time due to fatigue. It may show up suddenly.
- Engine problems are plenty in aircraft accidents and monitoring of engine is extremely important to avoid unplanned grounding of aircraft.

The major factors for errors from maintenance crew are provided in Table 4.

Bad Weather

Weather in the upper atmosphere is unpredictable and causes accidents resulting in injury to passengers and crew & damage to the aircraft. The occurrence of tornados,

Table 4. Maintenance factors in air accidents

Si no	Factor	Effect
1	Violations	Maintenance staff sometimes does not follow company policies, processes, and procedures while doing a job, which can ultimately result in an accident
2	Memorizing tasks	Memorizing tasks is a common phenomena observed in maintenance. The practice of using the maintenance manuals are not followed by many aircraft maintenance engineers and technicians
3	Un calibrated equipments	Many people use tools and equipments that are not calibrated to standards
4	Organizational pressure	To avoid events like flight cancellations, maintenance actions are compromised, which leads to accidents

turbulence, icing, hails, lightning are frequent in atmosphere. Aircrafts have to fly through these conditions, avoiding the extremes. Severe conditions of rain or hail has resulted in engine power loss, engine flame out, instability, and forced landings. Certain concentrations of rain and hail can be amplified through the engine core at certain combinations of flight speed and engine power resulting in engine anomalies such as surging, power loss, and engine flameout. Modern aircrafts use weather radars to circumvent the unfavorable weather conditions. But the reflectivity of the weather radar depends on the particle size of the object encountered. The reflectivity of radar signals to particles reduces with size of the particle as shown in Fig. 5.

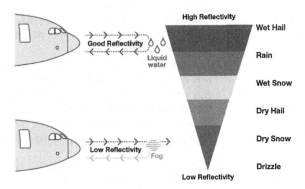

Fig. 5. Aircraft weather radar reflections

The weather radars can inform the pilots about the weather up to 320 nautical miles and provide accurate information up to 40 nautical miles. Weather radars can easily indicate the presence of liquid water. Dry snow, dry hail, drizzles, clear air turbulence and sandstorms are very difficult to identify, which results in accidents or incidents.

6 Potential of Artificial Intelligence in Air Safety

The correlation of the capabilities of AI and its scope in factors causing accidents indicated that AI with its data storage, data analysis and processing algorithms can improve air safety. AI has the capability to predict, remember, make decisions based on data, learn based on the training, analyze data and recognize objects based on training. The capabilities of prediction and recognition can be used to detect pilot fatigue. The analysis capabilities of AI can be very useful in identification of false alarms in the cockpit. The predictive capabilities can be used for predicting the weather, which is not provided by the existing weather radars. The scope is provided briefly in Table 5.

Table 5. Scope of AI in reducing air accidents

Si no	Area	Potential AI tools
1	Pilot fatigue/sleep monitoring	Pilot fatigue and sleep are two factors affecting air safety. Pilot fatigue can be identified by convolution neural networks, trained based on images of the eyes. Machine learning tools can be used to analyze the pilot images, especially of eyes and mouth in real time. The AI module can be trained to identify a potential pilot sleep and provide an alert. Combining images of the pilot with other parameters like circadian body clock, pilot history of sleep incidents as inputs for the model can predict sleep
2	Potential weather impacts on flight	Data can be collected from flights over various conditions like flight over the sea, flight at specific altitudes, flight in icing conditions and flight over volcanic areas. This data can be used to train models, which can predict weather hazards and provide warning to the pilot. Blunt impacts to composite structures from hail are a potential threat and can be avoided by predictions
3	Fault analysis	The experience of a test pilot can be bought in to assist a new un experienced pilot with fault tree analysis. A warning like "The aircraft is flying at 38000 feet above the Atlantic Ocean where chances of ice formation and blockage of Pitot tubes has occurred in the past. A warning of 'incorrect air speed' can appear which is temporary" can be very useful. The conditions in which a maintenance fault can result in a cockpit warning can be studied with the help of historical data. The cause for a warning can be an issue like a dry solder. The AI model has to take the maintenance information carried out on the aircraft. A message like "The aircraft reported issue related to angle of attack sensor during the last two flights, the warning could be result of the recent maintenance action. Fly aircraft manually monitoring other parameters" can be very useful to the pilot

7 AI Based Smart Cockpit Assistant

The concept proposed by this paper is named the "AI powered smart cockpit assistant" which can mitigate few of these hazards. The proposed implementation plan of this on Airbus A 320 is covered under this section.

Airbus A 320 has an Electronic Centralized Aircraft Monitor (ECAM) which gets the information from the various aircraft systems and sensors and displays the information to the pilots. In the event of any malfunction, the fault is displayed on the ECAM display, along with the steps for the remedial action. The ECAM system consists of Flight Warning Computer (FWC), System Data Acquisition Concentrators (SDAC), Display Management Computers (DMC) and the pilot interface in the cockpit which helps the pilot to view status of specific systems of the aircrafts. The architecture of the ECAM system is shown in Fig. 6.

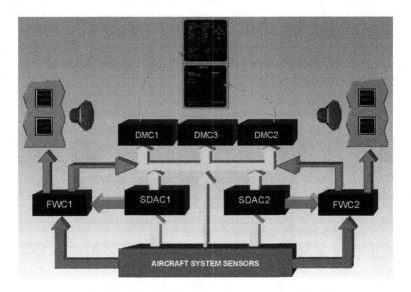

Fig. 6. Airbus electronic centralized aircraft monitor architecture

However, there are few drawbacks for this existing system:

- This is a dumb system which displays the error and provides the steps to rectify the error.
- This system cannot identify the root cause of an error. An interview with a highly experienced test pilot suggested that test pilots can understand the root cause of the error and reason for the warning, with their experience of systems. This experience and knowledge of systems are lacked by new pilots.

The block diagram for proposed smart cockpit assistant which can mitigate the factors associated with air safety is provided in Fig. 7.

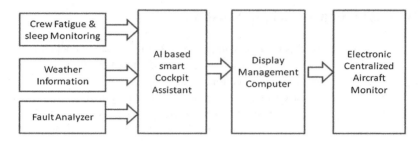

Fig. 7. AI based smart cockpit assistant for airbus A 320

The hardware of the proposed unit will be a graphical processing unit (GPU) and two cockpit cameras that can capture the images of the pilots in the cockpit. The, software, i.e. AI algorithms would be running on this hardware taking inputs from the camera, weather radar and data from aircraft sensors and maintenance information. Modular architecture is proposed for the system to implement functionalities as separate modules, which can be integrated together at a later stage. The detailed architecture for proposed smart cockpit assistant which can mitigate the factors associated with air safety is provided in Fig. 8.

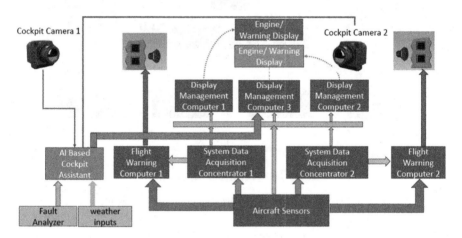

Fig. 8. Detailed architecture of smart cockpit assistant for airbus A 320

There are three AI systems proposed under the scope of smart cockpit assistant.

- The first module would be used for identification of pilot fatigue and sleep. The inputs to the system would be images from the camera installed on the cockpit and variables that can affect crew fatigue like crew age, workload etc.
- The second module would be using the data from the weather radar and with use of historical information, would be providing accurate weather data including hail prediction, turbulence predictions etc.

- The third module would be a fault analyzer that basically can identify a false warning. This system would bring the experience of a test pilot into the cockpit in analyzing the emergency situations and help the pilot to act safely. This would take into cognizance factors like recent maintenance of the component, historical failure of a component etc.

Module to Reduce Pilot Errors Due To Sleep and Fatigue

To reduce accidents related to human faults, the system should be able to detect sleep and fatigue. Sleep can be detected from images of the eye taken from the cockpit camera and combining with factors like crew age, time since awaken, circadian body block etc. using a random forest algorithms. Fatigue can be identified using convolutional neural network which can differentiate a fatigued eye from a normal eye. The input for the sleep monitoring system would be images on the pilot captured from the camera in the cockpit. This module would use reinforced learning, where the module is taught to identify a fatigued or sleepy eye with training data. At the first step the module would be taught to identify closure of the eye. This is based on Eye Aspect Ratio (EAR) shown in Fig. 9. The module uses a detector and a predictor. The detector detects the eye from the camera image and the predictor whether the person is sleepy or not. Closure of the eye alone cannot be identified as sleep and there are other parameters that need evaluation for a crew fatigue warning. Momentary closure of eyes cannot be misunderstood as a sleep. The times for which eye is closed also needs to be checked to correctly identify sleep. In case the eye remains closed for 30 frames (an assumption), it can be classified as a potential sleep and can become a hazard.

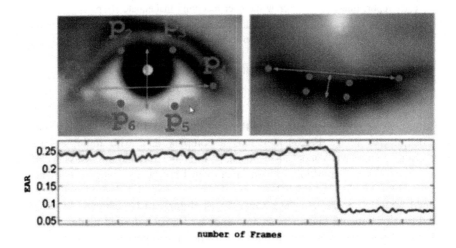

Fig. 9. Identification of eye closure and sleep

$$EAR = \{|P_2 - P_6| + |P_3 - P_5|\}/\{2|P_1 - P_4|\}$$

Additionally, the inputs provided in Table 6 also would be taken by the AI systems to correctly predict the fatigue. These factors will have to be made as a random forest algorithm to predict sleep.

Table 6. Factors for predicting sleep

Si no	Factor	Remarks
1.	Crew age	Sleep becomes more fragmented after about age 50–60 years. Older pilots take longer to fall asleep, gets less sleep overall, and had more fragmented sleep than young pilots
2.	Time since awaken (TSA)	The alertness and performance of crew deteriorates with longer the time they remain awake due to an increasing homeostatic pressure for sleep associated with the longer period of wakefulness
3.	Circadian body clock	The crew flying across time zones experience sudden shifts in the day/night cycle, and end up in landings where the body has the natural tendency to sleep
4.	Direction of flight	Body adapts faster to time zone changes for westward travel (phase delay) than after eastward travel (phase advance) across the same number of time zones
5.	Workload	Workload increases with the number of sectors in a flight duty period. Flying multiple sectors in high density airspace across long duty day increase the workload
6.	Unscheduled duty & early report time	An unscheduled duty or early report time may result in crew member receiving inadequate sleep
7.	Density of Airspace	Flight into high density airspace increase the fatigue for the pilots can result in incorrect responses
8.	Crew fatigue reports	Previous history of crew fatigue reported by the crew himself also would be used for AI system to predict fatigue

Fatigue also can be identified using the images captured by the camera installed in the cockpit. An image is considered as a complex data with multiple layers of abstraction. Neural Networks can be used to train the module and classify images. Neural networks with multiple hidden layers can be used for image processing and detection of pilot fatigue. Each layer can learn features and desired output can be obtained by training one layer at a time. This training can be achieved by training a special type of network known as an auto encoder for each desired hidden layer. First the hidden layers are to be trained individually in an unsupervised fashion using auto encoders. Then a final layer will be trained joining the layers together to form a deep network, which is trained one final time in a supervised fashion (Fig. 10).

Module to Reduce Impacts of Weather

The weather prediction module in the smart cockpit assistant predicts weather more accurately augmenting the existing systems. AI techniques in conjunction with a physical understanding of the environment can improve prediction for multiple types of

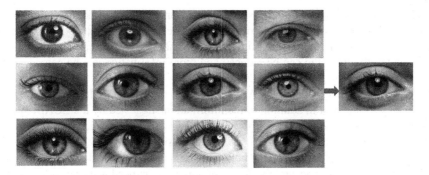

Fig. 10. Neural networks for identification of Fatigue

high-impact weather. This approach expands on traditional Model Output Statistics techniques. AI techniques provide a number of advantages, including easily generalizing spatially and temporally, handling large numbers of predictor variables, integrating physical understanding into the models, and discovering additional knowledge from the data. Weather radar data if complemented by knowledge of current atmospheric conditions can predict if the current atmosphere is conducive to hail development. Decision tree-based methods are very useful in predicting hails and turbulences augmenting the weather radar data. A sample decision tree for hail prediction has been provided in Fig. 11.

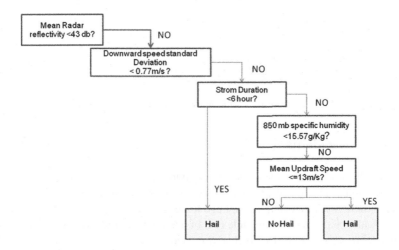

Fig. 11. Decision tree-based method for improved hail prediction

Fault Analyzer Module

The appearance of a warning in the cockpit adds more workload on the pilot. In many accidents analyzed, it was felt that the warnings appear on the cockpit does not correlate with the root cause of the problem. The experienced test pilots are capable on identifying the root cause, but a less experienced pilot finds it difficult to identify the root cause and fail to initiate the correct procedure. A warning has a lot of entropy associated with it, due to lot of reasons. With the use of machine learning, the entropy associated with a warning can be reduced and more information can be gained, which can assist the pilot to take a wiser decision.

The fault analyzer module runs AI algorithms at the back end. It can provide more information to the pilot in addition to the information suggested by the ECAM system. Decision trees can reduce the entropy associated with a warning, which brings the experience of the test pilot and the hazard analysis done by the designer into the system. The decision tree can handle both numerical and categorical data, which assists in decoding the warning accurately. A decision tree for airspeed warning for the case of Air France accident is provided in Fig. 12.

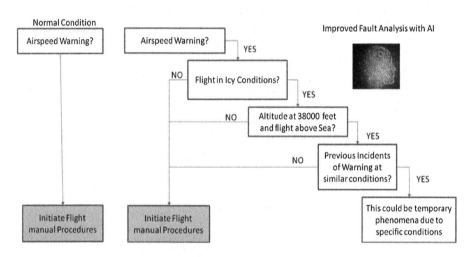

Fig. 12. Improved fault analysis based on decision trees

8   Cost of Accidents

Aviation collision/crash incidents are the second top cause of insured losses globally behind fire and explosion incidents [15]. Air accidents or incidents like hard landing, delays and faulty workmanship cause huge losses for the airlines. There are direct costs involved with accidents which include cost of damaged aircrafts, recovery costs, loss of third-party property, medical care costs for victims, legal costs and cost for accident investigation. Fatal accidents cause a huge of liability to the airlines (Fig. 13).

There are indirect costs arising out of accidents and incidents. The image and reputation of the airlines takes a hit as a result of accident and incidents. Passenger may perceive an airline as unsafe and opt for other airlines, resulting in revenue losses. Additional losses occur if a crew is injured or denied permission to fly after an incident and it affects the operations. Legal actions for compensation are initiated by the families of victims against the airlines. As the safety ratings of an airlines goes low, there

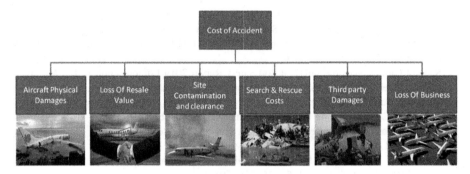

Fig. 13. Costs associated with accidents

are chances that the insurers charge more for providing insurance cover to the airlines. The cost range based on aircraft (type and age) and accident severity will be minimum of 4–211 million €; and maximum of 414–591 million €.

9 Conclusions

Air safety is of critical importance in aviation. A few accidents and incidents in the recent aviation history were analyzed for the purpose of the paper. The major contributing factors for accidents were also analyzed. Interactions were held with stakeholders in the industry including test pilots, commercial pilots and maintenance engineers to gain insight to the real operational scenario. The focus was to propose cost effective solutions with minimal changes to the aircraft. This concept based artificial intelligence can play a crucial role in increasing the air safety to a higher level. The system tries to mitigate three major hazards associated with safe flying, i.e. pilot fatigue/sleep, weather hazards and false warnings.

The concept presented in the paper can be implemented by OEMs who develops electronics systems for the aircraft, after extensive research, testing and validation. Combining the data from the aircraft level and system level hazard analysis carried out by the aircraft manufacturers, the system can be tested, validated and used in different aircrafts. The system proposed can be retrofitted on most of the aircrafts, with very few changes in the existing systems, which would make this a good value proposition for all the stake holders.

References

1. Artificail Intellegence Roadmap, A human-centric approach to AI in aviation, European Aviation Safety Agency, February 2020
2. Machine Learning Of Speech Recognition Models For Controller Assistance(MALORCA), SESAR Joint Undertaking, April 2018
3. Data-Driven AircraftTrajectory Prediction Exploratory Research, Data science in ATM, The DART project, SESAR Joint Undertaking, March 2017

4. Stroup, R.L., et. al. Application of AI in the NAS – the rationale forai-enhanced airspace management. In: Digital Avionics Systems Conference 2019, 8–12 September 2019
5. Big Data Analytics for Socioeconomic and Behavioural Research in ATM, State-of-the-art and Future Challenges May 2016
6. State of Global Aviation Safety, ICAO Safety Report 2019 Edition, Published in Montréal, Canada, International Civil Aviation Organization, July 2019
7. Statistical Summary of Commercial Jet Airplane Accidents Worldwide Operations, 1959 – 2018, 50th Edition, Boeing Commercial Airplanes, September 2019
8. MEDA Investigation Process, by William Rankin, Maintenance Human Factors Boeing Commercial Aeromagazine,Issue 26_Quarter 02|2007
9. Mazon et. al.: Influence of meteorological phenomena on worldwide aircraft accidents, 1967–2010. J. Meteorol. Appl. 5, 236–245 (2018)
10. Assumptions Used in the Safety Assessment Process and the Effects of Multiple Alerts and Indications on Pilot Performance, Safety Recommendation Report, ASR-19–01, National Transportation Safety Board, Washington, DC 20594, September 2019
11. Taxiway Overflight Air Canada Flight 759, Airbus A320–211, C-FKCK, San Francisco, California, July 7, 2017, AIR-18/01 Incident Report NTSB/AIR-18/01 PB2018-101561, National Transportation Safety Board, Washington, DC 20594, September 2018
12. Transportasi, K.N.K.: Aircraft Accident Investigation Report, Republic of Indonesia (2015)
13. et d'Analyses, B.D.E.: Final Report On the accident on Airbus A330–203 Air France flight AF 447 Rio de Janeiro - Paris pour la sécurité de l'aviation civile Published Jul 2012
14. https://flightsafety.org/asw-article/disoriented
15. https://www.agcs.allianz.com/news-and-insights/expert-risk-articles/global-claims-review-2018-aviation-claims-trends.html

A Creative Information System Based on the SCAMPER Technique

Rute Lopes[1], Pedro Malta[1], Henrique Mamede[2], and Vitor Santos[1(✉)]

[1] NOVA IMS – Information Management School, Universidade Nova de Lisboa, Lisbon, Portugal
{m2015143,pmalta,vsantos}@novaims.unl.pt
[2] INESC TEC, Departamento de Ciências e Tecnologia, Universidade Aberta, Lisbon, Portugal
hsmamede@gmail.com

Abstract. Nowadays, the use of creativity in business has been increasing drastically because it has been perceived to be important for the market to come up with new ways, focused on answers to the problems proposed by the users. Several different creativity techniques can be used in a myriad of contexts. One of the most important techniques is the SCAMPER technique, which is based on reorganizing, modifying, adding, and eliminating information. An automated system will provide answers and solutions to creativity problems and contribute to minimizing the cost of innovation in companies. The aim of this paper is, therefore, to design an architecture system for a creative information system based on the SCAMPER creativity technique, thus building an automated system of this technique.

Keywords: Creativity · Creativity techniques · Information systems architectures · SCAMPER · Creative information systems

1 Introduction

There are a variety of definitions and ways to use creativity. Over the years, we have studied the impact and uses in everyday life and business. The use of creativity techniques is a way to help improve and trigger creative thinking.

The scope of using these creative techniques is vast, although they all have advantages and disadvantages, depending on the situation, the schema can be useful.

The use of technology to recreate creativity using creativity techniques, where a system could help to increase creativity, providing different and original responses to different contexts, would be a significant step to be taken in this field of study.

We want to propose the best system architecture for the SCAMPER technique and understand which external systems the proposed system can use to support the answers given to the user.

© Springer Nature Switzerland AG 2020
M. Themistocleous et al. (Eds.): EMCIS 2020, LNBIP 402, pp. 595–606, 2020.
https://doi.org/10.1007/978-3-030-63396-7_40

2   Research on Creativity

In the early studies, creativity was quickly assumed to be an intrinsic characteristic of a person, although Guilford stated that the studies were inconclusive [5]. Subsequently, the term design thinking emerged, which is the way and strategies of thinking, where the different styles and characteristics of the individual have a great role in the process of creating something new [1, 2].

It is expected that a person who has an easier to approach design thinking will have a fluid, flexible, and original thinking. These characteristics are those that are tested when creativity is in focus. Nevertheless, researchers have come to conclude that there is a need for a more lateral thinking approach when looking for new solutions [3, 4, 16].

For years now, analytical thinking has been at the basis of problem-solving, where thinking is done in a recognition process, and solutions are based on hypotheses, analogies, or syntheses [9, 15]. These steps of vertical thinking can be accomplished not only by using data but also by using creative thoughts [5].

Many theories have been formulated around creativity, one of which is lateral thinking. Edward Bono described lateral thinking as a way of solving problems, moving from a known idea to a new one, based on standards and tools, as opposed to the traditional approach of finding solutions step by step [2].

Lateral thinking uses techniques that trigger people who are not so predisposed to creative thoughts and promotes creativity training in those who are, forcing the user to answer questions that would not generally come to mind, thereby rearranging information into new patterns, resulting in a problem and an opportunity [6, 7]. One of the most known techniques for lateral thinking is SCAMPER, the main subject of this article: supported by seven different interrogations, it helps generate ideas and can be used as a trigger for innovation in a way to promote products, services, solve problems, and create new ideas. In the next section, this technique is presented in detail.

2.1   SCAMPER Technique

The SCAMPER technique is one of the techniques that reorganizes and combines information to create different ideas according to a problem or situation. Created by Alex Osborn in 1953, it is among the most complex techniques, because each letter of the acronym represents a different method of use [8].

These methods are: Substitute (materials, components, people), Combine (mix, combine, integrate), Adapt (change function), Modify - (magnify, minify - increase or decrease the scale, change shape) added by Michalko, Put it to another use, Eliminate (remove, simplify, reduce) and Reverse – also Michalko Rearrange - (change components, change speed, turn inside out or upside down in order) [6].

The main advantage of the SCAMPER technique is that it promotes creative thinking when analyzing a problem and fosters the generation of new ideas. A weakness of the SCAMPER technique is that it only works in limited environments, those that encourage free thinking, and the fact that the technique discourages group thinking because it is a non-group technique. Although it could also be carried out in a group, this option can provoke discussions that can lead to dead ends [6].

2.2   Creative Information System

In recent studies, a "Creative Information System" (CIS) was created, which is an automated system that produces autonomous responses, using a creative technique as an intellectual basis. It is important to note that there are minimum requirements for entries, namely the problem specification, its context, and restrictions. Depending on the creativity technique, the system will generate responses through the chosen process [10].

Therefore, this system can recreate the original technique with a minimum of human interaction: the system will receive an entry with the context and restrictions of the problem and will generate answers or solutions to the problem that can be analyzed later [11].

The model presented in Santos et al. (2008) states how to plan and design an architecture for CIS [10]. In this model, the entry indicating the problem and the context must be specified by the user; then, the design is produced in two stages, the first representing the application of the creative technique and the second the generation of responses, resulting, ultimately, in the output for analysis.

This model was used to propose architectures for two different creative techniques: "Whiteboard" and "Brute thinking." These techniques are also explained by Michalko and are based on the random association of words. The process goes through three steps. The first is the introduction of a word (the model uses a dictionary and the Internet), the second step is the combination of a random word with the context provided, and the final step is a list of phrases (context and random words) [12–14].

In the CIS architecture for the Whiteboard technique, the user input is keywords using a random word combiner from a dictionary or the Internet. The results are a combination of keywords (context) and randomly generated words. The analysis of this list of combinations is done by the user, and its objective is to know which ones are valid or not [12].

The system for the Brute Thinking technique goes through approximately the same process, as explained above. The main difference between the two models is that the architecture of brute thinking is a collaborative semi-automatic system (more than one user at the same time). The first entry is made by users with all the necessary context. This context will be used by the other participants to generate and register keywords that can describe and classify the context. The same happens with an initial word. After these two steps, the system can generate a random combination of words with the following structure: keyword, verb (randomly generated), and a characteristic of the initial word [11].

3   Information System Architecture for the SCAMPER Technique

As shown in Fig. 1, the process starts when the user enters the information in the system. This set of phrases passes through the SCAMPER generator, which is the part of the system that makes changes to the input using the three different lists as an external source for changes: list of verbs (list V), list of subjects (list S), list of materials (list M),.

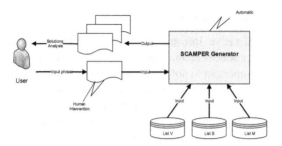

Fig. 1. CIS for the SCAMPER technique

The changes are documented in the output resulting in new sets of phrases in an equal or higher number as the input phrases.

The user can input as many sets of phrases as he wishes and can also leave one section of the phrases blank. However, in these case (phrases B or C), only some methods of the SCAMPER technique can be used (Fig. 2).

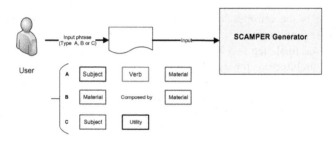

Fig. 2. Type of input for the system

The phrase A combines a subject that can be a specific product or person/name, a verb which is an action or a composition, and a material. The phrase B associates two, or more, types of materials, and the final phrase (phrase C) is a subject combined with a utility that can be a type of object or a name of an object.

There are three types of lists that are an external mid-system input, which can be filled with words from a dictionary. List V represents the list of verbs, and it has two different columns. The first column contains all the necessary verbs, and the second column has the opposite of the verbs in the first column. In this list, verbs can be repeated, as they can have more than one opposite, and the same verb can be in both columns of the list. The subject is represented in list S and only contains one column with the subject name. It can be a product, a person, or a category. List M consists of the name of the materials in the first column, and the usefulness of the materials from column one in the second column. The materials can have more than one utility and vice versa. Therefore, materials and utilities can be repeated.

The SCAMPER generator works in different ways for each possible method, following various actions using the inputs explained above. It is important to realize that all the changes in the input are randomly generated by the system.

The first method is "Substitution," and for that method, the generator can use three different actions. These actions directly change two elements of the phrases, the materials, and the subject, because the goal is to substitute materials to transform the final product and to change the subject to transform the way a task is performed.

One of the actions in this method is to change the material in phrase A for another from list M. Changing the materials will give different ways to have the same product but with distinct characteristics. As represented in Fig. 3, using list M the system will randomly choose the materials that differ from the one that is already in the phrase and substitute that one for an item of material from the list. In this action, the only focus is on the materials, and they can be changed regardless of their utility.

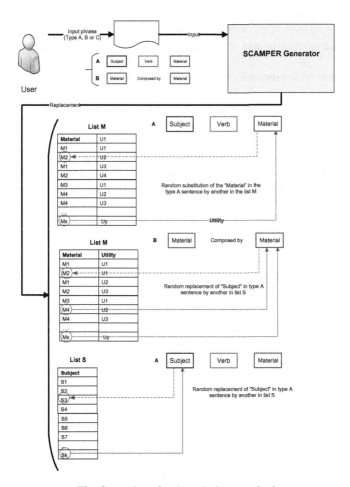

Fig. 3. Actions for the substitute method

The second action that we can list for the substitution method is also focused on the materials, but in this case, it uses phrase B. As shown in Fig. 3, the system will go through the list of materials and randomly choose a material that is not the same as the one that system is changing. The action is performed as many times as materials of the second instance exist as part of phrases B. The purpose of this action is to have other materials to be part of the composition of the final solution. Again, the usefulness of the materials is not crucial for this step, as it only provides other options for existing materials.

The final action for the substitution method is focused on the subject in the A phrases; in this case, the system will search for subjects in List S and will randomly choose one that differs from the one that is already there to replace in the sentence (Fig. 3). This action intends to maintain the subject's objective, maintaining the verb and the material, but changes what or who performs it, changing the subject in order to find new ways to perform the task.

The second method in the SCAMPER technique is "Combine." This method does not change the elements and instead combines different materials with the input of the phrases, as the goal is to add materials to transform the characteristics of the final product.

The system, as represented in Fig. 4, will go through the list of materials and randomly choose materials to add to the second instance of materials in sentence B. These materials are all different from those already included in the sentence in question. The number of materials to be added is a random number between zero and five, and it can create the same combinations in different phrases or all different combinations, as it is a random procedure. With this action, the SCAMPER generator will be able to supply different combinations of materials that may have the same utility or not; for this action, there is a focus on the different materials and not on their usefulness.

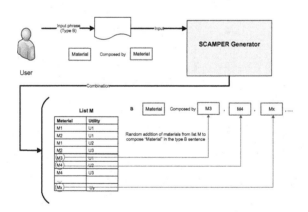

Fig. 4. Action for the combine method

Another SCAMPER method is "Adapt." In this case, the goal is to make changes to the materials or actions so that the initial product can be adapted to perform other actions or adapt materials to perform the actions of the initial product.

The first procedure used by the generator is related to the materials and verbs used in the entry in type A sentences. The objective is not to add or change the entry using the lists, but to adapt the materials and actions already used in sentences A to other subjects. This procedure can only be performed by the system if there are several phrases A greater than one, as the system, as shown in Fig. 4, changes the materials and/or verbs in a set of phrases A.

The second action to consider is centered on type B phrases and materials. The aim is to change the composition of the products. The system can change the materials in one or more B phrases so that the primary material becomes secondary and the same in reverse. As shown in Fig. 5, the system will make these changes so that at the exit, the materials are composed of different elements and, consequently, the solutions become more inventive.

Another action that the system can take when using the adapt method is to join the materials of the type A and B phrases with other phrases of these two types of entry. The objective is again to change the materials in a way that theoretically adapts them to other actions and compositions.

The system will select some of the materials from phrases A and B and change them, so that a material that, for example, is part of the composition, becomes a main part of the product. In addition, materials in different type A phrases can be added to type B phrases without changing materials, keeping the material in phrase A. To perform this action, there must be at least one type of phrase A and one type of phrase B at the entrance.

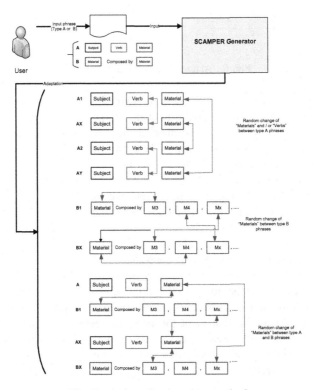

Fig. 5. Actions for the adapt method

The fourth method of the SCAMPER technique is "Modify." When using this method, changes are made to the materials, as the objective is to modify the attention that must fall on the usefulness of the different materials. There is only one action to be taken with this method, and it will change the materials in two different locations.

The action of this method is to change the materials in sentence A randomly and the materials of the second instance in sentence B. The system, as represented in Fig. 6, will go through the list of materials (list M) and will randomly choose some materials to be replaced in phrases A and B. The system will identify materials that are different from those that are already in the entry of the phrases in question and that have the same utility as those that are in the entry. With this action, the SCAMPER generator will be able to supply different combinations of materials that can have the same utility; for this action, there is a focus on different materials that have the same utility.

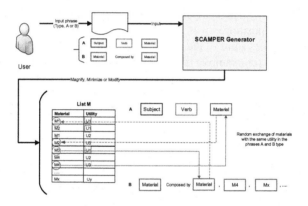

Fig. 6. Actions for the modify method

"Put to other use" is the next method in SCAMPER. Two actions can be performed with this method. In this case, the goal is to change the purpose of the entry, the actions it performs, and the utility it has. The main changes will occur in the utility and the verbs in the different types of sentences. These two actions will cause the output to change according to the essence of the method used for another use.

The first action is related to the verbs of sentence A. The objective is to change the action of the problem, placing the subject and the materials in different uses. The system, as represented in Fig. 7, will randomly search and find verbs in list V that are not the same as what is already in the input and will replace the input verb with these new verbs, creating new sentences. The only focus of this procedure is on verbs, and they can be changed regardless of their opposite.

The second procedure of this method is in the usefulness of the different materials. The objective is to change the utility so that it can give new ways to use the materials. The system, as shown in Fig. 7, will go through the first column of the list of materials and find the same material that is in the entry of sentence C, substituting for the usefulness of the materials found in the sentence, without repeating what is already there. The focus of this action is on utility and materials, as the system is looking for new uses for this material.

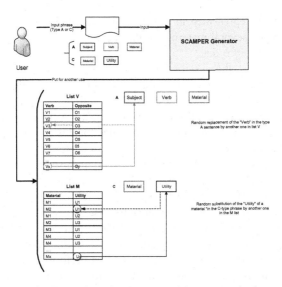

Fig. 7. Actions for the put to other use method

The next SCAMPER technique method is "Eliminate." There are two actions for the system to perform within this method. These actions have an impact on all elements of the system, regardless of their origin and according to the essence of the method "eliminate." The goal is to eliminate parts of the input so that, in the end, the output becomes something different in terms of materials, action, utility, or subjects.

The purpose of the first action of this method is to change the composition of the different products, so that the system eliminates the materials of phrase B. The rules for this elimination are: phrase B must have more than one material of the second instance at the entrance; it can eliminate a random number between one and the number of second instance materials minus one, so you cannot delete all materials from the second

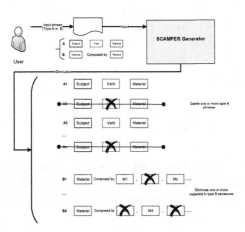

Fig. 8. Actions for the eliminate method

instance. The system, represented in Fig. 8, will go through all the B phrases at the entrance and eliminate several materials of the second instance; the materials will also be disposed of in random order.

In the second action, the system will need to modify the type A sentences and, consequently, the subject, verb, and materials. The objective is to eliminate parts of the entry so that the result of the system becomes different in different situations. To achieve this goal, the system, in Fig. 8, will recognize the A phrases and eliminate a set of arbitrary phrases, in a random number. The rules for this procedure are: the system can never delete all type A sentences; the number of sentences to be deleted is small and depends on how many type A sentences the entry has, so the system will eliminate several sentences between one and the total A phrases of the entry minus 1.

The last method in the SCAMPER technique is "Reverse." As the name demonstrates, the objective is to transform the entry into its opposite. In the system, there is only one action to be performed using this method; this action will manipulate the verbs, changing them. The goal is to replace the verbs to transform the actions that the final product produces, changing the main task to be performed.

The procedure in this final method is to change the verb in type A sentences by the opposite found in the verb list. The system, in Fig. 9, will identify the verb in the A phrases and look for the same verb in the column of verbs in list V and identify its opposite. The SCAMPER generator will replace the verbs in sentence A with the opposites found in the opposite column in list V. The purpose of this action is to cancel the action in the original entry and transform it into a different result, comparing it with the action performed in the SCAMPER technique.

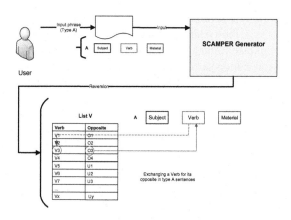

Fig. 9. Action for the reverse method

The output is organized by sets of phrases with the same structure as the input. For example, if the user types ten phrases, the output will be a selected number, greater than one, from a set of phrases with several phrases that have been changed by the system.

The number of sentence sets in the output is chosen by the user at the input to facilitate the analysis of the responses. Answers are provided in sets of phrases, and the number of sets is the result of the number of times the system makes separate changes to the entry. This way, the user will receive the number of possible outputs for him to analyze.

It is important to note that the system may not provide valid responses to the problem since what the system does is to provide several random responses that will later be analyzed by the user. As shown, the system can generate valid or invalid responses. Valid responses can be used as outputs from the system for further analysis.

4 Discussion

Due to the specificity of the topic, focus group discussion was organized with experts in creativity. The discussion goal was to promote a qualitative analysis and evaluation of the artefact. The focus group participants were the authors of the article to explain the artefact and two experts. One is a professor of bachelor's degree students and an expert in design thinking, marketing and innovation, and also a doctoral-level supervisor. In addition, to being a professor, he also has a career of over 15 years in senior marketing positions in various sectors and countries. The other person is an expert in information systems architecture and a professor for more than 15 years in the science and technology department of a Portuguese university, besides having written many papers in the area of information systems, including CIS, and worked in different sectors in the IT area.

The participants showed much interest in the solution, and both agreed on the importance of an automatic system that can replicate the SCAMPER technique. Both participants gave different perspectives on the system. These perspectives lead us to understand that the artefact can be useful for different types of people.

The focus group discussed how the system could be functional and concentrated on the practical side of the system, while also providing some tips on how it can be used for marketing proposes. Also, they focused more on what the future of the system could be, providing insight into the conceptual part of the system and the use it can achieve.

By the responses and suggestions made, the feeling at the end of the focus group meeting was that not only did we achieve the objectives of the research, but also that the work done could be put into practice. The crucial enthusiasm that all the parties showed at this meeting made us understand that the work presented in this paper is relevant and can lead to the creation of a useful and functional software system in the future.

5 Conclusion

This conceptual model of an information system architecture based on CIS and the SCAMPER creativity technique is a model that not only satisfies the objectives proposed at the beginning but also led some experts in the field.

An obvious development for this work is the construction of the system based on the architectural model for a broader application, for example, a web application that could be used as a tool to support enterprises' innovative projects.

In the topic of future work, there is still much to be studied. For instance, the system can be a web-based crowdsourcing platform to be used in groups or a system to use with artificial intelligence with the ability to learn the validation of many different responses. Moving away from artificial intelligence, the system can be reformulated by having pre-defined contexts.

References

1. Adams, K.: The Sources of Innovation and Creativity. National Center on Education and the Economy (2005)
2. De Bono, E.: Lateral Thinking. no. 416. Penguin Books, Harmondsworth (1989)
3. Cross, N.: Design Thinking: Understanding How Designers Think and Work. Berg Publishers, New York (2011)
4. Young, M., Binning, C., Young, M.: Motivating People: Using Management Agreements to Conserve Remnant Vegetation. CSIRO Wildlife and Ecology, Lyneham (1997)
5. Guilford, J.P.: Creative Talents: Their Nature, Uses and Development. Bearly limited Buffalo, New York (1986)
6. Michalko, M.: Thinkertoys: A handbook of business creativity for the 90s. Long Range Plann. **26**(3), 142 (1993)
7. Eberle, B.: SCAMPER - Games for Imagination Development. Prufrock Press Inc, Waco (1996)
8. Baecker, R.M.: Readings in Human-Computer Interaction: Toward the Year 2000. Elsevier, Menlo Park (1995)
9. Paulino, S., Reis, L.: Importância das Redes Sociais – Ambientes Comunitários como canal de transferência de Conhecimento nas organizações – estudo de caso. XXII Jornadas Luso-Espanholas de Gestão Científica, Universidade de Trás-os-Montes e Alto Douro, Bragança (2013)
10. Santos, V., Mamede, H.: Creative Information Systems. In: Encyclopedia of Internet Technologies and Applications, IGI Global, pp. 126–131 (2008)
11. Santos, V., Mamede, H.: Uma Arquitectura para um Sistema de Informação Criativo (2005)
12. Santos, V., Mamede, H.: Um Sistema de Informação Criativo baseado na técnica de criatividade whiteboard (2006)
13. Santos, V., Pereira, J., Martins, J., Gonçalves, R., Branco, F.: Creativity as a key ingredient of Information Systems (2015)
14. Santos, V., Mamede, H., Goncalves, R.: Creativity technique Brute Thinking application using computer mediation pp. 1–5 (2013)
15. Silveira, C., Faria, J., Aguiar, A., Vidal, R.: Wiki based requirements documentation of generic software products, In: Cox, K., Cybulski, J.L., Nguyen, L., Lamp, J.W., Smith, R., (eds.) Proceedings of The Tenth Australian Workshop on Requirements Engineering, pp. 42–51, Melbourne, Austrália (2005) ISBN: 1741560292
16. Gabora, L.: Research on Creativity. In: Carayannis, E.G., (ed.) Encyclopedia of Creativity, Invention, Innovation, and Entrepreneurship, pp. 1548–1558. New Delhi, Springer (2013)

Using Knowledge Graphs and Cognitive Approaches for Literature Review Analysis: A Framework

Samaa Elnagar[✉] and Kweku-Muata Osei-Bryson

Information Systems, Virginia Commonwealth University, Richmond, USA
{elnagarsa, kmosei}@vcu.com

Abstract. Advancements in research tools and databases have accelerated the scientific research life cycle. However, the chronological gap between published research, research in progress and emerging research topics is shrinking, thus putting pressure on researchers to find novel research ideas. The Literature Review (LR) process is a fundamental process that can identify gaps in the research literature and stimulate new research ideas. While many researchers adopt different methodologies conducting LR, there is no methodology that can comprehensively unveil innovative research ideas. This research aims to develop a search by concepts framework. The framework involves the use of Natural Language Processing (NLP), Knowledge Graphs (KGs), and Question Answering systems (QA) to ease finding relevant concepts related to a certain scientific topic along with associated files and citations that would in return maximize the efficiency of the scientific research. The framework also allows researchers to visualize the connection between different concepts similar to the cognitive imaging of the human mind.

Keywords: Literature review challenges · Concepts repository · Knowledge graphs · Question Answering systems · Cognitive theories · Information systems research · Thematic analysis

1 Introduction

The emergence of scientific databases such as Google Scholar and literature thematic coding software such as NVivo and Atlas has helped to facilitate the *Literature Review* (*LR*) process significantly [1]. These tools have accelerated the research life cycle by significantly decreasing the time gap between research in progress and emerging topics [2]. These tools also put increased pressure on researchers to promptly publish their research ideas [3]. Unfortunately, the *LR* process is time consuming and usually involves many search rounds to find content that is relevant to the research problem [4]. Moreover, no matter how comprehensive a research process is, there will be some missing captured knowledge [5]. However, knowledge gained by other researchers represents valuable knowledge that is not fully accessible using different databases. Moreover, searching by keywords turned out to be insufficient for achieving a comprehensive depiction of a research issue [6].

© Springer Nature Switzerland AG 2020
M. Themistocleous et al. (Eds.): EMCIS 2020, LNBIP 402, pp. 607–620, 2020.
https://doi.org/10.1007/978-3-030-63396-7_41

According to the *Cognitive load theory,* developed by John [7], the learning process could be enhanced by the proper presentation of information that would lead to superior task performance for individual users. Thematic analysis, specially coding, has been one of the valuable qualitative analysis approaches for *LR* analysis [8]. Coding research literature in the form of codes or concepts specially NVivo codes have been found to be an efficient representation of knowledge [9]. Therefore, sharing other researchers *LR* coding helps realize inaccessible knowledge from traditional research methodologies [10]. Ironically, while Information Systems (IS) researchers have been developing design science artifacts to solve various organizational problems, they rarely develop artifacts that help enhance their research process. We strongly argue that it is the role of IS research to build such an artifact, as the problem strongly relates to IS goal to resolve different society established problems in the light of rigorous technological advancement.

This research aims to build a scientific search concepts framework where previously generated *LR* codes or concepts are considered to be potential idea contributors. This framework is considered to be a design science artifact that could help researchers (designers) to develop innovative research ideas and facilitate the *LR* process. The framework saves the thematic coding of previous research projects in a repository where researchers can search on the concept level. The availability of the repository should accelerate the *LR* research process significantly as a researcher could browse all concepts created by other researchers and pull up the related content associated with those concepts. Searching by concepts offers the opportunity to maximize the value gained through the *LR* in terms of quality ideas through connecting different concepts that might not be accessible using traditional *LR* methods. Additionally, the repository connects different concepts graphically using *KG*s that mimic the human depiction of ideas in the working memory [11].

2 Literature Review Process Challenges

The basic motivation of this research is to overcome the researcher challenges in conducting *LR*. These challenges are external that emerge from limitations in Scientific Databases and software. Other challenges are internal, emerging from limitations in the researcher's cognitive abilities as discussed below.

2.1 Accessibility to Scientific Databases

Despite the plethora of scientific databases, some require paid subscription, which could limit access to important articles and slow down the research lifecycle [12]. However, the research won't violate the publishing rights to paid access. Otherwise, the developed framework will point out the research title where a certain code or concept has occurred. So, researchers will pay only for relevant articles to save time and money to download irrelevant articles.

2.2 Bias of Scientific Databases

Many researchers have reported discrepancies in their research results though using the same keywords [13]. Such discrepancies in results might be as a result of a problem in the *search and retrieve algorithms,* or an intentional behavior in the search engines. For example, a recent article showed how Google interferes with its search algorithms to change results [14]. This issue raises many questions about the significance of the retrieved articles to address the research problem. Building a repository that allows for sharing results of previous LRs, could increase the *likelihood* of finding relevant literature on a research topic.

2.3 Inefficient Search and Retrieve Algorithms

Many search engines are still using ordinary search by keywords and search cues where meta-tags and search keywords are used in retrieving relevant answers. Ordinary search algorithms might not retrieve all relevant answers because they lack semantics and inference in finding search answers [15]. In our research we will be using *Question Answering (QA)* systems that where the input search query is in the form of natural language. The *QA* uses advanced *NLP* algorithms so the output is inferred as candidate answers with confidence score [16].

2.4 Human Cognitive Limitations

Despite the valuable cognitive abilities of humans, they are still limited in their ability to recall and save knowledge. Human working memory is able to process a limited knowledge at a time. *"the limited attention span" is* phenomena where the most frequently visited and the easily accessed areas of the memory surface are activated [17]. Therefore, work developed by other researchers can serve as external memory that aids other researchers [18]. Researchers could benefit from each other's knowledge and expertise by sharing a repository of their thoughts in the form of concepts or thematic codes.

2.5 Approachability of New Ideas

Some valuable knowledge could be found between lines of unreachable research. This knowledge is usually captured by careful reading. However, in a large corpus of *LR*, careful reading of all articles might be challenging. Therefore, accessing concepts coded by other researchers will complement the missing careful reading of important concepts.

Ideas are generated by imaging connected concepts or issues in the working memory [19]. Given the limited cognitive abilities of humans and the large number of concepts found in the extant literature, it is hard to connect all concepts in the human mind which makes the cognitive imaging of ideas *probabilistic* and *incomplete* [20]. This research is using *KGs* to visualize the relationships between different concepts retrieved from the repository [21]. Visualizing concepts relations emulate the cognitive imaging of new scientific ideas.

3   Why to Reuse Thematic Codes?

Thematic Analysis (*TA*) tries to find common patterns (or "themes") within data. *TA* has the potential to exhibit strong interpretive power through exploring explicit and implicit significance in data [8]. One popular *TA* approach is coding by tagging elements of interest with a coding label in the form of thematic pattern or Nvivo code [22].

   TA has significant advantages such as theoretical flexibility for analyzing qualitative data, unlimited dataset size, and popularity across many scientific fields. However, *TA* suffers from limited interpretive power if it is not based on a clear theoretical basis. Therefore, in the design of the framework, we give weights to concepts or codes shared by more researchers because this decreases the subjectivity of a concept and establishes relevance to the topic of research.

4   Theoretical Lens

Kernel theories (prescriptive or a descriptive) help the design of the framework but not to constraint the design and the evaluation of the designed framework [23]. Therefore, kernel theories are used on the conceptual level. The role of theory in this research is to justify and guide the design. The selection of the kernel theories stemmed from the external and internal challenges of the *LR* process discussed earlier that can be summarized to: *accessibility issues, cognitive issues and representation issues*. To maximize the *accessibility* to relevant LR, a researcher should consider other researchers work. We found that the *Transactive memory theory* [24] asserts that other individuals could serve as external memory. This theory reinforces our position that other researchers' *LR*s are essential for generating new research ideas.

   In attempts to address the *representation issues* of LR, the *Cognitive fit theory* [25] claims that the presentation of information has a great impact on task performance. This theory supports the application of *KG*s to visualize concepts and their relations that mimic the cognitive imaging process of mind [26]. Representing LR codes or concepts in a form that is similar to how the human mind links different issues will definitely enhance the representation of LR knowledge. Lastly, we have to acknowledge the limitations of human cognition. The *Cognitive Load theory* [27] justify our assumption that human cognition is limited to certain capacity that might limit the depiction of a full image of the research problem. According to the *Cognitive Capacity theory* [28], which accentuate the human limited working memory capacity and the need for assistance to gain a comprehensive picture of the problem. These theories justify the need for external support represented in the concepts generated from previous LR. The depiction of how different theories contributed to the construction of our framework is shown in Fig. 1.

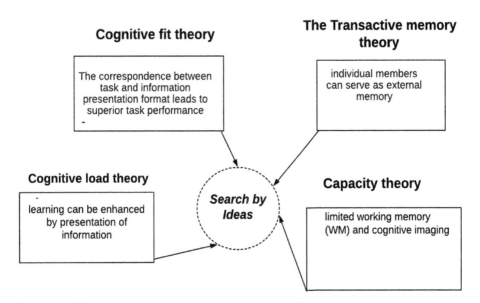

Fig. 1. The Contributing Theories in The Design of The Framework

5   Literature Review

Many previous researches have addressed the challenges in conducting LR, with several previous systems focused on building literature repositories using different types of databases. Those systems adopted the idea of clustering research topics by grouping related concepts using different clustering techniques. To provide an objective literature review and find the gap in literature, we conducted a comparison between previously published research on scientific research search systems as in Table 1.

Table 1. A Comparison between Different Research on Research Search Systems

Research	Objective	Technologies	Domain	Limitations	References
The MIMIC Code Repository, AI for medical	a centralized code base for generating reproducible studies	Relational database, SQL queries, LDA, PCA	Certain Medical domain of critical care, application of AI in medicine	The schema is fixed to certain medical terms, traditional search queries, no import export	[29, 30]
Topic Modeling of Research Fields	Classify/cluster research papers based on topic and language	Topic Modeling, LDA, Naive Bayes, NLP	Domain independent	No repository nor schema, No search and retrieval	[4, 31]
Recommending Scientific Articles	Recommender system for Scientific Articles	Topic Modeling, LDA, CTR,	Domain independent	No schema, limited repository of CiteULike articles, no issues	[6, 32]

(*continued*)

Table 1. (*continued*)

Research	Objective	Technologies	Domain	Limitations	References
Classifying Research Papers with the Computer Science Ontology	Classifier of Computer Science research	Ontologies, SPARQL	Computer Science	Only schema, no systems, no concepts to share	[33]
The Proposed Framework	Search by concepts in previous LR	NLP, KGs, QA systems	Domain independent	Still in initial design phase	

5.1   Gap in Literature

From the previous comparison, we can conclude that no previous related research has targeted the exchange and reuse of *LR* concepts or codes. In addition, most of such research provided schema (ontologies for LR classifying scientific papers) only, third party citation libraries, with no real-time search and retrieval mechanisms. Also, most of such research used *topic modelling* techniques, especially Latent Dirichlet allocation (LDA) to classify or recommend research topics. However, for building a general framework, it is infeasible to depend only on *topic modelling* across different scientific fields. So, the proposed research differs in its objective (i.e. help researchers reaching relevant literature and generate novel research ideas). The research also uses the cutting-edge *KG*s and *QA* systems that involve semantic search and retrieval mechanisms. In addition, the LR concepts should be categorized based on relevancy to the field of study. The framework inspires researchers to generate new research ideas by connecting different concepts stored in a repository of previous LR codes.

6   Research Methodology

We are following a *design thinking* perspective for the design of the *Search by Ideas* framework [34]. This perspective is built upon that a design should go through many design iterations in contact with the actual users of the system. Therefore, the proposed design as an initial iteration where the design is subject to change in each iteration.

To establish the rigor of the research, we built our model upon established IS theories. In addition, we developed a schema that could be saved as an ontology or any structured format such as plain RDF. The summary of the research activities of this research based on [35] design guidelines is summarized in Table 2:

Table 2. DSR Guidelines-based Activities of this Research.

DSR Guideline	Activity of this Research Project
Design as an Artifact	Development of a framework artifact for *Search by Ideas* framework
Design Evaluation	Functional evaluation and performance tests
Research Rigor	Building the artifact based on established theories and the utilization of established research coding schema
Design as a Search Process	Research on *Literature Review* (*LR*) process, *KGs*, *QA* systems and other relevant literature in order to identify appropriate techniques & other results that could be used to inform the design of the procedure

7   The Proposed Framework

The initial structure of the proposed framework is shown in Fig. 2. According to design thinking, the initial design is subject to change in each design iteration and the design should be decomposed into testable components. The framework consists of three main components: the user interface, the controlling system and the repository.

7.1   The User Interface

The user interface is responsible for interacting with users where there are three main functionalities to be supported

1- Interactively ask and answer the user about the research topic and concepts related to research problems.
2- Display and visualize results.
3- Allowing interface for import/export of code projects.

7.2   The Controlling System

We followed modular system design [34] where the system is decomposed to the fine-granular functional units according to design thinking perspective. The units are discussed below in detail.

The QA System: Receives the user questions and convert it into executable query format. The *QA* system is using advanced NLP methods that go beyond topic modelling to hypothesis building and ranking results based on event scoring [36].

The Code Project Parser: the parser search in the imported project for the concepts lists, related files, and citations list if any. In case there is no information provided in the research project description, the parser requests the user to provide the research problem, the scientific field, and the research purpose.

The File Copyright Checker: while parsing the code project file, each file is checked if it has an open access (free access) on the web. If the file has an open access, it will be saved in the repository. Otherwise, DOI and related information will be saved instead.

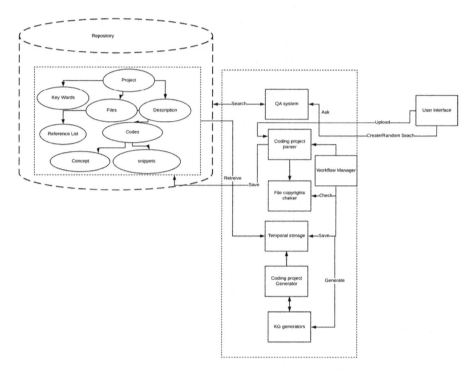

Fig. 2. The search by concepts framework initial design.

The Temporary Storage: it is used to store temporary search results to be visualized or exported as a code project.

The Workflow Manager: is responsible to coordinate between different units in the controlling system and manage the workflow activities *Search, Import, and Export* as shown in Fig. 3.

- *Search activity*: The workflow begins by choosing if the user is conducting a random search or creation of a *LR* project. In both cases, the user asks questions that represent the search queries to be retrieved from the projects repository.
- *The Export activity*: The question answering process will continue till the user is satisfied with the results. Then, the concepts retrieved from the repository along with files and citations are sent to the project generator to be converted to a code project to be downloaded by the user.
- *The Import activity*: In case the user is importing a code project, the project is parsed where the files, concepts, code list and citations are extracted. Then, files are checked for copyrights before they are saved to the coding repository.

The Coding Project Generator is used to convert the search activity codes, files and citations into a code project format so it could be exported and reused.

The KG generator: is used to visualize the relation between the concepts resulting from the search process that are saved in the temporary storage. Visualizing results will help build a cognitive image of the research problem and simulate researcher cognition.

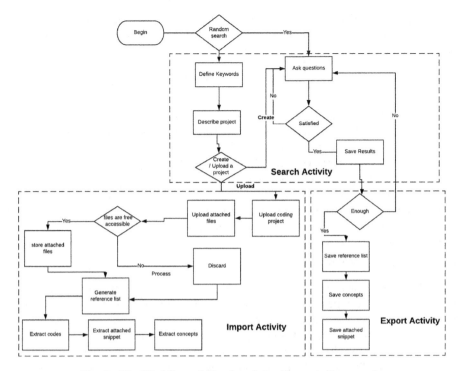

Fig. 3. The Workflow of The Search by Concepts Framework.

7.3   The Code Project Repository

This repository contains the code projects generated by other researchers. However, each code project should be stored in a predefined ontological schema to ease saving and retrieval [37]. The preliminary schema for the code project as shown in Fig. 2 is divided into three classes. The first is the *file class* which contains the list of the files used in the research project. The second class is the *description* class which encompasses the general description of the project and has a subclass of the *reference list* and the *codes* class. The *code class* encompasses the concepts(issues), Concepts weights (how often a concept is coded in research projects), and the corresponding text snippets that represent the concept. The last class is the *keywords class* which represents the meta-data about the research problem of interest to facilitate finding the right context for the search process.

8   Implementation

8.1   Building the Framework Components

The central component in the implementation of the framework is to build the coding repository. In the beginning, we will be using the code projects for a certain software "Nvivo" to avoid compatibility issues. The project itself should be decomposed into files, nodes (codes) with related descriptions that would be saved into the repository. The type of projects will be initially related to information systems research. Then, the design will be modified to include other sciences.

The second step is building the *QA* system. Platforms such as IBM Watson and Microsoft Cognitive services provide *QA* services that could be adjusted according to the project of interest [38]. However, the *QA* has to have full access to the knowledge base or repository to be able to semantically define the context of questions and adjust its performance. In the following step, we are trying to fit the research projects into the coding ontological schema. Then, perform pilot tests to make sure the search and retrieval process is working correctly. Most importantly is representing results from the search process in the form of *KG*s (nodes and edges) to be in the easily readable and simulating for a researcher. Next, *NLP* libraries are used to generate *KG*s of concepts and relations between them. Then, doing a pilot testing for the workflow manager to see if it is well integrated with other components.

8.2   Illustrative Scenario

An IS researcher wants to conduct a literature review about "*Convolutional Networks*" to study how they can be used in real-time object detection. At first, the researcher used the framework interface and wrote his question about *Convolutional Networks* as shown if Fig. 4. The framework allows the user to select multiple scientific disciplines to ensure precise search. The term itself might be used in mathematics and electrical engineering too. Therefore, the framework allows the user to select the main concepts associated with the question. So, The researcher excluded 5G and matrix multiplication from main concepts.

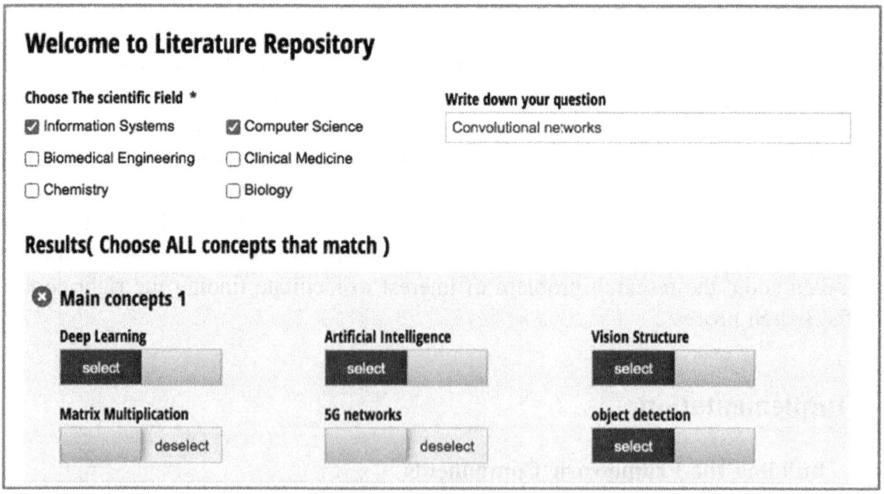

Fig. 4. Search by Concepts User Interface.

Next, the user interface displays available research along with publishing information. The interface also allows quick overview of the places where the concept was coded. If the research file has free access on the web, the researcher can download the file. Next, relevant concepts, parent and child concepts could be included as part of the total search as shown in Fig. 5. Additionally, the researcher could visualize the chosen concepts to be displayed in the form of a *KG* as shown in Fig. 6. A *KG* will display the relationships between concepts along with the weight of each concept (how often a concept appeared in other *LR* coding)

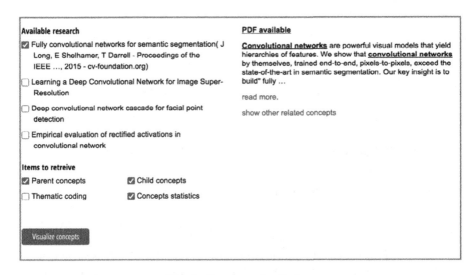

Fig. 5. Search results display.

The *KG* shown in Fig. 6 shows the concepts with strong weight in darker colors than concepts with weak weight or concepts which don't appear often as codes in *LR* thematic coding. We can conclude that the concepts "*Convolutional Networks*" and "*Deep Learning*" are the darkest nodes which appeared mostly in *LR* coding. In addition, the thicker is the line that connects two concepts, the stronger is the relationship between them. For example: "*Convolutional Networks*" and "*Deep Learning*" have strong (thick line) relation while "*Feature Vector*" and "*Activation Functions*" each have a weak (thin line) relation. Lastly, the researcher can decide to export all the search results along with a graph and concepts as a project file.

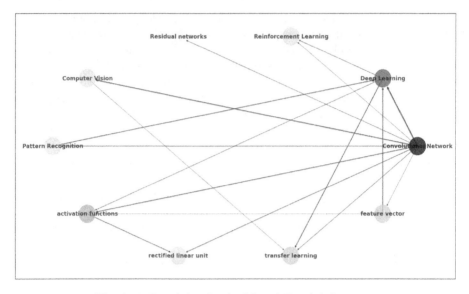

Fig. 6. A Knowledge Graph of Search Results' Concepts.

9   Discussion and Conclusion

This research aims to build a scientific research by concepts framework that reuses the thematic codes and concepts generated from previous research projects. Previous research concepts produced by previous researchers represent the transactive external memory for a researcher that maximizes finding relevant literature. Moreover, previously generated concepts complement the missing concepts needed for the creative cognitive imaging of research ideas. This research aims to build a *Search by Ideas* framework that allows the search, import and export of research projects where the concepts or codes are the central search goal. The retrieved concepts from previous research projects could be visualized in the form of *KG*s that simulates the cognitive imaging of ideas.

The framework is still in the first design iteration. Future work will include the engagement of researchers from different disciplines in the redesign of the framework, so that the design will be modified based on their requirements and suggestions. The evaluation of the framework should be performed by actual framework users. Evaluation should not only be technical/functional but also behavioral based users' feedback on the framework utility.

References

1. Stuckey, H.L.: Methodological issues in social health and diabetes research. J. Soc. Health Diabetes **1**, 56–59 (2013)
2. Luse, A., Mennecke, B.E., Townsend, A.M.: Selecting a research topic: a framework for doctoral students. Int. J. Doctoral Stud. **7**, 143 (2012)

3. Lordkipanidze, R.: Scientific invitation for conducting of researches to protect of honest competition. Int. Charity Sci. Res. Partnership Phys. Persons, **13** (2019)
4. Paul, M., Girju, R.: Topic modeling of research fields: an interdisciplinary perspective. In: Proceedings of the International Conference RANLP-2009 (2009)
5. Brereton, P., et al.: Lessons from applying the systematic literature review process within the software engineering domain. J. Syst. Software **80**(4), 571–583 (2007)
6. Wang, C., Blei, D.M.: Collaborative topic modeling for recommending scientific articles. In: Proceedings of the 17th ACM SIGKDD International Conference on Knowledge Discovery and Data Mining, ACM (2011)
7. Sweller, J.: Cognitive load during problem solving: effects on learning. Cogn. Sci. **12**(2), 257–285 (1988)
8. Braun, V., Clarke, V.: Thematic Analysis (2012)
9. Hilal, A.H., Alabri, S.S.: Using NVivo for data analysis in qualitative research. Int. Interdisciplinary J. Educ. **2**(2), 181–186 (2013)
10. Moghaddam, A.: Coding issues in grounded theory. Issues Educ. Res. **16**(1), 52–66 (2006)
11. Nijstad, B.A., Stroebe, W.: How the group affects the mind: a cognitive model of idea generation in groups. Personal. Soc. Psychol. Rev. **10**(3), 186–213 (2006)
12. Salager-Meyer, F.: Scientific publishing in developing countries: challenges for the future. J. English Acad. Purposes **7**(2), 121–132 (2008)
13. Beck, J.C., Perron, L.: Discrepancy-bounded depth first search. In: Proceedings of the Second International Workshop on Integration of AI and OR Techniques in Constraint Programming for Combinatorial Optimization Problems (CP-AI-OR 2000) (2000)
14. Grind, K.: How google interferes with its search algorithms and changes your results. wall street journal 2019. https://www.wsj.com/articles/how-google-interferes-with-its-search-algorithms-and-changes-your-results-11573823753?mod=djemalertNEWS<
15. Büttcher, S., Clarke, C.L., Cormack, G.V.: Information retrieval: implementing and evaluating search engines, MIT Press (2016)
16. Elnagar, S., Osei-Bryson, K.-M.A.: A Cognitive Ideation Support Framework using IBM Watson Services (2019)
17. Findley, N.: What do we mean by 'limited attention span'? Phi Delta Kappan **86**(9), 652–653 (2005)
18. Wegner, D.M., et al.: Paradoxical effects of thought suppression. J. Personality Soc. Psychol. **53**(1), 5 (1987)
19. Colom, R., et al.: Working memory and intelligence are highly related constructs, but why? Intelligence **36**(6), 584–606 (2008)
20. Smith, S.M.: The constraining effects of initial ideas. Group creativity: Innovation Through Collaboration, 15–31 (2003)
21. Elnagar, S., Weistroffer, H.R.: Introducing knowledge graphs to decision support systems design. In: Wrycza, S., Maślankowski, J. (eds.) SIGSAND/PLAIS 2019. LNBIP, vol. 359, pp. 3–11. Springer, Cham (2019). https://doi.org/10.1007/978-3-030-29608-7_1
22. Braun, V., Clarke, V.: Successful qualitative research: A practical guide for beginners. Sage (2013)
23. Hart, D., Gregor, S.: Information systems foundations: the role of design science. ANU E Press (2010)
24. Lewis, K.: Measuring transactive memory systems in the field: scale development and validation. J. Appl. Psychol. **88**(4), 587 (2003)
25. Vessey, I.: Cognitive fit: a theory-based analysis of the graphs versus tables literature. Decision Sci. **22**(2), 219–240 (1991)

26. Lin, J., Zhao, Y., Huang, W., Liu, C., Pu, H.: Domain knowledge graph-based research progress of knowledge representation. Neural Comput. Appl. **52**, 1–10 (2020). https://doi. org/10.1007/s00521-020-05057-5
27. Paas, F., Renkl, A., Sweller, J.: Cognitive load theory and instructional design: Recent developments. Educ. Psychol. **38**(1), 1–4 (2003)
28. McCutchen, D.: A capacity theory of writing: working memory in composition. Educ. Psychol. Rev. **8**(3), 299–325 (1996)
29. Johnson, A.E., et al.: The MIMIC Code Repository: enabling reproducibility in critical care research. J. Am. Med. Inf. Assoc. **25**(1), 32–39 (2017)
30. Tran, B.X., et al.: Modeling research topics for artificial intelligence applications in medicine: latent dirichlet allocation application study. J. Med. Internet Res. **21**(11), e15511 (2019)
31. Yau, C.-K., Porter, A., Newman, N., Suominen, A.: Clustering scientific documents with topic modeling. Scientometrics **100**(3), 767–786 (2014). https://doi.org/10.1007/s11192-014-1321-8
32. Pan, C., Li, W.: Research paper recommendation with topic analysis. In: 2010 International Conference On Computer Design and Applications, IEEE (2010)
33. Salatino, A., et al.: Classifying research papers with the computer science ontology (2018)
34. Brown, T.: Design thinking. Harvard Bus. Rev. **86**(6), 84 (2008)
35. Hevner, A., et al.: Design science research in information systems. MIS Q. **28**(1), 75–105 (2004)
36. Bouziane, A., et al.: Question answering systems: survey and trends. Procedia Comput. Sci. **73**, 366–375 (2015)
37. Bunnell, L., Osei-Bryson, K.-M., Yoon, V.Y.: RecSys issues ontology: a knowledge classification of issues for recommender systems researchers. Inf. Syst. Front. **9**(3), 1–42 (2019). https://doi.org/10.1007/s10796-019-09935-9
38. Su, D., et al.: Generalizing question answering system with pre-trained language model fine-tuning. In: Proceedings of the 2nd Workshop on Machine Reading for Question Answering (2019)

IT Governance and Alignment

The Influence of Cloud Computing on IT Governance in a Swedish Municipality

Parisa Aasi[(⊠)], Jovana Nikic, Melisa Li, and Lazar Rusu

Department of Computer and Systems Sciences, Stockholm University,
Stockholm, Sweden
{parisa,lrusu}@dsv.su.se, nikic.jovana95@gmail.com,
melisa.li@outlook.com

Abstract. Cloud computing is used to a greater extent in today's organizations and enables organizations to obtain on-demand network access to IT services. When cloud computing is adopted in an organization, the IT governance becomes more challenging, because organizations need to address business and IT-related processes as well as managing risks and maintaining the relationship with cloud computing vendors. This research aims at finding how cloud computing service model specifically Software as a Service (SaaS) influence IT governance structures, processes and relational mechanisms in a public organization. For this purpose a case study was conducted in a Swedish municipality and the data was collected through interviews with IT managers and from internal documents of municipality and was analyzed using thematic analysis. The results of this study shows that SaaS influences the IT governance structure by improving roles and responsibilities definition and speeds up the decision-making processes. Moreover, the communication with the vendors is more efficient due to the use of SaaS.

Keywords: Cloud computing · IT governance · Software as a service · Structures · Processes · Relational mechanisms · Municipality · Sweden

1 Introduction

Cloud computing is an evolution of IT outsourcing that is changing how organizations utilize, manage and deliver services over the Internet [1]. According to Mell & Grance [2, p. 2] "Cloud Computing is a model for enabling ubiquitous, convenient, on-demand network access to a shared pool of configurable computing resources (e.g., networks, servers, storage, applications, and services) that can be rapidly provisioned and released with minimal management effort or service provider interaction". For many organizations cloud computing has become a mainstream and strategic choice for differentiation among others [1].

IT governance or Enterprise governance of IT is defined as "an integral part of enterprise governance exercised by the board and address the definition and implementation of processes, structures and relational mechanisms in the organization that enable both business and IT people to execute their responsibilities in support of business/IT alignment and the creation of business value from IT-enabled business

© Springer Nature Switzerland AG 2020
M. Themistocleous et al. (Eds.): EMCIS 2020, LNBIP 402, pp. 623–639, 2020.
https://doi.org/10.1007/978-3-030-63396-7_42

investments" [3, p.3]. In opinion of Weill & Ross [4] enterprises with effective IT governance generate higher returns on their IT investments and also enhance their competitiveness". Moreover, according to Turedi & Zhu [5, p. 530] "organizations must institute effective IT governance mechanisms to maximally create business value from their IT investment".

IT plays a very important role in private organizations and is part of the business strategy, but has a lot to offer to public organizations as well that can benefit the most by using IT to achieve organizations strategies and improve their services [6]. Hoch & Payan [7] have noticed that IT governance is a critical capability for the leaders in the public sector that are looking to create IT value. Therefore, public organizations are very concern to improve their services that will require a focus on their efforts on having an effective IT governance in their organization [6]. In response to the increased cost of IT investments there is a need to effective IT governance otherwise an ineffective IT governance can lead to negative IT experiences, such as business losses, weakened competitive positions, higher cost of IT than expected with lower quality that will lead to enterprise inefficiency because of poor quality IT deliverables.

Cloud services in some form are used by approximately 74% of enterprises, which have grown 26% since 2009 [8]. According to Forrester Research "the public cloud market - cloud apps (software-as-a-service [SaaS]); cloud development and data platforms (platform-as-a-service [PaaS]); and cloud infrastructure (infrastructure-as-a-service [IaaS]) - will reach $411 billion by 2022" [9]. The benefits of cloud computing are mainly reduced IT costs, scalability, business continuity, collaboration efficiency, access to automatic updates [10]. However, when organizations are adopting cloud computing, IT governance becomes more complex and challenging for these organizations. This is because organizations need to address business and IT-related processes while maintaining the relationship, assess, and manage risks with the cloud-computing vendors [11]. In opinion of Jafarijoo & Joshi [12, p.2] "IT governance mechanisms have a positive and significant direct effect on cloud computing business value, thus influencing organizational performance". On the other hand, concerning research in the IT governance in public sector organizations there is still a need of more research in this area [13–16]. This because the majority of research studies concerning IT governance were conducted in the private sector organizations [16]. As we know, there are differences between the private and public sector organizations, where private organizations aim to generate financial returns and profits, while public organizations aim to improve public services and transparency. Nevertheless, according to Prasad et al. [17] and Vithayathil [18] there are a few research studies concerning how cloud computing is influencing IT governance. To address this problem this study has looked to investigate how cloud computing service model like Software as a Service (SaaS) is influencing IT governance in a public organization in Sweden, and the following research question has been defined: "How does Software as a Service influence IT governance in a Swedish municipality?". The next sections of the paper include the research background, research methodology, results and conclusions.

2   Research Background

2.1   Cloud Computing Service Models

Cloud computing is used by the organizations to gain on-demand network access to a shared pool of managed and scalable IT resource services, such as applications, storage and servers [19]. The cloud computing service model, defined by Mell & Grance [1] is composed of three service models (Infrastructure as a Service (IaaS), Platform as a Service (PaaS) and Software as a Service (SaaS)).

IaaS model provides virtualized computing resources such as servers, storage and networks for consumers to run arbitrary software, including applications and operating systems [1] and can be used to construct new cloud software environments [20]. Consumers have control over the operating systems, storage and deployed applications but does not have to manage or control the underlying cloud infrastructure [1]. The most common form of service model IaaS are virtual machines that enables consumers a new flexibility in configuring their settings while protecting the physical infrastructure of the provider's data center [20].

PaaS model implies that a consumer can deploy applications onto the cloud infrastructure using programming languages, libraries, services and tools that are supported by the provider. The consumer does not have to buy or manage the underlying cloud infrastructure but has control over the deployed applications [1]. Usually, the consumers of PaaS are cloud application developers that are deploying their applications onto the cloud. The PaaS vendors supplies the developers with programming-language environment to facilitate the interaction between the environments and the cloud applications [20].

SaaS model implies that a consumer uses the provider's applications on a cloud infrastructure. The consumer can access the applications from different devices through either a web browser or a program interface. The consumer does not own, manage or operate the underlying infrastructure platform [1]. The generic claimed benefits of cloud computing, which applies to SaaS, are automatic software integration, easy access to information, quick deployment, pay-per-use basis, low upfront capital investment, high degree of flexibility and up-to-date IT resources [19, 21, 22]. Although, there are some negative aspects of using SaaS which includes concerns about security, privacy and vendor lock-ins [22]. SaaS is an attractive choice for many consumers as it eases the burden of software maintenance and the ongoing operation and support costs. SaaS, as cloud computing solution, will be the focus in this study because public organizations are more likely to use SaaS over IaaS and PaaS. Because of IT knowledge shortage [14], SaaS can be used to ease the burden of software maintenance [20].

2.2   IT Governance Framework

Van Grembergen & De Haes [23] have introduced an IT governance framework that focuses on three significant components: structures, processes and relational mechanisms like is shown in Fig. 1. Compared to other frameworks like the one of five focus areas of ITGI [24], Van Grembergen and De Haes [23] framework is more delimited, and therefore, found to be more applicable to be used in this study. Moreover, similar studies of IT governance in public organizations have been used this ITG framework [25–28]. Thus, IT governance framework of Van Grembergen & De Haes [23], will be used in this study.

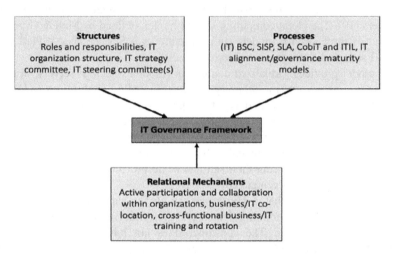

Fig. 1. IT governance framework of Van Grembergen & De Haes [23, p. 25]

IT Governance Structures
The structure component of the IT governance framework in Fig. 1, address where IT decision making authority is located and how the IT function is organized in the enterprise. For an effective IT governance framework, it is important for the board and executive management to define clear roles and responsibilities for the parties involved. It is important with continuous communication within the organization to keep knowledge of current business models, technologies; management techniques and potential risk up-to-date [29].

IT Governance Processes
The process component of the IT governance framework in Fig. 1, focus specifically on business and IT alignment and addresses different standards, methods and frameworks that can be used. For example, Balanced Scorecards (BSC), Strategic Information Systems Planning (SISP), Service Level Agreements (SLA), CobiT and IT Infrastructure Library (ITIL) [29]. By linking the Balanced Scorecard (BSC) and the IT BSC the IT governance can be supported by becoming an alignment method.

IT Governance Relational Mechanisms
The relational mechanisms of the IT governance framework in Fig. 1, is about communication, collaboration and participation between the business and the IT Department. This is to increase awareness of business in the IT Department and IT in the business departments [29]. According to Tonelli et al. [16, p. 607] "the relational mechanisms between IT and other organizational units are, in the IT governance

context, the determining factors for IT performance, and are also positively correlated with organizational performance". The relational mechanisms component in the IT governance ensures that knowledge is continuously shared across organization and departments to attain and sustain alignment between business and IT. To do this, it is also important with career cross-over, by having training, continuous education and rotation programs between the units. Here, balanced scorecards can be extended to include knowledge management initiatives as well.

2.3   Cloud Computing Influence on IT Governance

When a new technology, such as cloud computing is implemented in an organization, the IT governance of that organization will be affected [30]. Cloud computing is expected to be a disruptive technology, which means that adoption of it will entail the need for more rigorous governance strategies [21]. The impact of cloud computing on IT governance is according to Bounagui et al. [31] in the following domains: interoperability and portability; compliance and audit; roles and responsibilities; policy management; risks management; service level agreement; security and privacy. According to Winkler et al. [32] there is a critical need of a governance structure that is business-driven and includes senior managers and owners of business processes in an organization to achieve the payoffs coming out of cloud computing services. In fact, to manage cloud computing services, will be a need of a reconsideration of the IT governance, that will entail new competence developments to ensure that cloud computing services are aligned with the organization's strategic objectives [33]. In order to satisfy the cloud computing needs, the organizational structure will also have to support additional capabilities. The organizational structure will also be affected by cloud computing with regard to new positions and responsibilities [30]. For example, the organization could need the presence of a Chief Cloud Officer, Cloud Management Committee and a Cloud Relationship Center [17]. Cloud services will also affect the management and risk implications [30]. Moreover, by adopting cloud computing services new dimensions of information asymmetry will emerge with the cloud vendor. Information asymmetry occurs when two parties have private information that the other does not know about. For instance, the cloud provider could hold information, such as the availability of backup and disaster recovery, the security of the client's information and the potential for lock-in or high switching costs, that the client are not aware of. This brings new challenges to IT governance. Thus, the organization will need to ensure that formal processes are in place for information exchange between all parties; the IT department, the organization and the cloud vendors, through for example committees. By mitigating information asymmetry firms can increase benefits from cloud computing and add value by improving IT governance [18]. Regarding effective governance of cloud services, the organization need to manage relationships with cloud service vendors and other stakeholders. Cloud computing adoption can increase the number of stakeholders because of its impact on IT processes and other business units [33]. With cloud computing adoption, it is also important with clearly defined policies, IT strategies, and an established organizational structure with clear roles and responsibilities for business processes, IT management and the applications.

2.4   Research Conceptual Framework

The research conceptual framework shown in Fig. 2, will be used in this study to answer the research question: How does Software as a Service influence IT governance in a Swedish municipality?

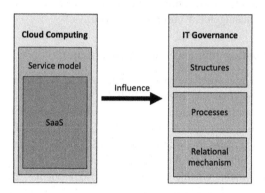

Fig. 2. Research conceptual framework

In Fig. 2, in the left part we have cloud computing service model that is represented by Software as a Service (SAAS) of Mell & Grance's [1]. In the right part of the research conceptual framework shown in Fig. 2 we have IT governance that is represented by IT governance framework of Van Grembergen & De Haes [23]. The research conceptual framework shown in Fig. 2, will be applied to study how cloud computing using SaaS, influence IT governance structures, processes and relational mechanisms in a Swedish municipality.

3   Research Methodology

To achieve the purpose of this study, and analyze how does SaaS influence IT governance in a public organization; a case study method has found to be the appropriate one [34]. Case study is the appropriate method when studying why and how questions [34, 35]. Myers and Avison [35, p. 81] defines case study as: "A case study examines a phenomenon in its natural setting, employing multiple methods of data collection to gather information from one or a few entities (people, groups, or organizations)". The case needs to have distinct boundaries and be a self-contained entity [36]. The choice of case was based on a matter of convenience; time and resource constraints, the applicability of the case in other organizations, and also the level of interest [36]. Case studies are used to focus on one instance of something being investigated and emphasizes relationships and processes, with the aim to explain the general by analyzing the particular [36]. The choice of case was based on a matter of convenience; the applicability of the case in other organizations, in this case municipalities or other public organizations and also the level of interest [36]. For this purpose, a large Swedish municipality with approximately 11000 employees was used as case study in this research. All the municipalities in Sweden work with social services, schools, emergency services, health and environmental protection, water and sewage, waste management, sanitation and planning and construction issues. They also arrange cultural and sport activities within the municipality area. The politicians of this Swedish municipality assembly take the decisions for the municipality. Apart from this assembly, there is also a Municipality Executive Committee, which is the highest executive body of the municipality. There are 20 different councils in the municipality that are responsible for ensuring that the decisions made in the municipality assembly are implemented within each department (Fig. 3). There are 14 departments in the municipality. The employees in the various departments have the task of implementing the council's decisions in practice. The employees in the departments also provide the politicians in the Municipality Assembly with supporting documents for the decisions that the councils should make. Each department is linked to one or more councils. In this municipality, there is a department for Information and Communication Technology (ICT), which is the largest department as well. ICT managers work with various IT related inquiries and also are responsible to inform the other departments for implementing the digitization plan in the municipality that has been produced by the Municipality Assembly.

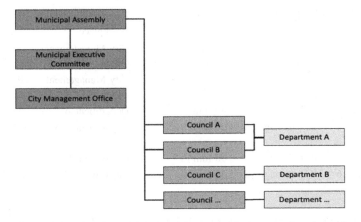

Fig. 3. Conceptualization of the municipality governance (Source: based on the governing model on the municipality's website)

The data was collected in the Swedish municipality through six semi-structured interviews with IT managers. Additionally, internal documents were also used in the data collection like the digitization plan and organizational structure of the municipality's to have multiple sources of evidence and assure data triangulation [34]. The interviewees were chosen based on non-probability sampling [36], and select the staff holding a position that could contribute with special knowledge within the area of IT governance and SaaS. The interviews were held in person at the municipality's office. The interviewees in this study have different IT management positions. Six people within the municipality were interviewed: the CDO (Chief Digital Officer), the IT

Security Manager and four ICT-managers that works in the five largest departments in the Swedish municipality. The semi-structured interviews were chosen because this type of interview is more flexible compared to structured interviews, since questions and topics can be asked in a different order than what may have been intended in the interview guide. This form of data collection also allows follow-up questions in response to the interviewee's answers [37]. Semi-structured interviews also give the interviewee the possibility to develop ideas and speak more freely [36]. An interview guide was used during these interviews that has included questions regarding how cloud computing influence IT governance in public organizations. The interviews have lasted approximately 30–60 min. During these six interviews, repeating answers from the interviewees were received. Thus, we have considered that we reached the level of saturation, so, no more interviewees were perceived to be further conducted in this organization. The anonymity of the participants and organization in this research is not disclose as the participants' in this study have requested. The participants, their generic positions (for anonymity), duration of the interviews, interviewees workplace and date of interviews are presented in Table 1.

Table 1. List of participants, their positions, duration of the interviews, interviewees' workplace, and dates of the interviews in the Swedish municipality

Participants	Position	Duration of interviews	Interviewees Workplace	Date of interviews
Interviewee 1	Chief Digital Officer	60 min	City Management Office	2018-12-05
Interviewee 2	IT security manager	30 min	City Management Office	2018-12-12
Interviewee 3	ICT manager	40 min	Department A	2018-12-14
Interviewee 4	ICT manager	60 min	Department B & C	2018-12-17
Interviewee 5	ICT manager	60 min	Department D	2018-12-21
Interviewee 6	ICT manager	60 min	Department E	2018-12-21

All the interviews were audio recorded and transcribed in English and then ana-lyzed using thematic analysis [38]. Thematic analysis is a data analyzing method used for systematically identifying, organizing and analyzing patterns in qualitative data [38]. When performing a thematic analysis, the data is examine in order to see and make sense of core themes that could be distinguished across qualitative data sets [37, 38]. The thematic analysis method was used in this study, because it focuses on meaning across data sets and it supports researchers in making sense of collective experiences and meaning. To analyze the data collected we have looked for keywords, codes and themes in relation with our research question and the concepts in cloud computing and IT governance. A thematic analysis was performed using Braun &

Clark [38] six-phase approach of thematic analysis that are the followings: familiarizing yourself with the data, generating initial codes, searching for themes, reviewing potential themes, defining and naming themes and producing the report [38]. The six phases mentioned before have been used in performing the thematic analysis of the qualitative data collected through the interviews. The main themes identified in this study are the followings: IT governance structures, processes and relational mechanisms in the Swedish municipality; SaaS influence on the IT governance structure; SaaS influence on the IT governance processes; and SaaS influence on the IT governance relational mechanisms. A presentation of the results under the main themes in this study is included in the next section.

4   Results

4.1   IT Governance Structures, Processes and Relational Mechanisms in the Swedish Municipality

IT Governance Structure in the Swedish Municipality
The structure component addresses the importance of continuous communication within the organization to keep knowledge of current business models, technologies, management techniques and potential risks up-to date. Therefore, an IT committee can be established in order to support the communication. The municipality has continuous communication within the organization by having a formal business forum once a month. They have defined a role as Chief Digital Officer (CDO) that holds the forum and all the ICT managers from the departments in the municipality as well as others from the unit for digitalization meet to ensure that everyone is working according to the digitalization plan. The purpose of the plan is to support the departments in their work towards the IT goals of the municipality. In the business forum various overall IT related questions are discussed, e.g., operating agreements, the scorecard for the central IT unit, budget and financing issues. The participants in the forum also update each other on the most important things that are going on in their departments: "The business forum is the only forum and collaboration space we have today, although we, the ICT managers, collaborate with each other based on different needs that emerge. If I know that a department has a function, some process or is working with some specific working method that I think is good or want to know more about, then I can contact that person directly. I work in such way that I contact the person I know is relevant to the question" (Interviewee 4). Additionally a process control group for business development and digitalization is formed. The participants in the process control group will include a number of different department directors that are most closely concerned. An evaluation panel or an activity forum is linked to this process control group. The ICT managers will then act as a preparatory organ for decision making in the process control group.

IT Governance Processes in the Swedish Municipality
The Swedish municipality uses different models, frameworks and guidelines to ensure that the business and IT is effectively aligned. For almost 10 years, the municipality has

used pm3 as their IT governance model, to manage business development. As a management model this depicts the stakeholders on both IT-side and business side and also the IT components to manage including the SaaS management. At this Swedish municipality, pm3 [39] also makes sure that manuals and proper education is in place for the employees. Moreover, ITIL framework is used by the organization's operating partner, since the municipality outsourced their IT operations to their operating partner. There are also security control processes designed regarding SaaS services.

IT Governance Relational Mechanisms in the Swedish Municipality
The Swedish municipality is a large organization with many different departments and it can be difficult to keep up with developments in the other departments. The employees that manage the software's in the departments according to pm3 have operational meetings to discuss common issues and to exchange information in general. These meetings are for sharing thoughts and knowledge between the departments and the meetings occur on a regular basis. The ICT managers in the various departments meet at the formal business forum, which is noticed as a strategic meeting. The meeting is for directing the focus and prioritization on where the municipality is heading regarding the IT that is common for all the departments across the municipality. On these meetings, ICT managers can also describe or illustrate things that they have done in their department, and if other departments finds it interesting, they often book informal meetings with key employees from that department. Even though it is up to every department in the municipality to handle their own IT, the software managers and the ICT managers in the various departments cooperate on a regular basis. The Swedish municipality practices concerning knowledge management is having formal operational meetings and formal strategic meetings, which can lead to informal meetings, in order to exercise knowledge creation, acquisition sharing and replenishment. By having these informal meetings, knowledge is shared between the employees in the different departments of this municipality.

4.2   SaaS Influence on IT Governance Structure, Processes and Relational Mechanisms in the Swedish Municipality

SaaS Influence on IT Governance Structure in the Swedish Municipality
The IT governance structure in the Swedish municipality addresses where the IT decision making authority is located. In the municipality every department controls their own IT and has their own IT budget. In the previous years, 20% of the municipality software was SaaS and approximately 80% was operated by a partner. Now, half of the software are in the cloud and half are operated by their partner. In the future years, the municipality is planning to have 80% SaaS and 20% of the software are going to be operated by their operating partner. Some departments in the municipality have adopted SaaS to a greater extent than others. This is mainly because some departments needs special software to suit their unique businesses and, in many cases, there are only a few vendors that offers this specific software. An ICT manager has stated that: "In our department we need very specific and custom made software, which are not available as SaaS solutions yet. Therefore, SaaS have not been adopted in a

large scale, but we are getting there" (Interviewee 6). On the other hand, all of the interviewees consider that there are numerous advantages of having SaaS, which could be a reason to why SaaS is used in a large extent in the municipality. The reason why the remaining 20% of the software are not being moved to the cloud is also because they are large, old and complex and it is not reasonable to move them. The municipality purchases SaaS to a greater extent today because the software vendors often provide SaaS solutions over software solutions requiring physical servers. Furthermore, the municipality wants to purchase features and services that can improve the municipality's own services. The decisions regarding IT in the departments are to be taken by the department's business along with the ICT manager. Although, the departments are obliged to consult the City Management Office, procurement office, legal department and safety. They have to do this in order to ensure that all departments are following laws. If there are decisions that have to be taken regarding basic IT prerequisites in the municipality, e.g., common storage, then the Chief Digital Officer (CDO) has the power to make the decisions. The CDO monitors the financing of what is common for all of the Departments in the municipality, e.g., the technical platforms and the entire operating agreement. The CDO has noticed that: "It could be a good idea to anchor IT decisions with the Municipality Assembly to get a political mandate and thus convey the reasoning to the politics" (Interviewee 1). Effective IT governance can be determined by the location of the IT decision making authority and the decision-making structure can be centralized, decentralized and federal [29]. The location of the decision-making structure in the municipality is not influenced by SaaS because the municipality is governed by politicians. Since the municipality is governed by politicians, the IT decision making structure can appear to be centralized. Although, because the municipality is a large organization that consists of 14 departments that can make their own IT decisions, the federal structure is a more suitable explanation of the municipality's IT decision making authority. The interviewees have explained that their roles and responsibilities have changed to some extent in regard to SaaS (see Fig. 4).

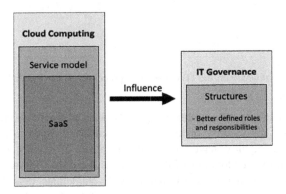

Fig. 4. SaaS influence on the IT governance structures in the Swedish municipality

For example, an ICT manager considers that roles have changed in regard to the fact that SaaS is more widely used, because now as ICT manager can focus on the right things and properly work with the development of the business, "Now, with SaaS it is less work for us, and we can do other things that are more important for the business, so our responsibilities have changed" (Interviewee 4).

SaaS Influence on IT Governance Processes in the Swedish Municipality
Using pm3 model as IT governance in the Swedish municipality has created a clear distinction between business related software management and IT related software management. The IT related software management is primarily about operating management, which is no longer required if you buy SaaS because the SaaS vendor operates the software. This means that IT related software management that pm3 [39] advocates is no longer in use with SaaS. The interviewees also explain that ITIL is not either developed for purchases of SaaS solutions. According to the interviewees they do not see the need for a new model to replace pm3 [39], instead they use what is relevant in the model that can be applied to the municipality, and to adjust and customize the model to better fit the municipality. Interviewee 4 noticed that: "Pm3 is not really adapted to organizations today, but I think that the model is really good because it creates structure and order, and it also makes costs more visible and so on. So, it is a good and clear model, but it is not the best for SaaS solutions, it needs to be adapted if used" (Interviewee 4). On the other hand the municipality uses pm3 and the operating vendor uses ITIL. In addition to pm3 [39] and ITIL each department can have their own guidelines, and IT governance frameworks or processes that they follow it (see Fig. 5).

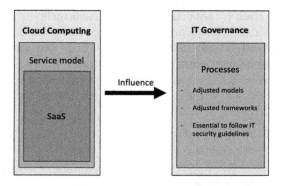

Fig. 5. SaaS influence on the IT governance processes in the Swedish municipality

Processes, guidelines and requirements are also in place in the Swedish municipality to make sure that the security of the software that are planned to be purchased are reliable. The municipality have guidelines in place containing different security requirements that the vendors must follow. For instance, they follow ISO/IEC 27000, which is an international standard that provide guidelines regarding information security. It can be utilized to assess the security of the internal organization or the security of an external organization. The municipality use ISO/ISO 27000 requires that the vendor have effective routines in place for their own IT security and also requires that the vendor's employees and their background are checked and that every party involved have signed a confidentiality agreement. Moreover, this municipality also demands that communications are encrypted, which is especially important when working with SaaS solutions because you can have access to the cloud wherever you are: "We do not know if the person are sitting here on our network or if he is sitting at home or wherever, so we want the SaaS solution to be encrypted, which you can get per automation" (Interviewee 2).

SaaS Influence on IT Governance Relational Mechanisms in the Swedish Municipality

The IT governance relational mechanisms of Van Grembergen & De Haes [23] framework is about collaboration, communication and participation between the business and IT department. The interviewees describe that the municipality, including all the departments, have cooperative agreements with their operating partner as well as the various SaaS vendors. In these agreements it is stated how often they should meet and what kind of expectations of proactive development there is. The City Management Office have meetings with important software vendors a couple of times per semester, at least 4 times per year. Important meaning bigger and more complex software which is used throughout the municipality or in certain departments. In these meetings, the City Management Office follow up on the vendors agreements and the content of the agreements. The City Management Office also have meetings every two week with their operating partner, this is because thousands of operating cases arises per week that needs to be followed up. The operating partner have stipulated a contract where they promise certain measuring points and delivery capacity. The meetings between the City Management Office and the operating partner is then often about overall operating issues, but also about the vendor showing that they are doing what was promised in the contract. Every department in the municipality can have their own SaaS vendor and therefore it is up to the department to have their own meetings with their SaaS vendor. Furthermore, with a SaaS solution fewer vendors needs to be involved, because the third party, the IT operating partner, is eliminated, since both the operation and software is included. This compared to the municipality having an operating partner and a software vendor, since they need to communicate and have meetings with both (see Fig. 6).

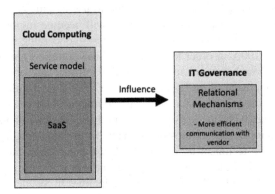

Fig. 6. SaaS influence on the IT governance relational mechanisms in the Swedish municipality

The influence of SaaS on IT governance relational mechanisms in the Swedish municipality is that makes communication and the use of the software more efficient and time effective. Otherwise, the municipality had to go through a software operating provider and the software provider had to communicate with the operating provider, and then the municipality had to be involved in some manner: "When a third party is eliminated you avoid people putting the blame on each other. That the software provider blames the operating provider and say that the issue is not with them but with the operating provider, and then the other party says, no it is not the operation but the software, i.e. you can avoid that, which is nice." (Interviewee 3). With the SaaS vendor the contact is more about planning, how do the SaaS vendor think, what kind of plans do they have to strategically move forward and what are the vendors planning to develop next. As example one of the interviewees has mentioned "With SaaS I believe we can plan more ahead at strategic level. We have more time to discuss development than to have to go into certain details and orders. SaaS vendors do not ask their customers if it is ok for them to replace a bad and old server. We can get this kind of question from our operating partner because they may want us to pay for it and that is a big difference between these vendors" (Interviewee 4).

5   Conclusions

This research has focused on how SaaS influence IT governance structures, processes and relational mechanisms in a Swedish municipality. The results shows that SaaS influence IT governance in different aspects like the roles and responsibilities in the ITG governance structure, making it possible for the departments in the municipality to better work with the development of the services. Moreover, ICT department have more time to focus on the development of the services in the Swedish municipality and SaaS could potentially speed up the decision-making processes in the various departments of this municipality. Apart from these findings, we have also found that there are new roles and responsibilities that are planned in regard to SaaS in the Swedish municipality that is currently investigating new forms of dialogue between the different departments regarding using SaaS. We have also found that SaaS influence IT governance processes and the IT governance model (pm3) used in the Swedish municipality needs to be adjusted if they will continue to use it. This is because pm3 is not developed for the use of SaaS. Furthermore, it will become important to follow the influence of the SaaS on the IT governance processes concerning information security like e.g. ISO/IEC 27000, in order to ensure that SaaS solutions are secure. In fact, by using SaaS in the Swedish municipality both the software and operation is included, which eliminates the need of an operating partner. This aspect influences the IT governance relational mechanisms by making the communication vender consumer more efficient. The contact with the SaaS vendor is in this case more about planning ahead which can add value for the various departments in the municipality. A limitation of this study is that the technical aspects of SaaS were not taken into account e.g. the cloud infrastructure. In order to generalize the findings of this study, a replication of this research will need to be done in other municipalities in Sweden. Cloud computing is now well spread in the public organizations in Sweden and will increase in the near future. According to ReportLinker (2019) "over 65% of Swedish organizations invest in digitization. The digitization trend is expected to continue during the forecast period, especially in the public sector. The demand is mostly driven by the adoption of new delivery models such as cloud computing, big data, and the Internet of Things (IoT)". Therefore, the results of this research are important for both researchers in this area as well for IT decision makers in public organizations for understanding how SaaS influence IT governance and identify the effective IT governance structures, processes and relational mechanisms that create value from this cloud computing service model.

References

1. Kathuria, A., Mann, A., Khuntia, J., Saldanha, T.J.V., Kauffman, R.J.: A strategic value appropriation path for cloud computing. J. Manage. Inf. Syst, **35**(3), 740–775 (2018)
2. Mell, P., Grance, T.: The NIST definition of Cloud Computing. National Institute of Standards and Technology, **53**, 20011 (2011)
3. Van Grembergen, W., De Haes, S.: Enterprise Governance of Information Technology: Achieving Strategic Alignment and Value. Springer, New York (2009)
4. Weill, P., Ross, J.W.: IT Governance: How Top Performers Manage IT Decision Rights for Superior Results. Harvard Business School Press, Boston (2004)
5. Turedi, S., Zhu, H.: How to generate more value from IT: the interplay of it investment, decision making structure, and senior management involvement in IT governance. Communi. Assoc. Inf. Syst. **44**, 511–536 (2019)
6. Rusu, L., Viscusi, G.: Preface. In: Rusu, L., Viscusi, G. (eds.) Information Technology Governance in Public Organizations - Theory and Practice. Springer International Publishing AG (2017)
7. Hoch, D., Payan, M.: Establishing good IT governance in the public sector, Transforming Government, McKinsey & Company, March 2008, 45–55 (2008)
8. Johansson, B., Muhic, M.: Relativism in the cloud: cloud sourcing in virtue of IS development outsourcing - a literature review. Int. J. Inf. Syst. Project Manage. **5**(4), 55–65 (2017)
9. Andriole, S.: Forrester Research Gets Cloud Computing Trends Right (2019). https://www.forbes.com/sites/steveandriole/2019/11/20/forrester-research-gets-cloud–computing-trends-right/#7853d09068a2
10. Queensland Government: Benefits of cloud computing (2017). https://www.business.qld.gov.au/running-business/it/cloud-computing/benefits
11. Prieto-González, L., Tamm, G., Stantchev, V.: Governance of Cloud Computing: semantic aspects and cloud service brokers. Int. J. Web and Grid Services, **11**(4), 377–389 (2015)
12. Jafarijoo, M., Joshi, K.D.: How do firms derive value from cloud computing investment? examining the role of information technology governance. In: AMCIS 2020 Proceedings. pp. 1–10, Association for Information Systems (2020)
13. Ali, S., Green, P.: IT governance mechanisms in public sector organizations: an Australian context. J. Global Inf. Manage. **15**(4), 41–63 (2007)
14. Campbell, J., McDonald, C., Sethibe, T.: Public and private sector it governance: identifying contextual differences. Australasian J. Inf. Syst. **16**(2), 5–18 (2009)
15. Al-Farsi, K., Haddadeh, R.E.: Framing information technology governance in the public sector: opportunities and challenges. Int. J. Electron. Govern. Res. **11**(4), 89–101 (2015)

16. Tonelli, A.O., de Souza Bermejo, P.H., Aparecida dos Santos, P., Zuppo, L., Zambalde, L. A.: IT governance in the public sector: a conceptual model. Inf. Syst. Front. **19**(3), 593–610 (2017)
17. Prasad, A., Green, P., Heales, J.: On governance structures for the Cloud Computing services and assessing their effectiveness. Int. J. Account. Inf. Syst. **15**, 335–356 (2014)
18. Vithayathil, J.: Will cloud computing make the information technology (IT) department obsolete? Inf. Syst. J. **28**(4), 634–649 (2017)
19. Schneider, S., Sunyaev, A.: Determinant factors of cloud-sourcing decisions: reflecting on the IT outsourcing literature in the era of cloud computing. J. Inf. Technol. **31**(1), 1–31 (2016)
20. Youseff, L., Butrico, M., Da Silva, D.: Toward a unified ontology of cloud computing. In: 2008 Grid Computing Environments Workshop, pp. 1–10, IEEE (2008)
21. Al-Ruithe, M., Benkhelifa, E.: Analysis and classification of barriers and critical success factors for implementing a cloud data governance strategy. Procedia Comput. Sci. **113**, 223–232 (2017)
22. Muhic, M., Johansson, B.: Cloud sourcing - next generation outsourcing? Procedia Technol. **16**, 553–561 (2014)
23. Van Grembergen, W., De Haes, S.: Implementing information technology governance: models. IGI Publishing, Practices and Cases (2008)
24. IT Governance Institute (ITGI): Board Briefing on IT Governance. Illinois: IT Governance Institute (2003). https://www.oecd.org/site/ictworkshops/year/2006/37599342.pdf
25. Nfuka, E., Rusu, L., Johannesson, P., Mutagahywa, B.: The state of IT governance in organizations from public sector in a developing country. In: Proceedings of HICSS-42 - Hawaii International Conference on System Sciences, pp. 1–12, IEEE (2009)
26. Winkler, T.J.: IT Governance Mechanisms and Administration/ IT Alignment in the Public Sector: A Conceptual Model and Case Validation, Wirtschaftsinformatik Proceedings 2013, pp. 831–845. Association for Information Systems (2013)
27. Al Qassimi, N., Rusu, L.: IT governance in a public organization in a developing country: a case study of a governmental organization. Procedia Comput. Sci. **64**, 450–456 (2015)
28. Bianchi, I., Sousa, R., Pereira, R., Hillegersberg, J.: Baseline mechanisms for IT governance at universities. In: Proceedings of the 25th European Conference on Information Systems (ECIS), pp. 1551–1567. Association for Information Systems (2017)
29. Van Grembergen, W., De Haes, S., Guldentops, E.: Structure, Processes and Relational Mechanisms for IT Governance. In: Van Grembergen, W. (ed.) Strategies for Information Technology Governance, pp. 1–36. Idea Group Publishing, Pennsylvania (2004)
30. Khalil, S., Fernandez, V., Fautrero, V.: Cloud impact on IT governance. In: 2016 IEEE 18th Conference on Business Informatics (CBI), pp. 255–261. IEEE (2016)
31. Bounagui, Y., Hafiddi, H., Mezrioui, A.: Challenges for IT based cloud computing governance. In: 2014 9th International Conference on Intelligent Systems: Theories and Applications (SITA-14), IEEE (2014)
32. Winkler, T.J., Benlian, A., Piper, M., Hirsch, H.: Bayer healthcare delivers a dose of reality for cloud payoff mantras in multinationals. MIS Quarterly Executive **13**(4), 193–208 (2014)
33. Prasad, A., Green, P.: Governing cloud computing services: reconsideration of IT governance structures. Int. J. Account. Inf. Syst. **19**, 45–58 (2015)
34. Yin, R.K.: Case Study Research: Design and Methods, 5th edn. Sage, London (2014)
35. Myers, M.D., Avison, D.E.: Qualitative Research in Information Systems: A Reader (Introducing Qualitative Methods). Sage Publications, London (2002)

36. Denscombe, M.: The Good Research Guide: For Small-scale Social Research Projects, 4th edn. Open University Press, Maidenhead (2010)
37. Bryman, A.: Social Research Methods, 4th edn. Oxford University Press, Oxford (2012)
38. Braun, V., Clarke, V.: Thematic analysis. In: Cooper, H. (ed.) The Handbook of Research Methods in Psychology. American Psychological Association, Washington (2012)
39. På pm3: pm3 model (2018). https://pm3.se/pm3-modellen/
40. ReportLinker: Sweden Asia Data Center Market - Investment Analysis and Growth Opportunities 2019–2024 (2019). https://www.reportlinker.com/p05796161/Sweden-Asia-Data-Center-Market-Investment-Analysis-and-Growth-Opportunities.html?utm_source=GNW

Cultural Barriers in Digital Transformation in a Public Organization: A Case Study of a Sri-Lankan Organization

Lazar Rusu[(⊠)], Prasanna B.L. Balasuriya, and Ousman Bah

Department of Computer and Systems Sciences, Stockholm University, Stockholm, Sweden
lrusu@dsv.su.se, prabalasuriya@yahoo.com, ousgaba@gmail.com

Abstract. Digital transformation is a sine qua non in the business operations in private and public sector organizations. However, in achieving digital transformation in public organizations of significance importance are the cultural barriers. Previous studies on the barriers in digital transformation have mainly focused on private organizations, and less attention has been given to cultural barriers in digital transformation in public organizations. Therefore, this research has focused on the case of a public organization like Inland Revenue Department (IRD) in Sri-Lanka to identify the cultural barriers in digital transformation. The data was collected through semi-structured interviews, and from internal documents (organizational publications and annual performance reports of IRD), and was analyzed using thematic analysis. The research has identified a number of twenty-one cultural barriers that were classified into five themes. Out of those twenty-one, twelve were recognized as new cultural barriers in digital transformation in public organizations. The results of this research are important for both researchers in this area as well as the managers in public organizations to focus their efforts, mitigate the identified cultural barriers, and improve the digital transformation implementation in their organizations.

Keywords: Digital transformation · Cultural barriers · Public organization · Developing Country · Sri-Lanka

1 Introduction

Due to the advancement of technology and the urgent need in addressing the challenges of businesses in fulfilling their operations, digital transformation has become a fundamental requirement in business organizations [1–5]. According to [6] cultural phenomenon and a creation of a business model for organizations had been the concern in defining the digital transformation. Henriette et al. [6, p. 3] have defined digital transformation as "a disruptive or incremental change process. It starts with the adoption and use of digital technologies, then evolving into an implicit holistic transformation of an organization or deliberate to pursue value creation". However, barriers in digital transformation is not only about the technological aspect but also concerning the cultural traditions such as; employee's resistant to change, lack of

© Springer Nature Switzerland AG 2020
M. Themistocleous et al. (Eds.): EMCIS 2020, LNBIP 402, pp. 640–656, 2020.
https://doi.org/10.1007/978-3-030-63396-7_43

sufficient resources, lack of required knowledge and practices, that are affecting negatively the digital transformation [2, 4]. According to [7] around 85% of digital transformation does not reach at a success and being successfully has been a consistent challenge in the implementation of digital transformation [8, 9]. With regard to the Sri-Lankan digital transformation failures, the attention has been focused mainly on financial sector [10] and transportation sector [11]. During colonialism, public sector organizations were more bureaucratic and hierarchical. Therefore, the employees thought that the head of the organization could only give solutions to their problems [11]. Moreover according to [11] digital transformation fails in public organizations due to cultural barriers; negative mind-set among employees, power distance (respecting people with power), resistant to change and absence of team culture. Furthermore, [11] also noted that a sense of superiority, and pride within the top management has created a strong power distance between the top and the junior management. Several researches on the barriers in digital transformation have been conducted [4, 6], [12–14], but a few studies have been carried out on the cultural barriers in digital transformation in developing countries [10, 11]. According to [15] public sector organizations should consider the central change challenges and barriers, prior the implementation of digital transformation process. Previous research studies conducted on digital transformation in organizations have given less attention to its cultural barriers and it still lacks a clear definition of them [16]. As noted by [17] less attention has been given to the research on digital transformation in developing countries that are different from that in the developed countries because of the cultural differences. According to [18] the growth of digital transformation in Sri-Lanka is far behind compared with countries like India, China and other developed countries. The prevailing culture in most of the public organizations in Sri-Lanka has become an obstacle for the implementation of digital transformation [18]. Compared with the private sector organizations, digital transformation in the public sector organizations is far behind [19]. Having considered the above factors, the problem addressed in this research is to identify the cultural barriers in digital transformation in a public organization in Sri-Lanka. To address this lack of knowledge the following research question was formulated; *"What are the cultural barriers in achieving digital transformation in a public organization in Sri-Lanka?"*. The next sections of the paper include the research background, research methodology, results and discussion, and conclusions.

2 Research Background

2.1 Culture and Barriers in Digital Transformation

According to [20, p.625] "business transformation is about bringing radical changes in organizational culture in terms of structure, processes and above all, people's attitudes, beliefs and behaviours". Therefore, in the process of successful digital transformation, cultural change becomes a mandatory element [20, 21]. Promoting the sharing of skills, knowledge, resources, development and learning are critical factors required for a strong organizational culture [22]. In encouraging the employees of an organization to absorb those critical factors [14] the role played by culture is rather significant in the process of digital transformation. Culture is including values, beliefs, life practices, language and behaviour of members of a society. It comprises of the behaviour, characteristics and values of citizens [23]. Therefore, there should be a thorough concern on the organizational culture within the organizational transformation [14]. Due to power distance, the employee's negative mind-set and the non-availability of team culture, digital transformation in public organizations in developing countries finds it rather difficult to prevail [11]. As per [24], culture is considered as the greatest challenge in the digital transformation and therefore the identification of cultural barriers in digital transformation is very important. Moreover, when there are cultural problems in an organization, it would even lead to the collapse of the best designed digital strategy, therefore organizational culture should be considered as a mandatory aspect in reaching a successful digital transformation [25]. Furthermore, for a successful digital transformation there is a need to start with a cultural transformation [26]. According to [27] the maturity of the digital transformation in organizations is acquired in four dimensions of the Forrester digital maturity model: culture, technology, organizations and insights. However, the main barriers in digital transformation are not technology, but the human factors such as; cultural traditions, lack of relevant knowledge and good practices, lack of motivation, risk taking, the effect of IT capability on digital transformation and employees' resistance to change [2], [28–30]. In opinion of [17] the adoption of digital transformation in an organization is influenced by the cultural barriers and the four dimensions of culture (uncertainty avoidance, power distance, individualism and masculinity). In Sri-Lanka as a developing country, public sector organizations are rather bureaucratic. In this country, [11] have noted that there is a power distance between the junior staff and the senior management. Furthermore, the senior management does not entertain the ideas of the junior staffers in the initiation of a digital transformation [11].

2.2 The Importance of Digital Transformation in Public Organizations

In the digital transformation of public sector organizations, the contribution given by web 2.0, social media and networks is considerable [31]. In a study done by [32] the authors have commented on three levels of maturity: *people, processes and preparedness* in connection with the digital transformation in the public sector organizations. In fact, public sector organizations should maintain ambidexterity with changes and strategies to have a successful digital transformation [13]. Digital transformation in a public organization needs an agile leadership, remedied cultural obstacles and changing government processes [31]. As found out by [19], digital transformation in public organizations is far behind as compared with the private organizations. However, digital transformation has already become a mandatory requirement in the public sector organizations since there is a growing need for development of information systems in the public departments while citizens are looking for agile and innovative services [33].

2.3 Factors Affecting Digital Transformation Identified in Research Literature

In a review of the research literature, we have identified a number of factors affecting digital transformation in organizations mapped into five main cultural dimensions and shown in Table 1. The five main cultural dimensions shown in Table 1 are those relevant to the factors that are affecting digital transformation, and are discussed below.

"**Knowledge Gaps**" is one of the cultural dimensions that negatively affect digital transformation. The lack of knowledge and the issues in the correct dissemination of knowledge stand as a barrier for the digital transformation. According to [2, 28, 30, 34, 35] lack of relevant knowledge, lack of qualified personnel and training, missing skills and lack of awareness and skills are the knowledge gaps which hinder the digital transformation. Depending on each other of the organization during the process of digital transformation is also a barrier.

"**Dependencies**" is one of the cultural dimensions that have a negative impact on the digital transformation process. As per [17, 25, 34] individualism, individual barriers and lack of competencies prevail within the constituent of dependencies. Previous researchers have also identified "**Bureaucracy**" as another cultural dimension that is one of the most significant in public sector organizational culture in the developing countries [11]. This phenomenon negatively affects with the digital transformation process. Bureaucratic culture gives power to the hierarchies. Bureaucracy considers that some people are very important; so that they should be respected [11]. "**Miscommunication**" is one of the cultural dimensions in the digital transformation because miscommunication with the employees, stakeholders and the citizens is a barrier for the digital transformation process. For example, resistant to change, lack of partnership and collaboration, and inescapable leadership, are in opinion of [11, 25, 28] involved with negative communication which create issues within the digital transformation process. In the dimension of "**Accomplishments**" that is another cultural dimension, it is highlighted that the digital transformation is successfully extinguished by mitigating all those barriers, discussed above. The previous research studies have identified also strategies, common elements, models, frameworks and benefits that can be used in accomplishing the digital transformation process [36–40]. Accomplishments stand as a barrier, because when the organizations did not embrace digitalization from the commencement, a successful implementation of digital transformation will not be attained. Moreover, when the organization did not support digital transformation, there cannot be a successful implementation of digital transformation, hence whatever strategies, aims and goals in place, digital transformation cannot be attained.

Table 1. Factors affecting the digital transformation found in research literature mapped into cultural dimensions

Authors	Research Focus	Factors Affecting Digital Transformation	Cultural Dimensions
[2]	Digital transformation in organizations	Cultural traditions	Bureaucracy
		Lack of relevant knowledge	Knowledge Gaps
		Employee's resistant to change	Miscommunication
		Lack of adequate resources	
		Lack of motivation	
[11]	Digital transformation failure in public sector	Power distance	Bureaucracy
		Negative mind-set	Knowledge Gaps
		Resistant to change	
		Absence of team culture	Miscommunication
		Role of leadership	Dependencies
[13]	Drivers, success factors and implications of digital transformation	A supportive organizational culture	Accomplishments
		Customer behaviour and expectations	
		Engage managers and employees	
		Reformed IS organization	
[14]	Developing a supportive culture in digital transformation	The importance of culture in change	Knowledge Gaps
		Building supportive culture	
		Digital organizational culture	
		Resistant to the technology	Bureaucracy
		Inadequate leadership skills	Dependencies
		Lack of vision	Miscommunication
[16]	Cultural values for digital transformation	Openness towards change	Accomplishments
		Innovation	
		Agility	
[17]	Digital transformation in SME's in a developing country	Power distance	Bureaucracy
		Masculinity	
		Individualism	Knowledge Gaps
		Uncertainty avoidance	
[21]	IT enabled business transformation	Business process redesign	Accomplishments
		Internal integration	

(continued)

Table 1. (*continued*)

Authors	Research Focus	Factors Affecting Digital Transformation	Cultural Dimensions
[22]	Managing organizational knowledge	Organizational perspective	Knowledge Gaps
		Team/Group perspective	
		Individual perspective	
[25]	Antithetic leadership	Inescapable leadership	Knowledge Gaps
		Impact of organizational culture	Miscommunication
[28]	Barriers of e-government implementation	ICT infrastructure	Accomplishments
		Privacy and security	
		Lack of qualified personnel and training	Knowledge Gaps
		Lack of partnership and collaboration	Miscommunication
		Leaders and management support	
		Cultural implications	Bureaucracy
[29]	Culture of change and innovation in digital transformation	Lack of imagination and strategy	Knowledge Gaps
		Lack of agility and innovation	
		Lack of competencies	
[30]	IT capability and digital transformation	The effect of IT capability on digital transformation	Knowledge Gaps
		The effect of IT capability on firm performance	
[31]	Digital transformation in public sector organizations	Organizational support	Accomplishments
		Web 2.0, social media and networks	
		Knowledge sharing organizational culture	Knowledge Gaps
[34]	Barriers to digital transformation	Missing skills	Knowledge Gaps
		Technical barriers	
		Individual barriers	Bureaucracy
		Organizational and cultural barriers	
[35]	Digital transformation: Is public sector following the enterprise 2.0	Culture and user focus	Miscommunication
		Lack of awareness and skills	Knowledge Gaps
		Characteristics of a digitally matured public organization	
[36]		Culture of innovation	Accomplishments

(*continued*)

Table 1. (*continued*)

Authors	Research Focus	Factors Affecting Digital Transformation	Cultural Dimensions
	Gearing up for successful digital transformation	Digital capability	
		Strategic alignment	
[37]	Digital transformation strategies	Use of technologies	Accomplishments
		Structural changes	
		Changes in value creation	
[38]	Five building blocks of digital transformation	Shared customer insights	Accomplishments
		Digital platform	
		Accountability framework	
[39]	Four dimensions of digital maturity	Culture: How company's approach to digital driven innovation	Accomplishments
		Technology: How company's use and adopt of technology	
		Organization: How to align company to support digital strategy	
		Insights: How company use customer and business data	
[40]	Embracing digital technology	Benefits of digital transformation	Accomplishments
		Attitudes of old workers	Knowledge Gaps
		Legacy technology	

3 Research Methodology

The study has focused on identifying the cultural barriers in digital transformation in a public organization in Sri-Lanka. The public organization selected in this research was The Inland Revenue Department (IRD) that is under the purview of the Ministry of Finance (MoF) of Sri-Lanka. The reason of selecting IRD was because Revenue Administration and Management Information System (RAMIS) assists IRD in simplifying its tax administration and tax compliance with the taxpayers and is on-going through a digital transformation, therefore, this was an important factor for the selection of this particular public organization. The research strategy is a plan of action designed in a layout to reach and achieve a specific goal of the study [41]. In this study, a case study research strategy was chosen to identify the cultural barriers in digital transformation at IRD. In acquiring meaningful data for the research, a non-probability sampling method was used to select the interview participants [41]. The selected participants

Table 2. List of participants, their positions in IRD, duration and dates of the interviews

Participants	The Position in IRD	Duration of interviews	Date of interviews
Respondent 1 (R1)	Top management	60 min	05 March 2020
Respondent 2 (R2)	Top management	60 min	06 March 2020
Respondent 3 (R3)	Top management	60 min	06 March 2020
Respondent 4 (R4)	Middle management	45 min	09 March 2020
Respondent 5 (R5)	Middle management	45 min	09 March 2020
Respondent 6 (R6)	Middle management	30 min	10 March 2020
Respondent 7 (R7)	Junior management	30 min	10 March 2020
Respondent 8 (R8)	Junior management	30 min	10 March 2020

in this study are those having the relevant experience with the ongoing RAMIS system, and involved in the process of digital transformation. They are from the top management, middle management and junior management of IRD. The interview questions were formulated using the factors affecting digital transformation shown in Table 1, and grouped into five dimensions (Knowledge Gaps, Dependencies, Bureaucracy, Communication and Accomplishments). The data collection was done through semi-structured interviews conducted with the selected participants at the head office in Colombo, Sri-Lanka. In order to achieve triangulation, the researchers have used multiple sources of information such as internal documents, annual performance reports and government publications [42]. The participants, their generic positions (for anonymity) in IRD, duration and date of interviews, are presented in Table 2.

In the consent form, we have agreed with the interviewees at IRD to keep their anonymity, and their names and positions in the public organization to not be disclosed. However, the Human Resource department of IRD gave its approval to use the name of their organization. The data collected was analyzed thematically and followed the step-by-step guidelines provided by [43] in conducting thematic analysis. By using the thematic analysis, in the transcribed interviews, were identified the patterns which reflect meanings and interest in the dataset and defined them into codes, sub-themes and themes. The thematic map generated through the above facts is shown in Fig. 1.

4   Results and Discussion

This study has looked to identify the cultural barriers in achieving the digital transformation in a public organization in Sri-Lanka. The identified cultural barriers are shown as sub-themes under five main themes (knowledge gap, dependencies, miscommunication, bureaucracy and accomplishments), are presented in thematic map in Fig. 1.

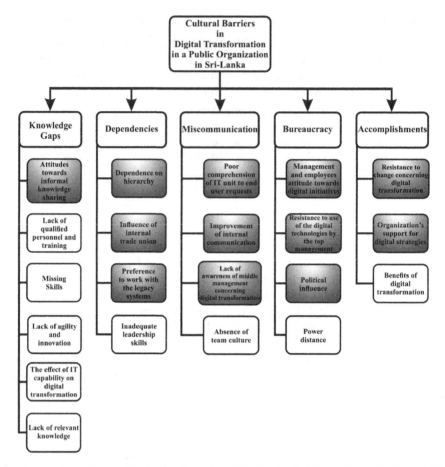

Fig. 1. The thematic map illustrating the cultural barriers in digital transformation in a public organization in Sri-Lanka

In Fig. 1, are shown twenty-one cultural barriers in digital transformation in a public organization in Sri-Lanka classified under five main themes. From these twenty-one cultural barriers, we have nine cultural barriers, identified through research literature (that they will not be discussed in this paper) and twelve new cultural barriers that were identified in a public organization (IRD) in Sri-Lanka and shown in the light grey color in Fig. 1. The twelve new cultural barriers in digital transformation identified in IRD, Sri-Lanka, are presented below under the five main themes.

"Attitudes towards informal knowledge sharing" is a new barrier, categorized under the theme of **Knowledge gaps**. As stated by most of the respondents, there are employees at IRD who have extra qualifications on IT, apart from that of the same in tax related matters. But as noted by R3, IRD never gets their service for any type of digital initiation.

"[......] frankly if the knowledge is shared, we can give an absolutely better service. It's in vain when we have to pay a great deal of money to a foreign company even when we have competent employees within the organization" (R3).

R5 noted that there are some officers who have a considerable knowledge on the functions of the RAMIS system. But, when an officer who does not have the same level of knowledge asks for the assistance of those officers, they refuse to assist.

"You know it's very funny to see that even when knowledge is already available some staffers are not willing to share it among the others who don't have it. I think that's something wrong in their cultural mind-set." (R5).

In order to address this barrier, knowledge on digital initiation should be shared among the employees.

"Dependence on hierarchy" is a new barrier under the theme of **Dependencies** and as noted by R3 a junior staff, despite the urgency of their workload, they have to remain silent until the senior officers of the top management give their consent on any matter related to digital transformation.

"[......] if there is a fault in the digital initiation, we are helpless, because the taxpayer has to wait for a long time until the boss himself rectifies the matters. You know sometimes those faults are very minor things. But you got to wait for a long time since you need the approval of the boss." (R3).

According to R7, if there are matters which cannot be remedied by the IT unit, it is notified to the Singaporean company. Generally, it is complained that it takes such a long time if the matters end up with the foreign company.

"[......] we inform the IT unit and at times it's so tired of waiting for long time until our matters are rectified. Sometimes even if we wait for a long time, the IT unit asks us to contact the Singaporean company." (R7).

In order to address this barrier, there is a need of an ad-hoc officer that should be appointed until the officer relevant returns. Moreover, there is a need for training like workshops concerning personality development that can be organized in order to avoid dependency on each other.

"Influence of internal trade union" is another new barrier under the theme of **Dependencies**. Whenever there is a digital transformation, some employees who dislike such a move often tend to complain to the trade union within IRD. R7 noted that by informing the trade union, the staffers try to take an upper hand on the suggested changes in the digital transformation.

"[......] whenever a word of digital transformation is heard they get panic and report it to the trade union. Trade union of course are in favour of the staffers and they make a big issue over the suggested digital transformation" (R7).

R2 noted that in his experience he has found out that trade union have been detrimental on the smooth function of public organizations. "Trade unions are the biggest troublemakers in public organizations. As you work digitally, it is better if trade unions are not involved [......]" (R2).

To address this barrier, trade union should be well convinced of the importance of digital transformation in providing better services for the citizens.

"Preference to work with the legacy systems" is a new barrier under the theme of **Dependencies**. As noted by R3 some of the senior officers are addicted to work on the legacy system, but hardly are they bothered to get adapted with the RAMIS system.

"There are many employees who still prefer to work with the legacy system. Those days it was rather difficult to convince them about the new RAMIS system [......]" (R3).

R5 has identified that some employees still give destructive criticism on the RAMIS system. Changing their deeply rooted attitudes on the RAMIS system was an absolutely difficult task.

"We never expected that our employees would resist the RAMIS system as much as they actually did. We had to speak to most of our employees individually [......]" (R5).

To address this barrier, the legacy system should be discharged in a period of time and the employees should be motivated to work with the RAMIS system.

"*Poor comprehension of IT unit to end user requests*" is a new barrier under the theme of **Miscommunication**. R3 stated that when the RAMIS system is updated with any changes introduced by the acts, sometimes it is inaccurately updated, where it is found that there is a poor understanding with the dissemination of information.

"When there are several parties they differently understand the actual nature of the initial information. End of the day you don't exactly get the true information. This is simply a miscommunication [......]" (R3).

According to R7, the end users generally face with difficulties in dealing with the taxpayers. Under these circumstances, the end user is well convinced of the issues, arise. However, though issues are asked to be remedied by the IT unit, the IT unit does not have a sound understanding on the issues.

"Even if the IT unit is informed of the issues that the end users face with, their understanding seems to be rather poor. And I believe their ignorance is due to the miscommunication" (R7).

To address this barrier, a communication officer should be appointed with the purpose to facilitate communication between the end user and the IT unit.

"*Improvement of internal communication*" is another new barrier under the theme of **Miscommunication**. As noted by R3, RAMIS system is having the interface in the English language. However, there are some senior officers whose English knowledge is not satisfactory and thus creates difficulties in understanding of working with the RAMIS system.

"There are some senior officers who have a poor understanding in English. But they are not willing to declare it. They keep it by themselves and that creates a nightmare [......]" (R3).

R2 stated that the Singaporean company is contacted for some upgrades in the RAMIS system. Sometimes it is found that the information, conveyed is not properly understood at the receiving end.

"When we speak to the Singapore company regarding the upgrades in RAMIS they take what we tell them differently [......]" (R2).

To address this barrier, the internal communication in the organization should be improved so all the employees can better understand each other's.

"*Lack of awareness of middle management concerning digital transformation*" is a new barrier under the theme of **Miscommunication**. As per R7, the top management keeps a low profile with the junior staffers in the decision making concerning the digital transformation. Therefore, the middle management does not get a proper awareness on digital transformation.

"Our bosses all of a sudden take decisions and implement them even without informing us. How good if they can inform everyone and get their ideas as well before any implementation [......]" (R7).

R4 stated that the training on digital transformation is not given to the relevant and competent officers.

"Actually, in our office, giving foreign training is heavily influenced. Therefore, the most relevant and suitable officers do not get it" (R4).

In order to address this barrier, the middle managers should be made well aware of the accomplishments of digital transformation as noted by [13]. Moreover, there is a need for a better selection of the employees who will be going on training in digital transformation.

"Management and employees attitude towards digital initiatives" is a new barrier under the theme of **Bureaucracy**. R4 noted that some of the officers in the top management generally refuse any initiation of a digital project.

"[......] the decisions taken by such officers hinder digital transformation. We can't influence them. They have a monopoly." (R4).

R2 said that some of the officers are not convinced of their contribution given to digital transformation. They are pessimistic on digital initiation.

"Most of the people in our culture are pessimistic. [......] People generally do not like to develop innovative ideas." (R2).

To address this barrier, the attitude of the employees and management should be changed for having a successful digital transformation [35].

"Resistance to use of the digital technologies by the top management" is a new barrier under the theme of **Bureaucracy**. As noted by most of the respondents, it is mandatory for IRD to be updated with digital transformation initiatives while being closely involved with new digital technologies. R4 noted that adding cloud computing into their digital transformation process would enhance the efficiency and effectiveness of the tax process.

"[......] it is absolutely good if we can have cloud computing in this process because we centrally deal with taxes, but since the top management is not concerned with new technologies still the matters remain in very primary level." (R4).

R5 revealed that some officers in the top management are difficult to be convinced with the benefits of new technologies.

"[......] anybody understands that in this digitalised world you can never survive without new technologies. But our top management is yet to understand this bitter truth." (R5).

To address this barrier, the benefits and value of using digital technologies for organization should be better explained by the IT unit to the top management.

"Political influence" is a new barrier under the theme of **Bureaucracy**. All the respondents noted that whenever a new government comes into power, the political hierarchy makes changes with the senior appointments in the departments and ministries.

"When a new minister comes in, the senior appointments in the ministry are changed [......]" (R3).

According to R2, the appointments made in the ministry are heavily politically influenced.

"If you were an ardent supporter of the elected political party, you have high possibilities of getting appointed as a top boss of a ministry or a department" (R2).

According to R4 as the government change, acts with regard to tax matters also get changed.

"When the government changes, we get burdened with many work. We got to entirely change our system of work according to the new acts introduced by the government." (R4).

To address this barrier, the public organizations should be made free of the political interferences.

"Resistance to change concerning digital transformation" is a new barrier under the theme of **Accomplishments**. R3 noted that most of the employees are pessimistic on the digital transformation and they keep on resisting from the very beginning of the digital initiation.

"[......] some officers seem little frightened over digital transformation. If all the officers also had given their contribution, the RAMIS could have been a huge success" (R3).

R4 also noted that generally at IRD, some officers in the top management as well as some junior employees oppose resistance whenever something innovative ways of working are introduced into their working area.

"[......] as I think I have felt that the employees in our organization have a different mind-set. Of course it is quite peculiar." (R4).

To address this barrier the employees should be well convinced of the importance and benefits of digital transformation as declared by [13] and the employees should be motivated to have thoughts on culture of innovation as noted by [36].

"Organization's support for digital strategies" is a new barrier under the theme of **Accomplishments**. According to R1, as the RAMIS system was initiated, IRD was well aligned to support digital strategies. However, the organization support did not last for long due to the negligence of the top management.

"RAMIS was initially in a very good form. But gradually it became slightly ineffective. I think that is exactly due to the fault of some of the officers in the top management [......]" (R1).

R7 noted that some of the officers who were about to retire were not highly knowledgeable and convinced of the benefits of the digital strategies.

"There are some officers who are eagerly waiting for their retirement and at the office mostly their work is quite less [......]" (R7).

In order to address this barrier as noted by [39] digital strategies should get the support of the organization.

5   Conclusions

To have a successful digital transformation it is very important to identify and mitigate the cultural barriers. Several research studies on the barriers in digital transformation have been conducted in different organizations [4, 6, 12, 13, 14], but only a few studies have been done on the cultural barriers in digital transformation in public organizations in the developing countries [11]. In fact, according to Gartner research [44] "the right culture is one of the most important requirements to achieve digital transformation". However, the public sector organizations in developing countries are facing a persistent challenge in reaching a successful implementation of digital transformation [11]. Therefore, in this study we have investigated *"What are the cultural barriers in achieving digital transformation in a public organization in Sri-Lanka?"*. The findings of this research study have identified twenty-one cultural barriers in digital transformation in a public organization in Sri-Lanka (IRD) that are important to be addressed for having a successful digital transformation implementation in this public organization. The new cultural barriers in digital transformation (in number of twelve) identified in this study are the followings: *"Attitudes towards informal knowledge sharing"*; *"Dependence on hierarchy"*; *"Influence of internal trade union"*; *"Preference to work with the legacy systems"*; *"Poor comprehension of IT unit to end users requests"*; *"Improvement of internal communication"*; *"Lack of awareness of middle management on digital transformation"*; *"Management and employees attitude towards digital initiatives"*; *"Resistance to use of the digital technologies by the top management"*; *"Political influence"*; *"Resistance to change concerning digital transformation"*; and *"Organization's support for digital strategies"*. There are possibilities for a future research due to the fact that this study has limited to one public organization like for example, the replication of this study in other public organizations in Sri-Lanka, in order to be able to generalize the results. However, the results of this research are still important for both researchers in this area as well as the managers in public organizations to focus their efforts, mitigate the identified cultural barriers, and improve the digital transformation implementation in their organizations.

Acknowledgements. The second and the third author of this paper are grateful to the Swedish Institute for their scholarships that have given them immense support in conducting this research work during their master's studies at Stockholm University.

References

1. Abolhassan, F.: Pursuing digital transformation driven by the cloud. In: Abolhassan, F. (ed.) The Drivers of Digital Transformation. MP, pp. 1–11. Springer, Cham (2017). https://doi.org/10.1007/978-3-319-31824-0_1
2. Schwertner, K.: Digital transformation of business. Trakia J. Sci. **15**(1), 388–393 (2017)
3. Ismail, M.H., Khater, M., Zaki, M.: Digital Business Transformation and Strategy: What Do We Know So Far? pp. 1–36, Cambridge Service Alliance, University of Cambridge (2017). https://cambridgeservicealliance.eng.cam.ac.uk/resources/Downloads/Monthly%20Papers/2017NovPaper_Mariam.pdf
4. Wolf, M., Semm, A., Erfurth, C.: Digital transformation in companies – challenges and success factors. In: Hodoň, M., Eichler, G., Erfurth, C., Fahrnberger, G. (eds.) I4CS 2018. CCIS, vol. 863, pp. 178–193. Springer, Cham (2018). https://doi.org/10.1007/978-3-319-93408-2_13
5. Porter, M., Heppelmann, J.: How smart, connected products are transforming competition. Harvard Bus. Rev. **92**(11), 1–23 (2014)

6. Henriette, E., Feki, M., Boughzala, I.: Digital transformation challenges. In: Proceedings of Mediterranean Conference on Information Systems (MCIS 2016), pp. 1–7. Association for Information Systems (2016)

7. Heeks, R.: Most e-Government-for-development projects fail: how can risks be reduced? iGovernment Working Paper no. 14. pp. 1–17 (2003). https://papers.ssrn.com/sol3/papers.cfm?abstract_id=3540052

8. Weerakkody, V., Baire, S., Choudrie, J.: E-Government: the need for effective process management in the public sector. In: Proceedings of the 39th Annual Hawaii International Conference on System Sciences (HICSS 2006), pp. 1–10. IEEE (2006)

9. Matt, C., Hess, T., Benlian, A., Wiesbock, F.: Options for formulating a digital transformation strategy. MIS Q. Executive 15(2), 123–139 (2015)

10. Fairooz, H., Wickramasinghe, C.: Innovation and development of digital finance: a review on digital transformation in banking & financial sector of Sri Lanka. Asian J. Econ. Finance Manage. 1(2), 69–78 (2019)

11. Syed, R., Bandara, W.: Public sector digital transformation failure: Insights from a revelatory case study in a developing country. https://qa-eprints.qut.edu.au/133406/

12. Châlons, C., Dufft, N.: The role of IT as an enabler of digital transformation. In: Abolhassan, F. (ed.) The Drivers of Digital Transformation. MP, pp. 13–22. Springer, Cham (2017). https://doi.org/10.1007/978-3-319-31824-0_2

13. Osmundsen, K., Iden, J., Bygstad, B.: Digital transformation: drivers, success factors, and implications. In: Proceedings of Mediterranean Conference on Information Systems (MCIS), pp. 1–15. Association for Information Systems (2018)

14. Çetin Gürkan, G., Çiftci, G.: Developing a supportive culture in digital transformation. In: Hacioglu, U. (eds.) Digital Business Strategies in Blockchain Ecosystems. Contributions to Management Science. pp. 83–102. Springer, Cham (2020)

15. Weerakkody, V., Janssen, M., Dwivedi, Y.K.: Transformational change and business process reengineering (BPR): lessons from the British and Dutch public sector. Govern. Inf. Q. 28(3), 320–328 (2011)

16. Hartl, E., Hess, T.: The role of cultural values for digital transformation: Insights from a Delphi study. Twenty-third Americas Conference on Information Systems (AMCIS). pp. 1–10. Association for Information Systems (2017)

17. Rassool, M., Dissanayake, D.: Digital transformation for small & medium enterprises (Smes): with special focus on sri lankan context as an emerging economy. Int. J. Bus. Manage. Rev. 7(4), 59–76 (2019)

18. De Bustis, A., Ganesan, V., Herath, G.: Unlocking Sri Lanka's digital opportunity, McKinsey & Company (2018). https://www.mckinsey.com/business-functions/mckinsey-digital/our-insights/unlocking-sri-lankas-digital-opportunity

19. Faro, B., Abedin, B., Kozanoglu, D.C.: Continuous transformation of public sector organisations in the digital era. In: Proceedings of the Americas Conference on Information Systems (AMCIS), pp. 1–5. Association for Information Systems (2019)

20. Philip, G., McKeown, I.: Business transformation and organizational culture. European Manage. J. 22(6), 624–636 (2004)

21. Venkatraman, N.: IT-enabled business transformation: from automation to business scope redefinition. Sloan Manage. Rev. 35(2), 73–87 (1994)

22. Bollinger, A., Smith, R.: Managing organizational knowledge as a strategic asset. J. Knowl. Manage. 5(1), 8–18 (2001)

23. Kreitner, R., Kinicki, A., Cole, N.: Fundamentals of Organizational Behavior: Key Concepts, Skills, and Best Practices, Second Canadian Edition. McGraw-Hill Ryerson, Whitby (2007)

24. Manyika, J., Lund, S., Bughin, J., Woetzel, J., Stamenov, K., Dhingra, D.: Digital globalization: the new era of global flows. Report, https://www.mckinsey.com/business-functions/mckinsey-digital/our-insights/digital-globalization-the-new-era-of-global-flows, McKinsey Global Institute (2016)
25. von Kutzschenbach, M., Mittemeyer, P., Wagner, W.: Antithetic leadership: designers are different, business people too. In: Oswald, G., Kleinemeier, M. (eds.) Shaping the Digital Enterprise. MP, pp. 93–107. Springer, Cham (2017). https://doi.org/10.1007/978-3-319-40967-2_4
26. CIO.Com: Successful Digital Transformation Begins with a Cultural Transformation (2019). https://www.cio.com/article/3402022/successful-digital-transformation-begins-with-a-cultural-transformation.html
27. Gill, M., VanBoskirk, S.: The Digital Maturity Model 4.0. Benchmarks: Digital Business Transformation Playbook, Forrester Research, Inc., Cambridge, USA (2016). https://forrester.nitro-digital.com/pdf/Forrester-s%20Digital%20Maturity%20Model%204.0.pdf
28. Alshehri, M., Drew, S.: E-Government fundamentals. In: Proceedings of the IADIS International Conference ICT, Society and Human Beings 2010, pp. 35–41. International Association for Development of the Information Society (IADIS) (2010). https://research-repository.griffith.edu.au/handle/10072/37709
29. Vey, K., Fandel-Meyer, T., Zipp, J.S., Schneider, C.: Learning & development in times of digital transformation: facilitating a culture of change and innovation. Int. J. Adv. Corporate Learn. (iJAC). 10(1), 22–30 (2017)
30. Nwankpa, J.K., Roumani, Y.: IT capability and digital transformation: a firm performance perspective. In: Thirty Seventh International Conference on Information Systems (ICIS), pp. 1–16. Association for Information Systems (2016)
31. Virkar, S., Edelmann, N., Hynek, N., Parycek, P., Steiner, G., Zenk, L.: Digital transformation in public sector organisations: the role of informal knowledge sharing networks and social media. In: Panagiotopoulos, P., Edelmann, N., Glassey, O., Misuraca, G., Parycek, P., Lampoltshammer, T., Re, B. (eds.) ePart 2019. LNCS, vol. 11686, pp. 60–72. Springer, Cham (2019). https://doi.org/10.1007/978-3-030-27397-2_6
32. Eggers, W.D., Bellman, J.: The journey to government's digital transformation, Deloitte University Press (2015). https://www2.deloitte.com/content/dam/Deloitte/uk/Documents/public-sector/deloitte-uk-government-digital-transformation-journey.pdf
33. da Rosa, I., de Almeida, J.: Digital transformation in the public sector. electronic procurement in Portugal. In: Shakya, R.K. (ed.) Digital Governance and E-Government Principles Applied to Public Procurement, pp. 99–125. IGI Global (2017)
34. Vogelsang, K., Liere-Netheler, K., Packmohr, S., Hoppe, U.: Barriers to digital transformation in manufacturing: development of a research agenda. In: Proceedings of the 52nd Hawaii International Conference on System Sciences (HICSS-52), pp. 4937–4944 (2019). http://hdl.handle.net/10125/59931
35. Kokkinakos, P., Markaki, O., Koussouris, S., Psarras, J.: Digital transformation: is public sector following the enterprise 2.0 paradigm? In: Chugunov, A.V., Bolgov, R., Kabanov, Y., Kampis, G., Wimmer, M. (eds.) DTGS 2016. CCIS, vol. 674, pp. 96–105. Springer, Cham (2016). https://doi.org/10.1007/978-3-319-49700-6_11
36. Gurbaxani, V., Dunkle, D.: Gearing up for successful digital transformation. MIS Q. Executive 18(3), 209–220 (2019)
37. Matt, C., Hess, T., Benlian, A.: Digital transformation strategies. Bus. Inf. Syst. Eng. 57(5), 339–343 (2015). https://doi.org/10.1007/s12599-015-0401-5
38. Ross, J., Mocker, M., Beath, C.: Five building blocks of digital transformation. MIT Sloan Center for Information Systems Research, 18, 6, 1–4 (2018). https://cisr.mit.edu/publication/2018_0601_BuildingBlocks_RossMockerBeath

39. Rajnai, Z., Kocsis, I.: Assessing industry 4.0 readiness of enterprises. In: 2018 IEEE 16th World Symposium on Applied Machine Intelligence and Informatics (SAMI), pp. 000225–000230 (2018)
40. Fitzgerald, M., Kruschwitz, N., Bonnet, D., Welch, M.: Embracing digital technology: a new strategic imperative. MIT Sloan Manage. Rev. 1–12 (2013). https://sloanreview.mit.edu/projects/embracing-digital-technology/
41. Denscombe, M.: The Good Research Guide: For Small-Scale Social Research Projects. McGraw-Hill/Open University Press, Maidenhead (2011)
42. Yin, R.: Case Study Research Design and Methods, 4th edn. Sage Publications Inc., Thousand Oaks (2009)
43. Braun, V., Clarke, V.: Using thematic analysis in psychology. Qualitative Res. Psychol. **3** (2), 77–101 (2006)
44. Hippold, S.: CIOs: Break Through Culture Barriers to Enable Digital Transformation (2019). https://www.gartner.com/smarterwithgartner/cios-break-through-culture-barriers-toenable-digital-transformation/

Strategic Alignment During Digital Transformation

Gideon Mekonnen Jonathan[1(✉)] 🆔 and Josue Kuika Watat[2] 🆔

[1] Department of Computer and Systems Sciences, Stockholm University,
Stockholm, Sweden
gideon@dsv.su.se
[2] AMBERO Consulting GmbH, Yaoundé, Cameroon
josuewatat@gmail.com

Abstract. The extant literature on digital transformation, as an emerging phenomenon, has grown in volume during the last decades. As organisations continue to embrace digital transformation, in pursuit of improved efficiency of their business processes as well as provision of better services and products to their customers, managing the necessary changes have become challenging for leaders. One of these challenges is the alignment between the IT strategy— including the introduction of new digital technologies—with the overall organisational strategy, also referred to as strategic alignment. Even though both digital transformation and strategic alignment have attracted the attention of IS researchers, there is a paucity of research exploring how strategic alignment issues play a role in the digital transformation processes undertaken by today's organisations. To address this gap, in this study we present the findings of an empirical qualitative study conducted in two countries. Our results indicate that the action organisations take to improve their strategic alignment is dependent on how far they have come to introduce new technologies, reconfigure their business processes, and redefined their overall organisational strategy. The study provides insights on how leaders plan and implement changes in response to the changes in external environment as well as the internal organisational dynamics.

Keywords: Digital transformation · Strategic alignment · IT alignment · Public organisations

1 Introduction

Digital transformation, "...*technology induced change on my levels in the organisation that includes both the exploitation of digital technologies to improve processes, and the exploration of digital innovation, which can transform the business model*" [1, p. 2] has become one of the hot topics garnering unprecedented interest among practitioners, researchers as well as policy makers and elected officials. Regardless of industries and sectors, digital transformation is seen as an enabler for innovation and a source of competitive advantage. However, from the leaders' point of view, digital transformation has brought about a challenging task of articulating and implementing simultaneous changes that touches upon multiple areas within an organisation. Among these

© Springer Nature Switzerland AG 2020
M. Themistocleous et al. (Eds.): EMCIS 2020, LNBIP 402, pp. 657–670, 2020.
https://doi.org/10.1007/978-3-030-63396-7_44

challenges, the alignment between IT strategies with the overall organisational (business) strategy has been brought to the fore [2].

Business-IT alignment (referred to as 'strategic alignment' in this study), defined as "...*the application of Information Technology (IT) in an appropriate and timely way, in harmony with business strategies, goals and needs*" [3, p. 3], has been recognised as one of the most researched topic in the IS and cognate disciplines. Even though the phenomenon has constantly ranked as one of the top concerns among practitioners [4], digital transformation has made the issue even more important. However, the widespread attention among researchers and practitioners, strategic alignment is still a challenging task for many organisations [2]. Moreover, the new trend of digital transformation coupled with the dynamic business environment has made strategic alignment more challenging. Given the relevance of strategic alignment for successful digital transformation [5, 6], researchers call for empirical studies that examine the relationship between the two constructs [5, 7, 8]. Thus, this study examines how organisations plan and implement strategies that could improve their strategic alignment while undertaking digital transformation.

The findings of prior studies indicate that IS studies focusing on both digital transformation and strategic alignment focus on private and commercial organisations [9]. However, the significant differences between private and public organisations that are relevant to IT management practices have been identified [10]. To address the lack of studies in the public organisations' context, this study is conducted in five public organisations.

To meet the objective of this study, the following research question is formulated: "*How can organisation pursue strategic alignment to successfully complete their digital transformation journey?*"

The paper is structured as follows. First, a brief review of the extant literature on digital transformation and strategic alignment is presented together with a theoretical framework underpinning the study. Next, the research strategy as well as the data collection and data analysis methods are described. The subsequent section presents the results and analysis of the study, starting with the description of the case organisations where the study was conducted. Finally, we conclude by summarising the findings of the study, research and practical implications and put forward suggestions for future research.

2 Prior Studies

2.1 Digital Transformation

Digital transformation, which has emerged as an important phenomenon among researchers and practitioners, has become an essential part of improving organisational performance in the literature [11, 12]. In addition to the recognition among academics and practitioners, the topic has also mobilised policy makers and elected officials [13]. Even though the concept has been around for a while, the literature does not clearly articulate what constitutes as digital transformation. For instance, according to Vial

[11], digital transformation has been characterised in more than 20 different ways in the literature. However, some common themes have also emerged in the recent years.

To start with, scholars agree that digital transformation calls for changes in the use of technologies where new and emerging digital solutions (e.g., Internet of things, cyber-physical systems, mobile technologies, big data) are introduce with the aim of improving the production and delivery of products and services. As we have noticed from prior studies in digital transformation, there are different view on which technologies are considered to be relevant to digital transformation. However, the introduction of digital tools and methods to exploit data (e.g., using business analytics and machine learning) is among the most important considered to be the most important benefit of digital transformation, particularly in the fast-paced business environment [11].

Second, digital transformation is seen as an organisation wide change of great magnitude affecting the business processes, employees and strategy in response to new developments. The new developments might come as a result of new business environments, or emergence of new digital technologies. According to Wessel [13] organisations undergoing digital transformation are simply rethinking how they configure the use of internal and external resources to further organisational objectives. Even though the new configurations require making adjustments to the whole aspects of organisations, in prior IS studies have ignored issues not directly related to new technologies [14]. Thus, scholars [1] argue that studies on non-IT organisational changes are also equally important for the success of digital transformation. Unfortunately, organisations still view digital transformation as an entirely technology phenomenon detached from organisational factors [2]. Most recent studies, on the other hand has identified several factors that are important for successful digital transformation, such as organisation structure [15], and organisational culture [16].

In sum, the digital transformation process involves formulating strategic directions, identifying activities that could lead to the realisation of overall organisational vision, and configuring resources appropriately. According to Berghaus and Back [1], and Kahre [2], organisations are struggling to align their business and IT strategies as the proliferation of IT increases where it is embedded with all aspects of organisations. Thus, identifying the stages of digital transformation is useful to help leaders prioritise the different activities that need to be acted upon. The digital maturity model we adopted [1] consists of five maturity stages—promote and support (stage 1), create and build (stage 2), commit and transform (stage 3), user centred and elaborated processes (stage 4), and data-driven enterprise (stage 5). These stages are characterised based on the strategic importance of It for organisations, the familiarity of employees to existing digital solutions, involvement of leaders as well as flexibility of work processes. Accordingly, those at the first stage have basic digital services that are designed to support existing support and products. On the higher end, organisations that managed to achieve stage 5 digital maturity are users of the most advanced data analytics for planning, real-time analysis, personalising interactions as well as identifying future opportunities and meet challenges of the dynamic environment.

2.2   Strategic Alignment in the Digital Transformation Era

The evolution of digital transformation, often presented in three generations (transformation to paperless procedures- generation 1, transformation to automated procedures- generation 2, and transformation to smart procedures- generation 3 [17]) calls for radical changes in organisations operational and strategic model which affects the IT and other functions. One of the challenges for leaders is the issue of IT management [2, 5, 16]. According to prior strategic alignment studies, the continuous introduction of digital technologies needs to be appropriately managed in such a way that organisations have made the necessary adjustments to accommodate the exploitation of new technologies. In other words, IT strategies need to be reformulated, and leaders have to make sure the organisational structures as well as the employees are ready for the transformation. Thus, aligning the IT strategies as well as overall organisational strategies requires leaders to comprehend the magnitude of organisational transformation.

A brief overview of prior strategic alignment studies might reveal how the digital transformation has brought about new approaches towards strategic alignment. For more than four decades, the IS as well as strategy and management literature adopted a consistent view of strategic alignment acknowledging the important role it plays to realise the value derived from IT, which in turn is reflected on organisational performance [3, 18]. Despite this rich volume of literature, several limitations have been noted. For instance, one criticism of prior studies is discussed along with digital transformation. According to these studies, there is a lack of acknowledgement of the dynamic business environment and its influence on strategic alignment [2, 11]. Accordingly, there were prior recognition that organisations might be able to find optimal arrangements where strategic, operational as well as tactical plans are formulated and implemented. This view assumes that strategic alignment is a function of well-articulated plan that might be sustained to improve organisational performance for a long run by applying IT solutions. This presupposition, however, has been labelled as 'outdated' [19].

On the other hand, new propositions acknowledging the environmental dynamics where both organisational as well as the emerging technological changes are inevitable, are gaining acceptance as appropriate approach towards reaching strategic alignment [2, 16, 20, 21]. Thus, strategic alignment researchers recognise the relevance of such contextual factors as environmental uncertainties and current trends and best practices when they attempt to reach strategic aligned position during digital transformation. It is also worth noting that there is a growing consensus among scholars that strategic alignment is a process, not as an outcome as previously thought [5]. One of the widely adopted model, Strategic Alignment Maturity Model (SAMM) places organisations in four different stages of maturity—(i.e., initial/ad-hock process- level 1, committed process- level 2, established focused process- level 3, improved/managed process- level 4, or optimised process- level 5) based on how well it has managed the six dimensions [3, 22]. The six dimensions of alignment assess Communications between IT and other units; Value Analytics (measuring the contribution of IT as understood by the IT and rest of the organisation); IT Governance (the IT decision-making arrangement); Partnering; Dynamic IT Scope (flexibility in terms of emerging technologies and provision of tailored solutions); and Business and IT Skills Development.

Benbya et al [23] argue that the IS studies still overlook the multi-faceted and co-evolutionary nature of strategic alignment and the relationship it has with various internal organisational aspects that might change over time. Digital transformation is one of the changes organisations undertake to help them exploit opportunities and meet challenges, particularly in the turbulent times. It is worth noting that the different stages of digital transformation require different levels of investment in IT infrastructure and setup, integration of IT, and changes in business processes. According to Vial [11], finding the right fit, between the adoption of new technologies and making adjustments gets complicated as organisations graduate to the next generation of digital transformation.

In sum, the findings of recent studies seem to suggest the invaluable role strategic alignment plays in the digital transformation process [2, 5, 11, 16]. Haffke et al [24] argue that, given the significant developments in terms of digital transformation, the pursuit for strategic alignment in the literature is no surprise. The fact that IT is now embedded with all aspects of organisations makes the alignment attempt more challenging. In the very early studies of strategic alignment [25], the message for organisations was to align their IT strategy subsequent to their business strategy. However, in the digital transformation era, as the adoption of new digital technologies drive organisational strategic directions, novel approaches to plan strategic alignment is of paramount importance. Accordingly, leaders are reminded the significance of paying attention to such areas as *organisational structure, organisational culture, skills development, organisational agility* [26, 27], *infrastructure flexibility*, and *rapid business process management* [5, 26–30].

2.3   Conceptual Research Framework

The conceptual framework shown in Fig. 1 is used to illustrate the research process. Based on the findings of prior studies, we attempt to examine how organisations prioritise activities related to strategic alignment to pursue successful digital transformation.

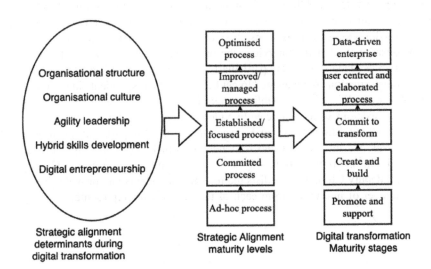

Fig. 1. Conceptual research framework

As the findings of recent studies suggest, for instance [5, 26–30], organisations undergoing digital transformation need to focus on specific organisational and managerial factors to improve their strategic alignment maturity [31]. Strategically aligned position, in turn, is considered to be invaluable to reach higher stage of digital transformation maturity [1].

3 Research Methodology

We chose an exploratory approach to investigate current developments in digital transformation and strategic alignment in the public sector. Among the exploratory research approaches, case study is one of the widely adopted research strategy in the IS research domain [32]. Particularly, strategic alignment studies in the public sector have been conducted applying single or multiple case study research approach [20]. According to Yin [33], case studies are best suited to explore a phenomenon in a complex natural setting. A multiple case study strategy, rather than a single case study, was deemed appropriate after assessment was made following the critical appraisal guidelines [34].

A qualitative case study is well established in IS research as that it provides a researcher with various forms of data collection methods improving the credibility of the findings [33]. In addition to interviews, observations, as well as internal organisational documents, as well as publicly available online materials were used to collect data. The documents obtained include meeting protocols, organisational charts, strategic plans (IT, and overall strategic documents), process description, role descriptions.

Attempts were made to examine organisations with similar organisational characteristics (size in terms of number of employees, stages of digital transformation, and organisational structure). Organisations participating in our study had at least 275 employees, have relatively centralised organisational structure, and report to their respective regional governments. In the first instance, one of the researchers approached CIOs of fifteen public organisations out of which four responded with confirmations for interview appointments with at least one CIO and two administrative leaders holding equivalent positions. The interview was conducted at the premises of the organisations. After the interview, the respondents were asked to refer us to more administrative leaders who are particularly assigned to work with areas related to digital transformation. We managed to get help from the respondents in recruiting other participants in additional one public organisation. Interviews with one of the participating organisations were conducted by video conference. In total, we gained access to five public organisations (three in Kenya and two in Ethiopia). Except in one of the organisations, we interviewed two respondents from IT and three from the administration side. In one organisation, we obtained three interviews from the IT side (CIO, CDO, and deputy CIO). Table 1 lists the role of respondents and provides information on the number of interviews from each of the departments represented.

Table 1. Respondents with their roles and department affiliations.

Departments	Role of Respondents	No. of Interviews
IT Department	CIO	5
	CDO	1
	Deputy CIO	4
Subtotal		*10*
Administration Departments	Administrative Head	5
	Logistics Head	1
	Finance Head	5
	HR Head	5
Subtotal		*16*
Total		**26**

Interview guides were used to conduct the semi-structured interviews with respondents from the administration and IT departments to ensure reliability and ease of comparing the results of the interviews. However, the interview questions were formulated differently taking the functional roles of the respondents into consideration. For instance, the CIOs were asked to provide their insights and opinions on the role of IT in their respective organisations, how their counterparts view IT and how they collaborate with other departments as well as how their relationship with the whole organisation plays a role in the success of the digital transformation. The interviews were conducted between November 2019 and March 2020. On the other hand, leaders of from the administration departments responds to questions pertaining their perception of the role of IT for their organisation and how they view the interaction between the IT unit and the rest of the organisation.

Even though all of the respondents were scheduled for an hour interviews, the actual interviews took between 45 and 70 min. Right after the interview, complementary quantitative data was collected from the respondents using questionnaires. The questionnaires were formulated to determine the level of strategic alignment and digital transformation maturity stages. The strategic alignment maturity in each of the participating organisations was measured according to the SAMM instrument [22, p. 40]. The assessment asks the respondents to rate the different criteria related to what Luftman et al [22] referred to as alignment dimensions. For instance, for the first dimension, i.e., communications, the respondents from the IT department assess how they understand their organisation's customers, processes, and partners. On the other hand, their counterparts from administration departments score the extent they understand the IT environment, its capabilities, etc. In total, the instrument contained 39 questions. The strategic alignment maturity level is then calculated as the average of the sum of the scores of the dimensions which were assessed using a 1 to 5 Likert scale. To determine the various stages of digital transformation, we formulated our questionnaires based on the Digital Maturity Model (DMM) [1].

The recorded interviews were transcribed by respective researchers who conducted the interviews. Seven of the interviews which were not in English, were translated into

English before coding the data. Prior research on digital transformation and strategic alignment was used as a basis for coding (i.e., inductive coding). Two of the researchers carried out the coding independently. Where inconsistencies were observed the literature was consulted and the data was recoded after discussions. We took sample of coded interview data and tested for objectivity and inter-coder reliability according to Krippendorff's alpha [35] and Cohen's kappa [36]. The test suggested that the reliability and objectivity of our coding was sufficient.

According to Yin [33], triangulation improves the reliability of case studies. Thus, we complemented the interview and questionnaire data with secondary data (the internal organisational documents we obtained, and publicly available data from websites). The data collected through the questionnaires was coupled with the thematically coded interview data from our respondents. Analysis was also made to compare participating organisations in terms of their similarities about the strategic alignment as well as strategic alignment maturity. Our justifications for the conclusion drawn came from the level of alignment and digital maturity with the coded responses from our interviews.

4   Results and Discussions

The result of the study is based on the empirical data we collected from five different public organisations. The section starts with the description of the case organisations.

4.1   The Case Organisations

The five case organisations investigated for this study are the mid-size municipalities and counties in Ethiopia and Kenya respectively. In Kenya the three counties selected are in the Eastern province in the former administration arrangement. The population size of these counties range between 250,000 and 350,000. The counties were selected from others due to the digital transformation they have been working on for the last few years. All of the counties, except one have centrally run IT department responsible for the provision of IT services for the different departments in the respective counties. The CIOs oversee the digital transformation projects together with steering committees selected from various departments. In one of the counties, the office for digitalisation is established to supervise the digital transformation. In Ethiopia, the data collection took place in two municipalities with the population size of about 250,000 each. Unlike the counties in Kenya, these municipalities work under the framework of the federal government to digitalise the public sector. However, the IT departments are responsible to provide IT services to other departments in the municipality, but also to other public organisations in the vicinity of the respective cities. The same criteria were used to select these municipalities—the digital transformation they are undergoing. We have also tried to examine organisations of similar size.

4.2 Digital Transformation- and Strategic Alignment Maturity

Using the responses from the questionnaire, we assessed the strategic alignment as well as the digital transformation maturity in the participating organisations. In the first glance, the average overall scores of the strategic alignment seems to suggest higher maturity value of digital transformation maturity. As shown in Table 2, three of the organisations seem to have reached the third stages in the digital transformation maturity stage. The result is not surprising given the late entry of public organisations to digitalisation. Previous empirical studies of digital transformation in well performing industries stands at about stage three [1]. As stated in the literature, organisations in this digital transformation maturity have organisational cultures and organisational structure that undergo considerable alterations.

Table 2. Results of the questionnaire assessing the strategic alignment maturity levels and digital transformation maturity stages

Maturity Assessment	ET1	KE1	ET2	KE2	KE3
Strategic Alignment					
Communications	2.3	2.3	4.0	3.1	3.2
Value Analytics	2.7	1.9	2.3	3.0	1.8
IT Governance	3.8	3.7	3.7	3.8	3.8
Partnering	2.0	3.2	1.3	1.9	3.0
Dynamic IT Scope	1.8	3.1	2.7	3.1	4.2
Skills Development	2.0	1.8	3.0	2.0	3.2
Average Score	2.4	2.7	2.8	2.8	3.2
Strategic Alignment Maturity Level	***Committed process***				***Established/ focused processes***
Digital Transformation Maturity Score	2.5	2.4	3.2	3.1	3.0
Digital Transformation Maturity Stage	***Create and build***		***Committee and transform***		

According to the responses obtained from the three organisations (ET2, KE2, and KE3) digital transformation is put forward as the top priority. One of the respondents (CDO) says *"...the private sector has already gone so far in transforming their businesses, so the pressure on us from our politicians and the citizens is overwhelming. That is why we have made it a top priority"*. A closer look into the strategic alignment assessment seem to reveal higher score in three of the strategic alignment dimensions (communications, IT Governance, and Dynamic IT Scope).

On the other hand, the analysis shows that two of the organisations (ET1, and KE1) appeared to be at stage two in the digital transformation maturity scale. According to the literature [1], organisations that did not pass the stage of experimenting with digital innovations. Our interviews with the CIOs and department heads also confirm the characterisation. For instance, in the word of the CIO *"...I can confidently say that the municipality understands digitalisation is something we have to do. However, you also need to appreciate that we have to consult with our staff and see what works and what not. As a public organisation, we do not have the big budget for RD".* The two organisations are also concerned about the digital competencies they have in house. As reflected in the skills development dimension, it is no surprise that the organisations exhibit the characteristics of stage 2 digital transformation maturity out of 5.

4.3   Determinant Factors for Strategic Alignment in the Digital Transformation Era

As shown in Table 2, organisations with relatively higher value on several dimensions of strategic alignment seem to do better in digital transformation maturity. Even though generalisations could not be drawn due to the sample size, prior studies acknowledge the important role of strategic alignment for digital transformation. Our respondents also confirm the association between the two constructs. However, or interviews have revealed several challenges that have influenced the levels of strategic alignment maturity which, in turn, is reflected on lower digital transformation maturity.

Organisational Agility: Recent literature reviews [18] show that strategic alignment as a construct has shifted from being an outcome at one point in time to a dynamic position that needs to be adjusted continuously to respond to the changes in the dynamic environment. One of such changes might be the emergence of new digital technologies or business processes. Our respondents acknowledge that the they are faced with volatile market and uncertainty. However, according to two of the finance heads (ET2, KE1), public organisations are huge bureaucratic machines that are not flexible to meet the necessary changes. In his own words, *"I have to turn down requests to make purchase in the fear that the procurement process alone takes long time that by the time we get the orders, it might be already obsolete".* Even though scholars agree that organisations need to develop the ability to detect and respond to change, in practice, this is easier said than done. Even though the respondents seem to agree organisational agility is difficult to maintain given the red tapes and centralised planning, the response to the questionnaire indicate that three of the organisations scored above 3 out of 5 points. It is also worth noting that KE3 which appears to have reached level three in strategic alignment scale have also managed to reach a digital transformation that is integrated with the county's overall strategic plan.

Organisational Culture: Consistent with the findings of previous literature, the response from our interviews reveal that organisational culture has important implication on how strategic alignment is pursued. According to the HR head at ET2, their top management has made it a point to embrace a culture of less hierarchy and open communication across departments and ranks. This has been reflected in the SAMM assessment where the organisation scores high in communication, IT governance and skills development. The literature is also clear on the significance of organisational culture in a formation of favourable mindset among leaders and other employees to embrace change [16, 37]. Besides, organisations with culture recognising IT as an essential element is likely to result in a relational leadership where the IT and the remaining units consider themselves as partners [38]. According to the CIO from KE3, the county has become a role model for others for mobilising the whole organisation under the slogan of 'digitalisation now' only made possible by the exceptional leadership skills of top management. Unfortunately, none of the organisations seems to have encouraged to their leaders to promoting an organisational culture which rewards employees with digital affinity, and digital commitment, digital entrepreneurship which is of paramount importance for digital transformation [39, 40]. Organisational cultures that encourage employees and leaders to engage in entrepreneurial behaviour bring flexibility and taking responsibility for transformations that benefit the organisation [41].

Organisational Structure: Strategic alignment and how it influences strategic alignment has been debated in the literature, particularly in relation to agility and adaptation of new digital technologies that have implication on business processes [26]. The respondents, even though acknowledge the important role of organisational structure on strategic alignment and digitalisation seems to be powerless in making changes. For instance, respondents from ET1 and KE1 argue that the communication between IT and other departments is being affected due to the unnecessary hierarchies and rigid structures at their respective departments. This may also be seen from the low score for skills development. On the other hand, respondents from ET2 and KE3 say that they have had the leeway to informally go around formal structures when time is of essence. The figures show that these organisations have better communications, IT governance, dynamic IT scope and skills development.

Skills Development: All of the organisations that participated in the study have raised concerns on the availability of skilled staff at different levels. This is consistent with prior studies that have identified the issue of access to trained personnel that could make the alignment of new technologies in the existing business processes [31]. Even though several internal and external factors determine how organisations manage their human resources, ET2 and KE3 indicate that their respective organisation requires those joining to possess both IT and other expertise. As the HR head puts it *"There is little we could do to attract talented experts. IT graduates are very popular in the private sector ... we have attempted to train our staff"*. The CIO from ET2 adds *"we no longer hire IT guys and expect them to have comprehension for our processes...it looks waste for them. We hire MBA graduates with some IT background"*. Recent strategic alignment studies have also recognised the benefit of having leaders and other staff with hybrid expertise. As IT becomes embedded with every aspect of an organisation undergoing digital transformation, some skill sets are becoming indispensable. For instance, leaders need to possess adaptive skills to new digital technologies such as digital security, rapid business design and management [24, 42]. Since external environment have influence on strategic alignment, in addition to managing the internal organisational factors, leaders should be able to identify both threats and opportunities and react accordingly [24].

5 Conclusion

This study was set out to explore how strategic alignment is pursued in public organisations where digital transformation in undertaken. The results of our study indicate that strategic alignment is still an important area of IT management during the digital transformation era. Our case studies suggest that organisations will be in a better position to make appropriate adjustments to their organisational as well as managerial factors when the various factors related to strategic alignment are appropriately dealt with. The analysis of our data has identified list of factors that improve strategic alignment as organisations undertake digital transformation.

In response to our research question, we argue that it is in organisations best interest to focus on activities that improve strategic alignment. Among others, designing organisational structure that can accommodate swift changes in technology and business processes as well as encourage organisational culture that embraces change and rewards entrepreneurial mindset were found to be important precursors. As the pace of change in technology and business environments, several sets of skills are also necessary to be possessed by leaders and employees.

The research findings are constrained by the small number of samples and case organisations represented. Even though case studies provide the benefit of in-depth observations, our results might not be generalised for other organisations. Future studies might explore the how strategic alignment is planned and executed to realise the objectives of digital transformation initiatives in more organisations. On the other hand, the data collection time frame might not be appropriate to provide a better insight on how the strategic alignment dimensions have evolved through time in response to the digital transformation processes in the selected organisations. As indicated in the literature [30], strategic alignment is a continuous process that changes over time. Future studies might take a longitudinal research approach. Quantitative research approach with large sample size might also be carried out to provide an overview of the developments across sectors and industries.

References

1. Berghaus, S., Back, A.: Stages in digital business transformation: results of an empirical maturity study. In: MCIS, p. 22 (2016)
2. Kahre, C., Hoffmann, D., Ahlemann, F.: Beyond business-it alignment-digital business strategies as a paradigmatic shift: a review and research agenda (2017)
3. Luftman, J.: Assessing business-it alignment maturity. Commun. Assoc. Inf. Syst. 4(1), 1–51 (2000)
4. Kappelman, L., Johnson, V.L., Maurer, C., Guerra, K., McLean, E., Torres, R., Snyder, M., Kim, K.: The 2019 sim it issues and trends study. MIS Q. Executive 19(1), 69–104 (2020)
5. Yeow, A., Soh, C., Hansen, R.: Aligning with new digital strategy: a dynamic capabilities approach. J. Strategic Inf. Syst. 27(1), 43–58 (2018)
6. Issa, A., Hatiboglu, B., Bildstein, A., Bauernhansl, T.: Industrie 4.0 roadmap: framework for digital transformation based on the concepts of capability maturity and alignment. In: Procedia CIRP 72, 973–978 (2018)

7. Zhang, N., Liu, B.: The key factors affecting RPA-business alignment. In: Proceedings of the 3rd International Conference on Crowd Science and Engineering, pp. 1–6 (2018)

8. Li, W., Liu, K., Belitski, M., Ghobadian, A., O'Regan, N.: e-leadership through strategic alignment: An empirical study of small-and medium-sized enterprises in the digital age. J. Inf. Technol. **31**(2), 185–206 (2016)

9. Winkler, T.: IT governance mechanisms and administration/IT alignment in the public sector: A conceptual model and case validation. In: Proceedings of the 11th International Conference on Wirtschaftsinformatik. WI 2013. pp. 831–845. Association for Information Systems. AIS Electronic Library (AISeL) (2013)

10. Caudle, S.L., Gorr, W.L., Newcomer, K.E.: Key information systems management issues for the public sector. MIS Q. **15**(2), 171–188 (1991)

11. Vial, G.: Understanding digital transformation: a review and a research agenda. J. Strategic Inf. Syst. **28**(2), 118–144 (2019)

12. Hess, T., Matt, C., Benlian, A., Wiesbock, F.: Options for formulating a digital transformation strategy. MIS Q. Executive **15**(2), 123–139 (2016)

13. Wessel, L., Baiyere, A., Ologeanu-Taddei, R., Cha, J., Jensen, T.: Unpacking the difference between digital transformation and it-enabled organizational transformation. J. Assoc. Inf. Syst. (2020, in press)

14. Berman, S.J.: Digital transformation: opportunities to create new business models. Strategy Leadership **40**(2), 16–24 (2012)

15. L'aszl'o, K., Andr'as, N., Akos, O., Andr'as, S.: Structuration theory and strategic alignment in information security management: introduction of a comprehensive research approach and program. AARMS–Acad. Appl. Res. Military Sci. **16**(1), 5–16 (2017)

16. Gajardo, P., Ariel, L.P.: The business-it alignment in the digital age. In: The 13th Mediterranean Conference on Information Systems (ITAIS & MCIS), Naples, Italy (2019)

17. Heilig, L., Lalla-Ruiz, E., Voß, S.: Digital transformation in maritime ports: analysis and a game theoretic framework. Netnomics: Econ. Res. Electron. Network. **18**(2–3), 227–254 (2017)

18. Galliers, R.D.: In celebration of diversity in information systems research. J. Inf. Technol. **26**(4), 299–301 (2011)

19. Chan, Y.E.: Why haven't we mastered alignment? The importance of the informal organization structure. MIS Q. Executive **22**(4), 97–112 (2002)

20. Jonathan, G.M., Rusu, L., Perjons, E.: Business-it alignment in the era of digital transformation: Quo vadis? In: Proceedings of the 53rd Hawaii International Conference on System Sciences, pp. 5563–5572 (2020)

21. Karpovsky, A., Galliers, R.D.: Aligning in practice: from current cases to a new agenda. J. Inf. Technol. **30**(2), 136–160 (2015)

22. Luftman, J., Lyytinen, K., Zvi, T.B.: Enhancing the measurement of information technology (IT) business alignment and its influence on company performance. J. Inf. Technol. **32**(1), 26–46 (2017)

23. Benbya, H., McKelvey, B.: Using coevolutionary and complexity theories to improve is alignment: a multi-level approach. J. Inf. Technol. **21**(4), 284–298 (2006)

24. Haffke, I., Kalgovas, B.J., Benlian, A.: The role of the cio and the cdo in an organization's digital transformation. In: Proceedings of the International Conference on Information Systems (2016)

25. Henderson, J.C., Venkatraman, H.: Strategic alignment: leveraging information technology for transforming organizations. IBM Syst. J. **38**(2.3), 472–484 (1999)

26. Jorfi, S., Nor, K.M., Najjar, L.: An empirical study of the role of IT flexibility and IT capability in IT-business strategic alignment. J. Syst. Inf. Technol. **19**(1/2), 2–21 (2017)

27. Liang, H., Wang, N., Xue, Y., Ge, S.: Unraveling the alignment paradox: How does business-IT alignment shape organizational agility? Inf. Syst. Res. **28**(4), 863–879 (2017)
28. Rahimi, F., Møller, C., Hvam, L.: Business process management and IT management: the missing integration. Int. J. Inf. Manage. **36**(1), 142–154 (2016)
29. Zhou, J., Bi, G., Liu, H., Fang, Y., Hua, Z.: Understanding employee competence, operational IS alignment, and organizational agility: an ambidexterity perspective. Inf. Manage. **55**(6), 695–708 (2018)
30. Panda, S., Rath, S.K.: Strategic IT-business alignment and organizational agility: from a developing country perspective. J. Asia Bus. Stud. **12**(4), 422–440 (2018)
31. Avila, O., Goepp, V., Kiefer, F.: Addressing alignment concerns into the design of domain-specific information systems. J. Manuf. Technol. Manage. **29**(5), 726–745 (2018)
32. Oates, B.J.: Researching Information Systems and Computing. Sage (2005)
33. Yin, R.K.: Case Study Research and Applications: Design and Methods. SAGE Publications (2017)
34. Atkins, C., Sampson, J.: Critical appraisal guidelines for single case study research. In: ECIS 2002 Proceedings, p. 15 (2002)
35. Hayes, A.F., Krippendorff, K.: Answering the call for a standard reliability measure for coding data. Commun. Methods Measures **1**(1), 77–89 (2007)
36. Cohen, J.: A coefficient of agreement for nominal scales. Educ. Psychol. Measurement **20**(1), 37–46 (1960)
37. Jonathan, G.M.: Digital transformation in the public sector: Identifying critical success factors. In: European, Mediterranean, and Middle Eastern Conference on Information Systems, pp. 223–235. Springer (2019)
38. Kude, T., Lazic, M., Heinzl, A., Neff, A.: Achieving IT-based synergies through regulation-oriented and consensus-oriented IT governance capabilities. Inf. Syst. J. **28**(5), 765–795 (2018)
39. Wagner, H.T., Meshtaf, J.: Individual IT roles in business–IT alignment and IT governance. In: Proceedings of the 49th Hawaii International Conference on System Sciences (HICSS), pp. 4920–4929. IEEE (2016)
40. Cˆamara, A.L., Maria da Costa Figueiredo, R., Canedo, E.D.: Analysis of conversation competencies in strategic alignment between business areas (external control) and information technology areas in a control body. Information **9**(7), 166 (2018)
41. Moon, Y.J., Choi, M., Armstrong, D.J.: The impact of relational leadership and social alignment on information security system effectiveness in korean governmental organizations. Int. J. Inf. Manage. **40**, 54–66 (2018)
42. Kritikos, K., Laurenzi, E., Hinkelmann, K.: Towards business-to-IT alignment in the cloud. In: Mann, Z.A., Stolz, V. (eds.) ESOCC 2017. CCIS, vol. 824, pp. 35–52. Springer, Cham (2018). https://doi.org/10.1007/978-3-319-79090-9_3

Management and Organisational Issues in Information Systems

A Chief Information Officer (CIO) Framework for Managing the Fourth Industrial Revolution (4IR): An Exploratory Research Synthesis

Joseph George and Grant Royd Howard$^{(\boxtimes)}$ ⓘ

University of South Africa (Unisa), Florida, South Africa
66036194@mylifeunisaac.onmicrosoft.com, howargr@unisa.ac.za

Abstract. The paper addressed the specific roles and corresponding capabilities required by Chief Information Officers (CIOs) to facilitate customer value development and organizational competitiveness and performance in the Fourth Industrial Revolution (4IR). The objective was to develop a CIO management framework with specific 4IR roles and capabilities. The study was an exploratory and theoretical literature synthesis that followed an interpretivist philosophy with qualitative analysis. It was evident that CIOs should fulfil the roles of customer value developer, technology entrepreneur and life-long learner in the 4IR. The paper made an original contribution to knowledge by developing a CIO framework for managing the 4IR comprising specific CIO roles and capabilities that were directly relevant to the 4IR. It also had value for CIOs and other industry leaders by highlighting the importance of the 4IR and its innovative technologies and the position of CIOs whose responsibility it is to convert the 4IR into value.

Keywords: Chief Information Officer (CIO) · CIO roles and capabilities · Fourth Industrial Revolution (4IR) · Industry 4.0 · Information and Communications Technology (ICT) · Information Systems (IS) · Information Technology (IT) · IT management · Theoretical literature synthesis

1 Introduction

An unprecedented convergence of advanced digital, physical and biological technologies is underway that promises to radically change the way we live, work, interact and even our environments [1, 2]. Examples of these technologies include additive manufacturing, Internet of Things, cloud computing, artificial intelligence, robotics, nanotechnology, cognitive augmentation, gene editing and maker communities. The current era of these unique, advanced and disruptive technologies is labelled the Fourth Industrial Revolution (4IR) and Industry 4.0, which has a typically narrower focus on manufacturing and production systems [3].

The impacts of the 4IR are expected to be extensive and include significant changes to manufacturing, information sharing, transportation, employment and labor, personal life, data production and consumption, privacy, cities and commerce [4]. Furthermore,

© Springer Nature Switzerland AG 2020
M. Themistocleous et al. (Eds.): EMCIS 2020, LNBIP 402, pp. 673–682, 2020.
https://doi.org/10.1007/978-3-030-63396-7_45

the 4IR is expected to drive the creation of new business models characterized by innovation, flexibility and rapid reorganization of processes for adaptation to increasingly competitive, global and dynamic environments [5]. Thus, technology investment management capabilities become essential in the 4IR [6] as do the competitiveness principles of interorganizational cooperation, decentralization of management processes, virtualization of business activities, service orientation, real-time assessment of organizational capabilities and modularity of services and products [7]. In addition, the areas within organizations that may be most affected by 4IR technologies are organizational strategy, culture, processes and employee education and training [8].

As businesses and business models become disrupted by 4IR technologies, there are unclear consequences for management, labor and organizational structures [9] and countries have indicated that skills shortages are expected to be major competitive barriers. Indeed, employability in the 4IR may require new conceptions of work spaces, tasks, time and pay and necessitate continual updates to technology skills for non-repetitive tasks, such as sensemaking, novel and adaptive thinking, social and cross-cultural competencies, new-media literacy, computational thinking, transdisciplinarity, cognitive load management and virtual collaboration [10].

Importantly, within organizations, senior management are ultimately responsible for setting the strategic goals and making decisions about how to utilize 4IR technologies competitively. In particular, the Chief Information Officer (CIO) role is a senior management role and often the highest Information Technology (IT) executive tasked with managing, setting the vision for, redesigning and shaping the strategy and operations with and creating business value from an organization's Information and Communications Technologies (ICTs) [11–13]. Therefore, the CIO role is a meaningful role for addressing an organization's response to the 4IR and deciding how to effectively employ 4IR technologies for organizational competitiveness, value creation and performance. In addition, research and theory to guide CIOs in the 4IR are relevant to and significant for economies, organizations, executive IT management and academics.

Consequently, a literature search was done during mid-2019 on 4IR and CIOs which returned 129 relevant and applicable peer-reviewed articles. Of the 129 articles, 18% focused on the duties, roles and capabilities of the CIO but were not directly related to the 4IR and the remaining 82% of the articles focused on 4IR and related technologies. None of the articles focused on the roles and capabilities of the CIO in the 4IR. Then, another search was conducted in July 2020 in the top journals in the Information Systems (IS) field as listed by the Association for Information Systems (AIS) [14]. Each journal was searched using the search keywords "fourth industrial revolution or industry 4.0 or 4th industrial revolution" and "CIO or chief information officer". Table 1 presents the search results and again demonstrates the lack of research on the roles and capabilities of the CIO in the 4IR.

Table 1. Search results from the top journals in the IS field.

Journal	Database that journal accessed from	Search date range	Article component searched on	No. of general CIO articles returned	No. of general 4IR articles returned	No. of CIO & 4IR articles returned
European Journal of Information Systems	Taylor & Francis Online	01/01/1991 - present	Keywords (abstract search not available)	2	0	0
Information Systems Journal	Wiley Online Library Database Model 2020	01/01/1997 - present	Abstract	1	0	0
Information Systems Research	INFORMS PubsOnline	01/03/1990 - present	Keywords (abstract search not available)	0	0	0
Journal of AIS	Business Premium Collection	01/01/2006 - present	Abstract	1	0	0
Journal of Information Technology	SAGE Premier 2020	01/03/1999 - present	Abstract	5	0	0
Journal of MIS	Business Source Ultimate	01/06/1984 - present	Abstract	10	0	0
Journal of Strategic Information Systems	ScienceDirect Freedom Collection	01/03/1995 - present	Title, abstract or author-specified keywords (abstract search not available)	6	0	0
MIS Quarterly	Business Source Ultimate	01/03/1977 - present	Abstract	17	0	0

The literature searches indicated that there was insufficient research about CIO roles and capabilities required for the 4IR. Furthermore, the 4IR was a relatively new phenomenon and the roles and capabilities of the CIO for this era have not been adequately developed but the technologies that are part of the 4IR have received considerable research attention. The study's research problem was the lack of knowledge about the roles and capabilities of the CIO in the 4IR.

Accordingly, the research question was: What are the new CIO roles and capabilities required in the era of the 4IR? Then, the research objective was to review research about CIOs and/or the 4IR to develop a literature-based framework to guide CIOs in the

4IR. Knowledge about roles and capabilities required for the 4IR would enable better decisions about investing in and utilizing 4IR technologies for business value creation, competitiveness and organizational performance. Hence, the study offers an original contribution to the academic body of knowledge relating to the roles and capabilities of the CIO in the 4IR.

The first section of the paper introduced the study's context and explained the research problem, question and objective. The next section explains and justifies the research design. Thereafter, the research synthesis is provided comprising analyzed and synthesized past research related to CIOs and the 4IR, which enable the study to answer the research question. Section Four concludes the study and highlights its contribution, limitations and opportunities for future research.

2   Methodology

The paper followed an interpretivist philosophy relating to ontology where the nature of existence is dependent on human perception and an epistemology where phenomena can be known through subjective social constructions such as language and context [15]. Accordingly, the study proceeded with a qualitative approach that facilitated interpretation, analysis and synthesis of the relevant phenomena using literature texts. The study was an exploratory and theoretical research synthesis of relevant and peer-reviewed literature, and made use of qualitative thematic analyses [16–18].

The research commenced with literature searches based on keywords from the research problem that filtered the literature for relevance [19–21]. Several search engines were used, including Google Scholar, but only articles accessible from the library of the University of South Africa (Unisa) were included in the study. This was done to ensure that any fake or predatory journal articles were excluded and only relevant, peer-reviewed and quality literature were part of the study.

Research syntheses make an important contribution to the scientific body of knowledge by progressing academic debate and developing meaningful, abstract patterns, features [22] and perspectives [23]. Furthermore, research syntheses expose key phenomena and theories, facilitating the development of new research questions and insights by other researchers.

3   Research Synthesis

3.1   CIO Roles and Capabilities not Directly Related to the 4IR

Twentieth century research presents CIO's roles as systems thinker, visionary, architect, deliverer, reformer, tactician, alliance manager and relationship builder [24]. In the late nineties, three areas of similar CIO responsibilities were reported, namely business and IT vision, design of IT architecture and delivery of Information Systems (IS) services, and nine IS capabilities were identified as leadership, business systems thinking, relationship building, architecture planning, making technology work, informed buying, contract facilitation, contract monitoring and vendor development [25]. It was also stated that the CIO role was evolving from a functional head delivering on promises to a strategic partner aligning IT with business and a business visionary driving change. Other developing CIO roles included IT problem firefighter, technical landscape cultivator, IT use opportunity seeker and technical solution innovator/creator, and labels such as Director of IT or Chief Innovation Officer were used instead of CIO [25].

By the twenty-tens, little seemed to have changed and CIO roles included leader, visionary, strategic thinker, relationship builder, diplomat, deliverer and market reader [12]. Furthermore, some of the general skills and personal traits that were mentioned as essential for a CIO were a solid business background, rational persuasion, good communication skills, personal appeal and good working relationships with peers [11].

More recent research shows that the CIO role has still not changed and continues to be a strategy-oriented executive focused on deploying IT and digital data in value-creating ways [26] with strategy, business model and governance emphasized. In addition, CIO roles have included global responsibilities and directing enterprise-wide IT strategies and policies, demand-side responsibilities that include prioritizing and constraining specific demands for IT-based business solutions and supply-side responsibilities that include provisioning, operating and maintaining the IT-based business solutions [27].

CIO role themes continue in this vein and one study reports that these roles fall into predominantly transformational roles that focus on new implementations, and functional roles focused on managing IT expenses, security, crises and operations, instead of strategic roles focused on strategy, growth and innovation [28]. In contrast, another recent study reveals CIO roles may be strategic, transformational or IT performance based and include technologist, enabler, innovator and strategist with objectives spanning IT efficiency, business transformation, strategic planning, business agility, reduced time to market, revenue generation and facilities management [29].

However, other recent studies have begun to demonstrate fundamental changes to the CIO roles and capabilities indicating the radical nature of 4IR disruption. For instance, it is stated that the CIO's objectives and capabilities are extending to less traditional IT roles including roles that have a large overlap with marketing and the Chief Marketing Officer (CMO) [30] and the CIO role has in some organizations been replaced by the Chief Digital Officer (CDO) role [31].

A further recent study has indicated that the CIO role involves distributed digital leadership that scans and monitors the technology ecosystem, builds digital platforms, manages data as an asset and leverages analytics for business insights [32]. Three CIO roles and corresponding capabilities were proposed, namely an implementer role with connecting capability, a business enabler role with modeling capability and a strategist role with weaving or shaping new contexts capability.

A study in the government sector suggests that CIOs possess the capabilities to align business and IT, manage digital transformation, renovate the IT-core, champion digital business strategy, create a flexible IT execution platform, balance exploitation and innovation, manage the portfolio budget, value or risk and develop talent [33] and the study also expressed the need to shift the CIO role from the traditional, control-oriented IT director to business innovator in the digital society.

While the literature acknowledges that the CIO role is increasingly complex requiring operational, organizational and strategic management capabilities for delivering business analytics and innovation, implementing digital transformation, mitigating cybersecurity threats and managing skill shortfalls, cost-cuts and new regulations [34], there is little explicit acknowledgement of the 4IR and the specific roles and capabilities required by the CIO to address the 4IR successfully.

Notably, in prior research the terms roles, responsibilities and capabilities appear to have been used somewhat interchangeably. For the purposes of the study, the term role is defined as a general, concise caption or category encompassing the activities, tasks and functions performed by a person in relation to their coworkers and the specific work environment, and the term capability is defined as experience, skills, knowledge and personal attributes that a person possesses for accomplishing the activities, tasks and functions required by a particular role. A role describes what a person is required to do, and a capability describes the qualities possessed by a person.

3.2   4IR Themes Relevant to CIO Roles and Capabilities

In relation to work environments, the 4IR is creating multicultural international work environments requiring intercultural communication abilities, lifelong learning and self-education skills [35]. The 4IR demands interdisciplinary skills and multidisciplinary knowledge. In particular, AI requires man-machine interaction for improved productivity, demanding non-technical or soft skills, including emotional intelligence, creativity, critical thinking, communication, innovation, leadership, collaboration and teamwork [36].

The complexity evident in the 4IR supports the need for a design-thinking approach that seeks to simplify work, balance technical, commercial and human requirements and manage feasibility, viability and desirability constraints [37] and the 4IR presents many risks necessitating preventive technological risk management [38]. The 4IR necessitates the effective division of human and technology labor to take advantage of efficiencies and effectiveness with large volumes of digital data and human creativity, ideas, critical analysis and decision-making [39].

In addition, product and service quality management evolve in the 4IR to include design and brand quality and the combination of quality experts and data scientists. New quality management approaches involve quality management in the planning stages, creative team-based thinking in the design stage, the replacement of sampling inspection with total inspection at the production stage and the creation of new customer value at the marketing and sales stages [40].

The 4IR emphasizes skills that are not easily automated, such as complex problem-solving, cognitive flexibility, critical thinking, judgement and decision-making, creativity, emotional intelligence, people management, negotiating, coordinating and service orientation [41]. Moreover, the 4IR stresses the importance of social skills including personal interaction, social intelligence, social perceptiveness, creativity [42], persuasion, caring, teaching and cooperating with technology [43] and requires people that can maintain and configure machines and continue to learn [44].

The 4IR calls for competitive intelligence supported by creativity, information literacy and collaborative innovation [45] and demands digital leaders in cross-hierarchical, team-oriented and cooperative roles focused on innovation [46].

The 4IR reiterates the requirement for continually updating professional skills and creating, maintaining and using digital networks with colleagues and employers [47]. The

4IR expects an entrepreneurial attitude in the implementation of its tools in organizations [9] and a single, end-to-end view of the customer [30] and demands global awareness and citizenship, innovation and creativity, analytical thinking, complex problem-solving, systems analysis, digital skills, interpersonal skills, negotiation, social awareness, leadership [48], perception and manipulation in unstructured processes, new ideas, social intelligence, persuasion and caring [49].

In addition, 4IR necessitates learnability, which is the aptitude and motivation to learn new skills, new knowledge and new ways to adapt to change, and typically involves critical thinking skills, decision making, creativity, innovation and emotional intelligence [50]. Importantly, the 4IR necessitates competitive intelligence supported by creativity, information literacy and collaborative innovation [45].

3.3   CIO Framework for Managing the Fourth Industrial Revolution (4IR)

Following analysis and synthesis of the preceding literature, Table 2 presents specific roles and corresponding capabilities required by CIOs in 4IR business environments for producing customer value, organizational competitiveness and performance. These roles and capabilities do not disregard the many other CIO roles and capabilities but are the roles and capabilities that appear pivotal for organizational survival in an unprecedented 4IR convergence of advanced digital, physical and biological technologies.

Table 2. CIO framework for managing the Fourth Industrial Revolution (4IR).

Specific 4IR roles	Role category	Corresponding specific 4IR capabilities
Customer value developer	Business and technical	• Has a single, end-to-end view of the customer
Technology entrepreneur		• Demonstrates competitive intelligence
		• Cooperates with ICT-driven machines
		• Divides labor between humans and ICT-driven machines
		• Uses a design-thinking approach
		• Is information literate
		• Applies creativity
		• Is flexible in how work time, wages, tasks, and workspace are perceived
Life-long learner	Research	• Exhibits learnability
		• Shows adaptability

4   Conclusion

The study addressed the research problem, being the lack of knowledge about CIO roles and capabilities in the 4IR, by conducting a research synthesis that produced a CIO framework for the 4IR. The framework answered the research question by exposing specific CIO roles and capabilities that were pivotal for success in the 4IR. These roles and capabilities provide important management guidance for CIOs in the 4IR and are considered a framework for managing the 4IR. This presents an original contribution to the scientific literature.

Furthermore, the framework provides scientists with a foundation from which to research and further develop CIO roles and capabilities in the 4IR and potentially other executive management roles and capabilities in the 4IR. This foundation supports both interpretivist and positivistic empirical epistemologies for advancing subjective and inductive, and objective and deductive scientific knowledge, respectively.

In addition, the CIO framework for managing the 4IR offers executive IT management with scientific evidence of the specific roles and capabilities required to create value, competitiveness and performance in the 4IR. Such knowledge is essential in an era of unprecedented radical and ambiguous change to our internal and external work and business environments.

A limitation was the exclusion of empirical data for supporting the concepts in the framework and the relationships among those concepts. However, these limitations provide worthwhile empirical research opportunities. Furthermore, other research opportunities may lie in adapting the framework for various other executive management positions that are also required to navigate and make high-value decisions in the 4IR.

References

1. Maynard, A.D.: Navigating the fourth industrial revolution. Nat. Nanotechnol. **10**, 1005–1006 (2015). https://doi.org/10.1038/nnano.2015.286
2. Philbeck, T., Davis, N.: The fourth industrial revolution: shaping a new era. J. Int. Aff. **72**, 17–22 (2019)
3. Xu, L.D., Xu, E.L., Li, L.: Industry 4.0: state of the art and future trends. Int. J. Prod. Res. **56**, 2941–2962 (2018). https://doi.org/10.1080/00207543.2018.1444806
4. Jeon, J., Suh, Y.: Analyzing the major issues of the 4th industrial revolution. Asian J. Innov. Policy **6**, 262–273 (2017). https://doi.org/10.7545/ajip.2017.6.3.262
5. Grabowska, S.: Industry 4.0 challenges for the business model. Sci. Notebooks Silesian Univ. Technol. Ser. Organ. Manag. **136**, 137–144 (2019). https://doi.org/10.29119/1641-3466.2019.136.11
6. Sotnyk, I., Zavrazhnyi, K., Kasianenko, V., Roubík, H., Sidorov, O.: Investment management of business digital innovations. Mark. Manag. Innov. 95–109 (2020). http://doi.org/10.21272/mmi.2020.1-07
7. Adamik, A.: Creating a competitive advantage in the age of industry 4.0. Manag. Issues – Probl. ZarzÈdzania **17**, 13–31 (2019). https://doi.org/10.7172/1644-9584.82.1
8. Kohnová, L., Papula, J., Salajová, N.: Internal factors supporting business and technological transformation in the context of industry 4.0. Bus. Theory Pract. **20**, 137–145 (2019). https://doi.org/10.3846/btp.2019.13
9. Ślusarczyk, B.: Industry 4.0 – are we ready? Polish J. Manag. Stud. **17**, 232–248 (2018). https://doi.org/10.17512/pjms.2018.17.1.19
10. Man, G.-M., Man, M.: Challenges in the fourth industrial revolution. Land Forces Acad. Rev. **24**, 303–307 (2019). https://doi.org/10.2478/raft-2019-0038
11. Banker, R.D., Hu, N., Pavlou, P.A., Luftman, J.: CIO reporting structure, strategic positioning, and firm performance. MIS Q. **35**, 487–504 (2011). https://doi.org/10.2307/23044053

12. Peppard, J.: Unlocking the performance of the Chief Information Officer (CIO). Calif. Manag. Rev. **52**, 73–99 (2010). https://doi.org/10.1525/cmr.2010.52.4.73
13. Karahanna, E., Preston, D.S.: The effect of social capital of the relationship between the CIO and top management team on firm performance. J. Manag. Inf. Syst. **30**, 15–55 (2013). https://doi.org/10.2753/MIS0742-1222300101
14. Members of the College of Senior Scholars: Senior Scholars' Basket of Journals. https://ais net.org/page/SeniorScholarBasket. Accessed 13 July 2020
15. Myers, M.D.: Qualitative Research in Business and Management. Sage Publications Ltd., London (2013)
16. Elsbach, K.D., van Knippenberg, D.: Creating high-impact literature reviews: an argument for 'integrative reviews'. J. Manag. Stud. 1–13 (2020). https://doi.org/10.1111/joms.12581
17. Schryen, G., Wagner, G., Benlian, A., Paré, G.: A knowledge development perspective on literature reviews: validation of a new typology in the IS field. Commun. Assoc. Inf. Syst. **46**, 134–186 (2020). https://doi.org/10.17705/1CAIS.04607
18. Onwuegbuzie, A.J., Leech, N.L., Collins, K.M.T.: Qualitative analysis techniques for the review of the literature. Qual. Rep. **17**, 1–28 (2012)
19. Klopper, R., Lubbe, S.: Using matrix analysis to achieve traction, coherence, progression and closure in problem-solution oriented research. Alternation **18**, 386–403 (2011)
20. Rowley, J., Slack, F.: Conducting a literature review. Manag. Res. News. **27**, 31–39 (2004). https://doi.org/10.1108/01409170410784185
21. Kitchenham, B.: Procedures for Performing Systematic Reviews. Keele, Newcastle (2004)
22. Suri, H., Clarke, D.: Advancements in research synthesis methods: from a methodologically inclusive perspective. Rev. Educ. Res. **79**, 395–430 (2009)
23. Boote, D.N., Beile, P.: Scholars before researchers: on the centrality of the dissertation literature review in research preparation. Educ. Res. **34**, 3–15 (2005)
24. Earl, M.J.: The Chief Information Officer: past, present and future. In: Earl, M.J. (ed.) Information Management: The Organizational Dimension, pp. 456–484. Oxford University Press, New York (1996)
25. Chun, M., Mooney, J.: CIO roles and responsibilities: twenty-five years of evolution and change. Inf. Manag. **46**, 323–334 (2009). https://doi.org/10.1016/j.im.2009.05.005
26. Dahlberg, T., Hokkanen, P., Newman, M.: How business strategy and changes to business strategy impact the role and the tasks of CIOs: an evolutionary model. In: Bui, T.X., Sprague, Jr., R.H. (eds.) 49th Hawaii International Conference on System Sciences (HICSS), pp. 4909–4919. IEEE Computer Society, Kauai (2016). https://doi.org/10.1109/HICSS.2016.609
27. Masli, A., Richardson, V.J., Watson, M.W., Zmud, R.W.: Senior executives' IT management responsibilities: serious IT-related deficiencies and CEO/CFO turnover. MIS Q. **40**, 687–708 (2016). https://doi.org/10.25300/MISQ/2016/40.3.08
28. Gonzaleza, P.A., Ashworth, L., McKeen, J.: The CIO stereotype: content, bias, and impact. J. Strateg. Inf. Syst. **28**, 83–99 (2019). https://doi.org/10.1016/j.jsis.2018.09.002
29. Jones, M.C., Kappelman, L., Pavur, R., Nguyen, Q.N., Johnson, V.L.: Pathways to being CIO: the role of background revisited. Inf. Manag. **57**, 1–14 (2020). https://doi.org/10.1016/j.im.2019.103234
30. Sleep, S., Hulland, J.: Is big data driving cooperation in the c-suite? The evolving relationship between the chief marketing officer and Chief Information Officer. J. Strateg. Mark. **27**, 666–678 (2019). https://doi.org/10.1080/0965254X.2018.1464496
31. Gerth, A.B., Peppard, J.: The dynamics of CIO derailment: how CIOs come undone and how to avoid it. Bus. Horiz. **59**, 61–70 (2016). https://doi.org/10.1016/j.bushor.2015.09.001
32. Korhonen, J.J.: Enterprise transformation capability for the digital era: demands for organizations and CIOs (2018). https://aaltodoc.aalto.fi/bitstream/handle/123456789/31309/isbn97 89526080130.pdf?sequence=1&isAllowed=y

33. Gong, Y., Janssen, M., Weerakkody, V.: Current and expected roles and capabilities of CIOs for the innovation and adoption of new technology. In: Chen, Y.-C., Salem, F., Zuiderwijk, A. (eds.) Proceedings of the 20th Annual International Conference on Digital Government Research, pp. 462–467. Association for Computing Machinery (ACM), Dubai, U.A.E. (2019). https://doi.org/10.1145/3325112.3325214

34. Kappelman, L., McLean, E., Johnson, V., Torres, R., Maurer, C., Kim, K.: The 2018 SIM IT issues and trends study. MIS Q. Exec. **18**, 51–84 (2019). https://doi.org/10.17705/2msqe.00008

35. de Andrade Régio, M.M., Gaspar, M.R.C., do Carmo Farinha, L.M., de Passos Morgado, M.M.A.: Forecasting the disruptive skillset alignment induced by the forthcoming industrial revolution. Rom. Rev. Precis. Mech. Opt. Mechatron. **49**, 24–29 (2016)

36. Maisiri, W., Darwish, H., van Dyk, L.: An investigation of industry 4.0 skills requirements. South Afr. J. Ind. Eng. **30**, 90–105 (2019). https://doi.org/10.7166/30-3-2230

37. Newton, J.: The urgent need to simplify work. Ind. Manag. **61**, 12–15 (2019)

38. Grigorievich, D.A.: The problem of preventive management of technological risks in the industry 4.0. Eur. Sci. Rev. **11–12**, 60–63 (2019)

39. Lobova, S.V., Alekseev, A.N., Litvinova, T.N., Sadovnikova, N.A.: Labor division and advantages and limits of participation in creation of intangible assets in industry 4.0: humans versus machines. J. Intellect. Cap. **21**, 623–638 (2020). https://doi.org/10.1108/JIC-11-2019-0277

40. Park, S.H., Shin, W.S., Park, Y.H., Lee, Y.: Building a new culture for quality management in the era of the fourth industrial revolution. Total Qual. Manag. **28**, 934–945 (2017). https://doi.org/10.1080/14783363.2017.1310703

41. Mfanafuthi, M., Nyawo, J., Mashau, P.: Analysis of the impact of artificial intelligence and robotics on human labour. Gend. Behav. **17**, 13877–13891 (2019). https://hdl.handle.net/10.10520/EJC-197549e03f

42. Kroh, M.: A Socio-economic context of the "Fourth Industrial Revolution". Educ. Sci. Without Borders **7**, 10–13 (2016)

43. Brougham, D., Haar, J.M., Tootell, B.: Service Sector employee insights into the future of work and technological disruption. New Zeal. J. Employ. Relat. **44**, 21–36 (2019)

44. Mayerová, K., Hyžová, S.: Development of information technologies and their impact on the labor markets. Soc. Econ. Rev. **17**, 70–79 (2019)

45. Ottonicar, S.L.C., Valentim, M.L.P., Mosconi, E.: A competitive intelligence model based on information literacy: organizational competitiveness in the context of the 4th Industrial Revolution. J. Intell. Stud. Bus. **8**, 55–65 (2018). http://hdl.handle.net/11449/185316

46. Oberer, B., Erkollar, A.: Leadership 4.0: digital leaders in the age of industry 4.0. Int. J. Organ. Leadersh. **7**, 404–412 (2018). https://doi.org/10.33844/ijol.2018.60332

47. Hirschi, A.: The fourth industrial revolution: issues and implications for career research and practice. Career Dev. Q. **66**, 192–204 (2018). https://doi.org/10.1002/cdq.12142

48. Singh, D., Sharma, D.: Employability skills to thrive during fourth industrial revolution: upskilling secondary school learners. Jaipuria Int. J. Manag. Res. **6**, 3–12 (2020). https://doi.org/10.22552/jijmr%2F2020%2Fv6%2Fi1%2F195903

49. Chinoracký, R., Turská, S., Madlenáková, L.: Does industry 4.0 have the same impact on employment in the sectors? Management **14**, 5–17 (2019). https://doi.org/10.26493/1854-4231.14.5-17

50. Živčicová, E., Gullerová, M.: Learnability as the key skill of the future. Soc. Econ. Rev. **17**, 75–80 (2019)

A Change and Constancy Management Approach for Managing the Unintended Negative Consequences of Organizational and IT Change

Grant Royd Howard$^{(\boxtimes)}$ (iD)

University of South Africa (Unisa), Florida, South Africa
howargr@unisa.ac.za

Abstract. The study focuses on large-scale planned organizational and IT changes because of their typical high costs and risks to organizations. The research gap was insufficient research relating to change management based on the ontological view that change and constancy exist in cohesion. The study contended that a change and constancy management approach would be worthwhile for addressing unintended negative consequences of changes. Thus, the aim was to empirically investigate these changes and determine whether actively managing change and constancy together could mitigate unintended negative consequences of changes and increase change success. A predominantly qualitative questionnaire survey was administered, and the resulting data were analyzed qualitatively and quantitatively. The data provided evidence of both change and constancy in these contexts, the failure rates reported in the literature, unintended negative consequences and their potential severity and the approach being worthwhile to mitigate any costly chasm between change conceptualization and actualization.

Keywords: Change and constancy · Change success and failure · Change management · Information Systems (IS) · Information Technology (IT) · Pragmatism · IT management · Organizational change · Qualitative · Quantitative · Unintended negative consequences of change

1 Introduction

As modern organizations compete in dynamic business environments, organizational and Information Technology (IT) change happen in various forms in every organization. These changes can differ greatly in scale and, while all types of change are important, it was the large-scale planned organizational and IT changes that were the focus of the paper due to their typical high costs and risks to organizations.

Large organizational and IT changes are defined as fundamental organization-wide changes that often involve changes to organizational strategy and business models, core operations and technologies and processes at many organizational levels [1].

This contrasts with minor changes such as hiring a new employee, updating a process or patching a computer system. In addition, the paper considered both organizational

© Springer Nature Switzerland AG 2020
M. Themistocleous et al. (Eds.): EMCIS 2020, LNBIP 402, pp. 683–697, 2020.
https://doi.org/10.1007/978-3-030-63396-7_46

change and IT change together because large organizational changes usually involve IT changes, and vice versa [2, 3].

In this context, the conspicuous real-world problem was the high failure rate of organizational [4, 5] and IT changes [6–9], reported to be well over fifty percent for both. Organizational and IT change failures have resulted in significant performance, market share, reputational, personnel and financial losses, extending to hundreds of millions of United States Dollars (USD) and even bankruptcy [10].

A pertinent consideration when studying organizational and IT change is the criteria for judging whether a change is a success or a failure. The literature reports that this judgement is based on criteria that are specific to each change, contextual, subjective and dependent on the particular evaluating stakeholders [10, 11–13].

Nevertheless, a change normally begins with planned or intended positive outcomes only. Planned or intended negative outcomes are not considered rational. Once a change is implemented there may be unintended negative or positive outcomes or consequences in addition to the planned or intended positive outcomes. Any unintended positive outcomes or consequences are not generally considered a problem and may be viewed as good fortune, but even unintended positive outcomes could potentially cause a change to be classified as a failure if not enough of the intended positive outcomes are achieved. However, unintended positive outcomes of changes were not a focus of the study since they are not typically reported as serious risks to organizations. It is the unintended negative outcomes or consequences of changes that present serious risks to organizations and were the focus of the study.

Generally, it can be argued that when a change goes according to its plan and the intended positive outcomes are achieved, then it may be regarded as a success. It follows that any unplanned or unintended negative consequences are not, by definition, part of any planned outcomes [14]. So, if they occur, they could cause a change to be classified as a failure [15]. In addition, it can be argued that not achieving an intended positive outcome is unintentional and negative. Thus, not achieving an intended positive outcome of a change can be regarded as an unintended negative outcome of the change. In addition, practically, minor unintended negative consequences could be easily ignored, accommodated or corrected, but major unintended negative consequences would be difficult to overlook and would likely cause a change to be classified as a failure.

Therefore, approaches to mitigate unintended negative consequences of changes, especially major unintended negative consequences, are relevant and significant to organizations globally and in Africa and their stakeholders and academics. In this regard, the literature provides many prevailing approaches and theories for managing and analyzing organizational and IT changes [16, 17], but these do not advocate managing change based on the ontological view that change and constancy exist in cohesion [18, 19]. This was the research problem or gap addressed by the paper.

The study contends that the ontological view of change and constancy existing in cohesion is vital for necessary insight into the realities of these organizational and IT change environments, where some aspects change at a particular time and others remain constant [20, 21]. The study maintains that this view is required to effectively mitigate unintended negative consequences of changes by managing change aspects and constancy aspects together, which requires proactively managing those aspects that should not change and could otherwise become the costly unintended consequences.

Subsequently, the research objective was to empirically investigate large organizational and IT changes and determine whether actively managing change and constancy together would be worthwhile for mitigating unintended negative consequences of changes and increasing the likelihood of change success. Hence, the research questions were:

1) Do experts in the field perceive elements of change and constancy in their organizational and IT environments and, if they do, what is the nature of these elements?
2) What are the perceived success rates of large organizational and IT changes and what are the main reasons for any successes and failures?
3) Have any unintended negative consequences occurred during large organizational and IT changes, and if so, how frequent are they and how severe are the consequences?
4) Do experts in the field consider it worthwhile to actively manage both the organizational and IT aspects that are intended for change and those not intended for change to mitigate any unintended negative consequences?
5) Do experts in the field consider IT and other organizational aspects so interdependent in today's organizations that large IT changes usually cause changes to organizational aspects and vice versa?

This introduction is followed by an analysis and synthesis of the relevant literature and prior research. Thereafter, the research design is detailed and justified. Then, the empirical results are presented, and the paper concludes with a discussion about the findings, knowledge contribution, limitations and future research directions.

2 Relevant Literature

The paper views change as difference and constancy as sameness over any selected time period [21]. Reasoning about change, constancy and existence dates back to ancient Greek philosophy [22]. Since then there have been varied ontological perspectives ranging from change being the only reality to constancy the only reality. Both ontological extremes have persuasive logic making it difficult to reject either one. It can be argued that both are valid and this is supported by convincing arguments that change and constancy exist in cohesion [19]. Therefore, the ontological perspective of the paper is that change and constancy exist in cohesion, which presents an epistemology where change is known in contrast to constancy and vice versa.

Change is intrinsically neither positive nor negative, and the same applies to constancy. For instance, change can be positive if it results in innovation, improvement, new business, competitiveness and improved performance [23] and negative when severe losses are experienced. Constancy can be positive through consistent, repeatable processes, stability and continuity and negative when business fails by not changing [24, 25].

Thus, it appears essential to diligently consider what to change and what to keep constant to achieve success and avoid failure because success and failure have occurred due to both change and constancy.

In organizations, there is often a pro-change bias which can create conditions for unintended negative consequences [26]. With a single focus on change, aspects that should not change are neglected and may become negatively and unintentionally altered. This pro-change bias is also evident in prominent studies on IT change initiatives or projects [27], business-IT alignment [28] and organizational change [16], where the idea of actively managing constancy is not apparent. Nonetheless, there is literature, although scant, reporting that managing change and constancy together leads to success [20].

The preceding two sections made an argument for actively managing change and constancy together for mitigating unintended negative consequences of changes. To empirically support or refute this argument, empirical evidence was gathered and analyzed. The next section details the study's empirical process or methodology and is followed by the empirical findings.

3 Methodology

3.1 Philosophy, Methodological Choice and Strategy

The study proceeded from the philosophical position of pragmatism to address the research problem and answer the research questions [29]. A pragmatist epistemology facilitates knowledge acquisition through both quantitative and qualitative data and analysis methods as are appropriate for answering the research questions. It views methods that may be considered antithetical as complementary and mutually beneficial for achieving research objectives.

Consequently, a predominantly qualitative questionnaire survey was administered to obtain rich data from a wide variety of applicable contexts [30] and the resulting data was analyzed qualitatively and quantitatively. The qualitative data was imported into qualitative data analysis software called QDA Miner Lite [31] and coded and categorized to answer the research questions rather than the development of new concepts, theory, models or frameworks. Then, descriptive quantitative analysis was performed using Microsoft Excel. The descriptive quantitative analyses provided numerical values to appropriately answer the research questions.

3.2 Data Selection and Collection

Data source selection was appropriately based on theoretical and purposive selection and was not related to statistical sampling, representativeness or generalizability [32]. Theoretical selection provided the underlying rationale for directing and adapting the subsequent purposive selection. The purposive selection implemented the focused criteria to obtain diverse and relevant expert information, experience and knowledge [33]. The specific selection inclusion criteria were English-speaking respondents with specialist and relevant knowledge, skills and experience in organizational and IT change from varied organizational types and sizes, industries and countries [30].

To discover and access these respondents, the study made use of the business and employment-oriented social media service called LinkedIn [34], which was designed for free and open professional networking [35]. The number of respondents or selection size was guided by the principle of theoretical saturation [30]. This was a subjective assessment by the researcher about whether new information and insights were evident or not as new data were collected [36]. After 74 responses were obtained between 31 January 2020 and 05 March 2020, it was apparent that the data were not providing any new theoretical insights and the data collection terminated. In addition, 74 responses exceeds the recommended flexible size estimates [32]. The study and both versions of the questionnaire were reviewed and approved by the University of South Africa's (Unisa's) School of Computing Research Ethics Committee.

Making use of LinkedIn to obtain data was time intensive and required a diligent and focused effort, but it did enable access to a vast number of relevant professionals and experts across many countries. In summary, 52% of connect requests sent to potential respondents were accepted, 12% of full survey invitations sent to relevant connections resulted in complete responses and, overall, 7% of connect requests sent to potential respondents resulted in complete responses.

4 Findings

4.1 Respondent Characteristics

Table 1 presents the respondents' management levels and occupational focus groupings. The most common occupational titles were Chief Information Officer (CIO) (34%), Chief Executive Officer (CEO) (7%), Organizational Development Consultant (4%) and Director (3%).

Table 1. Respondents' management level and occupational focus groupings.

Management level	Occupational focus	Number	Percentage (rounded)
Executive Management	IT and Related	29	39%
	Organization General	9	12%
Middle Management	IT and Related	9	12%
	Organization General	7	9%
Lower Management	IT and Related	6	8%
	Organization General	6	8%
Consultant	IT and Related	4	5%
	Organization General	4	5%
Totals		74	100%

Figure 1 presents the industries in which the respondents mainly worked. The industry categories were based on the standard industrial classification (SIC) of all economic activities from Statistics South Africa [37]. In addition, Fig. 2 presents the countries in which the respondents mostly worked.

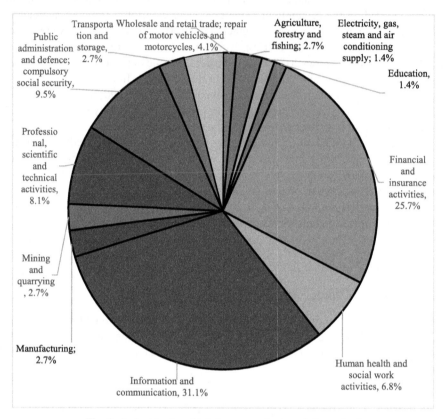

Fig. 1. Industries in which the respondents mainly worked

In addition, 24% of the respondents worked for small organizations (<50 employees), 12% worked for medium-sized organizations (50–250 employees) and 64% worked for large organizations (>250 employees).

The respondent characteristics demonstrated that a variety of English-speaking experts with specialist and relevant knowledge, skills and experience in organizational and IT change from varied organizational types and sizes, industries and countries were accessed and provided data for the study. Notably, most respondents worked in South Africa.

4.2 Perceptions of Change and Constancy

The first research question was about whether experts in the field perceived elements of constancy and change in their organizational and IT environments. Answers to this question were important for verifying or refuting the ontological basis of the study, that constancy and change exist in cohesion in these social and organizational contexts.

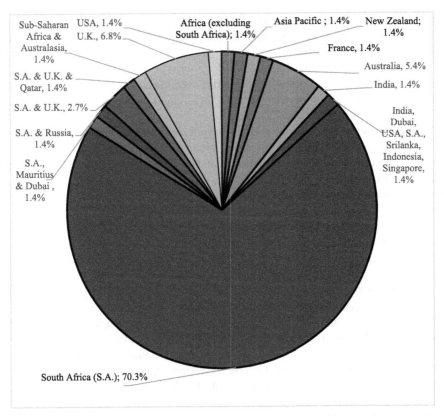

Sub-Saharan USA, 1.4%   Africa (excluding   Asia Pacific ; 1.4%   New Zealand;
Africa & U.K., 6.8%   South Africa); 1.4%   1.4%
Australasia,   France, 1.4%
1.4%
                                              Australia, 5.4%
S.A. & U.K. &
Qatar, 1.4%   India, 1.4%

S.A. & U.K., 2.7%   India,
                                              Dubai,
S.A. & Russia,   USA, S.A.,
1.4%   Srilanka,
                                              Indonesia,
S.A.,   Singapore,
Mauritius   1.4%
& Dubai ,
1.4%

South Africa (S.A.); 70.3%

Fig. 2. Countries in which the respondents mostly worked (a group with more than one country represents respondents who work in that group of countries)

In terms of the respondents' perceptions of medium to long-term historic change within their general organizational contexts, they perceived change as increased employee and customer centricity, efficiencies and external competition, increased IT innovations, internet connectedness and new work practices. In connection with perceptions of medium to long-term future change, they perceived change in increasing team-based work practices, customer centricity, sustainability, lower barriers to entry, more artificial intelligence (AI) technologies, innovations and remote work.

The respondents also perceived medium to long-term historic constancy within their general organizational contexts in traditional management practices, processes, organizational structure and culture, with risk aversion driving constancy. They perceived medium to long-term future constancy in the need for people, change resistance, business fundamentals and profit motive, competition and governance requirements. IT was not mentioned as part of medium to long-term historic or future constancy.

Regarding IT specifically, respondents perceived medium to long-term historic change as cloud and as-a-service computing, outsourcing, IT infrastructure, systems and applications, data and analysis, AI technologies, social media and IT innovations, with cost savings and IT skills driving the changes. They also perceived medium to long-term future IT change in AI technologies, information and data for competitiveness, cloud and as-a-service computing, internet of things (IoT), the merging of business and IT and blockchain technologies.

The respondents perceived medium to long-term historic IT constancy in core IT systems and management approaches, with risk aversion and IT/business misalignment driving constancy. In addition, they perceived medium to long-term future IT constancy in resistance to change and core IT systems.

Complementing this data were the data that referred to shorter term daily perceptions. 73% of the respondents indicated that, daily, within their general organizational contexts some aspects stayed the same while others changed. They explained that distinct aspects change at different rates and times, there is a need to balance stable operations and services against change risk associated with environmental adaptation and mentioned that changes can take time to cascade through larger organizations.

93% indicated that, daily, within the narrow scope of IT some aspects also stayed the same while others changed. They explained that this occurred through controlled changes for managing risk, internal requirements driving change, business innovation driving change and slow changes.

The remainder of the respondents perceived that, daily, either all general organizational and IT aspects changed at the same time or they all stayed the same. Specifically, 13% perceived that, daily, all general organizational aspects changed at the same time and 2% that all IT aspects changed at the same time. However, their explanations did not appear to fully support these answers and often suggested that some aspects change and others stay the same. In addition, 14% perceived that, daily, all general organizational aspects stay the same and 5% that, daily, all IT aspects stay the same. Similarly, the explanations did not strongly support these answers and these respondents seemed to refer to specific large aspects only, instead of all aspects.

Nevertheless, the number of respondents who perceived that, daily, all general organizational aspects change at the same time and that, daily, all organizational aspects stay the same, were similar, within 1%. Similarly, the number of respondents who perceived that, daily, all IT aspects change at the same time and that, daily, all IT aspects stay the same, were within 3%. Viewing this from a group perspective suggested a balancing support for the 73% and 93% majorities.

Thus, the perceptions across all time ranges provide verification for the ontological basis of the study, that constancy and change exist in cohesion in these general organizational and IT contexts.

4.3 Success Rates of Large Organizational and IT Changes

The second research question was about experts' success rate experiences of both large organizational and IT changes. Each respondent was asked to provide a percentage estimate for the success rate experienced and reasons for any successes and failures. This question was important to determine their reality of change success rates in relation to the reported rates in the literature.

For large organizational changes, just over a third of the respondents indicated a below 50% success rate, almost a quarter a 50% success rate and almost half an above

50% success rate, as per Fig. 3. No respondents provided a zero or hundred percent success rate.

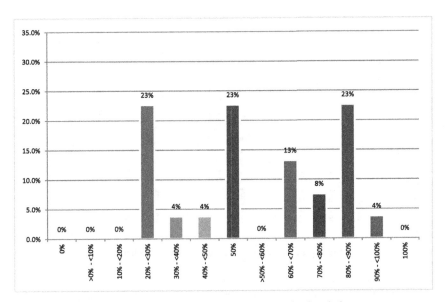

Fig. 3. Perceived success rates of large organizational changes

For large IT changes, almost a sixth of the respondents indicated a below 50% success rate, almost a quarter a 50% success rate and almost two thirds an above 50% success rate, as per Fig. 4. No respondents provided a zero or hundred percent success rate.

The data shows 16% more experiences of 50% and over success rates of large IT changes compared to large organizational changes. Nonetheless, it is evident that 54% of the respondents indicated that half or more organizational changes fail and 37% of the respondents that half or more IT changes fail, which could have resulted in material organizational losses and distress and was, therefore, a significant problem worth addressing.

The respondents' main reasons for successes, and the lack thereof could result in failures, were good change and project management and leadership practices, organizational and stakeholder buy-in, understanding and common purpose, top management support and commitment, defined business cases and success criteria, effective communication and engagement with stakeholders, correct technology choices, skilled and experienced people and manageable number, frequency and size of changes.

4.4 Unintended Negative Consequences of Large Organizational and IT Changes

The third research question was about experts' experiences of unintended negative consequences resulting from large organizational and IT changes, their frequency and severity. This question was important to determine whether unintended negative consequences were a problem in practice.

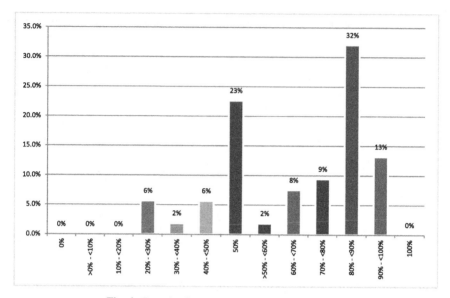

Fig. 4. Perceived success rates of large IT changes

Concerning the frequency of unintended negative consequences resulting from both large organizational and IT changes, 20% of the respondents indicated that none occurred, 30% a low frequency, 15% medium, 11% high and 24% varying. Then, 32% of the respondents indicated experiencing a low severity of unintended negative consequences, 18% medium, 34% high and 16% varying.

The respondents elaborated on their experiences stating that they had observed unintended negative consequences in the form of human, financial, productivity and external impacts. Human impacts included job loss, conflict, confusion, culture damage and stress. Financial impacts involved financial losses, project over-spending, resource wastage, costs to correct errors, costs to rehire, fraud and material organizational loss. Productivity impacts comprised loss of productivity, project delays, failure of core processes, change failure, general delays, errors, increased workloads, instability, loss of organizational knowledge, manual workarounds, reduced system functionality, slow adoption and system downtime. External impacts covered the loss of competitive advantage, loss of customers, customer complaints, impaired service delivery and lost revenue.

It was evident that the respondents did not have a uniform experience of unintended negative consequences, which appeared to be context dependent. Nevertheless, it was apparent that unintended negative consequences did occur, they could be severe and could impact many aspects of an organization. Therefore, developing approaches to reduce their occurrence was relevant and significant in practice and in academe.

4.5   Actively Managing Both the Organizational and IT Aspects that Are Intended for Change and Those not Intended for Change

The fourth research question was about whether experts consider it worthwhile to actively manage both the organizational and IT aspects that are intended for change and those not intended for change to mitigate any unintended negative consequences of changes. This question was important for assessing the perceived usefulness of the management approach presented by the study.

81% of the respondents agreed that it would be worthwhile to actively manage both the organizational and IT aspects that are intended for change and those not intended for change to prevent or minimize any unintended changes. 17% disagreed, 1% was indecisive and 2% welcomed positive unintended changes.

Of the respondents who agreed, one added that it was already happening, two presented concerns that it should not prevent growth through change and that it was often difficult to determine the exact scope of a change outcome before implementation, another indicated that it would have the added benefit of clarifying to the organization the reasons for a change and the rest suggested the addition of various management processes, including culture shift management, analyzing the whole value chain, requiring a team effort with good business processes, conducting the approach in the assessment phase, using impact analysis, stakeholder management and implementing the approach in a mature manner.

Of the respondents who disagreed, one interpreted constancy as business as usual processes and operations only and change as change programs and stated that they could not be managed together. However, while it is often the case in organizations and IT that management split logical parts into business/IT as usual or operations or run the business/IT and change the business/IT [38], there are always aspects that change and stay the same in both parts, but to different degrees. So, regardless of such splits, it can be argued that actively managing change and constancy would still be applicable.

Other disagreeing respondents stated that correct risk and change management should already minimize or predict unintended changes, any unintended changes that occur must be corrected and an individual made responsible, that unintended changes are normal and impossible to manage and an organization needs to be adaptive, there is no need to manage aspects that are not planned for change using change management which must focus on change only, it is not possible to forecast unintended changes, rather learn from negative unintended changes so they are not unintended the next time and rather monitor instead of manage change and constancy. While these arguments may be potentially feasible in specific contexts, they seem difficult to maintain considering the volume of reported change failures and unintended negative consequences and given the many other respondents who agree with actively managing change and constancy together.

4.6   Interdependence of Large Organizational and IT Changes

The fifth research question investigated whether experts consider IT and other organizational aspects so interdependent in today's organizations that large IT changes usually cause changes to other organizational aspects and vice versa. This question was important to determine if managing change and constancy should be applied differently to organizational and IT aspects.

88% of the respondents stated that organizational and IT aspects were so interdependent in today's organizations that large IT changes usually cause changes to other organizational aspects and vice versa. They supported this by disclosing that the business environment and IT drove change, IT was an enabler, IT was now the shop front, IT was used pervasively, organizations were dependent on IT, the IT aspects of cloud computing, AI, data and robotic process automation (RPA) were key to organizations, IT change at the structural level results in organizational change, IT change requires rethinking organizational processes, IT and organizations should be managed together and businesses were digital so there is no distinction between IT and the organization.

They also expressed some exceptions, such as the interdependence would not occur unless the organization is change ready and fit, when organizational change does not require IT adaptation, when IT only supports what business users, customers and suppliers require, when there is slower IT change due to older, more change resistant and less technically skilled staff and when there is less funding.

The remaining 12% were ambivalent and provided contingencies of interdependency, including that it depends on the industry and functional area and there are instances where IT is still a separate entity and cost center instead of a business partner.

5   Conclusion

The paper addressed the research problem and made an original contribution in the form of an evidence-based solution approach for mitigating unintended negative consequences of changes and improving control over intended goals, namely a change and constancy management approach. This approach is relevant and significant to practice in industry and theory in academe, given the potential for severe losses to organizations and their stakeholders.

The paper exposes an approach to managing organizational and IT changes based on a change and constancy ontology and an epistemology for developing further knowledge and insights in and from these environments, where change is known in contrast to constancy and vice versa. The change and constancy ontology is an efficient and parsimonious approach for conceptualizing and understanding typically multivariate and complex organizational and IT environments.

The research objective was achieved, and the research questions were answered. Specifically, most of the participating experts perceived elements of both change and constancy in their organizational and IT environments, which verified the ontological basis of the study, that constancy and change exist in cohesion in these social organizational and IT contexts.

They provided credibility to the reported failure rates in the literature for organizational changes with 54% of the respondents disclosing that half or more organizational changes fail and 37% that half or more IT changes fail. This data exposes the potential for material organizational losses.

Furthermore, a quarter of the respondents revealed that unintended negative consequences occurred with a medium to high frequency and over half of the respondents indicated that the negative consequences could have a medium to high severity. So, while their experiences vary there remains the potential for significant organizational losses, which is supported by the literature.

The paper's approach of actively managing change and constancy together for mitigating unintended negative consequences was put to the respondents and 81% agreed that it would be worthwhile. In addition, 88% stated that IT aspects and other organizational aspects are so interdependent in today's organizations that large IT changes usually cause changes to other organizational aspects and vice versa. Thus, there is reasonable support for considering both organizational change and IT change jointly and actively managing change and constancy together for mitigating unintended negative consequences and improving control over intended goals.

In addition, the paper recommends that the label of organizational and IT change be rebranded as organizational and IT improvement to create commitment and accountability on the part of change agents and management for positive change only and to remove any tacit gambling behavior.

Nonetheless, the paper did not prescribe detailed steps for operationalizing the change and constancy management approach. This was a limitation and an opportunity for future research. Although, the proposal was that the approach should not occur at change events only but be applied holistically and continuously since constancy and change are evident across all time ranges throughout an organization and should be actively managed. It is a high- and low-level management approach that should be applied from overall strategy to individual projects since changes and constancy can result in profits or losses at all levels.

The change and constancy management approach would enable improvement (change) agents and management to better understand, articulate, visualize and expose and measure more variables and details of changes, many of which may be unknown, intricate, interdependent, obscure and tacit, to mitigate any costly chasms between change conceptualization and actualization.

References

1. Malopinsky, L.V., Osman, G.: Dimensions of organizational change. In: Pershing, J.A. (ed.) Handbook of Human Performance Technology: Principles, Practices, and Potential, pp. 262–286. Pfeiffer, San Francisco (2006)
2. Besson, P., Rowe, F.: Strategizing information systems-enabled organizational transformation: a transdisciplinary review and new directions. J. Strateg. Inf. Syst. 21, 103–124 (2012). https://doi.org/10.1016/j.jsis.2012.05.001
3. Sligo, J., Gauld, R., Roberts, V., Villa, L.: A literature review for large-scale health information system project planning, implementation and evaluation. Int. J. Med. Inform. 97, 86–97 (2017)
4. Decker, P., Durand, R., Mayfield, C.O., McCormack, C., Skinner, D., Perdue, G.: Predicting implementation failure in organization change. J. Organ. Cult. Commun. Confl. 16, 29–49 (2012)
5. Jansson, N.: Organizational change as practice: a critical analysis. J. Organ. Chang. Manag. 26, 1003–1019 (2013). https://doi.org/10.1108/JOCM-09-2012-0152
6. Heeks, R.: Information systems and developing countries: failure, success, and local improvisations. Inf. Soc. 18, 101–112 (2002)

7. Cecez-Kecmanovic, D., Kautz, K., Abrahall, R.: Reframing success and failure of information systems: a performative perspective. MIS Q. **38**, 561–588 (2014)
8. The Standish Group: The CHAOS Report 2015 (2015)
9. Ebad, S.A.: An exploratory study of ICT projects failure in emerging markets. J. Glob. Inf. Technol. Manag. **21**, 139–160 (2018)
10. Dwivedi, Y.K., et al.: Research on information systems failures and successes: status update and future directions. Inf. Syst. Front. **17**, 143–157 (2014). https://doi.org/10.1007/s10796-014-9500-y
11. Dwivedi, Y.K., et al.: IS/IT project failures: a review of the extant literature for deriving a taxonomy of failure factors. In: Dwivedi, Y.K., Henriksen, H.Z., Wastell, D., De', R. (eds.) TDIT 2013. IAICT, vol. 402, pp. 73–88. Springer, Heidelberg (2013). https://doi.org/10.1007/978-3-642-38862-0_5
12. Janssen, M., van der Voort, H., van Veenstra, A.F.: Failure of large transformation projects from the viewpoint of complex adaptive systems: management principles for dealing with project dynamics. Inf. Syst. Front. **17**, 15–29 (2014). https://doi.org/10.1007/s10796-014-9511-8
13. Al-Ahmad, W., Al-Fagih, K., Khanfar, K., Alsamara, K., Abuleil, S., Abu-Salem, H.: A taxonomy of an IT project failure: root causes. Int. Manag. Rev. **5**, 93–104 (2009)
14. Jian, G.: Unpacking unintended consequences in planned organizational change: a process model. Manag. Commun. Q. **21**, 5–28 (2007). https://doi.org/10.1177/0893318907301986
15. Harrison, M.I., Koppel, R., Bar-Lev, S.: Unintended consequences of information technologies in health care-an interactive sociotechnical analysis. J. Am. Med. Inform. Assoc. **14**, 542–549 (2007). https://doi.org/10.1197/jamia.M2384
16. Al-Haddad, S., Kotnour, T.: Integrating the organizational change literature: a model for successful change. J. Organ. Change Manag. **28**, 234–262 (2015). https://doi.org/10.1108/JOCM-11-2013-0215
17. Howard, G.R.: A Change and constancy research and management framework for IT-related organisational change. In: 4th African Conference on Information Systems & Technology (ACIST), pp. 24–33. Department of Information Systems, University of Cape Town (UCT), Cape Town, South Africa (2018)
18. Talavera, I.: The fallacy of misplaced temporality in Western Philosophy, natural science, and Theistic religion. Forum Public Policy: J. Oxf. Round Table (2014). https://link.gale.com/apps/doc/A497796641/AONE?u=usa_itw&sid=AONE&xid=df5c9b24. GALE|A497796641
19. Loubser, A.: An ontological exploration of change and constancy. Koers – Bull. Christ. Scholarsh. **78**, 1–8 (2013)
20. Nasim, S., Sushil: Revisiting organizational change: exploring the paradox of managing continuity and change. J. Change Manag. **11**, 185–206 (2011). https://doi.org/10.1080/14697017.2010.538854
21. Howard, G.R.: Ontological solution for IT-organisational change problems: a change and constancy management approach. In: 15th European Conference on Management Leadership and Governance, ECMLG 2019, pp. 169–176. Academic Conferences and Publishing International Limited (ACPI), Porto, Portugal (2019)
22. Norton, B.: Change, constancy, and creativity: the new ecology and some old problems. First Ann. Cummings Colloq. Environ. Law Beyond Balanc. Nat. Environ. Law Faces New Ecol. **7**, 49–70 (1996)
23. Josefy, M.A., Harrison, J.S., Sirmon, D.G., Carnes, C.: Living and dying: synthesizing the literature on firm survival and failure across stages of development. Acad. Manag. Ann. **11**, 770–799 (2017)
24. Lucas Jr., H.C., Goh, J.M.: Disruptive technology: how Kodak missed the digital photography revolution. J. Strateg. Inf. Syst. **18**, 46–55 (2009)

25. Trahms, C.A., Ndofor, H.A., Sirmon, D.G.: Organizational decline and turnaround: a review and agenda for future research. J. Manag. **39**, 1277–1307 (2013)
26. Sveiby, K.-E.: Unattended consequences of innovation. In: Godin, B., Vinck, D. (eds.) Critical Studies of Innovation: Alternative Approaches to the Pro-Innovation Bias, pp. 137–155. Edward Elgar, Cheltenham (2017). https://doi.org/10.4337/9781785367229
27. Baghizadeh, Z., Cecez-Kecmanovic, D., Schlagwein, D.: Review and critique of the information systems development project failure literature: an argument for exploring information systems development project distress. J. Inf. Technol. **35**, 123–142 (2020). https://doi.org/10.1177/0268396219832010
28. Tallon, P.P., Queiroz, M., Coltman, T., Sharma, R.: Business process and information technology alignment: construct conceptualization, empirical illustration, and directions for future research. J. Assoc. Inf. Syst. **17**, 563–589 (2016). https://doi.org/10.17705/1jais.00438
29. Creswell, J.W.: Research Design: Qualitative, Quantitative, and Mixed Methods Approaches. Sage Publications Ltd., London (2009)
30. Myers, M.D.: Qualitative Research in Business & Management. Sage Publications Ltd., London (2013)
31. Provalis Research: QDA Miner Lite. https://provalisresearch.com/. Accessed 16 Apr 2020
32. Gentles, S.J., Charles, C., Ploeg, J., McKibbon, K.A.: Sampling in qualitative research: insights from an overview of the methods literature. Qual. Rep. **20**, 1772–1789 (2015)
33. Curtis, S., Gesler, W., Smith, G., Washburn, S.: Approaches to sampling and case selection in qualitative research: examples in the geography of health. Soc. Sci. Med. **50**, 1001–1014 (2000)
34. LinkedIn: LinkedIn. https://www.linkedin.com/. Accessed 11 Apr 2019
35. Sibona, C., Walczak, S.: Purposive sampling on Twitter: a case study. In: 45th Hawaii International Conference on System Sciences (HICSS), pp. 3510–3519. IEEE Computer Society, Maui (2012)
36. Sekaran, U., Bougie, R.: Research Methods for Business: A Skill Building Approach. Wiley, Chichester (2013)
37. Stats, S.A.: Standard Industrial Classification of all Economic Activities (SIC), 7th edn. Pretoria, South Africa (2012)
38. Murer, S., Bonati, B., Furrer, F.J.: Managed Evolution: A Strategy for Very Large Information Systems. Springer, Heidelberg (2011). https://doi.org/10.1007/978-3-642-01633-2

Evaluating the Impacts of IoT Implementation on Inter-organisational Value Co-creation in the Chinese Construction Industry

Zhen Sun[1] and Sulafa Badi[2(✉)]

[1] The Bartlett School of Construction and Project Management,
University College London, London, UK
ucbqzs0@ucl.ac.uk
[2] Faculty of Business and Law, The British University in Dubai, Dubai,
United Arab Emirates
Sulafa.badi@buid.ac.ae

Abstract. The increasing competition in the construction industry requires companies to cooperate and be actively involved in the dynamic management of multiple relationships and supply chains. To facilitate such dynamic supply chain management, some enterprises implement internet of things (IoT) technology and its smart devices. Through the utilisation of IoT technologies in supply chain cooperation, some enterprises have achieved the co-creation of values. However, few researchers evaluate the impacts of IoT implementation on the achievement of value co-creation in the Chinese construction context. To fill these gaps, this study concentrates on exploring the role of IoT implementation in enhancing value co-creation in terms of competency alignment (CA), behavioural alignment (BA), process alignment (PA) and congruence of expectation (CE) in Chinese supply chain collaboration. The data that informs the methodology is collected through a questionnaire and the findings illustrate that IoT implementation positively correlates with CA, BA, PA and CE. The paper concludes by summarising the study's findings and outlining the managerial implications and opportunities for future study.

1 Introduction

In the previous six decades, the growth of conventional supply chain management (SCM) has elevated the process of manual labour to modern automated production (Parkhi et al. 2015; Li et al. 2005). However, a company cannot both compete as an individual entity and develop as an active member of the supply chain network under the conditions of an unpredictable market and increasing competition (Lambert and Cooper 2000). To survive in this challenging environment, supply chain actors need to shift from conventional SCM to a dynamic approach (Krishnapriya and Baral 2014; Manavalan and Jayakrishna 2019). To achieve this goal, some companies cooperate to create value, which is known as supply chain collaboration (SCC) (Krishnapriya and Baral 2014; Fawcett et al. 2008). In the process of co-production and co-creation, issues such as poor tracking and incomplete alignments hinder the achievement of inter-firm value (Kim 2009; Gnimpieba et al. 2015). However, the advent of internet of things (IoT) technologies

© Springer Nature Switzerland AG 2020
M. Themistocleous et al. (Eds.): EMCIS 2020, LNBIP 402, pp. 698–714, 2020.
https://doi.org/10.1007/978-3-030-63396-7_47

provides an innovative approach to handling these difficulties (Gnimpieba et al. 2015; Wang and Alexander 2016). IoT technology, as a new extension of information technology (IT), helps to increase the communication between 'things' and people and to expand the possibility of autonomous collaboration among its smart devices and between supply chain entities (Ben-Daya et al. 2019). Such IoT implementation contributes to the internal and external integration of businesses and consumers (Ben-Daya et al. 2019). Furthermore, IoT technologies such as radio-frequency identification (RFID) tags increase a company's capacity for agility, visibility and supply chain adaptability; more practically, IoT technologies support smooth information exchange and data sharing between partners to facilitate the management of existing and potential risks (Ellis et al. 2015). While some researchers highlight the significance of IoT to supply chain development, its role in enhancing the achievement of value co-creation (VCC) is uncertain in the Chinese construction context (Forsström 2005).

To address this gap, this study focuses on investigating IoT implementation's role in promoting VCC between partners in the Chinese SCM context. More specifically, it explores the relationships between IoT implementation and competency alignment (CA), behavioural alignment (BA), process alignment (PA) and congruence of expectation (CE). The literature review initially organises this study, illustrating the concepts of IoT implementation, IoT and SCC, inter-organisational VCC and its four attributes (CA, BA, PA and CE). The sections that follow construct the conceptual framework, propose four reasonable hypotheses and explain the research methodology. Finally, the numerical results and findings, discussion, conclusion, managerial implications and limitations of the study are presented, along with opportunities for future research.

2   Literature Review

2.1   Internet of Things (IoT)

The concept of the IoT was first developed in the late twentieth century at MIT (Greengard 2015). Later, Ashton (2003) introduced the possibility of tracking industry supply chains by implementing RFID tags, and the concept has since received extensive attention (Schlick et al. 2013; Xu et al. 2014). Subsequently, some IoT technologies and smart devices were employed to support manufacturing and certain construction activities as outlined in Table 1.

Table 1. Examples of IoT technologies

IoT technology example	Description
Radio-frequency identification (RFID)	RFID is a fundamental IoT technology. It aims to tag different items and generate numerous operational and strategic data across the industry's value chain (Wang and Alexander 2016)
Wireless sensor networks (WSN)	WSN is defined as a self-configured wireless sensor network to monitor environmental or physical situations, such as pressure, temperature and pollution, and to pass these raw data via the network to a specific place where data could be modelled and measured (Matin and Islam 2012)
Cloud computing	Cloud computing is used to access data, files, information and third-party services from the online browser through the internet (Kim 2009)

IoT is often seen as a symbol of the digital future because it enables physical and digital properties to be linked to provide services with objects communicating through the internet (Uckelmann et al. 2011; Miorandi et al. 2012). Previous studies have illustrated that IoT implementation contributes to greater accessibility, interactivity, real-time synchronisation, greater monitoring, better connectedness, integration into the physical environment and increasing support for customer experience (Wünderlich et al. 2013; Hoffman and Novak 2015; Neuhofer et al. 2015). In practice, the implementation of IoT technologies provides significant efficiencies to the management of the supply chain and warehouses and increases the possibility for firms to collaborate and co-create value (Zorzi et al. 2010; Ding 2013; Gao and Bai 2014). Furthermore, the IoT expands the implementation of RFID tags to an automatic data identification and collection terminal. Possessing an RFID tag reader in the warehouse will make it easier to monitor the construction materials, manage the delivery time and enhance the flexibility of the supply chain (Kumar and Shoghli 2018).

2.2   Supply Chain Collaboration (SCC)

SCM has contributed to the transition from the primary process of manual labour to the current automatic management methods (Parkhi et al. 2015; Manavalan and Jayakrishna 2019; Li et al. 2005). SCM is the management of the interconnected services, materials, products, finance and information needed by end consumers (Harland 1996; Handfield and Linton 2017). However, increasing competition in construction markets requires firms to shift from a conventional to a dynamic form of SCM (Krishnapriya and Baral 2014). To achieve this objective, enterprises pursue cooperative relationship which entails SCC (Krishnapriya and Baral 2014; Fawcett et al. 2008). SCC is the extent to which supply chain actors strategically integrate with their partners and jointly manages the inter-organisational systems (Kumar and Dissel 1996; Lambert et al. 1999; Flynn et al. 2010).

In the process of SCC, the advent of IoT technologies such as cloud computing and RFID tags offers an innovative way to collect, transfer, store and share data to support better cooperation (Kim 2009; Gnimpieba et al. 2015; Wang and Alexander 2016). For example, the integration of the Electronic Product Code Information System (EPCIS), wireless sensor networks (WSN) and RFID tags enables enterprises to share location-related information and the status of services and products (Kumar and Shoghli 2018). It also supports the reading of information such as the Electronic Product Code (EPC) and product dangerousness (Kumar and Shoghli 2018). Thus, the data collected could be stored in the database, contributing to information-sharing and data-monitoring processes (Kim 2009; Wang and Alexander 2016). To measure the success of IoT implementation, companies commonly utilise the following four standards: sensitivity to latency, mobility of objects, smooth communication, and data storing and network performance (*OECD* 2018).

2.3   Inter-organisational Value Co-creation (VCC)

Academic research on VCC is developed from the concepts of service-dominant logic (SDL) (Vargo and Lusch 2004). SDL views service as the main focus of exchange in the market, whereas the traditional goods-dominant logic (GDL) believes the value of exchange is embedded in the exchange of goods (Lusch and Vargo 2006). Based on SDL, co-creation is the value that is more than the overall value created by individual enterprises themselves, indicating the importance of the establishment of relationships (Liu et al. 2014). Business-to-business VCC was regarded as the mechanism between industrial relationships and interdependence with the interaction between enterprises being crucial for partnership improvement (Forsström 2005; Ren et al. 2015).

Previous literature illustrates that misalignments will hinder the achievement of inter-organisational VCC (Park and Ungson 2001; Fawcett et al. 2008; Ng et al. 2010). Therefore, four alignment-related attributes should be considered: competency alignment (CA), behavioural alignment (BA), process alignment (PA) and congruence of expectations (CE) (Chakraborty et al. 2014). CA is the extent to which the supply chain partners provide competencies such as specialised skills and knowledge, expertise and judgment, and complementary resources (Stenroos and Jaakkola 2012). BA refers to the extent to which the collaborating enterprises' behaviours are appropriate and aligned to achieve VCC (Ng et al. 2010). To facilitate BA, partners must align their process to support a smooth exchange of information (Ng et al. 2011). PA indicates that the achievement of VCC needs to develop a synchronous process of collecting, transferring, sharing and storing information and of managing inventory (Yan and Huang 2009; Hung et al. 2007; Yusuf et al. 2004). CE is the extent to which the company's expectations of the partner match the partner's understandings of the firm's expectations (Zeithmal et al. 1993; Dean 2004; Ng et al. 2010).

2.4   IoT Implementation and Inter-organisational VCC

With the improvement of IT, IoT technology has also developed and become increasingly conspicuous in different fields (Balaji and Roy 2017). One of the most distinguished fields is the construction industry (Pantano and Timmermans 2014). Inspired by this new trend, innovative companies are exploring ways to exchange information during their operations; moreover, they desire to maintain an interrelationship with partners under support from IoT technologies (Liu et al. 2014). In practice, a firm can obtain real-time information related to the stock in the warehouse from the heads-up display, which could also support the retrieval and storage of in-time information, answer queries and enable deliveries without waiting in line (Balaji and Roy 2017; Ren et al. 2015). Thus, this approach involves more parties in one specific operational process and provides a possibility to facilitate inter-organisational VCC in the construction industry (Merlino and Sproge 2017; Kohli and Grover 2008; Ng et al. 2010). However, the literature seldom identifies the relationship between IoT implementation and its influence on inter-firm VCC. Furthermore, although Ng et al. (2010) conducted a prominent study about co-creating value for the business-to-business service, they did not consider the role of the IoT implementation in the construction industry.

3 Conceptual Framework and Hypothesis

3.1 IoT Implementation and Competency Alignment (CA)

IoT implementation contributes to better interaction between enterprises, and it essentially encourages the sharing of specialised knowledge (Chakraborty et al. 2014; Akter et al. 2016; Falcone et al. 2020). By connecting with partners' networks, IoT implementation could achieve the convergence of the following competencies: in-time information sharing, the capacity of storing data and specialised knowledge sharing (Neuhofer et al. 2015; Kumar and Shoghli 2018; Yusuf et al. 2004; Hanna 2007). More specifically, the integration of big data and cloud computing supplies the multi-dimensional information of one company to its partners, including competency skill sets, the capacity to access resources and their roles in the supply chain process (Wong et al. 1999; Stratman and Roth 2002; Liu et al. 2014; Kumar and Shoghli 2018). Consequently, IoT implementation facilitates greater accessibility to the technical information regarding partners' needs and their relative competencies (Hoffman and Novak 2015). The following hypothesis is thus proposed:

H1: The implementation of IoT technology positively influence the CA between supply chain actors.

3.2 IoT Implementation and Behavioural Alignment (BA)

Success in inter-organisational VCC highly depends on the interrelationship, which is mostly determined by the appropriate behaviours between enterprises (Ng et al. 2011). Aligning effective behaviours such as open information sharing and in-time communications is vital to deliver outcomes (Ren et al. 2015). For example, the integration of big data and RFID tags provides real-time information to all actors, ensuring the exchange of inventory information and contributing to the immediate communication between the supply chain actors (Lu et al. 2007; Ng et al. 2011). Therefore, the hypothesis postulated is as follows:

H2: The implementation of IoT technology positively influence the BA between supply chain actors.

3.3 IoT Implementation and Process Alignment (PA)

According to previous literature, IoT implementation enhances the ubiquitous connectedness between the partners, increases interactivity and contributes to closer integration into the physical situation, thereby further supporting PA (Yusuf et al. 2004; Hoffman and Novak 2015; Neuhofer et al. 2015). For instance, IoT technologies such as RFID tags can identify and support the real-time information, including the volume of inventory and picking optimisation in the delivery, which can critically affect the processes of decision-making and delivering between collaborating enterprises (Hung et al. 2007; Balaji and Roy 2017; Merlino and Sproge 2017; Kumar and Shoghli 2018). Thus, the following hypothesis is forwarded:

H3: The implementation of IoT technology positively influence the PA between supply chain actors.

3.4   IoT Implementation and Congruence of Expectations (CE)

If the collaborating enterprises have overlapping roles or capacities, it will easily cause role ambiguity (Ng et al. 2011). This confusion between the supply chain actors can lead to a mismatch of expectations (Ng et al. 2011). Thus, companies need to ensure that their expectations of the partners and their partners' understanding of these expectations match (Chakraborty et al. 2014). To facilitate the alignment of expectations, innovative firms implement IoT technologies in the process of collaboration (Ng et al. 2010). One example is the integration of big data and cloud computing technology. This integration could enable one party to analyse and predict its partners' expectations from the database (Dean 2004; Van Horn et al. 2012; Leventhal 2008). Thus, the following hypothesis is formulated:

H4: *The implementation of IoT technology positively influence the CE between supply chain actors.*

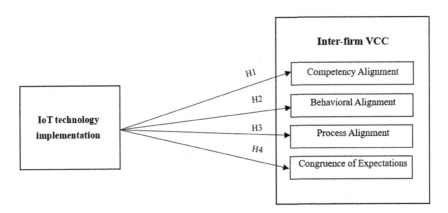

Fig. 1. Conceptual framework

Figure 1 illustrates the study's conceptual framework of the role of IoT implementation in enhancing value co-creation in terms of competency alignment (CA), behavioural alignment (BA), process alignment (PA) and congruence of expectation (CE). The methodology adopted to test the conceptual model in the Chinese construction industry will be outlined in the next section.

4   Methodology

This research mainly reflects the positivist approach that works in the tradition of the natural scientist (Saunders et al. 2009). A questionnaire was developed to gain insight into construction industry professionals' working experience in SCC and IoT implementation. It aimed to obtain participants' perceptions towards the achievement of four inter-firm VCC attributes: CA, BA, PA and CE. All items of these five variables can be found in Table 2, and they were all proposed by OECD (2018) and Ng et al. (2010).

Moreover, this questionnaire mainly utilised rating questions such as a Likert-style rating scale in which participants need to answer about how much they agree or disagree with the statement. This research used a five-point scale. The five categories of the agreement are strongly agree (5), agree (4), neither agree nor disagree (3), disagree (2) and strongly disagree (1) (Saunders et al. 2009). The study employed a cross-sectional approach and data collection was conducted in July and August 2020.

Table 2. The variables and measurement items

Variable	Items			
IoT implementation	Sensitivity to latency	Mobility of objects	Communication among devices	Data storage and network performance
Competency alignment	Skills	Roles	Resources	Technology
Behavioural alignment	Notification	Discuss plans	Discuss new ideas	Cooperate to apply ideas
	Share resources			
Process alignment	Gather information	Give information	Store information	Move information
	Collect material	Store material	Move material	Prepare material
	Install material			
Expectation alignment	What are partners doing	How they are doing it	What they will do	How they will do it
	What they should do	How they should do it		

This research required the participation of professionals who have experience in IoT implementation. Thus, this study distributed the online questionnaire to experienced SCC staff selected mainly from the two Chinese companies: Huangshan City Construction Group and Yantai Construction Group. The two companies were selected as sites for our investigation as they successfully implemented IoT in their supply chain processes. To contact potential experienced respondents, this study employed the snowball sampling method. The staff who answered this questionnaire also shared it with other experienced staff. The demographic information of the respondents can be found in Table 3. As the table indicates, nearly one-third of respondents are involved in the SCM process' sourcing and procurement department, while 32.05% work in the department of warehousing and transportation. Moreover, the portion of people who worked in SCM for under ten years is over 80%. This research employed three analysis techniques: reliability analysis, correlation analysis and regression analysis. The method used for assessing internal consistency was Cronbach's alpha. Next, correlation analysis was used to identify the relationships and relative intensity of IoT and CA, BA, PA and CE. Importantly, the Pearson correlation coefficient was selected as the indicator to analyse the intensity of these relations in this study (Zhang et al. 2017). Finally, simple linear regression analysis was utilised to predict the relationships between IoT and CA, BA, PA and CE.

Table 3. Demographic information of the sample

		Percentage (N = 78)
Department involved	Sourcing and procurement	33.33%
	Demand planning, order fulfilment and inventory	26.92%
	Warehousing and transportation	32.05%
	Logistics and information management	7.69%
Years of work	Under 5	44.87%
	6–10	35.9%
	11–15	7.69%
	16–20	5.13%
	Over 20	6.41%
Age	Under 20	2.56%
	21–30	12.82%
	31–40	30.77%
	41–50	39.74%
	Over 50	4.1%

5   Findings

5.1   Reliability Analysis and Results

This research implemented Cronbach's alpha to test the internal consistency of different variables. The results are presented in Tables 4, 5, 6, 7 and 8. IoT implementation contained four items and $\alpha = .947$, which was reliable. The CA subscale consisted of 4 items and $\alpha = .919$, which was reasonably reliable. BA was composed of five items ($\alpha = .942$), while the PA subscale consisted of nine items and $\alpha = .978$, which was highly reliable. Lastly, the CE subscale contained six items and $\alpha = .952$, indicating that the instrument was reliable.

Table 4. Reliability analysis of IoT implementation

IoT implementation	
A	N
.947	4

Table 5. Reliability analysis of competency alignment

Competency alignment	
A	N
.919	4

Table 6. Reliability analysis of behavioural alignment

Behavioural alignment	
A	N
.942	5

Table 7. Reliability analysis of process alignment

Process alignment	
A	N
.978	9

Table 8. Reliability analysis of expectation alignment

Expectation alignment	
A	N
.952	6

5.2   Correlation Analysis, Regression Analysis and Discussion

According to (Franzese and Iuliano 2019), correlation analysis is considered a means to measure the strength of the relations between two or more variables. One common and effective indicator is the Pearson correlation coefficient. Regarding regression analysis, linear regression is the most commonly used statistical technique to identify and predict relationships between different variables (Bacon 2013). This study identified four relationships: those between IoT implementation and CA, BA, PA and CE, respectively.

5.2.1   IoT Implementation and Competency Alignment

The results of the correlation analysis (Table 9) indicated there was a strongly positive relation between IoT implementation and CA ($r = .930, n = 78, p = .000 < .001$). The simple linear regression analysis (Table 10) demonstrated that the predictor (IoT implementation) showed 86.4% of the variance ($R^2 = .864, F = 483.218, p = .000 < .001$). These findings illustrated that IoT implementation and CA were strongly correlated. The high level of the implementation of IoT could enhance the achievement of CA between two or more enterprises. Furthermore, IoT was the vital predictor of CA in the

Chinese construction industry. Essentially, the results of the regression analysis indicated that the IoT implementation was responsible for 86.4% of the influence on CA.

These findings proved H1. Moreover, these results also supported previous studies about the relationship between IoT technology and the alignment of competency conducted by Chakraborty et al. (2014) and Hoffman and Novak (2015). Previous research proposed that IoT technologies could support the interaction between two or more supply chain actors and encourage specialised knowledge sharing (Chakraborty et al. 2014). Hoffman and Novak (2015) found that better performance in IoT implementation could lead to greater accessibility to technical information about partners' requirements and competencies.

Table 9. Correlation between IoT and competency alignment

Competency alignment			
	R	N	P
IoT implementation	.930	78	.000

Correlation is significant at the 0.01 level (2-tailed)

Table 10. Simple linear regression of IoT and competency alignment

			Coefficient		ANOVA
			Model		summary
B	P	F	P	R^2	
IoT	.930	.000	483.218	.000	.864

Dependent variable: Competency alignment

5.2.2 IoT Implementation and Behavioural Alignment

The results of the correlation analysis of IoT implementation and BA can be found in Table 11. It indicated that there is a strong relationship between these two variables, with $r = .955$, $n = 78$ and $p = .000 < .001$. From the outputs of the simple linear regression analysis in Table 12, the predictor (IoT implementation) showed 91.2% of the variance ($R^2 = .912$, $F = 784.909$, $p = .000 < .001$). These findings revealed that IoT implementation and BA were highly correlated and that IoT was an antecedent factor of BA. Moreover, the implementation of IoT could positively influence the process of BA between enterprises. Thus, these results demonstrated the validity of H2.

Considered theoretically, these findings were also consistent with the previous research indicating that the alignment of behaviours was associated with IoT implementations (Chakraborty et al. 2014). Moreover, concurring with the work of Ng et al. (2011), the supply chain actors were engaged in applying the right behaviours and integrating processes to further promote a smoother exchange of information. In this regard, this study's findings supported the above work, revealing that the implementation of IoT technologies and their smart devices could contribute to aligning the behaviours between two or more collaborating supply chain actors.

Table 11. Correlation between IoT and behavioural alignment

Behavioural alignment			
	R	N	P
IoT implementation	.955	78	.000

Correlation is significant at the 0.01 level (2-tailed)

Table 12. Simple linear regression of IoT and behavioural alignment

			Coefficient		ANOVA
			Model		summary
B	P	F	P	R^2	
IoT	.955	.000	784.909	.000	.912

Dependent variable: Behavioural alignment

5.2.3   IoT Implementation and Process Alignment

The results of the correlation analysis (Table 13) illustrated that IoT implementation and PA were positively connected, with $r = .87$, $n = 78$ and $p = .000 < .001$. The outcomes of the simple linear regression analysis of these two variables (Table 14) indicated that IoT implementation and PA were highly correlated and that IoT was the predictor and explained 75.7% variance of PA ($R^2 = .757$, $F = 236.881$, $p = .000 < .001$). These results demonstrated that the performance of IoT implementation could predict the achievement of PA. Specifically, the high level of IoT implementation in the SCC process contributed to the high level of PA. In other words, when corporations implement IoT technologies, they obtain more possibility to enhance ubiquitous connectedness with partners, increase interactivity and integrate more closely into the physical situation, thereby promoting the alignment of processes (Hoffman and Novak 2015; Neuhofer et al. 2015). Thus, these findings supported H3.

These outcomes also contributed to the existing research proposed by Hung et al. (2007) and Yan and Huang (2009). In previous studies, utilising IoT technologies such as RFID tags supported the collection, storage and exchange of extensive data and the exchange of real-time information (Hung et al. 2007; Balaji and Roy 2017; Merlino and Sproge 2017; Kumar and Shoghli 2018).

Table 13. Correlation between IoT and process alignment

Process alignment			
	R	N	P
IoT implementation	.87	78	.000

Correlation is significant at the 0.01 level (2-tailed)

Table 14. Simple linear regression of IoT and process alignment

			Coefficient		ANOVA
			Model		summary
β	P	F	P	R^2	
IoT	.870	.000	236.881	.000	.757

Dependent variable: Process alignment

5.2.4   IoT Implementation and Congruence of Expectation

The outcomes of the correlation analysis (Table 15) revealed there was a strong correlation between IoT implementation and CE ($r = .868$, $n = 78$, $p = .000 < .001$), while the results of the simple linear regression analysis (Table 16) indicated that these two factors were positively connected ($R^2 = .754$, $F = 232.386$, $p = .000 < .001$). These findings showed that the implementation of IoT was the predictor of the performance of CE and explained 75.4% of the variance in the Chinese construction context. The high level of IoT implementation promoted the high level of CE. Based on these results, H4 was supported.

These findings also confirmed the literature regarding the relationship between these two variables. Some innovative enterprises have implemented IoT technologies such as cloud computing and big data to clarify each other's respective expectations and requirements (Zeithmal et al. 1993; Dean 2004; Parasuraman et al. 1994). Specifically, IoT implementation supports one party in collecting and analysing their partners' expectations from the previous database; moreover, the level of IoT implementation positively influenced their capability to obtain data and information (Van Horn et al. 2012; Dean 2004; Leventhal 2008; Parasuraman et al. 1994; Zeithmal et al. 1993).

Table 15. Correlation between IoT and congruence of expectation

Congruence of expectation			
	R	n	P
IoT implementation	.868	78	.000

Correlation is significant at the 0.01 level (2-tailed)

Table 16. Simple linear regression of IoT and congruence of expectation

			Coefficient		ANOVA
			Model		summary
β	P	F	P	R^2	
IoT	.868	.000	232.386	.000	.754

Dependent variable: Congruence of expectation

6 Conclusion, Implications and Directions for Future Research

This study connects IoT implementation with the alignment of competency, behaviour, process and expectation. It aims to measure the impacts of IoT implementation on the achievement of inter-organisational VCC in the Chinese construction context. Accordingly, this study investigates and establishes the conceptual relationships between these five factors. The data analysis results reveal that IoT implementation positively correlates with competency, behavioural, process and expectation alignment in the process of SCC. Moreover, a high level of IoT implementation could boost the four alignments between two or more companies. These findings facilitate a more multi-dimensional understanding of IoT technologies' impacts on the SCC process and business-to-business VCC. Theoretically, this research also enriches the inter-organisational VCC literature. The previous studies about inter-firm VCC were mainly conducted by Ng et al. (2011) and Ren et al. (2015), while there is little literature that examines the influence of IoT implementation on inter-firm VCC in detail. Moreover, there is no research about co-creating value in SCC in the Chinese construction context. Thus, this study sheds light on the essential role of IoT implementation in the study of inter-firm VCC. It also provides an innovative perspective for corporations seeking to co-create value in practice.

The study has four managerial implications. The first is IoT implementation's role in enhancing CA. Some studies have proved that the integration of big data and cloud computing could provide multi-dimensional information to the partners. This research not only further corroborated previous findings about the strongly positive correlation between IoT implementation and CA but also supplied a numerical understanding of the strength of this relationship. Therefore, when supply chain actors utilise particular IoT technologies, they could gain greater access to their partners' specialised knowledge. Second, this research highlights the importance of relationships between the supply chain actors. Previous literature proposed that appropriate behaviour is the principal factor affecting the quality of the relationship. The findings of this study prove the significance of IoT technologies for the achievement of BA. Thus, companies could establish good relationships and achieve BA through implementing IoT technologies. The final two managerial implications concern the vital roles of IoT technologies in enhancing the alignments of process and expectation. The findings illustrate that IoT implementation could promote the ubiquitous connectedness between supply chain partners, increase interactivity and contribute to a smoother exchange of information and data, thus supporting the alignment of process. Moreover, the results suggest that the integration of big data and cloud computing technology supports one party in analysing and predicting its partners' expectations from the database. Hence, the study's findings prove the strong correlations between IoT implementation and PA and CE. Thus, based on these results, enterprises could promote IoT implementations such as RFID tags, WSN and cloud computing to create a smoother channel of information sharing.

This study is subject to two main limitations. First, this work only investigates the alignments of competency, behaviour, process and expectation in the construction industry, while other key attributes (perceived control, empowerment and behavioural transformation) of VCC are not taken into consideration (Ng et al. 2011). Thus, future research could study the impacts of IoT technologies on the performance of perceived control, empowerment and behavioural transformation in the Chinese supply chain context. In addition, the measurements used above for IoT implementation are possibly not sufficient. When evaluating IoT implementation, this research investigated its sensitivity to latency, mobility of objects, smooth communication among smart devices, and data storage and network performance. It did not develop multi-dimensions to explore the measurement of IoT implementation. This limitation may lead to bias and inaccurate results concerning the influence of IoT implementation. Future research could therefore explore more factors that affect IoT implementation.

References

Akter, S., Fosso Wamba, S., Gunasekaran, A., Dubey, R., Childe, S.: How to improve firm performance using big data analytics capability and business strategy alignment? Int. J. Prod. Econ. **182**, 113–131 (2016)

Ashton, K.: Auto-ID Center—The Big Picture. Presentation Delivered at the Sun/Mass e-Commerce Adoption Forum, 17 January 2003 (2003)

Bacon, C.R.: Practical Risk-Adjusted Performance Measurement. Wiley, Oxford (2013)

Balaji, M.S., Roy, S.K.: Value co-creation with Internet of things technology in the retail industry. J. Mark. Manag. **33**(2), 7–31 (2017)

Ben-Daya, M., Hassini, E., Bahroun, Z.: Internet of things and supply chain management: a literature review. Int. J. Prod. Res. **57**(15), 4719–4742 (2019)

Chakraborty, S., Bhattacharya, S., Dobrzykowski, D.D.: Impact of supply chain collaboration on value co-creation and firm performance: a healthcare service sector perspective. Proc. Econ. Finance **11**(2014), 676–694 (2014)

Dean, A.M.: Rethinking customer expectations of service quality: are call centres different? J. Serv. Mark. **18**(1), 60–78 (2004)

Ding, W.: Study of smart warehouse management system based on the IOT. In: Du, Z. (ed.) Intelligence Computation and Evolutionary Computation. AISC, vol. 180, pp. 203–207. Springer, Heidelberg (2013). https://doi.org/10.1007/978-3-642-31656-2_30

Ellis, S., Morris, H.D., Santagate, J.: IoT-enabled analytic applications revolutionize supply chain planning and execution. International Data Corporation (IDC) White Paper (2015). www.idc.com

Falcone, E., Kent, J., Fugate, B.: Supply chain technologies, interorganizational network and firm performance a case study of Alibaba Group and Cainiao. Int. J. Phys. Distrib. Logist. Manag. **50**(3), 333–354 (2020)

Fawcett, S.E., Magnan, G.M., McCarter, M.W.: Benefits, barriers, and bridges to effective supply chain management. Supply Chain Manag.: Int. J. **13**(1), 35–48 (2008)

Flynn, B.B., Huo, B., Zhao, X.: The impact of supply chain integration on performance: a contingency and configuration approach. J. Oper. Manag. **28**(1), 58–71 (2010)

Forsström, B.: Value Co-creation in Industrial Buyer-Seller Partnerships-Creating and Exploiting Interdependencies: An Empirical Case Study. Akadimi University Press, Turku (2005)

Franzese, M., Iuliano, A.: Correlation analysis. In: Encyclopedia of Bioinformatics and Computational Biology, pp. 706–721 (2019)

Gao, L., Bai, X.: A unified perspective on the factors influencing consumer acceptance of internet of things technology. Asia Pac. J. Mark. Logist. **26**(2), 211–231 (2014)

Gnimpieba, Z.D.R., Nait-Sidi-Moh, A., Durand, D., Fortin, J.: Using Internet of Things technologies for a collaborative supply chain: application to tracking of pallets and containers. Proc. Comput. Sci. **56**, 550–557 (2015)

Greengard, S.: The Internet of Things. MIT Press, Cambridge (2015)

Handfield, R., Linton, T.: GOOD! The ability to build balanced supply chains. In: The LIVING Supply Chain: The Evolving Imperative of Operating in Real Time, pp. 153–173 (2017)

Hanna, V.: Exploiting complementary competencies via inter-firm cooperation. Int. J. Technol. Manag. **37**(3/4), 247–258 (2007)

Hoffman, D.L., Novak, T.P.: Emergent experience and the connected consumer in the smart home assemblage and the Internet of things. The Center for the Connected Consumer: The George Washington University School of Business (2015)

Hung, R.Y., Chung, T., Lien, B.Y.: Organizational process alignment and dynamic capabilities in high-tech industry. Total Qual. Manag. **18**(9), 1023–1034 (2007)

Kim, W.: Cloud computing: "status and prognosis". J. Object Technol. **8**(1), 65–72 (2009)

Kohli, R., Grover, V.: Business value of IT: an essay on expanding research directions to keep up with the times. J. Assoc. Inf. Syst. **9**(1), 23–39 (2008)

Krishnapriya, V., Baral, R.: Supply chain integration - a competency based perspective. Int. J. Manag. Value Supply Chains (IJMVSC) **5**(3), 45–60 (2014)

Kumar, A., Shoghli, O.: A review of IoT applications in supply chain optimization of construction materials. In: International Symposium on Automation and Robotics in Construction, 35th International Symposium on Automation and Robotics in Construction, ISARC 2018, Berlin, Germany (2018)

Kumar, K., van Dissel, H.G.: Sustainable collaboration: managing conflict and cooperation in interorganizational systems. MIS Q. **20**(3), 279–300 (1996)

Lambert, D.M., Cooper, M.C.: Issues in supply chain management. Ind. Mark. Manag. **29**(1), 65–83 (2000)

Lambert, D.M., Emmelhainz, M.A., Gardner, J.T.: Building successful logistics partnerships. J. Bus. Logist. **20**(1), 118–165 (1999)

Leventhal, L.: The role of understanding customer expectations in aged care. Int. J. Health Care Qual. Assur. **21**(1), 50–59 (2008)

Li, S., Rao, S.S., Ragu-Nathan, T.S., Ragu-Nathan, B.: Development and validation of a measurement instrument for studying supply chain management practice. J. Oper. Manag. **23**(6), 618–641 (2005)

Liu, A.M., Fellows, R., Chan, I.Y.S.: Fostering value co-creation in construction: a case study of an airport project in India. Int. J. Archit. Eng. Constr. **3**(2), 120–130 (2014)

Manavalan, E., Jayakrishna, K.: A review of Internet of Things (IoT) embedded sustainable supply chain for industry 4.0 requirements. Comput. Ind. Eng. **127**, 925–953 (2019)

Matin, M.A., Islam, M.M.: Overview of Wireless Sensor Network (2012). https://www.intechopen.com/books/wireless-sensor-networks-technology-and-protocols/overview-of-wireless-sensor-network. Accessed 21 June 2020

Merlino, M., Sproge, I.: The augmented supply chain. Proc. Eng. **178**, 308–318 (2017)

Miorandi, D., Sicari, S., De Pellegrini, F., Chlamtac, I.: Internet of things: vision, applications and research challenges. Ad Hoc Netw. **10**(7), 1497–1516 (2012)

Neuhofer, B., Buhalis, D., Ladkin, A.: Smart technologies for personalized experiences: a case study in the hospitality domain. Electron. Mark. **25**(3), 243–254 (2015). https://doi.org/10.1007/s12525-015-0182-1

Ng, I., Nudurupati, S., Williams, J.: Redefining organisational capability for value co-creation in complex engineering service systems. In: Ng, I., Parry, G., Wild, P., McFarlane, D., Tasker, P. (eds.) Complex Engineering Service Systems. DECENGIN, pp. 109–128. Springer, London (2011). https://doi.org/10.1007/978-0-85729-189-9_6

Ng, I.C., Nudurupati, S.S., Tasker, P.: Value co-creation in the delivery of outcome-based contracts for business-to-business service. Aim Research Working Paper Series (2010). https://core.ac.uk/download/pdf/12824525.pdf. Accessed 14 April, June 2020

OECD: IoT measurement and applications (2018). https://iotbusinessnews.com/download/white-papers/OECD-IoT-Measurement-Applications.pdf. Accessed 14 Aug 2020

Pantano, E., Timmermans, H.: What is smart for retailing? Proc. Environ. Sci. **22**, 101–107 (2014)

Parasuraman, A., Zeithmal, V.A., Leonard, L.B.: Reassessment of expectations as a comparison standard in measuring service quality: implications for future research. J. Mark. **58**(January), 111–124 (1994)

Park, S.H., Ungson, G.R.: Inter-firm rivalry and managerial complexity: a conceptual framework of alliance failure. Organ. Sci. **12**(1), 37–53 (2001)

Parkhi, S., Joshi, S., Gupta, S., Sharma, M.: A study of evolution and future of supply chain management. Supply Chain Manag. **9**(2), 95–106 (2015)

Ramaswamy, V.: Competing through co-creation: innovation at two companies. Strat. Leadersh. **38**(2), 22–29 (2010)

Ren, S.J., Hu, C., Ngai, E.W.T., Zhou, M.: An empirical analysis of inter-organisational value co-creation in a supply chain: a process perspective. Prod. Plan. Control **26**(12), 969–980 (2015)

Saunders, M., Lewis, P., Thornhill, A.: Understanding research philosophies and approaches. Res. Methods Bus. Stud. **4**, 106–135 (2009)

Schlick, J., Ferber, S., Hupp, J.: IoT Applications – Value Creation for Industry. River Publisher, Aalborg (2013)

Stenroos, L., Jaakkola, E.: Value co-creation in knowledge intensive business services: a dyadic perspective on the joint problem-solving process. Ind. Mark. Manag. **41**(1), 15–26 (2012)

Stratman, J.K., Roth, A.V.: Enterprise resource planning (ERP) competence constructs: two-stage multi-item scale development and validation. Decis. Sci. **33**(4), 601–628 (2002)

Uckelmann, D., Harrison, M., Michahelles, F.: An architectural approach towards the future internet of things. In: Uckelmann, D., Harrison, M., Michahelles, F. (eds.) Architecting the Internet of Things, pp. 1–24. Springer, Berlin (2011). https://doi.org/10.1007/978-3-642-19157-2_1

Van Horn, D., Olewnik, A., Lewis, K.: Design analytics: capturing, understanding, and meeting customer needs using big data. In: ASME International Design Engineering Technical Conferences and Computers and Information in Engineering Conference (IDETC/CIE2011), Paper No. DETC2012-1038 (2012)

Vargo, S.L., Lusch, R.F.: Evolving to a new dominant logic for marketing. J. Mark. **68**(1), 1–17 (2004)

Wang, L., Alexander, C.A.: Big data analytics and cloud computing in internet of things. Am. J. Inf. Sci. Comput. Eng. **2**(6), 70–78 (2016)

Wong, A., Tjosvold, D.W., Wong, Y.L., Liu, C.K.: Relationships for quality improvement in the Hong Kong-China supply chain. Int. J. Qual. Reliab. Manag. **16**(1), 24–41 (1999)

Wünderlich, N.V., Wangenheim, F.V., Bitner, M.J.: High tech and high touch: a framework for understanding user attitudes and behaviours related to smart interactive services. J. Serv. Res. **16**(1), 3–20 (2013)

Xu, L.D., He, W., Li, S.: Internet of things in industries: a survey. IEEE Trans. Ind. Inf. **10**(4), 2233–2243 (2014)

Yan, B., Huang, G.: Supply chain information transmission based on RFID and internet of things. In: Computing, Communication, Control, and Management. ISECS International Colloquium, vol. 4, pp. 166–169 (2009)

Yusuf, Y.Y., Gunasekaran, A., Adeleye, E.O., Sivayoganathan, K.: Agile supply chain capabilities: determinants of competitive objectives. Eur. J. Oper. Res. **159**(2), 379–392 (2004)

Zhang, M., Zhong, Z., Luo, J., Zhu, M.: Online travel agent service and customer satisfaction based on correlation analysis: a marketing perspective in China. J. Mark. Consum. Res. **11**(1), 234–248 (2017)

Zeithmal, V.A., Berry, L.L., Parasuraman, A.: The nature and determinants of customer expectations of service. J. Acad. Mark. Sci. **21**(1), 1–12 (1993)

Zorzi, M., Gluhak, A., Lange, S., Bassi, A.: From today's intranet of things to a future internet of things: a wireless and mobility-related view. IEEE Wirel. Commun. **17**(6), 44–51 (2010)

Enhancing Decision-Making in New Product Development: Forecasting Technologies Revenues Using a Multidimensional Neural Network

Marie Saade[1]($\boxtimes$) (iD), Maroun Jneid[2], and Imad Saleh[1]

[1] Laboratoire Paragraphe (EA 349), Université Paris 8 Vincennes-Saint-Denis, Saint-Denis, France
marie.karam@etud.univ-paris8.fr,
imad.saleh@univ-paris8.fr
[2] TICKET Lab., Antonine University, Hadat-Baabda, Lebanon
maroun.jneid@ua.edu.lb

Abstract. Aiming to retain their position in the marketplace, organizations are constantly enhancing research and development-based digital innovation activities in order to constantly develop new products and deploy new technologies. However, innovative trends and products are prone to failure, leading to undesired repercussions. In addition, when evaluating a product life-cycle, many decision-makers confront unprecedented challenges related to the estimation of potential disruptive innovation. To address this gap and to tackle the opportunities of digitalization, we conduct quantitative study to investigate the usage of research and development activities that can represent a main economic driver for new product/service development. A new approach for predicting innovative technology-based product success is proposed using Neural Networks models and based on the analysis of patents, publications and technologies revenues which are considered major key performance indicators in measuring technology-based product power. The proposed methodology consists of two main steps: forecasting patents and publications growths separately for a specific candidate technology using a common predictive Neural Network regression model, then integrating the results into a Multi-dimensional Neural Network classifier model in order to predict future revenue growth for this candidate technology. The present methodology is applied using two different types of Neural Networks for comparison purpose: "Wide and Deep Neural Networks" and "Recurrent Neural Networks". Consequently, addressing this estimation represents a decision support and a crucial prerequisite step before proceeding with investments, where organizations can improve decision making in innovative technology-based product/service development. The findings show that the Recurrent Neural Networks models achieve higher prediction accuracy, and outperform the Wide and Deep Neural Networks, proving to be a more reliable model that can enhance digital innovation development.

Keywords: Innovative product development · Forecasting product revenues · Neural networks · Decision support

© Springer Nature Switzerland AG 2020
M. Themistocleous et al. (Eds.): EMCIS 2020, LNBIP 402, pp. 715–729, 2020.
https://doi.org/10.1007/978-3-030-63396-7_48

1 Introduction

Nowadays, with the intention to increase financial revenues and to determine competitiveness in the market, organizations are constantly enhancing research and development-based digital innovation activities which represent a main driver for new product/service development [1]. For instance, Jneid and Saleh stated in their study that innovation represents the main component that contributes to the success of new start-ups encountering a competitive environment [2]. However, despite the fact that organizations are constantly developing new products while increasing R&D investments and deploying new technologies, innovative trends are prone to failure, leading to undesired repercussions [3]. Furthermore, when evaluating a product life-cycle, the decision-makers of the organization first need to consider and estimate the potential disruptive innovation, in order to assess when a product is threatened to enter the decline phase [4]. For example, Apple with its innovative iPhone series and Samsung with its Android operating system forced Nokia phones to enter the decline phase of their life-cycle in 2007 [5].

Nevertheless, while innovation disruptiveness can threaten the existing product market performance, the adoption of this disruptive technology may improve and lead to a new product development [6].

The main problematic of the current study is to explore how disruptive innovation can be estimated quantitatively in an early stage, and therefore to examine how digital innovation development can be enhanced by forecasting new technology-based product success by applying a convenient predictive technique that can support the decision-making in the organizations.

Several previous studies proposed different methodologies to identify a potential disruptive innovation in order to improve efficiency during new product development process. Nagy, Schuessler and Dubinsky [7] suggested a qualitative study that can determine if a new candidate technology would be a potential disruptive innovation. This method highlights the importance of comparing the technical standards, the functionality and the ownership of this new candidate innovation with the existing technology currently used in the organization. In addition, Momeni and Rost [8] proposed a systematic tool that can analyze quantitatively the relationship between technological disruptiveness and highly cited patents. It is based on patent-development path, topic-modeling used for patent-citation analysis and k-core analysis to classify different subgroups of each technology. A quantitative study of a visualization bibliometric analysis has been elaborated as well to explore potential disruptive innovation [9].

However, each of those methodologies has limitations. For instance, the aforementioned qualitative procedure often rely on subjective judgments of decision-making experts, which may influence results [9]. The patent-development path solution and the bibliometrics-based analysis cover only single indicators, patents and bibliometrics dimensions respectively.

Consequently, to address this gap, the technologies-based products development process can be monitored by analyzing historical data of the related R&D activities and products revenues. Specifically, patents, publications and revenues are considered major key performance indicators and effective dimensions in measuring technology-based product power. In this regard, we propose a new methodology based on two main steps:

forecasting patents and publications growths separately for a specific candidate technology using a common predictive Neural Network regression, then integrating the results into a Multi-dimensional Neural Network classifier in order to predict the future revenue-volume for this candidate technology. The present methodology is applied using two different types of Neural Network models for comparison purpose: "Wide and Deep Neural Networks" and "Recurrent Neural Networks".

Consequently, addressing this estimation represents a decision support in technology-based product/service development and a prerequisite step before proceeding with investments.

The present study represents a proof of concept where it focuses on forecasting the patents, publications and revenues dimensions growth for a single candidate technology, noting that when this approach is to be applied on a real case study on organizational level, it can involve both a new technology representing a potential disruptive innovation, and an existing technology currently used in the organization, for comparison purposes.

In addition, given the fact that a single product may embed several combined technologies (such as a drone that can be composed of 3D mapping technology, Infrared cameras, etc.), and since patents and publications data are technology-bound whereas revenues data are product-bound, the current study focuses on a specific type of product which is based on one major trending technology.

The remainder of this paper is structured as following: Sect. 2 presents the related work on the patent, publication and revenues-based forecasting methods. Section 3 presents the research design and the proposed methodology. The experimental setting of the present study and the results are described in Sect. 4. Section 5 concludes the work and points to the study limitations and to future research directions.

2   Literature Review

R&D-based digital innovation activities represent a main driver for new product/service development. Patents data play a significant role in forecasting the success of trending technologies as justified in the paper "Predicting Technology Success based on Patent Data, using a Wide and Deep Neural Network and a Recurrent Neural Network" [10]. Publications data can be used as well to measure technological and scientific capabilities [11]. Furthermore, patents and publications data are considered among the most important dimensions that have potential benefits and reflection into the knowledge-based economy [12, 13].

Patent and Publication-Based Technology Forecasting Methods: Growth curves, scenario planning and analogies technology forecasting tools have been used based on patent and bibliometrics analysis, while focusing on food safety, fuel cell and optical storage technologies [14]. Moreover, patent analysis, bibliometric analysis and the technology roadmapping method have been combined to visualize and predict the future development of the Nanogenerator technology in China [15].

Revenue Forecasting Studies: Different revenue forecasting techniques are used to evaluate the product level and thus to support planning and decision making. An efficient solution based on three different machine learning models for regression and time series forecasting has been provided to predict revenues and applied on Microsoft's Finance organization real finance data [16]. The travel toll revenue forecasting has been applied and illustrated in a probability distribution, using a Neural Network model [17]. Moreover, an analysis on historical data has been conducted as well using a Neural Network model, in order to predict rental income for enterprises having several malls [18].

However, although several previous studies propose to identify future technology development, none of them rely on combining patents, publications and technologies revenues as key performance indicators. Accordingly, and based on our research, the current study has not been applied so far when evaluating and monitoring technology-based product development in this specific context.

3 Research Design

The analysis of patents, publications and revenues data is considered as a quantitative approach to assess their impact on the technology-based product success. Precisely, this study visualizes the historical growth of patents, publications and revenues dimensions, as well as their predictive future variation for a given candidate technology, using two separate types of Neural Networks for comparison purposes: a Wide and Deep Neural Network model and a Recurrent Neural Network model. These neural networks are to be implemented as following: The one-dimensional WDNN (ODWDNN) and RNN (ODRNN) models are employed to separately predict the patents and publications growth. Therefore, their predicted results, as well as the historical data of these two dimensions, will then be used as inputs in either a Multidimensional Wide and Deep Neural Network (MDWDNN) classifier for WDNN, or a Multidimensional Recurrent Neural Network (MDRNN) classifier for RNN. These multidimensional neural networks are designed to forecast future revenues ranges for specific trending technologies, and therefore evaluating and measuring technology-based product power.

Why Use a Neural Network Model: Based on different studies, Artificial Neural Network models can outperform traditional models, such as Linear Regression [19] and Autoregressive Integrated Moving Average [20] in the context of time series forecasting and obtaining higher accuracy. In addition, since this study model will eventually be targeting organizations in a future work, a predictive neural network can be trained and tested through historical Big Data for an unsupervised [21] and dynamic learning [22].

Why Use a Wide and Deep Neural Network Model: A wide and deep model can handle complex large-scale data, integrating heterogeneous input data [23]. Furthermore, Deep Learning algorithms can generalize the relationships in the data and the extracted representation, by extracting rare or new combinations by transitivity of correlations. However, deep neural network may over-generalize and extract less relevant features [24]. Accordingly, the exception rules and the memorization of features correlations or interactions in the historical data, is a crucial need to improve the neural network forecasting. Hence the power of combining a deep model for learning interactions within historical data and then generalizing the output on new data with a wide model for memorizing specific rules and learning exceptions [24].

Why Use a Recurrent Neural Network Model: A recurrent neural network can process sequences of inputs, which represent the time series of patents and publications in our case, with different lengths, to return a sequence of outputs [25]. In addition, LSTM (Long Short-Term Memory) can be used in the RNN to reduce the vanishing gradient problem that occurs in the basic recurrent neural networks [26].

3.1 Proposed Methodology

The current methodology relies on three dimensions: patents, publications and revenues. It first predicts the growth of the number of patents and the number of publications respectively, which will be used in the final prediction phase of revenues ranges. It covers different principle objectives explained in Table 1. Noting that these objectives and tasks are applied for both neural network types.

Table 1. Methodology design objectives.

Objective: Data Collection	
1	Listing new and old trending technologies based on different sources
2	Searching for related keywords for each technology
Objective: Database integration	
3	Inserting the collected data into a new integrated database
Objective: Data Collection	
4	Extracting patents, publications and revenues data for each technology from several sources based on keywords matching
Objective: Database integration	
5	Manipulating and inserting the collected data into the integrated database
Objective: Data manipulation	
6	Computing the total number of patents/publications per technology per year
Objective: Datasets creation	
7	Grouping patents/publications data by technology for *max* years. *max* represents the maximum number of years per technology where historical data is available in the training dataset
Objective: Neural Network 1 (NN1) implementation	
8	Training the first Neural Network (ODWDNN and ODRNN) with patents data
9	Testing the Neural Network (ODWDNN and ODRNN) with patents data
10	Predicting the number of patents for the candidate technology for the next p years
Objective: Database integration	
11	Inserting the output data of Neural Network 1 (ODWDNN and ODRNN) into the integrated database

(*continued*)

Table 1. (*continued*)

	Objective: Neural Network 1 (NN1) implementation
12	Training the first Neural Network (ODWDNN and ODRNN) with publications data
13	Testing the Neural Network (ODWDNN and ODRNN) with publications data
14	Predicting the number of publications for the candidate technology for the next p years
	Objective: Database integration
15	Inserting the output data of Neural Network 1 (ODWDNN and ODRNN) into the integrated database
	Objective: Dataset creation
16	Grouping patents, publications and revenues data by technology and by year
	Objective: Neural Network 2 (NN2) implementation
17	Training the second Neural Network (MDWDNN and MDRNN) based on the three dimensions
18	Testing the Neural Network (MDWDNN and MDRNN) with patents, publications and revenues data
19	Predicting the revenues classes for the candidate technology for future p years
	Objective: Database integration
20	Inserting the output data of Neural Network 2 (MDWDNN and MDRNN) into the integrated database
	Objective: Results visualization and Decision-making
21	Illustrating the revenues variation in statistical graphs
22	Evaluating the candidate technology based on business perspective

3.2   Neural Network Structures

The present Neural Networks are implemented using the TensorFlow[1] software library under Python. As previously mentioned, two Neural Network types are structured as following:

Neural Network 1. The first neural network is implemented using two different models for comparison purposes, in order to separately estimate the number of patents and the number of publications.

One-Dimensional WDNN (ODWDNN). This Neural Network is structured as a "DNN Linear Combined Regressor" where the predicted output represents a continuous variable. It is designed with the same architecture and configuration as the WDNN of the Saade, Jneid & Saleh paper [10]: ODWDNN contains h hidden layers, and each layer contains a specific number no of nodes. It is built based on the Adam optimization method which is designed for training deep neural networks and can outperform other stochastic optimization methods [27]. In addition, the number of patents/publications will be predicted for the technology in question for each future year separately, where each predicted output is serving as input for the next prediction until the number of future years p is reached.

---

[1] Tensorflow is an open-source API created by Google and is used for Machine Learning purposes.

One-Dimensional RNN (ODRNN). This Neural Network model is structured with the same architecture and configuration as the RNN in the study of Saade, Jneid & Saleh [10]: ODRNN contains h recurrent hidden layers, with a specific number *no* of nodes. It is built based on the following features:

- **Long Short-Term Memory (LSTM) cells:** they are activation cells that can outperform traditional recurrent layers.
- **Sequence-to-Sequence (seq2seq) neuronal architecture:** where the RNN encodes a variable-length sequence of inputs into a fixed-length vector representation and then decoding a fixed-length vector representation into a sequence of outputs [28]. Noting that the input sequences lengths vary according to the data availability of each technology.
- **Many-to-many structure:** where both the input and the output represent sequences of data with same or different lengths.
- **Adam optimizer:** can outperform other stochastic optimization methods [27].

In addition, the output layer represents a sequence of number of patents/publications forecasted in a single step from $Year_1$ till $Year_p$.

Neural Network 2. The second Neural Network is implemented using two different models for comparison purposes. They are designed as multidimensional neural networks and classification predictive models. Patents and publications data represent the inputs dimensions and the ranges of revenues represent the output classes. This classifier would return a probability distribution for each of the defined classes.

Multi-Dimensional WDNN (MDWDNN). MDWDNN is structured as a *"DNN Linear Combined Classifier"*. Adam is applied as well in the MDWDNN as an optimization method. This Neural Network consists of the following layers (Fig. 1):

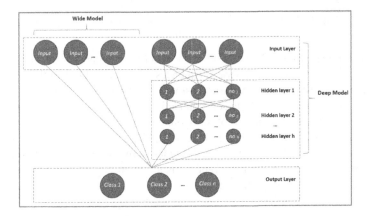

Fig. 1. Multi-dimensional Wide and Deep Neural Network (MDWDNN).

- **Input Layer:** The input layer represents the number of patents and publications for a technology for each available year.
- **Hidden Layers:** This neural network contains h hidden layers, and each layer contains no nodes.
- **Output layer:** represents the revenues ranges to be forecasted. Noting that each predicted output is serving as input for the next prediction until the number of future years p is reached.

Multi-Dimensional RNN (MDRNN). MDRNN processes time series sequences of multidimensional inputs, and predicts the probability distribution for each class for these sequences. In addition, it is based on encoder-decoder sub-models using LSTM and is structured as a Many-to-One model for classification usage, where the inputs represent sequences of data and the output represents a category. Moreover, Adam is applied as well in the MDRNN as an optimization method. Accordingly, it is built based on the following three layers (Fig. 2):

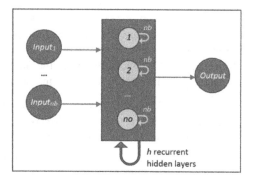

Fig. 2. Multi-dimensional Recurrent Neural Network (MDRNN).

- **Input Layers:** MDRNN consists of a specific number nb of input layers or dimensions. They take time series sequences with a variable length.
- **Hidden Layers:** Since a multidimensional recurrent neural network (MDRNN) consists of replacing the single self-connection in each node in a standard recurrent neural network with as many of self-connections as there are dimensions in the input data [29], MDRNN contains h recurrent hidden layers, with a specific number no of nodes, where each node in each hidden layer contains nb self-connections.
- **Output Layer:** The output layer represents a sequence of classes to be predicted in a single step from $Year_1$ till $Year_p$.

4   Experimentation

In order to train and test the neural networks, patents, publications and revenues data are collected for 15 trending technologies. Noting that since this study model will be targeting actual organizations in a future work, this predictive neural network can be eventually trained and tested using historical Big Data. The candidate technology's data are applied on the neural networks to predict its future patents, publications and its revenues ranges for the next four years.

4.1   Data Collection

Technologies Listing. Different web sources such as IEEE, Scientific American, Elsevier, etc. are used to list several trending technologies and their related keywords, such as the "Additive manufacturing" term for the "3D printing" technology.

Patent Data Source. Data of the granted patents applications that have been published before December 31, 2019, are extracted from the United States Patent and Trademark Office (USPTO) database which is considered among the richest intellectual property databases [30].

Publications Data Source. Publications data such as title, year, author name, etc. are extracted from Springer that includes a wide range of bibliometric resources.

Revenue Data Source. The revenues related to each technology for several years have been extracted from different web sources, such as: Statista web pages, Smart Insights and different reports and articles.

4.2   Training, Testing and Prediction Datasets Creation

Given that the amount of the collected data is limited in volume, it has been split manually into training and testing datasets. Furthermore, in order to compare the predicted values with the actual values and to visualize the accuracy of the Neural Networks, the validation dataset is also taken as the prediction dataset, where "Virtual Reality" represents the candidate technology for which its future values will be forecasted. In addition, the predicted outputs of ODWDNN and ODRNN are integrated into MDWDNN and MDRNN respectively, along with the historical data of patents, publications and revenues dimensions. Furthermore, given that Neural Network 2 (MDWDNN and MDRNN) represents a classifier model that predicts the future revenues ranges for a specific trending technology, revenues data have been grouped into 3 classes based on data availability, as following (Table 2):

Table 2. Revenues classes.

Class	Revenues ranges (in USD)
1	0 <= Revenue <= 10 Billion
2	10 Billion <= Revenue <= 50 Billion
3	Revenue > 50 Billion

4.3   Neural Networks Implementation

The configurations and the training parameters of the neural networks have been adjusted and tuned progressively and determined experimentally according to the most accurate results. In addition, in order to ensure a fair comparison, the number of training steps applied for both neural network types are similar, and equal to 1000 steps.

Neural Network 1. Regarding the results accuracy of the ODWDNN and ODRNN models, it is calculated based on the same steps and formulae employed in the Saade, Jneid & Saleh article [10].

One-Dimensional WDNN (ODWDNN). ODWDNN is implemented with the following main parameters, as defined in the Proposed Methodology section:

> $p = 4$ years; *max* $= 10$ years; $h = 5$ hidden layers; $no_1 = 1000$ nodes; $no_2 = 750$ nodes; $no_3 = 500$ nodes; $no_4 = 300$ nodes; $no_5 = 150$ nodes

One-Dimensional RNN (ODRNN). It represents a Sequence-to-Sequence Recurrent Neural Network. It has been built and implemented based on the following main parameters defined in the previous sections:

> $p = 4$ years; *max* $= 10$ years; $h = 2$ recurrent layers; $no = 250$ hidden nodes per layer

Neural Network 2. The results accuracy of the Multi-dimensional Neural Networks Classifiers MDWDNN and MDRNN are generated based on the built-in Softmax function that provides the probability distribution for output classes [31], which means Softmax takes the predicted output values and normalizes them into probabilities.

Multi-Dimensional WDNN (MDWDNN). MDWDNN is implemented with the following main parameters, as defined in the Proposed Methodology section:

> $p = 4$ years; *max* $= 10$ years; $h = 5$ hidden layers; $no_1 = 1000$ nodes; $no_2 = 750$ nodes; $no_3 = 500$ nodes; $no_4 = 300$ nodes; $no_5 = 150$ nodes

Multi-Dimensional RNN (MDRNN). The parameters of MDRNN are configured as following:

> $nb = 2$; $p = 4$ years; $h = 2$ recurrent layers; $no = 250$ hidden nodes per layer

4.4   Results

The following subsections represent the obtained results for the "Virtual reality" candidate technology using both types of Neural Networks, illustrating the predictions quality, where the ordinate axes represent the dimensions values and the abscissa axes represent the time.

Neural Network 1

As per the below graphs and Table 3, the ODRNN achieves a better performance and accuracy and outperforms the ODWDNN, given that the average prediction accuracy of the ODRNN is higher than that of the ODWDNN.

Table 3. Prediction accuracies of Neural Networks 1.

ODWDNN		ODRNN	
Patents prediction accuracy	Publications prediction accuracy	Patents prediction accuracy	Publications prediction accuracy
51.40%	83.58%	84.86%	70.18%
Average prediction accuracy: 67.49%		**Average prediction accuracy: 77.52%**	

One-Dimensional WDNN (ODWDNN) (Figs. 3 and 4)

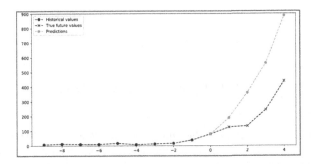

Fig. 3. Actual and predicted number of patents in the ODWDNN for the "Virtual reality" technology from 2006 to 2019.

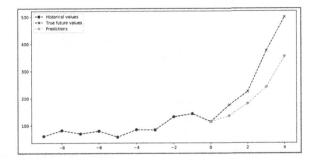

Fig. 4. Actual and predicted number of publications in the ODWDNN for the "Virtual reality" technology from 2006 to 2019.

One-Dimensional RNN (ODRNN) (Figs. 5 and 6)

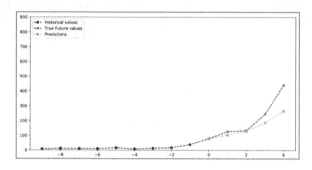

Fig. 5. Actual and predicted number of patents in the ODRNN for the "Virtual reality" technology from 2006 to 2019.

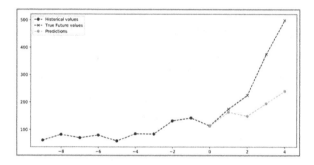

Fig. 6. Actual and predicted number of publications in the ODRNN for the "Virtual reality" technology from 2006 to 2019.

Neural Network 2. As per the following table, the MDRNN achieves a better performance and accuracy and outperforms the MDWDNN, given that the MDRNN was able to detect the actual revenue class of the fourth year by 39.94%, whereas the fourth probability of the MDWDNN was 0% (Table 4).

Table 4. Prediction accuracies of Neural Network 2.

Future years	MDWDNN			MDRNN		
	Actual Class	Predicted Class	**Actual Class Prediction Accuracy**	Actual Class	Predicted Class	**Actual Class Prediction Accuracy**
Year 1	1	1	99.50%	1	1	100%
Year 2	1	1	99.92%	1	1	99.99%
Year 3	1	1	99.99%	1	1	99.99%
Year 4	2	1	0%	2	1	39.94%
	Average prediction accuracy: 74.85%			**Average prediction accuracy: 84.98%**		

5   Conclusion/Discussion

Research and Development-based digital innovation activities represent a main driver for new product development and an added value in today's business economy. However, despite the fact that organizations are constantly developing new products while increasing the R&D investments and deploying new technologies, innovative trends are prone to failure. In addition, when evaluating a product life-cycle, the decision-makers of the organization first need to consider the potential disruptive innovation. Accordingly, predicting technology-based product success is a crucial need and a prerequisite step before proceeding with investments. A new quantitative approach has been proposed in the current paper, based on patents, publications and revenues dimensions analysis, and using Neural Network models that can evaluate and monitor a candidate technology-based product development. These dimensions are considered major key performance indicators to measure the technology power. Precisely, this paper covers two main steps: forecasting patents and publications growths separately using a common predictive Neural Network model, then integrating the results into a Multi-dimensional Neural Network classifier model in order to predict the future revenue-volume which can reflect the technology-based product success. The present methodology is applied using two different types of Neural Network models for comparison purpose: Wide and Deep Neural Networks and Recurrent Neural Networks. These neural networks have been implemented using United States Patent and Trademark Office data, Springer publications data and several web sources in order to collect technologies revenues data. In addition, this method has been experimented on 15 trending technologies to train the neural networks, then applied on one additional candidate technology, "Virtual reality", for the testing and prediction phases. The findings show that the Recurrent Neural Networks models achieve higher average prediction accuracy, and outperform the Wide and Deep Neural Networks in both steps, proving to be a valid model that can enhance digital innovation development.

Therefore, the proposed approach provides answers related to technology-based product success and reliable prediction models. The latter can be used by decision-makers in the organizations to evaluate and monitor a new trending innovation, in order to either measure its impact on existing product market performance, or to adopt this potential disruptive technology that may lead to a new product development.

Consequently, addressing this estimation is a crucial prerequisite step before proceeding with investments, where organizations can improve decision making in innovative technology-based product development. Furthermore, this method can be applied on several candidate technologies in order to prioritize and identify the most appropriate ones for a given investment project.

This methodology can be further developed by addressing its current limitations. For instance, accessing Big data represents the most challenging task faced in the current study where patents data are based uniquely on USPTO patents applications and publications information are extracted only from Springer. Moreover, the proposed methodology can be further evolved to include products composed of multiple major technologies to support all types of technologies-based products.

References

1. Distanont, A., Khongmalai, O.: The role of innovation in creating a competitive advantage. Kasetsart J. Soc. Sci. **41**, 15–21 (2018)
2. Jneid, M., Saleh, I.: Improving start-ups competitiveness and innovation performance: the case of Lebanon. In: ISPIM Conference Proceedings, p. 1. The International Society for Professional Innovation Management (ISPIM) (2015)
3. Christensen, C.M.: The Innovator's Dilemma: When New Technologies Cause Great Firms to Fail. Harvard Business Review Press, Brighton (2013)
4. Sun, J., Gao, J., Yang, B., Tan, R.: Achieving disruptive innovation-forecasting potential technologies based upon technical system evolution by TRIZ. In: 2008 4th IEEE International Conference on Management of Innovation and Technology, pp. 18–22. IEEE, September 2008
5. Sheffi, Y.: The Power of Resilience: How the Best Companies Manage the Unexpected. MIT Press, Cambridge (2015)
6. Obal, M., Ibrahim, S.: An investigation on the role of disruptive technology adoption on new product market performance and launch timeliness. In: Obal, M., Krey, N., Bushardt, C. (eds.) Let's Get Engaged! Crossing the Threshold of Marketing's Engagement Era. DMSPAMS, pp. 523–524. Springer, Cham (2016). https://doi.org/10.1007/978-3-319-11815-4_158
7. Nagy, D., Schuessler, J., Dubinsky, A.: Defining and identifying disruptive innovations. Ind. Mark. Manag. **57**, 119–126 (2016)
8. Momeni, A., Rost, K.: Identification and monitoring of possible disruptive technologies by patent-development paths and topic modeling. Technol. Forecast. Soc. Change **104**, 16–29 (2016)
9. Shang, T., Miao, X., Abdul, W.: A historical review and bibliometric analysis of disruptive innovation. Int. J. Innov. Sci. **11**, 208–226 (2019)
10. Saade, M., Jneid, M., Saleh, I.: Predicting technology success based on patent data, using a wide and deep neural network and a recurrent neural network. In: IBIMA 33 Conference proceedings. IBIMA (2019)
11. Geum, Y., Lee, S., Yoon, B., Park, Y.: Identifying and evaluating strategic partners for collaborative R&D: index-based approach using patents and publications. Technovation **33**(6–7), 211–224 (2013)
12. Han, F., Magee, C.L.: Testing the science/technology relationship by analysis of patent citations of scientific papers after decomposition of both science and technology. Scientometrics **116**(2), 767–796 (2018). https://doi.org/10.1007/s11192-018-2774-y
13. Wisła, R.: Patent data in economic analysis. Intellect. Property Rights 65 (2017)
14. Daim, T.H., Rueda, G., Martin, H., Gerdsri, P.: Forecasting emerging technologies: use of bibliometrics and patent analysis. World Sci. Ser. R&D Manag. 305 (2018)
15. Wang, B., Liu, Y., Zhou, Y., Wen, Z.: Emerging nanogenerator technology in China: a review and forecast using integrating bibliometrics, patent analysis and technology roadmapping methods. Nano Energy **46**, 322–330 (2018)
16. Gajewar, A., Bansal, G.: Revenue Forecasting for Enterprise Products. arXiv preprint, arXiv: 1701.06624 (2016)
17. Zhao, Y., Zhao, H.: Evaluating Toll Revenue Uncertainty Using Neural Network Models, pp. 2949–2956. ScienceDirect, Shanghai (2017)
18. Sanjaya, C., Iiana, M., Widodo, A.: Revenue Prediction Using Artificial Neural Network, pp. 97–99. IEEE (2010)

19. Gosasang, V., Chandraprakaikul, W., Kiattisin, S.: A comparison of traditional and neural networks forecasting techniques for container throughput at Bangkok port. Asian J. Shipp. Logist. **27**(3), 463–482 (2011)
20. Adebiyi, A.A., Adewumi, A.O., Ayo, C.K.: Comparison of ARIMA and artificial neural networks models for stock price prediction. J. Appl. Math. **2014**, 7 (2014)
21. Schmidhuber, J.: Deep learning in neural networks: an overview. Neural Netw. **61**, 85–117 (2015)
22. Alsheikh, M.A., Lin, S., Niyato, D., Tan, H.-P.: Machine learning in wireless sensor networks: algorithms, strategies, and applications. IEEE Commun. Surv. Tutor. **16**(4), 1996–2018 (2014)
23. Elaraby, N., Elmogy, M., Barakat, S.: Deep learning: effective tool for big data analytics. Int. J. Comput. Sci. Eng. (IJCSE) **5**, 254–262 (2016)
24. Cheng, H.-T., et al.: Wide & Deep Learning for Recommender Systems. Google (2016)
25. Zhou, S.K., Rueckert, D., Fichtinger, G. (eds.): Handbook of Medical Image Computing and Computer Assisted Intervention. Academic Press, Cambridge (2019)
26. Goyal, P., Pandey, S., Jain, K.: Deep learning for natural language processing. In: Deep Learning for Natural Language Processing: Creating Neural Networks with Python, pp. 138–143. Apress, Berkeley (2018)
27. Kingma, D.P., Ba, J.: Adam: a method for stochastic optimization. arXiv preprint arXiv: 1412.6980 (2014)
28. Sutskever, I., Vinyals, O., Le, Q.V.: Sequence to sequence learning with neural networks. In: Advances in Neural Information Processing Systems, pp. 3104–3112 (2014)
29. Graves, A., Fernández, S., Schmidhuber, J.: Multi-dimensional recurrent neural networks. In: de Sá, J.M., Alexandre, L.A., Duch, W., Mandic, D. (eds.) ICANN 2007. LNCS, vol. 4668, pp. 549–558. Springer, Heidelberg (2007). https://doi.org/10.1007/978-3-540-74690-4_56
30. USPTO: USPTO, June 2018. https://www.uspto.gov
31. Tang, D., Qin, B., Liu, T.: Document modeling with gated recurrent neural network for sentiment classification. In: Proceedings of the 2015 Conference on Empirical Methods in Natural Language Processing, pp. 1422–1432, September 2015

The Effects of Outsourcing on Performance Management in SMEs

Eisa Hareb Alneyadi and Khalid Almarri[✉]

The British University in Dubai, Dubai, UAE
khalid.almarri@buid.ac.ae

Abstract. Purpose - The purpose of this paper is to present a systemic review of the how outsourcing affects small and medium enterprises (SMEs). The paper achieves that purpose by focusing on outsourcing functions such as support activities, accounting, primary and back-office activities.

Methodology - This paper used secondary data. It relies on studies done by other researches to collect information related to the topic. This is presented through the competency theory, the transaction cost theory and the social view theory. The conceptual framework presented also relies on data collected from secondary sources.

Findings - The results of this research show that outsourcing in SMEs helps to improve business performance. Some SMEs are outsourcing their core activities to cut down on costs and offer better services.

Implications - The implications of the findings is that startups and SMEs will use the research to identify the best theories to rely on when outsourcing. The findings can also be used in framing policies for outsourcing.

Originality/value - The originality of the research is that it takes a new approach to address the issue of outsourcing in SMEs. It looks at the concept holistically instead of focusing on one function of outsourcing.

Keywords: Outsourcing · Small and medium enterprises (SME) · Theory · Performance

1 Introduction

The modern way of conducting business has been transformed by the increased complexity of business issues and a shift in the provision of goods and services. There is a rapid change in the dynamics of the industry forcing businesses to change their way of doing things. The most affected are SMEs that constitute more than 60% of the non-oil economy in the UAE (Gueraiche 2017). Data from the IMF estimates SME growth in the UAE to grow by close to 0.9% to hit 3.7% by the end of 2020. Similar scenarios are experienced across the globe, with most SMEs shifting gears to outsourcing both primary and support services. The basic underlying factor in all the changes is that all organizations have their goals. Ideally, the success of every business will be determined by how best it can achieve its goals. SMEs are welcoming the idea of outsourcing to

© Springer Nature Switzerland AG 2020
M. Themistocleous et al. (Eds.): EMCIS 2020, LNBIP 402, pp. 730–741, 2020.
https://doi.org/10.1007/978-3-030-63396-7_49

lower their costs. Most of the SMEs are startups or struggling to fit in the market. Outsourcing offers them a better way to spend money where it is required and improve their business models.

The majority of SMEs have been forced to look out for strategies to enhance their performance. There is increased pressure to achieve goals with the rapid changes in technology, the need for constant growth, and the knowledge explosion as well as the sophistication of business processes. Outsourcing has become the most viable option for SMEs. They can combine the efforts of their staff with those of third party contractors to achieve the required changes. Every firm wants to be on par with the rest in goal achievement and meeting the needs of customers (Sev 2009). Therefore, there is a need for companies to reflect on the capabilities of their staff, processes, and technical know-how, among other factors. There is a need for firms to ask themselves whether they can achieve their goals with what they have, or they need to go out for better complementary strategies (Isaksson and Lantz 2015). In that regard, enterprises are required to innovate on ways of becoming more competitive in meeting the demands of their customers. Organizations should focus on the reduction of their costs and core competencies. This presents outsourcing as the best strategy for improving business performance.

Most managers are using outsourcing to address business dynamics. It is a management tool that has become very popular in today's world. Outsourcing entails using the services of a third party to perform business functions (Dominguez 2006). In other words, it describes the process where companies use external service providers to perform in-house functions. Therefore, the management of the outsourced service becomes the responsibility of the external agent. Through outsourcing, enterprises can concentrate their core competencies on areas that provide unique experiences to their customers. It is worth noting that firms are no longer stuck to outsource cleaning, catering, and security services, as has always been the case. According to Laugen and Fleury (2012), outsourcing has grown to include critical areas such as information systems, manufacturing, design, distribution, and marketing. In the UAE, Transguard has entered into the business of white-collar outsourcing initiatives in payroll, healthcare human resource, and administration. Generally, there is an increased demand for outsourcing companies to cater for the more than 350, 000 SMEs in the country.

Globally, Kodak subcontracted its information and computing services to IBM. The effect was that Kodak recorded increased quality in operation, and computing systems ate reduced costs (Sev 2009; Ordonez 2017). Another company that has entered into outsourcing to improve its performance is Boeing. In 1997, it was the leading manufacturer of commercial jets enjoying more than 60% of global market share (Hill 2014). However, there was increased competition from Airbus industries in Europe. The competition increased operation costs at Boeing forcing it to look for ways of lowering the cost. Consequently, Boeing started outsourcing some of its spare parts from China, and it was able to survive in the market. It is the leading manufacturer of large commercial aircraft in the world.

Boeing is a big organization, and it is benefiting from outsourcing. The business of outsourcing is not unique to big firms only. SMEs have been receiving contracts from the customers and subcontracting them to other enterprises (Ordonez 2017). For instance, hotels outsource security services from security outfits since their core business is in the provision of hotel services. Pilot studies show that SMEs are currently outsourcing accounting functions to firms specializing in the provision of accounting services (Isaksson and Lantz 2015). They consider it to be cheaper in the long run than employing accountants. The companies employ one or two accountants for recording transactions. The external company handles all the other functions such as audits, computations and preparation of sophisticated accounts.

According to Cavusgil et al. (2015), SMEs are outsourcing services in advertising and staff training. Evidence shows that outsourcing is essential for SMEs to pave the way for professional services and concentrate more on core competencies. SMEs can benefit from outsourcing by responding in a better way to any changes in the market. Businesses can also benefit from better competitive strategies from suppliers aimed at ensuring that the services provided are of high quality and reduced costs. Other SMEs get access to diverse markets through outsourcing. They expand to new territories while removing barriers to their productivity. In that regard, several theories have been proposed to address issues so outsourcing. This paper focuses on the theories and suggests a conceptual framework that may be used to approach the whole idea of outsourcing.

1.1 Understanding the Concept of Outsourcing

The diverse nature of outsourcing and people who use it give it several definitions and dimensions. In that regard, there is no clear definition of outsourcing that has been agreed upon by researchers or economists. For this paper, the definition by Dominguez (2006) and Ordonez (2017) will be considered and adopted. According to Dominguez (2006), outsourcing is the practice of seeking the services of experts and professionals to handle enterprise functions that are not listed as part of the core business. In other words, outsourcing is the process of augmenting staff without increasing their numbers. Ordonez (2017) views outsourcing as a process of subcontracting services and operations to companies that have specialized in such services and operations. The outsourced firms are expected to offer the services and activities cheaper and better or both.

Based on the definitions given above, outsourcing is the process through which a firm subcontracts the operations and services of another firm. The definition of outsourcing agrees with the fact that some firms are specialists in the provision of certain products and services. For instance, a firm that performs both operational and administrative functions may not be efficient in all the services. That may lead to the delivery of low-quality services. The firm may benefit more by specializing in one area (either administration or operations) and outsource the other. Such a move would help in improving productivity.

2 Theoretical Framework

Researchers have failed to agree on the genesis of outsourcing either as a scientific concept or as a practice. However, most studies in supply chain management and manufacturing argue that outsourcing has evolved from the "make-or-buy" concept. This is a concept where manufacturers had the option of buying already manufactured products instead of making them if that was the cheapest option. This paper agrees with such researches and the theories underlying the evolution of outsourcing. The study by Jae et al. (2006)

revealed that the Core Competencies Theory and the Transaction Costs Theory are most often referred in outsourcing. However, other theories, such as resource dependence theory, the social exchange theory, the power theory, and the political theories have been developed. It focuses on the theories put forward by Jae et al. (2006) and the social view theory. The third theory will be a combination of aspects found in the social exchange theory, the political and the power theories.

2.1 The Core Competencies Theory

This theory is also known as the resource-based theory. According to this theory, all core functions of a firm should be done by the firm. The theory was conceptualized by Van (2010) based on the resources owned by an enterprise. According to Van (2010), core competencies are the knowledge and skills in a company that can be translated into strategies and integrated into multiple streams of technologies. The resource-based theory aims at developing and improving the core competencies in a firm to make it more competitive. Therefore, it tries to achieve what would have been achieved through outsourcing (Jae et al. 2006). The theory looks tangible and intangible resources in a firm and how valuable they are to the company.

The core competencies theory is aware that resources are rare and lack substitutes. The theory argues that an SME should try and obtain the most value from its available resources and capabilities (Van 2010). There are some products and services that are unique and associated with some SME. SMEs are considered to be leaders in the delivery of such products and services. They have the most loyal customers in regards to these products and services. The theory recommends that the SME should enhance its provision of those services and outsource the rest. According to Jae et al. (2006), a core competency may be a relationship with suppliers, a reliable process, or technical knowledge in a field of expertise. An SME may also be excellent in market coverage, management of human resources, or employee dedication. These should be considered to be strengths to the SME in comparison with others in the same industry.

Generally, SMEs have minimal resource bases. However, they can maximize on their core competencies and outsource other activities such as accounting, back-office, and support. The SME can also outsource some primary functions not related to the core competencies such as customer service, warehousing, and procurement (Goodyear 2014). However, firms should play to their strengths and functions they are competent. This helps to explain the need for outsourcing decisions for SMEs. In some instances, SMEs have the required resources and competencies but still go ahead to outsource. Some SMEs outsource in areas of their core competencies. For that reason, the core competency theory may not be sufficient to explain the effects of outsourcing for SMEs.

2.2 The Transaction Cost Theory

The baseline for this theory is that firms outsource services to lower their transaction costs. This theory works very well for SMEs in the manufacturing and supply chain industries. It relies on the perspective of Transaction Cost Analysis (TCA). The analysis looks at environmental factors affecting business performance. The environmental factors are then related to human factors and the results used to determine how organizations can reduce the costs associated with transactions (Williamson et al. 2016). According to the postulations of TCA, managers are expected to be rational, while stakeholders may be opportunists. This theory believes that SMEs should strive to minimize their operational costs through outsourcing. Therefore, they should evaluate their operations and identify those that can be outsourced. The SMEs can then redirect their efforts in customer service to improve customer satisfaction and get more loyal customers.

The transaction cost theory argues that firms can even outsource for functions they are in a position to offer. However, outsourcing becomes an option because it is considered to be cheaper compared to the firm offering the services. In that regard, some SMEs have shifted to outsourcing primary that may be seen as core operations in the mission and vision statements. Before outsourcing, a company will consider the transaction cost economics (TCE). Research by Lee (2018) shows that outsourcing becomes the best option where markets are incredibly competitive. Consider the example of Boeing given earlier. The more the suppliers in the market, the cheaper it becomes to outsource. Having more suppliers of service reduced pressure and the need to monitor supply. However, in contrast, suppliers would be exploitative and opportunistic.

The best thing to do is for an SME to carry out a market survey and determine the TCE of a service. There is no need to outsource when the supply is limited. In that case, the firm would need to go through stringent negotiations and supervision of the relationship, further increasing the transaction costs (Williamson et al. 2016). It is worth noting that the transaction theory is not sufficient in explaining the decisions of outsourcing. This is because there are SMEs that still prefer outsourcing even when it would have been cheaper to offer the service using in-house employees. For that reason, it is essential to consider the social view theory.

2.3   The Social View Theory

This theory is based on the aspects of power, cohesion, balance, and reciprocity. The theory is used to explain why some SMEs enter into close relationships with service providers. While engaging in their regular transactions, SMEs develop good relationships with service providers and begin to exchange valuable resources (May 2013; Daft 2016). With continued engagements, mutual and sequential trustworthiness develops, and the economic aspects of the relationships become foreseeable. The social view theory assumes organizations should keep on exchanging material and social-tangible resources as a basic form of human interaction. The theory believes that the interactions between SMEs and other firms should be a continuous process (Daft 2016). The relationship should be based on the rewarding reactions obtained from the other party. In other words, firms treat others as they are treated or would wish to be treated.

Social view theory is also based on the relationship between an SME and its stakeholders. For instance, employees will be committed to their tasks if they see a commitment from management to reward their efforts. The relationship is reciprocal. If an organization is not ready to invest in the training of its employees, they will not be competent in some areas, and this might call for outsourcing. According to Steers and Nardon (2014), social view theory requires SMEs to monitor their operations continuously and reinforce their relationships with others. In the social view theory, the most important thing to note is that some SMEs outsource services from large organizations to establish lasting relationships that are beneficial economically. Others outsource intending to gain recognition. Others outsource without necessarily seeking to increase profits but to have social relationships with the other firm.

Based on the analysis of the theories, it is clear that outsourcing decisions are made after consideration of many factors. The following theoretical framework is suggested for SMEs (Fig. 1).

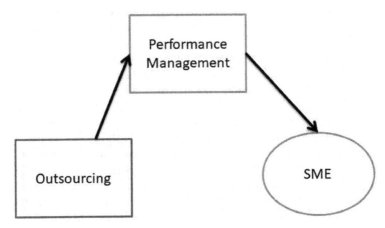

Fig. 1. Suggested theoretical framework

The structure shows that the performance of an SME can be improved using outsourcing strategies.

3 Conceptual Framework

Different scholars have classified outsourcing strategies differently. This section discusses the classifications and their relationship with organizational performance.

3.1 Classification, According to (Isaksson and Lantz 2015)

According to Isaksson and Lantz (2015), organizations may outsource primary activities, support activities, accounting activities, and back-office activities. The ability of an SME to outsource primary activities is based on cost advantage and availability of resources. Using the core competence and transaction cost theories, firms can have a comprehensive evaluation of what might lead them to outsource. Dimauro (2017) used the analysis of the two theories to understand why outsourcing has been a common practice recently. Research shows that some firms outsource primary functions. For instance, Nike, a leading footwear manufacturer, does not produce all its products but subcontracts independent suppliers to manufacture them (Clancy 2016). Firms are reported to outsource primary functions so that they can leverage available resources and reduce their asset base in the supply chain. Some of the primary functions that may be outsourced include customer service, salesforce, warehousing, purchases, and manufacturing.

SMEs are currently outsourcing most of the back-office activities. These are activities that form part of the day to day running of the enterprise. The back-office activities are not part of the core functions but contribute to the success of the core functions (Goldman 2013). Firms that outsource back-office services are those that do not have experience with the tasks or the technical know-how. The business may also lack the resources to perform the function or maybe hurt internally by the function. According to Isaksson and Lantz (2015), some of the back-office functions that may be outsourced include payment processing, order processing, billing, payroll, and bookkeeping. Organizations may also outsource security and cleaning services that require efficient functioning for better service to customers.

Most SMEs are now subcontracting cleaning companies to offer cleaning services to their offices. The cleaning companies come with their sophisticated equipment to ensure every corner of the office shines. The staff also do a garbage collection. SMEs are also contacting professional security companies that install CCTV and other surveillance systems, alarms, and carry out patrols (Fay 2006). If this were not part of the core business of a firm, it would be expensive in the long run. Research shows that outsourcing back-office functions help to improve the performance of a company (Goldman 2013; Lacity and Willcocks 2015). Besides the provision of better quality services, the outsourcing enterprise benefits from more enhanced service delivery and better customer satisfaction.

The outsourcing of support activities has been a norm, just like the back-office functions. Support functions are those that help an enterprise to run efficiently and effectively. SMEs may outsource support activities such as public relations, transport, legal services, advertising, training, information technology, and shipping, among others. There are specialist firms that handle social media, live chats, email, and telephone calls for SMEs satisfactorily (Chesterman and Fisher 2014). Their employees are trained to treat customers with high infectious enthusiasm and patience. Other support services that may be outsourced are technical support, scheduling appointments, handling complaints, event registration, and after-sales support.

SMEs are entering into the business of outsourcing not only to reduce costs but also to improve their performance. There is a growing need to transform the finance and accounting functions in SMEs, leading them to consider outsourcing. For instance, with the rapid changes in technology, budgetary pressures, and increased competition, firms may opt for outsourcing to ensure their accounts are in order (Kumaran 2013). Over the years, the outsourcing of accounting services has undergone significant transformations. SMEs can now forecast their expenses and plan their budgets. Through outsourcing, SMEs can monitor their routine operational costs and transactions. The service providers are using technology to provide customized services to SMEs. While some firms are using multi-agency teams to outsource for accounting functions, others are consolidating their outsourcing functions to increase efficiency and reduce complexity.

The increase in globalization has necessitated the outsourcing of accounting functions. The world has been reduced into a small village through globalization. Through globalization, there are more opportunities available for the outsourcing of accounting activities. Firms can now outsource one or more financial services benefiting from new expertise and talent. The study by Chesterman and Fisher (2014) revealed that SMEs are outsourcing accounting services to add value to their cash flow. The traditional notion where companies used to outsource accounting services just for payroll is being phased out. It is worth noting that accounting forms an integral part of the system functioning and operation of an enterprise. Consequently, it would be essential to outsource such services for organizations to streamline their operations. According to Kumaran (2013), outsourcing accounting services has the benefits of staying informed with trending accounting processes, saving up on processing time, offering cost-effective services, and avoiding penalties in times of tax processing, among others. This paper adopts the classification of outsourcing strategies by Isaksson and Lantz (2015). The classification for the services that may be outsourced is shown below (Fig. 2).

Fig. 2. Functions that SMEs can Outsource Source: Isaksson and Lantz 2015.

3.2 Classification, According to Harward (2010)

Harward (2010) classified outsourcing strategies into four different categories. He called them engagement models and divided them into two major divisions: Out-tasking models and business process outsourcing (BPO) models. Harward (2010) argued that the out-tasking models are mainly concerned with contracting and licensing. The understanding of this classification requires managers to see firms as a unit that has several processes run by the same person. For instance, in small enterprises, technology, delivery, content, and administrative functions are all managed by the business owner.

Differences in outsourcing strategies are determined by the time taken to manage such functions, the number of tasks to be controlled, and the complexity of their integration. According to Harward (2010), a BPO is a collection of all the processes that take longer time to manage, are most complex and may have challenges being integrated. On the other hand, out-tasking is a collection of all the functions that may be easier to handle. They may be more menial and tactical, but they are fewer and less complex.

Harward (2010) suggested that the most common form of outsourcing in SMEs is contracting. In some SMEs, it is referred to as "labor for hire." In such engagements, contractors are hired to perform a task within a given period. For instance, if a supplier is outsourced to manage a project and compensation is offered after project completion, which is an excellent example of contracting. After the completion of the project, the relationship between the two firms ends. Some SMEs prefer such types of arrangements because they are transactional and very flexible. The outsourcing firm sees it easier to manage the relationship. When things do not go well, it becomes easy to terminate the relationship.

4 Discussion

Researchers have conducted empirical studies intended to understand the impacts of outsourcing on SME performance. Most of the studies concluded that outsourcing has positive outcomes in business performance. All the theories discussed and the conceptual framework suggested in this paper show that SMEs should outsource to provide their customers with better quality services. A study by Suraju and Hamed (2013) relied on the core competencies theory and transaction cost theory to examine the effects of outsourcing strategies as strategic tools in organizational performance. They used the weighted and naive estimators in their analysis. The study modified the tools used by Dierks et al. (2013) to obtain better results. Questionnaires were administered to food and beverage companies in Nigeria for two weeks.

Secondary data was extracted from food databases in Nigeria and files contained in the websites of the selected companies. All the companies involved in the study were listed on the Nigeria Stock Exchange between 2005 and 2010. The results of the study showed that companies that outsourced more realized more benefits in organizational performance. Additionally, the study found that there was a close correlation between outsourcing and competitive advantage (Suraju and Hamed 2013). It was realized that companies that relied on outsourcing for support services had better results in labor productivity. They had an opportunity to engage their employees more, leading to service delivery. The study also revealed that through outsourcing, SMEs enhanced its financial economies and competitive advantage.

The study by Nazeri et al. (2012) was conducted to examine the propensity of outsourcing. The researchers wanted to understand how outsourcing affects objectives in operation such as improved quality, organizational performance, better service delivery, and cost reduction. The focus was on the role of outsourcing on the financial and non-financial performance of SMEs. The researchers administered questionnaires to the board of directors, lower managers, operational distributors, and quality managers in the selected SMEs. Using Minitab and SPSS software analysis tools, deductive and descriptive analytics was conducted on the obtained data. The analysis revealed that outsourcing led to a better financial and non-financial performance in SMEs. The results showed that SMEs could realize increased flexibility, better engagement with customers, and reduced costs through outsourcing.

Jiang et al. (2006) conducted a study to examine how outsourcing impacts the performance of firms. The study relied on annual reports sampled from trading firms in the United States. The researchers found that outsourcing impacted positively on the cost efficiency of firms. However, there was no evidence to show that outsourcing had any effect on the productivity or profitability of firms. There was no clear information provided on the size of the firms involved. However, the research applies to SMEs since it is in congruence with other analyses on SMEs in developing and developed countries.

In the exploration of the effects of outsourcing strategies on the performance of small manufacturing firms, a study was conducted by Isaksson and Lantz (2015). The researchers wanted to test how the outsourcing strategies in manufacturing companies were related to financial performance. They used a stratified technique to sample 700 small firms with less than 50 employees in Sweden. The collected data were analyzed using multiple regression strategies. The results of the analysis revealed that there was a direct correlation between outsourcing primary, support, accounting, and back-office functions with financial performance. Among the sample firms, those that used outsourcing strategies were performing better financially compared to those that used their staff to do everything.

Irefin et al. (2012) researched to ascertain the effects of outsourcing on the success of SME projects. Questionnaires were administered to SMEs that were selected using both stratified and random sampling techniques. The questionnaires were administered to middle-level employees while interviews were conducted on managers. Chi-Square and frequency distribution tools were used to analyze the obtained data. Based on the findings, the researchers concluded that most SMEs outsourced intending to increase sales turnover, reduce administrative burdens, reduce time to market. Other benefits include saving time for core activities, streamlining processes, managing costs, enhancing expertise, reducing staff, boosting the bottom line, and improving service quality, among others. The findings showed that outsourcing played a significant role in improving project success. The study provided a strong foundation for conducting future research on the profitability of SMEs using outsourcing strategies.

4.1 Research Gaps and Expansion of Existing Literature

Based on the outsourcing strategies reviewed, the success of SMEs is measured by their ability to outsource support, accounting, back-office, and primary activities. SMEs that use outsourcing strategies have witnessed increased profitability and better performance. Several researchers have come up with different theories of outsourcing. One such theory that is common in SMEs is the core competency theory that focuses on outsourcing services that are not in the core business of business (Goodyear 2014). Since most SMEs have minimal resources, they turn to external firms that have the expertise, knowledge, and skills in those areas. However, the core competencies theory does not explain why enterprises outsource for core competencies.

According to the core competency theory, some SMEs are still outsourcing in their core areas, even with the required resources. The transaction cost theory then comes in. The theory argues that firms only outsource after doing evaluations and concluding that outsourcing is the cheapest option. The transaction cost theory helps to explain why firms outsource on primacy functions that are considered core to a firm (Lee 2018). There is a need to do more research on the impacts of outsourcing options on SME performance. This paper provides the impacts of outsourcing on the performance of SMEs but focuses less on profitability. Additionally, the researches discussed in this paper did not address the effects of outsourcing on the performance of SMEs in either developing or developed countries. This is another area that future research should focus. With the increase in outsourcing and globalization, existing literature will likely be expanded.

5 Conclusion

The studies reviewed in this paper are in agreement that businesses, irrespective of their size, outsource. Over the years, large scale corporations, small and medium enterprises, have shifted to the outsourcing of accounting, support, back-office, and primary functions. It is also clear from the reviewed studies that all tasks in a company can be outsourced so long as the external firm has more expertise, knowledge, and skills, and the cost is lower than what the outsourcing firm would have spent. The reviewed studies, the theoretical framework, and the conceptual framework developed agree that outsourcing has enormous benefits in improving organizational performance. The studies by Jiang et al. (2006), Nazer et al. (2012), Suraju and Hamed (2013), and Irefin et al. (2012) have all presented positive effects of outsourcing on the performance of enterprises. These studies can be extrapolated to SMEs that are becoming the major players in the industry.

The paper has shown that outsourcing strategies may be classified based on outsourced functions or reasons for outsourcing. This paper concludes that outsourcing is beneficial to SMEs as it helps to provide better quality services improving business performance. It is worth noting that SMEs need to do a comprehensive evaluation of their operations and determine which services to outsource and which ones to continue providing. The baseline should be to meet customer expectations and improve customer satisfaction.

References

Cavusgil, S.T., Knight, G.A., Riesenberger, J.R., Rammal, H.G., Rose, E.L.: International Business: The New Realities. Pearson Australia, Frenchs Forest (2015)

Chesterman, S., Fisher, A.: Private Security, Public Order: The Outsourcing of Public Services and Its Limits. OUP, Oxford, Oxford (2014)

Clancy, M.: Sweating the Swoosh: Nike, The Globalization of Sneakers, and the Question on Sweatshop Labor. SAGE, London (2016)

Daft, R.L.: Organization Theory & Design. Cengage Learning, Boston (2016)

Dierks, A., Kuklinski, C.P.J.W., Moser, R.: How institutional change reconfigures successful value chains: the case of western pharma corporations in China. Thunderbird Int. Bus. Rev. **55**(2), 153–171 (2013)

DiMauro, L.: Encyclopedia of Small Business. Gale, Cengage Learning, Farmington Hills (2017)

Dominguez, L.: The Managers' Step-by-Step Guide to Outsourcing. McGraw Hill Companies, Boston (2006)

Fay, J.: Contemporary Security Management. Elsevier/Butterworth-Heinemann, Amsterdam (2006)

Goldman, T.F.: Technology in the Law Office. Pearson/Prentice Hall, Upper Saddle River (2013)

Goodyear, L.: Qualitative Inquiry in Evaluation: From Theory to Practice. Jossey-Bass, San Francisco (2014)

Guéraiche, W.: The UAE: Geopolitics, Modernity, and Tradition. IB Tauris, London (2017)

Harward, D.: 4 Sourcing Strategies – Which is best for your business? (2010). https://www.trainingindustry.com/blog/outsourcing/4-sourcing-strategies-which-is-best-for-your-business. Accessed 30 Mar 2020

Hill, C.W.L.: International Business: Competing in the Global Marketplace. McGraw Hill Education, New York (2014)

Irefin, I.A., Olateju, O.I., Hammed, G.O.: Effect of outsourcing strategy on project success. Transnatl. J. Sci. Technol. **2**(6), 128–143 (2012)

Isaksson, A., Lantz, B.: Outsourcing strategies and their impact on financial performance in small manufacturing firms in Sweden. Int. J. Bus. Finance Res. **9**, 11–20 (2015)

Jae, N.E., Minh, Q.H., Kwok, R.C., Shih, M.P.: The evolution of outsourcing research: what is the next issue. In: Proceedings of the 33rd Hawaii International Conference on System Sciences (2006)

Jiang, B., Frazier, G.V., Prater, E.L.: Outsourcing Effects on Firms' Operational Performance. Routledge, London (2006)

Kumaran, S.: Top 10 benefits of outsourcing accounting and payroll services (2013). https://www.invensis.net/blog/finance-andaccounting/top-10-benefits-of-outsourcing-accounting-and-payroll-services. Accessed 30 Mar 2020

Lacity, M., Willcocks, L.: Nine Keys to World-Class Business Process Outsourcing. Bloomsbury Publishing, London (2015)

Laugen, M., Fleury, S.: Small and medium scale enterprises (SMEs) in Nigeria: problems and prospects. A Ph.D. Dissertation Submitted to the Department of Management: St. Clements University (2012)

Lee, Y.H.: Vertical Integration and Technological Innovation: A Transaction Cost Approach. Routledge, London (2018)

May, S.: Case Studies in Organizational Communication: Ethical Perspectives and Practices. SAGE Publications, Los Angeles (2013)

Nazeri, A., Gholami, R., Rashidi, S.: Outsourcing and its impact on operational performance. In: Proceedings of the 2012 International Conference on Industrial Engineering and Operations Management, Istanbul, Turkey, 3–6 July 2012 (2012)

Ordóñez, P.P.: Managerial Strategies and Solutions for Business Success in Asia. Business Science Reference, Hershey (2017)

Sev, J.T.: An Empirical Assessment of Outsourcing: A strategy for Organizational effectiveness in the Nigerian corporate sector (a survey of some corporate Organizations in Nigeria). An Unpublished Research Survey (2009)

Steers, R.M., Nardon, L.: Managing in the Global Economy. Taylor and Francis, Hoboken (2014)

Suraju, R.F., Hamed, A.B.: Outsourcing services as a strategic tool for organizational performance: an exploratory study of Nigerian food, beverage, and tobacco industry. J. Manag. Policies Pract. **1**(1), 01–20 (2013)

Van, B.H.: International Finance and Open-Economy Macroeconomics: Theory, History, and Policy. World Scientific, Singapore (2010)

Williamson, O.E., Masten, S.E., Edward Elgar Publishing: Transaction Cost Economics: An Edward Elgar Research Review. Edward Elgar Publishing Limited, Cheltenham (2016)

The Attitude of Consumer Towards a Brand Source: Context of UAE

Omer Aftab and Khalid Almarri[(✉)]

The British University in Dubai, Dubai, United Arab Emirates
Khalid.almarri@buid.ac.ae

Abstract. Purpose – This study will examine to find out the solutions for the people who purchase certain products that are linked to a certain brand and at the same time, they are biased towards their sources, whereas, these sources are affiliated and endorsed by such brands.

Methodology – This study is based on quantitative research design method utilising convenience sampling method based on the existing literature in the field of business management.

Findings – The findings of this study will be congruent with the results of the previous literature, proving that the positive relationship among the different dependent and independent variables exist, respectively.

Implications – This study will examine the association between brand attractiveness, brand loyalty and celebrity endorsement in relation to the customer's attitude while purchasing a product, in the field of marking and business management.

Originality/value – This study is developed on the existing literature that will help the readers in understanding the consumer's attitude towards a brand source.

Keywords: Brand attractiveness · Brand loyalty · Celebrity endorsement · Social identification theory · Functional theory

1 Introduction

It is a common thing now days to follow the brands and their products. People like to affiliate themselves with bigger brands to have a better image. For instance, if one says the name of "Lionel Messi", the person will immediately think of Barcelona football club. Similarly, Lewis Hamilton is linked to Formula One sport. Hence, it can be concluded that those individuals carry with them the brands they have endorsed. The influence of endorsements is very high all over the world and it is associated with all sorts of activities and industries, which can be clothes, tennis, cosmetics, airlines and so on. People tend to follow such trends and brands, as it has already created a certain image in their minds which makes the customer a strong believer in those brands. We all know that to make a brand famous, they try to approach high profile celebrities or personalities in order to get their brand promoted and reach wider public. However, endorsing with a brand can have both positive as well as negative impact. Hafsa Lodhi stated in her article that affiliating brands with the celebrities creates a massive positive

© Springer Nature Switzerland AG 2020
M. Themistocleous et al. (Eds.): EMCIS 2020, LNBIP 402, pp. 742–753, 2020.
https://doi.org/10.1007/978-3-030-63396-7_50

impact to boost the sales not only over the social media, but also over the other digital marketing media. Therefore, people keep on purchasing and spending more on such brands that are endorsed by the celebrities (Lodi 2017).

On the contrary, there are also some celebrities who might be biased towards the brand, but they are still endorsing it. This can be due to the fact that they do not like the product source, but they like to utilise that brand and vice versa. An article issued by Mari Ouhan in 2014 highlighted the fact that in UAE, the newer generation are not at all inspired by high profile celebrity testimonials. They are more reluctant to purchase such products based on their own expertise and the use of such products (Swan 2014). In this report, the author will be trying to explore a person's attitude in relation to the source of the product and the product itself, in order to know how it intimidates to perceive about such brands. Furthermore, certain questions will also be explored with the help of this research, whether the attractiveness of brand, its loyalty and affiliation or association of the brand with a celebrity conveys any effect on the attitude of a customer or consumer, in purchasing a product or they do not have any influence on the decision making process of the consumer. Previous researches have covered different areas and different questions, in terms of customer attitude. This research will be following a framework made up of three different independent variables that have never been studied together, in respect to consumer attitude.

1.1 Problem of the Research

In this study, the author has defined the problem statement for this study as to discover about the probable resolutions for the individuals who purchase certain products that are linked to a certain brand and at the same time, they are biased towards their sources, whereas, these sources are affiliated and endorsed by such brands.

1.2 Aims of the Research

The aims of this research are as follows:

- Understanding customer's attitude regarding the purchase of a specific product regardless of the relation between the product and its source.
- Understanding how the factors such as the attractiveness of brand, loyalty to the brand and the affiliation of a celebrity with a brand assists in shaping consumer's attitude.

1.3 Objectives of the Research

Following are the objectives of this research:

- The effect of brand's attractiveness to influence an individual's attitude towards a brand.
- The effect of brand's loyalty to influence an individual's attitude towards a brand.
- The effect of celebrity affiliation/association to influence an individual's attitude towards a brand.

2   Literature Review

2.1   Brand Attractiveness and Customer's Attitude

Polyorat (2011) defined brand attractiveness in marketing terms as "the appearance of a brand to be prominent, reasonable and inimitable when associated or compared with other brands". If a brand has a constructive attractiveness, it affects the market shares positively to build and enhance its reputation (Kim, Han & Park 2002). Therefore, the author can conclude that a positive relation exists among the perceived brand attractiveness and the consumer.

So et al. (2017) claimed in their article that the satisfaction of a consumer's need is perceived by the positive assessment of the brand attractiveness. They further claimed that one must explore further the affects of brand attractiveness towards the consumer attitude for purchasing a certain product, in order to better understand about brand attractiveness and the benefit it carries with it for those particular brands (So et al. 2017). Hence, it can be concluded that when an individual purchases a certain brand, the person attributes himself with that brand, creating a positive attitude towards it (So et al. 2017). The author is of the view that an individual will never purchase such a product or brand which doesn't feel attractive, regardless of its price and convenience, only if it is a convenient product, for which we do not spend much time to purchase such products, like water, bread and so on.

In 1998, Till and Busler revealed in their research that an individual who endorses a brand, the packaging of the product or the attractiveness of the brand itself are enough to convince a person to purchase that brand. Hence, the right fit is required by the brand to be as attractive as possible in order to be sold as perceived by the brand itself. Moreover, the author can also conclude from this that when an individual is trying to make a purchase decision, the attractiveness of a brand is extremely vital for the final user.

Hurriyati and Setiawan (2016) mentioned in their report that the experts are also in favor of brand attractiveness as an extremely significant factor for the success of a brand, as it not only influences the success of it, but it helps in creating closer bonds and relations with the brands, along with creating a new space for the potential customers, which can assist in their decision making process through the brand's attractiveness. This in turn will assist the consumer in creating a positive attitude towards the brand. Another article argues that the perceived attractiveness of a brand becomes plausible and powerful as soon as the consumer starts purchasing such a brand more frequently and spending more on that brand due to its attractiveness (Hayes et al. 2006).

2.2   Brand Loyalty and Customer's Attitude

Brand loyalty is defined as "the buying behaviour of the consumer where he is positively biased towards the purchase of a certain brand or product" (Sheth & Park 1974). When an individual links himself or purchases a certain brand, he establishes a brand preference inexorably as compared to the other brands, as a result of it, creating a constructive attitude towards that brand. This helps in creating the brand loyalty for an individual (Sandy Zhang et al. 2014).

Different customer base of a particular brand appreciates the sales of its brand, be it locally or internationally, as it helps in creating a loyal customer base (Loi et al. 2015). In the western world, the brand loyalty is perceived differently than that in the eastern side of the world, as they have differences in their cultures, values and social norms, to name a few (Sandy Zhang et al. 2014). Hence, the author can conclude that the perceived value of the brand by purchasing it again and again, along with how the brand treats its costumer is vital in its decision making and durability.

One such research published by Hasan (2013) suggested that in order to establish more brand loyalty, the brands need to produce such a product that could be purchased more frequently by the end users; be it the committed buyer, a new customer, a gratified customer, a liker, or persistent customer. Hurriyati and Setiawan (2016) noted that by studying the close or strong proximity between the customer and the brand, it will give clear indications as to why people prefer some brands more over the other brands, hence creating a positive attitude towards their preferred brands. Therefore, the brands can understand it better how they could compete with their competitors in terms of the features and attributes they provide to their customers, in order to have a positive attitude from their loyal customers (Hurriyati & Setiawan 2016).

In 2018, Kim, Choe and Petrick claimed that a customer's brand loyalty can be tangible as well as intangible based on the type of product they are purchasing. For example, a person who purchases a car insurance with the same company for many years is loyal to that company for its services, which is an intangible service. On the other hand, a person purchasing just the Toyota brand is loyal to it, which is a tangible product. Such a strong is loyalty for many customers for their preferred brands that they will even order it from the other parts of the world or to travel to other parts of the world just to get their hands on that particular product (Kim, Choe & Petrick 2018).

2.3   Celebrity Endorsement and Customer's Attitude

Celebrity endorsement is described as "such an individual with notable achievements or accomplishments in different fields or activities, related to any industry" (Speck, Schumann & Thompson 1988). It is human nature to follow in the footsteps of one's favourite celebrity as to what he/she dons. One such famous definition given by McGuire (1985) which is widely used to define celebrity endorsement stated that "shared credit that is appreciated by a person on behalf of a customer acknowledging a brand by performing alongside it, in an announcement".

Celebrities and famous personalities from all over the world and from different fields endorse and affiliate themselves with different products at the same time. They act in such a way in order to convince their followers that they are an expert and trustworthy brand ambassadors of that particular product (Muda et al. 2014). Muda et al. (2014) also argued in the article that the famed star instantly becomes the face of the brand as soon as they endorse or affiliate with a certain brand. Hence it proves to be a win-win state for both sides, bringing success, publicity and a lot of money to the brand (Muda et al. 2014). Then there are those consumers who regardless of the endorsement, like to purchase certain products which are endorsed by famous celebrities, but have nothing to do with an individual's decision-making process.

Bergkvist and Zhou (2016) also argued that some brands also have celebrities endorsing their brand voluntarily, as they want to create trustworthiness among its followers, to make them feel comfortable while using such a product. Bergkvist and Zhou (2016) also argued that celebrities must be extra careful when they are being displayed or advertised internationally, as the cultural difference play an important role in it. For example, a female portrayed in the Eastern countries will be completely or some how different to that of how she will be displayed in the Western countries, keeping in mind that they still promote the overall image of the brand itself (Bergkvist & Zhou 2016). Therefore, it won't be wrong to say that the endorsers cannot neglect cultural differences, as cultural values play a vital role for many countries all over the world, especially the Eastern Region.

Furthermore, Mishra, Roy and Bailey (2015) argued that it is still a wide open debate that whether the celebrities should be paid a huge amount of money just to endorse or affiliate with a certain product, or it should be kept to minimum, to maintain balance among the company's operations and investment. Moreover, the research also shows that having a famous celebrity endorse with a certain brand has helped to expand and grow its market share, not to forget it also helps in increasing the number of customers an endorser can bring with him/her (Amos, Holmes & Strutton 2008). Therefore, it is highly recommended for a brand to choose such a celebrity who is well-known all over the world, who could be a celebrity, an expert in a field, a distinctive customer or a famous figure to name a few (Friedman et al. 1976).

3 Related Theories and Concepts

3.1 Social Identification Theory

Based on the literature mentioned above, many authors have successfully linked social identification theory with different variables mentioned in this report as well. The social identification theory is basically developed for social psychology which relates an individual's sense of belongingness with a certain brand or organization (Kim, Han & Park 2002). Consequently, it can be assumed that customer's attitude towards a certain brand helps the person to differentiate between various brands (Kim, Han & Park 2002).

In this research, social identification theory can also be applied for the two main constructs, brand loyalty and celebrity endorsements; since this theory deals with the brand expectation and prestige, as described in the previous literature (Mael & Ashforth 1992). This is also in accordance with the theme of this research, as it helps the consumers to associate themselves with the brands and the celebrities at the same time (Kim, Han & Park 2002).

3.2 Functional Theory

Then there is functional theory, which is completely based on the consumer's attitude. As stated and illustrated by various researchers, functional theory is a concept that relates attitude of an individual with a stored memory to associate them with particular objects and brands; hence evoking such memories at the time of decision-making or purchasing certain products that require some time to think (Argyriou & Melewar 2011). For instance, when an individual wants to take a decision based on the brand's attractiveness, an appropriate attitude will be stimulated to inform about the required decision (Katz 1960; Shavitt 1990; Eagly & Chaiken 1993).

This functional theory of attitude can also be expressed in the marketing terms, since it is dealing mostly with the customer's attitude towards a brand, be it the attractiveness, loyalty, or endorsement. As illustrated above in the literature review, this theory is integral to understand the concept and to link the various variables mentioned in this study. Therefore, it can be established that the concept of functional theory helps to organise, structure and summarise huge amount of information about a certain brand, primarily serving its purpose as a knowledge carrier (Grewal et al. 2004).

4 Conceptual Framework and Hypotheses

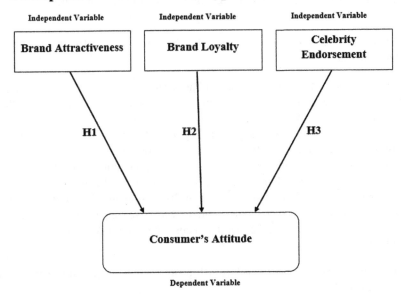

The author in this research identified four variables, as independent and dependent, respectively, which are as follows:

- **Independent variables** are *the attractiveness of a brand, loyalty towards a brand* and *the celebrity affirmations for a brand.*

- As for the **dependent variable**, it is just the *consumer's attitude towards a brand,* respectively.

Based on the conceptual framework figure shown above, it is clear to understand that what affect an individual autonomous variable will have on the subject variable, separately. Following three hypotheses were devised by the author based on the gathered literature and prior knowledge:

Hypothesis 1: There is a positive relationship between brand attractiveness and customer's attitude.

There exists a definite relationship between the brand attractiveness and the consumer attitude, as highlighted in the book "Marketing Management, Millenium Edition" by Kotler (2002). Another group of researchers agree with the fact that a solid positive relationship exists among the attractiveness of a brand and customer attitude, as cited by Ahearne, Bhattacharya and Gruen (2005). Consumer attitude and brand attractiveness go parallel with each other when purchasing a brand (Till & Busler 1998). In the Journal of Product and Brand Management, Hayes et al. (2006) mentioned that the packing and displaying of a brand is what helps a customer to purchase a product, hence the attractiveness of a brand has a positive relationship with the consumer's attitude. Therefore, the author can conclude that both brand attractiveness and consumer attitude have a positive relationship among each other.

Hypothesis 2: There is a positive relationship between the loyalty of a brand and customer's attitude.

A study published in 1974 by Sheth and Park argued that there is a comprehensive unanimity among the loyalty towards a brand and customer attitude which links them positively. It also means that brand loyalty is very important for a customer to show positive attitude towards a preferred brand (Sheth & Park 1974). Another study conducted by (Lowe & Corkindale 1998) had a similar opinion and understanding that brand loyalty creates a positive impact on the consumer attitude, regardless of the region (Eastern or Western). Furthermore, this hypothesis is also in congruency with the article published by Kim, Han and Park in 2002, showing a positive correlation between the brand loyalty and consumer attitude. Moreover, in an article published by Oliver in 1999, he also supports the fact that a customer's attitude is directly related to the brand's loyalty.

Hypothesis 3: There is a positive relationship between celebrity endorsement and customer's attitude.

Celebrity affirmations and affiliations create a definite influence on the customer attitude, as stated by Till and Busler (1998), since the celebrities are using those brands as well. The use of celebrity endorsers to improve the sales and brand image is highly followed by big brands, which in term helps them to achieve the consumer attitude through celebrity endorsements (Speck, Schumann & Thompson 1988). One such research published in 1976 by Friedman, Termini and Washington also stated the same fact that celebrity endorsement is absolutely associated to customer attitude, which is then followed by many prominent researchers throughout different decades. Lastly, the author can conclude that celebrity endorsers do have or help in creating a positive impact towards consumer attitude, as illustrated by Amos, Holmes and Strutton (2008) in their respective research. Hence, the formulation of this hypothesis is valid as well.

5   Research Methodology

5.1   Population, Sample Size and Selection

This study will be conducted within the environment of UAE, where the population of the research will be UAE inhabitants, purchasing products of various brands, from different places within UAE. The estimated sample size will be set at 150 respondents, a response anywhere near to such a sample size will be quite good. Furthermore, the participants will be chosen on random basis, utilising the convenience sampling method. As illustrated by Ackoff (1953) in his study, convenience sampling is good for the purpose of this research, as it can help the researcher to overcome many limitations associated with the data collection, especially for this study, where easy access to target unknown individuals is highly recommended (Taherdoost 2018).

5.2   Data Collection

In order to collect the data, the secondary as well as the primary methods will be used. The secondary data collection will help in formulating and gathering the required data for the literature review, hypotheses and the conceptual framework. Various journals in marketing, advertising, management, business review journal and journal of advertising will be used to gather the required information. Supporting the conceptual framework is vital for this research, hence the secondary data will also be utilised for it.

Furthermore, the primary data will consist of a questionnaire with close ended questions format, enabling the respondents to be more convenient and precise with their responses. There will be a proper division of the questionnaire; with the 1st segment covering the demographic characteristics of the respondents, while the 2nd segment will have 5 queries each about the three key concepts being tested for this research. The questions will be based on the format of 5-point Likert scale, with 1 being "strongly disagree" and 5 as "strongly agree". Google forms will be used to formulate the questionnaire and gather the required information for this quantitative study. It will then be distributed across several social media programs like Facebook, Instagram, Linkedin, Whatsapp and so on. The rationale behind using such online platforms is due to the current ongoing pandemic, along with easy access to wider outreach of the targeted population. A timeframe of two (2) months will be set to gather the required data through the questionnaire (Black 1999).

5.3   Data Analysis Method

Once the data is collected, SPSS software will then be used to analyse the collected data. Various tests will be conducted using the same software to find out about the

Reliability, Validity and Correlation of the constructs under investigation. Microsoft Excel will also be used to analyse the descriptive statistics. Furthermore, STATA software will be used to find SEM (Structural Equation Model) and to conduct the over all goodness of fit test for the subjected variables. Furthermore, various sorts of illustrations including tables and graphs will be displayed in this report in order to enable the reader to have a better understanding of the overall analysis (III 2010).

6   Discussion

6.1   Research Gaps

One of the main research gap mentioned for the brand attractiveness is its link with the brand identification, to find out if it is linked directly or has a mediating effect on the brand attractiveness, as highlighted by Kim, Han and Park (2002), since there is not much evidence supporting it. Hence, the author can conclude that it is important to study and examine the impact of brand identification on the brand's attractiveness, to come out with the right knowledge about it.

Furthermore, Kim, Han and Park (2002) pointed out the fact that brand loyalty is another area in relation to repurchasing behaviour or intention that needs further examination and in detailed study to understand its relationship better with the consumer attitude. Therefore, the author is of the view that the information related to brand loyalty and consumer's attitude is still very limited and requires further exploration.

Last but not the least, Argyriou and Melewar (2011) suggested in their research that consumer attitude is a broad area to be investigated, in terms of marketing; therefore, it is important to elaborate further on its relation with celebrity endorsements and brand attractiveness, respectively. Moreover, the above-mentioned gaps also give a clear guideline for the right direction to be chosen if one wants to conduct the research and explore further within the same field.

6.2   Expanding Existing Literature

Sandy Zhang, Van Doorn and Leeflang (2014) are in support of the study published by Kim, Han and Park (2002) that brand identification plays a crucial part in having a strong relation with the brand attractiveness, which creates or makes the brand more famous and sellable to its consumers. However, there are other factors as well that need to be explored to better understand the consumer's attitude.

Furthermore, investigation in the area of customer attitude towards a brand requires more saturated data, as suggested by Bergkvist, Hjalmarson and Mägi (2016) and So et al. (2017). Both these researches have emphasised on the fact that celebrity endorsements and brand attractiveness are not enough to establish a constructive consumer attitude about a brand. Hence, the author is of the view that more exploration within the field of consumer attitude can raise and open more gates to get a better understanding of the issues behind it. Moreover, the theories explained or linked in this study with the chosen variables are also supporting them, which means that there is a need to further explore the theories as well, to get the right information about the other variables that could be supported by different theories in the future.

6.3 Possible Research Questions

By looking at the research gaps, the author came up with the following possible research questions:

- Does brand identification have a mediating influence on brand attractiveness to achieve positive consumer attitude?
- How repurchasing behaviour or intention can assist a consumer in having a positive attitude towards a brand?
- Is it only celebrity endorsements that can establish an impression in the customer's mind or there are other factors as well?

7 Conclusion

The author can conclude that the three variables do seem linked with the dependent variable based on the literature review; however, it will be better if a person can conduct a proper qualitative or quantitative study on it. This will assist in reaching the right conclusion based on the gathered information from the various resources, be it an interview or a questionnaire. The relative theories supporting the variables are also in line with what previous literature has been stating so far. Moreover, the gaps are also in line with the literature review, where it is being supported by the conceptual framework. Lastly, the author recommends doing extensive research and study to come up with the right conclusion while conducting a proper research, including qualitative or quantitative study.

References

ACKOFF, R.L.: The Design of Social Research. University of Chicago Press, Chicago (1953)

Ahearne, M., Bhattacharya, C.B., Gruen, T.: Antecedents and consequences of customer-company identification: expanding the role of relationship marketing. J. Appl. Psychol. **90**(3), 574–585 (2005)

Amos, C., Holmes, G., Strutton, D.: Exploring the relationship between celebrity endorser effects and advertising effectiveness: a quantitative synthesis of effect size. Int. J. Advertising **27**(2), 209–234 (2008)

Argyriou, E., Melewar, T.C.: Consumer attitudes revisited: a review of attitude theory in marketing research. Int. J. Manage. Rev. **13**(4), 431–451 (2011)

Bergkvist, L., Hjalmarson, H., Mägi, A.W.: A new model of how celebrity endorsements work: attitude toward the endorsement as a mediator of celebrity source and endorsement effects. Int. J. Advertising **35**(2), 171–184 (2016)

Bergkvist, L., Zhou, K.Q.: Celebrity endorsements: a literature review and research agenda. Int. J. Advertising **35**(4), 642–663 (2016)

Black, T. R.: Doing Quantitative Research in the Social Sciences: An Integrated Approach to Research Design, Measurement and Statistics, Thousand Oaks (1999)

Eagly, A.H., Chaiken, S.: The Psychology of Attitudes. Harcourt Brace Jovanovich College Publishers, Fort Worth (1993)

Friedman, H.H., Termini, S., Washington, R.: The effectiveness of advertisements utilizing four types of endorsers. J. Advertising **5**(3), 22–24 (1976)

Grewal, R., Mehta, R., Kardes, F.R.: The timing of repeat purchases of consumer durable goods: the role of functional bases of consumer attitudes. J. Mark. Res. (JMR) **41**, 101–115 (2004)

Hasan, A.: Marketing dan Kasus-kasus Pilihan. Center for Academic Publishing Service (CAPS), Yogyakarta (2013)

Hayes, J.B., Alford, B.L., Silver, L., York, R.P.: Looks matter in developing consumer-brand relationships. J. Prod. Brand Manage. **15**(5), 306–315 (2006)

Hurriyati, R., Setiawan, R.: Destination personality analysis on brand attractiveness, brand awareness, and its impact on brand loyalty: a survey research in Indonesia. WSEAS Trans. Bus. Econo. **13**(1), 372–383 (2016)

Wagner III, W.E.: Using SPSS for Social Statistics and Research Methods (2010)

Katz, D.: The functional approach to the study of attitudes. Public Opin. Q. **24**, 163–204 (1960)

Kim, C.K., Han, D., Park, S.-B.: The effects of brand personality and brand identification on brand loyalty: applying the theory of social identification. In: Japanese Psychological Research, vol. 43, no. 4, pp. 195–206 (2002). https://onlinelibrary.wiley.com/doi/full/10.1111/1468–5884.00177

Kim, S.S., Choe, J.Y.J., Petrick, J.F.: The effect of celebrity on brand awareness, perceived quality, brand image, brand loyalty, and destination attachment to a literary festival. J. Destination Mark. Manage. **9**, 320–329 (2018)

Kotler, P.: Marketing Management, Millenium Edition: Custom Edition for University of Phoenix (2002)

Lodi, H.: Red-carpet looks and social-media posts: the truth behind celebrity endorsements. ARTS&CULTURE (2017). https://www.thenational.ae/arts-culture/red-carpet-looks-and-social-media-posts-the-truth-behind-celebrity-endorsements-1.47505

Loi, R., Lam, L.W., Ngo, H.Y., Cheong, S.: Young consumers' insights on brand equity effects of brand association, brand loyalty, brand awareness, and brand image. J. Manag. Psychol., **30**, 645–658 (2015)

Lowe, A.C.T., Corkindale, D.R.: Differences in cultural values and their effects on responses to marketing stimuli: a cross-cultural study between Australians and Chinese from the People's Republic of China. Eur. J. Mark. **32**(9/10), 843–867 (1998)

Mael, F., Ashforth, B.: Alumni and their alma mater: a partial test of the reformulated model of organizational identification. J. Organ. Behav. **13**(2), 103–123 (1992)

McGuire, W.J.: Attitudes and attitude change. Handbook of Social Psychology: Special Fields and Applications (1985)

Mishra, A.S., Roy, S., Bailey, A.A.: Exploring brand personality-celebrity endorser personality congruence in celebrity endorsements in the Indian context. Psychol. Mark. **32**(12), 1158–1174 (2015)

Muda, M., Musa, R., Mohamed, R.N., Borhan, H.: Celebrity entrepreneur endorsement and advertising effectiveness. Procedia – Soc. Behav. Sci. **130**, 11–20 (2014). Elsevier B.V

Oliver, R.L.: Whence consumer loyalty? J. Mark. **63**(May), 33 (1999)

Polyorat, K.: The influence of brand personality dimensions on brand identification and word-of-mouth: the case study of a university brand in Thailand. Asian J. Bus. Res. **1**(1), 54–69 (2011)

Sandy Zhang, S., Van Doorn, J., Leeflang, P.S.H.: Does the importance of value, brand and relationship equity for customer loyalty differ between Eastern and Western cultures? Int. Bus. Rev. **23**(1), 284–292 (2014)

Shavitt, S.: The role of attitude objects in attitude functions. J. Exp. Soc. Psychol. **26**, 124–148 (1990)

Sheth, J.N., Park, C.W.: A Theory of Multidimensional Brand Loyalty. Assoc. Consum. Res., **01**, 449–459 (1974). http://acrwebsite.org/volumes/5729/volumes/v01/NA-01

So, K.K.F., King, C., Hudson, S., Meng, F.: The missing link in building customer brand identification: The role of brand attractiveness. Tour. Manage. **59**, 640–651 (2017). Elsevier Ltd.

Speck, P.S., Schumann, D.W.,Thompson, C.: Celebrity endorsements-scripts, schema and roles: theoretical Framework and Preliminary tests. In: Advances in Consumer Research, vol. 15, pp. 69–76 (1988). http://acrwebsite.org/volumes/6799/volumes/v15/NA-15

Swan, M.: Young people in the UAE not influenced by celebrity endorsements (2014). https://www.thenational.ae/uae/education/young-people-in-the-uae-not-influenced-by-celebrity-endorsements-1.247564

Taherdoost, H.: Sampling Methods in Research Methodology; How to Choose a Sampling Technique for Research. SSRN Electronic Journal, September 2018

Till, B.D., Busler, M.: Matching products with endorsers: attractiveness versus expertise. J. Consum. Mark. **15**(6), 576–586 (1998)

Assessing the Success of the University Information System: A User Multi-group Perspective

Mariusz Grabowski[(⊠)], Jan Madej, and Adam Sagan

Cracow University of Economics, Krakow, Poland
{grabowsm, madejj, sagana}@uek.krakow.pl

Abstract. The purpose of the paper is to identify the key success factors that determine the perception of university information system based on latent dimensions of DeLone and McLean IS Success Models. These dimensions were identified on the basis of empirical data gathered on a sample of 759 university students and staff members. Two-group structural equation sub-models are constructed in the analysis of the measurement equivalence and estimation of two types of models: IS Success Model and Updated IS Success Model with feedback loop. The results show that parameters of IS Success Model differ significantly across groups, indicating the system quality for students, and information quality for staff members, as key factors shaping the satisfaction and individual and organizational impact of university information system. It is also noticeable that it was not possible to estimate sub-models of Updated IS Success Model due to unacceptable values of the stability index.

Keywords: University information system · IS success models · Multigroup SEM

1 Introduction

Computerized information systems (IT/IS) are the subject of many research approaches aiming at assessing the perceived quality, functionality and satisfaction of their users. Apart from its wide business use, IT/IS applications are increasingly used and are important for the functioning of universities and higher education institutions. These include socio-technical systems supporting the learning process, course management systems and its integrated forms like integrated university information systems.

The analysis of perceived effectiveness and success is most often based on attitude-behavior (A-B) models, used to assess the relationship between cognitive and affective dimensions of attitudes and behavior intentions or actual use of the system. These types of models include Theory of Reasoned Action (TRA) [1, 14] and Theory of Planned Behavior (TPB) [2, 3], which serve as the basis for many other behavioral models that were applied in the IT/IS domain. The best-known models are (among others) Technology Acceptance Model (TAM) [10, 11], The Unified Theory of Acceptance and Use of Technology (UTAUT) [32], DeLone and McLean IS Success Model [12] and DeLone and McLean Updated IS Success Model [13].

M. Themistocleous et al. (Eds.): EMCIS 2020, LNBIP 402, pp. 754–768, 2020.
https://doi.org/10.1007/978-3-030-63396-7_51

The aim of the paper is to assess the individual and organizational impact of University Study-Oriented System (USOS) system, resulting from the behavioral models of DeLone and McLean IS Success Model and Updated DeLone and McLean IS Success Model. These models were used to elaborate the relationship between individual and organizational effects and the perceived quality of the USOS system, perceived quality of information in the system, satisfaction and intentions of using the system. Taking into account that the system is used by different users, who have different expectations as to the system functionality, we took a multi-group perspective, in which the evaluation of the relationship between variables in the model is formed by students and staff group (lecturers and administrative staff supporting the education process).

The authors believe that such a comprehensive study of the functioning of the USOS system does not exist in the literature. There are numerous studies that compare DeLone and McLean IS success models conceptually, including DeLone and McLean paper, introducing the updated model [13]. There is, however, noticeable that the studies comparing empirically these models on the same data sample are at least scarce. The authors have had undertaken an excessive literature search[1] and according to the best knowledge, such studies do not exist at all in the university information systems context, which indicates research gap for our research.

In order to answer the research problem, several research questions have been developed:

- RQ1: What is the relationship between system quality and information quality with system use and user satisfaction?
- RQ2: What are the key determinants of individual and organizational impact of the system?
- RQ3: What are the mediation effects of system use and satisfaction?
- RQ4: What is the strength and direction of relationship between factors within particular groups (students and staff)?

Due to the exploratory nature of the research and the lack of existing research results in this regard, no research hypotheses were made, but two propositions were formulated for further testing:

- Satisfaction with the system and use significantly explain (mediate) the relationship between the perceived quality and individual and organizational effects.
- In the group of students there is a stronger relationship between system quality and satisfaction, while in staff group there is a stronger influence of information quality on satisfaction with the use of the USOS system.

The models were estimated using multi-group structural equation model (SEM) with assessment of measurement equivalence across groups. In order to grasp differences between IS success models two types of two-group models were developed. The first

---

[1] The literature query including keywords "DeLone", "McLean", "university" and "comparison" or "comparing", introduced to abstracts of the publications contained in the databases EBSCOhost, Emerald, ScienceDirect, Scopus and Web of Science did not return relevant papers (i.e. comparing both models empirically on the same data sample).

model was recursive DeLone and McLean IS Success Model with individual and organizational impact as the focal dependent variables. The second model was non-recursive (with feedback loop) Updated DeLone and McLean IS Success Model with Net Benefits as a focal dependent variable. The data was gathered through the sample of students and staff at Cracow University of Economics.

2   University Study-Oriented System

Educational institutions, such as universities deal with large volume of information in their organizational processes. The processing of this information is supported by massive automation and computerization of daily tasks. However, there is no universal solution that is commonly used as each university will choose its individual information system implementation. Universities use various classes and types of computerized tools devoted to performing specific tasks. They build heterogenous systems [15, 33] including student and course management system, library and distance learning system to mention the most popular. There are, however, attempts to put together many functions and implement an integrated solution covering various university activities. Integrated solutions are most commonly referenced as University Information Systems [5, 18, 23], Campus Information Systems [7, 27, 28] or Campus-Wide Information Systems [26].

The presented research relates to an integrated university information system implemented at Cracow University of Economics, Krakow, Poland. The University Study-Oriented System (USOS) is an integrated standard software for managing and operating processes related to the study of all levels and forms at the Polish universities (bachelor, master, postgraduate and doctoral studies). The system was launched in 2000 at the University of Warsaw as the result of cooperation between the largest Polish universities. The system is owned by MUCI (Interuniversity Information Center) – a consortium of Polish universities established in 2001. USOS is a non-profit undertaking implemented "by universities for universities." System developers are also its users. Consequently, people deploying the system have the necessary knowledge about processes and procedures in Polish universities. In addition, the universities that have implemented USOS cooperate with each other and provide mutual support – not only in IT/IS dimension, but also in matters related to higher education in general. The last remark is also associated with real influence on the decisions of the Ministry of Science and Higher Education.

The system includes a number of modules that handle various activities such as [8]: recruitment and enrolment, study schedule planning, handling student requests, student thesis archive and management, scholarships, tuition online payment service, and many others. The software is created in Oracle Forms and Java and consists mainly of Web-based applications. In order to integrate with other university systems, developers can also use USOS API, which allows developers to access the central database. Additionally, USOS exchange the data with various external systems (e.g. banking or public administration) enabling, i.a. [20]: managing international exchange (including in the Erasmus Without Paper and NAWA (National Agency for Academic Exchange programs)), export and import of money transfers to banking systems, internal reporting and reporting to the Central Statistical Office (CSO), sending data to The Integrated System of Information on Science and Higher Education POL-on as well as downloading results of high school final exams from the National Register of Matura (KReM). USOS is currently used in 37% of public universities (48 out of 130 all Polish public universities) and is interacted by 57% of all public university students (512 thousand out of 901 thousand) [9].

3 DeLone and McLean IS Success Model

The concept of information system success (IS success) is one of the most vital ideas, ever-present in the IT/IS literature. Its uniqueness comes from the fact that IS success is a complex phenomenon and includes various interrelated factors. It is impossible to judge on IS success purely in monetary categories as other non-material factors are equally important.

The most comprehensive multi-level information success model was for the first time presented by DeLone and McLean [12]. The authors have analyzed 180 papers on IS success published in IT/IS literature and identified six major interdependent success constructs (Fig. 1). They include [12, pp. 64, 66, 68, 69, 74]: System Quality (measure of information processing system itself), Information Quality (measure of information system output), Use (recipient consumption of the output of the information system), User Satisfaction (recipient response to the use of the output of an information system), Individual Impact (the effect of information on the behavior of the recipient) and Organizational Impact (the effect of information on organizational performance). The proposed model is considered to be a process construct including both, temporal and causal effects determining the overall IS success. System Quality and Information Quality jointly influence Use and User Behavior, which are mutually interdependent and together shape Individual Impact. Individual Impact, finely, determine Organizational Impact which is the focal outcome variable of the model.

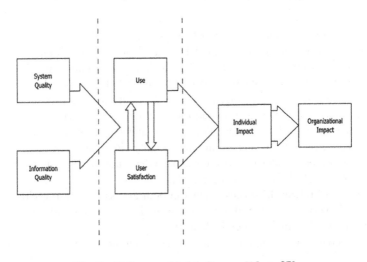

Fig. 1. IS Success Model. Source: [12, p. 87]

Ten years later after DeLone and McLean published their first paper, they published the second paper in which they modified the IS success original model [13] (Fig. 2). This modification was an answer to ongoing discussion present in the IT/IS literature concerning the model improvement.

The modification included several improvements. First, it was adding a new construct – Service Quality in order to measure the quality of the IT/IS service staff. This construct was inspired by a concept of SERVQUAL originating from marketing. Second, they divided original Use construct into two: Intention to Use and Use forming them into one construct. Third, two original constructs: Individual Impact and Organizational Impact were combined into one – Net Benefits, being a focal dependent variable of the model. Fourth, the model introduces the feedback loop connecting Net Benefits as the variable influencing Intention to Use and User satisfaction simultaneously.

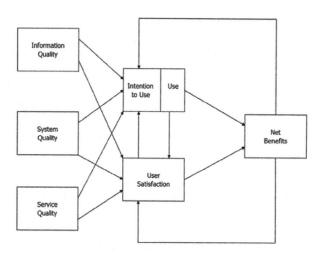

Fig. 2. Updated IS Success Model. Source: [13, p. 24]

Service Quality constitutes the third exogenous variable, together with the two already known from the previous model System Quality and Information Quality variables. They jointly influence User Satisfaction and Intention to Use/Use. User satisfaction strengthen or weakens Intention to Use while Use impact User satisfaction. Intention to Use is linked with exogenous variables (and endogenous User Satisfaction) while Use impacts User Satisfaction and the focal dependent variable – Net Benefits. Finally, Net Benefits influence Intention to Use and User Satisfaction. The original paper on IS success [12], belongs to the most highly cited papers of IT/IS community [30]. The IS success model is still a concept under study and builds the cumulative research tradition of IT/IS discipline [24, 31].

DeLone and McLean IS success model in both the original and modified versions was frequently verified and tested in various scenarios of different information systems implementations. Specific research includes knowledge management [29], information systems implemented in small and medium-sized enterprises (SMEs) [19], electronic brokerage systems in China [6], hospital information systems in a developing country [22], banking sector in Saudi Arabia [16] to mention some examples. The model has also been successfully used in the university information systems context in the developed [17, 25] and developing countries [21, 34].

4   Data and Scales Reliability

The survey was conducted at the Cracow University of Economics on January 16–31, 2020 (the original deadline for the survey availability January 16–24, was extended to January 31). The research frame has included total population of university system users. As the entire population of university employees and students was available, the questionnaires were sent to the entire population of system users (no random selection was made among system users). Technically, a link to the online survey form was sent by email to 10617 system users. Of these, 1279 people (12%) were university employees. Two callbacks (remainder contacts) were use to maximize the response rate. Finally, the survey was completed by 759 people (7.1%) including 643 students, 115 staff and 1 unidentified respondent. It is hard to evaluate whether the sample selected is biased to non-response error, but distribution of the sample approximates the structure of total population. The structure of sample is given in Table 1.

All survey questions were adjusted to USOS specifics and measured on 7-point Likert scale.

As conceptual models take into account latent variables and constitute the system of path relationships between constructs, the empirical estimation and evaluation of the two conceptual models, has involved structural equation modelling with latent variables (SEM). It allowed for a more complete evaluation of the model fit, assessment of measurement equivalence in multi-group analysis, evaluation of the reliability of scales based on the confirmatory factor analysis model, estimation of path coefficients and testing the mediation effects between constructs. Below are the measurement characteristics of the analysed constructs

System Quality construct was measured by 5 items: 1/ "The system is well adapted to my needs" (mean = 3.65, std. dev. = 1.66, alpha if deleted = 0.84, item-total correlation = 0.79), 2/ "The system is generally easy to use" (mean = 3.74, std. dev. = 1.82, alpha if deleted = 0.85, item-total correlation = 0.78), 3/ "The system has all the important functions" (mean = 3.70, std. dev. = 1.66, alpha if deleted = 0.87, item-total correlation = 0.67), 4/"The system is reliable" (mean = 2.93, std. dev. = 1.66, alpha if deleted = 0.89, item-total correlation = 0.60), 5/"It is easy to adapt to the specificity of the system" (mean = 3.69, std. dev. = 1.83, alpha if deleted = 0.85, item-total correlation = 0.77). The Cronbach's alpha = 0,885, rho reliability coefficient = 0.889, greatest lower bound reliability = 0.920, Bentler's dimension-free lower bound reliability = 0.920 and Shapiro's lower bound reliability for a weighted composite = 0.933. The optimal short scale consists of item 1, item 2, item 3 and item 5.

Information Quality construct was measured by 5 items: 1/ "The information in the system is complete" (mean = 3.48, std. dev. = 1.75, alpha if deleted = 0.83, item-total correlation = 0.75), 2/ "The information in the system is timely" (mean = 3.98, std. dev. = 1.72, alpha if deleted = 0.83, item-total correlation = 0.75), 3/ "The

Table 1. The structure of sample

Age	Below 20	21–30	31–40	41–50	51–60	61–70	Above 70
	17%	66%	4%	8%	3%	1%	1%
Gender	**Females**	**Males**					
	67%	33%					
Study type	**Regular students**	**Part time students**	**(Staff)**				
	52%	34%	(14%)				
Study level	**Under-graduate**	**Graduate**	**Doctoral**	**Unified master**	**(Staff)**		
	46%	37%	1%	2%	(14%)		
Study year	**1st year**	**2nd year**	**3rd year**	**4th year**	**5th year**	**(Staff)**	
	36%	34%	1%	4%	10%	(14%)	
Position	**Students**	**Administra-tive staff**	**Professors**	**Adjuncts**	**Lecturers**	**Others**	
	86%	3%	3%	4%	3%	1%	
Education	**Primary**	**Secondary**	**Higher**				
	2%	46%	52%				

information in the system is tailored to my personal needs" (mean = 3.62, std. dev. = 1.64, alpha if deleted = 0.81, item-total correlation = 0.81), 4/ "The information contained in the system is clear to me" (mean = 4.13, std. dev. = 1.72, alpha if deleted = 0.85, item-total correlation = 0.65), 5/ "The information in the system is securely stored" (mean = 4.59, std. dev. = 1.44, alpha if deleted = 0.88, item-total correlation = 0.52). The Cronbach's alpha = 0.871, rho reliability coefficient = 0.880, greatest lower bound reliability = 0.906, Bentler's dimension-free lower bound reliability = 0.906 and Shapiro's lower bound reliability for a weighted composite = 0.923. The optimal short scale consists of item 1, item 2 and item 3.

System Use construct was measured by 5 items: 1/ "I use the system almost every day" (mean = 2.66, std. dev. = 1.70, alpha if deleted = 0.61, item-total correlation = 0.52), 2/ "I use the system at all times regardless of the time of day" (mean = 3.83, std. dev. = 2.16, alpha if deleted = 0.61, item-total correlation = 0.51), 3/ "Navigation on the system's web pages is easy" (mean = 3.63, std. dev. = 1.78, alpha if deleted = 0.61, item-total correlation = 0.51), 4/ "I feel even addicted to the system" (mean = 1.56, std. dev. = 1.25, alpha if deleted = 0.68, item-total correlation = 0.35), 5/ "The system can be used on many devices (computer, tablet, smartphone)" (mean = 4.86, std. dev. = 1.73, alpha if deleted = 0.68, item-total correlation = 0.35). The Cronbach's alpha = 0,690, rho reliability coefficient = 0.704, greatest lower bound reliability = 0.766, Bentler's dimension-free lower bound reliability = 0.766 and Shapiro's lower bound reliability for a weighted composite = 0.775. All of 5 items are included in optimal scale (item 1 - item 5).

User Satisfaction construct was measured by 4 items: 1/ "I intend to constantly use the system" (mean = 3.62, std. dev. = 1.78, alpha if deleted = 0.86, item-total correlation = 0.72), 2/ "Generally, the system is worth recommending to anyone who has a relationship with the University" (mean = 3.54, std. dev. = 1.89, alpha if deleted = 0.82, item-total correlation = 0.81), 3/ "I feel satisfied that the system is implemented at my University" (mean = 3.78, std. dev. = 1.93, alpha if deleted = 0.81, item-total correlation = 0.84), 4/ "If the system stopped working it would be discomfort for me" (mean = 3.90, std. dev. = 1.97, alpha if deleted = 0.90, item-total correlation = 0.62). The Cronbach's alpha = 0,882, rho reliability coefficient = 0.887, greatest lower bound reliability = 0.908, Bentler's dimension-free lower bound reliability = 0.908 and Shapiro's lower bound reliability for a weighted composite = 0.931. The optimal short scale consists of item 2 and item 3.

Individual Impact was measured by 5 items: 1/ "The system increases the quality of my work/study" (mean = 3.04, std. dev. = 1.75, alpha if deleted = 0.89, item-total correlation = 0.81), 2/ "I achieve better results (work/learning) thanks to the system" (mean = 2.31, std. dev. = 1.47, alpha if deleted = 0.90, item-total correlation = 0.76), 3/ "The system allows more efficient decision making in my work/study" (mean = 2.91, std. dev. = 1.74, alpha if deleted = 0.89, item-total correlation = 0.84), 4/ "Thanks to the system, I achieve my goals related to work/studying faster" (mean = 2.72, std. dev. = 1.67, alpha if deleted = 0.88, item-total correlation = 0.87), 5/ "I save time by using the system" (mean = 3.82, std. dev. = 2.06, alpha if deleted = 0.92, item-total correlation = 0.69). The Cronbach's alpha = 0,916, rho reliability coefficient = 0.918, greatest lower bound reliability = 0.940, Bentler's dimension-free lower bound reliability = 0.940 and Shapiro's lower bound reliability for a weighted composite = 0.947. The optimal short scale consists of item 1, item 2 item 3 and item 4.

Organizational Impact was measured by 5 items: 1/ "The system reduces the operating costs of the University" (mean = 4.02, std. dev. = 1.54, alpha if deleted = 0.81, item-total correlation = 0.73), 2/ "The system allows attracting new students to the University" (mean = 3.23, std. dev. = 1.66, alpha if deleted = 0.84, item-total correlation = 0.63), 3/ "The system enables additional income for the University" (mean = 3.42, std. dev. = 1.40, alpha if deleted = 0.83, item-total correlation = 0.65), 4/ "The system shortens queues to the dean's office" (mean = 4.43, std. dev. = 1.92, alpha if deleted = 0.85, item-total correlation = 0.62), 5/ "The system reduces student service costs" (mean = 4.20, std. dev. = 1.62, alpha if deleted = 0.81, item-total correlation = 0.75). The Cronbach's alpha = 0,858, rho reliability coefficient = 0.861, greatest lower bound reliability = 0.902, Bentler's dimension-free lower bound reliability = 0.902 and Shapiro's lower bound reliability for a weighted composite = 0.916. All of 5 items are included in optimal scale (item 1 - item 5).

Service Quality construct was removed from the final scale because the USOS system does not enable the direct contact of end users (students and staff) with service providers (staff in IT department). Therefore, the items concerning service quality, credibility, empathy of service providers and reactivity are not valid in this case.

5   Comparison of USOS Success Models

5.1   Measurement Equivalence of Constructs

In multi-group analysis, the comparison of latent variables means, and variances requires the valid assumption of measurement equivalence. There are three levels of measurement equivalence – configural (congeneric), metric and scalar. In configural equivalence, constructs (latent factors) should be characterized by the same pattern of loadings across groups. In metric (weak) equivalence, each item should have the same factor loadings across groups (the contribution of items to the latent construct is the same). In scalar (strong) equivalence, the item intercepts should be equivalent in the groups.

Table 2. Tests of measurement invariance; Source: own based on Mplus 8.1

	Chi_Square, df, P-level	CFI, TLI	RMSEA
Configural model	1566.59, 388, 0.00	0.898, 0.871	0.090 (0.085-0.094)
Metric model	1591.35, 404, 0.00	0.888, 0.872	0.088 (0.084-0.093)
Scalar model	1728.40, 420, 0.00	0.876, 0.864	0.091 (0.086-0.095)
Metric vs. Configural	20.26, 16, 0.218	–	–
Scalar vs. Configural	165.11, 32, 0.000	–	–
Scalar vs. Metric	143.99, 16, 0.000	–	–

Additionally, the residual (strict) equivalence assumes the equality of residuals across groups. The two-group (students vs. staff) confirmatory factor analysis of IS success sub-models with invariance testing is given in Table 2.

The CFA model's goodness-of-fit is not so good. The Chi-Square test is significant (that means the rejection of exact fit). Comparative fit index (CFI) and Tucker-Lewis Index (TLI) seem to be too low and below the acceptance thresholds of 0.9. The Root Mean Square Error of Approximation (RMSEA) is near the level of approximate fit (0.08). The measurement invariance comparison indicates that the weak equivalence hypothesis is supported. The metric model is insignificantly worse than the configural one ($p > 0.05$). Comparison of scalar vs. metric enables to reject the hypothesis concerning strong measurement equivalence. Because metric equivalence is established, therefore it is possible to compare the structural sub-models across groups.

5.2   Comparison of Multi-group Models

Two empirical models (two sub-models for each model) were developed: IS Success Model and Updated IS Success Model. Having reliable and equivalent latent variable indicators, only structural parts of these models are presented and developed. IS Success Model, as is given in Fig. 1, has involved six constructs: System Quality (qual), Information Quality (qualinf), System Use (use), User Satisfaction (sat), Individual Impact (indimp) and Organizational Impact (orgimp). The structure of the sub-models, path coefficients and their standard errors (in brackets) for student and staff groups are given in Figs. 3 and 4.

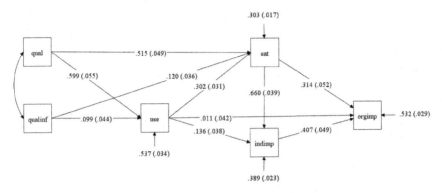

Fig. 3. Multi-group Structural IS Success Model – students group sub-model

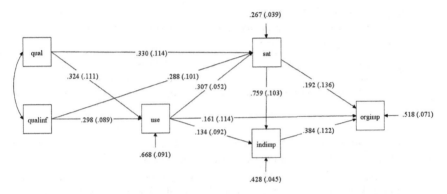

Fig. 4. Multi-group Structural IS Success Model – staff group sub-model

Chi-Square Test of Model Fit = 35.413, with 8° of freedom and p-level = 0.000. Scaling Correction Factor for MLR estimation method = 1.1570. Chi-Square contribution from student group is 22.017 and from staff group is 13.396. Comparative fit indices CFI/TLI are respectively 0.987 and 0.955. The RMSEA (Root Mean Square Error of Approximation) equals 0.095 (0.064–0.128). The SRMR (Standardized Root Mean Square Residual) equals 0.030.

Because of unequal group sizes, the standard error of the estimates was calculated using residual parametric Bollen-Stine bootstrap method with 500 bootstrap draws. In students' group, in comparison to staff group, there are relatively stronger relationships between System Quality and User Satisfaction (r = 0.515), System Quality and System Use (r = 0.599). The User Satisfaction has also a stronger relationship with Organizational Impact (r = 0.314).

In staff group, there is significant and stronger relationship between Information Quality and System Use (r = 0.298) and Information Quality and User Satisfaction (r = 0.288). System Use has also the significant and relatively strong relationship with Organizational Impact (r = 0.161).

The above results give the answers to RQ1 and RQ4.

5.3   Mediation Analysis

The path model contains several indirect paths and provides the answers to RQ2 and RQ3. Table 3 contains the significant parameters of total and specific indirect effects within the students' group.

Table 3. Mediation analysis of IS Success Model – student group

Effects from qual to orgimp			
	Estimate	Std. Err.	P-level
Total effect	0.446	0.032	0.000
qual-sat-orgimp specific indirect effect	0.162	0.030	0.000
qual-use-sat-orgimp specific indirect effect	0.057	0.012	0.000
qual-use-indimp-orgimp specific indirect effect	0.033	0.010	0.000
qual-sat-indimp-orgimp specific indirect effect	0.139	0.02	0.000
qual-use-sat-indimp-orgimp indirect effect	0.049	0.01	0.000
Effects from qualinf to orgimp			
	Estimate	Std. Err.	P-level
Total effect	0.094	0.026	0.000
qualinf-sat-orgimp specific indirect effect	0.038	0.014	0.009

The qual-orgimp and qualinf-orgimp total effects are significant for the students' group. The strongest specific indirect effect is related to qual-sat-orgimp and qual-sat-indimp-orgimp paths. Therefore, the User Satisfaction and Individual Impact significantly explain respectively the 36.3% and 31.2% of total effect in the relationship between Service Quality and Organizational Impact. On the other hand, the total effect for qualinf-orgimp is much weaker, but User Satisfaction explains the 40.4% of total effect between Information Quality and Organizational Impact.

Table 4 presents the significant parameters of total and specific indirect effects within the staff group.

Table 4. Mediation analysis of IS Success Model – staff group

Effects from qual to orgimp			
	Estimate	Std. Err.	P-level
Total effect	0.276	0.069	0.000
qual-sat-indimp-orgimp specific indirect effect	0.096	0.041	0.018
qual-use-sat-indimp-orgimp indirect effect	0.029	0.014	0.040
Effects from qualif to orgimp			
	Estimate	Std. Err.	P-level
Total effect	0.247	0.072	0.000
qualinf-sat-indimp-orgimp specific indirect effect	0.084	0.035	0.016

The qual-orgimp and qualinf-orgimp total effects are significant for the staff group. The strongest specific indirect effect is related to qual-sat-indimp-orgimp and qual-use-sat-indimp-orgimp paths. Therefore, the User Satisfaction/Individual Impact and System Use/User Satisfaction/Individual Impact significantly explains respectively the 34.8% and 10.51% of total effect in the relationship between Service Quality and Organizational Impact. The total effect for qualinf-orgimp is similar and User Satisfaction and Individual Impact explains the 34.0% of total effect between Information Quality and Organizational Impact among staff group.

The focal dependent variable of the Updated IS Success Model, as is given in Fig. 2, has direct feedback loop to User Satisfaction and System Use. The novelty of this model is to estimate parameters for non-recursive models. In order to solve simultaneous equation system with feedback loop, the stability indices were computed. The stability index is computed as the maximum modulus of the eigenvalues for the matrix of coefficients on endogenous variables predicting other endogenous variables. The results are stable if the eigenvalues of the coefficient matrix lie inside the unit circle [4]. However, the eigenvalue stability condition analysis of simultaneous equation systems showed that the stability index in the student group was equal to 6.601 and in the staff' group was equal to 5.192. Both sub-models (for students and staff groups) do not satisfy stability condition, therefore parameter estimations were unstable, and sub-models could not be estimated. For this reason, we were unable to evaluate the differences represented in both models. It should be, however, noted that it is unclear whether inability of Updated IS Success Model estimation was caused by the model itself or the character of our data. This opens the research direction which we are going to explore in the future.

6   Conclusions and Limitations

Original DeLone and McLean IS Success Model and Updated DeLone and McLean IS Success Model are very interesting theoretical frameworks for the measurement of components of IS perceptual effects of use. The Updated IS Success Model with feedback loop, although very interesting from a conceptual point of view, it was not correctly estimated in our study due to stability problems (stability index above 1). Service Quality was not used in the updated model because of specificity of the system, however, it would have no impact on instability of the model. As already stated, we want to explore this issue on the other data collections. We are going to examine what causes the model instability, the data or the model attributes (non-recursiveness).

Having the results of original USOS IS Success Model (both sub-models), we can conclude that among the students the system quality is the key factor that shapes students' satisfaction with USOS and USOS use, whereas among the staff members it is the information quality of USOS that has a crucial role for staff satisfaction and use of USOS (answers to RQ1 and RQ4). Students' satisfaction depends more on general characteristics of the system (adaptation, easiness of use, key features, system reliability). Among the staff members, user satisfaction is more related to informational content (completeness, timeliness, accuracy, understanding and information security). In both groups individual impact is significantly related to satisfaction and system use.

Finally, in the students' group, organizational impact is (in comparison to the staff group) more linked to satisfaction and individual impact. On the other hand, in the staff group organizational impact depends on system use (answer to RQ2).

The tested propositions were verified. Satisfaction with the system and use significantly explain (mediate) the relationship between the perceived system and information quality with individual and organizational effects (answer to RQ3). In the students' group there is a stronger relationship between system quality and satisfaction, while in the staff group, there is a stronger influence of information quality on satisfaction with the use of the USOS system.

The presented study has several limitations and we propose some suggestions for further research. Although, the USOS has relatively long tradition at universities, no excessive research was undertaken to assess the functionality and satisfaction with the system. Further development of domain-specific theories in the area of university information system are needed to be more grounded into empirical research and specifically SEM modelling. The sources of failure of non-recursive model estimation are not identified yet. It might be due to either one-university sample specificity, or specification error of theoretical model.

The proposed model was estimated on relatively large sample taken from only one university (Cracow University of Economics). Higher education system in Poland is very diverse (private and public universities of economics, general universities, polytechnics, etc.), therefore national complex sample is needed to ensure external validity of the model. Also, both student and staff samples need to be stratified due to possible heterogeneity of both populations. Students' needs and USOS use may be related to the enrolment status (full time vs. part time), experience in use (freshmen vs. graduates). Staff member should be divided at least into lecturers (scientists) and support staff (front-office and back-office). However, having in mind the level of standardization and comparability of USOS systems across universities, the results show some insightful and fruitful hints for identification of determinants of its individual and organizational impact.

Acknowledgements. The Project has been financed by the Ministry of Science and Higher Education within "Regional Initiative of Excellence" Programme for 2019-2022. Project no.: 021/RID/2018/19. Total financing: 11 897 131,40 PLN.

References

1. Ajzen, I., Fishbein, M.: Understanding Attitudes and Predicting Social Behavior. Prentice-Hall, Englewood Cliffs, NJ (1980)
2. Ajzen, I.: From intentions to actions: a theory of planned behavior. In: Kuhl, J., Beckmann, J. (eds.) Action Control. SSSSP, pp. 11–39. Springer, Heidelberg (1985). https://doi.org/10.1007/978-3-642-69746-3_2
3. Ajzen, I.: The theory of planned behavior. Organ. Behav. Hum. Decis. Process. **50**(2), 179–211 (1991)
4. Bentler, P.M., Freeman, E.H.: Tests for stability in linear structural equation systems. Psychometrika **48**, 143–145 (1983)

5. Bentley, Y., Cao, G., Lehaney, B.: The application of critical systems thinking to enhance the effectiveness of a university information system. Syst. Pract. Action Res. **26**(5), 451–465 (2013). https://doi.org/10.1007/s11213-012-9253-9

6. Chen, G.: The use of electronic brokerage systems in China: a modified e-commerce model. Can. J. Adm. Sci. **29**(1), 99–109 (2012)

7. Cobarsí, J., Bernardo, M., Coenders, G.: Campus information systems for students: classification in Spain. Campus-Wide Inf. Syst. **25**(1), 50–64 (2008)

8. Czerniak, M., Mincer-Daszkiewicz, J.: Uniwersytecki System Obsługi Studiów. Dokumentacja wdrożeniowa, Międzyuniwersyteckie Centrum Informatyzacji (2017). https://www.usos.edu.pl/sites/default/files/pl-usos-dokumentacja-wdrozeniowa_0.pdf. Accessed 10 Feb 2020

9. Czerniak, M.: Uniwersytecki System Obsługi Studiów w liczbach – stan na 31.12.2018. Międzyuniwersyteckie Centrum Informatyzacji (2019). https://www.usos.edu.pl/system/files/pdf/2020-USOS_w_liczbach_0.pdf. Accessed 10 Feb 2020

10. Davis, F.D., Bagozzi, R.P., Warshaw, P.R.: User acceptance of computer technology: a comparison of two theoretical models. Manage. Sci. **35**(8), 982–1003 (1989)

11. Davis, F.D.: Perceived usefulness, perceived ease of use, and user acceptance of information technology. MIS Q. **13**(3), 319–340 (1989)

12. DeLone, W.H., McLean, E.R.: Information systems success: the quest for the dependent variable. Inf. Syst. Res. **3**(1), 60–95 (1992)

13. DeLone, W.H., McLean, E.R.: The DeLone and McLean model of information systems success: a ten-year update. J. Manage. Inf. Syst. **19**(4), 9–30 (2003)

14. Fishbein, M., Ajzen, I.: Belief, Attitude, Intention, and Behavior: An Introduction to Theory and Research. Addison-Wesley, MA (1975)

15. Humphrey, M., Wasson, G.: The University of Virginia campus grid: integrating grid technologies with the campus information infrastructure. In: Sloot, P.M.A., Hoekstra, A.G., Priol, T., Reinefeld, A., Bubak, M. (eds.) EGC 2005. LNCS, vol. 3470, pp. 50–58. Springer, Heidelberg (2005). https://doi.org/10.1007/11508380_7

16. Jaafreh, A.B.: Evaluation information system success: applied DeLone and McLean information system success model in context banking system in KSA. Int. Rev. Manage. Bus. Res. **6**(2), 829–845 (2017)

17. Kim, K., Trimi, S., Park, H., Rhee, S.: The impact of CMS quality on the outcomes of e-learning systems in higher education: an empirical study. Deci. Sci. J. Innovative Educ. **10**(4), 575–587 (2012)

18. Kresimir, R., Marijana, B., Vlado, M.: Development of the intelligent system for the use of university information system. Procedia Eng. **69**, 402–409 (2014)

19. Lee, J.S., Kwon, Y.: Exploring key factors of application software services and their relationships for organizational success in SMEs. J. Small Bus. Manage. **52**(4), 753–770 (2014)

20. Mincer-Daszkiewicz, J.: Zintegrowane narzędzia informatyczne w projekcie USOS, Międzyuniwersyteckie Centrum Informatyzacji (2019). https://www.usos.edu.pl/sites/default/files/USOS6–5-0-All_0.pdf. Accessed 10 Feb 2020

21. Mtebe, J.S., Raisamo, R.: A model for assessing learning management system success in higher education in sub-saharan countries. Electron. J. Inf. Syst. Developing Countries **61**(7), 1–17 (2014)

22. Ojo, A.I.: Validation of the DeLone and McLean information systems success model. Healthc. Inform. Res. **23**(1), 60–66 (2017)

23. Özturan, M., Bozanta, A., Basarir-Ozel, B., Akar, E.: A roadmap for an integrated university information system based on connectivity issues: case of Turkey. Int. J. Manage. Sci. Inf. Technol. (IJMSIT), **17**, 1–22 (2015)

24. Petter, S., DeLone, W., McLean, E.: Measuring information systems success: models, dimensions, measures, and interrelationships. Eur. J. Inf. Syst. **17**(3), 236–263 (2008)
25. Rai, A., Lang, S., Welker, R.: Assessing the validity of IS success models: an empirical test and theoretical analysis. Inf. Syst. Res. **13**(1), 50–69 (2002)
26. Rothnie, L.: Campus wide information system development at three UK universities. Vine **23**(4), 18–30 (1993)
27. Saito, Y., Matsuo, T.: Decision support system based on computational collective intelligence in campus information systems. In: Nguyen, N.T., Kowalczyk, R. (eds.) Transactions on Computational Collective Intelligence II. LNCS, vol. 6450, pp. 108–122. Springer, Heidelberg (2010). https://doi.org/10.1007/978-3-642-17155-0_6
28. Sant-Geronikolou, S., Martínez-Ávila, D.: Prospects of library use data integration in campus information systems: a glocalized perspective. El profesional de la información, **28** (4) (2019). https://doi.org/10.3145/epi.2019.jul.10
29. Sarkheyli, A., Song, W.W.: Delone and McLean IS success model for evaluating knowledge sharing. In: Hacid, H., Sheng, Q., Yoshida, T., Sarkheyli, A., Zhou, R. (eds.), Data Quality and Trust in Big Data, Springer Nature Switzerland AG, pp. 125–136 (2019)
30. Straub, D.: Editor's comments: does MIS have native theories? MIS Q. **36**(2), iii–xii (2012)
31. Urbach, N., Müller, B.: The updated DeLone and McLean model of information systems success. In: Dwivedi, Y.K. et al. (eds.), Information Systems Theory: Explaining and Predicting Our Digital Society, Vol. 1, Integrated Series in Information Systems 28, Springer Science + Business Media, (2012). http://doi.org/10.1007/978-1-4419-6108-2_1
32. Venkatesh, V., Morris, M.G., Davis, G.B., Davis, F.D.: User acceptance of information technology: toward a unified view. MIS Q. **27**(3), 425–478 (2003)
33. Wang, F., Jia, Z.: Constructing digital campus using campus smart card system, instrumentation, measurement. In: Zhang, T. (ed.) Circuits and Systems. AISC 127, pp. 19–26. Springer-Verlag, Berlin Heidelberg (2012). https://doi.org/10.1007/978-3-642-27334-6_3
34. Yakubu, N., Dasuki, S.: Assessing eLearning systems success in Nigeria: an application of the DeLone and McLean information systems success model. J. Inf. Technol. Educ. Res. **17**, 183–203 (2018)

IS Project Management Success in Developing Countries

João Varajão[1] , António Trigo[1,2(✉)] , Isabel Moura[1] , and José Luís Pereira[1]

[1] Centro ALGORITMI, University of Minho, 4804-533 Guimarães, Portugal
{varajao,icm,jlmp}@dsi.uminho.pt, antonio.trigo@gmail.com
[2] Polytechnic Institute of Coimbra, ISCAC, Quinta Agrícola, Bencanta,
3040-316 Coimbra, Portugal

Abstract. The management of Information Systems (IS) projects occupies a prominent place in research given the need for continuously improve projects efficiency and efficacy. In the case of developing countries, this is even more important because projects success rates are typically lower than those of the so-called developed countries. Projects success is vital to development, because the countries not only need to use the scarce resources available in the best possible way, but also must gain trust from populations and investors to continue ensuring financing for future projects. Note that developing countries' governments many times depend on foreign investment to undertake large projects, for instance in the construction or IS infrastructure sectors. However, there are few known studies about the success of IS projects in developing countries. To help fill this gap, we carried out a questionnaire-based survey in four countries. The focus of our survey was on IS projects from the public sector. This enabled to identify quite low levels of success, as well as an urgent need for training and education programmes on project management.

Keywords: Information systems · Project management · Developing countries · Public sector

1 Introduction

Information Technology (IT) and Information Systems (IS) project management is one of the most researched topics, appearing in the fourth place in a study by Kwak and Anabari [1] on the most important research disciplines in the last 50 years in top project management journals. One of the main concerns is on how to ensure that projects are successful (which includes topics and lines of research related to success factors, the success of project management, the success of deliverables, among others) [2–4].

However, most of this research is on the private sector [5] and so-called developed countries [6, 7]. Developing countries (in contrast to such countries) have many limitations and specificities. For instance, in these countries resources are very scarce; and thus, developing countries depend on external financing to undertake large infrastructure projects [7, 8] such as projects on IS infrastructures [9, 10]. Typically, these projects involve the countries' governments.

© Springer Nature Switzerland AG 2020
M. Themistocleous et al. (Eds.): EMCIS 2020, LNBIP 402, pp. 769–780, 2020.
https://doi.org/10.1007/978-3-030-63396-7_52

In developing countries, the successful management of projects (which is perceived as having high failure rates [10–12]) is even more important, since it influences the capability for obtaining more funding to conduct new projects. Thus, it is important to characterize the success that has been achieved in IS projects and to identify the aspects that may hinder their success (e.g., the lack of project management practices) [10, 13–15].

Acknowledging the gap in the literature and eventual shortcomings of developing countries in IS project management is essential to help identify further research opportunities so the practices and culture of management can be improved in these demanding contexts. Therefore, we have defined the following research question: "what are the levels of success that have been achieved in the management of IS projects carried out in the public sector of developing countries?" To help answer our question, we carried out a questionnaire-based survey with senior public servants in the IS area from four developing countries (Cape Verde; Guinea-Bissau; São Tomé and Príncipe; and East Timor). The unit of analysis was the project.

The rest of the paper is structured as follows. Section 2 presents the background and related research. Then, Sect. 3 presents the research method. Section 4 presents and discusses the results. Finally, Sect. 5 presents some final considerations, main contributions, and directions for future work.

2 Background and Related Research

2.1 IS Project Management Success

Success in project management has been the subject of extensive research over the last years [16, 17], with IS being one of the main areas of interest [18] given their historical failure rate. Notwithstanding the increasing success of IS projects in recent years [12], it continues to be lower than desirable [19, 20]. For instance, regarding software development projects, the success rate has improved from 16.2% in 1994 [21] to 35% in the period of 2015-20 [22]. Another recent study, by the Project Management Institute (PMI), shows that a change is taking place in the way organizations approach project management. That is, organizations have been investing more and more in good management practices. This in turn has led to a considerable increase in success [23].

Project success and its management began to be studied in a more systemized way by the end of the eighties [24]. Along time, the studies presented new perspectives on project management including: (1) the definition of the Iron Triangle [25]; (2) the difference between the project's success and success of the project management [26, 27]; or (3) the identification of success factors for projects [28, 29]. As a result, new criteria emerged for the projects' success such as [24] the realization of client organization's strategic objectives and the satisfaction of end-users or other stakeholders.

Recent work points out to multiple criteria for evaluating IS project management success (and to some attempts of formalizing this evaluation [3, 30–34]) such as adherence to budget (cost), adherence to schedule (time), meeting functional and non-functional requirements (quality), process efficiency, client satisfaction, contractor satisfaction, and the end-users use of the system [35, 36].

2.2 IS Project Management Success in Developing Countries

United Nations define developing countries as those that have a Human Development Index below 0.8 (HDI < 0.800) [37]. According to their HDI value, these countries are further categorized as having a [37] low (HDI < 0.550), medium (0.550 < HDI < 0.699), or high (0.700 < HDI < 0.799) human development.

Developing countries differ from developed ones in several ways, as they often have, for instance [7, 10, 38, 39]: young working-age population; low-cost labour; rural life; poor income; gender gap; corruption; lack of Science, Technology, Education and Mathematics (STEM) education; and/or poor IT/IS literacy. Because of this, the scientific community has lines of research dedicated to developing countries in various research domains. It should be noted that these countries have come a long way in recent years and are trying to catch up in terms of IT/IS infrastructures and skills. However, they are still far behind with developed countries [15].

In general, developing countries projects' success rates are lower than developed countries [10]. Regarding IS projects in developing countries, governmental ones stand out as they are often financed by external countries. One example is China's investment to improve IT/IS access and connectivity in Africa [8]. Several others (e.g. "Enabling Digital Cape Verde and the Regional ICT Hub" in Cape Verde, worth 20 million dollars) are examples of projects financed by the International Monetary Fund (IMF) or the World Bank [40]. Funding for new projects, crucial to these countries' development, depends on the success of current projects [9].

Examples of related IS project management research topics are the existing gaps between developing and developed countries. Some of these gaps are in poor management practices (e.g. processes, tools and techniques), project managers competencies deficiencies, team members' insufficient skills and knowledge in IT, and poor project management maturity or poor risk management [10, 13–15]. As far as project management success is concerned, researchers' interests have been more focused on the identification of Critical Success Factors [11, 41–44]. To the best of our knowledge, there are currently no studies that report the success of IS projects in the public sector of developing countries. One exception is the study by Heeks [45], which states that only 15% of the projects are a success. But it focuses solely on eGovernment initiatives. Our study addresses this gap in the literature.

3 Method

The study involved a questionnaire-based survey administered to senior public servants in the IS field from the following countries: Cape Verde; Guinea-Bissau; São Tomé and Príncipe; and East Timor. We selected these countries because it was possible for us to collect data in person. Confidentiality of responses was ensured. We collected a total of 103 responses. Out of these 87 were valid. Table 1 shows demographic data from our sample.

Table 1. Respondents' characterization

	Frequency	Percent
Country		
Cape Verde	29	33.33
Guinea-Bissau	24	27.59
São Tomé and Príncipe	20	22.99
East Timor	14	16.09
Gender		
Male	61	70.11
Female	26	29.89
Age		
25–30	14	16.09
31–40	39	44.83
>40	19	21.84
DNK/NO	15	17.24
Organizational role		
Director (CIO/CTO/IT/Other)	25	28.74
Technical	18	20.69
Programmer	8	9.20
Analyst	6	6.90
Project Manager	3	3.45
Other	27	31.04
Academic degree		
Bachelor (three years)	5	5.75
Post-Bologna Degree (three years)	17	19.54
Pre-Bologna Degree (four/five years)	39	44.83
Postgraduate studies	6	6.90
Masters	10	11.49
PhD	1	1.15
Undergraduate	9	10.35
Experience in Project Management (years)		
<2	50	57.47
2–5	10	11.49
>5	5	5.75

(*continued*)

Table 1. (*continued*)

	Frequency	Percent
DNK/NO	22	25.29
Training in Project Management		
Yes	7	8.05
No	80	91.95

DNK/NO – Do not know/No opinion/No answer.

Regarding respondents' characteristics, about 70% of the participants are male and the majority (more than 66%) is over 30 years old (see Table 1). Concerning respondents' position in the organization, almost 30% have management roles, and more than 35% are analysts, programmers, or technicians. As for academic qualification, only about 10% have no higher education. In general, experience in project management is considerably low. The training in project management is also very limited, since only 8% of the participants mentioned it.

Table 2 shows the demographic characterization of our participants' organizations. Most organizations belong to the central administration (63.22%) and have a relatively low number of collaborators (up to 200 in 60.92% of the cases). It should also be noted that a Project Management Office (PMO) or similar does not exist in most of these organizations (83.91%). Literature suggests this as a success factor for project management success in developing countries [11].

Table 2. Characterization of respondent's organizations

	Frequency	Percent
Number of employees in the organization		
1 to 200	53	60.92
>201	6	6.90
DNK/NO	28	31.18
Organization type		
Local Administration	8	9.20
Central Administration	55	63.22
Other types of Administration	24	27.58
Project Management Office (or similar)		
Yes	14	16.09
No	73	83.91

DNK/NO – Do not know/No opinion.

Table 3 shows the global practice of project management in these organizations, where a general shortage of project management culture and project management practices can be noticed.

Table 3. Project management practices in the organizations

	Frequency	Percent
Approach/Methodology		
PMBOK	0	0.00
PRINCE2	0	0.00
Other (internal)	18	20.69
No formal methodology is used	69	79.31
Maturity Models in Project Management		
Yes	0	0.00
No	28	32.18
DNK/NO	59	67.82
Software for Project Management		
Yes	16	18.39
No	59	67.82
DNK/NO	12	13.79
If so, which one?		
MS Project	11	68.8
Other	5	31.2

DNK/NO – Do not know/No opinion.

4   Results and Discussion

Participants were asked about the last project they participated in, as shown in Table 4. It is worth mentioning the notorious difficulty participants felt characterizing projects: more than half of them were unable to indicate the type, duration, or budget of the project.

With regard to success achieved in projects (presented in Fig. 1), participants also felt serious difficulty reporting what happened in the last project in which they participated.

Table 4. Characterization of the last completed project, in which respondents participated

	Frequency	Percent
Project Type		
IS Project	29	33.34
Other	10	11.49
DNK/NO	48	55.17
Project Duration (in months)		
<12	22	25.29
12–24	9	10.34
>24	7	8.05
DNK/NO	49	56.32
Approximate budget (in Euros)		
<1.000.000	14	16.09
1.000.000–10.000.000	2	2.30
>10.000.000	2	2.30
DNK/NO	69	79.31

DNK/NO – Do not know/No opinion.

Charts (a) and (b) show that more than half (about 60%) of the participants could not answer the four questions they were asked about success: fulfilment of scope; fulfilment of time; fulfilment of budget; and overall success achieved in the project. In a way, this is understandable since success was not formally evaluated in 86% of the projects (refer to charts (c) and (d)); and, in a very similar percentage (83%), no criteria were even defined for this evaluation.

Overall, about 39% of the projects complied with scope (with or without changes), approximately 27% of the projects complied with time, and 32% managed to comply with budget. About 21% of the projects (circa one-fifth of all projects) met the scope, time, and budget (all criteria) regardless of whether these have changed during the project. The percentage drops to less than 5% considering the simultaneous fulfilment of the three criteria and no changes in these compared to the initially planned.

The lack of training and experience in project management (only 8% of the participants mentioned having it) may explain the overall low levels of success. This is consistent with the literature that suggests lack of training (in project management of those responsible for the projects) as one of the main factors that cause the low success levels of the projects in developing countries [10, 13–15].

Regarding project management practices in the organizations surveyed, our results acknowledge the findings described in the literature review, namely, the lack of use of adequate methodologies in project management [10, 13–15].

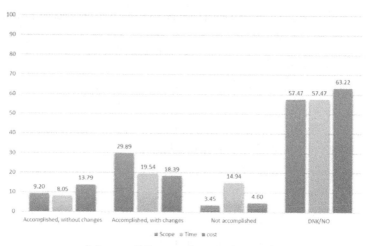

a) Accomplishment of scope, time, and cost.

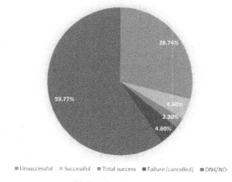

b) Project success.

c) The criteria for evaluating success   d) The success was formally evaluated.
were formally defined.

Fig. 1. Reported success in projects.

5 Conclusion

This study has several contributions. Although there are other studies focused on developing countries, as far as we know, this study focuses for the first time the management of IS projects in the public sector, addressing the success that has been achieved in project management. This is of paramount importance and deals with the two lowest groups of developing countries [37]: low human development (HDI < 0.55), the case of Guinea-Bissau; and medium human development (HDI < 0.7), the cases of Cape Verde, São Tomé and Príncipe, and East Timor, highlighting the needs of these countries regarding the management of IS projects.

It was possible to confirm the expectations that the research team had about the inexistence of adequate mechanisms for the management of IS projects, being able to point out as a very relevant data the quantity of "do not know" type responses, i.e., in which the senior public servants answered that they did not know, which confirms their lack of awareness in project management.

From the results, it was possible to notice low success rates, highlighting the lack of use of evaluation criteria (83%) and formal evaluation of projects (86%). Finally, two results should also be highlighted: no use of formal methodologies in project management (79.31%), and no training in project management, with 91.98% of the executives stating that they never received training in this area.

Nevertheless, there is a very positive aspect to highlight that is the education level of these executives (90% have higher education), which will allow them to evolve rapidly in the area of project management, if they receive training. Since the data was collected personally by the researchers, it was possible to notice the positive attitude from the participants toward the improvement of their activities and the will to learn new practices to improve performance. Thus, given this potential, one of the best investments that can be made in these countries is education and training in project management. As the Chinese proverb says: *"Give a man a fish, and you feed him for a day. Teach a man to fish, and you feed him for a lifetime"*.

This need for training was also recently reported by the PMI, which identified that currently there is a dramatic increase in the number of jobs requiring project management skills especially in developing countries with overall job growth expected to be around 33% [46].

One limitation of this study was the high number of "do not know" answers from the participants, which may influence results. As future research, it is recommended to address the project management current practice in these countries to get a better understanding (e.g., regarding project management processes), as well as the factors that influence success.

References

1. Kwak, Y.H., Anbari, F.T.: Analyzing project management research: perspectives from top management journals. Int. J. Proj. Manag. **27**(8), 435–446 (2009). https://doi.org/10.1016/j.ijproman.2008.08.004
2. Varajão, J., Trigo, A., Soto-Acosta, P.: An exploratory study on the influencers of the perceived relevance of CIO's activities. Int. J. Enterp. Inf. Syst. **12**(4) (2016). https://doi.org/10.4018/ijeis.2016100101
3. Varajão, J.: A new process for success management–bringing order to a typically ad-hoc area. J. Mod. Proj. Manag. **5**(3) (2018). https://doi.org/10.19255/jmpm01510
4. Diegmann, P., Basten, D., Pankratz, O.: Influence of communication on client satisfaction in information system projects: a quantitative field study. Proj. Manag. J. **48**(1), 81–99 (2017). https://doi.org/10.1177/875697281704800106
5. Rosacker, K.M., Rosacker, R.E.: Information technology project management within public sector organizations. J. Enterp. Inf. Manag. **23**(5), 587–594 (2010). https://doi.org/10.1108/17410391011083047
6. Fayaz, A., Kamal, Y., ul Amin, S., Khan, S.: Critical success factors in information technology projects. Manag. Sci. Lett. **7**(2), 73–80 (2017). https://doi.org/10.5267/j.msl.2016.11.012
7. Damoah, I.S., Akwei, C.A., Amoako, I.O., Botchie, D.: Corruption as a source of government project failure in developing countries. Proj. Manag. J. **49**(3), 17–33 (2018). https://doi.org/10.1177/8756972818770587
8. Wang, R., Bar, F., Hong, Y.: ICT aid flows from China to African countries: a communication network perspective. Int. J. Commun. **14**, 1–25 (2020)
9. World Bank: Annual report (2006)
10. Zhu, Y.-Q., Kindarto, A.: A garbage can model of government IT project failures in developing countries: the effects of leadership, decision structure and team competence. Gov. Inf. Q. **33**(4), 629–637 (2016). https://doi.org/10.1016/j.giq.2016.08.002
11. Ebad, S.A.: Influencing factors for IT software project failures in developing countries—A critical literature survey. J. Softw. **11**(11), 1145–1153 (2016). https://doi.org/10.17706/jsw.11.11.1145-1153
12. Hughes, D.L., Rana, N.P., Simintiras, A.C.: The changing landscape of IS project failure: an examination of the key factors. J. Enterp. Inf. Manag. **30**(1), 142–165 (2017). https://doi.org/10.1108/JEIM-01-2016-0029
13. Majeed, N., Shah, K.A., Qazi, K.A., Maqsood, M.: Performance evaluation of IT project management in developing countries. Int. J. Inf. Technol. Comput. Sci. **5**(4), 68–75 (2013). https://doi.org/10.5815/ijitcs.2013.04.08
14. Teklemariam, M.A., Mnkandla, E.: Software project risk management practice in Ethiopia. Electron. J. Inf. Syst. Dev. Countries **79**(1), 1–14 (2017). https://doi.org/10.1002/j.1681-4835.2017.tb00583.x
15. Kathuria, V., Oh, K.Y.: CT access: testing for convergence across countries. Inf. Soc. **34**(3), 166–182 (2018). https://doi.org/10.1080/01972243.2018.1438549
16. Söderlund, J.: Building theories of project management: past research, questions for the future. Int. J. Proj. Manag. **22**(3), 183–191 (2004). https://doi.org/10.1016/S0263-7863(03)00070-X
17. Padalkar, M., Gopinath, S.: Six decades of project management research: thematic trends and future opportunities. Int. J. Proj. Manag. **34**(7), 1305–1321 (2016). https://doi.org/10.1016/j.ijproman.2016.06.006
18. Kanwal, N., Zafar, M.S., Bashir, S.: The combined effects of managerial control, resource commitment, and top management support on the successful delivery of information systems projects. Int. J. Proj. Manag. **35**(8), 1459–1465 (2017). https://doi.org/10.1016/j.ijproman.2017.08.007

19. Iriarte, C., Bayona, S.: IT projects success factors: a literature review. Int. J. Inf. Syst. Proj. Manag. **8**(2), 49–78 (2020)
20. Bezdrob, M., Brkić, S., Gram, M.: The pivotal factors of IT projects' success – insights for the case of organizations from the Federation of Bosnia and Herzegovina. Int. J. Inf. Syst. Proj. Manag. **8**(1), 23–41 (2020)
21. Standish Group: CHAOS Report 1994 (1994)
22. Johnson J.: CHAOS 2020: Beyond Infinity (2020)
23. Project Management Institute: Success Rates Rise—Pulse of the Profession (2017)
24. Ika, L.A.: Project success as a topic in project management journals. Proj. Manag. J. **40**(4), 6–19 (2009). https://doi.org/10.1002/pmj.20137
25. Atkinson, R.: Project management: cost, time and quality, two best guesses and a phenomenon, its time to accept other success criteria. Int. J. Proj. Manag. **17**(6), 337–342 (1999). https://doi.org/10.1016/S0263-7863(98)00069-6
26. Baccarini, D.: The logical framework method for defining project success. Proj. Manag. J. **30**(4), 25–32 (1999). https://doi.org/10.1177/875697289903000405
27. Wit, A.: Measurement of project success. Int. J. Proj. Manag. **6**(3), 164–170 (1988). https://doi.org/10.1016/0263-7863(88)90043-9
28. Pinto, J.K., Covin, J.G.: Critical factors in project implementation: a comparison of construction and R&D projects. Technovation **9**(1), 49–62 (1989). https://doi.org/10.1016/0166-4972(89)90040-0
29. Sumner, M.: Critical success factors in enterprise wide information management systems projects. In: Proceedings of the 1999 ACM SIGCPR Conference on Computer Personnel Research, pp 297–303 (1999)
30. Trigo, A., Varajão, J., Soto-Acosta, P., Gonzálvez-Gallego, N., Molina, F.J.: Influence of firm size on the adoption of enterprise information systems: insights from Iberian firms. Int. J. Inf. Technol. Manag. **14**(4), 233–252 (2015). https://doi.org/10.1504/IJITM.2015.072046
31. Bannerman, P.L.: Defining project success: a multilevel framework. In: Proceedings of the Project Management Institute Research Conference, pp. 1–14. Citeseer (2008)
32. Bannerman, P.L., Thorogood, A.: Celebrating IT projects success: a multi-domain analysis. In: 2012 45th Hawaii International Conference on System Sciences, pp. 4874–4883. IEEE (2012)
33. Cruz-Cunha, M.M., Varajão, J., Trigo, A.: Sociotechnical Enterprise Information Systems Design and Integration. IGI Global (2013)
34. Varajão, J.: The many facets of information systems (+ projects) success. Int. J. Inf. Syst. Proj. Manag. **6**(4), 5–13 (2018)
35. Pankratz, O., Basten, D.: Opening the black box: managers' perceptions of IS project success mechanisms. Inf. Manag. **55**(3), 381–395 (2018). https://doi.org/10.1016/j.im.2017.09.005
36. Davis, K.: A method to measure success dimensions relating to individual stakeholder groups. Int. J. Proj. Manag. **34**(3), 480–493 (2016). https://doi.org/10.1016/j.ijproman.2015.12.009
37. United Nations: Human development report 2019: beyond income, beyond averages, beyond today (2019)
38. Bond-Barnarda, T.J., Steyna, H.: Project management in developing countries: implications for project trust, collaboration, and success. In: 3rd IPMA (International Project Management Association) Research Conference (2015)
39. Borrowman, M., Klasen, S.: Drivers of gendered sectoral and occupational segregation in developing countries. Feminist Econ. **26**(2), 62–94 (2020). https://doi.org/10.1080/13545701.2019.1649708
40. World Bank: Digital Governance Projects Database. In: Digital Governance Projects Database (2020). https://datacatalog.worldbank.org/dataset/digital-governance-projects-database

41. Khang, D.B., Moe, T.L.: Success criteria and factors for international development projects: a life-cycle-based framework. Proj. Manag. J. **39**(1), 72–84 (2008). https://doi.org/10.1002/pmj.20034

42. Ofori, D.F.: Project management practices and critical success factors–a developing country perspective. Int. J. Bus. Manag. **8**(21), 14–31 (2013). https://doi.org/10.5539/ijbm.v8n21p14

43. Almajed, A.I., Mayhew, P.: An empirical investigation of IT project success in developing countries. In: 2014 Science and Information Conference, pp. 984–990. IEEE (2014)

44. Trigo, A., Varajão, J.: IT project management critical success factors. In: Gervasi, O., et al. (eds.) ICCSA 2020. LNCS, vol. 12254, pp. 714–724. Springer, Cham (2020). https://doi.org/10.1007/978-3-030-58817-5_51

45. Heeks, R.: Success and failure rates of eGovernment in developing/transitional countries: overview (2008). http://www.egov4dev.org/success/sfrates.shtml. Accessed 2 June 2015

46. Project Management Institute: Job Growth and Talent Gap in Project Management (2017)

An Iterative Information System Design Process Towards Sustainability

Tobias Nyström[✉] and Moyen Mustaquim

Uppsala University, Uppsala, Sweden
tobias.nystrom@im.uu.se

Abstract. While bringing business and computer science into an improved alignment using the theoretical foundations of information and computation is one of the main aims of information science, improved design knowledge from other interdisciplinary research fields like human-computer interaction (HCI) could advance different information system (IS) design thinking and processes. Since structuring the IS design process for a sustainable result is challenging, a HCI viewpoint and focus on IS design could be beneficial due to the multi and interdisciplinary nature of HCI. In this paper an iterative design process for sustainable IS design conceptualized from HCI is proposed. The resulting design process highlighted the role of HCI in building knowledge in information science. This was achieved by showing the influence of different design choices on user behavior and in that way contributing towards generating reusable designs in different phases of the sustainable IS design process.

Keywords: Information system design · Iterative design process · Open innovation · Sustainability · Universal design

1 Introduction

Sustainability with its associated design and development problem is not a new issue in our society. The essence of sustainability is difficult to grasp if its complexity and multidimensionality are considered. Often the notion of sustainable development focuses on ecological design, a weakness of the modern approach to sustainability [10]. An IS can contribute to sustainable development in different ways. Since IS is a great force for productivity improvement [34] it can be designed in a sustainable manner and can act on its user to trigger sustainable behavior. One example is using persuasive technology to change the behavior of individuals through persuasion [28]. Nevertheless, the success of such an IS would typically depend on how it would be designed [47]. Since it is not possible to identify the boundaries of sustainability in an absolute way (a "wicked problem" [5]), it is a challenge to identify and select proper factors for sustainability in a system design scenario [12]. Therefore, the complexities of sustainability and its associated indicators bring new problems in the form of design challenges for IS.

© Springer Nature Switzerland AG 2020
M. Themistocleous et al. (Eds.): EMCIS 2020, LNBIP 402, pp. 781–795, 2020.
https://doi.org/10.1007/978-3-030-63396-7_53

While the importance of thinking sustainability outside the scope of environmental issues is obvious from previous research [6,7], designing at the same time introduces a multitude of new and complex sustainability indicators [52]. For example, complicated issues like time and thresholds have been claimed to be an important indicator for sustainability [33]. The right indicator selection for sustainability, typically can determine a system's behavior since it would then be built to reflect the associated behaviors with different selected indicators. While the addition of complex indicators could result in an improved designed system for sustainability, to do this successfully the relevant design process should incorporate the suggested design principles. This brings the challenge of defining an appropriate IS design process for sustainability. A reason for this is that IS is not only conceptualized within the limitations of the software systems, but the embedded concept of design is growing. Thus, it becomes a new challenge for IS design to align business and computer science using theoretical foundations of information and computation [17,23] to keep up with unexpected and continuous change [9]. Since new sustainability indicators may not be restricted within the basic pillar of sustainability, they could originate from any discipline. This breadth of origin is a challenge for IS because there is a clear disciplinary gap in the research of IS design, regardless of it being a multidiscipline practice, and IS research should thus be prepared to tackle such a challenge. This problem could be handled by pulling knowledge from other disciplines, namely HCI, which is an interdisciplinary research field [14,15]. This paper displays how knowledge tailored from HCI could be used to fill an identified disciplinary gap in IS design research. The identified gap is the need for a design process for sustainable system design where issues with indicators as stated above can be resolved. The underlying research question for this research paper is therefore "how can we structure and support an IS design aimed towards sustainability". As an answer to this question, a design process solution is developed in the form of a theoretical framework that is based on previously established research. It is argued that by placing more emphasis on interdisciplinary research like HCI, new knowledge could be built for the study of IS design for sustainability. This paper is organized in six sections. A short background in Sect. 2 presents the underlying concepts of sustainability, IS design and design process followed by Sect. 3 where a theoretical framework in the form of an iterative design process is explained in detail. Based on the structure of this theoretical framework some design principles for the addressed iterative design process for sustainable IS design are then formulated and presented in Sect. 4. An extensive discussion and future work prospect in Sect. 5 identifies and revisits different roles of sustainable HCI (SHCI) for sustainable IS design. Finally, conclusions are drawn in Sect. 6.

2   Background

2.1   Sustainability and Information System Design

ISs are considered as human designed artefacts [32]. This socio-technical system is created to blend and integrate processes, people, information technology and software to work towards a set goal [55]. The view of sustainability in this paper is based on the World Commission on Environment and Development's [53] definition of sustainable development to meet the needs of the present without compromising the ability of future generations to meet theirs. By reversing or diminishing the outcome of diverse human-induced processes, sustainability could be attained. One of humanity's challenges at present is how to achieve sustainability, one threat is global warming [24] and its impact on health [57], another threat is the rise of global obesity [25,39].

Watson et al. [56] wrote 2010 a seminal paper that called for more research from the IS community aimed at sustainability. In the same issue of MIS Q, Melville [34] put forward a research agenda on IS in the context of environmental sustainability. SHCI has mainly focused on reducing CO_2 through system design [8], though more significant changes are called for to secure the quality of life for humans [27]. IS is now ubiquitous and plays a larger role in the daily life of most humans, and therefore including sustainability in the design of these ISs is essential. The topic of sustainability is researched in different research fields such as information systems, environmental informatics, information technology, and human-computer interaction [20,41]. If sustainability is considered during the design of a system, it becomes possible to reach a set sustainability goal and increase the resulting impact. Previous research has noted that the inclusion of sustainability at the design stage is not acknowledging as important in the current SHCI research [3]. What is missing is a holistic view; currently, the approach is to simply look at the energy use of a certain artefact (e.g., computer, electronic device or house) and thus limit the scope to an often-delimited system [41]. A limited studied system can at first appear to be sustainable, but if studied in the context of a larger system can be viewed as unsustainable.

At first glance a thing often considered as sustainable is the smart home where electricity use is monitored and the household's behavior is directed towards conserving energy, water and heating [16,43,51]. Although conserving energy, water and heating could be a set sustainability goal, the cost of the whole system (e.g., manufacturing the smart hub, sensors, etc. and the power these artefacts consume, maintenance cost and the expected lifetime of the system before it needs to be replaced) must also be considered. This cost could be calculated in a life cycle assessment (for LCA see Hendrickson et al., [18]). The LCA could then be used to decide if the benefit of the smart house outweighs its cost. Both the direct and indirect impact of smart technologies need to be considered when assessing the sustainability of the system [21]. It is easy to pick low hanging fruits like the reduction of energy utilization in a device or system, but on the contrary, one might use the device and the system more and thereby as a whole act unsustainably i.e. Jevons' paradox [26]. Tomlinson et al. [54] saw similarities with more efficient IT. Another study of the impact of ICT on environmental sustainability modeling from 2000 to 2020 found benefits slightly outperform disadvantages [1,22]. A smart system with the goal of reducing fuel consumption by giving the best fuel saving route and avoiding traffic congestion by getting real time traffic data, might lead to more driving. Because the driving experience will become better (more enjoyable because less time is spent in traffic jams), people might be tempted to abandon public transport and use the car more. Thus, there are complexities associated with designing systems aimed towards sustainability. In addition, the analysis level from micro to macro, starting with the individuals followed by family, community, society and state, should be considered globally since optimization at one level could harm another.

2.2 Design Process

In different research fields the term "design" itself has a different meaning, and the understanding of "design process" is therefore contextual e.g., Herbert Simon [46] stated that everyone designs who takes action aimed at changing existing situations into preferred ones. Generally, the design process should reflect a set of processes in the form of a flow where the target is to produce a desired goal by following the involved set of processes. Consequently, when a series of steps are followed to achieving a specific solution, these steps could be seen in the form of a design process. While Simon is blending a scientific approach with design, other researchers have opposite ideas, e.g. Schön [44] is rooted in pragmatism and sees that design is about problem setting and not problem solving. It could be argued that this development reflects a move from understanding design through the lens of scientific and engineering tradition towards a designerly-oriented design practice [48]. This paper's objective can be categorized as the theoretical advancement to enhance the theoretical core of HCI [48,49], Stolterman & Wiberg describes this as developing "innovative concepts that lead to intellectual development through definitions, conceptual constructs, and theories." One of the sustainable design movement originators, Victor Papanek [42] stated, "All men are designers. All that we do, almost all the time, is design, for design is basic to all human activity. The planning and patterning of any act toward a desired, foreseeable end constitutes a design process...Design is the conscious effort to impose a meaningful order."

In this paper the design process is perceived as an IS design process that involves several steps. Nevertheless, designers and engineers often omit following these steps in a sequential manner and instead frequently return to a step as they require and then proceed over to the next step. This is the core idea behind an iterative process, as design is inherently an incremental and iterative activity [19]. One important challenge of the design process is designing the process itself. To be precise, to gain a successful outcome from a specific design process, the associated steps in that process need to be designed accordingly. Thus, in order to support an IS through specific factors, then the overall design process of that system should be tailored accordingly for the end system to act as a cause for those factors. The need of an IS for sustainability should thus take us back into an initial requirement of forming the prosper design process. As discussed in the introduction section, the interdisciplinary nature of HCI can give us a better understanding on how to do this. The following section illustrates and explains the proposed iterative system design process in detail.

3 Proposed Design Process

The proposed design process is shown in Fig. 1 in the form of a theoretical framework. The underlying concept and rationale behind this framework originates from the five previous studies referred to in Mustaquim and Nyström [35–38] and Nyström and Mustaquim [41]. The theoretical framework of this research is principally based on the notion of universal design (UD) and advancing its concept. UD was created as an answer to changes in demography; since people live longer, more people live with disabilities, and these limitations require the design and construction of environments and products that meets the need and rights of all citizens [50]. UD has already become a popular design philosophy in HCI for focusing on accessibility issues, outside of its traditional sphere, UD could also lead to user empowerment [29]. Frameworks, cognitive models and design principles were derived under the context of sustainability, open innovation (OI) and open sustainability innovation. The results of the addressed five published articles were condensed here in structuring the theoretical framework. The rationale behind the construction of this framework is described in Subsect. 3.1 while different phases of the framework are illustrated and described in detail in Subsect. 3.2.

Fig. 1. Proposed iterative design process for sustainable system design.

3.1 Foundation of the Design Phases

Fiksel [12] has exemplified several conventional sustainability indicators under the economical, ecological, and social dimensions of sustainability. These indicators are considered, and it is showed how they would fit within the context of the theoretical framework. The four triggers from the framework were derived and concluded from previous research [35–38, 41] shown in Table 1, where respective research articles are referred to with the identified triggers. Table 2 then shows a matrix of different sustainability indicators parallel with their corresponding triggers from the theoretical framework. The underlying rationale behind the selection of four triggers is principally focused on the concept of user-centered design. Increasing the possibility of including users in a design process would increase the possibility of the designed product to more appropriately fitting the needs of a desired user group. For sustainability, this user-centered concept can have a direct influence on the usability of a product and can therefore enable the designers to understand the associated interaction process and thereby assess any adverse effects caused by the use of the product [58].

Since the result of a sustainable system design can be benefited by adding complex requirements that are adaptable in the corresponding design phases, how each of the four different triggers are used as design phases in the proposed framework (Fig. 1) would reflect different indicators (Table 1) which will now be discussed here.

Table 1. Four triggers of the framework and their corresponding research.

Triggers of the Framework	Adapted From
OI	[35]
Open Sustainability Innovation	[38]
Sustainable System Design	[36, 41]
Cognitive Model and Persuasion Towards Sustainability	[37]

Table 2. A sustainability indicator matrix with associated triggers.

Sustainability Indicators [9]	Associated Triggers in Framework	Corresponding Life Cycle Phases
Customer Retention Business Interruption Direct Costs Revenues Contingent Costs	Open Innovation & Open Sustainability Innovation	Definition Level, Identifying the Target Design
Material Consumption Energy Consumption Local and Regional Impacts Global Impacts	Open Sustainability Innovation & Sustainable System Design	Development Level, Policy Alternation as Required
Quality of Life, Peace of Mind Safety Improvement Health, Wellness and Disease Reduction	Cognitive Model and Persuasion Towards Sustainability & Sustainable System Design	Operational Level, Action and New Problem Identification

Both OI, and open sustainability innovation consider stakeholders to build new knowledge in design for organizations where the latter specifically focuses on sustainable creation. Relationships with stakeholders and different interruptions of business due to the stakeholder involvement could be taken care of by the [35] policy. Several direct costs associated with product design and development could be controlled by advancing the marketing policy in an organization where open sustainability innovation can play new key roles. Similarly, for different types of tangible and intangible revenues, it will be possible to make stakeholders understand about the potentiality through open sustainability innovation. Organizations on the other hand, can have better control on different types of dependent costs too, when OI and open sustainability innovation are practiced. It is important to note here that the way OI and open sustainability innovation are perceived as a result of previous researches [35,38] does not mean only using stakeholders to generating new business or design ideas, but as part of an identification phase of any big design process where target design could be identified. Now, as discussed in Subsect. 2.2, the contextual meaning of design is very important to realize here and therefore for the trigger of OI and open sustainability innovation, a reasoned purpose (ex. sustainability) was seen to be the design problem.

Development and policy alternation as required could happen when a sustainable system design life cycle is followed. Different impacts on local and regional levels could be handled using open sustainability innovation principles, once again by looking at design from the perspective of a specific cause. Complex environmentally associated issues like material and energy consumptions together with broader global impact realization could be handled by policy alteration during the development phase. A system development life cycle, specifically meant for sustainable system design, [41] would allow this to happen smoothly.

At the operational level of a design process, proper actions should be taken to achieve a goal and thus new problems could be identified. Complex social issues like improving the quality of life, creating a trusting community and peace of mind, different safety improvement and health related issues are societal sustainability indicators that are not achievable in a short time. These issues could be reflected through the use of a design where action could take place by the practice of any improved designed cognitive model [37]. Persuasion and persuasive system design for sustainability could be considered to handle these complex long-term issues. On the other hand, a sustainable system design life cycle could be followed to identify and select these complex goals to be design challenges [37]. The selection of the right design principles [37] would help towards achieving these goals and if new problems arise, they could be addressed in an iterative manner by going back to the required design phase.

3.2 Structure of the Triggers as Design Phases

Four different triggers (see Table 1) were considered to be individual design phases in the proposed framework (see Fig. 1) and their structures are described here.

OI: Consider UD and its principles to generate required OI design principles. Increasing stakeholders' involvement for a successful OI is the challenge here. The business strategy must be aligned with the innovation strategy. By allowing stakeholder involvement in the innovation phase an organization will be able to better capture the added value that innovations can bring, innovated both internally and externally. If OI is practiced and implemented in the business strategy a business could thus gain a competitive advantage, e.g., the toy manufacturer Lego uses OI in their Lego Mindstorms product and allows the users to develop new features [2]. If more stakeholders are involved, the gap between research and development will be reduced since the research department will not be locked and isolated in secret research facilities limiting their scope and connection with user needs. When more stakeholders are involved the research network can be expanded and discover things that could otherwise not be realized as important to develop earlier.

Open Sustainability Innovation: To consider the improvement of marketing knowledge by selecting the correct design principles. Initiates open sustainability innovation by motivating stakeholders to participate in sustainable product or service development. The challenge here is the appropriate selection of design principles. The adoption is crucial for an innovation to become successful thus the marketing mechanism and the triggers of it must be understood, e.g., the video recorder system VHS was not technically superior to its main competitor Betamax (on the contrary) but was adopted by movie companies and consumers and hence became the standard video system [30]. Once this is understood and a marketing strategy is implemented it would be possible to use these triggers to enhance the marketing into a winning mix that will make the adoption of the innovation a success. The future participation in the open sustainable innovation will be assured since more people want to participate in the advancement of a successful and recognized innovation. Caution must be taken since the market is in constant change and a winning marketing mix today could be inappropriate tomorrow.

Sustainable System Design: Use UD principles to trigger sustainable system design. The challenge is to find out the correct system development life cycle for sustainability. Since the sustainable system design could be in constant flux due a dynamic and constantly changing world, it is necessary to use the UD principles for the sustainable design. The system could be developed following the SDLC. Different phases of SDLC need to be adjusted to fit the dominant goal of the sustainable system to be ready for changes and iterations due to goal changes as well as changing user behaviors.

Cognitive Model and Persuasion Towards Sustainability: Use design principles for persuasion and different cognitive models to persuade system development towards sustainability. A challenge is understanding what behavior that needs to be altered. The design of a system will be used to gain social transitions towards sustainability by acting as an agent and persuading users in one focused direction. It is therefore important to understand what drives and motivates the users of a system and then use appropriate design principles to persuade and motivate them towards a justified sustainability goal. The human mind is very complex and difficult to decipher and understand and if one behavior is changed, it could influence other behaviors that were not initially intended which could contribute to or be counterproductive in reaching a sustainable goal.

4   Design Principles

Norman [40] argued that regarding design, one important thing should not be forgotten and that is "Design is art... We do not know the best way to design something". Thus, design principle merits should work as guidance. The proposed design process contributes to understanding the complex sustainability achievement issues through IS design and the purpose of this paper is not to show empirical evidence to judge the success of the design process. However, with proper theoretical design process in hand it is still a big challenge for system designers to grasp the essence unless design principles exist as guidelines on how to practice a design process. In this section design principles are therefore proposed and discussed that would be ideal to successfully practice the iterative design process in Fig. 1 for sustainability. A matrix for identifying design principle's properties was drawn and shown in Table 3 followed by the descriptions of seven design principles in Subsect. 4.1.

Table 3. Identification of different design principle's properties.

Design Process Phases	Design Principle's Properties	Sustainability Identifiers
Open Innovation	Stakeholder involvement and design principles	Customer Retention, Business Interruption, Revenues
Open Sustainability Innovation	Marketing strategies and stakeholders' involvement	Direct and Contingent Costs
System Design Sustainable Design	Universal design and life cycle of sustainable system design	Material and Energy Consumption, Local, Regional and Global Impacts
Cognitive Model and Persuasion	Design principles for PSD and stakeholders	Quality of Life, Peace of Mind, Safety Improvement, Health and Wellness

4.1   Design Principles for Iterative Design Process for Sustainability

Factors and properties identified from Table 3 are summarized in the form of the following seven described design principles.

Principle 1: Use OI for a better control over tackling business interruption and customer retentions – By taking a holistic view on sustainability and using

OI, a business will be better prepared and perhaps gain absorption capacity for new innovations to understand customers better. Thus, it will be able to bridge interruptions and change/adjust the sustainability goal to fit future needs and maintain customer loyalty.

Principle 2: Practice OI at a small-scale system level for improved control on different associated costs and revenue – By limiting and scaling OI into smaller units it becomes easier to control, and therefore the associated risks will become lower and provide better predictions of costs and revenues.

Principle 3: Policy alternation on strategic marketing by involving stakeholders in the knowledge gathering process using open sustainability innovation – If the right marketing triggers are used the adoption of the innovation will be successful followed by customer retention and active participation in future sustainable innovations This will give a competitive advantage followed by revenue and profit.

Principle 4: Use UD and its extended concept for designing a system to enable ecological actions for sustainability – Using UD actively when designing systems should allow the designer to find and discover system generated actions that are beneficial for sustainability.

Principle 5: Follow the sustainable system development life cycle for designing a complex sustainable system reflecting on global sustainability triggers – SDLC is easy to understand and could be the foundation when designing sustainable systems, although other methodologies like agile development could be used if necessary, depending on the scale, complexity, time, and resources. Global sustainability triggers will also have an impact on the designing of the system.

Principle 6: Use a contextual cognitive model for persuading the involved stakeholders towards social sustainability – Stakeholder behavior is dependent on context and to frame the right contextual model will make it possible to relatively easily persuade the stakeholder in the right direction.

Principle 7: Design a persuasive system for stakeholders for changing their dissonance on complex social phenomena like community, health and wellness – If the right persuasion is used the stakeholder will feel liberated and committed to keep on acting towards a sustainable goal. This could have a positive impact on social life and health.

5   Discussions and Future Work

The proposed design process in this paper is unique since it is process focused. That is to say, the emphases is on how to design the process itself in an improved way. Existing design processes or system development life cycles found in the literature are very abstract and do not clearly specify what to do for a particular design challenge. For example, if a classical system development life cycle is followed then it is difficult to interpret what each stage of the life cycle would mean for a design aiming to overcome sustainability challenges. The strength of this paper is therefore the formulation of the iterative design process which could specifically tell the designer what to do in each of the different phases to reflect sustainability through design. In the introduction section it was mentioned that when the emphasis on sustainability is considered outside the scope of ecological dimensions, complexity arises, and design then becomes more challenging. One of the problems associated with this issue also therefore is, a shift towards product-focused sustainability and ignoring different associated processes. While IS design focuses on improving artefact design, it does not ignore the associated process. The use of the proposed framework can thus be crucial for looking into the issues of process related sustainability since each of the individual phases of the proposed framework considers sustainability as its separate outcome. That is, each phase is a trigger for sustainability and was shown to address a specific set of sustainability indicators. Also, Fiksel [12] argued that the success of a system's design with an explicit emphasis on sustainability would highly depend on the proper consideration of the associated subsystems. The proposed design process is considered to appropriately follow this argument, since individual design phases was taken into action as subsystems with an ambition of a comprehensive sustainability accomplishment.

The belief that human-computer interaction can be important when searching for a solution for complex and imminent problems that our society is challenged by can be traced back to Douglas Engelbart [11] who wrote about bootstrapping human intelligence; by doing this human capability would be extended (what he called augmentation). HCI could be considered as multidisciplinary [15] and have the possibility to challenge difficulties that humans are experiencing and find novel solutions that solve these problems. Sustainability in the form of sustainable IS design is an urgent task that could benefit from an approach based on sound HCI theorizing. The fundamental basis of this paper's theoretical framework is HCI based and is a good example of this argument. Norman [40] found a conflict between practice and research that he called a research-practice gap.

This paper is positioned as a theoretical paper with large connection to practice and with practical implications for the designing of sustainable ISs. This research does not focus on problems with new technology as Norman [40] described to be the predominant research in HCI; instead, an iterative design process was built to tackle an imminent important problem to drive the next needed product cycle. Since the pioneering research paper "Sustainable interaction design" by Blevis [4], the important role that HCI plays in sustainability has resulted in a steep increase of papers written in the SHCI research field [6, 41, 45]. This paper is adding to this accumulated knowledge and brings new perspectives on how to reach sustainability by using HCI. The shape of sociotechnical ISs and society as a whole is influenced by the social process of design. Fuchs and Obrist [13] and Mankoff et al. [31] highlights the importance of research that considers social, environmental and economic issues in design, evaluation and implementation issues and the developed theoretical framework considers these issues and brings a holistic and dynamic framework to use when designing sustainable ISs.

The next step is to evaluate and explore how the proposed iterative process would behave in a system design and how (and where) it could fit in an existing setup of a system. Design principles validation is also another important area that needs to be completed parallel to the design process verification. Only after doing these empirical studies, will it be possible to finetune a particular phase of the design process. One starting point of doing this could be to apply the framework in a small-scale setup and then test on a complex system. Existing design life cycles or processes can be compared together with this proposed design process and then conclusions could be drawn for justifying the feasibility of using a specific design process. This way the design process is a tool to quantify sustainability for an organization running a precise system. Finally, one long-term ambition of the proposed design process could be to measure and compare the sustainability of a system from where different policy makers of an organization could realize how to line up their available resources properly.

6   Conclusions

This paper has explored the scope of sustainable IS design by introducing an iterative design process. The theoretical framework is based on previously conducted research that evolved into an iterative design process in the form of a framework. The process was then explored and explained within the context of different complex sustainability identifiers. Seven design principles were then extracted and concluded from the design process theoretical framework. The role of SHCI concept was finally revisited to understand the perspective of sustainable IS design. The interdisciplinary nature of HCI is therefore concluded to play a crucial role in filling the disciplinary gap in IS research. Placing strong emphasis on describing different HCI design choices in order to understand its result on design process is thus needed. This would build cumulative reusable design knowledge for IS design as presented in this paper.

References

1. Ahmadi Achachlouei, M., Hilty, L.M.: Modeling the effects of ICT on environmental sustainability: revisiting a system dynamics model developed for the European commission. In: Hilty, L.M., Aebischer, B. (eds.) ICT Innovations for Sustainability, pp. 449–474. Springer, Cham (2015)
2. Antorini, Y.M., Muñiz Jr., A.M., Askildsen, T.: Collaborating with customer communities: Lessons from the lego group. MIT Sloan Manage. Rev. **53**(3), 73–95 (2012)
3. Bates, O., Thomas, V., Remy, C.: Doing good in HCI: can we broaden our agenda? Interactions **24**(5), 80–82 (2017)
4. Blevis, E.: Sustainable interaction design: invention & disposal, renewal & reuse. In: CHI 2007, pp. 503–512. ACM, New York (2007)
5. Blok, V., Gremmen, B., Wesselink, R.: Dealing with the wicked problem of sustainability: the role of individual virtuous competence. Bus. Prof. Ethics J. **34**(3), 297–327 (2016)
6. DiSalvo, C., Sengers, P., Brynjarsdóttir, H.: Mapping the landscape of sustainable HCI. In: CHI 2010, pp. 1975–1984. ACM, New York (2010)

7. DiSalvo, C., Sengers, P., Brynjarsdóttir, H.: Navigating the terrain of sustainable HCI. Interactions **17**(4), 22–25 (2010)
8. Dourish, P.: HCI and environmental sustainability: The politics of design and the design of politics. In: DIS 2010, pp. 1–10. Association for Computing Machinery, New York, NY, USA (2010)
9. Dove, R.: Knowledge management, response ability, and the agile enterprise. J. Knowl. Manage. **3**(1), 18–35 (1999)
10. Ehrenfeld, J.: Designing 'sustainable' product/service systems. In: Proceedings 2nd International Symposium on Environmentally Conscious Design and Inverse Manufacturing, pp. 12–23 (2001)
11. Engelbart, D.C.: Augmenting Human Intellect: A Conceptual Framework. SRI Summary Report AFOSR-3223. Stanford Research Institute, Menlo Park (1962)
12. Fiksel, J.: Designing resilient, sustainable systems. Environ. Sci.Technol. **37**(23), 5330–5339 (2003)
13. Fuchs, C., Obrist, M.: HCI and society: towards a typology of universal design principles. Int. J. Hum. Comput. Interact. **26**(6), 638–656 (2010)
14. Grudin, J.: Is HCI homeless?: in search of inter-disciplinary status. Interactions **13**(1), 54–59 (2006)
15. Hartson, H.R.: Human-computer interaction: interdisciplinary roots and trends. J. Syst. Softw. **43**(2), 103–118 (1998)
16. Heller, F., Borchers, J.: Physical prototyping of an on-outlet power-consumption display. Interactions **19**(1), 14–17 (2012)
17. Henderson, J.C., Venkatraman, H.: Strategic alignment: leveraging information technology for transforming organizations. IBM Syst. J. **32**(1), 4–16 (1993)
18. Hendrickson, C., Horvath, A., Joshi, S., Lave, L.: Peer reviewed: economic input-output models for environmental life-cycle assessment. Environ. Sci. Technol. **32**(7), 184A–191A (1998)
19. Hevner, A.R., March, S.T., Park, J., Ram, S.: Design science in information systems research. MIS Q. **28**(1), 75–105 (2004)
20. Hilty, L.M., Aebischer, B.: ICT for sustainability: an emerging research field. In: Hilty, L.M., Aebischer, B. (eds.) ICT Innovations for Sustainability, pp. 3–36. Springer, Cham (2015). https://doi.org/10.1007/978-3-319-09228-7_1
21. Hilty, L.M., Aebischer, B., Rizzoli, A.E.: Modeling and evaluating the sustainability of smart solutions. Environ. Model. Softw. **56**, 1–5 (2014)
22. Hilty, L.M., Arnfalk, P., Erdmann, L., Goodman, J., Lehmann, M., Wäger, P.A.: The relevance of information and communication technologies for environmental sustainability – a prospective simulation study. Environ. Model. Softw. **21**(11), 1618–1629 (2006)
23. Hinkelmann, K., Pasquini, A.: Supporting business and it alignment by modeling business and it strategy and its relations to enterprise architecture. In: 2014 Enterprise Systems Conference, pp. 149–154 (2014)
24. Intergovernmental Panel on Climate Change (IPCC): Special Report on Global Warming of 1.5 C. In: IPPC (2018)
25. James, W.: The epidemiology of obesity: the size of the problem. J. Intern. Med. **263**(4), 336–352 (2008)
26. Jevons, W.S.: The Coal Question: An Inquiry Concerning the Progress of the Nation, and the Probable Exhaustion of our Coal-mines. Macmillan & Co, London (1866)
27. Knowles, B., Bates, O., Håkansson, M.: This changes sustainable HCI. In: CHI 2018. Association for Computing Machinery, New York, USA (2018)

28. Knowles, B., Blair, L., Walker, S., Coulton, P., Thomas, L., Mullagh, L.: Patterns of persuasion for sustainability. In: Proceedings of the 2014 Conference on Designing Interactive Systems, pp. 1035–1044. ACM, New York (2014)
29. Ladner, R.E.: Design for user empowerment. Interactions **22**(2), 24–29 (2015)
30. Liebowitz, S.J., Margolis, S.E.: Path dependence, lock-in, and history. J. Law Econ. Organ. **11**(1), 205–226 (1995)
31. Mankoff, J.C., et al.: Environmental sustainability and interaction. In: CHI EA 2007, pp. 2121–2124. ACM, New York (2007)
32. March, S.T., Smith, G.F.: Design and natural science research on information technology. Decis. Support Syst. **15**(4), 251–266 (1995)
33. Meadows, D.H.: Indicators and Information Systems for Sustainable Development. The Sustainability Institute, Stellenbosch (1998)
34. Melville, N.P.: Information systems innovation for environmental sustainability. MIS Q. **34**(1), 1–21 (2010)
35. Mustaquim, M., Nyström, T.: Design principles of open innovation concept - universal design viewpoint. In: Stephanidis, C., Antona, M. (eds.) UAHCI, pp. 214–223. Springer, Berlin (2013). https://doi.org/10.1007/978-3-642-39188-0_23
36. Mustaquim, M., Nyström, T.: Designing sustainable IT system - from the perspective of universal design principles. In: Stephanidis, C., Antona, M. (eds.) UAHCI, pp. 77–86. Springer, Berlin (2013). https://doi.org/10.1007/978-3-642-39188-0_9
37. Mustaquim, M., Nyström, T.: Designing information systems for sustainability - the role of universal design and open innovation. In: Tremblay, M.C., VanderMeer, D., Rothenberger, M., Gupta, A., Yoon, V. (eds.) DESRIST 2014, pp. 1–16. Springer, Cham (2014). https://doi.org/10.1007/978-3-319-06701-8_1
38. Mustaquim, M., Nyström, T.: Open sustainability innovation–a pragmatic standpoint of sustainable HCI. In: Johansson, B., Andersson, B., Holmberg, N. (eds.) BIR 2014, pp. 101–112. Springer, Cham (2014). https://doi.org/10.1007/978-3-319-11370-8_8
39. Ng, M., Fleming, T., Robinson, M., et al.: Global, regional, and national prevalence of overweight and obesity in children and adults during 1980–2013: a systematic analysis for the global burden of disease study 2013. The Lancet **384**(9945), 766–781 (2014)
40. Norman, D.A.: The research-practice gap: the need for translational developers. Interactions **17**(4), 9–12 (2010)
41. Nyström, T., Mustaquim, M.: Sustainable information system design and the role of sustainable HCI. In: AcademicMindTrek 2014, pp. 66–73. ACM, New York (2014)
42. Papanek, V.: Design for the Real World: Human Ecology and Social Change, 2nd edn. Thames & Hudson, London (2016)
43. Pierce, J., Fan, C., Lomas, D., Marcu, G., Paulos, E.: Some consideration on the (in)effectiveness of residential energy feedback systems. In: DIS 2010, pp. 244–247. ACM, New York (2010)
44. Schön, D.A.: The Reflective Practitioner. Basic Books, New York (1983)
45. Silberman, M.S., et al.: What have we learned?: a SIGCHI HCI & sustainability community workshop. In: CHI EA 2014, pp. 143–146. ACM, New York (2014)
46. Simon, H.A.: The Sciences of The Artificial, 3rd edn. MIT Press, USA (1996)
47. Stegall, N.: Designing for sustainability: a philosophy for ecologically intentional design. Des. Issues **22**(2), 56–63 (2006)
48. Stolterman, E.: The nature of design practice and implications for interaction design research. Int. J. Des. **2**(1) (2008)
49. Stolterman, E., Wiberg, M.: Concept-driven interaction design research. Hum. Comput. Interact. **25**(2), 95–118 (2010)

50. Story, M.F., Mueller, J.L., Mace, R.L.: The universal design file: Designing for people of all ages and abilities. NC State University - The Center for Universal Design, revised edn. (1998)
51. Strengers, Y.: Smart energy in everyday life: are you designing for resource man? Interactions **21**(4), 24–31 (2014)
52. The Department of Economic and Social Affairs (DESA): Indicators of Sustainable Development: Guidelines and Methodologies, 3rd edn. United Nations, New York (2007)
53. The World Commission on Environment and Development (WCED): Our Common Future. Oxford University Press, Oxford (1987)
54. Tomlinson, B., Silberman, M.S., White, J.: Can more efficient it be worse for the environment? Computer **44**(1), 87–89 (2011)
55. Watson, R.T., Corbett, J., Boudreau, M.C., Webster, J.: An information strategy for environmental sustainability. Commun. ACM **55**(7), 28–30 (2012)
56. Watson, R.T., Boudreau, M.C., Chen, A.J.: Information systems and environmentally sustainable development: energy informatics and new directions for the is community. MIS Q. **34**(1), 23–38 (2010)
57. Watts, N., Adger, W.N., Ayeb-Karlsson, S., et al.: The lancet countdown: tracking progress on health and climate change. The Lancet **389**(10074), 1151–1164 (2017)
58. Wever, R., van Kuijk, J., Boks, C.: User-centred design for sustainable behaviour. Int. J. Sustain. Eng. **1**(1), 9–20 (2008)

Extensive Use of RFID in Shipping

Anna Karanika[1], Ioannis Filippopoulos[2,3], Angelika Kokkinaki[3],
Panagiotis Efstathiadis[1], Ioannis Tsilikas[4,5], and Yiannis Kiouvrekis[1,3(✉)]

[1] University of Thessaly, Volos, Greece
yianniskiouvrekis@gmail.com, kiouvrekis.y@uth.grs
[2] Hellenic American University, Nashua, USA
[3] University of Nicosia, Nicosia, Cyprus
[4] University of Athens, Athens, Greece
[5] National Technical University of Athens, Athens, Greece

Abstract. Radio Frequency Identification (RFID) Technology is a part
of supply chain systems but has not been fully integrated in the shipping industry to date. Port and terminal management teams already
make use of this technology to verify cargo information, reduce waiting
times and prevent bottlenecks. The adoption of RFID technology in the
shipping industry can provide invaluable real-time information about
a ship's crew and cargo. This study deals with RFID-based solutions
concerning issues of cargo security and handling, as well as tracking of
the crew in emergency situations. Although some maritime companies
have upgraded their fleet with modern management systems, there is
still much to be gained by the wide use of more RFID applications in
shipping. We will expound on some of the most useful RFID applications in the maritime sector and discuss their respective advantages and
disadvantages.

Keywords: Shipping · Containers · Radio Frequency Identification

1 Introduction

RFID technology is quite useful when it comes to automating all ship operations
concerning cargo and crew management. Before the advent and application of
RFID in the shipping industry, all essential activities and checking routines had
to be performed manually by the crew. This used to lead to time waste, which
is now avoidable. RFID technology allows us to remotely monitor data collected
from sensors and operate or plan future actions based on these data, allowing for
more effective decisions than were previously possible. In addition, much of the
work is performed by self-activating mechanisms which only require the appoval
of a crew member. Therefore, automation on a ship can reduce the number of
crew members that are required for seamless operation.

Concerning cargo safety, several issues can be addressed by making use of
automated systems. In many cases, crew members acting with malicious intent
or intruders are responsible for theft, loss or tampering with products. Similarly,

© Springer Nature Switzerland AG 2020
M. Themistocleous et al. (Eds.): EMCIS 2020, LNBIP 402, pp. 796–805, 2020.
https://doi.org/10.1007/978-3-030-63396-7_54

smuggling is another issue plaguing cargo transferring operations, since there is either an abundance of illegal and dangerous substances and products banned from import in certain or all countries, or the custom fees thereof are very high. A system must be put in place to prevent such instances.

Furthermore, correct handling of cargo, whether it involves loading, unloading or moving, can benefit from automation in a variety of ways. Up until now, stowage plans were made with previous knowledge concering which containers will be loaded on the ship, when and where they will come aboard and what their needs and restrictions will be. Based on this information, the best way in which to allocate containers to the appropriate position on the ship must be worked out by stowage coordinators before the process starts. Cargo repositioning is a process that occurs in almost every ship stop and the stowage plan must be designed in advance in such a way as to minimize it. It is also important to handle and position containers storing fragile products with caution so as to avoid damages.

In addition, a more sophisticated automated alerting system can prove quite useful because some materials are sensitive to specific environmental conditions that must be maintained to avert quality degradation.

Large sums of money are paid in the event of piracy, shipwreck or disease in compensation to crew members or their families in cases of post-traumatic stress disorders or death. In recent years and especially in the seas south of Africa, incidents of piracy have been increasingly common due to poverty and ongoing wars. There is also a need to reduce the transmission of viruses among crew members, treat illnesses fast and avoid negative repercussions on the health of recovering crew members. Automated monitoring of the location or biometrics of crew members can efficiently protect the crew and save them from extreme danger.

The use of RFID technology for building an efficient, low-cost and mature management system that logs all activities related to the cargo and extended information about the crew is an attractive option. The first official RFID patent was introduced in 1983 by Charles Walton [1]. Even though it is old technology, it is still commonly used thanks to its low cost, automatic collection of data without the need of human interaction, long reading range and high-speed data transactions.

This paper is organized as follows: In Sect. 2, we expound on research that has been conducted regarding the shipping industry. In Sect. 3, we describe the basic functionality of the RFID technology. Section 4 deals with established as well as proposed applications of the RFID technology in the shipping industry. Advantages and disadvantages of said applications are discussed in Sect. 5. Section 6 presents our conclusions.

2   Related Work

2.1   Cargo Safety

Up until now, containers on a ship have been locked using non-electronic means. The authors of [2] present a cable lock that is used to close a container. This lock cannot be opened unless the cord is cut. Therefore, the cable can be cut at any time and the container accessed, but it will become evident that there was unauthorized access.

2.2   Cargo Management and Positioning

The authors of [3] propose the use of two heuristic algorithms; one which formulates a stowage plan based on information about the containers that will be boarded on the ship and another that designs an efficient plan of loading and unloading containers at the different ports, where the ship will making stops, with the minimum amount of shifting, i.e. positional change of the containers, and taking into consideration the ship's stability.

The authors of [4] follow a similar approach, progressively refining the placement of containers within the cargo space of a container ship until each container is specifically allocated to a stowage location.

In [5] and [6], a system called iStow is presented, which produces several plan concepts based on inputs, from which the user can choose one and modify it taking into account their specific circumstances and cross checking it against requirements. Every completed planning task is stored in the database for future use. Some key features of the system are the ship stability calculation tool and other container load modules which help the planner to reach a final decision concerning the stowage plan. A similar system has also been proposed by [7] offering feasible stowage plans with reasonable crane intensity, taking into consideration the number of instances of rehandling and checks and adjustments before the stage of stability.

2.3   Quality Assurance

[8] mentions the need for systems that are responsible for the cargo's quality assurance without referring to specific systems. Nevertheless, it prioritizes accident reporting and analysis, regular and accurate management reviews of the systems and robust training programs.

As [9]'s authors posit, on-board and ongoing training, retraining and study leaves, testing and examination on their expertise, as well as internal quality audits of the cargo are a requirement for maintaining the quality of the seafaring labor in Korean ships and the cargo.

2.4   Emergency Tracking

In the event of a shipwreck alert, [10] proposes the use of a robotic team composed of an Unarmed Surface Vehicle (USV) and an Unarmed Aerial Vehicle (UAV) for search and rescue. In fact, the proposed cooperative system can search, track and provide basic life support, while also communicating the location and condition of human survivors to better-prepared manned rescue teams.

3   RFID Technology

An RFID system is divided into two key modules. The first module is the reader, which is equipped with an antenna, while the second module is the tag. An RFID reader transmits an encoded radio signal to interrogate the tag. When the second module (tag) receives an appropriate wave, it responds with its identification and other information to the RFID reader [11,12]. Other modules of an RFID system are the edge servers [13], the middleware [14], and the application software [15].

3.1   RFID Tags and Their Categories

There are three types of systems: passive, semi-passive and active. This classification is made based on the power source, as well as the read range of the tag. Passive tags use the power of the wave —emitted by a reader— that reaches them in order to respond. They are composed of a microchip attached to an antenna. The read range of passive tags is short —a few inches to 30 feet—, but their life is longer than that of active tags. This type of tag is characterized by a fast-reading rate (10 or more times a second). Additionally, they have the advantage of being exceptionally thin, which allows manufacturers to even place them between layers of paper, and of having very competitive prices (less than $ 0.05 in volumes of more than 10,000 pieces). Combined with the right packaging, they can be used under the harshest conditions. Semi-passive tags are the same as passive tags, with the exception of a small battery and a faster-reading ability.

Active tags have a power source/battery of their own. This feature enables them to emit their own signal, have a bigger memory, better noise protection and a wider range, which is why they are also called beacons. A reader in the vicinity of an active tag can receive its signals without having to initiate the message exchange itself. It is commonly used in environments such as water and metal which can hinder communication and thus require a strong signal, or cargo containers which have to be tracked over very long distances. However, the size of an active tag is considerably bigger than that of a passive one, its battery life lasts up to a number of years and its cost is higher than the cost of a passive tag.

3.2   RFID Readers

An RFID reader, also known as an interrogator, is composed of a control unit, a transceiver, and a link between the two. It can be mobile or fixed, depending on the needs of the user. Its purpose is to communicate with RFID tags, and report all received information to an edge server. The reader's antenna emits electromagnetic signals that trigger passive as well as active tags within the reader's reading range. Thus, it is capable of receiving information from all tags within range, without having to separately interrogate each and every one of them.

3.3 RFID Applications

RFID technology has proven useful in a wide area of every-day activities. First and foremost, a passport can be fitted with an RFID chip containing its owner's identification information, as well as some biometric information about them, a cryptographic signature that authenticates its legitimacy, thus verifying that it has not been altered [16,17].

Another field that encourages the use of RFID technology is that of retail; more specifically, every item is tagged with a microchip that describes it, enabling the customers to automatically be charged with the total amount that corresponds to the items they chose, since a reader at the exit records them as they leave the shop [18]. In addition, institutions can greatly benefit by the incorporation of RFID technology in their management systems; in the healthcare sector, patients can have wristbands or adhesive chips that hold their health history and can help not only with reducing waiting times and preventing bottlenecks, but also as a means of locating the patient [19]. In libraries and campuses, members can be identified and make use of available resources by swiping their RFID membership card and registering their transactions [20,21].

Furthermore, in the field of transportation, smart devices in combination with RFID technology facilitate passengers in purchasing tickets and drivers in automatically paying at the toll station. Nowadays, according to [22], traffic is monitored in smart cities and the data collected helps formulate decisions about the operation of traffic lights.

Another effective application of RFID systems is presented in large livestock facilities; breeders have their animals implanted with a tag that reports on the animal's information and whereabouts [23,24].

4 RFID Applications in Shipping

4.1 Electronic Container Seal

Nowadays, many cases have been observed where big companies or the state suffer financial losses due to the lack of security during the shipping of products. The following are some of the most frequently documennted security issues. First, product loss causes the largest economic harm to a company since the product is stolen on the way to its destination, thus leaving no choice to the recipient but to demand a full refund. Second, product tampering, which involves the illegal replacement of the product with a copycat product, or product altering which is also a common problem. Third, smugglers are constantly attempting to avoid custom control and transport illegal or mass destruction products without raising attention, taking advantage of legal transportation.

In order to address those kinds of issues, an RFID electronic seal is placed on a container. Its functionality entails keeping a record of the latest events, such as the time of its valid installation on the container, the managing operator and its current status. In fact, when an active RFID eSeal is used, the inspection with an RFID reader can be completed from a distance and in a very short time. Moreover, in case the seal's cable is cut or tampered with, the system logs the intrusion and alerts the system administrator. Therefore, such a seal can increase the security of a container and be useful in dealing with tampering [25–28].

4.2   Cargo Management and Positioning

RFID technology can have an effect on the loading and unloading process. Specifically, active RFID tags can be placed on every container and multiple RFID readers can collect the related identification and characteristics data and transmit them to a central system. After arriving at the port, they can be processed to produce a stowage plan that assigns the most appropriate position to every incoming container using allocation algorithms that take into account the characteristics of a container. This way, the pre-processing time can be minimized.

An efficient placement of containers on a ship entails several factors. First, ship stability is of paramount importance because it prevents the ship from tilting to the side and sinking. Second, minimizing the repositioning of cargo can save time and money for the ship owning companies. Furthermore, containers that carry sensitive content must have conditions that obey specific requirements and have to be placed in ideal positions to achieve that.

Ship stability is affected by the shift of the containers placed on it, the presence of wind or waves that can cause it to tilt to one side, as well as the removal of cargo mostly from one side of it. Lack of ship stability can lead to the ship sinking. To avoid problems that can arise regarding ship stability, necessary characteristics, such as weight, content and dimensions for each container are transmitted to the central system.

The time that is required for containers loading and, especially, unloading is valuable and, without special attention, can be increased greatly. Containers that are to be unloaded at the next port must be placed at the top, so that they are easily reachable and little to no repositioning is demanded. Thus, destination information is absolutely essential in minimizing repositioning operations.

More often than not, sensitive products are transported on ships. These products may be in danger of quality deterioration or can be destructive to the rest of the cargo and the ship's functioning systems. Refrigerated cargo units amount to one type of such cargo. In order to operate correctly, they should be placed close to power outlets. Hence, information about the need for power must be transmitted to the main system. Additionally, containers carrying dangerous materials should be kept away from direct sunlight and the engine to prevent fire and explosions that could prove catastrophic. Information concerning the content and danger it can cause must also be transmitted to the central system.

The containers' RFID tags may be updated to reflect their current position and, in case they change positions during their trip, the RFIDs should reflect that. In addition, the product manufacturers and customers are able to track the discussed products using the RFID technology, which is cheaper than GPS technology.

4.3 Quality Assurance

Transported goods or materials on ships are often fragile and require special attention to avoid damages. RFID tags installed on containers can include this information and inform the crane operator on how fast or slow to transfer the container from the port onto the ship and vice versa.

After the loading operations, materials inside containers that are sensitive to high or low temperature, humidity and pressure levels must be monitored at regular intervals to avoid quality degradation. Aiming to counter such dangers, sensor networks along with RFID tags are installed in containers, rendering them "Intelligent Containers" [29]. These sensors collect data related to the factors described above inside a container and send them out to a central management system by way of the connected RFID tag. If the collected data are not the desired, the management system alerts the crew to take action.

4.4 Emergency Tracking

As piracy and shipwrecks are a very real possibility for any ship itinerary, RFID technology could prove to be of great assistance to search and rescue operations. In such cases the ship's geo-locating and broadcasting systems can be shut down or broken down and be of no use to search and rescue teams trying to locate the ship and crew. Active RFID tags can be assigned to and placed on every crew member, in a wristband. Then, if a crew member disembarks from the ship, either because of being abducted or because of great danger on the ship that they are trying to avoid, they may be located through an RFID-based RTLS (Real-Time Location System) system [30] and rescued by the appropriate team. In addition, RFID tags can be embedded into life jackets and provide valuable information in the event of a shipwreck. This information can include pressure and altitude data that make clear whether the person wearing the wristband or life jacket is alive.

Finally, biometrics collected by a crew member's RFID wristband can be monitored for unusual or dangerous changes. For instance, high pressure can be a signal for an upcoming stroke and high temperature levels can be the symptom of a viral infection. An alert can be triggered if unexpected information comes through, possibly enabling the prevention of unwanted situations. If prevention is not feasible and a doctor is not present, biometrics should keep being monitored and sent to a doctor who can remotely instruct the rest of the crew on how to stabilize them. The provision of real-time medical data to the crew and doctor can be critical in preserving the patient's life or at least keeping them stable until the ship reaches the next port.

5   Advantages and Disadvantages

In this paper, we discuss the major benefits and drawbacks of using the RFID technology in the shipping industry.

5.1   Advantages

First of all, the use of RFID systems is undoubtedly a low-cost solution to many problems. Tags are mass produced and readers are extremely affordable especially compared to all other components of a ship. In addition, it is particularly easy to set up, thereby avoiding time and excessive costs. Moreover, the implementations that we propose in this paper concern dedicated active tags with a high frequency and a battery with a high energy capacity. Tags of this type offer us the ability to read them from a long distance. Importing RFID technology onto the ship can help the captain/company maintain more efficient control over both the crew and the cargo without the need of wasting any extra human resources for the main operations and procedures of the ship. Another positive effect of high-frequency active tags is their ability to transfer data they have stored in their internal memory in a very fast way, having a low probability of packet loss.

Due to the fact that RFID technology is mature enough, there are many communication means connecting it to other hardware or devices on the ship. These connections are very stable and easy to set up. Similarly, several commercial software solutions have embedded modules that are specifically created for the import of data from RFID readers.

5.2   Disadvantages

On the other hand, as technology evolves, especially in our day and age when the European Union has approved of bills involving the privacy of users' data, e.g. General Data Protection Regulation (GDPR), we cannot use so many data about the crew or the cargo without the consent of the affiliated parties because it is illegal.

Secondly, automated systems that the acceptance of RFID technology brings with it will have a negative impact on the job market. Specifically, maritime workers will encounter a great problem in keeping their job or finding a new one if and when the demand for their job position will plummet.

Last but not least, the high frequency required for the active tags to have a long reading range can be detrimental to crew health. In fact, even though it might not immediately cause obvious damage, it might be responsible for the long-term deterioration of their health, after their exposure for many and long periods of time.

6   Conclusions

As we have made abundantly clear, the shipping industry still has not made any big steps towards the acceptance and embrace of the RFID technology's applications. In most parts of a product's journey from the manufacturer to the consumer, such as customs, ports and terminals, these applications are already used quite successfully. Automation can boost the shipping industry by enabling the faster delivery of the transferred goods combining it with the highest possible safety of the products. We observe that many manufacturers have focused on creating smart containers which are modernized and on the same page with today's technology. RFID applications offer an evolution of the already existing management systems of a ship, even though they have their own disadvantages which do not seem sufficient to affect the essential operations. Smart containers and RFID-based automated systems are sufficient to modernize a merchant fleet and result in larger profits for all the companies involved.

References

1. Walton, C.A.: U.S. Patent No. 4,384,288. Washington, DC: U.S. Patent and Trademark Office (1983)
2. Natkins, E.: U.S. Patent No. 6,131,969. Washington, DC: U.S. Patent and Trademark Office (2000)
3. Kang, J.-G., Kim, Y.-D.: Stowage planning in maritime container transportation. J. Oper. Res. Soc. **53**(4), 415–426 (2002). https://doi.org/10.1057/palgrave.jors. 2601322
4. Wilson, I.D., Roach, P.A.: Container stowage planning: a methodology for generating computerised solutions. J. Oper. Res. Soc. **51**(11), 1248–1255 (2000)
5. Nugroho, S.: Case-based stowage planning for container ships. In: The International Logistics Congress, December 2004
6. Nugroho, S., Abidin, A., Zulkarnaen, F.: Stowage planning for container vessels: methodology development and implementation issues in the light of intelligent transportation systems implementation. Int. J. Bus. Econ. **2**, 119 (2010)
7. Low, M., Xiao, X., Liu, F., Huang, S.Y., Hsu, W.J., Li, Z.: An automated stowage planning system for large containerships. In: Proceedings of the International MultiConference of Engineers and Computer Scientists, pp. 17-19. Nanyang Technological University, School of Computer Engineering (2010)
8. Stewart, N.: Quality Assurance. The Implementation of Quality Management and Quality Assurance Standards: The Potential Effects on Shipping Agencies in Jamaica, pp. 33-37 (1999)
9. Lee, T. W.: A study on the introduction of quality management system for improving the international competitive power of the shipping companies in Korea. WIT Trans. Built Environ., **12** (1970)
10. Mendonça, R., Marques, M. M., Marques, F., Lourenco, A., Pinto, E., Santana, P., Barata, J.: A cooperative multi-robot team for the surveillance of shipwreck survivors at sea. In: OCEANS 2016 MTS/IEEE Monterey, pp. 1–6. IEEE, September 2016
11. Ahuja, S., Potti, P.: An introduction to RFID technology. Commun. Netw. **2**(3), 183–186 (2010)

12. Roberts, C.M.: Radio frequency identification (RFID). Comput. Secur. **25**(1), 18–26 (2006)
13. Sheng, Q.Z., Li, X., Zeadally, S.: Enabling next-generation RFID applications: solutions and challenges. Computer **41**(9), 21–28 (2008)
14. Floerkemeier, C., Lampe, M.: RFID middleware design: addressing application requirements and RFID constraints. In: Proceedings of the 2005 Joint Conference on Smart Objects and Ambient Intelligence: Innovative Context-aware Services: Usages and Technologies, pp. 219–224, October 2004
15. Floerkemeier, C., Roduner, C., Lampe, M.: RFID application development with the Accada middleware platform. IEEE Syst. J. **1**(2), 82–94 (2007)
16. Stanton, J.: ICAO and the biometric RFID passport: history and analysis. Playing the Identity card: Surveill. Secur. Ident. Glob. Perspect. **9**, 253–267 (2008)
17. Ezovski, G. M., Watkins, S. E.: The electronic passport and the future of government-issued RFID-based identification. In: 2007 IEEE International Conference on RFID, pp. 15–22. IEEE, March 2007
18. Schögel, M., Lienhard, S.D.: Cashierless stores-the new way to the customer? Mark. Rev. St. Gallen (2020)
19. Kaur, H., Atif, M., Chauhan, R.: An internet of healthcare things (IoHT)-based healthcare monitoring system. In: Mohanty, M.N., Das, S. (eds.) Advances in Intelligent Computing and Communication. LNNS, vol. 109, pp. 475–482. Springer, Singapore (2020). https://doi.org/10.1007/978-981-15-2774-6_56
20. Timoshenko, I.: RFID in Libraries: automatic identification and data collection technology for library documents. Chapters (2020)
21. Ahmad, N.A., Raziman, S.F., Baharum, Z., Rahman, F.A.: The secure authentication system using RFID system for institute of higher education: towards management perception (2020)
22. Chellani, N., Tahilyani, C.: Traffic congestion detection and control using RFID technology. In: International Journal of Engineering Research and Technology (IJERT) (2013)
23. Bonneau, M., Vayssade, J.A., Troupe, W., Arquet, R.: Outdoor animal tracking combining neural network and time-lapse cameras. Comput. Electron. Agric. **168**, 105150 (2020)
24. Adrion, F., et al.: Monitoring trough visits of growing-finishing pigs with UHF-RFID. Comput. Electron. Agric. **144**, 144–153 (2018)
25. Chin, L. P., Wu, C. L.: The role of electronic container seal (E-seal) with RFID technology in the container security initiatives. In: 2004 International Conference on MEMS, NANO and Smart Systems (ICMENS 2004), pp. 116–120. IEEE, August 2004
26. Rizzo, F., Barboni, M., Timossi, P., Azzalin, G., Sironi, M.: An innovative RFID sealing device to enhance the security of the supply chain. In: IWRT (2009)
27. Kadir, E. A., Rosa, S. L., Gunawan, H.: Application of RFID technology and e-seal in container terminal process. In: 2016 4th International Conference on Information and Communication Technology (ICoICT), pp. 1–6. IEEE, May 2016
28. Mullis, J., Kruest, J. R.: U.S. Patent No. 10,145,146. Washington, DC: U.S. Patent and Trademark Office (2018)
29. Lang, W., Jedermann, R., Mrugala, D., Jabbari, A., Krieg-Brückner, B., Schill, K.: The "intelligent container" –a cognitive sensor network for transport management. IEEE Sens. J. **11**(3), 688–698 (2010)
30. Park, D., Choi, Y., Nam, K.: RFID-based RTLS for improvement of operation system in container terminals. In: 2006 Asia-Pacific Conference on Communications (2006)

Author Index

Printed in the United States
By Bookmasters